RHS F/N 1 ~ 1 ~ 2D

GW00359457

Street by Street

SURREY

PLUS ALDERSHOT, BIGGIN HILL, BRACKNELL, CRAWLEY, EAST GRINSTEAD, EDENBRIDGE, FARNBOROUGH, GATWICK AIRPORT, HORSHAM, RICHMOND, SUTTON

Enlarged Areas Croydon, Farnham, Guildford, Kingston upon Thames, Woking

2nd edition September 2003
© Automobile Association Developments Limited 2003

Original edition printed May 2001

Ordnance Survey® This product includes map data licensed from Ordnance Survey ® with the permission of the Controller of Her Majesty's Stationery Office. © Crown copyright 2003. All rights reserved. Licence number: 399221.

Published by AA Publishing (a trading name of Automobile Association Developments Limited, whose registered office is Millstream, Maidenhead Road, Windsor, Berkshire SL4 5GD. Registered number 1878835).

Mapping produced by the Cartography Department of The Automobile Association. (A01711)

A CIP Catalogue record for this book is available from the British Library.

Printed by GRAFIASA S.A., Porto, Portugal

Key to map pages	ii–iii
Key to map symbols	iv–1
Enlarged map pages	2–11
Main map pages	12–195
Index – towns & villages	196–197
Index – streets	198–263
Index – featured places	263–275
Acknowledgements	275

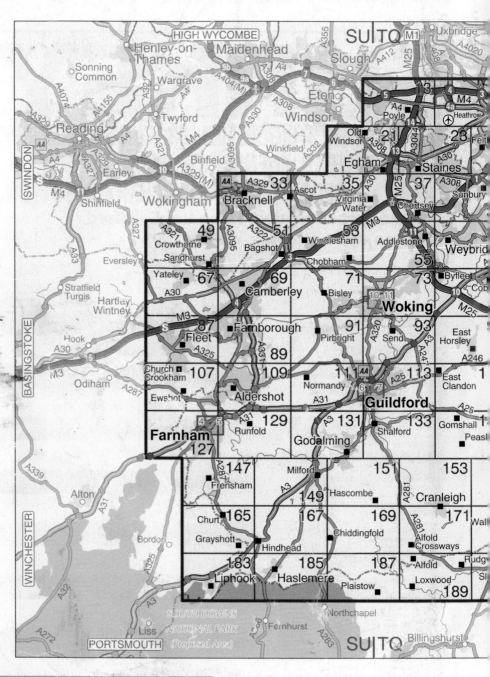

Scale of enlarged map pages 1:10,000 6.3 inches to 1 mile

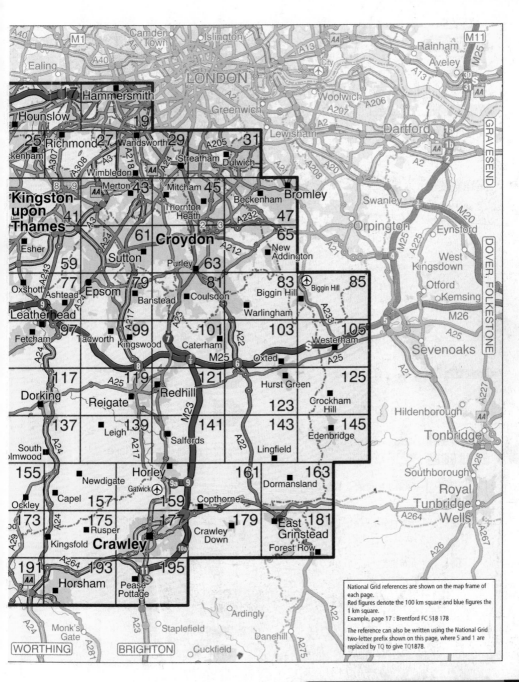

National Grid references are shown on the map frame of each page.
Red figures denote the 100 km square and blue figures the 1 km square.
Example, page 17 : Brentford FC 518 178
The reference can also be written using the National Grid two-letter prefix shown on this page, where 5 and 1 are replaced by TQ to give TQ1878.

2.5 inches to 1 mile   **Scale of main map pages**   1:25,000

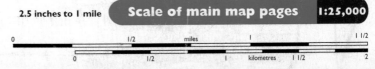

iv

Junction 9 Motorway & junction	⊖ Underground station
Services Motorway service area	⊖ Light railway & station
Primary road single/dual carriageway	++++++++++ Preserved private railway
Services Primary road service area	*LC* Level crossing
A road single/dual carriageway	●—●—●—● Tramway
B road single/dual carriageway	- - - - - - - Ferry route
Other road single/dual carriageway	·················· Airport runway
Minor/private road, access may be restricted	— · — · — County, administrative boundary
← One-way street	꙰꙰꙰꙰꙰ Mounds
Pedestrian area	**17** Page continuation 1:25,000
Track or footpath	**3** Page continuation to enlarged scale 1:10,000
Road under construction	River/canal, lake
Road tunnel	Aqueduct, lock, weir
AA AA Service Centre	465 ▲ Winter Hill Peak (with height in metres)
P Parking	Beach
P+🚌 Park & Ride	Woodland
🚌 Bus/coach station	Park
Railway & main railway station	Cemetery
Railway & minor railway station	Built-up area

	Featured building		Abbey, cathedral or priory
	City wall		Castle
A&E	Hospital with 24-hour A&E department		Historic house or building
PO	Post Office	Wakehurst Place NT	National Trust property
	Public library		Museum or art gallery
i	Tourist Information Centre		Roman antiquity
i	Seasonal Tourist Information Centre		Ancient site, battlefield or monument
	Petrol station, 24-hour Major suppliers only		Industrial interest
†	Church/chapel		Garden
	Public toilets		Garden Centre Garden Centre Association Member
	Toilet with disabled facilities		Garden Centre Wyevale Garden Centre
PH	Public house AA recommended		Farm or animal centre
	Restaurant AA inspected		Zoological or wildlife collection
Madeira Hotel	Hotel AA inspected		Bird collection
	Theatre or performing arts centre		Nature reserve
	Cinema		Aquarium
	Golf course	V	Visitor or heritage centre
▲	Camping AA inspected		Country park
	Caravan site AA inspected		Cave
▲	Camping & caravan site AA inspected		Windmill
	Theme park		Distillery, brewery or vineyard

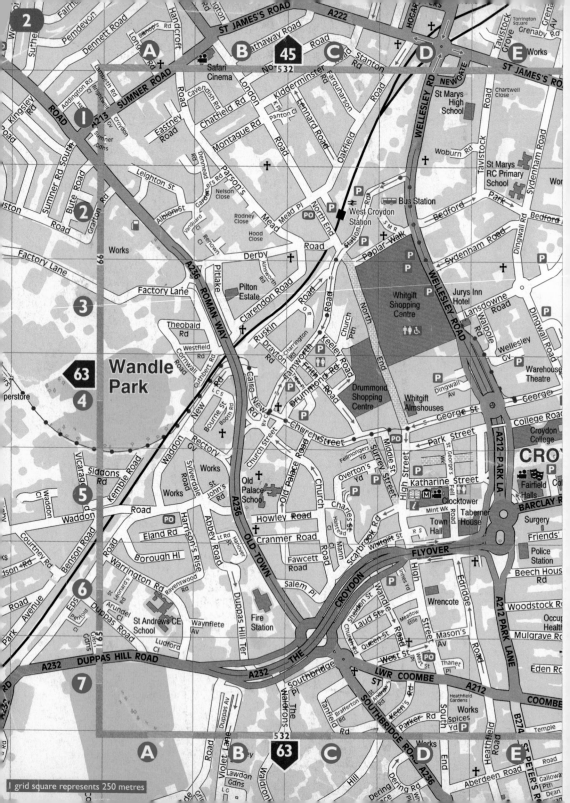

1 grid square represents 250 metres

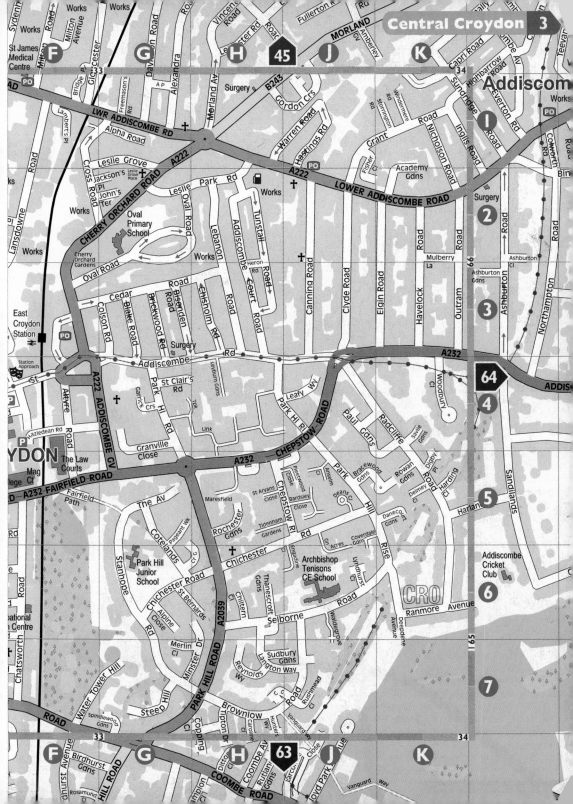

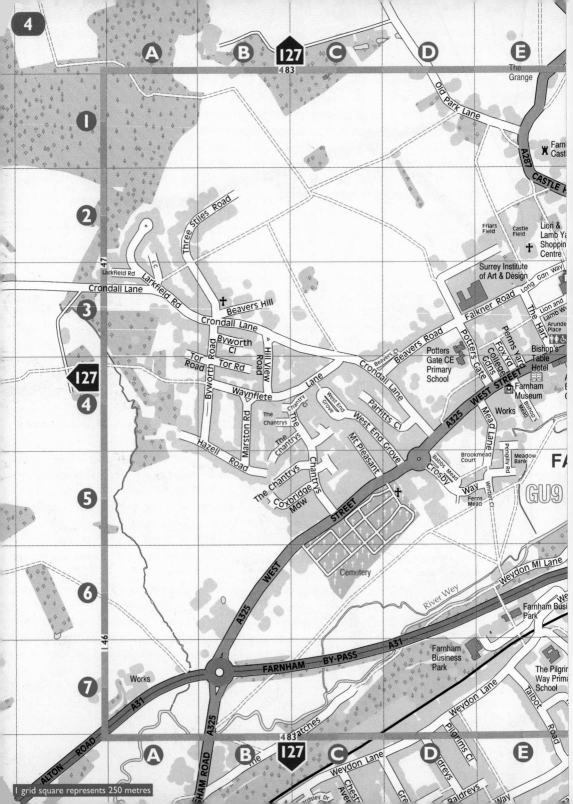

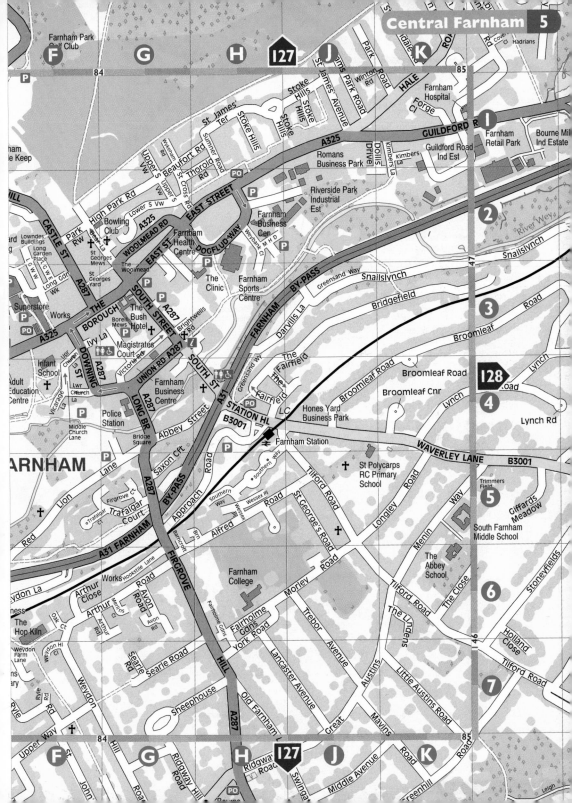

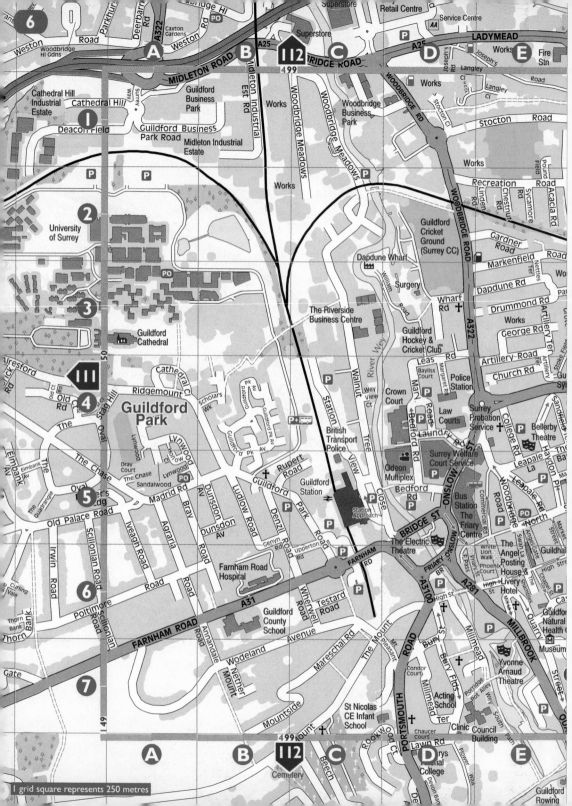

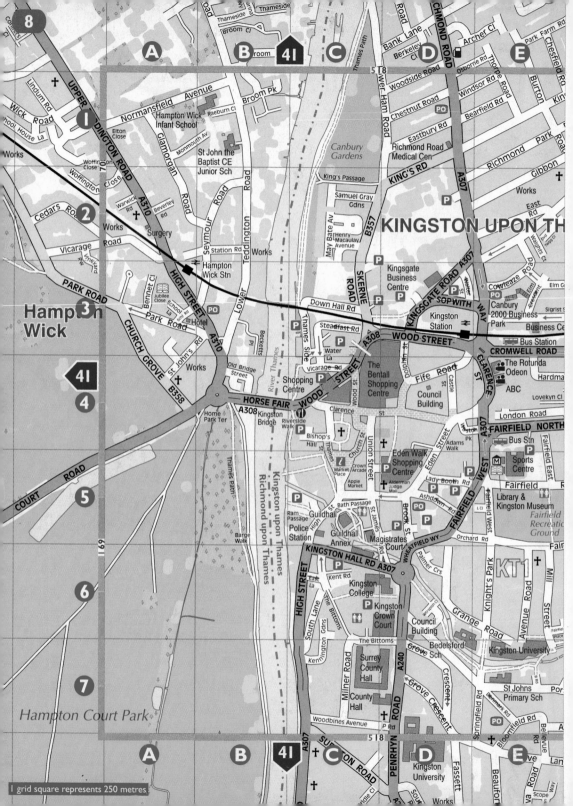

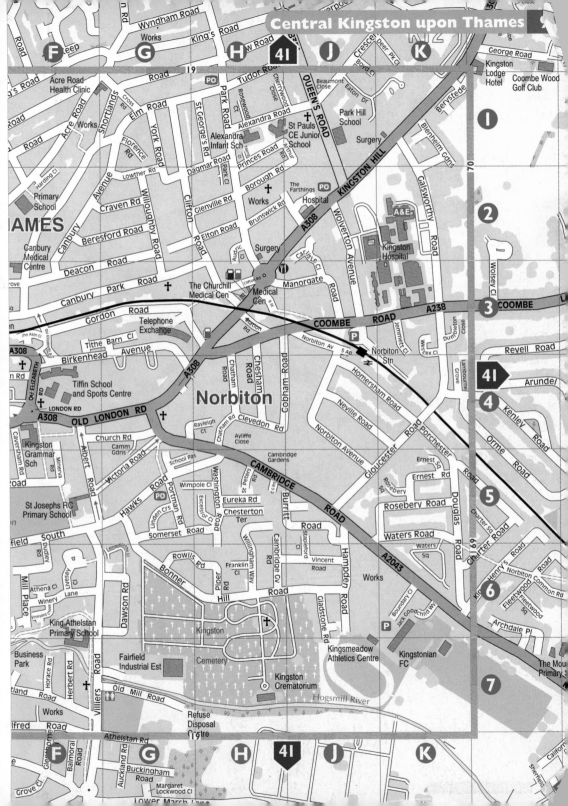

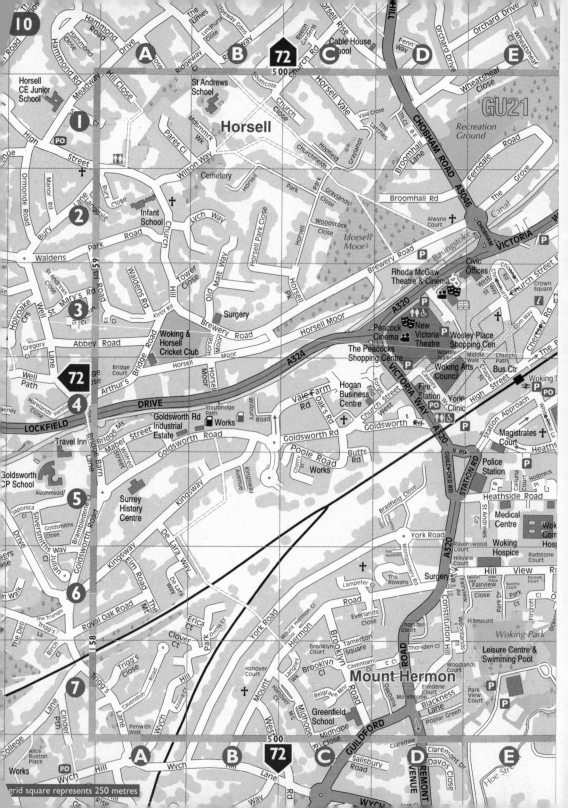

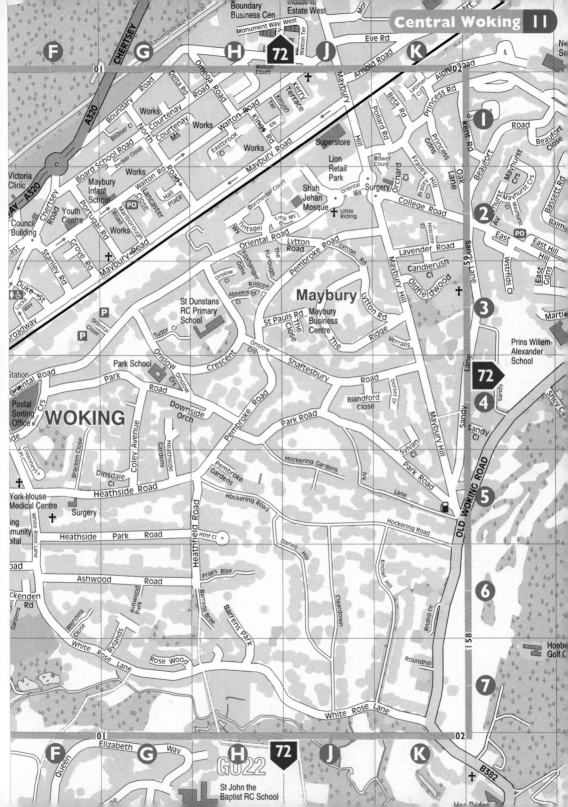

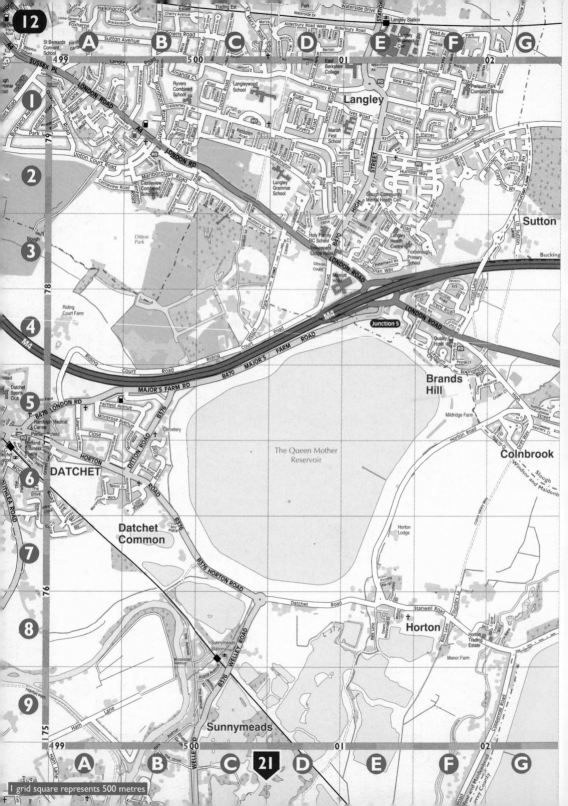

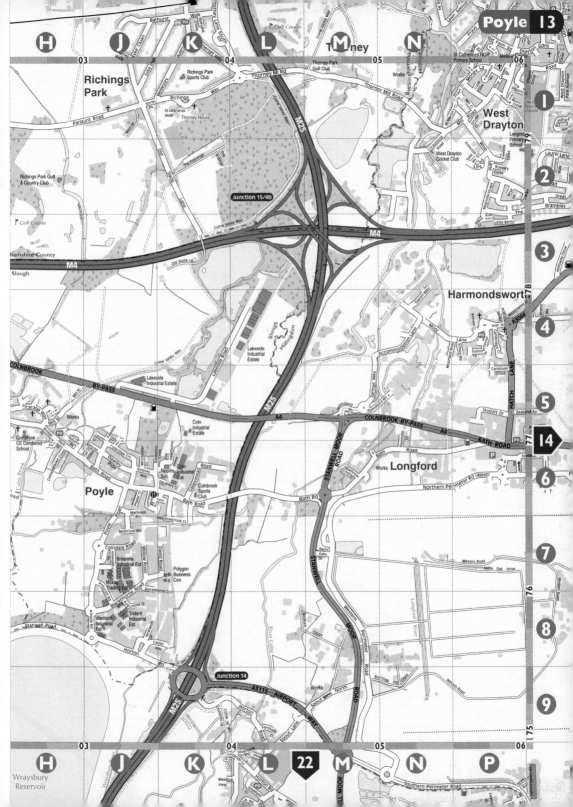

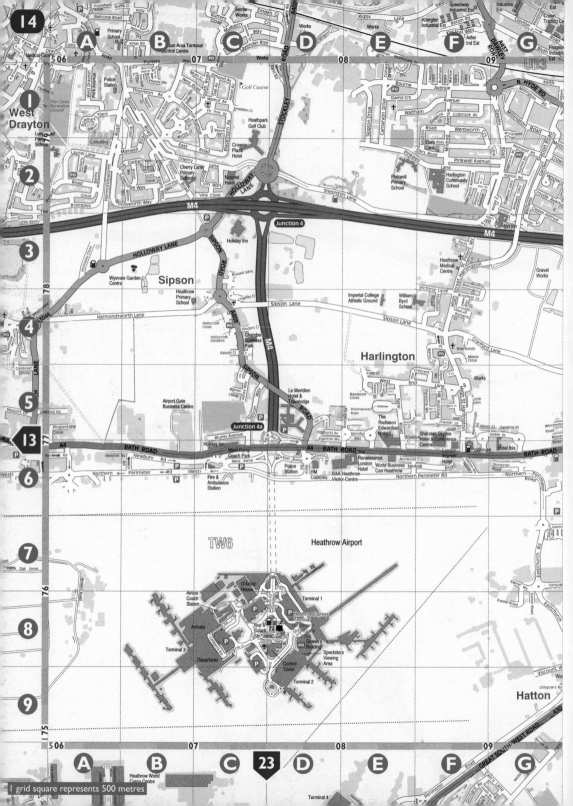

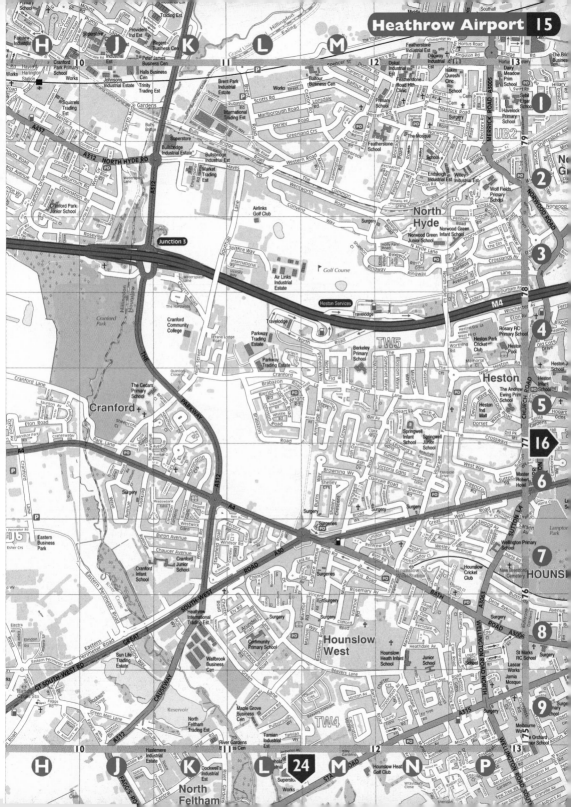

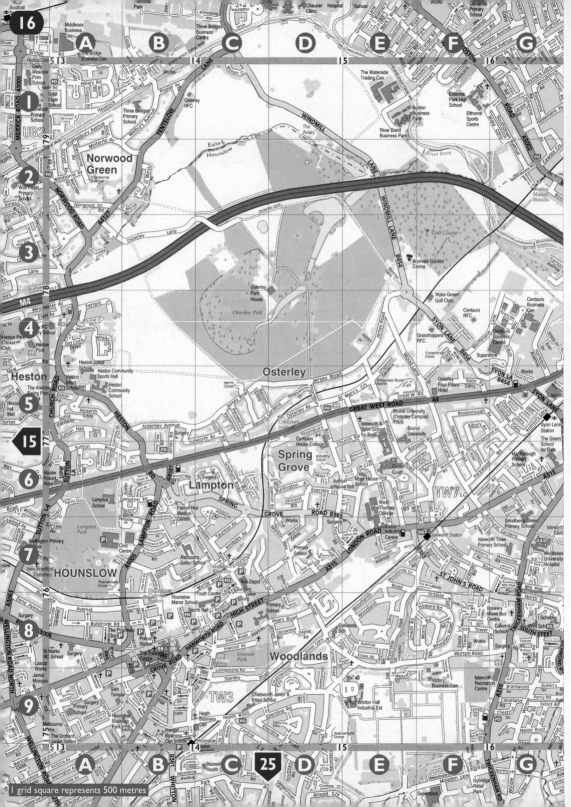

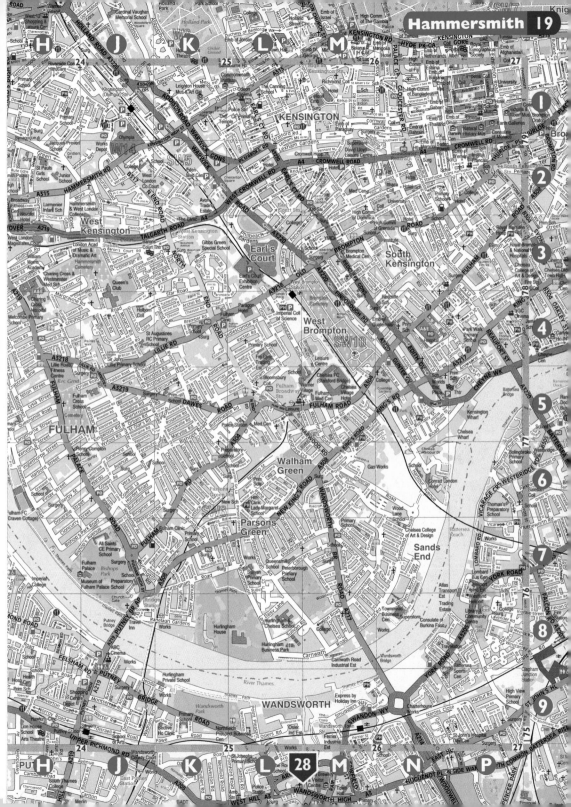

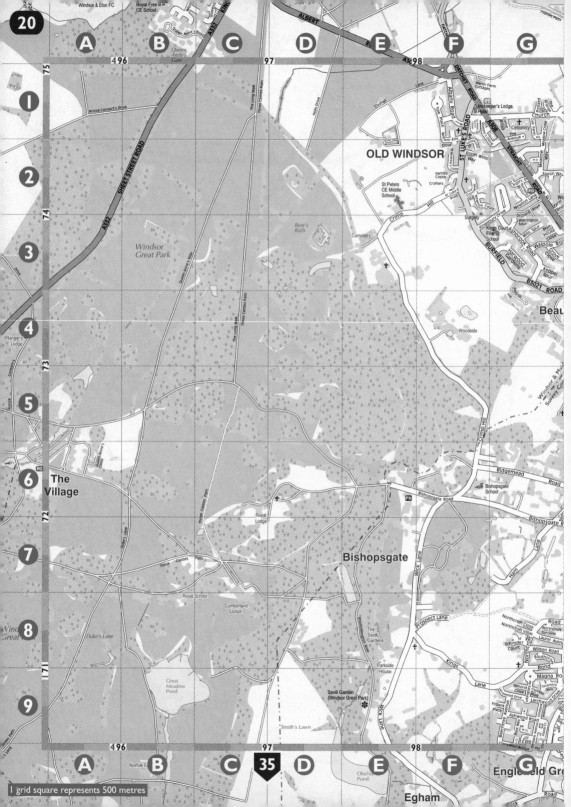

A 496 97 B C D E A3c98 F G

75

1 Prince Consort's Drive

Windsor & Eton FC
Royal Free Lane
CE School
Queen Anne's
Gate
ALBERT
Manor Farm
Cottages
Albany Road
Innkeeper's Lodge
Hotel
Church
Cemetery

OLD WINDSOR

2 74

St Peters
CE Middle
School
Hartley Copse
Crofters
St Luke's
Crimp Hill
Surgery
Newton Lane
Kings Court
First
School

SAXON ROAD
MEADOW WAY

3 Windsor
Great Park
Bear's
Rails
Cemetery
BURFIELD
Keppel
Spur
Walpole Grove
B3021 ROAD
Beau

4 Ranger's
Lodge
73
The Long Walk
Queen Anne's Ride
Three Castles Path
Woodside
Windsor &
Surrey

5 Crimp Hill

6 PO
The
Village
72
Royal
Lodge
Three Castles Path
PH
Bishopsgate Road
Bishopsgate
School
Ridgemead
Road
Bishopsgate R

7 Dukes Lane
Three Castles Path
Bishopsgate
Wick Lane
Ham Lane

8 Windsor
Great
Duke's Lane
Royal School
Cumberland
Lodge
The
Savill
Gardens
Parkside
House
Prospect Lane
Northcroft Close
Northcroft Villas
Laurel Road
Schroder
Court
Wilson Road
Northcroft
gardens
Northcroft
Road

9 171
Great
Meadow
Pond
Savill Garden
(Windsor Great Park)
Kings Lane
Magna Road
Ashwood Road

Smith's Lawn

A 496 B Norfolk F. C 97 35 D E Obelisk
Pond F G Englefield Gre

Egham

1 grid square represents 500 metres

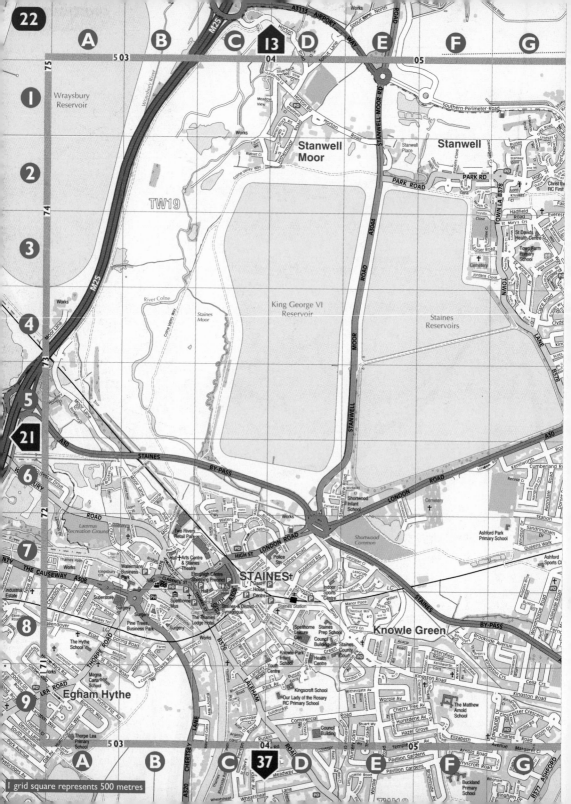

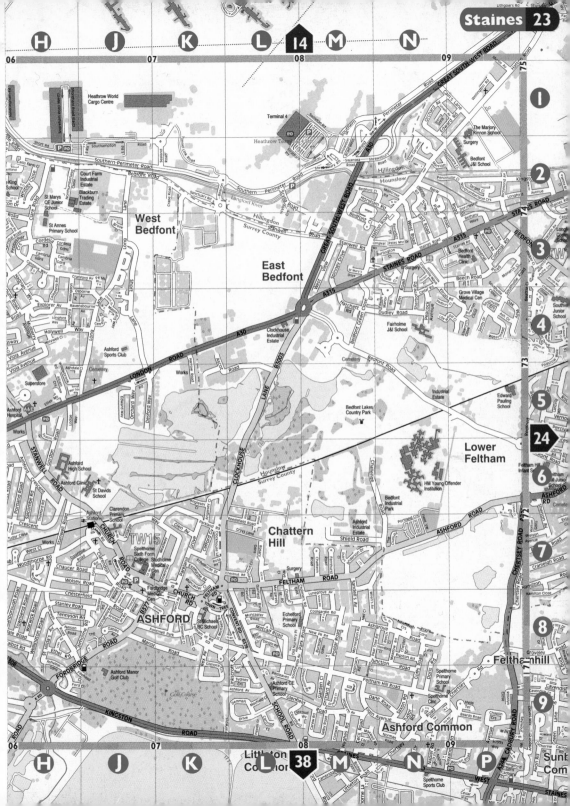

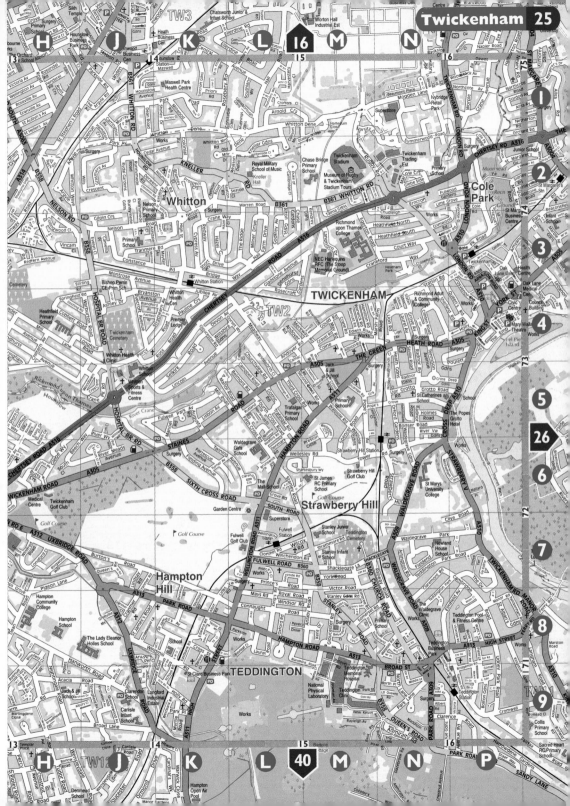

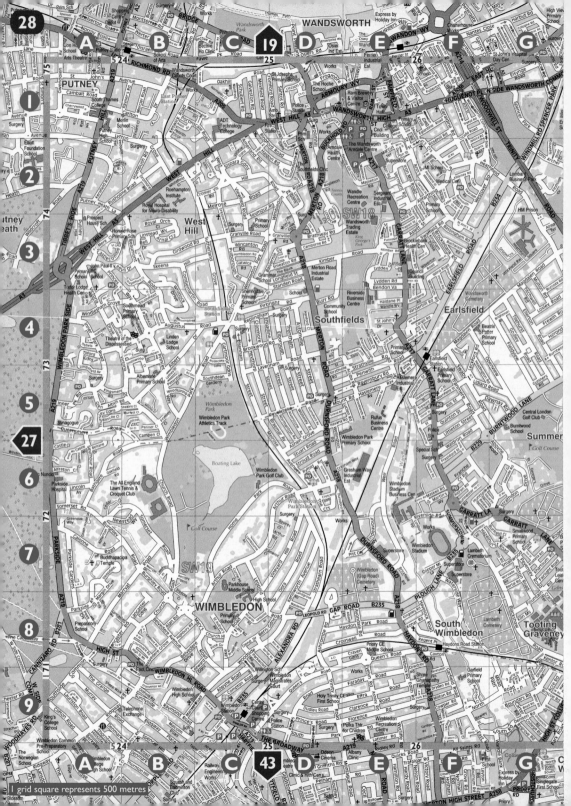

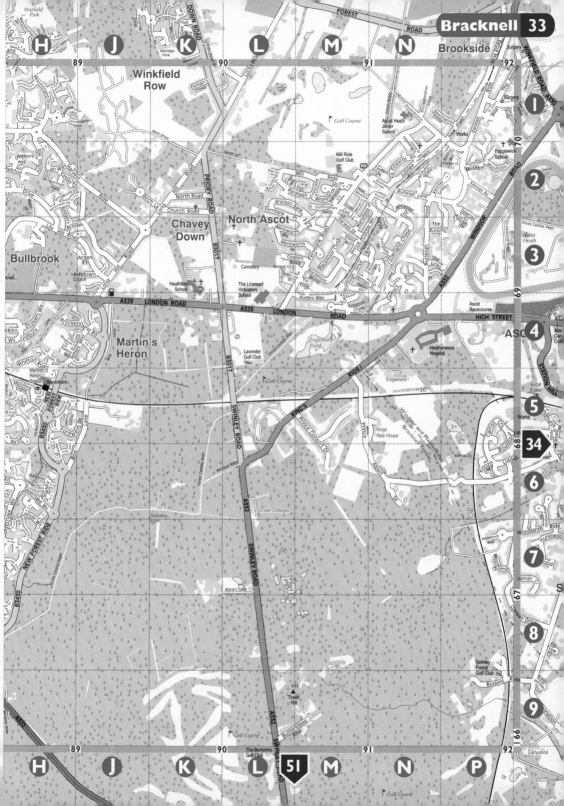

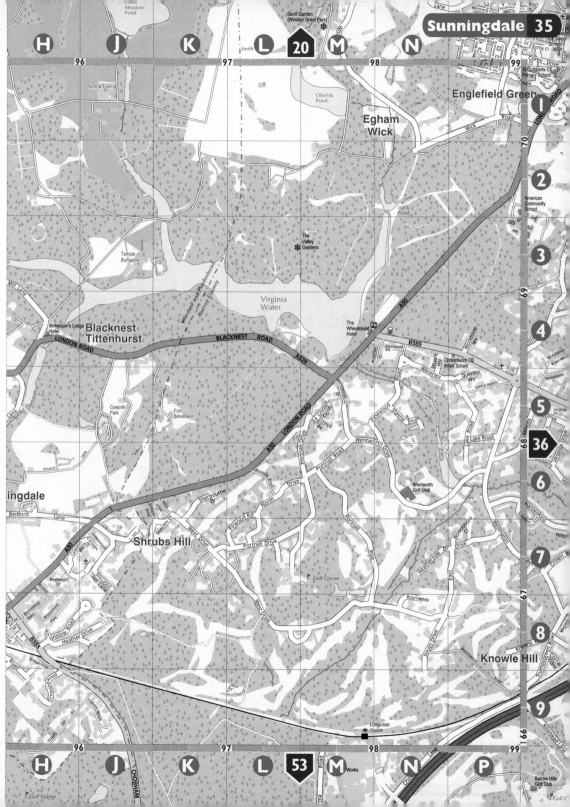

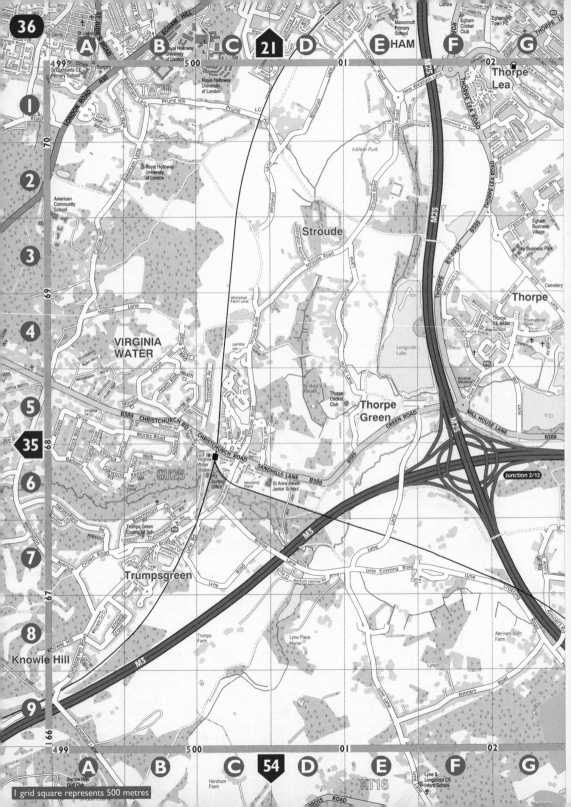

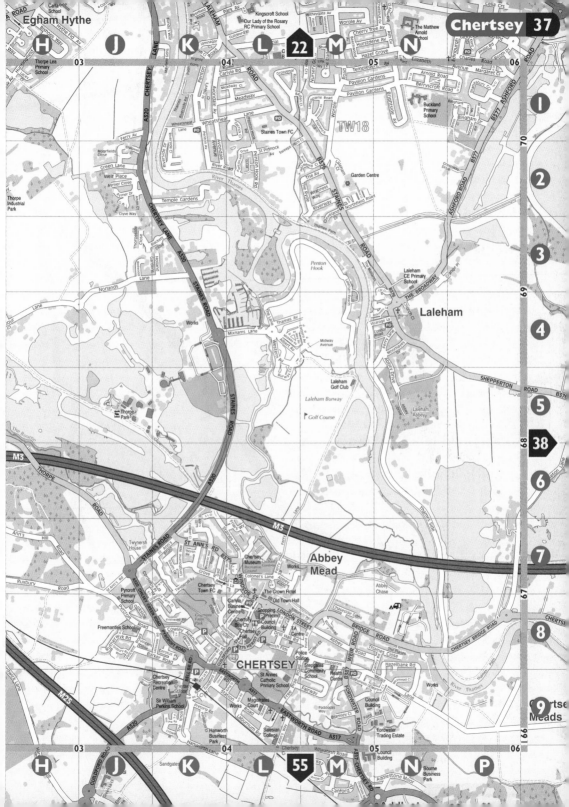

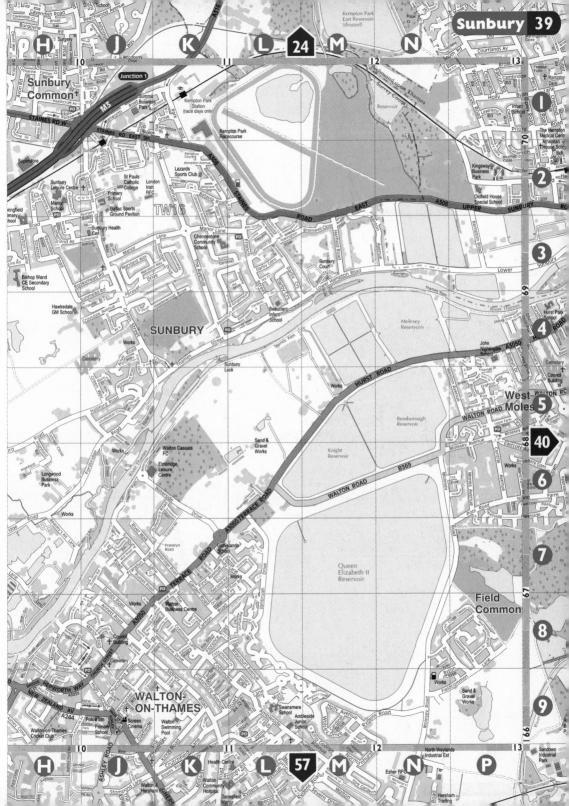

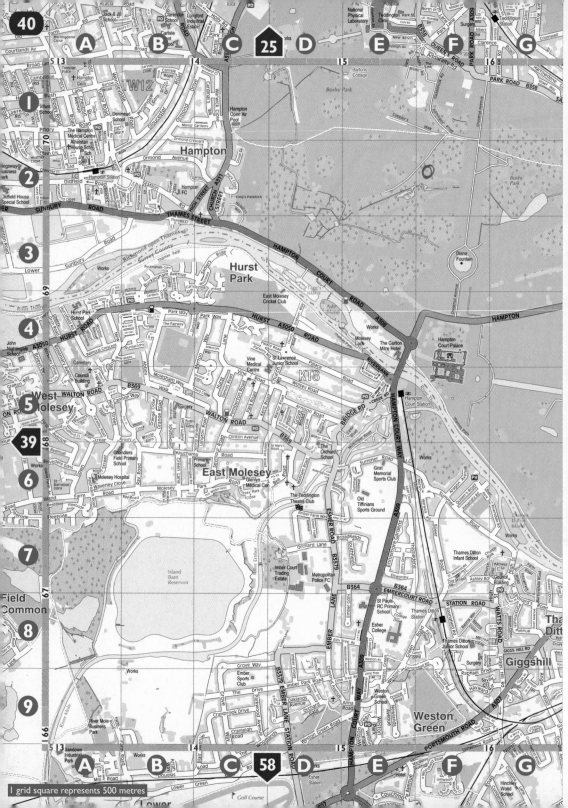

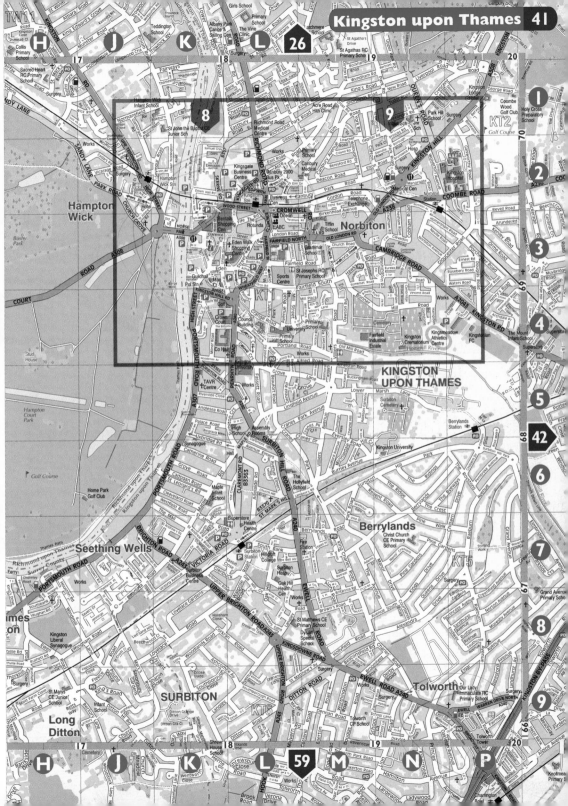

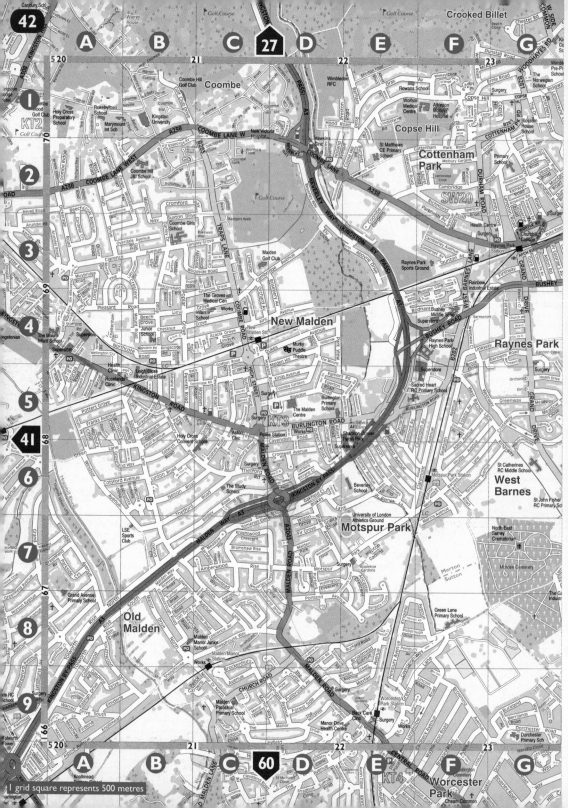

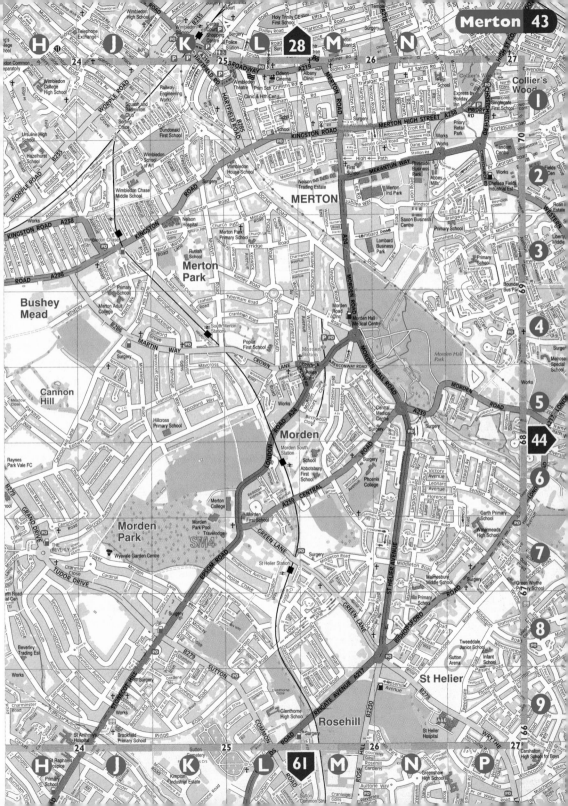

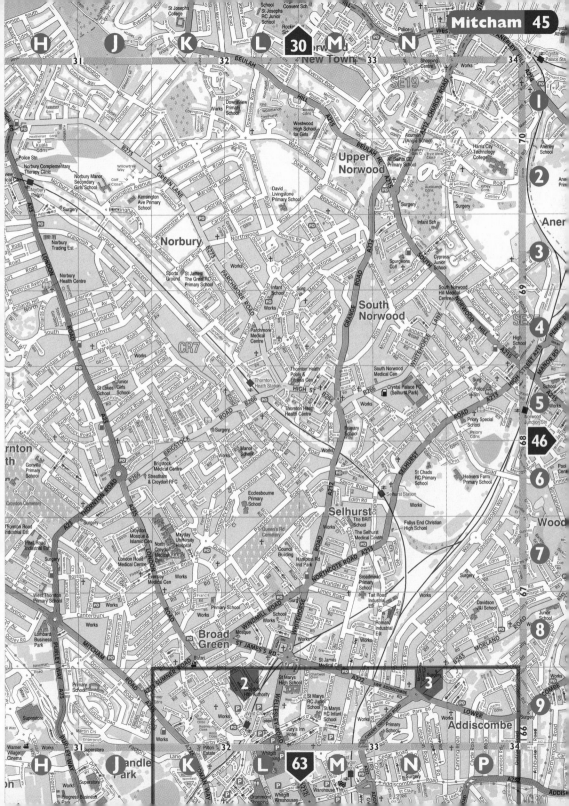

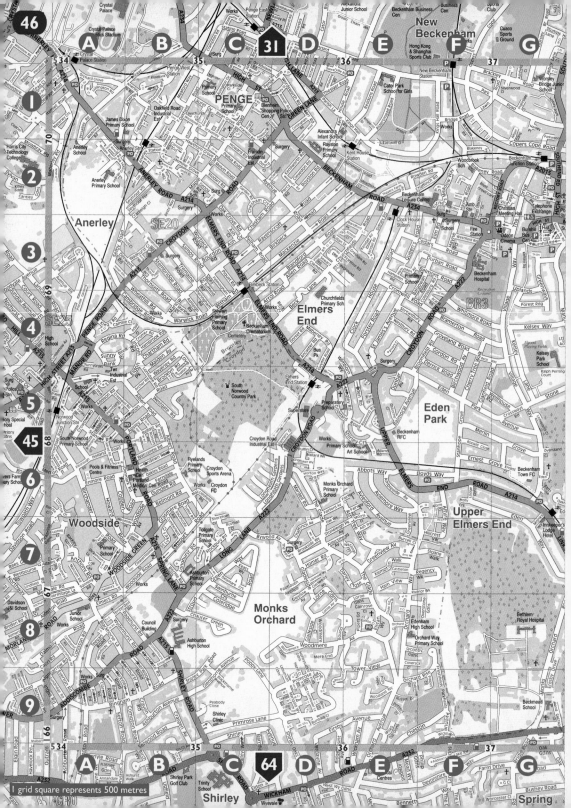

50

A B C **32** D E F G

66 485 86 87 88

65

BRACKNELL ROAD A3095 FORESTERS WAY

I

Crowthorne
Wood

2

3

RG45

Three Castles Path

64

4

Broadmoor
Hospital

5

Broadmoor

Broadmoor Farm

49

6

63

ROAD A3095

7

Wishmoor
Bottom

Owlsmoor

Owlsmoor
Primary
School

8

Surgery
Yeovil

62

College
Town

omprehensive
School

Oldden
Common

9

Junior
School

College
Infant
School

485 86 87 88

A B C **68** D E F **G** CAMBERLE

Royal Military
Academy

Cricket
Ground

I grid square represents 500 metres

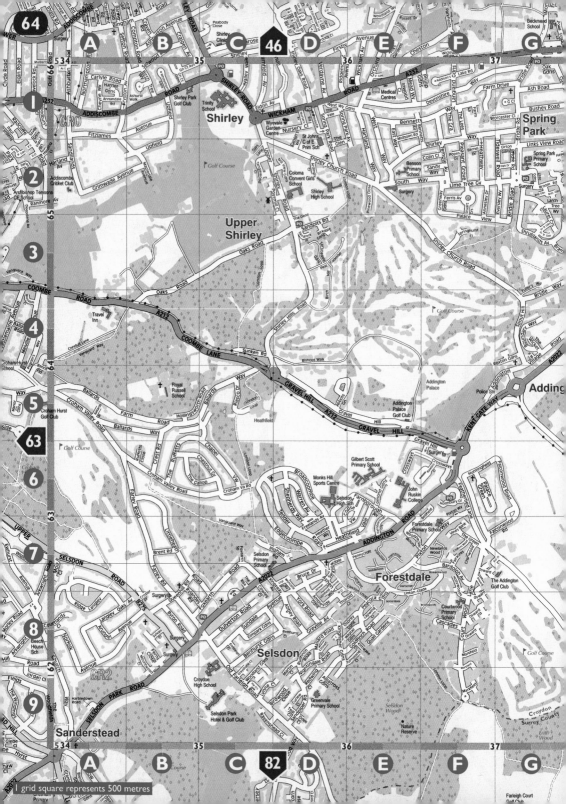

Fickleshole

Court

BIGGIN HILL

65

84

103

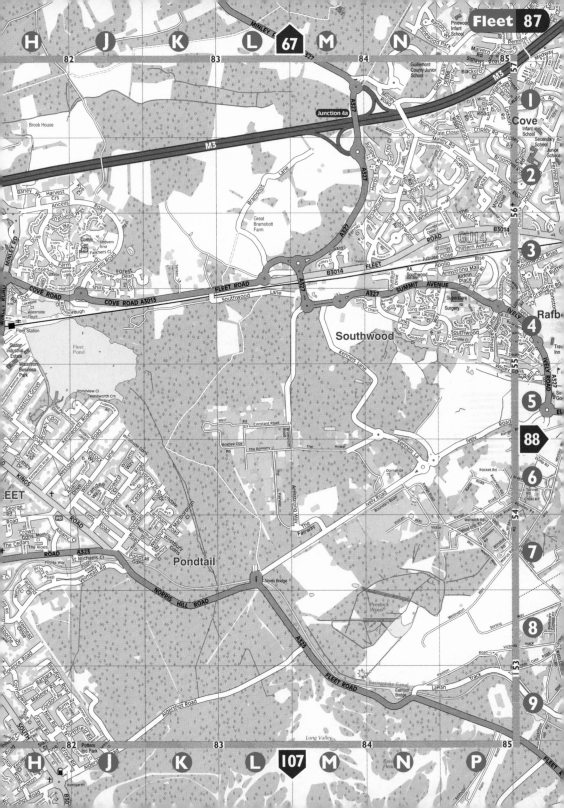

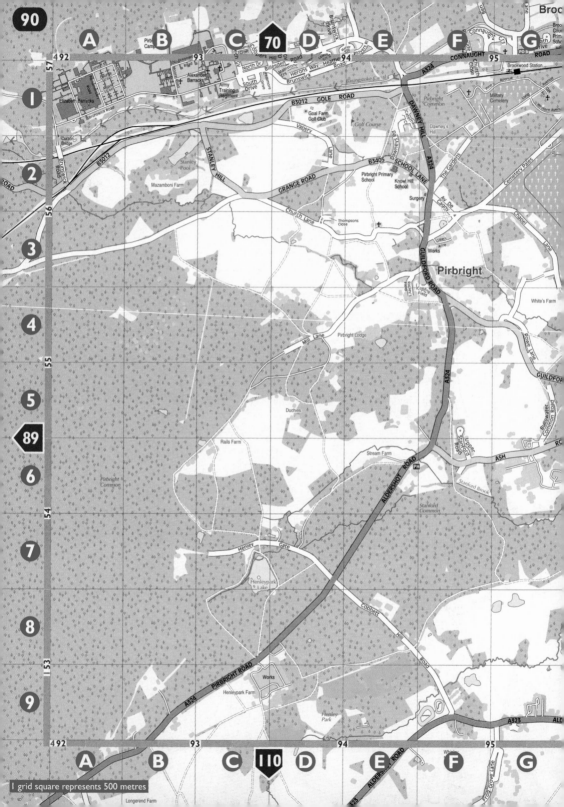

I grid square represents 500 metres

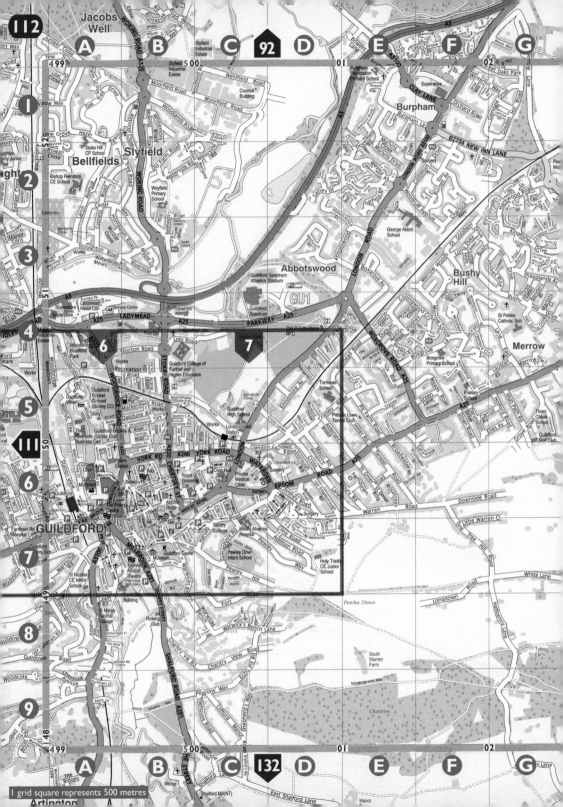

A B C **94** D E EPSOM ROAD F G

506 07 08 09

1

52

2

3

51

4

5

113 50

6

7

49

8

9

148 506 07 08 09

A B C **134** D E F G

Scale: 1 grid square represents 500 metres

East Clandon
Hatchlands Park (NT)
Back Lane
The Street
New Road
School La
Blossom Road
Staple Lane
Blake's Lane
Blake's Lane Farm
High Clandon
A246
Wix Farm
Wix Hill
Butter's Hill
PO
Cranmore Lane
Cranmore School
School La
Mount Pleasant
Centre
Business Centre
Elms Farm
Lark
The Sheepleas
Jeffries Road
Shere Road
Hook Wood
Fullers Farm
Killers Farm Road
Pebble Hill
Hillside Farm
Green Dene
Mountain House
Horsley
Clandon Downs
Old Scotland Farm
Woodcote Lodge
Shere Road
Shere Road
Combe Lane
Green Dene
Netley Heath
Staple Lane
North Downs Way
Combe Bottom
Combe Lane
Hollister Farm
North Downs Way
Colekitchen Farm
Colekitchen Lane
Silent Pool
Sherbourne Farm
SHERE ROAD A25
Netley House
A248
SHERBOURNE
Tilling Bourne
Shere
SHERE ROAD A25
Ubley Lane
Rectory La
Church La
Middle St
London La
Gravel Pits La
New Rd
Gosse Gn
Gomshall Station
STATION ROAD
Bennett Road
PO

124

A · B · C · 104 · D · E · F · G

541 | 42 | 43 | 44

Limpsfield Common

1

Stonewood Road · B269 · KENT HATCH ROAD · Ridlands Grove · Moorhouse Road · The High Chart · Goodley Stock

52

2

Pains Hill · Pastens Road · Tenchley's Lane · Tenchleys Park · Greenland Way · Carton Lane · Tally Road · Limpsfield Chart · Kent Hatch · Crockhamhill Common · KENT HATCH ROAD · B269

3

Short Lane · Boulthurst Farm · Chapel Road

Tenchleys Manor · Trevereux · Croc

RH8 · 51

4

Garst Lane · Itchingwood Common Road · Itchingwood Common · The Moat Farm · Vanguard Way · Oakdene Lane · Crockh Hill Co. Primary

LC

5

Stockenden Farm · Swaynesland Road · Swaynesland · Hurst Farm · Dairy Lane · Dennettsland Road · B2026 MAIN ROAD · SPOUT LANE · B269

123 · 50

6

Guildables Lane · Redlands · Earylands · B2026

7

Brills Farm · Langhurst · Guildables Wood · Rushett

49

High Farm

8

Staffhurst Wood Road · Black Robins Farm · Monks Lane · Staffhurst Wood · Gaywood · Hole Lane · Scamperdale · B2026 MAIN ROAD

9

White House · Caper's Farm · Batchelor's Farm · Troy Town · Homestead Road · Fairmead Road · Swan Lane Farm · Marlpit Hill

541 | 42 | 43 | 44

A · B · C · 144 · D · E · F · G

Bombers · Hilders Lane · Hilders · Marlinhurst · Meadow Lane · Little

1 grid square represents 500 metres

H J K L 105 M

45 46 48

French Street

117e Chart

The Philippines

Emmetts Road

Emmetts Garden (NT)

I

52

Horns Hill

Scords Wood

Id Hi

Hosey Common Lane

Mapleton Road

Greensand Way

2

Chartwell (NT)

Scords Lane

PH

Hill

3

51

Chartwell

Froghole

Puddledock Lane

Bardogs Farm

Toy's Hill

am Hill

Froghole Lane

Puddledock

4

ool

Tan House

5

50

Obriss Farm

Crockham Grange

B269

Mapleton Road

Boons Park

6

Coakham Farm

Toy's Hill

Mapleton

7

49

Chittende

Pootings

B2042 GREEN LANE

Holmwood Place

Roodlands Lane

8

Pootings Road

B269

Roodlands Farm

9

48

Broxham Manor

Four Elms

Stokes Close

Four Elms Primary School

Hillcrest

45 46 47 48

H J K L 145 M N P

Mowshurst

B2027

Broxham House

Four Elms Road

Five Fields Lane

Hill C

Furnace Ho Farm

Swan Lane

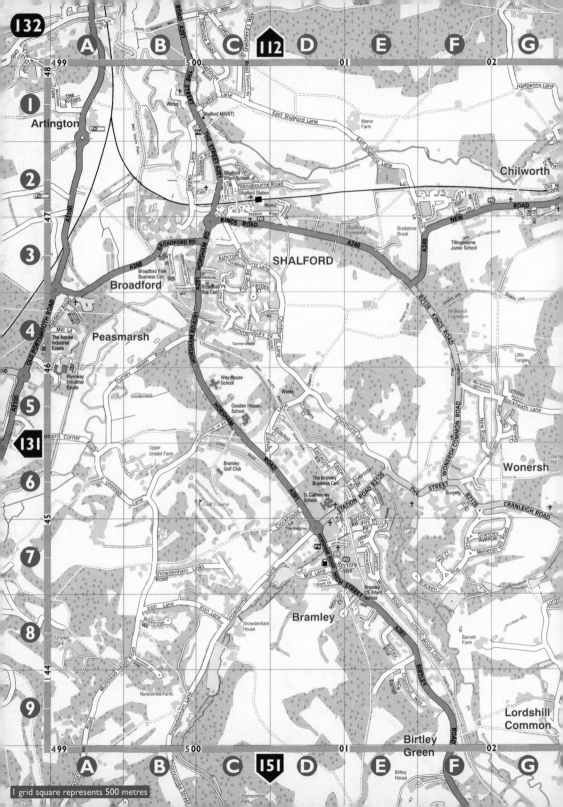

A B C **114** D E F G

5 06 48 07 SHERE 08 A25 09

SHERE ROAD A25

SHERE ROAD

1

2

3 Albury Heath

4 Brook

133

5

6 Farley Green

7

8

9

Burrows Cross

Gomshall

Abinger Hammer

Hoe

Peaslake

Hound House

Winterfold Wood

5 06 07 **153** 08 09

A B C **153** D E F G

I grid square represents 500 metres

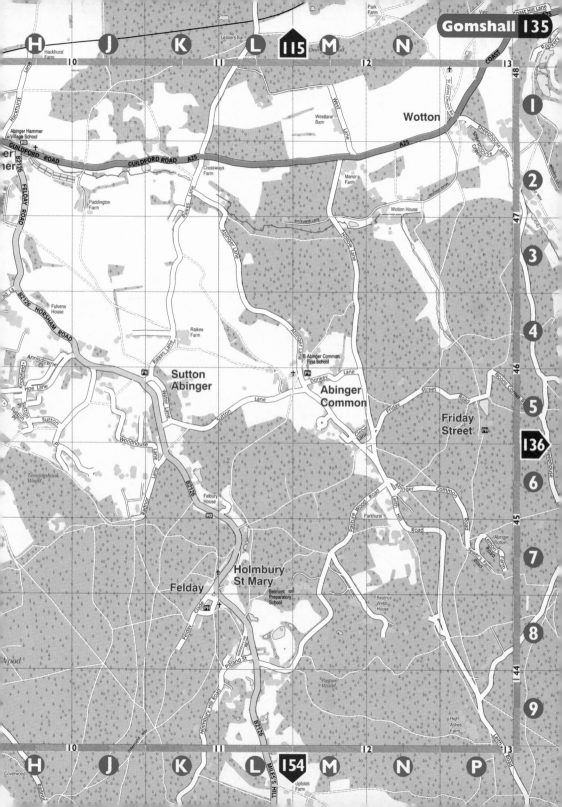

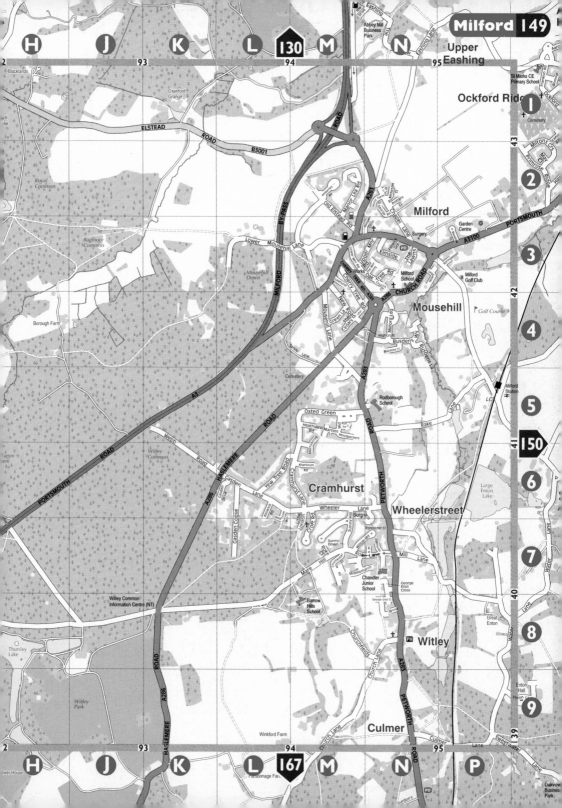

A **B** **C** **D** **E** **F** **G**

503 04 05

Stonards Brow
Sweetwater La
PH
PO
Woodhill
Woodhill
Woodlands
Farey H

Longacre
School
Longcroft
Chestnut Ave
First
Hullbrook
Hull
Greenland Way
Church La
Woodhill
Madgehole La

I
43
Hullbrook
House
Greenland Way
Church Hill B2128
Franklin's
Farm
Madgehole

2
Greenland Way
Greenland Way
Stroud Common
Willinghurst House

3
42
Rushett
Common
Upper
House
Run Common
Stroud
Guildford Road

4
Grafham
Down Link
Upper House Lane
East Whipley Lane
B2128
Smithwood
Common
Road
Algernbrook
Smithwood
Common

5
41
Whipley
Manor
Down Link
Wey South Path
Guildford Road B2128
Smithwood Av
Strathavon
Crescent

6
Palmers
Cross
A281 Horsham Road
Rowly
Farm
Rowly Drive
Restwell Av
PO
Rowly
Upfold

7
Fisny
Farm
Peppercorn Mews
Brooklands
Farm
Down Link
Manfield Pk
Cranleigh
School

8
40
Lane
Wey South Path
Down Link
Garden Centre
B2128
Woodcote
Cranleigh
Preparatory
School

9
39
Horsham Road
Rydinghurst
Elm Grove
Westbrook
Meadows
Lashmere
Bruton
College
Hewitts
Industrial
Estate
Little
Mead Industrial
Estate
B2130
Guildford Road
St James's Place
Regal
Cinema
East View
Downs Lane
B2128
Glebelands
School
Parsonage Rd
Middle Sch
Victoria Rd
High Street
Cranleigh
Health
Cranl
Field

Smithbrook
Clinic

A **B** **C** **D** **E** **F** **G**

503 04 05

A281
BARKLINE
B2130
ELMBRIDGE
Essex Drive
Nanhurst
Wey South Path

A   B   C   137   D   E   F   G

517   18   19

RHC
I
nickfold

43

Moorhurst Lane

Holmwood
Station

Horsham

Leith

Henfold
Henfold
Henfold Drive

The Weald CE
Primary School
Newdigate
Rd

Beare Green

Trouts
Farm

Gaterounds
Farm

2

A29

Arnolds

Parkgate Road

Knowle

Wigmore

A24

BOGNOR ROAD

Wigmore
Lane

Works

Village Street

Underhill
Road

Newdigate

Newdigate
Endowed CE
Infant School

A24 42

3

Hoyle Hill

Hoyle
Farm

Thunderfield

Trig

Kingsland

Winfield Gr

Church

Surgery

PH

D

4

Seaman's Green

Horsham Road

Hillhouse
Farm

Street

Rusper Road

Ryecroft
Lane

Misbrooks Green Road

Broomell's
Farm

5

The Street

Mizbrook Farm

Greens
Farm

Young'
Fa

155
41

Mortimer Road

Vicarage

Lane

Temple

Aldhurst
Farm

Tanhurst
Farm

6

PO

Scott
Broadwood
Infant School

Capel

Ockley
Station

Nursery
Bake

Temple
Lane

LANE

B2126

Cole's
Lane

Bennetts Wd

The Street

Woolvet Hill

Rushetts

Woodland
Drive

7

40

A24

8

Grenehurst
Park

Clark's
Green

Temple
Elfande

Road

9

139

Pleystowe
Farm

Rusper Road

517   18   19

A   B   C   174   D   E   F   G

HORSHAM

Taylors

Clock

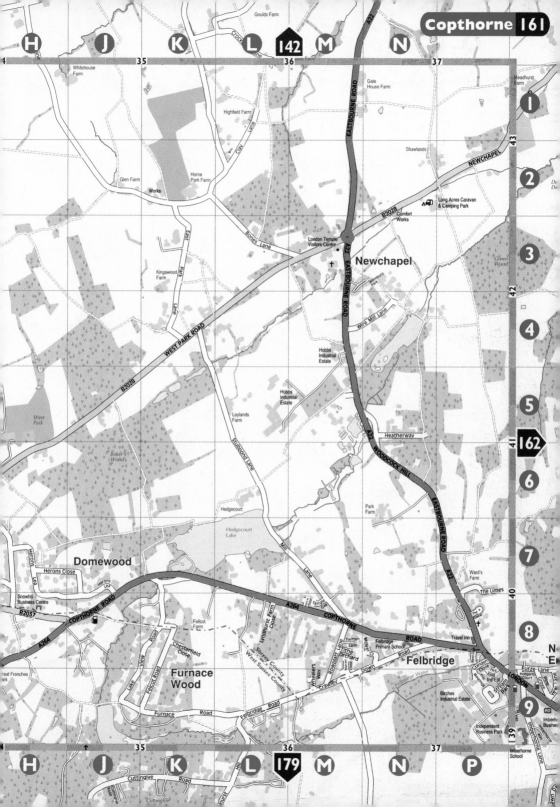

H J K L **142** M N

4 35 36 37

I

Goulds Farm

A22

Whitehouse Farm

Meadhurst Farm

Gate House Farm

1

EASTBOURNE ROAD

Highfield Farm

Shawlands

43

NEWCHAPEL

2

Glen Farm

Horne Park Farm

B2028

Long Acres Caravan & Camping Park

42

Works

Comfort Works

Clay Lane

Bones Lane

London Temple Visitors Centre

Newchapel

3

Green Wood

Kingswood Farm

A22

Park Lane

Stanbury Park

EASTBOURNE ROAD

4

East Park Lane

WEST PARK ROAD

Wire Mill Lane

Hobbs Industrial Estate

5

B2028

West Park

Laylands Farm

Hobbs Industrial Estate

Bakers Wood

Heatherway

41 **162**

A22

WOODCOCK HILL

6

Stumblehole Lane

Hedgecourt

Park Farm

EASTBOURNE ROAD

7

Hedgecourt Lake

Mill Lane

Ward's Farm

The Limes

Domewood

Herons Close

Herons Lea

Snowhill Business Centre

A22

40

8

B2037

COPTHORNE ROAD

A264

Lyndhurst Farm Close

A264

Tandridge Lane

Travel Inn

Fellcot Farm

Lake View Road

Felcot Road

Chesterfield Close

Furnace Wood

Surrey County

West Sussex County

Wheelers Way

Crawley

COPTHORNE ROAD

Tithe Orchard

Twitten Lane

Rowplatt Lane

Moat Road

Felbridge Primary School

Down Road

Felbridge

LONDON ROAD

Furze Lane

N E

9

Great Frenches Park

Furnace Road

Felbridge Road

Felbridge Water

Birches Industrial Park

Independent Business Park

Imberhorne Lane

139

Imberhorne School

H J K L **179** M N **P**

35 36 37

Cuttinglye Road

I grid square represents 500 metres

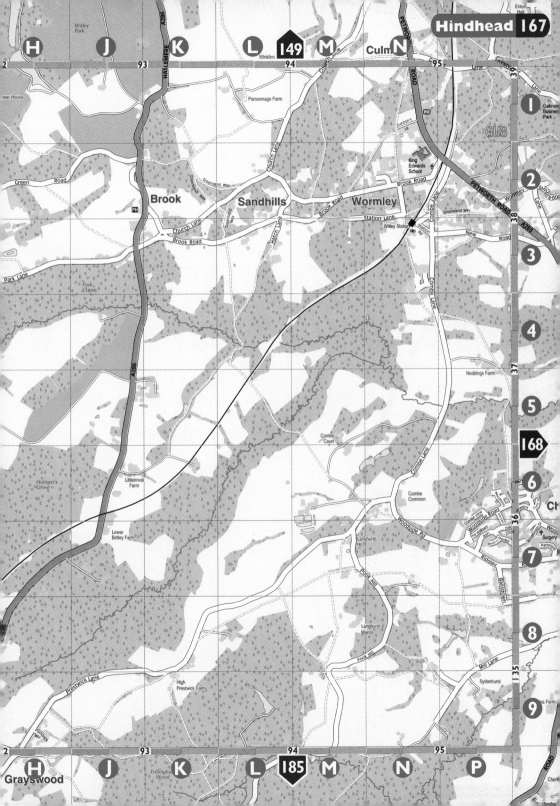

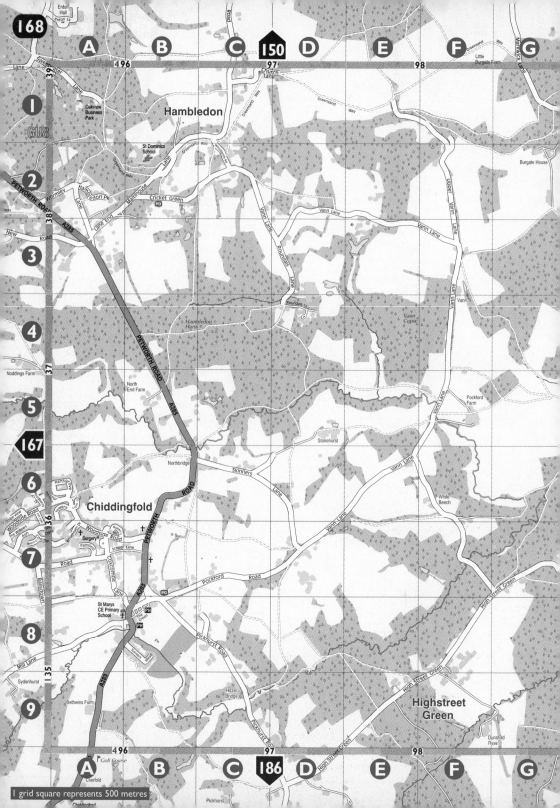

H J K L **151** M N

9 **5 00** 01 02 **39**

Smithbrook Clinic

The Hurtwood

GODALMING ROAD

B2130

1

STOVOLDS HILL BAR

The Raswell

Nore

Painshill Farm

2

Markwick Lane

Markwick Lane

B2130

Hookhouse Rd

Loxhill

GODALMING ROAD

DUNSFOLD ROAD

Park Hatch

STOVOLDS HILL

38

3

Park Farm

Peartree Green

Hookhouse Road

Windways

Dunsfold Common Road

High Loxley

High Billinghurst Farm

37

4

Field Place

Dunsfold Green

Holy Loxley Road

Works

5

170

Church Road

Church Road

Nuges Close

St Nicolas School

Binharns Lea

The Mews

Dunsfold

Dunsfold Aerodrome

6

36

PO

PH

Oak Tree Close

Dunsfold Common Road

Mill Lane

Sun Road

Alfold Road

Common House

7

Works

Barnfield

Chiddingfold Road

Blacknest Farm

Chiddingfold Road

Plaistow Road

Wrotham Hill

Knightons Lane

Chapel Hill

Dunsfold Common

Alfold Road

Wey South Path

8

35

9

Rams Lane

Lane

Hurlands

Hurlands

Sidney Wood

9 **5 00** 01 02

H J K L **187** M N P

Knightons

Wey South Path

169

152

188

1 grid square represents 500 metres

Alfold

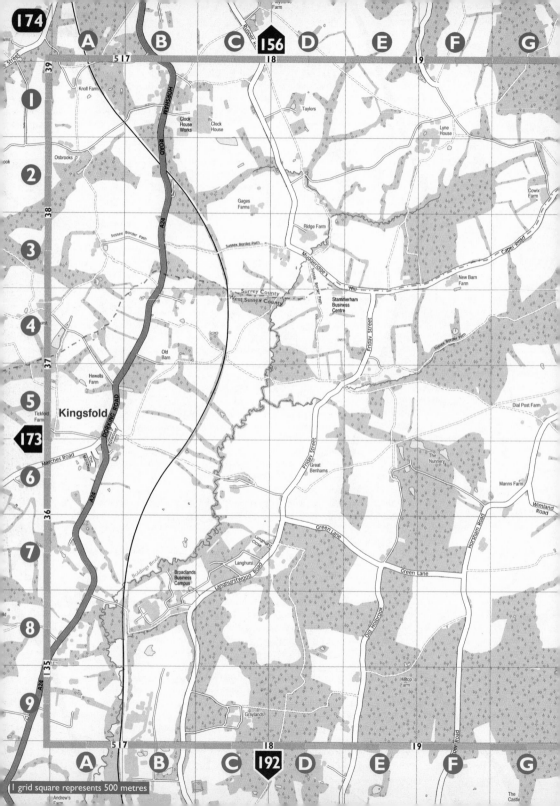

174

A   B   C 156 D   E   F   G

5 17   18   19

39

1

Knoll Farm

Clock House Works
Clock House

Taylors

Lyne House

38

2

Osbrooks

ook

Gages Farms

Cowix Farm

Ridge Farm

Capel Road

3

Sussex Border Path

Sussex Border Path

Murgeroge's

Sussex Border Path

New Barn Farm

Hill

37

4

HORSHAM ROAD

A24

urst

Old Barn

Surrey County
West Sussex County

Sussex Border Path

Stammerham Business Centre

Friday Street

Hewells Farm

5

Tickfold Farm

Kingsfold

173

DORKING ROAD

Dial Post Farm

6

Marches Road

Friday Street

Great Benhams

The Nunnery

Manns Farm

36

A24

Wimland Road

7

Bolding Brook

Langhurst Close

Langhurst

Green Lane

Green Lane

Broadlands Business Campus

Langhurstwood Road

Old Holbrook

Horsham Road

8

35

A24

Hilltop Farm

9

Graylands

Trev Road

A   B   C 192 D   E   F   G

5 17   18   19

Andrew's Farm

The Castle

1 grid square represents 500 metres

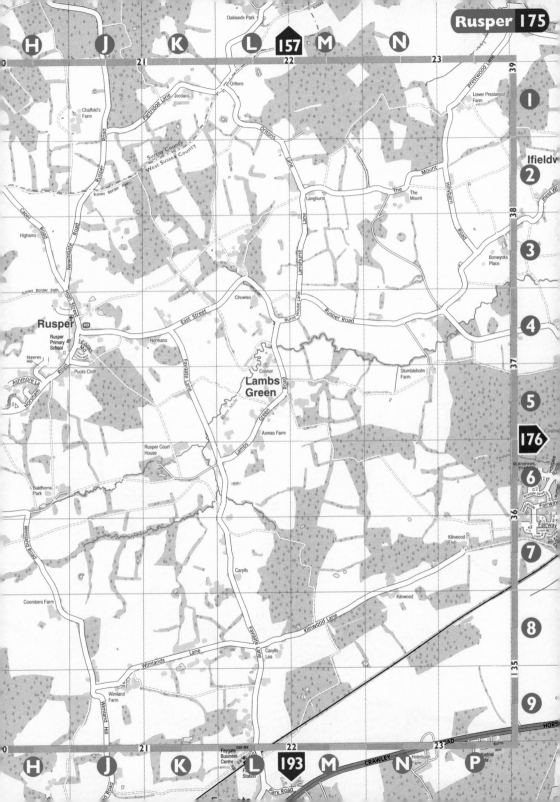

COPTHORNE

160

177

A B C D E F G

1 2 3 4 5 6 7 8 9

Junction 10a

RH10

Worth Abbey
Worth School

Copthorne Common
Copthorne Golf Club
Copthorne Hotel London Gatwick
Copthorne Squash Club
Pot Common
Golf Course
Old Rowfant
Ley House
Home Farm
Rowfant
Crabbet Park
Gatwick Worth Hotel
Hayheath
Worth Way
Wallage Lane
Works
Hundred Acres
Compasses Corner
Rowfant Business Centre
Miswells House
Worth Hall
Turners Hill Road
Tulleys Farm
Manor Hill
Worthlodge Forest
Standinghall Farm
The Grove
Paddockhurst Road
Coldharbour Farm
South Hill
Church Road

Copthorne Way
Turners Hill Road
Balcombe Road

Wakehurst Green Farm
Wymate Garden Centre
Burleigh Wood
Kelso Close
Hexham Close

Oak Close
Westway
Briggelands
The Meadow
Akehurst Close
Brookhill
Church Lane
Bramble Close
Spring Gardens

Shepherd's Farm
Turners Hill
Snow Hill
Barn Court

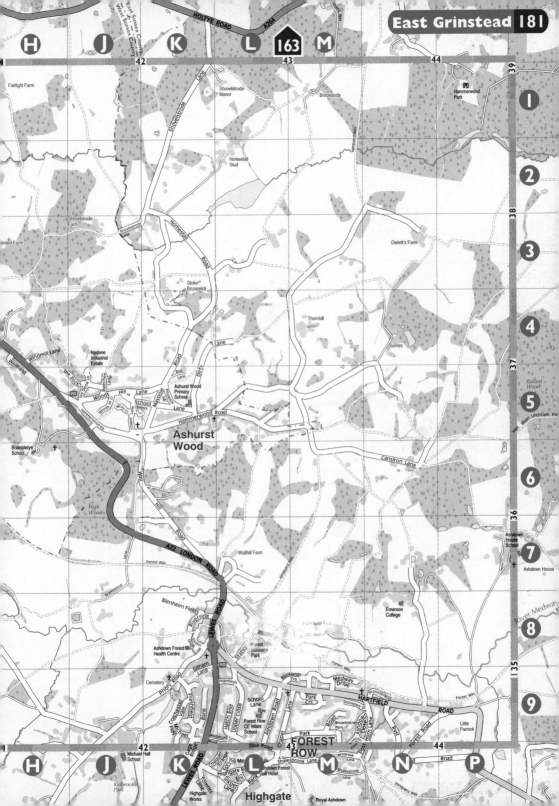

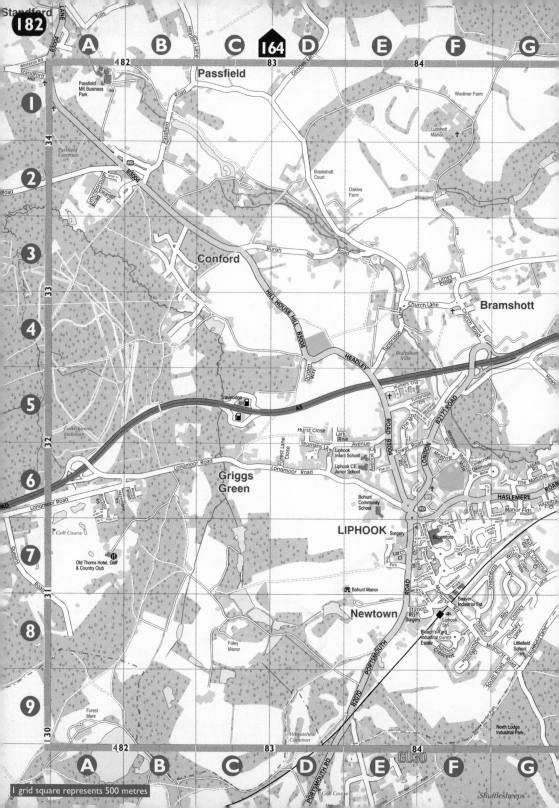

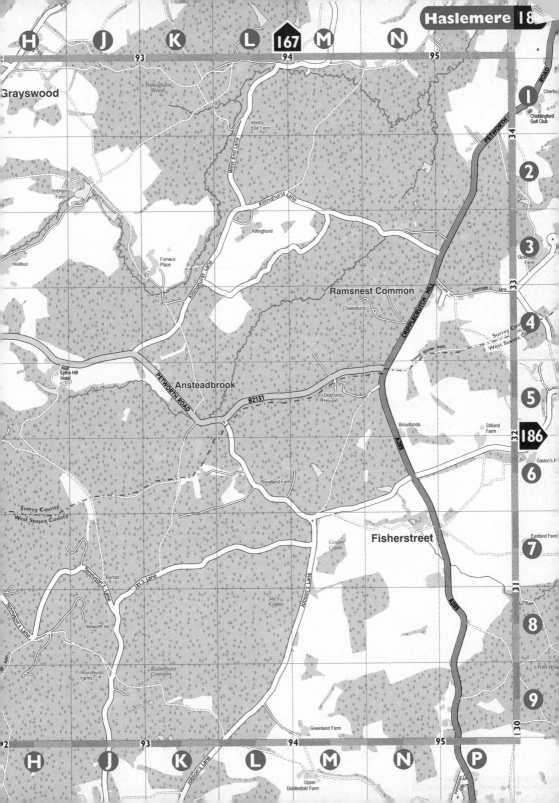

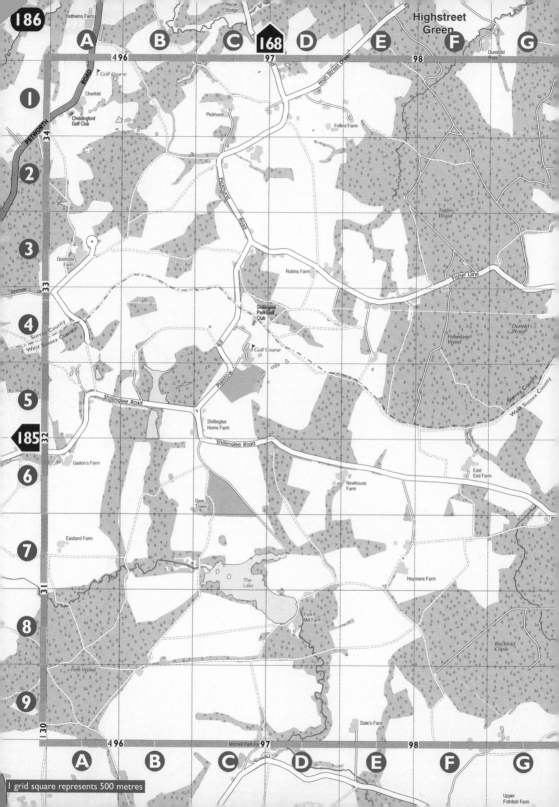

Aaron's Hill 131 H9
Abbey Mead 37 M7
Abbotswood 112 D3
Abinger Common 135 M5
Abinger Hammer 134 G2
Acton Green 18 B2
Addington 64 G5
Addlestone 55 N4
Addlestonemoor 45 P9
Addiscombe 133 N1
Albury 134 A3
Albury Heath 134 A3
Aldershot 108 E3
Alfold 188 C1
Alfold Bars 188 C3
Alfold Crossways 170 D8
Anerley 46 A5
Ansteadbrook 185 K5
Anthonys 72 E1
Aperfield 84 D6
Arford 164 B5
Artington 131 P1
Ascot 33 P4
Ash 109 J3
Ashford 23 J8
Ashford Common 23 N9
Ash Green 109 M6
Ashley Park 57 J2
Ashtead 77 L7
Ashurst Wood 181 K5
Ash Vale 89 J9
Badshot Lea 108 E8
Bagshot 51 L6
Bagshot Heath 51 N8
Baldwins Hill 162 B9
Balham 29 J5
Bandonhill 62 F4
Banstead 79 L5
Barford 165 H3
Barnes 18 F6
Barwell 59 J6
Batt's Corner 146 A5
Beacon Hill 165 N4
Beare Green 20 C4
Beaumont 47 H4
Beckenham 62 G1
Beddington 44 C8
Beddington Corner 18 D1
Bedford Park 112 A2
Bellfields 112 A2
Bell Green 31 N6
Bellingham 31 P7
Belmont 61 L7
Benhilton 61 M2
Berrylands 41 M7
Berry's Green 84 E5
Betchworth 118 A4
Bewbush 176 C8
Biggin Hill 83 P6
Binscombe 131 J5
Birch Hill 32 E8
Birtley Green 132 E9
Bishopsgate 20 E7
Bisley 71 H5
Blackbrook 137 L3
Black Corner 159 N8
Blackheath 133 J4
Blacknest 35 J4
Blackwater 67 P4
Blackwell 180 D1
Bletchingley 121 M5
Blindley Heath 142 D5
Boundstone 127 M9
The Bourne 127 N7
Bowlhead Green 166 F2
Bowling Alley 106 C6
Box Hill 117 N3
Bracknell 32 F5
Bramley 132 D8
Bramshott 182 F4
Brands Hill 12 F5
Brasted 105 M8
Brasted Chart 17 K4
Brentford 17 H4
Brentford End 17 H4
Brewer Street 121 L2
Brick Hill 53 J3
Bridge Hill 74 D9
Broadbridge Heath 191 J6
Broadfield 176 F9
Broadford 132 A3
Broad Green 45 K8
Broadham Green 123 J3
Broadmoor 136 B5
Brockham 117 N6
Brockham Park 138 A1
Brockley 31 N1
Bromley 47 P3
Bromley Park 47 L2
Brook 134 A4
Brook 167 K2
Brook Green 56 J7
Brooklands 70 C9
Brookwood 70 C9
Broomhall 34 F8
Buchan Hill 194 D2
Buckland 118 E4
Bucks Green 189 L4
Bullbrook 33 H3
Bunce Common 138 B3

Burgh Heath 79 H8
Burntcommon 93 K5
Burpham 112 E1
Burrowhill 53 M7
Burrows Cross 134 D3
Burstow 160 B5
Burwood Park 57 J4
Busbridge 150 F2
Bushbury 137 N1
Bushey Mead 43 H4
Bushy Hill 112 F3
Byfleet 73 P2
Camberley 68 G1
Camelsdale 184 B5
Cannon Hill 43 H5
Capel 156 C6
Carshalton 62 A3
Carshalton Beeches 62 A7
Carshalton on the Hill 62 B6
Cartbridge 92 F2
Castle Green 101 N3
Caterham 131 N7
Catteshall 101 K4
Chaldon 129 J8
Charleshill 129 J8
Charlton 38 E3
Charlwood 158 C5
The Chart 125 M1
Chattern Hill 23 L7
Chavey Down 33 K3
Cheam 61 K4
Cheapside 34 E3
Chelsham 82 G6
Chertsey 37 L8
Chertsey Meads 38 A9
Chessington 59 L5
Chiddingfold 168 A6
Chilworth 132 G2
Chipstead 80 C8
Chiswick 18 D2
Chobham 110 B6
Christmaspie 110 F1
Church Crookham 106 F1
Church End 94 B1
Church Town 122 C2
Churt 165 J2
Clapham Park 29 N2
Claremont Park 58 A6
Clark's Green 156 B8
Claygate 58 F5
Clock House 80 E3
Cobham 75 J3
Cold Ash Hill 183 H5
Coldharbour 136 D8
Cole Park 25 P2
Coles Meads 120 B2
Colgate 193 P4
College Town 50 A8
Collier's Wood 43 P7
Colnbrook 12 C6
The Common 128 B4
Compton 128 B4
Compton 130 G2
Coney Hall 65 L3
Conford 182 C3
Coombe 42 C1
Cooper's Hill 21 J6
Copse Hill 42 E1
Copthorne 160 C9
Cottenham Park 42 F2
Coulsdon 80 G5
Cove 88 A1
Cox Green 171 P9
Cramhurst 149 M6
Cranford 15 J5
Cranleigh 171 J2
Crawley 177 H4
Crawley Down 179 H6
Crawley Hill 68 G3
Cricket Hill 50 C4
Critchmere 183 P3
Crockham Hill 124 G4
Crondall 106 C7
Crooked Billet 27 N9
Crookham Village 86 C9
Crosswater 147 H8
Crossways 165 H2
Crowhurst 143 K2
Crowhurst Lane End 122 C9
Crownpits 150 D1
Crown Wood 32 F7
Crowthorne 49 J4
Croydon 2 E5
Crystal Palace 31 H8
Cudham 85 H4
Cudworth 157 K4
Culmer 149 N9
Darby Green 67 L2
Datchet Common 12 A7
Dawesgreen 138 C2
Deepcut 89 L1
Deepdene 117 K7
Denbies 116 D5
Dippenhall 127 H3
Dockenfield 146 C6
Dogmersfield 86 A9
Domewood 161 J7
Donkey Town 70 D2
Dora's Green 106 C9
Dorking 117 H8

Dormansland 162 G3
Dormans Park 162 D5
Doversgreen 119 M9
Down Park 179 H2
Downside 75 K8
Dulwich 30 C5
Dulwich Village 30 F3
Dunsfold 169 L6
Dunsfold Common 169 L7
Dunsfold Green 169 L5
Earl's Court 19 L3
Earlsfield 28 F4
Earlswood 120 B7
Eashing 130 F8
East Bedfont 23 L3
East Clandon 114 A2
East Dulwich 31 H1
East Ewell 61 H8
East Green 126 C7
East Grinstead 180 D1
Easthampstead 32 D5
East Horsley 94 F7
East Molesey 40 C6
East Sheen 27 J1
Edenbridge 144 E3
Eden Park 46 F5
Effingham 95 M7
Egham 21 M9
Egham Hythe 22 A9
Egham Wick 35 M1
Ellen's Green 171 P7
Elm Corner 74 C8
Elmers End 46 D4
Elstead 148 E1
Elvetham 86 B2
Elvetham Heath 86 E3
Englefield Green 150 A6
Enton Green 78 A3
Epsom 78 C3
Esher 58 C3
Eversley 48 B9
Eversley Centre 48 B9
Eversley Cross 48 C9
Ewell 60 F9
Ewhurst 153 P7
Ewhurst Green 153 P8
Ewshot 106 C6
Fairlands 111 K2
Fairmile 75 P1
Farleigh 82 F5
Farleigh Court 82 G3
Farley Green 134 A6
Farnborough 88 C3
Farnborough Green 88 B2
Farnborough Park 88 F4
Farnborough Street 88 E2
Farncombe 131 K5
Farnham 4 E5
Faygate 193 L3
Felbridge 161 N8
Felcourt 162 B4
Felday 135 K7
Feltham 24 C5
Felthamhill 23 P8
Fernhill 159 P5
Fetcham 96 D3
Fickleshole 83 L3
Field Common 39 P8
Finchampstead 48 B6
Fisherstreet 185 N7
Fleet 86 G6
Flexford 110 D5
Folly Hill 107 L9
Force Green 105 J4
Forestdale 64 E7
Forest Green 154 F5
Forest Hill 31 L4
Four Elms 125 L9
Fox Corner 91 J5
Fox Lane 68 B7
Fredley 97 H9
French Street 125 K1
Frensham 146 E5
Friday Street 135 P5
Frimley 69 J6
Frimley Green 69 H9
Frimley Ridge 69 J5
Frith Hill 131 K7
Frogholt 125 H5
Frogmore 67 M2
Fulham 19 H5
Furnace Green 177 K2
Furnace Wood 161 K9
Furzedown 29 L7
Gadbrook 118 B9
Gatton 100 B8
Giggshill 40 C8
Givons Grove 97 K5
Godalming 131 M9
Godstone 122 B2
Goldsworth Park 71 N5
Gomshall 134 E2
Goodley Stock 124 F1
Gossops Green 176 E6
Grafham 151 P4
Grayshott 165 L8
Grayswood 185 H1
Great Bookham 96 B6
Great Hollands 32 A7
Green Cross 165 L2
Griggs Green 182 C6

Grove Park 18 B6
Guildford 6 E7
Guildford Park 6 A4
Hackbridge 62 D1
Hale 107 P9
Ham 26 C6
Hambledon 168 B1
Hammer 183 M5
Hammer Bottom 183 L5
Hammersmith 18 F2
Hammerwood 181 M5
Hamm Moor 55 P5
Hampton 40 B2
Hampton Hill 25 K7
Hampton Wick 41 H2
Hamsey Green 82 C4
Hanworth 24 E6
Hanworth 32 C8
Harlington 14 E4
Harmans Water 32 F5
Harmondsworth 13 N4
Hascombe 151 K8
Haslemere 184 E4
Hatton 14 C9
Hatton Hill 52 D3
The Haven 189 N8
Hawk's Hill 96 F4
Hawley 68 A5
Hawley Lane 68 D9
Haxted 144 D5
Hayes 98 A6
Headley 164 A6
Headley 164 E7
Headley Down 164 E4
Hearn 107 P7
Heath End 107 P7
Heatherside 69 L4
Heathlands 49 K1
Herne Hill 30 D2
Hersham 57 L4
Heston 15 P5
Hever 145 N7
High Curley 51 M9
Highstreet Green 168 E9
Hill Park 104 F3
Hinchley Wood 58 F2
Hindhead 166 A4
Hoe 134 F5
Hog Hatch 107 K8
Holland 123 N4
Holloway Hill 150 D2
Holmbury St Mary 135 L7
Holmethorpe 120 D3
Holmwood Corner 137 K7
Holt Pound 127 H9
Honor Oak 31 L2
Honor Oak Park 31 M2
Hook 59 L4
Hook Heath 71 P9
Hookwood 158 F2
Hooley 100 C2
Horley 140 D8
Horne 141 P8
Horns Green 85 J6
Horsell 10 B1
Horsham 192 C6
Horton 12 E8
Hosey Hill 105 J8
Hounslow 16 A7
Hounslow West 15 M8
How Green 145 P3
Hurst Green 123 L3
Hurst Park 40 C3
Hurtmore 130 C6
Hydestile 150 D6
Hythe End 21 N6
Ifield 176 D3
Ifield Green 176 D2
Ifieldwood 176 A2
Ifold 187 P8
Irons Bottom 139 L4
Isleworth 17 H8
Jacobs Well 92 A9
Kenley 81 M5
Kensington 19 L1
Kew 17 P3
Kingfield 72 C9
Kingsfold 174 A5
Kingsley Green 184 A8
Kingston upon Thames 8 D2
Kingston Vale 27 J8
Kingswood 99 K3
Knaphill 71 J7
Knight's Hill 30 D4
Knockholt 85 L6
Knowle Green 22 E8
Knowle Hill 35 P8
Laker's Green 170 C7
Laleham 37 N4
Lambs Green 175 L5
Lampton 16 B6
Lane End 146 G5
Langley 12 D1
Langley Green 176 E1
Langley Vale 96 E1
Leatherhead 138 E3
Leigh 138 E5
Lett's Green 85 L3
Lightwater 52 C9
Limpsfield 103 M7

Limpsfield Chart 124 D2
Limpsfield Common 123 P1
Linchmere 183 K7
Lingfield 143 K9
Lingfield Common 143 K7
Liphook 182 D7
Little Bookham 95 H6
Littlefield Common 91 H9
Littlehaven 192 D5
Little Heath 75 P3
Little Sandhurst 49 L7
Littleton 38 D4
Littleton 131 N2
Littleton Common 38 D1
Littlewick 71 M5
Little Woodcote 62 C9
Logmore Green 136 B5
Longcross 53 P2
Long Ditton 41 H9
Longford 13 N6
Lordshill Common 132 G9
Lower Ashtead 77 J8
Lower Bourne 128 A7
Lower Feltham 23 P6
Lower Green 58 B1
Lower Halliford 57 H2
Lower Kingswood 99 L6
Lower Sydenham 31 L7
Lowfield Heath 159 J7
Loxhill 169 K3
Loxwood 188 B6
Lucas Green 70 D4
Luxted 84 E3
Maidenbower 177 M7
Malden Rushett 77 H1
Manor Royal 177 H1
Margery 99 P3
Marley Heights 184 A9
Marlpit Hill 144 F1
Marsh Green 144 F8
Martin's Heron 33 J4
Martyr's Green 74 G9
Maybury 11 J3
Mayes Green 154 F9
Mayford 92 A2
May's Green 75 H9
Mead Vale 119 N8
Meath Green 139 P8
Medhurst Row 145 M5
Merle Common 123 N7
Merrow 112 G4
Merstham 100 D8
Merton 43 L2
Merton Park 43 K3
Mickleham 97 H8
Middle Bourne 127 N9
Mid Holmwood 137 H4
Milford 149 N2
Millbridge 146 G3
Mill Lane 106 A5
Mimbridge 71 P2
Mitcham 44 D4
Mogador 99 D9
Monks Orchard 46 C8
Montgomery Lines 108 E2
Moorhouse Bank 104 E8
Moor Park 128 D4
Morden 43 L5
Morden Park 43 J7
Mortlake 18 A7
Motspur Park 42 E7
Mount Hermon 10 C7
Mousehill 149 N4
Mowshurst 145 J1
Mugswell 99 M5
Mytchett 88 G4
Mytchett Place 89 K3
Naldersward 138 G6
Nash 65 P5
New Addington 65 K6
New Beckenham 31 M9
Newchapel 161 M3
Newdigate 156 N6
New Haw 55 N6
Newlands Corner 113 M7
New Malden 42 D4
Newtown 182 E8
Norbiton 9 H4
Norbury 45 K3
Nork 79 H5
Norley Common 133 H8
Normandy 110 B2
Norney 130 E7
North Ascot 33 L3
North Camp 88 D9
North Cheam 61 H2
North End 162 A8
North Feltham 24 C1
Northgate 177 J3
North Holmwood 137 H6
North Hyde 15 N6
North Looe 78 G2
North Sheen 17 P2
North Town 108 G4
Norwood Green 16 A2
Norwood Hill 158 B1
Norwood New Town 30 E9
Nutcombe 165 N9
Nutfield 121 H5
Oakhill 192 E8

Oakwoodhill....172 G4	Reigate Hill....119 K3	Sidlow....139 M3	Three Bridges....177 J4	West End....57 P4
Oatlands Park....56 P3	Richings Park....13 J1	Sipson....14 B3	Thursley....148 D8	West End....70 F3
Ockford Ridge....149 P1	Richmond....26 D1	Slinfold....190 E7	Tilford....147 N1	West End....146 C4
Ockham....94 C2	Richmond Hill....26 D2	Slyfield....112 B2	Tilford Common....147 L3	Westerham....105 H7
Ockley....155 L7	Ridge Green....120 G8	Smallfield....160 B2	Tilford Reeds....147 L1	West Ewell....60 C6
Old Coulsdon....81 K9	Ripley....93 M1	South Ascot....34 A7	Tilgate....176 G8	Westfield....92 D2
Old Malden....42 B8	The Rise....34 E7	South Beddington....62 F5	Tilgate Forest Row....194 F5	West Green....176 F4
Old Windsor....20 E2	Roehampton....27 L1	South Croydon....63 K5	Tinsley Green....159 M8	West Heath....88 A2
Old Woking....72 F9	Roffey....192 F5	South Earlswood....140 A1	Tisman's Common....189 K5	West Hill....28 B3
Onslow Village....111 L7	Rosehill....43 M9	South Farnborough....88 F6	Titsey....104 A5	West Horsley....94 D8
Osterley....16 C5	Rose Hill....116 G7	Southfields....28 D4	Tittenhurst....35 J4	Westhumble....116 G2
Ottershaw....54 G4	Rotten Green....86 D2	Southgate....176 G7	Tolworth....41 N9	West Kensington....19 H5
Outwood....141 L5	Roundshaw....63 H5	South Godstone....122 F9	Tongham....109 H8	West Molesey....39 P5
Owlsmoor....49 P7	Rowhook....190 F1	South Holmwood....137 H7	Tooting....29 J8	West Norwood....30 D7
Oxshott....76 C2	Rowledge....146 C1	South Kensington....19 N3	Tooting Graveney....28 G8	Weston Green....40 E9
Oxted....103 K9	Rowly....152 E6	South Merstham....120 F1	Tower Hill....117 H9	West Wickham....47 K9
Pachesham Park....76 C5	Row Town....55 K5	South Norwood....45 M4	Toy's Hill....125 N3	Weybourne....108 B8
Pains Hill....124 A2	Rudgwick....189 M3	South Nutfield....120 C7	Troy Town....124 D9	Weybridge....56 K3
Palmers Cross....151 P6	Runfold....128 E2	South Park....119 J8	Trumpsgreen....36 A7	Wheelerstreet....149 N6
Park Barn....111 L4	Rushmoor....147 M5	South Street....84 D8	Tuesley....150 B4	Whitebushes....140 D1
Parkgate....138 B9	Rushmore Hill....85 N2	South Wimbledon....28 F8	Tulse Hill....30 C4	Whiteley Village....57 H7
Park Langley....47 J7	Rusper....175 H4	Southwood....87 M4	Turners Hill....179 H7	Whitton....25 K2
Park Street....190 D7	Russell Hill....63 H8	Spitals Cross....144 G2	Twickenham....25 M4	Whyteleafe....81 P7
Parsons Green....19 L7	Russ Hill....157 P7	Spreakley....146 E4	Tyler's Green....122 B1	Wick Hill....32 E1
Passfield....182 C1	Rydens....57 L1	Spring Grove....16 D6	Tyrell's Wood....97 N4	Wick Hill....48 E3
Paynes Green....173 K3	Rydeshill....111 K3	Spring Park....64 G1	Up Green....66 C2	Wildridings....32 B5
Pease Pottage....194 D3	St George's Hill....56 M7	Staines....22 C7	Upper Eashing....130 C9	Willey Green....110 D2
Peaslake....134 F7	St Helier....43 N9	Stanwell....22 F2	Upper Elmers End....46 F6	Wimbledon....28 B8
Peasmarsh....132 A4	Saint Hill....180 C7	Stanwell Moor....22 D2	Upper Hale....107 M8	Wimble Hill....126 E3
Penge....46 C1	St Johns....71 N8	Stoke D'Abernon....75 N4	Upper Halliford....38 F5	Windlesham....52 B5
Peper Harow....130 C8	St Margarets....26 B2	Stonebridge....137 K1	Upper Ifold....187 M3	Winkfield Row....33 J1
Petersham....26 D4	Salfords....140 D4	Stonehill....54 C5	Upper Norwood....45 M2	Wisley....74 A4
Pirbright....90 F3	Sanderstead....64 A9	Stoneleigh....60 D4	Upper Shirley....64 C3	Witley....149 N8
Pitch Place....91 M9	Sandhills....167 L2	Stonequarry....162 F9	Upper Sydenham....31 H7	Woking....11 F4
Pitch Place....148 B9	SANDHURST....49 M8	Stoughton....111 P2	Upper Tooting....29 H6	Woldingham....102 G3
Pixham....117 J4	Sands End....19 N7	Strawberry Hill....25 L6	Valley End....52 G4	Woldingham Garden
Plaistow....187 L8	The Sands....128 G3	Streatham....29 P8	The Village....20 A6	Village....102 F1
Pondtail....87 K7	Sandy Cross....129 H1	Streatham Hill....29 P4	Virginia Water....36 A4	Wonersh....132 G6
Pootings....125 J7	Scotswood....34 D9	Streatham Park....29 L7	Waddon....63 H1	Woodbridge Hill....111 N3
Pot Common....148 D2	Seale....129 K1	Streatham Vale....44 D1	Walham Green....19 L6	Woodcote....62 G9
Pound Hill....177 M3	Seething Wells....41 H7	Strood Green....191 J4	Wallington....62 C4	Woodcote....78 B5
Povey Cross....158 F3	Selhurst....45 M6	Stroude....36 D3	Walliswood....172 F2	Woodcote Green....62 D8
Poyle....13 J6	Selsdon....64 C8	Summerstown....28 G5	Walton-on-Thames....39 J9	Woodham....55 L8
Prey Heath....91 P3	Send....92 G4	Sunbury....39 J4	Walton on the Hill....98 D4	Woodhatch....119 L8
Priestwood....32 A3	Send Grove....92 F6	Sunbury Common....39 H1	Wanborough....110 B8	Woodlands....16 D8
Puddledock....125 L4	Send Marsh....93 K3	Sunningdale....34 G6	Wandle Park....2 A4	Woodmansterne....79 P4
Purley....81 J1	Shackleford....130 D6	Sunninghill....34 D6	Wandsworth....19 L9	Woodside....46 A7
Putney....28 A1	Shalford....132 D3	Sunnymeads....12 C9	Warlingham....82 D7	Wood Street Village....110 F4
Putney Heath....27 P5	Shamley Green....133 J8	Sunnyside....180 D5	Warnham....191 M2	Woolmer Hill....183 M3
Putney Vale....27 M6	Sheerwater....72 G2	Surbiton....41 K9	Warren Corner....106 C2	Worcester Park....60 F1
Puttenham....110 B9	Sheets Heath....70 F8	Sutton....12 G3	Warwick Wold....101 J9	Wormley....167 M2
Pyle Hill....92 B5	Shellwood Cross....138 C5	Sutton....61 L4	Wasp Green....141 L6	Worplesdon....91 K7
Pyrford....73 K4	Shepherd's Hill....184 D4	Sutton Abinger....135 K5	Waterside....143 M6	Worth....177 P6
Pyrford Green....73 M6	Shepperton....38 C7	Sutton Green....92 D5	Weatherhill....160 C1	Wotton....135 N1
Pyrford Village....73 J7	Shepperton Green....38 C5	Tadworth....98 G2	The Wells....77 M3	Wray Common....119 P3
Rafborough....88 A4	Shere....114 C9	Tandridge....122 C4	West Barnes....42 C6	Wraysbury....21 K3
Ramsnest Common....185 M4	Shipley Bridge....160 A6	Tatsfield....84 B9	West Bedfont....23 J5	Wrecclesham....127 K7
Ranmore Common....116 C4	Shirley....64 C1	Teddington....25 L9	West Brompton....19 M4	The Wythe....62 A1
Rapkyns....191 H6	Shortfield Common....146 E2	Thames Ditton....40 G8	Westbrook....131 J8	Wyke....109 P3
Ravenswood Village	Shortheath....127 M7	Thorncombe Street....151 H3	West Byfleet....73 M2	Yateley....67 H2
Settlement....49 J2	Shortlands....47 L4	Thornton Heath....44 G6	West Clandon....93 M9	York Town....68 C4
Raynes Park....42 G4	Shottermill....183 P4	Thorpe....36 B5	Westcott....116 B8	
Redhill....120 C3	Shrubs Hill....35 J7	Thorpe Green....36 E5	West Drayton....13 P1	
Reigate....119 K5		Thorpe Lea....36 G1	West Dulwich....30 E5	

USING THE STREET INDEX

Street names are listed alphabetically. Each street name is followed by its postal town or area locality, the Postcode District, the page number, and the reference to the square in which the name is found.

Standard index entries are shown as follows:

Aaron's HI *GODL* GU7 ....131 J9

Street names and selected addresses not shown on the map due to scale restrictions are shown in the index with an asterisk:

Abbeville Ms *CLAP* SW4 * 29 N1

GENERAL ABBREVIATIONS

ACC....ACCESS	CLFS....CLIFFS	DR....DRIVE	GDNS....GARDENS	INT....INTERCHANGE
ALY....ALLEY	CMP....CAMP	DRO....DROVE	GLD....GLADE	IS....ISLAND
AP....APPROACH	CNR....CORNER	DRY....DRIVEWAY	GLN....GLEN	JCT....JUNCTION
AR....ARCADE	CO....COUNTY	DWGS....DWELLINGS	GN....GREEN	JTY....JETTY
ASS....ASSOCIATION	COLL....COLLEGE	E....EAST	GND....GROUND	KG....KING
AV....AVENUE	COM....COMMON	EMB....EMBANKMENT	GRA....GRANGE	KNL....KNOLL
BCH....BEACH	COMM....COMMISSION	EMBY....EMBASSY	GRG....GARAGE	L....LAKE
BLDS....BUILDINGS	CON....CONVENT	ESP....ESPLANADE	GT....GREAT	LA....LANE
BND....BEND	COT....COTTAGE	EST....ESTATE	GTWY....GATEWAY	LDG....LODGE
BNK....BANK	COTS....COTTAGES	EX....EXCHANGE	HGR....HIGHER	LGT....LIGHT
BR....BRIDGE	CP....CAPE	EXPY....EXPRESSWAY	HL....HILL	LK....LOCK
BRK....BROOK	CPS....COPSE	EXT....EXTENSION	HLS....HILLS	LKS....LAKES
BTM....BOTTOM	CR....CREEK	F/O....FLYOVER	HO....HOUSE	LNDG....LANDING
BUS....BUSINESS	CREM....CREMATORIUM	FC....FOOTBALL CLUB	HOL....HOLLOW	LTL....LITTLE
BVD....BOULEVARD	CRS....CRESCENT	FK....FORK	HOSP....HOSPITAL	LWR....LOWER
BY....BYPASS	CSWY....CAUSEWAY	FLD....FIELD	HRB....HARBOUR	MAG....MAGISTRATE
CATH....CATHEDRAL	CT....COURT	FLDS....FIELDS	HTH....HEATH	MAN....MANSIONS
CEM....CEMETERY	CTRL....CENTRAL	FLS....FALLS	HTS....HEIGHTS	MD....MEAD
CEN....CENTRE	CTS....COURTS	FLS....FLATS	HVN....HAVEN	MDW....MEADOWS
CFT....CROFT	CTYD....COURTYARD	FM....FARM	HWY....HIGHWAY	MEM....MEMORIAL
CH....CHURCH	CUTT....CUTTINGS	FT....FORT	IMP....IMPERIAL	MKT....MARKET
CHA....CHASE	CV....COVE	FWY....FREEWAY	IN....INLET	MKTS....MARKETS
CHYD....CHURCHYARD	CYN....CANYON	FY....FERRY	IND EST....INDUSTRIAL ESTATE	ML....MALL
CIR....CIRCLE	DEPT....DEPARTMENT	GA....GATE	INF....INFIRMARY	ML....MILL
CIRC....CIRCUS	DL....DALE	GAL....GALLERY	INFO....INFORMATION	MNR....MANOR
CL....CLOSE	DM....DAM	GDN....GARDEN		MS....MEWS

MSN ....MISSION	PKWY ....PARKWAY	R ....RIVER	SP ....SPUR	UPR ....UPPER
MT ....MOUNT	PL ....PLACE	RBT ....ROUNDABOUT	SPR ....SPRING	V ....VALE
MTN ....MOUNTAIN	PLN ....PLAIN	RD ....ROAD	SQ ....SQUARE	VA ....VALLEY
MTS ....MOUNTAINS	PLNS ....PLAINS	RDG ....RIDGE	ST ....STREET	VIAD ....VIADUCT
MUS ....MUSEUM	PLZ ....PLAZA	REP ....REPUBLIC	STN ....STATION	VIL ....VILLA
MWY ....MOTORWAY	POL ....POLICE STATION	RES ....RESERVOIR	STR ....STREAM	VIS ....VISTA
N ....NORTH	PR ....PRINCE	RFC ....RUGBY FOOTBALL CLUB	STRD ....STRAND	VLG ....VILLAGE
NE ....NORTH EAST	PREC ....PRECINCT	RI ....RISE	SW ....SOUTH WEST	VLS ....VILLAS
NW ....NORTH WEST	PREP ....PREPARATORY	RP ....RAMP	TDG ....TRADING	VW ....VIEW
O/P ....OVERPASS	PRIM ....PRIMARY	RW ....ROW	TER ....TERRACE	W ....WEST
OFF ....OFFICE	PROM ....PROMENADE	S ....SOUTH	THWY ....THROUGHWAY	WD ....WOOD
ORCH ....ORCHARD	PRS ....PRINCESS	SCH ....SCHOOL	TNL ....TUNNEL	WHF ....WHARF
OV ....OVAL	PT ....PORT	SE ....SOUTH EAST	TOLL ....TOLLWAY	WK ....WALK
PAL ....PALACE	PT ....POINT	SER ....SERVICE AREA	TPK ....TURNPIKE	WKS ....WALKS
PAS ....PASSAGE	PTH ....PATH	SH ....SHORE	TR ....TRACK	WLS ....WELLS
PAV ....PAVILION	PZ ....PIAZZA	SHOP ....SHOPPING	TRL ....TRAIL	WY ....WAY
PDE ....PARADE	QD ....QUADRANT	SKWY ....SKYWAY	TWR ....TOWER	YD ....YARD
PH ....PUBLIC HOUSE	QU ....QUEEN	SMT ....SUMMIT	U/P ....UNDERPASS	YHA ....YOUTH HOSTEL
PK ....PARK	QY ....QUAY	SOC ....SOCIETY	UNI ....UNIVERSITY	

POSTCODE TOWNS AND AREA ABBREVIATIONS

ACT ....Acton	CHEL ....Chelsea	FRIM ....Frimley	LTWR ....Lightwater	STRHM/NOR ....Streatham/Norbury
ADL/WDHM ....Addlestone/Woodham	CHERT ....Chertsey	FROW ....Forest Row	MFD/CHID ....Milford/Chiddingfold	STWL/WRAY ....Stanwell/Wraysbury
ALDT ....Aldershot	CHOB/PIR ....Chobham/Pirbright	FSTH ....Forest Hill	MORT/ESHN ....Mortlake/East Sheen	SUN ....Sunbury
ASC ....Ascot	CHSGTN ....Chessington	FUL/PGN ....Fulham/Parsons Green	MRDN ....Morden	SURB ....Surbiton
ASHF ....Ashford (Surrey)	CHSWK ....Chiswick	GDST ....Godstone	MTCM ....Mitcham	SUT ....Sutton
ASHTD ....Ashtead	CLAP ....Clapham	GODL ....Godalming	NRWD ....Norwood	SWTR ....Southwater
ASHV ....Ash Vale	COB ....Cobham	GSHT ....Grayshott	NWDGN ....Norwood Green	SYD ....Sydenham
BAGS ....Bagshot	COUL/CHIP ....Coulsdon/Chipstead	GT/LBKH ....Great Bookham/Little Bookham	NWMAL ....New Malden	TEDD ....Teddington
BAL ....Balham	CRAN ....Cranleigh	GU ....Guildford	ORP ....Orpington	THDIT ....Thames Ditton
BARN ....Barnes	CRAWE ....Crawley east	GUW ....Guildford west	OXTED ....Oxted	THHTH ....Thornton Heath
BECK ....Beckenham	CRAWW ....Crawley west	HASM ....Haslemere	PECK ....Peckham	TOOT ....Tooting
BELMT ....Belmont	CROY/NA ....Croydon/New Addington	HAYES ....Hayes	PETW ....Petworth	TWK ....Twickenham
BF/WBF ....Byfleet/West Byfleet	CTHM ....Caterham	HEST ....Heston	PGE/AN ....Penge/Anerley	VW ....Virginia Water
BFOR ....Bracknell Forest/Windlesham	CWTH ....Crowthorne	HMSMTH ....Hammersmith	PUR/KEN ....Purley/Kenley	WAND/EARL ....Wandsworth/Earlsfield
BH/WHM ....Biggin Hill/Westerham	DORK ....Dorking	HNHL ....Herne Hill	PUT/ROE ....Putney/Roehampton	WARL ....Warlingham
BIL ....Billingshurst	DTCH/LGLY ....Datchet/Langley	HNWL ....Hanwell	RCH/KEW ....Richmond/Kew	WBPTN ....West Brompton
BLKW ....Blackwater	DUL ....Dulwich	HOR/WEW ....Horton/West Ewell	RCHPK/HAM ....Richmond Park/Ham	WDR/YW ....West Drayton/Yiewsley
BMLY ....Bromley	E/WMO/HCT ....East & West Molesey/Hampton Court	HORL ....Horley	RDKG ....Rural Dorking	WDSR ....Windsor
BNFD ....Binfield	EA ....Ealing	HORS ....Horsham	REDH ....Redhill	WEA ....West Ealing
BNSTD ....Banstead	EBED/NFELT ....East Bedfont/North Feltham	HPTN ....Hampton	REIG ....Reigate	WEY ....Weybridge
BOR ....Bordon	ECT ....Earl's Court	HSLW ....Hounslow	RFNM ....Rural Farnham	WHTN ....Whitton
BRAK ....Bracknell	EDEN ....Edenbridge	HSLWW ....Hounslow west	RGUE ....Rural Guildford east	WIM/MER ....Wimbledon/Merton
BRKHM/BTCW ....Brockham/Betchworth	EDUL ....East Dulwich	HTHAIR ....Heathrow Airport	RGUW ....Rural Guildford west	WKENS ....West Kensington
BROCKY ....Brockley	EGH ....Egham	HTWY ....Hartley Wintney	RHWH ....Rural Haywards Heath	WLGTN ....Wallington
BRXN/ST ....Brixton north/Stockwell	EGRIN ....East Grinstead	HYS/HAR ....Hayes/Harlington	RPLY/SEND ....Ripley/Send	WNWD ....West Norwood
BRXS/STRHM ....Brixton south/Streatham Hill	EHSLY ....East Horsley	ISLW ....Isleworth	RSEV ....Rural Sevenoaks	WOKN/KNAP ....Woking north/Knaphill
BRYLDS ....Berrylands	EPSOM ....Epsom	IVER ....Iver	RYNPK ....Raynes Park	WOKS/MYFD ....Woking south/Mayford
BTFD ....Brentford	ESH/CLAY ....Esher/Claygate	KENS ....Kensington	SAND/SEL ....Sanderstead/Selsdon	WOT/HER ....Walton-on-Thames/Hersham
BTSEA ....Battersea	EW ....Ewell	KUT ....Kingston upon Thames	SHB ....Shepherd's Bush	WPK ....Worcester Park
CAR ....Carshalton	EWKG ....Wokingham east	KUTN/CMB ....Kingston upon Thames north/Coombe	SHGR ....Shamley Green	WWKM ....West Wickham
CAT ....Catford	FARN ....Farnborough	KWD/TDW/WH ....Kingswood/Tadworth/Walton on the Hill	SHPTN ....Shepperton	YTLY ....Yateley
CBLY ....Camberley	FELT ....Feltham	LEW ....Lewisham	SHST ....Sandhurst	
CHEAM ....Cheam	FLEETN ....Fleet north	LHD/OX ....Leatherhead/Oxshott	SKENS ....South Kensington	
	FLEETS ....Fleet south	LING ....Lingfield	SNWD ....South Norwood	
	FNM ....Farnham	LIPH ....Liphook	STA ....Staines	

1

1st Av KWD/TDW/WH KT20 ....99 J5
2nd Av KWD/TDW/WH KT20 ....99 J5
3rd Av KWD/TDW/WH KT20 ....99 J5
4th Av KWD/TDW/WH KT20 ....99 J5
5th Av KWD/TDW/WH KT20 ....99 J5
6th Av KWD/TDW/WH KT20 ....99 J5
7th Av KWD/TDW/WH KT20 ....99 J5
8th Av KWD/TDW/WH KT20 ....99 J6
9th Av KWD/TDW/WH KT20 ....99 J6
10th Av KWD/TDW/WH KT20 ....99 J6
11th Av KWD/TDW/WH KT20 ....99 J6
12th Av KWD/TDW/WH KT20 ....99 J6
13th Av KWD/TDW/WH KT20 ....99 J6
14th Av KWD/TDW/WH KT20 ....99 J6
15th Av KWD/TDW/WH KT20 ....99 K6
16th Av KWD/TDW/WH KT20 ....99 J6

A

Aaron's HI GODL GU7 ....131 J9
Abbess CI BRXS/STRHM SW2 ....30 C4
Abbetts La CBLY GU15 ....68 D5
Abbeville Ms CLAP SW4 ....29 N1
Abbeville Rd CLAP SW4 ....29 M2
Abbey CI BRAK RG12 ....32 F6
  WOKS/MYFD GU22 ....73 J5
Abbey Ct CHERT KT16 * 37 M8
Abbey Dr STA TW18 ....37 N5
  TOOT SW17 ....29 K8
Abbeyfield CI MTCM CR4 ....44 A3
Abbey Gdns CHERT KT16 ....37 L7
  HMSMTH W6 ....19 J4

Abbey Gn CHERT KT16 ....37 L7
  KENS W8 * 19 M1
Abbey La BECK BR3 ....46 C1
Abbey Ms STA TW18 * 37 N4
Abbey Pk BECK BR3 ....46 C1
Abbey PI CHERT KT16 * 37 L4
Abbey Rd CHERT KT16 ....37 M8
  CROY/NA CRO 2 B5
  SAND/SEL CR2 ....64 D8
  SHPTN TW17 ....38 C9
  VW GU25 ....36 B6
  WIM/MER SW19 ....43 L1
  WOKN/KNAP GU21 ....72 A6
Abbey St FNM GU9 ....5 C5
Abbey Wk E/WMO/HCT KT8 ....40 B1
Abbey Wy FARN GU14 ....88 E3
Abbey Wd ASC SL5 ....34 C8
Abbeywood ASHV GU12 * 109 K2
Abbot CI BF/WBF KT14 * 55 P8
  STA TW18 ....37 P1
Abbot Rd GU GU1 ....7 G6
Abbots Av HOR/WEW KT19 ....59 N9
Abbotsbury BRAK RG12 ....32 B6
Abbotsbury Ct SWTR RH13 ....192 D1
Abbotsbury Rd MRDN SM4 ....43 M5
  WWKM BR4 ....65 M1
Abbots CI FLEETN GU51 ....86 C6
  GUW GU2 ....111 L8
Abbots Dr VW GU25 ....36 A5
Abbotsfield Rd
  CRAWW RH11 ....176 A6
Abbotsford CI
  WOKS/MYFD GU22 ....11 H3
Abbots Gn CROY/NA CRO 64 D5
Abbots La PUR/KEN CR8 ....81 L4
Abbotsleigh CI BELMT SM2 ....61 M6
Abbotsleigh Rd
  STRHM/NOR SW16 ....29 M7
Abbotsmede CI TWK TW1 ....25 N5
Abbots Pk BRXS/STRHM SW2 ....30 B4
Abbot's Ride FNM GU9 ....128 A5
Abbots Rd CHEAM SM3 ....61 J3
Abbotstone Rd
  PUT/ROE SW15 ....18 G8

Abbots Wk CTHM CR3 ....102 B2
Abbotswell Rd BROCKY SE4 ....31 N1
Abbotswood GU GU1 ....112 D3
Abbotswood CI RGUE GU4 ....112 D2
Abbotswood Dr WEY KT13 ....56 F8
Abbotswood Rd
  STRHM/NOR SW16 ....29 N6
Abbott Av RYNPK SW20 ....43 H3
Abbott CI HPTN TW12 ....24 F9
Abbotts Md
  RCHPK/HAM TW10 * 26 D7
Abbotts Ri REDH RH1 ....120 C3
Abbotts Rd MTCM CR4 ....44 E5
Abbotts Tilt WOT/HER KT12 ....57 N2
Abelia CI CHOB/PIR GU24 ....70 E2
Abercairn Rd
  STRHM/NOR SW16 ....44 E1
Aberconway Rd MRDN SM4 ....43 M4
Abercorn CI SAND/SEL CR2 ....82 D1
Abercorn Wy
  WOKN/KNAP GU21 ....71 N7
Aberdare CI WWKM BR4 ....65 J1
Aberdeen Rd CROY/NA CRO 63 L3
Aberdeen Ter GSHT GU26 * 165 N8
Aberfoyle Rd
  STRHM/NOR SW16 ....29 N9
Abingdon CI BRAK RG12 ....32 G6
  WIM/MER SW19 ....28 F9
  WOKN/KNAP GU21 ....71 P7
Abingdon Rd KENS W8 ....19 L1
  SHST GU47 ....49 N9
  STRHM/NOR SW16 ....44 C2
Abingdon Vls KENS W8 ....19 L1
Abinger Av BELMT SM2 ....60 G7
Abinger CI CROY/NA CRO 65 J5
  RDKG RH5 ....137 J2
  WLGTN SM6 ....62 G4
Abinger Common Rd
  RDKG RH5 ....135 N6

Abinger Gdns ISLW TW7 ....16 E8
Abinger La RDKG RH5 ....135 L4
Abinger Rd CHSWK W4 ....18 D1
  RDKG RH5 ....155 H3
  REDH RH1 ....120 A8
Abinger Wy RGUE GU4 ....92 F9
Aboyne Dr RYNPK SW20 ....42 E9
Aboyne Rd TOOT SW17 ....28 F6
Abrahams Rd CRAWW RH11 ....194 D1
Acacia Av BTFD TW8 ....17 H5
  SHPTN TW17 ....38 C6
  SHST GU47 ....49 P8
  STWL/WRAY TW19 ....12 C9
  WOKS/MYFD GU22 ....72 B9
Acacia CI ADL/WDHM KT15 ....55 K8
Acacia Ct BRAK RG12 ....32 D4
Acacia Dr ADL/WDHM KT15 ....55 K9
  CHEAM SM3 ....43 K9
  EW KT17 ....79 H3
Acacia Gdns WWKM BR4 ....65 J1
Acacia Gv DUL SE21 ....30 E5
  NWMAL KT3 ....42 B4
Acacia Ms WDR/YW UB7 ....13 P4
Acacia Rd BECK BR3 ....46 F4
  GU GU1 ....6 C2
  HPTN TW12 ....25 H9
  MTCM CR4 ....44 C3
  STA TW18 ....22 E8
  STRHM/NOR SW16 ....44 C4
Academy CI CBLY GU15 ....50 G9
Academy Gdns CROY/NA CRO 3 K2

Ackroyd Rd FSTH SE23 ....31 L3
Acorn CI EGRIN RH19 ....180 D3
  HORL RH6 ....140 E9
  HPTN TW12 ....24 A2
Acorn Gdns NRWD SE19 ....45 P2
Acorn Gv HYS/HAR UB3 ....15 H5
  KWD/TDW/WH KT20 ....99 K4
  WOKS/MYFD GU22 ....92 C1
Acorn Keep FNM GU9 ....107 P6
Acorn Rd BH/BLKW GU17 ....67 M3
Acorns SWTR RH13 ....192 F6
The Acorns CRAWW RH11 ....194 E1
  HORL RH6 ....160 C5
Acorns Wy ESH/CLAY KT10 ....58 C4
Acorn Wy FSTH SE23 ....31 L6
Acre La CAR SM5 ....62 C3
Acre Rd KUTN/CMB KT2 ....9 F1
  WIM/MER SW19 ....28 G9
Acres Gdns
  KWD/TDW/WH KT20 ....78 G8
Acres Platt CRAN GU6 ....153 J8
Acris St WAND/EARL SW18 ....28 F1
Acton La CHSWK W4 ....18 A2
Acuba Rd WAND/EARL SW18 ....28 E5
Adair CI SNWD SE25 ....46 B3
Adam & Eve Ms KENS W8 ....19 L1
Adams CI BRYLDS KT5 ....41 N7
Adams Cft CHOB/PIR GU24 ....70 C9
Adams Dr FLEETN GU51 ....87 H6
Adams Park Rd FNM GU9 ....127 P1
Adamsrill Rd SYD SE26 ....31 L7
Adams Rd BECK BR3 ....46 E6
Adams Wk KUT KT1 ....8 D4
Adam Wk FUL/PGN SW6 * 18 G5
Adare Wk STRHM/NOR SW16 ....29 P5
Adderley Gv BTSEA SW11 ....29 K1
Addington Gdns CROY/NA CRO 3 L2
Addington Rd CROY/NA CRO 45 J9
  SAND/SEL CR2 ....64 C7
  WWKM BR4 ....65 J3
Addington Village Rd
  CROY/NA CRO 64 F5

Addiscombe Av CROY/NA CR0 46 A8
Addiscombe Court Rd
　CROY/NA CR0 ....3 H2
Addiscombe Gv CROY/NA CR0 ..3 F4
Addiscombe Rd CROY/NA CR0 ..3 G4
　CWTH RG45 ......49 N5
Addison Bridge Pl
　WKENS W14 ......19 J2
Addison Av HSLW TW3 ......16 C6
Addison Crs WKENS W14 ......19 J1
Addison Gdns BRYLDS KT5 ...41 M5
　WKENS W14 ......19 H1
Addison Gv CHSWK W4 ......18 C1
Addison Rd CTHM CR3 ......101 M4
　FRIM GU16 ......68 C8
　GU GU1 ......7 J6
　SNWD SE25 ......46 A5
　TEDD TW11 ......25 N9
　WKENS W14 ......19 K1
Addison's Cl CROY/NA CR0 ...46 A7
Addison Ter CHSWK W4 * ...18 A2
Addlestone Moor
　ADL/WDHM KT15 ......55 N1
Addlestone Pk
　ADL/WDHM KT15 ......55 M4
Addlestone Rd
　ADL/WDHM KT15 ......56 B3
Adecroft Wy
　E/WMO/HCT KT8 ......40 C4
Adela Av NWMAL KT3 ......42 E6
Adelaide Cl CRAWW RH11 ..176 G2
　HORS RH12 ......192 G6
Adelaide Pl WEY KT13 ......56 E6
Adelaide Rd ASHF TW15 ......22 G8
　HEST TW5 ......15 N5
　NWDGN UB2 ......15 N2
　RCH/KEW TW9 ......17 M9
　SURB KT6 ......41 L6
　TEDD TW11 ......25 N9
　WOT/HER KT12 * ...57 J2
Adelaide Ter BTFD TW8 * ...17 K3
Adelina Ms BAL SW12 ......29 N4
Adelphi Cl CRAWE RH10 ......177 N7
Adelphi Rd HOR/WEW KT19 .78 D2
Adeney Cl HMSMTH W6 ......19 H4
Adenmore Rd CAT SE6 ......31 P3
Adie Rd HMSMTH W6 ......18 G1
Adlers La RDKG RH5 ......116 G3
Adlington St FARN GU14 ......88 C5
Admers Crs LIPH GU30 ......182 F8
Admiral Kepple Ct ASC SL5 * ..33 N1
Admiral Rd CRAWW RH11 ..176 D8
Admiral's Bridge La
　EGRIN RH19 ......180 B9
Admirals Ct GU GU1 ......7 H2
Admiral Sq WBPTN SW10 * ..19 N6
Admiralty Rd TEDD TW11 ...25 N9
Admiralty Wy CBLY GU15...68 D3
Adolf St CAT SE6 ......31 P7
Adrian Ms WBPTN SW10 ......19 M4
Advance Rd WNWD SE27 ...30 D7
Aerodrome Wy HEST TW5 ...15 L4
Aerospace Bvd ALDT GU11 ..88 C8
Agar La SURB KT6 ......6 A5
Agar Crs BNFD RG42 ......32 D1
Agate La HORS RH12 ......192 D5
Agate Rd HMSMTH W6 ......18 G1
Agates La ASHTD KT21 ......77 K7
Agincourt Pl ASC SL5 ......34 E4
Agnes Riley Gdns CLAP SW4 *..29 M3
Agnes Scott Ct WEY KT13 ...56 D2
Agnew Rd FSTH SE23 ......31 M1
Ailsa Av TWK TW1 ......25 P1
Ailsa Cl CRAWW RH11 ......176 E8
Ailsa Rd TWK TW1 ......26 A1
Ainger Cl ASHV GU12 ......108 A1
Ainsdale Wy
　WOKN/KNAP GU21 ......71 N6
Ainsworth Rd CROY/NA CR0 ..2 B3
Aintree Cl DTCH/LGLY SL3 ..13 K4
Aintree Rd CRAWE RH10 ...177 K7
Aintree St FUL/PGN SW6 ...19 J5
Aircraft Esp FARN GU14 ......88 C3
Airedale Av CHSWK W4 ......18 D3
Airedale Av South
　CHSWK W4 * 18 D3
Airedale Rd BAL SW12 ......29 J3
　EA W5 ......17 J1
Airport Wy HORL RH6 ......159 K4
　STWL/WRAY TW19 ......13 L3
Aisgill Av WKENS W14 ......19 K3
Aisne Rd FRIM GU16 ......69 N7
Aiten Pl HMSMTH W6 ......18 E2
Aitken Cl MTCM CR4 ......44 B8
Aitman Dr CHSWK W4 * ...17 N3
Akabusi Cl WNWD SE25 ......46 A1
Akehurst Cl CRAWE RH10 ..160 B9
Akehurst St PUT/ROE SW15 ..27 M7
Akerman Rd SURB KT6 ......41 J7
Alamein Rd ALDT GU11 ......108 D3
Alanbrooke Cl
　WOKN/KNAP GU21 ......71 J7
Alan Hilton Ct CHERT KT16 *..55 H5
Alan Rd WIM/MER SW19 ...28 B8
Alan Turing Rd GUW GU2 ...111 K5
Albain Crs ASHF TW15 ......23 H5
Albany Cl ESH/CLAY KT10 ...58 A7
　FLEETS GU51 ......87 H7
　MORT/ESHN SW14 ......26 C8
Albany Crs ESH/CLAY KT10 ..58 C5
Albany Ms SUT SM1 ......61 M4
Albany Pde BTFD TW8 * ...17 L4
Albany Pk Pl DTCH/LGLY SL3 ..13 H5
　FRIM GU16 ......68 C7
Albany Park Rd
　KUTN/CMB KT2 ......26 C9
　LHD/OX KT22 ......76 B8
Albany Pl BTFD TW8 * ...17 K4

EGH TW20 ......21 N7
Albany Rd BTFD TW8 ......17 K4
　CRAWW RH11 ......176 F5
　FLEETN GU51 ......86 G7
　NWMAL KT3 ......42 B5
　RCHPK/HAM TW10 * ...26 A1
　WDSR SL4 ......20 F1
　WIM/MER SW19 ......28 C8
　WOT/HER KT12 ......57 M3
The Albanys REIG RH2 ......119 L2
Albany Ter
　RCHPK/HAM TW10 * ...26 C9
The Albany KUTN/CMB KT2 ..26 C9
Albatross Gdns
　SAND/SEL CR2 ......64 D9
Albemarle Av WHTN TW2 ...24 C4
Albemarle Pk BECK BR3 * ...47 H2
Albemarle Rd BECK BR3 ......47 H2
Alberta Av SUT SM1 ......61 J3
Albert Carr Gdns
　STRHM/NOR SW16 ......29 N8
Albert Dr STA TW18 ......22 C8
　WIM/MER SW19 ......28 B5
　WOKN/KNAP GU21 ......72 F4
Albert Gv RYNPK SW20 ...43 H2
Albertine Cl EW KT17 ......78 F5
Albert Ms KENS W8 ......19 N1
Albert Rd ADL/WDHM KT15 ..55 P2
　ALDT GU11 ......108 C4
　ASHF TW15 ......23 J8
　ASHTD KT21 ......77 M7
　BELMT SM2 ......61 P4
　BNFD RG42 ......32 D2
　CBLY GU15 * 68 E2
　EGH TW20 ......21 J9
　EW KT17 ......78 D2
　HORL RH6 ......159 K1
　HPTN TW12 ......25 K8
　HSLW TW3 ......16 A9
　HYS/HAR UB3 ......14 C1
　KUT KT1 ......8 C4
　MTCM CR4 ......44 B4
　NWDGN UB2 ......15 M1
　NWMAL KT3 ......42 D5
　PGE/AN SE20 ......46 D1
　RCHPK/HAM TW10 ......26 D1
　REDH RH1 ......100 E4
　SNWD SE25 ......46 B5
　TEDD TW11 ......25 N9
　TWK TW1 ......25 N3
　WARL CR6 ......82 E6
Albert Rd North REIG RH2 ..119 K4
Albery Cl HORS RH12 ......192 A6
Albion Cl CRAWE RH10 ......177 N6
Albion Ms REIG RH2 * 119 N7
Albion Pde
　WOKN/KNAP GU21 * ...71 J7
Albion Pl HMSMTH W6 ......18 F2
Albion Villas Rd FSTH SE23 ..31 K6
Albion Wy EDEN TN8 ......144 C1
　HORS RH12 ......192 B6
Albury Av BELMT SM2 ......60 G7
　ISLW TW7 ......16 F5
Albury Cl CHERT KT16 ......53 N2
　HOR/WEW KT19 ......59 P7
　HPTN TW12 ......25 H9
Albury Keep HORL RH6 ......140 D9
Albury Rd CHSGTN KT9 ...59 L4
　GU GU1 ......7 K1
　REDH RH1 ......100 E3
　WOT/HER KT12 ......56 C5
Albury St SHGR GU5 ......133 L7
Alcester Rd WLGTN SM6 ...62 D3
Alcock Cl WLGTN SM6 ......62 F6
Alcock Rd HEST TW5 ......15 M5
Alcocks Cl
　KWD/TDW/WH KT20 ...79 J9
Alcocks La
　KWD/TDW/WH KT20 ...79 J9
Alcorn Cl CHEAM SM3 ......61 L1
Alcot Cl CWTH RG45 ......49 M5
Aldenham Ter BRAK RG12 ...32 E7
Aldenholme WEY KT13 ......56 G5
Aldensley Rd HMSMTH W6 ..18 F1
Alderbrook Cl CWTH RG45...49 M5
Alderbrook Rd BAL SW12 ...29 L2
　CRAN GU6 ......152 E5
Alderbury Rd BARN SW13 ...18 F2
Alder Cl ASHV GU12 ......89 J8
　CRAWE RH10 ......179 J3
　EGH TW20 ......21 K8
Aldercombe La CTHM CR3 ..101 N7
Alder Gv YTLY GU46 ......66 G3
Alderman Judge Ml KUT KT1...8 D5
Aldermead Rd BMLY BR1 ...47 M2
Aldermoor Rd CAT SE6 ......31 N6
Alders Av EGRIN RH19 ......162 C9
Aldersbrook Dr
　KUTN/CMB KT2 ......26 E9
Alders Cl EA W5 ......17 K1
Aldersey Rd GU GU1 ......7 K3
Aldersgrove
　E/WMO/HCT KT8 ......40 D6

Aldershot Rd ASHV GU12 ...109 H5
　CHOB/PIR GU24 ......90 E6
　FLEETN GU51 ......86 E8
　FLEETS GU52 ......106 F2
　RGUW GU3 ......110 E1
Alderside Wk EGH TW20 ...21 K8
Aldersmead Av CROY/NA CR0..47 H7
Aldersmead Rd BECK BR3 ...46 E1
Alders Rd REIG RH2 ......119 M3
Alderstead La REDH RH1 ..100 F5
The Alders BF/WBF KT14 ...73 N1
　FELT TW13 ......24 F8
　FNM GU9 ......108 C8
　HSLW TW3 ......15 P4
　STRHM/NOR SW16 * ...29 L7
　WWKM BR4 ......47 H9
Alders View Dr EGRIN RH19 .162 D9
Alderton Rd CROY/NA CR0 ..45 P8
Alderville Rd FUL/PGN SW6...19 K7
Alderwick Dr HSLW TW3 ...16 D8
Alderwood Cl CTHM CR3 ...101 N5
Aldingbourne Cl
　CRAWW RH11 ......176 C4
Aldis Ms TOOT SW17 ......29 H8
Aldis St TOOT SW17 ......29 H8
Aldren Rd TOOT SW17 ......28 F6
Aldrich Crs CROY/NA CR0 ...65 J7
Aldrich Gdns CHEAM SM3 ...61 K2
Aldrich Ter WAND/EARL SW18 .28 F5
Aldridge Ri NWMAL KT3 ......42 D9
Aldrington Rd
　STRHM/NOR SW16 ......29 M8
Aldrin Pl FARN GU14 ......87 P3
Aldwick Cl FARN GU14 ......88 C1
Aldwick Rd CROY/NA CR0 ...63 H2
Aldworth Cl BRAK RG12 ...32 C5
Aldworth Gdns CWTH RG45 .49 L4
Alexander Cl HAYES BR2 ...47 N9
　WHTN TW2 ......25 M5
Alexander Crs CTHM CR3 ...101 L1
Alexander Evans Ms
　FSTH SE23 ......31 L5
Alexander Godley Cl
　ASHTD KT21 ......77 M8
Alexander Rd
　COUL/CHIP CR5 ......80 D4
　EGH TW20 ......21 N8
　REIG RH2 ......119 L8
Alexanders Wk CTHM CR3 ..101 P6
Alexander Wk BRAK RG12 ...32 D6
Alexandra Av CBLY GU15 ...68 C3
　SUT SM1 ......61 L2
　WARL CR6 ......82 F6
Alexandra Cl ASHF TW15 ...38 F1
　STA TW18 ......22 G9
Alexandra Ct ASHF TW15 ...23 N9
　CRAWE RH10 * 176 G6
　FARN GU14 ......88 E6
Alexandra Dr BRYLDS KT5 ...41 N8
Alexandra Gdns CAR SM5 ...62 C7
　HSLW TW3 ......16 C7
　WOKN/KNAP GU21 ......71 J7
Alexandra Pl CROY/NA CR0 ...3 G1
　GU GU1 ......7 G2
　SNWD SE25 ......45 M6
Alexandra Rd
　ADL/WDHM KT15 ......55 P3
　ALDT GU11 ......108 B4
　ASHF TW15 ......23 N9
　ASHV GU12 ......109 H5
　BH/WHM TN16 ......84 C6
　BTFD TW8 * 17 K4
　CROY/NA CR0 ......3 G1
　EGH TW20 ......21 H9
　EW KT17 ......78 D2
　FARN GU14 ......88 E6
　HSLW TW3 ......16 B7
　KUTN/CMB KT2 ......9 H1
　MORT/ESHN SW14 ......18 B8
　RCH/KEW TW9 ......17 N7
　SYD SE26 ......31 L9
　THDIT KT7 ......40 F6
　TWK TW1 ......26 B2
　WARL CR6 ......82 E6
　WIM/MER SW19 ......44 A1
Alexandra Sq MRDN SM4 ...43 L6
Alexandra Ter ALDT GU11 * ..108 C4
Alexandra Wy
　HOR/WEW KT19 ......77 N1
Alfold By-Pass CRAN GU6 ..170 C5
Alfold Cl MFD/CHID GU8 ...169 L7
Alfonso Cl ASHV GU12 ......108 A8
Alford Cl RGUE GU4 ......112 D2
Alford Gn CROY/NA CR0 ...65 K5
Alfred Cl CHSWK W4 ......18 B2
　CRAWE RH10 ......177 P6
　FLEETN GU51 ......86 D5
Alfred Rd FELT TW13 ......24 D5
　FNM GU9 ......5 H5
　KUT KT1 ......8 E6
　SNWD SE25 ......46 B5
　SUT SM1 ......61 N4
Alfreton Cl WIM/MER SW19 ..28 A6
Alfriston BRYLDS KT5 ......41 M7
Alfriston Av CROY/NA CR0 ...45 M7
Alfriston Cl BRYLDS KT5 ...41 M7
Alfriston Rd CLAP SW4 ......29 J1
　FRIM GU16 ......68 E8
Algar Rd ISLW TW7 ......16 G8
Algarve Rd
　WAND/EARL SW18 ......28 E4
Alice Ms TEDD TW11 ......25 N8
Alice Rd ALDT GU11 ......108 C4
Alice Ruston Pl
　WOKN/KNAP GU22 ......72 A8
Alice Wy HSLW TW3 ......16 C9
Alicia Av CRAWE RH10 ......177 L5
Alington Gv WLGTN SM6 ...62 F7

Alison Cl CROY/NA CR0 ......46 D9
　FARN GU14 ......88 B4
　WOKN/KNAP GU21 ......72 C4
Alison Dr CBLY GU15 ......69 H3
Alison's Rd ALDT GU11 ......108 C1
Alison Wy ALDT GU11 ......108 A4
Alkerden Rd CHSWK W4 ...18 C2
Allan Cl NWMAL KT3 ......42 C6
Allbrook Cl TEDD TW11 ......25 M8
Allcard Cl HORS RH12 ......192 C5
Allcot Cl CRAWW RH11 ......176 B3
　EBED/NFELT TW14 ......24 A4
Allden Av ASHV GU12 ......108 F7
Allden Gdns ASHV GU12 ...108 F7
Allens La SHGR GU5 * 150 G2
Allder Wy SAND/SEL CR2 ...63 K6
Allee Dr LIPH GU30 ......182 E5
Allenby Av SAND/SEL CR2 ...63 L7
Allenby Rd BH/WHM TN16 ...84 C6
　CBLY GU15 ......68 C2
　FSTH SE23 ......31 M6
Allen Cl MTCM CR4 ......44 D2
　SUN TW16 ......39 K2
Allendale Cl SHST GU47 ......49 N8
　SYD SE26 ......31 L8
Allen House Pk
　WOKS/MYFD GU22 ......72 A9
Allen Rd BECK BR3 ......46 C3
　CROY/NA CR0 ......45 H8
　LTWR GU18 ......51 K9
　SUN TW16 ......39 K2
Allen's Cl EGRIN RH19 ......181 K5
Allen St KENS W8 ......19 M1
Allestree Rd FUL/PGN SW6 ..19 J5
Alleyn Crs DUL SE21 ......30 E5
Alleyn Pk DUL SE21 ......30 E5
　NWDGN UB2 ......15 P3
Alleyn Rd DUL SE21 ......30 E6
Allfarthing La
　WAND/EARL SW18 ......28 F2
Allgood Cl MRDN SM4 ......43 H7
All Hallows Av
　FSTH SE23 ......31 L5
Allingham Rd REIG RH2 ......119 L8
Allington Av SHPTN TW17 ...38 C4
Allington Ct FLEETN GU51 ...86 E8
Allison Gv DUL SE21 ......30 F4
Allnutt Wy CLAP SW4 ......29 N1
Alloway Cl WOKN/KNAP GU21..71 P7
All Saints Crs FARN GU14 ...68 A7
All Saints Dr SAND/SEL CR2...81 P1
All Saints Pas
　WAND/EARL SW18 * ...28 D1
All Saints Ri BNFD RG42 ...32 C1
All Saints Rd LTWR GU18 ...52 C8
　SUT SM1 ......61 N2
　WIM/MER SW19 ......43 N1
All Souls' La BRAK RG12 ...33 H4
All Souls Av PUR/KEN CR8 ..81 N1
All Souls' Rd ASC SL5 ......34 C4
Allum Gv KWD/TDW/WH KT20..98 F1
Allwood Cl SYD SE26 ......31 L7
Allyington Wy CRAWE RH10 ..177 N3
Allyn Cl STA TW18 ......22 C9
Alma Cl ASHV GU12 ......108 F5
　WOKN/KNAP GU21 ......71 J7
Alma Crs SUT SM1 ......61 J4
Alma Gdns FRIM GU16 ......69 H1
Alma La FNM GU9 ......107 N2
Alma Pl NRWD SE19 ......45 P1
　THHTH CR7 ......45 J6
Alma Rd BOR GU35 ......164 F6
　CAR SM5 ......62 A4
　ESH/CLAY KT10 ......40 E9
　REIG RH2 ......119 M4
　WAND/EARL SW18 ......28 F1
Alma Ter KENS W8 * 19 M1
　WAND/EARL SW18 * ...28 G3
Alma Wy FNM GU9 ......107 P7
Almer Rd RYNPK SW20 ......42 E1
Almners Rd CHERT KT16 ...36 D3
Almond Av CAR SM5 ......62 C1
　EA W5 ......17 J4
　WOKS/MYFD GU22 ......92 B1
Almond Cl CRAWW RH11 ..176 D6
　EGH TW20 ......21 K8
　FARN GU14 ......68 C8
　GU GU1 ......112 B1
　SHPTN TW17 ......38 E3
Almond Rd BTFD TW8 * 17 K4
Almond Wy MTCM CR4 ......44 F6
Almorah Rd HEST TW5 ......15 L6
Almsgate RGUW GU3 ......131 J3
Alms Heath RPLY/SEND GU23 ..94 H1
Almshouse La CHSGTN KT9...59 H7
Alnwick Gv MRDN SM4 ...43 M5
The Aloes FLEETN GU51 * ...87 H7
Alphabet Gdns CAR SM5 ...43 P7
Alpha Pl MRDN SM4 * 43 J7
Alpha Rd ASHV GU12 ......108 F5
　BRYLDS KT5 ......41 M7
　CHOB/PIR GU24 ......55 M8
　CRAWW RH11 ......176 F5
　CROY/NA CR0 ......3 H2
　HPTN TW12 ......25 H9
　WOKS/MYFD GU22 ......72 C6
Alpha Wy EGH TW20 ......36 G1
Alphea Cl WIM/MER SW19 ...44 C2
Alphington Av FRIM GU16 ...69 H7
Alphington Gn FRIM GU16 ...69 H7
Alpine Av BRYLDS KT5 ......42 B9
Alpine Cl CROY/NA CR0 ......3 J4
　FARN GU14 ......87 P4
Alpine Rd REDH RH1 ......120 C2
　WOT/HER KT12 ......39 J8
Alresford Rd GUW GU2 ......111 N6
Alric Av NWMAL KT3 ......42 C4
Alsford Cl LTWR GU18 ......69 P1

Alsom Av HOR/WEW KT19 ...60 D3
Alston Cl THDIT KT7 ......41 H8
Alston Rd TOOT SW17 ......28 C7
Altenburg Av WEA W13 ......17 H1
Alterton Cl
　WOKN/KNAP GU21 ......71 N6
Althea St FUL/PGN SW6 ...19 M7
Althorne Rd REDH RH1 ......120 C2
Althorp Rd TOOT SW17 ......29 J4
Alton Cl ISLW TW7 ......16 F7
Alton Ct STA TW18 ......37 J2
Alton Gdns BECK BR3 ......46 G1
　WHTN TW2 ......25 L2
Alton Ride BLKW GU17 ......67 N2
Alton Rd CROY/NA CR0 ......63 H1
　FLEETN GU51 ......87 J6
　PUT/ROE SW15 ......27 M4
　RCH/KEW TW9 ......17 L9
　RFNM GU10 ......127 H6
Altyre Cl BECK BR3 ......46 F6
Altyre Rd CROY/NA CR0 ......3 H4
Altyre Wy BECK BR3 ......46 F6
Alvernia Cl GODL GU7 ......150 B2
Alverstoke Gdns ALDT GU11 ..108 A5
Alverstone Av
　WAND/EARL SW18 ......28 E5
Alverstone Rd NWMAL KT3 ...42 E4
Alverston Gdns SNWD SE25 ..45 N6
Alvia Gdns SUT SM1 ......61 N3
Alwin Pl FNM GU9 ......107 N7
Alwyn Av CHSWK W4 ......18 B3
Alwyn Cl CROY/NA CR0 ......65 H6
Alwyne Ct WOKN/KNAP GU21 .10 D2
Alwyne Rd WIM/MER SW19 ...43 L9
Alwyns Cl CHERT KT16 ......37 L7
Alwyns La CHERT KT16 ......37 K7
Amalgamated Dr BTFD TW8 ..16 E4
Amanda Ct DTCH/LGLY SL3 ..12 F1
Ambarrow Crs SHST GU47 ...49 K8
Ambarrow La CWTH RG45 ...49 H7
Ambassador BRAK RG12 ...32 B6
Ambassador HSLW TW3 * ...15 N7
Ambercroft Wy
　COUL/CHIP CR5 ......81 K8
Amber Hl CBLY GU15 ......69 L4
Amberley Cl CRAWE RH10 ..177 M5
　HORS RH12 ......192 F4
　RPLY/SEND GU23 ......93 K5
Amberley Ct CRAWW RH11 *..158 G9
Amberley Dr
　ADL/WDHM KT15 ......55 M8
Amberley Gdns
　HOR/WEW KT19 ......60 D3
Amberley Gra ALDT GU11 ..108 B6
Amberley Gv CROY/NA CR0 ...46 B8
　SYD SE26 ......31 J7
Amberley Rd HORS RH12 ...192 F4
　MFD/CHID GU8 ......149 M2
Amberside Cl ISLW TW7 * ...25 J1
Amberwood Cl WLGTN SM6 ..62 G4
Amberwood Dr CBLY GU15 ...69 H1
Amberwood Ri NWMAL KT3 ...42 C7
Amblecote COB KT11 ......57 M9
Ambleside BECK BR3 * 46 E6
　STRHM/NOR SW16 ......29 N7
Ambleside Cl CRAWW RH11 ..176 A4
　FARN GU14 ......88 A3
　FRIM GU16 ......89 J3
　REDH RH1 ......140 D1
Ambleside Av BECK BR3 ...46 E6
　EBED/NFELT TW14 ......24 A4
Ambleside Gdns BELMT SM2 ..61 N5
　SAND/SEL CR2 ......64 D7
Ambleside Rd LTWR GU18 ...52 A9
Ambleside Wy EGH TW20 ...36 F1
Ambrey Wy WLGTN SM6 ...62 F7
Amerland Rd
　WAND/EARL SW18 ......28 C2
Amersham Rd CROY/NA CR0 .45 L7
Amesbury Av
　BRXS/STRHM SW2 ......29 N5
Amesbury Cl WPK KT4 ......42 G9
Amesbury Rd FELT TW13 ...24 E5
Amey Dr GT/LBKH KT23 ...96 C4
Amhurst Gdns ISLW TW7 ...16 F7
Amis Av HOR/WEW KT19 ...59 N5
　HOR/WEW KT19 ......59 N5
Amis Rd WOKN/KNAP GU21 ..71 J8
Amity Gv RYNPK SW20 ......42 G2
Amlets La CRAN GU6 ......152 G7
Amner Rd BTSEA SW11 ...29 K2
Amor Rd HMSMTH W6 ......18 G1
Ampere Wy CROY/NA CR0 ...44 G8
Amroth Cl FSTH SE23 ......31 J4
Amstel Wy
　WOKN/KNAP GU21 ......71 M7
Amundsen Rd HORS RH12 ..192 C4
Amyand Cottages TWK TW1 ..26 A2
Amyand Park Gdns TWK TW1 *..26 A3
Amyand Park Rd TWK TW1 ...25 P3
Amy Cl WLGTN SM6 ......62 G6
Amy Rd OXTED RH8 ......103 L9
Amyruth Rd BROCKY SE4 ...31 P1
Ancaster Dr ASC SL5 ......33 N2
Ancaster Rd BECK BR3 ......46 C4
Ancaster St WOOL/PLUM SE18 *..31 L1
Ancells Rd FLEETN GU51 ...87 J3
Anchorage Cl
　WIM/MER SW19 ......28 D2
Anchor Cl RGUW GU3 ......110 C2
Anchor Crs HORS RH12 * ...192 B9
Anchor Hl HORS RH12 ......71 K6
Anchor Meadow FARN GU14 ..88 B1
Ancill Cl HMSMTH W6 ......19 H4
Anders Cnr BNFD RG42 ...32 D1
Anderson Av GUW GU2 ......111 P6

Anderson Cl CHEAM SM3 43 L9
HOR/WEW KT19 77 P1
Anderson Dr ASHF TW15 23 M7
Anderson Pl BAGS GU19 51 N5
Anderson Rd WEY KT13 * 56 F2
Anderson's Pl HSLW TW3 16 B9
Andover Cl
EBED/NFELT TW14 24 A4
HOR/WEW KT19 60 B9
Andover Rd BLKW GU17 67 N2
WHTN TW2 25 L4
Andover Ter HMSMTH W6 * 18 F2
Andover Wy ALDT GU11 108 D7
Andrewartha Rd FARN GU14 88 G6
Andrew's Cl EW KT17 78 D3
FLEETS GU52 86 G9
WPK KT4 61 H1
Andrews Rd FARN GU14 88 A2
Andromeda Cl
CRAWW RH11 176 B7
Anerley Gv NRWD SE19 45 P1
Anerley Hl NRWD SE19 30 G9
Anerley Pk PGE/AN SE20 31 J9
Anerley Park Rd PGE/AN SE20 46 B1
Anerley Rd NRWD SE19 46 A1
Anerley Station Rd
PGE/AN SE20 46 B2
Anerley V NRWD SE19 45 P1
Anfield Cl BAL SW12 29 M3
Angelfield HSLW TW3 25 J1
Angel Ga GU GU1 6 E5
Angel Hl SUT SM1 61 M2
Angel Hill Dr SUT SM1 61 M2
Angelica Gdns CROY/NA CR0 46 D9
Angelica Rd CHOB/PIR GU24 70 G4
GUW GU2 111 N1
Angel Pl REIG RH2 * 119 M7
Angel Rd THDIT KT7 40 G9
Angel Wk HMSMTH W6 18 G2
Anglers Reach SURB KT6 * 41 K6
Anglesea Rd KUT KT1 41 K5
Anglesey Av FARN GU14 68 B9
Anglesey Cl ASHF TW15 23 K7
CRAWW RH11 176 F8
Anglesey Court Rd CAR SM5 62 C5
Anglesey Gdns CAR SM5 62 C5
Anglesey Rd ASHV GU12 108 F5
Angles Rd STRHM/NOR SW16 29 P7
Angora Wy FLEETN GU51 87 H3
Angus Cl CHSGTN KT9 59 N4
HORS RH12 192 C6
Anlaby Rd TEDD TW11 25 M8
Annandale Dr RFNM GU10 127 P7
Annandale Rd CHSWK W4 18 C2
CROY/NA CR0 64 A1
GUW GU2 6 B6
Anne Armstrong Cl
ALDT GU11 108 F1
Anne Boleyn's Wk
BELMT SM2 61 H6
KUTN/CMB KT2 26 D8
Anne Case Ms NWMAL KT3 * 42 B4
Anneforde Pl BNFD RG42 32 C1
Anners Cl EGH TW20 36 G4
Annesley Dr CROY/NA CR0 64 F2
Anne's Wk CTHM CR3 81 N9
Annes Wy FLEETS GU52 87 H9
Annett Cl SHPTN TW17 38 G5
Annettes Cft FLEETS GU52 106 E2
Annett Rd WOT/HER KT12 39 J8
Annie Brookes Cl STA TW18 22 A6
Anningsley Pk CHERT KT16 54 F8
Annisdowne Cl SHGR GU5 135 H4
Ann La WBPTN SW10 19 P5
Annsworthy Av THHTH CR7 45 M4
Ansdell St KENS W8 19 M1
Ansdell Ter KENS W8 19 M1
Ansell Gv CAR SM5 44 B9
Ansell Rd DORK RH4 117 H6
FRIM GU16 68 G8
TOOT SW17 29 H6
Anselm Cl CROY/NA CR0 3 J5
Anselm Rd FUL/PGN SW6 19 L4
Ansley Cl SAND/SEL CR2 82 B3
Anson Cl ALDT GU11 108 B3
PUR/KEN CR8 81 M9
Anstead MFD/CHID GU8 * 168 B8
Anstice Cl CHSWK W4 18 C5
Anstiebury Cl RDKG RH5 156 B1
Anstie Grange Dr RDKG RH5 137 H8
Anstie La RDKG RH5 136 F9
Anthony Pl GSHT GU26 * 184 A1
Anthony Rd SNWD SE25 46 A7
Anthony Wall BNFD RG42 33 H2
Antlands La HORL RH6 160 A7
Antlands La East HORL RH6 159 P7
Antlands La West HORL RH6 159 P8
Anton Crs SUT SM1 61 L2
Antrobus Cl SUT SM1 61 K4
Antrobus Rd CHSWK W4 18 A2
Anvil Cl STRHM/NOR SW16 44 E1
Anvil La COB KT11 75 J4
Anvil Rd SUN TW16 39 J4
Anyards Rd COB KT11 75 K3
Anzio Cl ALDT GU11 108 C4
Apeldoorn Dr WLGTN SM6 62 G7
Aperdele Rd LHD/OX KT22 76 F9
Aperfield Rd BH/WHM TN16 84 C6
Apers Av WOKS/MYFD GU22 92 D1
Apex Cl BECK BR3 47 H2
WEY KT13 56 F2
Apex Dr FRIM GU16 68 F7
Apley Rd REIG RH2 119 L8
Aplin Wy ISLW TW7 16 E6
LTWR GU18 52 A8
Apollo Av BMLY BR1 47 P2
Apollo Pl WBPTN SW10 * 19 P5
WOKN/KNAP GU21 * 71 N8
Apollo Ri FARN GU14 87 P3
Appostle Wy THHTH CR7 45 K3
Appach Rd
BRXS/STRHM SW2 30 B1
Appleby Cl WHTN TW2 25 L5
Appleby Gdns
EBED/NFELT TW14 * 24 A4
Appledore BRAK RG12 32 B7
Appledore Cl HAYES BR2 47 M6
TOOT SW17 29 J5
Appledore Ms FARN GU14 68 C9
Applefield CRAWE RH10 177 H4
Applegarth CROY/NA CR0 65 H6
ESH/CLAY KT10 58 F4
Applegarth Av GUW GU2 111 K5
Applegarth Rd WKENS W14 * 19 H1
Apple Garth BTFD TW8 17 K2
GODL GU7 131 J6
Apple Gv CHSGTN KT9 59 L3
Applelands Cl RFNM GU10 127 L9
Apple Market KUT KT1 8 C5
Appleton Gdns NWMAL KT3 42 E7
Apple Tree Cl GT/LBKH KT23 96 C4
Appletree Cl GODL GU7 150 E2
PGE/AN SE20 46 B2
Appletree Ct RGUE GU4 113 H3
Appletree La DTCH/LGLY SL3 12 A1
Appletree Pl BNFD RG42 32 C2
Apple Trees Pl
WOKS/MYFD GU22 * 72 A8
Apple Tree Wy SHST GU47 49 P8
Appley Dr CBLY GU15 68 D3
Approach Rd ASHF TW15 23 M9
E/WMO/HCT KT8 40 A6
FNM GU9 5 G5
PUR/KEN CR8 81 J1
RYNPK SW20 42 G3
WARL CR6 103 P2
The Approach EGRIN RH19 162 E6
April Cl ASHTD KT21 77 M7
CBLY GU15 68 E6
FELT TW13 24 B6
HORS RH12 192 B6
April Gln FSTH SE23 31 L6
Aprilwood Cl
ADL/WDHM KT15 55 K9
Apsey Ct BNFD RG42 32 A1
Apsley Rd NWMAL KT3 42 A4
SNWD SE25 46 B5
Aquarius TWK TW1 * 26 A4
Aquila Cl ASHTD KT21 97 L1
Arabella Dr PUT/ROE SW15 18 C9
Aragon Av EW KT17 60 F7
THDIT KT7 40 F6
Aragon Cl CROY/NA CR0 65 L8
SUN TW16 39 H1
Aragon Ct BRAK RG12 32 E5
Aragon Rd KUTN/CMB KT2 26 D8
MRDN SM4 43 H8
Aram Ct WOKS/MYFD GU22 * 72 F4
Arbor Cl BECK BR3 47 H3
Arborfield Cl
BRXS/STRHM SW2 30 A4
Arbour Cl LHD/OX KT22 96 F3
Arbrook La ESH/CLAY KT10 58 D5
Arbutus Cl REIG RH2 119 N7
Arbutus Rd REIG RH2 119 N7
Arcade Pde CHSGTN KT9 * 59 L3
The Arcade ALDT GU11 * 108 C4
REDH RH1 * 120 C4
Arcadia Cl CAR SM5 62 C3
Archbishop's Pl
BRXS/STRHM SW2 30 A2
Archdale Pl NWMAL KT3 41 P4
Archdale Rd EDUL SE22 30 G1
Archel Rd WKENS W14 19 K4
Archer Cl KUTN/CMB KT2 41 L1
Archer Rd SNWD SE25 46 B5
Arch Rd WOT/HER KT12 57 M2
Archway Cl CROY/NA CR0 * 62 G4
WIM/MER SW19 28 E7
Archway Ms DORK RH4 116 G6
Archway St BARN SW13 18 C8
Arcturus Rd CRAWW RH11 176 B7
Ardbeg Rd HNHL SE24 30 E2
Arden Cl BRAK RG12 33 J3
REIG RH2 119 M9
Arden Rd CRAWE RH10 177 J7
Ardenrun LING RH7 142 G5
Ardent Cl SNWD SE25 45 N4
Ardesley Wd WEY KT13 56 G3
Ardfern Av
STRHM/NOR SW16 45 J4
Ardingly BRAK RG12 32 C7
Ardingly Cl CRAWW RH11 176 E3
CROY/NA CR0 64 D2
Ardleigh Gdns CHEAM SM3 43 L9
Ardley Cl FSTH SE23 31 M6
Ardlui Rd WNWD SE27 30 D5
Ardmay Gdns SURB KT6 41 L6
Ardmore Av GUW GU2 111 P3
Ardmore Wy GUW GU2 111 P3
Ardrossan Av CBLY GU15 69 J4
Ardrossan Gdns WPK KT4 60 E2
Ardshiel Cl PUT/ROE SW15 19 H8
Ardshiel Dr REDH RH1 120 A7
Ardwell Cl CWTH RG45 49 J4
Ardwell Rd
BRXS/STRHM SW2 29 P5
Arena La ALDT GU11 108 A2
Arenal Dr CWTH RG45 49 L6
Arethusa Wy CHOB/PIR GU24 70 F5
Arford Common BOR GU35 164 D5
Arford Rd BOR GU35 164 C5
Argent Cl EGH TW20 21 P9
Argent Ct SURB KT6 * 59 N1
Argente Cl FLEETN GU51 87 H3
Argent Ter SHST GU47 * 50 A9
Argon Ms FUL/PGN SW6 19 L5
Argosy Gdns STA TW18 22 C9
Argosy La STWL/WRAY TW19 22 G3
Argus Wk CRAWW RH11 176 D8
Argyle Av HSLW TW3 25 H2
Argyle Pl HMSMTH W6 18 F2
Argyle Rd HSLW TW3 25 J1
Argyle St CHOB/PIR GU24 90 A1
Ariel Rd FARN GU14 88 C5
Ariel Wy HSLWW TW4 15 K8
Arkell Gv NRWD SE19 45 K1
Arkwright Rd DTCH/LGLY SL3 13 J7
SAND/SEL CR2 63 P8
Arlingford Rd
BRXS/STRHM SW2 30 B2
Arlington Cl BNFD RG42 32 C2
SUT SM1 61 L1
TWK TW1 * 26 B2
Arlington Ct HYS/HAR UB3 14 F3
Arlington Dr CAR SM5 62 B1
Arlington Gdns CHSWK W4 18 A3
Arlington Ldg WEY KT13 56 D3
Arlington Rd ASHF TW15 23 J8
RCHPK/HAM TW10 26 C5
SURB KT6 41 K7
TWK TW1 25 N7
TWK TW1 26 B2
Arlington Sq BRAK RG12 * 32 C3
Arlington Ter ALDT GU11 108 B4
Armadale Rd
EBED/NFELT TW14 24 B1
FUL/PGN SW6 19 L5
WOKN/KNAP GU21 71 N6
Armfield Cl E/WMO/HCT KT8 39 P6
Armfield Crs MTCM CR4 44 B3
Armitage Ct ASC SL5 34 C7
Armitage Dr FRIM GU16 69 H7
Armoury Wy
WAND/EARL SW18 28 D1
Armstrong Cl WOT/HER KT12 39 J7
Armstrong Ml FARN GU14 87 P3
Armstrong Rd EGH TW20 21 H9
FELT TW13 24 F8
Armstrong Wy FARN GU14 87 M6
Armytage Rd HEST TW5 15 M5
Arnal Crs WAND/EARL SW18 28 B3
Arncliffe BRAK RG12 32 C6
Arndale Wy EGH TW20 21 M8
Arne Cl CRAWW RH11 176 C8
Arne Gv HORL RH6 140 A8
Arnett Av EWKG RG40 48 C2
Arnewood Cl COB KT11 76 B3
PUT/ROE SW15 27 M4
Arney's La MTCM CR4 44 C7
Arnfield Cl CRAWW RH11 176 B6
Arnhem Dr CROY/NA CR0 65 K9
Arnison Rd E/WMO/HCT KT8 40 D5
Arnold Crs ISLW TW7 25 L1
Arnold Dr CHSGTN KT9 59 K5
Arnold Rd STA TW18 37 N1
TOOT SW17 44 B1
WOKN/KNAP GU21 11 J1
Arnott Cl CHSWK W4 18 B2
Arnull's Rd
STRHM/NOR SW16 30 C9
Arodene Rd
BRXS/STRHM SW2 30 A2
Arosa Rd TWK TW1 26 C2
Arragon Gdns
STRHM/NOR SW16 44 G1
WWKM BR4 65 H2
Arragon Rd TWK TW1 25 P4
WAND/EARL SW18 28 D4
Arragon Wk BF/WBF KT14 74 B2
Arran Cl CRAWW RH11 176 E8
WLGTN SM6 62 E3
Arran Wy ESH/CLAY KT10 58 B1
Arras Av MRDN SM4 43 N6
Arreton Md
WOKN/KNAP GU21 72 C3
Arrivals Rd HORL RH6 159 J4
Arrol Rd BECK BR3 46 C4
Arrow Rd FARN GU14 88 B5
Artel Cft CRAWE RH10 177 J5
Arterberry Rd RYNPK SW20 42 G1
Arthur Cl BAGS GU19 51 N8
FNM GU9 5 F6
Arthurdon Rd LEW SE13 31 P1
Arthur Rd BH/WHM TN16 84 A4
CRAWW RH11 176 B5
FNM GU9 5 F6
KUTN/CMB KT2 9 H1
NWMAL KT3 42 F6
SWTR RH13 192 C9
WIM/MER SW19 28 D7
Arthur's Bridge Rd
WOKN/KNAP GU21 10 A4
Arthur St ALDT GU11 108 D5
Artillery Rd ALDT GU11 88 F8
ALDT GU11 108 D4
GU GU1 6 E4
Artillery Ter GU GU1 6 E4
Arundel Av EW KT17 60 F8
MRDN SM4 43 K5
SAND/SEL CR2 64 A8
Arundel Cl BTSEA SW11 29 H1
CRAWE RH10 177 M5
CROY/NA CR0 2 A6
FLEETN GU51 87 H7
HPTN TW12 25 J8
LIPH GU30 182 A2
Arundel Ct DTCH/LGLY SL3 12 B2
Arundel Pl FNM GU9 4 E3
Arundel Rd BELMT SM2 61 K6
CBLY GU15 69 L4
CROY/NA CR0 45 M7
DORK RH4 116 G7
HSLWW TW4 15 L8
KUT KT1 41 P3
Arundel Ter BARN SW13 18 F4
Arunside HORS RH12 191 P9
Arun Wy SWTR RH13 192 D9
Aschurch Rd CROY/NA CR0 45 P8
Ascot Ct ALDT GU11 108 C5
Ascot Ga ASC SL5 * 34 F1
Ascot Ms WLGTN SM6 62 E7
Ascot Pk ASC SL5 * 33 N4
Ascot Rd ASHF TW15 23 K4
TOOT SW17 29 K9
Ashbourne BRAK RG12 32 B7
Ashbourne Cl ASHV GU12 109 L3
COUL/CHIP CR5 80 E7
Ashbourne Gv CHSWK W4 18 C3
EDUL SE22 30 G1
Ashbourne Rd MTCM CR4 29 K9
Ashbourne Ter
WIM/MER SW19 43 L1
Ashbrook Rd WDSR SL4 20 G3
Ashburn Gdns SKENS SW7 19 N2
Ashburnham Pk
ESH/CLAY KT10 58 C3
Ashburnham Rd
CRAWE RH10 177 K7
RCHPK/HAM TW10 26 A6
WBPTN SW10 * 19 N5
Ashburn Pl SKENS SW7 19 N2
Ashburton Av CROY/NA CR0 46 B9
Ashburton Cl CROY/NA CR0 46 A9
Ashburton Gdns
CROY/NA CR0 64 A1
Ashburton Rd CROY/NA CR0 64 A1
Ashbury Ct BMLY BR1 47 N1
Ashbury Crs RGUE GU4 112 G3
Ashbury Dr FARN GU14 68 C7
Ashbury Pl WIM/MER SW19 28 F9
Ashby Av CHSGTN KT9 59 N5
Ashby's Cl EDEN TN8 145 H5
Ashby Wk CROY/NA CR0 45 L7
Ashby Wy WDR/YW UB7 14 C5
Ashchurch Park Vls SHB W12 18 E1
Ash Church Rd ASHV GU12 109 K4
Ashchurch Ter SHB W12 18 D1
Ash Cl ASHV GU12 109 K3
BLKW GU17 67 N3
CAR SM5 62 B1
CRAWE RH10 179 K2
DTCH/LGLY SL3 12 F1
EDEN TN8 144 F4
KWD/TDW/WH KT20 118 A2
LING RH7 143 L8
NWMAL KT3 42 B3
PGE/AN SE20 46 C3
REDH RH1 120 E1
WOKS/MYFD GU22 72 C9
WOKS/MYFD GU22 73 L4
Ash Combe MFD/CHID GU8 167 P7
Ashcombe Av SURB KT6 41 K8
Ashcombe Dr EDEN TN8 144 F1
Ashcombe Pde
WOKS/MYFD GU22 * 72 E9
Ashcombe Rd CAR SM5 62 C5
DORK RH4 116 G5
REDH RH1 100 E7
WIM/MER SW19 28 D8
Ashcombe Sq NWMAL KT3 42 A4
Ashcombe St FUL/PGN SW6 * 19 M7
Ashcombe Ter
KWD/TDW/WH KT20 78 F9
Ash Ct HOR/WEW KT19 60 A3
Ashcroft RGUE GU4 132 C3
Ashcroft Pk COB KT11 75 N1
Ashcroft Ri COUL/CHIP CR5 80 G5
Ashcroft Rd CHSGTN KT9 59 M2
Ashdale GT/LBKH KT23 96 C6
Ashdale Cl STWL/WRAY TW19 23 H5
WHTN TW2 25 J3
Ashdale Pk EWKG RG40 48 G2
Ashdene Cl ASHF TW15 * 38 E1
Ashdene Crs ASHV GU12 109 J3
Ashdene Rd ASHV GU12 109 J3
Ashdown Av FARN GU14 88 G5
Ashdown Cl BECK BR3 47 H3
BRAK RG12 33 H3
FROW RH18 181 M9
REIG RH2 119 M9
Ashdown Ct CRAWE RH10 * 177 J8
Ashdown Dr CRAWE RH10 177 H9
Ashdown Gdns
SAND/SEL CR2 82 B4
Ashdown Pl THDIT KT7 40 G7
Ashdown Rd EW KT17 78 D2
FROW RH18 181 L9
KUT KT1 8 D5
REIG RH2 119 M9
Ashdown Vw EGRIN RH19 180 D4
Ashdown Wy TOOT SW17 29 K5
Ash Dr REDH RH1 120 C7
Ashenden Rd GUW GU2 111 M5
Ashen Gv WIM/MER SW19 28 D6
Ashen V SAND/SEL CR2 64 D7
Asher Dr ASC SL5 33 L2
Ashfield BIL RH14 187 K8
Ashfield Av FELT TW13 24 C4
Ashfield Cl BECK BR3 46 G1
RCHPK/HAM TW10 26 D4
Ashfield Gn YTLY GU46 67 K3
Ashford Av ASHF TW15 23 L9
Ashford Cl ASHF TW15 23 H7
Ashford Crs ASHF TW15 23 H6
Ashford Gdns COB KT11 75 M5
Ashford Rd FELT TW13 23 N7
SHPTN TW17 38 E1
STA TW18 37 P1
Ash Green La East
ASHV GU12 109 L6
Ash Green La West
ASHV GU12 109 H6
Ash Green Rd ASHV GU12 109 L5
Ash Gv EBED/NFELT TW14 23 P4
GUW GU2 111 N5
HEST TW5 15 M6
LIPH GU30 182 G7
PGE/AN SE20 46 C3
STA TW18 22 F9
WWKM BR4 65 J1
Ashgrove Rd ASHF TW15 23 M8
Ash Hill Rd ASHV GU12 109 L3
Ashington Rd
FUL/PGN SW6 * 19 K7
Ash Keys CRAWE RH10 177 H6
Ashlake Rd
STRHM/NOR SW16 29 P7
Ash La MFD/CHID GU8 148 D2
Ashleigh Av EGH TW20 36 G1
Ashleigh Cl HORL RH6 159 J1
Ashleigh Gdns SUT SM1 61 M1
Ashleigh Rd HORS RH12 192 B5
MORT/ESHN SW14 18 C8
PGE/AN SE20 46 B4
Ashley Av EPSOM KT18 78 B2
MRDN SM4 43 L6
Ashley Cl FRIM GU16 89 J1
GT/LBKH KT23 95 P5
RFNM GU10 106 D7
WEY KT13 38 G9
Ashley Cottages
ASHTD KT21 * 77 M8
Ashley Ct EPSOM KT18 78 B2
WOKN/KNAP GU21 * 71 M7
Ashley Dr BLKW GU17 67 M7
BNSTD SM7 79 L3
ISLW TW7 16 E4
WHTN TW2 25 J4
WOT/HER KT12 57 J2
Ashley Gdns
RCHPK/HAM TW10 26 C6
Ashley La CROY/NA CR0 63 K3
Ashley Park Av
WOT/HER KT12 39 H9
Ashley Park Crs
WOT/HER KT12 39 J9
Ashley Park Rd
WOT/HER KT12 57 J1
Ashley Ri WOT/HER KT12 57 J2
Ashley Rd DORK RH4 116 C8
EPSOM KT18 78 D6
FARN GU14 88 F3
HOR/WEW KT19 78 B2
HPTN TW12 40 A2
RCH/KEW TW9 17 L8
THDIT KT7 40 F7
THHTH CR7 45 H5
WIM/MER SW19 28 E9
WOKN/KNAP GU21 71 M7
WOT/HER KT12 57 H3
Ashley Wy CHOB/PIR GU24 70 D2
Ashling Rd CROY/NA CR0 46 A9
Ash Lodge Cl ASHV GU12 109 J5
Ash Lodge Dr ASHV GU12 109 J5
Ashlone Rd PUT/ROE SW15 18 G8
Ashlyn's Pk COB KT11 75 N2
Ashlyns Wy CHSGTN KT9 59 K5
Ashmead Rd
EBED/NFELT TW14 24 B4
Ashmere Av BECK BR3 47 K3
Ashmere Cl CHEAM SM3 61 H4
Ash Ms EPSOM KT18 78 C3
Ashmore La HORS RH12 175 H5
Ashmount Ter EA W5 * 17 K2
Ashness Rd BTSEA SW11 29 J1
Ashridge FARN GU14 68 B9
Ashridge Gn BNFD RG42 32 D2
Ashridge Wy MRDN SM4 43 K5
SUN TW16 24 B9
Ash Rd ASHV GU12 108 E6
BH/WHM TN16 105 H5
CHOB/PIR GU24 90 G6
CRAWE RH10 177 K3
CROY/NA CR0 64 G1
MRDN SM4 43 J9
SHPTN TW17 38 C5
WOKS/MYFD GU22 72 C9
Ash St ASHV GU12 109 J5
Ashtead La GODL GU7 150 C2
Ashtead Woods Rd
ASHTD KT21 77 J6
Ashton Cl SUT SM1 61 L3
WOT/HER KT12 57 K5
Ashton Gdns HSLWW TW4 15 P9
Ashton Rd WOKN/KNAP GU21 71 M6
Ashtree Av MTCM CR4 43 P3
Ash Tree Cl CROY/NA CR0 46 E7
FARN GU14 87 N4
HASM GU27 184 G1
SURB KT6 41 L9
Ashtrees CRAN GU6 171 H2
Ash Tree Wy CROY/NA CR0 46 E6
Ashurst Cl HORS RH12 192 F5
PGE/AN SE20 46 B2
PUR/KEN CR8 81 M4
Ashurst Dr CRAWE RH10 177 N5
KWD/TDW/WH KT20 117 P1
SHPTN TW17 38 A6
Ashurst Gdns
BRXS/STRHM SW2 * 30 B4
Ashurst Pk ASC SL5 * 34 D4
Ashurst Rd ASHV GU12 109 H2
KWD/TDW/WH KT20 98 F1
Ashurst Wk CROY/NA CR0 64 B1
Ash V MFD/CHID GU8 167 P6
Ashvale Rd TOOT SW17 29 J8
Ashview Cl ASHF TW15 23 H9
Ashview Gdns ASHF TW15 23 H8
Ashwell Av CBLY GU15 69 H2
Ashwood WARL CR6 82 C9
Ashwood Gdns CROY/NA CR0 65 H5
HYS/HAR UB3 15 H2
Ashwood Pk LHD/OX KT22 96 C3
WOKS/MYFD GU22 11 G6
Ashwood Rd EGH TW20 20 G9
WOKS/MYFD GU22 11 F6
Ashworth Pl GUW GU2 * 111 M5
Askill Dr PUT/ROE SW15 28 B1
Aslett St WAND/EARL SW18 28 E3
Asmar Cl COUL/CHIP CR5 80 G4
Aspen Cl COB KT11 75 N5
RGUE GU4 113 H2
STA TW18 22 C6
Aspen Gdns MTCM CR4 44 C6
Aspenlea Rd HMSMTH W6 19 H4
Aspen V CTHM CR3 81 P7
Aspen Wy EW KT17 79 H3
FELT TW13 24 C6
HORS RH12 192 D6

Aspin Wy BLKW GU17 ....67 M3
Aspley Rd WAND/EARL SW18 ..28 E1
Asprey Gv CTHM CR3 ....102 A4
Assembly Wk CAR SM5 ....44 A8
Assher Rd WOT/HER KT12 ......57 N2
Astleham Wy SHPTN TW17 ......38 A4
Aston Cl ASHTD KT21 ....77 J7
Aston Gn HEST TW5 ....15 L6
Aston Rd ESH/CLAY KT10 ....58 E4
RYNPK SW20 ....42 G3
Aston Ter BAL SW12 * 29 L2
Astonville St
WAND/EARL SW18 ....28 D4
Aston Wy EPSOM KT18 ....78 D5
Astor Cl ADL/WDHM KT15 ......55 P5
KUTN/CMB KT2 ....26 C9
Astoria Pde ASHF TW15 * 23 K7
STRHM/NOR SW16 * 29 P6
Astrop Ms HMSMTH W6 ....18 G1
Astrop Ter HMSMTH W6 ....18 G1
Astwood Ms SKENS SW7 ....19 M2
Atalanta Cl PUR/KEN CR8 ....63 J8
Atalanta St FUL/PGN SW6 ....19 H6
Atbara Rd FLEETS GU52 ....106 G2
TEDD TW11 ....26 A9
Atcham Rd HSLW TW3 ....16 C9
Atfield Gv BFOR GU20 ....52 D5
Atheldene Rd
WAND/EARL SW18 ....28 E4
Athelney St CAT SE6 ....31 P6
Athelstan Cl CRAWE RH10 ......177 P5
Athelstan Rd KUT KT1 ....41 M5
Athena Cl KUT KT1 ....9 F6
Athenlay Rd PECK SE15 ....31 L1
Atherfield Rd REDH RH1 ....119 H8
Atherley Wy HSLWW TW4 ....24 G3
Atherstone Ms SKENS SW7 * ...19 M2
Atherton Cl RGUE GU4 ....132 C2
STWL/WRAY TW19 ....22 G2
Atherton Dr WIM/MER SW19 ...28 A7
Atherton Rd BARN SW13 ....18 E5
Athlone ESH/CLAY KT10 ....58 E5
Athlone Rd
BRXS/STRHM SW2 ....30 A3
Atkins Cl WOKN/KNAP GU21 ...71 N7
Atkins Dr WWKM BR4 ....65 K2
Atkinson Ct HORL RH6 * 159 L2
Atkinson Rd CRAWE RH10 .....177 M7
Atkins Rd BAL SW12 ....29 L3
Atney Rd PUT/ROE SW15 ....19 J9
Atrebatti Rd SHST GU47 ....49 N8
Attebrouche Ct BRAK RG12 .....32 F8
Attenborough Cl
FLEETS GU51 ....87 H4
Atterbury Cl
BH/WHM TN16 ....105 H4
Attfield Cl ASHV GU12 ....109 H5
Attlee Cl CROY/NA CRO 45 L7
Attlee Gdns FLEETS GU52 .....106 F2
Attwood Cl SAND/SEL CR2 .....82 B3
Attwood GT/LBKH KT23 ....95 N4
Atwood Av RCH/KEW TW9 ....17 N2
Atwood Rd HMSMTH W6 ....18 F2
Aubyn HI NRWD SE27 ....30 D6
Aubyn Sq PUT/ROE SW15 ....18 E9
Auchinleck Ct
CRAWE RH10 * 179 J4
Auchinleck Wy ALDT GU11 ....108 A4
Auckland CI CRAWW RH11 ....176 C2
NRWD SE19 ....45 N2
Auckland HI WNWD SE27 ....30 D7
Auckland Ri NRWD SE19 ....45 N2
KUT KT1 ....41 M5
NRWD SE19 ....45 N2
Aucklands Gdns NRWD SE19 ..45 N2
Auden PI CHEAM SM3 * 61 J4
Audley Cl ADL/WDHM KT15 ....55 M4
Audley Dr SAND/SEL CR2 ....82 C4
Audley Firs WOT/HER KT12 .....57 K3
Audley PI BELMT SM2 ....61 M6
Audley Rd RCHPK/HAM TW10 ..26 E1
Audley Wy ASC SL5 ....33 M4
Audrey Cl BECK BR3 ....65 K3
Audric Cl KUTN/CMB KT2 ....9 H7
Augur Cl STA TW18 ....22 C8
Augusta Cl E/WMO/HCT KT8 ...39 P4
Augusta Rd WHTN TW2 ....25 K5
Augustine Cl DTCH/LGLY SL3 ...13 J8
Augustine Wy BNFD RG42 ....32 C1
Augustus Gdns CBLY GU15 ....69 H4
Augustus La SHGR GU5 ....133 P6
Augustus Rd WIM/MER SW19 ..28 A4
Aultone Wy CAR SM5 ....62 B2
SUT SM1 ....61 N1
Aurelia Gdns THHTH CR7 ....45 H6
Aurelia Rd CROY/NA CRO 44 C7
Auriol Cl EPSOM KT19 ....60 C2
Auriol Park Rd WPK KT4 ....60 C2
Auriol Rd WKENS W14 ....19 J2
Aurum Cl HORL RH6 ....159 L2
Austen Cl EGRIN RH19 ....180 F4
Austen Rd FARN GU14 ....88 C1
GU GU1 ....7 K5
Austin Cl CAT SE6 ....31 M3
PUR/KEN CR8 ....81 K7
Austyn Gdns BRYLDS KT5 * 41 P9
Autumn Cl WIM/MER SW19 .....28 F9
Autumn Dr BELMT SM2 ....61 M7
Avalon Cl RYNPK SW20 ....43 H3
Avalon Rd FUL/PGN SW6 ....19 M6
Avarn Rd TOOT SW17 ....29 J9
Avebury BRAK RG12 ....32 C5
Avebury Cl HORS RH12 ....192 F3
Avebury Pk SURB KT6 * 41 K7
Avebury Rd WIM/MER SW19 ....43 K1
Aveley La FNM GU9 ....127 N6
PUR/KEN CR8 ....81 H2
Aven Cl CRAN GU6 ....171 H1

Avening Rd
WAND/EARL SW18 ....28 D3
Avening Ter
WAND/EARL SW18 ....28 D2
Avenue C ADL/WDHM KT15 ....56 A2
Avenue Cl HEST TW5 ....15 K6
KWD/TDW/WH KT20 ....98 F2
LIPH GU30 ....182 D6
WDR/YW UB7 ....13 P1
Avenue Crs HEST TW5 ....15 J6
Avenue De Cagny
CHOB/PIR GU24 ....90 F2
Avenue Elmers SURB KT6 ....41 L6
Avenue Gdns HEST TW5 * 15 J5
HORL RH6 ....159 M2
MORT/ESHN SW14 ....18 C8
TEDD TW11 ....40 F1
Avenue One
ADL/WDHM KT15 ....56 A3
Avenue Pde SUN TW16 * 39 K4
Avenue Park Rd WNWD SE27 ..30 C5
Avenue Rd BELMT SM2 ....61 L8
BH/WHM TN16 ....84 C9
BNSTD SM7 ....79 M4
BTFD TW8 * 17 J3
COB KT11 ....75 M5
CRAN GU6 ....171 J2
CTHM CR3 ....101 M2
EPSOM KT18 ....78 B3
FARN GU14 ....88 F3
FELT TW13 ....24 A6
FLEETN GU51 ....86 F5
CSHT GU26 ....165 N8
HPTN TW12 ....40 B2
KUT KT1 ....41 M5
KUT KT1 ....8 E6
NWMAL KT3 ....42 C4
PGE/AN SE20 ....46 C2
RYNPK SW20 ....42 F3
SNWD SE25 ....46 A4
STA TW18 ....22 A8
SWTR RH13 ....192 E8
TEDD TW11 ....40 G1
WLGTN SM6 ....62 E6
Avenue South BRYLDS KT5 .....41 M8
Avenue Sucy GU15 ....68 C3
Avenue Ter NWMAL KT3 ....42 A4
The Avenue ADL/WDHM KT15..15 L8
ALDT GU11 ....108 E7
ASC SL5 ....33 P1
BECK BR3 ....47 H2
BELMT SM2 ....61 K7
BH/WHM TN16 ....104 E3
BRYLDS KT5 ....41 M7
CAR SM5 ....62 C6
CBLY GU15 ....68 D4
CHOB/PIR GU24 ....53 M7
CHSWK W4 ....18 C1
CLAP SW4 ....29 L2
COUL/CHIP CR5 ....80 F4
CRAN GU6 ....153 P6
CROY/NA CRO 45 N3
CTHM CR3 ....101 N7
CWTH RG45 ....49 L4
EGH TW20 ....21 N7
EGRIN RH19 ....162 F6
HEST TW5 ....15 L6
EW KT17 ....60 E5
FLEETN GU51 ....86 B8
GODL GU7 ....150 E2
GSHT GU26 ....165 N8
HEST TW5 ....15 J6
HORL RH6 ....159 J2
HPTN TW12 ....40 A2
HSLW TW3 ....16 E3
KUT KT1 ....41 M5
NRWD SE19 ....30 E9
RCH/KEW TW9 ....17 M7
RDKG RH5 ....117 N5
REDH RH1 ....140 A4
RFNM GU10 ....127 K9
RFNM GU10 ....146 G4
RGUW GU3 ....91 L7
STA TW18 ....37 M2
STWL/WRAY TW19 ....12 C9
SUN TW16 ....39 K3
TWK TW1 ....26 B1
WDSR SL4 ....20 C1
WPK KT4 ....60 D1
WWKM BR4 ....47 K8

Avenue Three
ADL/WDHM KT15 ....56 A3
Avenue Two
ADL/WDHM KT15 ....56 A3
Averil Gv STRHM/NOR SW16 ...30 C9
Averill St HMSMTH W6 ....19 H4
Avern Gdns E/WMO/HCT KT8 ..40 B5
Avern Rd E/WMO/HCT KT8 ......40 B5
Avery Cl EWKG RG40 ....48 B8
Aviary Rd WOKS/MYFD GU22 ..73 K2
Aviary Wy CRAWE RH10 ....179 K2
Aviemore Cl BECK BR3 ....46 E6
Aviemore Wy BECK BR3 ....46 E6
Avington Cl GU GU1 ....7 H2
Avington Gv PGE/AN SE20 ......46 C1
Avoca Rd TOOT SW17 ....29 P7
Avocet Crs SHST GU47 ....49 P9
Avon Cl ADL/WDHM KT15 ....55 L5
ASHV GU12 ....109 H5
FARN GU14 ....68 A3
SUT SM1 ....61 N3
WPK KT4 ....60 E1
Avondale ASHV GU12 ....109 H5
Avondale Av ESH/CLAY KT10 ..58 C2
STA TW18 ....37 K1
WPK KT4 ....60 E1
Avondale Cl HORL RH6 ....140 B8
WOT/HER KT12 ....57 L4

Avondale Gdns HSLWW TW4 ...24 G1
Avondale Rd ALDT GU11 ....108 D6
ASHF TW15 ....22 G6
FLEETN GU51 ....86 C5
MORT/ESHN SW14 ....18 B8
SAND/SEL CR2 ....63 L5
WIM/MER SW19 ....28 E8
Avon Gv BRAK RG12 ....32 E1
Avonmead
WOKN/KNAP GU21 ....72 A7
Avonmore Av GU GU3 ....7 K1
Avonmore Gdns
WKENS W14 * 19 K1
Avonmore PI WKENS W14 ....19 J2
Avonmore Rd WKENS W14 ......19 K2
Avon Rd FNM GU9 ....5 G6
SUN TW16 ....39 H1
Avon Wk CRAWW RH11 ....176 C6
Avonwick Rd HSLW TW3 ....16 B7
Avro Wy BF/WBF KT14 ....56 A8
WLGTN SM6 ....62 G6
Award Rd FLEETS GU52 ....106 D5
Axbridge BRAK RG12 ....32 G6
Axes La REDH RH1 ....140 E3
Axwood EPSOM KT18 ....78 A4
Ayebridges Av EGH TW20 ....36 E2
Ayesgarth FLEETS GU52 ....107 H1
Ayjay Cl ALDT GU11 ....108 D7
Aylesbury Rd HAYES SM20 * 66 C3
Aylesford Av BECK BR3 ....46 E6
Aylesham Wy YTLY GU46 ....66 F2
Aylesworth Sp WDSR SL4 ....20 G3
Aylett Rd ISLW TW7 ....16 E7
SNWD SE25 ....46 B5
Ayliffe Cl KUT KT1 ....9 H4
Ayling Ct FNM GU9 ....108 B7
Ayling Hi ALDT GU11 ....108 B5
Ayling La ALDT GU11 ....108 B6
Aylward Rd FSTH SE23 ....31 L5
RYNPK SW20 ....43 K3
Aymer Cl STA TW18 ....37 J2
Aymer Dr STA TW18 ....37 J2
Aynhoe Rd WKENS W14 ....19 H2
Ayrshire Gdns FLEETS GU51 ....87 H3
Ayrton Rd SKENS SW7 ....19 M3
Aysgarth BRAK RG12 ....32 B7
Aysgarth Rd DUL SE21 ....30 E2
Ayshe Court Dr SWTR RH13 ...192 D4
Azalea Ct WOKS/MYFD GU22 ..10 A7
Azalea Dr HASM GU27 ....184 D2
Azalea Gdns FLEETS GU52 ....107 H1
Azalea Wy CBLY GU15 ....69 K3

B

Babbacombe Cl CHSGTN KT9 ..59 K4
Babbacombe Rd BMLY BR1 .....47 P2
Babbs Md FNM GU9 ....4 C5
Baber Bridge Pde
EBED/NFELT TW14 * 24 D2
Baber Dr EBED/NFELT TW14 ...24 D2
Babington Rd
STRHM/NOR SW16 ....29 N8
Babs Fids RFNM GU10 ....126 A8
Babylon La
KWD/TDW/WH KT20 ....99 M7
Bachelor's La
RPLY/SEND GU23 ....94 C4
Back Dr CWTH RG45 * 49 M6
Back Gn WOT/HER KT12 ....57 L5
Back La BIL RH14 ....187 K8
BTFD TW8 * 17 K5
CRAWE RH10 ....178 D9
MFD/CHID GU8 ....129 M9
RCHPK/HAM TW10 ....26 B6
RGUE GU4 ....113 P2
Backley Gdns SNWD SE25 ....46 A7
Back Rd TEDD TW11 ....40 D1
Bacon Cl SHST GU47 ....67 P2
Bacon La RFNM GU10 ....146 F9
Badajos Rd ALDT GU11 ....108 B3
Baden Cl STA TW18 ....37 L1
Baden Dr HORL RH6 ....140 A4
Baden Powell Cl SURB KT6 .....59 M1
Baden Rd GUW GU2 ....111 N3
Bader Cl PUR/KEN CR8 ....81 M4
Badger Cl FELT TW13 ....24 C6
GUW GU2 ....111 P2
HSLWW TW4 ....15 L8
Badger Dr LTWR GU18 ....52 A8
Badgers Cl ASHF TW15 * 23 J8
FLEETS GU52 ....87 H3
GODL GU7 ....131 K5
HORS RH12 ....192 E4
WOKN/KNAP GU21 ....72 A7
Badgers Copse CBLY GU15 .....68 C5
WPK KT4 ....60 D1
Badgers Ct WPK KT4 * 60 D1
Badgers Cross
MFD/CHID GU8 ....149 N3
Badgers Hl VW GU25 ....36 B6
Badgers Hollow GODL GU7 ...131 K7
Badgers Holt YTLY GU46 ....66 F3
Badgers La WARL CR6 ....82 C8
Badgers Sett CWTH RG45 ....49 K4
Badgers Wk CTHM CR3 ....81 P7
NWMAL KT3 ....42 C3
PUR/KEN CR8 ....62 G9
Badgers Wy BIL RH14 ....188 D6
BRAK RG12 ....33 H2
EGRIN RH19 ....162 D9
Badgers Wd CTHM CR3 ....81 N7
Badger Wy RFNM GU10 ....107 H6
Badgerwood Dr FRIM GU16 .....68 F6
Badingham Dr LHD/OX KT22 ...96 E4
Badminton Rd BAL SW12 ....29 K2
Badshot Lea Rd FNM GU9 .....108 C9

Badshot Pk FNM GU9 ....108 C8
Bagley's La FUL/PGN SW6 ......19 M6
Bagot Cl ASHTD KT21 ....77 K5
Bagshot Gn BAGS GU19 ....51 N7
Bagshot Rd ASC SL5 ....34 B9
BRAK RG12 ....32 D4
CHOB/PIR GU24 ....53 H9
ENM GU10 ....5 G9
WOKN/KNAP GU21 ....71 H8
Bahram Rd HOR/WEW KT19 ....60 B8
Baigents La BFOR GU20 ....52 D5
Bailes La RGUW GU3 ....110 D4
Bailey Cl FRIM GU16 ....68 F8
REDH RH1 ....192 E3
Bailey Crs CHSGTN KT9 ....59 J9
Bailey Pl SYD SE26 ....31 K9
Bailey Rd DORK RH4 ....116 C8
Baileys Cl BLKW GU17 ....67 M4
Bailing HI HORS RH12 ....191 M4
Baillie Rd GU GU1 ....7 J5
Bain Av CBLY GU15 ....68 D7
Bainbridge Cl KUTN/CMB KT2 ..26 D8
Baines Cl SAND/SEL CR2 ....63 M4
Bainton Md
WOKN/KNAP GU21 ....71 N6
Baird Cl CRAWE RH10 ....177 K2
Baird Dr RGUW GU3 ....111 H4
Baird Gdns NRWD SE19 ....30 F7
Baird Rd FARN GU14 ....88 E1
Bakeham La EGH TW20 ....36 A1
Bakehouse Barn Cl
HORS RH12 ....192 D3
Bakehouse Ms ALDT GU11 * ...108 C4
Bakehouse Rd HORL RH6 ......140 B8
Baker La MTCM CR4 ....44 C2
Baker's Cl LING RH7 ....143 L8
Baker's La LING RH7 ....143 L9
Baker's Md GDST RH9 ....122 C1
Baker St WEY KT13 ....56 D3
Bakers Wy RDKG RH5 ....156 B7
Bakewell Wy NWMAL KT3 ....42 C3
Balaclava Rd SURB KT6 ....41 J8
Balchier Rd EDUL SE22 ....31 J2
Balchins La DORK RH4 ....116 A8
Balcombe Gdns HORL RH6 .....159 M2
Balcombe Rd CRAWE RH10 ....177 M4
CRAWE RH10 ....195 P1
HORL RH6 ....140 D9
Baldreys FNM GU9 ....127 L5
Baldry Gdns
STRHM/NOR SW16 ....29 P9
Baldwin Cl CRAWE RH10 ....177 M8
Baldwin Crs RGUE GU4 ....112 G3
Baldwin Gdns HSLW TW3 ....16 C6
Baldwins Fld EGRIN RH19 * ...162 B8
Balfern St BTSEA SW11 ....19 N7
Balfont Cl SAND/SEL CR2 ....82 A2
Balfour Av
WOKS/MYFD GU22 ....92 C2
Balfour Crs BRAK RG12 ....32 D6
Balfour Rd CAR SM5 ....62 B6
HSLW TW3 ....16 B8
NWDGN UB2 ....15 M1
SNWD SE25 ....46 A5
WEY KT13 ....56 B3
WIM/MER SW19 ....43 M1
Balgowan Cl NWMAL KT3 ....42 C5
Balgowan Rd BECK BR3 ....46 E4
Balham Gv BAL SW12 ....29 K3
Balham High Rd BAL SW12 ......29 L5
Balham Hi BAL SW12 ....29 L3
Balham New Rd BAL SW12 ......29 L3
Balham Park Rd TOOT SW17 ...29 J5
Balham Station Rd BAL SW12 ..29 L4
Balintore Ct SHST GU47 ....67 P1
The Ballands North
LHD/OX KT22 ....96 E2
The Ballands' South
LHD/OX KT22 ....96 E3
Ball & Wicket La FNM GU9 .....107 N7
Ballantine St
WAND/EARL SW18 ....19 N9
Ballantyne Rd FARN GU14 ....88 C1
Ballard Cl KUTN/CMB KT2 ....42 B1
Ballard Rd CBLY GU15 ....51 J9
Ballards Farm Rd
SAND/SEL CR2 ....64 A5
Ballards Gn
KWD/TDW/WH KT20 ....99 K1
Ballards La OXTED RH8 ....104 A9
Ballards Ri SAND/SEL CR2 ......64 A5
Ballards Wy SAND/SEL CR2 ....64 A4
Ballater Rd SAND/SEL CR2 ......63 P4
Ballencrieff Rd ASC SL5 ....34 F8
Ballfield Rd GODL GU7 ....131 K7
Ballina St FSTH SE23 ....31 L3
Ballingdon Rd BTSEA SW11 .....29 K2
Balliol Cl CRAWE RH10 ....177 J6
Balliol Wy SHST GU47 ....50 A8
Balloch Rd CAT SE6 ....31 P1
Ballsdown MFD/CHID GU8 .....167 P7
Balmoral Av BECK BR3 ....46 E5
Balmoral Cl PUT/ROE SW15 * ..28 A2
Balmoral Crs
E/WMO/HCT KT8 ....40 A2
FNM GU9 ....107 M8
Balmoral Dr FRIM GU16 ....68 G8
WOKS/MYFD GU22 ....72 G5
Balmoral Gdns HNWL W7 ....15 M8
SAND/SEL CR2 ....63 M8
Balmoral Ms SHB W12 ....18 D1
Balmoral Rd ASHV GU12 ....111 M5
KUT KT1 ....41 M5
WPK KT4 ....60 F2
Balmoral Wy BELMT SM2 ....61 L8
Balmuir Gdns PUT/ROE SW15 ..18 G9

Balquhain Cl ASHTD KT21 ....77 K6
Baltic Cl WIM/MER SW19 ....43 P1
Balvernie Gv
WAND/EARL SW18 ....28 C3
Bampfylde Cl WLGTN SM6 ......62 E2
Bampton Rd FSTH SE23 ....31 L6
Bampton Wy
WOKN/KNAP GU21 ....71 P7
Banavie Gdns BECK BR3 ....47 H2
Banbury BRAK RG12 ....32 G8
Banbury Cl FRIM GU16 ....69 H9
Banbury Ct BELMT SM2 * 61 L6
Bancroft Cl ASHF TW15 * 23 K8
Bancroft Ct REIG RH2 ....119 L5
Bancroft Rd CRAWE RH10 .....177 N5
REIG RH2 ....119 L5
Banders Ri GU GU1 ....112 G4
Band La EGH TW20 ....21 L8
Bandon Ri WLGTN SM6 ....62 F5
Bangalore St PUT/ROE SW15 ..18 G8
Banim St HMSMTH W6 ....18 F1
Bank Av MTCM CR4 ....43 P3
Bankhurst Rd CAT SE6 ....31 N3
Bank La CRAWE RH10 ....176 G5
KUTN/CMB KT2 ....41 L1
PUT/ROE SW15 ....27 K1
Bank Prec CRAWE RH10 * 177 K1
Bank Rd ALDT GU11 ....108 F1
Bank Side EWKG RG40 ....48 B7
Bankside FNM GU9 ....108 B7
SAND/SEL CR2 ....63 P5
WOKN/KNAP GU21 ....71 P7
Bankside Cl BH/WHM TN16.....84 A2
CAR SM5 ....62 A4
MFD/CHID GU8 ....148 E1
Bankside Dr THDIT KT7 ....59 H1
Bank's La EHSLY KT24 ....95 J2
Banks Rd CRAWE RH10 ....177 M6
Banks Wy RGUE GU4 ....112 D2
Bank Ter CRAWW RH11 * 176 D4
The Bank CRAWE RH10 * 179 H7
Bank Willow
RCHPK/HAM TW10 ....26 A6
Bannister Cl
BRXS/STRHM SW2 ....30 B4
MFD/CHID GU8 ....129 N8
Bannister Gdns HTWY RG27 ....48 C9
Bannister's Rd GUW GU2 ....111 M7
Bannow Cl HOR/WEW KT19 ....60 C3
Banstead Rd BELMT SM2 ....61 K6
BNSTD SM7 ....79 J3
CTHM CR3 ....101 M2
EW KT17 ....60 F8
PUR/KEN CR8 ....63 J3
Banstead Rd South
BELMT SM2 ....61 N8
Banstead Wy WLGTN SM6 ......62 G4
Barbara Cl FLEETS GU52 ....87 H3
SHPTN TW17 ....38 D6
Barber Cl CRAWE RH10 ....177 M9
Barber Dr CRAN GU6 ....153 H8
Barberry Cl FLEETS GU52 ....86 G9
Barberry Wy BLKW GU17 ....67 M5
Barb Ms HMSMTH W6 ....18 G1
Barbon Cl CBLY GU15 ....69 M5
Barchard St
WAND/EARL SW18 ....28 E1
Barclay Cl FUL/PGN SW6 * 19 L3
GT/LBKH KT23 ....96 E3
Barclay Rd CROY/NA CRO 2 E5
FUL/PGN SW6 ....19 L5
Barcombe Av
BRXS/STRHM SW2 ....29 P5
Bardney Rd MRDN SM4 ....43 M5
Bardolph Av CROY/NA CRO 64 E8
Bardolph Rd RCH/KEW TW9 ....17 M9
Bardon Wk
WOKN/KNAP GU21 ....71 P6
Bardsley Cl CROY/NA CRO 3 J5
Bardsley Dr FNM GU9 ....127 L5
Barfields REDH RH1 ....121 K4
Barford Cl FLEETN GU51 ....87 K7
Barfreston Wy PGE/AN SE20 ...46 B2
Bargate Cl NWMAL KT3 ....42 E8
Bargate Ri GODL GU7 ....131 J9
Barge Wk KUT KT1 ....8 B5
Bargrove Cl PGE/AN SE20 ....46 A1
Bargrove Crs CAT SE6 * 31 M5
Barham Cl WEY KT13 ....56 E3
Barham Rd CROY/NA CRO 2 E4
RYNPK SW20 ....42 G1
Barhatch La CRAN GU6 ....153 J3
Barhatch Rd CRAN GU6 ....153 J6
Baring Rd CROY/NA CRO 46 C9
Barker Cl KUT KT1 ....41 P5
Barker Rd CHERT KT16 ....37 J8
Barker Wk STRHM/NOR SW16 ..29 P5
Barkham Ride EWKG RG40 ......48 A7
Barkis Md SHST GU47 ....50 A7
Barkston Gdns ECT SW5 ....19 M3
Barlavington Wy
MFD/CHID GU8 ....149 P7
Barley Cl CRAWE RH10 ....176 G6
Barley Md BNFD RG42 ....32 G1
Barley Mow Cl
WOKN/KNAP GU21 ....71 K6
Barley Mow La
BRKHM/BTCW RH3 ....118 A5
Barley Mow Rd HI BOR GU35 ..164 C5
Barley Mow La
WOKN/KNAP GU21 ....71 K6
Barley Mow Pas CHSWK W4 ....18 B3
Barley Mow Wy SHPTN TW17 ..38 C5
Barley Wy FLEETS GU52 ....87 H2
Barlow Cl WLGTN SM6 ....62 G5
Barlow Rd CRAWW RH11 ....176 G6
HMSMTH W6 ....18 F2
HPTN TW12 ....40 A1
Barmouth Rd CROY/NA CRO ...64 D1
WAND/EARL SW18 ....28 F2
Barnaby Pl SKENS SW7 ....19 P2

Barnard Cl FRIM GU16 69 H8
SUN TW16 39 K1
WLGTN SM6 62 F6
Barnard Gdns NWMAL KT3 42 E5
Barnard Pl EW KT17 60 G8
Barnard Rd MTCM CR4 44 C4
WARL CR6 83 H8
Barnards Pl SAND/SEL CR2 63 K7
Barnard Wy ALDT GU11 108 B3
Barnato Cl BF/WBF KT14 74 A1
Barnby Rd WOKN/KNAP GU21 71 K6
Barn Cl ASHF TW15 23 L8
BNSTD SM7 79 P4
BRAK RG12 32 F3
CBLY GU15 68 G2
CRAWW RH11 194 E3
KWD/TDW/WH KT20 * 117 M3
Barn Ct CRAWE RH10 178 F1
Barn Crs PUR/KEN CR8 81 M2
Barncroft FNM GU9 5 G5
Barneby Cl WHTN TW2 25 M4
Barnes Av BARN SW13 18 E5
NWDGN UB2 15 P2
Barnes Br CHSWK W4 18 C7
Barnes Cl FARN GU14 88 F3
Barnes End NWMAL KT3 42 E6
Barnes High St BARN SW13 18 D7
Barnes Rd FRIM GU16 68 G8
GODL GU7 131 L5
Barnes Wallis Dr WEY KT13 56 A9
Barnett Cl LHD/OX KT22 77 H8
SHGR GU5 132 G5
Barnett Ct BRAK RG12 * 32 E3
Barnett Gn BRAK RG12 32 D7
Barnett La LTWR GU18 69 P1
SHGR GU5 132 F6
Barnett Rw RGUE GU4 92 B9
Barnett's Shaw OXTED RH8 103 K7
Barnett Wood La
ASHTD KT21 77 J7
Barnet Wood Rd
HAYES BR2 * 65 P2
Barn Fld BNSTD SM7 79 M3
Barnfield CRAN GU6 153 H9
NWMAL KT3 42 C7
YTLY GU46 67 H3
Barnfield Av CROY/NA CR0 46 C9
KUTN/CMB KT2 26 C7
MTCM CR4 44 D5
Barnfield Cl COUL/CHIP CR5 81 L8
Barnfield Gdns
KUTN/CMB KT2 26 D8
Barnfield Rd BH/WHM TN16 84 B9
CRAWE RH10 176 G4
SAND/SEL CR2 63 N7
Barnfield Wy OXTED RH8 123 N4
Barnfield Wood Cl BECK BR3 47 K7
Barnfield Wood Rd BECK BR3 47 K7
Barnhill Av HAYES BR2 47 N6
Barnlea Cl FELT TW13 24 F5
Barnmead CHOB/PIR GU24 53 M8
Barn Meadow Cl
FLEETS GU52 106 F3
Barn Meadow La
GT/LBKH KT23 95 P4
Barnmead Rd BECK BR3 46 D2
Barn Rd ADL/WDHM KT15 55 M7
Barnsbury Cl NWMAL KT3 42 A5
Barnsbury Crs BRYLDS KT5 42 A9
Barnsbury La BRYLDS KT5 59 P1
Barnscroft RYNPK SW20 42 F4
Barnsfold La HORS RH12 189 H4
Barnsford Crs
CHOB/PIR GU24 70 G1
Barnsley Cl FRIM GU16 89 K6
Barnsnap Cl HORS RH12 192 C4
Barnway EGH TW20 21 H8
Barnwell Rd HNHL SE24 30 B1
Barnwood Cl CRAWE RH10 177 M4
RGUW GU3 111 L3
Barnwood Ct GUW GU2 111 L3
Barnwood Rd GUW GU2 111 L4
The Barnyard
KWD/TDW/WH KT20 98 E4
Baron Cl BELMT SM2 61 M8
Baron Gv MTCM CR4 44 A5
Barons Court Rd WKENS W14 19 J3
Baronsfield Rd TWK TW1 * 26 A2
Baron's Hurst EPSOM KT18 78 A5
Barons Keep WKENS W14 * 19 J3
Baronsmead Rd BARN SW13 18 E6
The Barons TWK TW1 26 A2
Baron's Wk CROY/NA CR0 46 E7
Barons Wy EGH TW20 22 A9
REIG RH2 119 L9
Barossa Rd CBLY GU15 68 F1
Barracane Dr CWTH RG45 49 M5
Barrack Pth
WOKN/KNAP GU21 71 M7
Barrack Rd ALDT GU11 * 108 C4
GUW GU2 111 N3
HSLWW TW4 15 M9
Barrens Brae
WOKS/MYFD GU22 11 H6
Barrens Cl
WOKS/MYFD GU22 * 11 H7
Barrens Pk
WOKS/MYFD GU22 11 H6
Barrett Rd GT/LBKH KT23 96 C5
Barrhill Rd BRXS/STRHM SW2 29 P5
Barricane WOKN/KNAP GU21 71 P8
Barrie Cl COUL/CHIP CR5 80 E5
Barrie Rd FNM GU9 107 L7
Barrihurst La CRAN GU6 170 A1
Barringer Sq TOOT SW17 29 K7
Barrington Ct DORK RH4 116 G8
Barrington Ldg WEY KT13 56 E4
Barrington Rd CHEAM SM3 43 L9
CRAWE RH10 176 G7
DORK RH4 * 116 G8
PUR/KEN CR8 80 E1
SWTR RH13 192 D8
Barrington Wk
NRWD SE19 * 30 F9
Barrow Av CAR SM5 62 B6
Barrowgate Rd CHSWK W4 18 A3
Barrow Green Rd GDST RH9 122 G2
Barrow Hedges Cl CAR SM5 62 A6
Barrow Hedges Wy CAR SM5 62 A6
Barrow Hl WPK KT4 60 C1
Barrow Hill Cl WPK KT4 60 C1
Barrow Rd CROY/NA CR0 63 J4
STRHM/NOR SW16 29 N9
Barr's La WOKN/KNAP GU21 71 L5
Barry Cl CRAWE RH10 177 H8
Barry Rd EDUL SE22 31 H2
Barry Sq BRAK RG12 32 F8
Barry Ter ASHF TW15 * 23 J5
Barsons Cl PGE/AN SE20 46 C1
The Bars GU GU1 6 E5
Barston Rd WNWD SE27 30 D5
Barstow Crs
BRXS/STRHM SW2 30 A4
Bartholemew Ct
DORK RH4 * 116 G8
Bartholomew Cl
HASM GU27 184 D2
WAND/EARL SW18 19 N9
Bartholomew Pl BNFD RG42 32 C1
Bartholomew Wy
HORS RH12 192 F4
Bartlett Rd BH/WHM TN16 104 G6
Bartlett St SAND/SEL CR2 63 M4
Barton Cl ADL/WDHM KT15 55 L5
ALDT GU11 108 A5
SHPTN TW17 38 D7
Barton Crs EGRIN RH19 180 F3
Barton Gn NWMAL KT3 42 B3
Barton Pl RGUE GU4 * 112 F2
Barton Rd SHGR GU5 132 E7
WKENS W14 19 J3
Barton's Dr YTLY GU46 67 H4
Bartons Wy FARN GU14 67 N9
The Barton COB KT11 75 M1
Bartram Rd BROCKY SE4 31 M1
Barts Cl BECK BR3 46 G6
Barttelot Rd HORS RH12 192 B9
Barwell Cl CWTH RG45 49 K5
Barwell Ct CHSGTN KT9 * 59 J6
Barwood Av WWKM BR4 47 H9
Basden Gv FELT TW13 25 H5
Basemoors BRAK RG12 32 G3
Bashford Wy CRAWE RH10 177 N3
Basildene Rd HSLWW TW4 15 M8
Basildon Cl BELMT SM2 61 M7
Basildon Wy CRAWW RH11 176 B8
Basil Gdns CROY/NA CR0 46 D9
WNWD SE27 30 D8
Basingbourne Cl
FLEETS GU52 86 G9
Basingbourne Rd
FLEETS GU52 106 F1
Basing Cl THDIT KT7 40 F8
Basing Dr ALDT GU11 108 D7
Basingfield Rd THDIT KT7 40 F8
Basinghall Gdns BELMT SM2 61 M7
Basing Rd BNSTD SM7 79 K4
Basing Wy THDIT KT7 40 F8
Baskerville Rd
WAND/EARL SW18 29 H3
Bassano St EDUL SE22 30 G1
Basset Cl ADL/WDHM KT15 55 M8
Basset Dr REIG RH2 119 L4
Bassett Cl BELMT SM2 61 M7
FRIM GU16 68 G8
Bassett Gdns ISLW TW7 16 C5
Bassett Rd CRAWE RH10 177 N8
WOKS/MYFD GU22 72 G5
Bassetts Hl LING RH7 162 F2
Bassingham Rd
WAND/EARL SW18 28 F3
Baston Manor Rd
WWKM BR4 65 P2
Baston Rd HAYES BR2 65 P1
Basuto Rd FUL/PGN SW6 19 L6
Bat And Ball La FNM GU9 127 L7
Batavia Cl SUN TW16 39 L2
Batavia Rd SUN TW16 39 K2
Batcombe Md BRAK RG12 32 G8
Bateman Ct CRAWE RH10 * 177 K8
Batemans Cnr CHSWK W4 * 18 B2
Batemans Ct CRAWE RH10 177 K8
Bates Crs CROY/NA CR0 63 J5
STRHM/NOR SW16 44 E1
Bateson Wy
WOKN/KNAP GU21 72 G3
Bates Wk ADL/WDHM KT15 55 N5
Bathgate Rd WIM/MER SW19 28 A6
Bath House Rd CROY/NA CR0 44 G9
Bath Pas KUT KT1 8 C5
Bath Rd CBLY GU15 68 E2
CHSWK W4 18 C2
DTCH/LGLY SL3 13 J6
HEST TW5 15 M7
Baths Ap FUL/PGN SW6 * 19 K5
Bathurst Av WIM/MER SW19 43 M2
Batley Cl MTCM CR4 44 B8
Batoum Gdns HMSMTH W6 18 G1
Batsworth Rd MTCM CR4 43 P4
Batten Av WOKN/KNAP GU21 71 L8
Battersea Br BTSEA SW11 19 P5
Battersea Church Rd
BTSEA SW11 19 P6
Battersea High St
BTSEA SW11 19 P7
Battersea Ri BTSEA SW11 29 H1
Battlebridge La REDH RH1 120 D1
Battle Cl WIM/MER SW19 28 F9
Batts Hl REDH RH1 119 P3
The Baulk WAND/EARL SW18 28 D3
Bavant Rd STRHM/NOR SW16 44 G3
Bawdale Rd EDUL SE22 30 G1
Bawtree Cl BELMT SM2 61 N8
Bax Cl CRAN GU6 171 H1
Baxter Av REDH RH1 120 A5
Baxter Cl CRAWE RH10 177 L7
NWDGN UB2 16 B1
Bayards WARL CR6 82 C7
Bay Cl HORL RH6 140 A7
Bay Ct EA W5 * 17 L1
Bayeux KWD/TDW/WH KT20 99 H2
Bayfield Av FRIM GU16 68 G6
Bayfield Rd HORL RH6 140 A9
Bayford Cl FARN GU14 68 C7
Bayham Rd CHSWK W4 18 B1
MRDN SM4 43 M5
Bayhorne La HORL RH6 159 M3
Bayleaf Cl HPTN TW12 25 L8
Bayliss Ct GU GU1 6 D4
Baylis Wk CRAWW RH11 * 194 E1
Baynards Rd HORS RH12 171 K9
Bayonne Rd FUL/PGN SW6 19 J4
Bay Rd BRAK RG12 32 G3
Bays Cl SYD SE26 31 K8
Baysfarm Ct WDR/YW UB7 13 N6
Baythorn La HORL RH6 159 M3
Bay Tree Av LHD/OX KT22 76 G9
Baywood Cl FARN GU14 87 N2
Bazalgette Cl NWMAL KT3 42 A6
Bazalgette Gdns NWMAL KT3 42 B6
Beach Gv FELT TW13 25 H6
Beachy Rd CRAWW RH11 194 E1
Beacon Cl BNSTD SM7 79 H5
RFNM GU10 127 L8
Beacon Ct DTCH/LGLY SL3 12 G5
SWTR RH13 * 192 F6
Beacon Gdns FLEETN GU51 * 86 E6
Beacon Hl LING RH7 162 G4
WOKN/KNAP GU21 72 A8
Beacon Hill Ct GSHT GU26 165 N5
Beacon Hill Pk GSHT GU26 * 165 L6
Beacon Hill Rd FLEETS GU52 107 H2
GSHT GU26 165 M5
Beacon Pl CROY/NA CR0 62 G2
Beacon Rd FARN GU14 88 D7
HTHAIR TW6 23 K2
Beaconsfield Cl CHSWK W4 18 A3
Beaconsfield Gdns
ESH/CLAY KT10 58 E6
Beaconsfield Pl EW KT17 78 C1
Beaconsfield Rd BRYLDS KT5 41 M8
CHSWK W4 18 B1
CROY/NA CR0 45 M7
EPSOM KT18 78 B8
ESH/CLAY KT10 58 E6
NWMAL KT3 42 B3
TWK TW1 26 A3
WOKS/MYFD GU22 72 D9
Beaconsfield Terrace Rd
WKENS W14 19 J1
Beaconsfield Wk
FUL/PGN SW6 19 K6
Beacon View Rd
MFD/CHID GU8 148 D2
Beacon Wy BNSTD SM7 79 H5
Beadles La OXTED RH8 123 K1
Beadlow Cl MRDN SM4 43 P7
Beadman Pl WNWD SE27 * 30 C7
Beadman St WNWD SE27 30 C7
Beadnell Rd FSTH SE23 31 L4
Beadon Rd HAYES BR2 47 N5
HMSMTH W6 18 G2
Beaford Gv RYNPK SW20 43 J4
Beagle Cl FELT TW13 24 C7
Beales La RFNM GU10 127 K6
WEY KT13 56 D2
Beales Rd GT/LBKH KT23 96 B6
Bealeswood La RFNM GU10 146 B6
Beam Hollow FNM GU9 107 N7
Beardell St NRWD SE19 30 G9
Beard Rd RCHPK/HAM TW10 26 E8
Beard's Hl HPTN TW12 40 A2
Beard's Hill Cl HPTN TW12 40 A2
Beards Rd ASHF TW15 23 P9
Bearfield Rd KUTN/CMB KT2 8 D1
Bear La FNM GU9 5 F2
Bear Rd FELT TW13 24 E7
Bears Den
KWD/TDW/WH KT20 99 K2
Bearsden Wy HORS RH12 191 L7
Bearstead Ri BROCKY SE4 31 N1
Bearstead Ter BECK BR3 * 46 G2
Bearwood Cl
ADL/WDHM KT15 55 L5
Bearwood Gdns
FLEETN GU51 86 G6
Beasley's Ait SHPTN TW17 39 H7
Beasley's Ait La SUN TW16 39 H7
Beatrice Av
STRHM/NOR SW16 45 H4
Beatrice Pl KENS W8 19 M1
Beatrice Rd OXTED RH8 103 L8
RCHPK/HAM TW10 26 E1
Beattie Cl EBED/NFELT TW14 24 A4
GT/LBKH KT23 95 P4
Beatty Av GU GU1 112 E4
Beauchamp Rd
E/WMO/HCT KT8 40 B6
SUT SM1 61 L4
THHTH CR7 45 M2
TWK TW1 25 P3
Beauchamp Ter
PUT/ROE SW15 18 F8
Beauclare Cl ASHTD KT21 * 97 K1
Beauclerc Rd HMSMTH W6 18 F1
Beauclerk Cl FELT TW13 24 C4
Beaufighter Rd FARN GU14 88 C7
Beaufort Cl PUT/ROE SW15 27 P4
REIG RH2 119 K4
WOKS/MYFD GU22 72 G5
Beaufort Gdns ASC SL5 33 N2
HEST TW5 15 N6
STRHM/NOR SW16 45 H1
Beaufort Rd ASHV GU12 89 H9
FLEETS GU52 87 H8
FNM GU9 5 G2
KUT KT1 41 L5
RCHPK/HAM TW10 26 B7
REIG RH2 119 K4
TWK TW1 26 B3
WOKS/MYFD GU22 72 G5
Beauforts EGH TW20 21 H8
Beaufort St CHEL SW3 19 P4
Beaufort Wy EW KT17 60 E6
Beaufront Cl CBLY GU15 69 J1
Beaufront Rd CBLY GU15 69 J1
Beaulieu Av SYD SE26 31 J7
Beaulieu Cl BRAK RG12 33 H4
DTCH/LGLY SL3 12 A7
HSLWW TW4 24 G1
MTCM CR4 44 C2
TWK TW1 26 C2
Beaulieu Gdns BLKW GU17 67 N3
Beaulieu Pl CHSWK W4 18 A1
Beaumaris Pde FRIM GU16 69 H8
Beaumont Av RCH/KEW TW9 17 M8
WKENS W14 19 K3
Beaumont Cl CRAWW RH11 176 B6
KUTN/CMB KT2 9 J1
Beaumont Crs WKENS W14 19 K3
Beaumont Dr ASHF TW15 23 N8
Beaumont Gdns BRAK RG12 32 G6
Beaumont Gv ALDT GU11 108 A4
Beaumont Pl ISLW TW7 25 N1
Beaumont Rd CHSWK W4 18 A1
NRWD SE19 30 D9
PUR/KEN CR8 81 J2
WAND/EARL SW18 28 B3
Beaumonts REDH RH1 140 B4
Beauval Rd EDUL SE22 30 G2
Beaver Cl HORS RH12 192 D4
HPTN TW12 40 B2
PGE/AN SE20 * 46 A1
Beaver La YTLY GU46 67 J3
Beavers Cl FNM GU9 4 C4
GUW GU2 111 L4
Beavers Crs HSLWW TW4 15 M9
Beavers Hl FNM GU9 4 B3
Beavers La HSLWW TW4 15 L8
Beavers Rd FNM GU9 4 D4
Beavor La HMSMTH W6 18 E2
Beck Ct BECK BR3 46 D4
Beckenham Gv HAYES BR2 47 K3
Beckenham La HAYES BR2 47 L3
Beckenham Place Pk
BECK BR3 47 H1
Beckenham Rd BECK BR3 46 D2
WWKM BR4 47 H8
Beckenshaw Gdns
BNSTD SM7 80 A4
Becket Cl SNWD SE25 46 A7
WIM/MER SW19 * 43 M2
Beckett Av PUR/KEN CR8 81 K4
Beckett Cl STRHM/NOR SW16 29 N5
Beckett La CRAWW RH11 176 G2
Becketts Cl
EBED/NFELT TW14 24 C2
Becketts Pl KUT KT1 8 B3
Beckett Wk BECK BR3 31 M9
Beckett Wy EGRIN RH19 180 E3
Becket Wd RDKG RH5 138 A9
Beckford Av BRAK RG12 32 D7
Beckford Cl WKENS W14 19 K2
Beckford Rd CROY/NA CR0 45 P7
Beckford Wy CRAWE RH10 195 L1
Beck Gdns FNM GU9 107 L8
Beckingham Rd GUW GU2 111 N4
Beck La BECK BR3 46 D4
Beck River Pk BECK BR3 46 F2
Beck Wy BECK BR3 46 F4
Beckway Rd
STRHM/NOR SW16 44 F3
Beckwith Rd HNHL SE24 30 E2
Beclands Rd TOOT SW17 29 K9
Becmead Av
STRHM/NOR SW16 29 N7
Becondale Rd NRWD SE19 30 F8
Bective Rd PUT/ROE SW15 19 K9
Bedale Cl CRAWW RH11 176 F7
Beddington Farm Rd
CROY/NA CR0 44 G9
Beddington Gdns CAR SM5 62 C5
Beddington Gv WLGTN SM6 62 F4
Beddington La CROY/NA CR0 62 G1
MTCM CR4 44 E7
Beddington Ter
CROY/NA CR0 * 45 H8
Beddlestead La WARL CR6 83 M7
Bedfont Cl EBED/NFELT TW14 23 M2
MTCM CR4 44 C3
Bedfont Ct
STWL/WRAY TW19 13 L8
Bedfont Court Est
STWL/WRAY TW19 * 13 M9
Bedfont Green Cl
EBED/NFELT TW14 23 M4
Bedfont La
EBED/NFELT TW14 23 P3
Bedfont Rd FELT TW13 24 A6
STWL/WRAY TW19 23 J2
Bedford Av FRIM GU16 89 H2
Bedford Cl CHSWK W4 18 C4
WOKN/KNAP GU21 72 A4
Bedford Cnr CHSWK W4 * 18 C2
Bedford Crs FRIM GU16 88 G1
Bedford Hl BAL SW12 29 L5
Bedford La ASC SL5 35 H6
FRIM GU16 89 H1
Bedford Pk CROY/NA CR0 2 D2
Bedford Pl CROY/NA CR0 2 E2
Bedford Rd CHSWK W4 18 B1
GU GU1 6 D5
SWTR RH13 192 C9
WHTN TW2 25 L6
WPK KT4 60 G1
Bedford Vls KUT KT1 * 9 G5
Bedgebury Gdns
WIM/MER SW19 28 B5
Bedlow Wy CROY/NA CR0 63 H3
Bedser Cl THHTH CR7 45 L4
WOKN/KNAP GU21 11 G2
Bedster Gdns
E/WMO/HCT KT8 40 B3
Bedwardine Rd NRWD SE19 45 N1
Bedwell Gdns HYS/HAR UB3 14 G3
Beech Av BH/WHM TN16 84 B8
BTFD TW8 17 H5
CBLY GU15 68 F4
EHSLY KT24 115 M1
RFNM GU10 127 N8
SAND/SEL CR2 63 M9
Beechbrook Av YTLY GU46 67 H3
Beech Cl ASHF TW15 23 N8
BF/WBF KT14 74 A1
CAR SM5 62 B1
COB KT11 76 A1
DORK RH4 116 G6
EGRIN RH19 * 180 C1
EHSLY KT24 95 M8
LING RH7 142 E5
MFD/CHID GU8 167 P7
PUT/ROE SW15 27 M3
RYNPK SW20 27 P9
STWL/WRAY TW19 22 G3
SUN TW16 39 M3
WDR/YW UB7 14 C1
WOT/HER KT12 57 L3
Beech Close Ct COB KT11 57 P9
Beech Copse SAND/SEL CR2 63 N4
Beech Crs
KWD/TDW/WH KT20 118 A1
Beechcroft ASHTD KT21 77 M8
Beechcroft Av NWMAL KT3 42 A2
PUR/KEN CR8 81 M4
Beechcroft Cl ASC SL5 34 D5
HEST TW5 15 N5
LIPH GU30 182 A7
STRHM/NOR SW16 30 A8
Beechcroft Dr RGUW GU3 111 K8
Beechcroft Mnr WEY KT13 56 F2
Beechcroft Rd CHSGTN KT9 59 M3
MORT/ESHN SW14 * 18 A8
TOOT SW17 29 J6
Beechdale Rd
BRXS/STRHM SW2 30 A2
Beechdene
KWD/TDW/WH KT20 98 F2
Beech Dr BLKW GU17 67 P4
KWD/TDW/WH KT20 99 K2
REIG RH2 119 P5
RPLY/SEND GU23 93 K4
Beechen Cliff Wy ISLW TW7 16 F7
Beechen La
KWD/TDW/WH KT20 99 K5
Beechen Pl FSTH SE23 31 K5
The Beeches Av CAR SM5 62 A6
Beeches Cl
KWD/TDW/WH KT20 99 L3
PGE/AN SE20 46 C2
Beeches Crs CRAWE RH10 177 H7
Beeches La EGRIN RH19 181 J5
Beeches Rd CHEAM SM3 43 J9
TOOT SW17 29 H6
The Beeches ASHV GU12 89 H6
BNSTD SM7 79 M5
LHD/OX KT22 96 E4
SHGR GU5 132 D7
STA TW18 * 22 D8
Beeches Wk CAR SM5 61 P7
Beeches Wd
KWD/TDW/WH KT20 99 L2
Beechey Cl CRAWE RH10 160 C9
Beechey Wy CRAWE RH10 160 C9
Beech Farm Rd WARL CR6 83 K9
Beechfield BNSTD SM7 79 M2
Beechfield Rd CAT SE6 31 N4
Beech Flds EGRIN RH19 162 E9
Beech Gdns CRAWE RH10 179 H4
WOKN/KNAP GU21 72 C4
Beech Gln BRAK RG12 32 D5
Beech Gv ADL/WDHM KT15 55 M3
CHOB/PIR GU24 70 C9
CTHM CR3 101 N6
EPSOM KT18 78 F6
GT/LBKH KT23 96 A7
GUW GU2 111 M5
MTCM CR4 44 F6
NWMAL KT3 42 B4
Beech Hall CHERT KT16 * 54 G6
Beech Hanger End
GSHT GU26 165 L8
Beech Hl BOR GU35 164 E7
MFD/CHID GU8 166 G2
WOKS/MYFD GU22 92 B3
Beech Hill Rd ASC SL5 34 E7
BOR GU35 164 C5
Beech Holme CRAWE RH10 179 H3
Beech Holt LHD/OX KT22 97 J2
Beech House Rd
CROY/NA CR0 2 E6
Beeching Cl ASHV GU12 109 K3
Beeching Wy EGRIN RH19 180 C2
Beech La GSHT GU26 165 L7
GUW GU2 112 A8
RGUW GU3 110 A5
Beechlawn GU GU1 7 J4
Beechmeads COB KT11 * 75 M2
Beechmont Av VW GU25 36 B7
Beechmore Gdns
CHEAM SM3 61 H1
Beechnut Dr BLKW GU17 67 M2
Beechnut Rd ASHV GU12 108 D5
Beecholme EW KT17 * 79 J3
Beecholme Av MTCM CR4 44 D2
Beech Ride FLEETS GU52 86 F8
SHST GU47 49 M9
Beech Rd BH/WHM TN16 84 A6
EBED/NFELT TW14 23 P3
EPSOM KT18 78 D4
FARN GU14 68 D9

FRIM GU16 ....89 H1
HASM GU27 ....184 E3
HORS RH12 ....192 C5
REDH RH1 ....100 E6
REIG RH2 ....119 L3
STRHM/NOR SW16 ....44 G3
Beechrow KUTN/CMB KT2 ......26 D7
Beechside CRAWE RH10 ......177 H6
Beechtree Av ECH TW20 ....20 G9
Beech Tree Cl
  CRAWE RH10 * 176 G4
Beech Tree Dr FNM GU9 ....108 C9
Beech Tree La STA TW18 * 37 M3
Beech Tree Pl SUT SM1 ....61 M4
Beech V WOKS/MYFD GU22 ...10 E6
Beech Wk EW KT17 ....60 E9
Beechway GU GU1 ....112 F4
Beechwood
  KWD/TDW/WH KT20 * 117 P2
Beechwood Av
  COUL/CHIP CR5 ....80 D4
  KWD/TDW/WH KT20 ....99 L1
  RCH/KEW TW9 ....17 N6
  STA TW18 ....22 E9
  SUN TW16 ....24 B9
  THHTH CR7 ....45 K5
  WEY KT13 ....56 C3
Beechwood Cl ASC SL5 ....33 N1
  FLEETN GU51 ....86 F3
  SURB KT6 ....41 J8
  WEY KT13 ....56 C3
  WOKN/KNAP GU21 ....71 L6
Beechwood Dr COB KT11 ....58 A9
Beechwood Gdns
  CTHM CR3 ....102 A2
Beechwood La WARL CR6 ....82 D8
Beechwood Mnr WEY KT13 ...56 C3
Beechwood Pk LHD/OX KT22 ...97 J2
Beechwood Rd CTHM CR3 ...102 A2
  SAND/SEL CR2 ....63 N7
  VW GU25 ....35 P8
  WOKN/KNAP GU21 ....71 L7
Beechwood Vls REDH RH1 ...140 C6
Beecot La WOT/HER KT12 ...57 L1
Beecroft La BROCKY SE4 ...31 M1
Beecroft Ms BROCKY SE4 ...31 M1
Beecroft Rd BROCKY SE4 ...31 M1
Beeding Cl HORS RH12 ......192 F5
Beedingwood Dr
  HORS RH12 ....193 K4
Beehive Ring Rd
  CRAWE RH10 ....159 L8
Beehive Rd STA TW18 ....22 E8
Beehive Wy REIG RH2 ......119 M9
Beeleigh Rd MRDN SM4 ......43 M5
Beeston Wy
  EBED/NFELT TW14 ....24 D2
Beeton's Av ASHV GU12 ......109 J2
Beggarshouse La HORS RH6 ...157 P4
  CHOB/PIR GU24 ....53 J9
  SHGR GU5 ....133 K9
Beggar's Roost La SUT SM1 ...61 L5
Begonia Pl HPTN TW12 ....25 P3
Behenna Cl CRAWW RH11 ...176 B6
Beira St BAL SW12 ....29 L3
Belcroft Cl BMLY BR1 ......47 M1
Beldam Bridge Rd
  CHOB/PIR GU24 ....53 K8
Beldham Gdns
  E/WMO/HCT KT8 ....40 B4
Beldham Rd RFNM GU10 ...127 K6
Belfast Rd SNWD SE25 ......46 A6
Belfield Rd HOR/WEW KT19 ...60 B7
Belfry Ms SHST GU47 ....49 K9
The Belfry RH1 ....120 B4
Belgrade Rd HPTN TW12 ......40 B2
Belgrave Ct WOT/HER KT12 ...57 K4
Belgrave Cl BLKW GU17 ......67 D5
Belgrave Crs SUN TW16 ......39 K2
Belgrave Mnr
  WOKS/MYFD GU22 ....10 C7
Belgrave Rd BARN SW13 ......18 E5
  HSLWW TW4 ....15 P8
  SNWD SE25 ....45 P5
  SUN TW16 ....39 K2
Belgrave Wk MTCM CR4 ......44 A4
Belgravia Ms KUT KT1 ....41 K5
Bellamy Cl WKENS W14 ....19 K3
Bellamy Rd CRAWE RH10 ...177 M9
Belland Dr ALDT GU11 ......108 A5
Bel La FELT TW13 ....24 F6
Bellasis Av BRXS/STRHM SW2 ...29 P4
Bell Av WDR/YW UB7 ....14 B1
Bell Bridge Rd CHERT KT16 ...37 K9
Bell Cl FARN GU14 ....88 E1
Bell Crs COUL/CHIP CR5 ...100 D7
Bell Dr WAND/EARL SW18 ...28 B3
Bellever Hl CBLY GU15 ....68 G3
Belleville Rd BTSEA SW11 ...29 J1
Belle Vue Cl ASHV GU12 ...108 F4
  STA TW18 ....22 C9
Bellevue Pk THHTH CR7 ......45 L4
Bellevue Rd BARN SW13 ......18 E7
  KUT KT1 ....8 E7
  TOOT SW17 ....29 J3
Bellew Rd FRIM GU16 ....89 K1
Bellew St TOOT SW17 ....28 E7
Bellfields CROY/NA CR0 ......64 F7
Bellfields Rd GU GU1 ....112 B3
Bell Gn CAT SE6 ....31 N1
Bell Green La SYD SE26 ......31 N8
Bell Hammer EGRIN RH19 ...180 D3
Bellingham Cl CBLY GU15 ......69 L4
Bellingham Gn CAT SE6 ......31 P6

Bell La BLKW GU17 ....67 N3
  LHD/OX KT22 ....96 D3
  RFNM GU10 ....146 B1
  TWK TW1 ....25 P4
Bell Lane Cl LHD/OX KT22 ...96 D3
Bellmarsh Rd
  ADL/WDHM KT15 ....55 M3
Bell Meadow GDST RH9 ...122 C3
  NRWD SE19 ....30 F7
Belloc Cl CRAWE RH10 ......177 L4
Belloc Ct SWTR RH13 * 192 F7
Bello Cl BRXS/STRHM SW2 ...30 C4
Bell Pde HSLW TW3 * 16 B9
  WWKM BR4 * 47 J1
Bell Pl BAGS GU19 * 52 D6
Bell Rd E/WMO/HCT KT8 ......40 D6
  HASM GU27 ....184 B7
  HORS RH12 ....191 P2
  HSLW TW3 ....16 B9
Bells La DTCH/LGLY SL3 ......12 F3
Bell Rd REIG RH2 ....119 L5
Belltrees Gv
  STRHM/NOR SW16 ....30 A8
Bell Vale La HASM GU27 ...184 D6
Bell Weir Cl
  STWL/WRAY TW19 ....21 N5
Bellwether La REDH RH1 ...141 K5
Belmont Av GUW GU2 ......111 M2
  NWDGN UB2 ....15 N1
  NWMAL KT3 ....42 E6
Belmont Cl FARN GU14 ......88 D1
Belmont Gv CHSWK W4 ......18 B2
Belmont Ms CBLY GU15 ......68 E5
Belmont Ri BELMT SM2 ......61 J5
Belmont Rd BECK BR3 ......46 E3
  BELMT SM2 ....61 L8
  CBLY GU15 ....68 E4
  CWTH RG45 ....49 M3
  LHD/OX KT22 ....96 C2
  REIG RH2 ....119 N6
  SNWD SE25 ....46 B6
  WHTN TW2 ....25 L5
  WLGTN SM6 ....62 D3
Belmont Ter CHSWK W4 ......18 B2
Belmore Wk
  WOKS/MYFD GU22 ....73 H5
Beloe Cl BARN SW13 ....18 E9
Belsize Av WEA W13 ....17 H1
Belsize Gdns SUT SM1 ......61 M4
Belsize Rd FARN GU14 ......88 E6
Belstone Ms FARN GU14 ......68 C9
Beltane Dr WIM/MER SW19 ...28 A6
Beltham Crs BAL SW12 * 29 M3
Belton Rd FBLY GU14 ....88 B1
Beltran Rd FUL/PGN SW6 ...19 M7
Belvedere Av
  WIM/MER SW19 ....28 B8
Belvedere Cl ESH/CLAY KT10 ...58 B4
  FLEETN GU51 ....86 C6
  GUW GU2 ....111 P3
  TEDD TW11 ....25 M8
  WEY KT13 ....56 C4
Belvedere Ct BLKW GU17 ......67 P5
Belvedere Dr
  WIM/MER SW19 ....28 B8
Belvedere Gdns
  E/WMO/HCT KT8 ....39 P6
Belvedere Gv
  WIM/MER SW19 ....28 B8
Belvedere Rd BH/WHM TN16 ...84 D7
  FARN GU14 ....88 E5
  HNWL W7 ....16 E1
  NRWD SE19 ....30 G9
Belvedere Sq
  WIM/MER SW19 ....28 B8
The Belvedere
  WBPTN SW10 * 19 N6
Belvoir Cl FRIM GU16 ....69 H7
Belvoir Rd EDUL SE22 ....31 H3
Bembridge Ct CWTH RG45 ...49 H5
Bemish Rd PUT/ROE SW15 ...19 H8
Benbow La MFD/CHID GU8 ...169 P7
Benbow Rd HMSMTH W6 ......18 F1
Benbricke Gn BNFD RG42 ...32 C2
Benbrick Rd GUW GU2 ......111 N6
The Bence EGH TW20 ....36 F4
Bench Fld SAND/SEL CR2 ......63 P6
Benchfield Cl EGRIN RH19 ...180 G3
The Bench
  RCHPK/HAM TW10 * 26 B6
Bencombe Rd PUR/KEN CR8 ...81 J3
Bencroft Rd
  STRHM/NOR SW16 ....44 E5
Bencurtis Pk WWKM BR4 ...65 K1
Bendemeer Rd
  PUT/ROE SW15 ....19 H8
Bendon Va WAND/EARL SW18 ...28 E3
Benedict Dr
  EBED/NFELT TW14 ....23 N3
Benedict Gdn BNFD RG42 ...32 C1
Benedict Rd MTCM CR4 ......43 P4
Benedict Whf MTCM CR4 ......44 A4
Benen-Stock Rd
  STWL/WRAY TW19 ....22 D2
Benett Gdns
  STRHM/NOR SW16 ....44 G3
Benfleet Cl COB KT11 ....75 N1
  SUT SM1 ....61 N2
Benham Cl BTSEA SW11 ......19 P8
  CHSGTN KT9 ....59 J5
  COUL/CHIP CR5 ....81 K7
Benham Gdns HSLW TW3 ...24 D1
Benhams Dr HORL RH6 ...140 C8
Benhill Av SUT SM1 ....61 M3
Benhill Rd SUT SM1 ....61 N2
Benhill Wood Rd SUT SM1 ...61 N3
Benhilton Gdns SUT SM1 ...61 M2
Benhurst Cl SAND/SEL CR2 ...64 D8
Benhurst Gdns SAND/SEL CR2 ...64 C8
Benhurst La
  STRHM/NOR SW16 ....30 B8

Benin St LEW SE13 ....31 P5
Benjamin Cl CRAWE RH10 ...177 N7
Benner La CHOB/PIR GU24 ...70 F1
Bennerley Rd BTSEA SW11 ...29 J1
Bennet Cl KUT KT1 ....8 A3
Bennett Cl COB KT11 ....75 J2
  CRAWE RH10 ....177 L9
Bennett Ct CBLY GU15 ......68 E3
Bennetts Av CROY/NA CR0 ...64 E1
Bennetts Cl MTCM CR4 ......44 D2
Bennetts Farm Pl
  GT/LBKH KT23 ....95 P5
Bennetts Ri ALDT GU11 ......108 E6
Bennetts Rd SWTR RH13 ...192 D9
Bennett St CHSWK W4 ......18 C4
Bennetts Wy CROY/NA CR0 ...64 E1
Bennetts Wd RDKG RH5 ...156 B7
Bennett Wy RGUE GU4 ......93 L9
Bennings Cl BNFD RG42 ......32 C1
Bens Acre SWTR RH13 ......192 G7
Bensbury Cl PUT/ROE SW15 ...27 N3
Bensham Cl THHTH CR7 ......45 L5
Bensham Gv THHTH CR7 ......45 L3
Bensham La THHTH CR7 ......45 K5
Bensham Manor Rd
  THHTH CR7 ....45 L5
Benson Cl HSLW TW3 ....16 A9
Benson Rd CROY/NA CR0 ......63 J2
  CWTH RG45 ....49 H4
  FSTH SE23 ....31 K4
Benson's La HORS RH12 ...193 H1
Benthall Gdns PUR/KEN CR8 ...81 L5
Bentham Av
  WOKN/KNAP GU21 ....72 G4
Bentley Copse CBLY GU15 ...69 K4
Bentley Dr WEY KT13 ....56 C6
Benton's La WNWD SE27 ...30 D7
Benton's Ri WNWD SE27 ......30 F8
Bentsbrook Cl RDKG RH5 ...137 H2
Bentsbrook Pk RDKG RH5 ...137 H2
Benwell Ct SUN TW16 * 39 J2
Ben Well Rd CHOB/PIR GU24 ...53 J8
Benwell Rd CHOB/PIR GU24 ...70 C8
Beomonds Rw CHERT KT16 * ...37 L8
Berberis Cl GU GU1 ....112 A3
Berberis Wk WDR/YW UB7 ...14 A2
Berber Rd BTSEA SW11 ......29 J1
Berenger Wk WBPTN SW10 * ...19 P5
Beresford Av BRYLDS KT5 ...42 C7
  TWK TW1 ....26 B2
Beresford Cl FRIM GU16 ......89 H1
Beresford Gdns HSLWW TW4 ...24 C1
Beresford Rd BELMT SM2 ......61 K6
  DORK RH4 ....117 H7
  KUTN/CMB KT2 ....9 F2
  NWMAL KT3 ....41 P5
Berestede Rd HMSMTH W6 ...18 D3
Bergenia Ct CHOB/PIR GU24 ...70 E2
Berghem Ms WKENS W14 ...19 H1
Berisford Ms
  WAND/EARL SW18 ....28 F2
Berkeley Av HEST TW5 ......15 L6
Berkeley Cl CRAWW RH11 ...176 A9
  FLEETN GU51 ....87 H6
  KUTN/CMB KT2 ....41 L1
  STWL/WRAY TW19 ....22 A5
Berkeley Ct WEY KT13 ......56 F1
Berkeley Crs FRIM GU16 ......89 H1
Berkeley Dr E/WMO/HCT KT8 ...39 M4
Berkeley Gdns BF/WBF KT14 ...73 P3
  ESH/CLAY KT10 ....58 G6
  WOT/HER KT12 ....39 H8
Berkeley Ms SUN TW16 ......39 L4
Berkeley Pl EPSOM KT18 ......78 B4
  WIM/MER SW19 ....27 P3
Berkeley Rd BARN SW13 ......18 E6
Berkeley Waye HEST TW5 ...15 L5
Berkeley Wy WHTN TW2 * ...25 M6
Berkley Cl GU GU1 ....7 J2
Berkshire Cl CTHM CR3 ...101 M2
Berkshire Corpse Rd
  ALDT GU11 ....88 A8
Berkshire Rd CBLY GU15 ...51 H9
Berkshire Wy BRAK RG12 ...32 C4
  MTCM CR4 ....44 G5
Bermadine Cl BNFD RG42 ...32 C1
Bernard Av WEA W13 ....17 H1
Bernard Gdns
  WIM/MER SW19 ....28 C8
Bernard Rd WLGTN SM6 ......62 D4
Bernel Dr CROY/NA CR0 ......64 F2
Berne Rd THHTH CR7 ....45 K6
Bernersh Cl SHST GU47 ......49 N8
Berney Rd CROY/NA CR0 ......45 M7
Berridge Rd NRWD SE19 ......30 E8
Berrington Dr EHSLY KT24 ...94 H4
Berrybank SHST GU47 ....68 A2
Berrycroft BNFD RG42 ......32 F2
Berrylands BRYLDS KT5 ......41 N6
  RYNPK SW20 ....42 G7
Berrylands Rd BRYLDS KT5 ...41 M7
Berry La DUL SE21 ....30 E7
  RGUW GU3 ....91 K4
Berryman's La SYD SE26 ......31 L7
Berry Meade ASHTD KT21 ...77 M6
Berry Meade Cl ASHTD KT21 ...77 M6
Berrymeade Rd CHSWK W4 ...18 B1
Berryscroft Rd STA TW18 ...37 N1
Berry's Green Rd
  BH/WHM TN16 ....84 F5
Berry's Hl BH/WHM TN16 ...84 F4
Berry's La BF/WBF KT14 ......73 P8
Berry Wk ASHTD KT21 ....77 M8
Bertal Rd TOOT SW17 ....28 G7
Bertie Rd SYD SE26 ....31 L9
Bertram Cl KUTN/CMB KT2 ...41 N1
Bert Rd THHTH CR7 ....45 L6

Berwyn Av HSLW TW3 ....16 B6
Berwyn Rd HNHL SE24 ......30 C4
  RCHPK/HAM TW10 ....17 P9
Beryl Rd HMSMTH W6 ....19 H3
Berystede KUTN/CMB KT2 ......9 K1
Bessant Dr RCH/KEW TW9 ...17 P6
Bessborough Rd
  PUT/ROE SW15 ....27 M4
Beswick Gdns BRAK RG12 ...33 H2
Beta Rd CHOB/PIR GU24 ......53 M8
  FARN GU14 ....88 B2
  WOKS/MYFD GU22 ....11 K1
Betchets Green Rd
  RDKG RH5 ....137 J7
Betchley Cl EGRIN RH19 ...162 D9
Betchworth Cl SUT SM1 ......61 P4
Betchworth Wy
  CROY/NA CR0 ....65 J7
Bethany Pl
  WOKN/KNAP GU21 * 10 A5
Bethany Waye
  EBED/NFELT TW14 ....23 P3
Bethel Cl FNM GU9 ....107 P8
Bethel Rd FNM GU9 ....107 P8
Bethersden Cl BECK BR3 ......46 F1
Bethune Cl CRAWE RH10 ...177 L6
Bethune Rd SWTR RH13 ...192 D9
Betjeman Cl COUL/CHIP CR5 ...81 H6
Betjeman Wk YTLY GU46 ......66 F4
Betley Ct WOT/HER KT12 ......57 K2
Betony Cl CROY/NA CR0 ......46 D9
Bettridge Rd FUL/PGN SW6 ...19 K7
Betts Cl BECK BR3 ....46 E3
Betts Wy CRAWE RH10 ......176 C1
  PGE/AN SE20 ....46 B3
  SURB KT6 ....41 H9
Betula Cl PUR/KEN CR8 ......81 M4
Between Streets COB KT11 ...75 K3
Beulah Av THHTH CR7 * 45 L3
Beulah Crs THHTH CR7 ......45 L3
Beulah Gv CROY/NA CR0 ......45 K7
Beulah Hl NRWD SE19 ......30 D9
Beulah Rd SUT SM1 ....61 L3
  THHTH CR7 ....45 L4
  WIM/MER SW19 ....43 J1
Beulah Wk CTHM CR3 ....82 E9
Bevan Ct CROY/NA CR0 ......63 H4
Bevan Ga BNFD RG42 ....32 C2
Bevan Pk EW KT17 ....60 D9
Beveren Cl FLEETN GU51 ......87 H3
Beverley Av ADL/WDHM KT15 ...55 P4
  FARN GU14 ....88 A2
Beverley Cl
  ADL/WDHM KT15 ....55 M3
  BARN SW13 ....18 D8
  BTSEA SW11 ....19 J9
  CHSGTN KT9 ....59 J3
  EPSOM KT18 ....78 E3
  FARN GU14 ....88 A2
Beverley Crs FARN GU14 ......88 B4
Beverley Gdns BARN SW13 ...18 D8
  WPK KT4 ....42 E9
Beverley Hts REIG RH2 ......119 M3
Beverley La KUTN/CMB KT2 ...42 B1
Beverley Ms CRAWE RH10 ...177 K6
Beverley Rd BARN SW13 ......18 D8
  CHSWK W4 ....18 D3
  CTHM CR3 ....81 N6
  KUT KT1 ....8 A2
  MTCM CR4 ....44 E5
  NWDGN UB2 ....15 N2
  NWMAL KT3 ....42 D5
  PGE/AN SE20 ....46 B3
  SUN TW16 ....39 H2
  WHTN TW2 ....25 L3
  WPK KT4 ....61 H1
Beverley Wy NWMAL KT3 ...42 D2
Beverley Wy (Kingston by Pass)
  NWMAL KT3 ....42 D2
Beverstone Rd
  BRXS/STRHM SW2 ....30 A1
  THHTH CR7 ....45 J5
Bevill Cl SNWD SE25 ....46 A4
Bevington Rd BECK BR3 ......47 H3
Bevin Sq TOOT SW17 ....29 J6
Bewbush Dr CRAWW RH11 ...176 A7
Bewley St WIM/MER SW19 ...28 F9
Bewlys Rd WNWD SE27 ......30 C8
Bexhill Cl FELT TW13 ....24 F5
Bexhill Rd BROCKY SE4 ......31 N2
  MORT/ESHN SW14 ....18 A8
Beynon Rd CAR SM5 ....62 B4
Bicester Rd RCH/KEW TW9 ...17 N7
Bickersteth Rd TOOT SW17 ...29 J9
Bickerton St TOOT SW17 ......29 H9
Bicknell Rd FRIM GU16 ......68 G6
Bickney Wy LHD/OX KT22 ...96 C2
Bicknoller Cl BELMT SM2 ......61 M8
Bidborough Cl HAYES BR2 ...47 M6
Biddulph Rd SAND/SEL CR2 ...63 M7
Bideford Cl FELT TW13 ......24 G6
Bidhams Crs
  KWD/TDW/WH KT20 ....98 G1
The Bield REIG RH2 ....119 J7
Big Barn Gv BNFD RG42 ......32 F1
Big Common La REDH RH1 ...121 K4
Biggin Av MTCM CR4 ....44 B1
Biggin Cl CRAWW RH11 ......176 C9
Biggin Hl NRWD SE19 ....45 K1
Biggin Wy NRWD SE19 ......45 K1
Bigginwood Rd
  STRHM/NOR SW16 ....45 K1
Bigg's Rw PUT/ROE SW15 ...19 H8
Bignor Cl HORS RH12 ......192 F4
Bilberry Cl CRAWW RH11 ...176 E6
Billesden Rd CHOB/PIR GU24 ...90 C1
Billing Av EWKG RG40 ......48 C3
Billingbear La BNFD RG42 ...33 H1
Billing Rd WBPTN SW10 * ...19 M5

Billingshurst Rd HORS RH12 ...191 K7
Billing St WBPTN SW10 * 19 M5
Billinton Dr CRAWE RH10 ...177 L5
Billockby Cl CHSGTN KT9 ...59 M5
Bilton Centre LHD/OX KT22 * ...76 F8
Bina Gdns ECT SW5 ....19 N2
Binden Rd SHB W12 ....18 C3
Binfield Rd BF/WBF KT14 ......74 A1
  BNFD RG42 ....32 C1
  SAND/SEL CR2 ....63 P4
Bingham Dr STA TW18 ....37 P1
  WOKN/KNAP GU21 ....71 M7
Bingham Rd CROY/NA CR0 ...46 A9
Bingley Rd SUN TW16 ....39 J1
Binhams Lea MFD/CHID GU8 ...169 L6
Binhams Meadow
  MFD/CHID GU8 ....169 L6
Binney Ct CRAWE RH10 ...177 L6
Binns Rd CHSWK W4 ....18 C3
Binscombe GODL GU7 ......131 K5
Binscombe Crs GODL GU7 ...131 L6
Binscombe La GODL GU7 ...131 K5
Binstead Cl CRAWW RH11 ...176 E3
Binsted Dr BLKW GU17 ......67 P4
Binton La RFNM GU10 ......128 C3
Birchanger GODL GU7 ......131 L6
Birchanger Rd SNWD SE25 ...46 A6
Birch Av CTHM CR3 ....101 M4
  FLEETN GU51 ....86 F3
Birch Cir GODL GU7 ....131 M5
Birch Cl ADL/WDHM KT15 ...55 M7
  BTFD TW8 * 17 H5
  CBLY GU15 ....50 G9
  CRAWE RH10 ....179 K3
  HSLW TW3 ....16 D8
  RFNM GU10 ....127 L9
  RPLY/SEND GU23 ....93 K5
  TEDD TW11 ....25 P8
  WOKN/KNAP GU21 ....72 A8
Birchcroft Cl CTHM CR3 ...101 L5
Birchdale Cl BF/WBF KT14 ...73 N3
Birch Dr BLKW GU17 ....67 P5
Birchend Cl SAND/SEL CR2 ...63 M5
Birches Cl EPSOM KT18 ......78 C4
  MTCM CR4 ....44 B4
Birches Rd HORS RH12 ......192 G5
The Birches BLKW GU17 ......67 M3
  CRAWE RH10 ....177 K4
  EHSLY KT24 ....94 G6
  FARN GU14 ....87 J3
  HSLWW TW4 * 24 C3
  WOKS/MYFD GU22 ....10 E5
Birchett Rd ALDT GU11 ......108 C4
  FARN GU14 ....88 A2
Birchetts Cl BNFD RG42 ......32 D2
Birchfield Cl
  ADL/WDHM KT15 ....55 M3
  COUL/CHIP CR5 ....81 H5
Birchfield Est HORL RH6 * ...158 A8
Birchfields CBLY GU15 ....68 E4
Birchgate Ms
  KWD/TDW/WH KT20 * 98 G1
Birch Gn STA TW18 * 22 C8
Birchgrove COB KT11 ....75 L4
Birch Gv BRAK RG12 ....32 E5
  GU GU1 ....112 A2
  KWD/TDW/WH KT20 ....99 K4
  SHPTN TW17 ....38 C3
  WOKS/MYFD GU22 ....73 H4
Birch Hl CROY/NA CR0 ....64 D4
Birch Hill Rd BRAK RG12 ......32 D8
Birchington Rd BRYLDS KT5 ...41 M8
Birchlands Av BAL SW12 ......29 J3
Birch La ASC SL5 ....33 J2
  CHOB/PIR GU24 ....70 D1
  PUR/KEN CR8 ....62 G9
Birch Lea CRAWE RH10 ......177 K2
Bircholt Rd LIPH GU30 ......182 A6
Birch Platt CHOB/PIR GU24 ...70 C2
Birch Rd BFOR GU20 ....52 D5
  BOR GU35 ....164 G5
  EWKG RG40 ....48 C2
  FELT TW13 ....24 F4
  GODL GU7 ....131 M5
Birch Side CWTH RG45 ......49 K3
Birch Tree Av WWKM BR4 ...65 K6
Birch Tree Vw LTWR GU18 ...52 A8
Birch V COB KT11 ....76 A2
Birchvale Ct YTLY GU46 ......66 C4
Birch Wk MTCM CR4 ....44 C1
Birch Wy ASHV GU12 ....89 J8
  WARL CR6 ....82 E7
Birchway REDH RH1 ....120 D7
Birchwood Av BECK BR3 ......46 F6
  WLGTN SM6 ....62 C2
Birchwood Cl CRAWE RH10 ...177 M8
  HORL RH6 ....140 D9
  MRDN SM4 ....43 M4
Birchwood Dr BF/WBF KT14 ...73 L3
  LTWR GU18 ....52 C8
Birchwood Gv HPTN TW12 ...25 H9
Birchwood La CTHM CR3 ...101 K5
Birchwood Rd
  ADL/WDHM KT15 ....73 L1
  TOOT SW17 ....29 L8
Birdham Cl CRAWW RH11 ...176 E3
Birdhaven RFNM GU10 ......127 L8
Bird House La ORP BR6 ......84 E3
Birdhurst Av SAND/SEL CR2 ...63 M3
Birdhurst Gdns
  SAND/SEL CR2 ....63 M3
Birdhurst Ri SAND/SEL CR2 ...63 N4
  WAND/EARL SW18 ....19 N9
Birdhurst Rd
  WIM/MER SW19 ....28 G8
Bird-in-hand Pas FSTH SE23 * ...31 K5
Birds Gv WOKN/KNAP GU21 ...71 N7
Birds Hill Dr LHD/OX KT22 ...76 D2
Birds Hill Ri LHD/OX KT22 ...76 D2
Birds Hill Rd LHD/OX KT22 ...76 D1

Birdswood Dr
  WOKN/KNAP GU21 ....71 L8
Bird Wk *WHTN* TW2.................24 G4
Birdwood Cl *SAND/SEL* CR2...64 C9
  TEDD TW11 ....25 M7
Birdwood Rd *EBLY* GU15 ......68 B2
Birkbeck Hl *DUL* SE21............30 C5
Birkbeck Pl *DUL* SE21............30 C4
  SHST GU47 ....50 A8
Birkbeck Rd *BECK* BR3...........46 D3
  EA W5.................................17 J2
  WIM/MER SW19 ....29 M7
Birkdale *BRAK* RG12 ....32 C5
Birkdale Dr *CRAWW* RH11 ...176 A6
Birkdale Gdns *CROY/NA* CR0...64 D5
Birkenhead Av *KUTN/CMB* KT2..9 F4
Birkenholme Cl *BOR* GU35.....166 F7
Birkheads Rd *REIG* RH2 ....119 L4
Birkwood Cl *BAL* SW12 ....29 N3
Birnham Cl *RPLY/SEND* GU23..95 L4
Birtley Ri *SHGR* GU5 ....132 E8
Birtley Rd *SHGR* GU5 ....132 E8
Biscay Rd *HMSMTH* W6 ....19 H3
Biscoe Cl *HEST* TW5 ....5 H6
Bisenden Rd *CROY/NA* CR0 ......3 J3
Bisham Cl *CRAWE* RH10 ....177 N7
  MTCM CR4 ....44 B8
Bishop Cl *RCHPK/HAM* TW10..26 C6
Bishopdale *BRAK* RG12............32 C5
Bishop Duppas Pk
  SHPTN TW17 ....38 F8
Bishop Fox Wy
  E/WMO/HCT KT8 ....39 F5
Bishop Kings Rd *WKENS* W14..19 J2
Bishopric *HORS* RH12 ....192 D3
Bishopric Ct *HORS* RH12 ......192 D3
Bishop's Av *FUL/PGN* SW6 .....19 H7
Bishops Cl *CHSWK* W4 ....18 A3
  COUL/CHIP CR5 ....81 J7
  FLEETS GU52 ....86 G8
  SUT SM1 ....61 L2
Bishops Dr
  EBED/NFELT TW14 ....23 N2
Bishopsford Rd *MRDN* SM4...43 N8
Bishopsgate Rd *WDSR* SL4 ...20 F6
Bishops Gv *BFOR* GU20 ....52 C5
  HPTN TW12 ....25 J5
Bishop's Hall KT1 * 8 C4
Bishop's Hl *WOT/HER* KT12...39 J8
Bishop's Md *FARN* GU14...........6 D3
Bishopsmead Cl *EHSLY* KT24..95 H8
  HOR/WEW KT19 ....60 B2
Bishopsmead Dr *EHSLY* KT24..95 H9
Bishop's Park Rd
  FUL/PGN SW6 ....19 H7
  STRHM/NOR SW16 ....44 G2
Bishop's Pl *SUT* SM1 ....61 N4
Bishop's Rd *CROY/NA* CR0 .....45 K8
  FNM GU9 ....107 M8
  FUL/PGN SW6 ....19 K6
Bishopsthorpe Rd *SYD* SE26...31 K7
Bishop Summer Dr *FNM* GU9..107 N8
Bishops Wk *CROY/NA* CR0....64 D4
Bishops Wy *EGH* TW20 ....22 A9
Bishops Wd
  WOKN/KNAP GU21 ....71 M6
Bisley Cl *WPK* KT4.................43 G9
Bitmead Cl *CRAWW* RH11 *..176 B6
Bittams La *CHERT* KT16 ....155 H3
Bittern Cl *CRAWW* RH11 ....176 A6
  SHST GU47 ....49 P9
Bitterne Dr
  WOKN/KNAP GU21 ....71 M6
Bittoms Ct *KUT1/1* * 8 C6
The Bittoms *KUT1/1* 8 C7
Bixley Cl *NWDGN* UB2 ....15 P2
Blackberry Cl *GU* CU21 ....111 P2
  SHPTN TW17 ....38 G5
Blackberry Farm Cl
  HEST TW5 ....15 N5
Blackberry La *LING* RH7 ......162 C2
Blackberry Rd *EGRIN* RH19..162 B4
Blackbird Cl *SHST* GU47 ....49 P9
Blackbird Hl *CRAWE* RH10 ..179 K6
Blackborough Cl *REIG* RH2 ..119 N5
Blackborough Rd
  REDH RH1 ....119 P5
Blackbridge La *HORS* RH12..191 P9
Blackbridge Rd
  WOKS/MYFD GU22 ....72 C5
Blackbrook Rd *RDKG* RH5 ..137 L3
The Blackburn *GT/LBKH* KT23..95 P4
Blackburn Cl *BELMT* SM2....61 N6
Blackburn Pk *PYTLY* GU46 *..66 G3
Blackbushes Rd
  FLEETN GU51 ....86 E1
  HTWY RG27 ....66 C7
Blackcap Cl *CRAWW* RH11..176 F7
Blackcap Pl *SHST* GU47 ....50 A9
Black Dog Wk *CRAWE* RH10..177 H3
Blackdown Av
  WOKS/MYFD GU22 ....73 J4
Blackdown Cl
  WOKS/MYFD GU22 ....72 C5
Blackdown Rd *FRIM* GU16....69 G9
Black Eagle Cl
  BH/WHM TN16 ....104 C7
Blackenham Rd *TOOT* SW17...29 J7
Blackett Cl *EGH* TW20 ....37 J3
Blackett Rd *CRAWE* RH10 ..177 M6
Blackett St *PUT/ROE* SW15..19 H8
Blackfold Rd *CRAWE* RH10 ..177 K6
Blackford Cl *SAND/SEL* CR2..63 K7
Blackheath *CRAWE* RH10 ....177 M4
Blackheath Gv *SHGR* GU5 ..132 F5
Blackheath La *SHGR* GU5 ..132 G5
  SHGR GU5 ....133 M3
Blackheath Rd *FNM* GU9....107 L7
Blackhills *ESH/CLAY* KT10 ....57 P7
Blackhorse La *CROY/NA* CR0..46 A1
  REIG RH2 ....99 M9

Blackhorse Rd
  WOKS/MYFD GU22 ....71 K9
Black Horse Wy *HORS* RH12..192 B8
Blackhouse Rd *SWTR* RH13..193 P4
Blacklands Crs *FROW* RH18..181 L9
Blacklands Meadow
  REDH RH1 ....120 C4
Black Lion La *HMSMTH* W6...18 E2
Blackman Gdns *ALDT* GU11..108 D6
Blackman's La *WARL* CR6......83 L3
Blackmeadows *BRAK* RG12...32 E7
Blackmoor Cl *ASC* SL5..........33 M3
Blackmoor Wd *ASC* SL5........33 M3
Blackmore Crs
  WOKN/KNAP GU21 ....72 C3
Blackmore's Gv *TEDD* TW11..25 P9
Blackness La
  WOKS/MYFD GU22 ....10 D7
Blackness Rd *ASC* SL5..........35 K4
Black Pond La *RFNM* GU10..127 N7
Black Prince Cl *BF/WBF* KT14..74 B5
Black Rd Cl *HYS/HAR* UB3 ....15 H1
Blackshaw La *TOOT* SW17....28 C8
Blacksmith La *RGUE* GU4 ..132 C1
Blacksmith Rw
  DTCH/LGLY SL3 ....12 E2
Blacksmiths Hl
  SAND/SEL CR2 ....82 B2
Blacksmiths La *CHERT* KT16...37 L8
  SWTR RH13 ....37 M4
Black's Rd *HMSMTH* W6......19 H1
Blackstone Cl *FARN* GU14....87 P1
  REIG RH2 ....120 A6
Blackstroud La East
  LTWR GU18 ....52 D9
Blackstroud La West
  LTWR GU18 ....52 D9
Black Swan Cl *CRAWW* RH11..194 E3
Blackthorn Av *WDR/YW* UB7..14 C2
Blackthorn Cl *CRAWW* RH11..176 F3
  REIG RH2 ....119 N7
  SWTR RH13 ....192 E8
Blackthorn Crs *FARN* GU14...68 B8
Blackthorn Dell
  DTCH/LGLY SL3 ....12 A1
Blackthorn Dr *LTWR* GU18....70 B1
Blackthorne Av
  CROY/NA CR0 ....46 C9
Blackthorne Crs
  DTCH/LGLY SL3 ....13 J7
Blackthorne Rd
  DTCH/LGLY SL3 ....13 J8
  GT/LBKH KT23 ....96 C6
Blackthorn Pl *GU* GU1 * 112 A2
Blackthorn Rd
  BH/WHM TN16 ....84 C5
  REIG RH2 ....119 N7
Blackwater Cl *ASHV* GU12 ..109 J5
Blackwater La *CRAWE* RH10..177 M6
Blackwater Pk *ASHV* GU12 ..108 G5
Blackwater Vw *EWKG* RG40..48 E7
Blackwell Av *GUW* GU2 ......111 K5
Blackwell Farm Rd
  EGRIN RH19 ....162 E9
Blackwell Hollow
  EGRIN RH19 ....180 E1
Blackwell Rd *EGRIN* RH19 ..180 E1
Blackwood Cl *BF/WBF* KT14..74 N1
Bladen Cl *WEY* KT13............56 F5
Blades Cl *LHD/OX* KT22........77 K9
Bladon Cl *GU* GU1 ....112 E4
Blagdon Cl *NWMAL* KT3......42 D5
Blagdon Wk *TEDD* TW11 ....26 B9
Blair Av *ESH/CLAY* KT10 ......58 C1
Blair Cl *HYS/HAR* UB3 ....15 J2
Blairderry Rd
  BRXS/STRHM SW2 ....29 P5
Blaire Pk *YTLY* GU46 ....48 F9
Blaise Cl *FARN* GU14 ....88 F4
Blake Cl *CAR* SM5 ....44 A9
  CRAWE RH10 ....177 J9
  CTHM CR3 ....45 N5
Blakeden Dr *ESH/CLAY* KT10..58 F6
Blakehall Rd *CAR* SM5 ....62 B5
Blakemore Rd
  STRHM/NOR SW16 ....29 P6
  THHTH CR7 ....45 H6
Blakeney Av *BECK* BR3........46 E1
Blakeney Cl *HOR/WEW* KT19..60 B9
Blakeney Rd *BECK* BR3........46 E1
Blake Rd *CROY/NA* CR0 ....3 G3
  MTCM CR4 ....44 A4
Blakes Av *NWMAL* KT3 ......42 D6
Blake's Gn *WWKM* BR4 ......47 J8
Blakes La *NWMAL* KT3 ......42 C6
  RGUE GU4 ....114 D2
Blakes Ride *YTLY* GU46........66 F1
Blakes Ter *NWMAL* KT3 ......42 E6
Blakewood Cl *FELT* TW13....24 D7
Blanchards Hl *RGUE* GU4 ....92 C7
Blanchland Rd *MRDN* SM4 ..43 M6
Blanchman's Rd *WARL* CR6..82 E7
Blandfield Rd *BAL* SW12 ....29 J3
Blandford Av *BECK* BR3......46 E3
  WHTN TW2 ....25 J4
Blandford Cl *CROY/NA* CR0 ..62 G2
  DTCH/LGLY SL3 ....12 B1
  WOKS/MYFD GU22 ....11 J4
Blandford Rd *BECK* BR3......46 D3
  CHSWK W4 ....18 C1
  NWDGN UB2 ....16 A2
  TEDD TW11 ....25 L8
Blandford Rd North
  DTCH/LGLY SL3 ....12 B1
Blandford Rd South
  DTCH/LGLY SL3 ....12 B1

Blane's La *ASC* SL5..............33 'L7
Blanford Rd *REIG* RH2 ......119 N6
Blanks La *HORL* RH6..........157 M1
Blantyre St *WBPTN* SW10 ....19 P5
Blantyre Wk *WBPTN* SW10 *..19 P5
Blatchford Rd *SWTR* RH13..192 E7
Blays Cl *EGH* TW20 ....21 H9
Blay's La *EGH* TW20 ....20 G9
Blean Gv *PGE/AN* SE20........46 C1
Blegborough Rd
  STRHM/NOR SW16 ....29 M9
Blencarn Cl
  WOKN/KNAP GU21 ....71 N5
Blenheim Cl *BF/WBF* KT14 ..73 K2
  CRAWE RH10 ....177 N1
  EGRIN RH19 ....162 F9
  RFNM GU10 ....108 G7
  RYNPK SW20 ....42 G4
  WLGTN SM6 ....62 E6
Blenheim Ct *FARN* GU14......88 F5
Blenheim Crs *FNM* GU9 ....107 L8
  SAND/SEL CR2 ....63 L6
Blenheim Flds *FROW* RH18..181 K8
Blenheim Gdns
  BRXS/STRHM SW2 ....30 A2
  KUTN/CMB KT2 ....9 K1
  SAND/SEL CR2 ....82 A5
  WLGTN SM6 ....62 E5
  WOKS/MYFD GU22 ....71 P8
Blenheim Pk *ALDT* GU11 ......88 E8
Blenheim Park Rd
  SAND/SEL CR2 ....81 P5
Blenheim Rd *ALDT* GU11 ....88 E8
  CHSWK W4 ....18 C1
  DTCH/LGLY SL3 ....12 B1
  HOR/WEW KT19 ....60 B9
  HORS RH12 ....192 C5
  PGE/AN SE20 ....46 C1
  RYNPK SW20 ....42 G4
  SUT SM1 ....61 L2
Blenheim Wy *ISLW* TW7......16 G6
Blenkarne Rd *BTSEA* SW11...29 J2
Bleriot Rd *HEST* TW5 ....15 J5
Bletchingley Cl *REDH* RH1..100 E9
  THHTH CR7 ....45 K5
Bletchingley Rd *GDST* RH9..122 A2
  REDH RH1 ....100 E9
  REDH RH1 ....121 J4
Bletchingly Cl *THHTH* CR7 ..45 K5
Bletchmore Cl *HYS/HAR* UB3..14 F3
Blewburton Wk *BRAK* RG12..32 G5
Blewfield *GODL* GU7..........150 E2
Bligh Cl *CRAWE* RH10 ......177 J8
Blighton La *RFNM* GU10 ....128 F3
Blincoe Cl *WIM/MER* SW19...28 A5
Blindley Ct *LING* RH7 * 162 C2
Blindley Rd *CRAWE* RH10 ..177 N2
Blithfield St *KENS* W8..........19 M1
Blondell Cl *WDR/YW* UB7 ..13 P4
Blondin Av *EA* W5................17 J2
Bloomfield Cl
  WOKN/KNAP GU21 ....71 L7
Bloomfield Dr *BRAK* RG12....32 E1
Bloomfield Rd *KUT* KT1 ....41 L5
Bloom Gv *WNWD* SE27 ......30 C6
Bloomhall Rd *NRWD* SE19...30 E8
Bloom Park Rd
  FUL/PGN SW6 ....19 K5
Bloomsbury Cl
  HOR/WEW KT19 ....60 B8
Bloomsbury Wy *BLKW* GU17..67 N5
Bloor Cl *HORS* RH12..........192 C3
Blossom Cl *SAND/SEL* CR2..63 P4
Blossom Wy *WDR/YW* UB7 ..14 C2
Blossom Waye *HEST* TW5 ....15 N4
Blount Av *EGRIN* RH19 ......180 B2
Blount Crs *BNFD* RG42........32 A1
Bloxham Crs *HPTN* TW12 ....39 J7
Bloxham Rd *CRAN* GU6 ......153 K9
Bloxworth Cl *BRAK* RG12....33 H5
  WLGTN SM6 ....44 E9
Blue Ball La *EGH* TW20 ......21 L8
Blue Barn Wy *WEY* KT13......56 C9
Bluebell Cl *CRAWW* RH11 *..176 E8
  EGRIN RH19 ....180 D2
  HORS RH12 ....192 D5
  SYD SE26 ....30 G7
Bluebell Ct
  WOKS/MYFD GU22 * 10 A7
Bluebell Hl *BRAK* RG12 ......32 G2
Bluebell La *EHSLY* KT24......94 G9
Bluebell Ri *LTWR* GU18......52 D4
Blueberry Gdns
  COUL/CHIP CR5 ....81 H5
Blueberry La *RSEV* TN14......85 N5
Blue Cedars *BNSTD* SM7 ....79 H3
Blue Cedars Pl *COB* KT11 ....75 M1
Blue Coat Wk *BRAK* RG12....32 F4
Bluefield Cl *HPTN* TW12 ....25 H8
Bluegates *EW* KT17..............60 E6
Bluehouse Gdns *OXTED* RH8..103 N8
Bluehouse La *OXTED* RH8 ..103 L8
Blue Leaves Av
  COUL/CHIP CR5 ....80 G8
Blue Prior Ct *FLEETS* GU52..106 E3
Blue Riband Est
  CROY/NA CR0 * 2 A3
Bluethroat Cl *SHST* GU47 ....50 B9
Bluff Cove *ALDT* GU11......108 E5
Blundel La *COB* KT11 ....75 P5
Blundell Av *HORL* RH6 ......159 J1
Blunden Rd *FARN* GU14......88 B2
Blunt Rd *CROY/NA* CR0 ....3 G7
Blunts Av *WDR/YW* UB7......14 D4
Blunts Wy *HORS* RH12......192 B7
Blyth Cl *TWK* TW1 ....25 N2
Blythe Cl *CAT* SE6 ....31 N3
Blythe Hl *CAT* SE6 ....31 N3
Blythe Hill La *CAT* SE6........31 N3
Blythe Hill Pl *FSTH* SE23 *..31 M3
Blythe Ms *WKENS* W14 * 19 H1

Blythe Rd *WKENS* W14........19 H1
Blythe V *CAT* SE6 ....31 N4
Blythewood La *ASC* SL5......33 M4
Blythe Rd *BMLY* BR1..........47 M2
Blythwood Dr *FRIM* GU16....68 G8
The Blytons *EGRIN* RH19 ..180 A2
Board School Rd
  WOKN/KNAP GU21 ....11 F2
Boar Hl *RDKG* RH5 ....136 E6
Bockhampton Rd
  KUTN/CMB KT2 ....9 M1
Boddicott Cl *WIM/MER* SW19..28 B5
Bodens Ride *ASC* SL5 ....33 P9
Bodiam Cl *CRAWE* RH10 ..177 M5
Bodiam Rd
  STRHM/NOR SW16 ....44 F2
Bodley Cl *NWMAL* KT3 ......42 C6
Bodley Rd *NWMAL* KT3......42 C7
Bodmin Gv *MRDN* SM4......43 M5
Bodmin St *WAND/EARL* SW18..28 D4
Bodnant Gdns *RYNPK* SW20..42 E4
Boeing Wy *NWDGN* UB2 ....15 K1
Bofors Rd *FARN* GU14..........88 C2
Bog La *BRAK* RG12 ....33 H6
Bognor Rd *HORS* RH12 *......52 B2
  RDKG RH5 ....155 N4
  RDKG RH5 ....173 K4
Boileau Rd *BARN* SW13 ......18 E5
Bois Hall Rd *ADL/WDHM* KT15..55 N4
Bolderwood Wy *WWKM* BR4..65 H1
Bolding House La
  CHOB/PIR GU24 ....70 F2
Boleyn Av *EW* KT17..............60 E8
Boleyn Cl *CRAWE* RH10 ....177 N8
  STA TW18 ....22 B8
Boleyn Dr *E/WMO/HCT* KT8...39 P4
Boleyn Gdns *WWKM* BR4 ....65 H1
Boleyn Wk *LHD/OX* KT22......76 G9
Bolingbroke Gv *BTSEA* SW11..29 J2
Bolingbroke Rd *WKENS* W14..19 H1
Bolingbroke Wk
  BTSEA SW11 * 19 P5
Bollo Bridge Rd *ACT* W3......17 P1
Bollo La *ACT* W3................17 P1
  CHSWK W4 ....18 A2
Bolney Ct *CRAWW* RH11 ....176 C9
Bolsover Gv *REDH* RH1 ....100 D9
Bolstead Rd *MTCM* CR4 ....44 D2
Bolters La *BNSTD* SM7........79 K4
Bolters Rd *HORL* RH6........140 D8
Bolters Rd South *HORL* RH6..140 D8
Bolton Cl *CHSGTN* KT9........59 K5
Boltons Gdns *CH EST5*........19 M3
  TEDD TW11 ....25 N8
Bolton Gardens Ms
  WBPTN SW10 ....19 M3
Bolton Rd *CHSGTN* KT9......59 K5
  CHSWK W4 ....18 A5
Boltons Cl *WOKS/MYFD* GU22..73 L4
Boltons La *BNFD* RG42 ....32 A1
  WDR/YW UB7 ....14 A1
  WOKS/MYFD GU22 ....73 L5
Boltons Pl *WBPTN* SW10 ....19 M3
The Boltons *WBPTN* SW10 *..19 M3
  WPK KT4................................42 D9
Bomber Cl *WDR/YW* UB7 ....14 C5
Bomers Fld *BRXS/STRHM* SW2..30 A1
Bond Cl *RSEV* TN14............85 P4
Bond Gdns *WLGTN* SM6 ....62 E3
Bond Rd *MTCM* CR4............44 A3
  SURB KT6 ....59 M1
  WARL CR6 ....82 F7
Bond's La *RDKG* RH5..........137 H6
Bond St *EGH* TW20 ....21 L8
Bondy Wy *BRAK* RG12........32 B3
Bonehurst Rd *HORL* RH6 ..140 C6
Bone Mill La *GDST* RH9 ....122 C5
Bones La *HORL* RH6 ....142 A9
Bonham Rd
  BRXS/STRHM SW2 ....30 A1
Bonner Hill Rd *KUT* KT1........41 M1
Bonners Cl
  WOKS/MYFD GU22 ....92 D2
Bonners Fld *RFNM* GU10 ..126 A8
Bonnetts La *CRAWW* RH11..158 D9
Bonneville Gdns *CLAP* SW4..29 P2
Bonnys Rd *REIG* RH2........119 H5
Bonser Rd *TWK* TW1............25 N5
Bonsey Cl *WOKS/MYFD* GU22..92 C1
Bonsey's La *CHOB/PIR* GU24..54 C7
Bonsor Dr
  KWD/TDW/WH KT20..........99 J2
Bookham Cl *GT/LBKH* KT23..95 P5
Bookham Gv *GT/LBKH* KT23..96 B6
Bookham Rd *COB* KT11 ......75 M1
Bookhurst Hl *CRAN* GU6 ..153 L8
Bookhurst Rd *CRAN* GU6 ..153 J8
Boole Hts *BRAK* RG12 ....32 C6
Booth Dr *STA* TW18 ....22 G9
Booth Rd *CRAWE* RH10 ....176 B8
  CROY/NA CR0 ....2 C4
Booth Wy *SWTR* RH13 * 192 D7
Borage Cl *CRAWW* RH11 ..176 C7
Border Cha *CRAWE* RH10 ..177 M8
Border Ct *EGRIN* RH19 ......162 B8
Border Gdns *CROY/NA* CR0..65 H3
Border Ga *MTCM* CR4........44 B2
Border Gdns *CROY/NA* CR0..65 H3
Border Rd *HASM* GU27........183 N4
  SYD SE26 ....31 H8
Borderside *YTLY* GU46........66 F1
Borders La *LOU* IG10 ....43 M5
Bordon Wk *PUT/ROE* SW15..27 M1
The Boreen *BOR* GU35......164 E6
Borelli Ms *FNM* GU9 ....5 H5
Borers Arms Rd
  CRAWE RH10 ....160 C8
Borers Cl *CRAWE* RH10 * ..160 D9
Borland Rd *TEDD* TW11......26 A9

Borneo St *PUT/ROE* SW15..18 G8
Borough Hl *CROY/NA* CR0 ....2 A6
Borough Rd *BH/WHM* TN16..104 B1
  GODL GU7 ....131 K8
  ISLW TW7 ....16 E6
  KUTN/CMB KT2 ....9 K2
  MTCM CR4 ....44 A3
The Borough *FNM* GU9..........5 F3
  RDKG RH5 ....117 N6
  RGUE GU4 ....100 C8
Borrodale Rd
  WAND/EARL SW18 ....28 E2
Borrowdale Cl
  CRAWW RH11 ....176 E2
  EGH TW20 ....36 F1
  SAND/SEL CR2 ....81 P2
Borrowdale Dr
  SAND/SEL CR2 ....81 P1
Boscombe Cl *EGH* TW20 * ..36 G1
Boscombe Rd *TOOT* SW17...29 K9
  WIM/MER SW19 ....43 L2
  WPK KT4................................42 G9
Bosham Rd *CRAWE* RH10 ..177 M8
Boston Gdns *EGH* TW20......21 J3
Boston Av *BFOR* GU20........52 B2
Bostock Av *HORS* RH12 ....192 F6
Boston Gdns *BTFD* TW8 ......16 C2
  CHSWK W4 ....18 C4
Boston Manor Rd *BTFD* TW8..16 A2
Boston Rd *CROY/NA* CR0 ....45 J7
Boston Park Rd *BTFD* TW8 ..17 J4
Boston V *HNWL* W7 * 16 G2
Boswell Rd *CRAWE* RH10 ..177 M8
  THHTH CR7 ....45 L5
Botany Hl *RFNM* GU10......128 F4
Boterys Cross *REDH* RH1 *..121 K4
Bothwell Rd *CROY/NA* CR0..65 H8
Bothwell St *HMSMTH* W6 ..19 H4
Botley's Pk *CHERT* KT16 * 54 G4
Botsford Rd *RYNPK* SW20....43 H3
Bottom Harrow Rd *VW* GU25..36 D7
Boucher Cl *TEDD* TW11......25 N8
Boughton Av *HAYES* BR2 ....47 M8
Bouldih Farm Rd *ASC* SL5 ..33 K6
The Boulevard *CRAWE* RH10..176 G5
Boulevard *CROY/NA* CR0 ....45 L7
Boulters Rd *ASHV* GU12 ..108 D5
Boulthurst Wy *OXTED* RH8..123 N3
Boundaries Rd *BAL* SW12 ..29 J5
  FELT TW13 ....24 D4
Boundary Cl *CRAWE* RH10..177 H6
  KUT KT1................................9 K6
  NWDGN UB2 ....16 A3
Boundary Rd *ASHF* TW15 ....22 F8
  CRAWE RH10 ....177 H4
  FARN GU14 ....88 E5
  GSHT GU26 ....165 N8
  RFNM GU10 ....146 B5
  WIM/MER SW19 ....28 G9
  WLGTN SM6 ....62 C4
  WOKN/KNAP GU21 ....11 G1
Boundary Rd East
  ADL/WDHM KT15..............55 M7
Boundary Rd North
  ADL/WDHM KT15..............55 M7
Boundary Rd West
  ADL/WDHM KT15..............55 M7
Boundary Wy *CROY/NA* CR0..64 G4
  FARN GU14 ....72 F4
Boundless La
  MFD/CHID GU8 ....166 D4
Boundstone Cl *RFNM* GU10..127 M8
Boundstone Rd *RFNM* GU10..127 K9
Bourdon Rd *PGE/AN* SE20...46 C3
Bourg-de-Peage Av
  EGRIN RH19 ....180 F2
Bourke Cl *CLAP* SW4..........29 P2
Bourke Hl *COUL/CHIP* CR5..80 B7
Bourley La *RFNM* GU10 ....107 K4
Bourley Rd *FLEETS* GU52 ..107 J2
  HYS/HAR UB3 ....14 E1
Bourne Av *CHERT* KT16 ......37 L4
  ESH/CLAY KT10 ....58 F1
  RGUE GU4 ....132 F2
Bourne Cl *ALDT* GU11 ......108 C6
  BF/WBF KT14 ....74 A2
Bourne Dene *RFNM* GU10..127 L8
Bourne Dr *MTCM* CR4 ....43 P3
Bournefield Rd *CTHM* CR3...81 M3
Bourne Firs *RFNM* GU10 ..127 P9
Bourne Gv *ASHTD* KT21 ......77 K8
  RFNM GU10 ....128 A6
Bourne Grove Cl *FNM* GU9..128 A6
Bourne Grove Dr
  RFNM GU10 ....128 A6
Bourne Ms *FARN* GU14 * ..127 N5
Bourne St *CROY/NA* CR0 ......2 B5
The Bourne *FLEETS* GU52....86 G9
Bourne V *HAYES* BR2..........47 N9
Bournevale Rd
  STRHM/NOR SW16 ....29 N7
Bourne Vw *PUR/KEN* CR8 ..81 M4
Bourne Wy *ADL/WDHM* KT15..55 N4
  HAYES BR2 ....65 N1

HOR/WEW KT19 60 A3
SUT SM1 61 K4
WOKS/MYFD GU22 92 B2
Bournville Rd CAT SE6 31 P3
Bousley Ri CHERT KT16 55 H6
Bouverie Gdns
COUL/CHIP CR5 80 G3
Bouverie Rd COUL/CHIP CR5 80 C7
Bouverie Wy DTCH/LGLY SL3 12 C3
Boveney Rd FSTH SE23 31 L3
Bovill Rd FSTH SE23 31 L3
Bovingdon Rd FUL/PGN SW6 19 M6
Bowater Cl
BRXS/STRHM SW2 29 P2
Bowater Rdg WEY KT13 56 F8
Bowater Rd CRAWE RH10 177 M8
Bowcott Hl BOR GU35 164 C6
Bowden Cl
EBED/NFELT TW14 23 P4
Bowden Rd ASC SL5 34 C6
Bowen Dr DUL SE21 30 F6
Bowenhurst Gdns
FLEETS GU52 106 G2
Bowenhurst La RFNM GU10 106 B5
Bowenhurst Rd
FLEETS GU52 106 G1
Bowens Wd CROY/NA CR0 * 64 F7
Bowenswood CROY/NA CR0 64 F7
Bower Ct WOKS/MYFD GU22 11 K1
Bowerdean St FUL/PGN SW6 19 M6
Bower Hill Cl REDH RH1 120 G7
Bower Hill La REDH RH1 120 F6
Bowerland La LING RH7 143 K5
Bower Rd RFNM GU10 127 L8
Bowers Cl RGUE GU4 112 E1
Bowers Farm Dr RGUE GU4 112 E1
Bowers La RGUE GU4 92 E9
Bowers Pl CRAWE RH10 179 J3
Bowes Cl SWTR RH13 192 D7
Bowes Rd STA TW18 22 B9
WOT/HER KT12 57 K1
Bowfell Rd HMSMTH W6 18 G4
Bowie Cl CLAP SW4 29 N3
Bowland Dr BRAK RG12 32 G8
Bowley Cl NRWD SE19 * 30 G9
Bowley La NRWD SE19 30 G8
Bowlhead Green Rd
MFD/CHID GU8 166 G2
Bowling Court Gn FRIM GU16 68 G9
Bowling Green Cl
PUT/ROE SW15 27 N3
Bowling Green La
HORS RH12 192 C7
Bowling Green Rd
CHOB/PIR GU24 53 L7
Bowman Ct CRAWE RH10 * 176 G4
CWTH RG45 49 J5
Bowman Ms
WAND/EARL SW18 28 C4
Bowmans Lea FSTH SE23 31 K3
Bowman's Meadow
WLGTN SM6 62 D2
Bowness Crs PUT/ROE SW15 27 K8
Bowness Dr HSLWW TW4 15 N9
Bowry Dr STWL/WRAY TW19 21 L2
Bowsley Ct FELT TW13 24 B5
The Bowsprit COB KT11 75 L4
Bowyers Cl ASHTD KT21 77 M7
Bowyer Wk ASC SL5 33 N2
Boxall Rd DUL SE21 30 F2
Boxall's Gv ALDT GU11 108 C7
Boxall's La ALDT GU11 108 C7
Boxall Wk SWTR RH13 192 C9
Box Cl CRAWW RH11 194 F1
Boxford Cl SAND/SEL CR2 82 D1
Boxford Rdg BRAK RG12 32 D4
Boxgrove Av GU GU1 112 E3
Boxgrove La GU GU1 112 E4
Boxgrove Rd GU GU1 112 E4
Boxhill Rd DORK RH4 117 L4
KWD/TDW/WH KT20 118 B1
Boxhill Wy
BRKHM/BTCW RH3 117 P9
Box La EGRIN RH19 181 K5
Boxley Rd MRDN SM4 43 N5
Box Ridge Av PUR/KEN CR8 81 H1
Box Tree Wk REDH RH1 119 N8
Boxwood Wy WARL CR6 82 D6
Boyd Cl KUTN/CMB KT2 41 N1
Boyd Ct BNFD RG42 32 C2
Boyd Rd WIM/MER SW19 28 G9
Boyle Farm Rd THDIT KT7 40 G7
Brabazon Av WLGTN SM6 62 G7
Brabazon Rd HEST TW5 15 L5
Brabon Rd FARN GU14 88 B2
Brabourne Cl NRWD SE19 30 F8
Brabourne Ri BECK BR3 47 K6
Bracebridge CBLY GU15 68 C3
Bracewood Gdns
CROY/NA CR0 3 J5
Bracken Av BAL SW12 29 K2
CROY/NA CR0 64 G2
Bracken Bank ASC SL5 33 L2
Brackenbury Gdns
HMSMTH W6 18 F1
Brackenbury Rd
HMSMTH W6 18 F1
Bracken Cl CRAWE RH10 177 H3
CRAWE RH10 178 C1
GT/LBKH KT23 95 P4
SHGR GU5 132 F7
SUN TW16 * 24 A9
WHTN TW2 25 H3
WOKS/MYFD GU22 11 F5
Brackendale Cl FRIM GU16 68 G5
HEST TW5 16 B6
Brackendale Rd CBLY GU15 68 F4
Brackendene ASHV GU12 109 L3
Brackendene Cl
WOKN/KNAP GU21 72 E4
Bracken End ISLW TW7 25 L1
Bracken Gdns BARN SW13 18 E7
Bracken Gv HORS RH12 192 G5
Brackenhill COB KT11 58 A9
Bracken Hill Cl BMLY BR1 47 M2
Bracken Hill La BMLY BR1 47 M2
Bracken La YTLY GU46 66 E2
Brackenlea GODL GU7 131 K6
Bracken Pth EPSOM KT18 77 P2
Brackenside HORL RH6 140 D9
The Brackens ASC SL5 * 33 K4
CWTH RG45 49 L2
Bracken Wy CHOB/PIR GU24 53 M8
RGUW GU3 111 L3
Brackenwood CBLY GU15 69 M3
SUN TW16 39 J2
Brackenwood Rd
WOKN/KNAP GU21 71 K8
Bracklesham Cl FARN GU14 68 C9
Brackley WEY KT13 56 F4
Brackley Cl WLGTN SM6 62 G6
Brackley Rd BECK BR3 46 F1
CHSWK W4 18 C2
Brackley Ter CHSWK W4 18 C3
Bracklyn Av EGRIN RH19 * 162 F6
Bracknell Beeches
BRAK RG12 * 32 D4
Bracknell Cl CBLY GU15 51 H8
Bracknell Rd BAGS GU19 51 M3
CBLY GU15 51 J7
CWTH RG45 49 N4
Bracondale ESH/CLAY KT10 58 C4
Bradbourne St FUL/PGN SW6 19 L7
Bradbury Cl NWDGN UB2 15 P2
Bradbury Rd CRAWE RH10 177 M8
Braddock Cl ISLW TW7 16 F8
Braddon Rd RCH/KEW TW9 17 M8
Bradenhurst Cl CTHM CR3 101 P6
Bradfield Cl RGUE GU4 112 E2
WOKS/MYFD GU22 10 D5
Bradfields BRAK RG12 32 F6
Bradford Cl SYD SE26 31 J7
Bradford Dr HOR/WEW KT19 60 D5
Brading Rd
BRXS/STRHM SW2 30 A3
CROY/NA CR0 45 H7
Brading Ter SHB W12 18 E1
Bradley La DORK RH4 117 H3
Bradley Rd NRWD SE19 30 D9
Bradmore Park Rd
HMSMTH W6 18 F1
Bradmore Wy
COUL/CHIP CR5 80 G7
Bradshaw Cl WIM/MER SW19 28 D9
Bradshaws Cl SNWD SE25 46 A4
Bradstock Rd EW KT17 60 F4
Braemar Av SAND/SEL CR2 63 L8
THHTH CR7 45 K4
WAND/EARL SW18 28 D5
Braemar Cl FRIM GU16 69 H8
GODL GU7 150 C1
Braemar Gdns WWKM BR4 47 J9
Braemar Rd BTFD TW8 17 K4
WPK KT4 60 F2
Braeside ADL/WDHM KT15 55 M9
BECK BR3 31 P8
Braeside Av
WIM/MER SW19 43 J2
Braeside Cl HASM GU27 184 A2
Braeside Rd
STRHM/NOR SW16 44 E1
Braes Md REDH RH1 120 G6
Brafferton Rd CROY/NA CR0 2 C7
Bragg Rd TEDD TW11 40 E1
Braid Cl FELT TW13 24 G5
Brailsford Cl WIM/MER SW19 44 A1
Brailsford Rd
BRXS/STRHM SW2 30 B2
Brainton Av
EBED/NFELT TW14 24 C3
Brair Bank CAR SM5 62 C7
Brake Rd FARN GU14 88 A6
Brakey Hl REDH RH1 121 N5
Bramber Cl CRAWE RH10 177 H3
Bramber Rd WKENS W14 19 K4
Bramble Acres Cl BELMT SM2 61 L6
Bramble Bank FRIM GU16 89 J1
Bramble Banks CAR SM5 62 C7
Bramble Cl BECK BR3 47 J6
CRAWE RH10 160 C9
CROY/NA CR0 64 G3
REDH RH1 120 C7
RGUW GU3 111 L3
SHPTN TW17 38 F5
Brambledene Cl
WOKN/KNAP GU21 72 A7
Brambledown STA TW18 37 M2
Brambledown Cl HAYES BR2 47 L7
Brambledown Rd CAR SM5 62 C6
SAND/SEL CR2 63 N6
Bramblegate CWTH RG45 49 L3
Bramble Hall La
KWD/TDW/WH KT20 * 117 M3
Bramble La HPTN TW12 24 G9
Bramble Ri COB KT11 75 L4
Brambles Cl ASHV GU12 109 K5
BTFD TW8 17 H5
CTHM CR3 101 N2
Brambles Pk SHGR GU5 132 D7
The Brambles CWTH RG45 49 H3
GODL GU7 131 K6
RFNM GU10 * 106 C8
SUT SM1 61 P1
WDR/YW UB7 13 P3
WIM/MER SW19 * 28 C8
Brambleton Av FNM GU9 127 M6
Brambletye La FROW RH18 181 J8
Brambletye Park Rd
REDH RH1 120 B7
Brambletye Rd CRAWE RH10 177 K6
Bramble Wk EPSOM KT18 77 P3
REDH RH1 * 120 C7
Bramble Wy
RPLY/SEND GU23 93 K4
Bramblewood REIG RH2 100 D9
Bramblewood Cl CAR SM5 44 A9
Bramblewood Pl
FLEETN GU51 86 E6
Brambling Cl SWTR RH13 192 F9
Brambling Rd SWTR RH13 192 F9
Bramcote CBLY GU15 69 L3
Bramcote Av MTCM CR4 44 B5
Bramcote Rd PUT/ROE SW15 18 F9
Bramerton Rd BECK BR3 46 F4
Bramfield Rd BTSEA SW11 29 H2
Bramford Rd
WAND/EARL SW18 19 N9
Bramham Gdns
CHSGTN KT9 * 59 K4
ECT SW5 19 M3
Bramley Av COUL/CHIP CR5 80 E4
SHPTN TW17 38 G4
Bramley Cl CHERT KT16 37 M9
CRAWE RH10 177 J5
REDH RH1 120 A7
SAND/SEL CR2 63 K4
STA TW18 22 F9
WHTN TW2 25 K2
Bramley Gv CWTH RG45 49 H4
Bramley Hl SAND/SEL CR2 63 L3
Bramley Hyrst
SAND/SEL CR2 * 63 L4
Bramley La BLKW GU17 67 M3
Bramley Rd BELMT SM2 61 H7
CBLY GU15 68 D6
EA W5 17 J1
SUT SM1 61 P4
Bramley Wk HORL RH6 159 M1
Bramley Wy ASHTD KT21 77 M6
HSLWW TW4 24 G1
WWKM BR4 65 H1
Bramling Av YTLY GU46 66 F2
Brampton Gdns
WOT/HER KT12 57 L4
Brampton Rd CROY/NA CR0 45 P8
Bramshaw Ri NWMAL KT3 42 C7
Bramshot Dr FLEETN GU51 86 G5
Bramshot La FLEETN GU51 87 L2
Bramshott Ct LIPH GU30 * 182 D2
Bramshott Rd FARN GU14 87 L5
Bramswell Rd GODL GU7 131 M7
Bramwell Cl SUN TW16 39 M3
Brancaster La PUR/KEN CR8 63 L9
Brancaster Rd
STRHM/NOR SW16 29 P6
Brandlehow Rd
PUT/ROE SW15 19 K9
Brandon Cl CBLY GU15 69 M4
CRAWE RH10 177 N7
Brandon Rd FLEETS GU52 106 E2
NWDGN UB2 15 P3
SUT SM1 61 M3
Brandreth Rd TOOT SW17 29 L5
The Brandries WLGTN SM6 62 F2
Brandsland REIG RH2 119 M9
Brands Rd DTCH/LGLY SL3 12 F4
Brandy Bottom BLKW GU17 * 67 J5
Brandy Wy BELMT SM2 61 L6
Brangwyn Crs
WIM/MER SW19 43 P3
Branksea St FUL/PGN SW6 19 J5
Branksome Cl CBLY GU15 68 G2
WOT/HER KT12 57 M1
Branksome Hill Rd
SHST GU47 68 A1
Branksome Park Rd
CBLY GU15 68 G2
Branksome Rd
BRXS/STRHM SW2 29 P1
WIM/MER SW19 43 L2
Branksome Wy NWMAL KT3 42 A3
Branksomewood Rd
FLEETN GU51 86 E6
Bransby Rd CHSGTN KT9 59 L6
Branstone Rd RCH/KEW TW9 17 M6
Brantridge La RHWH RH17 195 K8
Brantridge Rd CRAWE RH10 177 J7
Brants Br BRAK RG12 32 G3
Brantwood Av ISLW TW7 16 G9
Brantwood Dr BF/WBF KT14 73 K2
Brantwood Gdns
BF/WBF KT14 73 K2
Brantwood Rd HNHL SE24 30 D1
SAND/SEL CR2 63 L7
Brasenose Dr BARN SW13 18 G4
Brassey Cl
EBED/NFELT TW14 * 24 B4
Brassey Hl OXTED RH8 103 N9
Brassey Rd OXTED RH8 103 N9
Brasted Cl BELMT SM2 61 L8
SYD SE26 31 K7
Brasted Hl RSEV TN14 85 L9
Brasted Hill Rd
BH/WHM TN16 105 N2
Brasted La RSEV TN14 85 L8
Brasted Rd BH/WHM TN16 105 J6
Brathway Rd
WAND/EARL SW18 28 D3
Bravington Cl SHPTN TW17 38 B6
Braxted Pk
STRHM/NOR SW16 30 A9
Braybourne Dr ISLW TW7 16 F5
Braybrooke Gdns
NRWD SE19 45 N1
Braybrooke Rd BNFD RG42 32 D1
Bray Cl CRAWE RH10 177 N7
Braycourt Av WOT/HER KT12 39 L8
Braye Cl SHST GU47 49 N8
Bray Gdns WOKS/MYFD GU22 73 J5
Bray Rd COB KT11 75 N5
GUW GU2 6 A5
Braywood Av EGH TW20 21 L9
Breakfield COUL/CHIP CR5 80 G5
Breamore Cl PUT/ROE SW15 27 M4
Breamwater Gdns
RCHPK/HAM TW10 26 A6
Breasley Cl PUT/ROE SW15 18 F9
Brechin Pl SKENS SW7 19 N3
Brecon Cl FARN GU14 67 P9
MTCM CR4 44 G5
WPK KT4 60 G1
Brecon Rd HMSMTH W6 19 J4
Bredhurst Cl PGE/AN SE20 31 K9
Bredon Rd CROY/NA CR0 45 P8
Bredune PUR/KEN CR8 81 M4
Breech La
KWD/TDW/WH KT20 98 E5
The Breech CBLY GU15 68 A1
Breer St FUL/PGN SW6 19 M8
Breezehurst Dr
CRAWW RH11 176 C8
Bregsells La RDKG RH5 137 K9
Bremer Rd
STWL/WRAY TW19 22 D6
Bremner Av HORL RH6 140 B9
Bremner Rd SKENS SW7 * 19 N1
Brenchley Cl HAYES BR2 47 M6
Brenchley Gdns FSTH SE23 31 K2
Brenda Rd TOOT SW17 29 J5
Brende Gdns
E/WMO/HCT KT8 40 B5
Brendon Cl ESH/CLAY KT10 58 C5
HYS/HAR UB3 14 E5
Brendon Dr ESH/CLAY KT10 58 C5
Brendon Rd FARN GU14 67 P9
Brenley Cl MTCM CR4 44 C4
Brent Lea BTFD TW8 17 J5
Brentmoor Rd
CHOB/PIR GU24 70 C2
Brent Rd BTFD TW8 17 J4
NWDGN UB2 15 L1
SAND/SEL CR2 64 B7
Brentside BTFD TW8 17 J4
Brent Wy BTFD TW8 17 K5
Brentwick Gdns BTFD TW8 17 L2
Bret Harte Rd FRIM GU16 68 G7
Bretlands Rd CHERT KT16 55 J1
Brettgrave HOR/WEW KT19 60 A8
Brettingham Cl
CRAWW RH11 * 176 B8
Brewer Rd CRAWE RH10 176 G7
Brewers Cl FARN GU14 88 C2
Brewer St REDH RH1 121 L2
Brewery La BF/WBF KT14 74 A2
Brewery Rd
WOKN/KNAP GU21 10 B3
Brew House Rd
BRKHM/BTCW RH3 117 P9
Brewhouse St
PUT/ROE SW15 19 J9
Brewhurst La BIL RH14 188 D8
Brian Av SAND/SEL CR2 81 N1
Briane Rd HOR/WEW KT19 60 A8
Briar Av LTWR GU18 69 P1
STRHM/NOR SW16 45 H1
Briar Cl BF/WBF KT14 55 M9
CRAWW RH11 176 F2
HPTN TW12 24 G8
ISLW TW7 25 N1
Briar Gdns HAYES BR2 47 M9
Briar Gv SAND/SEL CR2 82 A2
Briar Hl PUR/KEN CR8 62 G9
Briar La CAR SM5 62 C7
CROY/NA CR0 65 H3
Briar Patch GODL GU7 131 K7
Briar Rd RPLY/SEND GU23 92 F4
SHPTN TW17 38 B6
STRHM/NOR SW16 44 G4
WHTN TW2 25 M4
Briars Cl FARN GU14 87 P4
Briars Ct LHD/OX KT22 76 D3
The Briars ASHV GU12 109 K5
DTCH/LGLY SL3 12 D3
Briars Wd HORL RH6 140 E9
Briarswood Cl CRAWE RH10 177 N3
Briar Wk BF/WBF KT14 73 L1
PUT/ROE SW15 18 F9
Briar Wy RGUE GU4 112 F1
Briarwood Cl FELT TW13 23 P6
Briarwood Ct WPK KT4 * 42 E9
Briarwood Dr EWKG RG40 48 C3
Briarwood Rd CLAP SW4 29 N1
EW KT17 60 E5
WOKN/KNAP GU21 71 K8
Brickbarn Cl WBPTN SW10 * 19 N5
Brick Farm Cl RCH/KEW TW9 17 P6
Brickfield Cl BTFD TW8 17 J5
Brickfield La HYS/HAR UB3 14 F4
Brickfield Rd REDH RH1 141 L5
THHTH CR7 45 K2
WIM/MER SW19 28 E7
Brickfields Wy WDR/YW UB7 14 B1
Brickfield Vls SUT SM1 * 62 A2
Brickhouse La GDST RH9 142 C8
Brick Kiln La OXTED RH8 124 A1
Bricklands CRAWE RH10 179 J4
Brick La FLEETN GU51 86 G5
Brick Quarters ALDT GU11 * 108 F1
Bricksbury Hl FNM GU9 107 N7
Brickwood Cl SYD SE26 31 J6
Brickwood Rd CROY/NA CR0 3 G3
Brickyard Copse RDKG RH5 155 K8
Brickyard La CRAWE RH10 179 J3
RDKG RH5 135 M3
Brideake Cl CRAWW RH11 176 D8
Bridge Av HMSMTH W6 18 G3
Bridge Barn La
WOKN/KNAP GU21 72 A6
Bridge Cl BF/WBF KT14 74 B1
STA TW18 22 B7
WOKN/KNAP GU21 72 A6
WOT/HER KT12 39 H8
Bridge Ct WOKN/KNAP GU21 10 A4
Bridge End CBLY GU15 68 D4
Bridgefield FNM GU9 5 J3
Bridgefield Cl BNSTD SM7 78 G4
Bridgefield Rd SUT SM1 61 L5
Bridge Gdns ASHF TW15 38 E1
E/WMO/HCT KT8 40 D5
Bridgeham Cl WEY KT13 56 C4
Bridgeham Wy HORL RH6 160 C2
Bridgehill Cl GUW GU2 111 N3
Bridgelands CRAWE RH10 160 A9
Bridge La VW GU25 36 C7
Bridgeman Rd TEDD TW11 25 P9
Bridgemead FRIM GU16 68 F8
Bridge Ms WOKN/KNAP GU21 10 A4
Bridge Pde
STRHM/NOR SW16 * 29 P8
Bridge Pk RGUE GU4 * 112 G2
Bridge Pl CROY/NA CR0 3 F1
Bridge Rd ALDT GU11 108 C6
ASC SL5 34 D6
BAGS GU19 51 N5
BECK BR3 46 F1
CBLY GU15 68 D5
CHERT KT16 37 M8
CHSGTN KT9 59 L4
COB KT11 75 K4
CRAN GU6 171 H1
E/WMO/HCT KT8 40 E5
EW KT17 78 D1
FARN GU14 88 B3
GODL GU7 131 L8
HASM GU27 184 D3
HORS RH12 189 N3
HSLW TW3 16 D8
SUT SM1 61 M5
TWK TW1 26 A2
WEY KT13 56 B3
WLGTN SM6 62 D4
Bridge Rw CROY/NA CR0 * 3 F1
Bridges Cl HORL RH6 159 N1
Bridges Ct BTSEA SW11 19 P8
Bridges La CROY/NA CR0 62 G3
Bridge Sq FNM GU9 5 G4
Bridge St CHSWK W4 18 B2
DTCH/LGLY SL3 13 H5
GODL GU7 131 L9
GU GU1 6 D5
LHD/OX KT22 96 G2
TWK TW1 26 C2
WOT/HER KT12 39 H9
Bridgetown Cl NRWD SE19 30 F8
Bridge Vw ASC SL5 35 H8
Bridgeview HMSMTH W6 18 G3
Bridge Vls WIM/MER SW19 * 28 D8
Bridge Wk YTLY GU46 67 H1
Bridgewater Ct
DTCH/LGLY SL3 12 E3
Bridgewater Rd WEY KT13 56 F5
Bridge Wy COUL/CHIP CR5 80 A8
WHTN TW2 25 K3
Bridgewood Cl PGE/AN SE20 46 B1
Bridgewood Rd
STRHM/NOR SW16 44 F1
WPK KT4 60 E3
Bridgford St
WAND/EARL SW18 28 F6
Bridgman Rd CHSWK W4 18 A1
Bridle Cl GSHT GU26 165 K8
HOR/WEW KT19 60 A3
KUT KT1 41 K5
SUN TW16 39 J4
Bridle La COB KT11 76 B4
TWK TW1 26 A2
Bridle Pth CROY/NA CR0 62 G2
The Bridle Pth EW KT17 60 G8
Bridlepath Wy
EBED/NFELT TW14 23 P3
Bridle Rd CROY/NA CR0 64 G2
ESH/CLAY KT10 59 H5
EW KT17 78 D2
The Bridle Rd PUR/KEN CR8 62 G8
Bridle Wy CRAWE RH10 177 N4
CROY/NA CR0 64 G4
Bridleway Cl EW KT17 60 G8
The Bridle Wy WLGTN SM6 62 E3
Bridlington Cl BH/WHM TN16 83 P8
Bridport Rd THHTH CR7 45 J4
Brier Lea KWD/TDW/WH KT20 99 K6
Brierley CROY/NA CR0 65 H5
Brierley Cl SNWD SE25 46 A5
Brierley Rd BAL SW12 29 M5
Brierly Cl GUW GU2 111 N3
Brier Rd KWD/TDW/WH KT20 78 F8
Brigade Pl CTHM CR3 101 L2
Briggs Cl MTCM CR4 44 D2
Bright Hl GU GU1 7 G6
Brightlands Rd REIG RH2 119 N3
Brightling Rd BROCKY SE4 31 N2
Brightman Rd
WAND/EARL SW18 28 G4
Brighton Cl ADL/WDHM KT15 55 N4
Brighton Rd
ADL/WDHM KT15 55 N3
ALDT GU11 108 E6
BELMT SM2 61 M8
BNSTD SM7 79 K3
COUL/CHIP CR5 80 E7
CRAWW RH11 194 F2
GODL GU7 131 L9
HORL RH6 140 C9
KWD/TDW/WH KT20 99 L7
MFD/CHID GU8 150 G3
PUR/KEN CR8 80 G3
REDH RH1 120 B5
REDH RH1 140 C4
SURB KT6 41 J7
Brighton Ter REDH RH1 * 120 B6
Brightside Av STA TW18 37 N1
Brightwell Cl CROY/NA CR0 45 J9
Brightwell Crs TOOT SW17 29 J8
Brightwells Rd FNM GU9 5 G3
Brigstock Rd COUL/CHIP CR5 80 D4
THHTH CR7 45 L5
Brimshot La CHOB/PIR GU24 53 L7
Brindle Cl ALDT GU11 108 D7
The Brindles BNSTD SM7 79 K6
Brinkley Rd WPK KT4 60 F1

Brinksway FLEETN GU51 86 G7
Brinn's La BLKW GU17 67 N3
Brinsworth Cl WHTN TW2 25 L4
Brisbane Av
WIM/MER SW19 43 M2
Brisbane Cl CRAWW RH11 176 C2
Briscoe Rd WIM/MER SW19 28 G9
Brisson Cl ESH/CLAY KT10 57 P5
Bristol Cl CRAWE RH10 177 N2
STWL/WRAY TW19 23 H2
WLGTN SM6 62 G7
Bristol Rd MRDN SM4 43 N6
Bristow Rd CBLY GU15 68 D5
CROY/NA CR0 62 G3
HSLW TW3 16 B8
NRWD SE19 30 F8
Britannia Rd BRYLDS KT5 41 M8
FUL/PGN SW6 19 M5
Britannia Wy FUL/PGN SW6 19 M5
STWL/WRAY TW19 22 G3
British Gv CHSWK W4 18 D3
British Grove Pas
CHSWK W4 * 18 D3
Briton Cl SAND/SEL CR2 63 N9
Briton Crs SAND/SEL CR2 63 N9
Briton Hill Rd SAND/SEL CR2 63 N8
Brittain Rd WOT/HER KT12 57 M4
Britten Cl ASHV GU12 109 K4
CRAWW RH11 176 C8
Brittens Cl GUW GU2 91 N9
Brixton Hl BRXS/STRHM SW2 30 A2
Brixton Hill Pl
BRXS/STRHM SW2 29 P3
Brixton Water La
BRXS/STRHM SW2 30 B1
Broadacre STA TW18 22 D8
Broadacres FLEETN GU51 86 D7
Broad Acres GODL GU7 131 L5
Broadacres GUW GU2 111 L3
Broadbridge Heath Rd
HORS RH12 191 L6
Broadbridge La HORL RH6 160 B2
Broad Cl WOT/HER KT12 57 M2
Broadcoombe SAND/SEL CR2 64 D6
Broadeaves Cl SAND/SEL CR2 63 N4
Broadfield Cl
KWD/TDW/WH KT20 78 G9
Broadfield Dr CRAWW RH11 176 F9
Broadfield Pk
CRAWW RH11 * 176 G9
Broadfield Pl CRAWW RH11 176 E9
Broadfield Rd SHGR GU5 134 F4
Broadfields E/WMO/HCT KT8 40 D7
Broadford La
CHOB/PIR GU24 71 L1
Broadford Pk RGUE GU4 132 B3
Broadford Rd RGUE GU4 132 B3
Broadgates Rd
WAND/EARL SW18 28 G4
Broad Green Av
CROY/NA CR0 45 K8
Broadham Green Rd
OXTED RH8 123 K4
Broadham Pl OXTED RH8 123 K3
Broad Ha'penny
RFNM GU10 127 L8
Broad Hwy COB KT11 75 M3
Broadhurst ASHTD KT21 77 L5
FARN GU14 87 N3
Broadhurst Gdns REIG RH2 119 M8
Broadlands FARN GU14 88 C5
FELT TW13 24 G6
FRIM GU16 69 H8
HORL RH6 140 E9
Broadlands Av SHPTN TW17 38 E7
STRHM/NOR SW16 29 P5
Broadlands Cl
STRHM/NOR SW16 29 P5
Broadlands Dr ASC SL5 34 C8
WARL CR6 82 C8
Broadlands Wy NWMAL KT3 42 D7
Broad La BRAK RG12 32 E4
HPTN TW12 39 P1
RDKG RH5 138 B8
Broadley Gn BFOR GU20 52 D6
Broadmead ASHTD KT21 77 L7
CAT SE6 31 P6
FARN GU14 87 P4
HORL RH6 140 E9
REDH RH1 * 100 E8
Broadmead Av WPK KT4 42 E8
Broadmead Cl HPTN TW12 25 H9
Broadmeads
RPLY/SEND GU23 92 F2
Broad Oak SUN TW16 24 A9
Broad Oaks SURB KT6 41 P9
Broadoaks Crs BF/WBF KT14 73 M3
Broad Oaks Wy HAYES BR2 47 M6
Broad Platts DTCH/LGLY SL3 12 B1
Broadrick Heath BNFD RG42 32 F1
Broadstone Pk FROW RH18 181 M9
Broad St CHOB/PIR GU24 70 D1
RGUW GU3 111 K3
TEDD TW11 25 N9
Broadview Rd
STRHM/NOR SW16 44 F1
Broadwalk CRAWE RH10 176 G5
Broad Wk COUL/CHIP CR5 100 C2
CRAN GU6 171 J2
CTHM CR3 101 P2
EPSOM KT18 78 G8
FRIM GU16 68 G6
HEST TW5 15 M6
RCH/KEW TW9 17 M5
Broadwater Cl
STWL/WRAY TW19 21 K3
WOKN/KNAP GU21 73 H1
WOT/HER KT12 57 J4
Broadwater Ri GU GU1 112 E6
Broadwater Rd TOOT SW17 29 H7
Broadwater Rd North
WOT/HER KT12 57 H4
Broadwater Rd South
WOT/HER KT12 57 J4
Broad Wy FARN GU14 88 C7
Broadway BRAK RG12 32 E3
STA TW18 * 22 E8
SURB KT6 41 P9
SUT SM1 61 N3
WOKN/KNAP GU21 71 H8
Broadway Av CROY/NA CR0 45 M6
TWK TW1 26 A2
Broadway Cl SAND/SEL CR2 82 B3
Broadway Ct
WIM/MER SW19 * 28 D9
Broadway Gdns MTCM CR4 44 A5
Broadway Rd
CHOB/PIR GU24 52 D7
The Broadway
ADL/WDHM KT15 55 L8
CHEAM SM3 61 J5
CRAWE RH10 176 G5
SHST GU47 67 M1
STA TW18 37 N4
THDIT KT7 40 E9
WIM/MER SW19 28 C9
WOKN/KNAP GU21 10 E3
Broadwell Rd RFNM GU10 127 K7
Broadwood Cl HORS RH12 192 F5
Broadwood Ri
CRAWW RH11 194 D1
Broadwood Ter
WKENS W14 * 19 K2
Brockenhurst
E/WMO/HCT KT8 39 P6
Brockenhurst Av WPK KT4 42 C9
Brockenhurst Cl
WOKN/KNAP GU21 72 D3
Brockenhurst Dr YTLY GU46 67 H3
Brockenhurst Rd
ALDT GU11 108 D6
ASC SL5 34 B6
BRAK RG12 33 H4
CROY/NA CR0 46 B8
Brockenhurst Wy
STRHM/NOR SW16 44 F3
Brockham Cl WIM/MER SW19 28 C8
Brockham Crs CROY/NA CR0 65 K6
Brockham Dr
BRXS/STRHM SW2 30 A3
Brockham Hill Pk
KWD/TDW/WH KT20 118 A2
Brockhamhurst Rd
BRKHM/BTCW RH3 137 P3
Brockham La
BRKHM/BTCW RH3 117 N5
Brockhill WOKN/KNAP GU21 * 71 N6
Brockhurst Cl HORS RH12 191 N9
Brockhurst Ldg FNM GU9 127 M6
Brocklands YTLY GU46 66 F4
Brocklebank Rd
WAND/EARL SW18 28 E3
Brocklesby Rd SNWD SE25 46 B5
Brockley Combe WEY KT13 56 F4
Brockley Gv BROCKY SE4 31 N1
Brockley Hall Rd BROCKY SE4 31 M2
Brockley Ms BROCKY SE4 31 M1
Brockley Pk FSTH SE23 31 M3
Brockley Ri FSTH SE23 31 M3
Brockley Rd BROCKY SE4 31 N1
Brockley Vw FSTH SE23 31 M3
Brockley Wy FSTH SE23 31 L1
Brock Rd CRAWW RH11 176 E2
Brock's Cl GODL GU7 131 N8
Brocks Dr CHEAM SM3 61 J2
RGUW GU3 111 J1
Brockshot Cl BTFD TW8 17 K4
Brock Wy VW GU25 36 A6
Brockway Cl GU GU1 112 F4
Brockwell Park Gdns
HNHL SE24 30 C3
Brodie Rd GU GU1 7 G5
Brodrick Gv GT/LBKH KT23 96 A6
Brodrick Rd TOOT SW17 29 J4
Brograve Gdns BECK BR3 47 H3
Broke Ct RGUE GU4 112 G2
Brokes Crs REIG RH2 119 L3
Brokes Rd REIG RH2 119 L3
Brokle Cl FLEETS GU52 106 E2
Bromford Cl OXTED RH8 123 N4
Bromley Av BMLY BR1 47 L1
Bromley Crs HAYES BR2 47 M4
Bromley Gdns HAYES BR2 47 M3
Bromley Gv HAYES BR2 47 K3
Bromley Hl BMLY BR1 47 M1
Bromley Rd BECK BR3 46 G2
BECK BR3 47 H2
Brompton Cl HSLWW TW4 24 G1
Brompton Cottages
WBPTN SW10 * 19 N4
Brompton Park Crs
FUL/PGN SW6 19 M4
Bronsart Rd FUL/PGN SW6 19 J5
Bronson Rd RYNPK SW20 43 H3
The Brontes EGRIN RH19 * 180 C2
Brook Av FNM GU9 108 B7
Brook Cl DORK RH4 117 J5
EGRIN RH19 180 G2
FLEETN GU51 86 G7
HOR/WEW KT19 60 C7
RYNPK SW20 42 F4
SHST GU47 50 A8
STWL/WRAY TW19 23 J3
TOOT SW17 29 K5
Brook Ct BECK BR3 * 46 F2
Brook Dr BRAK RG12 * 32 G5
Brooke End OXTED RH8 * 123 N4
Brooke Forest RGUW GU3 111 J1
Brookers Cl ASHTD KT21 77 J6
Brookers Cnr CWTH RG45 49 N4
Brookers Rw CWTH RG45 49 N3
Brook Farm Rd COB KT11 75 M4
Brookfield GODL GU7 131 N5
WOKN/KNAP GU21 71 P5
Brookfield Av SUT SM1 62 A2
Brookfield Cl CHERT KT16 55 H5
REDH RH1 140 C2
Brookfield Gdns
ESH/CLAY KT10 58 F5
Brookfield Rd ASHV GU12 108 G4
Brookfields Av MTCM CR4 44 A6
Brook Gdns BARN SW13 18 D8
FARN GU14 88 B5
KUTN/CMB KT2 42 A2
Brook Gn BNFD RG42 32 B2
HMSMTH W6 18 G1
Brook Hl OXTED RH8 123 J1
SHGR GU5 133 P5
Brookhill Cl CRAWE RH10 160 B9
Brookhill Rd CRAWE RH10 178 B1
Brookhouse Rd FARN GU14 88 B4
Brookhurst Fld
HORS RH12 * 189 N2
Brookhurst Rd
ADL/WDHM KT15 55 M5
Brooklands GDST RH9 * 142 C3
Brooklands Av
WAND/EARL SW18 28 E5
Brooklands Cl COB KT11 75 N4
FNM GU9 107 P7
RFNM GU10 126 B8
SUN TW16 38 G2
Brooklands La WEY KT13 56 B5
Brooklands Rd
CRAWW RH11 194 F1
FNM GU9 108 A7
THDIT KT7 40 F9
WEY KT13 56 D7
Brooklands Ter SUN TW16 * 39 J5
The Brooklands ISLW TW7 * 16 D6
Brooklands Wy EGRIN RH19 180 C3
FNM GU9 108 A7
REDH RH1 120 A3
Brook La CHOB/PIR GU24 53 K9
HORS RH12 193 J3
RPLY/SEND GU23 93 J2
SHGR GU5 134 A4
Brook La North BTFD TW8 17 K3
Brookley Cl RFNM GU10 128 D2
Brookleys CHOB/PIR GU24 53 M8
Brookly Gdns FLEETN GU51 87 H6
Brooklyn Av SNWD SE25 46 B5
Brooklyn Cl CAR SM5 62 A1
WOKS/MYFD GU22 10 C7
Brooklyn Ct
WOKS/MYFD GU22 10 C7
Brooklyn Gv SNWD SE25 46 B5
Brooklyn Rd SNWD SE25 46 B5
WOKS/MYFD GU22 10 C6
Brooklyn Wy WDR/YW UB7 13 P1
Brook Md HOR/WEW KT19 60 C5
Brookmead MTCM CR4 44 E7
Brookmead Ct CRAN GU6 171 H1
FNM GU9 4 D5
Brookmead Rd CROY/NA CR0 44 E7
Brook Rd BAGS GU19 51 N7
CBLY GU15 68 D4
HORS RH12 192 D4
MFD/CHID GU8 167 K3
REDH RH1 100 E8
REDH RH1 120 B6
RGUE GU4 132 G2
SURB KT6 59 L1
THHTH CR7 45 L5
TWK TW1 25 P2
Brook Rd South BTFD TW8 17 L4
Brooksby Cl BLKW GU17 67 M3
Brooks Cl WEY KT13 56 C8
Brookscroft CROY/NA CR0 64 F8
Brookside CAR SM5 62 C4
CHERT KT16 37 J8
CRAN GU6 153 H9
CRAN GU6 171 H2
CRAWE RH10 160 B9
CRAWE RH10 177 J4
DTCH/LGLY SL3 12 C5
FNM GU9 107 N8
GDST RH9 122 D9
RDKG RH5 137 M7
RGUE GU4 92 B9
SHST GU47 67 N1
Brookside Av ASHF TW15 22 F8
STWL/WRAY TW19 12 B8
Brookside Cl FELT TW13 24 B6
Brookside Crs WPK KT4 42 E8
Brookside Pk FARN GU14 * 68 C7
Brookside Wy CROY/NA CR0 46 D7
Brooks La CHSWK W4 17 N4
Brooks Rd CHSWK W4 17 N3
Brook St KUT KT1 8 D6
Brookswood RGUE GU4 132 G3
The Brook CRAWE RH10 176 G4
Brook Va RDKG RH5 137 H4
Brookview CRAWE RH10 160 B9
Brookview Rd
STRHM/NOR SW16 29 M8
Brookville Rd FUL/PGN SW6 19 K5
Brook Wy LHD/OX KT22 76 G7
Brookwell La SHGR GU5 151 N2
Brookwood HORL RH6 140 D9
Brookwood Av BARN SW13 18 D8
Brookwood Br
WOKN/KNAP GU21 71 H9
Brookwood Cl HAYES BR2 47 M5
Brookwood Lye Rd
WOKS/MYFD GU22 71 J9
Brookwood Rd FARN GU14 88 F3
HSLW TW3 16 B7
WAND/EARL SW18 28 C4
Broom Acres FLEETS GU52 86 F9
SHST GU47 49 M9
Broom Bank WARL CR6 83 J8
Broom Cl ESH/CLAY KT10 58 B4
TEDD TW11 41 K1
Broomcroft Dr
WOKS/MYFD GU22 73 H4
Broomdashers Rd
CRAWE RH10 177 J4
Broome Cl EPSOM KT18 98 B6
HORS RH12 192 C5
YTLY GU46 66 G1
Broome Ct BRAK RG12 32 D4
Broomehall Rd RDKG RH5 155 L2
Broome Rd HPTN TW12 39 P2
Broomers La CRAN GU6 153 P7
Broom Fld LTWR GU18 70 A1
Broomfield GUW GU2 111 L4
MFD/CHID GU8 129 N9
SUN TW16 39 J2
Broomfield Cl RGUW GU3 111 L3
WOKS/MYFD GU22 73 H5
Broomfield Ct WEY KT13 56 C5
Broomfield La RFNM GU10 146 D3
Broomfield Pk ASC SL5 35 H8
DORK RH4 116 C8
Broomfield Ride
LHD/OX KT22 76 D1
Broomfield Rd
ADL/WDHM KT15 55 M9
BECK BR3 46 E5
BRYLDS KT5 41 M9
RCH/KEW TW9 17 M6
TEDD TW11 26 B9
Broomfields ESH/CLAY KT10 58 C4
Broom Gdns CROY/NA CR0 64 G2
Broom Hall LHD/OX KT22 76 C3
Broomhall End
WOKN/KNAP GU21 10 D1
Broomhall La ASC SL5 34 F7
WOKN/KNAP GU21 10 D2
Broomhall Rd SAND/SEL CR2 63 M7
WOKN/KNAP GU21 10 D2
Broomhill RFNM GU10 107 H6
Broomhill Rd FARN GU14 87 P2
WAND/EARL SW18 28 D1
Broomhouse La
FUL/PGN SW6 19 L7
Broomhouse Rd
FUL/PGN SW6 19 L7
Broomhurst Ct DORK RH4 117 H9
Broomlands La OXTED RH8 104 E8
Broom La CHOB/PIR GU24 53 L7
Broomleaf Cnr FNM GU9 5 K4
Broomleaf Rd FNM GU9 5 K3
Broomloan La SUT SM1 61 L1
Broom Lock TEDD TW11 * 26 B8
Broom Pk KUT KT1 8 B1
TEDD TW11 41 K1
Broomrigg Rd FLEETN GU51 86 E5
Broom Rd CROY/NA CR0 64 G2
TEDD TW11 26 B9
Broomsquires Rd BAGS GU19 51 N7
Broom Water TEDD TW11 26 B9
Broom Water West
TEDD TW11 26 B8
Broom Wy BLKW GU17 67 P4
WEY KT13 56 F3
Broomwood Cl CROY/NA CR0 46 D6
Broomwood Rd BTSEA SW11 29 J2
Broomwood Wy
RFNM GU10 127 N7
Broseley Gv SYD SE26 31 M8
Broster Gdns SNWD SE25 45 P4
Brougham Pl FNM GU9 107 M7
Brough Cl KUTN/CMB KT2 * 26 C8
Broughton Av
RCHPK/HAM TW10 26 B7
Broughton Ms FRIM GU16 69 H7
Broughton Rd FUL/PGN SW6 19 M8
THHTH CR7 45 J7
Broughton Road Ap
FUL/PGN SW6 * 19 M7
Browell's La FELT TW13 24 D5
Brown Cl WLGTN SM6 62 F6
Browngraves Rd
WDR/YW UB7 14 E5
Browning Av SUT SM1 62 A3
WPK KT4 42 F9
Browning Cl CBLY GU15 69 L4
CRAWE RH10 177 M4
HPTN TW12 24 G7
Browning Rd FLEETS GU52 106 E3
LHD/OX KT22 96 D5
Brownings EDEN TN8 144 G1
The Brownings EGRIN RH19 180 B2
Browning Wy HEST TW5 15 M6
Brownlow Dr BNFD RG42 32 E1
Brownlow Rd CROY/NA CR0 3 H7
REDH RH1 120 A5
Brownrigg Crs BRAK RG12 32 G2
Brownrigg Rd ASHF TW15 23 K7
Brown's Hl REDH RH1 141 M3
Browns La EHSLY KT24 95 M7
Brownsover Rd FARN GU14 87 N3
Brown's Rd BRYLDS KT5 41 M8
Browns Wk RFNM GU10 127 K8
Browns Wd EGRIN RH19 162 D8
The Brow REDH RH1 140 C1
Broxash Rd BTSEA SW11 29 K2
Broxholm Rd WNWD SE27 30 B6
Brox La ADL/WDHM KT15 55 H7
Brox Rd CHERT KT16 54 G7
Broxted Rd CAT SE6 31 N5
Bruce Av SHPTN TW17 38 E7
Bruce Cl BF/WBF KT14 73 P2
Bruce Dr SAND/SEL CR2 64 D7
Bruce Rd MTCM CR4 44 C1
SNWD SE25 45 M5
Brudenell Rd TOOT SW17 29 J6
Brumana Cl WEY KT13 56 D5
Brumfield Rd
HOR/WEW KT19 60 A4
Brunel Cl HEST TW5 15 K5
NRWD SE19 30 G9
Brunel Pl CRAWE RH10 177 H6
Brunel Wk WHTN TW2 25 H3
Brunner Ct CHERT KT16 54 G4
Brunswick BRAK RG12 32 C8
Brunswick Cl CRAWE RH10 177 K7
THDIT KT7 40 F9
WHTN TW2 25 L6
WOT/HER KT12 57 L1
Brunswick Dr
CHOB/PIR GU24 70 D9
Brunswick Gv COB KT11 75 L2
Brunswick Ms
STRHM/NOR SW16 29 N9
Brunswick Pl NRWD SE19 46 A1
Brunswick Rd
CHOB/PIR GU24 90 D1
FRIM GU16 89 L1
KUTN/CMB KT2 9 H2
SUT SM1 61 M3
Bruntile Cl FARN GU14 88 F6
Brushfield Wy
WOKN/KNAP GU21 71 J7
Brushwood Rd HORS RH12 192 G4
Brussels Rd BTSEA SW11 19 P9
Bruton Rd MRDN SM4 43 N5
Bruton Wy BRAK RG12 32 G8
Bryan Cl SUN TW16 39 J1
Bryanston Av WHTN TW2 25 J4
Bryanston Cl NWDGN UB2 15 P2
Bryanstone Av GUW GU2 111 M1
Bryanstone Cl FLEETS GU52 86 G9
GUW GU2 111 M2
Bryanstone Gv GUW GU2 111 M1
Bryce Cl HORS RH12 192 F5
Bryce Gdns ALDT GU11 108 E7
Bryden Cl SYD SE26 31 M8
Brympton Cl DORK RH4 116 G9
Brynford Cl
WOKN/KNAP GU21 72 C4
Bryn Rd RFNM GU10 127 K6
Bryony Rd GU GU1 112 F2
Bryony Wy SUN TW16 24 B9
Buchanan Dr EWKG RG40 48 C2
Buchans Lawn
CRAWW RH11 176 E9
The Buchan CBLY GU15 51 J9
Bucharest Rd
WAND/EARL SW18 28 F3
Buckfast Rd MRDN SM4 43 M5
Buckham Thorns Rd
BH/WHM TN16 104 G6
Buckhold Rd
WAND/EARL SW18 28 D2
Buckhurst Av CAR SM5 44 A9
Buckhurst Cl EGRIN RH19 162 B9
REDH RH1 120 A3
Buckhurst Hl BRAK RG12 33 H5
Buckhurst La ASC SL5 34 F4
Buckhurst Rd ASC SL5 34 F3
BH/WHM TN16 84 F9
FRIM GU16 89 H1
Buckhurst Wy EGRIN RH19 162 B9
Buckingham Av
E/WMO/HCT KT8 40 B3
EBED/NFELT TW14 24 C2
THHTH CR7 45 J2
Buckingham Cl GU GU1 7 K1
HPTN TW12 24 G8
Buckingham Ct
BELMT SM2 * 61 L7
Buckingham Dr EGRIN RH19 180 F4
Buckingham Gdns
E/WMO/HCT KT8 40 B3
THHTH CR7 45 J3
Buckingham Ga HORL RH6 159 M4
Buckingham La FSTH SE23 31 M3
Buckingham Rd FELT TW13 24 G7
KUT KT1 41 M5
MTCM CR4 44 G6
RCHPK/HAM TW10 26 C5
RDKG RH5 137 J6
Buckingham Wy WLGTN SM6 62 E7
Buckland Cl FARN GU14 68 E9
Buckland La
BRKHM/BTCW RH3 118 F2
Buckland Rd BELMT SM2 60 G8
CHSGTN KT9 59 M4
KWD/TDW/WH KT20 99 K9
REIG RH2 119 H4
Bucklands Rd TEDD TW11 26 B9
Bucklands Whf KUT KT1 * 8 C4
Buckland Wk MRDN SM4 43 N5
Buckland Wy WPK KT4 42 G9
Bucklebury BRAK RG12 32 C8
Buckleigh Av RYNPK SW20 43 K4
Buckleigh Rd
STRHM/NOR SW16 29 N9
Buckleigh Wy NRWD SE19 * 45 P1
Bucklers' Wy CAR SM5 62 B2
Buckles Wy BNSTD SM7 79 J5
Buckley Pl CRAWE RH10 179 H3
Buckmans Rd CRAWW RH11 176 G5
Bucknall Wy BECK BR3 47 J5
Bucknills Cl EPSOM KT18 78 A3
Bucks Cl BF/WBF KT14 73 M3
Buckstone Cl FSTH SE23 31 K2
Buckswood Dr
CRAWW RH11 176 D7
Buckthorne Rd BROCKY SE4 31 M2
Buckthorns BNFD RG42 32 A1
Budebury Rd STA TW18 22 C8
Budge La MTCM CR4 44 B8
Budgen Cl CRAWE RH10 177 N2
Budgen Dr REDH RH1 120 C2
Budgin's Hl ORP BR6 85 M1
Budham Wy BRAK RG12 32 D7
Buer Rd FUL/PGN SW6 19 J7
Buff Av BNSTD SM7 79 M4
Buffbeards La HASM GU27 183 P3
Buffers La LHD/OX KT22 76 G8
Bug Hl WARL CR6 82 D9
Bugkingham Wy FRIM GU16 69 H8
Bulganak Rd THHTH CR7 45 L5
Bulkeley Cl EGH TW20 21 H8
Bullard Rd TEDD TW11 * 25 N9
Bullbeggars La GDST RH9 122 C3

WOKN/KNAP GU21 71 P5
Bullbrook Dr BRAK RG12 32 G2
Bullbrook Rw BRAK RG12 32 G3
Buller Ct FARN GU14 88 E6
Buller Rd ALDT GU11 108 D2
THHTH CR7 45 M4
Bullers Rd FNM GU9 108 A8
Bullfinch Cl HORL RH6 140 A9
HORS RH12 192 B3
SHST GU47 50 A9
Bullfinch Rd SAND/SEL CR2 64 D8
Bull Hl LHD/OX KT22 96 G1
Bull La BRAK RG12 32 D2
RGUE GU4 92 D6
Bullrush Cl CROY/NA CR0 45 N7
Bulls Aly MORT/ESHN SW14 * 18 B8
Bull's Br HYS/HAR UB3 15 J1
Bulls Bridge Rd NWDGN UB2 15 K1
Bullswater Common Rd
CHOB/PIR GU24 90 G5
Bulstrode Av HSLW TW3 15 P8
Bulstrode Gdns HSLW TW3 16 A8
Bulstrode Rd HSLW TW3 16 A8
Bunbury Wy EW KT17 78 F5
Bunce Common Rd
REIG RH2 138 B3
Bunce Dr CTHM CR3 101 M3
Bunch La HASM GU27 184 B3
Bunch Wy HASM GU27 184 B4
Bundy's Wy STA TW18 22 C9
Bungalow Rd FARN GU14 88 D5
SNWD SE25 45 N5
The Bungalows
STRHM/NOR SW16 44 D1
Bunting Cl MTCM CR4 44 B6
SWTR RH13 192 E7
Bunyan Cl CRAWW RH11 176 B8
Bunyard Dr
WOKN/KNAP GU21 72 G3
Burbage Gn BRAK RG12 33 H6
Burbage Rd HNHL SE24 30 E2
Burbeach Cl CRAWW RH11 176 E8
Burberry Cl NWMAL KT3 42 C3
Burbidge Rd SHPTN TW17 38 C5
Burbury Woods CBLY GU15 68 G2
Burchets Hollow SHGR GU5 134 F6
Burchett Coppice
EWKG RG40 48 D1
Burchetts Wy SHPTN TW17 38 D7
Burcote WEY KT13 56 F5
Burcote Rd
WAND/EARL SW18 28 G4
Burcott Gdns
ADL/WDHM KT15 55 P5
Burcott Rd PUR/KEN CR8 81 J3
Burden Cl BTFD TW8 17 J3
Burdenshot Hl RGUW GU3 91 N5
Burdenshott Av
RCHPK/HAM TW10 17 P9
Burdenshott Rd RGUE GU4 92 A7
RGUW GU3 91 N4
Burden Wy GUW GU2 91 P9
Burdett Av RYNPK SW20 42 E2
Burdett Cl CRAWE RH10 177 N6
Burdett Rd CROY/NA CR0 45 M7
RCH/KEW TW9 17 M7
Burdock Cl CRAWW RH11 176 D9
CROY/NA CR0 46 D9
LTWR GU18 52 B9
Burdon La BELMT SM2 61 K7
Burdon Pk BELMT SM2 61 K7
Burfield Cl TOOT SW17 28 F7
Burfield Dr WARL CR6 82 C8
Burfield Rd WDSR SL4 20 F3
Burford La EW KT17 60 G9
Burford Lea MFD/CHID GU8 129 N9
Burford Rd BTFD TW8 17 L3
CAT SE6 31 N5
CBLY GU15 68 D4
SUT SM1 61 L1
SWTR RH13 192 D8
WPK KT4 42 E8
Burford Wk FUL/PGN SW6 * 19 M5
Burford Wy CROY/NA CR0 65 J6
Burges Gv BARN SW13 18 F5
Burges Rd STA TW18 22 D9
Burgess Cl FELT TW13 24 F7
Burgess Rd SUT SM1 61 M3
Burgh Cl CRAWE RH10 177 N2
Burghead Cl SHST GU47 67 P1
Burghfield EW KT17 78 D4
Burgh Heath Rd EW KT17 78 D4
Burgh Hill Rd LIPH GU30 182 C3
Burghill Rd SYD SE26 31 L7
Burghley Av NWMAL KT3 42 B2
Burghley Hall Cl
WIM/MER SW19 * 28 B4
Burghley Pl MTCM CR4 44 B5
Burghley Rd WIM/MER SW19 28 B7
Burgh Mt BNSTD SM7 79 K4
Burgh Wd BNSTD SM7 79 J4
Burgos Cl CROY/NA CR0 63 J5
Burgoyne Rd CBLY GU15 69 J2
SNWD SE25 45 P5
SUN TW16 24 A9
Burham Cl PGE/AN SE20 46 C1
Burhill Rd WOT/HER KT12 57 K7
Burke Cl PUT/ROE SW15 18 C9
Burket Cl NWDGN UB2 15 N2
Burland Rd BTSEA SW11 29 J1
Burlands CRAWW RH11 176 D2
Burlea Cl WOT/HER KT12 57 K4
Burleigh Av WLGTN SM6 62 C2
Burleigh Cl ADL/WDHM KT15 55 M4
CRAWE RH10 179 J3
Burleigh Gdns ASHF TW15 23 M8
WOKN/KNAP GU21 * 11 F2
Burleigh La ASC SL5 33 N2
CRAWE RH10 179 K4
Burleigh Pk COB KT11 75 N1
Burleigh Pl PUT/ROE SW15 28 A1
Burleigh Rd ADL/WDHM KT15 55 M3
ASC SL5 33 N3
CHEAM SM3 43 J9
FRIM GU16 68 F8
Burleigh Wy CRAWE RH10 179 J3
Burley Cl BIL RH14 188 D6
STRHM/NOR SW16 44 F3
Burleys Rd CRAWE RH10 177 N5
Burley Wy BLKW GU17 67 N2
Burlingham Cl RGUE GU4 113 H3
Burlings La RSEV TN14 85 K6
The Burlings ASC SL5 33 N3
Burlington Av RCH/KEW TW9 17 N6
Burlington Cl
EBED/NFELT TW14 23 N3
Burlington Ct ALDT GU11 108 B5
BLKW GU17 67 N5
Burlington Gdns CHSWK W4 18 A3
Burlington La CHSWK W4 18 A5
Burlington Pl FUL/PGN SW6 19 J7
REIG RH2 119 L4
Burlington Rd CHSWK W4 * 18 A3
FUL/PGN SW6 19 J7
ISLW TW7 16 D6
NWMAL KT3 42 D5
THHTH CR7 45 L3
Burlsdon Wy BRAK RG12 32 G2
Burma Rd CHOB/PIR GU24 53 M1
Burma Ter NRWD SE19 * 30 F8
Burmester Rd TOOT SW17 28 F6
Burnaby Crs CHSWK W4 17 P4
Burnaby Gdns CHSWK W4 17 P4
Burnaby St WBPTN SW10 19 N5
Burnbury Rd BAL SW12 29 M4
Burn Cl ADL/WDHM KT15 55 P3
LHD/OX KT22 76 C4
Burne-jones Dr SHST GU47 67 P2
Burnell Av RCHPK/HAM TW10 26 B8
Burnell Rd SUT SM1 61 M3
Burnet Av GU GU1 112 F2
Burnet Cl CHOB/PIR GU24 70 E2
Burnet Gv HOR/WEW KT19 78 A2
Burney Av BRYLDS KT5 41 M6
Burney Cl GT/LBKH KT23 96 C5
Burney Rd RDKG RH5 116 G2
Burnfoot Av FUL/PGN SW6 19 J6
Burnham Cl
WOKN/KNAP GU21 71 K7
Burnham Dr REIG RH2 119 L4
WPK KT4 61 H1
Burnham Gdns CROY/NA CR0 45 P8
HEST TW5 15 K6
HYS/HAR UB3 14 F1
Burnham Gv BNFD RG42 32 E1
Burnham Pl SWTR RH13 * 192 C9
Burnham Rd MRDN SM4 43 M6
WOKN/KNAP GU21 71 K7
Burnhams Rd GT/LBKH KT23 95 N4
Burnham St KUTN/CMB KT2 9 H3
Burnham Wy SYD SE26 31 N8
WEA W13 17 H2
Burnhill Rd BECK BR3 46 G3
Burn Moor Cha BRAK RG12 32 G8
Burnmoor Meadow
EWKG RG40 48 C7
Burnsall Cl FARN GU14 88 D1
Burns Av EBED/NFELT TW14 24 B2
FLEETS GU52 87 H9
Burns Cl FARN GU14 88 B1
HORS RH12 192 D3
WIM/MER SW19 28 G9
Burns Dr BNSTD SM7 79 J3
Burnside ASHTD KT21 77 M7
FLEETN GU51 86 G6
Burnside Cl TWK TW1 25 P2
Burns Rd CRAWE RH10 177 M3
Burns Wy EGRIN RH19 180 B2
HEST TW5 15 M6
HORS RH12 193 P1
Burntcommon Cl
RPLY/SEND GU23 93 K5
Burntcommon La
RPLY/SEND GU23 93 L5
Burnt Hill Rd RFNM GU10 127 L7
Burnt Hill Wy RFNM GU10 127 M8
Burnthouse Gdns BNFD RG42 32 G1
Burnt House La HORS RH12 175 L4
Burnthwaite Rd
FUL/PGN SW6 19 K5
Burnt Oak EWKG RG40 48 D1
Burnt Oak La RDKG RH5 157 K4
Burnt Pollard La
CHOB/PIR GU24 52 E8
Burntwood Cl CTHM CR3 102 A1
WAND/EARL SW18 * 28 G4
Burntwood Grange Rd
WAND/EARL SW18 28 G4
Burntwood La CTHM CR3 102 A1
TOOT SW17 28 G5
Burntwood Vw NRWD SE19 * 30 G8
Burnwood Park Rd
WOT/HER KT12 57 K3
Burpham La RGUE GU4 92 E9
Burrell Cl CROY/NA CR0 46 E7
Burrell Rd FRIM GU16 68 E8
Burrell Rw BECK BR3 46 G3
The Burrell DORK RH4 116 C8
Burr Hill La CHOB/PIR GU24 53 L7
Burritt Rd KUT KT1 9 H5
Burroway Rd DTCH/LGLY SL3 12 F1
Burrow Hill Gn
CHOB/PIR GU24 53 K7
Burrows Cl GT/LBKH KT23 95 P4
GUW GU2 111 M4
Burrows Hill Cl
STWL/WRAY TW19 13 M9
Burrows La SHGR GU5 134 E2
Burr Rd WAND/EARL SW18 28 D4
Burrwood Gdns ASHV GU12 109 J2
Burstead Cl COB KT11 75 M2
Burstock Rd PUT/ROE SW15 19 J9
Burston Gdns EGRIN RH19 162 C8
Burston Rd PUT/ROE SW15 28 A1
Burstow Rd RYNPK SW20 43 J2
Burtenshaw Rd THDIT KT7 40 G8
Burton Cl CHSGTN KT9 59 K6
HORL RH6 159 K2
THHTH CR7 45 M4
Burton Gdns HEST TW5 15 P6
Burton Rd KUTN/CMB KT2 8 E1
Burtons Ct HORS RH12 * 192 B8
Burton's Rd HPTN TW12 25 J7
Burtwell La WNWD SE27 30 E7
Burwash Rd CRAWE RH10 177 K6
Burway Crs CHERT KT16 37 L5
Burwood Av HAYES BR2 65 P1
PUR/KEN CR8 81 K3
Burwood Cl GU GU1 112 G4
REIG RH2 119 P5
SURB KT6 41 N9
WOT/HER KT12 57 L5
Burwood Rd WEY KT13 56 F6
WOT/HER KT12 57 H6
Bury Cl WOKN/KNAP GU21 10 A2
Bury Flds GUW GU2 6 D7
Bury Gv MRDN SM4 43 M6
Bury La WOKN/KNAP GU21 72 A5
Bury Ms GUW GU2 * 6 D7
The Burys GODL GU7 131 L8
Bury St GUW GU2 6 D7
Busbridge La GODL GU7 150 D1
Busch Cl ISLW TW7 17 H6
Busdens Cl MFD/CHID GU8 149 N4
Busdens La MFD/CHID GU8 149 N4
Busdens Wy MFD/CHID GU8 149 N4
Bushbury La
BRKHM/BTCW RH3 137 N1
Bush Cl ADL/WDHM KT15 55 N4
Bush Cottages
WAND/EARL SW18 28 D1
Bushell Cl BRXS/STRHM SW2 30 A5
Bushetts Gv REIG RH2 100 D9
Bushey Cl PUR/KEN CR8 81 P5
Bushey Cft OXTED RH8 123 J1
Bushey La SUT SM1 61 L2
Bushey Rd CROY/NA CR0 64 G1
HYS/HAR UB3 14 G2
RYNPK SW20 42 G3
SUT SM1 61 M3
Bushey Wy BECK BR3 47 K7
Bushfield BIL RH14 187 L8
Bushfield Dr REDH RH1 140 C1
Bush La RPLY/SEND GU23 93 H4
Bushnell Rd TOOT SW17 29 L5
Bush Rd RCH/KEW TW9 17 M4
SHPTN TW17 38 B6
Bushwood Rd RCH/KEW TW9 17 N4
Bushy Hill Dr GU GU1 112 G4
Bushy Park Gdns
HPTN TW12 * 25 L8
Bushy Park Rd TEDD TW11 41 H1
Bushy Rd GT/LBKH KT23 96 B2
TEDD TW11 25 M9
Bushy Shaw ASHTD KT21 77 J6
Busk Crs FARN GU14 88 B4
Bute Av RCHPK/HAM TW10 26 D5
Bute Gdns HMSMTH W6 19 H2
RCHPK/HAM TW10 * 26 D4
WLGTN SM6 62 E4
Bute Gdns West WLGTN SM6 62 E4
Bute Rd CROY/NA CR0 45 J9
WLGTN SM6 62 E3
Bute St SKENS SW7 * 19 P2
Butler Rd BAGS GU19 51 P7
CWTH RG45 49 M3
Butlers Dene Rd CTHM CR3 82 F9
Butlers Hl EHSLY KT24 114 D1
Butlers Rd SWTR RH13 192 F6
Butt Cl CRAN GU6 153 H8
Buttercup Sq
STWL/WRAY TW19 * 22 G4
Butterfield CBLY GU15 68 D4
EGRIN RH19 162 A9
Butterfield Cl TWK TW1 25 N2
Butterfly Wk WARL CR6 82 C9
Butter Hl DORK RH4 116 G7
WLGTN SM6 62 C2
Buttermer Cl RFNM GU10 127 J6
Buttermere Cl
EBED/NFELT TW14 24 A4
FARN GU14 88 A3
HORS RH12 192 G4
MRDN SM4 43 H7
Buttermere Ct ASHV GU12 * 109 H2
Buttermere Dr CBLY GU15 69 M4
PUT/ROE SW15 28 B1
Buttermere Gdns BRAK RG12 32 E4
PUR/KEN CR8 81 M2
Buttermere Wy EGH TW20 36 F1
Buttersteep Ri ASC SL5 33 L9
Butterwick HMSMTH W6 18 G2
Butts Cl CRAWW RH11 176 E4
Butts Crs FELT TW13 25 H6
Butts Rd WOKN/KNAP GU21 10 C5
The Butts BTFD TW8 17 K4
Buxton Av CTHM CR3 101 N1
Buxton Crs CHEAM SM3 61 J3
Buxton Dr NWMAL KT3 42 B3
Buxton La CTHM CR3 101 N1
Buxton Rd ASHF TW15 22 G8
MORT/ESHN SW14 18 C8
THHTH CR7 45 K6
Byam St FUL/PGN SW6 19 N7
Byards Cft STRHM/NOR SW16 44 F2
Bychurch End TEDD TW11 * 25 N8
Bycroft St PGE/AN SE20 46 D1
Bycroft Wy CRAWE RH10 177 L3
Byerley Wy CRAWE RH10 177 P4
Byers La GDST RH9 142 C4
Bye Ways WHTN TW2 25 J6
The Byeways BRYLDS KT5 41 N6
The Byeway
MORT/ESHN SW14 18 A8
Byfeld Gdns BARN SW13 18 E6
Byfield Rd ISLW TW7 16 G8
Byfleet Rd ADL/WDHM KT15 55 P8
COB KT11 74 D1
Byfleets La HORS RH12 191 L5
Bygrove CROY/NA CR0 65 H5
Bygrove Rd WIM/MER SW19 28 G9
Bylands WOKS/MYFD GU22 11 G7
Byne Rd CAR SM5 62 A1
SYD SE26 31 K9
Bynes Rd SAND/SEL CR2 63 M6
Byrd Rd CRAWW RH11 176 C8
Byrefield Rd GUW GU2 111 M2
Byrne Rd BAL SW12 29 L4
Byron Av COUL/CHIP CR5 80 G4
FRIM GU16 69 K5
HSLWW TW4 15 K7
NWMAL KT3 42 E6
SUT SM1 61 P3
Byron Av East SUT SM1 61 P3
Byron Cl CRAWE RH10 177 L4
FLEETN GU51 86 G7
HORS RH12 192 D4
HPTN TW12 24 G7
PGE/AN SE20 * 46 B4
SYD SE26 * 31 M7
WOKN/KNAP GU21 71 L6
WOT/HER KT12 39 N9
YTLY GU46 66 F4
Byron Dr CWTH RG45 49 M6
Byron Gdns SUT SM1 61 P3
Byron Gv EGRIN RH19 180 B3
Byron Pl LHD/OX KT22 97 H2
Byron Rd ADL/WDHM KT15 55 P3
SAND/SEL CR2 64 B8
Byron Wy WDR/YW UB7 14 B2
Byton Rd TOOT SW17 29 J9
Byttom Hl RDKG RH5 97 J7
Byward Av
EBED/NFELT TW14 24 D2
Byways YTLY GU46 66 F3
The Byways HOR/WEW KT19 60 D3
The Byway BELMT SM2 61 P7
Bywood BRAK RG12 32 C8
Bywood Av CROY/NA CR0 46 C7
Bywood Cl PUR/KEN CR8 81 K4
Byworth Cl FNM GU9 4 B3
Byworth Rd FNM GU9 4 B4

C

Cabbell Pl ADL/WDHM KT15 55 N3
Cabell Rd GUW GU2 111 L4
Caberfeigh Pl REDH RH1 * 119 P5
Cabin Moss BRAK RG12 32 G8
Cabrera Av VW GU25 36 B6
Cabrera Cl VW GU25 36 A7
Cabrol Rd FARN GU14 88 C2
Caburn Ct CRAWW RH11 176 F7
Caburn Hts CRAWW RH11 176 F7
Cacket's La RSEV TN14 85 H4
The Cackstones
CRAWE RH10 * 177 N4
Cadbury Cl ISLW TW7 16 G6
SUN TW16 38 G1
Cadbury Rd SUN TW16 38 G1
Caddy Cl EGH TW20 21 M8
Cader Rd WAND/EARL SW18 28 F2
Cadet Wy FLEETS GU52 107 H2
Cadmer Cl NWMAL KT3 42 C5
Cadnam Cl ALDT GU11 108 E8
Cadogan Cl TEDD TW11 25 M8
Cadogan Ct BELMT SM2 61 M5
Cadogan Rd ALDT GU11 88 F8
SURB KT6 41 K6
Caenshill Rd WEY KT13 56 C6
Caenswood Hl WEY KT13 56 C8
Caenwood Cl WEY KT13 56 C5
Caen Wood Rd ASHTD KT21 77 J7
Caerleon Cl ESH/CLAY KT10 59 H6
GSHT GU26 165 M5
Caernarvon FRIM GU16 69 H8
Caernarvon Cl MTCM CR4 44 G4
Caesar's Camp Rd CBLY GU15 51 J9
Caesar's Cl CBLY GU15 51 J9
Caesars Ga BNFD RG42 32 G1
Caesars Wk MTCM CR4 44 B6
Caesar's Wy SHPTN TW17 38 F7
Caffins Cl CRAWE RH10 177 H3
Cage Farm Cottages
OXTED RH8 * 123 H5
Cage Yd REIG RH2 * 119 L5
Caillard Rd BF/WBF KT14 55 P9
Cain Rd BRAK RG12 32 A3
Cain's La EBED/NFELT TW14 23 N1
Cairn Cl FRIM GU16 69 K5
Cairndale Cl BMLY BR1 47 M1
Cairngorm Pl FARN GU14 68 A9
Cairns Rd BTSEA SW11 29 H1
Cairo New Rd CROY/NA CR0 2 B4
Caistor Rd BAL SW12 29 L3
Caithness Dr EPSOM KT18 78 B3
Caithness Rd MTCM CR4 44 D1
WKENS W14 19 H1
Calbourne Rd BAL SW12 29 J3
Calcott Pk YTLY GU46 66 G2
Caldbeck Av WPK KT4 60 F1
Calder Ct DTCH/LGLY SL3 12 D3
Calderdale Cl CRAWW RH11 176 E7
Calder Rd MRDN SM4 43 N6
Caldervale Rd CLAP SW4 29 N1
Calder Wy DTCH/LGLY SL3 13 J8
Caldwell Rd BFOR GU20 52 D4
Caledonian Wy HORL RH6 * 159 L4
Caledonia Rd
STWL/WRAY TW19 23 H4
Caledon Pl GU GU1 112 E2
Caledon Rd WLGTN SM6 62 C3
Calfridus Wy BRAK RG12 32 G4
Calidore Cl
BRXS/STRHM SW2 * 30 A2
California Rd NWMAL KT3 42 A5
Calley Down Crs
CROY/NA CR0 65 K8
Callis Farm Cl
STWL/WRAY TW19 23 H2
Callisto Cl CRAWW RH11 176 B8
Callow Fld PUR/KEN CR8 81 J2
Callow Hl VW GU25 36 A3
Callow St CHEL SW3 19 N4
Calluna Ct WOKS/MYFD GU22 10 E5
Calluna Dr CRAWE RH10 178 B1
Calonne Rd WIM/MER SW19 28 A7
Calshot Rd HTHAIR TW6 14 D7
Calshot Wy FRIM GU16 69 J9
HTHAIR TW6 14 C7
Calthorpe Gdns SUT SM1 61 N2
Calthorpe Rd FLEETN GU51 86 E5
Calton Av DUL SE21 30 F2
Calton Gdns ALDT GU11 108 E7
Calvecroft LIPH GU30 182 F6
Calverley Rd EW KT17 60 E5
Calvert Cl ASHV GU12 108 F5
Calvert Crs DORK RH4 117 H5
Calvert Rd DORK RH4 117 H5
EHSLY KT24 95 K8
Calvin Cl CBLY GU15 69 K4
Camac Rd WHTN TW2 25 L4
Cambalt Rd PUT/ROE SW15 28 A1
Camber Cl CRAWE RH10 177 M5
Camberley Av RYNPK SW20 42 F3
Camberley Cl CHEAM SM3 61 H2
Camberley Rd HTHAIR TW6 14 C8
Camborne Cl HTHAIR TW6 14 C8
Camborne Crs HTHAIR TW6 14 C8
Camborne Rd BELMT SM2 61 L6
CROY/NA CR0 46 A8
MRDN SM4 43 H7
WAND/EARL SW18 28 D3
Camborne Wy HEST TW5 16 A6
Cambray Rd BAL SW12 29 M4
Cambria Cl HSLW TW3 16 A9
Cambria Ct
EBED/NFELT TW14 24 C3
Cambria Gdns
STWL/WRAY TW19 23 H3
Cambrian Cl CBLY GU15 68 D3
WNWD SE27 30 C6
Cambrian Rd FARN GU14 67 P9
RCHPK/HAM TW10 26 E2
Cambrian Wy EWKG RG40 48 E1
Cambria St FUL/PGN SW6 19 M5
Cambridge Av NWMAL KT3 42 D3
Cambridge Cl HSLWW TW4 15 N9
RYNPK SW20 42 F2
WDR/YW UB7 13 P4
WOKN/KNAP GU21 71 M7
Cambridge Crs TEDD TW11 * 25 P8
Cambridge Gdns KUT KT1 9 H5
Cambridge Gv HMSMTH W6 18 F2
PGE/AN SE20 * 46 B2
Cambridge Grove Rd KUT KT1 9 H5
Cambridge Lodge Pk
HORL RH6 * 140 C7
Cambridge Pk TWK TW1 26 C3
Cambridge Rd ALDT GU11 108 B4
ASHF TW15 38 E1
BARN SW13 18 D7
BMLY BR1 47 N1
CAR SM5 62 A5
CWTH RG45 49 N5
HPTN TW12 39 P1
HSLWW TW4 15 N9
KUT KT1 9 H5
MTCM CR4 44 E4
NWMAL KT3 42 B5
PGE/AN SE20 46 A4
RCH/KEW TW9 17 N5
RYNPK SW20 42 F2
SHST GU47 50 A8
SWTR RH13 192 C8
TEDD TW11 25 P7
TWK TW1 26 C2
WOT/HER KT12 39 K7
Cambridge Rd East
FARN GU14 88 E6
Cambridge Rd North
CHSWK W4 17 P3
Cambridge Rd South
CHSWK W4 17 P3
Cambridge Rd West
FARN GU14 88 E6
Cambridgeshire Cl
BNFD RG42 33 H1
Cambridge Sq REDH RH1 120 C8
Camden Av FELT TW13 24 D5
Camden Gdns SUT SM1 61 M4
THHTH CR7 45 K4
Camden Hill Rd NRWD SE19 30 F9
Camden Rd CAR SM5 62 B3
LING RH7 162 C1
SUT SM1 61 M4
Camden Wk FLEETN GU51 87 J6
Camden Wy THHTH CR7 45 K4
Camel Gv KUTN/CMB KT2 26 C8
Camellia Ct CHOB/PIR GU24 70 F2
Camellia Pl WHTN TW2 25 J3
Camelot Cl BH/WHM TN16 84 A5
WIM/MER SW19 28 C7
Camelsdale Rd HASM GU27 184 A5
Camel Wy FARN GU14 88 C7
Camera Pl WBPTN SW10 19 P4
Cameron Cl CRAN GU6 171 H2
Cameron Rd ALDT GU11 88 F8
CAT SE6 * 31 N5
CROY/NA CR0 45 K7
HAYES BR2 47 N6
Camilla Cl GT/LBKH KT23 96 B5
SUN TW16 * 23 P9
Camilla Dr RDKG RH5 116 G1
Camille Cl SNWD SE25 46 A4

Camm Gdns *KUT* KT1 ....9 G4
THDIT KT7 ....40 E8
Camomile Av *MTCM* CR4 ......44 B2
Campana Rd *FUL/PGN* SW6...19 L6
Campbell Av
WOKS/MYFD GU22 ....92 D1
Campbell Cl *ALDT* GU11 ......108 D7
FLEETN GU51 ....86 E6
STRHM/NOR SW16 * 29 N8
WHTN TW2 ....25 L4
YTLY GU46 ....67 K2
Campbell Cottages
MTCM CR4 * 44 C3
Campbell Crs *EGRIN* RH19 ...180 A4
Campbell Pl *FRIM* GU16 ....69 H5
Campbell Rd *ALDT* GU11 ......108 C3
CRAWE RH10 ....177 M7
CROY/NA CR0 ....45 K8
CTHM CR3 ....56 C6
WEY KT13 ....56 C6
WHTN TW2 ....25 L5
Campden Rd *SAND/SEL* CR2 ...63 N4
Campden Ter *CHSWK* W4 * ...18 C3
Campen Cl *WIM/MER* SW19 ...28 B5
Camp End Rd *WEY* KT13 ....56 F7
Camp Farm Rd *ALDT* GU11 ...108 F1
Camp Hi *RFNM* GU10 ....128 E5
Camphill Ct *BF/WBF* KT14 .....73 L1
Camphill Rd *BF/WBF* KT14 .....73 L1
Campion Cl *BLKW* GU17 ....68 B5
SAND/SEL CR2 ....63 N3
Campion Dr
KWD/TDW/WH KT20 ....78 F9
Campion Rd *ISLW* TW7 ....16 F6
PUT/ROE SW15 ....18 G9
Camp Rd *CTHM* CR3 ....102 E1
FARN GU14 ....88 E7
WIM/MER SW19 ....27 N8
Camp Vw *WIM/MER* SW19 ....27 N8
Camrose Av *FELT* TW13 ....24 C7
Camrose Cl *CROY/NA* CR0 ....46 E8
MRDN SM4 ....43 L5
Camus Cl *FLEETS* GU52 ......106 D1
Canada Av *REDH* RH1 ....120 C9
Canada Dr *REDH* RH1 ....120 C9
Canada Rd *BF/WBF* KT14 ......55 P9
COB KT11 ....75 K3
FRIM GU16 ....69 M8
Canada Wy *LIPH* GU30 ....182 F7
Canal Cl *ALDT* GU11 ....108 F1
Canal Wk *CROY/NA* CR0 ......45 N7
Canal Yd *NWDGN* UB2 * 15 K2
Canberra Cl *CRAWW* RH11 ...176 G2
HORS RH12 ....192 E6
HTWY RG27 ....66 E1
Canberra Pl *HORS* RH12 * ...192 E6
Canberra Rd *HTHAIR* TW6 ....14 C8
Canberra Wy *ALDT* GU11 ......88 B7
Canbury Av *KUTN/CMB* KT2 ....9 F2
Canbury Ms *SYD* SE26 ....31 H6
Canbury Park Rd
KUTN/CMB KT2 ....9 F3
Candleford Cl *BRAK* RG12 .....32 E1
Candleford Ga–*LIPH* GU30 * ...182 E6
Candler Ms *TWK* TW1 ....25 P3
Candlerush Cl
WOKS/MYFD GU22 ....72 G9
Candover Cl *WDR/YW* UB7 ....13 P5
Candy Cft *GT/LBKH* KT23 ......96 B6
Canewden Cl
WOKS/MYFD GU22 ....72 A1
Canford Cl *ENC/FH* EN2 ....xx xx
Canford Dr *ADL/WDHM* KT15 ...55 M1
Canford Gdns *NWMAL* KT3 ....42 C7
Canford Pl *TEDD* TW11 ....26 B9
Canham Rd *SNWD* SE25 ....45 N4
Can Hatch
KWD/TDW/WH KT20 ....79 J7
Canmore Gdns
STRHM/NOR SW16 ....44 E1
Canning Pl *KENS* W8 ....19 N1
Canning Place Ms *KENS* W8 * ..19 N1
Canning Rd *ALDT* GU12 ....108 F4
CROY/NA CR0 ....3 J3
Cannizaro Rd
WIM/MER SW19 ....27 P9
Cannon Cl *HPTN* TW12 ....25 J9
RYNPK SW20 ....42 G4
SHST GU47 ....50 D9
Cannon Crs *CHOB/PIR* GU24 ...53 L9
Cannon Gv *LHD/OX* KT22 .....96 E2
Cannon Hi *BRAK* RG12 ....32 E7
Cannon Hill La *MRDN* SM4 .....43 H6
Cannon Side *LHD/OX* KT22 ....96 E2
Cannon Wy *E/WMO/HCT* KT8 ...40 A5
LHD/OX KT22 ....96 E1
Canonbie Rd *FSTH* SE23 ......31 K3
Canons Cl *REIG* RH2 ....119 J4
Canon's Hi *COUL/CHIP* CR5 ...81 J7
Canons La
KWD/TDW/WH KT20 ....79 J8
Canon's Wk *CROY/NA* CR0 ....64 D2
Canopus Wy
STWL/WRAY TW19 ....23 H3
Cansiron La *FROW* RH18 .....181 N6
Cantelupe Ms *EGRIN* RH19 * ..180 D2
Cantelupe Rd *EGRIN* RH19 ...180 E2
Canterbury Cl *BECK* BR3 ......47 H2
Canterbury Ct *DORK* RH4 * ...116 C6
Canterbury Gv *WNWD* SE27 ...30 C6
Canterbury Rd *ASHV* GU12 ...109 J3
CRAWE RH10 ....177 M9
CROY/NA CR0 ....45 H8
FARN GU14 ....88 D5
FELT TW13 ....24 F5
MRDN SM4 ....43 N6
The Canter *CRAWE* RH10 ....177 P4
Cantley Gdns *SNWD* SE19 ....45 P2
Cantley Rd *HNWL* W7 ....16 G1
Capel Av *WLGTN* SM6 ....63 H4

Capel La *CRAWW* RH11 ....176 C6
Capel Rd *HORS* RH12 ....175 H2
Capern Rd *WAND/EARL* SW18 ...28 F4
Capital Interchange Wy
CHSWK W4 ....17 N3
Capper Rd *CBLY* GU15 ....68 C1
Capri Rd *CROY/NA* CR0 ....45 P8
Capricorn Cl *CRAWW* RH11 ...176 A7
Capsey Rd *CRAWW* RH11 .....176 B6
Capstans Whf
WOKN/KNAP GU21 ....71 M7
Caradon Ct
WOKN/KNAP GU21 ....71 P7
Caraway Cl *CRAWW* RH11 ....176 G2
Caraway Pl *GUW* GU2 ....91 N9
WLGTN SM6 * 62 D2
Carberry Rd *NRWD* SE19 ......30 F9
Carbery La *ASC* SL5 ....34 B4
Cardamom Cl *GUW* GU2 ......111 N1
Cardiff Rd *HNWL* W7 ....16 G1
Cardigan Cl
WOKN/KNAP GU21 ....71 L7
Cardigan Rd *BARN* SW13 .....18 E5
RCHPK/HAM TW10 ....26 D2
WIM/MER SW19 ....28 D8
Cardinal Av *KUTN/CMB* KT2 ...26 D8
MRDN SM4 ....43 J7
WPK KT4 ....60 E3
Cardinal Cl *MRDN* SM4 ....43 J7
WPK KT4 ....60 E3
Cardinal Crs *NWMAL* KT3 ......42 A3
Cardinal Dr *WOT/HER* KT12 ...39 M9
Cardinal Pl *PUT/ROE* SW15 ...19 H9
Cardinal Rd *FELT* TW13 ....23 N4
The Cardinals *BRAK* RG12 * ...32 D5
Cardinal's Wk *HPTN* TW12 .....40 C1
Cardinal's Wk *HPTN* TW12 .....23 P9
Cardingham
WOKN/KNAP GU21 ....71 N6
Cardington Sq *HSLWW* TW4 ...15 M9
Cardross St *HMSMTH* W6 .....18 F1
Cardwell Crs *ASC* SL5 ....34 C6
Cardwells Keep *GUW* GU2 ....111 N2
Carew Cl *COUL/CHIP* CR5 .....81 K8
Carew Rd *ASHF* TW15 ....23 M9
MTCM CR4 ....44 C3
THHTH CR7 ....45 K4
WLGTN SM6 ....62 E5
Careys Copse *HORL* RH6 * ...160 C1
Carey's Wd *HORL* RH6 ....160 C1
Carfax *HORS* RH12 ....192 B8
Carfax Av *RFNM* GU10 ....109 H6
Carfax Rd *HYS/HAR* UB3 ......15 J5
The Carfax *SYD* SE26 * 31 K6
Cargate Av *ALDT* GU11 ....108 B5
Cargate Gv *ALDT* GU11 ....108 B5
Cargate Hl *ALDT* GU11 ....108 B5
Cargate Ter *ALDT* GU11 ....108 B5
Cargo Forecourt Rd
HORL RH6 ....158 G5
Cargo Rd *HORL* RH6 ....158 G4
Cargreen Rd *SNWD* SE25 .....45 P5
Carholme Rd *FSTH* SE23 ......31 N4
Carisbrooke *FRIM* GU16 ....69 H8
Carisbrooke Rd *MTCM* CR4 ...44 G5
Carleton Av *WLGTN* SM6 ......62 F7
Carleton Cl *ESH/CLAY* KT10 ...40 D9
Carlingford Rd *MRDN* SM4 .....43 H7
Carlin Pl *CBLY* GU15 ....68 E4
Carlinwark Dr *CBLY* GU15 .....69 H1
Carlisle Cl *KUTN/CMB* KT2 .....9 J2
Carlisle Rd *HPTN* TW12 ....40 B1
RFNM GU10 ....147 L5
SUT SM1 ....61 K5
Carlos St *GODL* GU7 ....131 L9
Carlton Av *EBED/NFELT* TW14 ...24 D2
SAND/SEL CR2 ....63 M6
Carlton Cl *CHSGTN* KT9 ....59 K5
FRIM GU16 ....69 K5
WOKN/KNAP GU21 ....72 D3
Carlton Ct *HORL* RH6 * 140 D8
Carlton Crs *CHEAM* SM3 ....61 J3
Carlton Dene *EW* KT17 * 60 D3
Carlton Dr *PUT/ROE* SW15 ...28 A1
Carlton Gn *REDH* RH1 ....120 A2
Carlton Park Av *RYNPK* SW20 ...42 G3
Carlton Pl *WEY* KT13 * 56 D3
Carlton Rd *BOR* GU35 ....164 F1
EW KT17 ....60 D5
MORT/ESHN SW14 ....18 A8
NWMAL KT3 ....42 C3
REDH RH1 ....119 P3
SAND/SEL CR2 ....63 M6
SUT SM1 ....61 H5
WOKN/KNAP GU21 ....72 D3
WOT/HER KT12 ....39 L9
Carlton Ter *SYD* SE26 * 31 K6
Carlton Tye *HORL* RH6 ....159 N1
Carlwell St *TOOT* SW17 ....29 H8
Carlyle Cl *E/WMO/HCT* KT8 ...40 B3
Carlyle St *WBPTN* SW10 * 19 P3
Carlyle Rd *CROY/NA* CR0 ......64 A1
FARN GU14 ....89 H3
STA TW18 ....37 K1
Carlyle Sq *CHEL* SW3 ....19 P3
Carlyon Cl *FARN* GU14 ....88 D4
Carlys Cl *BECK* BR3 ....46 D2
Carmalt Gdns *PUT/ROE* SW15 ...18 G9
WOT/HER KT12 ....57 L4
Carmarthen Cl *FARN* GU14 ....88 B9
Carmel Cl
WOKS/MYFD GU22 ....10 D6
Carmichael Cl *BTSEA* SW11 * ...19 P8
Carmichael Rd *SNWD* SE25 ...46 A6
Carminia Rd *BAL* SW12 ....29 L5
Carmino Ter *LIPH* GU30 * 182 E6

Carnac St *WNWD* SE27 ....30 E7
Carnarvon Dr *HYS/HAR* UB3 ...14 E1
Carnation Cl *EWKG* RG40 ......49 H1
Carnegie Cl *SURB* KT6 ....59 M1
Carnforth Cl *HOR/WEW* KT19 ...59 P5
Carnforth Rd
STRHM/NOR SW16 ....44 F1
Carnoustie *BRAK* RG12 ....32 A8
Carolina Pl *EWKG* RG40 ....48 C2
Carolina Rd *THHTH* CR7 ....45 K3
Caroline Cl *CROY/NA* CR0 ......3 H7
STRHM/NOR SW16 ....30 A7
Caroline Ct *ASHF* TW15 ....23 K9
CRAWW RH11 ....176 G6
Caroline Pl *HYS/HAR* UB3 ......14 G5
Caroline Rd *WIM/MER* SW19 ...43 K1
Caroline Wk *HMSMTH* W6 .....19 J4
Caroline Wy *FRIM* GU16 ....69 H8
Carolyn Cl *WOKN/KNAP* GU21 ...71 M8
The Carriageway
RSEV TN14 ....105 P4
Carrick Cl *ISLW* TW7 ....16 G8
Carrick Ga *ESH/CLAY* KT10 ...58 C2
Carrick La *YTLY* GU46 ....67 J2
Carrington Av *HSLW* TW3 ....25 J1
Carrington Cl *CROY/NA* CR0 ...46 E8
REDH RH1 ....120 B4
Carrington La *ASHV* GU12 .....89 H7
Carrington Pl
ESH/CLAY KT10 * 58 B3
Carrington Rd
RCHPK/HAM TW10 ....17 N9
Carroll Av *GU* GU1 ....112 F5
Carroll Crs *ASC* SL5 ....34 B5
Carrow Rd *WOT/HER* KT12 ....57 M2
Carshalton Gv *SUT* SM1 ....61 P3
Carshalton Park Rd *CAR* SM5 ...62 C5
Carshalton Pl *CAR* SM5 ....62 C4
Carshalton Rd *BNSTD* SM7 ....80 B2
CBLY GU15 ....51 J8
MTCM CR4 ....44 C4
SUT SM1 ....61 N4
Carslake Rd *PUT/ROE* SW15 ...27 P2
Carson Rd *DUL* SE21 ....30 D5
Cartbridge Cl
RPLY/SEND GU23 ....92 F3
Carter Cl *WLGTN* SM6 ....62 F6
Carter Rd *CRAWE* RH10 ....177 N8
WIM/MER SW19 ....28 G9
Carters Cl *GU* GU1 ....112 C1
Carters La
WOKS/MYFD GU22 ....72 G9
Carterslodge La
RHWH RH17 ....193 P9
Cartersmead Cl *HORL* RH6 ...140 D9
Carter's Rd *EW* KT17 ....78 D4
Carters Wk *FNM* GU9 ....107 P6
Carter's Yd
WAND/EARL SW18 ....18 E2
Carthew Rd *HMSMTH* W6 .....18 F1
Carthew Vls *HMSMTH* W6 .....18 F1
Carthona Dr *FLEETS* GU52 ....86 F8
Carthouse La
WOKN/KNAP GU21 ....71 L3
Cartmel Cl *REDH* RH1 ....120 A4
Cartmel Gdns *MRDN* SM4 .....43 N6
Cartwright Wy *BARN* SW13 ....18 F5
Carver Rd *HNHL* SE24 ....30 D2
Carville Crs *BTFD* TW8 ....17 L3
Cascades *CROY/NA* CR0 ....64 F8
Caselden Cl *ADL/WDHM* KT15 ...55 N4
Casewick Rd *WNWD* SE27 .....30 C8
Casher Rd *CRAWE* RH10 .....177 M8
Casino Av *HNHL* SE24 ....30 D1
Cassidy Rd *FUL/PGN* SW6 ....19 K5
Cassilis Rd *TWK* TW1 ....26 A2
Cassino Cl *ALDT* GU11 ....108 D4
Cassiobury Av
EBED/NFELT TW14 ....24 A3
Cassland Rd *THHTH* CR7 ......45 M5
Cassilee Rd *CAT* SE6 ....31 N3
Castello Av *PUT/ROE* SW15 ...27 P1
Castelnau *BARN* SW13 ....18 F5
Castlands Rd *CAT* SE6 ....31 N5
Castle Av *EW* KT17 ....60 E5
Castle Cl *CBLY* GU15 ....68 C3
HAYES BR2 ....47 P4
REDH RH1 ....121 L4
REIG RH2 ....119 M9
WIM/MER SW19 ....28 A6

WOKN/KNAP GU21 ....72 D3
Castle Rw *CHSWK* W4 * 18 B3
Castle Sq *REDH* RH1 ....121 L4
Castle St *FLEETS* GU52 ....86 F8
FNM GU9 ....5 F2
GU GU1 ....6 E7
KUT KT1 ....8 C1
REDH RH1 ....121 K4
The Castle *HORS* RH12 ....192 D3
Castleton Cl *BNSTD* SM7 ....79 L4
CROY/NA CR0 ....46 E7
Castleton Rd *BNSTD* SM7 ......79 J1
Castletown Rd *WKENS* W14 ...19 J3
Castleview Rd
DTCH/LGLY SL3 ....12 A2
Castle View Rd *WEY* KT13 .....56 D3
Castle Wk *SUN* TW16 * 39 L4
Castle Wy *EW* KT17 ....60 E8
FELT TW13 ....24 B6
Castle Yd *RCHPK/HAM* TW10 ...26 C1
YTLY GU46 ....66 F1
Castor Ct *FLEETS* GU52 ......107 H1
Castor La *CROY/NA* CR0 ....3 J6
Caswall Cl *FARN* GU14 ....87 N3
Catalina Rd *HTHAIR* TW6 ......14 D8
Catalpa Cl *GU* GU1 * 112 A3
Catena Ri *LTWR* GU18 ....52 A8
Caterfield La *LING* RH7 ....143 H5
Caterham By-Pass
CTHM CR3 ....102 B3
Caterham Cl
CHOB/PIR GU24 ....90 E1
Caterham Rd
COUL/CHIP CR5 ....81 L8
Caterways *HORS* RH12 ....191 P7
Catesby Gdns *YTLY* GU46 .....66 E3
Catford Hl *CAT* SE6 ....31 M3
Catford Rd *CAT* SE6 ....31 M1 *
Cathcart Rd *WBPTN* SW10 * ...19 M4
Cathedral Cl *GU* GU2 ....111 N4
Cathedral Hl *GUW* GU2 ....111 N4
Cathedral Vw *GUW* GU2 ......111 M5
Catherine Cl *BF/WBF* KT14 ....74 A3
Catherine Dr *RCH/KEW* TW9 ...17 L9
SUN TW16 ....39 H1
Catherine Gdns *HSLW* TW3 ...16 D3
Catherine Howard Ct
WEY KT13 ....56 D2
Catherine Rd *SURB* KT6 ....41 K6
Catherine Vis *RYNPK* SW20 * ...42 F1
Catherine Wheel Rd
BTFD TW8 ....17 K5
Cathill La *RDKG* RH5 ....155 P9
Cathles Rd *BAL* SW12 ....29 L2
Catlin Crs *SHPTN* TW17 ....38 F6
Catlin Gdns *GDST* RH9 ....122 B2
Catling Cl *FSTH* SE23 ....31 K6
Cator Cl *CROY/NA* CR0 ....65 L9
Cator Crs *CROY/NA* CR0 ....65 L9
Cator La *BECK* BR3 ....46 F3
Cator Rd *CAR* SM5 ....62 C5
SYD SE26 ....31 L9
Catteshall Hatch *GODL* GU7 ...131 N7 *
Catteshall La *GODL* GU7 ......131 M8
Catteshall Rd *GODL* GU7 .....131 N7
Caudwell Ter
WAND/EARL SW18 * 28 G2
Causeway *EBED/NFELT* TW14 ...15 N9 *
HORS RH12 ....192 B9
The Causeway *BELMT* SM2 ....61 N7
CAR SM5 ....62 C2
CHSGTN KT9 ....59 L3
ESH/CLAY KT10 ....58 F6
HORS RH12 ....192 B9
STA TW18 ....21 P7
TEDD TW11 ....25 N9
WAND/EARL SW18 ....28 G2
WIM/MER SW19 ....27 L9
WOKS/MYFD GU22 ....71 P9
Cavalier Wy *EGRIN* RH19 .....180 E4
Cavalry Ct *ALDT* GU11 ....108 A4
Cavalry Crs *HSLWW* TW4 ......15 J5
Cavaye Pl *WBPTN* SW10 * 19 N4
Cavell Wy *CRAWE* RH10 ......177 M6
HOR/WEW KT19 ....59 N4
WOKN/KNAP GU21 ....71 J7
Cavendish Av *NWMAL* KT3 ....42 F6
Cavendish Rd *CRAWE* RH10 ...192 C3 *
SUN TW16 ....24 A9
Cavendish Cl *BLKW* GU17 .....xx A9
SUN TW16 ....24 A9
Cavendish Dr *ESH/CLAY* KT10 ...58 C4
FLEETS GU52 xx
REDH RH1 ....120 C4
Cavendish Gdns *CLAP* SW4 ...29 M2
FLEETS GU52 ....106 F1
REDH RH1 ....120 C4
Cavendish Meads *ASC* SL5 ...34 D7
Cavendish Ms *ALDT* GU11 ...108 C5
Cavendish Pde *HSLWW* TW4 * ...15 N7
Cavendish Rd *ALDT* GU11 ...108 C5
BAL SW12 ....29 M3
BELMT SM2 ....61 N6
CHSWK W4 ....18 A6
CROY/NA CR0 ....45 H9
FLEETS GU52 ....106 F1
NWMAL KT3 ....42 D6
REDH RH1 ....120 C5
SUN TW16 ....39 H3
WEY KT13 ....56 D7
WIM/MER SW19 ....44 A1
WOKS/MYFD GU22 ....10 C7
Cavendish Ter *FELT* TW13 * ...24 B5
Cavendish Wy *WWKM* BR4 ...47 H7
Cavenham Cl
WOKS/MYFD GU22 ....10 C7
Caverleigh Wy *WPK* KT4 ....42 G9
Cave Rd *RCHPK/HAM* TW10 ...26 B7
Caversham Av *CHEAM* SM3 ...61 J1

Caversham Rd *KUT* KT1 ....9 F4
Caves Farm Cl *SHST* GU47 ....49 L9
Cawdor Crs *HNWL* W7 ....16 G2
Cawnpore St *NRWD* SE19 .....30 F8
Cawsey Wy
WOKN/KNAP GU21 ....10 D4
Caxton Av *ADL/WDHM* KT15 ...55 L5
Caxton Cl *CRAWE* RH10 ......176 G8
Caxton Gdns *GUW* GU2 ......111 P4
Caxton La *OXTED* RH8 ....124 C2
Caxton Ms *BTFD* TW8 * 17 K5
Caxton Rd *REDH* RH1 ....120 C4
WIM/MER SW19 ....28 F8
Caygill Cl *HAYES* BR2 ....47 M5
Cayley Rd *NWDGN* UB2 ....16 B1
Cayton Rd *COUL/CHIP* CR5 ...100 E2
Cearn Wy *COUL/CHIP* CR5 ....81 H5
Cecil Cl *ASHF* TW15 ....23 M9
CHSGTN KT9 ....59 K3
Cecil Pl *MTCM* CR4 ....44 B6
Cecil Rd *ASHF* TW15 ....38 E1
CROY/NA CR0 ....44 G7
HSLW TW3 ....16 C8
SUT SM1 ....61 K5
Cedar Av *BLKW* GU17 ....xx G6 *
COB KT11 ....75 K3
WHTN TW2 ....25 J2
Cedar Cl *ALDT* GU12 ....108 G6
BAGS GU19 ....51 N6
CAR SM5 ....62 B5
CRAWW RH11 ....176 F2
DORK RH4 ....117 H7
DUL SE21 ....30 D4
ESH/CLAY KT10 ....57 P6
EW KT17 ....78 C2
HORS RH12 ....192 B8
KUTN/CMB KT2 ....xx J7
REIG RH2 ....119 N7
STA TW18 ....37 N3
WARL CR6 ....82 E7
Cedar Ct *ADL/WDHM* KT15 ...55 N3
EGH TW20 ....21 M7
HASM GU27 ....184 E6
WIM/MER SW19 ....28 A6
Cedarcroft Rd *CHSGTN* KT9 ...59 M3
Cedar Dr *ASC* SL5 ....34 G8
BNFD RG42 ....32 E1
EDEN TN8 ....144 F3
FLEETN GU51 ....87 J2
LIPH GU30 ....182 E6
PIN HA5 xx
Cedar Gdns *BELMT* SM2 ......61 N5
WOKN/KNAP GU21 ....71 P7
Cedar Gv *CHOB/PIR* GU24 ....70 G4
EA W5 ....17 K1
WEY KT13 ....56 D3
Cedar Hts *RCHPK/HAM* TW10 ...26 A4
Cedar Hl *EPSOM* KT18 ....78 A4
Cedarhurst *BMLY* BR1 * 47 L1
Cedar Ldg *HASM* GU27 * 184 D5
Cedarne Rd *FUL/PGN* SW6 ...19 L5
Cedar Pk *CTHM* CR3 ....101 N1
Cedar Rd *BELMT* SM2 ....61 N5
COB KT11 ....75 K3
CROY/NA CR0 ....3 K5
E/WMO/HCT KT8 ....40 C5
EBED/NFELT TW14 ....23 N4
FARN GU14 ....88 E4
HEST TW5 ....15 L7
TEDD TW11 ....25 P8
WEY KT13 ....56 D4
WOKS/MYFD GU22 ....71 P9
Cedars *BNSTD* SM7 ....80 B3
Cedars Av *MTCM* CR4 ....44 C5
Cedars Cl *SHST* GU47 ....49 K9
Cedars Cottages
PUT/ROE SW15 * 27 M2
Cedars Ct *GU* GU1 * 112 E2
Cedars Rd *BARN* SW13 ....18 D7
BECK BR3 ....46 E3
CROY/NA CR0 ....63 J2
E/WMO/HCT KT8 ....40 C4
MRDN SM4 ....43 L5
The Cedars *BF/WBF* KT14 .....74 B1
FLEETN GU51 xx
LHD/OX KT22 ....97 K1
MFD/CHID GU8 ....149 M4
REIG RH2 ....119 P5
RGUE GU4 ....112 G2
TEDD TW11 ....25 P8
Cedar Ter *RCH/KEW* TW9 .....17 L9
Cedar Tree Gv *WNWD* SE27 ...30 C8
Cedarville Gdns
STRHM/NOR SW16 ....30 A9
Cedar Wk *ESH/CLAY* KT10 ....58 F5
KWD/TDW/WH KT20 ....99 K1
PUR/KEN CR8 ....81 L5
Cedar Wy *DTCH/LGLY* SL3 ....12 C2
GU GU1 ....112 A2
SUN TW16 ....38 C1
Cedarways *FNM* GU9 ....127 M6
Celandine Cl *CRAWW* RH11 * ...176 D9
CWTH RG45 ....49 L1
Celandine Rd *WOT/HER* KT12 ...57 N3
Cell Barn Av *WDSR* SL4 ....20 C1
Celtic Av *HAYES* BR2 ....47 L4
Celtic Rd *BF/WBF* KT14 ....73 L3
Cemetery La *SHPTN* TW17 ....38 D8
Cemetery Pales
CHOB/PIR GU24 ....90 G2
Cemetery Rd *FLEETS* GU52 ...86 E8
Centaur Ct *BTFD* TW8 * 17 L3
Centennial Ct *BRAK* RG12 * ...32 C3
Central Av *ASHF* TW15 ....23 P9
E/WMO/HCT KT8 ....39 P6
HSLW TW3 ....16 C8
WLGTN SM6 ....62 G4
Central Hl *NRWD* SE19 ....30 D9

Central Pde *CROY/NA* CR0........65 J8
E/WMO/HCT KT8 *............39 P5
HORL RH6 *.............159 K2
PGE/AN SE20 *...........46 D1
STRHM/NOR SW16 *.......29 P6
SURB KT6 *.............41 L7
Central Park Est
HSLWW TW4 *...........15 M9
Central Pl SNWD SE25.........46 A5
Central Rd MRDN SM4.........43 M6
WPK KT4...............60 E1
Central Sq E/WMO/HCT KT8....39 P5
Central Ter BECK BR3 *........4 A6
Central Wy CAR SM5...........62 A6
EBED/NFELT TW14.........24 C1
OXTED RH8.............103 K7
Centre Terrace Rd
FARN GU14.............88 C7
The Centre FELT TW13.........24 B5
Centurion Cl SHST GU47........49 P9
Centurion Ct WLGTN SM6 *.....62 D1
Century Rd EGH TW20........21 P8
Cerne Rd MRDN SM4..........43 N7
Cerotus Pl FLEET KT16.........37 K8
Ceylon Rd EW KT17..........60 H1
Chadhurst Cl RDKG RH5......137 K1
Chadwick Av
WIM/MER SW19...........28 D9
Chadwick Cl CRAWW RH11....194 D8
TEDD TW11.............25 P9
Chadwick Pl SURB KT6 *.......41 J7
Chadworth Wy
ESH/CLAY KT10...........58 D4
Chaffers Md ASHTD KT21......77 M5
Chaffinch Av CROY/NA CR0.....46 D7
Chaffinch Cl CRAWW RH11....176 C3
CROY/NA CR0...........46 C6
HORS RH12.............192 C3
SWTR GU47.............50 A9
SURB KT6.............59 N2
Chaffinch Rd BECK BR3........46 E2
Chaffinch Wy HORL RH6.......140 A9
Chailey Cl CRAWW RH11.....176 D8
HEST TW5.............15 M5
Chailey Pl WOT/HER KT12.....57 N3
Chalcot Cl BELMT SM2........61 L6
Chalcot Ms
STRHM/NOR SW16........29 P6
Chalcott Gdns SURB KT6 *.....41 J9
Chalcraft Cl LIPH GU30......182 D6
Chaldon Cl REDH RH1........120 A7
Chaldon Common Rd
CTHM CR3.............101 L4
Chaldon Rd CRAWW RH11....194 F2
CTHM CR3.............101 M3
FUL/PGN SW6...........19 J5
Chaldon Wy COUL/CHIP CR5...80 G6
Chale Rd BRXS/STRHM SW2....29 P2
Chalet Dr FARN GU14........88 E5
Chalfont Rd SNWD SE25.......46 A5
Chalfont Wy WEA W13........17 H1
Chalford Cl E/WMO/HCT KT8...40 A5
Chalford Rd DUL SE21........30 E7
Chalgrove Av MRDN SM4......43 L6
Chalgrove Rd BELMT SM2.....61 N6
Chalice Cl WLGTN SM6........62 F5
Chalkenden Cl PGE/AN SE20...46 B1
Chalk Hill Rd HMSMTH W6....19 H2
Chalcot Cl BELMT SM2........61 L6
Chalk La ASHTD KT21........77 N8
EHSLY KT24.............115 H2
EPSOM KT18.............78 C5
MFD/CHID GU8..........130 D5
Chalkley Cl MTCM CR4........44 B3
Chalk Paddock EPSOM KT18...78 B4
Chalkpit La
BRKHM/BTCW RH3.......117 H7
DORK RH4.............116 D5
OXTED RH8.............103 J7
Chalkpit Ter DORK RH4.......116 C5
Chalkpit Wd OXTED RH8.....103 K7
Chalk Rd BIL RH14..........187 P7
GODL GU7.............131 L8
Chalky La CHSGTN KT9........59 K7
Challenge Ct LHD/OX KT22....77 H3
Challenge Rd ASHF TW15......23 M6
Challenor Cl EWKG RG40......48 D2
Challice Wy
BRXS/STRHM SW2........30 A4
Challin St PGE/AN SE20.......46 C2
Challis Rd BNFD RG42.........32 A2
Challis Rd BTFD TW8..........17 K3
Challock Cl BH/WHM TN16....84 A5
Challoner Crs WKENS W14.....19 K3
Challoners Cl
E/WMO/HCT KT8..........40 D5
Challoner St WKENS W14......19 K3
Chalmers Cl HORL RH6.......158 B6
Chalmers Rd ASHF TW15......23 L7
BNSTD SM7.............79 M3
Chalmers Rd East ASHF TW15..23 L7
Chalmers Wy
EBED/NFELT TW14........24 C1
Chamberlain Crs WWKM BR4..47 H9
Chamberlain Gdns
HSLW TW3.............16 C6
Chamberlain Wy SURB KT6....41 L8
Chamber La RFNM GU10.....126 G5
Chamomile Gdns
FARN GU14.............87 N2
Champion Crs SYD SE26.......31 M7
Champion Rd SYD SE26.......31 M7
Champ ness Wy WNWD SE27..30 E7
Champney Cl DTCH/LGLY SL3..12 E8

Champneys Cl BELMT SM2 *...61 K6
Chancellor Gdns
SAND/SEL CR2..........63 K7
Chancellor Gv DUL SE21.......30 D5
Chancellor's Rd HMSMTH W6..18 G3
Chancellors St HMSMTH W6...18 G3
Chancellors Whf
HMSMTH W6 *...........18 G3
Chancery La BECK BR3.........47 H1
Chanctonbury Cha
REDH RH1.............120 D6
Chanctonbury Dr ASC SL5.....34 E8
Chanctonbury Gdns
BELMT SM2.............61 M6
Chanctonbury Wy
CRAWW RH11...........176 F7
Chandler Cl CRAWE RH10....176 G7
HPTN TW12.............39 P2
Chandlers Cl
EBED/NFELT TW14........24 A3
Chandlers La YTLY GU46......66 C5
Chandlers Rd ASHV GU12....109 K2
Chandos Av EA W5...........17 J2
Chandos Rd STA TW18.........22 A8
Chanel CI HEST TW5...........16 A6
Channings WOKN/KNAP GU21..72 C4
Chanters Cl EGRIN RH19.....180 B1
Chanton Dr BELMT SM2.......60 G8
Chantrey Cl ASHTD KT21......77 J8
Chantrey Rd CRAWE RH10...177 H8
Chantreys FLEETN GU51.......86 D7
Chantry Cl FNM GU9..........4 B4
HORL RH6.............140 B9
SUN TW16.............39 H9
Chantry Hurst EPSOM KT18...78 B4
Chantry La SHGR GU5.......134 B1
Chantry Rd BAGS GU19.......51 M7
CHERT KT16.............37 M9
CHSGTN KT9...........59 M4
RGUE GU4.............132 F2
Chantry Sq KENS W8 *........19 L1
The Chantrys FNM GU9........4 B5
Chantry View Rd GU GU1.....112 B8
Chantry Wy MTCM CR4........43 P4
Chapel Av ADL/WDHM KT15...55 M3
CHOB/PIR GU24..........91 H1
Chapel Cl MFD/CHID GU8....149 N2
Chapel Ct DORK RH4 *.......116 G7
Chapel Gn PUR/KEN CR8......81 J2
Chapel Gv ADL/WDHM KT15..55 M3
EPSOM KT18.............78 C8
Chapel Hi EHSLY KT24........95 M7
Chapel La BAGS GU19........169 L8
CHOB/PIR GU24..........90 G3
CRAWE RH10...........160 G8
DORK RH4.............116 C8
EGRIN RH19.............181 J5
FARN GU14.............88 G8
LIPH GU30.............182 D7
LT/LBKH KT23...........96 C8
MFD/CHID GU8........149 N2
Chapel Md HTWY RG27........48 C9
Chapel Pk
ADL/WDHM KT15........55 M3
Chapel Rd CBLY GU15.........68 D3
HORL RH6.............158 B5
HORL RH6.............160 C1
HSLW TW3.............16 B8
KWD/TDW/WH KT20......98 C13
OXTED RH8.............124 A1
REDH RH1.............120 B5
RFNM GU10.............146 B1
TWK TW1.............26 A3
WARL CR6.............82 D7
WNWD SE27............30 C7
Chapel Sq CBLY GU15.........68 D3
VW GU25.............36 C4
Chapel St FARN GU14.........88 F1
GU GU1.................6 E6
WOKN/KNAP GU21........10 D4
Chapel Wy SAND/SEL CR2....64 C6
Chapel Wy EPSOM KT18......78 C8
Chaplain's Hl CWTH RG45.....49 P5
Chaplin Crs SUN TW16........23 P9
Chapman Pl CRAWE RH10....177 J9
CROY/NA CR0............45 J9
Chapman's La EGRIN RH19...180 A5
Chapman Sq
WIM/MER SW19..........28 A5
Chappell Cl LIPH GU30......182 F6
Chapter Wy HPTN TW12.......25 H7
Chara Pl CHSWK W4 *.........18 C3
Chasefield Rd TOOT SW17.....29 J7
Chargate Cl WOT/HER KT12...57 J5
Charlbury Cl BRAK RG12.......33 J3
Charlecote Cl FARN GU14.....88 F4
Charlecote Gv SYD SE26......31 J6
Charles Babbage Cl
CHSGTN KT9............59 J6
Charles Cobb Gdns
CROY/NA CR0...........63 J4
Charles Dickens Ter
PGE/AN SE20 *..........46 C1
Charlesfield Rd HORL RH6....140 A8
Charles Haller St
BRXS/STRHM SW2........30 B3
Charles HI RFNM GU10......128 C7
Charles Rd STA TW18.........22 C9
WIM/MER SW19..........43 L2
Charles Sq BRAK RG12.........32 E3
Charles St BARN SW13........18 C3
CBLY GU15.............68 E3
CHERT KT16.............37 L9
CROY/NA CR0............2 C5
HSLW TW3.............15 P7
Charleston Cl FELT TW13.....24 B6
Charleston Ct CRAWE RH10...177 L8
Charleville Circ SYD SE26.....31 H6
Charleville Rd WKENS W14....19 J3
Charlmont Rd TOOT SW17....29 H9

Charlock Wy GU GU1.........112 F3
Charlotte Cl FNM GU9.......107 P6
Charlotte Gv HORL RH6......141 J9
Charlotte Ms
ESH/CLAY KT10 *.........58 B3
Charlotte Pde
FSTH SE23 *............31 M5
Charlotte Rd BARN SW13.....18 D6
WLGTN SM6.............62 E5
Charlow Cl FUL/PGN SW6.....19 N7
Charlton Av WOT/HER KT12...57 K3
Charlton Cl EWKG RG40......48 D1
Charlton Ct SHST GU47.......49 P8
Charlton Dr BH/WHM TN16...84 B6
Charlton Gdns
COUL/CHIP CR5..........80 E7
Charlton Kings WEY KT13.....56 G3
Charlton La SHPTN TW17......38 E4
Charlton Rd SHPTN TW17.....38 E3
Charlwood CROY/NA CR0.....64 F7
Charlwood Cl GT/LBKH KT23..96 B3
Charlwood Dr LHD/OX KT22...76 D4
Charlwood Rd RDKG RH5.....157 M7
Charlwood Rd
CRAWW RH11...........176 C1
HORL RH6.............158 F4
HORL RH6.............158 G7
PUT/ROE SW15..........19 H9
Charlwood Ter
PUT/ROE SW15..........19 H9
Charlwood Wk
CRAWW RH11...........176 E2
Charman Rd REDH RH1.......120 A5
Charmans Cl HORS RH12 *...192 C5
Charm Cl HORL RH6..........140 A9
Charminster Av
WIM/MER SW19..........43 L3
Charminster Rd WPK KT4.....43 H9
Charnwood ASC SL5..........34 F7
Charnwood Av
WIM/MER SW19..........43 L3
Charnwood Cl NWMAL KT3...42 C5
Charnwood Rd SNWD SE25....45 N6
Charrington Rd CROY/NA CR0..2 B4
Charrington Wy HORS RH12..191 K7
Charta Rd EGH TW20.........21 P8
Chart Cl CROY/NA CR0........46 C2
HAYES BR2.............47 L2
Chart Downs RDKG RH5.....117 J9
Charter Crs HSLWW TW4......15 N8
Charterhouse Cl BRAK RG12..32 C6
Charterhouse Rd GODL GU7..131 K7
Charter Pl STA TW18.........22 D9
Charter Rd KUT/HW KT1......41 P3
Charter Sq KUT KT1..........41 P3
Charters Cl NRWD SE19......30 F8
Charters La ASC SL5..........34 D6
Charters Rd ASC SL5.........34 E8
Charters Wy ASC SL5.........34 F8
Charter Wk HASM GU27 *...184 D4
Chartfield Av PUT/ROE SW15..27 N1
Chartfield Rd REIG RH2.......119 N6
Chartfield Sq
PUT/ROE SW15..........28 A1
Chart Gdns RDKG RH5........137 J1
Chartham Gv WNWD SE27....30 B6
Chartham Rd SNWD SE25.....46 B4
Chart House Rd ASHV GU12...89 J8
Chart La BH/WHM TN16......84 B6
DORK RH4.............117 H7
REIG RH2.............119 N5
Chart La South RDKG RH5...117 K9
Charts Cl CRAN GU6.........171 H1
Chart Wy HORS RH12........192 B6
Chartway REIG RH2..........119 N5
Chartwell FNM GU9 *........127 K7
FRIM GU16.............88 G2
Chartwell Cl CROY/NA CR0 *....2 E1
Chartwell Gdns ALDT GU11...108 B8
Chartwell Pl CHEAM SM3.....61 J3
EPSOM KT18.............78 C3
Chartwell Wy PGE/AN SE20...46 B2
Chase End HOR/WEW KT19...78 B1
Chasefield Cl RGUE GU4.....112 G2
Chaseley Dr CHSWK W4......17 P3
Chaseley Dr SAND/SEL CR2...63 N8
Chasemore Cl MTCM CR4.....44 B8
Chasemore Gdns
CROY/NA CR0...........63 J4
Chase Pln GSHT GU26 *.....183 M1
Chase Rd HOR/WEW KT19.....78 B1
Chaseside Av RYNPK SW20...43 J2
Chaseside Gdns CHERT KT16..37 M8
The Chase ASHTD KT21.......77 J7
BMLY BR1.............47 P4
COUL/CHIP CR5..........80 E7
CRAWE RH10...........177 K6
CWTH RG45.............49 L4
EHSLY KT24.............95 H6
FARN GU14.............105 H3
GUW GU2...............6 A5
GUW GU2.............111 N6
KWD/TDW/WH KT20......99 N1
REIG RH2.............119 P5
STRHM/NOR SW16........45 H1
SUN TW16.............39 K2
WLGTN SM6.............62 G4

Chatfield Dr RGUE GU4......112 G3
Chatfield Rd BTSEA SW11.....19 N8
Chatham Av HAYES BR2.......47 N8
Chatham Cl CHEAM SM3......43 K6
Chatham Rd BTSEA SW11.....29 J2
KUT KT1...............9 H4
Chatsfield EW KT17..........60 E8
Chatsworth Av HASM GU27..184 D2
RYNPK SW20............43 J2
Chatsworth Cl CHSWK W4....18 A4
WWKM BR4.............47 N1
Chatsworth Crs HSLW TW3....16 D9
Chatsworth Gdns
NWMAL KT3............42 E7
Chatsworth Gv FNM GU9....107 M8
Chatsworth Hts CBLY GU15...69 J1
Chatsworth Pl LHD/OX KT22...76 D1
MTCM CR4.............44 C3
TWK TW1.............25 P7
Chatsworth Rd CHEAM SM3..61 H1
CHSWK W4.............18 A4
CROY/NA CR0...........2 D7
FARN GU14.............88 C4
Chatsworth Wy WNWD SE27..30 D5
Chattern Hl ASHF TW15......23 M7
Chattern Rd ASHF TW15......23 N7
Chatton Rw CHOB/PIR GU24..70 G6
Chatto Rd BTSEA SW11.......19 N4
Chaucer Av E/WMO/HCT KT8..39 M5
HSLWW TW4.............15 K7
RCH/KEW TW9...........17 N7
WEY KT13.............56 C4
Chaucer Cl BNSTD SM7.......79 J3
Chaucer Ct GU GU1..........7 G6
Chaucer Gdns SUT SM1......61 L2
CROY/NA CR0...........66 B8
Chaucer Gv CBLY GU15.......68 F3
Chaucer Rd ASHF TW15......23 H7
CRAWE RH10...........177 L3
CWTH RG45.............49 M5
FARN GU14.............88 B4
HNHL SE24.............30 C1
SUT SM1...............61 J3
Chaucer Wy
ADL/WDHM KT15........55 L5
Chaundlers Cft RFNM GU10..106 D9
Chave Cft EPSOM KT18 *......78 C8
Chavecroft Ter
EPSOM KT18 *..........78 C8
Chaworth Cl CHERT KT16.....54 C5
Chaworth Rd CHERT KT16....54 C5
Chawton Cl FLEETN GU51.....86 C4
Cheam Cl BRAK RG12.........32 D6
KWD/TDW/WH KT20......98 F1
Cheam Common Rd
WPK KT4...............60 F1
Cheam Man CHEAM SM3 *....61 J5
Cheam Park Wy CHEAM SM3..61 H5
Cheam Rd BELMT SM2.......61 H7
EW KT17...............60 F8
Cheapside Rd ASC SL5........34 C4
Cheeseman Cl HPTN TW12...24 F9
Cheesemans Ter
WKENS W14.............19 K3
Cheetah Rd FARN GU14.......88 D8
Chellows La LING RH7.......145 M3
Chelmsford Cl BELMT SM2....61 L7
HMSMTH W6.............19 H4
Chelsea Cl HPTN TW12........25 K9
WPK KT4...............42 E9
Chelsea Crs WBPTN SW10 *...19 N6
Chelsea Gdns CHEAM SM3....61 J3
Chelsea Harbour Dr
WBPTN SW10............19 N6
Chelsea Park Gdns
WBPTN SW10............19 N6
Chelsea Sq CHEL SW3........19 P3
Chelsea Village
WBPTN SW10 *..........19 M5
Chelsfield Gdns SYD SE26.....31 K6
Chelsham Court Rd
WARL CR6.............83 K7
Chelsham Rd SAND/SEL CR2..63 N6
WARL CR6.............82 F6
Cheltenham Av TWK TW1.....25 P3
Cheltenham Cl NWMAL KT3...42 A4
Chelverton Rd
PUT/ROE SW15..........19 H9
Chelwood Cl COUL/CHIP CR5..80 E9
CRAWE RH10...........177 J7
EW KT17...............78 D1
Chelwood Gdns
RCH/KEW TW9...........17 N7
Chelwood Wk
DTCH/LGLY SL3.........12 F4
Cheniston Cl BF/WBF KT14....73 L2
Cheniston Gdns KENS W8 *...19 M1
Chennells Brook Cottages
HORS RH12.............192 E5
Chepstow Cl CRAWE RH10...177 P5
Chepstow Ri CROY/NA CR0.....3 H5
Chepstow Rd CROY/NA CR0....3 H5
Chequer Rd EGRIN RH19.....180 E2
Chequers Cl HORL RH6......140 C9
KWD/TDW/WH KT20......98 E5
Chequers Dr HORL RH6......140 C9
Chequers La HTWY RG27 *....48 C9
Chequers Pl DORK RH4......117 H7

Cheriton Ct WOT/HER KT12...39 L9
Cheriton Sq TOOT SW17......29 K5
Cheriton Wy BLKW GU17......67 P7
Cherkley RDKG RH5..........97 K6
Cherkley Hl RDKG RH5.......97 J6
Cherrimans Orch
HASM GU27............184 A4
Cherry Cl BRXS/STRHM SW2 *..30 B3
CAR SM5...............62 B1
EW KT17...............60 H1
EW KT17...............79 H3
MRDN SM4.............43 J5
Cherry Crs BTFD TW8.........17 H5
Cherry Crs BTFD TW8.........17 H5
Cherrydale Rd CBLY GU15....69 M3
Cherry Garth BTFD TW8......17 K3
Cherry Green Cl REDH RH1...120 D7
Cherry Hill Gdns
CROY/NA CR0...........63 H3
Cherryhurst
MFD/CHID GU8 *........168 A3
Cherry La CRAWW RH11.....176 F2
WDR/YW UB7...........14 B2
Cherry Lodg ASHV GU12 *...108 D5
Cherry Orch ASHTD KT21.....77 P7
STA TW18.............22 D8
Cherry Orchard Gdns
CROY/NA CR0...........3 F2
E/WMO/HCT KT8.........39 P4
Cherry Orchard Rd
CROY/NA CR0...........3 F2
E/WMO/HCT KT8.........40 A4
Cherry St WOKN/KNAP GU21..10 C5
Cherry Tree Av GUW GU2....111 N5
HASM GU27............184 A3
STA TW18.............22 D8
Cherry Tree Cl CRAWE RH10..177 N3
FARN GU14.............87 N2
SHST GU47.............49 P8
Cherry Tree Ct
COUL/CHIP CR5..........81 H7
Cherry Tree Dr BRAK RG12....32 F4
STRHM/NOR SW16........29 P6
Cherry Tree Gn
SAND/SEL CR2..........82 B3
Cherry Tree La GODL GU7...131 K5
Cherry Tree Rd
MFD/CHID GU8 *........149 M3
RFNM GU10............146 B1
Cherry Tree Wk BECK BR3....46 E5
WWKM BR4.............65 M3
Cherry Wy HAYES BR2 *......47 N9
Cherry Wy DTCH/LGLY SL3....12 D8
HOR/WEW KT19..........60 B5
SHPTN TW17............38 B5
Cherrywood Av EGH TW20....20 C9
Cherrywood Cl
KUTN/CMB KT2..........9 H1
Cherrywood Dr
PUT/ROE SW15..........28 A1
Cherrywood La MRDN SM4...43 J5
Cherrywood Rd FARN GU14..104 D4
Chertsey Bridge Rd
CHERT KT16............37 P8
Chertsey Cl PUR/KEN CR8....81 K4
Chertsey Crs CROY/NA CR0...65 J8
Chertsey Dr CHEAM SM3.....61 J1
Chertsey La STA TW18........22 C9
Chertsey Rd
ADL/WDHM KT15........55 N2
ASHF TW15.............38 F1
BF/WBF KT14...........55 N5
BFOR GU20.............52 E5
CHOB/PIR GU24.........53 N8
FELT TW13.............38 A8
SHPTN TW17...........38 A4
TWK TW1.............25 L3
WOKN/KNAP GU21.......10 E3
WOKN/KNAP GU21.......72 E2
Chertsey Sq GU GU1..........7 F4
TOOT SW17.............29 K8
Chertsey Wk CHERT KT16 *...37 K8
Chervil Cl FELT TW13........24 B6
Cherwell Cl DTCH/LGLY SL3...12 F4
Cherwell Ct HOR/WEW KT19..60 A6
Cherwell Wk CRAWW RH11..176 F6
Cheryls Cl FUL/PGN SW6.....19 N6
Cheselden Rd GU GU1.........7 H4
Cheseman St SYD SE26.......31 J4
Chesfield Rd KUTN/CMB KT2..41 L1
Chesham Cl BELMT SM2 *....61 J8
Chesham Crs PGE/AN SE20...46 C2
Chesham Ms GU GU1.........7 H5
Chesham Rd GU GU1.........7 H5
KUTN/CMB KT2..........9 K5
PGE/AN SE20...........46 C2
WARL CR6.............82 G5
Cheshire CI CHERT KT16......55 H5
Cheshire Gdns CHSGTN KT9..59 J5
Chesilton Rd FUL/PGN SW6..19 K6
Chesnut Ct FUL/PGN SW6 *..19 K6
Chesney Crs CROY/NA CR0...65 J7
Chessholme Rd ASHF TW15..23 M9
Chessington Cl
HOR/WEW KT19..........60 A5
Chessington Hall Gdns
CHSGTN KT9............59 K6
Chessington Hill Pk
CHSGTN KT9............59 N4
Chessington Pde
CHSGTN KT9 *..........59 K4
Chessington Rd CHSGTN KT9..59 N5
Chessington Wy WWKM BR4..65 H1
Chesson Rd WKENS W14.....19 K4
Chester Av
RCHPK/HAM TW10........26 E2
WHTN TW2.............25 H3
Chesterblade La BRAK RG12..32 F6
Chester Cl ASHF TW15........23 N8

ASHV GU12 109 K4
BARN SW13 * 18 F8
DORK RH4 117 J5
GUW GU2 111 M3
SUT SM1 61 L1
Chesterfield Cl CRAWE RH10 161 K8
Chesterfield Dr
ESH/CLAY KT10 58 G1
Chesterfield Gv EDUL SE22 30 G1
Chesterfield Rd ASHF TW15 23 H8
CHSWK W4 18 A4
HOR/WEW KT19 60 B6
Chester Gdns MRDN SM4 43 N6
Chester Rd ASHV GU12 109 K3
EHSLY KT24 95 K8
HSLWW TW4 15 K8
HTHAIR TW6 14 C8
WIM/MER SW19 27 P9
Chesters HORL RH6 140 A8
Chesters Rd CBLY GU15 69 K3
The Chesters NWMAL KT3 42 C2
Chesterton Cl EGRIN RH19 180 E4
WAND/EARL SW18 28 D1
Chesterton Ct SWTR RH13 192 F6
Chesterton Dr REDH RH1 100 G8
STWL/WRAY TW19 23 J4
Chesterton Sq WKENS W14 19 K2
Chesterton Ter KUT KT1 9 H5
Chester Wy RFNM GU10 109 H8
Chestnut Aly FUL/PGN SW6 * 19 K4
Chestnut Av ASHV GU12 108 G7
BH/WHM TN16 104 B2
BTFD TW8 17 K3
CBLY GU15 69 J2
E/WMO/HCT KT8 40 F4
ESH/CLAY KT10 40 D8
FNM GU9 127 L5
GUW GU2 112 A9
HASM GU27 184 D3
HOR/WEW KT19 60 C3
HPTN TW12 40 A1
MORT/ESHN SW14 * 18 B8
TEDD TW11 40 F1
VW GU25 35 M5
WEY KT13 56 E6
WOT/HER KT12 56 G7
WWKM BR4 65 L4
Chestnut Cl ADL/WDHM KT15 55 P4
ASHF TW15 23 L7
BLKW GU17 * 68 A3
CAR SM5 44 B9
EDEN TN8 144 F3
EGH TW20 20 G9
EGRIN RH19 180 F2
FLEETN GU51 87 J3
GSHT GU26 165 L8
KWD/TDW/WH KT20 99 L3
LIPH GU30 182 G7
REDH RH1 120 D7
RPLY/SEND GU23 93 L5
STRHM/NOR SW16 30 B7
SUN TW16 24 A9
WDR/YW UB7 14 D5
Chestnut Copse OXTED RH8 123 P4
Chestnut Ct ASHV GU12 108 F4
Chestnut Dr EGH TW20 21 J9
Chestnut End BOR GU35 164 C7
Chestnut Gdns HORS RH12 192 B5
Chestnut Gv BAL SW12 29 K3
EA W5 17 K1
FLEETN GU51 87 H5
ISLW TW7 16 G9
MTCM CR4 44 F6
NWMAL KT3 42 B4
SAND/SEL CR2 64 B6
STA TW18 22 F9
WOKS/MYFD GU22 72 C9
Chestnut La CHOB/PIR GU24 53 J5
WEY KT13 56 D4
Chestnut Mnr WLGTN SM6 62 D3
Chestnut Manor Cl STA TW18 22 E8
Chestnut Md REDH RH1 120 A4
Chestnut Pl ASHTD KT21 77 L8
SYD SE26 30 G7
WEY KT13 * 56 D4
Chestnut Rd ASHF TW15 23 K7
FARN GU14 88 C2
GU GU1 6 E2
HORL RH6 140 C8
KUTN/CMB KT2 8 D1
RYNPK SW20 43 H3
WHTN TW2 25 M5
WNWD SE27 30 C6
The Chestnuts BECK BR3 * 46 D4
WOT/HER KT12 57 J1
Chestnut Ter SUT SM1 * 61 M3
Chestnut Wk CRAWW RH11 176 F2
EGRIN RH19 162 B5
SHPTN TW17 38 G6
Chestnut Wy FELT TW13 24 C6
GODL GU7 150 E2
SHGR GU5 132 E9
Cheston Av CROY/NA CR0 46 E9
Cheswell Gdns FLEETN GU51 86 E9
Chesworth Crs SWTR RH13 192 B9
Chesworth Gdns
SWTR RH13 192 B9
Chesworth La SWTR RH13 192 B9
Chetwode Dr EPSOM KT18 79 H7
Chetwode Pl ALDT GU11 108 E7
Chetwode Rd EPSOM KT18 78 G8
KWD/TDW/WH KT20 79 H8
TOOT SW17 29 J6
Chetwode Ter ALDT GU11 108 A5
Chetwood Rd HORS RH12 176 A9
Cheveney Wk HAYES BR2 47 N4
Chevening Cl CRAWW RH11 194 F1
Chevening Rd NRWD SE19 45 M1
Cheviot Cl BELMT SM2 61 P7
BNSTD SM7 79 M4
CBLY GU15 69 L4
FARN GU14 68 A9
HYS/HAR UB3 14 F5
Cheviot Dr FLEETN GU51 87 H3
Cheviot Rd DTCH/LGLY SL3 12 E3
SHST GU47 49 K8
WNWD SE27 30 C8
Cheviot Wk CRAWW RH11 * 176 E5
Chewter La BFOR GU20 52 B3
Cheyham Gdns BELMT SM2 61 H8
Cheyham Wy BELMT SM2 61 J8
Cheylesmore Dr FRIM GU16 69 M5
Cheyne Av WHTN TW2 24 G4
Cheyne Ct BNSTD SM7 79 M4
Cheyne Hl BRYLDS KT5 41 M5
Cheyne Rd ASHF TW15 23 N9
Cheyne Wk CROY/NA CR0 64 A1
HORL RH6 159 K2
WBPTN SW10 19 P5
Cheyne Wy FARN GU14 68 B9
Chichele Gdns CROY/NA CR0 3 H7
Chichele Rd OXTED RH8 103 L8
Chichester Cl CRAWE RH10 177 H9
DORK RH4 117 H5
HPTN TW12 24 G9
MFD/CHID GU8 149 M7
Chichester Ct EW KT17 * 60 D7
Chichester Dr PUR/KEN CR8 81 H1
Chichester Rd ASHV GU12 109 J3
CROY/NA CR0 3 H6
DORK RH4 117 H4
Chichester Ter SWTR RH13 192 C8
Chichester Wy
EBED/NFELT TW14 24 D3
Chiddingfold Rd
MFD/CHID GU8 169 H8
Chiddingly Cl CRAWE RH10 177 K6
Chiddingstone Cl BELMT SM2 61 L8
Chiddingstone St
FUL/PGN SW6 19 L7
Chilberton Dr REDH RH1 120 E1
Chilbrook Rd COB KT11 75 J7
Chilcroft La HASM GU27 184 C9
Chilcroft Rd HASM GU27 184 A3
Chilcrofts Rd HASM GU27 184 B9
Childebert Rd TOOT SW17 29 L5
Childerley St FUL/PGN SW6 19 J6
Childerstone Cl LIPH GU30 182 E6
Childs Hall Dr GT/LBKH KT23 95 P5
Childs Hall Rd GT/LBKH KT23 95 P5
Childs La NRWD SE19 * 30 F9
Child's Pl ECT SW5 19 L2
Child's St ECT SW5 19 L2
Child's Wk ECT SW5 * 19 L2
Chilham Cl FRIM GU16 69 H8
Chilham Wy HAYES BR2 47 N8
Chillerton Rd TOOT SW17 29 K8
Chillingham Wy CBLY GU15 68 E4
Chillingworth Gdns
TWK TW1 * 25 N5
Chilmans Dr GT/LBKH KT23 96 B5
Chilmark Gdns NWMAL KT3 42 D7
REDH RH1 100 G9
Chilmark Rd
STRHM/NOR SW16 44 F3
Chilmead REDH RH1 * 120 B4
Chilmead La REDH RH1 120 F3
Chilsey Green Rd CHERT KT16 37 J7
Chiltern WOKS/MYFD GU22 92 A2
Chiltern Av FARN GU14 87 P3
WHTN TW2 25 H4
Chiltern Cl CRAWW RH11 176 E5
CROY/NA CR0 3 H6
FARN GU14 87 N3
FLEETS GU52 107 H1
HASM GU27 184 C5
STA TW18 22 D8
WPK KT4 60 G1
Chiltern Dr BRYLDS KT5 41 P7
Chiltern Gdns HAYES BR2 47 M5
Chiltern Rd BELMT SM2 61 N8
SHST GU47 49 K8
The Chilterns BELMT SM2 * 61 M7
Chilthorne Cl CAT SE6 31 N3
Chiltlee Cl LIPH GU30 182 F6
Chiltlee Mnr LIPH GU30 182 F6
Chiltley La LIPH GU30 182 G8
Chiltley Wy LIPH GU30 182 F8
Chilton Av EA W5 17 K2
Chilton Cl CRAN GU6 170 C9
Chilton Farm Pk FARN GU14 * 87 N3
Chilton Rd RCH/KEW TW9 17 N8
Chiltons Cl BNSTD SM7 79 M4
Chilvers Cl WHTN TW2 25 M5
Chilworth Gdns SUT SM1 61 N2
Chilworth Rd SHGR GU5 133 L1
Chinchilla Dr HSLWW TW4 15 L7
Chineham Cl FLEETN GU51 86 C4
The Chine DORK RH4 * 117 H6
RFNM GU10 127 K8
Chingford Av FARN GU14 88 E2
Chinnock Cl FLEETS GU52 86 F8
Chinthurst La RGUE GU4 132 C3
Chinthurst Pk RGUE GU4 132 C4
Chippendale Rd
CRAWW RH11 194 E1
Chipstead Av THHTH CR7 45 K5
Chipstead Cl BELMT SM2 61 M7
COUL/CHIP CR5 80 C6
NRWD SE19 45 P1
REDH RH1 120 B6
Chipstead Ct
WOKN/KNAP GU21 71 L6
Chipstead La COUL/CHIP CR5 99 M4
Chipstead Rd BNSTD SM7 79 K6
Chipstead Station Pde
COUL/CHIP CR5 80 B7
Chipstead St FUL/PGN SW6 19 L6
Chipstead Valley Rd
COUL/CHIP CR5 80 D5
Chipstead Wy BNSTD SM7 80 B5
Chirton Wk
WOKN/KNAP GU21 71 N7
Chisbury Cl BRAK RG12 32 G7
Chisholm Rd CROY/NA CR0 3 H3
RCHPK/HAM TW10 26 E2
Chislehurst Rd
RCHPK/HAM TW10 26 D2
Chislet Cl BECK BR3 46 G1
Chiswick Br
MORT/ESHN SW14 18 A7
Chiswick Cl CROY/NA CR0 63 H2
Chiswick Common Rd
CHSWK W4 18 B2
Chiswick High Rd CHSWK W4 17 P3
Chiswick House Grounds
CHSWK W4 * 18 B4
Chiswick La CHSWK W4 18 C3
Chiswick La South
CHSWK W4 18 D4
Chiswick Ml CHSWK W4 18 D4
Chiswick Pk CHSWK W4 * 18 A1
Chiswick Pier CHSWK W4 * 18 D5
Chiswick Quay CHSWK W4 18 A6
Chiswick Rd CHSWK W4 18 A2
Chiswick Sq CHSWK W4 18 C4
Chiswick Staithe CHSWK W4 17 P6
Chiswick Village CHSWK W4 17 N4
Chithurst La HORL RH6 160 F5
Chitterfield Ga
WDR/YW UB7 14 C5
Chitty's Wk RGUW GU3 111 M1
Chivalry Rd BTSEA SW11 29 H1
Chivenor Gv KUTN/CMB KT2 26 C8
Chivers Dr EWKG RG40 48 C2
Chives Pl BNFD RG42 32 F1
Chobham Cl CHERT KT16 54 F5
Chobham Gdns
WIM/MER SW19 28 A5
Chobham La CHERT KT16 53 N1
Chobham Park La
CHOB/PIR GU24 53 N8
Chobham Rd CHERT KT16 54 E6
CHOB/PIR GU24 53 J1
FRIM GU16 68 G6
WOKN/KNAP GU21 10 D1
WOKN/KNAP GU21 71 H7
Choir Gn WOKN/KNAP GU21 71 L6
Cholmley Rd THDIT KT7 41 H7
Cholmley Ter THDIT KT7 * 41 H8
Cholmley Vls THDIT KT7 * 41 H8
Chrislaine Cl
STWL/WRAY TW19 22 G2
Chrismas Av ASHV GU12 108 E5
Chrismas Pl ASHV GU12 108 E5
Christabel Cl ISLW TW7 16 E8
Christchurch Av TEDD TW11 25 P8
Christchurch Cl
FLEETS GU52 106 F2
WIM/MER SW19 43 P1
Christchurch Dr BLKW GU17 67 N2
Christ Church Mt
HOR/WEW KT19 59 P9
Christchurch Pk BELMT SM2 61 N6
Christ Church Rd BECK BR3 * 46 G3
BRYLDS KT5 41 M8
EPSOM KT18 77 L1
Christchurch Rd
BRXS/STRHM SW2 30 A4
MORT/ESHN SW14 26 G1
PUR/KEN CR8 63 K9
VW GU25 36 C5
WIM/MER SW19 43 P1
Christchurch Wy
WOKN/KNAP GU21 10 E3
Christian Flds
STRHM/NOR SW16 45 J1
Christie Cl GT/LBKH KT23 95 P5
LTWR GU18 52 B8
Christie Dr SNWD SE25 46 A6
Christies EGRIN RH19 180 C3
Christie Wk YTLY GU46 66 G4
Christine Cl ASHV GU12 109 H5
Christmas Hl SHGR GU5 132 F4
Christmaspie Av RGUW GU3 110 B5
Christopher Av HNWL W7 16 G1
Christopher Rd EGRIN RH19 180 D2
NWDGN UB2 15 K2
Christy Est ASHV GU12 * 108 G4
Christy Rd BH/WHM TN16 84 A4
Chrystie La GT/LBKH KT23 96 B6
Chuck's La
KWD/TDW/WH KT20 98 F4
Chudleigh Gdns SUT SM1 61 N2
Chudleigh Rd BROCKY SE4 31 N1
WHTN TW2 25 M2
Chulsa Rd SYD SE26 31 J8
Chumleigh Wk BRYLDS KT5 41 M5
Church Ap DUL SE21 30 E6
EGH TW20 36 G4
Church Av BECK BR3 46 G2
FARN GU14 88 E5
MORT/ESHN SW14 18 B9
NWDGN UB2 15 N1
Church Cir FARN GU14 88 E6
Church Cl ADL/WDHM KT15 55 M3
CHOB/PIR GU24 70 F9
EW KT17 * 78 C2
HASM GU27 166 G9
HSLW TW3 15 P7
KWD/TDW/WH KT20 99 K7
LHD/OX KT22 96 D4
MFD/CHID GU8 149 N3
STA TW18 37 N4
WDR/YW UB7 14 A1
WOKN/KNAP GU21 10 B1
Church Ct FLEETN GU51 86 F6
REIG RH2 119 M5
Churchcroft Cl BAL SW12 * 29 K3
Church Dr WWKM BR4 65 L2
Church Farm La CHEAM SM3 61 J5
Church Fld EDEN TN8 145 H4
Churchfield Rd REIG RH2 119 K4
WEY KT13 56 C3
WOT/HER KT12 39 J9
Church Flds BOR GU35 164 B6
Churchfields
E/WMO/HCT KT8 40 A4
MFD/CHID GU8 149 M8
RGUE GU4 92 E9
WOKN/KNAP GU21 10 C1
Churchfields Av FELT TW13 24 G6
WEY KT13 56 D3
Churchfields Rd BECK BR3 46 D3
Church Gdns LHD/OX KT22 * 77 H9
Church Ga FUL/PGN SW6 19 J8
Church Gn
KWD/TDW/WH KT20 * 98 E4
WOT/HER KT12 57 L5
Church Green Cottages
HASM GU27 * 184 D3
Church Gv FLEETN GU51 86 E6
KUT KT1 8 A3
Church Hams EWKG RG40 48 B3
Church Hl ALDT GU11 108 D6
BH/WHM TN16 104 B2
CAR SM5 62 B4
CBLY GU15 68 G3
CTHM CR3 101 P4
PUR/KEN CR8 62 G8
REDH RH1 100 D6
REDH RH1 121 H4
RSEV TN14 84 G4
SHGR GU5 134 C1
SHGR GU5 152 B1
WIM/MER SW19 28 C8
WOKN/KNAP GU21 10 A2
WOKS/MYFD GU22 73 K6
Church Hill Rd CHEAM SM3 61 H3
SURB KT6 41 L6
Church Hill Ter
RFNM GU10 * 106 D8
Churchill Av ASHV GU12 108 E6
HORS RH12 192 A7
Churchill Cl
EBED/NFELT TW14 24 A4
LHD/OX KT22 96 E3
WARL CR6 82 C6
Churchill Ct CRAWE RH10 177 J2
Churchill Crs BOR GU35 164 C7
FARN GU14 68 D9
Churchill Dr WEY KT13 56 E2
Churchill Rd ASC SL5 33 P3
DTCH/LGLY SL3 12 D2
GU GU1 7 H4
HOR/WEW KT19 59 N9
HORL RH6 160 C1
SAND/SEL CR2 63 L7
Churchill Wy BH/WHM TN16 84 B4
BMLY BR1 47 N3
SUN TW16 24 B8
Church La ASC SL5 34 D5
ASC SL5 34 G4
ASHV GU12 109 K4
BOR GU35 164 A5
CHOB/PIR GU24 70 G4
CHOB/PIR GU24 90 D2
CHSGTN KT9 59 M5
COUL/CHIP CR5 100 C2
CRAN GU6 152 G9
CRAWE RH10 177 J4
CRAWE RH10 178 B1
CTHM CR3 101 J3
EGRIN RH19 180 E2
EPSOM KT18 98 A5
EWKG RG40 48 C5
FARN GU14 88 A3
GDST RH9 122 D3
GSHT GU26 165 M8
HASM GU27 184 D3
HORL RH6 159 P6
HORS RH12 191 L7
LIPH GU30 182 E4
MFD/CHID GU8 167 K3
MFD/CHID GU8 168 C1
OXTED RH8 103 L9
OXTED RH8 123 K1
RDKG RH5 172 G2
REDH RH1 121 M4
RFNM GU10 107 H7
RFNM GU10 126 A7
RFNM GU10 127 K6
RFNM GU10 146 B1
RGUW GU3 91 L7
RPLY/SEND GU23 92 F6
SHGR GU5 133 M1
SHGR GU5 134 C1
TEDD TW11 25 N8
THDIT KT7 40 F7
TOOT SW17 29 L7
TWK TW1 25 P4
WARL CR6 82 D6
WARL CR6 83 J5
WEY KT13 56 C3
WIM/MER SW19 43 L3
WLGTN SM6 62 F2
Church Lane Av
COUL/CHIP CR5 100 D2
Church Lane Dr
COUL/CHIP CR5 100 D2
Church La East ALDT GU11 108 D6
Church La West ALDT GU11 108 B5
Churchley Rd SYD SE26 31 J7
Church Meadow SURB KT6 59 J1
Church Ms ADL/WDHM KT15 55 N3
Churchmore Rd
STRHM/NOR SW16 44 E2
Church Paddock Ct
WLGTN SM6 62 F2
Church Pde ASHF TW15 * 23 J7
Church Pk CRAWW RH11 * 176 D4
Church Pth ASHV GU12 109 J3
CHSWK W4 18 A1
CROY/NA CR0 2 C3
MTCM CR4 44 A4
RYNPK SW20 43 K3
WOKN/KNAP GU21 10 E3
Church Pl MTCM CR4 44 A4
Church Ri CHSGTN KT9 59 M5
FSTH SE23 31 L4
Church Rd ADL/WDHM KT15 55 L4
ALDT GU11 108 E6
ASC SL5 33 K2
ASC SL5 34 A5
ASC SL5 34 G7
ASHF TW15 23 K8
ASHTD KT21 77 K7
BAGS GU19 51 M6
BARN SW13 18 E7
BF/WBF KT14 74 A2
BFOR GU20 52 B5
BH/WHM TN16 84 B6
BH/WHM TN16 105 M4
BRAK RG12 32 E3
CBLY GU15 68 B1
CHEAM SM3 61 J5
CHOB/PIR GU24 70 F1
CRAWE RH10 160 C9
CRAWE RH10 177 P5
CRAWE RH10 178 G8
CROY/NA CR0 2 C6
CTHM CR3 81 P7
CTHM CR3 101 P3
CTHM CR3 102 D1
CTHM CR3 102 E3
E/WMO/HCT KT8 40 D5
EGH TW20 21 M8
ESH/CLAY KT10 58 F5
EW KT17 78 C2
FELT TW13 24 D8
FLEETN GU51 86 E5
FLEETN GU51 86 G6
FRIM GU16 68 F8
GT/LBKH KT23 95 P3
GU GU1 6 E4
HASM GU27 184 D3
HAYES BR2 47 L4
HAYES BR2 47 N3
HEST TW5 15 K3
HEST TW5 16 A5
HOR/WEW KT19 60 B6
HORL RH6 141 P8
HORL RH6 159 H7
HORL RH6 159 J2
HORL RH6 160 B5
HORS RH12 191 L7
HORS RH12 192 G5
ISLW TW7 16 D6
KUT KT1 9 F4
LHD/OX KT22 97 H2
LING RH7 143 K9
LIPH GU30 182 F4
MFD/CHID GU8 149 N4
MFD/CHID GU8 151 K9
MFD/CHID GU8 169 K6
MTCM CR4 43 P3
NRWD SE19 45 N1
NWDGN UB2 15 P1
PUR/KEN CR8 62 G8
PUR/KEN CR8 81 M4
RCHPK/HAM TW10 26 D1
RCHPK/HAM TW10 26 D7
RDKG RH5 156 G3
RDKG RH5 157 H3
REDH RH1 120 A7
REIG RH2 119 L7
SHPTN TW17 38 D8
SHST GU47 49 K8
SHST GU47 49 P8
SURB KT6 41 J9
TEDD TW11 25 M7
WARL CR6 82 D6
WDSR SL4 20 G1
WIM/MER SW19 28 B8
WLGTN SM6 62 E2
WOKN/KNAP GU21 10 C1
WOKN/KNAP GU21 71 N8
WPK KT4 42 C9
Church Rd East CWTH RG45 49 M4
FARN GU14 88 F6
Church Rd West CWTH RG45 49 M5
FARN GU14 88 E6
Church Rw FUL/PGN SW6 * 19 M5
RPLY/SEND GU23 * 93 N1
WAND/EARL SW18 * 28 D1
Church Side EPSOM KT18 77 P2
Churchside Cl BH/WHM TN16 84 A7
Church Sq SHPTN TW17 38 D8
Church St ALDT GU11 108 B5
BRKHM/BTCW RH3 118 C6
CHSWK W4 18 C4
COB KT11 75 K4
CRAWW RH11 176 F5
CROY/NA CR0 2 B5
CWTH RG45 49 M5
DORK RH4 116 G7
EDEN TN8 145 H4
EHSLY KT24 95 M7
EPSOM KT18 78 C2
ESH/CLAY KT10 58 B3
EW KT17 60 E7
GODL GU7 131 K9
HORS RH12 189 N2
HORS RH12 189 P2
HORS RH12 191 N3
HPTN TW12 40 C2
HSLW TW3 25 K1
ISLW TW7 17 H8
KUT KT1 8 C5
LHD/OX KT22 97 H2
REIG RH2 119 M5
RFNM GU10 106 C8
STA TW18 22 B7
SUN TW16 39 J4
TWK TW1 25 P4
WEY KT13 56 C3
WOKS/MYFD GU22 92 G1
WOT/HER KT12 39 J9
Church St East
WOKN/KNAP GU21 10 E3

Church St West
WOKN/KNAP GU21 ....10 C4
Church Ter FUL/PGN SW6 * ...19 M7
RCHPK/HAM TW10 ....26 C1
RDKG RH5 ....137 J7
Church V FSTH SE23 ....31 K5
Church Vw ASHV GU12 ....109 J4
YTLY GU46 ....67 H1
Church View Cl HORL RH6 ..159 J3
Churchview Rd WHTN TW2 ...25 L4
Church Wk BTFD TW8 ....17 J4
CRAWE RH10 ....176 G5
CTHM CR3 ....102 A4
HORL RH6 ....159 J2
LHD/OX KT22 ....97 H2
REIG RH2 ....119 M5
RYNPK SW20 ....42 G4
STRHM/NOR SW16 ....40 E7
WEY KT13 ....56 C2
WOT/HER KT12 ....39 J9
Church Wy OXTED RH8 ....123 M3
SAND/SEL CR2 ....63 P8
Churston Cl
CROY/NA CRO * 44 G8
Churston Dr MRDN SM4 ......43 H6
Churton Pl CHSWK W4 * 17 P4
Churt Rd BOR GU35 ....164 E3
RFNM GU10 ....10 C8
Churt Wynde GSHT GU26 .....165 N4
Cinnamon Cl
CROY/NA CRO * 44 G8
Cinnamon Gdns GUW GU2 ....91 N9
Cintra Pk NRWD SE19 ....45 P1
Circle Gdns BF/WBF KT14 ....74 B2
WIM/MER SW19 ....43 L3
Circle Hill Rd CWTH RG45 ....49 N4
Circle Rd WOT/HER KT12 .....56 G8
The Circle GODL GU7 ....131 M7
The Circus LHD/OX KT22 * 77 H9
Cissbury Cl HORS RH12 ....192 F4
Cissbury Hl CRAWW RH11 ....176 F7
Clacket La BH/WHM TN16 ...104 C4
Clacy Gn BNFD RG42 ....32 C1
Clairvale Rd HEST TW5 ....15 M6
Clairview Rd TOOT SW17 * ...29 L8
Clairvile MFD/CHID GU8 * ...167 P7
Clancarty Rd FUL/PGN SW6 ...19 L7
Clandon Av EGH TW20 ....36 G1
Clandon Cl EW KT17 ....60 D5
Clandon Ct FARN GU14 ....88 F4
Clandon Rd GU GU1 ....7 H4
RPLY/SEND GU23 ....95 L6
Clandon Ter RYNPK SW20 * ...43 H3
Clanfield Ride BLKW GU17 ....67 P3
Clapgate La SWTR RH13 .....190 D5
Clapham Common South Side
CLAP SW4 ....29 L2
Clapham Common West Side
CLAP SW4 ....29 K1
Clapham Court Ter
BRXS/STRHM SW2 * 29 P1
Clapham Park Est
CLAP SW4 ....29 N3
Clapham Park Rd
BRXS/STRHM SW2 * 29 P1
Clappers Ga CRAWE RH10 ....176 C4
Clappers La CHOB/PIR GU24 ..53 J9
Clappers Meadow
CRAN GU6 ....170 D9
Clappers Orch CRAN GU6 * ..170 D8
Clare Cl BF/WBF KT14 ....73 L2
CRAWE RH10 ....177 K2
Clare Cr CTHM CR3 ....102 C3
Clare Crs LHD/OX KT22 ....76 C7
Claredale WOKS/MYFD GU22 ..72 C8
Clare Gdns EGH TW20 ....21 M8
Clare Hl HEST TW5 ....15 M6
Clare Hl (No 2) ESH/CLAY KT10..58 B4
Clare Lawn Av
MORT/ESHN SW14 ....27 J1
Clare Md RFNM GU10 ....146 C1
Clare Ms FUL/PGN SW6 ....19 M5
Claremont Av CBLY GU15 ......69 H3
ESH/CLAY KT10 ....57 P5
NWMAL KT3 ....42 E5
SUN TW16 ....39 K2
WOKS/MYFD GU22 ....72 C8
WOT/HER KT12 ....57 M3
Claremont Cl
BRXS/STRHM SW2 * 30 A4
SAND/SEL CR2 ....82 B3
WOT/HER KT12 ....57 M3
Claremont Ct DORK RH4 .....117 H8
Claremont Dr ESH/CLAY KT10..58 B6
SHPTN TW17 ....38 D7
WOKS/MYFD GU22 ....72 C8
Claremont End
ESH/CLAY KT10 ....58 B5
Claremont Gdns SURB KT6 ...41 L5
Claremont Gv CHSWK W4 .....18 C5
Claremont La ESH/CLAY KT10..58 A4
Claremont Park Rd
ESH/CLAY KT10 ....58 B5
Claremont Rd BF/WBF KT14 ..73 L1
CROY/NA CRO 46 C9
EBED/NFELT TW14 ....24 B3
REDH RH1 ....120 C2
STA TW18 ....22 A8
SURB KT6 ....41 L6
TEDD TW11 ....25 N8
TWK TW1 ....26 A3
Claremont Ter THDIT KT7 * ...41 H8
Claremont Vls KUT KT1 * 9 G5
Claremount Cl EPSOM KT18 ...78 G6

Claremount Gdns
EPSOM KT18 ....78 G6
Clarence Av CLAP SW4 ....29 N3
NWMAL KT3 ....41 P3
WOT/HER KT12 ....57 K3
Clarence Cl ASHV GU12 .....108 E4
WOT/HER KT12 ....57 K3
Clarence Crs CLAP SW4 ....29 N2
Clarence Dr CBLY GU15 ....69 K1
EGH TW20 ....21 M6
EGRIN RH19 ....180 F1
Clarence La PUT/ROE SW15 ...27 L2
Clarence Rd BH/WHM TN16 ..84 D7
CHSWK W4 ....17 N3
CROY/NA CRO 45 M8
FLEETN GU51 ....86 E7
RCH/KEW TW9 ....17 M6
REDH RH1 ....119 P8
SUT SM1 ....61 M3
SWTR RH13 ....192 C9
TEDD TW11 ....25 N9
WIM/MER SW19 ....28 E9
WLGTN SM6 ....62 D4
WOT/HER KT12 ....57 K3
Clarence St EGH TW20 ....21 C4
KUT KT1 ....8 E4
NWDN UB2 ....15 M1
RCH/KEW TW9 ....17 L9
STA TW18 ....22 B7
Clarence Ter HSLW TW3 ......16 C9
Clarence Vls KUT KT1 * 9 G5
Clarence Wk REDH RH1 .....119 P8
Clarence Wy HORL RH6 .....159 N1
Clarendon Cl BLKW GU17 .....67 P5
Clarendon Crs WHTN TW2 ....25 M5
Clarendon Dr PUT/ROE SW15 ..18 G9
Clarendon Ga CHERT KT16 ...55 H5
Clarendon Gv MTCM CR4 .....44 B4
Clarendon Ms ASHTD KT21 * ..77 L8
Clarendon Rd ASHF TW15 ....23 J7
CROY/NA CRO 2 B3
REDH RH1 * 120 B4
WIM/MER SW19 ....44 A1
WLGTN SM6 ....62 D5
Clarens St CAT SE6 ....31 N5
Clare Rd HSLW TW4 ....15 P8
STWL/WRAY TW19 ....22 G4
The Clares CTHM CR3 ....102 A4
Claret Gdns SNWD SE25 ......45 N5
Clareville Grove Ms
SKENS SW7 * 19 N2
Clareville Rd CTHM CR3 .....102 A4
Clareville St SKENS SW7 * 19 N2
Clare Wd LHD/OX KT22 ....76 D7
Clarewood Dr CBLY GU15 .....68 G2
Clarice Wy WLGTN SM6 ....62 G7
Claridge Gdns LING RH7 .....162 F2
Claridge Md LING RH7 ....162 F2
Clarke Crs CBLY GU15 ....68 A1
Clarkes Av WPK KT4 ....43 H9
Clark Rd CRAWW RH11 ......194 D1
Clarks Hl RFNM GU10 ....126 C3
Clarks La WARL CR6 ....105 P3
Clark Wy HEST TW5 ....15 M5
Claudia Pl WIM/MER SW19 ...28 B4
Claverdale Rd
BRXS/STRHM SW2 ....30 A3
Claverdon BRAK RG12 ....32 C8
Clavering Av BARN SW13 ......18 F4
Clavering Cl TWK TW1 ....25 P7
Claxton Crv HMSMTH W6 ......19 J1
Clay Av MTCM CR4 ....44 D3
Claybrook Rd HMSMTH W6 ....19 H4
Claycart Rd ALDT GU11 ......107 P3
Claydon Dr CROY/NA CRO 62 G3
Claydon Gdns FARN GU14 ....68 C7
Claydon Rd
WOKN/KNAP GU21 ....71 N5
Clayford LING RH7 ....162 F2
Claygate Crs CROY/NA CRO ...65 J5
Claygate La ESH/CLAY KT10 ..58 C2
THDIT KT7 ....40 G9
Claygate Lodge Cl
ESH/CLAY KT10 ....58 E6
Claygate Rd DORK RH4 ......117 H9
WEA W13 ....17 H1
Clay Hall La CRAWE RH10 ...160 D8
Clayhall La REIG RH2 ....119 J4
WDSR SL4 ....20 E1
Clayhanger RGUE GU4 ....112 G3
Clayhill Cl BRAK RG12 ....33 H4
REIG RH2 ....138 D4
Clayhill Rd REIG RH2 ....138 D4
Clay La EPSOM KT18 ....97 P4
LING RH7 ....161 L2
REDH RH1 ....120 E6
RGUE GU4 ....92 B8
Claymore Cl MRDN SM4 ....43 L8
Claypole Dr HEST TW5 ....15 N6
Clayponds Av BTFD TW8 ....17 L2
Clayponds Gdns EA W5 ....17 L3
Clayponds La BTFD TW8 ....17 L3
Clays Cl EGRIN RH19 ....180 D3
Clayton Barracks
ALDT GU11 ....108 F2
Clayton Ct FNM GU9 * 5 F4
Clayton Crs BTFD TW8 ....17 K2
Clayton Dr GUW GU2 ....111 M2
Clayton Gv BRAK RG12 ....32 G2
Clayton Md GDST RH9 ....122 H4
Clayton Pde DTCH/LGLY SL3 * ..12 F3
Clayton Rd CHSGTN KT9 ......59 J4
EW KT17 ....78 C1
FARN GU14 ....88 D5
ISLW TW7 ....16 E8
Cleardene DORK RH4 ....117 H7
Cleardown
WOKS/MYFD GU22 ....11 J6
Clearsprings LTWR GU18 .....51 P9
The Clears REIG RH2 ....119 J3

Clearwater Pl SURB KT6 ....41 J7
Cleave Av HYS/HAR UB3 ....14 C2
Cleaveland Rd SURB KT6 ......41 K6
Cleave Prior COUL/CHIP CR5 ..80 A8
Cleaverholme Cl SNWD SE25 ..46 B7
Cleeve Hl FSTH SE23 ....31 J4
Cleeve Rd LHD/OX KT22 ....76 G9
The Cleeve GU GU1 ....112 E5
Clem Attlee Ct
FUL/PGN SW6 * 19 K4
Clem Attlee Pde
FUL/PGN SW6 * 19 K4
Clement Cl CHSWK W4 ....18 B2
PUR/KEN CR8 ....81 K5
Clement Gdns HYS/HAR UB3 ..14 C3
Clement Rd BECK BR3 ....46 E3
WIM/MER SW19 ....28 B8
Clements Pl BTFD TW8 ....17 K3
Clements Rd WOT/HER KT12 ..57 K1
Clensham La SUT SM1 ....61 L1
Cleopatra Pl BNFD RG42 ......32 C1
Clerks Cft REDH RH1 ....121 M4
Clevedon WEY KT13 ....56 F4
Clevedon Cr FARN GU14 ....88 F4
Clevedon Gdns HEST TW5 .....15 K7
Clevedon Rd KUT KT1 ....9 H4
PGE/AN SE20 ....46 C2
TWK TW1 ....25 P3
Cleveland Av CHSWK W4 ......18 D2
HPTN TW12 ....39 P1
Cleveland Cl WOT/HER KT12 ..57 K2
Cleveland Dr STA TW18 ....37 M3
Cleveland Gdns BARN SW13 ...18 D7
WPK KT4 ....60 C1
Cleveland Ri MRDN SM4 ......43 H8
Cleveland Rd BARN SW13 .....18 D7
CHSWK W4 ....18 A1
ISLW TW7 ....16 F9
NWMAL KT3 ....42 C5
WPK KT4 ....60 C1
Cleves Av EW KT17 ....60 F7
Cleves Cl COB KT11 ....75 K3
Cleves Crs CROY/NA CRO 65 M8
Cleves Rd RCHPK/HAM TW10 ..26 D6
Cleves Wy HPTN TW12 ....39 P1
SUN TW16 ....24 A9
Cleves Wd WEY KT13 ....56 G2
Clewborough Dr CBLY GU15 ..69 K2
Clews La CHOB/PIR GU24 ......53 N5
Clifden Rd BTFD TW8 ....17 K4
TWK TW1 ....25 N4
Cliff End PUR/KEN CR8 ....81 K1
Cliffe Rd GODL GU7 ....150 B2
Cliffe Rd SAND/SEL CR2 ......63 M4
Clifford Av MORT/ESHN SW14..18 A7
RCH/KEW TW9 ....26 G1
WLGTN SM6 ....62 E3
Clifford Gdns HYS/HAR UB3 ..14 A2
Clifford Manor Rd
RGUE GU4 ....112 C9
Clifford Rd HSLW TW4 ....15 M8
RCHPK/HAM TW10 ....26 C5
SNWD SE25 ....46 A5
Clifton Av BELMT SM2 ....61 M9
FELT TW13 ....24 D6
Clifton Cl ADL/WDHM KT15 ...55 M1
CTHM CR3 ....101 M3
HORL RH6 ....159 L1
RFNM GU10 ....127 J9
Clifton Ga WBPTN SW10 * 19 N4
Clifton Gdns CHSWK W4 ....18 B2
FRIM GU16 ....89 H1
Clifton Ms SNWD SE25 ....45 N5
Clifton Pde FELT TW13 * 24 E7
Clifton Park Av RYNPK SW20 ..42 G4
Clifton Pl BNSTD SM7 ....79 L4
KUTN/CMB KT2 * 9 J1
WBPTN SW10 * 19 N4
Clifton Rd COUL/CHIP CR5 ....80 D4
CRAWE RH10 ....177 M6
HNHL TW6 * 14 D9
ISLW TW7 ....16 E7
KUTN/CMB KT2 ....9 H1
NWDGN UB2 ....15 M3
SNWD SE25 ....45 N5
TEDD TW11 ....25 M7
WIM/MER SW19 ....28 B9
WLGTN SM6 ....62 D4
Clifton Ter DORK RH4 * 117 H8
Cliftonville DORK RH4 ....117 J8
Clifton Wy WOKN/KNAP GU21..71 K7
Climping Rd CRAWW RH11 ...176 E3
Cline Rd GU GU1 ....7 J6
Clinton Av E/WMO/HCT KT8 ..40 C5
Clinton Cl WEY KT13 ....56 C2
WOKN/KNAP GU21 ....71 K7
Clinton Hl LING RH7 ....162 F3
Clinton Rd LHD/OX KT22 ......97 J3
Clintons Gn BNFD RG42 ....32 C1
Clinton Ter SUT SM1 * 61 N3
Clippesby Cl CHSGTN KT9 ....59 M5
Clipstone Rd HSLW TW3 ....16 A8
Clitherow Rd FARN GU14 ......67 K7
Clitherow Av HNWL W7 ....16 G1
Clitherow Gdns
CRAWE RH10 ....177 M6
Clitherow Rd BTFD TW8 ....17 H3
Cliveden Pl SHPTN TW17 ......38 D7
Cliveden Rd WIM/MER SW19 ..43 K3
Clive Gn BRAK RG12 ....32 D6
Clive Rd ASHV GU12 ....108 G5
DUL SE21 ....30 F6
EBED/NFELT TW14 ....24 B2
ESH/CLAY KT10 ....58 B3
TWK TW1 ....25 N7
WIM/MER SW19 ....29 H9

Clive Wy CRAWE RH10 ....177 M5
Clock Barn La
MFD/CHID GU8 ....150 E5
Clock House Cl
BF/WBF KT14 ....74 B1
Clockhouse Cl
WIM/MER SW19 ....27 P6
Clock House Ct
HASM GU27 * 184 D4
Clockhouse La ASHF TW15 ....23 L6
SHGR GU5 ....132 D7
Clockhouse La East
EGH TW20 ....36 E1
Clockhouse La West
EGH TW20 ....36 E1
Clock House Md COB KT11 ....76 B3
Clockhouse Pl
PUT/ROE SW15 ....28 B1
Clock House Rd BECK BR3 .....46 E4
Clockhouse Rd FARN GU14 ....88 D3
Clock Tower Rd ISLW TW7 .....16 F8
Clodhouse Hl
WOKS/MYFD GU22 ....91 K2
Cloister Cl TEDD TW11 ....26 A8
Cloister Gdns SNWD SE25 .....46 B7
The Cloisters FRIM GU16 ......68 F7
WOKS/MYFD GU22 ....72 C8
Cloncurry St FUL/PGN SW6 ...19 H7
Clonmel Rd FUL/PGN SW6 .....19 L6
TEDD TW11 ....25 L7
Clonmore St
WAND/EARL SW18 ....28 C4
The Close ASC SL5 ....33 M3
BECK BR3 ....46 E5
BF/WBF KT14 ....73 L2
BH/WHM TN16 ....187 P7
BRAK RG12 ....32 E5
BRKHM/BTCW RH3 ....117 P9
CAR SM5 ....62 A7
CHEAM SM3 ....43 M8
EGRIN RH19 ....180 C5
FRIM GU9 ....5 K6
FRIM GU16 ....68 E8
GODL GU7 ....150 E1
HORL RH6 ....159 M3
ISLW TW7 ....16 D7
LTWR GU18 ....52 A8
MTCM CR4 ....44 A3
NWMAL KT3 ....41 M2
PUR/KEN CR8 ....63 H8
RCH/KEW TW9 ....17 N8
REIG RH2 ....119 M6
SHGR GU5 ....132 D7
SHST GU47 ....50 A9
SURB KT6 ....41 L8
VW GU25 ....36 B6
WOKS/MYFD GU22 ....11 J8
Closeworth Rd FARN GU14 ....88 G7
Cloudesdale Rd TOOT SW17 ...29 L5
Clouston Cl WLGTN SM6 ....62 G4
Clouston Rd FARN GU14 ....88 A2
Clovelly Av WARL CR6 ....82 B7
Clovelly Dr GSHT GU26 ....165 M4
Clovelly Rd GSHT GU26 ....165 M5
HSLW TW3 ....16 A8
Clover Cl WOKS/MYFD GU22 ..10 D9
Cloverfields HORL RH6 ....140 D9
Clover Hl COUL/CHIP CR5 ....100 D1
Cloverlands CRAWE RH10 ....177 J3
Clover La YTLY GU46 ....66 E2
Clover Lea GODL GU7 ....131 L5
Clover Rd GUW GU2 ....111 L4
Clovers End HORS RH12 ......193 J5
Clover Wy HORL RH6 ....160 B1
WLGTN SM6 ....44 C9
Clowders Rd CAT SE6 ....31 N6
Clowser Cl SUT SM1 ....61 N4
Club Gardens Rd HAYES BR2 ..47 N8
Clubhouse Rd ALDT GU11 ....108 B1
Club La CWTH RG45 ....49 P4
Clump Av
KWD/TDW/WH KT20 ....118 A2
Clumps Rd RFNM GU10 ....128 A9
The Clumps FELT TW13 ....25 H7
Clunbury Av NWDGN UB2 .....15 P3
Cluny Ms ECT SW5 ....19 L2
Clyde Av SAND/SEL CR2 ....82 E4
Clyde Cl REDH RH1 ....120 C4
Clyde Flats FUL/PGN SW6 * ...19 K5
Clyde Rd CROY/NA CRO 3 J3
STWL/WRAY TW19 ....22 G4
SUT SM1 ....61 L4
WLGTN SM6 ....62 E4
Clydesdale Cl ISLW TW7 ......16 F8
Clydesdale Gdns
RCHPK/HAM TW10 ....17 P9
Clyde Ter FSTH SE23 ....31 K5
Clyde V FSTH SE23 ....31 K5
Clymping Dene
EBED/NFELT TW14 ....24 C3
Clyve Wy STA TW18 ....37 J2
Coach House Cl FRIM GU16 ...68 G5
Coach House Gdns
FLEETN GU51 ....86 C4
Coach House La
WIM/MER SW19 ....28 A7
Coach House Ms
FSTH SE23 ....31 K2
REDH RH1 * 120 B6
Coach House Yd
WAND/EARL SW18 * 19 M9
Coachlads Av GUW GU2 ....111 M5
Coachmans Dr
CRAWW RH11 ....176 E9
Coach Rd ASC SL5 ....33 N1
BRKHM/BTCW RH3 ....117 N7
CHERT KT16 ....54 C5
HORL RH6 ....159 L5

RDKG RH5 ....117 L5
Coalecroft Rd
PUT/ROE SW15 ....18 G9
Coast Hill RDKG RH5 ....115 P9
Coast Hill La DORK RH4 ......116 A9
Coates Av WAND/EARL SW18 ..29 H2
Cobb Cl DTCH/LGLY SL3 ....12 B6
Cobbets Rdg RFNM GU10 ....128 C8
Cobbets Wy EDEN TN8 ....144 G5
Cobbett Cl CRAWE RH10 .....177 M3
Cobbett Hl Rd RGUW GU3 .....90 B8
Cobbett Rd GUW GU2 ....111 L4
WHTN TW2 ....25 H4
Cobbetts Cl
WOKN/KNAP GU21 ....71 P5
Cobbetts Farm
CHOB/PIR GU24 * 70 G4
Cobbetts Hl WEY KT13 ....56 D6
Cobbetts Ms BLKW GU17 ......67 K4
Cobbetts Wk CHOB/PIR GU24..70 G5
Cobbetts Wy FNM GU9 * 127 K7
Cobbler's Wd TEDD TW11 .....40 E1
Cobbles Crs CRAWE RH10 ....177 H4
Cobblestone Pl
CROY/NA CRO * 2 C3
Cobb's Rd HSLW TW4 ....15 P9
Cob Cl CRAWE RH10 ....179 K3
Cobden La HASM GU27 ....184 E5
Cobden Ms SYD SE26 ....31 J8
Cobden Rd SNWD SE25 ....46 A6
Cobham Av NWMAL KT3 ....42 E6
Cobham Cl BTSEA SW11 * 29 H2
WLGTN SM6 ....62 G5
Cobham Park Rd COB KT11 ...75 K6
Cobham Rd COB KT11 ....15 L5
HEST TW5 ....15 K5
KUT KT1 ....9 J4
Cobham Wy CRAWE RH10 ....159 L8
EHSLY KT24 ....94 G3
Cobnor Cl CRAWW RH11 ......176 C7
Cobs Wy ADL/WDHM KT15 .....55 N8
Coburg Crs
BRXS/STRHM SW2 ....30 A4
Cob Wk CRAWW RH11 ....176 B6
Cochrane Pl BFOR GU20 ....52 D4
Cochrane Rd WIM/MER SW19..43 J1
Cock-a-Dobby SHST GU47 .....49 L9
Cockcrow Hl SURB KT6 * 41 K9
Cockett Rd DTCH/LGLY SL3 ...12 C1
Cock La LHD/OX KT22 ....96 C2
Cocks Crs NWMAL KT3 ....42 E5
Cockshot Hl REIG RH2 ....119 M7
Cockshot Rd REIG RH2 ....119 M7
The Coda Centre
FUL/PGN SW6 * 19 J6
Codrington Ct
WOKN/KNAP GU21 ....71 M7
Codrington Hl FSTH SE23 ......31 M3
Cody Cl ASHV GU12 ....109 H1
WLGTN SM6 ....62 F6
Cody Rd FARN GU14 ....88 B4
Coe Av SNWD SE25 ....46 A7
Coe Cl ALDT GU11 ....108 C5
Cokenor Rd RFNM GU10 ....127 K7
Cockcrow Hl SURB KT6 * 41 K9
Cokers La DUL SE21 ....30 D4
Colbeck FLEETS GU52 ....107 H2
Colborne Wy WPK KT4 ....60 F2
Colbred Cnr FLEETN GU51 ....87 J3
Colbrook Av HYS/HAR UB3 ....14 F1
Colbrook Cl HYS/HAR UB3 ....14 F1
Colburn Av CTHM CR3 ....101 P4
Colburn Crs RGUE GU4 ....112 E2
Colburn Wy SUT SM1 ....61 P2
Colby Rd NRWD SE19 ....30 F9
WOT/HER KT12 ....39 J9
Colchester V FROW RH18 ....181 K9
Colcokes Rd BNSTD SM7 ....79 L5
Coldharbour Cl EGH TW20 ....36 C4
Coldharbour La
CHOB/PIR GU24 ....52 F9
DORK RH4 ....116 G9
EGH TW20 ....36 C4
Cold Harbour La FARN GU14 ..88 E5
Coldharbour La
PUR/KEN CR8 ....63 J3
RDKG RH5 ....136 F5
REDH RH1 ....121 P7
WOKS/MYFD GU22 ....73 K4
Coldharbour Rd
BF/WBF KT14 ....73 K3
CROY/NA CRO 63 J4
Coldharbour Wy
CROY/NA CRO 63 J4
Coldshott OXTED RH8 ....123 N4
Coldsteam Rd CTHM CR3 .....101 L2
Coldstream Gdns
PUT/ROE SW15 ....28 C2
Cole Av ALDT GU11 ....108 B3
Colebrook CHERT KT16 ....55 H5
Colebrooke Pl CHERT KT16 * ..54 G4
Colebrooke Rd REDH RH1 ....120 A3
Colebrook Rd HAYES BR2 * 47 L9
Colebrook Rd
STRHM/NOR SW16 ....44 G2
Cole Cl CRAWW RH11 ....194 E1
Coleford Bridge Rd
FRIM GU16 ....88 H4
Coleford Cl FRIM GU16 ....89 H4
Coleford Paddocks
FRIM GU16 ....89 H4
Coleford Rd
WAND/EARL SW18 ....19 F1
Cole Gdns HEST TW5 ....15 J5
Coleherne Ms WBPTN SW10 ..19 M3
Coleherne Rd WBPTN SW10 ...19 M3
Colehill Gdns FUL/PGN SW6 ..19 J7
Colehill La FUL/PGN SW6 ......19 K7
Colekitchen La SHGR GU5 ....114 E9
Coleman Cl SNWD SE25 ....46 A3
Coleman Rd ASHV GU12 ......109 H1

Cole Park Gdns TWK TW1 .....25 P2
Cole Park Rd TWK TW1 ....25 P3
Coleridge Av SUT SM1 ....62 A3
  YTLY GU46 ....67 J3
Coleridge Cl CWTH RG45 .....49 N5
  HORS RH12 ....192 D4
Coleridge Crs DTCH/LGLY SL3 ..13 J5
Coleridge Rd ASHF TW15 .....23 H7
  CROY/NA CRO 64 C8
Coleridge Wy WDR/YW UB7 ....14 B2
Cole Rd TWK TW1 ....25 P2
Colesburg Rd BECK BR3 .....46 F4
Colescroft Hl PUR/KEN CR8 ..81 J4
Coleshill Rd TEDD TW11 .....25 M9
Coles La BH/WHM TN16 .....105 N5
  RDKG RH5 ....156 A7
Colesmead Rd REDH RH1 ....120 B2
Coleson Hill Rd RFNM GU10 ..127 K8
Colet Gdns WKENS W14 ....19 H1
Colet Rd CRAWE RH10 ....176 G8
Colette Rd BECK BR3 ....46 B2
Coley Av WOKS/MYFD GU22 ...11 G5
Colfe Rd FSTH SE23 ....31 M4
Colgate Cl CRAWW RH11 ....176 E3
Colin Cl CROY/NA CRO 64 F2
Colin Rd CTHM CR3 ....102 A3
Coliston Rd
  WAND/EARL SW18 ....28 D3
Collamore Av
  WAND/EARL SW18 ....29 H4
Collards Ga HASM GU27 * ...184 E4
Collards La HASM GU27 .....184 E6
College Av EGH TW20 ....21 N9
  EW KT17 ....78 D3
College Cl ADL/WDHM KT15 ..55 P2
  CBLY GU15 ....50 F9
  EGRIN RH19 ....180 E2
  LING RH7 ....143 K9
  RHWH RH17 ....194 F8
  WHTN TW2 ....25 L4
College Crs REDH RH1 ......120 C2
College Dr THDIT KT7 ......40 E8
College Gdns FNM GU9 ....4 E3
  HASM GU27 ....184 D4
  KT3 ....42 D6
  TOOT SW17 ....29 J5
The College EW KT17 * 78 E4
College HI GODL GU7 ....150 B1
  HASM GU27 ....184 D4
College Hill Ter HASM GU27 ..184 D4
College La EGRIN RH19 .....180 E2
  WOKS/MYFD GU22 ....11 K6
College Pl WBPTN SW10 * ...19 L7
College Ride BAGS GU19 ....51 L7
  CBLY GU15 ....51 J3
College Rd ASHV GU12 .....109 J3
  BMLY BR1 ....47 N2
  BRAK RG12 ....32 E5
  CRAWE RH10 ....177 H5
  CRO 2 E4
  DUL SE21 ....30 F3
  DUL SE21 ....30 G6
  EW KT17 ....78 E3
  GU GU1 ....6 E5
  ISLW TW7 ....16 F6
  SHST GU47 ....68 A1
  WIM/MER SW19 ....28 G9
  WOKS/MYFD GU22 ....11 K2
The College EW KT17 * 78 E4
College Wy ASHF TW15 ......23 J7
Collendean La HORL RH6 ....139 K9
Collins Fld CHOB/PIR GU24 ..90 E4
Colley La REIG RH2 ....119 J3
Colley Manor Dr REIG RH2 ..119 H4
Colley Wy REIG RH2 ....119 J2
Collier Cl FARN GU14 ......24 B7
  HOR/WEW KT19 ....59 N5
Collier Rw CRAWE RH10 ....176 C8
Colliers CTHM CR3 ....102 A5
Colliers Cl WOKN/KNAP GU21 ..71 P6
Colliers Water La THHTH CR7 ..45 K6
Collier Wy RGUE GU4 ......113 H3
Collingdon CRAN GU6 * 171 J2
Collingdon Ct CRAN GU6 * ..171 J2
Collingham Gdns ECT SW5 ..19 M2
Collingham Pl ECT SW5 ....19 M2
Collingham Rd ECT SW5 ....19 M2
Collingsbourne
  ADL/WDHM KT15 * 55 M3
Collingtree Rd SYD SE26 ...31 K7
Collingwood Av BRYLDS KT5 ..42 A9
Collingwood Cl EGRIN RH19 ..180 E4
  RDKG RH6 ....140 D9
  HSLW TW3 ....35 H3
Colling Wood Cl PGE/AN SE20 ..46 B2
Collingwood Crs GU GU1 ....112 E4
Collingwood Grange Cl
  CBLY GU15 ....50 F9
Collingwood Ri CBLY GU15 ..69 J3
Collingwood Rd
  HORS RH12 ....177 N6
  HORS RH12 ....192 A5
  MTCM CR4 ....44 A3
  SUT SM1 ....61 L3
Collins Gdns ASHV GU12 ...109 K4
Collins Rd CRAWW RH11 ....176 B7
Collyer Av CROY/NA CRO 62 G5
Collyer Rd CROY/NA CRO 62 G3
Collyers Crs LIPH GU30 ....183 H6
Colman Cl EPSOM KT18 .....78 C6
Colmans HI SHGR GU5 ......134 F6
Colman Wy REDH RH1 ......120 A3
Colmer Rd
  STRHM/NOR SW16 ....44 G1
Colnbrook By-Pass
  DTCH/LGLY SL3 ....12 C5
  WDR/YW UB7 ....13 M5
Colndale Rd DTCH/LGLY SL3 ..13 J7

Colne Bank STWL/WRAY TW19 ..12 G8
Colne Ct EWKG RG40 * 60 A3
Colne Dr WOT/HER KT12 .....57 M2
Colne Rd WHTN TW2 ....25 M4
Colne Valley Wy
  STWL/WRAY TW19 ....22 B4
Colne Wy ASHV GU12 ....109 J5
  STWL/WRAY TW19 ....21 P6
Cologne Rd BTSEA SW11 .....19 H9
Colonel's La CHERT KT16 ...37 L7
Colonial Av HSLW TW3 ......15 J2
Colonial Dr CHSWK W4 .....18 A2
Colonial Rd
  EBED/NFELT TW14 ....23 H7
Colonsay Rd CRAWW RH11 ..176 E8
Colson Rd CROY/NA CRO 3 F5
Colson Wy STRHM/NOR SW16 ..29 M7
Colston Av CAR SM5 ....62 A3
Colston Rd
  MORT/ESHN SW14 ....18 A9
  SUT SM1 ....61 M1
Coltash Rd CRAWE RH10 ....177 K6
Coltsfoot Dr GU GU1 ......112 F2
  HORS RH12 ....192 C5
Coltsfoot La OXTED RH8 ....123 M4
Columbia Av WPK KT4 ......42 D8
Columbia Ct EWKG RG40 ....48 C2
Columbine Av SAND/SEL CR2 ..63 K6
Columbus Dr FARN GU14 ....87 N4
Colville Gdns LTWR GU18 ...52 C9
Colville Rd ACT W3 ....17 P1
Colvin Cl SYD SE26 ....31 K9
Colvin Rd THHTH CR7 ......45 J6
Colwell Rd EDUL SE22 .....30 C1
Colwith Rd HMSMTH W6 .....18 G4
Colwood Gdns
  WIM/MER SW19 ....43 P1
Colworth Rd CROY/NA CRO ..46 A9
Colwyn Cl CRAWW RH11 ....176 B7
  STRHM/NOR SW16 ....29 M8
  YTLY GU46 ....66 F2
Colwyn Crs HSLW TW3 ......16 C6
Colyton Cl WOKN/KNAP GU21 ..72 A7
Colyton La
  STRHM/NOR SW16 ....29 P8
Colyton Rd EDUL SE22 .....31 J1
Combe La FARN GU14 ....87 P6
  MFD/CHID GU8 ....151 J2
  MFD/CHID GU8 ....167 N6
  SHGR GU5 ....114 C2
  SHGR GU5 ....151 K2
  WOT/HER KT12 ....57 H7
Combemartin Rd
  WAND/EARL SW18 ....28 B3
Combe Ri RFNM GU10 ......127 P8
Combermere Rd MRDN SM4 ..43 M7
Combe Rd GODL GU7 ....131 L5
Combe Vw MFD/CHID GU8 * ..167 P7
Comeragh Cl
  WOKS/MYFD GU22 ....71 J8
Comeragh Ms WKENS W14 * ..19 J3
Comeragh Rd WKENS W14 ....19 J3
Comet Rd STWL/WRAY TW19 ..22 G3
Comforts Farm Av
  OXTED RH8 ....123 M4
Comfrey Cl FARN GU14 .....87 N2
Commerce Rd BTFD TW8 ....17 J4
Commerce Wy CROY/NA CRO ..63 H2
Commercial Rd ASHV GU12 ..108 E5
  GU GU1 ....6 E5
  STA TW18 ....22 D9
Commercial Wy
  WOKN/KNAP GU21 ....10 E3
Commodore Pde
  STRHM/NOR SW16 * 45 H1
Common Cl
  WOKN/KNAP GU21 ....72 B3
Commondale PUT/ROE SW15 ..18 G7
Commonfield Rd BNSTD SM7 ..79 L3
Commonfields
  CHOB/PIR GU24 ....70 F2
Common La ADL/WDHM KT15 ..55 N1
  ESH/CLAY KT10 ....58 C6
  DTCH/LGLY SL3 ....12 E2
  REDH RH1 ....58 G5
Common Side EPSOM KT18 ...77 N4
Commonside GT/LBKH KT23 ..96 A3
Commonside CR BELMT SM2 ..61 M9
  COUL/CHIP CR5 ....81 K9
Commonside East
  MTCM CR4 ....44 C4
The Common NWDGN UB2 ....15 M2
Commonwealth Rd
  CTHM CR3 ....102 A3
Community Cl HEST TW5 ....15 K6
Como Rd FSTH SE23 ....31 M5
Compass HI
  RCHPK/HAM TW10 ....26 C2
Compassion Cl
  CRAWW RH11 ....176 B6
Compton Cl CRAWW RH11 ...176 B7
Compton Gn CROY/NA CRO ...83 L1
Compound Rd FARN GU14 ...88 C5
Compton Cl BRAK RG12 ....32 A7
Compton Crs CHSWK W4 ....18 A3
  FLEETS GU52 ....106 F7
  HOR/WEW KT19 ....78 A2
  SHST GU47 ....49 N8
Compton Crs CHSGTN KT9 ...59 L5
  CHSWK W4 ....18 A4
Compton Rd CROY/NA CRO ...46 B9
  FLEETS GU52 ....107 H1
  WIM/MER SW19 ....28 C9
Commons Brow La
  SWTR RH13 ....192 E7
Comptons Cl SWTR RH13 ...192 E7
Comptons La SWTR RH13 ...192 E7
Compton Wy RFNM GU10 ...128 C3
Comsaye Wk BRAK RG12 ....32 E6
Conaways Cl EW KT17 .....60 E8
Concorde Cl HSLW TW3 ....16 B7
Condor Cl GUW GU2 ....6 D7
Condor Rd FARN GU14 .....88 D5

STA TW18 ....37 N4
Conduit La DTCH/LGLY SL3 ..12 C3
  SAND/SEL CR2 ....64 C5
The Conduit REDH RH1 ....101 M9
Coney Acre DUL SE21 ......30 D4
Coneyberry REDH RH1 .....119 N9
Coneybury BRAK RG12 .....32 E5
Coneybury Cl WARL CR6 ....82 B8
Coney Cft HORS RH12 .....192 C5
Coney Cl CRAWW RH11 ....176 E3
Coney Hall Pde WWKM BR4 * ..65 L2
Coney Hill Rd WWKM BR4 ...65 L1
Coneyhurst La CRAN GU6 ...153 M5
Conford Dr RGUE GU4 .....132 C3
Coniers Wy RGUE GU4 .....112 F2
Conifer Cl FLEETS GU52 ...106 F1
  REIG RH2 ....119 J3
Conifer Dr CBLY GU15 .....69 J2
Conifer Gdns
  STRHM/NOR SW16 ....30 A6
  SUT SM1 ....61 M1
Conifer La EGH TW20 ......21 P8
Conifer Pk EW KT17 ....60 C9
Conifers WEY KT13 ....56 G3
Conifers Cl HORS RH12 ...192 C4
  TEDD TW11 ....41 H1
The Conifers CWTH RG45 ..49 L2
Coniger Rd FUL/PGN SW6 ...19 L7
Coningsby BRAK RG12 .....32 E5
Coningsby Rd SAND/SEL CR2 ..63 M7
Conista Ct WOKN/KNAP GU21 ..71 M5
Coniston Cl BARN SW13 ...18 D5
  CBLY GU15 ....51 J8
  CHSWK W4 ....18 A6
  CRAWW RH11 ....176 A7
  FARN GU14 ....88 A4
  HORS RH12 ....192 C5
  MRDN SM4 ....43 H7
Coniston Ct BELMT SM2 * ..61 P5
Coniston Dr FNM GU9 .....107 L8
Coniston Rd COUL/CHIP CR5 ..80 E5
  CROY/NA CRO 46 D8
  WHTN TW2 ....25 J2
  WOKS/MYFD GU22 ....72 F9
Coniston Wy CHSGTN KT9 ...59 L2
  EGH TW20 ....36 A9
  FLEETS GU52 ....106 E1
  REIG RH2 ....119 J3
Connaught Av ASHF TW15 ...23 H7
  HSLW TW3 * 24 A1
  MORT/ESHN SW14 ....18 A8
Connaught Barracks
  ALDT GU11 ....88 F9
Connaught Cl CWTH RG45 ...49 K6
  SUT SM1 ....61 P1
  YTLY GU46 ....66 F2
Connaught Crs
  CHOB/PIR GU24 ....70 F9
Connaught Dr WEY KT13 ...56 B9
Connaught Gdns
  CRAWE RH10 ....176 G3
  MRDN SM4 ....43 N5
Connaught Ms
  FUL/PGN SW6 * 19 J6
Connaught Rd ALDT GU11 ...108 E5
  BAGS GU19 ....51 L6
  CBLY GU15 ....69 H3
  CHOB/PIR GU24 ....70 F9
  HPTN TW12 ....25 P8
  NWMAL KT3 ....42 C5
  RCHPK/HAM TW10 ....26 E1
  SUT SM1 ....61 P1
Connop Wy FRIM GU16 .....69 H5
Conquest Rd
  ADL/WDHM KT15 ....55 L4
Conrad Dr WPK KT4 ....42 G5
Consfield Av NWMAL KT3 ...42 E5
Consort Dr CBLY GU15 ....69 L1
Consort Ms ISLW TW7 .....25 L2
Consort Wy HORL RH6 ....159 K1
Consort Wy East HORL RH6 ..159 L2
Constable Gdns ISLW TW7 ..25 L2
Constable Rd CRAWE RH10 ..177 J9
Constable Wy SHST GU47 ...68 A2
Constance Cres HAYES BR2 ..47 M9
Constance Rd CROY/NA CRO ..45 H8
  SUT SM1 ....61 N3
  WHTN TW2 ....25 H3
Constant Rd FARN GU14 ...87 L5
Constitution HI
  WOKS/MYFD GU22 ....10 D6
Control Tower Rd
  HTHAIR TW6 ....14 C8
Convent Cl BECK BR3 .....47 J1
Convent Gdns EA W5 ......17 J2
Convent HI NRWD SE19 ....30 D9
Convent Rd ASHF TW15 ....23 L8
Convent Wy NWDGN UB2 ...15 L2
Conway Dr ASHF TW15 ....23 M9
  BELMT SM2 ....61 M5
  FARN GU14 ....87 P2
  HYS/HAR UB3 ....14 F1
Conway Gdns MTCM CR4 ...44 F5
Conway Rd FELT TW13 .....24 E8
  HSLW TW3 ....24 G3
  RYNPK SW20 ....42 G2
Conyers Cl WOT/HER KT12 ..57 M4
Conyer's Rd
  STRHM/NOR SW16 ....29 N8
Cooden Cl BMLY BR1 ......47 P1
Cookes La CHEAM SM3 ....61 H5
Cookham Cl NWDGN UB2 ...16 B1
  SHST GU47 ....49 N8
Cookham Rd BRAK RG12 ...32 A2
Cook Rd CRAWE RH10 .....177 H7
  HORS RH12 ....192 C4
Cooks HI HORS RH12 .....189 J1
Cooks Md HORS RH12 ....175 J4

Cooks Meadow HORS RH12 ..175 J4
Coolarne Ri CBLY GU15 ....69 J2
Coolgardie Rd ASHF TW15 ..23 M8
Coolhurst La SWTR RH13 ..192 F9
Coombe Av CROY/NA CRO 63 M3
Coombe Bank NWMAL KT3 ..42 C2
  FRIM GU16 ....68 F8
  HSLW TW3 ....16 A9
Coombe Crs HPTN TW12 ...39 N1
Coombe Dr ADL/WDHM KT15 ..55 K5
  FLEETS GU51 ....87 J6
Coombe End KUTN/CMB KT2 ..42 B1
Coombefield Cl NWMAL KT3 ..42 C6
Coombe Gdns NWMAL KT3 ...42 E5
  RYNPK SW20 ....42 E3
Coombe Hill Gld
  KUTN/CMB KT2 ....42 C1
Coombe Hill Rd EGRIN RH19 ..180 B5
  KUTN/CMB KT2 ....42 C1
Coombe House Cha
  NWMAL KT3 ....42 A1
Coombelands La
  KUTN/CMB KT2 ....55 L5
Coombe La CROY/NA CRO 64 A5
  RGUW GU3 ....91 J8
  RYNPK SW20 ....42 E5
Coombe Mnr CHOB/PIR GU24 ..71 H4
Coombe Neville
  KUTN/CMB KT2 ....42 A1
Coombe Pk KUTN/CMB KT2 ..27 H8
Coombe Pine BRAK RG12 ...32 F7
Coombe Ridings
  KUTN/CMB KT2 ....27 H8
Coombe Rd CHSWK W4 .....18 C3
  CROY/NA CRO 2 E7
  HPTN TW12 ....24 G9
  KUTN/CMB KT2 ....9 J3
  NWMAL KT3 ....42 C4
  SYD SE26 ....31 J7
  WEA W13 ....17 H1
  YTLY GU46 ....66 F1
Coomber Wy CROY/NA CRO ..44 G8
The Coombes SHGR GU5 ....132 E8
The Coombe
  BRKHM/BTCW RH3 ....118 B2
Coombe Vis
  WAND/EARL SW18 * 28 D3
Coombe Wy BF/WBF KT14 ..74 B1
Coombe Wood HI
  PUR/KEN CR8 ....81 L1
Coombe Wood Rd
  KUTN/CMB KT2 ....27 H8
Coomb Fld EDEN TN8 .....144 G5
Coomer Ms FUL/PGN SW6 * ..19 K4
Coomer Pl FUL/PGN SW6 ...19 K4
Cooper Cr HORL RH6 ......160 B1
Cooper Crs CAR SM5 ......62 B2
Cooper Rd BFOR GU20 ....52 D5
  CROY/NA CRO 63 J4
  GU GU1 ....7 K4
Cooper Rw CRAWE RH10 ...176 D8
Coopers Cl STA TW18 .....22 B8
Coopers Hl HTWY RG27 ....66 B5
Coopers Hill Dr
  CHOB/PIR GU24 ....70 C9
Coopers Hill La EGH TW20 ..21 H6
Coopers Hill Rd REDH RH1 ..121 H4
Coopers Ri GODL GU7 .....150 A1
Coopers Yd NRWD SE19 ....30 F9
Cootes Av HORS RH12 ....191 P7
Copeland Cl DTCH/LGLY SL3 ..69 M4
Copeman Cl SYD SE26 ....31 K8
Copenhagen Wy
  WOT/HER KT12 ....57 K2
Cope PI KENS W8 ....19 L1
Copers Cope Rd BECK BR3 ..46 F1
Copgate Pth
  STRHM/NOR SW16 ....30 A9
Copleigh Dr
  KWD/TDW/WH KT20 ....79 J9
  WOKN/KNAP GU21 ....71 L8
Copley Cl REDH RH1 ......120 A3
  WOKN/KNAP GU21 ....71 L8
Copley Pk STRHM/NOR SW16 ..30 A8
Copley Wy
  KWD/TDW/WH KT20 ....79 H9
Copnall Wy HORS RH12 ...192 B8
Coppard Gdns CHSGTN KT9 ..59 J5
Copped Hall Dr CBLY GU15 ..69 J3
Copped Hall Wy CBLY GU15 ..69 J3
Copper Beech
  WOKS/MYFD GU22 ....91 P1
Copperfield Av SHST GU47 ..49 N7
Copperfield Cl
  PUR/KEN CR8 ....63 L9
Copperfield Pl HORS RH12 ..192 A7
Copperfield Ri
  ADL/WDHM KT15 ....55 K4
Copperfields LHD/OX KT22 ..96 C2
  SUN TW16 * 23 K4
Coppergate Cl BMLY BR1 ...47 P2
Copper Mill Dr ISLW TW7 ..16 F7
Coppermill Rd
  STWL/WRAY TW19 ....21 N2
Coppice Cl BECK BR3 .....47 H5
  FNM GU9 ....127 K4
  GUW GU2 ....111 K4
  RYNPK SW20 ....42 G6
Coppice Gdns BNFD RG42 ..32 B1
Coppice La REIG RH2 .....119 K3
Coppice Rd HORS RH12 ...192 C5
The Coppice ASHF TW15 ...23 L9
  CRAWE RH10 ....179 J3
Coppice Wk CRAWE RH10 ..177 K4
Copping Cl CROY/NA CRO 3 K7
The Coppins CROY/NA CRO ..65 H5

Coppsfield E/WMO/HCT KT8 ..40 C1
Copse Av FNM GU9 ....108 A3
  WWKM BR4 ....65 H2
Copse Cl CBLY GU15 ......51 J3
  CRAWE RH10 ....179 J3
  EGRIN RH19 ....162 E9
  HORS RH12 ....192 A4
  RGUE GU4 ....132 G2
  WDR/YW UB7 ....13 P1
Copse Crs CRAWW RH11 ...176 F4
Copse Edge CRAN GU6 ....153 J8
  MFD/CHID GU8 ....167 P4
  WOT/HER KT12 * 57 G2
Copse Edge Av EW KT17 ...78 D2
Copse End CBLY GU15 .....69 H2
Copse Gld SURB KT6 ......41 K9
Copse HI BELMT SM2 ......61 M6
  PUR/KEN CR8 ....80 G2
  RYNPK SW20 ....42 G2
Copse La HORL RH6 ....140 E9
Copsem Dr ESH/CLAY KT10 ..58 C5
Copsem La LHD/OX KT22 ...58 C5
Copsem Wy ESH/CLAY KT10 ..58 C5
Copse Rd COB KT11 ....75 H2
  HASM GU27 ....183 N5
  REIG RH2 ....119 N7
  WOKN/KNAP GU21 ....71 M7
Copse Side GODL GU7 .....131 K5
The Copse BRAK RG12 * ...32 F4
  CTHM CR3 ....102 A6
  FARN GU14 ....88 A3
  GT/LBKH KT23 ....96 B3
  REDH RH1 ....120 C7
  RFNM GU10 ....127 K9
Copse Vw SAND/SEL CR2 ...64 E7
Copse Wy EWKG RG40 .....48 C2
Copsleigh Av REDH RH1 ..140 C5
Copsleigh Cl REDH RH1 ...140 C5
Copsleigh Wy REDH RH1 ..140 C2
Copthall Gdns TWK TW1 ...25 P4
Copthall Wy
  ADL/WDHM KT15 ....55 K8
Copt Hill La
  KWD/TDW/WH KT20 ....79 J9
Copthorne Av BAL SW12 ...29 N3
Copthorne Bank
  CRAWE RH10 ....160 G3
  HORL RH6 ....160 G6
Copthorne Cl SHPTN TW17 ..38 E7
Copthorne Common Rd
  CRAWE RH10 ....178 C1
Copthorne Ct LHD/OX KT22 * ..96 C1
Copthorne Dr LTWR GU18 ...52 B8
Copthorne Ms HYS/HAR UB3 ..14 C2
Copthorne Ri PUR/KEN CR8 ..81 M1
Copthorne Rd CRAWE RH10 ..161 J8
  CRAWE RH10 ....177 N3
  LHD/OX KT22 ....96 C2
Copthorne Wy CRAWE RH10 ..178 A1
Copyhold Rd EGRIN RH19 ..180 C3
Corban Rd HSLW TW3 .....16 A8
Corbet Cl WLGTN SM6 ....44 C9
Corbet Rd EW KT17 ......60 C8
Corbett Cl CROY/NA CRO ...83 K1
Corbett Dr LTWR GU18 ....69 P1
Corby Cl EGH TW20 ......21 H9
Corby Dr EGH TW20 ......21 H9
Cordelia Cft BNFD RG42 ...32 C2
Cordelia Gdns ASHV GU12 ..89 H7
  STWL/WRAY TW19 ....23 H3
Cordelia Rd
  STWL/WRAY TW19 ....23 H3
Cordrey Gdns
  COUL/CHIP CR5 ....80 G4
Cordwalles Rd CBLY GU15 ..51 H9
Coresbrook Wy
  WOKN/KNAP GU21 ....71 H7
Corfe Cl ASHTD KT21 .....77 J7
Corfe Gdns FRIM GU16 ....69 H7
Corfe Wy FARN GU14 .....88 C6
Corfield Cl EWKG RG40 ...48 C6
Coriander Cl FARN GU14 ..87 N3
Coriander Crs GUW GU2 ...91 N9
Corkran Rd SURB KT6 ....41 K8
Corkscrew HI WWKM BR4 ..65 J1
Cormongers La REDH RH1 ..121 F4
Cormorant Pl SHST GU47 ..50 A9
Cornbunting Cl SHST GU47 ..67 P1
Corn Cft BNFD RG42 .....32 F1
Corner Farm Cl
  KWD/TDW/WH KT20 ....98 G2
Cornelia Cl FARN GU14 * ..87 P4
Corner Fielde
  BRXS/STRHM SW2 * 30 A4
Cornerside ASHF TW15 ....38 E1
Corney Reach Wy
  CHSWK W4 ....18 C5
Corney Rd CHSWK W4 .....18 C4
Cornfield Rd REIG RH2 ...119 N6
Cornfields GODL GU7 .....131 M5
  YTLY GU46 ....66 F3
Cornflower La CROY/NA CRO ..46 D9
Cornflower Ter EDUL SE22 ..31 J2
Cornford Cl HAYES BR2 ....47 N6
Cornford Gv BAL SW12 ....29 L5
Cornhill Cl ADL/WDHM KT15 ..55 M1
Cornish Gv PGE/AN SE20 ..46 B2
Cornwall Av BF/WBF KT14 ..74 B3
  ESH/CLAY KT10 ....58 F6
Cornwall Cl CBLY GU15 ...69 H1
Cornwall Gdns EGRIN RH19 ..180 C3
  SKENS SW7 ....19 M1
  SNWD SE25 * 45 P5
Cornwall Gardens Wk
  SKENS SW7 ....19 M1
Cornwall Gv CHSWK W4 ...18 C3
Cornwallis Cl CTHM CR3 ..101 L2
Cornwall Ms South
  SKENS SW7 ....19 N1

Cornwall Ms West
SKENS SW7 * 19 M1
Cornwall Rd BELMT SM2 .....61 K6
CROY/NA CR0 .....2 A3
TWK TW1 .....25 P3
Cornwall Wy STA TW18 .....22 B9
Cornwall Rd WDSR SL4 .....20 F2
Coronation Av ALDT GU11 ...108 D7
ASC SL5 .....34 A7
EGRIN RH19 .....180 D4
HYS/HAR UB3 .....15 H2
YTLY GU46 .....67 H1
The Coronet HORL RH6 .....159 M3
Corporation Av HSLWW TW4 ..15 N9
Corrib Dr SUT SM1 .....62 A4
Corrie Gdns VW GU25 .....36 A8
Corrie Rd ADL/WDHM KT15 ..55 P3
WOKS/MYFD GU22 .....72 F9
Corrigan Av COUL/CHIP CR5 ..80 C4
Corringway FLEETS GU52 .....87 P4
Corry Rd GSHT GU26 .....165 M5
Corsair Cl STWL/WRAY TW19 ..22 G3
Corsair Rd STWL/WRAY TW19 ..23 H3
Corscombe Cl KUTN/CMB KT2 ..27 N4
Corsehill St
STRHM/NOR SW16 .....29 M9
Corsham Wy CWTH RG45 .....49 M4
Corsletts Av HORS RH12 .....191 L7
Cortayne Rd FUL/PGN SW6 * ..19 K7
Cortis Rd PUT/ROE SW15 .....27 N1
Cortis Ter PUT/ROE SW15 .....27 N1
Corunna Dr SWTR RH13 .....192 E8
Cosbycote Av HNHL SE24 .....30 D1
Cosdach Av WLGTN SM6 .....62 F6
Cosedge Crs CROY/NA CR0 .....63 J4
Cosford Rd MFD/CHID GU8 ...148 F4
Cosmur Cl SHB W12 .....18 D1
Costells Meadow
BH/WHM TN16 .....105 H6
Coteford St TOOT SW17 .....29 J7
Cotelands CROY/NA CR0 .....3 J5
Cotford Rd THHTH CR7 .....45 L5
Cotherstone Rd
BRXS/STRHM SW2 .....30 A4
Cotland Acres REDH RH11 ...119 P7
Cotsford Av NWMAL KT3 .....42 A6
Cotsford Rd NWMAL KT3 .....42 A6
Cotswold Cl CRAWW RH11 ...176 E5
ESH/CLAY KT10 .....58 F1
FARN GU14 .....68 A9
STA TW18 .....22 D8
Cotswold Cl SWTR RH13 .....192 D8
Cotswold Rd BELMT SM2 .....61 M8
HPTN TW12 .....49 K8
SHST GU47 .....49 K8
Cotswold St WNWD SE27 .....30 C1
Cotswold Wy WPK KT4 .....60 G1
Cottage Cl CHERT KT16 .....54 C5
HORS RH12 .....192 G4
Cottage Farm Wy
EGH TW20 * 50 A6
Cottage Gdns FARN GU14 .....88 B3
Cottage Gv SURB KT6 .....41 K7
Cottage Pl CRAWE RH10 * ...176 G5
Cottage Rd HOR/WEW KT19 ..60 B6
Cottenham Dr RYNPK SW20 ..42 F1
Cottenham Park Rd
RYNPK SW20 .....42 F1
Cottenham Pl RYNPK SW20 ..42 F1
Cottenhams LING RH7 .....142 G2
Cotterell Cl BNFD RG42 .....32 D1
Cotterill Rd SURB KT6 .....59 M1
Cottesbrooke Cl
DTCH/LGLY SL3 .....13 H6
Cottesloe Cl CHOB/PIR GU24 ..70 F5
Cottesmore BRAK RG12 .....32 C8
Cottesmore Gdns KENS W8 ..19 M1
Cottimore Av WOT/HER KT12 ..39 K9
Cottimore Crs
WOT/HER KT12 .....39 K8
Cottimore La WOT/HER KT12 ..39 L9
Cottimore Ter
WOT/HER KT12 .....39 K8
Cottingham Av HORS RH12 ...192 C3
Cottingham Rd PGE/AN SE20 ..46 D1
Cottington Rd FELT TW13 .....24 E7
Cotton Cl ALDT GU11 .....108 B3
Cottongrass Cl CROY/NA CR0 ..46 D9
Cotton Rw BTSEA SW11 .....19 N8
RDKG RH5 .....154 D4
Cotts Wood Dr RGUE GU4 .....92 D2
Couchmore Av
ESH/CLAY KT10 .....58 E1
Coulsdon Court Rd
COUL/CHIP CR5 .....81 H5
Coulsdon La COUL/CHIP CR5 ..80 C4
Coulsdon Pl CTHM CR3 .....101 M2
Coulsdon Ri COUL/CHIP CR5 ..80 G5
Coulsdon Rd COUL/CHIP CR5 ..81 H5
Coulter Rd HMSMTH W6 .....18 F1
Countisbury Gdns
ADL/WDHM KT15 .....55 M4
Country Wy FELT TW13 .....24 D8
Country Oak La CRAWE RH10 ..158 G9
Country Oak Wy
WIM/MER SW19 .....176 G1
Country Pde BTFD TW8 * 17 H1
County Rd THHTH CR7 .....45 K3
Courland Rd
ADL/WDHM KT15 .....55 N4
Course Rd ASC SL5 .....34 A4
Court Av COUL/CHIP CR5 .....81 H7
Court Bushes Rd CTHM CR3 ..82 A8
Court Cl EGRIN RH19 .....180 E2
FELT TW13 .....24 A6
LIPH GU30 .....182 E7
Court Close Av FELT TW13 .....25 J6
Court Crs CHSGTN KT9 .....59 K5
EGRIN RH19 .....180 E2
Court Downs Rd BECK BR3 .....47 H3
Court Dr CROY/NA CR0 .....63 H3

SUT SM1 .....61 J4
Courtenay Av BELMT SM2 .....61 J7
COUL/CHIP CR5 .....81 H7
Courtenay Dr BECK BR3 .....47 L3
Courtenay Ms
WOKN/KNAP GU21 .....11 L1
Courtenay Rd FNM GU9 .....108 A8
PGE/AN SE20 .....46 D1
WOKN/KNAP GU21 .....11 L1
WPK KT4 .....60 G2
Court Farm Av
HOR/WEW KT19 .....60 B4
Court Farm Gdns
HOR/WEW KT19 .....60 B4
Court Farm Pk WARL CR6 * ..82 A5
Court Farm Rd WARL CR6 .....82 A7
Courtfield Gdns ECT SW5 .....19 M2
Courtfield Ms SKENS SW5 * ..19 N2
Courtfield Ri WWKM BR4 .....65 K2
Courtfield Rd ASHF TW15 .....23 L9
SKENS SW5 .....19 N2
Court Gdns CBLY GU15 .....68 F3
Court Haw BNSTD SM7 .....80 A4
Court Hi COUL/CHIP CR5 .....80 A7
Court La EGH TW20 * 21 N1
DUL SE21 .....30 G3
Court Lane Gdns DUL SE21 ..30 F3
Courtleas COB KT11 .....76 A2
Court Lodge Rd HORL RH6 ..140 A9
Courtmead Cl HNHL SE24 .....30 D2
Courtmoor Av FLEETS GU52 ..86 F8
Courtney Crs CAR SM5 .....61 P7
Courtney Pl COB KT11 .....75 P1
Courtney Rd CROY/NA CR0 ..63 J2
HTHAIR TW6 .....14 A3
WIM/MER SW19 .....44 A1
Courtney Wy HTHAIR TW6 ..14 C8
Courtrai Rd BROCKY SE4 .....31 M2
Court Rd ALDT GU11 .....108 C4
BNSTD SM7 .....79 L4
CTHM CR3 .....101 M3
GDST RH9 .....122 C2
NWDGN UB2 .....15 P2
SNWD SE25 .....45 P3
Courts Hill Rd HASM GU27 ...184 C4
Courts Mount Rd
HASM GU27 .....184 C4
The Courts
STRHM/NOR SW16 .....44 G1
Court St BMLY BR1 .....47 N3
The Court GUW GU2 * 6 D7
WARL CR6 .....82 A5
Court Wy WHTN TW2 .....25 P5
Court Wood La CROY/NA CR0 ..64 F8
The Courtyard BF/WBF KT14 ..73 L1
BH/WHM TN16 .....105 H6
CRAWE RH10 * 176 G6
EGRIN RH19 .....180 C2
HORS RH12 * 192 B8
Coutts Av CHSGTN KT9 .....59 L4
Coval Gdns
MORT/ESHN SW14 .....17 P9
Coval La MORT/ESHN SW14 ..18 A9
Coval Rd MORT/ESHN SW14 ..17 P9
Coveham Crs COB KT11 .....75 J2
Coventry Rd SNWD SE25 .....46 A5
Coverack Cl CROY/NA CR0 .....46 E9
Coverdale Gdns CROY/NA CR0 ..3 J5
Cove Rd FARN GU14 .....88 C3
FLEETN GU51 .....87 J4
Covert Cl CRAWE RH10 .....177 H4
Covert La BRAK RG12 .....32 D5
Coverton Rd TOOT SW17 .....29 H7
Coverts Cl FNM GU9 .....108 B3
Coverts Rd ESH/CLAY KT10 ..58 F6
The Covert ASC SL5 .....34 B8
FARN GU14 .....68 A8
NRWD SE19 * 45 P1
Covey Cl FARN GU14 .....68 C8
WIM/MER SW19 .....43 K9
The Covey CRAWE RH10 .....177 N5
Covington Gdns
STRHM/NOR SW16 .....45 K1
Covington Wy
STRHM/NOR SW16 .....30 B9
Cowden St CAT SE6 .....31 P7
Cowdray Cl CRAWE RH10 .....177 H4
Cowdrey Rd WIM/MER SW19 ..28 E9
Cowfold Cl CRAWW RH11 .....176 C8
Cowick Rd TOOT SW17 .....29 J7
Cow La GODL GU7 .....131 K9
Cowleaze Rd KUTN/CMB KT2 ..8 E3
Cowley Av CHERT KT16 .....37 K8
Cowley Cl SAND/SEL CR2 .....64 B7
Cowley Crs WOT/HER KT12 ..57 L3
Cowley La CHERT KT16 .....37 K8
Cowley Rd MORT/ESHN SW14 ..18 C8
Cowper Av SUT SM1 .....61 P3

Cowper Cl CHERT KT16 .....37 K7
Cowper Gdns WLGTN SM6 ..62 E5
Cowper Rd
RCHPK/HAM TW10 .....26 E8
WIM/MER SW19 .....28 F9
Cowshot Crs CHOB/PIR GU24 ..70 D9
Cowslip La RDKG RH5 .....96 C8
Coxbridge Mdw FNM GU9 .....4 D9
Coxcombe La
MFD/CHID GU8 .....168 A7
Coxdean EPSOM KT18 .....78 G8
Coxes Av SHPTN TW17 * 38 G4
Coxgreen SHST GU47 .....67 P2
Cox Green Rd HORS RH12 .....171 J4
Coxheath Rd FLEETS GU52 ..86 E9
Cox La CHSGTN KT9 .....59 M3
HOR/WEW KT19 .....59 P4
Coxley Ri PUR/KEN CR8 .....81 L2
Coxmoor Cl FLEETS GU52 .....107 J1
Coxs Av SHPTN TW17 .....38 G4
Coxs Cottages WARL CR6 * ..83 L3
Coxwell Rd NRWD SE19 .....45 N1
Crabbet Rd CRAWE RH10 .....177 L4
Crab Hi BECK BR3 .....47 K1
Crab Hill La REDH RH1 .....140 C4
Crabtree Cl GT/LBKH KT23 ..96 C6
Crabtree Dr LHD/OX KT22 .....97 J5
Crabtree La BOR GU35 .....164 B6
FUL/PGN SW6 .....19 H5
GT/LBKH KT23 .....96 C6
LHD/OX KT22 .....98 A6
RDKG RH5 .....116 F1
Crabtree Rd CBLY GU15 .....68 D6
CRAWW RH11 .....176 F4
EGH TW20 .....36 C3
Cradocks Av ASHTD KT21 .....77 M5
Cradhurst Cl DORK RH4 .....116 D8
Craigans CRAWW RH11 .....176 D5
Craigen Av CROY/NA CR0 .....46 B9
Craignair Rd
BRXS/STRHM SW2 .....30 A3
Craignish Av
STRHM/NOR SW16 .....45 H3
Craig Rd RCHPK/HAM TW10 ..26 B7
Craigwell Av FELT TW13 .....24 B6
Craigwell Cl STA TW18 .....37 J2
Crakell Rd REIG RH2 .....119 N6
Crake Pl SHST GU47 .....49 P9
Cramhurst La
MFD/CHID GU8 .....149 M6
Crammond Cl HMSMTH W6 ..19 J4
Crampshaw La ASHTD KT21 ..77 M9
Crampton Rd PGE/AN SE20 ..31 K9
Cranborne Av NWDGN UB2 ..16 A2
Cranborne Wk CRAWE RH10 ..177 J7
Cranbourne Cl HORL RH6 .....140 A9
STRHM/NOR SW16 .....44 G4
Cranbrook Cl HAYES BR2 .....47 N7
Cranbrook Ct FLEETN GU51 ..86 C4
Cranbrook Dr ESH/CLAY KT10 ..40 A9
WHTN TW2 .....25 J4
Cranbrook Rd CHSWK W4 .....18 C3
DEPT SE8 .....31 P1
HSLWW TW4 .....15 L3
THHTH CR7 .....45 L3
WIM/MER SW19 .....43 J1
Cranbury Rd FUL/PGN SW6 ..19 M7
Crane Av ISLW TW7 .....25 P1
Cranebank Ms TWK TW1 * ..26 A1
Cranebrook WHTN TW2 .....25 K5
Crane Ct MORT/ESHN SW14 * ..18 A9
SHST GU47 .....49 P9
Craneford Cl WHTN TW2 .....25 N3
Craneford Wy WHTN TW2 .....25 N3
Crane Gdns HYS/HAR UB3 ..15 H2
Crane Lodge Rd HEST TW5 .....15 K4
Crane Park Rd WHTN TW2 .....25 J5
Crane Rd STWL/WRAY TW19 ..23 H1
WHTN TW2 .....25 M4
Cranes Dr BRYLDS KT5 .....41 L5
Cranes Pk SURB KT6 .....41 L5
Cranes Park Av SURB KT6 .....41 L5
Cranes Park Crs BRYLDS KT5 ..41 M5
Craneswater HYS/HAR UB3 ..15 H5
Craneswater Pk NWDGN UB2 ..16 A3
Crane Wy WHTN TW2 .....25 K3
Cranfield Rd East CAR SM5 ..62 C7
Cranfield Rd West CAR SM5 * ..62 B7
Cranford Av FLEETS GU52 .....106 E1
STWL/WRAY TW19 .....23 H3
Cranford Cl PUR/KEN CR8 .....81 L2
RYNPK SW20 .....42 F1
STWL/WRAY TW19 .....23 H3
Cranford Dr HYS/HAR UB3 ..15 H2
Cranford La HEST TW5 .....15 L5
HTHAIR TW6 .....14 B4
HYS/HAR UB3 .....14 F4
Cranford Park Dr YTLY GU46 ..67 H2
Cranford Park Rd
HYS/HAR UB3 .....15 H2
Cranford Ri ESH/CLAY KT10 ..58 C4
Cranleigh Cl PGE/AN SE20 ..46 B3
SAND/SEL CR2 .....82 A1
Cranleigh Ct FARN GU14 .....88 B3
Cranleigh Gdns
KUTN/CMB KT2 .....26 E9
SAND/SEL CR2 .....82 A1
SNWD SE25 .....45 N4
SUT SM1 .....61 M1
Cranleigh Md CRAN GU6 .....171 J1
Cranleigh Rd CRAN GU6 .....153 N8
ESH/CLAY KT10 .....40 C9
FELT TW13 .....24 A6
SHGR GU5 .....132 G6
WIM/MER SW19 .....43 L4
Cranley Cl GU GU1 .....112 C5
Cranley Gdns SKENS SW7 .....19 N3
WLGTN SM6 .....62 E6
Cranley Ms SKENS SW7 .....19 N3
Cranley Pl SKENS SW7 .....19 P2

WOKN/KNAP GU21 * 71 K7
WIM/MER SW19 .....28 D6
WWKM BR4 .....47 L7
YTLY GU46 .....67 H1
Cranley Rd GU GU1 .....7 K3
WIM/MER SW19 .....28 D6
Cranmer Av WEA W13 .....17 H1
Cranmer Cl MRDN SM4 .....43 H7
WARL CR6 .....82 E6
WEY KT13 .....56 C6
Cranmer Ct HPTN TW12 .....25 J8
Cranmer Farm Cl MTCM CR4 ..44 B5
Cranmer Gdns WARL CR6 .....82 E6
Cranmer Rd CROY/NA CR0 ..2 B5
HPTN TW12 .....25 J8
KUTN/CMB KT2 .....26 D8
MTCM CR4 .....44 B5
Cranmer Ter TOOT SW17 .....28 G8
Cranmore Cl ALDT GU11 .....108 A5
Cranmore Gdns ALDT GU11 ..108 A5
Cranmore La ALDT GU11 .....108 A5
EHSLY KT24 .....94 D9
Cranmore Rd FRIM GU16 .....89 H3
Cranston Cl HSLW TW3 .....15 N7
REIG RH2 .....119 N7
Cranston Rd EGRIN RH19 .....180 E1
FSTH SE23 .....31 L4
Cranstoun Cl RGUW GU3 .....111 H1
Cranwell Gv LTWR GU18 .....51 P9
SHPTN TW17 .....38 B5
Craster Rd BRXS/STRHM SW2 ..30 A3
Cravan Av FELT TW13 .....24 B5
Craven Cl RFNM GU10 .....127 N1
Craven Gdns WIM/MER SW19 ..28 E8
Craven Rd CRAWE RH10 .....177 L6
CROY/NA CR0 .....46 B9
KUTN/CMB KT2 .....8 G3
The Cravens HORL RH6 .....160 B1
Crawford Cl ISLW TW7 .....16 E7
Crawford Gdns CBLY GU15 ..68 D3
SWTR RH13 .....192 D7
Crawfurd Wy EGRIN RH19 .....180 E1
Crawley Av CRAWE RH10 .....177 M1
CRAWW RH11 .....176 E8
Crawley Down Rd
EGRIN RH19 .....161 M9
Crawley Dr CBLY GU15 .....69 H3
Crawley Goods Yd
CRAWE RH10 .....177 L1
Crawley Hi CBLY GU15 .....69 H2
Crawley La CRAWE RH10 .....177 N2
RHWH RH17 .....195 N5
Crawley Market
CRAWE RH10 .....176 G5
Crawley Rdg CBLY GU15 .....69 H2
Crawley Rd HORS RH12 .....192 A5
Crawley Wood Cl CBLY GU15 ..69 H3
Crawshaw Rd CHERT KT16 ..55 H5
Crawters Cl CRAWE RH10 .....177 J4
Cray Av ASHTD KT21 .....77 M5
Crayke Hi CHSGTN KT9 .....59 L6
Crayonne Cl SUN TW16 .....38 G2
Crealock St
WAND/EARL SW18 .....28 E2
Creasys Dr CRAWW RH11 .....194 E2
Crebor St EDUL SE22 .....31 H2
Credenhill St
STRHM/NOR SW16 .....29 M9
Crediton Wy ESH/CLAY KT10 ..58 G3
Credon Cl FARN GU14 .....88 A2
Creek Cottages
E/WMO/HCT KT8 * 40 E5
Creek Rd E/WMO/HCT KT8 ..40 E5
The Creek SUN TW16 .....39 H6
Creeland Gv CAT SE6 .....31 N4
Cree's Meadow BFOR GU20 * ..52 D6
Crefeld Cl FUL/PGN SW6 .....19 K1
Creighton Rd EA W5 .....17 K1
Cremorne Est WBPTN SW10 * ..19 P4
Cremorne Gdns
HOR/WEW KT19 .....60 B7
Cremorne Rd WBPTN SW10 ..19 N5
Crescent Ct HORL RH6 * 159 K3
Crescent Gdns
WIM/MER SW19 .....28 D6
Crescent Gv MTCM CR4 .....44 A5
Crescent La ASHV GU12 .....109 K1
CLAP SW4 .....29 N1
Crescent Rd BECK BR3 .....47 H3
BMLY BR1 .....47 N1
CTHM CR3 .....102 A4
EGRIN RH19 .....162 B4
REDH RH1 .....121 L4
REIG RH2 .....119 L2
RYNPK SW20 .....28 D9
SHPTN TW17 .....38 E6
The Crescent ASHF TW15 .....23 J8
BARN SW13 .....18 D7
BECK BR3 .....46 G2
BELMT SM2 .....61 L9
BRAK RG12 .....32 E5
CBLY GU15 .....68 F4
CTHM CR3 .....102 C3
E/WMO/HCT KT8 .....39 P5
EGH TW20 .....21 L9
EGRIN RH19 .....162 B4
EPSOM KT18 .....78 C3
FARN GU14 .....88 E4
FLEETN GU51 .....86 D9
FNM GU9 .....107 P6
GUW GU2 .....111 N6
HORL RH6 .....159 K3
HORS RH12 .....191 P8
HYS/HAR UB3 .....15 H3
LHD/OX KT22 .....97 H2
NWMAL KT3 .....42 A3
REDH RH1 .....119 P6
REIG RH2 .....119 M3
SHPTN TW17 .....38 E6
SNWD SE25 .....45 M7
SURB KT6 .....41 L6
SUT SM1 .....61 P4
WEY KT13 .....56 C2
Crescent Wy HORL RH6 .....159 K3
STRHM/NOR SW16 .....45 H1
Crescent Wood Rd SYD SE26 ..31 H6
Cresford Rd FUL/PGN SW6 ..19 M6
Cressall Cl LHD/OX KT22 .....77 H1
Cressall Md LHD/OX KT22 .....77 H9
Cressida Cha BNFD RG42 .....32 G3
Cressingham Gv SUT SM1 ..61 N3
Cresswell Rd NRWD SE19 .....45 N8
FELT TW13 .....24 F6
SNWD SE25 .....45 A5
TWK TW1 .....26 C2
Cressy Ct HMSMTH W6 .....18 F1
Cressys Cnr HSLW TW3 * 16 B8
Cresta Dr ADL/WDHM KT15 ..55 K8
Creston Av
WOKN/KNAP GU21 .....71 L6
Creston Wy WPK KT4 .....43 H9
Crest Rd HAYES BR2 .....47 M8
SAND/SEL CR2 .....63 N6
The Crest BRYLDS KT5 .....41 N6
Crestway PUT/ROE SW15 .....27 L2
Crestwood Wy HSLWW TW4 ..24 G1
Creswell WOKN/KNAP GU21 * ..71 K6
Creswell Cnr
WOKN/KNAP GU21 * 71 K6
Crewdson Rd HORL RH6 .....159 L1
Crewe's Av WARL CR6 .....82 C5
Crewe's Cl WARL CR6 .....82 C5
Crewe's La WARL CR6 .....82 D5
Crichton Av WLGTN SM6 .....62 F4
Crichton Rd CAR SM5 .....62 A6
Cricket Ct EGRIN RH19 .....162 D9
Cricketers Cl CHERT KT16 .....59 K4
RDKG RH5 .....155 K8
Cricketers La BFOR GU20 .....52 D4
Cricketers Wk SYD SE26 .....31 J8
Cricket Field Gv CWTH RG45 ..49 P5
Cricket Field Rd HORS RH12 ..192 A9
Cricketfield Rd WDR/YW UB7 ..13 N2
Cricket Gn MFD/CHID GU8 ...168 B2
MTCM CR4 .....44 B5
Cricket Hill La BLKW GU17 ..67 H5
Cricket La BECK BR3 .....31 M9
REDH RH1 .....121 H7
Cricket Vw WEY KT13 .....56 G1
Cricklade Av
BRXS/STRHM SW2 .....30 A5
Crieff Rd WAND/EARL SW18 ..28 F2
Criffel Av BRXS/STRHM SW2 ..29 N5
Crimea Rd ALDT GU11 .....108 C3
FRIM GU16 .....69 M8
Cripley Rd FARN GU14 .....87 P2
Cripplecroft H
MFD/CHID GU8 .....185 N4
Crispen Rd FELT TW13 .....24 F7
Crisp Gdns BNFD RG42 .....32 A3
Crispin Crs CROY/NA CR0 .....45 J1
Cristowe Rd FUL/PGN SW6 ..19 K7
Critchmere Hl HASM GU27 ..183 P5
Critchmere La HASM GU27 ..183 N4
Critchmere V HASM GU27 .....183 N4
Critten La RDKG RH5 .....115 M3
Cricket Cl GSHT GU26 .....165 N5
Cricketers Ms
WAND/EARL SW18 .....28 E1
Crocker Cl ASC SL5 .....33 N2
Crockers La LING RH7 .....142 D9
Crockerton Rd TOOT SW17 ..29 J5
Crockford Cl
ADL/WDHM KT15 .....55 N4
Crockford Park Rd
ADL/WDHM KT15 .....55 N4
Crockham Cl CRAWW RH11 ..176 F7
Crocknorth Rd EHSLY KT24 ..115 N2
Crocus Cl CROY/NA CR0 .....46 D9
Croffets KWD/TDW/WH KT20 ..99 H1
WWKM BR4 .....47 H5
Croft Cl HYS/HAR UB3 .....14 E5
Crofton ASHTD KT21 .....77 L7
Crofton Av CHSWK W4 .....18 B5
WOT/HER KT12 .....57 L2
Crofton Cl BRAK RG12 .....32 C6
CHERT KT16 .....54 C6
Crofton Gate Wy
BROCKY SE4 .....31 M1
Crofton Park Rd BROCKY SE4 ..31 N2
Crofton Ter RCH/KEW TW9 ..17 N9
Croft Rd ALDT GU11 .....108 D6
BH/WHM TN16 .....104 F6
CTHM CR3 .....102 F2
GODL GU7 .....131 K9
MFD/CHID GU8 .....149 M7
STRHM/NOR SW16 .....45 J1
SUT SM1 .....61 P4
WIM/MER SW19 .....43 N1
Crofts Cl MFD/CHID GU8 .....168 A6
The Crofts SHPTN TW17 .....38 G5
Croft Ter BNFD RG42 .....32 D1
The Croft BNFD RG42 .....32 D1
CRAWW RH11 .....176 D5

HEST TW5 ....15 N5
Croft Wy FRIM GU16 ....69 H7
HORS RH12 ....191 P7
RCHPK/HAM TW10 ....26 A5
Croham Manor Rd
SAND/SEL CR2 ....63 N6
Croham CI SAND/SEL CR2 ....63 N5
Croham Mt SAND/SEL CR2 ....63 P4
Croham Park Av
SAND/SEL CR2 ....63 N4
Croham Rd SAND/SEL CR2 ....63 N4
Croham Valley Rd
SAND/SEL CR2 ....64 A5
Croindene Rd
STRHM/NOR SW16 ....44 G2
Cromer Hyde MRDN SM4 * 43 M6
Cromer Rd HTHAIR TW6 ....14 C8
SNWD SE25 ....46 B4
TOOT SW17 ....29 K9
Cromer Rd West HTHAIR TW6 ..14 C8
Cromer Villas Rd
WAND/EARL SW18 ....28 C1
Cromford CI ORP BR6 ....28 C2
Cromford Wy NWMAL KT3 ......42 B2
Crompton Flds
CRAWE RH10 ....177 H2
Crompton Wy CRAWE RH10 ..177 H2
Cromwell Av HAYES BR2 ....47 P5
HMSMTH W6 ....18 F2
NWMAL KT3 ....42 D6
Cromwell CI CHSWK W4 * 17 P3
WOT/HER KT12 ....39 K9
Cromwell Crs ECT SW5 ....19 L2
Cromwell Gv CTHM CR3 ....101 L1
HMSMTH W6 ....18 G1
Cromwell Ms SKENS SW7 ......19 P2
Cromwell PI CRAN GU171 ......171 J2
ECRIN RH19 ....180 E4
MORT/ESHN SW14 ....18 A7
SKENS SW7 ....19 P2
Cromwell Rd ASC SL5 ....34 B5
BECK BR3 ....46 E3
CBLY GU15 ....68 F1
CROY/NA CRO 45 M8
CTHM CR3 ....101 L1
ECT SW5 ....19 M2
FELT TW13 ....24 C4
HSLW TW3 ....16 B3
KUT KT1 ....8 E3
REDH RH1 ....120 B5
TEDD TW11 ....25 P9
WIM/MER SW19 ....28 D8
WOT/HER KT12 ....39 K9
WPK KT4 ....60 B2
Cromwell St HSLW TW3 * 16 A9
Cromwell Ter HSLW TW3 * 16 A9
Cromwell Wy FARN GU14 ......68 D9
Crondace Rd FUL/PGN SW6 ..19 L6
Crondall Ct CBLY GU15 ....68 B8
Crondall End YTLY GU46 ....66 G3
Crondall La RFNM GU10 ......126 C3
Crondall Rd FLEETN GU51 ..106 C6
RFNM GU10 ....126 E6
Cronks HI REIG RH2 ....119 N6
Cronks Hill CI REDH RH1 ......119 P7
Cronks Hill Rd REIG RH2 ......119 P7
Crookham Reach
FLEETS GU52 ....106 E1
Crookham Rd FLEETN GU51 ..86 E9
FUL/PGN SW6 ....19 K6
Crooksbury Rd RGUW GU10 ..128 D2
Crosby CI FELT TW13 ....24 F7
Crosby Hill Dr CBLY GU15 ......69 H1
Crosby Wy FNM GU9 ....4 D5
Crossacres
WOKS/MYFD GU22 ....73 J5
Cross Deep TWK TW1 ....25 N6
Cross Deep Gdns TWK TW1 ..25 N5
Cross Feli BRAK RG12 ....32 C5
Crossfield PI WEY KT13 ....56 D6
Cross Gdns FRIM GU16 ....69 H1
Cross Gates CI BRAK RG12 ....33 H4
Cross Keys CRAWE RH10 ....176 G5
Cross Lances Rd HSLW TW3 ..16 B9
Crossland Rd REDH RH1 ......120 C5
THHTH CR7 ....45 L6
Crosslands Av NWMAL UB2 ..15 P3
Crosslands Pde
NWMAL UB2 ....16 A3
Crosslands Rd
HOR/WEW KT19 ....60 B5
Cross La CHERT KT16 ....54 F8
FRIM GU16 ....89 H1
HORL RH6 ....160 D4
Cross Lanes GU 7 J3
Crossley CI BH/WHM TN16 ....84 A9
Cross Oak La REDH RH1 ......140 G8
Crosspath CRAWE RH10 * 177 H4
Cross Rd ASC SL5 ....34 F9
ASHV GU12 ....109 K3
BELMT SM2 ....61 L8
CROY/NA CRO 3 F1
FARN GU14 ....88 A4
FELT TW13 ....24 F7
KUTN/CMB KT2 ....9 G1
PUR/KEN CR8 ....81 K2
SUT SM1 ....61 N6
WEY KT13 ....56 D3
WIM/MER SW19 ....43 L1
The Crossroads EHSLY KT24 ..95 M8
Cross St BARN SW13 ....18 C7
FARN GU14 ....88 B4
HPTN TW12 ....25 J9
Crosswater La RFNM GU10 ..147 H8
Crossway BRAK RG12 * 32 F3
NWMAL KT3 ....42 G5
WOT/HER KT12 ....39 K9
Crossways ASHV GU12 ....108 G3
BELMT SM2 ....61 P7

BH/WHM TN16 ....84 A9
CRAWE RH10 ....177 K4
EGH TW20 ....22 A9
EHSLY KT24 ....95 M7
RFNM GU10 ....19 P4
SAND/SEL CR2 ....64 F6
SUN TW16 ....39 N7
Crossways Av EGRIN RH19 ..180 B2
Crossways CI CRAWE RH10 ..177 J4
Crossways La REIG RH2 ....99 H8
Crossways Rd BECK BR3 ......165 N5
OSHT GU26 ....30 C6
MTCM CR4 ....44 D4
The Crossways BRYLDS KT5 * ..41 P9
COUL/CHIP CR5 ....81 H8
GUW GU2 ....111 M7
HEST TW5 ....15 P5
HEST TW5 ....15 P5
Crosswell CI SHPTN TW17 ....38 E5
Crossweys GUW GU2 * 6 C6
Crouch CI BECK BR3 ....31 P9
Crouch House Rd EDEN TN8 ..144 E12
Crouchmans CI SYD SE26 ......30 C6
Crouch Oak La
ADL/WDHM KT15 ....65 J4
Crowberry CI CRAWW RH11 ..176 D9
Crowborough La WARL CR6 ....82 E7
Crowborough Rd WARL CR6 ..82 E7
Crowborough Rd TOOT SW17 ..29 K8
Crowhurst La CRAWE RH10 ..177 P5
Crowhurst La LING RH7 ....123 K9
Crowhurst Md GDST RH9 ......122 C1
Crowhurst Rd LING RH7 ....143 K7
Crowhurst Village Rd
LING RH7 ....143 L3
Crowland Rd HYS/HAR UB3 ..14 A2
Crowland Rd THHTH CR7 * 45 M5
Crowland Wk MRDN SM4 ......43 M7
Crowley Crs CROY/NA CRO 63 J4
Crown Ar KUT KT1 ....8 C5
Crownbourne Ct SUT SM1 * ..61 M3
Crown CI DTCH/LGLY SL3 ......12 C5
WOT/HER KT12 ....39 L8
Crown DI NRWD SE19 ....30 D9
Crown Dr FNM GU9 ....108 C9
Crown Gdns FLEETN GU51 ....87 H7
Crown Hts GU GU1 ....112 C8
Crown HI CROY/NA CRO * 2 D4
Crown Hill Ct ASC SL5 ....34 B6
Crown La FNM GU9 ....108 C9
STRHM/NOR SW16 ....30 B8
VW GU25 ....36 B7
WIM/MER SW19 ....43 L4
Crown Lane Gdns
WNWD SE27 * 30 B8
Crown Meadow
DTCH/LGLY SL3 ....12 F5
Crown Pde MRDN SM4 * 43 M6
Crownpits La GODL GU7 ......150 D1
Crown PI SHST GU47 * 49 P8
Crown RI CHERT KT16 ....37 K9
Crown Rd EDEN TN8 ....145 H2
NWMAL KT3 ....42 A2
SUT SM1 ....61 M8
TWK TW1 ....26 A2
VW GU25 ....36 A7
WIM/MER SW19 ....43 L5
Crown Rw BRAK RG12 ....32 F7
Crown Sq WOKN/KNAP GU21 ..10 E3
Crownstone Rd
BRXS/STRHM SW2 ....30 B1
Crown St EGH TW20 ....21 M8
Crown Ter RCH/KEW TW9 ......17 M8
Crowntree CI ISLW TW7 ....16 F4
Crown Yd HSLW TW3 * 16 B8
Crowther Av BTFD TW8 ....17 L3
Crowther Rd SNWD SE25 ......46 A5
Crowthorne Cl
WAND/EARL SW18 ....27 N4
Crowthorne Rd BRAK RG12 ..32 B9
SHST GU47 ....49 M9
Crowthorne Rd North
BRAK RG12 ....32 D4
Croxden Wk MRDN SM4 ....43 N7
Croxted CI DUL SE21 ....30 D3
Croxted Rd DUL SE21 ....30 D4
Croyde CI FARN GU14 ....68 C3
Croyde CI FARN GU14 ....88 A4
Croydonbarn La GDST RH9 ..142 A9
The Croydon F/O
CROY/NA CRO 2 C7
Croydon Gv CROY/NA CRO 2 A4
Croydon La BNSTD SM7 ....79 P7
Croydon La South
BNSTD SM7 ....79 P8
Croydon Rd BH/WHM TN16 ..104 C6
CTHM CR3 ....102 A2
MTCM CR4 ....44 D6
PGE/AN SE20 ....46 B3
REIG RH2 ....119 N4
WARL CR6 ....82 A3
WLGTN SM6 ....62 D3
WWKM BR4 ....65 L2
Croylands Dr SURB KT6 ....41 L8
Croysdale Av SUN TW16 ....39 J4
Crozier Dr SAND/SEL CR2 ....64 A7
Cruikshank Lea SHST GU47 ..68 A2
Crunden Rd SAND/SEL CR2 ..63 N6
Crusader Gdns CROY/NA CRO ..3 K6
Crusoe Rd MTCM CR4 ....44 B1
Crutchfield La HORL RH6 ......139 L7
WOT/HER KT12 ....39 K9
Crystal Palace Pde
NRWD SE19 * 30 G9
Crystal Palace Park Rd
SYD SE26 ....31 H8
Crystal Palace Rd EDUL SE22 ..30 D2
Crystal Ter NRWD SE19 ....30 E9
Cubitt St CROY/NA CRO 65 H3
Cubitt Wy WOKN/KNAP GU21 ..71 K7
Cuckfield CI CRAWW RH11 ..176 C8

Cuckmere Crs CRAWW RH1 ......RH1
Cuckoo La CHOB/PIR GU2 ......GU2
Cuckoo V CHOB/PIR GU2 ....GU2
Cuda's CI AH/WEW KT1 ....KT1
Cuddington Av WPK KT4 ......KT4
Cuddington CI
KWD/TDW/WH KT20 ....KT20
Cuddington Gld
HOR/WEW KT19 ....KT19
Cuddington Park CI
BNSTD SM7 ....79 K2
Cuddington La BELMT SM2 ....29 H1
Cudham CI BELMT SM2 ....61 L8
Cudham Dr CROY/NA CRO 65 H8
Cudham La North RSEV TN14 ..84 G3
Cudham La South RSEV TN14 ..84 G4
Cudham Rd BH/WHM TN16 ....84 C8
Cudworth La RDKG RH5 ....157 H3
Cudworth Pk RDKG RH5 ......157 K4
Cuffs HI CRAWE RH10 ....177 P9
Cullen CI YTLY GU46 ....66 G3
Cullens Ms ALDT GU11 * 108 C5
Cullerne CI EW KT17 ....78 C4
Cullesden Rd PUR/KEN CR8 ..81 K4
Cull's Rd RGUW GU3 ....110 B5
Culmer La MFD/CHID GU8 ....149 N9
Culmington Rd
SAND/SEL CR2 ....63 L6
Culmstock Rd BTSEA SW11 ..29 K1
Culsac Rd SURB KT6 ....59 L1
Culver CI WAND/EARL SW18 ..32 A1
Culverden Rd BAL SW12 ....29 M6
Culverden Ter WEY KT13 ....56 F2
Culver Dr OXTED RH8 ....123 L1
Culverhay ASHTD KT21 ....77 L5
Culverhouse Gdns
STRHM/NOR SW16 ....30 A7
Culverlands Crs ASHV GU12 ..109 H3
Culver Rd SHST GU47 ....49 P8
Culvers AV CAR SM5 ....62 B1
Culvers Retreat CAR SM5 ......44 B9
Culverstone CI HAYES BR2 ....47 M7
Culvers Wy CAR SM5 ....62 B1
Cumberland Av GUW GU2 ......91 N9
Cumberland Cl
HOR/WEW KT19 ....60 C8
RYNPK SW20 ....43 H1
TWK TW1 ....26 A2
Cumberland Dr BRAK RG12 ..32 F2
CHSGTN KT9 ....59 L2
ESH/CLAY KT10 ....58 D1
Cumberland Rd ASHF TW15 ..23 H6
BARN SW13 ....18 D6
CBLY GU15 ....69 L4
HAYES BR2 ....47 L5
RCH/KEW TW9 ....17 N6
SNWD SE25 ....46 A4
Cumberland Ter
PGE/AN SE20 * 46 B1
Cumberlow Av SNWD SE25 ....46 A4
Cumbernauld Gdns
SUN TW16 ....24 A8
Cumbrian Gdns SURB KT6 * ..41 K9
Cumbria Ct FARN GU14 ....88 G6
Cumnor Gdns EW KT17 ....60 E5
Cumnor Ri PUR/KEN CR8 ......81 L6
Cumnor Rd BELMT SM2 ....61 N5
Cumnor Wy BRAK RG12 ....32 G5
Cunliffe CI EPSOM KT18 ....78 A9
Cunliffe Rd HOR/WEW KT19 ..60 D3
Cunliffe St STRHM/NOR SW16 ..29 M9
Cunningham Av GU GU1 ......112 E4
Cunningham CI WWKM BR4 ..65 H1
Cunningham Rd BNSTD SM7 ..79 P4
Cunnington Rd FARN GU14 ....88 G6
Cunnington St CHSWK W4 ....18 A1
Cunworth Ct BRAK RG12 ....32 A7
Curfew Bell Rd CHERT KT16 ..37 K8
Curlew CI SAND/SEL CR2 ......64 D9
Curlew Gdns RGUE GU4 ......113 H3
Curley Hill Rd LTWR GU18 ......69 N1
Curling CI COUL/CHIP CR5 ....81 H8
Curley V GUW GU2 ....111 N7
Curry Bridge CI FARN GU14 ..68 B8
Currie Hill CI WIM/MER SW19 ..28 C2
Curtis CI BOR GU35 ....164 B5
CBLY GU15 ....69 H1
Curtis Field Rd
STRHM/NOR SW16 ....30 A7
Curtis La BOR GU35 ....164 B5
Curtis Rd DORK RH4 ....116 F6
HOR/WEW KT19 ....60 A3
HSLWW TW4 ....24 G3
Curvan CI EW KT17 ....60 D6
Curzon Av HORS RH12 ....192 A6
Curzon Br CHOB/PIR GU24 ....90 A2
Curzon CI WEY KT13 ....56 C3
Curzon Dr FLEETS GU52 ......106 E1
Curzon Rd THHTH CR7 ....45 J7
WEY KT13 ....56 C3
Cusack CI TWK TW1 * 25 N7
Cuthbert Gdns SNWD SE25 ..45 N4
Cuthbert Rd ASHV GU12 ....89 J9
CROY/NA CRO 2 B2
Cuttinglye La CRAWE RH10 ..179 H1
Cuttinglye Rd CRAWE RH10 ..179 J1
Cutts Rd ALDT GU11 ....88 F8
Cyclamen CI HPTN TW12 ......25 H9
Cyclamen Wy
HOR/WEW KT19 ....60 A4
Cygnet Av
EBED/NFELT TW14 ....24 D3
The Cygnets FELT TW13 ....24 F7
STA TW18 ....22 G4
Cypress FARN GU14 ....68 B7
Cypress Av WHTN TW2 ....25 K3
Cypress CI EWKG RG40 ....48 E1

/W GU25 ....36 D5
FLEETN GU51 ....87 J6
Cypress La EGH TW20 ....RH20
Dacres Est FSTH SE23 * 31 L6
Dacres Rd FSTH SE23 ....31 L6
Dade Wy NWDGN UB2 ....15 P3
HPTN TW12 ....25 H9
Daffodil CI CROY/NA CRO 44 G9
Daffodil Dr CHOB/PIR GU24 ..70 G5
Dafforne Rd TOOT SW17 ....29 K7
Dagden Rd RGUE GU4 ....132 C2
Dagley La RGUE GU4 ....132 B2
Dagmar Rd KUTN/CMB KT2 ......9 H1
NWDGN UB2 ....15 N1
SNWD SE25 ....45 N5
Dagnall Pk SNWD SE25 ....45 N6
Dagnall Rd SNWD SE25 ....45 N6
Dagnan Rd BAL SW12 ....29 L3
Dahlia Gdns MTCM CR4 ....44 F5
Dahomey Rd
STRHM/NOR SW16 ....29 M9
Daimler Wy WLGTN SM6 ....62 G6
Dairy CI BMLY BR1 * 47 P1
Dairyfields CRAWW RH11 ....176 D6
Dairy Gate Rd FARN GU14 ......88 D2
Dairy La EDEN TN8 ....124 F5
Dairymans Wk RGUE GU4 ......93 J7
Daisy CI CROY/NA CRO 46 D9
Daisy La FUL/PGN SW6 ....19 L8
Dakin CI CRAWE RH10 ....177 M9
The Dakins EGRIN RH19 ......180 D3
Dakota CI CROY/NA CRO 63 H6
Dalberg Rd
BRXS/STRHM SW2 ....30 B2
Dalby Rd WAND/EARL SW18 ..19 N9
Dalcross BRAK RG12 ....32 C7
Dalcross Rd HEST TW5 ....15 N7
Dale Av HSLWW TW4 ....15 N8
Dalebury Rd TOOT SW17 ....29 J5
Dale CI ADL/WDHM KT15 ......55 M4
ASC SL5 ....34 A9
HORS RH12 ....192 E5
RFNM GU10 ....127 K6
Dale Gdns SHST GU47 ....49 L9
Dalegarth Gdns
PUR/KEN CR8 ....81 M2
Daleham Av EGH TW20 ....21 M9
Dale Lodge Rd ASC SL5 ....34 C6
Dale Park Av CAR SM5 ....62 B1
Dale Park Rd NRWD SE19 ....45 L2
Daleside ORP BR6 ....81 J1
SUN TW16 ....39 H3
SUT SM1 ....61 K3
WOT/HER KT12 ....39 H4
Daleside Rd HOR/WEW KT19 ..60 B5
STRHM/NOR SW16 ....29 K9
Dale St CHSWK W4 ....18 C2
Dale Vw EPSOM KT18 ....97 P3
HASM GU27 ....184 A5
WOKN/KNAP GU21 ....71 N7
Dalewood Gdns
CRAWE RH10 ....177 J3
WPK KT4 ....60 F1
Dalkeith RG DUL SE21 ....30 D4
Dallas Rd CHEAM SM3 ....61 J7
SYD SE26 ....31 J7
Dallas Ter HYS/HAR UB3 * 15 H2
Dallaway Gdns EGRIN RH19 ..180 D2
Dalley Ct SHST GU47 ....49 N8
Dalling Rd HMSMTH W6 ....18 F2
Dallinger Rd DUL SE21 ....31 K1
Dalmain Rd FSTH SE23 ....31 L4
Dalmally Rd CROY/NA CRO 45 P7
Dalmeny Av
STRHM/NOR SW16 ....45 J3
Dalmeny Crs HSLW TW3 ....16 D9
Dalmeny Rd CAR SM5 ....62 D5
EW KT17 ....60 G7
Dalmore Av ESH/CLAY KT10 ..58 F5
Dalmore Rd DUL SE21 ....30 E3
Dalston CI CBLY GU15 ....69 K4
Dalton Av MTCM CR4 ....44 A3
Dalton CI CRAWW RH11 ....176 A5
PUR/KEN CR8 ....81 L2
Dalton St WNWD SE27 ....30 C5
Damask CI CHOB/PIR GU24 ..70 E2
Damer Ter WBPTN SW10 * 19 N5
Damien St
CROY/NA CRO 3 K5
Dampier Wk CRAWW RH11 * ..194 E1
Damsonwood Rd
NWDGN UB2 ....16 A1
Danbrook Rd
STRHM/NOR SW16 ....44 G2
Danbury Ms CAR SM5 ....62 B3
Dancer Rd FUL/PGN SW6 ......19 K6
RCH/KEW TW9 ....17 N9
Dandridge CI DTCH/LGLY SL3 ..12 E4
Danebury CROY/NA CRO 65 H5
Danebury Av PUT/ROE SW15 ..27 H2
Dane Ct WOKS/MYFD GU22 ..73 K4
Danecourt Gdns
CROY/NA CRO 3 K5
Danecroft Rd HNHL SE24 * 30 D1

Danehurst CI EGH TW20 ....21 K9
Danehurst Crs SWTR RH13 ..192 E8
Danehurst St FUL/PGN SW6 ..19 H4
Danemere St PUT/ROE SW15 ..18 G8
Danemore La GDST RH9 ......142 E13
Dane Rd ASHF TW15 ....23 M9
WARL CR6 ....82 D6
WIM/MER SW19 ....43 N2
Danesbury Rd FELT TW13 ......24 C4
Danes CI LHD/OX KT22 ....76 C5
Danescourt Crs SUT SM1 ......45 K1
Danesfield RPLY/SEND GU23 ..93 K3
Danesfield CI WOT/HER KT12 ..57 H2
Danes HI WOKS/MYFD GU22 ..11 H5
Daneshill CI REDH RH1 ....120 A4
Daneshill La REDH RH1 ....120 A4
Danes Hill School Dr
LHD/OX KT22 * 76 D7
Danesmead COB KT11 ....58 A9
Danes Rd GU GU1 ....7 J4
Daneswood CI WEY KT13 ......56 B4
Danetree CI HOR/WEW KT19 ..60 A6
Danetree Rd HOR/WEW KT19 ..60 A6
Daniel CI HSLWW TW4 ....24 G3
WIM/MER SW19 ....29 N9
Daniell Wy CROY/NA CRO 44 G9
Daniels La WARL CR6 ....82 F5
Daniel Wy BNSTD SM7 ....79 M6
Danley La HASM GU27 ....183 K7
Danses CI RGUE GU4 ....113 H3
Danvers Dr FLEETS GU52 ....106 E2
Danvers St CHEL SW3 ....19 P4
Danvers Wy CTHM CR3 ....101 L3
Dapdune RG GU GU1 ....7 F4
Daphne Dr FLEETS GU52 ......28 F2
Daphne St WAND/EARL SW18 ..28 F2
Darby Crs SUN TW16 ....39 L3
Darby Gdns SUN TW16 ....39 L3
Darby Green La BLKW GU17 ..67 M9
Darby Green Rd BLKW GU17 ..67 L3
Darcy CI COUL/CHIP CR5 ......81 K8
Darcy PI ASHTD KT21 ....77 M6
HAYES BR2 ....47 N5
Darcy Rd ASHTD KT21 ....77 M6
CHEAM SM3 ....61 H3
ISLW TW7 ....16 G6
STRHM/NOR SW16 ....44 G3
Darell Rd RCH/KEW TW9 ......17 N8
Darenth Gdns
BH/WHM TN16 ....105 H6
Darenth Wy HORL RH6 ....140 B8
Dare's La RFNM GU10 ....106 E5
Darfield Rd BROCKY SE4 ......31 N1
RGUE GU4 ....112 E2
Darfur St PUT/ROE SW15 ......19 H8
Dargate CI NRWD SE19 ....45 P1
Darien CI RD BTSEA SW11 ....19 K5
Dark La BROCKY SE4 ....130 B1
Darlan Rd FUL/PGN SW6 ......19 K5
Darley CI ADL/WDHM KT15 ..55 N4
CROY/NA CRO 47 H6
Darley Dene Ct
ADL/WDHM KT15 * 55 N3
Darley Dr NWMAL KT3 ....42 B3
Darley Gdns MRDN SM4 ....43 M7
Darlaston Rd BTSEA SW11 ....29 C8
Darlington Rd WNWD SE27 ....30 C8
Darmaine CI SAND/SEL CR2 ..63 L6
Darnley Pk WEY KT13 ....56 D2
Darracott CI CBLY GU15 ....69 K1
Darrell CI DTCH/LGLY SL3 ....12 D2
Darrell Rd EDUL SE22 ....31 H1
Darset Av FLEETS GU52 ......106 C5
Dart CI DTCH/LGLY SL3 ....12 F4
EWKG RG40 ....48 D2
Dartmouth Av
WOKN/KNAP GU21 ....72 G3
Dartmouth CI BRAK RG12 ....32 G4
Dartmouth PI CHSWK W4 ......18 C4
FSTH SE23 ....31 J6
Dartmouth Rd HAYES BR2 ....47 N8
SYD SE26 ....31 J6
Dartnell Av W/BF KT14 ....73 M1
Dartnell CI W/BF KT14 ....73 M1
Dartnell Crs W/BF KT14 ....73 M1
Dartnell Park Rd
BF/WBF KT14 ....73 M1
Dartnell PI BF/WBF KT14 ......73 M1
Dartnell Rd CROY/NA CRO 46 A8
Dartrey Wk WBPTN SW10 * ..19 N5
Dart Rd FARN GU14 ....87 P1
Darvel CI WOKN/KNAP GU21 ..5 H4
Darvill Hts FNM GU9 * 5 H4
Darvills La FNM GU9 ....5 H4
Darwall Dr ASC SL5 ....33 M3
Darwin CI HORS RH12 ....192 G6
Darwin Gdns WOT/HER KT12 ..108 E5
Darwin Rd EA W5 ....17 J3
Daryngton Dr GU GU1 ....112 F5
Dashwood CI BF/WBF KT14 ..73 N3
BRAK RG12 ....32 F2
DTCH/LGLY SL3 ....12 A2
Daubeny Ms CAR SM5 ....62 B4
DTCH/LGLY SL3 ....62 B4
WDSR SL4 ....20 F1
Dault Rd WAND/EARL SW18 ..28 F2
Datchet Rd CAT SE6 ....31 M4
DTCH/LGLY SL3 ....12 D2
Davenant Rd CROY/NA CRO 2 C7
Davenport CI TEDD TW11 ......25 P9
Davenport Rd BRAK RG12 ....32 G2
Daventry CI DTCH/LGLY SL3 ..13 J6
Daventry Ct BNFD RG42 ....32 D2
David CI HYS/HAR UB3 ....14 F5

David Rd DTCH/LGLY SL3 .....13 K7
Davidson Rd CROY/NA CR0 .....3 G1
David's Rd FSTH SE23.....31 K4
David Twigg Cl
  KUTN/CMB KT2 .....8 E2
Davies Cl GODL GU7 .....131 K6
  SNWD SE25 .....45 P7
Davies Wk ISLW TW7 .....16 D6
Davis Cl CRAWW RH11 .....194 D1
Davis Gdns SHST GU47 .....68 A1
Davis Rd CHSGTN KT9 .....59 N3
  WEY KT13 .....56 D8
Davos Cl WOKS/MYFD GU22 .....72 C8
Dawell Dr BH/WHM TN16 .....84 A6
Dawes Av ISLW TW7 .....16 D7
Dawes Ct ESH/CLAY KT10.....58 B3
Dawes Rd FUL/PGN SW6 .....19 K5
Dawley Ride DTCH/LGLY SL3 .....14 G2
Dawley Rd HYS/HAR UB3.....14 C2
Dawlish Av
  WAND/EARL SW18 .....28 E5
Dawnay Cl ASC SL5 .....33 P2
Dawnay Gdns
  WAND/EARL SW18 .....28 G5
Dawnay Rd CBLY GU15 .....50 D9
  GT/LBKH KT23 .....96 B6
  WAND/EARL SW18 .....28 F5
Dawn Cl HSLWW TW4 .....15 N8
Dawney HI CHOB/PIR GU24.....90 E1
Dawneys Rd CHOB/PIR GU24 .....90 E2
Dawn Redwood Cl
  DTCH/LGLY SL3 .....12 E8
Dawsmere Cl CBLY GU15 .....69 L3
Dawson Rd BF/WBF KT14 .....55 P9
  KUT KT1 .....9 G6
Daybrook Rd
  WIM/MER SW19 .....43 M3
Daylesford Av
  PUT/ROE SW15 .....18 E9
Daymerslea Rdg
  LHD/OX KT22 .....97 J1
Day's Acre SAND/SEL CR2 .....63 P8
Daysbrook Rd
  BRXS/STRHM SW2 .....30 A4
Dayseys HI REDH RH1 .....140 A3
Dayspring GUW GU2 .....111 P1
Deacon Cl CDST KT11 .....75 K8
  CTHM CR3 .....101 L3
  PUR/KEN CR8 .....62 G7
Deacon Ct LING RH7 .....143 P5
Deacon Fld GUW GU2 .....111 N4
Deacon Rd KUTN/CMB KT2 .....9 F3
Deacons Wk HPTN TW12 .....25 G7
Deadbrook La ASHV GU12 .....108 G3
Deal Rd TOOT SW17 .....29 K9
Dealtry Rd PUT/ROE SW15 .....18 G7
Dean Cl WOKS/MYFD GU22 .....73 J5
  GODL GU7 .....131 L8
Deanfield Gdns
  CROY/NA CR0 *.....63 M3
Deanhill Ct
  MORT/ESHN SW14 *.....17 P9
Deanhill Rd
  MORT/ESHN SW14 .....17 N9
Dean La
  KWD/TDW/WH KT20 .....98 F5
  REDH RH1 .....121 J4
Deans Rd REDH RH1 .....121 L4
  SUT SM1 .....61 M2
Deans Wk COUL/CHIP CR5.....81 J7
De'arn Gdns MTCM CR4 .....44 A4
Debden Cl KUTN/CMB KT2 .....26 C8
Deborah Cl ISLW TW7 .....16 E6
De Broome Rd FELT TW13 .....24 D4
De Burgh Gdns
  KWD/TDW/WH KT20 .....79 H8
De Burgh Pk BNSTD SM7 .....79 K3
Deburgh Rd WIM/MER SW19 .....43 N1
Decimus Cl SNWD SE25 *.....45 M5
Decouttere Cl FLEETS GU52...106 E1
Dedisham Cl CRAWE RH10.....177 K6
Dedswell Dr RGUE GU4 .....93 L9
Deedman Cl ASHV GU12 .....109 J4
Deepcut Bridge Rd
  FRIM GU16.....69 M7
Deepdale BRAK RG12 .....32 C5
  WIM/MER SW19 .....28 A7
Deepdene Av HAYES BR2 .....47 M5
Deepdene Av CROY/NA CR0 .....3 K6
  RDKG RH5 .....117 J7
Deepdene Avenue Rd
  DORK RH4 .....117 J5
Deepdene Gdns
  BRXS/STRHM SW2 .....30 A3
  DORK RH4 .....117 H6
Deepdene Park Rd
  RDKG RH5 .....117 J6
Deepdene V DORK RH4 .....117 J5
Deepdene Wd BRAK RG12 .....32 C5
Deepfield HORL RH6 .....140 B8
Deepfield Wy
  COUL/CHIP CR5 .....80 G5

Deep Pool La CHOB/PIR GU24...62 A3
Deeprose Cl GUW GU2 .....
Deepwell Cl ISLW TW7 .....
Deep Well Dr CBLY GU15.....
Deerbarn Rd GUW GU2 .....
Deerbrook Rd
  BRXS/STRHM SW2 .....
Deerhurst Cl FELT TW13 .....
Deerhurst Crs HPTN TW12.....
Deerhurst Rd
  THHTH/NOR SW16 .....30 A3
Deerings Rd REIG RH2 .....119 M5
Deerleap Rd RSEV TN14 .....
Deer Leap LTWR GU18 .....52 A9
Deerleap La DORK RH4 .....
Deerleap Rd DORK RH4 .....116 B8
Dee Pd RCH/KEW TW9 .....17 M9
Deer Park Cl KUTN/CMB KT2...41 P1
Deer Park Gdns MTCM CR4 *..43 P5
Deer Rock Hl BRAK RG12 .....32 E7
Deers Farm Cl
  RPLY/SEND GU23 .....74 A5
Deerswood Cl CRAWW RH11..176 E4
  CTHM CR3 .....102 E4
Deerswood Rd
  CRAWW RH11 .....176 E4
Deeside Rd TOOT SW17 .....28 G6
Dee Wy HOR/WEW KT19 .....60 C8
Defiant Rd FARN GU14 .....88 B7
Defiant Wy WLGTN SM6 .....62 G6
Defoe Av RCH/KEW TW9 .....17 N5
Defoe Cl WIM/MER SW19.....29 H9
De Frene Rd SYD SE26 .....31 L7
De Lara Wy
  WOKN/KNAP GU21 .....10 A6
De La Warr Rd EGRIN RH19..180 E2
Delawyk Crs HNHL SE24 .....30 E2
Delcombe Av WPK KT4 .....42 G9
Delderfield ASHTD KT21 .....77 K9
Delfont Cl CRAWE RH10 .....177 N7
Delia St WAND/EARL SW18...28 E3
Delius Gdns CRAWW RH13..192 G6
Dell Bow Rd
  EBED/NFELT TW14 .....24 C1
Dell Campus BRAK RG12 *.....32 A3
Dell Cl HASM GU27 .....184 B8
  LHD/OX KT22 .....96 D5
  RDKG RH5 .....
  WLGTN SM6 .....62 E3
Dell Se BNFD RG42 .....32 B1
Dellfield Cl BECK BR3 .....47 J2
Dell Gv FRIM GU16 .....69 H6
Dell La EW KT17 .....60 E4
Dell Rd EW KT17 .....60 E5
The Dell BECK BR3 * 46 C1
  BTFD TW8 .....17 J4
  EBED/NFELT TW14 .....24 C3
  EGRIN RH19 .....180 G2
  FNM GU9 .....107 N7
  HORL RH6 .....140 D9
  KWD/TDW/WH KT20 .....98 C1
  NRWD SE19 * 45 P2
  REIG RH2 * 119 L4
  WOKN/KNAP GU21 .....72 A8
  YTLY GU46 .....66 G3
Dellwood NWMAL KT3 .....
Delmey Cl CROY/NA CR0 .....3 J5
Delorme St HMSMTH W6 .....19 H4
Delta Cl CHOB/PIR GU24 .....53 M8
  WPK KT4 .....60 C2
Delta Dr HORL RH6 .....159 K3
Delta Rd CHOB/PIR GU24.....53 M8
  WOKN/KNAP GU21 .....10 A1
  WPK KT4 .....60 C2
Delta Wy EGH TW20 .....36 C2
Delves KWD/TDW/WH KT20...99 H1
Delville Cl FARN GU14 .....87 P4
Delvino Rd FUL/PGN SW6 .....19 L6
Demesne Rd WLGTN SM6.....62 F3
De Montfort Pde
  STRHM/NOR SW16 * 29 P6
De Montfort Rd
  STRHM/NOR SW16 .....29 P5
De Morgan Rd FUL/PGN SW6..19 M8
Dempster Rd
  WAND/EARL SW18 .....28 F1
Denbigh Cl SUT SM1 .....61 K4
Denbigh Gdns
  RCHPK/HAM TW10 * 26 E1
Denbigh Rd HASM GU27.....184 E5
  HSLW TW3 .....16 B7
Denby Rd COB KT11 .....75 L1
Denchers Plat CRAWW RH11..176 E4
Dencliffe ASHF TW15 * 23 K8
Den Cl BECK BR3 .....47 K5
Dendy Cl BAL SW12 .....29 N5
Dene Av HSLW TW3 .....15 P8
Dene Cl ASHV GU12 .....109 L4
  BRAK RG12 .....32 E2
  COUL/CHIP CR5 .....80 A3
  HASM GU27 .....184 D4

...SR2 .....47 M9
...10 .....140 A8
...RFNM GU10.....127 P7
...(faded) 60 D1
...PUR/KEN CR8...84 M4
Dene Gdns THDIT KT7 .....58 C1
Denehurst Gdns
  RCHPK/HAM TW10 .....17 N9
  WHTN TW2 .....25 L3
Dene La W RFNM GU10.....127 P7
Dene M WOKN/KNAP GU21...71 P7
Dene Rd ASHTD KT21 .....77 M8
  FARN GU14 .....88 D4
  GU GU1 .....7 H5
Dene St DORK RH4 .....117 H7
Dene St Gdns
  DORK RH4 .....117 H7
  CROY/NA CR0 .....64 D3
  E/WMO/HCT KT8 .....39 P6
Dene Tye CRAWE RH10.....177 M4
Dene Wk RFNM GU10 .....127 P7
Denfield DORK RH4 .....117 H9
Denham Crs MTCM CR4 .....44 B4
Denham Dr YTLY GU46 .....67 H3
Denham Gv BRAK RG12 * 32 E7
Denham Rd PDKG RH5 * 137 K9
Denham Rd
  EBED/NFELT TW14 .....24 D3
  EGH TW20 .....21 M7
  EW KT17 .....78 D1
Denholm Gdns RGUE GU4 .....112 E2
Denison Rd FELT TW13 .....24 A7
  WIM/MER SW19 .....43 P1
Denleigh Gdns THDIT KT7 * 40 E7
Denly Wy LTWR GU18 .....52 B9
Denman Cl FLEETN GU51 .....87 J6
Denman Dr ASHF TW15 .....23 L9
  ESH/CLAY KT10 .....58 C4
Denmans CRAWE RH10 .....177 N4
Denmark Av WIM/MER SW19...43 J1
Denmark Ct MRDN SM4 .....43 L6
Denmark Gdns CAR SM5 .....62 B2
Denmark Rd BMLY BR1 .....47 P2
  CAR SM5 .....62 B2
  KUT KT1 .....8 E6
  SNWD SE25 .....46 A6
  WHTN TW2 .....25 L6
  WIM/MER SW19 .....28 A9
Denmark Sq ASHV GU12.....108 G4
Denmark St ASHV GU12 .....108 E4
Denmead Ct BRAK RG12 .....32 C7
Denmead Rd CROY/NA CR0 .....63 J4
Dennan Rd SURB KT6 .....41 M9
Denne Pde CRAWW RH11 .....176 G6
Denne Rd CRAWW RH11.....176 G6
The Dennings WPK KT4 .....60 C1
Dennis Cl REDH RH1 .....120 A3
Dennis Park Crs RYNPK SW20..43 J2
Dennis Reeve Cl MTCM CR4...44 B2
Dennis Rd E/WMO/HCT KT8...40 C5
Dennistoun Cl CBLY GU15 .....68 F3
Dennis Wy GU GU1 .....92 C9
Denny Rd DTCH/LGLY SL3 * 12 D2
Den Rd HAYES BR2 .....47 K4
Densham Dr PUR/KEN CR8...81 H4
Densole Cl BECK BR3 * 46 F1
Denton Cl REDH RH1 .....140 C1
Denton Gv WOT/HER KT12...57 N1
Denton Rd TWK TW1 .....26 C2
Denton Wy FRIM GU16 .....68 F6
  WOKN/KNAP GU21 .....71 N6
Dents Gv KWD/TDW/WH KT20..99 H8
Dents Rd BTSEA SW11 .....29 J3
Denvale Wk
  WOKN/KNAP GU21 .....71 N7
Denzil Rd GUW GU2 .....6 C5
Deodar Rd PUT/ROE SW15...19 J9
Depot Cl CRAWE RH10 .....177 H6
Depot Rd CRAWE RH10 .....176 G6
  EW KT17 .....78 E3
  HSLW TW3 .....16 C8
  SWTR RH13 .....192 D8
Derby Arms Rd EPSOM KT18..78 F8
Derby Cl EPSOM KT18 .....78 F8
Derby Hill Crs FSTH SE23 .....31 K5
Derby Hill FSTH SE23 .....31 K5
Derby Rd BRYLDS 41 N9
  CROY/NA CR0 .....2 C2
  GUW GU2 .....111 M5
  HASM GU27 .....184 C3
  HSLW TW3 .....16 B9
  MORT/ESHN SW14 .....17 J1
  SUT SM1 .....61 K5
  WIM/MER SW19 .....43 L1
Derbyshire Gn BNFD RG42.....33 H1
Derby Stables Rd
  EPSOM KT18 .....78 C6
Derek Av HOR/WEW KT19...59 N5
  WLGTN SM6 .....62 D2
Derek Cl HOR/WEW KT19 .....59 P4
Derek Walcott Cl
  HNHL SE24 *.....30 C1
Deri Dene Cl
  STWL/WRAY TW19 * 23 H2
Dering Rd CROY/NA CR0 .....63 J3
Derinton Rd TOOT SW17 .....29 K7
Derley Rd NWDGN UB2 .....15 L1
Deronda Rd
  BRXS/STRHM SW2 .....30 C4
Deroy Cl CAR SM5 .....62 B5
Derrick Av SAND/SEL CR2 .....63 L8
Derrick Rd BECK BR3 .....46 F4

Derry Cl ASHV GU12 .....109 H1
Derrydown
  WOKS/MYFD GU22 .....91 P1
Derry Rd CROY/NA CR0 .....62 C2
  FARN GU14 .....68 B7
Derwent Av ASHV GU12 .....109 H2
  PUT/ROE SW15 .....27 K7
Derwent Cl ADL/WDHM KT15 ..55 P4
  CRAWW RH11 .....176 C6
  EBED/NFELT TW14 .....24 A4
  ESH/CLAY KT10 .....58 E5
  FARN GU14 .....87 P5
  FNM GU9 .....108 A2
  HORS RH12 .....192 G4
Derwent Dr PUR/KEN CR8.....81 M3
Derwent Rd EA W5 .....17 J1
  EGH TW20 .....21 N9
  LTWR GU18 .....52 B9
  MRDN SM4 .....43 H7
  PGE/AN SE20 .....46 A3
  WHTN TW2 .....25 J2
Derwent Yd EA W5 *.....17 J1
Desborough Cl SHPTN TW17..38 C8
Desenfans Rd DUL SE21 .....30 F2
Desford Wy ASHF TW15 .....23 J5
Detillens La OXTED RH8.....103 N1
Detling Rd CRAWW RH11.....194 F1
Dettingen Rd FRIM GU16 .....69 N8
Devana End CAR SM5 .....62 B2
Devas Rd RYNPK SW20 .....42 G2
Devenish La ASC SL5 .....34 D7
Devenish Rd ASC SL5 .....34 C7
De Vere Ms KENS W8 * 19 N1
Devereux La BARN SW13 .....18 F5
Devereux Rd BTSEA SW11 .....29 J2
Deverills Wy DTCH/LGLY SL3...12 G2
Devey Cl KUTN/CMB KT2 .....42 D1
The Devil's Hwy CWTH RG45...45 J4
Devil's La EGH TW20 .....21 P9
  UPH QU30 .....183 H7
Devitt Cl ASHTD KT21 .....77 N5
Devoil Cl RGUE GU4 .....112 F1
Devoke Wy WOT/HER KT12...57 N1
Devon Bank GUW GU2 .....112 A8
Devon Cl FLEETN GU51 .....87 J6
  HOR/WEW KT19 .....77 N1
  PUR/KEN CR8 .....81 N5
  SHST GU47 .....67 P1
Devon Crs REIG RH2 .....119 P3
Devonhurst Cl CHSWK W4 * ..18 B3
Devonhurst Pl CHSWK W4 *...18 B3
Devon Rd BELMT SM2 .....61 J7
  REDH RH1 .....120 E1
  WOT/HER KT12 .....57 L3
Devonshire Av BELMT SM2...61 N6
  KWD/TDW/WH KT20 .....118 A2
  WOKN/KNAP GU21 .....72 C3
Devonshire Dr SURB KT6 .....41 J8
Devonshire Gdns CHSWK W4..18 A5
Devonshire Pl ALDT GU11 .....108 B5
  KENS W8 * 19 M1
Devonshire Rd BELMT SM2...61 N6
  CAR SM5 .....62 C3
  CHSWK W4 .....18 C3
  CROY/NA CR0 .....45 J7
  EA W5 .....17 J1
  FELT TW13 .....24 F6
  FSTH SE23 .....31 K3
  SWTR RH13 .....192 G9
  WEY KT13 * 56 A4
  WIM/MER SW19 .....44 A1
Devonshire Sq HAYES BR2.....47 N3
Devonshire St CHSWK W4 .....18 C3
Devonshire Wy
  CROY/NA CR0 .....64 F1
  HOR/WEW KT19 .....60 C6
Devon Waye HEST TW5 .....15 P5
Dewar Cl CRAWW RH11 * 176 B6
Dewey St TOOT SW17 .....29 J8
Dewhurst Rd WKENS W14.....19 H1
Dewlands GDST RH9 .....122 C2
Dewlands Cl CRAN GU6 .....153 H9
Dewlands La CRAN GU6 .....153 H8
Dewsbury Gdns WPK KT4 .....60 E2
Dexter Dr EGRIN RH19 .....180 B4
Dexter Wy FLEETN GU51 .....87 H3
Diamedes Av
  STWL/WRAY TW19 .....22 G3
Diamond Cl CBLY GU15 .....68 G1
Diamond Rdg CBLY GU15 .....68 A8
Diamond Wy FARN GU14 .....88 A7
Diana Gdns SURB KT6 .....59 M1
Dianthus Cl CHERT KT16 .....37 H8
Dianthus Ct
  WOKS/MYFD GU22 .....10 B2
Dibdin Cl SUT SM1 .....61 L2
Dibdin Rd SUT SM1 .....61 L2
Diceland Rd BNSTD SM7 .....79 K5
Dickens Cl EGRIN RH19 .....180 D2
  HYS/HAR UB3 .....14 G2
Dickens Dr ADL/WDHM KT15..55 N5
Dickenson Rd FELT TW13 .....24 D8
Dickenson's La SNWD SE25...46 A7
Dickenson's Pl SNWD SE25...46 A7
Dickens Rd CRAWE RH10.....176 B5
Dickens Wy YTLY GU46 .....66 G3
Dickens Wood Cl NRWD SE19..45 K1
Dickerage La NWMAL KT3.....41 P3
Dickerage Rd KUT KT1 .....42 A2
Dick Turpin Wy
  EBED/NFELT TW14 .....13 K9
Digby Cl CROY/NA CR0 .....3 K5
Digby Wy BF/WBF KT14 .....74 B2
Digdens Ri EPSOM KT18 .....78 A4
Dighton Rd WAND/EARL SW18..28 F1

Dillwyn Cl SYD SE26 .....31 M7
Dilston Rd LHD/OX KT22 .....76 G8
Dimes PI HMSMTH W6 .....18 F2
Dingle Cl CRAWW RH11 .....176 E4
Dingle Rd ASHF TW15 .....23 L8
The Dingle CRAWW RH11.....176 E5
Dingley La
  STRHM/NOR SW16 .....29 N5
Dingley Wy FARN GU14 .....88 C7
Dingwall Av CROY/NA CR0 .....2 D7
Dingwall Rd CAR SM5 .....62 B7
  CROY/NA CR0 .....2 E3
  WAND/EARL SW18 .....28 F3
Dinorben Av FLEETS GU52.....86 E8
Dinorben Beeches
  FLEETS GU52 .....86 E8
Dinorben Cl FLEETS GU52.....86 F8
Dinsdale Cl
  WOKS/MYFD GU22 .....11 F5
Dinsdale Gdns SNWD SE25 .....45 N5
Dinsmore Rd BAL SW12 .....29 L3
Dinton Rd KUTN/CMB KT2.....41 M1
  WIM/MER SW19 .....44 C1
Dippenhall Rd RFNM GU10..126 F5
Dippenhall St RFNM GU10..106 C9
Dirdene Cl EW KT17 .....78 D1
Dirdene Gdns EW KT17 .....78 D1
Dirdene Gv EW KT17 .....78 C1
Dirtham La EHSLY KT24 .....95 K9
Dirty La EGRIN RH19 .....181 K6
Disbrowe Rd HMSMTH W6.....19 J4
Discovery Pk CWTH RG45 * 32 F9
Disraeli Ct DTCH/LGLY SL3 * ..12 F4
Disraeli Rd PUT/ROE SW15...19 L6
Distillery La HMSMTH W6 .....18 G3
Distillery Rd HMSMTH W6 .....18 G3
Ditches La COUL/CHIP CR5...80 E6
Ditchfield La EWKG RG40 .....48 C1
Ditchling BRAK RG12 .....32 C8
Ditchling HI CRAWW RH11....176 F8
Ditton Cl THDIT KT7 .....40 G8
Dittoncroft Cl SAND/SEL CR2...63 N3
Ditton Grange Cl SURB KT6...41 K9
Ditton Grange Dr SURB KT6...41 K9
Ditton Hill Rd SURB KT6 .....41 J9
Ditton Lawn THDIT KT7 .....40 G9
Ditton Park Rd
  DTCH/LGLY SL3 .....12 C4
Ditton Pl PGE/AN SE20 * 46 B2
Ditton Rd DTCH/LGLY SL3.....12 B6
  NWDGN UB2 .....15 P3
  SURB KT6 .....41 L9
The Dittons EWKG RG40 .....48 C3
Dixon Dr WEY KT13 .....56 B8
Dixon Pl WWKM BR4 .....47 H9
Dixon Rd SNWD SE25 .....45 N4
Dobbins Pl CRAWW RH11.....176 A6
Dobson Rd CRAWE RH10 .....176 G2
Dockenfield St RFNM GU10..146 A6
Dockett Eddy La
  SHPTN TW17 .....38 B7
Dockett Moorings
  SHPTN TW17 .....38 B8
Dock Rd BTFD TW8 * 17 K5
Dockwell Cl
  EBED/NFELT TW14 .....15 J9
Doctors La CTHM CR3 .....101 J4
Dodbrooke Rd WNWD SE27...30 B6
Dodds Crs BF/WBF KT14 .....73 M3
Dodd's La BF/WBF KT14 .....73 L3
Dodds Pk
  BRKHM/BTCW RH3 .....117 P7
Dodsells Well EWKG RG40 * ..48 D1
Doel Cl WIM/MER SW19 .....43 N1
Dogflud Wy FNM GU9 .....5 H2
Doggett Rd CAT SE6 .....31 P3
Doggetts Cl EDEN TN8 .....144 G6
Doghurst Av WDR/YW UB7...14 D5
Doghurst Dr WDR/YW UB7...14 D5
Doghurst La COUL/CHIP CR5..80 D9
Dolby Rd FUL/PGN SW6 .....19 K7
Dolby Ter HORL RH6 * 158 B6
Doley Pde KUT KT1 * 9 K6
Dollis Cl CRAWE RH10 .....177 M6
Dollis Dr FNM GU9 .....5 J1
Dolman Rd CHSWK W4 .....18 B2
Dolphin Cl HASM GU27 .....183 P4
  SURB KT6 .....41 K7
Dolphin Cl Br CRAWE RH12...32 E5
  STWL/WRAY TW19 .....22 D6
Dolphin Ct North
  STWL/WRAY TW19 * 22 D6
Dolphin Est SUN TW16 .....38 G2
Dolphin Rd SUN TW16 .....38 G2
Dolphin Rd North SUN TW16..38 G2
Dolphin Rd South SUN TW16...38 F2
Dolphin Rd West SUN TW16...38 F2
Dolphin St KUT KT1 .....8 D4
Doman Rd CBLY GU15 .....68 C4
Dome Buildings
  RCHPK/HAM TW10 * 26 C1
Dome Hill CTHM CR3 .....101 N7
Dome Hill Pk SYD SE26.....30 G7
Dome Peak CTHM CR3 .....101 N6
Dome Wy REDH RH1 .....120 B4
Dominion Rd CROY/NA CR0...45 P8
  NWDGN UB2 .....15 N1
Donald Rd CROY/NA CR0 .....45 H7
Donald Woods Gdns
  BRYLDS 59 P1
Doncaster Wk CRAWE RH10...177 K7
Doncastle Rd BRAK RG12 .....32 B4
Donkey Aly EDUL SE22 .....31 H3
Donkey La HORL RH6 .....159 N5
  RDKG RH5 .....135 M5
Donlan Dr FARN GU14 .....87 N6

Donnafields CHOB/PIR GU24 ...70 G5
Donne CI CRAWE RH10 ...177 L3
Donne Gdns
  WOKS/MYFD GU22 ...73 J4
Donne PI MTCM CR4 ...44 D5
Donnington CI CBLY GU15 ...68 D4
Donnington Ct
  CRAWW RH11 ...176 C8
Donnington Rd WPK KT4 ...60 E1
Donnybrook BRAK RG12 ...32 C8
Donnybrook Rd
  STRHM/NOR SW16 ...44 E1
Donovan CI HOR/WEW KT19 ...60 D1
Doods Park Rd REIG RH2 ...119 N5
Doods PI REIG RH2 * ...119 N4
Doods Wy REIG RH2 ...119 N4
Doomsday Gdn SWTR RH13 ...192 E9
Doone CI TEDD TW11 ...25 P8
Doral Wy CAR SM5 ...62 B5
Doran Dr REIG RH2 ...119 P5
Doran Gdns REIG RH2 * ...119 P5
Dora Rd WIM/MER SW19 ...28 C8
Dora's Green La RFNM GU10..126 F3
Dorcas Ct CBLY GU15 ...68 D5
Dorchester Ct HNHL SE24 ...30 D1
  WOKS/MYFD GU22 ...11 H2
Dorchester Dr
  EBED/NFELT TW14 ...23 P2
  HNHL SE24 ...30 D1
Dorchester Gv CHSWK W4 ...18 C4
Dorchester Ms TWK TW1 ...26 B2
Dorchester Pde
  STRHM/NOR SW16 * ...29 N6
Dorchester Rd MRDN SM4 ...43 M8
  WEY KT13 ...56 D2
  WPK KT4 ...42 G9
Doreen CI FARN GU14 ...67 P8
Dore Gdns MRDN SM4 ...43 M8
Dorian Ct WARL CR6 * ...82 B8
Dorian Dr ASC SL5 ...34 E2
Doria Rd FUL/PGN SW6 ...19 K7
Doric Dr KWD/TDW/WH KT20 ...79 K9
Dorin Ct WARL CR6 * ...82 B9
  WOKS/MYFD GU22 ...73 J4
Doris Rd ASHF TW15 ...23 H8
Dorking CI WPK KT4 ...60 H1
Dorking Rd EPSOM KT18 ...77 P4
  GT/LBKH KT23 ...96 B7
  HORS RH12 ...173 P9
  KWD/TDW/WH KT20 ...98 F6
  LHD/OX KT22 ...97 H3
  RGUE GU4 ...133 H2
Dorcote Rd
  WAND/EARL SW18...28 G3
Dorling Dr EW KT17 ...78 D1
Dorly CI SHPTN TW17 ...38 C5
Dormans CRAWW RH11 ...176 D6
Dormans CI LING RH7 ...162 F2
Dormans La LING RH7 ...162 F4
Dormans High St LING RH7...162 F5
Dormans Park Rd
  EGRIN RH19 ...162 C9
Dormans Rd LING RH7 ...162 F2
Dormans Station Rd
  LING RH7 ...162 E1
Dormay St WAND/EARL SW18..28 F1
Dormer CI CRAWE RH10 ...177 L3
Dormers CI GODL GU7 ...131 K6
Dorncliffe Rd FUL/PGN SW6 ...19 J7
Dorney Gv WEY KT13 ...56 D1
Dorney Wy HSLWW TW4 ...24 F1
Domford Gdns
  COUL/CHIP CR5 ...81 L8
Domton Rd BAL SW12 ...29 L5
  SAND/SEL CR2 ...63 N4
Dorrit Crs RGUW GU3 ...111 L3
Dorset Av EGRIN RH19 ...162 B9
  NWDGN UB2 ...16 A1
Dorset Dr WOKS/MYFD GU22 ...11 K4
Dorset Gdns EGRIN RH19 ...162 B9
  STRHM/NOR SW16 ...45 H6
Dorset Rd ASHF TW15 ...22 G6
  ASHV GU12 ...109 J1
  BECK BR3 ...46 D4
  BELMT SM2 ...61 L8
  EA W5 ...17 J1
  MTCM CR4 ...44 A3
  WIM/MER SW19 ...43 L2
Dorset Wy BF/WBF KT14 ...55 P9
  WHTN TW2 ...25 J3
Dorset Waye HEST TW5 ...15 P5
Dorton Wy RPLY/SEND GU23 ...93 M1
Dorville Crs HMSMTH W6 ...18 F1
Douai CI FARN GU14 ...
Douai Gv HPTN TW12 ...40 C2
Douglas Av NWMAL KT3 ...42 F5
Douglas CI RGUE GU4 ...92 B8
  WLGTN SM6 ...62 G5
Douglas Ct CTHM CR3 * ...101 L2
Douglas Dr CROY/NA CR0 ...64 G2
  GODL GU7 ...131 M8
Douglas La
  STWL/WRAY TW19 ...21 L1
Douglas Ms BNSTD SM7 ...79 K5
Douglas Rd ADL/WDHM KT15..55 M2
  ESH/CLAY KT10 ...58 D1
  HSLW TW3 ...16 B8
  KUT KT1 ...9 K5
  REIG RH2 ...119 L4
  STWL/WRAY TW19 ...21 L1
  SURB KT6 ...59 M1
Douglas Vis KUT KT1 * ...9 K5
The Doultons STA TW18 ...22 D9
Dounesforth Gdns
  WAND/EARL SW18 ...28 E4
Douro PI KENS W8 ...19 M1
Dove CI CRAWW RH11 ...176 C6
  CROY/NA CR0 ...63 H6
  SAND/SEL CR2 ...64 D9

Dovecote CI WEY KT13 ...56 D2
Dovedale CI RGUE GU4 ...112 E2
  SHST GU47 * ...49 P8
Dovedale Crs CRAWW RH11 ...176 E7
Dovedale Ri MTCM CR4 ...44 B1
Dovedale Rd EDUL SE22 ...31 J1
Dovehouse Gn WEY KT13 ...56 F3
Dove Ms ECT SW5 ...19 N2
Dover Ct CRAN GU6 ...153 K9
Dovercourt Av THHTH CR7 ...45 J5
Dovercourt La SUT SM1 ...61 N2
Dovercourt Rd EDUL SE22 ...30 F2
Doverfield Rd
  BRXS/STRHM SW2 ...29 P2
  RGUE GU4 ...112 E2
Dover Gdns CAR SM5 ...62 B2
Dover House Rd
  PUT/ROE SW15 ...18 E9
Dover Park Dr
  PUT/ROE SW15 ...27 N2
Dover Rd NRWD SE19 ...30 E9
Dovers Green Rd REIG RH2 ...119 M9
Doversmead
  WOKN/KNAP GU21 ...71 L5
Dover Ter RCH/KEW TW9 * ...17 N7
Doverton Rd SAND/SEL CR2 ...63 M4
Dowdeswell CI
  PUT/ROE SW15 ...18 C9
Dowding Ct CWTH RG45 ...49 N3
Dowding Rd BH/WHM TN16 ...84 B4
Dower Av WLGTN SM6 ...62 D7
Dower Wk CRAWW RH11 ...176 D6
Dowlands La HORL RH6 ...160 G2
Dowlans CI GT/LBKH KT23 ...96 A7
Dowlans Rd GT/LBKH KT23 ...96 B7
Dowman CI WIM/MER SW19 ...43 M1
Downe Av RSEV TN14 ...84 C1
Downe CI HORL RH6 ...140 A8
Downer Meadow GODL GU7 ...131 L5
Downe Rd MTCM CR4 ...44 B5
  RSEV TN14 ...84 G3
Downes CI TWK TW1 ...26 A2
Downfield WPK KT4 ...42 D9
Down Hall Rd KUTN/CMB KT2 ...8 C3
Downham CI
  CRAWE RH10 * ...57 L2
Downhurst Rd CRAN GU6 ...153 P6
Downing Av GUW GU2 ...111 M6
Downing St FNM GU9 ...5 F3
Downland CI COUL/CHIP CR5 ...80 D5
  EPSOM KT18 ...78 F7
Downland Dr CRAWW RH11 ...176 F7
Downland Gdns EPSOM KT18 ...78 F7
Downland PI CRAWW RH11 ...176 F7
Downlands Rd PUR/KEN CR8 ...80 F2
Downland Wy EPSOM KT18 ...78 F7
Down La RGUW GU3 ...111 H9
Downmill Rd BRAK RG12 ...32 B3
Downs Av EPSOM KT18 ...78 D4
Downs Bridge Rd BECK BR3 ...47 K2
Downs Court Rd
  PUR/KEN CR8 ...81 L2
Downs Hill BECK BR3 ...47 K1
Downs Hill Rd EPSOM KT18 * ...78 C4
Downshire Wy BRAK RG12 ...32 C4
Downside BECK BR3 ...46 G2
  CHERT KT16 ...37 K9
  EPSOM KT18 ...78 C3
  GSHT GU26 ...165 N4
  SUN TW16 ...39 J2
  TWK TW1 ...25 N6
Downs Lodge Ct
  EPSOM KT18 * ...78 C3
Downs Rd BECK BR3 ...47 H5
  BELMT SM2 ...61 M9
  COUL/CHIP CR5 ...80 F7
  EPSOM KT18 ...78 A4
  EPSOM KT18 ...78 C4
  PUR/KEN CR8 ...63 K9
  WWKM BR4 ...47 L2
Downs Side BELMT SM2 ...61 K9
The Downs LHD/OX KT22...97 J5
  RYNPK SW20 ...43 H1
Down St E/WMO/HCT KT8 ...40 A6
Down Vw DORK RH4 ...117 J5
  ISLW TW7 ...16 F6
  KWD/TDW/WH KT20 * ...98 F1
Downsview Av
  WOKS/MYFD GU22 ...92 D1
Downsview CI COB KT11 ...75 J6
Downsview Gdns DORK RH4..117 H8
  NRWD SE19 ...45 L1
Downs View Rd
  GT/LBKH KT23 ...96 C7
  HORS RH12 ...192 G4
Downs Wy EPSOM KT18 ...78 D5
  GT/LBKH KT23 ...96 C6

  KWD/TDW/WH KT20 ...98 F1
  OXTED RH8 ...103 L7
Downsway CTHM CR3 ...81 P5
  GU GU1 ...113 H5
  SAND/SEL CR2 ...63 N9
Downsway CI
  KWD/TDW/WH KT20 ...98 E1
The Downsway BELMT SM2 ...61 N7
Downs Wd EPSOM KT18 ...78 F6
Downswood REDH RH1 ...119 P3
Downton Av
  BRXS/STRHM SW2 ...30 A5
Downview CI GSHT GU26 ...165 N5
Down Yhonda
  MFD/CHID GU8 ...148 D1
Doyle Gdns YTLY GU46 * ...66 G3
Doyle Rd SNWD SE25 ...46 A5
Draco Ga PUT/ROE SW15 * ...18 G8
Dragon La WEY KT13 ...56 C8
Drake Av CTHM CR3 ...101 L2
  DTCH/LGLY SL3 ...12 B2
  FRIM GU16 ...89 H8
  STA TW18 ...22 C8
Drake CI BRAK RG12 ...32 D6
  EWKG RG40 ...48 C2
  HORS RH12 ...192 D4
Drakefield Rd TOOT SW17 ...29 K6
Drake Rd CHSGTN KT9 ...59 N4
  CRAWE RH10 ...177 H8
  CROY/NA CR0 ...45 H8
  HORL RH6 ...159 H1
  MTCM CR4 ...44 C7
Drake's CI EFSH/CLAY KT10 ...58 A4
Drakes Wy
  WOKS/MYFD GU22 ...92 B2
Drakewood Rd
  STRHM/NOR SW16 ...44 F1
Draven CI HAYES BR2 ...47 M6
Drax Av RYNPK SW20 ...42 E1
Draxmont WIM/MER SW19 ...28 B9
Draycot Rd SURB KT6 ...41 N9
Draycott BRAK RG12 ...32 C6
Dray Ct GUW GU2 ...6 C3
Drayhorse Dr BAGS GU19 ...51 N7
Draymans Wy ISLW TW7 ...16 F8
Drayton CI BRAK RG12 ...32 F3
  HSLWW TW4 ...24 G1
  LHD/OX KT22 ...97 H3
Drayton Ct WDR/YW UB7 * ...14 B2
Drayton Gdns WBPTN SW10 ...19 N3
Drayton Rd CROY/NA CR0 ...2 B3
Dresden Wy WEY KT13 ...56 E4
Dressington Av BROCKY SE4...31 P1
Drew PI CTHM CR3 ...101 M3
Drews Cottages BAL SW12 * ...29 L1
Drewstead Rd
  STRHM/NOR SW16 ...29 N5
The Drift COB KT11 ...94 C4
Drift Wy DTCH/LGLY SL3 ...13 H2
The Driftway BNSTD SM7 ...78 G4
  LHD/OX KT22 ...97 J3
  MTCM CR4 ...44 C2
Driftwood PI PUR/KEN CR8 ...81 L6
Drill Hall Rd CHERT KT16 ...37 L8
Drive Rd COUL/CHIP CR5 ...81 H9
Drivers Md LING RH7 ...162 B1
The Drive ASHF TW15 ...38 F1
  BECK BR3 ...46 G3
  BELMT SM2 ...61 K9
  BIL RH14 ...188 A4
  BNSTD SM7 ...78 F5
  COB KT11 ...75 N3
  COUL/CHIP CR5 ...80 G3
  CRAN GU6 ...171 H1
  CRAWE RH10 ...160 D9
  EBED/NFELT TW14 ...24 C3
  ESH/CLAY KT10 ...40 C9
  FNM GU9 ...127 M6
  GODL GU7 ...130 E9
  GODL GU7 ...150 D2
  GUW GU2 ...111 M5
  GUW GU2 ...111 M7
  HOR/WEW KT19 ...60 D5
  HORL RH6 ...159 L2
  HSLW TW3 ...16 D7
  KUTN/CMB KT2 ...42 A1
  KWD/TDW/WH KT20 * ...96 E2
  LHD/OX KT22 ...97 J3
  LHD/OX KT22 ...97 N4
  MFD/CHID GU8 ...130 E9
  MRDN SM4 ...43 N6
  RGUW GU3 ...111 P9
  RYNPK SW20 ...42 G1
  SHGR GU5 ...132 D5
  STWL/WRAY TW19 ...21 J7
  SURB KT6 ...41 P9
  THHTH CR7 ...45 M5
  WLGTN SM6 ...62 G7
  WOKS/MYFD GU22 ...71 P9
  WWKM BR4 ...47 L4
Dr Johnson Av TOOT SW17 ...29 L6
Drodges CI SHGR GU5 ...132 D5
Droitwich CI BRAK RG12 ...32 F4
  SYD SE26 ...31 H6
Dromore Rd PUT/ROE SW15 ...28 B2
Drove Rd RGUE GU4 ...113 L7
Drovers End FLEETN GU51 ...87 J3
Drovers Rd SAND/SEL CR2 ...63 M4
Drovers Wy ASHV GU12 ...109 L3
  BRAK RG12 ...33 H4
  FNM GU9 ...107 J2
Druce Rd DUL SE21 ...30 F3
Druid's CI ASHTD KT21 ...77 M9
Drummond CI BRAK RG12 ...33 H2
Drummond Rd
  CRAWW RH11 ...176 B6
  CROY/NA CR0 ...2 C3
  GU GU1 ...6 E3
Drummonds PI RCH/KEW TW9..17 L9

Drungewick La BIL RH14 ...188 G9
Drury CI CRAWE RH10 ...177 N7
Drury Crs CROY/NA CR0 ...63 J1
Dryad St PUT/ROE SW15 ...19 H8
Dry Arch Rd ASC SL5 ...34 F8
Dryburgh Rd
  PUT/ROE SW15 ...18 G9
Dryden BRAK RG12 ...32 C8
Dryden Rd FARN GU14 ...88 B1
  WIM/MER SW19 ...28 F9
Drynham Pk WEY KT13 ...56 G2
Duchess CI CWTH RG45 ...56 C2
  SUT SM1 ...61 N3
Duchess of Kent Barracks
  ALDT GU11 ...108 D3
Dudley CI ADL/WDHM KT15 ...55 M2
Dudley Dr MRDN SM4 ...43 J9
Dudley Gv EPSOM KT18 ...78 B3
Dudley Rd ASHF TW15 ...23 J8
  EBED/NFELT TW14 ...23 N4
  KUT KT1 ...9 F5
  RCH/KEW TW9 ...17 M7
  WIM/MER SW19 ...28 D1
  WLGTN SM6 ...62 D4
  WOT/HER KT12 ...39 J7
Dudmaston Ms CHEL SW3 ...19 P3
Dudset La HEST TW5 ...15 J6
Duffield Rd
  KWD/TDW/WH KT20 ...98 F4
Duffins Orch CHERT KT16 ...54 C6
Duke CI CRAWE RH10 ...177 M9
Duke of Cambridge CI
  WHTN TW2 ...25 L2
Duke of Cornwall Av
  CBLY GU15 ...50 F8
Duke of Edinburgh Rd
  SUT SM1 ...61 P2
Duke Rd CHSWK W4 ...18 B3
Dukes Av CHSWK W4 ...18 B3
  HSLWW TW4 ...15 N9
  NWMAL KT3 ...42 D3
  RCHPK/HAM TW10 ...26 B7
Dukes CI ASHF TW15 ...23 M7
  CRAN GU6 ...171 K1
  FNM GU9 ...107 L8
  HPTN TW12 ...24 G8
Dukes Covert BAGS GU19 ...51 N3
Dukes Dr GODL GU7 ...131 H6
Dukes Ga CHSWK W4 * ...18 A2
Dukes HI BAGS GU19 ...51 N4
Dukeshill Rd BNFD RG42 ...32 D2
Dukes La ASC SL5 ...34 F1
Dukes Md FLEETN GU51 ...86 E5
Dukes Pk ALDT GU11 ...88 F7
Dukes Ride CWTH RG45 ...49 K5
  RDKG RH5 ...137 K1
Dukes Rd RDKG RH5 ...156 G6
  WOT/HER KT12 ...57 H4
Dukesthorpe Rd SYD SE26 ...31 L7
Duke St RCH/KEW TW9 * ...26 C1
  SUT SM1 ...61 P3
  WOKN/KNAP GU21 ...11 F3
Dukes Wd CWTH RG45 ...49 M4
Dulka Rd BTSEA SW11 ...29 J2
Dulverton Rd SAND/SEL CR2 ...64 C8
Dulwich Common DUL SE21 ...30 G4
The Dulwich Oaks DUL SE21 *..30 G6
Dulwich Village DUL SE21 ...30 F2
Dulwich Wood Av
  NRWD SE19 ...30 F7
Dulwich Wood Pk
  NRWD SE19 ...30 F7
Dumas CI YTLY GU46 ...66 G3
Du Maurier CI FLEETS GU52 ..106 C3
Dumbarton Rd
  BRXS/STRHM SW2 ...29 P2
Dumbleton CI KUT KT1 ...9 K3
Dump Rd FARN GU14 ...88 A1
Dumville Dr GDST RH9 ...122 B2
Dunally Pk SHPTN TW17 ...38 F7
Dunbar Av BECK BR3 ...46 E5
  STRHM/NOR SW16 ...45 J3
Dunbar Ct WOT/HER KT12 ...57 L1
Dunbar Rd FRIM GU16 ...69 H9
  NWMAL KT3 ...42 A5
Dunbar St WWNWD SE27 ...30 D6
Dunboe PI SHPTN TW17 ...38 E8
Duncan Dr GU GU1 ...112 E4
Duncan Gdns STA TW18 ...22 D8
Duncan Rd
  KWD/TDW/WH KT20 ...79 J8
  RCH/KEW TW9 ...17 L9
Duncombe Hi FSTH SE23 ...31 M3
Duncombe Rd GODL GU7 ...150 C2
Duncroft CI REIG RH2 ...119 K5
Dundaff CI CBLY GU15 ...69 J3
Dundas CI BRAK RG12 ...32 D5
Dundas Gdns
  E/WMO/HCT KT8 ...40 B4
Dundee Rd SNWD SE25 ...46 B6
Dundela Gdns WPK KT4 ...60 F3
Dundonald Rd
  WIM/MER SW19 ...43 K1
Dundrey Crs REDH RH1 ...100 G9
Dunedin Dr CTHM CR3 ...101 H5
Dunelm Gv WNWD SE27 ...30 D7
Dunfee Wy BF/WBF KT14 ...74 A1
Dunford Dr
  WOKN/KNAP GU21 ...54 F9
Dunford PI BNFD RG42 ...32 A1
Dungarvan Av
  PUT/ROE SW15 ...18 E9
Dungates La
  BRKHM/BTCW RH3 ...118 E4
Dungells Farm CI YTLY GU46..66 F4
Dungells La YTLY GU46 ...66 G4
Dunheved CI THHTH CR7 ...45 J7
Dunheved Rd North
  THHTH CR7 ...45 J7

Dunheved Rd South
  THHTH CR7 ...45 J7
Dunheved Rd West
  THHTH CR7 ...45 J7
Dunkeld Rd SNWD SE25 ...45 M5
Dunkirk St WNWD SE27 * ...30 D7
Dunleary CI HSLWW TW4 ...24 C3
Dunley Dr CROY/NA CR0 ...65 J5
Dunlin CI REDH RH1 ...140 A1
Dunlin Ri RGUE GU4 ...113 H1
Dunmail Dr PUR/KEN CR8 ...81 N3
Dunmore GUW GU2 ...111 K4
Dunmore Rd RYNPK SW20 ...42 G2
Dunmow CI FELT TW13 * ...24 F7
Dunmow HI FLEETN GU51 ...87 J3
Dunnets WOKN/KNAP GU21 ...71 L6
Dunnings Rd EGRIN RH19 ...180 D5
Dunnymans Rd BNSTD SM7 ...79 K4
Dunoon Gdns FSTH SE23 * ...31 L3
Dunoon Rd FSTH SE23 ...31 K3
Dunottar CI REIG RH2 ...119 H7
Dunraven Av REDH RH1 ...140 D4
Dunsany Rd WKENS W14 ...19 H1
Dunsbury CI BELMT SM2 * ...61 M7
Dunsdon Av GUW GU2 ...6 A5
Dunsfold CI CRAWW RH11 ...176 G8
Dunsfold Common Rd
  MFD/CHID GU8 ...169 L4
Dunsfold Ri COUL/CHIP CR5 ...80 F2
Dunsfold Rd BIL RH14 ...187 K7
  MFD/CHID GU8 ...188 B3
  MFD/CHID GU8 ...170 B8
  MFD/CHID GU8 ...187 H3
Dunsfold Wy CROY/NA CR0 ...65 J6
Dunsmore Gdns YTLY GU46 ...66 E3
Dunsmore Rd WOT/HER KT12..39 K6
Dunstable Rd
  E/WMO/HCT KT8 ...39 P5
  RCH/KEW TW9 ...17 L9
Dunstall Pk FARN GU14 ...68 C9
Dunstall Rd RYNPK SW20 ...42 G1
Dunstan Rd COUL/CHIP CR5 ...80 F6
Dunstans Gv EDUL SE22 ...31 J2
Dunstan's Rd EDUL SE22 ...31 H3
Dunster Av MRDN SM4 ...43 H6
Dunton CI SURB KT6 ...41 L9
Duntshill Rd
  WAND/EARL SW18 ...28 E4
Dunvegan CI
  E/WMO/HCT KT8 ...40 B5
Dupont Rd RYNPK SW20 ...43 H3
Duppas Av CROY/NA CR0 ...2 B7
Duppas CI SHPTN TW17 ...38 F6
Duppas Hill La CROY/NA CR0 ...2 B6
Duppas Hill Rd CROY/NA CR0..63 J3
Duppas Hill Ter CROY/NA CR0..2 B6
Dura Den CI BECK BR3 ...47 H1
Durban Rd BECK BR3 ...46 F3
  WNWD SE27 ...30 D7
Durbin Rd CHSGTN KT9 ...59 L3
Durfold Dr REIG RH2 ...119 N5
Durfold Rd HORS RH12 ...192 D3
Durford Crs PUT/ROE SW15 ...27 M4
Durham Av HAYES BR2 ...47 N5
  HEST TW5 ...15 P4
Durham CI CRAWE RH10 ...177 H9
  GUW GU2 ...111 M3
Durham Rd EA W5 ...17 K1
  EBED/NFELT TW14 ...24 B3
  HAYES BR2 ...47 N5
  SHST GU47 ...50 A7
Durham Ter PGE/AN SE20 * ...46 B1
Durkins Rd EGRIN RH19 ...162 C9
Durleston Park Dr
  GT/LBKH KT23 ...96 C5
Durley Md BRAK RG12 ...33 H6
Durning Rd NRWD SE19 ...30 E8
Durnsford Av FLEETS GU52 ...86 C8
  WAND/EARL SW18 ...28 D5
Durnsford Rd
  WAND/EARL SW18 ...28 D5
Durnsford Wy CRAN GU6 ...171 J1
Durrell Rd FUL/PGN SW6 ...19 J6
Durrell Wy SHPTN TW17 ...38 F7
Durrington Av RYNPK SW20 ...42 G2
Durrington Park Rd
  RYNPK SW20 ...42 G2
Dutch Barn CI
  STWL/WRAY TW19 ...22 G2
Dutchells Copse HORS RH12..192 G4
Dutch Gdns KUTN/CMB KT2 ...26 G9
Dutch Yd WAND/EARL SW18 ...28 D1
Duval PI BAGS GU19 ...51 M5
Duxhurst La HORL RH6 ...139 M6
Dwelly La LING RH7 ...144 E1
Dyehouse Rd
  MFD/CHID GU8 ...148 B8
Dyer's Fid HORL RH6 ...160 C1
Dyer's La PUT/ROE SW15 ...18 F8
Dykes Pth WOKN/KNAP GU21..72 G4
Dykes Wy HAYES BR2 ...47 M4
Dymock St FUL/PGN SW6 ...19 L9
Dynevor PI RGUW GU3 ...111 J1
Dynevor Rd
  RCHPK/HAM TW10 ...26 D1
Dysart Av KUTN/CMB KT2 ...26 B8
Dyson Ct DORK RH4 * ...116 G7
Dyson Wk CRAWW RH11 * ...194 E1

E

Eady Cl SWTR RH13 192 E8
Eagle Cl CWTH RG45 49 L2
WLGTN SM6 62 G5
Eagle Hl NRWD SE19 30 E9
Eagle Pl WBPTN SW10 19 N3
Eagle Rd FARN GU14 88 D5
GU GU1 7 F3
HTHAIR TW6 15 H8
Eagles Dr BH/WHM TN16 84 B7
Eagles Nest SHST GU47 49 L8
Ealing Park Gdns EA W5 17 J2
Ealing Rd EA W5 17 K2
Eardley Crs ECT SW5 19 L3
Eardley Rd
STRHM/NOR SW16 29 M9
Earldom Rd PUT/ROE SW15 18 G9
Earle Cft BNFD RG42 32 E1
Earle Gdns KUTN/CMB KT2 41 L1
Earles Meadow HORS RH12 192 G4
Earleswood COB KT11 75 M1
Earleydene ASC SL5 34 B9
Earl Rd MORT/ESHN SW14 18 A9
Earlsbourne FLEETS GU52 107 H2
Earlsbrook Rd REDH RH1 120 B7
Earls Court Gdns ECT SW5 19 M2
Earl's Court Rd ECT SW5 19 L2
Earl's Court Sq ECT SW5 19 M3
Earlsfield Rd
WAND/EARL SW18 28 F4
Earls Gv CBLY GU15 68 G2
Earls Ter KENS W8 19 L1
Earlsthorpe Ms BAL SW12 29 K2
Earlsthorpe Rd SYD SE26 31 L7
Earls Wk KENS W8 19 L1
Earlswood BRAK RG12 32 D8
Earlswood Av THHTH CR7 45 J6
Earlswood Cl SWTR RH13 192 E6
Earlswood Rd REDH RH1 120 B7
Early Commons
CRAWE RH10 177 J4
Earsby St WKENS W14 19 J2
Easby Crs MRDN SM4 43 M7
Eashing La GODL GU7 130 F9
Easington Pl GU GU1 7 K4
East Av CROY/NA CR0 63 H4
FNM GU9 107 P8
Eastbank Rd HPTN TW12 25 K8
Eastbourne Gdns
MORT/ESHN SW14 18 A8
Eastbourne Rd BTFD TW8 17 K3
CHSWK W4 18 A4
EGRIN RH19 161 N6
FELT TW13 24 E5
GDST RH9 122 D4
TOOT SW17 29 K9
Eastbrook Cl
WOKN/KNAP GU21 11 H1
Eastbury Ct BNFD RG42 32 B1
Eastbury Gv CHSWK W4 18 C3
Eastbury La RGUW GU3 130 G2
Eastbury Rd KUTN/CMB KT2 8 D1
Eastchurch Rd HTHAIR TW6 14 G8
Eastcote Av E/WMO/HCT KT8 39 P6
East Ct EGRIN RH19 * 180 E1
Eastcroft Rd HOR/WEW KT19 60 C6
Eastdean Av EPSOM KT18 77 P2
East Dr CAR SM5 62 A7
VW GU25 35 P7
East Dulwich Gv EDUL SE22 30 F1
Eastern Av CHERT KT16 37 L4
CHOB/PIR GU24 91 H1
Eastern La CWTH RG45 50 B5
Eastern Perimeter Rd
HTHAIR TW6 14 G7
Eastern Rd ASHV GU12 108 G4
BRAK RG12 32 F3
Eastern Vw BH/WHM TN16 84 A6
Easter Wy GDST RH9 122 F9
Eastfield Rd REDH RH1 120 E7
Eastfields MFD/CHID GU8 149 N7
Eastfields Rd MTCM CR4 44 C3
East Flexford La RGUW GU3 110 F8
East Gdns WIM/MER SW19 29 H9
WOKS/MYFD GU22 72 G6
Eastgate BNSTD SM7 79 K3
Eastgate Ct GU GU1 * 7 G5
Eastgate Gdns GU GU1 7 G4
East Gn BLKW GU17 67 N4
East Grinstead Rd LING RH7 162 C1
Easthampstead Rd
BRAK RG12 32 C3
East Hl BH/WHM TN16 83 P7
EGRIN RH19 162 D6
OXTED RH8 103 M9
SAND/SEL CR2 63 N8
WAND/EARL SW18 28 F1
WOKS/MYFD GU22 72 G5
East Hill La CRAWE RH10 160 E6
East Hill Rd OXTED RH8 103 L9
Eastlands Cl OXTED RH8 103 K7
Eastlands Crs EDUL SE22 30 G2
Eastlands Wy OXTED RH8 103 K7
East La EHSLY KT24 94 E6
KUT KT1 8 C6
Eastleigh Cl BELMT SM2 61 M6
Eastleigh Wy
EBED/NFELT TW14 24 B4
Eastmead FARN GU14 88 D4
WOKN/KNAP GU21 71 P6
East Meads GUW GU2 111 M6
Eastmearn Rd DUL SE21 30 D5
East Ms HORS RH12 * 192 B8
Eastmont Rd ESH/CLAY KT10 58 F1
Eastney Rd CROY/NA CR0 2 A1
Eastnor Pl REIG RH2 * 119 L7
Eastnor Rd REIG RH2 119 K7
East Pk CRAWE RH10 176 G6
East Park La LING RH7 161 K3
East Pl WNWD SE27 30 D7
East Rp HTHAIR TW6 14 D6
East Ring RFNM GU10 109 J7
East Rd EBED/NFELT TW14 23 N3
KUTN/CMB KT2 8 E2
REIG RH2 119 K4
WDR/YW UB7 14 B2
WEY KT13 56 F6
WIM/MER SW19 28 F9
Eastry Av HAYES BR2 47 M7
East Shalford La RGUE GU4 132 E1
East Sheen Av
MORT/ESHN SW14 27 J1
East Stanley Gn
DTCH/LGLY SL3 12 D2
East Station Rd ASHV GU12 108 D5
East Stratton Cl BRAK RG12 33 H6
East St BMLY BR1 47 N3
BTFD TW8 17 J5
CRAWE RH10 179 J7
EW KT17 78 C1
FNM GU9 5 G3
GT/LBKH KT23 96 B5
HORS RH12 175 K4
HORS RH12 192 B9
East View La CRAN GU6 152 F9
East Wk REIG RH2 119 M5
East Wy CROY/NA CR0 64 E1
Eastway GUW GU2 111 M5
HAYES BR2 47 N8
HOR/WEW KT19 78 A1
HORL RH6 159 L5
MRDN SM4 43 H6
WLGTN SM6 62 E3
Eastwell Cl BECK BR3 46 E2
East Whipley La SHGR GU5 152 C6
Eastwick Dr GT/LBKH KT23 96 B4
Eastwick Park Av
GT/LBKH KT23 96 B4
Eastwick Rd GT/LBKH KT23 96 B5
WOT/HER KT12 57 K5
Eastwood CRAWE RH10 177 J5
Eastwood Ldg SHGR GU5 * 132 D6
Eastwood Rd SHGR GU5 132 D6
Eastwood St
STRHM/NOR SW16 29 M9
Eastworth Rd CHERT KT16 37 L9
Eaton Dr KUTN/CMB KT2 9 J1
Eaton Pk COB KT11 75 N3
Eaton Park Rd COB KT11 75 N3
Eaton Rd BELMT SM2 61 P5
CBLY GU15 68 D4
ISLW TW7 16 D9
Eatonville Rd TOOT SW17 29 J5
Eatonville Vls TOOT SW17 29 J5
Ebba's Wy EPSOM KT18 77 P4
Ebbisham La
KWD/TDW/WH KT20 98 D1
Ebbisham Rd EPSOM KT18 77 P4
WPK KT4 60 G1
Ebenezer Wk MTCM CR4 44 E2
Ebner St WAND/EARL SW18 28 E1
Ebsworth St FSTH SE23 31 L3
Ecclesbourne Rd THHTH CR7 45 L6
Eccleshill RDKG RH5 137 J2
Echelforde Dr ASHF TW15 23 K7
Echo Barn La RFNM GU10 127 J8
Echo Pit Rd RGUE GU4 112 C9
Ecob Cl RGUW GU3 111 M1
Ecton Rd ADL/WDHM KT15 55 M3
Eddeys Cl BOR GU35 164 E5
Eddeys La BOR GU35 164 E6
Eddington Hl CRAWW RH11 194 D1
Eddington Rd BRAK RG12 32 A7
Eddiscombe Rd
FUL/PGN SW6 19 K7
Eddy Rd ASHV GU12 108 E5
Eddystone Rd BROCKY SE4 31 M1
Ede Cl HSLW TW3 15 P8
Edenbrook LING RH7 143 L9
Eden Cl ADL/WDHM KT15 55 M8
DTCH/LGLY SL3 12 E3
KENS W8 19 L1
Edencourt Rd STRHM/NOR
SW16 29 L9
Edencroft SHGR GU5 132 E6
Edenfield Gdns WPK KT4 60 D2
Eden Grove Rd BF/WBF KT14 74 A2
Edenhurst Av FUL/PGN SW6 19 K8
Eden Pde BECK BR3 * 46 E5
Eden Park Av BECK BR3 46 G6
Eden Rd BECK BR3 46 E5
CRAWW RH11 176 C7
CROY/NA CR0 2 E7
WNWD SE27 30 C8
Edenside Rd GT/LBKH KT23 95 P4
Edensor Rd CHSWK W4 18 C5
Eden St KUT KT1 8 D5
Eden V EGRIN RH19 162 D8
Edenvale Rd MTCM CR4 44 C1
Edenvale St FUL/PGN SW6 19 M7
Eden Valley Wk EDEN TN8 144 D7
Eden Wy BECK BR3 46 G6
WARL CR6 82 E7
Ederline Av
STRHM/NOR SW16 45 H4
Edes Cottages ASHTD KT21 * 77 K8
Edgar Cl CRAWE RH10 177 P6
Edgarley Ter FUL/PGN SW6 * 19 J6
Edgar Rd BH/WHM TN16 104 B1
HSLWW TW4 24 G3
SAND/SEL CR2 63 M8
Edgbarrow Ct CWTH RG45 * 49 L6
Edgbarrowhill Star
CWTH RG45 49 L6
Edgbarrow Ri SHST GU47 49 L7
Edgcumbe Park Dr
CWTH RG45 49 L4
Edgeborough Ct GU GU1 * 7 K5
Edge Cl WEY KT13 56 C6
Edgecombe Cl KUTN/CMB KT2 42 B1
Edgecoombe SAND/SEL CR2 64 D7
Edgedale Cl CWTH RG45 49 M5
Edgefield Cl CRAN GU6 152 F8
REDH RH1 140 C1
Edge Hl WIM/MER SW19 43 H1
Edgehill Ct WOT/HER KT12 * 39 L9
Edgehill Rd MTCM CR4 44 D3
PUR/KEN CR8 63 J8
Edgeley GT/LBKH KT23 95 N4
Edgell Cl VW GU25 36 D4
Edgell Rd STA TW18 22 C9
Edgel St WAND/EARL SW18 19 M9
Edgemoor Rd FRIM GU16 69 L5
Edgepoint Cl WNWD SE27 * 30 C8
Edgewood Cl CWTH RG45 49 L2
Edgewood Gn CROY/NA CR0 46 D9
Edgeworth Cl CTHM CR3 82 A7
Edgington Rd
STRHM/NOR SW16 29 N9
Edinburgh Ct KUT KT1 * 8 D6
Edinburgh Dr STA TW18 22 G9
Edinburgh Rd SUT SM1 61 N1
Edinburgh Wy EGRIN RH19 180 E4
Edison Rd HAYES BR2 47 N3
Edith Gdns BRYLDS KT5 41 P8
Edith Gv WBPTN SW10 19 N4
Edith Rd SNWD SE25 45 M6
WIM/MER SW19 28 E9
WKENS W14 19 J2
Edith Rw FUL/PGN SW6 19 M6
Edith Ter WBPTN SW10 * 19 N5
Edith Vls WKENS W14 19 K2
Edmonds Ct BRAK RG12 * 32 E2
Edmund Gv FELT TW13 24 G5
Edmund Rd MTCM CR4 44 A4
Edna Rd RYNPK SW20 43 H3
Edney Cl FLEETS GU52 87 H9
Edrich Rd CRAWW RH11 194 D1
Edridge Rd CROY/NA CR0 2 D6
Edward Av CBLY GU15 68 C3
MRDN SM4 43 P6
Edward Cl HPTN TW12 25 K8
Edward Ct STA TW18 22 F9
Edwardes Pl WKENS W14 19 K1
Edwardes Sq KENS W8 19 K1
Edward Ii Av BF/WBF KT14 74 B3
Edward Rd BFOR GU20 52 D5
BH/WHM TN16 84 C7
BMLY BR1 47 P1
COUL/CHIP CR5 80 F4
CROY/NA CR0 45 N8
EBED/NFELT TW14 23 N1
FNM GU9 127 N6
HPTN TW12 25 K8
PGE/AN SE20 46 D1
Edwards Cl WPK KT4 61 H1
Edward St ALDT GU11 108 B4
Edward Wy ASHF TW15 23 J5
Edwin Cl EHSLY KT24 94 F5
Edwin Rd EHSLY KT24 94 E5
WHTN TW2 25 M4
Eelmoor Br ALDT GU11 87 N9
Eelmoor Plain Rd
ALDT GU11 107 P2
Eelmoor Rd ALDT GU11 107 P1
FARN GU14 88 B5
Effie Pl FUL/PGN SW6 19 L5
Effie Rd FUL/PGN SW6 19 L5
Effingham Cl BELMT SM2 61 M6
Effingham Common Rd
EHSLY KT24 95 L5
Effingham Ct
WOKS/MYFD GU22 * 10 D7
Effingham La CRAWE RH10 160 F7
Effingham Pl EHSLY KT24 95 M7
Effingham Rd CROY/NA CR0 45 H8
HORL RH6 160 D6
REIG RH2 119 M6
SURB KT6 41 H8
Effort St TOOT SW17 29 H8
Effra Pde BRXS/STRHM SW2 30 B1
Effra Rd BRXS/STRHM SW2 30 B1
WIM/MER SW19 28 E9
Egerton Pl WEY KT13 56 E5
Egerton Rd GUW GU2 111 M5
NWMAL KT3 42 D5
SHST GU47 68 A2
SNWD SE25 45 N4
WEY KT13 56 E5
WHTN TW2 25 M3
Egerton Wy WDR/YW UB7 14 D5
Eggars Fld RFNM GU10 126 B8
Eggar's Hl ALDT GU11 108 C6
Eggleton Cl FLEETS GU52 106 E1
Egham By-pass EGH TW20 21 L7
Egham Cl CHEAM SM3 61 J1
Egham Crs CHEAM SM3 61 H2
Egham Hl EGH TW20 21 J9
Eglantine Rd
WAND/EARL SW18 28 F1
Egleston Rd MRDN SM4 43 M7
Egley Dr WOKS/MYFD GU22 92 B2
Egley Rd WOKS/MYFD GU22 92 B2
Eglinton Rd RFNM GU10 147 L6
Eglise Rd WARL CR6 82 E6
Egliston Ms PUT/ROE SW15 18 G8
Egliston Rd PUT/ROE SW15 18 G8
Egmont Av SURB KT6 41 N9
Egmont Park Rd
KWD/TDW/WH KT20 98 E5
Egmont Rd BELMT SM2 61 N6
NWMAL KT3 42 D5
SURB KT6 41 M9
WOT/HER KT12 39 K8
Egmont Wy
KWD/TDW/WH KT20 79 J8
Egremont Rd WNWD SE27 30 B6
Egret Gdns ALDT GU11 108 C7
Eight Acres GSHT GU26 165 M4
Eighteenth Rd MTCM CR4 44 G5
Eighth Av
KWD/TDW/WH KT20 * 99 K6
Eileen Rd SNWD SE25 45 M6
Eindoven Cl MTCM CR4 44 C9
Eland Rd ASHV GU12 108 F5
CROY/NA CR0 2 A5
Elberon Av CROY/NA CR0 44 E7
Elbe St FUL/PGN SW6 19 N7
Elborough Rd SNWD SE25 46 A6
Elborough St
WAND/EARL SW18 28 D4
Elbow Meadow
DTCH/LGLY SL3 * 13 K6
Elcho Rd CHOB/PIR GU24 70 C8
Elder Cl RGUE GU4 112 E2
Eldergrove FARN GU14 88 G5
Elder Oak Cl PGE/AN SE20 46 B2
Elder Rd CHOB/PIR GU24 70 G4
WNWD SE27 30 D8
Eldersley Cl REDH RH1 120 B3
Eldersley Gdns REDH RH1 120 B3
Elderslie Cl BECK BR3 46 G7
Elderton Rd SYD SE26 31 M7
Eldertree Wy MTCM CR4 44 D2
Elder Wy RDKG RH5 137 J2
Eldon Av CROY/NA CR0 64 C1
HEST TW5 16 A5
Eldon Dr RFNM GU10 127 P8
Eldon Pk SNWD SE25 46 B5
Eldon Rd CTHM CR3 101 M1
KENS W8 19 M1
Eldridge Cl
EBED/NFELT TW14 24 B4
Eleanora Ter SUT SM1 * 61 N4
Eleanor Av HOR/WEW KT19 60 B8
Eleanor Cl LIPH GU30 182 A2
Eleanor Gv BARN SW13 18 C8
Electra Av HTHAIR TW6 15 H8
Electric Pde SURB KT6 41 K7
Elers Rd HYS/HAR UB3 14 E2
Eleventh Av
KWD/TDW/WH KT20 * 99 K6
Elfindale Rd HNHL SE24 30 D1
Elfin Gv TEDD TW11 25 N8
Elfrida Crs CAT SE6 31 P7
Elgar Av BRYLDS KT5 41 P9
CWTH RG45 49 M3
STRHM/NOR SW16 44 G4
Elgarth Dr EWKG RG40 48 D1
Elgar Wy HORS RH12 192 G6
Elger Wy CRAWE RH10 160 B8
Elgin Av ASHF TW15 23 M9
SHB W12 18 F1
Elgin Crs CTHM CR3 102 A2
HTHAIR TW6 14 G7
Elgin Gdns GU GU1 112 E4
Elgin Pl WEY KT13 * 56 E5
Elgin Rd BLKW GU17 67 J7
CROY/NA CR0 3 K3
SUT SM1 61 N2
WEY KT13 56 C5
WLGTN SM6 62 E5
Elgin Wy FRIM GU16 69 H9
Eliot Bank FSTH SE23 31 J5
Eliot Cl CBLY GU15 69 K1
Eliot Dr HASM GU27 183 P4
Eliot Gdns PUT/ROE SW15 18 E9
Elizabethan Wy
CRAWE RH10 177 M6
STWL/WRAY TW19 22 G3
Elizabeth Av BAGS GU19 51 P7
STA TW18 22 F9
Elizabeth Barnes Ct
FUL/PGN SW6 * 19 M7
Elizabeth Cl BRAK RG12 32 E5
SUT SM1 61 K3
Elizabeth Cottages
RCH/KEW TW9 17 M6
Elizabeth Ct GODL GU7 131 L6
HORL RH6 * 159 K1
Elizabeth Crs EGRIN RH19 162 E9
Elizabeth Dr FLEETS GU52 106 G1
Elizabeth Gdns ASC SL5 34 B6
SUN TW16 39 L4
Elizabeth Rd GODL GU7 131 L6
Elizabeth Wy FELT TW13 24 D7
NRWD SE19 45 M1
Elkins Gdns RGUE GU4 112 E2
Elkins Gv RFNM GU10 * 4 A4
Ellaline Rd HMSMTH W6 19 H4
Elland Rd WOT/HER KT12 57 M1
Ellenborough Cl BRAK RG12 32 F2
Ellenborough Pl
PUT/ROE SW15 18 E9
Ellenbridge Wy
SAND/SEL CR2 63 N7
Ellen Dr FLEETN GU51 87 H3
Elleray Ct ASHV GU12 109 J1
Elleray Rd TEDD TW11 25 N9
Ellerby St FUL/PGN SW6 19 H6
Ellerdine Rd HSLW TW3 16 C9
Ellerker Gdns
RCHPK/HAM TW10 26 D2
Ellerman Av WHTN TW2 24 G4
Ellerton Rd BARN SW13 * 18 E6
RYNPK SW20 42 E1
SURB KT6 59 M1
WAND/EARL SW18 28 G4
Ellery Cl CRAN GU6 171 H2
Ellery Rd NRWD SE19 45 M1
Elles Av GU GU1 112 F5
Elles Cl FARN GU14 88 D4
Ellesfield Av BRAK RG12 32 A5
Ellesmere Av BECK BR3 47 H3
Ellesmere Dr SAND/SEL CR2 82 B3
Ellesmere Pl WEY KT13 56 G4
Ellesmere Rd TWK TW1 26 B2
WEY KT13 56 G5
Elles Rd FARN GU14 88 A5
Ellice Rd OXTED RH8 103 M9
Ellies Ms ASHF TW15 23 H5
Ellingham Rd CHSGTN KT9 59 K5
Ellington Rd FELT TW13 24 A7
HSLW TW3 16 B7
Ellington Wy EPSOM KT18 78 F6
Elliot Cl CRAWE RH10 177 M6
Elliot Ri ASC SL5 33 M3
Elliott Ct WOKN/KNAP GU21 * 11 H2
Elliott Gdns SHPTN TW17 38 C5
Elliott Rd CHSWK W4 18 C2
THHTH CR7 45 K5
Elliotts La BH/WHM TN16 105 N4
Ellis Av GUW GU2 111 M7
Ellis Cl COUL/CHIP CR5 81 H9
Ellis Farm Cl
WOKS/MYFD GU22 92 B2
Ellisfield Dr PUT/ROE SW15 27 L3
Ellison Gdns NWDGN UB2 15 P2
Ellison Rd BARN SW13 18 D7
STRHM/NOR SW16 44 F1
Ellison Wy RFNM GU10 109 H7
Ellis Rd COUL/CHIP CR5 81 H9
CWTH RG45 49 M3
MTCM CR4 44 B7
Ellman Rd CRAWW RH11 176 C7
Ellora Rd STRHM/NOR SW16 29 N8
Ellson Cl CRAWE RH10 177 M7
Ellwood Pl CRAWW RH11 * 176 C5
Elm Bank CHOB/PIR GU24 * 53 L9
YTLY GU46 66 G1
Elmbank Av EGH TW20 20 G9
GUW GU2 111 N6
Elm Bank Gdns BARN SW13 18 C7
Elmbourne Rd TOOT SW17 29 L6
Elmbridge Av BRYLDS KT5 42 A7
Elmbridge La
WOKS/MYFD GU22 72 D8
Elmbridge Rd CRAN GU6 170 C1
Elmbrook Cl SUN TW16 39 K2
Elmbrook Rd SUT SM1 61 K3
Elm Cl BRYLDS KT5 42 A8
CAR SM5 44 B9
KWD/TDW/WH KT20 118 A1
LHD/OX KT22 97 H2
RYNPK SW20 42 G5
SAND/SEL CR2 63 M5
STWL/WRAY TW19 22 G4
WARL CR6 82 D6
WHTN TW2 25 J5
WOKN/KNAP GU21 72 B4
Elm Cottages GDST RH9 * 122 B1
MTCM CR4 * 44 B3
Elm Ct WOKN/KNAP GU21 71 K6
Elmcourt Rd WNWD SE27 30 C5
Elm Crs FNM GU9 107 P7
KUTN/CMB KT2 8 E3
Elm Cft DTCH/LGLY SL3 12 A6
Elmcroft GT/LBKH KT23 * 96 A4
Elmcroft Cl CHSGTN KT9 * 59 L2
EBED/NFELT TW14 24 A2
FRIM GU16 69 H9
Elmcroft Dr ASHF TW15 * 23 K8
CHSGTN KT9 59 L2
Elmdene BRYLDS KT5 42 A9
Elmdene Cl BECK BR3 46 F6
Elmdene Ct
WOKS/MYFD GU22 10 D7
Elmdon Rd HEST TW5 15 M7
HTHAIR TW6 15 H8
Elm Dr CHOB/PIR GU24 53 M8
EGRIN RH19 180 F2
LHD/OX KT22 97 H2
SUN TW16 39 L3
Elmer Cottages
LHD/OX KT22 * 96 G3
Elmer Gdns ISLW TW7 16 D8
Elmer Ms LHD/OX KT22 96 G3
Elmer's Dr TEDD TW11 26 A9
Elmers End Rd BECK BR3 46 C4
Elmerside Rd BECK BR3 46 E5
Elmers Rd CROY/NA CR0 46 A8
RDKG RH5 155 K8
Elmfield GT/LBKH KT23 96 A3
Elmfield Av MTCM CR4 44 C2
TEDD TW11 25 N8
Elmfield Pk BMLY BR1 47 N4
Elmfield Rd BAL SW12 29 L5
BMLY BR1 47 N4
NWDGN UB2 15 N1
Elmfield Wy SAND/SEL CR2 63 P7
Elm Gdns EPSOM KT18 78 G8
ESH/CLAY KT10 58 F5
MTCM CR4 44 F5
Elmgate Av FELT TW13 24 C6
Elm Gv CHOB/PIR GU24 70 G5
CRAN GU6 152 D9
CTHM CR3 101 N2
EPSOM KT18 78 A3
FNM GU9 107 N7
KUTN/CMB KT2 8 E3
SUT SM1 61 M3
SWTR RH13 192 D9
WIM/MER SW19 43 J1
Elmgrove Cl
WOKN/KNAP GU21 71 K6
Elm Grove Pde WLGTN SM6 62 C2
Elm Grove Rd BARN SW13 18 E6
COB KT11 75 M5
FARN GU14 88 D3
Elmgrove Rd CROY/NA CR0 46 B8
WEY KT13 56 C3
Elmhurst Av MTCM CR4 44 C1
Elmhurst Ct GU GU1 * 7 K4
Elmhurst Dr DORK RH4 117 H9
Elmhurst Rd DTCH/LGLY SL3 12 E1
Elm La CAT SE6 31 N5
RFNM GU10 109 H6
RPLY/SEND GU23 74 B8
Elmore Rd COUL/CHIP CR5 100 B1
Elm Pk ASC SL5 34 E9
BRXS/STRHM SW2 30 A2
Elmpark Gdns SAND/SEL CR2 64 C8
Elm Park Gdns WBPTN SW10 19 P3
Elm Park La CHEL SW3 19 P4
Elm Park Rd CHEL SW3 19 P4
SNWD SE25 45 P4

Elm Pl ALDT GU11 108 E6
SKENS SW7 19 P3
Elm Rd BECK BR3 46 F3
BH/WHM TN16 105 J5
CHSGTN KT9 59 L3
EBED/NFELT TW14 23 N4
ESH/CLAY KT10 58 F5
EW KT17 60 D5
FNM GU9 107 P7
GODL GU7 131 M5
KUTN/CMB KT2 9 G1
LHD/OX KT22 97 H2
MORT/ESHN SW14 18 A8
NWMAL KT3 42 B4
PUR/KEN CR8 81 K2
REDH RH1 120 A5
THHTH CR7 45 L5
WARL CR6 82 D6
WLGTN SM6 44 C9
WOKN/KNAP GU21 10 A6
Elm Rd West MRDN SM4 43 K8
Elms Crs CLAP SW4 29 M2
Elmshaw Rd PUT/ROE SW15 27 M1
Elmshorn EW KT17 78 G5
Elmside CROY/NA CR0 65 H5
GUW GU2 111 N6
MFD/CHID GU8 149 N3
Elmsleigh Rd FARN GU14 88 C3
STA TW18 22 C8
WHTN TW2 25 L5
Elmslie Cl EPSOM KT18 78 A3
Elms Rd ALDT GU11 108 C5
CLAP SW4 29 M1
FLEETN GU51 87 J6
Elmstead Cl HOR/WEW KT19 60 C4
Elmstead Gdns WPK KT4 60 E2
Elmstead Rd BF/WBF KT14 73 L2
The Elms BARN SW13 18 D8
BLKW GU17 * 67 P4
ESH/CLAY KT10 * 58 F6
RFNM GU10 109 H7
TOOT SW17 * 29 K6
WLGTN SM6 * 62 E3
Elmstone Rd FUL/PGN SW6 19 L6
Elmsway ASHF TW15 23 J8
Elmswood GT/LBKH KT23 95 P4
Elmsworth Av HSLW TW3 16 B7
Elm Tree Av ESH/CLAY KT10 40 D8
Elm Tree Cl ASHF TW15 23 L8
CHERT KT16 55 J1
HORL RH6 * 140 C9
Elmtree Cl BF/WBF KT14 74 A2
Elmtree Rd TEDD TW11 25 M8
Elm Vw ASHV GU12 109 K3
Elm Wk RYNPK SW20 42 G5
Elm Wy HOR/WEW KT19 60 B4
WPK KT4 60 G2
Elmwood Av FELT TW13 24 C6
Elmwood Cl EW KT17 60 E6
WLGTN SM6 62 D1
Elmwood Ct ASHTD KT21 77 K6
Elmwood Dr EW KT17 60 E6
Elmwood Rd CHSWK W4 18 A4
CROY/NA CR0 45 K8
HNHL SE24 30 E1
MTCM CR4 44 B4
REDH RH1 120 C1
WOKN/KNAP GU21 71 K8
Elmworth Gv DUL SE21 30 E5
Elruge Cl WDR/YW UB7 13 P1
Elsdon Rd WOKN/KNAP GU21 71 N7
Elsenham St
WAND/EARL SW18 28 C4
Elsenwood Crs CBLY GU15 69 J2
Elsenwood Dr CBLY GU15 69 J1
Elsiemaud Rd BROCKY SE4 31 N1
Elsinore Av
STWL/WRAY TW19 * 23 H3
Elsinore Rd FSTH SE23 31 M4
Elsinore Wy RCH/KEW TW9 17 P8
Elsley Cl FRIM GU16 89 H1
Elsrick Av MRDN SM4 43 L6
Elstan Wy CROY/NA CR0 46 E8
Elstead Rd MFD/CHID GU8 149 J1
RFNM GU10 109 J9
Elsted Cl CRAWW RH11 176 E3
Elston Pl ASHV GU12 108 E6
Elston Rd ASHV GU12 108 E6
Elstree Hl BMLY BR1 47 L1
Elswick St FUL/PGN SW6 19 N7
Elsworth Cl
EBED/NFELT TW14 23 P4
Elsworthy THDIT KT7 40 E7
Elsynge Rd
WAND/EARL SW18 28 G1
Elthiron Rd FUL/PGN SW6 19 L6
Elthorne Ct FELT TW13 24 D4
Elthorne Park Rd HNWL W7 16 F1
Elton Cl E/WMO/HCT KT8 8 A1
Elton Rd KUTN/CMB KT2 9 H2
PUR/KEN CR8 80 E1
Eltringham St
WAND/EARL SW18 19 N9
Elvaston Ms SKENS SW7 * 19 N1
Elvaston Pl SKENS SW7 19 N1
Elveden Cl WOKS/MYFD GU22 73 M6
Elveden Pl
WOKS/MYFD GU22 * 73 M6
Elveden Rd COB KT11 57 K9
Elvetham Cl FLEETN GU51 86 F4
Elvetham Crs FLEETN GU51 86 D4
Elvetham Heath
FLEETN GU51 86 D4
Elvetham Heath Wy
FLEETN GU51 86 D4
Elvetham Pl FLEETN GU51 86 E4
Elvetham Rd FLEETN GU51 86 E5
Elvington Gn HAYES BR2 47 M6
Elvino Rd SYD SE26 31 L8
Elwell Cl EGH TW20 21 M9
Elwill Wy BECK BR3 47 K5
Ely Cl CRAWE RH10 177 J9
FRIM GU16 69 J9
NWMAL KT3 42 D3
Ely Pl GUW GU2 * 111 M3
Ely Rd CROY/NA CR0 45 M6
HSLWW TW4 15 L8
HTHAIR TW6 15 H7
Elysium Pl FUL/PGN SW6 19 K7
Elysium St FUL/PGN SW6 19 K7
Elystan Cl WLGTN SM6 62 E7
Embankment PUT/ROE SW15 19 H8
The Embankment
STWL/WRAY TW19 21 H3
TWK TW1 25 P4
Embassy Ct WLGTN SM6 * 62 D5
Ember Cl ADL/WDHM KT15 55 P4
Embercourt Rd THDIT KT7 40 E7
Ember Farm Av
E/WMO/HCT KT8 40 D7
Ember Farm Wy
E/WMO/HCT KT8 40 D6
Ember Gdns ESH/CLAY KT10 40 E8
Ember La ESH/CLAY KT10 40 D9
Ember Rd DTCH/LGLY SL3 12 F1
Emberwood CRAWW RH11 * 176 G3
Embleton Rd BOR GU35 164 E5
Emden St FUL/PGN SW6 19 M6
Emerald Sq NWDGN UB2 15 M1
Emerton Rd LHD/OX KT22 76 C9
Emery Down Cl BRAK RG12 33 J4
Emery Down Dr
FLEETN GU51 86 C4
Emily Davison Dr
EPSOM KT18 78 F7
Emley Rd ADL/WDHM KT15 55 L2
Emlyn La LHD/OX KT22 96 G2
Emlyn Rd HORL RH6 140 A9
REDH RH1 120 C7
Emmanuel Cl GUW GU2 111 N2
Emmanuel Rd BAL SW12 29 M4
Emma Ter RYNPK SW20 * 42 G1
Emmetts Cl
WOKN/KNAP GU21 10 A3
Emmetts Rd BH/WHM TN16 125 N1
Emperor's Ga SKENS SW7 19 M1
Empire Vls REDH RH1 140 C6
Empress Av FARN GU14 88 D2
Empress Pl ECT SW5 19 L3
Emsworth Cl CRAWE RH10 * 177 M8
Emsworth St
BRXS/STRHM SW2 30 A5
Ena Rd STRHM/NOR SW16 44 G4
Enborne Gdns BRAK RG12 32 F1
Endale Cl CAR SM5 62 B1
Endeavour Wy CROY/NA CR0 44 G8
WIM/MER SW19 28 E7
Endlesham Rd BAL SW12 29 K3
Endsleigh Cl SAND/SEL CR2 64 C8
Endsleigh Gdns SURB KT6 41 J7
WOT/HER KT12 57 L4
Endsleigh Rd NWDGN UB2 15 N2
REDH RH1 100 E9
Ends Pl HORS RH12 * 191 K3
Endway BRYLDS KT5 41 N8
Endymion Rd
BRXS/STRHM SW2 30 A3
Enfield Rd ASHV GU12 109 K1
BTFD TW8 17 K3
CRAWW RH11 176 E9
HTHAIR TW6 14 G7
Engadine Cl CROY/NA CR0 3 J6
Engadine St
WAND/EARL SW18 28 C4
Engalee EGRIN RH19 180 B1
England Wy NWMAL KT3 41 P5
Englefield HORS RH12 191 N8
Englefield Cl CROY/NA CR0 45 L7
EGH TW20 21 H9
Englefield Rd
WOKN/KNAP GU21 * 71 J6
Engleheart Dr
EBED/NFELT TW14 24 A2
Englehurst EGH TW20 21 H9
Englemere Pk ASC SL5 33 M5
COB KT11 76 B3
Englemere Rd BNFD RG42 32 B1
Englesfield CBLY GU15 69 L3
Englewood Rd BAL SW12 29 L2
Engliff La WOKS/MYFD GU22 73 K5
English Gdns
STWL/WRAY TW19 12 B9
Enmore Av SNWD SE25 46 A6
Enmore Gdns
MORT/ESHN SW14 27 J1
Enmore Rd PUT/ROE SW15 18 G9
SNWD SE25 46 A6
Ennerdale BRAK RG12 32 C5
Ennerdale Cl CRAWW RH11 176 E7
EBED/NFELT TW14 24 A4
SUT SM1 61 K3
Ennerdale Gv FNM GU9 107 L8
Ennerdale Rd RCH/KEW TW9 17 M7
Ennismore Av CHSWK W4 18 D2
GU GU1 7 J3
Ennismore Gdns THDIT KT7 40 E7
Ennismore Gardens Ms
SKENS SW7 19 P1
Ensign Cl PUR/KEN CR8 63 J8
STWL/WRAY TW19 22 G4
Ensign Wy STWL/WRAY TW19 22 G4
Ensor Ms SKENS SW7 19 P3
Enterdent Rd GDST RH9 122 C5
Enterprise Cl CROY/NA CR0 45 J9
Enterprise Est GU GU1 * 112 C1
Enterprise Wy EDEN TN8 144 F2
TEDD TW11 25 N8
WAND/EARL SW18 19 L9
Enton La MFD/CHID GU8 150 A9
Envis Wy RGUW GU3 111 J1
Eothen Cl CTHM CR3 102 A4
Epirus Ms FUL/PGN SW6 19 L5
Epirus Rd FUL/PGN SW6 19 K5
Epping Wk CRAWE RH10 177 J7
Epping Wy BRAK RG12 33 H5
Epple Rd FUL/PGN SW6 19 K6
Epsom Cl CBLY GU15 50 E9
Epsom College EW KT17 * 78 E3
Epsom La North
KWD/TDW/WH KT20 78 F8
Epsom La South
KWD/TDW/WH KT20 98 G1
Epsom Pl CRAN GU6 153 J9
Epsom Rd ASHTD KT21 77 M7
CRAWE RH10 177 K7
CROY/NA CR0 63 J3
EHSLY KT24 94 F9
EW KT17 60 D9
GU GU1 7 H5
LHD/OX KT22 97 H1
MRDN SM4 43 K8
RGUE GU4 113 J4
Epsom Sq HTHAIR TW6 * 15 H7
Epts Rd FARN GU14 88 C7
Epworth Rd ISLW TW7 17 H5
Eresby Dr BECK BR3 46 G9
Erica Cl CHOB/PIR GU24 70 E2
Erica Ct WOKS/MYFD GU22 10 A6
Erica Gdns CROY/NA CR0 65 H3
Erica Wy CRAWE RH10 160 A9
HORS RH12 192 C5
Ericcson Cl WAND/EARL SW18 28 D1
Eridge Cl CRAWE RH10 177 M5
Eridge Rd CHSWK W4 18 B1
Erin Cl BMLY BR1 47 L1
Eriswell Crs WOT/HER KT12 57 H5
Eriswell Rd WOT/HER KT12 57 H3
Erkenwald Cl CHERT KT16 37 J7
Erlesmere Gdns HNWL W7 16 G1
Erles Rd LIPH GU30 182 F6
Ermine Cl HSLWW TW4 15 L7
Ermyn Cl LHD/OX KT22 97 K1
Ermyn Wy LHD/OX KT22 97 K1
Erncroft Wy TWK TW1 25 N2
Ernest Av WNWD SE27 30 C7
Ernest Cl BECK BR3 46 G6
RFNM GU10 127 M7
Ernest Gdns CHSWK W4 17 P4
Ernest Gv BECK BR3 46 F6
Ernest Rd KUT KT1 9 K5
Ernest Sq KUT KT1 9 K5
Ernle Rd RYNPK SW20 42 F1
Ernshaw Pl PUT/ROE SW15 28 B1
Erpingham Rd
PUT/ROE SW15 18 G8
Erridge Rd WIM/MER SW19 43 L3
Errol Gdns NWMAL KT3 42 E5
Erskine Cl CRAWW RH11 176 B9
SUT SM1 62 A2
Erskine Rd SUT SM1 61 P3
Esam Wy STRHM/NOR SW16 30 B8
Escombe Dr GUW GU2 91 P9
Escot Rd SUN TW16 38 G1
Escott Pl CHERT KT16 54 G5
Esher Av CHEAM SM3 61 H2
WOT/HER KT12 39 K9
Esher Cl ESH/CLAY KT10 58 B4
Esher Crs HTHAIR TW6 15 H7
Esher Gn ESH/CLAY KT10 58 B3
Esher Green Dr
ESH/CLAY KT10 58 A2
Esher Ms MTCM CR4 44 C4
Esher Park Av
ESH/CLAY KT10 58 C4
Esher Place Av
ESH/CLAY KT10 58 B3
Esher Rd CBLY GU15 51 J8
E/WMO/HCT KT8 40 D7
WOT/HER KT12 57 N3
Eskdale Ct ASHV GU12 * 109 H2
Eskdale Gdns PUR/KEN CR8 81 M3
Eskdale Wy CBLY GU15 69 L4
Eskmont Rdg NRWD SE19 45 N1
Esmond Gdns CHSWK W4 * 18 B2
Esmond Rd CHSWK W4 18 B1
Esmond St PUT/ROE SW15 19 J9
Esparto St WAND/EARL SW18 28 E3
Essendene Cl CTHM CR3 101 N3
Essendene Rd CTHM CR3 101 N3
Essenden Rd SAND/SEL CR2 63 N6
Essex Av ISLW TW7 16 E8
Essex Cl ADL/WDHM KT15 55 N3
FRIM GU16 69 J9
MRDN SM4 43 H8
Essex Ct BARN SW13 18 D7
Essex Dr CRAN GU6 170 C1
Essex Gv NRWD SE19 30 E9
Essex Pl CHSWK W4 18 B2
Essex Place Sq CHSWK W4 * 18 B2
Essex Ri BNFD RG42 33 H1
Essex Rd CHSWK W4 18 B2
Estcots Dr EGRIN RH19 180 F2
Estcourt Rd FUL/PGN SW6 19 K5
SNWD SE25 46 B7
Estella Av NWMAL KT3 42 F5
Estoria Cl BRXS/STRHM SW2 30 B3
Estreham Rd
STRHM/NOR SW16 29 N9
Estridge Cl HSLW TW3 16 A9
Eswyn Rd TOOT SW17 29 J7
Ethelbert Cl HAYES BR2 47 N3
Ethelbert Rd BMLY BR1 47 N4
RYNPK SW20 43 H2
Ethelbert St BAL SW12 29 L4
Ethel Rd ASHF TW15 23 H8
Etherley Hl RDKG RH5 155 H5
Etherow St EDUL SE22 31 H2
Etherstone Rd
STRHM/NOR SW16 30 A7
Eton Av HEST TW5 15 P4
NWMAL KT3 42 B6
Eton Cl WAND/EARL SW18 28 E3
Eton Ct STA TW18 22 C8
Eton Pl FNM GU9 107 M7
Eton Rd HYS/HAR UB3 15 H5
Eton St RCHPK/HAM TW10 26 C1
Etps Rd FARN GU14 88 D7
Etton Rd HSLW TW3 25 K1
Etwell Pl BRYLDS KT5 41 M7
Eureka Rd KUT KT1 9 H5
Europa Park Rd GU GU1 112 A4
Eustace Rd FUL/PGN SW6 19 L5
RGUE GU4 113 H3
Euston Rd CROY/NA CR0 45 J9
Evans Cl CRAWE RH10 177 N6
Evans Gv FELT TW13 25 H5
Evedon BRAK RG12 32 D8
Evelina Rd PGE/AN SE20 46 C1
Eveline Rd MTCM CR4 44 B2
Evelyn Av ALDT GU11 108 D6
Evelyn Cl WHTN TW2 25 J3
WOKS/MYFD GU22 72 B9
Evelyn Crs SUN TW16 39 H2
Evelyn Gdns GDST RH9 122 C1
RCH/KEW TW9 17 L9
WBPTN SW10 19 N3
Evelyn Rd CHSWK W4 18 B1
RCH/KEW TW9 17 L8
RCHPK/HAM TW10 26 B6
WIM/MER SW19 28 E8
Evelyn Ter RCH/KEW TW9 17 L8
Evelyn Wk CRAWE RH10 177 H8
Evelyn Wy COB KT11 75 P5
HOR/WEW KT19 59 N9
SUN TW16 39 H2
WLGTN SM6 62 F3
Evelyn Woods Rd ALDT GU11 88 E8
Evenlode Wy SHST GU47 49 N9
Evenwood Cl
PUT/ROE SW15 * 28 B1
Everard Av HAYES BR2 47 N9
Everatt Cl
WAND/EARL SW18 * 28 C2
Everdon Rd BARN SW13 18 E4
Everest Ct WOKN/KNAP GU21 71 L5
Everest Rd CBLY GU15 50 F9
CWTH RG45 49 M3
STWL/WRAY TW19 22 G3
Everglade BH/WHM TN16 84 B7
The Everglades HSLW TW3 * 16 C8
Evergreen Cl PGE/AN SE20 46 C1
Evergreen Ct
STWL/WRAY TW19 * 22 G3
Evergreen Rd FRIM GU16 69 H6
Evergreen Wy
STWL/WRAY TW19 22 G3
Everington St HMSMTH W6 19 H4
Everlands Cl
WOKS/MYFD GU22 10 C6
Eve Rd ISLW TW7 16 G9
WOKN/KNAP GU21 72 F4
Eversfield Rd RCH/KEW TW9 17 M7
REIG RH2 119 M5
SWTR RH13 192 D9
Eversley Crs ISLW TW7 16 D6
Eversley Dr FLEETN GU51 86 C4
Eversley Pk WIM/MER SW19 27 N8
Eversley Rd BRYLDS KT5 41 M5
NRWD SE19 45 M1
Eversley Wy CROY/NA CR0 64 G2
EGH TW20 36 G3
Everton Rd CROY/NA CR0 46 A9
Evesham Cl BELMT SM2 61 L6
REIG RH2 119 K4
Evesham Gn MRDN SM4 43 M7
Evesham Rd MRDN SM4 43 M7
REIG RH2 119 K4
Evesham Rd North
REIG RH2 119 K4
Evesham Ter SURB KT6 * 41 K7
Evesham Wk SHST GU47 49 N8
Ewald Rd FUL/PGN SW6 19 K7
Ewart Rd FSTH SE23 31 L3
Ewelands HORL RH6 140 E9
Ewell By-Pass EW KT17 60 E8
Ewell Court Av
HOR/WEW KT19 60 C4
Ewell Downs Rd EW KT17 60 E9
Ewell House EW KT17 * 60 D8
Ewell House Gv EW KT17 60 D8
Ewell House Pde EW KT17 * 60 D8
Ewell Park Gdns EW KT17 60 E6
Ewell Park Wy EW KT17 60 E5
Ewell Rd CHEAM SM3 61 H5
SURB KT6 41 M7
THDIT KT7 41 H8
Ewelme Rd FSTH SE23 31 K4
Ewen Crs BRXS/STRHM SW2 30 B3
Ewhurst Av SAND/SEL CR2 63 P8
Ewhurst Cl BELMT SM2 60 G7
CRAWW RH11 176 F5
Ewhurst Rd BROCKY SE4 31 N2
CRAN GU6 153 H9
CRAWW RH11 176 E5
SHGR GU5 134 F7
Ewins Cl ASHV GU12 109 J4
Ewood La RDKG RH5 137 M7
Ewshot La FLEETS GU52 106 F3
Exbury Rd CAT SE6 31 P5
Excalibur Cl CRAWW RH11 176 B5
Excelsior Cl KUT KT1 9 H5
Exchange Rd ASC SL5 34 C6
CRAWE RH10 177 H5
Exeforde Av ASHF TW15 23 K7
Exeter Cl CRAWE RH10 177 H9
Exeter Gdns YTLY GU46 66 F1
Exeter Ms FUL/PGN SW6 * 19 L5
Exeter Pl GUW GU2 * 111 M3
Exeter Rd ASHV GU12 109 J3
CROY/NA CR0 45 N8
FELT TW13 24 G6
HTHAIR TW6 14 G8
Exeter Wy HTHAIR TW6 14 G7
Exhibition Rd FARN GU14 88 C7
SKENS SW7 * 19 P2
Explorer Av
STWL/WRAY TW19 23 H4
Eyhurst Cl KWD/TDW/WH KT20 99 K4
Eyhurst Pk
KWD/TDW/WH KT20 * 99 N3
Eyhurst Sp
KWD/TDW/WH KT20 99 K4
Eyles Cl HORS RH12 192 A6
Eylewood Rd WNWD SE27 30 D8
Eynella Rd DUL SE21 30 G3
Eyot Gdns HMSMTH W6 18 D3
Eyston Dr WEY KT13 56 C8

F

Fabian Rd FUL/PGN SW6 19 K5
The Facade FSTH SE23 * 31 K5
REIG RH2 119 L4
Factory La CROY/NA CR0 2 A3
Fagg's Rd EBED/NFELT TW14 15 J9
Fairacre ISLW TW7 * 16 D6
NWMAL KT3 42 C4
Fair Acres HAYES BR2 47 N6
Fairacres COB KT11 75 M1
CROY/NA CR0 64 F7
KWD/TDW/WH KT20 98 G1
RFNM GU10 * 127 K9
Fairbairn Cl PUR/KEN CR8 81 J2
Fairborne Wy GUW GU2 111 N2
Fairbourne COB KT11 75 M2
Fairbourne Cl
WOKN/KNAP GU21 71 N6
Fairbourne La CTHM CR3 101 L2
Fairchild Cl BTSEA SW11 19 P7
Fairchildes Av CROY/NA CR0 83 K1
Fairchildes Rd WARL CR6 83 K4
Faircross BRAK RG12 32 D4
Fairdale Gdns PUT/ROE SW15 18 F9
Fairdene Rd COUL/CHIP CR5 80 F7
Fairey Av HYS/HAR UB3 15 H1
Fairfax BNFD RG42 32 C2
Fairfax Av EW KT17 60 F7
REDH RH1 120 B4
Fairfax Cl WOT/HER KT12 39 K9
Fairfax Ms FARN GU14 88 F5
PUT/ROE SW15 18 G9
Fairfax Pl WKENS W14 19 J1
Fairfax Rd CHSWK W4 18 C1
FARN GU14 68 D9
TEDD TW11 40 G1
WOKS/MYFD GU22 72 F9
Fairfield Ap
STWL/WRAY TW19 21 J2
Fairfield Av DTCH/LGLY SL3 12 A5
HORL RH6 159 K3
STA TW18 22 C7
WHTN TW2 25 J4
Fairfield Cl GT/LBKH KT23 96 B5
HOR/WEW KT19 60 C4
WIM/MER SW19 44 A1
Fairfield Cnr KUT KT1 * 9 F5
Fairfield Dr DORK RH4 117 H5
FRIM GU16 68 G5
WAND/EARL SW18 28 E1
Fairfield East KUT KT1 8 E4
Fairfield La CHOB/PIR GU24 70 F1
Fairfield North KUT KT1 8 E4
Fairfield Pk COB KT11 75 M3
Fairfield Pth CROY/NA CR0 3 F5
Fairfield Pl KUT KT1 8 E6
Fairfield Ri GUW GU2 111 M4
Fairfield Rd BECK BR3 46 G3
BMLY BR1 47 N1
CROY/NA CR0 3 F5
EGRIN RH19 180 E3
KUT KT1 8 E5
LHD/OX KT22 97 H1
STWL/WRAY TW19 21 J2
Fairfields CHERT KT16 * 37 M9
Fairfield South KUT KT1 8 E6
Fairfield St
WAND/EARL SW18 28 E1
The Fairfield FNM GU9 5 H4
Fairfield Wy COUL/CHIP CR5 80 F3
HOR/WEW KT19 60 C4
Fairfield West KUT KT1 8 E5
Fairford Av CROY/NA CR0 46 D6
Fairford Cl BF/WBF KT14 73 K2
CROY/NA CR0 46 D6
REIG RH2 119 N3
Fairford Ct BELMT SM2 * 61 M6
Fairford Gdns WPK KT4 60 D2
Fairgreen Rd THHTH CR7 45 K6
Fairhaven EGH TW20 21 L8
Fairhaven Av CROY/NA CR0 46 D7
Fairhaven Rd REDH RH1 120 C1
Fairholme EBED/NFELT TW14 23 N3
Fairholme Crs ASHTD KT21 77 J6
Fairholme Gdns FNM GU9 5 H6
Fairholme Rd ASHF TW15 23 H8
CROY/NA CR0 45 J8
SUT SM1 61 K5
WKENS W14 19 J3
Fairland Cl FLEETS GU52 87 H7
Fairlands Av RGUW GU3 111 J1
SUT SM1 61 L1
THHTH CR7 45 H5
Fairlands Rd RGUW GU3 91 J9
Fair La COUL/CHIP CR5 99 N5
Fairlawn GT/LBKH KT23 95 P4
WEY KT13 * 56 G4
Fairlawn Av CHSWK W4 18 A2
Fairlawn Cl ESH/CLAY KT10 58 F5
FELT TW13 24 G7
KUTN/CMB KT2 27 H9
Fairlawn Crs EGRIN RH19 180 A1
Fairlawn Dr EGRIN RH19 180 A1
REDH RH1 120 A7
Fairlawn Gv BNSTD SM7 79 P2
CHSWK W4 18 A2

Fairlawn Pk SYD SE26 ....31 M8
WOKN/KNAP GU21 ....72 C4
Fairlawn Rd BELMT SM2 ....61 N9
WIM/MER SW19 ....43 K1
Fairlawns ADL/WDHM KT15 ....55 K9
HORL RH6 ....159 L2
SUN TW16 ....24 B7
TWK TW1 ....26 B2
Fairlawns CI STA TW18 ....22 E9
Fairlight CI WPK KT4 ....60 C3
Fairlight Rd TOOT SW17 ....28 G7
Fairmead SURB KT6 ....41 P9
WOKN/KNAP GU21 ....72 A7
Fairmead CI HEST TW5 ....15 M5
NWMAL KT3 ....42 B4
SHST GU47 ....68 A1
Fairmead Ct CBLY GU15 ....68 E4
Fairmead Rd CROY/NA CRO 45 J8
EDEN TN8 ....124 F9
Fairmeads COB KT11 ....75 P7
Fairmile Av COB KT11 ....75 N3
STRHM/NOR SW16 ....29 N8
Fairmile Ct COB KT11 ....75 N1
Fairmile Hts COB KT11 ....76 A2
Fairmile La COB KT11 ....75 N1
Fairmile Park Copse
COB KT11 ....75 P1
Fairmile Park Rd COB KT11 ....75 P7
Fairmount Rd
BRXS/STRHM SW2 ....30 A2
Fair Oak CI LHD/OX KT22 ....58 D9
Fairoak CI PUR/KEN CR8 ....81 K4
Fairoak La LHD/OX KT22 ....58 E9
Fairoaks RGUW GU3 * 90 C5
Fairs Rd LHD/OX KT22 ....76 G8
Fairstone Ct HORL RH6 ....140 D9
Fair Vw HSLW TW3 ....16 C8
Fairtrough Rd ORP BR6 ....85 M2
Fairview EW KT17 ....60 C9
Fair Vw HORS RH12 ....191 P7
Fairview Av
WOKS/MYFD GU22 ....10 C6
Fairview CI SYD SE26 * 31 M7
WOKS/MYFD GU22 ....10 C6
Fairview Dr SHPTN TW17 ....38 B6
Fairview Gdns FNM GU9 ....107 P8
Fairview PI
BRXS/STRHM SW2 ....30 A3
Fairview Rd ASHV GU12 ....109 K3
BOR GU35 ....164 E6
EW KT17 ....60 D9
STRHM/NOR SW16 ....45 H2
SUT SM1 ....61 P4
Fairview Ter BOR GU35 * 164 D5
Fairwater Dr
ADL/WDHM KT15 ....55 P7
Fairway CAW SM5 ....61 N9
CHERT KT16 ....37 M9
CRAWE RH10 ....177 J4
CRAWW RH11 ....176 A6
GU GU1 ....113 H5
RYNPK SW20 ....42 G4
Fairway CI CRAWE RH10 ....178 B1
CROY/NA CRO 46 E6
HOR/WEW KT19 ....60 A6
LIPH GU30 ....182 A7
WOKS/MYFD GU22 ....71 P8
Fairway Hts CBLY GU15 ....69 K2
Fairways ASHF TW15 ....23 K9
GSHT GU26 ....165 L5
ISLW TW7 ....16 E6
PUR/KEN CR8 ....81 J1
TEDD TW11 ....41 K1
The Fairways REDH RH1 ....119 P8
The Fairway CHOB/PIR GU24 ..91 J4
E/WMO/HCT KT8 ....40 B4
FARN GU14 ....87 M7
FRIM GU16 ....107 P7
GODL GU7 ....150 E2
LHD/OX KT22 ....76 C7
NWMAL KT3 ....42 B2
WEY KT13 ....56 C9
Fairwell La EHSLY KT24 ....94 F8
Fairwyn Rd SYD SE26 ....31 M6
Fakenham Wy SHST GU47 ..49 P8
Falaise EGH TW20 ....21 K8
Falaise CI ALDT GU11 ....108 D3
Falcon CI CHSWK W4 ....17 P4
CRAWW RH11 ....176 C3
LTWR GU18 ....51 P9
Falcon Dr STWL/WRAY TW19 ..12 A6
Falconhurst LHD/OX KT22 ..57 H4
Falcon Rd GU GU1 ....7 F3
HPTN TW12 ....39 P1
Falcons CI BH/WHM TN16 ..84 B6
Falcon Wy HORS RH12 ....38 G3
YTLY GU46 * 66 F2
Falconwood EGH TW20 ....21 K8
Falconwood Rd
CROY/NA CRO 64 G6
Falcourt CI SUT SM1 ....61 M3
Falkland Gv DORK RH4 ....116 G8
Falkland Park Rd SNWD SE25 ..45 N4
Falkland Rd DORK RH4 ....116 G8
Falkner CI FNM GU9 ....4 D1
Falkners CI FLEETS GU51 ..87 J3
Fallow Deer CI SWTR RH13 ..192 G7
Fallowfield FLEETN GU51 ..87 J3
YTLY GU46 ....66 F1
Fallowfield Wy HORL RH6 ..140 D9
Fallsbrook Rd
STRHM/NOR SW16 ....29 L9
Falmer CI CRAWW RH11 ..176 G7
Falmouth CI CBLY GU15 ....51 H9
Falmouth Rd WOT/HER KT12 ..57 L3

Falstone WOKN/KNAP GU21 ..71 P7
Famet Av PUR/KEN CR8 ....81 L2
Famet CI PUR/KEN CR8 ....81 L2
Famet Wk PUR/KEN CR8 ....81 L2
Fanes CI BNFD RG42 ....32 B2
Fane St WBHS W14 ....19 K4
Fanshawe Rd
RCHPK/HAM TW10 ....26 B7
Fanthorpe St PUT/ROE SW15 ..18 G8
Faraday Av EGRIN RH19 ..180 E5
Faraday Rd CRAWE RH10 ..177 J1
E/WMO/HCT KT8 ....40 A5
FARN GU14 ....88 A1
WIM/MER SW19 ....28 E9
Farcrosse CI SHST GU47 * ..49 P9
Fareham Rd
EBED/NFELT TW14 ....24 D3
Farewell PI MTCM CR4 ....43 P2
Farhalls Crs HORS RH12 ..192 E4
Faringdon CI SHST GU47 ..49 N8
Faringdon Dr BRAK RG12 ..32 F6
Faris Barn Dr
ADL/WDHM KT15 ....73 K1
Faris La ADL/WDHM KT15 ..55 K9
Farleigh Av HAYES BR2 ....47 M8
Farleigh Court Rd WARL CR6 ..82 F3
Farleigh Dean Crs
CROY/NA CRO 65 H9
Farleigh Rd ADL/WDHM KT15 ..55 L9
WARL CR6 ....82 E6
Farleton CI WEY KT13 ....56 F5
Farley Copse BNFD RG42 ....32 A2
Farley Ct FARN GU14 * 88 F5
Farleycroft BH/WHM TN16 ..104 F6
Farley Heath Rd SHGR GU5 ..133 M9
Farley La BH/WHM TN16 ..104 F7
Farley Nursery
BH/WHM TN16 ....104 C3
Farley Pk OXTED RH8 ....123 K1
Farley PI SNWD SE25 ....46 A5
Farleys CI SAND/SEL CR2 ....64 B6
Farlington PI PUT/ROE SW15 ..27 N3
Farlow Rd PUT/ROE SW15 ..19 H8
Farlton Rd WAND/EARL SW18 ..28 E3
Farm Av HORS RH12 ....192 A2
STRHM/NOR SW16 ....29 P7
Farm CI ASC SL5 ....34 C6
BELMT SM2 ....61 P6
BF/WBF KT14 ....74 B1
BIL RH14 ....188 D2
BNFD RG42 ....32 B2
CHERT KT16 ....37 H7
CRAWE RH10 ....177 J4
CWTH RG45 ....49 N2
EGRIN RH19 ....180 C3
EHSLY KT24 ....94 H8
HORS RH12 ....19 L5
LHD/OX KT22 ....96 D4
RGUW GU3 ....91 J9
SHPTN TW17 ....38 C8
STA TW18 ....22 B8
WLGTN SM6 ....62 E8
WWKM BR4 ....65 M2
YTLY GU46 ....67 H3
Farm Cottages
E/WMO/HCT KT8 * 40 C5
Farm Ct FRIM GU16 ....69 H6
Farmdale Rd CAR SM5 ....62 A6
Farm Dr CROY/NA CRO 64 F1
FLEETN GU51 ....87 H3
PUR/KEN CR8 ....80 F1
WDSR SL4 ....20 G2
Farmer's Rd STA TW18 ....22 B8
Farmfield Dr DORL RH6 ..158 E4
Farm Flds SAND/SEL CR2 ....63 P9
Farmhouse CI
STRHM/NOR SW16 ....44 E1
Farm La ADL/WDHM KT15 ..55 L5
ASHTD KT21 ....77 P7
CROY/NA CRO 64 F1
EHSLY KT24 ....95 H8
FUL/PGN SW6 ....19 L5
PUR/KEN CR8 ....62 E8
RFNM GU10 ....106 C9
RPLY/SEND GU23 ....92 G3
Farmleigh CI CRAWE RH10 ..177 M3
Farmleigh Gv WOT/HER KT12 ..57 H4
Farm Rd ASHV GU12 ....108 G5
BELMT SM2 ....61 P6
ESH/CLAY KT10 ....40 A9
FRIM GU16 ....68 G6
HSLWW TW4 ....24 F4
MRDN SM4 ....43 M6
STA TW18 ....22 E9
WARL CR6 ....82 E9
WOKS/MYFD GU22 ....72 F9
Farmstead Dr EDEN TN8 ..144 G2
The Farm WIM/MER SW19 * ..28 A3
Farmview CQB KT11 ....75 M5
Farm Vw YTLY GU46 ....67 H3
Farm Wk ASHV GU12 ....109 L6
GUW GU2 ....111 M7
Farm Wy STWL/WRAY TW19 ..22 G2
WPK KT4 ....60 G2
Farnaby Rd BMLY BR1 ....47 L2
Farnan Rd STRHM/NOR SW16 ..29 P8
Farnborough Av
SAND/SEL CR2 ....64 E6
Farnborough Crs HAYES BR2 ..47 M9
SAND/SEL CR2 ....64 E7
Farnborough Ga
FARN GU14 * 68 E3
Farnborough Rd ALDT GU11 ..107 P5
FARN GU14 ....88 E4

Farnborough St FARN GU14 ..88 F2
Farncombe HI GODL GU7 ..131 K6
Farncombe St GODL GU7 ..131 L6
Farnell Ms ECT SW5 ....19 M3
Farnell Rd ISLW TW7 ....16 D8
STA TW18 ....22 D6
Farnham CI BRAK RG12 ....32 F1
CRAWW RH11 ....194 F2
Farnham Gdns RYNPK SW20 ..42 F3
Farnham La HASM GU27 ..184 B1
Farnham Park CI FNM GU9 ..107 M8
Farnham Rd FLEETG GU51 ..87 K6
GUW GU2 ....6 C6
MFD/CHID GU8 ....129 L9
Farnhurst La CRAN GU6 ..170 C7
Farningham BRAK RG12 ....32 G7
Farningham Crs CTHM CR3 ..102 A3
Farningham Rd CTHM CR3 ..102 A3
Farnley WOKN/KNAP GU21 ..71 M6
Farnley Rd WKENS W14 ....19 H1
SNWD SE25 ....45 J5
Farquhar Rd NRWD SE19 ..30 G8
WIM/MER SW19 ....28 E6
Farquharson Rd
CROY/NA CRO 45 L8
Farrell CI CBLY GU15 ....68 E5
Farren Rd FSTH SE23 ....31 M5
Farriers CI EW KT17 ....60 C9
The Farriers SHGR GU5 ..132 E8
Farrier Wk WBPTN SW10 * ..19 N4
Farrington Acres WEY KT13 * ..56 F2
Farriers Rd EW KT17 ....60 C9
Farthing Flds BOR GU35 ..164 B6
Farthingham La CRAN GU6 ..153 P6
Farthings WOKN/KNAP GU21 ..71 L5
The Farthings HORS RH12 * ..192 A9
Farthing Wk HORS RH12 ..191 N7
Farwig La BMLY BR1 ....47 N2
Fassett Rd KUT1 ....41 L5
Fauconberg Rd CHSWK W4 ..18 A4
Faulkner CI CRAWW RH11 ..194 F2
Faulkner PI BAGS GU19 ....51 N5
Faulkner's Rd WOT/HER KT12 ..57 L5
Favart Rd FUL/PGN SW6 ....19 L6
Faversham Rd BECK BR3 ....46 F3
CAT SE6 ....31 N3
MRDN SM4 ....43 M7
SHST GU47 ....49 P9
Fawcett CI BTSEA SW11 ....19 P7
STRHM/NOR SW16 ....30 B7
Fawcett Rd CROY/NA CRO ..2 C6
Fawcett St WBPTN SW10 ..19 N4
Fawcus CI ESH/CLAY KT10 ..58 E1
Fawe Park Rd
PUT/ROE SW15 ....19 K9
Fawler Md EGH TW20 * 33 H5
Fawnbrake Av HNHL SE24 ..30 C1
Fawns Manor Rd
EBED/NFELT TW14 ....23 N4
Fawsley CI DTCH/LGLY SL3 ..13 J5
Faygate La GDST RH9 ....142 C2
Faygate Rd
BRXS/STRHM SW2 ....30 A5
Fayland Av
STRHM/NOR SW16 ....29 M8
Fay Rd HORS RH12 ....192 A2
Fearn CI EHSLY KT24 ....94 G9
Fearnley Crs HPTN TW12 ..24 G9
Featherbed La CROY/NA CRO ..64 F6
Feathercombe La
MFD/CHID GU8 ....150 C8
Feathers La
STWL/WRAY TW19 ....21 M5
Featherstone Av FSTH SE23 ..31 J5
Featherstone Rd
NWDGN UB2 ....15 N1
Featherstone Ter
NWDGN UB2 ....15 N1
Fee Farm Rd ESH/CLAY KT10 ..58 F6
Felbridge Av CRAWE RH10 ..177 N4
Felbridge CI BELMT SM2 ....61 M7
EGRIN RH19 ....162 B9
FRIM GU16 ....69 H6
STRHM/NOR SW16 ....30 B7
Felbridge Ct EGRIN RH19 ..161 K9
Felbridge PI EGRIN RH19 * ..161 L9
Felbridge Rd EGRIN RH19 ..161 J9
Felcot Rd CRAWE RH10 ..161 K9
Felcott CI WOT/HER KT12 ..57 L2
Felcott Rd WOT/HER KT12 ..57 L2
Felcourt La EGRIN RH19 ..162 A5
Felcourt Rd EGRIN RH19 ..162 B5
Felday Gld RDKG RH5 ....135 K8
Felday Rd RDKG RH5 ....135 J7
Felden St FUL/PGN SW6 ....19 K6
The Feld EGRIN RH19 ..161 P9
Felgate Ms HMSMTH W6 ..18 F2
Felix Dr RGUE GU4 ....93 L8
Felix La SHPTN TW17 ....38 G7
Felix Rd WOT/HER KT12 ..39 J7
Felland Wy REDH RH1 ....119 P9
Fellbrigg Rd EDUL SE22 ....30 G1
Fellbrook RCHPK/HAM TW10 ..26 A6
Fellcott Wy HORS RH12 ..191 N9
Fellmongers Yd CROY/NA CRO ..2 C5
Fellow Gn CHOB/PIR GU24 ..70 F2
Fellow Green Rd
CHOB/PIR GU24 ....70 F2
Fellows Rd FARN GU14 ....88 F6
Fell Rd CROY/NA CRO 2 D5
Felmingham Rd
PGE/AN SE20 ....46 C3
Felsberg Rd
BRXS/STRHM SW2 ....29 P2
Felsham Rd PUT/ROE SW15 ..18 G8
Felstead Rd HOR/WEW KT19 ..60 B9
Feltham Av E/WMO/HCT KT8 ..40 E5

Felthambrook Wy FELT TW13 ..24 C7
Feltham Hill Rd ASHF TW15 ..23 K8
Feltham Rd ASHF TW15 ....23 K7
MTCM CR4 ....44 B3
REDH RH1 ....140 B1
Fenby CI SWTR RH13 ....192 G5
Fenchurch Rd CRAWE RH10 ..177 L2
Fencote BRAK RG12 ....32 F8
Fendall Rd HOR/WEW KT19 ..60 A4
Fendon Pl WKENS W14 ....19 K2
Fengates Rd REDH RH1 ....120 A5
Fenhurst CI HORS RH12 ..191 N9
Fennel CI CROY/NA CRO 46 D9
FARN GU14 ....87 M3
GU GU1 ....112 F2
Fennel Crs CRAWW RH11 ..176 B8
Fennells Md HOR/WEW KT19 ..60 D7
Fenner Sq BTSEA SW11 * ..19 P8
Fennscombe Ct
CHOB/PIR GU24 ....70 E2
Fenns La CHOB/PIR GU24 ..70 E3
Fenn's Wy WOKN/KNAP GU21 ..72 C4
Fenton Av STA TW18 ....22 F9
Fenton CI REDH RH1 ....120 C5
Fenton Rd REDH RH1 ....120 C5
Fentum Rd GUW GU2 ....111 N3
Fenwick CI
WOKN/KNAP GU21 ....71 P7
Fenwick PI SAND/SEL CR2 ..63 K6
Ferbies FLEETS GU51 * 87 J6
Ferguson Av BRYLDS KT5 ..41 M6
Ferguson CI BECK BR3 ....47 J4
Fermandy La CRAWE RH10 ..179 J2
Fermor Dr ALDT GU11 ....108 B3
Fermor Rd FSTH SE23 ....31 M4
Fern Av MTCM CR4 ....44 F5
Fernbank EWKG RC40 ....48 B3
Fernbank Av WOT/HER KT12 ..39 N8
Fernbank Crs ASC SL5 ....33 M2
Fernbank Ms CLAP SW4 ....29 L2
Fernbank PI ASC SL5 ....33 L2
Fernbank Rd
ADL/WDHM KT15 ....55 M4
ASC SL5 ....33 M3
Fernbrae CI RFNM GU10 ..146 E2
Fern CI CWTH RG45 ....49 M2
FRIM GU16 ....69 H6
WARL CR6 ....82 E7
Ferndale GUW GU2 ....111 L3
Ferndale Av CHERT KT16 ....55 J2
HSLWW TW4 ....15 N8
Ferndale Rd ASHF TW15 ....23 H9
BNSTD SM7 ....79 K5
FLEETS GU51 ....106 F1
SNWD SE25 ....46 B6
Ferndell Av FELT TW14 ....24 E7
Fernden La HASM GU27 ..184 E9
Ferndown CRAWE RH10 ..177 N1
HORL RH6 ....140 C8
Ferndown CI BELMT SM2 ..61 P5
GU GU1 ....112 E6
Ferndown Gdns COB KT11 ..75 J3
FARN GU14 ....88 A3
Ferne CI FLEETN GU51 ....86 G9
The Fernery STA TW18 ....22 B8
Ferney Meade Wy ISLW TW7 ..16 G7
Fern Gv EBED/NFELT TW14 ..24 C3
Fernham Rd THHTH CR7 ....45 L5
Fernhill CI LHD/OX KT22 ....76 F6
Fernhill CI BNFD RG42 ....32 B1
CRAWE RH10 ....179 J2
FARN GU14 ....68 A3
FNM GU9 ....107 M8
WOKS/MYFD GU22 ....72 A9
Fernhill Dr FARN GU14 ....68 A9
HORL RH6 ....159 N6
Fernhill Gdns KUTN/CMB KT2 ..26 C8
Fernhill La FARN GU14 ....68 A9
FNM GU9 ....107 M7
WOKS/MYFD GU22 ....72 A9
Fernhill Pk
WOKS/MYFD GU22 ....72 A9
Fernhill Rd FARN GU14 ....68 A9
HORL RH6 ....159 N6
Fernhill Wk FARN GU14 ....68 B9
Fernhurst CI CRAWW RH11 ..176 B3
Fernhurst Rd ASHF TW15 ..23 H9
CROY/NA CRO 46 B8
FUL/PGN SW6 ....19 J6
Fernihough CI WEY KT13 ....56 C9
Fernlands CI CHERT KT16 ..55 J2
Fern La HNDGN UB2 ....15 P3
Fernlea GT/LBKH KT23 ....96 B4
Fernlea Rd BAL SW12 ....29 L4
MTCM CR4 ....44 C3
Fernleigh CI CROY/NA CRO ..63 J3
WOT/HER KT12 ....57 K2
Fernleigh Ri FRIM GU16 ....69 L9
Fern Rd GODL GU7 ....131 M7
Ferns CI SAND/SEL CR2 ....64 C6
Fernshaw CI WBPTN SW10 * ..19 N4
Fernshaw Rd WBPTN SW10 ..19 N4
Fernside Av FELT TW13 ....24 C7
Fernside Rd BAL SW12 ....29 J4
The Ferns FNM GU9 * 107 N7
Fernthorpe Rd
STRHM/NOR SW16 ....29 M9
Fern Towers CTHM CR3 ..102 A5
Fern Wk ASHF TW15 ....22 G8
Fern Wy HORS RH12 ....192 C5
Fernwood
CROY/NA CRO 65 H8
Fernwood Av
STRHM/NOR SW16 ....29 N7
Fernwood PI ESH/CLAY KT10 ..58 F6
Ferraro CI HEST TW5 ....16 A4
Ferrard CI ASC SL5 ....33 M3
Ferraro CI HEST TW5 ....16 A4
Ferrers Av WLGTN SM6 ....62 F3
Ferrers Rd STRHM/NOR SW16 ..29 M9

Ferrier St WAND/EARL SW18 ..19 M9
Ferriers Wy EPSOM KT18 ....78 G8
Ferrings DUL SE21 ....30 F5
Ferris Av CROY/NA CRO 64 F3
Ferry Av STA TW18 ....37 J1
Ferry La BARN SW13 ....18 D4
BTFD TW8 ....17 L3
CHERT KT16 ....37 L7
GUW GU2 ....112 A9
SHPTN TW17 ....38 C9
STA TW18 ....37 N4
STWL/WRAY TW19 ....21 N5
Ferrymoor
RCHPK/HAM TW10 ....26 A6
Ferry Rd BARN SW13 ....18 E5
E/WMO/HCT KT8 ....40 A4
TEDD TW11 ....26 A8
THDIT KT7 ....41 H7
TWK TW1 ....26 A4
Ferry Sq BTFD TW8 * 17 L4
Festing Rd PUT/ROE SW15 ..19 H8
Fetcham Common La
LHD/OX KT22 ....96 B1
Fetcham Park Dr
LHD/OX KT22 ....96 E3
Fettes Rd CRAN GU6 ....153 K9
Fiddicroft Av BNSTD SM7 ..79 L3
Field CI CHSGTN KT9 ....59 J4
E/WMO/HCT KT8 ....40 B6
HSLWW TW4 ....15 K6
HYS/HAR UB3 ....14 E5
GUW GU2 ....113 H3
SAND/SEL CR2 ....82 B3
Fieldcommon La
WOT/HER KT12 ....39 N9
Field Cottages
FUL/PGN SW6 * 19 K7
Field Ct OXTED RH8 ....103 L8
Field Dr EDEN TN8 ....145 H2
Field End CHOB/PIR GU24 ..70 F3
COUL/CHIP CR5 ....80 F3
FNM GU9 ....128 B1
Fielden HORS RH12 ....192 G5
TEDD TW11 ....25 N7
Fieldend Rd
STRHM/NOR SW16 ....44 N1
Fielden PI BRAK RG12 ....32 F5
Fielders Gn GU GU1 ....112 E5
The Fielders HTWY RG27 ..48 C9
Fieldfare Av YTLY GU46 ....66 E2
Field House CI ASC SL5 ....34 A9
Fieldhouse Rd BAL SW12 ..29 M4
Fieldhouse Vis BNSTD SM7 * ..80 A4
Field Hurst DTCH/LGLY SL3 ..12 D2
Fieldhurst CI
ADL/WDHM KT15 ....55 M4
Fielding Av WHTN TW2 ....25 K6
Fielding Gdns CWTH RG45 ..49 L5
Fielding Rd CHSWK W4 ....18 C1
SHST GU47 ....68 A2
WKENS W14 ....19 H1
The Fieldings BNSTD SM7 ..79 K6
FSTH SE23 ....31 K4
HORL RH6 ....140 D9
WOKN/KNAP GU21 ....71 M5
Field La BTFD TW8 ....17 J3
FRIM GU16 ....69 H6
GODL GU7 ....131 M6
TEDD TW11 ....25 P8
Field Pk BRAK RG12 ....32 F2
Field PI LIPH GU30 ....182 E7
NWMAL KT3 ....42 D7
Field Rd EBED/NFELT TW14 ..24 C2
FARN GU14 ....88 D4
HMSMTH W6 ....19 J4
Fieldsend Rd CHEAM SM3 ..61 J4
Field Stores Ap ALDT GU11 ..108 E3
Field Vw EGH TW20 ....21 P8
FELT TW13 ....23 N7
Fieldview HORL RH6 ....140 D9
WAND/EARL SW18 ....28 G4
Field Wk HORL RH6 ....141 L9
Field Wy ASHV GU12 ....108 G4
CROY/NA CRO 65 H6
RFNM GU10 ....109 H7
RPLY/SEND GU23 ....93 K5
Fie Yard Rd FARN GU14 ....88 C5
Fifehead CI ASHF TW15 ....23 H9
Fife Rd KUT KT1 ....8 D4
MORT/ESHN SW14 ....27 H1
Fife Wy GT/LBKH KT23 ....96 A5
Fifield La RFNM GU10 ....146 F2
Fifield Pth FSTH SE23 ....31 L6
Fifteenth Av
KWD/TDW/WH KT20 * ..99 K6
Fifth Av
KWD/TDW/WH KT20 * ..99 K6
Fifth Cross Rd WHTN TW2 ..25 L5
Figge's Rd MTCM CR4 ....44 C1
Filbert Crs CRAWW RH11 ..176 D5
Filby Rd CHSGTN KT9 ....59 M5
Filey CI BELMT SM2 ....61 N6
BH/WHM TN16 ....83 P8
CRAWW RH11 ....176 C7
Filmer Chambers
FUL/PGN SW6 * 19 K6
Filmer Gv GODL GU7 ....131 L8
Filmer Rd FUL/PGN SW6 ..19 K6
Finborough Rd TOOT SW17 ..44 B1
WBPTN SW10 ....19 M4
Fincham End Dr CWTH RG45 ..49 K5
Finchampstead Rd
EWKG RG40 ....48 C5
Finch Av WWLW SE27 ....30 E7
Finch CI WOKN/KNAP GU21 ..71 J6
Finch Crs CRAWE RH10 ..179 K6
Finch Dr EBED/NFELT TW14 ..24 E3
Finches Ri GU GU1 ....112 F3
Finch Rd GU GU1 ....7 F3
Findhorn CI SHST GU47 ....67 P1

The Findlay *FARN* GU14 .....68 A8
Findlay Dr *RGUW* GU3 .....111 M1
Findon CI *WAND/EARL* SW18 ...28 D2
Findon Rd *CRAWW* RH11 .....176 E3
Findon Wy *REDH* RH12 .....191 L7
Finlay Gdns *ADL/WDHM* KT15 ..55 N3
Finlays CI *CHSGTN* KT9 .....59 N4
Finlay St *PUT/PGN* SW6 .....19 H6
Finmere *BRAK* RG12 .....32 E7
Finnart CI *WEY* KT13 .....56 E3
Finney Dr *BFOR* GU20 .....52 D5
Finsbury CI *CRAWW* RH11 ...176 F9
Finstock Gn *BRAK* RG12 .....33 H5
Fintry PI *FARN* GU14 .....68 A9
Fiona CI *GT/LBKH* KT23 .....96 A4
Fir Acre Rd *ASHV* GU12 .....89 J9
Firbank Dr *WOKN/KNAP* GU21 ..71 P8
Firbank La *WOKN/KNAP* GU21 ..71 P8
Firbank PI *EGH* TW20 .....20 G9
Fir CI *FLEETN* GU51 .....86 F7
    WOT/HER KT12 .....39 J8
Fir Cottage Rd *EWKG* RG40 ...48 C1
Fircroft CI *WOKS/MYFD* GU22 ..10 E6
Fircroft CI *WOKN/KNAP* GU22 ..10 E6
Fircroft Rd *CHSGTN* KT9 .....59 J6
Fircroft Wy *EDEN* TN8 .....144 G2
Firdene *BRYLDS* KT5 .....42 A9
Fir Dr *BLKW* GU17 .....67 P5
Fireball HI *ASC* SL5 .....34 D8
Fire Bell Aly *SURB* KT6 .....41 L7
Firebell Ms *SURB* KT6 .....41 L7
Fire Station Rd *ALDT* GU11 ..108 D3
Fire Thorn CI *FLEETS* GU52 ...86 F9
Firfield Rd *ADL/WDHM* KT15 ..55 L3
    FNM GU9 .....127 L6
Firfields *WEY* KT13 .....56 D6
Firglen Dr *YTLY* GU46 .....67 H1
Fir Grange Av *WEY* KT13 .....56 C4
Fir Gv *NWMAL* KT3 .....42 D7
Firgrove *WOKN/KNAP* GU21 ...71 N8
Firgrove CI *FNM* GU9 .....5 G5
Firgrove HI *FNM* GU9 .....5 G6
Firgrove Pde *FARN* GU14 * ...88 D3
Firgrove Rd *FARN* GU14 .....88 D2
    HTWY RG27 .....66 E2
Firhill Rd *CAT* SE6 .....31 P6
Firlands *BRAK* RG12 .....32 E6
    HORL RH6 .....140 D9
    WEY KT13 .....56 C5
Firlands Av *CBLY* GU15 .....68 F3
Firle CI *CRAWE* RH10 .....177 H5
Firle CI *EW* KT17 * 21 D1
Fir Rd *CHEAM* SM3 .....43 K9
    FELT TW13 .....24 E8
Firs Av *MORT/ESHN* SW14 .....18 A9
    SHGR GU5 .....132 E7
Firsby Av *CROY/NA* CRO 46 D9
Firs CI *DORK* RH4 .....116 G9
    ESH/CLAY KT10 .....58 E5
    EWKG RG40 .....48 D2
    FARN GU14 .....88 E5
    FSTH SE23 .....31 L3
    MTCM CR4 .....44 D3
Firsdene CI *CHERT* KT16 .....55 H5
Firs Dr *HEST* TW5 .....15 J5
Firs La *SHGR* GU5 .....133 H9
Firs Rd *PUR/KEN* CR8 .....81 K4
First Av *E/WMO/HCT* KT8 .....40 B3
    E/WMO/HCT KT8 .....39 P5
    HOR/WEW KT19 .....60 C6
    KWD/TDW/WH KT20 * 99 G6
    MORT/ESHN SW14 .....18 A9
    WOT/HER KT12 .....39 K7
First CI *E/WMO/HCT* KT8 .....40 C5
First Cross Rd *WHTN* TW2 .....25 M5
The Firs *BF/WBF* KT14 * 73 P1
    EBED/NFELT TW14 * 23 P2
    GT/LBKH KT23 .....96 B5
    LIPH GU30 .....182 E7
    RGUW GU3 .....111 P9
First Quarter
    HOR/WEW KT19 * 60 C9
Firstway *RYNPK* SW20 .....42 G3
Firsway *GUW* GU2 .....111 L6
Firswood Av *HOR/WEW* KT19 ..60 C4
Firth Gdns *FUL/PGN* SW6 .....19 J6
Fir Tree Av *HASM* GU27 .....183 N4
Fir Tree Av *MTCM* CR4 .....44 C3
Fir Tree Av *WOT/HER* KT12 ...14 C1
Fir Tree CI *ASC* SL5 .....34 A8
    CRAWW RH11 .....176 E2
    ESH/CLAY KT10 .....58 E1
    EW KT17 .....78 C4
    HOR/WEW KT19 .....60 D3
    LHD/OX KT22 .....97 J3
Firtree CI *SHST* GU47 .....49 H8
Fir Tree La *EW* KT17 .....78 F5
Fir Tree Gdns *CROY/NA* CRO ..64 C3
Fir Tree PI *ASHF* TW15 * 23 J7
Fir Tree Rd *EW* KT17 .....78 F5
    GU GU1 .....112 A2
    HSLWW TW4 .....15 N9
    LHD/OX KT22 .....97 J3
Fir Tree Wk *REIG* RH2 .....119 P7
Firtree Wy *FLEETS* GU51 .....87 H1
Fir WK *EW* KT17 * 61 H5
Firway *GSHT* GU26 .....165 N4
Firwood CI
    WOKN/KNAP GU21 .....71 L9
Firwood Dr *CBLY* GU15 .....68 C3
Firwood Rd *VW* GU25 .....35 J7
Fisher CI *CRAWE* RH10 .....177 H7
    .....3 J2
    WOT/HER KT12 .....57 K3
Fisherdene *ESH/CLAY* KT10 ..58 G6
Fisher La *MFD/CHID* GU8 .....186 F5
Fisherman CI
    RCHPK/HAM TW10 .....26 B7
Fishermen's CI *ALDT* GU11 ..108 G1
Fisher Rowe CI *SHGR* GU5 ..132 E7

Fishers Ct *HORS* RH12 .....192 B6
Fisher's La *CHSWK* W4 .....18 A1
Fishers Wd *ASC* SL5 .....35 J9
Fishponds Rd *TOOT* SW17 .....29 J7
Fitchet CI *CRAWW* RH11 .....176 E3
Fitzalan Rd *ESH/CLAY* KT10 ..58 E6
    HORS RH12 .....192 H6
Fitzgeorge Av *WKENS* W14 ...19 J2
Fitzgerald Av
    MORT/ESHN SW14 .....18 C8
Fitzgerald Rd
    MORT/ESHN SW14 .....18 B8
    THDIT KT7 .....40 G7
Fitzhugh Gv
    WAND/EARL SW18 .....28 G2
Fitz-James Av *CROY/NA* CR0 ..64 A1
Fitz-James Av *WKENS* W14 ...19 J2
Fitzjohn CI *RGUE* GU4 .....112 G2
Fitzrobert PI *EGH* TW20 .....21 M9
Fitzroy Av *BRAK* RG12 .....32 C7
Fitzroy Crs *CHSWK* W4 * 18 B5
Fitzroy Rd *FLEETN* GU51 .....86 E6
Fitzroy Gdns *NRWD* SE19 .....45 N1
Fitzwilliam Av *RCH/KEW* TW9 ..17 M7
Fitz Wygram Ct *HPTN* TW12 ...25 K8
Fiveacre Ct *THHTH* CR7 .....45 J7
Five Acres *CRAWE* RH10 .....177 H3
Five Fields La *EDEN* TN8 .....145 N1
Five Oaks CI
    WOKN/KNAP GU21 .....71 K8
Five Oaks Rd *SWTR* RH13 .....191 H9
Flag CI *CROY/NA* CRO 46 D9
Flambard Wy *GODL* GU7 .....131 K9
Flamborough CI
    BH/WHM TN16 .....83 P8
Flamsteed Hts
    CRAWW RH11 * 194 E1
Flanchford Rd *REIG* RH2 .....118 G1
    SHB W12 .....18 D1
Flanders Crs *TOOT* SW17 .....44 B7
Flanders Rd *CHSWK* W4 .....18 C2
The Flats *BLKW* GU17 .....67 M4
Flaxley Rd *MRDN* SM4 .....43 M7
Fleece Rd *SURB* KT6 .....41 J9
Fleet CI *E/WMO/HCT* KT8 .....39 P6
Fleet HI *EWKG* RG40 .....48 A7
Fleet Rd *ALDT* GU11 .....87 M9
    FARN GU14 .....87 M3
    FLEETN GU51 .....86 C1
    FLEETN GU51 .....87 H3
    HTWY RG27 .....86 A2
Fleetside *E/WMO/HCT* KT8 .....39 P7
Fleetway *EGH* TW20 .....36 G4
Fleetwood CI *CHSGTN* KT9 .....59 K6
    CROY/NA CRO 3 J5
    KWD/TDW/WH KT20 .....99 J6
Fleetwood Ct *BF/WBF* KT14 ...73 J2
Fleetwood Rd *NWMAL* KT3 .....41 P4
Fleetwood Sq *NWMAL* KT3 .....41 P4
Fleming CI *FARN* GU14 .....88 F1
    WBPTN SW10 * 19 N4
Fleming Ct *CROY/NA* CRO 63 J4
Fleming Md *WIM/MER* SW19 ..44 A1
Fleming Wy *CRAWE* RH10 .....177 J4
    ISLW TW7 .....16 F8
Flemish Flds *CHERT* KT16 .....57 L8
Flemish PI *BRAK* RG12 .....32 F1
Fletcher CI *CHERT* KT16 .....55 H5
    CRAWE RH10 .....177 H7
Fletcher Rd *CHERT* KT16 .....55 H5
    CHSWK W4 .....18 A1
Fletchers La *HAYES* BR2 .....47 P5
    SWTR RH13 .....192 D9
Flexford Gn *BRAK* RG12 .....32 A7
Flexford Rd *RGUW* GU3 .....110 B6
Flint CI *BNSTD* SM7 .....79 M3
    CRAWE RH10 * 177 J8
    GT/LBKH KT23 .....96 C6
    REDH RH1 .....120 C6
Flint Cottages *LHD/OX* KT22 * ..97 H1
Flintgrove *BRAK* RG12 .....32 F2
Flint HI *DORK* RH4 .....117 H9
Flint Hill CI *DORK* RH4 .....137 H1
Flintlock CI
    STWL/WRAY TW19 .....13 L9
Flitwick Ct *MFD/CHID* GU8 .....149 N3
Flock Mill PI
    WAND/EARL SW18 .....28 E4
Flood La *TWK* TW1 * 25 P4
Flora Gdns *CROY/NA* CRO 65 J9
Florence Av *ADL/WDHM* KT15 ..55 L9
    MRDN SM4 .....43 N6
Florence CI *WOT/HER* KT12 ..39 K8
    YTLY GU46 .....66 G2
Florence Gdns *CHSWK* W4 ...18 A4
    STA TW18 .....37 M1
Florence Rd *BECK* BR3 .....46 D3
    BMLY BR1 .....47 N2
    CHSWK W4 .....18 B1
    FELT TW13 .....24 C4
    FLEETS GU52 .....87 H9
    KUTN/CMB KT2 .....9 J2
    NWDGN UB2 .....15 M2
    SAND/SEL CR2 .....63 N6
    SHST GU47 .....68 A1
    WIM/MER SW19 .....28 E9
    WOT/HER KT12 .....39 K8
Florence Wy *BAL* SW12 .....29 J4
    WOKN/KNAP GU21 .....71 J7
Florian Av *SUT* SM1 .....61 P3
Florian Rd *PUT/ROE* SW15 .....19 J9
Florida Rd *RGUE* GU4 .....132 C2
    THHTH CR7 .....45 K2
Floss St *PUT/ROE* SW15 .....19 M8
Flower Crs *CHERT* KT16 .....54 F5
Flower La *GDST* RH9 .....102 D9
Flower Wk *GUW* GU2 .....112 A8
Floyds La *WOKS/MYFD* GU22 ..73 L5
The Flyers Wy
    BH/WHM TN16 .....105 H6

Foden Rd *ALDT* GU11 .....108 C5
Folder's La *BRAK* RG42 .....32 E1
Foley Ms *ESH/CLAY* KT10 .....58 E5
Foley Rd *BH/WHM* TN16 .....84 B7
    ESH/CLAY KT10 .....58 E5
Folkestone Ct *DTCH/LGLY* SL3 ..12 E3
Follet CI *WDSR* SL4 .....20 C2
Folly CI *FLEETS* GU52 .....86 G8
Follyfield Rd *BNSTD* SM7 .....79 L3
Folly HI *FNM* GU9 .....107 L9
Folly La *RDKG* RH5 .....137 H6
Folly La North *FNM* GU9 .....107 L8
Folly La South *FNM* GU9 .....107 L8
The Folly *LTWR* GU18 * 70 B1
Fontaine Rd
    STRHM/NOR SW16 .....30 A9
Fontana CI *CRAWE* RH10 .....177 N6
Fontenoy Rd *BAL* SW12 .....29 L5
Fontley Wy *PUT/ROE* SW15 ...27 M3
Fontmell CI *ASHF* TW15 .....23 K8
Fontmell Pk *ASHF* TW15 .....23 J8
Fontwell CI *ASHV* GU12 .....108 F4
Fontwell Rd *CRAWE* RH10 .....177 K8
The Footpath
    PUT/ROE SW15 * 27 M1
Forbes CI *CRAWE* RH10 .....177 L9
Forbes CI *CRAWE* RH10 .....177 L9
Force Green La
    BH/WHM TN16 .....105 H4
Fordbridge Rd *ASHF* TW15 ...23 H9
    SHPTN TW17 .....38 C7
Ford CI *ASHF* TW15 .....23 J7
    SHPTN TW17 .....38 C6
    THHTH CR7 .....45 K7
Fordingbridge CI
    CHERT KT16 * 37 M9
    HORS RH12 .....192 B9
Ford La *RFNM* GU10 .....127 M7
Ford Manor Rd *LING* RH7 .....162 G2
Fordmill Rd *CAT* SE6 .....31 P5
Ford Rd *ASHF* TW15 .....23 J7
    CHERT KT16 .....37 M9
    CHOB/PIR GU24 .....39 J8
    CHOB/PIR GU24 .....70 F4
    WOKS/MYFD GU22 .....72 F9
Fordwater Rd *CHERT* KT16 ...37 M9
Fordwells Dr *BRAK* RG12 .....33 H5
Foreman Pk *ASHV* GU12 .....109 K4
Foreman Rd *ASHV* GU12 .....109 K5
Forest CI *ASC* SL5 .....18 L4
    CRAWE RH10 .....179 J3
    EHSLY KT24 .....95 H5
    SWTR RH13 .....192 G6
    WOKS/MYFD GU22 .....73 H4
Forestdale *GSHT* GU26 .....165 N8
Forest Dean *FLEETS* GU52 ...87 J3
Forest Dr
    KWD/TDW/WH KT20 * 99 L1
    RFNM GU10 .....127 N9
    SUN TW16 .....39 H1
Forest End *FLEETS* GU52 .....87 J3
Forest End Rd *SHST* GU47 ...49 K8
Forest Ga *CRAWE* RH10 .....177 H7
Foresters CI *WLGTN* SM6 .....62 F6
    WOKN/KNAP GU21 .....71 M7
Foresters Dr *WLGTN* SM6 .....62 F6
Foresters Sq *BRAK* RG12 .....32 G4
Foresters Wy *CRWH* RG45 .....50 B2
Forestfield *CRAWE* RH10 .....177 M6
    SWTR RH13 .....192 F7
Forest Gld *RFNM* GU10 .....146 A1
Forest Gra *SWTR* RH13 .....193 K6
Forest Gn *BRAK* RG12 .....32 F3
Forest Hill Rd *EDUL* SE22 .....31 J2
Forest Hills *CBLY* GU15 .....68 D4
Foresthome CI *FSTH* SE23 * ...31 K4
Forest La *EHSLY* KT24 .....94 D6
Forest Lane CI *LIPH* GU30 .....182 D6
Forest Oaks *SWTR* RH13 .....192 G6
Forest Rdg *BECK* BR3 .....46 G4
Forest Rd *CHEAM* SM3 .....43 L9
    CWTH RG45 .....49 N3
    EHSLY KT24 .....95 H5
    FELT TW13 .....24 D6
    HORS RH12 .....192 G6
    RCH/KEW TW9 .....17 N1
    WOKS/MYFD GU22 .....73 H4
The Forestry Rd *BIL* RH14 .....187 N6
Forest Side *WPK* KT4 .....42 D9
Forest Vw *CRAWE* RH10 .....177 J8
Forest View Rd *EGRIN* RH19 .180 D5
Forest Wy *ASHTD* KT21 .....77 N6
    EGRIN RH19 .....180 G6
Forge Av *COUL/CHIP* CR5 .....81 J9
Forge Bridge La
    COUL/CHIP CR5 .....100 D2
Forge CI *FNM* GU9 .....5 K1
Forge Cft *EDEN* TN8 .....144 G4
Forge CI *ESH/CLAY* KT10 .....58 B8
Forge End *WOKN/KNAP* GU21 ..10 C4
Forgefield *BH/WHM* TN16 .....84 B5
Forge La *ALDT* GU11 .....61 J6
    CRAWE RH10 * 177 K4
    FELT TW13 .....24 F8
    HORS RH12 .....191 M2
    MRDN SM4 .....43 K6
    SUN TW16 .....39 J4
Forge Ms *CROY/NA* CRO 64 G4
    SUN TW16 * 39 J4
Forge Rd *CRAWE* RH10 .....177 H4
The Forge *HORL* RH6 * 158 B5
    HORS RH12 .....191 M3
Forge Wd *CRAWE* RH10 .....159 N9
Formby CI *DTCH/LGLY* SL3 .....12 G2
Forrester Pth *SYD* SE26 .....31 K7
Forrest Gdns
    STRHM/NOR SW16 .....45 H4
Forstal CI *HAYES* BR2 .....47 N4
Forster Rd *BECK* BR3 .....46 E4

BRXS/STRHM SW2 .....29 P3
Forsyte Crs *NRWD* SE19 .....45 N4
Forsythia PI *GU* GU1 * 112 A3
Forsyth Rd
    WOKN/KNAP GU21 .....72 G4
Fortescue Av *WHTN* TW2 .....25 K6
Fortescue Rd *WEY* KT13 .....56 B5
    WIM/MER SW19 .....43 P1
Forth CI *FARN* GU14 .....87 M2
Fort La *REIG* RH2 .....119 M1
Fort Rd *GU* GU1 .....112 C8
    KWD/TDW/WH KT20 .....117 P2
Fortrose CI *SHST* GU47 .....67 P1
Fortrose Gdns
    BRXS/STRHM SW2 .....29 P4
Fort Rd *CRAN* GU6 .....171 H2
Fortyfoot Rd *LHD/OX* KT22 ...97 J1
The Forum *E/WMO/HCT* KT8 ...40 B5
Forval CI *MTCM* CR4 .....44 B6
Foskett Rd *FUL/PGN* SW6 .....19 K7
Foss Av *CROY/NA* CRO 63 J4
Fosse Wy *BF/WBF* KT14 .....73 K2
Fosseway *CWTH* RG45 .....49 K4
Fossewood Dr *CBLY* GU15 .....50 F9
Foss Rd *TOOT* SW17 .....29 H7
Fosterdown *GDST* RH9 .....102 B9
Foster Rd *CHSWK* W4 .....18 B3
Fosters Gv *BFOR* GU20 .....52 B3
Fosters La *WOKN/KNAP* GU21 ..71 J6
Foulis Ter *SKENS* SW7 .....19 P3
Foulser Rd *TOOT* SW17 .....29 K6
Foulsham Rd *THHTH* CR7 .....45 L4
Founders Gdns *NRWD* SE19 ..45 L1
Foundry CI *SWTR* RH13 .....192 D6
Foundry Ct *CHERT* KT16 .....37 L8
Foundry La *DTCH/LGLY* SL3 ..12 F8
    HASM GU27 .....183 L6
    SWTR RH13 .....192 D7
Fountain Dr *CAR* SM5 .....62 B7
    NRWD SE19 .....30 G7
Fountain Rd *REDH* RH1 .....120 A7
    THHTH CR7 .....45 L3
    TOOT SW17 .....28 G8
Fountains Av *FELT* TW13 .....24 G6
Fountains CI *CRAWW* RH11 ..176 D7
    FELT TW13 .....24 G5
Fountains Garth *BRAK* RG12 ..32 C4
Four Acres *COB* KT11 .....75 N2
    GU GU1 .....112 E3
Four Elms Rd *EDEN* TN8 .....145 K1
Four Seasons Crs
    CHEAM SM3 .....61 K1
Fourteenth Av
    KWD/TDW/WH KT20 * 99 K6
Fourth Av
    KWD/TDW/WH KT20 * 99 K6
Fourth Cross Rd *WHTN* TW2 ...25 L5
Fourth Dr *COUL/CHIP* CR5 .....80 F5
Four Wents *COB* KT11 .....75 L4
Fowler Av *FARN* GU14 .....88 D5
Fowler CI *BTSEA* SW11 * 19 P1
    CRAWE RH10 .....177 M7
Foxacre *COB* KT11 .....75 N2
Foxborough CI
    DTCH/LGLY SL3 .....12 E3
Foxborough Gdns
    BROCKY SE4 .....31 P2
Foxborough Hill Rd
    MFD/CHID GU8 .....151 H1
    SHGR GU5 .....132 C5
Foxbourne Rd *TOOT* SW17 ...29 K5
Foxbridge La *BIL* RH14 .....187 P9
Foxburrows Av *GUW* GU2 .....111 M5
Fox CI *CRAWW* RH11 .....176 E3
    WEY KT13 .....56 E5
    WOKS/MYFD GU22 .....73 H4
Foxcombe *CROY/NA* CRO 65 H5
Foxcote *EWKG* RG40 .....48 E2
Fox Covert *LHD/OX* KT22 .....96 D4
    LTWR GU18 .....52 A9
Fox Covert CI *ASC* SL5 .....34 C6
Fox Cft *FLEETS* GU52 .....106 G1
Fox Dene *GODL* GU7 .....150 B2
Foxdown CI *CBLY* GU15 .....68 E3
Fox Dr *YTLY* GU46 .....67 H1
Foxearth CI *BH/WHM* TN16 ...84 C7
Foxearth Rd *SAND/SEL* CR2 ..64 C7
Foxearth Sp *SAND/SEL* CR2 ..64 C7
Foxenden Rd *GU* GU1 * 7 G4
Foxes Dr *HAYES* BR2 .....47 K4
Foxes Pth *RGUE* GU4 .....92 D6
Foxglove Av *HORS* RH12 .....192 D4
Foxglove CI
    STWL/WRAY TW19 .....22 C4
Foxglove Gdns *PUR/KEN* CR8 ..62 G9
    RGUE GU4 .....112 G3
Foxglove La *CHSGTN* KT9 .....59 N3
Foxglove Wy *WLGTN* SM6 .....44 C8
Fox Gv *WOT/HER* KT12 .....39 K8
Foxgrove Av *BECK* BR3 .....47 H1
Foxgrove Dr
    WOKN/KNAP GU21 .....72 D4
Foxgrove Rd *BECK* BR3 .....47 J1
Foxhanger Gdns
    WOKS/MYFD GU22 .....11 H2
Fox Heath *FARN* GU14 .....87 N4
Fox HI *NRWD* SE19 .....45 N1
Foxhill Crs *CBLY* GU15 .....51 K9
Fox Hill Gdns *NRWD* SE19 .....45 N2
Foxhills *WOKN/KNAP* GU21 ...72 A7
Foxhills Ct *CHERT* KT16 .....54 F5
Fox Hills La *ASHV* GU12 .....109 L3
Fox Hills Rd *CHERT* KT16 .....54 E4
Foxholes *HORS* RH12 .....189 N2
    WEY KT13 .....45 H3
Foxhurst Rd *ASHV* GU12 .....109 J1

Foxlake Rd *BF/WBF* KT14 .....74 B1
Fox La *GT/LBKH* KT23 .....95 P4
    HAYES BR2 .....65 P4
    HTWY RG27 .....87 J9
    REIG RH2 .....119 M2
Fox La North *CHERT* KT16 .....37 K9
Fox La South *CHERT* KT16 * ..37 K9
Foxleigh Cha *HORS* RH12 .....192 E6
Foxley CI *BLKW* GU17 .....67 N1
    REDH RH1 .....140 C1
Foxley Gdns *PUR/KEN* CR8 ...81 K1
Foxley Hill Rd *PUR/KEN* CR8 ..81 J1
Foxley La *PUR/KEN* CR8 .....62 G8
Foxley Rd *PUR/KEN* CR8 .....81 K4
    THHTH CR7 .....45 K5
Foxoak HI *WEY* KT13 .....56 G8
Foxon CI *CTHM* CR3 .....101 N1
Foxon La *CTHM* CR3 .....101 M1
Foxon Lane Gdns
    CTHM CR3 .....101 N1
Fox Rd *BRAK* RG12 .....32 E5
    DTCH/LGLY SL3 .....12 B3
    HASM GU27 .....183 P4
    RFNM GU10 .....127 N7
Foxton Gv *MTCM* CR4 .....43 P5
Foxwarren *ESH/CLAY* KT10 ...58 D7
Fox Wy *RFNM* GU10 .....107 H6
Foxwood *FLEETN* GU51 .....87 J4
    HORS RH12 .....174 A6
Foxwood CI *FELT* TW13 .....24 C6
Fox Yd *FNM* GU9 .....4 E3
Foye La *FLEETS* GU52 .....107 H1
Frailey CI *WOKS/MYFD* GU22 ..11 K2
Frailey HI *WOKS/MYFD* GU22 ..11 K1
Framfield CI *CRAWW* RH11 ..176 D3
Framfield Rd *MTCM* CR4 .....44 C1
Frampton CI *BELMT* SM2 .....61 L6
Frampton Rd *HSLWW* TW4 ....24 F1
France Hill Dr *CBLY* GU15 .....68 B3
Frances Av *LEW* SE13 .....31 P1
Franche Court Rd
    TOOT SW17 .....28 F6
Francis Av *FELT* TW13 .....24 B6
Francis Barber CI
    STRHM/NOR SW16 * 30 A7
Franciscan Rd *TOOT* SW17 ...29 P7
Francis Chichester CI *ASC* SL5 ..34 B6
Francis CI *HOR/WEW* KT19 ...60 B3
    SHPTN TW17 .....38 C5
Francis Ct *GUW* GU2 * 111 P3
Francis Edwards Wy
    CRAWW RH11 .....176 B9
Francis Gv *WIM/MER* SW19 ...28 C9
Francis Rd *CROY/NA* CRO 45 K8
    CTHM CR3 .....101 M2
    HSLWW TW4 .....15 M7
    WLGTN SM6 .....62 E5
Franconia Rd *CLAP* SW4 .....29 M1
Frank Dixon CI *DUL* SE21 .....30 F3
Frank Dixon Wy *DUL* SE21 ...30 F4
Frankfurt Rd *HNHL* SE24 .....30 F1
Frankland Rd *SKENS* SW7 * ..19 P1
Franklands Dr
    ADL/WDHM KT15 .....55 K6
Franklin CI *KUT* KT1 .....9 H8
    WNWD SE27 .....30 C6
Franklin Ct *GUW* GU2 * 111 M5
Franklin Crs *MTCM* CR4 .....44 G5
Franklin Rd *CRAWE* RH10 .....177 M6
    PGE/AN SE20 .....46 C1
Franklin Sq *WKENS* W14 .....19 K3
Franklin Wy *CROY/NA* CRO ...44 G9
Franklyn Rd *GODL* GU7 .....150 H2
    WOT/HER KT12 .....39 K7
Franks Av *NWMAL* KT3 .....42 A5
Franksfield *SHGR* GU5 .....134 G7
Franks Rd *GUW* GU2 .....111 N2
Fransfield Gv *SYD* SE26 .....31 J8
Frant CI *PGE/AN* SE20 .....46 C1
Frant Fld *EDEN* TN8 .....144 G4
Frant Rd *THHTH* CR7 .....45 K6
Fraser Md *SHST* GU47 .....68 A1
Fraser Rd *BNFD* RG42 .....32 D2
Fraser St *CHSWK* W4 .....18 C3
Frays CI *WDR/YW* UB7 .....13 P1
Frederick CI *SUT* SM1 .....61 K3
Frederick Gdns *CROY/NA* CR0 ..45 K7
    SUT SM1 .....61 K4
Frederick Rd *SUT* SM1 .....61 K4
Frederick Sanger Rd
    GUW GU2 .....111 K6
Frederick St *ALDT* GU11 .....108 C4
Freeborn Wy *BRAK* RG12 .....32 G2
Freedown La *BELMT* SM2 .....79 M2
Freelands Av *SAND/SEL* CR2 .64 C7
Freelands Dr *FLEETS* GU52 .....106 E1
Freelands Gv *BMLY* BR1 .....47 P2
Freelands Rd *BMLY* BR1 .....47 P2
    COB KT11 .....75 K3
Freeman CI *SHPTN* TW17 .....38 C5
Freeman Dr *E/WMO/HCT* KT8 ..39 P5
Freeman Rd *HORS* RH12 .....191 M2
    MRDN SM4 .....43 P6
Freemantle Rd *BAGS* GU19 ..51 P6
Freemason's Rd
    CROY/NA CRO 3 G1
Free Prae Rd *CHERT* KT16 ...37 L9
Frees Dr *CHOB/PIR* GU24 .....70 C5
Freestone Yd
    DTCH/LGLY SL3 * 45 J7
Freethorpe CI *NRWD* SE19 ...45 M1
Frenchaye *ADL/WDHM* KT15 ..55 N4
Frenches Rd *REDH* RH1 .....120 D2
The Frenches *REDH* RH1 .....120 C2
French Gdns *BLKW* GU17 .....67 P4
    COB KT11 .....75 L3
Frenchlands Hatch
    EHSLY KT24 .....94 G7
French La *MFD/CHID* GU8 .....166 F4
Frenchmans Creek
    FLEETS GU52 .....106 E2
French St *SUN* TW16 .....39 L2

French's Wls
WOKN/KNAP GU21 71 P6
Frensham *BRAK* RG12 32 F7
Frensham Av *FLEETN* GU51 87 J6
Frensham Cl *YTLY* GU46 66 F2
Frensham Ct *RFNM* GU10 127 M9
Frensham Dr *CROY/NA* CR0 65 J6
PUT/ROE SW15 27 M6
Frensham Heights Rd
RFNM GU10 146 D2
Frensham La *BOR* GU35 164 D1
Frensham Rd *CWTH* RG45 49 M2
PUR/KEN CR8 81 K3
Frensham V *RFNM* GU10 127 N9
Frensham Wy *EW* KT17 78 G5
Frere Av *FLEETN* GU51 86 E8
Freshborough Ct *GU* GU1 7 J4
Freshfield Bank *FROW* RH18 181 K9
Freshfield Cl *CRAWE* RH10 177 K6
Freshfields *CROY/NA* CR0 46 F8
Freshford St *TOOT* SW17 28 F6
Freshmount Gdns
HOR/WEW KT19 59 P9
Freshwater Cl *TOOT* SW17 29 K9
Freshwater Pde
HORS RH12 * 192 A8
Freshwater Rd *TOOT* SW17 29 K9
Freshwood Cl *BECK* BR3 47 H2
Freshwood Dr *YTLY* GU46 66 G4
Freshwoods *HORS* RH12 189 N2
Freshwood Wy *WLGTN* SM6 62 E7
Frewin Rd *WAND/EARL* SW18 28 G4
Friar Ms *WNWD* SE27 30 C6
Friars Av *PUT/ROE* SW15 27 L6
Friars Cft *RGUE* GU4 112 G2
Friars Fld *FNM* GU9 4 E2
Friar's Ga *GUW* GU2 111 N7
Friars Keep *BRAK* RG12 32 D5
Friars La *RCH/KEW* TW9 26 C1
Friars Orch *LHD/OX* KT22 96 D1
Friars Ri *WOKS/MYFD* GU22 11 H6
Friars Rd *VW* GU25 36 B5
Friars Rookery *CRAWE* RH10 177 H5
Friars Stile Rd
RCHPK/HAM TW10 26 D2
Friars Wy *CHERT* KT16 37 L7
Friars Wd *CROY/NA* CR0 * 64 E7
Friarswood *CROY/NA* CR0 64 E7
Friary Br *GU* GU1 6 D6
Friary Ct *WOKN/KNAP* GU21 71 M7
Friary Pas *GU* GU1 6 D6
Friary Rd *ASC* SL5 34 B7
STWL/WRAY TW19 21 H2
Friary St *GU* GU1 6 D6
The Friary *GU* GU1 * 6 D5
STWL/WRAY TW19 21 H2
Friary Wy *CRAWE* RH10 176 G6
Friday Rd *MTCM* CR4 44 B1
Friday St *HORS* RH12 174 D6
HORS RH12 191 M3
RDKG RH5 155 L8
Friday Street Rd *RDKG* RH5 135 N5
Friend Av *ASHV* GU12 108 F5
Friends Cl *CRAWW* RH11 176 G2
Friendship Wy *BRAK* RG12 32 D4
Friends' Rd *CROY/NA* CR0 2 E5
PUR/KEN CR8 81 K1
Friern Rd *EDUL* SE22 31 H2
Friesian Cl *FLEETN* GU51 87 H3
Frimley Av *WLGTN* SM6 62 G4
Frimley Cl *CROY/NA* CR0 65 J6
WIM/MER SW19 28 B5
Frimley Crs *CROY/NA* CR0 65 J6
Frimley Gdns *MTCM* CR4 44 A4
Frimley Green Rd *FRIM* GU16 68 G9
Frimley Grove Gdns
FRIM GU16 68 F7
Frimley Hall Dr *CBLY* GU15 69 H2
Frimley High St *FRIM* GU16 68 E8
Frimley Rd *ASHV* GU12 89 J7
CBLY GU15 68 D4
CHSGTN KT9 59 K4
Frinton Rd *TOOT* SW17 29 K9
Friston St *FUL/PGN* SW6 19 M7
Friston Wk *CRAWW* RH11 176 D4
Fritham Cl *NWMAL* KT3 42 C7
Frith Hill Rd *FRIM* GU16 69 J7
GODL GU7 131 K7
Frith Knowle *WOT/HER* KT12 57 K4
Frith Pk *EGRIN* RH19 162 D9
Frith Rd *CROY/NA* CR0 2 C4
Friths Dr *REIG* RH2 119 M2
Frithwald Rd *CHERT* KT16 37 K8
Frobisher *BRAK* RG12 32 E8
Frobisher Cl *PUR/KEN* CR8 81 L6
Frobisher Crs
STWL/WRAY TW19 23 H3
Frobisher Gdns *GU* GU1 112 E4
Frodsham Wy *SHST* GU47 50 A7
Froggetts La *CRAN* GU6 172 D2
Frog Grove La *RGUW* GU3 110 F2
Froghole La *EDEN* TN8 125 J4
Frog La *BRAK* RG12 32 C4
RGUE GU4 92 C5
Frogmore *WAND/EARL* SW18 28 D1
Frogmore Cl *CHEAM* SM3 61 H2
Frogmore Gdns *CHEAM* SM3 61 J3
Frogmore Gv *BLKW* GU17 67 N4
Frogmore Park Dr
BLKW GU17 67 P4
Frogmore Rd *BLKW* GU17 67 N4
Frome Cl *FARN* GU14 87 P1
Fromondes Rd *CHEAM* SM3 61 J4
Fromow Gdns *BFOR* GU20 52 D5
Fromows Cnr *CHSWK* W4 * 18 A3
Froxfield Down *BRAK* RG12 33 H6
Fruen Rd *EBED/NFELT* TW14 24 A3
Fry Cl *CRAWW* RH11 194 E1
Fryern Wd *CTHM* CR3 101 L4
Fry's La *YTLY* GU46 67 J1
Fryston Av *COUL/CHIP* CR5 80 D3
CROY/NA CR0 64 A1
Fuchsia Wy *CHOB/PIR* GU24 70 E2
Fugelmere Rd *FLEETN* GU51 87 J5
Fulbourne Cl *REDH* RH1 120 A3
Fulbrook La *MFD/CHID* GU8 129 M7
Fulford Rd *CTHM* CR3 101 M1
HOR/WEW KT19 60 B6
Fulham Broadway
FUL/PGN SW6 19 L5
Fulham Cl *CRAWW* RH11 176 E9
Fulham Est *FUL/PGN* SW6 19 L4
Fulham High St
FUL/PGN SW6 19 J8
Fulham Palace Rd
FUL/PGN SW6 19 H5
Fulham Park Gdns
FUL/PGN SW6 19 K7
Fulham Park Rd
FUL/PGN SW6 19 K7
Fulham Rd *FUL/PGN* SW6 19 J7
Fullbrook Av
ADL/WDHM KT15 55 L9
Fullbrooks Av *WPK* KT4 42 D9
Fullers Av *SURB* KT6 59 M1
Fullers Farm Rd *EHSLY* KT24 114 D4
Fullers Hl *BH/WHM* TN16 105 H6
Fullers Rd *RFNM* GU10 127 H9
Fullers V *BOR* GU35 164 C6
Fullers Wy North *SURB* KT6 59 M2
Fullers Wy South
CHSGTN KT9 59 L3
Fuller's Wd *CROY/NA* CR0 64 G4
Fullers Wood La *REDH* RH1 120 E5
Fullerton Cl *BF/WBF* KT14 74 B3
Fullerton Dr *BF/WBF* KT14 74 A3
Fullerton Rd *BF/WBF* KT14 74 A3
CAR SM5 62 A7
CROY/NA CR0 45 P8
WAND/EARL SW18 28 F1
Fullerton Wy *BF/WBF* KT14 74 A3
Fuller Wy *HYS/HAR* UB3 15 H3
Fullmer Wy *ADL/WDHM* KT15 55 K8
Fulmar Cl *CRAWW* RH11 * 176 A6
Fulmar Ct *BRYLDS* KT5 41 M7
Fulmar Dr *EGRIN* RH19 162 F9
Fulmead St *FUL/PGN* SW6 19 M6
Fulmer Cl *HPTN* TW12 24 F8
Fulmer Wy *WEA* W13 17 H1
Fulstone Cl *HSLWW* TW4 15 P9
Fulvens *SHGR* GU5 134 G5
Fulwell Park Av *WHTN* TW2 25 K5
Fulwell Rd *HPTN* TW12 25 L7
Fulwood Gdns *TWK* TW1 25 N2
Fulwood Wk *WIM/MER* SW19 28 B4
Furber St *HMSMTH* W6 18 F1
Furlong Cl *WLGTN* SM6 44 D9
Furlong Rd *DORK* RH4 116 C8
Furlong Wy *HORL* RH6 159 J4
The Furlough
WOKS/MYFD GU22 11 H2
Furmage St
WAND/EARL SW18 28 E3
Furnace Dr *CRAWE* RH10 177 J7
Furnace Farm Rd
CRAWE RH10 * 177 K7
Furnace Pde *CRAWE* RH10 177 K7
Furnace Pl *CRAWE* RH10 177 K7
Furnace Rd *CRAWE* RH10 161 K9
Furneaux Av *WNWD* SE27 30 C8
Furness Rd *FUL/PGN* SW6 19 M7
MRDN SM4 43 M7
Furnival Cl *VW* GU25 36 B7
Furrows Pl *CTHM* CR3 101 P3
The Furrows *WOT/HER* KT12 57 L1
Furse Cl *CBLY* GU15 69 K4
Furtherfield Cl
CROY/NA CR0 45 J7
Further Vell-Mead
FLEETS GU52 106 E2
Furzebank *ASC* SL5 34 D5
Furze Cl *ASHV* GU12 89 J8
REDH RH1 120 B4
Furzedown Cl *EGH* TW20 21 K9
Furzedown Dr *TOOT* SW17 29 L8
Furzedown Rd *BELMT* SM2 61 N9
TOOT SW17 29 L8
Furzefield *CRAWW* RH11 176 E4
Furze Fld *LHD/OX* KT22 76 D2
Furzefield Cha *EGRIN* RH19 162 D6
Furzefield Crs *REIG* RH2 119 N7
Furzefield Rd *EGRIN* RH19 162 C8
HORS RH12 192 C5
REIG RH2 119 N7
Furze Gv *KWD/TDW/WH* KT20 99 K1
Furze Hl *KWD/TDW/WH* KT20 99 K1
PUR/KEN CR8 62 G9
Furzehill *REDH* RH1 120 A4
Furze Hill Crs *CWTH* RG45 49 N5
Furze Hill Rd *BOR* GU35 164 F7
Furze La *EGRIN* RH19 162 A9
GODL GU7 131 M5
PUR/KEN CR8 62 G9
Furzemoors *BRAK* RG12 32 D6
Furzen La *HORS* RH12 172 B8
Furze Pl *REDH* RH1 * 120 B4
Furze Rd *ADL/WDHM* KT15 55 K5
HORS RH12 189 N2
THHTH CR7 45 L4
Furze Vale Rd *BOR* GU35 164 E7
Furzewood *SUN* TW16 39 J2
Fyfe Wy *BMLY* BR1 47 N3
Fyfield Cl *BECK* BR3 47 N5
BLKW GU17 67 P3

G

Gable Ct *SYD* SE26 31 J7
Gable End *FARN* GU14 * 88 D3
Gables Av *ASHF* TW15 23 J8
Gables Cl *ASHV* GU12 109 J1
FARN GU14 88 C3
WOKS/MYFD GU22 72 D9
Gables Rd *FLEETS* GU52 106 F2
The Gables *BNSTD* SM7 79 K6
HORS RH12 192 C6
LHD/OX KT22 76 C1
NRWD SE19 * 45 N2
WEY KT13 56 E4
WOKS/MYFD GU22 * 10 B7
Gables Wy *BNSTD* SM7 79 K5
Gabriel Cl *FELT* TW13 24 F7
Gabriel Dr *CBLY* GU15 69 K4
Gabriel Rd *CRAWE* RH10 177 M9
Gabriel St *FSTH* SE23 31 L3
Gadbridge La *CRAN* GU6 153 P8
Gadbrook Rd
BRKHM/BTCW RH3 138 A2
Gadesden Rd
HOR/WEW KT19 60 A5
Gaffney Cl *ALDT* GU11 88 F8
Gage Cl *CRAWE* RH10 179 K2
Gainsborough *BRAK* RG12 32 E7
Gainsborough Cl *BECK* BR3 46 G1
CBLY GU15 69 H1
ESH/CLAY KT10 * 40 D9
FARN GU14 88 F5
Gainsborough Ct
WOT/HER KT12 57 J3
Gainsborough Dr *ASC* SL5 33 M4
SAND/SEL CR2 82 A2
Gainsborough Gdns
HSLW TW3 25 L1
Gainsborough Rd *CHSWK* W4 18 D2
CRAWE RH10 177 J9
HOR/WEW KT19 60 A8
NWMAL KT3 42 B7
RCH/KEW TW9 17 M7
Gainsborough Ter
BELMT SM2 * 61 K6
Gaist Av *CTHM* CR3 102 B2
Galahad Rd *CRAWW* RH11 176 B5
Galata Rd *BARN* SW13 18 E5
Gale Barracks *ALDT* GU11 * 108 D2
Gale Cl *HPTN* TW12 24 F9
MTCM CR4 43 P4
Gale Crs *BNSTD* SM7 79 L6
Gale Dr *LTWR* GU18 52 A8
Galena Rd *HMSMTH* W6 18 F2
Galen Cl *HOR/WEW* KT19 59 N9
Galesbury Rd
WAND/EARL SW18 28 F2
Gales Cl *RGUE* GU4 * 113 H2
Gales Dr *CRAWE* RH10 177 J5
Gales Pl *CRAWE* RH10 177 J5
Galgate Cl *WIM/MER* SW19 28 B4
The Galleries *ALDT* GU11 * 108 C4
Gallery Rd *DUL* SE21 30 E4
Galleymead Rd
DTCH/LGLY SL3 13 K6
The Gallop *BELMT* SM2 61 P7
SAND/SEL CR2 64 B6
YTLY GU46 67 H1
Galloway Cl *FLEETN* GU51 87 J3
Galloway Pth *CROY/NA* CR0 63 M3
Gallwey Rd *ALDT* GU11 108 E3
Gally Hill Rd *FLEETS* GU52 106 F2
Galpin's Rd *THHTH* CR7 44 G5
Galsworthy Rd *CHERT* KT16 * 37 L8
KUTN/CMB KT2 9 K2
Galton Rd *ASC* SL5 34 F7
Galveston Rd *PUT/ROE* SW15 28 C1
Gambles La *RPLY/SEND* GU23 93 N5
Gambole Rd *TOOT* SW17 29 H7
Gamlen Rd *PUT/ROE* SW15 19 H9
Gander Green Crs
HPTN TW12 40 A2
Gander Green La *CHEAM* SM3 61 J1
Gangers Hl *GDST* RH9 102 F7
Ganghill *GU* GU1 112 E3
Gapemouth Rd *FRIM* GU16 89 N2
Gap Rd *WIM/MER* SW19 28 D8
Garbetts Wy *RFNM* GU10 108 G8
Garbrand Wk *EW* KT17 60 D7
Garden Av *MTCM* CR4 44 D1
Garden Cl *ADL/WDHM* KT15 55 P3
ASHF TW15 23 M9
BNSTD SM7 79 L4
EGRIN RH19 180 E4
FARN GU14 88 A5
HPTN TW12 24 G8
LHD/OX KT22 97 J4
PUT/ROE SW15 27 N3
SHGR GU5 133 H9
WLGTN SM6 62 G4
Gardeners Cl *HORS* RH12 191 M2
Gardeners Gn *HORS* RH12 175 H5
Gardener's Hill Rd
RFNM GU10 127 M9
Gardeners Rd *CROY/NA* CR0 2 B2
Gardener's Wk *GT/LBKH* KT23 96 B6
Garden Flats *HMSMTH* W6 * 19 H4
Garden House La
EGRIN RH19 180 E4
Gardenia Ct *CHOB/PIR* GU24 70 F2
Garden La *BRXS/STRHM* SW2 30 A4
Garden Pl *HORS* RH12 * 192 B6
Garden Rd *BMLY* BR1 47 P1
PGE/AN SE20 46 C2
RCH/KEW TW9 17 N8
WOT/HER KT12 39 K7
The Gardens *BECK* BR3 47 J3
CHOB/PIR GU24 90 F2
COB KT11 * 74 E8
EBED/NFELT TW14 23 N2
ESH/CLAY KT10 58 A3
RFNM GU10 109 H7
Garden Vls *ESH/CLAY* KT10 * 58 F6
Garden Wk *BECK* BR3 46 F2
COUL/CHIP CR5 100 D3
CRAWW RH11 176 F5
Garden Wood Rd
EGRIN RH19 180 B2
Gardner La *CRAWE* RH10 179 H3
Gardner Pl *EBED/NFELT* TW14 24 C2
Gardner Rd *GU* GU1 6 E2
Garendon Gdns *MRDN* SM4 43 M8
Garendon Rd *MRDN* SM4 43 M8
Gareth Cl *WPK* KT4 61 H1
Garfield Rd *ADL/WDHM* KT15 55 N4
CBLY GU15 68 E3
TWK TW1 25 P4
WIM/MER SW19 28 F9
Garibaldi Rd *REDH* RH1 120 B6
Garland Ct *EGRIN* RH19 * 180 C2
Garland Rd *EGRIN* RH19 180 C2
Garlands Rd *LHD/OX* KT22 97 H1
REDH RH1 120 B5
Garland Wy *CTHM* CR3 101 M2
Garlichill Rd *EPSOM* KT18 78 F6
Garlies Rd *FSTH* SE23 31 M6
Garnet Fld *YTLY* GU46 66 E3
Garnet Rd *THHTH* CR7 45 L5
Garrad's Rd
STRHM/NOR SW16 29 N6
Garrard Rd *BNSTD* SM7 79 L5
Garratt Cl *CROY/NA* CR0 62 G3
Garratt La *WAND/EARL* SW18 28 E3
Garratts La *BNSTD* SM7 79 K5
Garratt Ter *TOOT* SW17 29 H7
Garrett Cl *CRAWE* RH10 177 M7
Garrett Rd *EWKG* RG40 48 C1
Garrick Cl *BTSEA* SW11 19 N9
RCH/KEW TW9 26 B1
STA TW18 37 L1
WOT/HER KT12 57 K3
Garrick Crs *CROY/NA* CR0 3 G4
Garrick Gdns
E/WMO/HCT KT8 40 A4
Garrick Rd *RCH/KEW* TW9 17 N7
Garrick Wk *CRAWE* RH10 177 H8
Garrick Wy *FRIM* GU16 88 G1
Garrison Cl *HSLWW* TW4 24 G1
Garrison La *CHSGTN* KT9 59 L6
The Garrones
CRAWE RH10 * 177 P4
Garsdale Ter *WKENS* W14 * 19 K3
Garside Cl *HPTN* TW12 40 B1
Garson La *STWL/WRAY* TW19 21 J3
Garson Rd *ESH/CLAY* KT10 57 P4
Garston La *PUR/KEN* CR8 81 M4
The Garstons *GT/LBKH* KT23 95 P5
Garswood *BRAK* RG12 32 F7
Garth Cl *FNM* GU9 127 L6
KUTN/CMB KT2 26 E8
MRDN SM4 43 H8
Garthorne Rd *FSTH* SE23 31 L3
Garth Rd *CHSWK* W4 18 B3
KUTN/CMB KT2 26 E8
MRDN SM4 43 H9
Garthside *KUTN/CMB* KT2 26 D8
Garth Sq *BNFD* RG42 32 D1
The Garth *ASHV* GU12 109 H5
COB KT11 75 N2
FARN GU14 88 F3
HPTN TW12 25 J9
Gartmoor Gdns
WIM/MER SW19 28 C4
Garton Cl *CRAWW* RH11 176 B6
Garton Pl *WAND/EARL* SW18 28 F2
Gartons Wy *BTSEA* SW11 19 N8
Gascoigne Rd *CROY/NA* CR0 65 J8
WEY KT13 56 D2
Gasden Copse
MFD/CHID GU8 149 L7
Gasden Dr *MFD/CHID* GU8 149 L6
Gasden La *MFD/CHID* GU8 149 L6
Gaskarth Rd *BAL* SW12 29 L2
Gaskyns Cl *HORS* RH12 189 N3
Gaspar Ms *ECT* SW5 19 M2
Gassiot Rd *TOOT* SW17 29 J7
Gassiot Wy *SUT* SM1 61 P2
Gasson Wood Rd
CRAWW RH11 176 B7
Gastein Rd *HMSMTH* W6 19 H4
Gaston Bell Cl *RCH/KEW* TW9 17 M8
Gaston Bridge Rd
SHPTN TW17 38 G6
Gaston Rd *MTCM* CR4 44 C4
Gaston Wy *SHPTN* TW17 38 F6
Gateford Dr *HORS* RH12 192 E4
Gatehouse Cl *KUTN/CMB* KT2 42 A1
Gates Cl *CRAWE* RH10 177 M9
Gatesden Cl *LHD/OX* KT22 96 C3
Gatesden Rd *LHD/OX* KT22 96 C3
Gates Green Rd *WWKM* BR4 65 N3
Gateside Rd *TOOT* SW17 29 J6
The Gates *FLEETN* GU51 87 J3
Gatestone Rd *NRWD* SE19 30 F9
Gateways *GU* GU1 112 F6
The Gateways
RCH/KEW TW9 * 17 K9
The Gateway
WOKN/KNAP GU21 72 F3
Gatfield Gv *FELT* TW13 25 H5
Gatley Av *HOR/WEW* KT19 59 P4
Gatley Dr *RGUE* GU4 112 D2
Gatton Bottom *REIG* RH2 100 B8
Gatton Cl *BELMT* SM2 * 61 M7
REIG RH2 119 N2
Gatton Park Rd *REDH* RH1 119 P2
Gatton Rd *REIG* RH2 119 N2
TOOT SW17 29 H7
Gatwick Rd *CRAWE* RH10 177 K1
HORL RH6 159 K8
WAND/EARL SW18 28 C3
Gatwick Wy *HORL* RH6 159 J4
Gauntlet Crs *PUR/KEN* CR8 81 M8
Gauntlett Rd *SUT* SM1 61 P4
Gavell Rd *COB* KT11 75 J2
Gaveston Cl *BF/WBF* KT14 74 B2
Gaveston Rd *LHD/OX* KT22 76 G9
Gavina Cl *MRDN* SM4 44 A6
Gayfere Rd *EW* KT17 60 E4
Gayhouse La *REDH* RH1 141 N6
Gayler Cl *REDH* RH1 121 P5
Gaynesford Rd *CAR* SM5 62 B6
FSTH SE23 31 L5
Gayton Cl *ASHTD* KT21 77 L7
Gayville Rd *BTSEA* SW11 29 J2
Gaywood Cl
BRXS/STRHM SW2 30 A4
Gaywood Rd *ASHTD* KT21 77 M7
Geary Cl *HORL* RH6 160 C3
Geffers Ride *ASC* SL5 33 N4
Gemini Cl *CRAWW* RH11 176 A7
Genesis Cl *STWL/WRAY* TW19 23 J4
Geneva Cl *SHPTN* TW17 38 G3
Geneva Rd *KUT* KT1 41 L5
THHTH CR7 45 L6
Genoa Av *PUT/ROE* SW15 27 P1
Genoa Rd *PGE/AN* SE20 46 C2
Gentles La *LIPH* GU30 182 D1
Genyn Rd *GUW* GU2 6 B6
George Denyer Cl
HASM GU27 184 D3
George Eliot Cl
MFD/CHID GU8 149 N8
George Gdns *ALDT* GU11 108 E7
George Groves Rd
PGE/AN SE20 46 A2
Georgeham Rd *SHST* GU47 49 P7
George Horley Pl
RDKG RH5 * 156 G3
Georgelands
RPLY/SEND GU23 93 M1
George La *HAYES* BR2 47 P9
George Rd *FLEETN* GU51 87 H6
GODL GU7 131 L6
GU GU1 6 E3
KUTN/CMB KT2 41 P1
MFD/CHID GU8 149 N2
NWMAL KT3 42 D5
George's Rd *BH/WHM* TN16 84 B9
Georges Ter *CTHM* CR3 101 M2
George St *CHOB/PIR* GU24 90 A1
CROY/NA CR0 2 E4
HSLW TW3 15 P7
NWDGN UB2 15 N2
RCHPK/HAM TW10 26 C1
STA TW18 22 C7
Georgetown Cl *NRWD* SE19 30 E8
George Wyver Cl
WAND/EARL SW18 28 B3
Georgian Cl *CBLY* GU15 68 G1
CRAWE RH10 177 N6
HAYES BR2 47 P9
STA TW18 22 E7
Georgia Rd *NWMAL* KT3 42 A5
THHTH CR7 45 K2
Geraldine Rd *CHSWK* W4 17 N4
WAND/EARL SW18 28 F1
Gerald's Gv *BNSTD* SM7 79 H3
Geranium Cl *CWTH* RG45 49 M1
Gerard Av *HSLWW* TW4 25 H3
Gerard Rd *BARN* SW13 18 D6
Germander Dr
CHOB/PIR GU24 70 G5
Gerrards Md *BNSTD* SM7 79 K5
Gertrude St *WBPTN* SW10 19 N4
Ghent St *CAT* SE6 31 P5
Giant Arches Rd *HNHL* SE24 30 D3
Gibbet La *CBLY* GU15 69 J1
Gibbon Rd *KUTN/CMB* KT2 8 E2
Gibbons Cl *CRAWE* RH10 * 177 M8
SHST GU47 67 N1
Gibbon Wk *PUT/ROE* SW15 * 18 E9
Gibb's Acre *CHOB/PIR* GU24 90 F3
Gibbs Av *NRWD* SE19 30 E9
Gibbs Brook La *OXTED* RH8 123 K5
Gibbs Cl *EWKG* RG40 48 C3
NRWD SE19 * 30 E8
Gibbs Gn *WKENS* W14 * 19 K3
Gibbs Sq *NRWD* SE19 * 30 E8
Gibbs Wy *YTLY* GU46 66 F4
Giblets La *HORS* RH12 192 E3
Giblets Wy *HORS* RH12 192 D3
Gibraltar Crs *HOR/WEW* KT19 60 C8
Gibson Cl *CHSGTN* KT9 * 59 J4
ISLW TW7 16 D8
Gibson Ct *DTCH/LGLY* SL3 12 D3
Gibson Pl *STWL/WRAY* TW19 22 F2
Gibson Rd *SUT* SM1 61 M4
Gibson's Hl
STRHM/NOR SW16 30 B9
Gidd Hl *COUL/CHIP* CR5 80 C5
Giffard Dr *FARN* GU14 88 B1
Giffards Cl *EGRIN* RH19 180 E2
Giffards Meadow *FNM* GU9 128 A4
Giffard Wy *GUW* GU2 111 N2
Giggs Hill Gdns *THDIT* KT7 40 G9
Giggs Hill Rd *THDIT* KT7 40 G8
Gilbert Cl *WIM/MER* SW19 * 43 M2
Gilbert Rd *BMLY* BR1 47 N1
FRIM GU16 68 E7
WIM/MER SW19 43 N1
Gilbert St *HSLW* TW3 16 C8
Gilbert Wy *EWKG* RG40 48 C1
Gilbey Rd *TOOT* SW17 29 H7
Gilders Rd *CHSGTN* KT9 59 M6
Giles Coppice *NRWD* SE19 30 G7
Giles Md *EPSOM* KT18 * 78 C3
Giles Travers Cl *EGH* TW20 36 G4
Gilham La *FROW* RH18 181 K9
Gilham's Av *BNSTD* SM7 79 H1
Gilhams Cottages
BNSTD SM7 * 79 J1
Gilkes Crs *DUL* SE21 30 F2
Gilkes Pl *DUL* SE21 30 F2
Gill Av *GUW* GU2 111 [illegible]
Gillet Ct *SWTR* RH13 * 192 [illegible]
Gillett Ct *SWTR* RH13 192 [illegible]
Gillett Rd *THDIT* KT7 [illegible]
Gillham's La *HASM* GU27 [illegible]
Gilliam Gv *PUR/KEN* CR8 [illegible]

Gillian Av ASHV GU12 ....108 E6
Gillian Cl ASHV GU12 ....108 F6
Gillian Park Rd CHEAM SM3 ...43 K9
Gillian Ter BRYLDS KT5 * 41 M7
Gilliat Dr RGUE GU4 ....113 H3
Gilligan Cl HORS RH12 ....192 A8
Gilmais GT/LBKH KT23 ....96 C5
Gilmore Crs ASHV GU12 ....23 K8
Gilpin Av MORT/ESHN SW14 ...18 B9
Gilpin Cl MTCM CR4 ....44 A3
Gilpin Crs HSLW TW3 ....25 J3
Gilpin Wy HYS/HAR UB3 ....14 F5
Gilsland Rd THHTH CR7 ....45 M5
Gilson Ct STWL/WRAY TW19 ...21 H3
Gilstead Rd FUL/PGN SW6 ....19 M7
Gilston Rd WBPTN SW10 ....19 N3
Gimcrack HI LHD/OX KT22 ...97 H2
Ginhams Rd CRAWW RH11 ...176 E5
Gipsy HI NRWD SE19 ....30 E8
Gipsy La BARN SW13 ....18 E8
   BRAK RG12 ....32 F4
Gipsy Rd WNWD SE27 ....30 E7
Gipsy Road Gdns WNWD SE27 ...30 D7
Girdlers Rd WKENS W14 ....19 H2
Girdwood Rd WAND/EARL SW18 ....28 B3
Girling Wy EBED/NFELT TW14..15 J8
Gironde Rd FUL/PGN SW6 ....19 K5
Girton Cl SHST GU47 ....50 A8
Girton Gdns CROY/NA CRO...64 C2
Girton Rd SYD SE26 ....31 L8
Gisbourne Cl WLGTN SM6....62 F2
Glade Cl SURB KT6 ....59 K1
Glade Gdns CROY/NA CRO...46 E8
Gladeside CROY/NA CRO 46 D8
Glade Sp KWD/TDW/WH KT20 ..99 M1
The Glades EGRIN RH19 ...180 G2
Glade The ASC SL5 ....34 C6
   BELMT SM2 ....61 J7
   BF/WBF KT14 ....73 J2
   COUL/CHIP CR5 ....81 J8
   CRAWE RH10 ....177 K7
   CROY/NA CRO 46 D6
   EW KT17 ....60 E5
   FNM GU9 ....107 P7
   FRIM GU16 ....89 H5
   KWD/TDW/WH KT20 ....99 M1
   LHD/OX KT22 ....96 B2
   STA TW18 ....37 M1
   SWTR RH13 ....192 F1
   WWKM BR4 ....65 H2
Gladiator St FSTH SE23 ....31 M2
Gladiator Wy FARN GU14...88 C7
Gladioli Cl HPTN TW12 ....25 H9
Gladsmuir Cl WOT/HER KT12...57 L1
Gladstone Av EBED/NFELT TW14 ....24 B2
   WHTN TW2 ....25 L2
Gladstone Gdns HSLW TW3...16 C6
Gladstone Ms PGE/AN SE20 ..46 C1
Gladstone Pl E/WMO/HCT KT8 * 40 E6
Gladstone Rd ASHTD KT21...77 K7
   CHSWK W4 ....18 B1
   CROY/NA CRO 45 M8
   HORS RH12 ....192 C7
   KUT KT1 ....9 J6
   SURB KT6 ....59 K1
   WIM/MER SW19 ....43 L1
Gladstone Ter WNWD SE27 *..30 D7
Gladwyn Rd PUT/ROE SW15...19 H8
Glamis Cl FRIM GU16 ....69 H9
Glamis Crs HYS/HAR UB3....14 E1
Glamorgan Cl MTCM CR4...44 G4
Glamorgan Rd KUT KT1 ....8 A1
Glanfield Rd BECK BR3 ....46 F5
The Glanty EGH TW20.....21 P7
Glanville Rd BRXS/STRHM SW2 ....29 N1
   HAYES BR2 ....47 P4
Glasbrook Av WHTN TW2 ....24 G4
Glasford St TOOT SW17 ....29 J9
Glassmill La HAYES BR2 ....47 M3
Glastonbury Rd MRDN SM4 ..43 L8
Glaston Hill Rd HTWY RG27 ...86 A1
Glayshers HI BOR GU35 ...164 D5
Glazbury Rd WKENS W14 ....19 J2
Glazebrook Cl DUL SE21....30 E5
Glazebrook Rd TEDD TW11...40 F2
Glaziers La RGUW GU3 ....110 C4
Gleave Cl EGRIN RH19 ....180 F1
Glebe Av MTCM CR4 ....44 A3
Glebe Cl CHSWK W4 * 18 C3
   CRAN GU6 ....176 G4
   FNM GU9 ....108 C7
   GT/LBKH KT23 ....96 A6
   LTWR GU18 ....52 C8
   SAND/SEL CR2 ....81 P1
Glebe Cottages RGUE GU4 ..113 M3
Glebe Ct FLEETS GU51 ....86 E6
Glebe Gdns BF/WBF KT14 ....73 P5
   NWMAL KT3 ....42 C8
Glebe House Dr HAYES BR2..47 P9
Glebe Hyrst SAND/SEL CR2..81 P1
Glebeland Gdns SHPTN TW17 ..38 E7
Glebeland Rd CBLY GU15....68 B3
Glebelands BIL RH14 ....188 C6
   CRAWE RH10 ....179 H5
   E/WMO/HCT KT8 ....40 B6
   ESH/CLAY KT10 ....58 F7
Glebelands Meadow CRAN GU6 * ...188 C1
Glebelands Rd EBED/NFELT TW14 ....24 B3
Glebe La RDKG RH5 ....135 M5
   RFNM GU10 ....147 M7
Glebe Pth ASHTD KT21 ....77 K7
   BARN SW13 ....18 A4
   BELMT SM2 ....61 J7
   BMLY BR1 ....47 N2
   BOR GU35 ....164 B6
   CAR SM5 ....62 B5
   COUL/CHIP CR5 ....100 D4
   CRAN GU6 ....153 H8
   DORK RH4 ....116 F7
   ECH TW20 ....21 P9
   FARN GU14 ....88 B2
   FARN RG10 ....106 D8
   RGUE GU4 ....82 D6
   STA TW18 ....22 E8
   WARL CR6 ....82 D6
   WDSR SL4 ....
Glebe Side TWK TW1 ....25 N2
Glebe Sq MTCM CR4 ....44 B4
Glebe St CHSWK W4 ....18 B3
The Glebe BLKW GU17 ....68 A4
   CRAN GU6 ....153 P6
   CRAWE RH10 ....160 C9
   EGRIN RH19 ....161 P8
   HSLW TW3 ....16 D7
   REIG RH2 ....138 E3
   STRHM/NOR SW16 ....29 N7
   WDR/YW UB7 ....14 A2
   WPK KT4 ....42 D9
Glebe Wy FELT TW13 ....25 H6
   SAND/SEL CR2 ....81 P1
   WWKM BR4 ....65 J1
Gledhow Rd BRAK RG12 ....32 E6
Gledhow Gdns ECT SW5 ....19 N2
Gledhow Wd KWD/TDW/WH KT20 ....99 M2
Gledstanes Rd WKENS W14...19 J3
Glegg Pl PUT/ROE SW15 * ...19 H9
Glen Albyn Rd WIM/MER SW19 ....28 A5
Glena Mt SUT SM1 ....61 N3
Glen Av ASHF TW15 ....23 K7
Glenavon Cl ESH/CLAY KT10..58 G5
Glenavon Gdns DTCH/LGLY SL3 ....12 A2
   YTLY GU46 ....67 H4
Glenbuck Rd SURB KT6....41 K7
Glenburnie Rd TOOT SW17...29 J6
Glencairn Rd STRHM/NOR SW16 ....44 G1
Glen Cl CGSHT GU26 ....165 M5
   KWD/TDW/WH KT20 ....99 J3
   SHPTN TW17 ....38 C5
Glencoe Cl FRIM GU16 ....69 H8
Glencoe Rd WEY KT13 ....56 C2
Glen Ct ADL/WDHM KT15 *....53 K4
Glenavon Rd DRGUE GU4 ....112 G1
   WOKN/KNAP GU21 ....72 A7
Glendale Cl HORS RH12 ....192 F4
Glendale Dr RGUE GU4 ....112 G1
   WIM/MER SW19 ....28 C8
Glen Dale Ms BECK BR3 ....47 H2
Glendale Pk FLEETN GU51...86 C5
Glendale Rd PUR/KEN CR8...81 K4
Glendarvon St PUT/ROE SW15 ....19 H8
Glendene Av EHSLY KT24....94 G6
Glendower Gdns MORT/ESHN SW14 ....18 B8
Glendower Rd MORT/ESHN SW14 ....18 B8
Glendyne Cl EGRIN RH19...180 F3
Glendyne Wy EGRIN RH19...180 F3
Gleneagle Ms STRHM/NOR SW16 ....29 N8
Gleneagle Rd STRHM/NOR SW16 ....29 N8
Gleneagles Cl HTHAIR TW6...22 F2
Gleneagles Ct CRAWE RH10 * 176 G6
Gleneagles Dr FARN GU14 ..87 N4
Glenelon Ms STRHM/NOR SW16 ....29 N7
Glenelon Rd STRHM/NOR SW16 ....29 N7
Glenelg Rd BRXS/STRHM SW2..29 P1
Glenfield Cl BRKHM/BTCW RH3 ....117 P8
Glenfield Rd ASHF TW15 ....23 L9
   BAL SW12 ....29 M4
   BNSTD SM7 ....79 M4
   BRKHM/BTCW RH3 ....117 P9
Glen Gdns CROY/NA CRO....63 J2
Glenheadon Cl LHD/OX KT22..97 K3
Glenheadon Ri LHD/OX KT22..97 K3
Glenhurst BFOR GU20 ....52 A3
Glenhurst Cl BLKW GU17....68 A4
Glenhurst Ri NRWD SE19...45 L1
Glenhurst Rd BTFD TW8 ....17 J4
Glen Innes SHST GU47 ....50 B8
Glenister Park Rd STRHM/NOR SW16 ....44 F1
Glenlea CGSHT GU26 ....183 P1
Glenlea Hollow CGSHT GU26..183 P2
Glenmore Cl ADL/WDHM KT15 ....55 M2
Glenmount Rd FRIM GU16...89 J5
Glenn Av PUR/KEN CR8 ....63 K9
Glennie Rd WNWD SE27....30 B6
Glen Rd CHSGTN KT9 ....59 L2
   FLEETN GU51 ....86 F7
   CGSHT GU26 ....165 M5
   CSHT GU26 ....165 M5
   WLGTN SM6 ....62 D7
Glenrosa St FUL/PGN SW6 ...19 N7
Glentanner Wy TOOT SW17..29 H8
Glentham Cottages BARN SW13 * 18 E4
Glentham Gdns BARN SW13 ..18 F3
Glentham Rd BARN SW13....18 E3
The Glen ADL/WDHM KT15....55 K4
   ASC SL5 ....34 D5
   BELMT SM2 ....61 N5
   CROY/NA CRO 64 D2
   DTCH/LGLY SL3 ....12 A2
   FNM GU9 ....107 N8
   HAYES BR2 ....47 L3
   NWDGN UB2 ....15 P3
Glenthorne Av CROY/NA CRO..46 C9
Glenthorne Cl CHEAM SM3...43 L9
Glenthorne Gdns CHEAM SM3 ....43 L9
Glenthorne Rd HMSMTH W6..18 G2
   KUT KT1 ....41 M5
Glenthorpe Rd MRDN SM4...43 H8
Glenville Gdns CSHT GU26 ..166 A1
Glenview Ct CRAWE RH10...177 J3
Glenville Rd KUTN/CMB KT2...9 H2
Glen Vue EGRIN RH19 ....180 E2
Glenwood BRAK RG12 ....32 C5
   RDKG RH5 ....117 J9
Glenwood Rd CAT SE6 ....31 N4
   EW KT17 ....60 E5
   HSLW TW3 ....16 D8
Glenwood Rw NRWD SE19 *...45 N2
Glenwood Wy CROY/NA CRO...46 D7
Gliddon Rd WKENS W14 ....19 J2
Globe Farm La BLKW GU17...67 M3
Glomey Md FNM GU9 ....108 C8
Glory Md DORK RH4 ....137 J1
Glossop Rd SAND/SEL CR2..63 M7
Gloster Rd NWMAL KT3 ....42 C5
   WOKS/MYFD GU22 ....73 H7
Gloucester Cl FRIM GU16....88 G1
   THDIT KT7 * 40 C9
Gloucester Crs STA TW18 ...22 G9
Gloucester Dr STWL/WRAY TW19 ....21 P6
Gloucester Gdns SUT SM1..61 M1
Gloucester Pde HYS/HAR UB3 * 14 E1
Gloucester Pl BNFD RG42...33 H1
Gloucester Rd ALDT GU11 ..108 E7
   BAGS GU19 ....51 N6
   CRAWE RH10 ....177 H9
   CROY/NA CRO 3 F1
   FELT TW13 ....24 D4
   GUW GU2 ....111 M3
   HPTN TW12 ....40 B1
   HSLWW TW4 ....15 N9
   KUT KT1 ....41 L4
   RCH/KEW TW9 ....17 N5
   REDH RH1 ....120 B4
   SKENS SW7 ....19 N2
   TEDD TW11 ....25 M8
   WHTN TW2 ....25 K4
Glover's Rd HORL RH6 ....158 A5
   REIG RH2 ....119 M6
Glyn Cl EW KT17 ....60 E7
   SNWD SE25 ....45 N3
Glynde Pl HORS RH12 ....192 B9
Glynde St BROCKY SE4 ....31 N2
Glyn Rd WPK KT4 ....61 H1
Glynswood CBLY GU15 ....69 H5
   RFNM GU10 ....127 L9
Goaters Rd ASC SL5 ....33 L3
Goat Rd MTCM CR4 ....44 C8
Goatsfield Rd BH/WHM TN16..84 A9
Goat Wharf BTFD TW8 ....17 L4
Godalming Av WLGTN SM6...62 G4
Godalming Rd GODL GU7...151 K9
Goddard Cl CRAWE RH10...177 L8
Goddard Rd BECK BR3 ....46 D5
Goddards La CBLY GU15....68 D5
Godfrey Av WHTN TW2 ....25 L3
Godfrey Cl SHST GU47 ....67 P1
Godfrey Wy HSLWW TW4...24 G1
Godley Rd BF/WBF KT14....74 B2
   WAND/EARL SW18 ....28 C4
Godolphin Cl BELMT SM2 ...61 K9
Godolphin Rd WEY KT13....56 F5
Godric Crs CROY/NA CRO...65 K8
Godson Rd CROY/NA CRO...63 J2
Godstone Green Rd GDST RH9 ....122 B2
Godstone HI GDST RH9 ....102 B8
Godstone HI PUR/KEN CR8 *..81 K1
Godstone Mt PUR/KEN CR8 *..81 K1
Godstone Rd CTHM CR3....101 M2
   LING RH7 ....143 J8
   PUR/KEN CR8 ....81 K2
   PUR/KEN CR8 ....81 N4
   REDH RH1 ....121 N4
   SUT SM1 ....61 N3
   TWK TW1 ....25 P1
Godwin Cl HOR/WEW KT19...60 A5
Godwin Wy HORS RH12 ....192 E6
Goffs Cl CRAWW RH11 ....176 F6
Goffs La CRAWW RH11 ....176 E5
Goffs Park Rd CRAWW RH11..176 F6
Goffs Rd ASHF TW15 ....23 N9
Gogmore Farm Cl CHERT KT16 ....37 J8
Gogmore La CHERT KT16....37 J8
Goidel Cl WLGTN SM6 ....62 F3
Goldcliff Cl MRDN SM4 ....43 L8
Goldcrest Cl HORL RH6 ....139 P9
   YTLY GU46 ....66 F2
Goldcrest Wy CROY/NA CRO..65 K8
   PUR/KEN CR8 ....62 F8
Gold Cup La ASC SL5 ....33 M2
Goldenfield Cl LIPH GU30 ..182 C4
Golden Flds LIPH GU30 ....182 G1
Goldfinch Cl ALDT GU11 ....108 B6
   CRAWW RH11 ....176 G5
   HORS RH12 ....192 D3
Goldfinch Gdns RGUE GU4 ..113 H4
Goldfinch Rd SAND/SEL CR2..64 E8
Goldhawk Rd HMSMTH W6...18 D2
Goldhill RFNM GU10 ....127 N7
Golding Cl CRAWE RH10 ....177 M6
The Goldings WOKN/KNAP GU21 ....71 M5
Gold La ALDT GU11 ....108 G2
Goldney Rd CBLY GU15 ....69 K4
Goldrings Rd LHD/OX KT22...76 C2
Goldsmith Cl WOKN/KNAP GU21 ....72 A7
Goldsmith Wy CWTH RG45...49 M5
Goldstone Farm Vw GT/LBKH KT23 * 96 A7
Goldsworth Orch WOKN/KNAP GU21 ....71 N7
Goldsworth Rd WOKN/KNAP GU21 ....10 A5
Goldwell Rd THHTH CR7 ....45 H5
Gole Rd CHOB/PIR GU24....90 D1
Golf Cl STRHM/NOR SW16...45 J2
   WOKS/MYFD GU22 ....73 J3
Golf Club Dr KUTN/CMB KT2..27 K7
Golf Club Rd WEY KT13 ....56 D8
Golf Dr CBLY GU15 ....69 H4
Golf Links Av CSHT GU26 ..165 L5
Golf Rd PUR/KEN CR8 ....81 N4
Golf Side BELMT SM2 ....61 J9
   WHTN TW2 ....25 L6
Golf Side Cl NWMAL KT3....42 C3
Gomer Gdns TEDD TW11 ...25 P9
Gomer Pl TEDD TW11 ....25 P9
Gomshall Av WLGTN SM6...62 G4
Gomshall Gdns PUR/KEN CR8..81 N2
Gomshall La SHGR GU5 ....134 C1
Gomshall Rd BELMT SM2...60 G8
Gondreville Gdns FLEETS GU52 ....106 E2
Gong HI RFNM GU10 ....146 G1
Gong Hill Dr RFNM GU10...127 P9
Gonston Cl WIM/MER SW19...28 B5
Gonville Rd THHTH CR7 ....45 H6
Gonville St FUL/PGN SW6...19 J8
Goodden Crs FARN GU14....88 B5
Goodenough Cl COUL/CHIP CR5 ....81 J9
Goodenough Wy COUL/CHIP CR5 ....81 H9
Goodhart Wy WWKM BR4...47 L2
Goodhew Rd SNWD SE25....46 A7
Gooding Cl NWMAL KT3....42 A5
Goodley Stock Rd EDEN TN8 ....104 F9
Goodman Crs BRXS/STRHM SW2 ....29 N5
Goodrich Rd EDUL SE22....30 G2
Goodways Dr BRAK RG12...32 E3
Goodwin Cl CRAWW RH11..176 B8
   MTCM CR4 ....43 P4
Goodwin Gdns CROY/NA CRO..63 K5
Goodwin Rd CROY/NA CRO...63 K5
Goodwins Cl EGRIN RH19...162 C9
Goodwood Cl CBLY GU15....68 G4
   CRAWE RH10 ....177 K8
   MRDN SM4 ....43 L5
Goodwood Pde BECK BR3 *..46 E5
Goodwood Pl FARN GU14 ...88 E5
Goodwood Rd REDH RH1...120 B3
Goodwyns Rd DORK RH4 ..137 H1
Goose Green Cl STRHM/NOR SW16 ....29 J6
Goose Green Cl HORS RH12..192 C5
Goose La WOKS/MYFD GU22..91 P2
Goose Rye Rd RGUW GU3...91 K6
Goossens Cl SUT SM1 ....61 N4
Gordon Av CBLY GU15 ....68 D4
   FLEETS GU52 ....87 H9
   MORT/ESHN SW14 ....18 C9
   PUR/KEN CR8 ....63 L8
   TWK TW1 ....25 P1
Gordonbrook Rd BROCKY SE4 ....31 P1
Gordon Cl CHERT KT16 ....55 J3
   STA TW18 ....22 E9
Gordon Ct REDH RH1 * 120 B7
Gordon Crs CBLY GU15 ....68 E4
   CROY/NA CRO 3 H1
   HYS/HAR UB3 ....15 J2
Gordondale Rd WIM/MER SW19 ....28 D5
Gordon Dr CHERT KT16 ....55 J2
   SHPTN TW17 ....38 F7
Gordon Rd ALDT GU11 ....108 C5
   ASHF TW15 ....23 H6
   BECK BR3 ....46 F4
   BRYLDS KT5 ....41 M8
   CAR SM5 ....62 B5
   CBLY GU15 ....68 E4
   CHSWK W4 ....18 B1
   HPTN TW12 ....25 H9
   MTCM CR4 ....44 C6
   PUR/KEN CR8 ....81 J2
   WIM/MER SW19 ....43 K1
Gorse Dr HORL RH6 ....141 K9
Gorse End HORS RH12 ....192 C5
Gorse Hill La VW GU25 ....36 B5
Gorse Hill Rd VW GU25....36 B5
Gorselands YTLY GU46 ....66 G4
Gorselands Cl ASHV GU12 ..109 P3
   BF/WBF KT14 ....55 N9
   BOR GU35 ....164 F7
Gorse La CHOB/PIR GU24....53 L6
   RFNM GU10 ....127 L7
Gorse Pl BNFD RG42 * 33 K1
Gorse Ride North EWKG RG40..48 C2
Gorse Ride South EWKG RG40 ....48 C2
Gorse Ri TOOT SW17 ....29 K8
Gorse Rd CROY/NA CRO....64 G2
   FRIM GU16 ....89 H8
Gorseway FLEETS GU52....86 G8
Gorsewood Rd WOKN/KNAP GU21 ....71 K8
Gorst Rd BTSEA SW11 ....29 J1
Gort Cl ALDT GU11 ....108 G2
Gosberton Rd BAL SW12 ...29 J4
Gosbury HI CHSGTN KT9 ...59 L3
Gosden Cl CRAWE RH10...177 K6
   SHGR GU5 ....132 D5
Gosden Hill Rd RGUE GU4...112 G3
Gosden Rd CHOB/PIR GU24..70 F2
Gosfield Rd HOR/WEW KT19..78 B1
Gosling Gn DTCH/LGLY SL3...12 C1
Gosling Rd DTCH/LGLY SL3...12 C1
Gosnell Cl FRIM GU16 ....69 N5
Gossops Dr CRAWW RH11 ..176 D6
Gossops Green La CRAWW RH11 ....176 D6
Gostling Rd WHTN TW2 ....25 H4
Goston Gdns THHTH CR7...45 J4
Gostrode La MFD/CHID GU8..185 N3
Gothic Ct HYS/HAR UB3 ....14 F4
Gothic Rd WHTN TW2 ....25 L5
Goudhurst Cl CRAWE RH10..177 P5
Gough Rd FLEETN GU51 ....86 F5
Gough's La BRAK RG12 ....32 F1
Gough's Meadow SHST GU47..67 N1
Gould Ct RGUE GU4 ....113 H3
Goulding Gdns THHTH CR7...45 L3
Gould Rd EBED/NFELT TW14..23 P3
   WHTN TW2 ....25 M4
Government House Rd ALDT GU11 * 88 C2
Government Rd ALDT GU11..108 G2
Governor's Rd CBLY GU15...68 B2
Govett Av SHPTN TW17 *...38 E6
Govett Gv BFOR GU20 ....52 D4
Gowan Av FUL/PGN SW6 ...19 J6
Gower Cl CLAP SW4 ....29 M2
Gower Pk SHST GU47 ....67 P1
Gower Rd HORL RH6 ....159 H1
   ISLW TW7 ....16 F4
   WEY KT13 ....56 F6
The Gower EGH TW20 ....36 F4
Gowland Pl BECK BR3 ....46 F3
Gowrie Pl CTHM CR3 ....101 L2
Graburn Wy E/WMO/HCT KT8 ....40 D4
Grace Bennett Cl FARN GU14 * 68 C3
Gracedale Rd STRHM/NOR SW16 ....29 L8
Gracefield Gdns STRHM/NOR SW16 ....29 P6
Grace Rd CRAWW RH11 ...194 D1
   CROY/NA CRO 45 L7
Gracious Pond Rd CHOB/PIR GU24 ....53 M6
The Gradient SYD SE26 ....31 H7
Graemesdyke Av MORT/ESHN SW14 ....17 P8
Graffham Cl CRAWW RH11..176 E3
Grafton Cl BF/WBF KT14....73 K2
   HSLWW TW4 ....24 F4
   WPK KT4 ....60 C1
Grafton Park Rd WPK KT4...60 C1
Grafton Rd CROY/NA CRO...63 J1
   NWMAL KT3 ....42 C5
   WPK KT4 ....60 C2
Grafton Wy E/WMO/HCT KT8..39 P4
Graham Av MTCM CR4 ....44 C2
Graham Cl CROY/NA CRO...64 G1
Graham Gdns SURB KT6....41 L9
Graham Rd BFOR GU20 ....52 C5
   CHSWK W4 ....18 B1
   HPTN TW12 ....25 H7
   MTCM CR4 ....44 C2
   PUR/KEN CR8 ....81 J2
   WIM/MER SW19 ....43 K1
Grainger Rd ISLW TW7 ....16 F5
Grampian Cl BELMT SM2 ...61 N6
   HYS/HAR UB3 ....14 F5
Grampian Rd SHST GU47 ...49 N8
Granada St TOOT SW17 ....29 J8
Granard Av PUT/ROE SW15..27 N1
Granard Rd BAL SW12 ....29 H3
Granary Cl HORL RH6 ....140 C6
Granary Wy HORS RH12 ...191 N9
Grand Av BRYLDS KT5 ....41 P7
   CBLY GU15 ....68 E2
Grand Dr RYNPK SW20 ....42 G5
Grandison Rd CLAP SW4 ...29 J1
   WPK KT4 ....60 G1
Grand Pde CRAWE RH10 *..176 G5
   MORT/ESHN SW14 * 18 A9
   SURB KT6 ....41 N8
Grand Stand Rd EPSOM KT18..78 D6
Grand Union Canal Wk HNWL W7 ....16 E1
   NWDGN UB2 ....15 K1
Grand View Av BH/WHM TN16 ....84 A6

Granfield St BTSEA SW11 * 19 P6
Grange Av CWTH RG45 ....45 K9
 SNWD SE25 ....45 M3
 WHTN TW2 ....25 M5
Grangecliffe Gdns
 SNWD SE25 ....45 N3
Grange CI BH/WHM TN16 * 104 C6
 CRAWE RH10 ....177 K3
 E/WMO/HCT KT8 ....40 B5
 EDEN TN8 ....144 C4
 GODL GU7 ....131 N8
 GUW GU2 ....111 P1
 LHD/OX KT22 ....77 K9
 NWDGN UB2 ....15 P3
 REDH RH1 ....121 M4
 REIG RH2 ....100 D8
 STWL/WRAY TW19 ....21 K2
Grange Ct BELMT SM2 * 61 M6
 EGH TW20 ....21 L8
 GDST RH9 ....122 E9
 GU GU1 ....111 P1
 RFNM GU10 ....108 G8
 WLGTN SM6 * 62 D2
 WOT/HER KT12 ....57 J1
Grange Cres CRAWE RH10 ....179 J4
 WOKN/KNAP GU21 ....72 C4
Grange End HORL RH6 ....160 B1
Grange Farm Rd ASHV GU12 ....109 J3
Grangefields Rd RGUE GU4 ....92 B8
Grange Gdns BNSTD SM7 ....79 M2
 SNWD SE25 ....45 N3
Grange La DUL SE21 ....30 C5
Grange Meadow BNSTD SM7 ....79 M2
Grange Ms FELT TW13 * 25 N6
Grangemill Rd CAT SE6 ....31 P6
Grangemill Wy CAT SE6 ....31 P5
Grangemount LHD/OX KT22 ....77 K9
Grange Pk CRAN GU6 ....153 J9
Grange Park PI RYNPK SW20 ....42 F1
Grange Park Rd THHTH CR7 ....45 M4
Grange PI STA TW18 ....37 N3
 WOT/HER KT12 ....57 J1
Grange Rd ADL/WDHM KT15 ....55 L8
 ASHV GU12 ....109 K5
 BARN SW13 ....18 E4
 BELMT SM2 ....61 L6
 BRAK RG12 ....32 C3
 CBLY GU15 ....68 G3
 CHOB/PIR GU24 ....90 D2
 CHSGTN KT9 ....59 L3
 CHSWK W4 ....17 P3
 CRAWE RH10 ....179 H4
 CTHM CR3 ....102 A5
 E/WMO/HCT KT8 ....40 B5
 EGH TW20 ....21 L8
 FARN GU14 ....68 D9
 FLEETS GU52 ....106 F1
 KUT KT1 ....8 D6
 LHD/OX KT22 ....77 K9
 RFNM GU10 ....108 G8
 RGUW GU3 ....91 P9
 SAND/SEL CR2 ....63 L8
 SNWD SE25 ....45 M4
 WOKN/KNAP GU21 ....72 C4
 WOT/HER KT12 ....57 N3
The Grange CHOB/PIR GU24 ....53 L8
 CROY/NA CR0 ....64 F1
 HOR/WEW KT19 * 60 B7
 NWMAL KT3 * 42 E6
 WDSR SL4 ....20 C1
 WIM/MER SW19 ....28 A9
 WKENS W14 ....19 K2
 WOT/HER KT12 ....57 K1
Grange W BELMT SM2 * 61 M6
Grangeway HORL RH6 ....160 B1
Grangewood La BECK BR3 ....31 N9
Granston Wy CRAWE RH10 ....179 K3
Grantchester KUT KT1 * 9 H5
Grant CI SHPTN TW17 ....38 D7
Grantham CI SHST GU47 ....50 D8
Grantham Rd CHSWK W4 ....18 C5
Grantley Av SHGR GU5 ....132 F7
Grantley CI RGUE GU4 ....112 B2
Grantley Ct FNM GU9 ....127 K7
Grantley Dr FLEETS GU52 ....86 F8
Grantley Gdns GUW GU2 ....111 N4
Grantley PI ESH/CLAY KT10 ....58 B4
Grantley Rd GUW GU2 ....111 N4
 HSLWW TW4 ....15 L7
Granton Rd
 STRHM/NOR SW16 ....44 E2
Grant Rd BTSEA SW11 ....19 P7
 CROY/NA CR0 ....3 J1
 CWTH RG45 ....49 N6
Grants La OXTED RH8 ....124 B8
 OXTED RH8 ....124 B8
Grant Wk ASC SL5 ....34 C4
Grant Wy ISLW TW7 ....16 G4
Grantwood CI REDH RH1 ....140 C1
Granville Av FELT TW13 ....24 B5
 HSLW TW3 ....15 J1
Granville Gdns
 STRHM/NOR SW16 ....45 H2
Granville Rd BFN FUL/PGN SW6 * 19 M5
 HYS/HAR UB3 ....15 H2
 OXTED RH8 ....103 M9
 WAND/EARL SW18 ....28 D3
 WEY KT13 ....56 E6
 WIM/MER SW19 ....43 L1
 WOKS/MYFD GU22 ....11 G6
Grapsome CI CHSGTN KT9 ....59 J6
Grasholm Wy DTCH/LGLY SL3 ....12 G2
Grasmere Av HSLW TW3 ....25 J2
 PUT/ROE SW15 ....27 J7
 WIM/MER SW19 ....43 L4

Grasmere CI
 EBED/NFELT TW14 ....24 A4
 EGH TW20 ....36 F1
 GU GU1 ....112 F4
Grasmere Gdns HORS RH12 ....192 G4
Grasmere Rd BMLY BR1 ....47 M2
 FARN GU14 ....88 A4
 FNM GU9 ....107 L8
 LTWR GU18 ....52 B8
 PUR/KEN CR8 ....63 H4
 SNWD SE25 ....46 B7
 STRHM/NOR SW16 ....30 A8
Grasmere Wy BF/WBF KT14 ....74 B1
Grasslands HORL RH6 ....160 B1
Grassmere HORL RH6 ....140 D9
Grassmount FSTH SE23 ....31 J5
 WLGTN SM6 ....62 E3
Grassway WLGTN SM6 ....62 E3
Gratton Rd WKENS W14 ....19 J1
Grattons Dr CRAWE RH10 ....177 M2
The Grattons SWTR RH13 ....190 F7
Gravel Hi CROY/NA CR0 ....64 D5
Gravel Hill Rd RFNM GU10 ....126 E8
Gravelly Hi REDH RH1 ....101 P8
Gravel Pits La SHGR GU5 ....134 E1
Gravel Rd FARN GU14 ....88 F7
 FLEETS GU52 ....87 H9
 FNM GU9 ....107 M7
 WHTN TW2 ....25 M4
Gravenel Gdns TOOT SW17 * 29 H8
Graveney Gv PGE/AN SE20 ....46 C1
Graveney Rd CRAWE RH10 ....177 M6
 TOOT SW17 ....29 H7
Gravetts La RGUW GU3 ....111 L2
Graveney CI CRAWE RH10 ....177 K7
Grayham Crs NWMAL KT3 ....42 B5
Grayham Rd NWMAL KT3 ....42 B5
Graylands WOKN/KNAP GU21 ....10 C1
Graylands CI
 WOKN/KNAP GU21 ....10 C2
Gray PI CHERT KT16 ....55 H5
Grays Ct HASM GU27 * 184 F2
Grayscroft Rd
 STRHM/NOR SW16 ....44 F1
Grayshot Dr BLKW GU17 ....67 N3
Grayshott Rd BOR GU35 ....164 F6
Grays La ASHF TW15 ....23 L7
 ASHTD KT21 ....77 M8
Grays Rd BH/WHM TN16 ....104 F1
 GODL GU7 ....131 M6
Grays Wd HORL RH6 ....159 M1
Grayswood Gdns
 RYNPK SW20 ....42 F3
Grayswood Ms
 HASM GU27 * 166 G9
Grayswood Rd HASM GU27 ....184 E2
Great Austins FNM GU9 ....127 P5
Great Benty WDR/YW UB7 ....14 A2
Great Brownings SYD SE26 ....31 M6
Great Chertsey Rd
 CHSWK W4 ....18 B6
 FELT TW13 ....24 G6
Great Church La
 HMSMTH W6 ....19 H3
Great Elshams BNSTD SM7 ....79 L5
Great Ellshams EW KT17 * 60 D9
Greatfield CI FARN GU14 ....68 D8
Greatfield Rd FARN GU14 ....68 C8
Greatford Dr GU GU1 ....113 H5
Great Gatton CI
 CROY/NA CR0 ....46 E8
Great George St GODL GU7 ....131 L9
Great Goodwin Dr GU GU1 ....112 F3
Greatham Rd CRAWE RH10 ....177 M8
Great Hollands Rd
 BRAK RG12 ....32 B7
Great Hollands Sq
 BRAK RG12 ....32 B7
Great House Ct
 EGRIN RH19 * 180 C1
Greatlake Ct HORL RH6 ....140 D9
Great Oaks Pk RGUE GU4 ....112 F1
Great Quarry GU GU1 ....112 B8
Great South-West Rd
 EBED/NFELT TW14 ....15 H9
 EBED/NFELT TW14 ....14 F3
Great Tattenhams
 EPSOM KT18 ....78 G7
Great West Rd CHSWK W4 ....18 A4
 HEST TW5 ....15 N7
 HMSMTH W6 ....18 F3
 ISLW TW7 ....16 G4
Great West Rd Chiswick
 CHSWK W4 ....18 D4
Great West Rd Ellesmere Rd
 CHSWK W4 ....18 A4
Great West Rd Hogarth La
 CHSWK W4 ....18 B4
Greatwood CI CHERT KT16 ....54 G7
Great Woodcote Dr
 PUR/KEN CR8 ....62 F8
Great Woodcote Pk
 PUR/KEN CR8 ....62 F8
Greaves PI TOOT SW17 ....29 H7
Grebe Ct SUT SM1 ....61 K4
Grebe Crs SWTR RH13 ....192 F9
Grebe Ter KUT KT1 * 8 D6
Grecian Crs NRWD SE19 ....30 D9
Green Acre ALDT GU11 ....108 B5
Greenacre Ct EGH TW20 * 21 H9
Greenacre PI WLGTN SM6 ....62 C1
Greenacres CRAWE RH10 ....177 L6
Green Acres CROY/NA CR0 ....3 J5
Greenacres GT/LBKH KT23 ....96 A4
 HORS RH12 ....192 B6
 OXTED RH8 ....103 L7
 RFNM GU10 ....128 E3
Green Av WEA W13 ....17 H1
Greenbush La CRAN GU6 ....171 J2

Green Chain Wk BECK BR3 ....47 J1
 SYD SE26 ....31 L9
Green CI CAR SM5 ....62 B1
 FELT TW13 ....24 F8
 HAYES BR2 ....47 L3
Green Court Av
 CROY/NA CR0 ....64 B1
Green Court Gdns
 CROY/NA CR0 ....64 B1
Greencroft Rd HEST TW5 ....15 P6
Green Cross La RFNM GU10 ....165 K2
Green Curve BNSTD SM7 ....79 K4
Green DI EDUL SE22 ....30 D4
Green Dene EHSLY KT24 ....114 C6
Green Dragon La BTFD TW8 ....17 L3
Green Dr RPLY/SEND GU23 ....93 K3
Greene Fielde End STA TW18 ....37 P1
Green End CHSGTN KT9 ....59 K3
Green Farm Rd BAGS GU19 ....51 P6
Greenfield EDEN TN8 ....145 H4
Greenfield Av BYRLDS KT5 ....41 P8
Greenfield CI LIPH GU30 ....182 F5
Greenfield Link
 COUL/CHIP CR5 ....80 G4
Greenfield Rd FNM GU9 ....127 K6
 SWTR RH13 ....190 E7
Greenfields CI HORL RH6 ....140 A8
 HORS RH12 ....192 F4
Greenfields PI RDKG RH5 ....157 K9
Greenfields Rd HORL RH6 ....140 A8
 HORS RH12 ....192 F5
Greenfields Wy HORS RH12 ....192 F4
Green Finch CI CWTH RG45 * 49 K3
Greenfinch Wy HORS RH12 ....192 C3
Greenford Rd SUT SM1 ....61 M3
Green Glades FLEETS GU52 ....106 F1
Greenham Wk
 WOKN/KNAP GU21 ....72 A7
Greenhanger RFNM GU10 ....165 J3
Greenhaven YTLY GU46 ....66 F3
Greenhayes Av BNSTD SM7 ....79 L4
Greenhayes CI REIG RH2 ....119 N5
Greenhayes Gdns
 BNSTD SM7 ....79 L4
Green Hedges Av
 EGRIN RH19 ....180 C1
Green Hedges CI
 EGRIN RH19 ....180 C1
Green Heights Ct
 WOKS/MYFD GU22 ....72 A9
Greenheys PI
 WOKS/MYFD GU22 ....11 F4
Green Hill HAYES BR2 ....84 C1
Greenhill Av CTHM CR3 ....102 B1
Green Hill CI CBLY GU15 ....69 L2
Greenhill CI FNM GU9 ....127 L6
 GODL GU7 ....150 C1
Greenhill Gdns RGUE GU4 ....112 C2
Greenhill La WARL CR6 ....82 E6
Green Hill Rd CBLY GU15 ....69 L2
Greenhill Wy FNM GU9 ....127 P5
Greenholme CBLY GU15 ....69 M3
Greenhow BRAK RG12 ....32 C4
Greenhurst La OXTED RH8 ....123 N5
Greenhurst Rd WNWD SE27 ....30 B8
Greening Wd GSHT GU26 * 166 A6
Greenlake Ter STA TW18 * 37 L1
Greenlands Crs NWDGN UB2 ....15 L1
Greenlands CHERT KT16 ....54 C2
 HOR/WEW KT19 ....59 P4
Greenlands Rd CBLY GU15 ....68 D7
 STA TW18 ....37 M2
 WEY KT13 ....56 D2
Green La ASC SL5 ....34 E2
 ASHTD KT21 ....77 K5
 BAGS GU19 ....51 P7
 BF/WBF KT14 ....74 B1
 BLKW GU17 ....68 A4
 CHERT KT16 ....55 J1
 CHOB/PIR GU24 ....53 M8
 CHSGTN KT9 ....59 L7
 COB KT11 ....75 N1
 CRAN GU6 ....153 P8
 CRAWE RH10 ....160 G9
 CRAWE RH10 ....177 H3
 CROY/NA CR0 ....46 D9
 CTHM CR3 ....102 G3
 EGH TW20 ....21 H7
 EW KT17 ....78 E1
 FELT TW13 ....24 C5
 FNM GU9 ....107 M1
 FNM GU9 ....108 D9
 FRIM GU16 ....69 H3
 GDST RH9 ....122 B3
 HAYES BR2 ....47 N8
 HEST TW5 ....16 A4
 KWD/TDW/WH KT20 ....99 H3
 KWD/TDW/WH KT20 ....99 H3
 LHD/OX KT22 ....96 G4
 MFD/CHID GU8 ....149 M4
 MRDN SM4 ....43 J5
 NWMAL KT3 ....42 A4
 RCH/KEW TW9 ....17 H1
 RDKG RH5 ....157 J4
 REDH RH1 ....120 A8
 REDH RH1 ....140 C1
 REDH RH1 ....141 H4
 REIG RH2 ....119 K5

 REIG RH2 ....138 C5
 RFNM GU10 ....128 F7
 RFNM GU10 ....146 D6
 RFNM GU10 ....165 J3
 RGUE GU4 ....95 L7
 RGUW GU3 ....110 G3
 SHGR GU5 ....133 K7
 SHPTN TW17 ....38 F7
 SHST GU47 ....49 N9
 SUN TW16 ....37 J2
 SUN TW16 ....39 H1
 THHTH CR7 ....45 K2
 WOT/HER KT12 ....42 F8
 YTLY GU46 ....66 F1
Green Lane Av
 WOT/HER KT12 ....57 K4
Green Lane CI BF/WBF KT14 ....74 B1
 CBLY GU15 ....68 E1
 CHERT KT16 ....55 J1
Green La East RGUW GU3 ....110 A6
Green Lane Gdns THHTH CR7 ....45 L2
Green Lanes HOR/WEW KT19 ....60 C7
Green Leas SUN TW16 ....39 H1
Green Leas CI SUN TW16 ....24 A9
Greenleas CI YTLY GU46 ....66 G1
Greenleaves Ct ASHF TW15 * 23 L9
Green Leys FLEETS GU52 ....106 F2
Green Man La
 EBED/NFELT TW14 ....15 J9
Green Md ESH/CLAY KT10 ....57 P5
Greenmead CI SNWD SE25 ....46 A6
Greenmeads
 WOKS/MYFD GU22 ....92 C2
Green Oaks NWDGN UB2 * 15 M2
Greenoak Wy
 WIM/MER SW19 ....28 A7
Greenock Rd ACT W3 ....17 P1
 STRHM/NOR SW16 ....44 F2
Greeno Crs SHPTN TW17 ....38 C6
Green Pde HSLW TW3 * 25 J2
Green Rd CHERT KT16 ....36 F5
Greensand CI REDH RH1 ....100 F8
Greensand Rd REDH RH1 ....120 B5
Greensand Wy
 BRKHM/BTCW RH3 ....118 A6
 EDEN TN8 ....124 G2
 FNM GU9 ....5 H4
 GDST RH9 ....122 B3
 GSHT GU26 ....166 B9
 HASM GU27 ....184 D3
 MFD/CHID GU8 ....148 D9
 MFD/CHID GU8 ....151 K8
 OXTED RH8 ....105 L6
 OXTED RH8 ....123 L2
 REDH RH1 ....120 B8
 REDH RH1 ....121 K5
 REIG RH2 ....119 J3
 SHGR GU5 ....151 M6
Greenside CWTH RG45 ....49 K4
 RPLY/SEND GU23 * 93 N1
Greenside CI RGUE GU4 ....112 C2
Greenside Dr ASHTD KT21 ....77 H6
Greenside Rd CROY/NA CR0 ....45 J8
Green Springs RFNM GU10 ....106 D7
Greenstead Gdns
 PUT/ROE SW15 ....27 M1
Greenstede Av EGRIN RH19 ....162 E5
Green St SUN TW16 ....39 J2
The Green ASHF TW15 * 22 G8
 BH/WHM TN16 ....105 H6
 BRAK RG12 ....32 D5
 CAR SM5 * 62 C3
 CRAN GU6 ....153 P8
 CRAWE RH10 ....177 J6
 CRAWW RH11 ....176 F4
 CROY/NA CR0 ....64 G9
 CTHM CR3 ....102 G3
 EGH TW20 ....21 H7
 EW KT17 ....78 E1
 FELT TW13 ....24 C5
 FNM GU9 ....107 M1
 FNM GU9 ....108 D9
 FRIM GU16 ....69 H3
 GODL GU7 ....131 L9
 HASM GU27 ....184 C3
 HAYES BR2 ....47 M3
 HEST TW5 ....16 A4
 HPTN TW12 ....25 J9
 KWD/TDW/WH KT20 ....99 H3
 LHD/OX KT22 ....96 G4
 MRDN SM4 ....43 J5
 NWMAL KT3 ....42 A4
 RCH/KEW TW9 ....17 H1
 RFNM GU10 ....128 C8
 STWL/WRAY TW19 ....21 K2
 SUT SM1 * 61 M3
 WDR/YW UB7 ....13 P1
 WHTN TW2 ....25 M4
Greenvale Rd
 WOKN/KNAP GU21 ....71 K8
Green Vw CHSGTN KT9 ....59 M6
Greenview Av BECK BR3 ....46 E7
Green Wk CRAWE RH10 ....177 H8
 NWDGN UB2 ....16 A3
 REDH RH1 ....120 A3
Green Wy ASHV GU12 ....108 G3

 SUN TW16 ....39 J5
Greenway BH/WHM TN16 ....84 A9
 GT/LBKH KT23 ....96 B3
 HORS RH12 ....191 P7
 RYNPK SW20 ....42 G5
 WLGTN SM6 ....62 E3
Greenway CI BF/WBF KT14 ....73 L2
Greenway Dr STA TW18 ....37 N2
Greenway Gdns
 CROY/NA CR0 ....64 F2
Greenways BECK BR3 ....46 G3
 EGH TW20 ....21 K9
 ESH/CLAY KT10 ....58 E3
 FLEETS GU52 ....86 F9
 KWD/TDW/WH KT20 ....98 E5
 SHST GU47 ....49 M8
Greenways Dr ASC SL5 ....34 E9
The Greenways TWK TW1 * 25 P2
The Greenway EPSOM KT18 ....77 N4
 HSLWW TW4 * 15 P9
 OXTED RH8 ....123 N4
Greenway Wk GDST RH9 ....122 B1
Greenwich CI CRAWW RH11 ....176 F9
Green Wd ASC SL5 ....33 L2
Greenwood CI
 ADL/WDHM KT15 ....55 K9
 MRDN SM4 ....43 J5
 THDIT KT7 ....40 G9
Greenwood Cottages ASC SL5 * 35 J7
Greenwood Ct
 CRAWW RH11 * 194 E1
Greenwood Dr REDH RH1 ....140 C1
Greenwood Gdns
 CTHM CR3 ....102 A5
Greenwood La HPTN TW12 ....25 J8
Greenwood Pk
 KUTN/CMB KT2 ....42 C1
Greenwood Rd
 CHOB/PIR GU24 ....90 B1
 CROY/NA CR0 ....45 K8
 CWTH RG45 ....49 L3
 ISLW TW7 ....16 E8
 MTCM CR4 ....44 F4
 THDIT KT7 ....40 G9
 WOKN/KNAP GU21 ....71 J6
The Greenwood GU GU1 ....112 E5
Green Wrythe La CAR SM5 ....44 A8
Green Wrythe La MRDN SM4 ....43 P7
Gregory CI CRAWE RH10 ....177 M9
 WOKN/KNAP GU21 ....72 A6
Gregory Dr WDSR SL4 ....20 G2
Gregory Rd NWDGN UB2 ....16 A1
Gregsons HORS RH12 ....191 M2
Grenaby Av CROY/NA CR0 ....45 M8
Grenaby Rd CROY/NA CR0 ....45 M8
Grenadier PI CTHM CR3 ....101 L2
Grenadier Rd ASHV GU12 ....109 K2
Grenadiers Wy FARN GU14 ....87 N4
Grena Gdns RCH/KEW TW9 ....17 M9
Grena Rd RCH/KEW TW9 ....17 M9
Grendon CI HORL RH6 ....140 D9
Grenfell Rd TOOT SW17 ....29 J9
Grennell CI SUT SM1 ....61 P1
Grennell Rd SUT SM1 ....61 N1
Grenside CI WEY KT13 ....56 C9
Grenville CI BRYLDS KT5 ....42 A2
 COB KT11 ....75 N2
 LIPH GU30 ....182 F6
Grenville Dr FLEETN GU51 ....86 E8
Grenville Gdns FRIM GU16 ....88 G1
Grenville Ms HPTN TW12 ....25 J8
Grenville PI BRAK RG12 ....32 E3
 SKENS SW7 * 19 N1
Grenville Rd CROY/NA CR0 ....65 J8
 MFD/CHID GU8 ....130 D6
Gresham Av WARL CR6 ....82 E7
Gresham CI OXTED RH8 ....103 M9
Gresham Rd BECK BR3 ....46 E3
 HEST TW5 ....16 C6
 HPTN TW12 ....25 H8
 OXTED RH8 ....103 M9
 SNWD SE25 ....46 A5
 STA TW18 ....22 G8
Gresham Wk CRAWE RH10 ....177 H8
Gresham Wy FRIM GU16 ....88 G1
 WIM/MER SW19 ....28 D6
Gressenhall Rd
 WAND/EARL SW18 ....28 C2
Greswell St FUL/PGN SW6 ....19 H6
Greta Bank EHSLY KT24 ....94 G6
Gretton Rd SAND/SEL CR2 ....64 C8
Greville CI ALDT GU11 ....108 B4
 ASHTD KT21 ....77 L8
 GUW GU2 ....111 L5
 TWK TW1 ....26 A3
Greville Park Av ASHTD KT21 ....77 L7
Greville Park Rd ASHTD KT21 ....77 L7
Greville Rd
 RCHPK/HAM TW10 ....26 E2
Grey Alders KWI KT17 ....78 C3
Greybury La EDEN TN8 ....163 N1
Greycot Rd BECK BR3 ....31 P8
Greyfields CI PUR/KEN CR8 ....81 K2
Greyfriars Dr ASC SL5 ....34 C4
 CHOB/PIR GU24 ....70 G4
Greyfriars Rd
 RPLY/SEND GU23 ....93 N4
Greyhound La
 STRHM/NOR SW16 ....29 P9
Greyhound Rd SUT SM1 ....61 N4
Greyhound Slip
 CRAWE RH10 ....177 N4
Greyhound Ter
 STRHM/NOR SW16 ....44 E2
Greys Ct ALDT GU11 ....108 A4
Greystead Rd FSTH SE23 ....31 J3
Greystoke Rd BRAK RG12 32

Greystoke Ct CWTH RG45 .....49 L5
Greystone Cl SAND/SEL CR2 ...64 C9
Greystones Cl REIG RH2 ....119 P7
Greystones Dr REIG RH2 ......119 N3
Greyswood St
  STRHM/NOR SW16 ....29 L9
Greythorne Rd
  WOKN/KNAP GU21 ....71 N7
Greywaters SHGR GU5 ....132 E2
Grice Av BH/WHM TN16 ....83 P2
Grier Cl CRAWW RH11 ....176 B6
Grierson Rd FSTH SE23 ....31 M1
Grieve Cl RFNM GU10 ....108 G7
Griffin Cl ASHTD KT21 * 77 L8
Griffin Wy GT/LBKH KT23 .....96 A6
  SUN TW16 ....39 J3
Griffiths Rd WIM/MER SW19 ...43 L1
Griffon Cl FARN GU14 ....87 P4
Griggs Meadow
  MFD/CHID GU8 ....169 L4
Grimston Rd FUL/PGN SW6 ....19 K7
Grimwade Av CROY/NA CR0 ....64 J2
Grimwood Rd TWK TW1 ....25 N3
Grindall Cl CROY/NA CR0 ......63 K3
Grindley Gdns
  CROY/NA CR0 * 45 P7
Grindstone Crs
  WOKN/KNAP GU21 ....71 H7
Grisedale Cl CRAWW RH11 ....176 F7
  PUR/KEN CR8 ....81 N3
Grisedale Gdns PUR/KEN CR8 ..81 N3
Grobars Av
  WOKN/KNAP GU21 ....72 A4
Groombridge Cl
  WOT/HER KT12 ....57 K4
Groombridge Wy
  HORS RH12 ....191 N9
Groom Cl HAYES BR2 ....47 P5
Groom Crs WAND/EARL SW18 ..28 C3
Groomfield Cl TOOT SW17 .....29 K7
The Grooms CRAWE RH10 ....177 N3
Grosse Wy PUT/ROE SW15 ....27 N2
Grosvenor Av CAR SM5 ....62 B5
  MORT/ESHN SW14 ....18 C8
Grosvenor Ct BLKW GU17 .....67 P5
Grosvenor Gdns
  KUTN/CMB KT2 ....26 C9
  MORT/ESHN SW14 ....18 C8
  WLGTN SM6 ....62 E6
Grosvenor Hl
  WIM/MER SW19 ....28 B9
Grosvenor Ms REIG RH2 .....119 M8
Grosvenor Pl WEY KT13 ....56 F2
Grosvenor Rd ALDT GU11 ....108 C4
  BTFD TW8 ....17 K4
  CHOB/PIR GU24 ....71 K2
  CHSWK W4 ....18 A3
  EGRIN RH19 ....180 C2
  EPSOM KT18 ....78 C8
  GODL GU7 ....150 D1
  HSLW TW3 ....15 P8
  NWDGN UB2 ....15 P1
  RCHPK/HAM TW10 ....26 D1
  SNWD SE25 ....46 A5
  STA TW18 ....37 L1
  TWK TW1 ....25 P3
  WLGTN SM6 ....62 D5
  WWKM BR4 ....65 H1
Groton Rd WAND/EARL SW18 ..28 E5
Grotto Rd TWK TW1 ....25 N5
  WEY KT13 ....56 E3
Grouse Rd SWTR RH13 ....193 P7
Grove Av EW KT17 ....78 C4
  SUT SM1 ....61 L5
  TWK TW1 ....25 N4
Grove Cl CRAN GU6 ....171 J2
  EWKG RG40 ....49 J2
  FSTH SE23 ....31 M1
  HAYES BR2 ....65 N1
  HOR/WEW KT19 ....78 N8
  KUT KT1 ....41 L5
  WDSR SL4 ....20 C3
Grove Cottages CHSWK W4 * ..18 C4
  COB KT11 * 75 M5
Grove Ct E/WMO/HCT KT8 ....40 D6
  EGH TW20 ....21 M8
Grove Crs FELT TW13 ....24 F7
  KUT KT1 ....8 D7
  WOT/HER KT12 ....39 K8
Grove Cross Rd FRIM GU16 ...89 H7
Grove End BAGS GU19 ....51 P5
Grove End La ESH/CLAY KT10 ..40 D9
Grove End Rd FNM GU9 .....127 M6
Grove Farm Pk FRIM GU16 * ..89 H6
Grovefields Av FRIM GU16 .....68 F7
Grove Footpath SURB KT6 ....41 L5
Grove Gdns TEDD TW11 ......25 P7
Grove Heath La
  RPLY/SEND GU23 ....93 N4
Grove Heath North
  RPLY/SEND GU23 ....93 M2
Grovehill Rd REDH RH1 .....120 A5
Groveland Av
  STRHM/NOR SW16 ....45 H1
Groveland Rd BECK BR3 ......46 F4
Grovelands E/WMO/HCT KT8 ..40 A6
  RFNM GU10 ....128 A6
Grovelands Rd PUR/KEN CR8 ..81 H1
Groveland Wy NWMAL KT3 ...42 A6
Grove La COUL/CHIP CR5 .....80 D4
  KUT KT1 ....41 L5
Groveley Rd SUN TW16 ....24 A8
Grove Ms HMSMTH W6 * 18 F2
Grove Park Av FARN GU14 ....88 A5
Grove Park Gdns CHSWK W4 ..18 A5
Grove Park Rd CHSWK W4 ....17 P5
Grove Park Ter CHSWK W4 ....17 P5
Grove Pl BAL SW12 ....29 L1
  WEY KT13 ....56 E4
Grove Rd ASHTD KT21 ....77 M7
  ASHV GU12 ....109 J3
  BARN SW13 ....18 D7

BH/WHM TN16 ....84 A9
BTFD TW8 ....17 J3
CBLY GU15 ....68 G5
CHERT KT16 ....51 K7
CRAN GU6 ....171 J2
E/WMO/HCT KT8 ....40 D5
EPSOM KT18 ....78 C2
FLEETS GU52 ....107 H1
GODL GU7 ....150 B1
GSHT GU26 ....165 M5
GU GU1 ....112 G5
HORL RH6 ....140 A9
HSLW TW3 ....16 B6
ISLW TW7 ....16 E6
LING RH7 ....143 L8
MTCM CR4 ....44 D3
RCHPK/HAM TW10 ....26 E2
SHPTN TW17 ....38 E7
SURB KT6 ....41 K6
SUT SM1 ....61 M5
THHTH CR7 ....45 J5
WHTN TW2 ....25 L6
WIM/MER SW19 ....43 N1
Grovers Farm Cottages
  ADL/WDHM KT15 * 55 J9
Groveside GT/LBKH KT23 ......96 A1
Groveside Cl CAR SM5 ....62 A1
  GT/LBKH KT23 ....96 A1
Grovestile Waye
  EBED/NFELT TW14 ....23 N3
Grove Ter TEDD TW11 ....25 P5
The Grove ADL/WDHM KT15 ...55 M4
  ALDT GU11 ....108 E1
  ASC SL5 ....33 L2
  BH/WHM TN16 ....84 B7
  COUL/CHIP CR5 ....80 F4
  CRAWW RH11 ....176 F5
  CTHM CR3 ....101 K1
  EGH TW20 ....21 M8
  EW KT17 ....78 C3
  FARN GU14 ....88 F6
  FRIM GU16 ....89 J7
  GU GU1 * 7 J2
  HORL RH6 ....159 L2
  ISLW TW7 ....16 B6
  LIPH GU30 ....182 E6
  TEDD TW11 ....25 P5
  WOKN/KNAP GU21 ....10 E2
  WOT/HER KT12 ....39 K8
  WWKM BR4 ....65 J2
Grove Wd Hl
  COUL/CHIP CR5 ....80 F3
Grub St OXTED RH8 ....104 A9
Guardian Cl MFD/CHID GU8 .148 D1
Guards Av CTHM CR3 ....101 L2
Guards Ct ASC SL5 ....35 H8
Gubyon Av HNHL SE24 ....30 D1
Guerdon Pl BRAK RG12 ......32 F8
Guernsey Cl CRAWW RH11 ...176 D9
  HEST TW5 ....15 N6
  RGUE GU4 ....92 E9
Guernsey Dr FLEETN GU51 ...87 H3
Guernsey Farm Dr
  WOKN/KNAP GU21 * 72 B4
Guernsey Gv HNHL SE24 .....30 D3
Guildables La OXTED RH8 ...124 C5
Guildcroft GU GU1 ....112 E5
Guildford Business Park Rd
  GUW GU2 * 6 A1
Guildford La SHGR GU5 .....113 L9
Guildford Park Av GUW GU2 ...6 A5
Guildford Park Rd GUW GU2 ...6 A5
Guildford Rd ALDT GU11 ....108 F7
  ASHV GU12 ....109 M3
  BAGS GU19 ....51 M5
  BIL RH14 ....188 C5
  CHERT KT16 ....54 F8
  CHOB/PIR GU24 ....70 E1
  CHOB/PIR GU24 ....70 G5
  CHOB/PIR GU24 ....90 F3
  CRAN GU6 ....152 E8
  CROY/NA CR0 ....45 K6
  DORK RH4 ....116 D9
  FLEETN GU51 ....87 J6
  FNM GU9 ....89 J2
  GODL GU7 ....131 N7
  GT/LBKH KT23 ....95 P8
  HORS RH12 ....189 J2
  HORS RH12 ....190 C3
  HORS RH12 ....191 J4
  HORS RH12 ....191 N7
  LHD/OX KT22 ....96 E4
  RDKG RH5 ....135 J2
  RFNM GU10 ....128 C1
  RGUE GU4 ....92 A5
  RGUW GU3 ....91 J5
  SHGR GU5 ....152 C2
  WOKS/MYFD GU22 ....10 D1
Guildford Rd East
  FARN GU14 ....88 E6
Guildford Rd West
  FARN GU14 ....88 E6
Guildford St CHERT KT16 .....37 J8
  STA TW18 ....22 D9
Guildford Wy WLGTN SM6 ....62 G4
Guildown Av GUW GU2 ......111 P8
Guildown Rd GUW GU2 .....111 P8
Guileshill La RPLY/SEND GU23 .94 A12
Guilford Av BRYLDS KT5 ......41 M6
Guillemont Flds FARN GU14 ...87 H2
Guinevere Rd CRAWW RH11 ..176 B5
Guinness Cl HYS/HAR UB3 ....14 F1
Guinness Ct CROY/NA CR0 * ..3 J6
Guion Rd FUL/PGN SW6 ......19 K7
Gull Cl WLGTN SM6 ....62 G6

Gulley Rd FARN GU14 ....88 C7
Gumbrells Cl RGUW GU3 ....111 J1
Gumleigh Rd EA V5 ....47 J2
Gumley Gdns ISLW TW7 ......16 G8
Gunnell Cl CROY/NA CR0 ....108 D3
Gunnell Cl SNWD SE25 ....45 P7
  SYD SE26 * 31 H7
Gunnersbury Av ACT W3 .....17 N1
Gunnersbury Av (N Circular Rd)
  ACT W3 ....17 N1
Gunnersbury Cl CHSWK W4 * .17 N2
Gunners Rd
  WAND/EARL SW18 ....28 G5
Gunning Cl CRAWW RH11 ...176 D8
Gunns Farm LIPH GU30 .....182 F8
Gun Pit Rd LING RH7 ....143 J9
Gunter Gv WBPTN SW10 .....19 N4
Gunters Md LHD/OX KT22 * ..58 C9
Gunterstone Rd
  WKENS W14 ....19 J3
Gunton Rd TOOT SW17 ......29 K9
Gurdon's La MFD/CHID GU8 .167 N1
Gurney Cr CROY/NA CR0 .....45 H8
Gurney Rd CAR SM5 ....62 C3
  FUL/PGN SW6 ....19 N8
Gurney's Cl REDH RH1 ....120 B6
Guyatt Gdns MTCM CR4 ......44 C3
Guy Rd CROY/NA CR0 ....62 G2
Gwalior Rd PUT/ROE SW15 ...19 H6
Gwendolen Av
  PUT/ROE SW15 ....28 A1
Gwendwr Rd WKENS W14 .....19 J3
Gwydor Rd BECK BR3 ....46 D5
Gwydyr Rd HAYES BR2 ....47 M4
Gwyn Cl FUL/PGN SW6 ....19 N5
Gwynne Av CROY/NA CR0 .....46 D8
Gwynne Rd BTSEA SW11 ......19 P7
Gwynne Rd EGRIN RH19 .....180 D1
  CTHM CR3 ....101 M3
Gwynne Vaughan Av
  GUW GU2 ....111 N1
Gwynne Whf CHSWK W4 .....18 D1

H

Haarlem Rd WKENS W14 ......19 H1
Habershon Dr FRIM GU16 ....69 M6
Haccombe Rd
  WIM/MER SW19 ....28 F9
Hackbridge Park Gdns
  CAR SM5 ....62 B1
Hackbridge Rd CAR SM5 .....62 C1
Hackenden Cl EGRIN RH19 ..162 D9
Hackenden Cottages
  EGRIN RH19 * 162 D9
Hackenden La EGRIN RH19 ..162 E8
Hacketts La
  WOKS/MYFD GU22 ....73 K3
Hackhurst La RDKG RH5 ....135 H1
Hackington Crs BECK BR3 ....31 P9
Haddon Cl NWMAL KT3 ....42 D6
Haddon Rd SUT SM1 ....61 M3
Hadfield Rd
  STWL/WRAY TW19 ....22 C2
Hadleigh Cl RYNPK SW20 ....43 K3
Hadleigh Dr BELMT SM2 ......61 L7
Hadley Gdns CHSWK W4 ......18 B3
  NWDGN UB2 ....15 P3
Hadley Pl WEY KT13 ....56 C6
Hadley Rd MTCM CR4 ....44 F5
Hadleys RFNM GU10 ....146 B1
Hadley Wood Ri
  PUR/KEN CR8 ....81 K4
Hadmans Cl HORS RH12 ....192 B9
Hadrian Cl STWL/WRAY TW19 .23 H3
Hadrians CRM GU16 * 128 A1
Hadrian Wy
  STWL/WRAY TW19 ....22 G3
Haggard Rd TWK TW1 ....26 A3
Hagley Rd FLEETN GU51 .....25 B5
Haigh Crs REDH RH1 ....120 D7
Haig La FLEETS GU52 ....107 H1
Haig Rd ASHV GU12 ....108 E5
  BH/WHM TN16 ....84 C6
  CBLY GU15 ....68 B2
Hailes Cl WIM/MER SW19 .....28 F9
Hailsham Av
  BRXS/STRHM SW2 ....30 A5
Hailsham Cl SHST GU47 ......49 P8
  SURB KT6 ....41 K8
Hailsham Rd TOOT SW17 ....29 K9
Haines Ct WEY KT13 ....56 F4
Haines Wk MRDN SM4 ....43 M8
Haining Cl CHSWK W4 ....17 N3
Haining Gdns FRIM GU16 ....89 J1
Hainthorpe Rd WNWD SE27 ..30 C6
Haldane Pl WAND/EARL SW18 .28 E4
Haldane Rd FUL/PGN SW6 ....19 K5
  WNWD SE27 ....30 E6
Halebourne La
  CHOB/PIR GU24 ....52 G8
Hale End BRAK RG12 ....33 H5
Hale Ends WOKS/MYFD GU22 .91 P1
Hale House La RFNM GU10 ..165 K2
Hale Pit Rd GT/LBKH KT23 ...96 C6
Hale Pl FNM GU9 ....108 A9
Hale Reeds FNM GU9 ....5 K1
Hale Rd FNM GU9 ....108 A9
Hales Fld HASM GU27 ......184 D4
Hales Oak GT/LBKH KT23 ....96 C6
Halesowen Rd MRDN SM4 ....43 M8
Hale St STA TW18 ....22 B7
Halesweod COB KT11 ....75 L5
Hale Wy FRIM GU16 ....89 J2
Halewood BRAK RG12 ....32 B7
Half Acre BTFD TW8 ....17 K4
Half Acre Ms BTFD TW8 ......17 K5

Half Moon Hl HASM GU27 ...184 D4
Half Moon La HNHL SE24 .....30 E1
Halford Rd FUL/PGN SW6 .....19 L4
  RCHPK/HAM TW10 ....26 D1
Halfpenny Cl RGUE GU4 .....133 H2
Halfpenny La ASC SL5 ....34 G8
  RGUE GU4 ....112 G8
Halfway Gn WOT/HER KT12 ...57 K2
Halfway La GODL GU7 ....131 J9
Haliburton Rd TWK TW1 .....25 P1
Halifax Cl CRAWE RH10 .....177 P2
  FARN GU14 ....88 B4
Halifax St SYD SE26 ....31 J6
Halifax Wy FARN GU14 ....88 B8
Halimote Rd ALDT GU11 ....108 C5
Haliwell Cl CRAWE RH10 ....177 K4
Haling Gv SAND/SEL CR2 .....63 M5
Haling Park Gdns
  SAND/SEL CR2 ....63 K5
Haling Park Rd
  SAND/SEL CR2 ....63 K5
Haling Rd SAND/SEL CR2 .....63 M5
Hallam Rd GODL GU7 ....131 M7
Halland Cl CRAWE RH10 ....177 K4
Hallbrooke Gdns BNFD RG42 .32 A1
Hall Cl CBLY GU15 ....68 G2
  GODL GU7 ....131 L6
Hall Ct TEDD TW11 ....25 N8
Hall Dene Cl GU GU1 ....113 J3
Hall Dr SYD SE26 ....31 K8
Halley Cl CRAWW RH11 .....194 E1
Halley Dr ASC SL5 ....33 M3
Halley's Ap
  WOKN/KNAP GU21 ....71 N7
Halley's Ct
  WOKN/KNAP GU21 * 71 N7
Halley's Wke ADL/WDHM KT15 .55 N6
Hall Farm Crs YTLY GU46 .....66 G3
Hall Farm Dr WHTN TW2 .....25 L3
Hall Hl OXTED RH8 ....123 K3
The Halliards WOT/HER KT12 .39 J7
Halliford St SHPTN TW17 .....38 G4
Halliford Rd SHPTN TW17 ....38 G6
Hallington Cl
  WOKN/KNAP GU21 ....71 P6
Halliwell Rd
  BRXS/STRHM SW2 ....30 A2
Hall La HYS/HAR UB3 ....14 F5
  YTLY GU46 ....66 C5
Hallmark Ct SHST GU47 ......50 A9
Hallmead Rd SUT SM1 ....61 M2
Hallowell Av CROY/NA CR0 ...62 G3
Hallowell Cl MTCM CR4 ......44 C4
Hallowfield Wy MTCM CR4 ....44 P4
Hall Pl WOKN/KNAP GU21 ....11 G2
Hall Place Dr WEY KT13 ......56 G5
Hall Rd FARN GU14 ....88 D5
  ISLW TW7 ....25 L1
  SHGR GU5 ....132 D6
  WLGTN SM6 ....62 D7
Halls Farm Cl
  WOKN/KNAP GU21 ....71 K6
Hallsland CRAWE RH10 .....179 K3
Hallsland Wy OXTED RH8 ...123 M4
Halnaker Wk
  CRAWW RH11 * 176 C8
Halsford La EGRIN RH19 .....179 N5
Halsford Park Rd
  EGRIN RH19 ....180 B1
Halstead Cl CROY/NA CR0 ....2 C5
Halters End GSHT GU26 .....165 K8
Hambalt Rd CLAP SW4 ....29 M1
Hamble Av BLKW GU17 ....67 P3
Hamble Cl WOKN/KNAP GU21 .71 N6
Hambledon Gdns SNWD SE25 .46 A4
Hambledon Hl EPSOM KT18 ..78 A5
Hambledon Pk
  MFD/CHID GU8 ....168 A2
Hambledon Pl DUL SE21 .....30 G4
  GT/LBKH KT23 ....96 A3
Hambledon Rd CTHM CR3 ...101 M3
  MFD/CHID GU8 ....150 D8
  WAND/EARL SW18 ....28 C5
Hambledon V EPSOM KT18 ...78 A5
Hambledown Rd SNWD SE25 .46 B4
Hambro Av HAYES BR2 ....47 N3
Hambro Rd
  STRHM/NOR SW16 ....29 N9
Hamburgh Av HAYES BR2 ...131 N9
Hamesmoor Rd FRIM GU16 ..89 H3
Hamesmoor Wy FRIM GU16 ..89 H3
Ham Farm Rd
  RCHPK/HAM TW10 ....26 E7
Hamfield Cl OXTED RH8 .....103 J7
Hamilton Av CHEAM SM3 .....43 H7
  SURB KT6 ....59 N1
  WOKS/MYFD GU22 ....73 J5
Hamilton Cl CHERT KT16 .....57 K9
  FELT TW13 ....24 A8
  GUW GU2 * 6 B2
  PUR/KEN CR8 ....81 K1
Hamilton Crs HSLW TW3 .....25 J1
Hamilton Dr ASC SL5 ....34 D7
  GUW GU2 ....91 N9
Hamilton Gordon Ct GU GU1 ..6 G1
Hamilton Ms WEY KT13 * 56 C3
Hamilton Pde FELT TW13 * ...24 B7
Hamilton Pl ALDT GU11 .....108 B5
  GUW GU2 ....91 N9
  KWD/TDW/WH KT20 ....99 K3
  SUN TW16 ....39 K1

Hamilton Rd BTFD TW8 ....17 K4
  CHSWK W4 ....18 C1
  FELT TW13 ....23 P8
  FLEETS GU52 ....87 H9
  HORS RH12 ....192 A3
  THHTH CR7 ....45 M4
  WHTN TW2 ....25 M4
  WIM/MER SW19 ....43 M1
  WNWD SE27 ....30 E7
Hamilton Road Ms
  WIM/MER SW19 ....43 M1
Hamilton Rd BTFD 62 F7
Ham La EGH TW20 ....20 C7
  MFD/CHID GU8 ....129 N9
  WDSR SL4 ....12 A9
Hamlash La RFNM GU10 ....146 F3
Hamlet Gdns HMSMTH W6 ...18 E2
Hamlet Rd NRWD SE19 ....45 P1
Hamlyn Gdns NRWD SE19 ...45 N1
Hammelton Rd BMLY BR1 ....47 N2
Hammerfield Dr RDKG RH5 ..135 J1
Hammer Hl HASM GU27 ....183 M6
Hammer La GSHT GU26 .....165 J4
  LIPH GU30 ....183 K4
Hammersley Rd ALDT GU11 ..88 E5
Hammersmith Br
  HMSMTH W6 ....18 E3
Hammersmith Bridge Rd
  BARN SW13 ....18 F4
Hammersmith Broadway
  HMSMTH W6 ....18 G2
Hammersmith Emb
  HMSMTH W6 ....18 G3
Hammersmith F/O
  HMSMTH W6 ....18 G2
Hammersmith Gv
  HMSMTH W6 ....18 F1
  WKENS W14 ....19 H2
Hammersmith Ter
  HMSMTH W6 ....18 E3
Hammerwood Copse
  HASM GU27 ....183 N5
Hammerwood Rd
  EGRIN RH19 ....181 K5
Hammer Yd CRAWW RH11 * .176 C6
Hamm Moor La
  ADL/WDHM KT15 ....56 A4
Hammond Av MTCM CR4 .....44 D3
Hammond Cl HPTN TW12 ....40 A2
  WOKN/KNAP GU21 ....72 A4
Hammond Rd CRAWW RH11 .194 E2
  WOKN/KNAP GU21 ....15 N1
Hammond Wy LTWR GU18 ....52 B8
Hamond Cl SAND/SEL CR2 ...63 K7
Hampden Av BECK BR3 ....46 E4
Hampden Cl CRAWE RH10 ...177 P2
Hampden Rd BECK BR3 ....46 E3
  DTCH/LGLY SL3 ....12 D1
  KUT KT1 ....8 E6
Hampers La SWTR RH13 ....192 F8
Hampshire Cl ASHV GU12 ...108 F7
Hampshire Hog La
  HMSMTH W6 ....18 F2
Hampshire Rd CBLY GU15 ...51 H9
Hampstead La DORK RH4 ...116 F8
Hampstead Rd DORK RH4 ...116 G8
Hampstead Wk
  CRAWW RH11 ....176 F9
Hampton Cl FLEETS GU52 ..106 G2
  RYNPK SW20 ....42 G1
Hampton Court Av
  E/WMO/HCT KT8 ....40 D7
Hampton Court Crs
  E/WMO/HCT KT8 * 40 D6
Hampton Court Est
  THDIT KT7 * 40 D7
Hampton Court Rd
  E/WMO/HCT KT8 ....40 D7
Hampton Court Wy
  ESH/CLAY KT10 ....58 E1
  THDIT KT7 ....40 E8
Hampton Gv EW KT17 ....60 D9
Hampton La FELT TW13 ......24 F7
Hampton Rd CROY/NA CR0 ...45 L8
  FELT TW13 ....24 F7
  HPTN TW12 ....40 F8
  REDH RH1 ....140 B1
  WHTN TW2 ....25 L6
  WPK KT4 ....60 E1
Hampton Rd East FELT TW13 .24 C7
Hampton Rd West
  FELT TW13 ....24 C7
Hampton Wy EGRIN RH19 ...180 E4
Ham Ridings
  RCHPK/HAM TW10 ....26 E8
Hamsey Green Gdns
  WARL CR6 ....82 C5
Hamsey Wy SAND/SEL CR2 ...82 B4
Ham St RCHPK/HAM TW10 ...26 B6
Hanbury Dr BH/WHM TN16 ...85 P2
Hanbury Rd CRAWW RH11 ..176 B6
Hanbury Wy CBLY GU15 ......68 E5
Hancock Rd NRWD SE19 ......30 F9
Hancocks Mt ASC SL5 ....34 G7
Handcroft Rd CROY/NA CR0 ..45 K9
Handcross Rd RFNM GU10 ..106 D6
Handcross Rd RHWH RH17 ..195 M7
Handford La YTLY GU46 ......66 G3
Handley Page Rd
  WLGTN SM6 ....63 H6
Handside Cl WPK KT4 ....43 H9
Hanford Cl WAND/EARL SW18 .28 D4
Hangerfield Cl YTLY GU46 ....66 G3
Hanger Hl WEY KT13 ....56 E4
The Hanger BOR GU35 ......164 B9

Hang Grove Hl ORP BR6 ......84 F2
Hanley Pl BECK BR3 ....46 A5
Hannah Cl BECK BR3 ....47 H4
Hannans Farm RFNM GU3.106 C8
Hannell Rd FUL/PGN SW6 ....19 J5
Hannen Rd W/NWD SE27 * ..30 C6
Hannibal Rd
  STWL/WRAY TW19 ....23 H3
Hannibal Wy CROY/NA CR0 ..63 H4
Hanover Av FELT TW13 ....24 B4
Hanover Ct CHEAM SM3 ......61 K1
  CRAWE RH10 ....177 J7
  EGH TW20 ....20 G9
  FRIM GU16 ....29 K2
  RCH/KEW TW9 ....17 N5
  REDH RH1 ....100 E8
  YTLY GU46 ....67 H1
Hanover Dr DORK RH4 ....116 F7
  WOKS/MYFD GU22 ....10 B7
Hanover Dr FLEETN GU51 ....87 J3
Hanover Gdns BRAK RG12 ...32 B8
  FARN GU14 ....88 A1
Hanover Rd WIM/MER SW19 .43 N1
Hanover St CROY/NA CR0 ......2 B5
Hanover Wk WEY KT13 ....56 E5
Hansler Gv E/WMO/HCT KT8 .40 D6
Hansler Rd EDUL SE22 ....30 C1
Hansom Ter BMLY BR1 * 47 J7
Hanson Cl BAL SW12 ....29 L3
  CBLY GU15 ....69 K1
  MORT/ESHN SW14 ....18 A8
  RGUE GU4 ....J1
  WDR/YW UB7 ....23 L8
Hanworth Cl BRAK RG12 ......32 E7
Hanworth La CHERT KT16 .....37 K9
Hanworth Rd BRAK RG12 ......32 C8
  FELT TW13 ....24 C4
  HPTN TW12 ....24 G7
  HSLW TW3 ....16 B8
  HSLWW TW4 ....24 C2
  REDH RH1 ....140 B1
  SUN TW16 ....39 J1
Hanworth Ter HSLW TW3 ......16 B9
Harberson Rd BAL SW12 ......29 L4
Harbledown Rd
  FUL/PGN SW6 ....19 L6
  SAND/SEL CR2 ....64 A9
Harborough Rd
  STRHM/NOR SW16 ....30 A7
Harbour Av WBPTN SW10 .....19 N6
Harbour Cl FARN GU14 ....68 C2
Harbourfield Rd BNSTD SM7..79 M4
Harbour Yd WBPTN SW10 * ..19 N6
Harbridge Av PUT/ROE SW15 .27 L3
Harbury Rd CAR SM5 ....62 A7
Harbut Rd BTSEA SW11 ....19 P9
Harcourt CWL/WRAY TW19 ...21 K2
Harcourt Av WLGTN SM6 ......62 G3
Harcourt Cl EGH TW20 ....21 P3
  ISLW TW7 ....16 G8
Harcourt Fld WLGTN SM6 .....62 D3
Harcourt Rd BRAK RG12 ......32 D3
  CBLY GU15 ....68 D3
  THHTH CR7 ....45 J7
  WIM/MER SW19 ....43 L1
  WLGTN SM6 ....62 D3
Harcourt Ter WBPTN SW10 ...19 M3
Hardcastle Cl SNWD SE25 ....46 A7
Hardcourts Cl WWKM BR4 ....65 H3
Hardell Ct EGH TW20 ....20 E8
Hardel Wk
  BRXS/STRHM SW2 ....30 B3
Harden Farm Cl
  COUL/CHIP CR5 ....100 E1
Hardham Cl CRAWW RH11 ...176 D3
Harding Cl CROY/NA CR0 ....3 K5
  KUTN/CMB KT2 ....9 J7
Harding Rd EPSOM KT18 ......78 C8
Hardman Rd KUTN/CMB KT2...8 E4
Hardwell Wy BRAK RG12 ......32 C5
Hardwick Cl LHD/OX KT22 ....56 A4
Hardwicke Av HEST TW5 * 16 A6
Hardwicke Rd CHSWK W4 .....18 A2
  RCHPK/HAM TW10 ....26 B7
Hardwick La CHERT KT16 .....54 B6
Hardwick Rd REDH RH1 ....119 P7
Hardwick's Wy
  WAND/EARL SW18 ....28 D1
Hardy Av YTLY GU46 ....68 C4
Hardy Cl CRAWE RH10 ....177 M4
  HORL RH6 ....159 H1
  HORS RH12 ....192 A6
  RDKG RH5 ....137 H2
Hardy Gn CWTH RG45 ....49 M5
Hardy Rd WIM/MER SW19 ....43 M1
Harebell Hl COB KT11 ....75 M3
Harecroft DORK RH4 ....137 J1
  GT/LBKH KT23 ....96 B3
Haredon Cl FSTH SE23 ....31 K3
Harefield ESH/CLAY KT10 .....58 E2
Harefield Av BELMT SM2 ......61 J7
Harefield Rd
  STRHM/NOR SW16 ....45 H1
Hare Hill ADL/WDHM KT15 ...55 K5
Harelands Cl
  WOKN/KNAP GU21 ....73 L4
Hare La CRAWW RH11.............72 A6
  ESH/CLAY KT10 ....58 E5
  GODL GU7 ....131 M7
  LING RH7 ....142 D8
Harendon
  KWD/TDW/WH KT20 ....98 C1
Hares Bank CROY/NA CR0 ....65 H5
Harestone Dr CTHM CR3 .....101 P6
Harestone La CTHM CR3 .....101 N5

Harestone Valley Rd
  CTHM CR3 ....101 P5
Harewood Cl CRAWE RH10 ..177 K2
  REIG RH2 ....119 N3
Harewood Gdns
  SAND/SEL CR2 ....82 B4
Harewood Rd ISLW TW7 ....16 F5
  RGUE GU4 ....112 C2
  SAND/SEL CR2 ....63 N5
  WIM/MER SW19 ....29 H9
Harewood Ter NWDGN UB2 ..15 P1
Harfield Gdns CMBW SE5 * ..30 E3
Harington Pl REIG RH2 ....119 L3
Harkness Cl EW KT17 ....78 C5
Harland Av CROY/NA CR0 ......3 K5
Harland Cl WIM/MER SW19 ..43 M4
Harlech Gdns HEST TW5 ....15 L4
Harlech Rd BLKW GU17 ....67 P2
Harlequin Av BTFD TW8 ....16 C4
Harlequin Centre
  NWDGN UB2 * 15 L2
Harlequin Cl ISLW TW7 ....25 M1
Harlequin Rd TEDD TW11 * ..41 K1
Harleyford BMLY BR1 ....47 P2
Harley Gdns WBPTN SW10 ..19 N3
Harlington Cl HYS/HAR UB3 ..14 E5
Harlington Rd East
  EBED/NFELT TW14 ....24 C3
Harlington Rd West
  EBED/NFELT TW14 ....24 C2
Harlington Wy FLEETN GU51..86 E2
Harman Pl FUL/PGN SW6 .....63 H3
Harmans Md EGRIN RH19 ....180 C2
Harmans Md EGRIN RH19 ....180 F2
Harmans Water Rd
  BRAK RG12 ....32 F6
Harmondsworth La
  WDR/YW UB7 ....14 A4
Harmondsworth Rd
  WDR/YW UB7 ....14 A1
Harmony Cl CRAWW RH11 ...176 B7
  WLGTN SM6 ....62 G7
Harms Gv RGUE GU4 ....93 J2
Harold Av HYS/HAR UB3 ......15 H1
Harold Rd CRAWE RH10 ......177 P6
  NRWD SE19 ....45 M1
  SUT SM1 ....61 P3
Haroldslea Cl HORL RH6 ......159 P2
Haroldslea Dr HORL RH6 .....159 M3
Haroldslea Dr HORL RH6 .....159 N5
Harpdon Pde YTLY GU46 ......67 H1
Harpenden Rd W/NWD SE27 .30 C5
Harper Dr CRAWE RH10 ....177 M9
Harper's Rd ASHV GU12 ......109 L4
Harpers Yd ISLW TW7 * 16 F7
Harpesford Av VW GU25 ......36 A6
Harps Oak La REDH RH1 ......100 B5
Harpton Cl YTLY GU46 ....67 H1
Harpurs KWD/TDW/WH KT20 .98 H1
Harrier Cl CRAN GU6 ....153 H8
Harriet Cl BRXS/STRHM SW2 .30 B3
Harriet Gdns CROY/NA CR0 ..64 A1
Harrington Cl CROY/NA CR0 .62 C1
  REIG RH2 ....138 E3
Harrington Gdns ECT SW5 ...19 M2
Harrington Rd SKENS SW7 ...19 P2
  SNWD SE25 ....46 A5
Harriotts Cl ASHTD KT21 ......77 K9
Harriotts La ASHTD KT21 .....77 J8
Harris Cl CRAWW RH11 ....176 B8
  HEST TW5 ....15 L5
Harrison Cl REIG RH2 ....119 M6
Harrison Ct SHPTN TW17 * ...38 D6
Harrison's Ri CROY/NA CR0 ...2 A5
Harris Pth CRAWW RH11 .....176 E8
Harris Wy SUN TW16 ....38 G2
Harrogate Ct DTCH/LGLY SL3.12 E3
Harroway Rd BTSEA SW11 ...19 P7
Harrowdene Ct ADL/WDHM KT15 ..55 M1
  CHSGTN KT9 ....59 K6
  DORK RH4 ....116 G8
Harrowdene Gdns
  TEDD TW11 ....40 G1
Harrowlands Pk DORK RH4 ..117 H8
Harrow La GODL GU7 ....131 L6
Harrow Rd ASHF TW15 ....23 K8
  CAR SM5 ....62 A5
  DTCH/LGLY SL3 ....12 E4
  WARL CR6 ....82 F4
Harrow Rd East DORK RH4 ..117 H9
Harrow Rd West DORK RH4 ..116 G9
Harrowsley Ct HORL RH6 .....159 M2
Harrowsley Gn La HORL RH6.160 D5
Harrow Wy SHPTN TW17 ......38 E3
Hart Cl BNFD RG42 ....32 C1
  FARN GU14 ....88 A3
  REDH RH1 ....121 P4
Hart Dene Ct BAGS GU19 ....51 N5
Harte Rd HSLW TW3 ....15 P7
Hartfield Crs WIM/MER SW19.43 K1
  WWKM BR4 ....65 N2
Hartfield Gv PGE/AN SE20 ...46 B2
Hartfield Rd CHSGTN KT9 ....59 K4
  EDEN TN8 ....145 L9
  FROW RH18 ....181 M9
  WIM/MER SW19 ....28 C9
  WWKM BR4 ....65 N3
Hartford Bridge Flats
  HTWY RG27 ....66 A7
Hartford Ri CBLY GU15 ....68 D2
Hartford Rd HOR/WEW KT19 .59 N5
Hart Gdns DORK RH4 ....117 H6
Hartham Cl ISLW TW7 ....16 F6
Hartham Rd ISLW TW7 ....16 F6
Harting Ct CRAWW RH11 .....176 C8
Hartington Pl REIG RH2 * 119 L3
Hartington Rd CHSWK W4 ....17 P5
  NWDGN UB2 * 15 N1
  TWK TW1 ....26 B2
Hartismere Rd FUL/PGN SW6.19 K5

Hartland Cl ADL/WDHM KT15 .55 N8
Hartland Rd FARN GU14 ....68 C9
Hartland Rd
  ADL/WDHM KT15 ....55 L6
  HPTN TW12 ....25 J7
  ISLW TW7 ....16 G8
  MRDN SM4 ....43 L8
The Hartlands HEST TW5 ......15 K4
Hartland Wy CROY/NA CR0 ...64 E1
  MRDN SM4 ....43 J8
Hartley Cl BLKW GU17 ....67 M3
Hartley Copse WDSR SL4 .....20 F4
Hartley Down
  COUL/CHIP CR5 ....81 H4
Hartley Farm PUR/KEN CR8 .81 H4
Hartley Hl PUR/KEN CR8 ......81 H4
Hartley Old Rd PUR/KEN CR8.81 H4
Hartley Rd BH/WHM TN16 ...105 H5
  CROY/NA CR0 ....45 L8
Hartley Wy PUR/KEN CR8 ....81 H4
Hart Rd BF/WBF KT14 ....74 A2
  DORK RH4 ....117 J1
Hartscroft CROY/NA CR0 ......64 E7
Harts Gdns GUW GU2 ....111 P2
Hartshill CRAWE RH10 ....111 K4
Hart's La GDST RH9 ....122 D7
Hartsleaf Cl FLEETN GU51 ....86 F7
Harts Leap Cl SHST GU47 .....49 L9
Harts Leap Rd SHST GU47 ....49 L9
Hartspiece Rd REDH RH1 .....120 C5
Hartswood CROY/NA CR0 .....65 H7
Hartswood Av REIG RH2 ......119 L9
Hartswood Gdns SHB W12 * .18 D1
The Hart FRIM GU16 ....8 A4
Harvard Hl CHSWK W4 ....17 P3
Harvard Rd CHSWK W4 ....17 P3
  ISLW TW7 ....16 E6
  SHST GU47 ....50 B8
Harvest Bank Rd WWKM BR4 .65 N2
Harvest Cl YTLY GU46 ....66 F4
Harvest Crs FLEETN GU51 ....87 H2
Harvester Rd
  HOR/WEW KT19 ....60 B8
Harvesters HORS RH12 ....192 C6
Harvesters Cl ISLW TW7 ......25 L1
Harvest Hl EGRIN RH19 ....180 D3
  GODL GU7 ....131 K9
Harvest La THDIT KT7 ....40 G8
Harvest Ride BNFD RG42 .....32 C1
Harvest Rd CRAWE RH10 .....177 J3
  EGH TW20 ....21 J8
  FELT TW13 ....24 B7
Harvey Cl CRAWW RH11 .....194 D1
Harvey Dr HPTN TW12 ....40 B2
Harvey Gdns GU GU1 * 7 F6
Harvey Rd DTCH/LGLY SL3 ..12 F1
  FARN GU14 ....87 N2
  GU GU1 ....7 G6
  HSLWW TW4 ....24 C3
  WOT/HER KT12 ....39 L3
Harwarden Cl CRAWE RH10..179 K3
Harwood Av BMLY BR1 ....47 P3
  MTCM CR4 ....44 A4
Harwood Gdns WDSR SL4 ...20 C9
Harwood Pk REDH RH1 ....140 C5
Harwood Rd FUL/PGN SW6 ..19 M5
  SWTR RH13 ....192 D7
Harwoods Cl EGRIN RH19 ....180 E4
Harwood's Rd EGRIN RH19 ..180 E4
Harwood Ter FUL/PGN SW6 .19 N6
Haseley End FSTH SE23 * 31 K3
Haseltine Rd SYD SE26 ....31 N7
Haslam Av CHEAM SM3 ....43 J9
Hasle Dr HASM GU27 ....184 C5
Haslemere Av HEST TW5 ......15 L7
  HNWL W7 ....16 C1
  MTCM CR4 ....43 N3
  WAND/EARL SW18 ....28 E5
Haslemere Cl FRIM GU16 .....69 L5
  HPTN TW12 ....24 G9
  WLGTN SM6 ....62 G4
Haslemere Heathrow Est
  HSLWW TW4 * 15 K7
Haslemere Rd FNM GU9 ......5 C4
  THHTH CR7 ....45 K6
  WIM/MER SW19 ....43 M2
Haslett Av East
  CRAWE RH10 ....177 K5
Haslett Av West
  CRAWE RH10 ....176 G6
Haslett Rd SHPTN TW17 ....38 G3
Hassocks Cl SYD SE26 ....31 J6
Hassocks Ct CRAWW RH11 ..176 C8
Hassocks Rd
  STRHM/NOR SW16 ....44 F2
Hassock Wd KES BR2 ....66 G2
Haste Hl HASM GU27 ....184 B8
Haste Hill Top HASM GU27 * .184 E5
Hastings Cl FRIM GU16 ....69 J6
Hastings Dr SURB KT6 ....41 J7
Hastings Rd CRAWE RH10 ...177 L5
  CROY/NA CR0 ....3 J1
Hatch Cl ADL/WDHM KT15 ...55 M2
  CRAN GU6 ....170 D8
Hatch End BFOR GU20 ....52 B6
The Hatches FNM GU9 ....127 K5
  FRIM GU16 ....88 D3
Hatchett Rd
  EBED/NFELT TW14 ....23 M4
Hatch Gdns
  KWD/TDW/WH KT20 ....79 H9
Hatchgate HORL RH6 ....159 H2
Hatchgate Copse BRAK RG12.32 A7
Hatch Hl HASM GU27 ....184 C9
Hatchlands HORS RH12 ....192 F3

Hatchlands Rd REDH RH1 ....120 A5
Hatch La HASM GU27 ....184 C9
  MFD/CHID GU8 ....167 L8
  REDH RH1 ....141 H2
  RPLY/SEND GU23 ....74 D9
  WDR/YW UB7 ....13 P5
Hatch Pl RCHPK/HAM TW10 .26 E8
Hatch Ride EWKG RG40 ....49 K1
Hatch Rd STRHM/NOR SW16..44 G3
Hatfield Cl BELMT SM2 ....61 L7
  BF/WBF KT14 * 73 M1
  MTCM CR4 * 43 P5
Hatfield Ct CBLY GU15 ....68 D3
Hatfield Gdns FARN GU14 ....88 G4
Hatfield Rd ASHTD KT21 ......77 M8
Hathaway Rd CROY/NA CR0 .45 K8
Hatherleigh Cl CHSGTN KT9 .59 K4
  MRDN SM4 ....43 L5
Hatherley Rd RCH/KEW TW9 .17 M6
Hatherop Rd HPTN TW12 .....24 G9
Hathersham Cl HORL RH6 ....141 J9
Hathersham La HORL RH6 ...141 H7
Hatherwood ASHTD KT21 ....77 K9
  YTLY GU46 * 66 F4
Hatton Cross Set
  HTHAIR TW6 * 15 H9
Hatton Gdns MTCM CR4 ......44 B6
Hatton Gn EBED/NFELT TW14.15 J9
Hatton Hl BFOR GU20 ....52 C4
Hatton Rd CROY/NA CR0 ....3 K5
  EBED/NFELT TW14 ....23 M3
  STRHM/NOR SW16 ....23 H9
Hatton Rd North
  HTHAIR TW6 ....14 F6
Havana Cl WIM/MER SW19 ..28 D5
Havelock Rd CROY/NA CR0 ...3 K3
  WIM/MER SW19 ....28 F8
Haven Cl WIM/MER SW19 ....28 A6
  CT BRYLDS KT5 * 41 M7
Haven Gdns CRAWE RH10 ...179 H2
Havengate HORS RH12 ....192 E5
Haven Rd ASHF TW15 ....23 L7
  BIL RH14 ....189 N7
The Haven MFD/CHID GU8 *.168 A2
  RCH/KEW TW9 ....17 N8
  SUN TW16 ....39 H1
Haven Wy FNM GU9 ....127 P1
Haverfield Gdns
  RCH/KEW TW9 ....17 N5
Haverhill Rd BAL SW12 ....29 M4
Haversham Cl CRAWE RH10 .177 J5
  TWK TW1 ....26 C3
Haversham Dr BRAK RG12 ...32 D7
Hawarden Gv HNHL SE24 ....30 D3
Hawarden Rd CTHM CR3 .....101 L1
Hawes La WWKM BR4 ....65 J9
Hawes Rd BMLY BR1 * 47 P2
  KWD/TDW/WH KT20 ....79 H9
Haweswater Ct
  ASHV GU12 *.....................109 H2
Hawke Rd NRWD SE19 ....30 E9
Hawker Rd ASHV GU12 ....109 H1
Hawkesbourne Rd
  HORS RH12 ....192 E5
Hawkesfield Rd FSTH SE23 ...31 M5
Hawkes Leap BFOR GU20 * ..52 B3
Hawkesley Cl TWK TW1 ....25 P7
Hawkesmoore Dr
  RDKG RH5 ....156 B2
Hawkesmoor Rd
  CRAWW RH11 ....176 B7
Hawkes Rd
  EBED/NFELT TW14 ....24 B3
  MTCM CR4 ....44 A3
  WAND/EARL SW18 * 28 E5
Hawkesworth Dr BAGS GU19.51 M8
Hawkewood Rd SUN TW16 ...39 K4
Hawkfield Ct ISLW TW7 * 16 E7
Hawkhirst Rd PUR/KEN CR8 .81 M5
Hawkhurst COB KT11 ....76 A3
Hawkhurst Rd
  STRHM/NOR SW16 ....44 F2
Hawkhurst Wk
  CRAWE RH10 ....177 L7
Hawkhurst Wy NWMAL KT3 ..42 B6
  WWKM BR4 ....65 J1
Hawkins Cl BRAK RG12 ....33 J3
Hawkins Gv FLEETN GU51 ....86 D9
Hawkins Rd CRAWW RH11 ...176 G7
  TEDD TW11 ....25 P9
Hawkins Wy CAT SE6 ....31 P8
Hawk La BRAK RG12 ....32 F5
Hawkley Gdns W/NWD SE27 .30 C5
Hawksbrook La BECK BR3 ....47 J5
Hawkshaw Cl
  BRXS/STRHM SW2 ....29 P2
Hawkshead Cl BMLY BR1 .....47 L4
Hawkshead Rd CHSWK W4 ..18 C1
Hawks Hl LHD/OX KT22 ....96 F3
Hawkshill Cl ESH/CLAY KT10 .58 A5
Hawks Hill Cl LHD/OX KT22 ..96 F3
Hawkshill Cl ESH/CLAY KT10 .58 A5
Hawkslade Rd PECK SE15 ....31 L1
Hawksmoor St HMSMTH W6 .19 H4
Hawks Rd KUT KT1 ....41 M2
Hawksview COB KT11 ....76 A1
Hawksway STA TW18 ....22 C6
Hawkswell Cl
  WOKN/KNAP GU21 ....71 M6
Hawkswood Av FRIM GU16 ...69 H9
Hawkwell CHOB/PIR GU24 ...70 G5
Hawkwood Dell
  GT/LBKH KT23 ....96 A6
Hawkwood Ri GT/LBKH KT23 .96 A6
Hawley Cl HPTN TW12 ....24 G8

Hawley Gn BLKW GU17 ....68 A5
Hawley Gv BLKW GU17 ....68 A6
Hawley La FARN GU14 ....68 E2
Hawley Rd BLKW GU17 ....68 A5
Hawley Wy ASHF TW15 ....23 K8
Hawmead CRAWE RH10 ......179 K3
Haworth Rd CRAWE RH10 ....177 L6
Hawth Av CRAWE RH10 ....177 K6
Hawth Cl CRAWE RH10 ....177 H7
Hawthorn Av THHTH CR7 .....45 L2
Hawthorn Cl ASHV GU12 .....108 C9
  BNFD RG42 ....32 B4
  BNSTD SM7 ....79 J3
  CRAWW RH11 ....176 F2
  EDEN TN8 ....144 F3
  HEST TW5 ....15 K5
  HORS RH12 ....192 B6
  HPTN TW12 ....25 H8
  REDH RH1 * 140 C5
  WOKS/MYFD GU22 ....72 C9
Hawthorn Crs SAND/SEL CR2.64 C9
Hawthorndene Cl
  HAYES BR2 ....65 M1
Hawthorndene Rd
  HAYES BR2 ....65 N1
Hawthorn Dr WWKM BR4 ....65 L3
Hawthorne Av
  BH/WHM TN16 ....84 B4
  CAR SM5 ....62 C6
  MTCM CR4 ....43 P3
Hawthorne Ct
  STWL/WRAY TW19 * 22 C3
Hawthorne Crs BLKW GU17 .68 A4
Hawthorne Pl EW KT17 ....78 C1
Hawthorne Wy RGUA GU4 ...112 F1
Hawthorn Gdns EA W5 ....17 K1
Hawthorn Hatch BTFD TW8 ..17 H5
Hawthorn La RFNM GU10 ....109 L7
Hawthorn Pl RGUE GU4 ....93 B9
Hawthorn Rd BTFD TW8 ....16 G5
  FRIM GU16 ....69 H6
  GODL GU7 ....150 A2
  RPLY/SEND GU23 ....93 K4
  SUT SM1 ....62 B8
  WLGTN SM6 ....62 C9
  WOKS/MYFD GU22 ....72 C9
The Hawthorns
  DTCH/LGLY SL3 ....13 K6
  EW KT17 ....60 D5
  OXTED RH8 ....123 N4
Hawthorn Ter WEY KT13 * 56 A4
Hawthorn Wy
  ADL/WDHM KT15 ....55 M8
  CHOB/PIR GU24 ....70 G5
  REDH RH1 ....120 D7
  SHPTN TW17 ....38 F5
Haxted Rd BMLY BR1 ....47 P2
  LING RH7 ....143 L6
Hayborn Dr HORS RH12 ......192 G3
Haycroft Cl PUR/KEN CR8 ....81 K8
Haycroft Rd
  BRXS/STRHM SW2 ....29 P1
  SURB KT6 ....41 J6
Hayden Ct ADL/WDHM KT15 .55 M8
Haydn Av PUR/KEN CR8 ....81 J4
Haydon Park Rd
  WIM/MER SW19 ....28 D8
Haydon Pl GU GU1 ....6 E4
Haydon Rd WIM/MER SW19 ..28 D8
Haydon Wy BTSEA SW11 .....19 N9
Hayes Barton
  WOKS/MYFD GU22 ....73 H5
Hayes Cha WWKM BR4 ....47 J7
Hayes Cl HAYES BR2 ....65 N1
Hayes Crs CHEAM SM3 ....61 H3
Hayesford Park Dr
  HAYES BR2 ....47 M6
Hayes Gdn HAYES BR2 ....65 N1
Hayes Hl HAYES BR2 ....47 L9
Hayes Hill Rd HAYES BR2 ....47 L9
Hayes La BECK BR3 ....47 K4
  HAYES BR2 ....47 L9
  PUR/KEN CR8 ....81 K6
  SWTR RH13 ....190 D9
Hayes Mead Rd HAYES BR2 .47 L9
Hayes Rd HAYES BR2 ....47 N5
  NWDGN UB2 ....15 L2
Hayes St HAYES BR2 ....47 N9
The Hayes EPSOM KT18 ....78 B8
Hayes Wk HORL RH6 ....141 J9
Hayes Wy BECK BR3 ....47 J4
Hayes Wood Av HAYES BR2 ..47 N9
Hayfields HORL RH6 ....140 F9
Haygarth Pl WIM/MER SW19 .28 A8
Haygreen Cl KUTN/CMB KT2 .26 G9
Hayling Av FELT TW13 ....24 C5
Hayling Ct CRAWW RH11 .....176 A6
  SUT SM1 ....61 H4
Haymeads Dr ESH/CLAY KT10.58 C5
Haymer Gdns WPK KT4 ....60 E2
Hayne Rd BECK BR3 ....46 F3
Haynes Cl DTCH/LGLY SL3 ...12 D3
  RPLY/SEND GU23 ....93 M2
Hayne Wk HORS RH12 ....192 F3
Hayse Hill RYNPK SW20 ....28 G9
Hays Wk BELMT SM2 ....61 H8
Hayter Rd BRXS/STRHM SW2.29 P1
The Haywain OXTED RH8 .....123 K1
Hayward Cl WIM/MER SW19 .43 M1
Hayward Gdns
  PUT/ROE SW15 ....27 P2
Hayward Rd THDIT KT7 ....40 G8
Haywards CRAWE RH10 ....177 N2
Haywood BRAK RG12 ....32 C8
Haywood Dr FLEETS GU52 ...86 C8
Hazel Av FARN GU14 ....88 C1
  GU GU1 ....112 A1

Hazel Bank BRYLDS KT5 ....42 A9
Hazelbank EWKG RG40 ....48 B3
Hazelbank CI LIPH GU30 ....182 G6
Hazelbank Rd CHERT KT16 ....37 N8
Hazelbourne Rd BAL SW12 ......29 L2
Hazelbury CI WIM/MER SW19.43 L3
Hazel CI BTFD TW8 * 17 H5
  CRAWE RH10 ....179 K3
  CRAWW RH11 ....176 F2
  CROY/NA CR0 ....46 D6
  EGH TW20 ....20 G9
  MTCM CR4 ....44 F5
  REIG RH2 ....119 N7
  WHTN TW2 ....25 K3
Hazeldene ADL/WDHM KT15...55 N4
Hazeldene Ct PUR/KEN CR8 .....81 M4
Hazeldene Rd LIPH GU30 ....182 G6
Hazeldon Rd BROCKY SE4 ....31 M1
Hazel Dr RPLY/SEND GU23 ......93 K5
Hazel Gv GSHT GU26 ....165 P8
  STA TW18 ....22 E9
  SYD SE26 ....31 L7
Hazelhurst BECK BR3 ....47 K2
  HORL RH6 ....160 G2
Hazelhurst CI RGUE GU4 ....92 A9
Hazelhurst Crs HORS RH12 .....191 N9
Hazelhurst Dr CRAWE RH10 ..177 P5
Hazelhurst Rd TOOT SW17......29 P7
Hazell Hl BRAK RG12 ....32 E4
Hazel Md EW KT17 ....60 E8
Hazelmere ADL/WDHM KT15...55 N4
  EBED/NFELT TW14 ....23 N2
  LHD/OX KT22 * 77 H8
Hazelmere Wy HAYES BR2.......47 N7
Hazel Pde LHD/OX KT22 * 96 C2
  BF/WBF KT14 ....73 L3
  FRIM GU16 ....89 J5
  REIG RH2 ....119 N7
Hazel Wy COUL/CHIP CR5 ....80 B8
  CRAWE RH10 ....179 J3
  LHD/OX KT22 ....96 C2
Hazelwick Av CRAWE RH10....177 L3
Hazelwick Mill La
  CRAWE RH10 ....177 L3
Hazelwick Rd CRAWE RH10 ....177 K4
Hazelwood CRAWW RH11 ....176 D5
  DORK RH4 ....117 H9
Hazelwood Av MRDN SM4 ....43 M5
Hazelwood CI CRAWE RH10 ....177 L1
Hazelwood Ct SURB KT6 ....41 L7
Hazelwood Gv SAND/SEL CR2 ..82 B3
Hazelwood Hts OXTED RH8...123 N2
Hazelwood La
  COUL/CHIP CR5 ....80 B8
Hazelwood Rd OXTED RH8 ....123 P3
  RSEV TN14 ....85 H1
  WOKN/KNAP GU21 ....11 L7
Hazlebury Rd FUL/PGN SW6 ...19 M7
Hazledean Rd CROY/NA CR0 ......3 F4
Hazledene Rd CHSWK W4 ....18 A4
Hazlemere Gdns WPK KT4 ....42 E9
Hazlewell Rd PUT/ROE SW15 ..27 P7
Hazlewood MFD/CHID GU8 ....149 M8
Hazlitt CI FELT TW13 * 24 F7
Hazlitt Ms WKENS W14 * 19 J1
Hazlitt Rd WKENS W14 ....19 J1
Hazon Wy HOR/WEW KT19 ....78 B1
Headcorn Rd THHTH CR7..........45 H5
Headington Rd
  WAND/EARL SW18..................28 F4
Headlam Rd CLAP SW4..............29 N3
Headland Wy LING RH7 ....143 J9
Headley Av WLGTN SM6 ....63 H4
Headley CI CHSGTN KT9 ....59 N5
  CRAWE RH10 ....177 N3
Headley Common Rd
  EPSOM KT18 ....98 B7
Headley Dr CROY/NA CR0.........65 J6
  EPSOM KT18 ....78 F8
Headley Flds BOR GU35 ....164 B9
Headley Gv
  KWD/TDW/WH KT20 ....78 F9
  KWD/TDW/WH KT20 ....98 B8
Headley Heath Ap
  KWD/TDW/WH KT20 ....117 P1
Headley Hill Rd BOR GU35 ....164 B9
Headley La LIPH GU30 ....164 B9
Headley Pde EPSOM KT18 * 78 F8
Headley Rd ASHTD KT21 ....78 A7
  GSHT GU26 ....165 J7
  LHD/OX KT22 ....182 D4
  RDKG RH5 ....116 C7
Headway CI
  RCHPK/HAM TW10 ....26 B7
The Headway EW KT17 ....60 D7
Hearmon CI YTLY GU46 ....67 H2
Hearn Rd CHSWK W4 ....17 N3
Hearn V BOR GU35 ....164 D4
Hearnville Rd BAL SW12 ....29 K4
Hearsey Gdns BLKW GU17.......47 N7
Heatham Pk WHTN TW2 ....25 N5
Heathbridge WEY KT13 * 56 C5
Heath CI BNSTD SM7 ....79 M3
  FNM GU9 ....107 N2
  GSHT GU26 ....165 M4
  HORS RH12 ....191 M7
  HYS/HAR UB3 ....14 F5
  SAND/SEL CR2 ....63 K5
  STWL/WRAY TW19 ....22 F2
  VW GU25 ....36 B5
Heathcote
  KWD/TDW/WH KT20 ....78 F9
Heathcote CI ASHV GU12 ....109 K3
Heathcote Dr EGRIN RH19 ......180 A1
Heathcote Rd ASHV GU12 ....109 K3
  CBLY GU15 ....68 E3
  EPSOM KT18 ....78 B3
  TWK TW1 ....26 A2

Heath Cottages
  GSHT GU26 * 165 M5
Heathcroft Av SUN TW16 ....39 H1
Heathdale Av HSLWW TW4 ....15 N3
Heathdene
  KWD/TDW/WH KT20 ....79 J8
Heathdene Rd
  STRHM/NOR SW16 ....45 H1
  WLGTN SM6 ....62 D6
Heathdown Rd
  WOKS/MYFD GU22 ....73 H4
Heath Dr BELMT SM2 ....61 N7
  CHOB/PIR GU24 ....70 G9
  KWD/TDW/WH KT20 ....98 F6
  RPLY/SEND GU23 ....92 F3
  RYNPK SW20 ....42 J5
Heathedge SYD SE26 * 31 J5
Heatherbank CI COB KT11 ....57 M9
Heather CI ADL/WDHM KT15...55 M8
  ALDT GU11 ....108 A5
  ASHV GU12 ....109 K1
  CRAWE RH10 ....178 C1
  EWKG RG40 ....48 A2
  FNM GU9 ....127 K7
  GUW GU2 ....111 P3
  HORS RH12 ....192 C5
  HPTN TW12 ....39 P2
  ISLW TW7 ....25 L1
  KWD/TDW/WH KT20 ....99 J2
  REDH RH1 ....120 D2
  WOKN/KNAP GU21 ....72 A4
Heatherdale CI
  KUTN/CMB KT2 ....26 F9
Heatherdeane EHSLY KT24 ....94 F5
Heatherdene Av CWTH RG45 ....49 J5
Heatherdene La CRAWE RH10 ..43 P5
Heather Dr ASC SL5 ....35 H8
  FLEETS GU52 ....106 F1
Heather Gdns BELMT SM2 ....61 L5
  FARN GU14 ....88 C3
Heatherley CI FRIM GU16 ....69 H6
Heatherley Rd FRIM GU16 ....69 H6
Heather Md FRIM GU16 ....69 H6
Heathermount Dr
  CWTH RG45 ....49 K3
Heather PI ESH/CLAY KT10 ....58 B3
Heatherset CI ESH/CLAY KT10 ..58 C4
Heatherset Gdns
  STRHM/NOR SW16 ....45 H1
Heatherside CI
  GT/LBKH KT23 * 95 P5
Heatherside Dr VW GU25.........35 N7
The Heathers
  STWL/WRAY TW19 ....23 J3
Heathervale Rd
  ADL/WDHM KT15 ....55 M8
Heather Wk CHOB/PIR GU24....90 D1
  HORL RH6 ....160 D1
Heather Wy CHOB/PIR GU24....55 L6
  HORL RH6 ....160 D1
Heatherway CWTH RG45 ....49 L4
Heatherway GSHT GU26 ....166 A7
Heatherway LING RH7 ....143 J9
Heather Wy SAND/SEL CR2 ....64 D7
Heathfield COB KT11 ....75 M8
  CRAWE RH10 ....177 N3
Heathfield Av ASC SL5 ....34 E6
  WAND/EARL SW18 ....28 G3
Heathfield CI ASHTD KT21 ....77 P8
  GODL GU7 ....150 C2
  WOKS/MYFD GU22 ....11 H5
Heathfield Dr MTCM CR4 ....44 A3
  REDH RH1 ....140 A1
Heathfield Gdns CHSWK W4 ....18 A3
  CROY/NA CR0 ....2 D7
  WAND/EARL SW18 ....28 G2
Heathfield North WHTN TW2 ...25 M3
Heathfield Rd BMLY BR1 ....47 M1
  CROY/NA CR0 ....2 D7
  WAND/EARL SW18 ....28 F2
  WOKS/MYFD GU22 ....11 H6
  WOT/HER KT12 ....57 N3
Heathfield South
  WHTN TW2 ....25 N3
Heathfield Sq
  WAND/EARL SW18 ....28 G3
Heathfield Ter CHSWK W4 ....18 A3
  WAND/EARL SW18 * 28 C7
Heath Gdns TWK TW1 ....25 P5
Heath Gv PGE/AN SE20 ....46 C1
  SUN TW16 ....39 H1
Heath Hl DORK RH4 ....117 H7
Heath Hill Rd North
  RFNM GU10 ....146 B9
Heath Hill Rd South
  RFNM GU10 ....49 M4
Heathhurst Rd
  SAND/SEL CR2 ....63 N7
Heathlands
  KWD/TDW/WH KT20 ....99 H2
Heathlands CI SUN TW16 ....39 H1
  TWK TW1 ....25 N5
  WOKN/KNAP GU21 ....72 B7
Heathlands Ct HSLWW TW4 .....24 F1
Heathland St ALDT GU11 ....108 C4
Heathlands Wy HSLWW TW4....24 F1
Heath La FNM GU9 ....107 N7
  GODL GU7 ....150 F2
  RFNM GU10 ....99 N6
  SHGR GU5 ....134 A3
Heatman's Rd
  FUL/PGN SW6 * 19 K6
Heath Md WIM/MER SW19 ....28 A6

Heath Mill La RGUW GU3 ....91 J5
Heathmoors BRAK RG12 ....32 E6
Heathpark Dr BFOR GU20 ....52 E5
Heath PI BAGS GU19 * 51 N6
Heath Ride CWTH RG45 ....49 H5
  EWKG RG40 ....48 D9
Heath Ri CBLY GU15 ....68 D1
  DORK RH4 ....116 C9
  HAYES BR2 ....47 N7
  PUT/ROE SW15 ....27 N2
Heathrise RPLY/SEND GU23 .....93 M3
Heath Ri VW GU25 ....36 A5
Heath Rd BAGS GU19 ....51 N6
  CTHM CR3 ....101 M3
  HASM GU27 ....183 N5
  HSLW TW3 ....16 C9
  LHD/OX KT22 ....76 C1
  THHTH CR7 ....45 L4
  TWK TW1 ....25 N4
  WOKN/KNAP GU21 ....72 D4
Heathrow SHGR GU5 ....134 E1
Heathrow CI WDR/YW UB7 ......13 M6
Heathside ESH/CLAY KT10 ....58 E2
  HSLWW TW4 ....24 C3
  WEY KT13 ....56 D4
Heathside CI ESH/CLAY KT10 ...58 E2
Heathside Ct
  KWD/TDW/WH KT20 ....98 F3
Heathside Crs
  WOKS/MYFD GU22 ....11 G4
Heathside Gdns
  WOKS/MYFD GU22 ....11 G4
Heathside La GSHT GU26 ....165 N5
Heathside Pk CBLY GU15 ....69 L1
Heathside Park Rd
  WOKS/MYFD GU22 ....11 F5
Heathside PI EPSOM KT18 ....79 H7
Heathside Rd
  WOKS/MYFD GU22 ....10 E5
The Heath CTHM CR3 ....101 L4
Heathvale Bridge Rd
  ASHV GU12 ....89 J9
Heath Vw EHSLY KT24 ....95 J5
Heathview Gdns
  PUT/ROE SW15 ....27 P3
Heathview Rd
  MFD/CHID GU8 ....149 M5
  THHTH CR7 ....45 J5
Heath Vls
  WAND/EARL SW18 * 28 F4
Heath Wy HORS RH12 ....192 C5
Heathway ASC SL5 ....33 N2
  CBLY GU15 ....68 D1
  CROY/NA CR0 ....64 F2
  CTHM CR3 ....101 L5
  EHSLY KT24 ....94 H4
  NWDGN UB2 * 15 M2
Heathway CI CBLY GU15 ....68 F3
Heathwood CI YTLY GU46 ....67 H1
Heathyfields Rd FNM GU9 ......107 K8
Heaton Rd MTCM CR4 ....44 C1
Heaver Rd BTSEA SW11 * 19 P8
Hebdon Rd TOOT SW17 ....29 H6
Heber Rd EDUL SE22 ....30 G2
Hebron Rd HMSMTH W6 ....18 F1
Heckfield PI FUL/PGN SW6 ....19 L1
Hectors La EGRIN RH19 ....181 H4
Heddon CI ISLW TW7 ....16 C9
Heddon Wk FARN GU14 ....68 C9
Hedgecourt PI EGRIN RH19 ....161 M8
Hedgecroft YTLY GU46 ....66 F2
Hedgehog La HASM GU27 ....184 C5
Hedgerley Ct
  WOKN/KNAP GU21 ....72 A6
Hedgeside CRAWW RH11 ....194 F1
Hedgeway GUW GU2 ....111 N3
Hedingham CI HORL RH6 ....140 E9
Hedley Rd WHTN TW2 ....25 H3
Heenan CI FRIM GU16 ....68 G9
Heidegger Crs BARN SW13 ....18 F5
Heighton Gdns CROY/NA CR0...63 K4
Heights CI BNSTD SM7 ....79 J5
  RYNPK SW20 ....42 F1
The Heights BECK BR3 * 47 J1
  WEY KT13 * 56 C8
Helby Rd CLAP SW4 ....29 N2
Helder St SAND/SEL CR2 ....63 M5
Heldmann CI HSLW TW3 ....16 D9
Helen Av EBED/NFELT TW14 .....24 C3
Helen CI E/WMO/HCT KT8 ....40 B5
Helen Ct FARN GU14 ....88 D3
Helford Wk
  WOKN/KNAP GU21 ....71 N7
Helgiford Gdns SUN TW16........38 G1
Helix Gdns BRXS/STRHM SW2 .30 A2
Helix Rd BRXS/STRHM SW2 ......30 A2
Helksham CI SHST GU47 ....49 P8
Helm CI HOR/WEW KT19 ....77 N1
Helme CI WIM/MER SW19 ....28 C8
Helmsdale BRAK RG12 ....32 G6
Helmsdale Rd
  STRHM/NOR SW16 ....44 E2
Helvellyn CI EGH TW20 ....36 F1
Helvetia St CAT SE6 ....31 N5
Hemingford Rd CHEAM SM3 .....60 C3
Hemlock CI
  KWD/TDW/WH KT20 ....99 J3
Hemming CI HPTN TW12 ....40 A2
Hempshaw Av BNSTD SM7 ....80 E5
Hempson Av DTCH/LGLY SL3 ...12 A1
Hemsby Rd CHSGTN KT9 ....59 M5
Henbit CI EPSOM KT18 ....78 F8
Henchley Dene RGUE GU4 ......113 H2
Henderson Av GUW GU2 ....91 P9
Henderson Rd
  BH/WHM TN16 ....84 A1
  CRAWW RH11 ....194 E1
  CROY/NA CR0 ....45 M7
  WAND/EARL SW18 ....29 H3

Hendham Rd TOOT SW17 ....29 H5
Hendon Gv HOR/WEW KT19 .....59 H9
Hendon Ter ASHF TW15 * 23 N9
Hendon Wy
  STWL/WRAY TW19 ....22 C3
Hendrick Av BAL SW12 ....29 J1
Heneage Crs CROY/NA CR0 ......65 J8
Henfield Rd WIM/MER SW19....43 K2
Henfold Dr RDKG RH5 ....156 D1
Henfold La RDKG RH5 ....137 L6
Hengelo Gdns MTCM CR4 ....43 P5
Hengist Dr HORS RH12 ....191 P9
Hengist Wy HAYES BR2 ....47 K5
Hengrave Rd FSTH SE23 ....31 K3
Hengrove Crs ASHF TW15 ....22 G6
Henhurst Cross La
  RDKG RH5 ....155 P1
Henley Av CHEAM SM3 ....61 J2
Henley Bank GUW GU2 ....111 N7
Henley CI CRAWE RH10 ....68 A8
  FARN GU14 ....16 F8
  ISLW TW7 ....16 B1
Henley Ct WOKS/MYFD GU22 ..72 G9
Henley Dr FRIM GU16 ....68 G9
  KUTN/CMB KT2 ....27 L5
Henley Gdns YTLY GU46 ....67 H3
Henley Ga CHOB/PIR GU24 ......90 C7
Henley Pk RGUW GU3 * 90 D9
Henley Wy FELT TW13 ....24 E8
Hennel CI FSTH SE23 ....31 K6
Hennessy Ct
  WOKN/KNAP GU21 ....72 G2
Henniker Ms CHEL SW3 ....19 P4
Henry Doulton Dr
  TOOT SW17 ....29 K7
Henry Jackson Rd
  PUT/ROE SW15 ....27 P3
Henry Macaulay Av
  KUTN/CMB KT2 ....8 C2
Henry Peters Dr TEDD TW11....25 M8
Henryson Rd BROCKY SE4 ....31 P1
Henry St BMLY BR1 ....47 P2
Hensford Gdns SYD SE26 ....31 J7
Henshaw CI CRAWW RH11 .....176 C7
Henslowe Rd EDUL SE22 ....31 H1
Henslow Wy
  WOKN/KNAP GU21 ....73 H3
Henson Rd CRAWE RH10 ....177 L6
Hensworth Rd ASHF TW15 ....22 G9
Henty CI CRAWW RH11 ....176 B8
Henty Wk PUT/ROE SW15 ....27 N1
Henville Rd BMLY BR1 ....47 P2
Hepburn Gdns HAYES BR2 ....47 M9
Hepple CI ISLW TW7 ....17 H7
Hepplewhite CI
  CRAWW RH11 ....194 E1
Hepworth Cft SHST GU47 ....68 A2
Hepworth Rd
  WOT/HER KT12 ....39 H9
Herald Gdns WLGTN SM6 ....62 D2
Herbert CI BRAK RG12 ....32 E6
Herbert Crs
  WOKN/KNAP GU21 ....71 L7
Herbert Gdns CHSWK W4 ....17 P4
Herbert Rd FLEETN GU51 ....87 H3
  KUT KT1 .... 8 F7
  WIM/MER SW19 ....43 K1
Herbs End FARN GU14 ....87 N2
Hereford CI CRAWE RH10 ....177 H9
  EPSOM KT18 ....78 B2
  GUW GU2 ....111 M3
  STA TW18 ....22 E9
Hereford Copse
  WOKS/MYFD GU22 ....71 P8
Hereford Gdns WHTN TW2 * 25 K4
Hereford La FNM GU9 ....107 M8
Hereford Rd FLEETN GU51 ....87 H3
  FELT TW13 ....24 D4
Hereford Rd BED AL W5 ....17 J1
Hereford Sq SKENS SW7 * 19 N2
Hereward Av PUR/KEN CR8 ....63 J8
Hereward Rd TOOT SW17 ....29 J7
Heriot Rd CHERT KT16 ....37 L8
Heritage La HORL RH6 ....140 D9
Heritage PI
  WAND/EARL SW18 * 29 J7
Herm CI CRAWW RH11 * 176 D9
  ISLW TW7 ....16 C5
Hermes CI FLEETN GU51 ....87 J6
Hermes Wy WLGTN SM6 ....62 F6
Hermitage CI DTCH/LGLY SL3 ..12 A1
  ESH/CLAY KT10 ....58 G5
  FARN GU14 ....88 E6
  FRIM GU16 ....69 H8
  RCHPK/HAM TW10 * 26 C5
  SHPTN TW17 ....38 C1
Hermitage Dr ASC SL5 ....33 N3
Hermitage Gdns NRWD SE19 ...45 L1
Hermitage La CROY/NA CR0 .....45 P8
  EGRIN RH19 ....180 E3
  STRHM/NOR SW16 ....45 H1
Hermitage Pde ASC SL5 * 34 A4
Hermitage Rd EGRIN RH19 .....162 C9
  NRWD SE19 ....45 L1
  PUR/KEN CR8 ....81 L5
  WOKN/KNAP GU21 ....71 J1
The Hermitage BARN SW13 * ...18 D6
  FELT TW13 * 24 A6
  FSTH SE23 ....31 K3
  KUT KT1 * 8 E6
  RCHPK/HAM TW10 * 26 D1
Hermitage Woods Crs
  WOKN/KNAP GU21 ....71 K9
Hermits Rd CRAWE RH10 ....177 H4
Hermonger La HORS RH12 .....172 A9
Herndon CI EGH TW20 ....21 M1
Herndon Rd
  WAND/EARL SW18 ....28 F1

Herne HI HNHL SE24 ....30 D1
Herne Hl HNHL SE24 ....30 C2
Herne Rd SURB KT6 ....59 K1
Heron CI ASC SL5 ....33 M2
  CRAWW RH11 ....176 F3
  FLEETS GU52 ....107 J1
  FRIM GU16 ....89 H3
  GUW GU2 ....111 P2
Heron Dr ADL/WDHM KT15 ......55 H4
Heron Dl DORK RH4 * 116 G6
  KUT KT1 * 8 D7
Heron Dl ADL/WDHM KT15 ......55 H4
Herondale BRAK RG12 ....32 E8
  HASM GU27 ....183 P4
  SAND/SEL CR2 ....64 D7
Herondale Av
  WAND/EARL SW18 ....28 G4
Heron Dr DTCH/LGLY SL3 ....12 F2
Heronfield EGH TW20 ....20 G9
Heron PI EGRIN RH19 ....180 E3
Heron Rd CROY/NA CR0 ....3 H3
  TWK TW1 ....16 E6
The Heronry WOT/HER KT12....57 H9
Herons CI CRAWE RH10 ....161 H7
Heronscourt LTWR GU18 ....52 C9
Heronscroft LTWR GU18 ....52 C9
Herons Cft WEY KT13 ....56 E5
Heron Shaw CRAN GU6 ....171 H2
Herons Lea CRAWE RH10 ....161 J7
Herons PI ISLW TW7 ....17 H8
Herons Wy CHOB/PIR GU24 ......90 D1
Herons Wood Ct
  HORL RH6 * 140 D9
Herontye Dr EGRIN RH19 ....180 E3
Heron Wy EBED/NFELT TW14 ...15 J9
  SWTR RH13 ....192 F8
Heron Wood Rd ASHV GU12 ...108 F4
Herretts Gdns ASHV GU12 ......108 F5
Herrett St ASHV GU12 ....108 F6
Herrick CI CRAWE RH10 ....177 M3
  FRIM GU16 ....89 H3
Herrings La BFOR GU20 ....52 D4
Herriot Ct YTLY GU46 ....66 G4
Herschell Rd FSTH SE23 ....31 L3
Herschel Wk CRAWW RH11 * ...194 E1
Herschens Ct PUT/ROE SW15...27 M5
Hersham Gdns
  WOT/HER KT12 * 57 M4
Hersham PI WOT/HER KT12 * ...57 M4
Hersham Rd WOT/HER KT12 ....57 K1
Hershell Ct
  MORT/ESHN SW14 * 17 P9
Hertford Av
  MORT/ESHN SW14 ....27 J1
Hertford CI CRAWE RH10 ....177 J1
Hesiers Hl WARL CR6 ....85 L6
Hesiers Rd WARL CR6 ....85 L5
Hesketh CI CRAN GU6 ....153 H9
Heslop Rd BAL SW12 ....29 J4
Hesper Ms ECT SW5 * 19 M3
Hesse Gv EW KT17 * 60 B7
Hestercombe Av
  FUL/PGN SW6 ....19 J7
Hesterman Wy CROY/NA CR0...44 G9
Hester Ter RCH/KEW TW9 ....17 N8
Heston Av HEST TW5 ....15 P4
Heston Grange La HEST TW5 ....15 P6
Heston Rd HEST TW5 ....16 A5
  REDH RH1 ....140 B1
Hetherington Rd
  SHPTN TW17 ....38 E3
Hethersett CI REIG RH2 ....119 N2
Hever Rd EDEN TN8 ....145 L6
Hevers Av HORL RH6 ....140 B9
Hewers Wy
  KWD/TDW/WH KT20 ....78 F9
Hewett CI CROY/NA CR0 ....64 C2
Hewlett PI BAGS GU19 ....51 N6
Hewshott Gv LIPH GU30 ....183 H5
Hewshott La LIPH GU30 ....182 G5
Hexham CI CRAWE RH10 ....177 P5
  SHST GU47 ....49 P7
Hexham Gdns ISLW TW7 ....16 G5
Hexham Rd MRDN SM4 ....43 M9
  WNWD SE27 ....30 D5
Hextalls La REDH RH1 ....101 M3
Heybridge Av
  STRHM/NOR SW16 ....30 A9
Heyford Av RYNPK SW20 ....43 K4
Heyford Rd MTCM CR4 ....44 A3
Heymede LHD/OX KT22 ....97 J3
Heythorpe CI
  WOKN/KNAP GU21 ....71 M6
Heythorp St
  WAND/EARL SW18 ....28 C4
Heywood Dr BAGS GU19 ....51 J3
Hibbert St BTSEA SW11 ....19 N8
Hibernia Gdns HSLW TW3 ....25 H1
Hibernia Rd HSLW TW3 ....16 A3
Hichisson Rd PECK SE15 ....33 K1
Hickmans CI GDST RH9 ....122 C3
Hicks La BLKW GU17 ....67 J4
Hidcote CI WOKS/MYFD GU22..11 K1
Hidcote Gdns RYNPK SW20 ......42 G5
Higgs La BAGS GU19 ....51 M6
Highacre DORK RH4 ....137 H1
Highams Hl CRAWW RH11 ......176 C6
Highams Hill Cottages
  HAYES BR2 * 52 L5
Highams La CHOB/PIR GU24 ....52 G3
Highbank PI
  WAND/EARL SW18 * 28 E3
High Barn Rd EHSLY KT24 ....95 N8
Highbarrow Rd CROY/NA CR0...46 P9
High Beech BRAK RG12 ....33 K5
  SAND/SEL CR2 ....64 D7
High Beeches EW KT17 ....79 H3
  FRIM GU16 ....68 F6
High Beeches CI
  PUR/KEN CR8 ....62 F8
High Beeches La
  RHWH RH17 ....194 G8
High Broom Crs WWKM BR4 ....47 H8

Highbury Av THHTH CR7 ....45 J3
Highbury CI NWMAL KT3 ....42 A5
    WWKM BR4 ....65 H5
Highbury Crs CBLY GU15 ....69 J1
Highbury Gv HASM GU27 ....184 D2
Highbury Rd WIM/MER SW19 ...28 B8
High Cedar Dr RYNPK SW20 ......42 F1
Highclere ASC SL5 ....34 D6
    GU GU1 ....112 E2
Highclere CI BRAK RG12 ....32 C3
    PUR/KEN CR8 ....81 L4
Highclere Ct
    WOKN/KNAP GU21 ....71 J6
Highclere Dr CBLY GU15 ....69 J1
Highclere Gdns
    WOKN/KNAP GU21 ....71 J6
Highclere Rd ASHV GU12 ....108 F6
    NWMAL KT3 ....42 B4
    WOKN/KNAP GU21 ....71 J6
Highclere St SYD SE26 ....31 N7
Highcliffe Dr PUT/ROE SW15 ....27 L2
High Coombe PI
    KUTN/CMB KT2 ....42 B1
Highcotts La RGUE GU4 ....93 L6
Highcroft MFD/CHID GU8 ....149 N4
    SHGR GU5 ....133 J9
Highcroft Ct GT/LBKH KT23 .....96 D4
Highcroft Dr HORS RH12 ....189 P1
Highdaun Dr
    STRHM/NOR SW16 ....45 H5
Highdown FLEETN GU51 ....86 G5
    WPK KT4 ....60 C3
Highdown Ct CRAWE RH10 ......177 L8
High Down Rd BELMT SM2 ....61 M9
Highdown Rd
    PUT/ROE SW15 ....27 N2
Highdown Wy HORS RH12 ....192 E3
High Dr CTHM CR3 ....102 F2
Highfield BNSTD SM7 ....79 H2
    NWMAL KT3 ....42 A2
Higher Alham BRAK RG12 ....32 C8
Highercombe Rd
    HASM GU27 ....184 F2
Higher Dr BNSTD SM7 ....79 H2
    EHSLY KT24 ....94 G7
    PUR/KEN CR8 ....81 J2
Higher Gn KT17 ....78 E2
Highfield BNSTD SM7 ....80 A6
    BRAK RG12 ....32 B7
    RGUE GU4 ....132 D4
Highfield Av ALDT GU11 ....108 C6
Highfield CI ALDT GU11 ....108 D6
    FNM GU9 ....127 M6
    LHD/OX KT22 ....58 D9
    SURB KT6 ....41 J9
Highfield Crs GSHT GU26 ....165 P7
Highfield Dr HAYES BR2 ....47 L1
    WIM/MER KT19 ....60 B5
    WWKM BR4 ....65 H2
Highfield Gdns ALDT GU11 ......108 C6
Highfield HI NRWD SE19 ....45 M1
Highfield La LIPH GU30 ....182 G8
    MFD/CHID GU8 ....166 C2
    RGUE GU4 ....130 A2
Highfield Pth FARN GU14 ....88 B3
Highfield Rd BF/WBF KT14 ....73 L2
    BH/WHM TN16 ....84 A6
    BRYLDS KT5 ....42 A8
    CHERT KT16 ....37 L9
    CTHM CR3 ....102 A2
    EGH TW20 ....21 J9
    EGRIN RH19 ....162 C9
    FARN GU14 ....88 B3
    FELT TW13 ....24 B4
    ISLW TW7 ....16 F6
    PUR/KEN CR8 ....62 A8
    SUN TW16 ....39 H6
    SUT SM1 ....62 A4
    WOT/HER KT12 ....39 J9
High Fids ASC SL5 ....34 F6
Highfields ASHTD KT21 ....77 K8
    EHSLY KT24 ....94 F8
    FROW RH18 ....181 J3
    LHD/OX KT22 ....96 D4
Highfields Rd EDEN TN8 ....124 G9
High Foleys ESH/CLAY KT10 ......59 H6
High Garth ESH/CLAY KT10 ....58 C5
Highgate La FARN GU14 ....88 E2
Highgrove FARN GU14 ....68 D9
Highgrove Ms CAR SM5 ....62 A2
Highland Cottages
    WLGTN SM6 * 62 D3
Highland Dr FLEETN GU51 ....87 H4
Highland Pk FELT TW13 ....24 A7
Highland Rd ASHV GU12 ....108 F8
    BMLY BR1 ....47 M2
    CBLY GU15 ....50 C9
    NRWD SE19 ....30 F7
    PUR/KEN CR8 ....81 J3
    RDKG RH5 ....156 B1
Highlands Av LHD/OX KT22 ....97 J2
    SWTR RH13 ....192 D6
Highlands CI FNM GU9 ....127 M6
    HSLW TW3 ....16 B6
    LHD/OX KT22 ....97 H2
Highlands Crs SWTR RH13 .....192 D8
Highlands La
    WOKS/MYFD GU22 ....92 E5
Highlands Rd FNM GU9 ....107 N7
    LHD/OX KT22 ....97 J2
    REDH RH1 ....119 P4
    SWTR RH13 ....192 D8
The Highlands EHSLY KT24 ....94 G5
High La HASM GU27 ....184 D2
    WARL CR6 ....82 F9
High Level Dr SYD SE26 ....31 H7
High Limes NRWD SE19 * 30 F9
High Loxley Rd
    MFD/CHID GU8 ....169 N5

High Md WWKM BR4 ....65 K1
High Meadow CI DORK RH4 ....117 H8
High Meadow PI CHERT KT16 ...37 K7
High Oaks CRAWW RH11 ....176 E7
The High Pde
    STRHM/NOR SW16 * 29 P6
High Park Av EHSLY KT24 ....95 H6
High Park Rd FNM GU9 ....5 F2
    RCH/KEW TW9 ....17 N6
High Pth WIM/MER SW19 ....43 M2
High Path Rd GU GU1 ....112 C5
High Pewley GU GU1 ....7 G7
High Pine CI WEY KT13 ....56 E4
High Pines WARL CR6 ....82 C8
High Pitfold GSHT GU26 ....165 N9
Highpoint WEY KT13 ....56 C4
High Rdg GODL GU7 ....150 C2
Highridge CI EPSOM KT18 * 78 C4
High Rd BF/WBF KT14 ....74 B2
    COUL/CHIP CR5 ....100 A4
High Standing CTHM CR3 ....101 L5
High St ADL/WDHM KT15 ....55 M3
    ALDT GU11 ....108 D4
    ASC SL5 ....33 P4
    ASC SL5 ....34 B6
    BAGS GU19 ....51 N6
    BECK BR3 ....46 G3
    BELMT SM2 ....61 N6
    BH/WHM TN16 ....104 C7
    BIL RH14 ....188 C7
    BNFD RG42 ....32 A1
    BOR GU35 ....164 B6
    BRAK RG12 ....32 D3
    BTFD TW8 ....17 J5
    CAR SM5 ....62 B4
    CBLY GU15 ....68 F2
    CHEAM SM3 ....61 J5
    CHOB/PIR GU24 ....53 L9
    CHOB/PIR GU24 ....70 E1
    COB KT11 ....75 K3
    CRAN GU6 ....152 G9
    CRAWE RH10 ....176 G6
    CROY/NA CR0 ....2 C4
    CTHM CR3 ....101 N3
    CWTH RG45 ....49 N5
    DORK RH4 ....117 H7
    DTCH/LGLY SL3 ....12 E2
    DTCH/LGLY SL3 ....12 C5
    E/WMO/HCT KT8 ....40 E1
    EDEN TN8 ....144 G4
    EGH TW20 ....21 M8
    EGRIN RH19 ....180 E3
    ESH/CLAY KT10 ....58 F5
    EW KT17 ....60 D8
    FARN GU14 ....88 E2
    FELT TW13 ....24 B5
    GDST RH9 ....122 C2
    GODL GU7 ....131 K9
    GODL GU7 ....150 C1
    GT/LBKH KT23 ....96 B5
    GU GU1 ....6 F5
    HASM GU27 ....184 E3
    HEST TW5 ....15 K5
    HOR/WEW KT19 ....78 F2
    HORL RH6 ....159 L1
    HORS RH12 ....175 H3
    HPTN TW12 ....25 K9
    HPTN TW12 ....40 B2
    HSLW TW3 ....16 C8
    HYS/HAR UB3 ....14 F4
    KUT KT1 ....8 B3
    KWD/TDW/WH KT20 ....98 G3
    LHD/OX KT22 ....76 D2
    LHD/OX KT22 ....97 H2
    LING RH7 ....143 K9
    NWMAL KT3 ....42 C5
    OXTED RH8 ....103 P8
    OXTED RH8 ....123 M1
    PGE/AN SE20 ....46 C1
    PUR/KEN CR8 ....63 J9
    REDH RH1 ....100 D8
    REDH RH1 ....120 B5
    REDH RH1 ....121 H5
    REDH RH1 ....121 M4
    REIG RH2 ....119 L5
    RFNM GU10 ....146 B1
    RHWH RH17 ....195 L6
    RHWH RH17 ....195 P4
    RPLY/SEND GU23 ....93 N1
    SHGR GU5 ....132 D2
    SHPTN TW17 ....38 E7
    SHST GU47 ....49 P6
    SNWD SE25 ....45 P5
    STA TW18 ....22 C7
    STWL/WRAY TW19 ....21 K2
    STWL/WRAY TW19 ....22 G2
    SUT SM1 ....61 M3
    TEDD TW11 ....25 P8
    THDIT KT7 ....40 D6
    THHTH CR7 ....45 L5
    WDR/YW UB7 ....13 P4
    WEY KT13 ....56 C3
    WIM/MER SW19 ....28 A8
    WOKN/KNAP GU21 ....10 C4
    WOKN/KNAP GU21 ....71 J7
    WOKS/MYFD GU22 ....92 E1
    WOT/HER KT12 ....39 J9
High Street Collier's Wd
    WIM/MER SW19 ....43 P1
High Street Gn
    MFD/CHID GU8 ....186 D1
High Street Harlington
    HYS/HAR UB3 ....14 F5
High Street Ms
    WIM/MER SW19 ....28 B8
High Thicket Rd RFNM GU10 ..146 A8

High Tor CI BMLY BR1 ....47 P1
High Tree CI ADL/WDHM KT15 ..55 L4
High Trees BRXS/STRHM SW2 ...30 B4
    CROY/NA CR0 ....46 E9
High Trees CI CRAWE RH10 .....177 K3
High Trees Rd REIG RH2 ....119 P6
High Vw SHGR GU5 ....134 E1
    BELMT SM2 ....61 K9
Highview CTHM CR3 ....101 N4
    WOKN/KNAP GU21 * 71 L6
High View Av WLGTN SM6 ....63 H4
High View CI FARN GU14 ....88 C3
    NRWD SE19 ....45 N5
High View Ct REIG RH2 * 119 P5
High View Rd FARN GU14 ....88 C3
    GUW GU2 ....111 K8
    LTWR GU18 ....51 N9
    NRWD SE19 ....30 E9
Highway CWTH RG45 ....49 L4
Highwayman's Rdg
    BFOR GU20 ....52 B3
The Highway BELMT SM2 ....61 N7
High Weald Landscape Trail
    EGRIN RH19 ....180 C4
Highwold COUL/CHIP CR5 ....80 C7
Highwood D PUR/KEN CR8 ....81 L6
    YTLY GU46 ....66 G4
Highwoods CTHM CR3 ....101 N5
    LHD/OX KT22 ....97 J1
Highworth SWTR RH13 * 192 E9
Hilary Av MTCM CR4 ....44 C4
Hilary CI FUL/PGN SW6 * 19 L5
Hilary Dr CWTH RG45 ....49 M3
Hilbert Rd CHEAM SM3 ....61 H3
Hilborough CI
    WIM/MER SW19 ....43 N1
Hildenlea PI HAYES BR2 ....47 L3
Hildenley CI REDH RH1 ....100 F8
The Hildens DORK RH4 ....116 C6
Hilder Gdns FARN GU14 ....88 F4
Hilders La EDEN TN8 ....144 F1
Hilders La EDEN TN8 ....144 D1
Hildreth St BAL SW12 ....29 L4
Hildyard Rd FUL/PGN SW6 ....19 L4
Hilfield BLKW GU17 ....67 K3
Hilgay GU GU1 ....7 J3
Hilgay CI GU GU1 ....7 J3
Hilland Ri BOR GU35 ....164 C7
Hillars Heath Rd
    COUL/CHIP CR5 ....80 G4
Hillary CI EGRIN RH19 ....180 F1
    FNM GU9 ....127 M6
Hillary Crs WOT/HER KT12 ....39 L9
Hillary Dr ISLW TW7 ....16 F9
Hillary Rd DTCH/LGLY SL3 ....12 C1
    FNM GU9 ....127 M6
    NWDGN UB2 ....16 A1
Hillbarn SAND/SEL CR2 ....63 N9
Hillberry BRAK RG12 ....32 E8
Hillborne Ct HYS/HAR UB3 ....15 J3
Hillborough CI
    WIM/MER SW19 ....43 N1
Hillbrook Gdns WEY KT13 ....56 C6
Hillbrook Ri FNM GU9 ....107 L8
Hillbrook Rd TOOT SW17 ....29 J6
Hillbrow NWMAL KT3 ....42 D4
Hillbrow CI RGUW GU3 ....111 H4
Hillbrow Rd BMLY BR1 ....47 L1
    ESH/CLAY KT10 ....58 C5
Hillbury CI WARL CR6 ....82 B7
Hillbury Gdns WARL CR6 ....82 C7
Hillbury Rd TOOT SW17 ....29 L6
    WARL CR6 ....82 A6
Hill CI COB KT11 ....76 A1
    PUR/KEN CR8 ....81 L1
    SHGR GU5 ....132 F7
Hillcote Av
    STRHM/NOR SW16 ....45 J1
Hill Ct FARN GU14 ....68 B7
Hillcourt Rd EDUL SE22 ....31 J2
Hill Crs BRYLDS KT5 ....41 M6
    WPK KT4 ....60 C1
Hillcrest EDEN TN8 ....125 M9
    FLEETN GU51 ....86 G4
    VW GU25 ....36 C3
    WEY KT13 * 107 P6
    WOKS/MYFD GU22 ....92 A4
Hillcrest Av CHERT KT16 ....55 P2
Hillcrest CI BECK BR3 ....46 F7
    CRAWE RH10 ....177 N5
    EPSOM KT18 ....78 D4
    SYD SE26 ....31 H7
Hill Crest Dr RFNM GU10 ....127 K7
Hillcrest Gdns ESH/CLAY KT10 ..58 F3
Hillcrest Rd BH/WHM TN16 ......84 B5
    CBLY GU15 ....68 B1
    CTHM CR3 ....81 P6
    EDEN TN8 ....144 G1
    GUW GU2 ....111 M4
    HORS RH12 ....192 C5
    PUR/KEN CR8 ....81 K3
    SUT SM1 ....61 K3
Hilldale Rd SUT SM1 ....61 J4
Hilldeane Rd PUR/KEN CR8 ......63 J8
Hilldown Rd HAYES BR2 ....47 L9
    STRHM/NOR SW16 ....44 G1
Hill Dr STRHM/NOR SW16 ....44 G1
Hillersdon Av BARN SW13 ....18 E7
Hilley Field La LHD/OX KT22 .....96 C2
Hill Farm CI HASM GU27 * 184 A5
Hillfield Av MRDN SM4 ....44 A5
Hillfield CI GU GU1 ....112 G3
    REDH RH1 ....120 C5

Hillfield Pde MRDN SM4 * 43 P7
Hill Field Rd HPTN TW12 ....39 P1
Hillfield Rd REDH RH1 ....120 C5
Hilford PI REDH RH1 ....140 C2
Hillgarth GSHT GU26 ....165 N6
Hillgate PI BAL SW12 ....29 L2
Hill Gv FELT TW13 ....24 G5
Hillhampton ASC SL5 ....34 F8
Hill House CI CRAWE RH10 .....179 H7
Hill House Dr HPTN TW12 ....40 A2
    REIG RH2 ....119 M7
    WEY KT13 ....56 C9
Hill House HI LIPH GU30 ....182 C3
Hillhouse La HORS RH12 ....189 H1
Hill House Rd
    STRHM/NOR SW16 ....30 A8
Hillhurst Gdns CTHM CR3 ....81 N1
Hillier Gdns CROY/NA CR0 ....63 J4
Hillier PI CHSGTN KT9 ....59 K5
Hillier Rd BTSEA SW11 ....29 J2
    GU GU1 ....112 E5
Hillier's La CROY/NA CR0 ....62 G2
Hillingdale BH/WHM TN16 ....83 P7
    CRAWW RH11 ....194 F1
Hillingdon Av
    STWL/WRAY TW19 ....23 H4
Hillingdon Trail HYS/HAR UB3 ...15 J3
Hill La KWD/TDW/WH KT20 ......99 J1
Hillmead CRAWW RH11 ....176 C5
Hill Md HORS RH12 ....191 P7
Hillmont Rd ESH/CLAY KT10 .....58 E2
Hillmore Gv SYD SE26 ....31 L8
Hill Pk LHD/OX KT22 * 76 D8
Hill Park Ct LHD/OX KT22 * 76 F8
Hill PI CRAWW RH11 ....176 F5
Hillrise ESH/CLAY KT10 ....58 F5
Hill Ri DORK RH4 ....116 C5
Hill Ri ESH/CLAY KT10 ....59 H1
    RCHPK/HAM TW10 ....26 C5
Hill Rd CAR SM5 ....62 A5
    FNM GU9 ....107 P7
    CSHT GU26 ....165 M8
    GT/LBKH KT23 ....96 B2
    HASM GU27 ....184 D4
    MTCM CR4 ....44 D2
    PUR/KEN CR8 ....81 H1
    SUT SM1 ....61 M4
Hillsboro Rd EDUL SE22 ....30 F1
Hillsborough Ct FARN GU14 ......88 A4
Hillsborough Pk CBLY GU15 .....69 L3
Hill School ASC SL5 * 34 C6
    BNSTD SM7 ....79 J4
    CBLY GU15 ....88 B1
    CRAWE RH10 ....177 N6
    ESH/CLAY KT10 ....58 B4
    HORS RH12 ....191 P8
    VW GU25 ....36 A9
    WIM/MER SW19 ....28 D9
    WOKS/MYFD GU22 ....72 B9
    WOKN/KNAP GU21 ....71 K6
Hillside Av BNSTD SM7 ....79 J5
    BOR GU35 ....164 C5
    CRAWW RH11 ....194 D1
    EGRIN RH19 ....66 C9
    FLEETN GU51 ....86 D9
    MRDN SM4 ....44 A3
    RDKG RH5 ....117 N6
    WOKN/KNAP GU21 ....71 K6
Hillside Cottages
    BNSTD SM7 * 80 B2
Hillside Crs FRIM GU16 ....69 H9
Hillside Gdns
    ADL/WDHM KT15 ....55 K4
    BRKHM/BTCW RH3 ....117 N5
    BRXS/STRHM SW2 * 30 C4
    WLGTN SM6 ....62 E6
Hillside La FNM GU9 ....107 P7
    HAYES BR2 ....65 L3
Hillside Pk ASC SL5 ....34 F9
Hillside Rd ASHTD KT21 ....77 K3
    ASHV GU12 ....109 K3
    BELMT SM2 ....61 K6
    BH/WHM TN16 ....84 C8
    BRXS/STRHM SW2 * 30 B5
    COUL/CHIP CR5 ....80 G7
    CROY/NA CR0 ....63 K4
    CTHM CR3 ....82 A7
    EW KT17 ....78 A8
    FNM GU9 ....107 A7
    HASM GU27 ....184 A5
    HAYES BR2 ....65 L3
    WNWD SE27 ....30 E1
Hillside Wy GODL GU7 ....131 K6
Hillsmead Wy SAND/SEL CR2 ...82 A3
Hills PI HORS RH12 ....191 P8
Hillspur CI GUW GU2 ....111 M4
Hillspur Rd GUW GU2 ....111 M4
Hill St RCHPK/HAM TW10 ....26 B3
Hillswood Dr CHERT KT16 ....54 C3
The Hill CTHM CR3 ....101 N4
Hill Top MRDN SM4 ....43 K8
Hilltop CI ASC SL5 ....34 E3
    LHD/OX KT22 ....97 J3
    RGUW GU3 ....111 H3
Hilltop Cottages SYD SE26 * 31 J6
Hilltop La CTHM CR3 ....101 J6
Hilltop Ri GT/LBKH KT23 ....96 C6
Hilltop Rd CTHM CR3 ....81 N6
    REIG RH2 ....119 M7
Hilltop Wk CTHM CR3 ....82 B6
Hill Vw CHOB/PIR GU24 ....54 F7
Hill View CI ASC SL5 ....34 F7
Hill View Crs GUW GU2 ....111 M3
Hillview REDH RH1 ....120 C6
Hillview Dr REDH RH1 ....120 C6
Hillview Gdns CRAWW RH11 ...194 F2
Hill View Rd ESH/CLAY KT10 .....58 C6
    FNM GU9 ....4 B3
    STWL/WRAY TW19 ....21 J2
    TWK TW1 ....25 P2
    WOKS/MYFD GU22 ....72 B9
Hillview Rd SUT SM1 ....61 N2
Hillworth BECK BR3 * 47 H3
Hillworth Rd
    BRXS/STRHM SW2 ....30 B3
Hillybarn Rd CRAWW RH11 .....175 P2
Hilsea St WAND/SEL CR2 ....82 H8
Himley Rd TOOT SW17 ....29 H8
Hinaidi Wy FARN GU14 ....88 B7
Hinchley CI ESH/CLAY KT10 ....58 F2
Hinchley Dr ESH/CLAY KT10 ......58 F2
Hinchley Wy ESH/CLAY KT10 .....58 F2
Hindell CI FARN GU14 ....68 E1
Hindhead CI CRAWW RH11 ....176 F7
Hindhead Rd HASM GU27 ......183 P2
Hindhead Wy WLGTN SM6 ....62 G4
Hindmans Rd EDUL SE22 ....31 H1
Hindsley's PI FSTH SE23 ....31 K5
Hinkler CI WLGTN SM6 * 62 G7
Hinksey CI DTCH/LGLY SL3 ......12 F1
Hinstock CI FARN GU14 ....88 C4
Hinton Av HSLWW TW4 ....15 M9
Hinton CI CWTH RG45 ....49 M3
Hinton Dr CWTH RG45 ....49 M3
Hinton Rd WLGTN SM6 ....62 E5
Hipley St WOKS/MYFD GU22 ....92 F3
Hitchcock CI SHPTN TW17 ....38 D4
Hitches La FLEETN GU51 ....86 C8
Hitchings Wy REIG RH2 ....119 L9
Hitherbury CI GUW GU2 ....112 A8
Hitherfield Rd
    STRHM/NOR SW16 ....30 A5
Hitherhooks HI BNFD RG42 ....32 A2
Hithermoor Rd
    STWL/WRAY TW19 ....22 D2
Hitherwood CRAN GU6 ....171 H1
Hitherwood CI REDH RH1 ....119 P3
Hitherwood Dr DUL SE21 ....30 G7
H Jones Crs ALDT GU11 ....108 E3
Hoadly Rd STRHM/NOR SW16 ...29 N6
Hobart Gdns THHTH CR7 ....45 M4
Hobart PI RCHPK/HAM TW10 ....26 E3
Hobart Rd WPK KT4 ....60 F2
Hobbes Wk PUT/ROE SW15 ......27 N1
Hobbs CI BF/WBF KT14 ....73 M2
Hobbs Rd CRAWW RH11 ....194 D1
    WNWD SE27 ....30 D7
Hobury St WBPTN SW10 ....19 N4
Hocken Md CRAWE RH10 ....177 N3
Hockering Gdns
    WOKS/MYFD GU22 ....11 J5
Hockering Rd
    WOKS/MYFD GU22 ....11 H5
Hockford CI RGUW GU3 ....91 H6
Hodgkin CI CRAWE RH10 ....177 L6
Hodgson Gdns RGUE GU4 ....112 E2
Hoebrook CI
    WOKS/MYFD GU22 ....92 C1
Hoe La MFD/CHID GU8 ....151 J8
    SHGR GU5 ....134 G5
Holland Rd WKENS W14 ....19 J1
Hogarth Av ASHF TW15 ....25 M9
Hogarth Crs CROY/NA CR0 ....45 L7
Hogarth Ct SHST GU47 ....68 A2
Hogarth Crs CROY/NA CR0 ....45 L7
    WIM/MER SW19 ....43 P2
Hogarth Gdns HEST TW5 ....16 A5
Hogarth PI ECT SW5 * 19 M2
Hogarth Rd CRAWE RH10 ....177 J8
    ECT SW5 ....19 M2
Hogarth Ter CHSWK W4 * 18 C4
Hogarth Wy HPTN TW12 ....40 C2
Hogbatch La FNM GU9 ....107 J2
Hogscross La
    COUL/CHIP CR5 ....100 B2
Hogshill La COB KT11 ....75 L3
Hogsmill Wy HOR/WEW KT19 ...60 A4
Hogspudding La RDKG RH5 ....156 G2
Hogtrough HI
    BH/WHM TN16 ....105 L4
Hogtrough La OXTED RH8 ....103 H8
    REDH RH1 ....120 F6
Hogwood Rd BIL RH14 ....187 P7
Holbeach Rd CAT SE6 ....31 N2
Holbeche CI YTLY GU46 ....66 E3
Holbeck BRAK RG12 ....32 B7
Holbein Rd CRAWE RH10 ....177 J6
Holborn Wy MTCM CR4 ....44 B3
Holbreck PI
    WOKS/MYFD GU22 ....10 E5
Holbrook CI FNM GU9 ....108 B6
Holbrook Meadow
    EGH TW20 ....21 P9
Holbrook School La
    HORS RH12 ....192 C3
Holcombe Wy ALDT GU11 ....108 D7
Holcombe CI BH/WHM TN16 ...105 H6
Holcombe St HMSMTH W6 ....18 F3
Holcon Ct REDH RH1 ....120 C2
Holdenby Rd BROCKY SE4 ....31 M1
Holdenhurst Rd ISLW TW7 ....16 G6
    TOOT SW17 * 29 H8
Holderness Wy WNWD SE27 .....30 C1
Holdfast La HASM GU27 ....184 G2
Hole CI CRAWE RH10 ....116 P7
Hole La EDEN TN8 ....124 E8
    RFNM GU10 ....126 A4
Holford Rd GU GU1 ....112 G5
Holgate Rd BTSEA SW11 ....19 P8
Holland Av BELMT SM2 ....61 L6
    RYNPK SW20 ....42 D2
Holland CI FNM GU9 ....128 A4
    HAYES BR2 ....65 M1
    REDH RH1 ....120 B5

Holland Crs OXTED RH8 ...123 N4
Holland Dr FSTH SE23 ...31 M6
Holland Gdns EGH TW20 ...37 K3
  FLEETN GU51 ...86 C2
  WKENS W14 ...19 J1
Holland La OXTED RH8 ...123 N4
Holland Park Rd
  WKENS W14 ...19 K1
Holland Pines BRAK RG12 ...32 B8
Holland Rd OXTED RH8 ...123 N4
  SNWD SE25 ...46 A6
Hollands Rd HORS RH12 ...191 M6
The Hollands
  WOKS/MYFD GU22 ...10 D6
  WPK KT4 ...42 D9
Hollands Wy EGRIN RH19...162 F8
  HORS RH12 ...191 N2
Holland Wy HAYES BR2 ...65 M1
Holliday Sq BTSEA SW11 ...19 P8
Hollies Av BF/WBF KT14 ...73 K2
Hollies Cl STRHM/NOR SW16...30 B9
  TWK TW1 ...25 N5
Hollies Ct ADL/WDHM KT15...55 N4
Hollies Rd EA W5 ...17 J2
The Hollies
  ADL/WDHM KT15 * ...55 N4
  FARN GU14 * ...68 B7
  WOKN/KNAP GU21 * ...71 K6
Holligrave Rd BMLY BR1 ...47 H2
Hollin Ct CRAWE RH10 ...177 L2
Hollingbourne Crs
  CRAWW RH11 ...194 F2
Hollingbourne Rd HNHL SE24..30 D1
Hollingsworth Rd
  SAND/SEL CR2 ...64 B5
Hollington Crs NWMAL KT3 ...42 D7
Hollingworth Cl
  E/WMO/HCT KT8 ...39 P5
Hollingworth Wy
  BH/WHM TN16 ...105 H6
Hollis Rw REDH RH1 * ...120 B7
Hollis Wood Dr RFNM GU10..127 J8
Hollman Gdns
  STRHM/NOR SW16 ...30 C9
Holloway Av YEAD UB4 ...13 A3
Holloway Dr VW GU25 ...56 C5
Holloway Hl CHERT KT16 ...54 E2
  GODL GU21 * ...13 K9
Holloway La WDR/YW UB7 ...13 M4
  WDR/YW UB7 * ...14 C2
Holloway St HSLW TW3 ...16 B8
Hollow Cl GUW GU35 ...164 B5
Hollow La BOR GU35 ...164 B5
  LING RH7 ...162 G4
  RDKG RH5 ...135 M3
  VW GU25 ...36 A4
The Hollow CRAWW RH11 ...176 C6
  GODL GU2 ...13 J9
Hollowfield ADL/WDHM KT15...55 L8
  FRIM GU16 ...69 K5
  WOT/HER KT12 ...39 M9
Hollybank CHOB/PIR GU24 ...70 F2
Hollybank Cl HPTN TW12 ...25 H8
Hollybank Rd BF/WBF KT14 ..73 J3
Holly Bank Rd
  WOKS/MYFD GU22 ...91 P1
Hollybush Cl CRAWE RH10 ...177 H4
Holly Bush La HPTN TW12 ...39 F1
Hollybush La ALDT GU11 ...108 E9
  HTWY RG27 ...48 C9
Hollybush Ride BFOR GU20...51 P2
  EWKG RG40 ...48 G4
Hollybush Rd CRAWE RH10..177 H4
  KUTN/CMB KT2 ...26 D8
Hollybush Ter NRWD SE19 * ..30 F9
Holly Cl ASHV GU12 ...108 E4
  BECK BR3 ...47 J5
  BOR GU35 ...164 F6
  CHERT KT16 ...55 N2
  CRAWE RH10 ...177 K3
  EGH TW20 ...20 C9
  FARN GU14 ...88 C3
  FELT TW13 ...24 F7
  HORS RH12 ...192 C5
  WOKN/KNAP GU21 ...71 P8
Hollycombe EGH TW20 ...21 J7
Hollycombe Cl LIPH GU30..182 F8
Holly Ct WEY KT13 * ...49 K4
Holly Crs BECK BR3 ...46 F6
Hollycroft Cl SAND/SEL CR2 ..63 N4
  WDR/YW UB7 ...14 C4
Hollycroft Gdns
  WDR/YW UB7 ...14 C4
Holly Dr WDSR SL4 ...20 D1
Holly Farm Rd NWDGN UB2 ..15 N3
Hollyfield BRYLDS KT5 ...41 M8
Hollyfields Cl CBLY GU15 ...68 D3
Holly Gn WEY KT13 ...56 F3
Hollygrove Cl HSLW TW3 ...25 H9
Holly Hedge Cl FRIM GU16...68 G6
Holly Hedge La COB KT11 ...75 K3
  FRIM GU16 ...68 G6
Holly Ldg
  WOKN/KNAP GU21 * ...71 L6
Hollymead CAR SM5 ...62 B2
Hollymead Rd
  COUL/CHIP CR5 ...80 C7
Holly Ms WBPTN SW10 ...19 N3
Hollymoor La
  HOR/WEW KT19 ...60 B8

Holly Pde COB KT11 ...75 K4
Hollyridge HASM GU27...184 D4
Holly Rd ASHV GU12 ...108 E5
  CHSWK W4 * ...18 B2
  FARN GU14 ...88 D3
  HPTN TW12 ...25 K9
  HSLW TW3 ...16 B9
  REIG RH2 ...119 M7
  TWK TW1 ...25 P4
Holly Spring La BRAK RG12 ..32 F2
Hollytree Cl WIM/MER SW19..28 A4
Holly Tree Gdns FRIM GU16...68 F8
Holly Tree Rd CTHM CR3 ...101 N2
Hollytrees FLEETN GU51 ...86 D9
Holly Vls HMSMTH W6 * ...18 F1
Holly Wy BLKW GU17 ...67 P4
  MTCM CR4 ...44 F5
Hollywood Ms
  WBPTN SW10 * ...19 N4
Hollywood Rd WBPTN SW10..19 N4
Hollywoods CROY/NA CRO ...64 F8
Holman Cl CRAWW RH11 ...194 E2
Holman Ct EW KT17 * ...60 E7
Holman Rd BTSEA SW11 ...19 P7
  HOR/WEW KT19 ...60 A4
Holmbank Dr SHPTN TW17 ..38 G5
Holmbrook Cl FARN GU14 ...87 N3
Holmbury Av CWTH RG45 ...49 L2
Holmbury Cl CRAWW RH11..194 A1
Holmbury Dr RDKG RH5 ...137 J1
Holmbury Gv CROY/NA CRO...64 F6
Holmbury Hl Rd RDKG RH5..135 L8
Holmbury Rd CRAN GU6 ...158 B3
  RDKG RH5 ...154 F3
Holmbush Ct RDKG RH5 * ..193 N1
Holmbush Rd PUT/ROE SW15..28 B2
Holm Cl ADL/WDHM KT15 ...73 J1
Holmcroft CRAWE RH10 ...177 H6
  KWD/TDW/WH KT20 * ...98 D6
Holmdene Av HNHL SE24 ...30 D1
Holmdene Cl BECK BR3 ...47 J3
Holmead Rd FUL/PGN SW6 ..19 M5
Holme Cl CWTH RG45 ...49 L2
Holmes Cl ASC SL5 ...34 C7
  WOKS/MYFD GU22 ...92 D1
Holmesdale Av
  MORT/ESHN SW14 * ...17 P8
Holmesdale Cl GU GU1 ...112 F4
  SNWD SE25 ...45 N4
Holmesdale Pk REDH RH1 * .121 H5
  RCH/KEW TW9 ...17 M6
Holmesdale Rd
  RDKG RH5 ...137 H1
  REDH RH1 ...121 H7
  REIG RH2 ...119 M4
  TEDD TW11 ...26 B4
Holmesdale Ter RDKG RH5 * .137 H2
Holmesley Rd BROCKY SE4 ..31 M2
Holmes Rd TWK TW1 ...25 N5
  WIM/MER SW19 ...43 N1
Holmethorpe Av REDH RH1..120 D2
Holmewood Gdns
  BRXS/STRHM SW2 ...30 A3
Holmewood Rd
  BRXS/STRHM SW2 ...29 P3
  SNWD SE25 ...45 N5
Holming End HORS RH12 ...192 G3
Holmlea Rd DTCH/LGLY SL3 ..12 B6
Holmlea Wk DTCH/LGLY SL3 ..12 B6
Holm Oak Cl PUT/ROE SW15 ..28 C2
Holmshaw Cl SYD SE26 ...31 M7
Holmside Rd BAL SW12 ...29 K2
Holmsley Cl NWMAL KT3 ...42 D7
Holmwood Av SAND/SEL CR2..81 P2
Holmwood Cl
  ADL/WDHM KT15 ...55 L4
  BELMT SM2 ...61 H7
  EHSLY KT24 ...94 C8
Holmwood Gdns WLGTN SM6..62 D5
Holmwood Rd BELMT SM2...60 G7
  CHSGTN KT9 ...59 L4
Holmwood View Rd
  RDKG RH5 ...137 H4
Holne Cha MRDN SM4 ...43 L7
Holroyd Rd ESH/CLAY KT10 ..58 C7
  PUT/ROE SW15 ...18 G9
Holstein Av WEY KT13 ...56 C3
Holsworthy Wy CHSGTN KT9..59 J4
Holt Cl FARN GU14 ...68 E9
Holton Heath BRAK RG12 ...33 H5
Holt Pound La RFNM GU10..126 G8
The Holt MRDN SM4 * ...43 L5
  SUTN SM1 ...61 M5
Holtye Av EGRIN RH19 ...162 F1
Holtye Rd EGRIN RH19 ...163 K9
  EGRIN RH19 ...180 E1
Holtye Wk CRAWE RH10 * ..177 K7
Holwood Cl WOT/HER KT12 ..57 L1
Holybourne Av
  PUT/ROE SW15 ...27 M3
Holyoake Av
  WOKN/KNAP GU21 ...72 A6
Holyoake Crs
  WOKN/KNAP GU21 ...72 A6
Holyport Rd FUL/PGN SW6 ..18 G5
Holyrood Pl CRAWW RH11..176 E9
Holywell Cl FARN GU14 ...68 E3
  STWL/WRAY TW19 ...23 H4
Holywell Wy
  STWL/WRAY TW19 ...23 H4
Hombrook Dr BRAK RG42 ...32 A2
Home Cl CAR SM5 ...62 B1
  CRAWE RH10 ...177 M3
  LHD/OX KT22 ...96 D1
  VW GU25 ...36 B7
Home Ct FELT TW13 * ...24 B4
  SURB KT6 * ...41 K6

Homecroft Rd SYD SE26 ...31 K8
Home Farm Cl
  BRKHM/BTCW RH3 ...118 C6
  CHERT KT16 ...54 E6
  EPSOM KT18 ...79 H6
  ESH/CLAY KT10 ...58 D8
  FSH/CLAY KT10 ...88 F1
  SHPTN TW17 ...38 G5
  THDIT KT7 ...40 F8
Home Farm Gdns
  WOT/HER KT12 ...57 L1
Home Farm Rd GODL GU7...150 E2
  HTWY RG27 ...66 B9
Homefield MFD/CHID GU8 *..148 D9
Homefield Cl
  ADL/WDHM KT15 ...73 J1
  HORL RH6 ...140 D9
  LHD/OX KT22 ...97 J1
Homefield Gdns
  KWD/TDW/WH KT20 ...78 G9
  WIM/MER SW19 ...43 N3
Homefield Ms BECK BR3 ...46 G2
Homefield Rd CHSWK W4 ...18 D2
  COUL/CHIP CR5 ...81 K9
  WARL CR6 ...82 C7
  WIM/MER SW19 ...28 B9
  WOT/HER KT12 ...39 P8
Home Mdw BNSTD SM7 ...79 L5
Home Meadow BNSTD SM7 ..79 L5
Homemead Rd CROY/NA CRO..44 E7
Home Pk OXTED RH8 ...123 N3
Home Park Cl SHGR GU5 ...132 D7
Home Park Ct KUT KT1 * ...41 K5
Home Park Rd
  WIM/MER SW19 ...28 C7
  YTLY GU46 ...66 C2
Home Park Ter KUT KT1 * ...8 B4
Home Park Wk SURB KT6 ...41 K5
Homer Rd CROY/NA CRO ...46 D7
Homersham Rd KUT KT1 ...9 J4
Homershaw Rd CTHM CR3 ..101 M3
Homestall GUW GU2 ...111 K5
Homestall Rd EDUL SE22 ...31 K1
  EGRIN RH19 ...181 K3
Homestead CRAN GU6 ...153 H7
Homestead Gdns
  ESH/CLAY KT10 ...58 E4
Homestead Rd CTHM CR3 ..101 M3
  EDEN TN8 ...124 F9
  FUL/PGN SW6 ...19 K5
  STA TW18 ...22 E9
Homestead Wy
  CROY/NA CRO ...65 J9
Homewaters Av SUN TW16...39 H2
Homewood CRAN GU6 ...153 K9
Homewood Gdns SNWD SE25 *..45 N6
Hone Hl SHST GU47 ...67 M1
Honeybrook Rd BAL SW12 ..29 M3
Honeycrock La REDH RH1...140 C3
Honeyhill Rd BNFD RG42 ...32 C2
Honeypot La LING RH7 ...144 B1
Honeypots Rd
  WOKS/MYFD GU22 ...92 B2
Honeysuckle Bottom
  EHSLY KT24 ...114 G5
Honeysuckle Gdns
  CROY/NA CRO ...46 D8
Honeysuckle La BOR GU35...164 E6
  CRAWW RH11 ...176 F2
Honeysuckle Wk
  HORS RH12 ...192 F5
Honeywell Rd BTSEA SW11...29 H2
Honeywood La RDKG RH5...172 F6
Honeywood Rd ISLW TW7 * ..16 G9
  SWTR RH13 ...192 F6
Honeywood Wk CAR SM5 ...62 B3
Honister Gdns FLEETN GU51 ..87 J5
Honister Hts PUR/KEN CR8 ..81 M3
Honnor Gdns ISLW TW7 ...16 D7
Honnor Rd STA TW18 ...37 P1
Honor Oak Pk FSTH SE23 ...31 L2
Honor Oak Ri FSTH SE23 ...31 K2
Honor Oak Rd FSTH SE23 ...31 K4
Hood Av MORT/ESHN SW14 ..27 H1
Hood Cl CROY/NA CRO ...2 B2
Hood Rd RYNPK SW20 ...42 D1
Hooke Rd EHSLY KT24 ...95 H4
Hookfield HOR/WEW KT19 ...78 A2
Hook Heath Av
  WOKS/MYFD GU22 ...91 M1
Hook Heath Gdns
  WOKS/MYFD GU22 ...91 J2
Hook Heath Rd
  WOKS/MYFD GU22 ...91 M1
Hook Hill La
  WOKS/MYFD GU22 ...91 M1
Hook Hill Pk
  WOKS/MYFD GU22 ...91 M1
Hookhouse Rd
  MFD/CHID GU8 ...169 K5
Hook La CHOB/PIR GU24 ...70 C2
  RGUW GU3 ...130 D5
  SHGR GU5 ...134 C5
Hookley Cl MFD/CHID GU8 ..148 F1
Hookley La MFD/CHID GU8 ..148 F1
Hook Mill La CHOB/PIR GU24..52 D7
Hook Ri North SURB KT6 ...59 N2
Hook Ri South CHSGTN KT9..59 M2
Hook Rd CHSGTN KT9 ...59 K4

HOR/WEW KT19 ...60 A8
Hookstile La FNM GU9 ...5 G6
Hookstone La
  CHOB/PIR GU24 ...52 F9
Hook Underpass
  (Kingston By-Pass)
  SURB KT6 ...59 K2
Hookwood Cnr OXTED RH8...103 P8
Hooley La REDH RH1 ...120 B6
Hope Av BRAK RG12 ...32 G8
Hope Cl BTFD TW8 ...17 L3
  SUT SM1 ...61 N4
Hope Ct CRAWW RH11 * ...194 E1
Hope Fountain CBLY GU15 ...69 H4
Hope Grant's Rd
  ALDT GU11 ...108 C2
Hope La FNM GU9 ...107 M8
Hopeman Cl SHST GU47 ...49 P1
Hopes Cl HEST TW5 ...16 A4
Hope St BTSEA SW11 ...19 P8
  MFD/CHID GU8 ...149 M3
Hope Wy ALDT GU11 ...108 B4
Hopfield WOKN/KNAP GU21 ..71 N6
Hopfield Av BF/WBF KT14 ...74 A1
Hop Gdn FLEETS GU52 ...106 E2
Hophurst Cl CRAWE RH10..179 J3
Hophurst Dr CRAWE RH10..179 J3
Hophurst Hl CRAWE RH10 ..179 L1
Hophurst La CRAWE RH10..179 L3
Hopkins Ct CRAWW RH11 * ..194 E1
Hopper V BRAK RG12 ...32 C7
The Hoppety
  KWD/TDW/WH KT20 ...99 H2
Hoppingwood Av
  NWMAL KT3 ...42 C4
Hopton Gdns NWMAL KT3 ...42 E7
Hopton Pde
  STRHM/NOR SW16 * ...29 N8
Hopton Rd
  STRHM/NOR SW16 ...29 N8
Hopwood Cl TOOT SW17 ...28 F6
Horace Rd KUT KT1 ...9 H5
Horatio Av BNFD RG42 ...32 G2
Horatius Wy CROY/NA CRO ..63 H5
Horder Rd FUL/PGN SW6 ...19 J6
Horewood Rd BRAK RG12 ...32 D7
Horley Lodge La REDH RH1..140 B5
Horley Rd HORL RH6 ...158 D5
  REDH RH1 ...120 B8
Horley Rw HORL RH6 ...140 C9
Hormer Cl SHST GU47 ...49 P8
Hornbeam Cl ADL/WDHM KT15 *..55 N4
  SHST GU47 ...49 N7
  SWTR RH13 ...192 E5
Hornbeam Crs BTFD TW8 ...17 H5
Hornbeam Rd GU GU1 ...112 A2
  REIG RH2 ...119 N8
Hornby Av BRAK RG12 ...32 E8
Hornchurch Cl
  KUTN/CMB KT2 ...26 C8
Horncastle Cl CRAWE RH10..177 N1
  PUT/ROE SW15 ...27 M4
Horndean Cl CRAWE RH10..177 N1
Horndean Rd BRAK RG12 ...33 H7
Homecourt Rd CROY/NA CRO..141 P6
Homer La MTCM CR4 ...43 P3
Horne Rd SHPTN TW17 ...38 B5
Home Wy PUT/ROE SW15 ...18 G7
Homhatch RGUE GU4 ...132 F3
Homhatch Cl RGUE GU4 ...132 F2
Homhatch La RGUE GU4 ...132 E2
Horniman Dr FSTH SE23 ...31 J4
Hominan Gdns FSTH SE23 * .31 J4
Horn Rd FARN GU14 ...88 A2
Hornshill La HORS RH12 ...189 J1
Horsebrass Dr BAGS GU19 ..51 N7
Horsecroft BNSTD SM7 * ...79 L5
Horsecroft Mdw
  BNSTD SM7 * ...79 L5
Horse Fair KUT KT1 ...8 C3
Horse Gate Ride ASC SL5 ...34 A7
Horse Hl HORL RH6 ...139 M9
Horsell Birch
  WOKN/KNAP GU21 ...71 N4
Horsell Common Rd
  WOKN/KNAP GU21 ...72 A3
Horsell Ct CHERT KT16 ...37 M8
Horsell Moor
  WOKN/KNAP GU21 ...10 B3
Horsell Pk WOKN/KNAP GU21..10 C3
Horsell Park Cl
  WOKN/KNAP GU21 ...10 B3
Horsell Ri WOKN/KNAP GU21..10 B2
Horsell Rise Cl
  WOKN/KNAP GU21 ...10 C1
Horsell Wy
  WOKN/KNAP GU21 ...72 A5
Horsemoor Cl DTCH/LGLY SL3..12 A5
Horseshoe Bend GSHT GU26..165 K8
Horseshoe Cl CBLY GU15 ...51 N9
  CRAWE RH10 ...177 N4
Horseshoe Crs CBLY GU15 ...51 N9
Horseshoe La ASHV GU12 ...89 J9
  CRAN GU6 ...152 F8
Horseshoe La West GU GU6..112 F4
Horseshoe Rdg WEY KT13 ..56 E6
The Horseshoe BNSTD SM7 ..79 L5
  COUL/CHIP CR5 ...80 F2
  GODL GU7 ...150 D1
Horsford Rd
  BRXS/STRHM SW2 ...30 A1
Horsham Gates
  HORS RH13 * ...192 D7
Horsham Rd BIL RH14 ...188 G1
  CRAN GU6 ...152 A9
  CRAN GU6 ...153 P9
  CRAN GU6 ...171 J2
  CRAWW RH11 ...194 B4
  CRAWW RH11 ...194 D4
  DORK RH4 ...116 C4

EBED/NFELT TW14 ...23 M1
  HORS RH13 ...174 F7
  HORS RH13 ...176 A9
  RDKG RH5 ...154 D2
  RDKG RH5 ...155 C3
  RDKG RH5 ...156 C5
  RDKG RH5 ...172 E5
  RDKG RH5 ...174 B1
  SHGR GU5 ...132 C5
  SHGR GU5 ...135 H4
  SHGR GU5 ...152 A8
Horshoe La East GU GU1 ...112 F4
Horsley Cl HOR/WEW KT19 ..78 B2
Horsley Dr CROY/NA CRO ...65 J6
  KUTN/CMB KT2 ...26 C8
Horsley Rd BMLY BR1 ...47 P2
  COB KT11 ...75 K8
Horsmonden Rd BROCKY SE4..31 N1
Horsmele La BNFD RG42 ...32 D2
Hortensia Rd WBPTN SW10 ..19 N4
Horticultural Pl CHSWK W4 ..18 B3
Horton Gdns
  DTCH/LGLY SL3 * ...12 B8
  HOR/WEW KT19 ...60 A9
Horton La HOR/WEW KT19 ..59 N9
Horton Pl BH/WHM TN16 ...105 H6
Horton Rd DTCH/LGLY SL3 ..12 A6
  STWL/WRAY TW19 ...13 H9
Hortons Wy BH/WHM TN16 .105 H6
Horton Wy CROY/NA CRO ...46 D6
Horvath Cl WEY KT13 ...56 F3
Hosack Rd BAL SW12 ...29 J5
Hosey Common La
  BH/WHM TN16 ...125 J1
Hosey Common Rd
  BH/WHM TN16 ...105 J9
Hosey Hl BH/WHM TN16 ...105 J7
Hoskins Cl HYS/HAR UB3 ...15 J3
Hoskins Pl EGRIN RH19 ...162 E8
Hoskins Rd OXTED RH8 ...103 L9
Hoskins Wk OXTED RH8 ...103 L9
Hospital Bridge Rd
  WHTN TW2 ...25 J5
Hospital Hl ALDT GU11 ...108 C3
Hospital Rd ALDT GU11 ...108 C3
  HSLW TW3 ...16 A8
Hostel Rd FARN GU14 ...88 D7
Hotham Cl E/WMO/HCT KT8 ..40 A4
Hotham Rd PUT/ROE SW15 ..18 G8
  WIM/MER SW19 ...43 N1
Houblon Rd
  RCHPK/HAM TW10 ...26 D1
Houghton Cl HPTN TW12 ...24 F9
Houghton Rd
  CRAWE RH10 * ...177 M3
Houlder Crs CROY/NA CRO ..63 K5
Houlton Ct BAGS GU19 ...51 N7
Hound House Rd SHGR GU5..134 C3
Houndown La
  MFD/CHID GU8 ...148 B7
Hounslow Av HSLW TW3 ...25 J1
Hounslow Gdns HSLW TW3 ..25 J1
Hounslow Rd
  EBED/NFELT TW14 ...24 C3
  FELT TW13 ...24 G5
  HSLW TW3 ...25 J2
Houseman Rd FARN GU14 ...88 B1
Houston Rd FSTH SE23 ...31 M5
  SURB KT6 ...41 H7
Hove Gdns SUT SM1 ...43 N9
Howard Av EW KT17 ...60 E8
Howard Cl ASHTD KT21 ...77 M7
  EHSLY KT24 ...94 B5
  FLEETN GU51 ...87 J6
  HPTN TW12 ...40 C1
  KWD/TDW/WH KT20 ...98 D5
  LHD/OX KT22 ...97 J3
  SUN TW16 ...24 A8
Howard Cole Wy ALDT GU11..108 A4
Howard Dr FARN GU14 ...87 M3
Howard Gdns GU GU1 ...112 E4
Howard Pl REIG RH2 ...119 L3
Howard Rdg RGUE GU4 ...112 E1
Howard Rd ASHTD KT21 ...77 M7
  BMLY BR1 ...47 N1
  COUL/CHIP CR5 ...80 E5
  CRAWW RH11 ...176 A9
  DORK RH4 ...116 C7
  EHSLY KT24 ...95 J2
  GT/LBKH KT23 ...96 B7
  ISLW TW7 ...16 F8
  NWMAL KT3 ...42 C2
  PGE/AN SE20 ...46 C2
  RDKG RH5 * ...137 J2
  REIG RH2 ...119 M6
  SNWD SE25 ...46 A6
  SWTR RH13 ...192 F6
Howards Cl
  WOKS/MYFD GU22 ...72 D9
Howard St THDIT KT7 ...41 H8
Howberry Rd THHTH CR7 ...45 N2
Howden Rd SNWD SE25 ...45 P3
Howe Dr CTHM CR3 ...101 M2
Howell Hl BELMT SM2 * ...60 G8
Howell Hill Cl EW KT17 ...60 G9
Howell Hill Gv EW KT17 ...60 G8
Howes Gdns FLEETN GU51 ..86 E9
Howgate Rd
  MORT/ESHN SW14 ...18 B2
How Green La EDEN TN8 ...145 N4
Howitts Cl ESH/CLAY KT10 ..58 A5
How La COUL/CHIP CR5 ...80 C7
Howley Rd CROY/NA CRO ...2 B5

Howsman Rd BARN SW13 ...18 E4
Howson Ter
  RCHPK/HAM TW10 * ...26 D2
Hoylake Cl CRAWW RH11 ...176 A6
Hoylake Gdns MTCM CR4 ...44 E4
Hoyle Hi RDKG RH5 ...156 C3
Hoyle Rd TOOT SW17 ...29 H8
Hubbard Dr CHSGTN KT9 ...59 J5
Hubbard Rd WNWD SE27 ...30 D1
Hubberholme BRAK RG12 ...32 C4
Hubert Rd DTCH/LGLY SL3 ...12 B1
Huddington Gld HTWY RG27 ...66 E3
Huddleston Crs REDH RH1 ...100 F8
Hudson Cl LIPH GU30 ...182 F7
Hudson Rd GUW GU2 ...111 M5
Hudson Rd CRAWE RH10 ...177 H7
  HYS/HAR UB3 ...14 F4
Hugh Dalton Av
  FUL/PGN SW6 * ...19 K4
Hughenden Rd WPK KT4 ...42 E8
Hughes Rd ASHF TW15 ...23 M6
Hughes Wk CROY/NA CR0 ...45 L8
Hugh Gaitskell Cl
  FUL/PGN SW6 * ...19 K4
Hugon Rd FUL/PGN SW6 ...19 M8
Huguenot Pl
  WAND/EARL SW18 ...28 F1
Hullbrook La SHGR GU5 ...133 H9
Hullmead SHGR GU5 ...133 J9
Hulton Cl LHD/OX KT22 ...97 J3
Hulverston Cl BELMT SM2 ...61 M8
Humber Dr DTCH/LGLY SL3 ...12 L2
  SHST GU47 ...49 P9
Humbolt Cl GUW GU2 ...111 L5
Humbolt Rd HMSMTH W6 ...19 J4
Hummer La ASHV GU12 ...16 F1
Hummer Rd EGH TW20 ...21 M7
Humphrey Cl LHD/OX KT22 ...96 F1
Hungerford Cl SHST GU47 ...49 N9
Hungry Hill La
  RPLY/SEND GU23 ...93 N6
Hunnels Cl FLEETS GU52 ...106 E3
Hunstanton Cl
  CRAWW RH11 ...176 A6
  DTCH/LGLY SL3 ...12 C5
Hunston Rd MRDN SM4 ...43 M9
Hunter Cl BAL SW12 ...29 K4
Hunter Rd CRAWE RH10 ...176 D8
  FARN GU14 ...88 B4
  GU GU1 ...7 K7
  RYNPK SW20 ...42 G2
  THHTH CR7 ...45 M4
Hunters Cha GDST RH9 ...122 F8
  LIPH GU30 ...182 F7
Hunters Cl ESH/CLAY KT10 ...58 A3
Hunters Ct RCH/KEW TW9 ...26 C1
Hunters Cft HOR/WEW KT19 ...78 A2
Hunters Cl REIG RH2 ...119 N2
Hunters Meadow
  NRWD SE19 ...30 F7
Hunters Wy CHSGTN KT9 ...59 L2
Hunters Wy CROY/NA CR0 ...3 J7
Hunting Cl ESH/CLAY KT10 ...58 A3
Huntingdon Cl MTCM CR4 ...44 G5
Huntingdon Gdns
  CHSWK W4 ...18 A5
  WPK KT4 ...60 G2
Huntingdon House Dr
  GSHT GU26 ...165 P7
Huntingdon Rd REDH RH1 ...120 B5
  WOKN/KNAP GU21 ...71 L6
Huntingfield CROY/NA CR0 ...64 F6
Huntingfield Rd
  PUT/ROE SW15 ...18 E3
Huntingfield Wy EGH TW20 ...37 H1
Huntingford Cl GSHT GU26 *.165 M4
Hunting Gate Ms
  WHTN TW2 ...25 M4
Huntington Pl
  DTCH/LGLY SL3 ...12 F1
Huntley Wy RYNPK SW20 * ...42 E3
Huntly Rd SNWD SE25 ...45 N5
Hunt Rd NWDGN UB2 ...16 A1
Hunts Cl GUW GU2 ...111 K4
Huntsgreen Ct BRAK RG12 ...32 C4
Hunts Hill Rd RGUW GU3 ...110 A1
Huntsman Cl FELT TW13 ...24 C7
Huntsmans Cl WARL CR6 ...82 C8
Huntsmans Meadow ASC SL5 ...33 P2
Huntsman's Ms FRIM GU16 ...89 H3
Huntsmoor Rd
  HOR/WEW KT19 ...60 B4
Huntspill St TOOT SW17 ...28 F6
Hunts Slip Rd DUL SE21 ...30 F6
Hurland La BOR GU35 ...164 C7
Hurlands Cl FNM GU9 ...128 E3
Hurlands La MFD/CHID GU8 .187 L1
Hurlands Pl FNM GU9 ...128 E3
Hurley Cl WOT/HER KT12 ...57 K1
Hurley Gdns RGUE GU4 ...112 E2
Hurlford WOKN/KNAP GU21 ...71 N6
Hurlingham Gdns
  FUL/PGN SW6 ...19 K8
Hurlingham Pk
  FUL/PGN SW6 * ...19 K7
Hurlingham Rd
  FUL/PGN SW6 ...19 K7
Hurlingham Sq
  FUL/PGN SW6 * ...19 L8
Hurlstone Rd SNWD SE25 ...45 M6
Hurn Court Rd HEST TW5 ...15 M7
Hurnford Cl SAND/SEL CR2 ...63 N8
Huron Dr LIPH GU30 ...182 C7
Huron Rd TOOT SW17 ...29 K5
Hurricane Rd WLGTN SM6 ...63 H6
Hurricane Wy FARN GU14 ...88 B8
Hurst Av HORS RH12 ...192 C7
Hurstbourne FSTH SE23 ...31 M4
Hurst Cl BRAK RG12 * ...32 C6

CHSGTN KT9 ...59 N4
CRAWW RH11 ...176 C7
EPSOM KT18 ...98 A4
HAYES BR2 ...47 N6
LIPH GU30 ...182 D5
WOKS/MYFD GU22 ...72 A9
Hurst Dr KWD/TDW/WH KT20 ...
Hurstcourt Rd SUT SM1 ...43 M9
Hurst Cft GU GU1 ...112 C8
Hurstdene Av HAYES BR2 ...47 M9
  STA TW18 ...22 E9
Hurst Dr KWD/TDW/WH KT20 .98 E6
Hurst Farm Cl EGRIN RH19 ...180 D8
Hurst Farm Rd EGRIN RH19 .180 C3
Hurstfield HAYES BR2 ...47 N6
Hurstfield Rd
  E/WMO/HCT KT8 ...40 A4
Hurst Green Cl OXTED RH8 .123 N3
Hurst Green Rd OXTED RH8 .123 N3
Hurst La E/WMO/HCT KT8 ...40 C5
  EGH TW20 ...36 D4
  EPSOM KT18 ...98 E8
Hurstleigh Cl REDH RH1 ...120 B3
Hurstleigh Dr REDH RH1 ...120 B3
Hurstmere Cl GSHT GU26 ...165 N6
Hurst Rd ALDT GU11 ...108 E3
  CROY/NA CR0 ...63 M4
  E/WMO/HCT KT8 ...40 C4
  EPSOM KT18 ...78 B8
  FARN GU14 ...68 D8
  HOR/WEW KT19 ...60 B9
  HORL RH6 ...140 A9
  HORS RH12 ...192 C7
  WOT/HER KT12 ...39 M5
Hurst St HNHL SE24 ...30 P2
Hurst View Rd SAND/SEL CR2 .63 N6
Hurst Wy SAND/SEL CR2 ...63 N5
  WOKS/MYFD GU22 ...73 J3
Hurstwood ASC SL5 ...34 A7
Hurtmore Cha GODL GU7 ...131 H5
Hurtmore Rd GODL GU7 ...130 C5
  MFD/CHID GU8 ...130 D7
Hurtwood Rd WOT/HER KT12 .39 P8
Hurworth Av DTCH/LGLY SL3 .12 A1
Huson Rd BNFD RG42 ...32 E1
Hussar Ct ALDT GU11 ...108 A4
Hussars Cl HSLWW TW4 ...15 M8
Husseywell Crs HAYES BR2 ...47 N9
Hutchingson's La
  CROY/NA CR0 ...65 J3
Hutchins Wy HORL RH6 ...140 B8
Hutton Cl BFOR GU20 ...52 D6
Hutton Rd ASHV GU12 ...89 J9
Huxbear St BROCKY SE4 ...31 N1
Huxley Cl GODL GU7 ...131 K6
Huxley Rd GUW GU2 ...111 K6
Hyacinth Cl HPTN TW12 ...25 H9
Hyacinth Rd PUT/ROE SW15 .27 M4
Hyde Dr CRAWW RH11 ...176 B6
Hyde Farm Ms BAL SW12 ...29 N4
Hyde La RFNM GU10 ...106 B7
  RFNM GU10 ...165 N2
Hyde Park Ga SKENS SW7 * .19 P3
Hyde Rd RCHPK/HAM TW10 .26 E1
  SAND/SEL CR2 ...81 N7
Hyde Ter SUN TW16 ...23 P9
Hydethorpe Rd BAL SW12 ...29 M4
Hyde Wk MRDN SM4 ...43 L8
Hyde Wy HYS/HAR UB3 ...15 H2
Hylands Cl CRAWE RH10 ...177 K6
Hylands Ms EPSOM KT18 ...78 A4
Hylands Rd EPSOM KT18 ...78 A4
Hyndewood FSTH SE23 ...31 L6
Hyndman Cl CRAWW RH11 ...194 E2
Hyperion Ct CRAWW RH11 .176 B7
Hyperion Pl HOR/WEW KT19 .60 B7
Hythe Cl BRAK RG12 ...32 C6
Hythe End Rd
  STWL/WRAY TW19 ...21 M5
Hythe Field Av EGH TW20 ...22 A9
Hythe Park Rd EGH TW20 ...21 P8
Hythe Rd STA TW18 ...22 A8
  THHTH CR7 ...45 M3
The Hythe STA TW18 ...22 B8

I

Iberian Av WLGTN SM6 ...62 F3
Iberian Wy CBLY GU15 ...69 J2
Ibis La CHSWK W4 ...18 A6
Ibsley Gdns PUT/ROE SW15 ...27 M4
Icehouse Wd OXTED RH8 ...123 M2
Icklingham Rd COB KT11 ...75 L1
Iden Cl HAYES BR2 ...47 L4
Idlecombe Rd TOOT SW17 ...29 K9
Idmiston Rd WNWD SE27 ...30 D6
  WPK KT4 ...42 D8
Idmiston Sq WPK KT4 ...42 D8
Iffley Rd HMSMTH W6 ...18 F1
Ifield Av CRAWW RH11 ...176 C1
Ifield Cl REDH RH1 ...120 A8
Ifield Dr CRAWW RH11 ...176 B5
Ifield Pk CRAWW RH11 *...176 C5
Ifield Rd CRAWW RH11 ...176 E4
  HORL RH6 ...158 B7
  WBPTN SW10 ...19 M4
Ifield St CRAWW RH11 ...176 A1
Ifield Wd CRAWW RH11 ...176 A2
Ifold Bridge La BIL RH14 ...187 P6
Ifoldhurst BIL RH14 ...187 P8
Ifold Rd REDH RH1 ...120 C7

Ikona Ct WEY KT13 * ...56 E4
Ilchester Pl WKENS W14 ...19 K1
Ildersly Gv DUL SE21 ...30 D3
Ilex Cl EGH TW20 ...35 P1
  SUN TW16 ...39 L3
  YTLY GU46 ...66 F7
Ilex Wy STRHM/NOR SW16 ...30 B8
Ilkley Cl NRWD SE19 * ...30 E9
Illingworth Cl MTCM CR4 ...43 P4
Illingworth Gv BRAK RG12 ...33 H2
Imber Cross THDIT KT7 * ...40 F8
Imber Gv ESH/CLAY KT10 ...40 D8
Imberhorne La EGRIN RH19 .179 P4
Imberhorne Wy EGRIN RH19.162 A9
Imber Park Rd
  ESH/CLAY KT10 ...40 D9
Imjin Cl ALDT GU11 ...108 D3
Imperial College Rd
  SKENS SW7 ...19 P3
Imperial Gdns MTCM CR4 ...44 D4
Imperial Pk LHD/OX KT22 * ...76 G9
Imperial Rd
  EBED/NFELT TW14 ...23 P3
  FUL/PGN SW6 ...19 M6
Imperial Sq FUL/PGN SW6 ...19 M6
Imperial Wy CROY/NA CR0 ...63 J5
Imran Ct ASHV GU12 ...108 C1
Ince Rd WOT/HER KT12 ...56 G4
Inchmead BRAK RG12 ...32 E9
  CROY/NA CR0 ...65 H3
Ingatestone Rd SNWD SE25 .46 B7
Ingham Cl SAND/SEL CR2 ...64 D7
Ingham Rd SAND/SEL CR2 ...64 C7
Ingleboro Dr PUR/KEN CR8 ...81 M2
Ingleby Wy WLGTN SM6 ...62 F7
Ingle Dell CBLY GU15 ...68 G5
Ingle Gln EWKG RG40 ...48 E2
Inglehurst ADL/WDHM KT15 .55 M8
Inglemere Rd FSTH SE23 ...31 L6
  MTCM CR4 ...29 N8
Ingleside DTCH/LGLY SL3 ...13 P8
Ingleside Cl BECK BR3 ...46 G1
Inglethorpe St FUL/PGN SW6 .19 H6
Ingleton BRAK RG12 ...32 C4
Ingleton Rd CAR SM5 ...62 A7
Inglewood CHERT KT16 ...55 K2
  CROY/NA CR0 ...64 E7
  WOKN/KNAP GU21 ...71 P7
Inglewood Av CBLY GU15 ...69 L4
Inglis Rd CROY/NA CR0...3 K1
Ingram Cl HORS RH12 ...191 K8
Ingram Rd THHTH CR7 ...45 L2
Ingrams Cl WOT/HER KT12 ...57 L4
Ingrave St BTSEA SW11 ...19 P8
Ingress St CHSWK W4 ...18 C2
Inholms La RDKG RH5 ...137 J2
Inkerman Pde
  WOKN/KNAP GU21 ...71 L7
Inkerman Rd
  WOKN/KNAP GU21 ...71 L7
Inkerman Wy
  WOKN/KNAP GU21 ...71 L7
Inman Rd WAND/EARL SW18.28 F3
Inner Park Rd
  WIM/MER SW19 ...28 A5
Inner Ring East HTHAIR TW6 .14 D8
Innes Cl RYNPK SW20 ...43 J3
Innes Gdns PUT/ROE SW15 .27 N2
Innes Rd HORS RH12 ...192 E6
Innes Yd CROY/NA CR0 ...2 D6
Innings La BNFD RG42 ...32 F1
Institute Rd ASHV GU12 ...109 C8
  DORK RH4 ...116 C8
Instow Gdns FARN GU14 ...68 D8
International Av HEST TW5 ...15 J3
Inval Hi HASM GU27 ...184 D2
Inveresk Gdns WPK KT4 ...60 D2
Inverness Rd HSLW TW3 ...15 P9
  NWDGN UB2 ...15 P2
  WPK KT4 ...43 H9
Inverness Wy SHST GU47 ...67 P1
Invicta Cl EBED/NFELT TW14..24 A4
Invincible Rd FARN GU14 ...88 C5
Inwood Av COUL/CHIP CR5 ...81 J9
  HSLW TW3 ...16 C8
Inwood Cl CROY/NA CR0 ...64 E9
Inwood Rd HSLW TW3 ...16 C9
Iona Cl CAT SE6 ...31 P3
  CRAWW RH11 ...176 E8
  MRDN SM4 ...43 M8
Ipswich Rd TOOT SW17 ...29 K9
Irene Rd COB KT11 ...76 B3
  ORP BR6 ...19 L6
Ireton Av WEY KT13 ...57 H1
Iris Cl CROY/NA CR0 ...46 D9
  SURB KT6 * ...41 M8
Iris Rd CHOB/PIR GU24 ...70 G4
  HOR/WEW KT19 ...59 P4
Iron La SHGR GU5 ...132 G9
Iron Mill La
  WAND/EARL SW18 * ...28 E2
Iron Mill Rd
  WAND/EARL SW18 ...28 E2
Ironsbottom REIG RH2...159 K6
Irvine Dr FARN GU14 ...68 A1
Irvine Pl VW GU25 ...36 C5
Irving Rd WKENS W14 ...19 H1
Irving Wk CRAWE RH10 ...177 H8
Irwin Dr HORS RH12 ...191 P8
Irwin Rd GUW GU2 ...111 N6
Isabella Ct RCHPK/HAM TW10.26 E7
Isbells Dr REIG RH2...119 M7
Isham Rd STRHM/NOR SW16.44 F3
Isis Cl CRAWW RH11 ...176 G6
Isis St WAND/EARL SW18 ...28 F5
Isis Wy SHST GU47 ...49 P9
Island Cl STA TW18 ...22 A7
Island Farm Av
  E/WMO/HCT KT8 ...39 P6
Island Farm Rd
  E/WMO/HCT KT8 ...39 P6
Island Rd MTCM CR4 ...44 B1

Islay Gdns HSLWW TW4 ...24 E1
Itchel La RFNM GU10 ...106 B7
Itchingwood Common Rd
  OXTED RH8 ...124 A4
Ivanhoe Cl CRAWW RH11 ...194 E1
Ivanhoe Rd HSLWW TW4 ...15 M8
Ivatt Pl WKENS W14 ...19 K3
Iveagh Cl CRAWW RH11 ...194 E1
Iveagh Rd GUW GU2 ...6 A5
Ively Rd FARN GU14 ...88 A6
Iverna Ct KENS W8 ...19 L1
Iverna Gdns
  EBED/NFELT TW14 ...23 N1
  KENS W8 ...19 L1
Ivers Wy CROY/NA CR0 ...65 H6
Ives Cl YTLY GU46 ...66 F1
Ivor Cl GU GU1 ...7 K4
Ivory Ct FELT TW13 ...24 B5
Ivory Wk CRAWW RH11 ...176 B8
Ivybank GODL GU7 ...131 L7
Ivybridge Cl TWK TW1 ...25 P2
Ivychurch Cl PGE/AN SE20 ...46 B1
Ivy Cl SUN TW16 ...39 L3
Ivy Crs CHSWK W4 ...18 A2
Ivydale Rd CAR SM5 ...62 B1
Ivydene Gv STRHM/NOR SW16.30 A6
Ivydene Cl REDH RH1 ...140 D1
  SUT SM1 ...61 N3
Ivy Dene La EGRIN RH19 ...181 J5
Ivy Dr LTWR GU18 ...52 B3
Ivy Gdns MTCM CR4 ...44 F4
Ivyhole Hi HTWY RG27 ...66 C5
Ivy La FNM GU9 ...5 J9
  HSLWW TW4 ...15 P9
  WOKS/MYFD GU22 ...11 J5
Ivy Mill Cl GDST RH9 ...122 B3
Ivy Mill La REDH RH1 ...122 A3
Ivymount Rd WNWD SE27 ...30 B6
Ivy Rd ASHV GU12 ...108 G4
  HSLW TW3 ...16 B9
  SURB KT6 * ...59 N1
  TOOT SW17 ...29 H8

J

Jacaranda Cl NWMAL KT3 ...42 C4
Jackass La GDST RH9 ...122 F2
  HAYES BR2 ...47 N9
Jackdaw Cl CRAWW RH11 ...176 F3
Jackdaw La HORS RH12 ...192 D5
Jack Good Child Wy KUT KT1.9 K6
Jackman's La
  WOKN/KNAP GU21 ...71 N8
Jackson Cl BRAK RG12 ...32 D6
  EPSOM KT18 ...78 B3
Jackson Crs CRAWW RH11 .194 E2
Jackson's Pl CROY/NA CR0...3 J3
Jacobean Cl CRAWE RH10 .177 M6
Jacob Rd CBLY GU15 ...68 C1
Jacobs Well Rd RGUE GU4 ...92 E9
Jaggard Wy BAL SW12 ...29 J3
Jaguar Rd FARN GU14 ...88 D5
Jail La BH/WHM TW16 ...84 B4
Jamaica Rd THHTH CR7 ...45 K7
James Rd ALDT GU11 ...88 F8
  CBLY GU15 ...68 D6
  RGUW GU3 ...132 A4
James St HSLW TW3 ...16 C8
Jameston BRAK RG12 ...32 E9
Janeway Hill La
  WOKN/KNAP GU21 ...72 A8
Japonica Cl
  WOKN/KNAP GU21 ...72 A7
Jarrett Cl BRXS/STRHM SW2 .30 C4
Jarrow Cl MRDN SM4 ...43 M6
Jarvis Cl HTWY RG27 ...66 B2
Jarvis Rd SAND/SEL CR2 ...63 M5
Jasmine Cl REDH RH1 ...140 C1
  WOKN/KNAP GU21 ...71 M5
Jasmine Ct HORS RH12 ...192 B8
Jasmine Gdns CROY/NA CR0.65 H2
Jasmine Gv PGE/AN SE20 ...46 B2
Jasmine Rd HOR/WEW KT19 .59 P5
Jasmin Rd HOR/WEW KT19 ...59 P5
Jason Cl REDH RH1 ...140 A1
  WEY KT13 ...56 E4
Jasons Dr RGUE GU4 ...112 G2
Jasper Rd NRWD SE19 ...30 G9
Jay Av ADL/WDHM KT15 * ...56 A2
Jay's La HASM GU27 ...185 J7
Jay Wk CRAWE RH10 * ...179 K6
Jean Batten Cl CROY/NA CR0.63 H6
Jebb Av BRXS/STRHM SW2 ...29 P1
Jefferson Cl DTCH/LGLY SL3 .12 E2
Jeffreys Pas GU GU1 ...7 H1
Jeffries Rd EHSLY KT24 ...114 D2
Jeffs Cl HPTN TW12 * ...25 J1
Jeffs Rd SUT SM1 ...61 K3
Jelf Rd BRXS/STRHM SW2 ...30 B1
Jengar Cl SUT SM1 ...61 M3
Jenkins' Hill London Rd
  BAGS GU19 ...51 L8
Jenner Dr CHOB/PIR GU24 ...70 G2
Jenner Rd CRAWE RH10 ...159 K9
  GU GU1 ...7 G5

Jenners Cl LING RH7 ...143 K9
Jennett Rd CROY/NA CR0 ...63 J2
Jennings Cl ADL/WDHM KT15.55 N7
  SURB KT6 ...41 J8
Jennings Rd EDUL SE22 ...30 C2
Jennings Wy HORL RH6 ...159 N3
Jenny La LING RH7 ...143 J9
Jenny's Wk YTLY GU46 ...67 J2
Jenny Wy COUL/CHIP CR5 ...100 E2
Jenson Wy NRWD SE19 ...45 P1
Jephtha Rd
  WAND/EARL SW18 ...28 D2
Jeppo's La MTCM CR4 ...44 B5
Jerdan Pl FUL/PGN SW6 ...19 L5
Jerome Cnr CWTH RG45 ...49 N6
Jerrymoor Hi EWKG RG40 ...48 C3
Jersey Brow Rd FARN GU14 ...88 C5
Jersey Cl CHERT KT16 ...55 K2
  FLEETN GU51 ...87 H3
  RGUE GU4 ...92 F9
Jersey Rd CRAWW RH11 ...176 D9
  HEST TW5 ...16 B6
  TOOT SW17 ...44 D1
Jerviston Gdns
  STRHM/NOR SW16 ...30 B9
Jesmond Cl MTCM CR4 ...44 D4
Jesmond Rd CROY/NA CR0 ...45 P8
Jessamy Rd WEY KT13 ...56 C1
Jesse Cl BLKW GU17 ...67 K3
Jesses La SHGR GU5 ...134 E5
Jessett Dr FLEETS GU52 ...106 F2
Jessica Rd WAND/EARL SW18 .28 F2
Jessiman Ter SHPTN TW17 ...38 C6
Jessop Av NWDGN UB2 ...15 P2
Jessops Wy MTCM CR4 ...44 E1
Jevington BRAK RG12 ...32 E8
Jewels Hi WARL CR6 ...83 N1
Jews Rw WAND/EARL SW18 ...19 M9
Jews Wk SYD SE26 ...31 J7
Jeypore Rd
  WAND/EARL SW18 ...28 F3
Jig's La South BNFD RG42 ...32 G2
Jillian Cl HPTN TW12 ...40 A1
Jobson's La HASM GU27 ...185 M8
Jocelyn Rd RCH/KEW TW9 ...17 L8
Jockey Md BRAK RG12 ...191 P9
Jock's La BNFD RG42 ...32 A2
Jodrell Cl ISLW TW7 ...16 G6
John Archer Wy
  WAND/EARL SW18 ...28 G2
John Ashby Cl
  BRXS/STRHM SW2 ...29 P2
John Austin Cl KUTN/CMB KT2.9 K4
John Cl ALDT GU11 ...108 A6
John Cobb Rd WEY KT13 ...56 C6
John Parker Sq
  BTSEA SW11 * ...19 P8
John Russell Cl GUW GU2 ...111 N2
John Smith Av FUL/PGN SW6 .19 K5
Johnsdale OXTED RH8 ...103 M9
Johns La MRDN SM4 ...43 N6
Johnson Rd CROY/NA CR0 ...45 M8
  HEST TW5 ...15 L5
Johnson's Cl CAR SM5 ...62 B2
Johnsons Dr HPTN TW12 ...40 C2
Johnsons Wy St NWDGN UB2 .15 L1
Johnson Wk CRAWE RH10 ...176 G8
Johnson Wy FLEETS GU52 ...86 F9
John's Ter CROY/NA CR0 ...3 G2
Johnston Wk GUW GU2 ...111 N1
John St HSLW TW3 ...15 N7
  SNWD SE25 ...46 A5
Johns Wk CTHM CR3 ...82 A8
John Wiskar Dr CRAN GU6...170 C1
Joinville Pl ADL/WDHM KT15.55 P3
Jolesfield CRAWW RH11 ...176 C8
Jolive Ct GU GU1 * ...112 E6
Jolliffe Rd REDH RH1 ...100 E6
Jones Cnr ASC SL5 ...33 N2
Jonson Cl MTCM CR4 ...44 E4
Jordan Cl SAND/SEL CR2 ...64 B8
Jordans Cl CRAWW RH11 ...176 G3
  GU GU1 ...112 E4
  REDH RH1 ...140 C1
  STWL/WRAY TW19 ...22 F3
Jordans Crs CRAWW RH11 ...176 G2
Jordans Ms WHTN TW2 ...25 M5
The Jordans EGRIN RH19 ...180 D3
Josephine Av
  BRXS/STRHM SW2 ...30 A1
  KWD/TDW/WH KT20 ...99 K7
Josephine Cl
  KWD/TDW/WH KT20 ...99 K7
Joseph Locke Wy
  ESH/CLAY KT10 ...58 A1
Joseph Powell Cl BAL SW12 ...29 M2
Joseph's Rd GU GU1 ...112 B4
Joshua Cl SAND/SEL CR2 ...63 K6
Jubilee Av ASC SL5 ...33 N2
  FARN GU14 ...87 N3
  KUT KT1 ...41 J8
  STWL/WRAY TW19 ...22 F3
Jubilee Cl ADL/WDHM KT15...55 J9
  GU GU1 ...
Jubilee Crs ADL/WDHM KT15.55 P4
Jubilee Dr ASHV GU12 ...89 J9
Jubilee Est HORS RH12 ...192 B6
Jubilee Hall Rd FARN GU14 ...88 E4
Jubilee La FNM GU9 ...128 C6
  RFNM GU10 ...127 L8
Jubilee Rd ALDT GU11 ...108 C7
  CHEAM SM3 ...61 H4
  EWKG RG40 ...48 D4
  FARN GU14 ...88 E4
  HORS RH12 ...189 N2
Jubilee Ter
  BRKHM/BTCW RH3 ...118 A9
  DORK RH4 ...117 H6
  FUL/PGN SW6 * ...19 J7

Jubilee Vls ESH/CLAY KT10 * 40 E9
Jubilee Wk CRAWE RH10 ....177 K5
Jubilee Wy CHSGTN KT9 ....59 P2
EBED/NFELT TW14 ....24 B4
WIM/MER SW19 ....43 M2
Judge's Ter EGRIN RH19 ....180 D3
Judge Wk ESH/CLAY KT10 ....58 E5
Julian Cl WOKN/KNAP GU21 ....72 A7
Julian Hl WEY KT13 ....56 C6
Julian Tayler Pth FSTH SE23 * 31 J5
Julien Rd COUL/CHIP CR5 ....80 E4
EA W5 ....17 J1
Juliet Gdns BNFD RG42 ....33 H1
Julius Hl BNFD RG42 ....33 H2
Jumps Rd RFNM GU10 ....147 J9
Junction Rd ASHF TW15 ....23 M8
DORK RH4 ....116 G7
EA W5 ....17 J2
LTWR GU18 ....52 B8
SAND/SEL CR2 ....63 M5
June Cl COUL/CHIP CR5 ....80 D3
June La REDH RH1 ....140 D3
Junewood Cl
ADL/WDHM KT15 ....55 K9
Juniper Cl BRAK RG12 ....32 E9
Juniper Ct BH/WHM TN16 ....84 C6
CHSGTN KT9 ....59 M4
GU 91 P9
REIG RH2 ....119 N7
Juniper Dr CHOB/PIR GU24 ....70 G4
Juniper Gdns MTCM CR4 ....44 E2
SUN TW16 ....24 A9
Juniper Rd CRAWW RH11 ....176 F2
FARN GU14 ....88 B1
REIG RH2 ....119 N7
Jura Cl CRAWW RH11 ....176 G6
Justin Cl BTFD TW8 ....17 K5
Jutland Pl EGH TW20 ....21 P8
Juxon Cl CRAWW RH11 ....176 C7

K

Kambala Rd BTSEA SW11 ....19 P7
Kangley Bridge Rd SYD SE26 ..31 N8
Karen Ct BMLY BR1 ....47 M2
Kashmir Cl ADL/WDHM KT15 ...55 P7
Katharine St CROY/NA CRO 2 D5
Katherine Cl
ADL/WDHM KT15 ....55 L5
Katherine Rd EDEN TN8 ....144 G5
Kay Av ADL/WDHM KT15 ....56 A2
Kay Crs BOR GU35 ....164 E5
Kaye Don Wy WEY KT13 ....56 C8
Kayemoor Rd BELMT SM2 ....62 A6
Kaynes Pk ASC SL5 ....33 K4
Kaywood Cl DTCH/LGLY SL3 ...12 A1
Keable Rd RFNM GU10 ....127 K6
Kearton Cl PUR/KEN CR8 ....81 L6
Keates Gn BNFD RG42 ....32 D2
Keats Av REDH RH1 ....120 C5
Keats Cl HORS RH12 ....192 D3
WIM/MER SW19 ....28 C9
Keats Pl EGRIN RH19 ....180 C2
Keats Wy CROY/NA CRO 46 C7
CWTH RG45 ....49 M2
WDR/YW UB7 ....14 B2
YTLY GU46 ....66 F4
Keble Cl CRAWE RH10 ....177 N2
WPK KT4 ....42 D2
Keble Pl BARN SW13 ....18 F4
Keble St TOOT SW17 ....28 F7
Keble Wy SHST GU47 ....50 A7
Kechill Gdns HAYES BR2 ....47 N8
Keeley Rd CROY/NA CRO 2 C3
Keens Cl STRHM/NOR SW16 ...29 N8
Keens Park Rd RGUW GU3 .....111 M1
Keen's Rd CROY/NA CRO 2 D7
Keepers Cl RGUE GU4 ....113 H2
Keepers Combe BRAK RG12 ...32 F7
Keepers Ms TEDD TW11 ....26 B9
Keepers Wk VW GU25 ....36 B6
The Keep KUTN/CMB KT2 ....26 E9
Keevil Dr WIM/MER SW19 ....27 N5
Keith Lucas Rd FARN GU14 .....88 B5
Keith Park Crs
BH/WHM TN16 ....84 A1
Keith Rd HYS/HAR UB3 ....14 C1
Keldholme BRAK RG12 ....32 C4
Kelling Gdns CROY/NA CRO 45 K7
Kellino St TOOT SW17 ....29 J7
Kelly Cl SHPTN TW17 ....38 G3
Kelmscott Gdns SHB W12 ......18 E1
Kelmscott Ri CRAWW RH11 ...194 E2
Kelmscott Rd BTSEA SW11 ....29 J1
Kelsey Av EWKG RG40 ....48 C5
Kelsey Cl HORL RH6 ....159 J1
Kelsey Gv YTLY GU46 ....67 J3
Kelsey La BECK BR3 ....46 G4
Kelsey Park Av BECK BR3 ....47 H4
Kelsey Park Rd BECK BR3 ....46 G3
Kelsey Sq BECK BR3 ....46 G3
Kelsey Wy BECK BR3 ....46 G4
Kelso Cl CRAWE RH10 ....177 N5
Kelso Pl KENS W8 ....19 M1
Kelso Rd CAR SM5 ....43 N8
Kelton Vls KUT KT1 * 9 G5
Kelvedon Av WOT/HER KT12 ...56 G6
Kelvedon Cl KUTN/CMB KT2 ...26 F9
Kelvedon Rd FUL/PGN SW6 ...19 K5
Kelvin Av LHD/OX KT22 ....76 F9
Kelvinbrook
E/WMO/HCT KT8 ....40 B4
Kelvin Cl HOR/WEW KT19 ....59 N5
Kelvin Dr TWK TW1 ....26 A2
Kelvin Gdns CROY/NA CRO 44 G8
Kelvin Gv SURB KT6 ....59 K2

SYD SE26 ....31 J6
Kelvington Cl CROY/NA CRO ...46 E8
Kelvington Rd PECK SE15 ....31 L1
Kelvin La CRAWE RH10 ....177 J1
Kelvin Wy CRAWE RH10 ....177 J1
Kemble Cl WEY KT13 ....56 F3
Kemble Rd CROY/NA CRO 2 A5
FSTH SE23 ....31 L4
Kembleside Rd
BH/WHM TN16 ....84 A7
Kemerton Rd BECK BR3 ....47 H3
CROY/NA CRO 45 P8
Kemishford
WOKS/MYFD GU22 ....91 N3
Kemnal Pk HASM GU27 ....184 E2
Kemp Ct BAGS GU19 ....51 P7
Kempe Cl DTCH/LGLY SL3 .....12 G2
Kemp Gdns CROY/NA CRO 45 L7
Kempsford Gdns ECT SW5 .....19 L3
Kempshott Rd HORS RH12 ...192 A6
STRHM/NOR SW16 ....44 G1
Kempson Rd FUL/PGN SW6 ...19 L6
Kempton Av SUN TW16 ....39 K2
Kempton Ct FARN GU14 ....88 B5
SUN TW16 ....39 J2
Kempton Pk SUN TW16 * 39 J3
Kempton Rd HPTN TW12 ....39 P3
Kempton Wk CROY/NA CRO ...46 E7
Kemsing Cl BH/WHM TN16 .....84 B8
Kemsley Rd BH/WHM TN16 ....84 B8
Kendal Cl EBED/NFELT TW14 ...24 A4
FARN GU14 * 88 A3
REDH RH1 ....119 P4
Kendale Cl CRAWE RH10 ....177 M9
Kendal Gdns SUT SM1 ....61 N1
Kendal Gv CBLY GU15 ....69 M4
Kendall Av BECK BR3 ....46 E3
SAND/SEL CR2 ....63 M7
Kendall Av South
SAND/SEL CR2 ....63 L8
Kendal Rd BECK BR3 ....46 E3
ISLW TW7 ....16 C7
Kendal Pl PUT/ROE SW15 ....28 C1
Kendor Av HOR/WEW KT19 .....60 A7
Kendra Hall Rd
SAND/SEL CR2 ....63 K6
Kendrey Gdns WHTN TW2 .....25 M2
Kendrick Ms SKENS SW7 ....19 P2
Kendrick Pl SKENS SW7 ....19 P2
Keniford Rd BAL SW12 ....29 L3
Kenilworth Av BRAK RG12 .....32 E2
COB KT11 ....75 H2
WIM/MER SW19 ....28 D9
Kenilworth Cl BNSTD SM7 .....79 M5
CRAWW RH11 ....176 F8
Kenilworth Dr
WOT/HER KT12 ....57 M2
Kenilworth Gdns STA TW18 ...22 F8
Kenilworth Rd ASHF TW15 .....22 G6
EW KT17 ....60 E5
FARN GU14 ....87 N2
FLEETN GU51 ....87 H6
PGE/AN SE20 ....46 D2
Kenilworth Ter BELMT SM2 * ...61 L6
Kenley Aerodrome
PUR/KEN CR8 ....81 M3
Kenley Cl BH/WHM TN16 ....84 C5
Kenley Gdns THHTH CR7 ....45 K5
Kenley La PUR/KEN CR8 ....81 L4
Kenley Rd BOR GU35 ....164 E6
KUT KT1 ....41 P3
TWK TW1 ....25 P2
WIM/MER SW19 ....43 L4
Kenley Wk CHEAM SM3 ....61 H3
Kenlor Rd TOOT SW17 ....28 C8
Kenmara Cl CRAWE RH10 .....177 L1
Kenmara Ct CRAWE RH10 ....177 K1
Kenmare Dr MTCM CR4 ....44 B1
Kenmare Rd THHTH CR7 ....45 J7
Kenmore Cl FLEETS GU52 .....107 H1
FRIM GU16 ....68 F8
Kenmore Rd PUR/KEN CR8 ....81 K3
Kennard Ct FROW RH18 * 181 K8
Kennedy Av EGRIN RH19 .....162 C9
Kennedy Cl MTCM CR4 ....44 C3
Kennedy Rd SWTR RH13 .....192 C9
Kennel Av ASC SL5 ....33 P2
Kennel Cl GT/LBKH KT23 ....96 C4
Kennel Gn ASC SL5 ....33 N2
Kennel La BFOR GU20 ....52 C2
BNFD RG42 ....32 D1
HORL RH6 ....158 G2
LHD/OX KT22 ....96 C3
RFNM GU10 ....146 F2
Kennel Ride ASC SL5 ....34 A1
Kennels La FARN GU14 ....87 M4
FARN GU14 ....87 N4
Kennel Wd ASC SL5 ....33 P2
Kennel Wood Crs
CROY/NA CRO 65 K9
Kennet Cl ASHV GU12 ....109 J5
BTSEA SW11 ....19 P9
CRAWW RH11 ....176 C6
FARN GU14 ....88 C1
Kenneth Rd BNSTD SM7 ....79 P4
Kennet Rd ISLW TW7 ....16 F8
Kennett Rd DTCH/LGLY SL3 ....12 F1
Kennington Av THHTH CR7 ....45 J7
Kenny Dr CAR SM5 ....62 C7
Kenrick Sq REDH RH1 ....121 N5
Kensington Av THHTH CR7 .....45 J2
Kensington Court Gdns
KENS W8 * 19 M1
Kensington Court Ms
KENS W8 * 19 M1
Kensington Court Pl
KENS W8 ....19 M1
Kensington Ga KENS W8 ....19 M1
Kensington Hall Gdns
WKENS W14 * 19 K3
Kensington High St
WKENS W14 ....19 J2

Kensington Rd
CRAWW RH11 ....176 E9
Kensington Ter
SAND/SEL CR2 ....63 M6
Kent Cl STA TW18 ....22 C9
STRHM/NOR SW16 ....44 G5
Kent Dr TEDD TW11 ....25 M8
Kent Gate Wy CROY/NA CRO ..64 F5
Kent Hatch Rd OXTED RH8 ...124 A1
Kent House La BECK BR3 ....31 M9
Kent House Rd BECK BR3 ....31 M9
Kentigern Dr CWTH RG45 ....50 A4
Kentish Wy BMLY BR1 ....47 P3
Kenton Av SUN TW16 ....39 M3
Kenton Cl BRAK RG12 ....32 F3
FRIM GU16 ....69 H6
Kenton Wy
WOKN/KNAP GU21 ....71 M6
Kent Rd BFOR GU20 ....52 D4
CHSWK W4 ....18 A1
E/WMO/HCT KT8 ....40 C5
FLEETN GU51 ....87 H6
KUT KT1 ....8 C6
RCHPK/HAM TW10 ....17 K5
WOKS/MYFD GU22 ....11 K9
WWKM BR4 ....47 H9
Kent Wy SURB KT6 ....59 L2
Kentwode Gn BARN SW13 .....18 E5
Kentwyns Ri REDH RH1 ....121 H6
Kenway Rd ECT SW5 ....19 M2
Kenwith Av FLEETN GU51 ....87 J6
Kenwood Cl WDR/YW UB7 ....14 C4
Kenwood Dr BECK BR3 ....47 J4
WOT/HER KT12 ....57 K5
Kenwood Pk WEY KT13 ....56 F5
Kenwood Rdg PUR/KEN CR8 ..81 K6
Kenworth Gv LTWR GU18 ....51 P8
Kenwyn Rd RYNPK SW20 ....42 G2
Kenya Ct HORL RH6 * 140 B9
Kenyngton Dr SUN TW16 ....24 B6
Kenyons EHSLY KT24 ....94 D8
Kenyon St FUL/PGN SW6 ....19 H6
Keogh Barracks FRIM GU16 ...89 J7
Keogh Cl FRIM GU16 ....89 K6
Keppel Rd DORK RH4 ....117 H5
Keppel Sq WDSR SL4 ....12 G9
Kepple Pl BAGS GU19 ....51 N6
Kerill Ct LU GU1 * 6 C2
Kerria Wy CHOB/PIR GU24 .....70 F7
Kerrill Av COUL/CHIP CR5 ....81 J8
Kerry Cl FLEETN GU51 ....87 H2
Kerry Ter WOKN/KNAP GU21 ..11 K9
Kersey Dr SAND/SEL CR2 .....82 C5
Kersfield Rd PUT/ROE SW15 ..28 A2
Keston Av ADL/WDHM KT15 ...55 L9
COUL/CHIP CR5 ....81 J8
Keston Gdns HAYES BR2 ....47 N7
Keston Pk WEY KT13 * 56 G6
Kestrel Av HNHL SE24 ....30 C1
Kestrel Cl CRAWW RH11 .....176 F5
HOR/WEW KT19 ....59 N9
HORS RH12 ....192 D5
KUTN/CMB KT2 ....26 C7
RFNM GU10 ....107 H7
RGUE GU4 ....113 H3
Kestrel Rd FARN GU14 ....88 A1
Kestrel Wk CRAWE RH10 * 179 K6
WOKN/KNAP GU21 ....71 P4
Kestrel Wy CROY/NA CRO 65 K7
WOKN/KNAP GU21 ....71 P4
Keswick Av KUTN/CMB KT2 ....27 K8
SHPTN TW17 ....38 C4
WIM/MER SW19 ....43 L3
Keswick Cl CBLY GU15 ....69 J4
CRAWW RH11 ....176 A7
SUT SM1 ....61 N3
Keswick Dr LTWR GU18 ....52 B9
Keswick Rd EGH TW20 ....36 F1
GT/LBKH KT23 ....96 C5
MFD/CHID GU8 ....149 L6
PUT/ROE SW15 ....28 B7
WHTN TW2 ....25 K2
WWKM BR4 ....65 L1
Kettering St
STRHM/NOR SW16 ....29 L9
Kettlewell Cl
WOKN/KNAP GU21 ....72 C4
Kettlewell Hl
WOKN/KNAP GU21 ....72 C4
Kevan Dr RPLY/SEND GU23 ...93 J5
Kevin Cl HSLWW TW4 ....15 M7
Kevins Dr YTLY GU46 ....67 J1
Kevins Gv FLEETN GU51 ....87 H6
Kew Br RCH/KEW TW9 ....17 N4
Kew Bridge Arches
RCH/KEW TW9 ....17 N4
Kew Bridge Rd BTFD TW8 .....17 M4
Kew Crs CHEAM SM3 ....61 K2
Kew Foot Rd RCH/KEW TW9 ...17 L9
Kew Gardens Rd
RCH/KEW TW9 ....17 M5
Kew Meadow Pth
RCH/KEW TW9 ....17 P6
Kew Rd RCH/KEW TW9 ....17 L9
Keymer Cl BH/WHM TN16 .....84 A5
Keymer Rd
BRXS/STRHM SW2 ....30 A5
CRAWW RH11 ....176 C7
Keynes Cl FLEETS GU52 .....107 H2
Keynsham Rd MRDN SM4 .....43 M9
Keynsham Wy SHST GU47 .....49 P7
Keysham Av HEST TW5 ....15 H5
The Key FLEETN GU51 ....86 D4
Keywood Dr SUN TW16 ....24 B9
Khama Rd TOOT SW17 ....29 H7
Khartoum Rd
MFD/CHID GU8 ....149 M6
TOOT SW17 ....28 G7
Kibble Gn BRAK RG12 ....32 E7
Kidborough Down
GT/LBKH KT23 ....96 A7
Kidborough Rd CRAWW RH11 .176 C7

Kidderminster Pl
CROY/NA CRO 2 B1
Kidderminster Rd
CROY/NA CRO 2 B1
Kidmans Cl HORS RH12 ....192 E5
Kidworth Cl HORL RH6 ....160 B8
Kier Pk ASC SL5 ....34 C4
Kilberry Cl ISLW TW7 ....16 D7
Kilcorral Cl EW KT17 ....78 E3
Kildoran Rd
BRXS/STRHM SW2 ....29 P1
Kilgour Rd FSTH SE23 ....31 M2
Kilkie St FUL/PGN SW6 ....19 N7
Killarney Rd
WAND/EARL SW18 ....28 F2
Killburns Mill Cl WLGTN SM6 ..62 D1
Killiester Gdns EW KT17 ....60 F3
Killicks CRAN GU6 ....153 J8
Killieser Av
BRXS/STRHM SW2 ....29 P5
Killinghurst La HASM GU27 ..185 K4
Kilmaine Rd FUL/PGN SW6 ....19 J6
Kilmarnock Pk REIG RH2 .....119 M4
Kilmarsh Rd HMSMTH W6 ....18 G2
Kilmartin Av
STRHM/NOR SW16 ....45 J4
Kilmartin Gdns FRIM GU16 ....69 H7
Kilmington Cl BRAK RG12 .....32 G8
Kilmington Rd BARN SW13 ....18 E4
Kilmiston Av SHPTN TW17 ....38 E5
Kilmore Dr CBLY GU15 ....69 K4
Kilmorey Gdns TWK TW1 ....16 A1
Kilmorey Rd TWK TW1 ....17 H9
Kilmorie Rd FSTH SE23 ....31 M4
Kilmuir Cl SHST GU47 ....67 P1
Kiln Cl HYS/HAR UB3 ....14 F4
Kiln Copse CRAN GU6 ....153 H8
Kilnfield Rd HORS RH12 .....189 N2
Kiln Flds HASM GU27 ....184 D2
Kiln La ASC SL5 ....34 G6
BRAK RG12 ....32 C3
BRKHM/BTCW RH3 ....118 A5
EW KT17 ....60 F3
HORL RH6 ....140 B8
RFNM GU10 ....127 N7
RPLY/SEND GU23 ....93 M4
Kilnmead CRAWE RH10 ....177 H4
Kilnmead Cl CRAWE RH10 ....177 H4
Kiln Mdw RGUW GU3 ....111 J1
Kiln Ms TOOT SW17 ....28 G8
Kiln Ride EWKG RG40 ....48 E2
Kiln Ride Extension
EWKG RG40 ....48 E3
Kiln Rd FARN GU14 ....179 J4
Kilnside ESH/CLAY KT10 ....58 G6
ESH/CLAY KT10 ....58 G6
The Kilns FNM GU9 * 107 P9
Kiln Wy ALDT GU11 ....108 D7
GSHT GU26 ....165 H6
Kilnwood La HORS RH12 .....175 M8
Kilross Rd EBED/NFELT TW14 ..23 N4
Kilrue La WOT/HER KT12 ....57 H3
Kilrush Ter WOKN/KNAP GU21 .11 H1
Kilsha Rd WOT/HER KT12 ....39 K7
Kimbell Gdns FUL/PGN SW6 ..19 H6
Kimber Ct RGUE GU4 * 113 H5
Kimberley BRAK RG12 ....32 C9
FLEETS GU52 ....107 H2
Kimberley Cl DTCH/LGLY SL3 ..12 D2
HORL RH6 ....159 H1
Kimberley Pl PUR/KEN CR8 ...63 J9
Kimberley Ride COB KT11 .....76 B2
Kimberley Rd BECK BR3 ....46 D3
CRAWW RH11 ....176 A1
CROY/NA CRO 45 K7
Kimber Rd WAND/EARL SW18 ..28 E3
Kimbers La FNM GU9 ....5 K1
Kimble Rd WIM/MER SW19 ....28 G9
Kimmeridge BRAK RG12 ....32 G7
Kimpton Dr FLEETN GU51 .....86 C4
Kimpton Rd CHEAM SM3 ....61 K2
Kinburn Dr EGH TW20 ....21 K8
Kindersley Cl EGRIN RH19 ...162 C6
Kinfauns Rd
BRXS/STRHM SW2 ....30 B5
King Alfred Av CAT SE6 ....31 P7
King Charles Crs BRYLDS KT5 .41 M8
King Charles Rd BRYLDS KT5 .41 M7
King Charles Wk
WIM/MER SW19 * 28 B4
Kingcup Cl CROY/NA CRO 46 D9
Kingcup Dr CHOB/PIR GU24 ...70 G4
King Edward Dr SURB KT6 ....59 L2
King Edwards Cl ASC SL5 * ...33 N2
King Edward's Gv
TEDD TW11 ....26 A9
King Edwards Ri ASC SL5 * ...33 N1
King Edwards Rd ASC SL5 * ..33 N2
Kingfield Cl
WOKS/MYFD GU22 ....72 D9
Kingfield Dr
WOKS/MYFD GU22 ....72 D9
Kingfield Gdns
WOKS/MYFD GU22 ....72 D9
Kingfield Rd
WOKS/MYFD GU22 ....72 D9
Kingfisher Cl CRAWE RH10 ...177 K2
FARN GU14 ....87 N1
FLEETS GU52 ....106 C1
WOT/HER KT12 ....57 N4
Kingfisher Dr
RCHPK/HAM TW10 ....26 B7
REDH RH1 ....120 C2
RGUE GU4 ....112 G3
STA TW18 ....22 B9
YTLY GU46 ....66 F2
Kingfisher Gdns
SAND/SEL CR2 ....64 D8
Kingfisher La CRAWE RH10 ...179 K6
Kingfisher Ri EGRIN RH19 ....180 E3
Kingfisher Wk ASHV GU12 ...109 H3

Kingfisher Wy CROY/NA CRO ..46 D6
HORS RH12 ....192 B5
King Gdns CROY/NA CRO 63 K4
King Garth Ms FSTH SE23 .....31 K5
King George Av EGRIN RH19 .162 D9
WOT/HER KT12 ....57 N1
King George Cl FARN GU14 ...88 F5
SUN TW16 ....23 P8
King George's Dr
ADL/WDHM KT15 ....55 L8
King George Sq
RCHPK/HAM TW10 ....26 E2
King George VI Av
MTCM CR4 ....44 B5
Kingham Cl
WAND/EARL SW18 ....28 F3
King Henry's Dr
CROY/NA CRO 65 J7
King Henry's Rd KUT KT1 ....41 P4
King John's Cl
STWL/WRAY TW19 ....21 H2
Kingpost Pde RGUE GU4 * ...112 F1
Kings App CBLY GU15 ....68 E4
Kings Arbour NWDGN UB2 ....15 K3
Kings Av BAL SW12 ....29 N4
BF/WBF KT14 ....73 P1
CAR SM5 ....62 A6
CHOB/PIR GU24 ....70 D8
HEST TW5 ....16 B6
NWMAL KT3 ....42 C4
REDH RH1 ....120 A7
RFNM GU10 ....108 G6
SUN TW16 ....24 A8
Kingsbridge Rd MRDN SM4 ....43 H8
NWDGN UB2 ....15 P2
WOT/HER KT12 ....57 J8
Kingsbrook LHD/OX KT22 ....76 G7
Kingsbury Crs STA TW18 ....22 A8
Kingsbury Dr WDSR SL4 ....13 J9
Kings Cha E/WMO/HCT KT8 ....40 C4
Kingsclear Pk CBLY GU15 .....69 H4
Kingsclere Cl PUT/ROE SW15 .27 M3
Kingscliffe Gdns
WIM/MER SW19 ....28 C4
Kings Cl STA TW18 ....37 P1
THDIT KT7 ....40 G7
WOT/HER KT12 ....39 K9
Kings Copse EGRIN RH19 * ..180 E3
Kingscote Hl CRAWW RH11 ..176 E7
Kingscote Rd CHSWK W4 .....18 B1
CROY/NA CRO 46 C8
NWMAL KT3 ....42 B4
Kingscourt Rd
STRHM/NOR SW16 ....29 N6
Kings Crs CBLY GU15 ....50 E9
Kingscroft FLEETN GU51 ....86 C7
Kingscroft Rd BNSTD SM7 .....79 P4
LHD/OX KT22 ....77 H9
Kings Cross La REDH RH1 ...121 H8
Kingsdale Rd PGE/AN SE20 ...46 D2
Kingsdene
KWD/TDW/WH KT20 ....98 C2
Kingsdown Av SAND/SEL CR2 .63 L7
Kingsdown Rd SURB KT6 ....41 L8
EW KT17 ....78 E2
Kingsdown Wy HAYES BR2 ....47 N8
Kings Dr BRYLDS KT5 ....41 N8
THDIT KT7 ....41 H7
The Kings Dr WOT/HER KT12 ..57 P7
Kings Farm Av
RCHPK/HAM TW10 ....17 N9
Kingsfold Cl HORS RH12 * ...174 A6
Kingsford Av WLGTN SM6 .....62 G6
Kingsgate CRAWE RH10 * 177 H5
Kingsgate Rd KUT KT1 ....8 D3
Kings Hall Rd BECK BR3 ....46 D1
King's Head La BF/WBF KT14 ..55 P9
Kingshill Av WPK KT4 ....42 E8
Kings Keep FLEETS GU52 .....86 G9
HAYES BR2 * 47 L4
SHST GU47 ....49 M8
SURB KT6 * 41 L5
Kingsland RDKG RH5 ....156 F3
Kingsland Ct CRAWE RH10 * ..177 J1
Kings La BFOR GU20 ....52 E4
EGH TW20 ....20 F8
RFNM GU10 ....127 K7
Kingslawn Cl PUT/ROE SW15 .27 H3
Kingslea LHD/OX KT22 ....76 G9
SWTR RH13 ....192 D7
Kingsleigh Pl MTCM CR4 ....44 B4
Kingsleigh Wk HAYES BR2 ....47 M5
Kingsley Av BNSTD SM7 ....79 L4
CBLY GU15 ....68 G5
EGH TW20 ....20 D8
HSLW TW3 ....16 C7
HSLW TW3 ....16 C7
SUT SM1 ....62 A3
WDSR SL4 ....13 H6
WIM/MER SW19 ....28 F9
Kingsley Cl CWTH RG45 ....49 M6
HORL RH6 ....140 B8
Kingsley Dr WPK KT4 ....42 D2
Kingsley Gv REIG RH2 ....119 L8
Kingsley Ms KENS W8 * 19 M1
Kingsley Rd CRAWW RH11 ...176 D8
CROY/NA CRO 45 H8
FARN GU14 ....88 B1
HORL RH6 ....140 B8
HSLW TW3 ....16 C7
HTHW RG27 ....85 J4
WIM/MER SW19 ....28 E9
Kingslyn Crs NRWD SE19 .....45 N2
Kings Ml HMSMTH W6 * 18 G3
Kings Md HORL RH6 ....160 C1
REDH RH1 ....100 F4
Kingsmead BH/WHM TN16 ....84 F6
Kings Md GU 153 H9
FARN GU14 ....88 D3
FRIM GU16 ....89 G9

RCHPK/HAM TW10 ....26 E2
WOKN/KNAP GU21 ....11 H1
Kingsmead Av MTCM CR4 ....44 E4
SUN TW16 ....39 L4
SURB KT6 ....59 N1
WPK KT4 ....60 F2
Kingsmead Cl
HOR/WEW KT19 ....60 B6
TEDD TW11 ....26 A9
Kings Mead Pk
ESH/CLAY KT10 ....58 E6
Kingsmead Pl HORS RH12 ...191 K7
Kingsmead Rd
BRXS/STRHM SW2 ....30 B5
HORS RH12 ....191 K7
Kingsmere Cl PUT/ROE SW15 .19 H8
Kingsmere Rd BNFD RG42 ....32 B2
WIM/MER SW19 ....28 A5
Kings Ms HORS RH12 ....192 A8
King's Pas ALDT TL REDH RH1 .120 F9
Kingsnympton Pk
KUTN/CMB KT2 ....47 P1
Kings Paddock HPTN TW12 ...40 C1
Kings Pde CAR SM5 * 62 A2
FLEETN GU51 ....86 C5
SHB W12 * 18 E1
King's Pas KUTN/CMB KT2 ....8 C2
The Kings Peace
GSHT GU26 * 165 M8
Kings Pl CHSWK W4 ....18 A3
King's Quay WBPTN SW10 * ..19 N6
King's Ride ASC SL5 ....33 L5
CBLY GU15 ....50 F8
Kings Rd ADL/WDHM KT15 ....55 M8
ALDT GU11 ....108 A5
ASC SL5 ....34 E6
BELMT SM2 ....61 L8
BH/WHM TN16 ....84 A6
CHEL SW3 ....19 P4
CHOB/PIR GU24 ....70 G3
CRAN GU6 ....171 J1
CWTH RG45 ....45 L5
EGH TW20 ....21 J9
FELT TW13 ....24 D4
FLEETN GU51 ....87 H6
FUL/PGN SW6 ....19 N5
GODL GU27 ....131 M7
HASM GU27 ....184 B4
HORL RH6 ....159 K1
KUTN/CMB KT2 ....8 E1
MORT/ESHN SW14 ....18 B8
RCHPK/HAM TW10 ....26 D1
RGUE GU4 ....132 C3
SNWD SE25 ....46 A4
SURB KT6 ....41 J9
SWTR RH13 ....192 D7
TEDD TW11 ....25 L8
TWK TW1 * 26 A2
WIM/MER SW19 ....28 D9
WOKN/KNAP GU21 ....11 H1
WOT/HER KT12 ....57 K1
Kings Shade Wk
HOR/WEW KT19 * 78 B2
King's Rd GU GU1 ....7 F7
Kingsthorpe Rd SYD SE23 ...31 M5
Kingston Av CHEAM SM3 .....61 J2
EBED/NFELT TW14 ....23 P2
EHSLY KT24 ....95 H6
LHD/OX KT22 ....97 H1
Kingston Cl TEDD TW11 .....26 A9
Kingston Crs ASHF TW15 ....22 F8
BECK BR3 ....47 J7
Kingston Gdns CROY/NA CRO .62 G2
Kingston Hall Rd KUT KT1 ...8 C6
Kingston Hill KUTN/CMB KT2 ..9 J1
Kingston Hill Pl
KUTN/CMB KT2 ....27 H7
Kingston House Est
SURB KT6 ....41 H7
Kingston House Gdns
LHD/OX KT22 ....97 H1
Kingston La EHSLY KT24 ....94 C7
TEDD TW11 ....25 P8
Kingston Ldg NWMAL KT3 * ..42 C4
Kingston Ri ADL/WDHM KT15 .55 L8
Kingston Rd BRYLDS KT5 ....59 P6
CBLY GU15 ....51 J8
HOR/WEW KT19 ....60 C4
LHD/OX KT22 ....60 D2
NWMAL KT3 ....42 B5
PUT/ROE SW15 ....27 N4
RYNPK SW20 ....43 J3
STA TW18 ....22 D7
TEDD TW11 ....26 A9
Kingston Sq NRWD SE19 .....30 E8
Kingston V PUT/ROE SW15 ...27 J7
Kings St KERT KT16 ....37 L9
HMSMTH W6 ....18 F3
NWDGN UB2 ....15 N1
RCH/KEW TW9 ....94 C6
TWK TW1 ....25 P4
King Street Cloisters
HMSMTH W6 * 8 F3
King Street Pde TWK TW1 * .25 P4
King's Wk CBLY GU15 ....68 B2
SAND/SEL CR2 ....82 B3
Kings Wy CROY/NA CRO 62 G2
Kingsway ALDT GU11 ....108 B5
MORT/ESHN SW14 ....42 P3
NWMAL KT3 ....42 C4
STWL/WRAY TW19 ....22 A9
WWKM BR4 ....65 M2
Kingsway Av SAND/SEL CR2 ..64 C7

Kingsway Rd CHEAM SM3 .....61 J6
Kingsway Ter WEY KT13 .....56 C6
The Kingsway EW KT17 ......60 D8
Kingswick Cl ASC SL5 ......34 E5
Kingswick Dr ASC SL5 ......34 E5
Kingswood Av HAYES BR2 ....47 L4
HEST TW5 ....15 P7
HPTN TW12 ....25 J9
SAND/SEL CR2 ....82 B4
THHTH CR7 ....45 J4
Kingswood Cl CRAWW RH11 ..194 F12
ECH TW20 ....21 J7
GU GU1 ....112 G4
NWMAL KT3 ....42 C5
SURB KT6 ....41 L8
WEY KT13 ....56 D6
Kingswood Creek
STWL/WRAY TW19 ....21 J1
Kingswood Dr BELMT SM2 ...61 M7
CAR SM5 ....44 B9
NRWD SE19 ....30 E7
Kingswood Firs GSHT GU26 .165 M9
Kingswood La GSHT GU26 ...165 M9
WARL CR6 ....82 C4
Kingswood Ri EGH TW20 .....21 J8
Kingswood Rd
BRXS/STRHM SW2 ....29 P2
CHSWK W4 ....18 A1
HAYES BR2 ....47 L4
KWD/TDW/WH KT20 ....98 F1
PGE/AN SE20 ....31 K9
WIM/MER SW19 ....43 K2
Kingswood Ter CHSWK W4 ...18 A1
Kingswood Wy
SAND/SEL CR2 ....82 D1
WLGTN SM6 ....62 G4
Kingsworth Cl BECK BR3 ....46 E6
Kingsworthy Cl KUT KT1 .....9 G5
Kings Yd ASC SL5 * 33 N5
PUT/ROE SW15 * 19 H8
Kingwood Rd FUL/PGN SW6 ..19 J5
Kinloss Rd CAR SM5 ....43 N8
Kinnaird Av CHSWK W4 ......18 A5
Kinnersley Mnr REIG RH2 * .139 N4
Kinnersley Wk REIG RH2 ...139 L1
Kinnibrugh Dr LING RH7 ...162 F3
Kinnoul Rd HMSMTH W6 .....19 J4
Kinross Av ASC SL5 ....34 B5
WPK KT4 ....60 E1
Kinross Cl SUN TW16 ....24 A8
Kinross Ct ASC SL5 ....33 P6
Kinross Dr SUN TW16 ....24 A8
Kintyre Cl STRHM/NOR SW16 .45 H3
Kinver Rd SYD SE26 ....31 K7
Kipings KWD/TDW/WH KT20 ...99 H2
Kipling Cl SWTR RH13 .....192 F6
YTLY GU46 ....66 C4
Kipling Dr WIM/MER SW19 ...28 C9
Kipling Wy EGRIN RH19 ....180 B2
Kirby Cl HOR/WEW KT19 .....60 D4
Kirby Rd WOKN/KNAP GU21 ..11 N7
Kirdford Cl CRAWW RH11 ...176 D3
Kirkdale SYD SE26 ....31 J5
Kirkdale Cnr SYD SE26 * ...31 K7
Kirkfields GUW GU2 ....111 N2
Kirkham Cl SHST GU47 ......49 P7
Kirk Knoll BOR GU35 ......164 C6
Kirkland Av
WOKN/KNAP GU21 ....71 L5
Kirkleas Rd SURB KT6 ......41 L9
Kirklees Rd THHTH CR7 .....45 J6
Kirkley Rd WIM/MER SW19 ...43 L2
Kirkly Ct SAND/SEL CR2 ....63 N7
Kirkstall Gdns
BRXS/STRHM SW2 ....29 N4
Kirkstall Rd
BRXS/STRHM SW2 ....29 N4
Kirksted Rd MRDN SM4 ......43 M9
Kirkstone Cl CBLY GU15 ....69 M4
Kirkstone Wy BMLY BR1 * ...47 L1
Kirrane Cl NWMAL KT3 ......42 C5
Kirriemuir Gdns ASHV GU12 .109 M3
Kirtley Rd SYD SE26 ....31 M7
Kirton Cl CHSWK W4 ....18 B2
Kirton Gdns
WAND/EARL SW18 * 28 E2
Kitchener Rd ALDT GU11 ....88 F9
THHTH CR7 ....45 M4
Kites Cl CRAWW RH11 ......176 F1
Kithurst Cl CRAWW RH11 ...176 F7
Kitley Gdns NRWD SE19 .....45 P1
Kitsmead CRAWE RH10 ......178 B1
Kitsmead La CHERT KT16 ....36 A4
Kitson Rd BARN SW13 ....18 E4
Kittiwake Cl CRAWW RH11 ..176 A7
SAND/SEL CR2 ....64 E8
Kitts La MFD/CHID GU8 ....169 J3
Klea Av CLAP SW4 ....29 M2
Kingston Sq NRWD SE19 .....31 J5
Knapmill Rd CAT SE6 ....31 P5
Knapmill Wy CAT SE6 ....31 P5
Knapp Rd ASHF TW15 ....23 L8
Knapton Ms TOOT SW17 .....29 K9
Knaresborough Dr
WAND/EARL SW18 * 28 A4
Knaresborough Pl ECT SW5 ..19 M2
Kneller Gdns ISLW TW7 .....25 L2
Kneller Rd NWMAL KT3 ......42 C8
WHTN TW2 ....25 J1
Knepp Cl CRAWE RH10 .....177 M5
Knight Cl FLEETN GU51 .....86 C9
Knighton Cl CRAWE RH10 ..177 N1
SAND/SEL CR2 ....63 K7
Knighton Park Rd SYD SE26 .31 L8
Knighton Rd REDH RH1 .....120 C7
Knightons La
MFD/CHID GU8 ....169 L7
Knightsbridge Crs STA TW18 .22 E9
Knightsbridge Rd CBLY GU15 .68 G1
Knights Cl EGH TW20 * 22 A9

Knight's Hl WNWD SE27 .....30 C8
Knight's Hill Sq WNWD SE27 .30 C7
Knights Pk KUT KT1 ....8 E6
Knights Pl REDH RH1 ......120 C4
Knightswood CROY/NA CRO ..64 A7
Kingswood BRAK RG12 ....32 D9
WOKN/KNAP GU21 ....71 M7
Knightwood Cl REIG RH2 ...119 J7
Knightwood Crs NWMAL KT3 .42 C7
Knipp Hl COB KT11 ....75 P2
Knivet Rd FUL/PGN SW6 .....19 L1
Knobfield SHGR GU5 ....135 H5
Knob Hl HORS RH12 ....191 P1
Knockhundred La
GSHT GU26 ....183 L2
Knole Gv EGRIN RH19 ......177 N4
CROY/NA CRO 47 L7
Knole Cv EGRIN RH19 .....160 C6
Knoll Cl FLEETN GU51 ......86 C5
Knoll Cl FLEETN GU51 ......86 C4
Knollmead BRYLDS KT5 .....42 A9
Knoll Park Rd CHERT KT16 ..37 K9
Knoll Quarry GODL GU7 ....131 L7
Knoll Rd CAR SM5 ....62 C4
DORK RH4 ....116 C9
FLEETN GU51 ....86 C5
GODL GU7 ....131 K7
WAND/EARL SW18 ....28 F1
Knolls Cl WPK KT4 ....60 E2
The Knolls EW KT17 ....78 C5
The Knoll BECK BR3 ....47 H1
CHERT KT16 ....37 K9
COB KT11 ....76 A2
HAYES BR2 ....65 N1
LHD/OX KT22 ....97 J1
Knoll Wd GODL GU7 ....131 L7
Knolly's Cl STRHM/NOR SW16 .30 B6
Knollys Rd ALDT GU11 .....108 B3
STRHM/NOR SW16 ....30 B6
The Knook SHST GU47 * 67 P1
Knowle Cl CRAWE RH10 ....160 C6
Knowle Dr CRAWE RH10 ....160 C6
Knowle Gdns BF/WBF KT14 ..73 K2
Knowle Gn STA TW18 ....22 D8
Knowle Gv VW GU25 ....36 A8
Knowle Grove Cl VW GU25 ..36 A8
Knowle Hl VW GU25 ....35 P8
Knowle La CRAN GU6 ......170 C3
HORS RH12 ....189 J1
Knowle Pk COB KT11 ....75 N4
Knowle Park Av STA TW18 ...22 E9
Knowle Rd WHTN TW2 ....25 N4
Knowles Av CWTH RG45 .....49 K5
The Knowle
KWD/TDW/WH KT20 * 98 F1
Knowl Hl WOKS/MYFD GU22 *.11 K6
Knowlton Gn HAYES BR2 ....47 M6
Knowsley Ter
MFD/CHID GU8 * 167 P7
Knox Cl FLEETN GU52 ......106 E1
Knox Rd GUW GU2 ....111 P1
Kohat Ct ALDT GU11 * 108 B4
Kohat Rd WIM/MER SW19 ....28 E8
Kohima Cl ALDT GU11 .....108 D4
Koonowla Cl BH/WHM TN16 ..84 B4
Kooringa WARL CR6 ....82 B8
Korda Cl SHPTN TW17 ......37 P6
Korea Cottages COB KT11 * .75 M5
Kramer Ms ECT SW5 * 19 L3
Krooner Rd CBLY GU15 ......68 D5
Kuala Gdns
STRHM/NOR SW16 ....45 H2
Kyle Cl BRAK RG12 ....32 D4
Kynance Ms KENS W8 ....19 M1
Kynance Pl SKENS SW7 .....19 N1
Kynaston Av THHTH CR7 .....45 L6
Kynaston Ct CTHM CR3 * ...101 N5
Kynaston Crs THHTH CR7 ....45 L6
Kynaston Rd THHTH CR7 ....45 L6
Kynersley Cl CAR SM5 ......62 B2
Kyrle Rd BTSEA SW11 ......29 K2

L

Laburnum Av SUT SM1 ......62 A2
Laburnum Cl GU GU1 ......112 A2
Laburnum Crs SUN TW16 ....39 M4
Laburnum Gdns
CROY/NA CRO 46 D8
Laburnum Gv DTCH/LGLY SL3 .12 E4
HSLW TW5 ....15 P9
NWMAL KT3 ....42 B3
Laburnum Pl EGH TW20 .....20 F7
Laburnum Rd ALDT GU11 ...108 C5
CHERT KT16 ....37 L9
EPSOM KT18 ....78 C2
FNM GU9 ....108 A7
HYS/HAR UB3 ....15 H2
MTCM CR4 ....44 C3
WIM/MER SW19 ....43 N1
WOKS/MYFD GU22 ....72 B9
The Laburnums BLKW GU17 * .67 M3
Laburnum Wy
STWL/WRAY TW19 ....23 J4
Lacey Av COUL/CHIP CR5 ....80 F1
Lacey Cl EGH TW20 ....37 H1
Lacey Dr COUL/CHIP CR5 ....80 B7
HPTN TW12 ....39 P2
Lackford Rd COUL/CHIP CR5 .80 B7
Lacock Cl WIM/MER SW19 ...28 F9
Lacrosse Wy
STRHM/NOR SW16 ....44 F2
Lacy Gn COUL/CHIP CR5 .....81 H3
Lacy Rd PUT/ROE SW15 .....19 H9
Ladas Rd WNWD SE27 ....30 D8

Ladbroke Gv REDH RH1 ....120 C4
Ladbroke Hurst LING RH7 ..162 F3
Ladbroke Rd EPSOM KT18 ...78 C3
HORL RH6 ....140 C8
REDH RH1 ....140 C4
Ladbrook Rd SNWD SE25 ....45 M4
Ladderstile Ride
RCHPK/HAM TW10 ....27 H8
Ladybank BRAK RG12 ....32 D9
Lady Booth Rd KUT KT1 ......8 D5
Ladycross MFD/CHID GU8 ..149 M4
Ladygate Cl RDKG RH5 ....117 J7
Ladygate Rd RDKG RH5 ....117 J7
Lady Forsdyke Wy
HOR/WEW KT19 ....59 N7
Ladygate Dr GSHT GU26 ...165 K8
Ladygrove CROY/NA CRO 64 E7
Ladygrove Dr RGUE GU4 .....92 F9
Lady Harewood Wy
HOR/WEW KT19 ....59 N7
Lady Hay WPK KT4 ....60 D1
Lady Margaret Rd ASC SL5 ..34 B3
CRAWW RH11 ....176 D4
Ladymead GU GU1 ....111 N2
Ladymead Cl CRAWE RH10 .177 M8
Ladymount WLGTN SM6 ......62 F2
Ladyship Ter EDUL SE22 * ..31 J3
Ladythorpe Cl
ADL/WDHM KT15 ....55 M3
Ladywell Rd LEW SE13 .....31 P1
Ladywood Av FARN GU14 ...108 A1
Ladywood Rd SURB KT6 .....59 N1
Laffan's Rd ALDT GU11 ....108 A1
Laffan Tr ALDT GU11 ....87 N9
Lafone Av FELT TW13 ......24 D4
Lagham Ct GDST RH9 * 122 E9
Lagham Pk GDST RH9 ......122 E8
Lagham Rd GDST RH9 ......122 E9
Laglands Ct REIG RH2 .....119 N3
Laings Av MTCM CR4 ....44 B3
Lainlock Pl HSLW TW3 ......16 B6
Lainson St WAND/EARL SW18 .28 D2
Lairdale Cl DUL SE21 ......30 D4
Laird Ct BAGS GU19 ....51 N8
Laitwood Rd BAL SW12 .....29 L3
Lake Cl BF/WBF KT14 ....73 P1
Lake End Wy CWTH RG45 ....49 L5
Lake Gdns RCHPK/HAM TW10 .26 A6
WLGTN SM6 ....62 D2
Lakehall Gdns THHTH CR7 ...45 K6
Lakehall Rd THHTH CR7 ....45 K6
Lakehurst Rd
HOR/WEW KT19 ....60 C4
Lakeland Dr FRIM GU16 .....68 G7
Lake La HORL RH6 ....140 B6
RFNM GU10 ....146 B6
Lake Rd CROY/NA CRO 64 D1
FRIM GU16 ....89 J1
RDKG RH5 ....155 K6
VW GU25 ....35 P6
WIM/MER SW19 ....28 B8
Lakers Ri BNSTD SM7 ....80 B6
Lakes Cl RGUE GU4 ....132 F2
Lakeside BECK BR3 ....47 H4
BNFD RG42 ....32 E1
HOR/WEW KT19 ....60 D4
HORS RH12 ....192 A5
REDH RH1 ....120 C5
WEY KT13 ....56 E4
WLGTN SM6 ....62 D3
WOKN/KNAP GU21 ....71 L4
Lakeside Cl ASHV GU12 ....109 M2
SNWD SE25 ....46 A3
WOKN/KNAP GU21 ....71 L4
Lakeside Dr ESH/CLAY KT10 .58 A5
Lakeside Gdns FARN GU14 ..68 A9
Lakeside Gra WEY KT13 .....56 E2
Lakeside Rd ALDT GU11 ....88 C3
ASHV GU12 ....109 M2
DTCH/LGLY SL3 ....13 K5
WDR/YW UB7 ....13 P3
The Lake Side BLKW GU17 * .67 M4
Lake Vw RDKG RH5 ....137 J1
Lake View Rd CRAWE RH10 .161 J9
EGRIN RH19 ....162 F2
Lakeview Rd WNWD SE27 ....30 B8
SNWD SE25 ....46 A6
Laleham Abbey STA TW18 * ..37 N5
Laleham Cl STA TW18 ....37 M2
Laleham Ct SUT SM1 * 61 N4
WOKN/KNAP GU21 ....10 D1
Laleham Reach CHERT KT16 .37 M3
Laleham Rd SHPTN TW17 ....37 K5
CAT SE6 ....31 N4
STA TW18 ....22 D8
Lalor St FUL/PGN SW6 ......19 J7
Lamberhurst Rd WNWD SE27 .30 B7
Lamberhurst Wk
CRAWE RH10 ....177 K6
Lambert Av DTCH/LGLY SL3 ..12 E4
RCH/KEW TW9 ....17 N1
Lambert Cl BH/WHM TN16 ...84 B5
Lambert Crs BLKW GU17 ....67 N4
Lambert Rd BNSTD SM7 .....79 N2
BRXS/STRHM SW2 ....29 P1
Lambert's Pl CROY/NA CRO ..45 N9
Lambert's Rd SURB KT6 .....41 L6
Lambeth Cl CRAWW RH11 ..176 E6
Lambeth Rd CROY/NA CRO ...45 L9
Lambeth Wk
CRAWW RH11 * 176 E6
Lambly Hl VW GU25 ....35 P5
Lamborne Cl SHST GU47 ....49 L8
Lambourn Cl EGRIN RH19 ..162 D9
Lambourne Av
WIM/MER SW19 ....28 C7
Lambourne Cl CRAWE RH10 .177 J7
Lambourne Crs
WOKN/KNAP GU21 ....73 H2
Lambourne Dr BAGS GU19 ...51 N7
COB KT11 ....75 P4
Lambourne Gv BRAK RG12 ...32 G3
KUT KT1 ....9 K4

Lambourne Wy RFNM GU10 .108 G7
Lambrook Ter FUL/PGN SW6 .19 J6
Lambs Cl FLEETN GU51 ....192 E5
Lambs Farm Cl HORS RH12 .192 E5
Lambs Farm Rd HORS RH12 .192 D4
Lambs Green Rd HORS RH12 .175 L8
Lamb's Ms RCHPK/HAM TW10 .42 G3
Lamby Cft ALDT RH6 ......140 E9
Lamington St HMSMTH W6 ...18 F2
Lammas Av MTCM CR4 ......44 C2
Lammas Cl GODL GU7 ......131 N7
STA TW18 ....22 B6
Lammas Dr STA TW18 ....22 A7
Lammas La ESH/CLAY KT10 ..58 A3
Lammas Md BNFD RG42 .....32 A1
Lammas Rd GODL GU7 .....131 N8
RCHPK/HAM TW10 ....26 A6
Lammermoor Rd BAL SW12 * .29 L3
Lamont Rd WBPTN SW10 ....19 N4
Lamont Road Pas
WBPTN SW10 * 19 P4
Lamorna WOKS/MYFD GU22 *.10 D6
Lampard La RFNM GU10 ....164 C1
Lampeter Cl
WOKS/MYFD GU22 ....10 C5
Lampeter Sq HMSMTH W6 ...19 J4
Lampton Av HEST TW5 ......16 A6
Lampton House Cl
WIM/MER SW19 ....28 A8
Lamorra WOKS/MYFD GU22 *.10 D6
Lamport Cft ALDT RH6 .....140 E9
Lamington St HMSMTH W6 ...18 F2
Lammas Av MTCM CR4 ......44 C2
Lammas Cl GODL GU7 ......131 N7
STA TW18 ....22 B6
Lammas Dr STA TW18 ....22 A7
Lanark Cl FRIM GU16 ......68 G6
SWTR RH13 ....192 D8
Lancaster Av ASHV GU12 ...109 H1
CRAWE RH10 ....177 N2
EGH TW20 ....21 J8
HAYES BR2 ....47 M5
STWL/WRAY TW19 ....21 J2
WOKN/KNAP GU21 ....11 G2
Lancaster Ct WOT/HER KT12 .39 J8
Lancaster Dr CBLY GU15 ....68 F2
EGRIN RH19 ....162 F9
Lancaster Gdn
KUTN/CMB KT2 ....26 C8
Lancaster Gdns
WIM/MER SW19 ....28 B8
Lancaster Ms
RCHPK/HAM TW10 ....26 D2
WAND/EARL SW18 * 28 E1
Lancaster Pk
RCHPK/HAM TW10 ....26 D1
Lancaster Pl TW TWK TW1 ...25 P3
WIM/MER SW19 ....28 A8
Lancaster Rd FARN GU14 ...88 D6
SNWD SE25 ....46 A3
WIM/MER SW19 ....28 A8
Lancaster Wy FARN GU14 ...68 E9
Lancaster Rd WLGTN SM6 ...62 G6
Lancelot Cl CRAWW RH11 ..176 B5
Lancer Ct ALDT GU11 * 108 A4
Lancing Cl CRAWW RH11 ...176 D4
Lancing Rd CROY/NA CRO ...45 H7
FELT TW13 ....24 A5
Landcroft Rd EDUL SE22 ....30 C2
Landells Rd EDUL SE22 .....30 G2
Landen Pk HORL RH6 ......140 A8
Landford Rd PUT/ROE SW15 .18 G8
Landgrove Rd WIM/MER SW19 .28 B8
Landon Wy ASHF TW15 * 23 L9
Landridge Rd FUL/PGN SW6 .19 J7
Landscape Rd WARL CR6 ...82 B8
Landseer Cl SHST GU47 * ...50 A9
WIM/MER SW19 ....43 N2
Landseer Rd NWMAL KT3 ....42 B8
SUT SM1 ....61 L5
Lane Cl ADL/WDHM KT15 ....55 L4
Lane End EPSOM KT18 ....77 P3
MFD/CHID GU8 ....168 A3
Lane End Dr
WOKN/KNAP GU21 ....71 J6
Lanercost Rd
BRXS/STRHM SW2 ....30 B5
CRAWW RH11 ....176 G6
The Lane BIL RH14 ....187 P6
CHERT KT16 ....37 L9
VW GU25 ....36 C4
Laneway PUT/ROE SW15 .....27 N1
Lanfrey Pl WKENS W14 .....19 K3
Langaller La LHD/OX KT22 ..96 B1
Langbourne Wy
ESH/CLAY KT10 ....58 E5
Lang Cl LHD/LBKH KT23 ....96 B3
Langcroft Cl CAR SM5 ......62 B2
Langdale Av MTCM CR4 .....44 B4
Langdale Cl FARN GU14 ....88 A3
MORT/ESHN SW14 ....17 P9
WOKN/KNAP GU21 ....72 A5
Langdale Ct ASC SL5 ......33 N3
Langdale Dr ASC SL5 ......33 N3
Langdale Rd CRAWW RH11 ..176 A7
THHTH CR7 ....45 J5
Langdon Cl CBLY GU15 .....69 L4
Langdon Pl
MORT/ESHN SW14 ....18 A8
Langdon Rd HAYES BR2 .....47 P4
MRDN SM4 ....43 N6
Langdon Wk MRDN SM4 .....43 N6
Langdon Dene FUL/PGN SW6 .19 M7
Langham Cl GODL GU7 ....131 M8
Langham Dene
PUR/KEN CR8 * 81 K4
Langham Gdns
RCHPK/HAM TW10 ....26 B7
Langham House Cl
RCHPK/HAM TW10 ....26 C7

Langham Pk GODL GU7 .....131 M8
Langham Park Pl HAYES BR2 ..47 M5
Langham Pl CHSWK W4 .....18 C1
  EGH TW20 .....21 L8
Langham Rd RYNPK SW20.....42 G2
  TEDD TW11 .....26 A8
Langhorn Cl BAL SW12.....29 N5
Langhorn Dr WHTN TW2 .....25 M3
Langhurst Cl HORS RH12 .....174 C7
Langhurst La CRAWW RH11...175 M3
Langhurstwood Rd
  HORS RH12 .....174 C7
Langland Gdns CROY/NA CRO..64 F1
Langlands Ri HOR/WEW KT19 ..78 A2
Langley Av SURB KT6.....41 K9
  WPK KT4.....61 H1
Langley Broom
  DTCH/LGLY SL3 .....12 D3
Langley Cl EPSOM KT18.....78 B8
  FLEETS GU52 .....106 F2
  .....6 E1
Langley Crs HYS/HAR UB3.....15 H5
Langley Dr ALDT GU11.....98 D2
  CBLY GU15.....68 F2
  CRAWW RH11.....176 F3
Langley Gv NWMAL KT3.....42 B3
Langley La CRAWW RH11.....176 D5
Langley Oaks Av
  SAND/SEL CR2.....64 A8
Langley Pde CRAWW RH11 ...176 F2
Langley Park Rd BELMT SM2 ..61 N5
Langley Pl CRAWW RH11 .....176 F2
  DTCH/LGLY SL3 .....12 A1
  ISLW TW7 .....16 F7
  SAND/SEL CR2.....64 D7
  STA TW18 .....22 C9
  SURB KT6.....41 L8
  WIM/MER SW19 .....43 K2
Langley Vale Rd EPSOM KT18..78 B7
Langley Wk CRAWW RH11...176 F2
  WOKS/MYFD GU22.....10 C7
Langley Wy WWKM BR4.....47 K9
Langley Wd BECK BR3 * 47 L6
Langmans
  WOKN/KNAP GU21.....71 L5
Langmead St WNWD SE27.....30 C7
Langport Ct WOT/HER KT12 ...39 L9
Langridge Dr EGRIN RH19 .....180 D3
Langridge Ms HPTN TW12.....24 C9
Langroyd Rd TOOT SW17.....29 J5
Langshott HORL RH6.....140 F9
Langshott Cl
  ADL/WDHM KT15.....55 J9
Langshott La HORL RH6.....140 G8
Langside Av PUT/ROE SW15 ...18 E9
Langsmead LING RH7.....142 E5
Langstone Cl CRAWE RH10 ...177 M8
Langthorne St FUL/PGN SW6 ..19 H6
Langton Av EW KT17.....60 D9
Langton Cl ADL/WDHM KT15..55 J8
  WOKN/KNAP GU21.....71 M6
Langton Dr BOR GU35.....164 D4
Langton Ri FSTH SE23.....31 J3
Langton Rd E/WMO/HCT KT8..40 C6
Langton St WBPTN SW10.....19 N4
Langton Wy CROY/NA CRO.....3 H7
  EGH TW20 .....21 P9
Langtry Pl FUL/PGN SW6.....19 L4
Langwood Cha TEDD TW11.....26 B9
Langwood Cl ASHTD KT21.....77 N6
Lanigan Dr HSLW TW3.....25 J1
Lankton Cl BECK BR3.....47 J2

Lansbury Av
  EBED/NFELT TW14.....24 C2
Lansbury Rd CRAWW RH11..194 E1
Lansdell Rd MTCM CR4.....44 C3
Lansdown GU GU1.....112 E5
Lansdown Cl HORS RH12.....192 G4
  WOT/HER KT12.....39 L9
Lansdowne Cl BRYLDS KT5 ...59 P7
  RYNPK SW20.....43 H1
  TWK TW1.....26 A5
Lansdowne Copse WPK KT4 *..60 E1
Lansdowne Ct WPK KT4.....60 E1
Lansdowne Hl WNWD SE27 ...30 C6
Lansdowne Pl NRWD SE19.....45 P1
Lansdowne Rd ALDT GU11 ...108 C5
  BMLY BR1.....47 N1
  CROY/NA CRO 2 D3
  FRIM GU16.....69 J8
  HOR/WEW KT19.....60 A6
  HSLW TW3.....16 B8
  PUR/KEN CR8.....81 J1
  RYNPK SW20.....42 G1
  STA TW18.....37 M1
Lansdowne Wood Cl
  WNWD SE27.....30 C6
Lantern Cl PUT/ROE SW15....18 E9
Lanyon Ms HORS RH12 *.....192 G4
Lanyon Wk HORS RH12 *.....192 G4
Lapse Wood Wk FSTH SE23...31 J4
Lapwing Cl CROY/NA CRO.....64 E8
  HORS RH12.....192 E7
Lapwing Gv RGUE GU4.....113 H3
Lara Cl CHSGTN KT9.....59 L6
Larbert Rd
  STRHM/NOR SW16.....44 E2
Larby Pl EW KT17.....60 C8
Larch Av ASC SL5.....34 E6
  GU GU1.....112 A3
Larch Cl BAL SW12.....29 L5
  CBLY GU15.....50 G8
  KWD/TDW/WH KT20.....99 H1
  LIPH GU30.....182 E7
  REIG RH2.....119 N7
  WARL CR6.....82 E8
Larch Crs HOR/WEW KT19 ...59 P5
Larch Dr CHSWK W4.....17 N3
Larch End HORS RH12.....192 A7

Larches Av
  MORT/ESHN SW14.....18 B9
The Larches EGRIN RH19.....162 F8
  HORS RH12.....193 N4
  WOKN/KNAP GU21.....10 D1
Larches Wy CRAWE RH10.....179 K3
Larchfield Rd FLEETS GU52 ...86 E8
Larch Rd BOR GU35.....164 F6
Larch Tree Wy CROY/NA CRO..64 G2
Larch Wy FARN GU14.....88 A7
Larchwood Cl BNSTD SM7.....79 J5
Larchwood Dr EGH TW20.....21 J9
Larchwood Gld CBLY GU15 ...69 J1
Larchwood Rd
  WOKN/KNAP GU21.....71 K9
Larcombe Cl CROY/NA CRO...63 P3
Larges Bridge Dr BRAK RG12 ..32 E4
Larges La BRAK RG12.....32 E3
Largewood Av SURB KT6.....59 N1
Lark Av STA TW18.....22 C1
Larkbere Rd SYD SE26.....31 N7
Larkfield COB KT11.....75 J2
  CRAN GU6.....153 P8
Larkfield Cl FNM GU9.....4 A2
Larkfield Rd HORL RH6.....160 B1
Larkfield Rd FNM GU9.....4 A1
  RCH/KEW TW9.....17 L9
Larkham Cl FELT TW13.....23 P6
Larkin Cl COUL/CHIP CR5.....81 H6
Larkins Rd HORL RH6.....158 G5
Lark Ri CRAWE RH10.....179 K5
  CRAWW RH11.....176 F3
  EHSLY KT24.....114 C2
  LIPH GU30.....182 C5
Larksfield EGH TW20.....35 P1
  HORL RH6.....140 D9
Larkspur Cl ALDT GU11.....108 C7
Larkspur Wy HOR/WEW KT19..60 A4
  RDKG RH5.....137 K1
Larks Wy WOKN/KNAP GU21 ..71 J5
Larkswood Cl SHST GU47.....49 L8
Larkswood Dr CWTH RG45 ...49 M4
Lark Wy CAR SM5.....44 A8
Larmer Cl FLEETN GU51.....106 D8
Larnach Rd HMSMTH W6.....19 H4
La Roche Cl DTCH/LGLY SL3 ...12 A1
Larpent Av PUT/ROE SW15...27 P1
Lascombe La RGUW GU3.....130 A1
Lasham Rd FLEETN GU51.....86 C3
Lashmere CRAN GU6.....152 D9
  CRAWE RH10.....160 A8
Lasswade Rd CHERT KT16.....37 K8
Latchmere Cl
  RCHPK/HAM TW10.....26 D8
Latchmere La KUTN/CMB KT2..26 E9
Latchmere Rd
  KUTN/CMB KT2.....26 D9
Latchwood La FARN GU10 ...127 P8
Lateward Rd BTFD TW8.....17 K4
Latham Av FRIM GU16.....68 G8
Latham Cl BH/WHM TN16.....84 A5
Latham Rd TWK TW1.....25 N3
Latham's Wy CROY/NA CRO...45 H3
Latimer BRAK RG12.....32 D9
Latimer Cl CRAWW RH11.....176 C2
  WOKS/MYFD GU22.....11 K1
  WPK KT4.....60 F3
Latimer Rd CROY/NA CRO.....2 B5
  GODL GU7.....131 L9
  TEDD TW11.....25 N8
  WIM/MER SW19.....28 E9
  WOT/HER KT12.....39 P8
Latton Cl ESH/CLAY KT10.....58 B3
  WOT/HER KT12.....39 P8
Lauder Cl FRIM GU16.....68 G6
Lauderdale FARN GU14.....87 P5
Lauderdale Dr
  RCHPK/HAM TW10.....26 C6
Laud St CROY/NA CRO.....2 C6
Laughton Rd HORS RH12.....192 E5
Launceston Pl KENS W8.....19 N1
Laundry La ASC SL5.....34 D5
Laundry Rd GU GU1.....6 D3
  HMSMTH W6.....19 J4
Laundry Wy RDKG RH5.....156 B2
Lauradale BRAK RG12.....32 C5
Laurel Av EGH TW20.....20 G8
  TWK TW1.....25 N4
Laurel Bank
  CHOB/PIR GU24 *.....53 L9
Laurel Bank Gdns
  FUL/PGN SW6.....19 K7
Laurel Cl CBLY GU15.....68 F2
  CRAWE RH10.....177 K8
  DTCH/LGLY SL3.....13 J5
  FARN GU14.....88 A7
  TOOT SW17.....29 H8
Laurel Crs CROY/NA CRO.....64 G2
  WOKN/KNAP GU21.....72 C2
Laurel Dene EGRIN RH19.....180 E2
Laureldene RGUW GU3.....110 E5
Laurel Dr OXTED RH8.....123 M2
Laurel Gdns ALDT GU11.....108 C7
  HSLW TW4.....15 N9
Laurel Gv PGE/AN SE20.....46 B1
  SYD SE26.....31 L8
Laurel La WDR/YW UB7.....14 A1
Laurel Rd BARN SW13.....18 E7
  HPTN TW12.....24 G8
  RYNPK SW20.....42 G2
The Laurels BNSTD SM7.....79 L4
  COB KT11.....75 N4
  CRAWE RH10 *.....177 K2
  FLEETN GU51.....86 E6
  FNM GU9.....108 B7
Laurel Wk WSKR RH13.....192 E9
Laurier Rd CROY/NA CRO.....45 P8
Lauriston Cl WOKN/KNAP GU21..71 K6

Lauriston Rd WIM/MER SW19..28 A9
Lauser Rd STWL/WRAY TW19 ..22 F3
Laustan Cl GU GU1.....112 G5
Lavant Cl CRAWW RH11.....176 C6
Lavender Av MTCM CR4.....44 A2
  WPK KT4.....60 G2
Lavender Cl CAR SM5.....62 C4
  CHEL SW3.....19 P4
  COUL/CHIP CR5 *.....80 E8
  CTHM CR3.....101 L5
  REDH RH1.....140 D1
Lavender Cottages
  LHD/OX KT22.....97 J2
Lavender Ct E/WMO/HCT KT8..40 B4
Lavender Ga LHD/OX KT22.....76 B2
Lavender Gv MTCM CR4.....44 A2
Lavender La FRNM GU10.....127 K9
Lavender Park Rd
  BF/WBF KT14 *.....73 L2
Lavender Rd BTSEA SW11.....19 P9
  CAR SM5.....62 C4
  CROY/NA CRO.....45 H7
  HOR/WEW KT19.....59 P4
  SUT SM1.....61 P3
  WOKS/MYFD GU22.....11 K2
Lavender V WLGTN SM6.....62 F5
Lavender Wy CROY/NA CRO...46 D7
Lavengro Rd WNWD SE27.....30 D5
Lavenham Rd
  WAND/EARL SW18.....28 C5
Laverstoke Gdns
  PUT/ROE SW15.....27 L3
Laverton Ms ECT SW5.....19 M2
Laverton Pl ECT SW5.....19 M2
Lavington Cl CRAWW RH11 ...176 C4
Lavington Rd CROY/NA CRO...63 H2
Lawbrook La SHGR GU5.....134 E5
Lawday Link FNM GU9.....107 L7
Lawday Pl FNM GU9.....107 L7
Lawday Place La FNM GU9...107 L7
Lawdon Gdns CROY/NA CRO...63 H3
Lawford Cl WLGTN SM6.....62 G7
Lawford Crs YTLY GU46.....67 H2
Lawford Gdns PUR/KEN CR8...81 L5
Lawford Rd CHSWK W4.....18 A5
Lawford's Hill Rd RGUW GU3...91 J4
Lawn Cl BMLY BR1.....47 P1
  DTCH/LGLY SL3.....12 B3
  NWMAL KT3.....42 C3
Lawn Crs RCH/KEW TW9.....17 N7
Lawn Rd BECK BR3.....46 G1
  GUW GU2.....112 A8
Lawnsmead SHGR GU5.....132 F6
Lawns Rd HORS RH12.....171 K8
The Lawns BELMT SM2 *.....61 J6
  DTCH/LGLY SL3 *.....13 J6
  FARN GU14.....88 A4
  MFD/CHID GU8.....149 N3
  NRWD SE19.....45 M5
  SNWD SE25.....45 P5
  WWKM BR4.....65 H3
Lawrence Av CBLY GU15.....68 B6
  NWMAL KT3.....42 C9
  PGE/AN SE20.....46 C2
Lawrence Cl GU GU1.....112 F3
  RGUE GU4.....92 F9
Lawrence Ct BFOR GU20.....52 D5
Lawrence La
  BRKHM/BTCW RH3.....118 F5
Lawrence Pde ISLW TW7 *.....17 H8
Lawrence Rd EA W5.....17 J2
  FLEETS GU52.....86 F7
  HPTN TW12.....39 P1
  HSLWW TW4.....15 L9
  RCHPK/HAM TW10.....26 B7
  SNWD SE25.....45 P5
  WWKM BR4.....65 H3
Lawrence Wy CBLY GU15.....68 B6
Lawrie Park Av SYD SE26.....31 J8
Lawrie Park Crs SYD SE26.....31 J8
Lawrie Park Gdns SYD SE26...31 J7
Lawrie Park Rd SYD SE26.....31 K9
Lawson Cl WIM/MER SW19.....28 A6
Lawson Ter SHGR GU5 *.....132 F6
Lawson Wk CAR SM5.....62 B8
Lawson Wy ASC SL5.....35 H7
Laws Ter ALDT GU11.....108 E3
Laxton Gdns REDH RH1.....100 F8
Layard Rd THHTH CR7.....45 M3
Layburn Crs DTCH/LGLY SL3 ...12 F4
Layham Ct WEY KT13.....56 D3
Layton Crs CROY/NA CRO.....63 J4
Layton Pl RCH/KEW TW9.....17 N6
Layton Rd BTFD TW8.....17 K3
  HSLW TW3.....16 B9
Layton's La SUN TW16.....39 H3
Lea Cl ASHV GU12.....109 J5
  CRAWW RH11.....176 C6
  FNM GU9.....108 A3
  WHTN TW2.....24 G3
Lea Cottages MTCM CR4 *.....44 C3
Lea Ct FNM GU9.....108 A3
Leacroft ASC SL5.....34 G6
Lea Cft CWTH RG45.....49 M5
Leacroft EGRIN RH19.....180 C1
  STA TW18.....22 E8
Leacroft Av BAL SW12.....29 J3
Leacroft Cl PUR/KEN CR8.....81 L5
  STA TW18.....22 E7
Leaf Cl THDIT KT7.....40 E7
Leaf Gv STRHM/NOR SW16.....30 B8
Leafield Cl
  STRHM/NOR SW16.....30 C9
  WOKN/KNAP GU21.....71 P7
Leafield Copse BRAK RG12 ...33 H5
Leafield Rd RYNPK SW20.....43 K4
  SUT SM1.....61 L1
Leafy Wy CROY/NA CRO.....3 M3
Leamington Av MRDN SM4.....43 K5
Leamington Cl HSLW TW3.....25 L1
Leamington Rd NWDGN UB2...15 M2
Leamore St HMSMTH W6.....18 F2

Leander Rd
  BRXS/STRHM SW2.....30 A2
  THHTH CR7.....45 H5
Leapale La GU GU1.....6 E5
Leapale Rd GU GU1.....6 E5
Lea Rd BECK BR3.....46 G4
  CBLY GU15.....68 D6
  NWDGN UB2.....15 N2
Leas Cl CHSGTN KT9.....59 M6
Leaside GT/LBKH KT23.....96 C6
Leas La WARL CR6.....82 D7
Lea Springs FLEETN GU51.....86 D8
Leas Rd GUW GU2.....6 D4
  WARL CR6.....82 D7
The Leas STA TW18 *.....22 C7
The Lea EGH TW20.....36 F1
  EWKG RG40.....48 D1
  FLEETN GU51.....86 E8
Leather Cl EDEN TN8.....144 G5
  MTCM CR4.....44 C3
Leatherhead By-Pass Rd
  LHD/OX KT22.....77 H9
Leatherhead Rd ASHTD KT21 ..77 K9
  GT/LBKH KT23.....96 C6
  LHD/OX KT22.....96 G2
Leather La SHGR GU5.....133 E1
Leaveland Cl BECK BR3.....46 G5
Leavesden Rd WEY KT13.....56 D4
Leaves Gn BRAK RG12.....32 F7
Lea Wy ASHV GU12.....109 H3
Leaway FNM GU9 *.....108 C9
Leawood Rd FLEETN GU51.....86 E8
Lea Wood Rd FLEETN GU51 ...86 E8
Leazes Av CTHM CR3.....101 J3
Lebanon Av FELT TW13.....24 E8
Lebanon Dr COB KT11.....76 A2
Lebanon Gdns
  BH/WHM TN16.....84 B6
  WAND/EARL SW18.....28 A3
Lebanon Rd CROY/NA CRO.....3 H2
  WAND/EARL SW18.....28 D1
Le Borowe FLEETS GU52.....106 D2
Lechford Rd HORL RH6.....159 J3
Leckford Rd
  WAND/EARL SW18.....28 D5
Lecky St SKENS SW7.....19 P3
Leconfield Av BARN SW13.....18 D8
Ledbury Rd CROY/NA CRO.....63 L3
  REIG RH2.....119 L5
Ledger Cl GU GU1.....112 F3
Ledger Dr ADL/WDHM KT15 ...55 K5
Ledgers Rd WARL CR6.....82 G5
Ledrington Rd NRWD SE19 ...30 G9
Lee Acre DORK RH4 *.....137 J1
Leechcroft Rd WLGTN SM6.....62 C2
Leech La LHD/OX KT22.....98 A6
Leechpool La SWTR RH13.....192 H6
Lee Ct ALDT GU11.....108 D6
Leehurst MFD/CHID GU8.....149 N4
Lee Rd ALDT GU11.....108 A4
  WIM/MER SW19.....43 M2
Leeside HORS RH12 *.....175 H5
Leeson Rd BRXN/ST SW9 *.....30 B1
The Lees CROY/NA CRO.....64 F1
Lee St HORL RH6.....140 A9
Leeward Gdns
  WIM/MER SW19.....28 B9
The Leeways CHEAM SM3 *.....61 J5
Leewood Wy EHSLY KT24.....95 L7
Lefroy's Fld RFNM GU10.....106 D6
Leger Cl FLEETS GU51.....106 E1
Legge Crs ALDT GU11.....108 A5
Legrace Av HSLWW TW4.....15 L9
Leicester BRAK RG12.....32 F8
Leicester Av MTCM CR4.....44 G5
Leicester Cl WPK KT4.....60 G3
Leicester Rd CROY/NA CRO...45 N8
Leigham Av
  STRHM/NOR SW16.....29 P6
Leigham Court Rd
  STRHM/NOR SW16.....29 P6
Leigham Dr ISLW TW7.....16 E5
Leigham Hall Pde
  STRHM/NOR SW16 *.....29 P6
Leigham V
  STRHM/NOR SW16.....30 B6
Leigh Cl ADL/WDHM KT15.....55 K6
  NWMAL KT3.....42 B5
Leigh Court Cl COB KT11.....75 L3
Leigh Crs CROY/NA CRO.....65 H6
Leigh Hill Rd COB KT11.....75 L4
Leighlands CRAWE RH10.....177 M3
Leigh Orchard Cl
  STRHM/NOR SW16.....30 B5
Leigh Pl DTCH/LGLY SL3 *.....12 A5
Leigh Place La GDST RH9.....122 D3
Leigh Place Rd REIG RH2.....138 E2
Leigh Rd BRKHM/BTCW RH3...118 B7
  COB KT11.....75 K2
  HSLW TW3.....16 D9
Leighton Gdns SAND/SEL CR2..82 B2
Leighton St CROY/NA CRO.....2 A2
Leighton Wy EPSOM KT18.....78 B3
Leinster Av
  MORT/ESHN SW14.....18 A8
Leipzig Barracks
  FLEETS GU52.....107 H4
Leipzig Rd FLEETS GU52.....107 H3
Leisure La BF/WBF KT14.....73 M1
Leith Cl CWTH RG45.....49 L2
Leithcote Gdns
  STRHM/NOR SW16.....30 A6
Leithcote Pth
  STRHM/NOR SW16.....30 A5
Leith Dr ALDT GU11.....108 D6
Leith Gv RDKG RH5.....137 K9
Leith Hill Rd RDKG RH5.....135 N6
Leith Lea RDKG RH5 *.....137 K9
Leith Rd EPSOM KT18.....78 C3
Leith Rd EW KT17.....78 C1

  RDKG RH5.....137 J3
Leith Towers BELMT SM2 *.....61 M6
Leith Vw RDKG RH5.....137 J2
Leith View Rd HORS RH12.....192 F5
Leith Av HSLWW TW4.....15 P7
Le Marchant Rd FRIM GU16 ...69 H5
Le May Cl HORL RH6.....140 C9
Lemington Gv BRAK RG12.....32 D7
Lemmington Wy
  HORS RH12.....192 E3
Lemon's Farm Rd
  RDKG RH5.....135 P7
Lena Gdns HMSMTH W6.....18 G1
Lendore Rd FRIM GU16.....68 F8
Lenelby Rd SURB KT6.....41 N9
Len Freeman Pl
  FUL/PGN SW6.....19 K4
Lenham Rd SUT SM1.....61 M3
  THHTH CR7.....45 M5
Lennard Cl WWKM BR4.....65 L1
Lennard Av WWKM BR4.....65 L1
Lennard Rd CROY/NA CRO.....2 C2
  PGE/AN SE20.....31 L9
Lennard Ter SYD SE26 *.....31 L9
Lennel Gdns FLEETS GU52 ...87 J3
Lennox Gdns CROY/NA CRO...63 J4
Lenten Cl SHGR GU5.....134 F4
Lenton Ri RCH/KEW TW9.....17 L8
Leominster Rd MRDN SM4.....43 N7
Leominster Wk MRDN SM4.....43 N7
Leonard Av MRDN SM4.....43 N6
Leonard Cl FRIM GU16.....68 F8
Leonard Ct KENS W8.....19 L1
Leonard Rd MTCM CR4.....44 C4
  NWDGN UB2.....15 M1
Leonardslee Ct
  CRAWE RH10 *.....177 L8
Leonard Wy SWTR RH13.....192 E8
Leopold Av FARN GU14.....88 D2
  WIM/MER SW19.....28 C8
Leopold Rd CRAWW RH11.....176 E5
  WIM/MER SW19.....28 C8
Le Personne Rd CTHM CR3 ...101 M2
Leppington BRAK RG12.....32 C7
Leppoc Rd CLAP SW4.....29 N1
Leret Wy LHD/OX KT22.....96 G1
Lerry Cl WKENS W14.....19 K4
Lesbourne Rd REIG RH2.....119 M6
Lescombe Cl FSTH SE23.....31 M6
Lescombe Rd FSTH SE23.....31 M6
Leslie Gdns BELMT SM2.....61 L6
Leslie Gv CROY/NA CRO.....3 G2
Leslie Grove Pl CROY/NA CRO...3 G2
Leslie Park Rd CROY/NA CRO...3 G2
Leslie Rd CHOB/PIR GU24.....53 K8
  DORK RH4.....117 K5
Lessar Av CLAP SW4.....29 M1
Lessingham Av TOOT SW17.....29 J7
Lessing St FSTH SE23.....31 M3
Lessness Rd MRDN SM4.....43 N7
Lestock Wy FLEETN GU51.....87 G2
Letchworth Av
  EBED/NFELT TW14.....24 A3
Letchworth Cl HAYES BR2.....47 N6
Letchworth Dr HAYES BR2 ...47 N6
Letchworth St TOOT SW17.....29 J7
Letcombe Sq BRAK RG12.....33 J5
Letterstone Rd FUL/PGN SW6..19 K5
Lettice St FUL/PGN SW6.....19 K7
Levana Cl WIM/MER SW19.....28 A4
Levendale Rd FSTH SE23.....31 M5
Leveret Cl CROY/NA CRO.....65 K9
Leveret La CRAWW RH11.....176 C4
Leverkusen Rd BRAK RG12.....32 D4
Levern Dr FNM GU9.....107 N8
Leverson St
  STRHM/NOR SW16.....29 M9
Levett Rd LHD/OX KT22.....77 H9
Levignen Cl FLEETS GU52.....106 D1
Levylsdene GU GU1.....113 H5
Lewes Cl CRAWE RH10.....177 M5
Lewesdon Cl WIM/MER SW19..28 A4
Lewes Rd EGRIN RH19.....180 F3
  FROW RH18.....181 K8
Lewin Rd MORT/ESHN SW14 ...18 B8
  STRHM/NOR SW16.....29 N9
Lewins Rd EPSOM KT18.....77 P3
Lewis Cl ADL/WDHM KT15.....55 N6
Lewisham Cl CRAWW RH11 ...176 F9
Lewisham Wy SHST GU47.....49 N8
Lewis Rd MTCM CR4.....44 A3
  RCHPK/HAM TW10.....26 C1
  SUT SM1.....61 M3
Lexden Rd MTCM CR4.....44 F5
Lexham Gdns ECT SW5.....19 M2
Lexham Ms KENS W8.....19 L2
Lexington Ct PUR/KEN CR8 ...63 L8
Lexton Gdns
  BRXS/STRHM SW2.....30 A3
Leybourne Pk RCH/KEW TW9..17 N7
Leybourne Av BF/WBF KT14...74 D2
Leybourne Cl BF/WBF KT14 ...74 D2
  CRAWW RH11.....194 F1
  HAYES BR2.....47 N6
Leyburn Gdns CROY/NA CRO...3 K4
Leycester Cl BFOR GU20.....52 C4
Leyfield WPK KT4.....60 C1
Leylands La
  STWL/WRAY TW19.....12 C8
Ley Rd FARN GU14.....68 C8
Leyside CWTH RG45.....49 K4
Leys LHD/OX KT22.....76 D1
The Leys WOT/HER KT12 *.....57 N1
Leyton Rd WIM/MER SW19.....43 N1
Leywood Cl ASHV GU12.....109 H3
Liberty Hall Rd
  ADL/WDHM KT15.....55 L4
Liberty La ADL/WDHM KT15 ...55 M4
Liberty Ri ADL/WDHM KT15 ...55 L5
Library Rd FARN GU14.....88 D5
Lichfield Gdns
  RCH/KEW TW9 *.....26 D1

Lichfield Rd HSLWW TW4 .....15 L8
  RCH/KEW TW9 .....17 M6
Lichfields BRAK RG12 .....52 F7
Lichfield Ter
  RDPK/HAM TW10 * 26 D1
Lichfield Wy SAND/SEL CR2.....64 D8
Lickfolds Rd RFNM GU10 .146 B2
Liddell Cl EWKG RG40 .....48 C6
Liddell Wy ASC SL5 .....33 P6
Liddington Hall Dr
  RGUW 111 L2
Liddington New Rd
  RGUW 111 L2
Lidiard Rd WAND/EARL SW18 ..28 F5
Lido Rd GU GU1 .....7 K5
Lidsey Cl CRAWE RH10 .....177 M7
Lidstone Cl
  WOKN/KNAP GU21 .....71 P6
Lilford St PUT/ROE SW15 .....19 H9
Lightwater Meadow
  LTWR GU18.....52 B9
Lightwater Rd LTWR GU18 .....52 B9
Lightwood BRAK RG12 .....32 F7
Lilac Av WOKS/MYFD GU22 ....72 B9
Lilac Cl GU GU1 .....112 A1
Lilac Gdns CROY/NA CRO 64 C2
  EA W5 .....17 K1
Lilian Rd MTCM CR4 .....44 E2
Lille Barracks ALDT GU11 .....87 P7
Lilleshall Rd MRDN SM4 .....43 P7
Lilley Dr KWD/TDW/WH KT20 ..99 M2
Lilley Rd BARN SW13 .....18 C4
Lillie Rd BH/WHM TN16 .....88 B7
  FUL/PGN SW6 .....19 H4
Lillie Yd FUL/PGN SW6 .....19 L4
Lilliott's La LHD/OX KT22 .....76 G8
Lily Cl WKENS W14 * 19 J2
Lily Dr WDR/YW UB7 .....13 P4
Lilyfields Cha CRAN GU6.....153 P9
Lily Hill Dr BRAK RG12 .....33 G3
Lily Hill Rd BRAK RG12 .....33 H3
Lilyville Rd FUL/PGN SW6 .....19 K6
Lime Av CBLY GU15 .....19 M9
  HORS RH12 .....192 F6
Limebush Cl
  ADL/WDHM KT15.....55 N7
Lime Cl CRAWE RH10 .....160 C9
  CRAWW RH11 .....176 F2
  REIG RH2 .....119 M8
  RGUE GU4 .....93 M8
Lime Crs SUN TW16 .....39 L3
Limecroft Cl GU GU46 .....66 B6
Limecroft Cl HOR/WEW KT19 .60 B6
Limecroft Rd
  WOKN/KNAP GU21 .....71 H6
Lime Dr FLEETN GU51 .....87 H3
Lime Gv ADL/WDHM KT15 .....55 L3
  GU GU1 .....111 P1
  NWMAL KT3 .....42 B4
  RGUE GU4 .....93 M8
  TWK TW1 .....25 N2
  WARL CR6 .....82 E8
  WOKS/MYFD GU22 .....92 C1
Lime Meadow Av
  SAND/SEL CR2 .....82 A2
Limerick Cl BAL SW12 .....29 M3
  BNFD RG42.....32 C3
Limerston St WBPTN SW10 ..19 N4
Limes Av BARN SW13 .....18 D7
  CAR SM5 .....44 B9
  CROY/NA CRO 45 H2
  HORL RH6.....159 L3
  PGE/AN SE20 .....46 B1
Limes Cl ASHF TW15 .....23 J8
  CAR SM5 .....62 B1
  LIPH GU30 .....182 F3
Limes Field Rd BARN SW13 ..18 C8
Limes Gdns
  WAND/EARL SW18.....28 D2
Limes Rd BECK BR3 .....47 H3
  CROY/NA CRO 45 H2
  EGH TW20 .....21 L8
  FARN GU14.....88 D3
  WEY KT13.....56 C3
The Limes CRAN TN8 .....144 C4
  EGRIN RH19 .....161 P7
  LHD/OX KT22 .....97 H3
  WAND/EARL SW18 * 28 D2
  WOKN/KNAP GU21 .....72 B4
Lime St ALDT GU11 .....108 B8
Lime Tree Av THDIT KT7 .....40 E9
Limetree Cl
  BRXS/STRHM SW2 .....30 A4
Lime Tree Cl GT/LBKH KT23 ...96 A4
Lime Tree Gv CROY/NA CRO.....64 A4
Limetree Pl MTCM CR4 .....44 D2
Lime Tree Rd HEST TW5 .....16 B6
Lime Tree Ter CAT SE6 * 31 N4
Lime Tree Wk VW GU25 .....36 A5
  WWKM BR4 .....65 M3
Lime Wk BRAK RG12 .....32 E5
Limeway Ter DORK RH4 .....116 G5
Limewood Cl BECK BR3 .....47 J6
  WOKN/KNAP GU21 .....71 K9
Limpsfield Av THHTH CR7 .....45 K6
  WIM/MER SW19 .....28 A5
Limpsfield Rd SAND/SEL CR2 .82 A1
  WARL CR6.....82 C8
Lince La DORK RH4 .....116 D7
Linchfield Rd DTCH/LGLY SL3 .12 A6
Linchmere Pl CRAWW RH11..176 B6
Linchmere Rd HASM GU27 ..183 M7
Lincoln Av WHTN TW2 .....25 H4
  WIM/MER SW19 .....28 A4
Lincoln Cl ASHV GU12 .....109 J1
  CBLY GU15 .....69 J2
  CRAWE RH10 .....177 H8
Lincoln Dr WOKS/MYFD GU22 .73 J4
  FARN GU14.....88 C3
  FELT TW13 .....24 C6

GUW GU2 .....111 M3
  MTCM CR4 .....44 C6
  NWMAL KT3 .....42 A4
  SNWD SE25 .....46 B4
  WFT TW4.....42 F9
Lincolnshire Gdns
  BNFD RG42.....32 C3
Lincolns Md LING RH7 .....162 B1
Lincoln Ter BELMT SM2 * 61 L6
Lincoln Wy SUN TW16 .....38 G2
Lindale Cl VW GU25 .....35 M5
Lindal Rd BROCKY SE4 .....31 N1
Lindbergh Rd WLGTN SM6.....62 G7
Linden Av COUL/CHIP CR5.....80 D5
  EGRIN RH19 .....180 B1
  HSLW TW3 .....25 J1
  THHTH CR7 .....45 K4
Linden Cl ADL/WDHM KT15 ...55 L9
  CRAWE RH10 .....177 K8
  HORS RH12 .....192 D6
  KWD/TDW/WH KT20 .....79 H9
  THDIT KT7 .....40 E8
Linden Cottages
  WIM/MER SW19 * 28 B9
Linden Ct CBLY GU15 .....69 H1
  EGH TW20 .....21 J8
  LHD/OX KT22 .....97 H1
Linden Crs KUT KT1 .....9 G5
Linden Dr CTHM CR3 .....101 L4
Linden Gdns CHSWK W4 .....18 B3
  LHD/OX KT22 .....97 J1
Linden Gv NWMAL KT3 .....42 C4
  SYD SE26 .....31 K9
  WARL CR6.....82 E7
  WOT/HER KT12 .....57 H1
Lindenhill Rd BNFD RG42.....32 B2
Linden Lea DORK RH4 * 117 J9
Linden Leas WWKM BR4 .....65 K1
Linden Pit Pth LHD/OX KT22 ..97 H1
Linden Rd EHSLY KT24 * 94 A6
  GU GU1 .....6 E2
  HPTN TW12 .....40 A2
  LHD/OX KT22 .....97 H1
  WEY KT13 .....56 C5
Lindens Cl EHSLY KT24 .....95 N8
The Lindens CHSWK W4 .....18 A6
  CRAWE RH10 .....160 C9
  CROY/NA CRO 65 J5
  FNM GU9.....5 K6
Linden Wy RPLY/SEND GU23 ..95 K5
  SHPTN TW17 .....38 E6
  WLGTN SM6.....62 E8
  WOKS/MYFD GU22 .....92 D1
Lindfield Gdns GU GU1 .....7 J1
Lindfield Rd CROY/NA CRO 45 P7
Lindfield Ter
  WOKN/KNAP GU21 * 72 A5
Lindgren Wk
  CRAWW RH11 * 194 E1
Lindisfarne Rd RYNPK SW20 ..42 F1
Lindley Pl RCH/KEW TW9 .....17 N6
Lindley Rd GDST RH9 .....122 C1
  WOT/HER KT12 .....57 N2
Lindores Rd CAR SM5 .....43 N8
Lind Rd SUT SM1 .....61 N4
Lindrop St FUL/PGN SW6 .....19 N7
Lindsay Cl CHSGTN KT9 .....59 L6
  HOR/WEW KT19 .....78 A2
  STWL/WRAY TW19 .....22 G2
Lindsay Dr SHPTN TW17 .....38 F7
Lindsay Rd ADL/WDHM KT15...55 L9
  HPTN TW12 .....25 H8
  WPK KT4.....60 F1
Lindsey Cl MTCM CR4 .....44 G6
Lindsey Gdns
  EBED/NFELT TW14 * 23 N3
Lindum Dene ALDT GU11.....108 C5
Lindum Rd TEDD TW11 .....41 J1
Lindway WNWD SE27 .....30 C9
Linersh Dr SHGR GU5 .....132 E7
Linersh Wood SHGR GU5 ..132 E8
Linfield Cl WOT/HER KT12 * ...57 H4
Ling Crs BOR GU35 .....164 E5
Ling Dr LTWR GU18 .....69 P1
Lingfield Av BRYLDS KT5 .....41 L5
Lingfield Common Rd
  LING RH7 .....143 J9
Lingfield Dr CRAWE RH10 ..177 P4
Lingfield Gdns
  COUL/CHIP CR5 .....81 K8
Lingfield Rd EDEN TN8.....144 E5
  EGRIN RH19 .....162 C7
  WIM/MER SW19 .....27 P2
  WPK KT4.....60 G2
Lingmala Gv FLEETS GU52 ...107 H1
Lingwell Rd TOOT SW17 .....29 H6
Lingwood BRAK RG12.....32 E7
Lingwood Gdns ISLW TW7 ....16 E5
Link 10 CRAWE RH10.....177 K2
Linkfield E/WMO/HCT KT8.....40 A4
Linkfield Gdns REDH RH1 ..120 A5
Linkfield La REDH RH1 .....120 A3
Linkfield Rd ISLW TW7 .....16 F7
Linkfield St REDH RH1 .....120 A5
Link La WLGTN SM6.....62 G5
Link Rd ADL/WDHM KT15.....56 A3
  DTCH/LGLY SL3 .....12 C5
  EBED/NFELT TW14 .....24 A3
  FARN GU14.....87 P7
  WLGTN SM6.....44 C9
Links Av MRDN SM4 .....43 L5
Links Brow LHD/OX KT22 .....96 E3
Links Cl ASHTD KT21 .....77 J6
  CRAN GU6.....153 N2
Linkscroft Av ASHF TW15.....23 L9
Links Gdns
  STRHM/NOR SW16 .....45 J1

Links Green Wy COB KT11 .....76 A3
Linkside NWMAL KT3 .....42 C3
Linkside East GSHT GU26 ..165 L4
Linkside North GSHT GU26 .165 L4
Linkside South GSHT GU26 .165 M5
Linkside West GSHT GU26 ..165 L4
Links Pl ASHTD KT21 .....77 K6
Links Rd ASHF TW15 .....23 H8
  ASHTD KT21 .....77 H6
  EW KT17 .....78 E2
  SHGR GU5.....132 C6
  TOOT SW17 .....29 K9
  WOKS/MYFD GU22 .....72 D8
The Links ASC SL5 .....33 N3
  WOT/HER KT12 .....57 J1
Links View Av RDKG RH5 ....117 N5
Linksview Ct HPTN TW12 * ...25 L7
Links View Rd CROY/NA CRO...64 C2
  HPTN TW12 .....25 L8
Links Wy BECK BR3 .....46 G7
  EHSLY KT24 .....94 N8
  FARN GU14.....87 N4
The Link CRAWW RH11 .....176 C5
  TEDD TW11 .....25 N9
  YTLY GU46 .....66 C1
Link Wy RCH/KEW TW9 .....26 C5
  STA TW18 .....22 B9
Linkway CBLY GU15 .....68 E4
  CWTH RG45.....49 K4
  FLEETS GU52 .....86 F9
  GUW GU2 .....111 M5
  HORL RH6.....159 M5
  RYNPK SW20 .....42 F5
The Linkway BELMT SM2 .....61 N7
Linnell Cl CRAWW RH11 .....194 E2
Linnell Rd REDH RH1 .....120 C6
Linnet Cl CRAWE RH10 .....179 K6
  SAND/SEL CR2 .....64 D8
Linnet Gv RGUE GU4 .....113 H5
Linnet Ms BAL SW12 .....29 K3
Linnett Cl CRAWE RH10 * 179 K5
Linsford La FRIM GU16 .....89 H4
Linslade Cl HSLWW TW4 .....24 F1
Linstead Rd FARN GU14 .....68 A8
Linstead Wy
  WAND/EARL SW18.....28 B9
Linsted La BOR GU35 .....164 A4
Lintaine Cl FUL/PGN SW6 * ...19 J4
Linton Cl CAR SM5.....44 B8
Linton Gld CROY/NA CRO 64 E8
Linton's La EW KT17 .....78 C1
Lintott Ct STWL/WRAY TW19 ..22 G2
Lintott Gdns SWTR RH13.....192 D7
Linver Rd FUL/PGN SW6.....19 K7
Lion & Lamb Wy FNM GU9.....4 E3
Lion & Lamb Yd FNM GU9.....5 F3
Lion Av TWK TW1 .....25 N4
Lion Cl BROCKY SE4 .....31 P2
  SHPTN TW17 .....38 A4
Lionel Rd North BTFD TW8 ....17 L1
Lionel Rd South BTFD TW8 ...17 M1
Lion Gate Gdns
  RCH/KEW TW9 .....17 M8
Lion Green Rd
  COUL/CHIP CR5 .....80 F4
Lion La CRAWE RH10 .....179 H7
  GSHT GU26.....184 A1
Lion Md HASM GU27 .....184 A4
Lion Park Av CHSGTN KT9 .....59 N3
Lion Rd CROY/NA CRO 45 L6
  FARN GU14.....88 D5
  WHTN TW2 .....25 N4
Lion Wy BTFD TW8 .....17 L5
  FLEETS GU52 .....107 H1
Lion Wharf Rd ISLW TW7 .....17 H8
Liphook Crs FSTH SE23.....31 K3
Liphook Rd BOR GU35 .....164 B8
  HASM GU27 .....183 H6
  HASM GU27 .....183 P4
Lipsham Cl BNSTD SM7 .....79 P2
Lisbon Av WHTN TW2 .....25 K5
Liscombe BRAK RG12.....32 D8
Lisgar Ter WKENS W14.....19 K2
Liskeard Dr FARN GU14 .....88 C1
Lisle Cl TOOT SW17 .....29 L7
Lismore WIM/MER SW19 * 28 C8
Lismore Cl ISLW TW7 .....16 G7
Lismore Crs CRAWW RH11 ..176 E8
Lismore Rd SAND/SEL CR2 ...63 N5
Lismoyne Cl FLEETN GU51 ...86 F5
Lissant Cl SURB KT6 .....41 J8
Lissoms Rd COUL/CHIP CR5...80 C7
Lister Av EGRIN RH19 .....180 D5
Lister Cl MTCM CR4 .....44 B1
Litchfield Av MRDN SM4 .....43 K8
Litchfield Rd SUT SM1 .....61 N3
Litchfield Wy GUW GU2.....111 M7
Lithgow's Rd HTHAIR TW6.....14 G9
Little Acre BECK BR3.....46 G4
Little Aly EDEN TN8.....144 F9
Little Austins Rd FNM GU9.....5 K7
Little Benty WDR/YW UB7.....13 P3
Little Birch Cl
  ADL/WDHM KT15.....55 P7
The Little Boltons
  WBPTN SW10.....19 M3
Little Bookham St
  GT/LBKH KT23 .....95 P4
Little Bornes DUL SE21.....30 F7
Little Borough
  BRKHM/BTCW RH3.....117 N6
Littlebrook Cl CROY/NA CRO...46 D7
Little Browns La EDEN TN8...144 C1
Little Chesters
  KWD/TDW/WH KT20.....98 E5
Little Collins REDH RH1 * 141 K6
Littlecombe Cl
  PUT/ROE SW15 * 28 A2
Little Common La
  REDH RH1 .....121 K3

Little Comptons
  SWTR RH13 .....192 E8
Little Copse FLEETS GU52 .....86 F8
  YTLY GU46 .....66 G1
Littlecote Cl WIM/MER SW19 ..28 A3
Little Ct WWKM BR4 .....65 L1
Little Crabtree
  CRAWW RH11.....176 F4
Little Cranmore La
  EHSLY KT24 .....94 D8
Littlecroft Rd EGH TW20 .....21 L8
Littledale Cl BRAK RG12 .....32 G4
Little Dimocks BAL SW12 .....29 L5
Little Ealing La EA W5 .....17 J2
Little Elms HYS/HAR UB3 .....14 F5
Little Ferry Rd TWK TW1 * 26 A4
Littlefield Cl ASHV GU12 .....109 J5
  KUT KT1 .....8 E5
  RGUW GU3 .....130 C1
Littlefield Gdns ASHV GU12..109 J5
Littlefield Wy RGUW GU3.....111 J1
Littleford La RGUE GU4.....133 K7
  SHGR GU5.....133 K7
Little Frith EWKG RG40.....48 A7
Little Grebe HORS RH12.....192 B5
Little Green La CHERT KT16 ...55 J2
  FNM GU9.....4 C1
Little Gv DORK RH4 * 117 J9
Little Hatch HORS RH12.....192 E5
Little Haven La HORS RH12..192 E5
Littlehaven La HORS RH12 ..192 E5
Littleheath La COB KT11 .....76 A3
Little Heath Rd
  CHOB/PIR GU24.....53 L7
Littleheath Rd SAND/SEL CR2..64 B7
Little Hide GU GU1 .....112 E3
Little Kiln GODL GU7 .....131 L5
Little King St EGRIN RH19 ...180 D2
Little London
  MFD/CHID GU8 .....149 M7
  SHGR GU5.....134 A3
Little Lullenden LING RH7.....143 K8
Little Manor Gdns
  CRAN GU6.....170 G1
Littlemead ESH/CLAY KT10...58 D3
Little Md WOKN/KNAP GU21...71 M5
Little Moor SHST GU47 .....49 P3
Little Moreton Cl
  BF/WBF KT14 * 73 M1
Little Orch ADL/WDHM KT15...55 L9
  WOKN/KNAP GU21 .....72 E3
Little Orchards EPSOM KT18...78 C3
Little Orchard Wy
  RGUE GU4.....132 C3
Little Paddock CBLY GU15 .....51 J9
Little Park Dr FELT TW13 .....24 E5
Little Platt GUW GU2 .....111 K4
Little Queens Rd TEDD TW11...25 N9
Little Riding
  WOKS/MYFD GU22 .....11 J2
Little Ringdale BRAK RG12.....32 G5
Little Roke Av PUR/KEN CR8...81 K3
Little Roke Rd PUR/KEN CR8...81 L3
Little Rownings FSTH SE23 * ..31 J3
Littlers Cl WIM/MER SW19 .....43 P2
Little St Leonards
  MORT/ESHN SW14 .....18 A8
Littlestone Cl BECK BR3 .....31 P9
Little St GUW GU2.....111 P1
Little Sutton La
  DTCH/LGLY SL3 .....12 C3
Little Thatch GODL GU7 .....131 M7
Little Thurbans Cl FNM GU9 ..127 J7
Littleton La REIG RH2 .....119 J7
  RGUW GU3 .....131 N2
  STA TW18 .....38 A6
Littleton Rd ASHF TW15 .....38 E1
Littleton St
  WAND/EARL SW18.....28 F5
Little Tumners Ct GODL GU7..131 L6
Little Vigo YTLY GU46 .....66 F4
Little Warren Cl RGUE GU4 ..112 F7
Little Wellington St
  ALDT GU11 .....108 C4
Littlewick Rd
  WOKN/KNAP GU21 .....71 K5
Littlewood CRAN GU6.....153 J9
Littlewood Cl WEA W13 .....17 H1
Little Woodcote La CAR SM5...80 D7
Littleworth Av
  ESH/CLAY KT10.....58 D4
Littleworth Common Rd
  ESH/CLAY KT10.....58 D2
Littleworth La
  ESH/CLAY KT10.....58 D3
Littleworth Pl ESH/CLAY KT10..58 D3
Littleworth Rd
  ESH/CLAY KT10.....58 D4
  MFD/CHID GU8 .....149 N6
  RFNM GU10.....129 H4
Litten Hallards
  WOT/HER KT12 * 39 J7
Liverpool Rd KUTN/CMB KT2...41 N1
  THHTH CR7 .....45 L4
Livesey Cl KUT KT1 .....9 F6
Livingstone Rd BTSEA SW11 ..19 P8
  CTHM CR3 .....101 M3
  CTHM CR3 .....101 N3
  HSLW TW3 .....16 C9
  SWTR RH13 .....192 C9
  THHTH CR7 .....45 M2

Lloyd Rd WPK KT4 .....60 G2
Lloyds Ct CRAWE RH10 * 177 H2
Lloyds Wy BECK BR3 .....46 E6
Loats Rd BRXS/STRHM SW2...29 P2
Lobelia Rd CHOB/PIR GU24...70 G4
Lochaline St HMSMTH W6.....18 G4
Lochinvar St BAL SW12 .....29 L3
Lochinver BRAK RG12.....32 D8
Lock Cl WOKN/KNAP GU21.....73 J1
Locke-king Cl WEY KT13.....56 C6
Locke King Rd WEY KT13.....56 C6
Locke Rd LIPH GU30 .....182 G6
Lockesley Sq SURB KT6 * 41 K7
Locke Wy WOKN/KNAP GU21 ..11 F5
Lockfield Dr
  WOKN/KNAP GU21 .....71 L6
Lockhart Rd COB KT11 .....75 L2
Lockhursthatch La
  SHGR GU5.....134 A7
Lock La WOKS/MYFD GU22.....73 M5
Lock Rd ALDT GU11 .....108 F1
  GU GU1 .....112 B1
  RCHPK/HAM TW10 .....26 B7
Lock's La MTCM CR4.....44 C2
Locksley Dr
  WOKN/KNAP GU21 .....71 M6
Locksmeade Rd
  RCHPK/HAM TW10 .....26 A7
Locks Meadow LING RH7.....162 F3
Locks Ride ASC SL5 .....33 L1
Lockswood CHOB/PIR GU24 ..71 H9
Lockton Cha ASC SL5.....33 M4
Lockwood Cl FARN GU14.....68 A8
  HORS RH12 .....192 G1
  SYD SE26 .....31 L7
Lockwood Pth
  WOKN/KNAP GU21 .....73 H2
Lockwood Wy CHSGTN KT9 ...59 N4
Lockyer Pl BH/WHM TN16 * ..105 H6
Locomotive Dr
  EBED/NFELT TW14 .....24 B4
Loddon Cl CBLY GU15 .....69 J2
Loddon Rd FARN GU14.....87 P1
Loddon Wy ASHV GU12 .....109 J3
Loder Cl WOKN/KNAP GU21...73 H2
Lodge Av CROY/NA CRO 63 L1
Lodgebottom Rd RDKG RH5...97 N7
Lodge Cl
  CRAWW RH11.....176 F5
  EGH TW20 .....21 J8
  EGRIN RH19 .....180 B2
  EW KT17 .....60 G8
  ISLW TW7 .....17 H6
  LHD/OX KT22 .....96 G2
  RDKG RH5 .....137 M6
  WLGTN SM6 .....44 C9
Lodge Gdns BECK BR3.....46 F5
Lodge Hl PUR/KEN CR8 .....81 J4
Lodge Hl Cl RFNM GU10.....127 P7
Lodge Hill Rd RFNM GU10 ...127 P6
Lodge La BH/WHM TN16.....104 C7
  CROY/NA CRO 65 J5
  RDKG RH5 .....137 M6
  REDH RH1 .....140 A4
Lodge Pl SUT SM1 .....61 M4
Lodge Rd CROY/NA CRO.....45 K2
  FNM GU9.....128 B3
  SUT SM1 .....61 M4
  WLGTN SM6 .....62 D4
Lodge Wk WARL CR6 .....82 G5
  SHPTN TW17 .....38 E3
Lodge Wy ASHF TW15 .....23 H5
  SHPTN TW17 .....38 E2
Lodsworth FARN GU14 .....87 P4
Lofthouse Pl CHSGTN KT9.....59 J5
Logan Cl HSLWW TW4 .....15 P9
Logan Ms KENS W8 .....19 L2
Logan Pl ECT SW5 .....19 L2
Logans La DORK RH4.....136 E3
Lois Dr SHPTN TW17 .....38 D6
Loisworth La EHSLY KT24.....94 E6
Loman Rd FRIM GU16.....89 L2
Lomas Cl CROY/NA CRO 65 J6
Lombard Rd BTSEA SW11 ....19 P7
  WIM/MER SW19 .....43 M3
Lombard St MFD/CHID GU8...128 P7
Lombardy Cl
  WOKN/KNAP GU21 .....71 M6
Lomond Gdns SAND/SEL CR2..64 G6
Loncin Mead Av
  ADL/WDHM KT15.....55 N7
Londiandes FLEETS GU52...106 C3
London La BMLY BR1.....47 N1
  SHGR GU5.....134 C1
London Loop BNSTD SM7 .....79 K2
  COUL/CHIP CR5 .....80 C8
  CROY/NA CRO 64 D2
  PUR/KEN CR8 .....81 N4
  SAND/SEL CR2 .....64 D7
  WARL CR6.....65 K2
London Rd ASC SL5.....34 C4
  BFOR GU20.....52 A6
  BH/WHM TN16.....104 C3
  BLKW GU17 .....68 A4
  BMLY BR1.....47 M1
  BRAK RG12.....32 F3
  CBLY GU15 .....51 J9
  CHEAM SM3.....61 J1
  CTHM CR3 .....101 M3
  CROY/NA CRO 176 G4
  CROY/NA CRO 45 J2
  CTHM CR3 .....101 M3
  DORK RH4 .....117 H6
  DTCH/LGLY SL3 .....12 A1
  DTCH/LGLY SL3 .....12 B1
  EGH TW20 .....36 A1
  EW KT17 .....60 D7
  FROW RH18 .....181 K7
  FSTH SE23.....31 K4
  GU GU1 .....7 G5
  HORL RH6.....159 L5

HORS RH12 ...192 B8
ISLW TW7 ...16 E7
KUT KT1 ...9 G4
KUTN/CMB KT2 ...8 E1
LIPH GU30 ...182 F6
MRDN SM4 ...41 L6
MRDN SM4 ...44 A6
MTCM CR4 ...44 B3
REDH RH1 ...120 C2
REIG RH2 ...119 L5
RPLY/SEND GU23 ...93 J6
STA TW18 ...22 C7
STRHM/NOR SW16 ...15 P4
TWK TW1 ...25 P4
WLGTN SM6 ...62 D1
London Rd North REDH RH1..100 D6
London Rd South
  REDH RH1 ...100 D9
London Sq GU GU1 * ...7 F3
London Stile CHSWK W4 ...17 N3
London St CHERT KT16 ...37 L8
Loneacre BFOR GU20 * ...52 C2
Lone Oak HORL RH6 ...160 C3
Lonesome La WOK RH6 ...119 N9
Longacre ASHV GU12 ...109 J4
Long Acre CRAWE KT1 ? ...145 G5
Longacre Pl CAR SM5 *...62 C5
Long Av CHOB/PIR GU24 ...90 G1
Long Beech Dr FARN GU14 ...87 N4
Longbourne Wy CHERT KT16 ..37 K7
Longboyds COB KT11 ...75 K4
Long Br FNM GU9 ...5 F2
Longbridge Rd HORL RH6 ..159 J3
Longbridge Wk HORL RH6 ..159 J3
Longchamp Cl HORL RH6 ..159 M1
Long Copse Cl GT/LBKH KT23 ..96 B3
Longcroft RFNM GU10...126 A8
Longcroft Av BNSTD SM7 ...79 N3
Long Cross HI BFOR GU35 ..168 B6
Longcross Rd CHERT KT16...53 P2
Longdene Rd HASM GU27 ..184 C4
Longdown Cl RFNM GU10 ...86 F9
Longdown La RFNM GU10 ..127 N7
Longdown La North EW KT17..78 E2
Longdown La South
  EW KT17 ...78 E4
Longdown Rd CAT SE6 ...31 P7
  EW KT17 ...78 E2
  RFNM GU10 ...127 M8
  RGUE GU4 ...112 F8
  SHST GU47 ...49 L8
Long Dyke GU GU1 ...112 F5
Longfellow Rd WPK KT4 ...42 E9
Longfield BRLY DR1 ...47 M7
Longfield Av WLGTN SM6...44 C1
Longfield Cl FARN GU14 ...68 C8
Longfield Crs
  KWD/TDW/WH KT20 ...78 G9
  SYD SE26 ...31 K6
Longfield Dr
  MORT/ESHN SW14 ...26 G1
  WIM/MER SW19 ...29 J5
Longfield Rd ASHV GU12 ..109 J4
  DORK RH4 ...116 F8
Longfield St
  WAND/EARL SW18 ...28 D3
Longford
  EBED/NFELT TW14 ...23 P2
  STWL/WRAY TW19 ...23 H4
Longford Cl CBLY GU15 ...68 F4
  FELT TW13 ...24 F6
  HPTN TW12 ...25 J8
Longford Ct HOR/WEW KT19 ..60 A6
  HPTN TW12 ...25 J8
Longford Gdns SUT SM1 ...61 N2
Longford Rd WHTN TW2 ...25 H4
Longford Wy
  STWL/WRAY TW19 ...23 H4
Long Garden Pl FNM GU9 ...5 F2
Long Garden Wk FNM GU9 ...5 F3
Long Garden Wk East
  FNM GU9 ...5 F3
Long Garden Wk West
  FNM GU9 ...5 F2
Long Garden Wy FNM GU9 ....4 E3
Long Gore GODL GU7 ...131 L5
Long Grove Rd
  HOR/WEW KT19 ...59 P8
Longheath Dr GT/LBKH KT23 ..95 N4
Longheath Gdns
  CROY/NA CRO ...46 C6
Long Hi CTHM CR3 ...102 E1
  RFNM GU10 ...128 G4
Long Hill Rd ASC SL5 ...33 K2
Longhope Dr RFNM GU10 ..127 L7
Longhurst Rd CRAWW RH11 ..194 D1
  CROY/NA CRO ...46 D9
  EHSLY KT24 ...94 G9
Longlands Av
  COUL/CHIP CR5 ...80 D3
Long La CROY/NA CRO ...46 C5
  STWL/WRAY TW19 ...23 J4
Longleat Sq FARN GU14 ...88 G4
Longleat Wy
  EBED/NFELT TW14 ...23 M3
Longley Rd CROY/NA CRO ...45 K8
  FNM GU9 ...5 J5
  TOOT SW17 ...29 J9
Long Lodge Dr
  WOT/HER KT12 ...57 L2
Longmead FLEETS GU52 ...86 C8
  GU GU1 ...112 G5
Longmead Cl CTHM CR3 ...101 N1
  Longmeadow FRIM GU16 ...69 H5
  GT/LBKH KT23 ...95 P5
Long Meadow Cl BECK BR3...47 J8
Longmead Rd
  HOR/WEW KT19 ...60 C8

THDIT KT7 ...40 F8
TOOT SW17 ...29 J8
Longmere Gdns
  KWD/TDW/WH KT20 ...78 G8
Longmere Rd CRAWE RH10..176 G3
Long Mickle SHST GU47 ...49 L8
Longmoor Cl EWKG RG40...48 C2
Longmoor Dr LIPH GU30 ..182 A6
Longmoor Rd LIPH GU30 ..182 B6
Longmoors BNFD RG42 ...32 A2
Longmoor Rd WOT/HER KT12..57 N3
Longpoles Rd CRAN GU6 ..171 J1
Longport Rd EHSLY KT24 ...94 D4
Longridge Gv
  WOKS/MYFD GU22 ...73 J3
Longridge Rd ECT SW5 ...19 L2
Longs Cl WOKS/MYFD GU22...73 L5
Longsdon Wy CTHM CR3...102 A4
Long Shaw LHD/OX KT22 ...76 G8
Longshot La BRAK RG12 ...32 A5
Longside Cl EGH TW20 ...36 C2
Longstaff Crs
  WAND/EARL SW18 ...28 D2
Longstaff Rd
  WAND/EARL SW18 ...28 D2
Longstone Rd
  STRHM/NOR SW16 ...29 L8
Longthornton Rd
  STRHM/NOR SW16 ...44 E3
Longton Av SYD SE26 ...31 H7
Longton Gv SYD SE26 ...31 J7
Long Wk EPSOM KT18 ...78 G8
  NWMAL KT3 ...41 N4
  WDSR SL4 * ...20 C1
The Long Wk WDSR SL4 ....20 C4
Longwater La EWKG RG40 ...48 C7
Longwater Rd BRAK RG12 ...32 E7
  HTWY RG27 ...48 D9
Longwood Ct WPK KT4 ...60 E1
Longwood Dr
  PUT/ROE SW15 ...27 M2
Longwood Rd PUR/KEN CR8 ..81 M5
Longwood Vw CRAWW RH10..177 K8
Lonsdale Gdns
  STRHM/NOR SW16 ...45 H5
Lonsdale Ms RCH/KEW TW9 *..17 N6
Lonsdale Rd BARN SW13 ...18 D5
  DORK RH4 ...117 H6
  NWDGN UB2 ...15 M1
  SNWD SE25 ...46 B5
  WEY KT13 ...56 C6
Loop Rd EPSOM KT18 ...78 A8
  WOKS/MYFD GU22 ...72 D9
Loppets Rd CRAWE RH10...177 J7
Loraine Gdns ASHTD KT21 ...77 L6
Loraine Rd CHSWK W4 ...17 P4
Lord Chancellor Wk
  KUTN/CMB KT2 ...42 A2
Lord Chatham's Ride
  RSEV TN14 ...85 P6
Lord Knyvett Cl
  STWL/WRAY TW19 ...23 H2
Lord Knyvetts Ct
  STWL/WRAY TW19 * ...23 H2
Lord Napier Pl HMSMTH W6 ..18 E3
Lord Roberts Ms
  FUL/PGN SW6 * ...19 M5
Lordsbury Fld WLGTN SM6 ...62 E8
Lords Cl DUL SE21 ...30 D5
  FELT TW13 ...24 F5
Lordsgrove Cl
  KWD/TDW/WH KT20 ...78 F9
Lords Hill Cottages
  SHGR GU5 * ...132 C9
Lordshill Rd SHGR GU5 ...132 G8
Lordship La EDUL SE22 ...30 C2
Loretto Cl CRAN GU6 ...153 J9
Lorian Dr REIG RH2 ...119 N4
Loriners CRAWE RH10...176 G8
Loriners Cl COB KT11 ...75 J3
Loring Rd ISLW TW7 ...16 F7
Loris Rd HMSMTH W6...18 G1
Lorne Av CROY/NA CRO ...46 D9
Lorne Gdns CROY/NA CRO ...46 E8
  WOKN/KNAP GU21 ...71 K8
Lorne Rd RCHPK/HAM TW10 ..26 E1
The Lorne GT/LBKH KT23 ....96 A6
Lorraine Rd CBLY GU15 ...51 H9
Lorry Rdg BAGS GU19 ...51 N5
Loseberry Rd ESH/CLAY KT10 ..58 D4
Loseley Rd GODL GU7 ...131 L5
Lothian Wd
  KWD/TDW/WH KT20 ...98 F2
Lots Rd WBPTN SW10 ...19 N5
Lotus Rd BH/WHM TN16 ...84 D7
Loubet St TOOT SW17 ...29 J9
Loudwater Cl SUN TW16 ...39 J5
Loughborough BRAK RG12 ...32 F7
Louise Margaret Rd
  ALDT GU11 ...108 E4
Louis Flds RGUW GU3 ...111 J1
Louisville Rd TOOT SW17 ...29 K6
Louvaine Rd BTSEA SW11 ...19 P9
Lovedean Ct BRAK RG12 ...32 G7
Lovekyn Cl KUTN/CMB KT2 ....8 E4
Lovelace Cl EHSLY KT24 ...95 J3
Lovelace Dr
  WOKS/MYFD GU22 ...73 K4
Lovelace Gdns SURB KT6 ...41 K8
  WOT/HER KT12 ...57 L4
Lovelace Rd BRAK RG12 ...32 A5
  DUL SE21 ...30 D5
  SURB KT6 ...41 J8
Lovelace Vls THDIT KT7 *...41 H8
Lovelands La CHOB/PIR GU24..70 D2
  KWD/TDW/WH KT20 ...99 M7
Love La CHAM SM3 ...61 J5
  GDST RH9 ...122 C3
  KWD/TDW/WH KT20 ...98 E5

MRDN SM4 ...43 L8
MTCM CR4 ...44 A4
SNWD SE25 ...46 A5
SURB KT6 ...59 K1
Loveletts CRAWW RH11 ...176 D6
Lovell Rd RCHPK/HAM TW10 ..26 B6
Lovells Cl LTWR GU18 ...52 B8
Lovelock Cl PUR/KEN CR8 ...81 L6
Lovers La RFNM GU10 ...146 F5
Lovett Dr CAR SM5 ...43 N8
Lovett Rd EGH TW20 ...21 N7
Lowbury Rd BRAK RG12 ...32 G5
Lowburys DORK RH4 ...136 G1
Lowdells Cl EGRIN RH19 ..162 D8
Lowdells Dr EGRIN RH19 ..162 D8
Lowdells La EGRIN RH19 ..162 D9
Lowe Cl ALDT GU11 ...108 B8
  CRAWW RH11...194 E2
Lower Addiscombe Rd
  CROY/NA CRO ...3 F1
Lower Barn Cl HORS RH12...192 E5
Lower Barn Rd PUR/KEN CR8..81 L1
Lower Breache Rd
  CRAN GU6 ...154 D8
Lower Bridge Rd REDH RH1 ..120 B5
Lower Broadmoor Rd
  CWTH RG45 ...49 P5
Lower Canes YTLY GU46...66 E2
Lower Church La FNM GU9 ....5 F3
Lower Church Rd SHST GU47 ..49 J8
Lower Church St
  CROY/NA CRO ...2 B4
Lower Common South
  PUT/ROE SW15 ...18 F8
Lower Coombe St
  CROY/NA CRO ...2 C7
Lower Ct HOR/WEW KT19 ...60 B9
Lower Court Rd
  HOR/WEW KT19 ...60 A9
Lower Dene EGRIN RH19 ...180 F2
Lower Downs Rd
  RYNPK SW20 ...43 H2
Lower Dunnymans
  BNSTD SM7 ...79 K3
Lower Eashing GODL GU7 ..130 E9
Lower Edgeborough Rd
  GU GU1 ...7 J4
Lower Farm Rd EHSLY KT24 ...95 K4
Lower Farnham Rd
  ALDT GU11 ...108 E7
Lower Forecourt HORL RH6 ..159 L5
Lower Green Gdns WPK KT4 ..42 E9
Lower Green Rd
  ESH/CLAY KT10 ...58 B1
Lower Gn West MTCM CR4 ...44 A4
Lower Grove Rd
  RCHPK/HAM TW10 ...26 E2
Lower Guildford Rd
  WOKN/KNAP GU21 ...71 K6
Lower Ham La
  MFD/CHID GU8 ...129 N9
Lower Hampton Rd
  SUN TW16 ...39 M3
Lower Ham Rd
  KUTN/CMB KT2 ...26 C9
Lower Hanger HASM GU27 ..183 M4
Lower Hill Rd
  HOR/WEW KT19 ...77 P1
Lower House Rd
  MFD/CHID GU8 ...166 G2
Lower Manor Rd GODL GU7 ..131 L7
  MFD/CHID GU8 ...149 M3
Lower Marsh La KUT KT1 ...41 M5
Lower Mere EGRIN RH19 ...180 E3
Lower Mill Fld BAGS GU19 ...51 N7
Lower Moor YTLY GU46 ...67 H3
Lower Morden La MRDN SM4 ..42 G7
Lower Mortlake Rd
  RCH/KEW TW9 ...17 M8
Lower Mount St
  FLEETN GU51 ...86 C4
Lower Mousehill La
  MFD/CHID GU8 ...149 L3
Lower Newport Rd
  ASHV GU12 ...108 G8
Lower Northfield BNSTD SM7..79 K3
Lower Park Rd BNSTD SM7 ...80 A7
Lower Peryers EHSLY KT24 ...94 G8
Lower Pillory Down CAR SM5..80 C2
Lower Richmond Rd
  PUT/ROE SW15 ...18 G8
  RCH/KEW TW9 ...17 N8
Lower Rd GT/LBKH KT23 ...95 P6
  HASM GU27 ...166 G9
  LHD/OX KT22 ...96 D3
  PUR/KEN CR8 ...81 J3
  REIG RH2 ...119 P7
  SUT SM1 ...61 P4
Lower Sandfields
  RPLY/SEND GU23 ...93 H3
Lower Sand Hills SURB KT6 ...41 J8
Lower Sandhurst Rd
  EWKG RG40 ...48 E7
Lower Sawleywood
  BNSTD SM7 ...79 K3
Lower Shott GT/LBKH KT23...96 B6
Lower South St GODL GU7 ..131 K9
Lower South Vw FNM GU9 ....5 G2
Lower St HASM GU27 ...184 D4
  SHGR GU5 ...134 C1
Lower Sunbury Rd
  HPTN TW12 ...39 P3
Lower Tanbridge Wy
  HORS RH12 ...192 A8
Lower Teddington Rd
  KUT KT1 ...8 A3
Lower Terrace Rd FARN GU14..88 C7
Lower Village Rd ASC SL5 ....34 C6
Lower Weybourne La
  FNM GU9 ...108 B8
Lower Wokingham Rd
  EWKG RG40 ...49 H3

Lower Wood Rd
  ESH/CLAY KT10 ...58 G5
Lowfield Cl LTWR GU18 ...52 B4
Lowfield Heath Rd
  HORL RH6 ...158 C6
Lowfield Rd RCHR/HAM TW13 ..190 E7
Lowfield Wy HORL RH6 ...159 H7
Lowicks Rd RFNM GU10 ...147 L6
Lowlands Rd BLKW GU17...67 N4
  STWL/WRAY TW19 ...22 C7
Low La FNM GU9 ...108 D8
Lowndes Buildings FNM GU9 ...5 F2
Lowry Cl SHST GU47 ...49 L8
Lowry Crs MTCM CR4 ...44 A3
Lowther Hl FSTH SE23 ...31 M1
Lowther Rd BARN SW13 ...18 E6
  KUTN/CMB KT2 ...9 G1
Lowthorpe CTHM CR3 ...101 P5
Loxford Wy CTHM CR3 ...101 P5
Loxley Cl SYD SE26 ...31 L8
Loxley Rd HPTN TW12 ...24 G4
  WAND/EARL SW18 ...28 G4
Loxton Rd FSTH SE23 ...31 L1
Loxwood Av FLEETN GU51 ...86 E8
Loxwood Cl
  EBED/NFELT TW14 ...23 N4
Loxwood Farm Pl BIL RH14 ..188 D6
Loxwood Rd BIL RH14 ...187 M8
  BIL RH14 ...188 C6
  CRAN GU6 ...188 B2
Loxwood Wk CRAWW RH11 ..176 C4
Lucan Dr STA TW18 ...37 P1
Lucas Cl EGRIN RH19 * ...180 E2
  YTLY GU46 ...66 G2
Lucas Green Rd
  CHOB/PIR GU24 ...70 D4
Lucas Rd HORS RH12 ...191 M2
  PGE/AN SE20 ...31 K9
Lucerne Cl
  WOKS/MYFD GU22 ...72 C9
Lucerne Dr CRAWE RH10 ...177 N7
Lucerne Rd THHTH CR7 ...45 K6
Lucie Av ASHF TW15 ...23 L9
Lucien Rd TOOT SW17 ...29 K7
  WAND/EARL SW18 ...28 G6
Lucilina Dr EDEN TN8 ...144 G5
Luddington Av EGH TW20 ...36 D3
Ludford Cl CROY/NA CRO ...2 C7
Ludlow BRAK RG12 ...32 D8
Ludlow Cl FRIM GU16 ...69 J9
  HAYES BR2 ...47 N4
Ludlow Rd FELT TW13 ...24 B6
  GUW GU2 ...6 A5
Ludovick Wk PUT/ROE SW15 ..18 C9
Ludshott Gv BOR GU35 ...164 E6
Luke Rd ALDT GU11 ...108 A6
Luke Rd East FNM GU9 ...108 A6
Lullarook Cl BH/WHM TN16...84 A5
Lullington Garth BMLY BR1 * ..47 L1
Lullington Rd PGE/AN SE20...46 A1
Lulworth Av HEST TW5 ...16 B5
  FARN GU14 ...68 C9
Lulworth Crs MTCM CR4 ...44 A3
Lumley Gdns CHEAM SM3 ...61 J5
Lumley Rd CHEAM SM3 ...61 J5
  HORL RH6 ...159 K1
Lunar Cl BH/WHM TN16...84 B5
Luna Rd THHTH CR7 ...45 L4
Lundy Cl CRAWW RH11 ...176 B8
Lundy Dr HYS/HAR UB3 ...14 G2
Lunghurst Rd CTHM CR3 ...102 C1
Lunham Rd NRWD SE19 ...30 F9
Lupin Cl BAGS GU19 ...51 L8
  BRXS/STRHM SW2 ...30 C5
  CROY/NA CRO ...46 D9
  WDR/YW UB7 ...13 P3
Lupin Ride CWTH RG45 ...49 M1
Lurgan Av HMSMTH W6 ...19 H4
Lushington Dr COB KT11 ...75 K3
Lusted Hall La BH/WHM TN16..84 A4
Lusteds Cl DORK RH4 ...137 J1
Lutterworth Cl BRAK RG42...32 E1
Luttrell Av PUT/ROE SW15...27 N1
Lutwyche Rd FSTH SE23 ...31 N5
Lutyens Cl CRAWW RH11 ...176 B7
Luxemburg Gdns
  HMSMTH W6 ...19 H2
Luxford Cl HORS RH12 ...192 E5
Luxfords La EGRIN RH19 ...180 D4
Luxted Rd ORP BR6 ...84 E1
Lyall Av DUL SE21 ...30 E4
Lyall Pl FNM GU9 ...107 M7
Lych Gate Cl SHST GU47 ...49 K9
Lych Wy WOKN/KNAP GU21 ..71 K6
Lyconby Gdns CROY/NA CRO..46 E8
Lydbury BRAK RG12 ...33 H4
Lydden Gv WAND/EARL SW18..28 E3
Lydden Rd WAND/EARL SW18..28 E3
Lydens La EDEN TN8 ...145 K7
Lydford Cl FARN GU14 ...69 J9
  FRIM GU16 ...69 J9
Lydhurst Av
  BRXS/STRHM SW2 ...30 A5
Lydney BRAK RG12 ...32 D8
Lydney Cl WIM/MER SW19 ...28 B5
Lye Copse Av FARN GU14 ...68 D8
Lyefield La CRAN GU6 ...153 M6
The Lye KWD/TDW/WH KT20 ..98 G2
Lyfield LHD/OX KT22 ...76 B3
Lyford Rd WAND/EARL SW18..28 G4
Lyham Cl BRXS/STRHM SW2 ..29 P1
Lyham Rd BRXS/STRHM SW2..29 P1
Lymden Gdns REIG RH2 ...119 N7
Lymer Av NRWD SE19 ...30 G8
Lyme Regis Rd BNSTD SM7 ...79 K6
Lymescote Gdns SUT SM1 ...61 L1

Lyminge Gdns
  WAND/EARL SW18 ...29 H4
Lymington Av YTLY GU46...66 G3
Lymington Cl
  STRHM/NOR SW16 ...44 F3
Lymington Gdns
  HOR/WEW KT19 ...60 D4
Lynams FLEETS GU52 ...106 E3
Lynchborough Rd
  LIPH GU30 ...182 A2
Lynchen Cl HEST TW5 ...15 H4
Lynchford La FARN GU14...88 G6
Lynchford Rd ALDT GU11...88 F7
Lynch Rd FNM GU9 ...5 J3
Lyncroft Gdns EW KT17 ...60 D7
  HSLW TW3 ...25 K1
Lyndale ESH/CLAY KT10 * ...40 E8
Lyndale Dr FLEETN GU51 ...87 K6
Lyndale Hampton Court Wy
  ESH/CLAY KT10 ...40 D8
Lyndale Rd REDH RH1 ...120 B2
Lyndford Ter FLEETS GU52 ...86 F8
  WAND/EARL SW18 ...28 G4
  BRYLDS KT5 ...41 P9
  FNM GU9 ...108 E8
  STRHM/NOR SW16 ...44 F3
  SUN TW16 ...39 J4
  WHTN TW2 ...24 G4
Lyndhurst Cl BRAK RG12 ...33 J4
  CRAWW RH11 ...176 G6
  CROY/NA CRO ...3 J5
  WOKN/KNAP GU21 ...72 B4
Lyndhurst Dr NWMAL KT3 ...42 C7
Lyndhurst Farm Cl
  EGRIN RH19 ...161 L8
Lyndhurst Leys HAYES BR2 *..47 K3
Lyndhurst Prior SNWD SE25 *..45 N4
Lyndhurst Rd ASC SL5 ...34 A5
  COUL/CHIP CR5 ...80 C5
  FLEETN GU51 ...86 F8
  REIG RH2 ...119 L8
  THHTH CR7 ...45 H5
Lyndhurst Wy BELMT SM2 ...61 L6
  CHERT KT16 ...55 J2
Lyndon Av WLGTN SM6 ...62 C2
Lyndon Yd TOOT SW17 ...28 F7
Lyndsey Cl FARN GU14 ...87 M3
Lyndwood Dr WDSR SL4 ...20 D7
Lyndwood Pde WDSR SL4 *...20 D7
Lyne Cl VW GU25 ...36 D7
Lyne Crossing Rd
  CHERT KT16 ...36 F7
Lynegrove Av ASHF TW15 ...23 M8
Lyneham Rd CWTH RG45 ...49 M4
Lyne La CHERT KT16 ...36 E7
Lyne Rd VW GU25 ...36 C5
Lynette Av CLAP SW4 ...29 L2
Lynmead Cl EDEN TN8 ...144 F1
Lynmouth Av MRDN SM4 ...43 H8
Lynmouth Gdns HEST TW5...15 M6
Lynn Cl ASHF TW15 ...23 M8
Lynne Cl SAND/SEL CR2 ...64 C9
Lynn Rd BAL SW12 ...29 L3
Lynn Wk REIG RH2 ...119 M9
Lynn Wy FARN GU14 ...87 P5
Lynscott Wy SAND/SEL CR2 ..63 K7
Lynsted Ct BECK BR3 ...46 E3
Lynton Cl CHSGTN KT9 ...59 L3
  FNM GU9 ...127 L6
  ISLW TW7 ...16 F9
Lynton Park Av EGRIN RH19 ..180 F1
Lynton Rd CROY/NA CRO ...45 J7
  NWMAL KT3 ...42 B6
Lynwick St HORS RH12 ...189 N1
Lynwood GUW GU2 ...6 A5
Lynwood Av COUL/CHIP CR5...80 D6
  DTCH/LGLY SL3 ...12 B1
  EGH TW20 ...21 K9
  EW KT17 ...78 D3
Lynwood Cha BRAK RG12 ...32 E1
Lynwood Cl
  WOKN/KNAP GU21 ...73 H2
Lynwood Ct HORS RH12 ...192 B7
Lynwood Crs ASC SL5 ...34 E7
Lynwood Dr FRIM GU16 ...89 J4
  WPK KT4 ...60 E1
Lynwood Gdns
  CROY/NA CRO ...63 H3
Lynwood Rd ESH/CLAY KT10...58 F1
  EW KT17 ...78 D3
  REDH RH1 ...120 C3
  TOOT SW17 ...29 J6
Lyonsdene
  KWD/TDW/WH KT20 ...99 K7
Lyons Dr GUW GU2 ...91 N9
Lyons Rd SWTR RH13 ...190 F7
Lyons Wk WKENS W14 ...19 J2
Lyon Wy FRIM GU16 ...89 H3
Lyric Cl CRAWE RH10 ...177 N7
Lyric Ms SYD SE26 ...31 K4
Lyric Rd BARN SW13 ...18 D6
Lysander Gdns SURB KT6 ...41 L7
Lysander Rd CROY/NA CRO ...63 H5
Lysander Wy FNM GU9 ...108 D6
Lysias Rd BAL SW12 ...29 L2
Lysia St FUL/PGN SW6 ...19 H5
Lysons Av ASHV GU12 ...108 G3
Lysons Dr WOT/HER KT12 ...57 H3
Lysons Rd ALDT GU11 ...108 C5
Lysons Wk PUT/ROE SW15 *..27 M1
Lyster Ms COB KT11 ...75 L2
Lytchet Minster Cl BRAK RG12..33 H6

Lytchet Rd BMLY BR1 .....47 N1
Lytchgate CI SAND/SEL CR2 ...63 N6
Lytcott Dr EDUL SE22 ....39 P4
Lytcott Gv EDUL SE22 .....30 G1
Lytham BRAK RG12 ....32 A7
Lytton Dr CRAWE RH10 ....177 N4
Lytton Gdns WLGTN SM6 .....62 F3
Lytton Gv PUT/ROE SW15 ....28 A1
Lytton Pk COB KT11 ......75 P1
Lytton Rd WOKS/MYFD GU22 ..11 J3
Lyveden Rd WIM/MER SW19 ..29 H9
Lywood CI
  KWD/TDW/WH KT20 ....98 G2

M

Mabbotts
  KWD/TDW/WH KT20 ....99 H1
Mabel St WOKN/KNAP GU21 ...10 A5
Maberley Crs NRWD SE19 .....46 A1
Maberley Rd BECK BR3 ....46 B6
  NRWD SE19 ....45 P2
Mablethorpe Rd
  FUL/PGN SW6 ....19 J5
Macadam Av CWTH RG45 * 49 Q2
Macaulay Av ESH/CLAY KT10 ..58 E1
Macaulay Rd CTHM CR3 .....101 N2
Macbeth Ct BNFD RG42 ......32 C2
Macbeth St HMSMTH W6 ......18 F3
Macclesfield Rd SNWD SE25 ..46 B6
Macdonald Rd FNM GU9 .....107 M7
  LTWR GU18 ....51 P9
Mace La RSEV TN14 ....85 H2
Macfarlane La ISLW TW7 ....16 F4
Mackenzie Rd BECK BR3 ......46 C4
Mackie Rd BRXS/STRHM SW2 ..30 B3
Mackies HI SHGR GU5 ......134 C7
Maclean Rd FSTH SE23 ......31 M1
Macleod Rd SWTR RH13 ....192 D9
Maclise Rd WKENS W14 ......19 J1
Macrae Rd YTLY GU46 ....66 C2
Madan CI MALDN TN16 .....105 J5
Madan Rd BH/WHM TN16 ....105 H5
Maddison CI TEDD TW11 .....25 N9
Maddox La GT/LBKH KT23 .....95 N4
Maddox Pk GT/LBKH KT23 ....95 N3
Madehurst Ct CRAWW RH11 ..176 C8
Madeira Av BMLY BR1 ....47 L2
  HORS RH12 ....192 B8
Madeira Crs BF/WBF KT14 ....73 K2
Madeira Rd BF/WBF KT14 ....73 K2
  MTCM CR4 ....44 B5
  STRHM/NOR SW16 ....29 P8
  REIG RH2 ....119 P4
Madeley Rd FLEETS GU52 .....87 H9
Madeline Rd PGE/AN SE20 ....46 A1
Madgehole La SHGR GU5 ....133 M9
Madingley BRAK RG12 ....32 D9
Madox Brown End
  SHST GU47 ....68 A2
Madrid Rd BARN SW13 ....18 E6
  GUW GU2 ....6 A5
Maesmaur Rd
  BH/WHM TN16 ....104 B1
Mafeking Av BTFD TW8 ......17 L4
Mafeking Rd
  STWL/WRAY TW19 ....21 N5
Magazine PI LHD/OX KT22 ....97 H2
  FARN GU14 ....88 B7
Magdala Rd ISLW TW7 ....16 G8
  SAND/SEL CR2 ....63 M6
Magdalen CI BF/WBF KT14 ....74 A3
Magdalen Ct BF/WBF KT14 ...36 A8
Magdalene CI CRAWW RH10 ..177 M2
Magdalene Rd SHPTN TW17 ..38 B5
  SHST GU47 ....50 B7
Magdalen Rd
  WAND/EARL SW18 ....28 E4
Magellan Ter CRAWE RH10 * ..177 K1
Magna Carta La
  STWL/WRAY TW19 ....21 K4
Magna CI EGH TW20 ....20 C9
Magnolia CI KUTN/CMB KT2 ..9 K1
  SHST GU47 ....49 P8
Magnolia Ct HORL RH6 .....159 K1
Magnolia Dr BH/WHM TN16 ..84 B5
Magnolia PI CLAP SW4 ......29 P1
  GU GU1 * 112 A2
Magnolia Rd CHSWK W4 ......17 P4
Magnolia St WDR/YW UB7 ....13 P2
Magnolia Wy FLEETS GU52 ...68 G8
  HOR/WEW KT19 ....60 A5
  RDKG RH5 ....157 K1
Magnolia Whf CHSWK W4 * ...17 P4
Magpie CI COUL/CHIP CR5 ....81 H7
  RFNM GU10 ....107 H6
Maguire Dr FRIM GU16 ......69 L5
  RCHPK/HAM TW10 ....26 B5
Mahonia CI CHOB/PIR GU24 * .70 F2
Maida Rd ALDT GU11 ....108 D2
Maidenbower Dr
  CRAWE RH10 ....177 M7
Maidenbower La
  CRAWE RH10 ....177 L7
Maidenbower PI
  CRAWE RH10 ....177 M7
Maiden La CRAWW RH11 ....176 F3
Maidenshaw Rd
  HOR/WEW KT19 ....78 D1
Main Dr BNFD RG42 ....33 K1
  IVER SL0 ....13 P1
Main Gate Rd FARN GU14 ....88 D5
Mainprize Rd BRAK RG12 ....32 G2
Main Rd BH/WHM TN16 ......84 A2
  EDEN TN8 ....124 G5

RSEV TN14 ....85 L7
Mainstone CI FRIM GU16 ....69 L9
Mainstone Crs
  CHOB/PIR GU24 ....90 D1
Mainstone Rd
  CHOB/PIR GU24 ....70 F5
Main St ADL/WDHM KT15 .....56 A2
  FELT TW13 ....24 E8
Maise Webster CI
  STWL/WRAY TW19 * 22 G3
The Maisonettes SUT SM1 * ..61 M4
Maitland CI BF/WBF KT14 ....73 L2
  HSLWW TW4 ....15 J3
  WOT/HER KT12 ....57 N1
Maitland Rd FARN GU14 .....88 D7
  SYD SE26 ....31 L9
Maitlands CI RFNM GU10 ...108 G8
Maizecroft HORL RH6 ......140 E9
Major's Farm Rd
  DTCH/LGLY SL3 ....12 C5
Major's HI CRAWE RH10 ....178 E7
Makepiece Rd BNFD RG42 ....32 C1
Malacca Farm RGUE GU4 .....93 M8
Malan CI BH/WHM TN16 .....84 D3
Malbrook Rd PUT/ROE SW15 ..18 F7
Malcolm CI PGE/AN SE20 * ...46 C1
Malcolm Dr SURB KT6 ....41 K9
Malcolm Gdns HORL RH6 ...158 C3
Malcolm Gavin CI TOOT SW17 .29 H5
Malcolm Rd COUL/CHIP CR5 ..80 F4
  PGE/AN SE20 ....46 C1
  SNWD SE25 ....46 A7
Malden Av SNWD SE25 ......46 B5
Malden Green Av WPK KT4 ...42 D9
Malden HI NWMAL KT3 ....42 C3
Malden Hill Gdns NWMAL KT3 .42 D4
Malden Pk NWMAL KT3 ......42 D7
Malden Rd CHEAM SM3 ......61 H3
  NWMAL KT3 ....42 B7
Malden Wy (Kingston By-Pass)
  NWMAL KT3 ....42 C7
Maldon Rd WLGTN SM6 ......62 C4
Malet CI EGH TW20 * 22 A9
Maley Av WNWD SE27 ....30 C5
Malham Cl CRAWE RH10 ....177 M8
Malham Fell BRAK RG12 .....32 C5
Malham Rd FSTH SE23 ......31 L4
Mallard Cl ASHV GU12 .....109 H4
  HASM GU27 ....183 P4
  HORL RH6 ....140 C8
  HORS RH12 ....192 B5
  REDH RH1 ....120 C2
  WHTN TW2 ....25 H3
Mallard Ct EGRIN RH19 ....180 E3
  TWK TW1 ....25 P6
Mallard Rd SAND/SEL CR2 ...64 D8
Mallard's Reach WEY KT13 ...56 F1
The Mallards FRIM GU16 ....69 H6
  STA TW18 ....22 G9
Mallards Wy LTWR GU18 .....52 A9
Mallard Wk WLGTN SM6 .....62 E7
  YTLY GU46 ....66 F2
Malling CI CROY/NA CR0 .....46 C7
Malling Gdns MRDN SM4 ....43 N7
Mallinson Rd BTSEA SW11 ...29 H1
  CROY/NA CR0 ....62 F2
Mallord St CHEL SW3 ....19 P4
Mallow CI CROY/NA CR0 .....46 D9
  HORS RH12 ....192 D4
  KWD/TDW/WH KT20 ....78 F8
Mallow Crs RGUE GU4 ......112 F2
Mallowdale Rd BRAK RG12 ...32 F8
Mall Rd HMSMTH W6 ....18 F3
Malmains CI BECK BR3 ......47 K6
Malmains Wy BECK BR3 .....47 J5
Malmesbury Rd MRDN SM4 ...43 N8
Malmstone Av REDH RH1 ...100 E8
Malta Rd FRIM GU16 ....68 E1
Maltby Rd CHSGTN KT9 ......59 N5
Malt HI EGH TW20 ....21 K8
Malthouse CI FLEETS GU52 ..106 E1
Malt House CI WDSR SL4 ....20 C3
Malthouse Ct
  CHOB/PIR GU24 * 70 F1
  RGUW GU3 ....91 J4
Malthouse Dr FELT TW13 ....24 E8
Malthouse La
  CHOB/PIR GU24 ....70 F1
  RGUW GU3 ....91 J4
Malthouse Md
  MFD/CHID GU8 ....149 N7
Malthouse Mdw LIPH GU30 ..182 F6
Malthouse Rd CRAWE RH10 ..176 G6
Maltings PI FUL/PGN SW6 ...19 M6
The Maltings BF/WBF KT14 ..74 A2
  LIPH GU30 ....182 G6
  OXTED RH8 ....123 M2
  SHGR GU5 ....134 E4
  SNWD SE25 ....45 N4
  STA TW18 ....22 B7
Maltings Wy ISLW TW7 ......17 H8
Malthouse La
  MFD/CHID GU8 ....168 B2
Malus CI ADL/WDHM KT15 ...55 K6
Malus Dr ADL/WDHM KT15 ...55 K6
Malva CI WAND/EARL SW18 ...28 E1
Malvern CI BF/WBF KT16 ....54 E2
  MTCM CR4 ....44 E4
  SURB KT6 ....41 L9
Malvern Dr FELT TW13 ......24 E8
Malvern Rd BLKW GU17 .....67 K7
  CRAWW RH11 ....176 F7
  FARN GU14 ....67 P9

HPTN TW12 ....40 A2
HYS/HAR UB3 ....14 G5
SURB KT6 ....59 L1
THHTH CR7 ....45 J5
Malwood Rd BAL SW12 ......29 L2
The Malyons SHPTN TW17 * ..38 F7
Manbre Rd HMSMTH W6 ......18 G4
Manchester Rd THHTH CR7 ...45 L4
Manchuria Rd BTSEA SW11 ...29 K2
Mandalay Rd CLAP SW4 .....29 M1
Mandeville CI GUW GU2 ....111 N2
  SNWD SE25 ....46 A3
Mandeville Dr SURB KT6 ....41 K9
Mandeville Rd ISLW TW7 ....16 G7
  SHPTN TW17 ....38 C6
Mandora Rd ALDT GU11 ....108 D2
Mandrake Rd TOOT SW17 ....29 J6
Mandrell Rd
  BRXS/STRHM SW2 ....29 P1
Manfield Pk CRAN GU6 .....152 E7
Manfield Rd ASHV GU12 ...109 J4
Mangles Ct GU GU1 ....6 C5
Mangles Rd GU GU1 ....112 B3
Manley Bridge Rd
  RFNM GU10 ....127 J9
Manmead EPSOM KT18 ......78 C8
Mannamead CI DTCH/LGLY SL3 .12 D2
Mann CI CRAWW RH11 ......194 E2
  CROY/NA CR0 ....2 C5
Manning CI EGRIN RH19 ....180 C1
Manning PI
  RCHPK/HAM TW10 ....26 E2
Mannings CI CRAWE RH10 ..177 N2
Manningtree CI
  WIM/MER SW19 ....28 B4
Mann's CI ISLW TW7 ....25 N1
Manoel Rd WHTN TW2 ....25 K5
Manor Av CTHM CR3 ....101 N4
  HSLWW TW4 ....15 M8
Manor Cha WEY KT13 ....56 E3
Manor Ct BNFD RG42 ....32 C1
  EHSLY KT24 ....94 C8
  GDST RH9 ....122 F9
  HASM GU27 ....183 P4
  HORL RH6 ....159 J1
  RFNM GU10 ....109 H7
  WARL CR6 ....82 C9
  WOKS/MYFD GU22 ....73 K5
  WPK KT4 ....42 C9
Manor Ct ACT W3 * 17 N2
  E/WMO/HCT KT8 * 40 A5
  FLEETS GU52 ....106 G2
  HORS RH12 * 192 A6
  KUTN/CMB KT2 * 9 J5
  WEY KT13 ....56 D3
Manor Crs BF/WBF KT14 .....74 B2
  BRYLDS KT5 ....41 N7
  CHOB/PIR GU24 ....70 D9
  GUW GU2 ....111 P3
  HOR/WEW KT19 ....77 N1
Manorcrofts Rd EGH TW20 ...21 M9
Manor Dr ADL/WDHM KT15 ...55 L8
  BRYLDS KT5 ....41 N7
  FELT TW13 ....24 E8
  HOR/WEW KT19 ....60 C5
  SUN TW16 ....39 J3
Manor Dr North NWMAL KT3 ..42 B8
The Manor Dr WPK KT4 ......42 C9
Manor Farm Av SHPTN TW17 .38 D7
Manor Farm CI ASHV GU12 * .109 H5
Manor Farm Cottages
  WDSR SL4 ....20 F1
Manor Farm Ct EGH TW20 * ..21 M8
Manor Farm La EGH TW20 * ..21 M8
Manor Farm Rd
  STRHM/NOR SW16 ....45 J3
Manorfields CRAWW RH11 ..176 E8
Manor Flds LIPH GU30 .....182 G6
  SWTR RH13 ....192 F6
Manor Gdns ACT W3 * 17 N2
  EHSLY KT24 ....95 M6
  CODL GU7 ....131 L6
  GUW GU2 ....111 P3
  HPTN TW12 ....40 B1
  RCH/KEW TW9 ....17 M9
  RFNM GU10 ....127 P8
  RYNPK SW20 ....43 K3
  SAND/SEL CR2 ....63 P5
  SUN TW16 ....39 J2
Manorgate Rd KUTN/CMB KT2 .9 H1
Manor Green Rd
  HOR/WEW KT19 ....78 A1
Manor Gv BECK BR3 ....47 H3
  RCH/KEW TW9 ....17 N9
Manor HI BNSTD SM7 ....80 B4
Manor House Ct
  EPSOM KT18 ....78 A2
  SHPTN TW17 ....38 D8
Manor House Dr ASC SL5 ....34 A1
Manor House Gdns
  EDEN TN8 ....144 G4
Manorhouse La
  GT/LBKH KT23 ....95 N6
Manor House Wy ISLW TW7 ..17 H8
Manor La FELT TW13 ....24 B5
  HYS/HAR UB3 ....14 D8
  KWD/TDW/WH KT20 ....99 L9
  SHGR GU5 ....152 B1
  SUN TW16 ....39 K3
  SUT SM1 ....61 N4
Manor Lea Rd
  MFD/CHID GU8 ....149 M2
Manor Leaze EGH TW20 .....21 N8
Manor Ldg GUW GU2 ....111 P3
Manor Mt FSTH SE23 ....31 K4
Manor Pk RCH/KEW TW9 ....17 M9
  STA TW18 ....22 A9
Manor Park CI WWKM BR4 ...47 H9
Manor Park Dr EWKG RG40 ..48 C3

YTLY GU46 ....67 J3
Manor Park Est
  ASHV GU12 * 108 E5
Manor Park Rd SUT SM1 .....61 N4
  WWKM BR4 ....47 H9
Manor PI EBED/NFELT TW14 ..24 A4
  GT/LBKH KT23 ....96 A6
  MTCM CR4 ....44 E4
  STA TW18 ....22 E8
  SUT SM1 ....61 M4
Manor Rd ALDT GU11 ......108 C6
  ASHF TW15 ....23 J8
  ASHV GU12 ....109 H5
  BECK BR3 ....46 G3
  BELMT SM2 ....61 K6
  BH/WHM TN16 ....84 C9
  EDEN TN8 ....144 F4
  EGRIN RH19 ....180 B1
  FARN GU14 ....88 A3
  FNM GU9 ....128 A1
  GUW GU2 ....111 P3
  HORS RH12 ....192 E5
  MTCM CR4 ....44 E4
  RCH/KEW TW9 ....17 M8
  REDH RH1 ....120 B9
  REIG RH2 ....119 K3
  RPLY/SEND GU23 ....93 K3
  RSEV TN14 ....85 L4
  RYNPK SW20 ....43 K3
  SNWD SE25 ....46 A5
  TEDD TW11 ....25 P8
  WHTN TW2 ....25 J5
  WLGTN SM6 ....62 D5
  WOKN/KNAP GU21 ....72 A5
  WOT/HER KT12 ....57 J1
  WWKM BR4 ....65 H1
Manor Rd North
  ESH/CLAY KT10 ....58 F2
  WLGTN SM6 ....62 C4
Manor Rd South
  ESH/CLAY KT10 ....58 E3
Manor Royal CRAWE RH10 ..177 H2
Manorside CI RFNM GU10 ...109 H6
The Manor MFD/CHID GU8 ..149 N5
Manor V BFBD TW8 ....17 J3
Manor Wk ALDT GU11 ......108 D5
  WEY KT13 ....56 D4
Manor Wy BAGS GU19 ....51 N7
  BECK BR3 ....80 B5
  BNSTD SM7 ....80 B5
  EGH TW20 ....21 L9
  GUW GU2 ....111 P3
  LHD/OX KT22 ....76 C5
  MTCM CR4 ....44 E4
  NWDGN UB2 ....15 M2
  PUR/KEN CR8 ....81 L6
  SAND/SEL CR2 ....63 N5
  WOKS/MYFD GU22 ....72 F9
  WPK KT4 ....42 C9
Manor Wood Rd
  PUR/KEN CR8 ....80 G2
Manresa Rd CHEL SW3 * 19 P3
Mansard Beeches
  TOOT SW17 ....29 K8
Manse CI HYS/HAR UB3 ......14 F4
Mansel CI GUW GU2 ....91 P9
Mansell Wy CTHM CR3 .....101 L2
Mansel Rd WIM/MER SW19 ...28 B9
Mansfield CI ASC SL5 ......33 M3
Mansfield Crs BRAK RG12 ...32 D7
Mansfield Dr REDH RH1 ....100 E8
Mansfield Rd ASC SL5 ......33 M3
  CHSGTN KT9 ....59 J4
  SAND/SEL CR2 ....63 N5
Manship Rd MTCM CR4 .....44 C2
The Mansions ECT SW5 * 19 M3
Manson Ms SKENS SW7 * 19 N2
Manson PI SKENS SW7 * 19 N2
Manston Av NWDGN UB2 ....15 M2
Manston CI PGE/AN SE20 ....46 C2
Manston Dr BRAK RG12 .....32 D7
Manston Gv KUTN/CMB KT2 ...8 C8
Manston Rd RGUE GU4 .....112 E1
Mantilla Rd TOOT SW17 .....29 L7
Mantlet CI STRHM/NOR SW16 .44 E1
Manton Ter
  ADL/WDHM KT15 * 55 N3
Mantua St BTSEA SW11 .....19 P8
Manville Gdns TOOT SW17 ...29 L6
Manville Rd TOOT SW17 .....29 K5
Manwood Rd BROCKY SE4 ...31 N2
Manygate La SHPTN TW17 ...38 E7
Many Gates BAL SW12 ......29 L5
Maori Rd GU GU1 ....7 K3
Maple CI ASHV GU12 ....89 H8
  BLKW GU17 ....67 K2
  CLAP SW4 ....29 M1
  CRAWW RH11 ....176 F7
  CTHM CR3 ....101 P3
  HORS RH12 ....192 F6
  HPTN TW12 ....24 G9
  MTCM CR4 ....44 E1
  SHST GU47 ....49 P8
Maple Ct EGH TW20 ....20 G9
  NWMAL KT3 ....42 B4
  YTLY GU46 ....67 H3
Maple Gv BTFD TW8 ....17 H6
  GU GU1 ....7 K1
  WOKS/MYFD GU22 ....72 D1
Maplehatch CI GODL GU7 ..150 D2
Maplehurst CI KUT/HW KT1 ...41 L5
Maplehurst Rd RCH/KEW TW9 .17 N8

Maple Ldg HASM GU27 * 184 F6
Maple Ms STRHM/NOR SW16 ..30 A8
Maple PI EW KT17 ....79 H3
Maple Rd ASHTD KT21 ......77 K8
  CTHM CR3 ....81 P6
  PGE/AN SE20 ....46 B2
  REDH RH1 ....120 B9
  RPLY/SEND GU23 ....93 L4
  SURB KT6 ....41 L6
Maplestead Rd
  BRXS/STRHM SW2 ....30 A3
The Maples BNSTD SM7 .....79 M2
  CHERT KT16 ....54 F5
  E/WMO/HCT KT8 * 39 P1
  ESH/CLAY KT10 * 58 G6
Maplethorpe Rd THHTH CR7 ..45 J5
Mapleton CI HAYES BR2 .....47 N6
Mapleton Crs
  WAND/EARL SW18 ....28 E2
  BH/WHM TN16 ....125 J3
  EDEN TN8 ....125 L6
  WAND/EARL SW18 ....28 E2
Maple Wk ASHV GU12 ......108 F6
Maple Wy BOR GU35 ....164 E5
  COUL/CHIP CR5 ....100 D1
Maplin CI PUR/KEN CR8 .....81 N9
Maplin Pk DTCH/LGLY SL3 ...12 F1
Marble Hill CI TWK TW1 .....26 A3
Marble Hill Gdns TWK TW1 ...26 A3
Marbles Wy
  KWD/TDW/WH KT20 ....79 H8
Marchbank Rd WKENS W14 ..19 K4
Marchecia CI BRAK RG12 * ..32 D7
Marches Rd HORS RH12 ....173 L7
The Marches HORS RH12 ...174 A6
Marchmont Rd
  RCHPK/HAM TW10 ....26 E1
  WLGTN SM6 ....62 E7
March Rd TWK TW1 ....25 N3
  WLGTN SM6 ....62 C4
Marcilly Rd
  WAND/EARL SW18 ....28 G1
Marco Rd HMSMTH W6 ......18 F1
Marcus Ct
  WOKS/MYFD GU22 ....10 E5
Marcus Ct CTHM CR3 ......101 L3
Marcus Garvey Ms
  EDUL SE22 ....31 J2
Marcus St WAND/EARL SW18 .28 E2
Mardale CBLY GU15 ....69 L4
Mardell Rd CROY/NA CR0 ....46 D6
Marden Av HAYES BR2 ......47 N7
Marden Crs CROY/NA CR0 ...45 H7
Marden Rd CROY/NA CR0 ....45 H7
The Mardens CRAWW RH11 ..176 F4
Mare Hill MFD/CHID GU8 ...149 M7
Mare La MFD/CHID GU8 ....150 G8
Mareschal Rd GUW GU2 ......6 C7
Mareth CI ALDT GU11 .....108 D4
Marfleet CI CAR SM5 ....62 A1
Margaret Ct STA TW18 * P1
Margaret Ingram CI
  FUL/PGN SW6 ....19 K4
Margaret Lockwood CI
  KUT KT1 * 41 M5
Margaret Rd GU GU1 ....7 J4
Margaret Wy PUR/KEN CR8 ..81 K8
Margate Rd
  BRXS/STRHM SW2 ....29 P1
Margery La
  KWD/TDW/WH KT20 ....99 J9
Margin Dr WIM/MER SW19 ...28 A8
Margravine Gdns
  HMSMTH W6 ....19 H3
Margravine Rd HMSMTH W6 ..19 H4
Marguerite Vs
  RYNPK SW20 * 42 F1
Marham Gdns MRDN SM4 ....43 N8
  WAND/EARL SW18 ....29 H4
Maria Theresa CI NWMAL KT3 .42 B6
Mariette CI WLGTN SM6 .....62 C7
Marigold Ct GU GU1 ....112 C2
Marigold Dr CHOB/PIR GU24 .90 E4
Marigold Wy CROY/NA CR0 ..46 D9
Marina Av NWMAL KT3 ......42 G6
Marina CI CHERT KT16 ......37 K5
Marina Dr FNM GU9 ....107 L7
  RCH/KEW TW9 ....45 L6
Marinefield Rd FUL/PGN SW6 .19 M4
Mariner Gdns
  RCHPK/HAM TW10 ....26 A6
Mariners Dr RGUW GU3 ....110 B3
Marion Av SHPTN TW17 .....38 D6
Marion Rd CRAWE RH10 ....177 L8
  THHTH CR7 ....45 L6
  CROY/NA CR0 ....45 J6
Marius Rd TOOT SW17 ......29 L5
Marjoram CI FARN GU14 ....87 M3
  GUW GU2 ....111 N1
Markedge La
  COUL/CHIP CR5 ....100 B3
Markenfield Rd GU GU1 ......6 E3
Markenhorn GODL GU7 .....131 K6
Market Field Rd REDH RH1 ..120 C5
Marketfield Wy REDH RH1 ..120 B5
Market La DTCH/LGLY SL3 ...12 C1
Market Pde BMLY BR1 * 47 N2
  EW KT17 * 60 D7
  FELT TW13 * 24 E5
  PGE/AN SE20 * 46 B2
Market PI BRAK RG12 ....32 D4
  BTFD TW8 ....17 H3
  DTCH/LGLY SL3 * 12 C5
  KUT KT1 ....8 C5
Market Rd RCH/KEW TW9 ....17 N8
Market Sq BH/WHM TN16 ...104 C7

BMLY BR1 ....47 N3
HORS RH12 * 192 B9
Market St BRAK RG12 ....32 D3
GU GU1 ....6 E5
The Market CAR SM5 * 17 L4
RCH/KEW TW9 ....26 C1
Market Wy BH/WHM TN16 ....105 H6
Markfield CROY/NA CR0 ....64 F9
Markfield Rd CTHM CR3 ....102 B6
Markham Ct CBLY GU15 ....68 F2
Markham Rd RDKG RH5 ....156 N7
Markhole CI HPTN TW12 ....59 P1
Mark Oak La LHD/OX KT22 ......96 A1
Marksbury Av RCH/KEW TW9 ..17 N8
Marks Rd WARL CR6 ....82 E7
Mark St REIG RH2 ....119 M4
Markville Gdns CTHM CR3 ....102 A5
Mark Wy GODL GU7 ....131 H5
The Markway SUN TW16 ....39 L3
Markwell CI SYD SE26............31 K7
Markwick La LHD/OX KT22 ......31 H5
Marlborough CI
   CRAWW RH11 ....176 F9
   FLEETN GU51 ....87 K7
   HORS RH12 ....192 C5
   WIM/MER SW19 ....29 J9
   WOT/HER KT12 ....57 M2
Marlborough Dr WEY KT13 ....56 E2
Marlborough Ri CBLY GU15 ......68 C2
Marlborough Rd ASHF TW15 ....38 H8
   CHSWK W4 ....18 A3
   DORK RH4 ....117 H7
   DTCH/LGLY SL3 ....12 B2
   FELT TW13 ....25 H9
   HPTN TW12 ....25 H9
   HYS/HAR UB3 ....14 F5
   NWDGN UB2 ....15 L1
   RCHPK/HAM TW10 ....26 D2
   SAND/SEL CR2 ....63 L6
   SUT SM1 ....61 L2
   WIM/MER SW19 ....29 H9
   WOKN/KNAP GU21 ....11 G2
Marlborough Vw FARN GU14 ....87 N2
The Marld ASHTD KT21 ....77 M7
Marler Rd FSTH SE23 ....31 N4
Marles La BIL RH14 ....189 N9
Marley CI ADL/WDHM KT15 .....55 K5
Marley Combe Rd
   HASM GU27 ....184 A5
Marley Hanger HASM GU27 ....184 B5
Marley La HASM GU27 ....183 P5
Marley Ri DORK RH4 ....136 G1
Marlhurst EDEN TN8 ....144 F1
Marlin CI SUN TW16................23 H9
Marlingdene CI HPTN TW12 .....25 H9
Marlings CI CTHM CR3 ....81 N6
Marlins CI SUT SM1 * 61 N4
Marloes Rd KENS W8 ....19 M1
Marlow Ct PGE/AN SE20 ....46 B4
Marlow Cr CRAWE RH10 ....176 G4
Marlow Crs TWK TW1 ....25 N2
Marlow Dr CHEAM SM3.............61 H2
Marlow Wy CROY/NA CR0.........62 C1
Marlow Gdns HYS/HAR UB3 ....14 F1
Marlow Rd NWDGN UB2 ....15 P1
   PGE/AN SE20 ....46 B4
Marlpit CI COUL/CHIP CR5 ....80 D6
Marlpit CI EDEN TN8 ....144 C1
   EGRIN RH19 ....162 D9
Marlpit La COUL/CHIP CR5 ....80 D7
Marl Rd WAND/EARL SW18 ....19 M9
Marlyns CI RGUE GU4 ....112 G2
Marmora Rd EDUL SE22 ....31 K2
Marmot Rd HSLWW TW4 ....15 M8
Marnell Wy HSLWW TW4 ....15 M8
Marneys CI EPSOM KT18 ....77 N4
Marnfield Crs
   BRXS/STRHM SW2 * 30 A4
Marnham PI
   ADL/WDHM KT15..................55 N3
Marnock Rd BROCKY SE4...........31 N1
Maroons Wy CAT SE6 ....33 P8
Marrick CI PUT/ROE SW15 ....18 E9
Marriott CI
   EBED/NFELT TW14 ....23 N2
Marriott Lodge CI
   ADL/WDHM KT15..................55 N3
Marrowbrook CI FARN GU14 ....88 C4
Marrowbrook La FARN GU14 ....88 C4
Marrowells WEY KT13 ....56 G2
Marryat PI WIM/MER SW19 ......28 D7
Marryat Rd WIM/MER SW19 ....28 A8
Marryat Sq FUL/PGN SW6 * 19 J6
Marshall CI FARN GU14 ....68 B8
   FRIM GU16 ....69 M6
   HSLWW TW4 ....24 G1
   SAND/SEL CR2 ....82 A2
   WAND/EARL SW18 ....28 F2
Marshall Pde
   WOKS/MYFD GU22 * 73 K4
Marshall Rd ADL/WDHM KT15 ..55 N7
   GODL GU7 ....131 L7
   SHST GU47 ....67 P1
Marshalls CI LHD/OX KT22 ....19 J3
Marshall's Rd SUT SM1 ....61 M3
Marsh Av HOR/WEW KT19 ....60 D8
   MTCM CR4 ....44 B3
Marsh Farm Rd WHTN TW2 .....25 N4
Marshfield DTCH/LGLY SL3 .....12 A6
Marsh Green Rd EDEN TN8 .....144 F9
Marsh La ADL/WDHM KT15 .....55 M3
   HTWY RG27 .... B
Marshwood Rd LTWR GU18 ......52 D9
Marston HOR/WEW KT19 * 60 A5
Marston Av CHSGTN KT9 ....59 L5
Marston Dr FARN GU14 ....68 D9
   WARL CR6 ....82 E7
Marston Rd FNM GU9 ....4 B5
   TEDD TW11 ....26 A8
   WOKN/KNAP GU21 ....71 P6
Marston Wy ASC SL5.................33 N3
   NRWD SE19 ....45 K1
Martel CI CBLY GU15 ....68 F4
Martell Rd DUL SE21 ....30 E6
Martens PI GODL GU7 ....131 L7
Martin CI CRAWW RH11 ....176 D3
   SAND/SEL CR2 ....64 D9
   WARL CR6 ....82 B5
Martin Crs CROY/NA CR0..........45 H9
Martindale
   MORT/ESHN SW14 ....27 H1
Martindale Av CBLY GU15 ....69 L5
Martindale Rd RGUE GU4 ....113 H3
Martindale PI
   MFD/CHID GU8 * 167 P7
Martindale Rd BAL SW12 ....29 L3
   HSLWW TW4 ....15 N9
   WOKN/KNAP GU21 ....71 M7
Martineau CI ESH/CLAY KT10 ...58 D3
Martineau Dr DORK RH4 ....117 H9
Martingale CI SUN TW16 ....39 J5
Martingale Ct ALDT GU11 ....108 A4
Martingales CI
   RCHPK/HAM TW10 ....26 C6
Martin Gv WIM/MER SW19 ....43 L4
Martins CI BLKW GU17 ....67 P4
   GU GU1 ....112 G4
   WWKM BR4 ....65 K1
Martins Dr BRAK RG12 ....32 G4
Martins Pk FARN GU14 * 67 P9
Martin's Rd HAYES BR2 ....47 L3
The Martins CRAWE RH10 ....179 K3
   SYD SE26 ....31 J8
Martinsyde
   WOKS/MYFD GU22 ....72 G6
Martin Wy FRIM GU16 ....68 G7
   RYNPK SW20 ....43 J4
   WOKN/KNAP GU21 ....71 N7
Martlets CI HORS RH12 ....192 B5
The Martlets CRAWE RH10 ......177 H5
Martlets Cnr HORS RH12 * 189 N3
Marton CI CAT SE6..................32 P4
The Marts HORS RH12 ....189 N3
Martyns PI EGRIN RH19 ....180 F3
Martyr Rd GU GU1 ....6 E5
Martyrs Av CRAWW RH11 ....176 F2
Martyrs La WOKN/KNAP GU21 ..72 H1
Marville Rd FUL/PGN SW6 ....19 K5
Marwell BH/WHM TN16 ....104 F6
Marwell CI WWKM BR4 ....65 M1
Marwell CI FLEETN GU51 ....86 C3
Mary Adelaide CI
   PUT/ROE SW15 ....27 K6
Maryland CI PL/KEN CR8 ....81 L6
Maryland Rd EWKG RG40 ....48 D3
Maryland Wy SUN TW16 ....39 J3
Mary Rd GU GU1 ....6 D3
Mary Rose CI HPTN TW12 ....40 A2
Mary's Ter TWK TW1 ....25 P3
Mary V GODL GU7 ....150 C2
Masbro' Rd WKENS W14 ....19 H1
Masdar Gdns EWKG RG40 ....48 C3
Masefield CI CRAWW RH11 ....176 B8
   FELT TW13 ....24 C7
Masefield Wy
   STWL/WRAY TW19 ....23 J4
Maskall CI
   BRXS/STRHM SW2 * 30 B4
Maskell Rd TOOT SW17 ....28 F6
Maskell Wy FARN GU14 ....87 N4
Mason CI EGRIN RH19 ....180 D1
   HPTN TW12 ....39 P2
   RYNPK SW20 ....43 J2
   YTLY GU46 * 66 F3
Masonic Hall Rd CHERT KT16 ...57 K7
Mason PI SHST GU47 ....49 K9
Mason Rd CRAWE RH10 ....177 H1
   FARN GU14 ....88 A1
Mason's Av CROY/NA CR0............2 D6
Mason's Bridge Rd
   REDH RH1 ....140 D1
Masons Ct EW KT17 * 60 E7
Masons HI HAYES BR2 ....47 N4
Masons Paddock DORK RH4 ...116 C6
Mason's PI MTCM CR4 ....44 B2
Mason Wy ALDT GU11 ....108 D7
Massetts Rd HORL RH6 ....159 J2
Massingberd Wy TOOT SW17 ...29 J7
Master CI OXTED RH8 ....105 L9
Masters CI STRHM/NOR SW16 ..29 M9
Maswell Park Crs HSLW TW3 ....25 K1
Maswell Park Rd HSLW TW3 ....25 J1
Matfield CI HAYES BR2 ....47 N6
Matham Rd E/WMO/HCT KT8 ..40 D6
Matheson Rd WKENS W14 ....19 H2
Mathews Ter ALDT GU11 * 108 B4
Mathias CI EPSOM KT18 ....78 A2
Mathisen Wy DTCH/LGLY SL3 ...13 J6
Matilda CI NRWD SE19 ....45 K6
Matlock Crs CHEAM SM3 ....61 J3
Matlock Gdns CHEAM SM3 ....61 J3
Matlock PI CHEAM SM3 ....61 J3
Matlock Rd CTHM CR3 ....101 N2
Matlock Wy NWMAL KT3 ....42 C2
Matthew Arnold CI COB KT11 ...75 J3
   STA TW18 ....22 C7
Matthew Ct MTCM CR4 ....44 F6
Matthew Rd ALDT GU11 ....108 A6
Matthews Cha BENFD RG42 ......32 B1
Matthews Dr CRAWE RH10 .....177 M9
Matthew's Gdns
   CROY/NA CR0.......................65 K9
Matthews La STA TW18 ....22 C7
Matthews Rd CBLY GU15 ....50 E9
Matthew's St REIG RH2 ....119 L9
Mauleverer Rd
   BRXS/STRHM SW2 ....29 P1
Maultway CI CBLY GU15 ....51 K9
Maultway Crs CBLY GU15 ....51 K8
Maultway North CBLY GU15 .....51 K8
The Maultway CBLY GU15 ....51 L9
Maunsell Pk CRAWE RH10 ......177 L5
Maurice Av CTHM CR3 ....101 M2
Mavins Rd FNM GU9 ....4 C6
Mavis Av HOR/WEW KT19 ....60 C4
Mavis CI HOR/WEW KT19 ....60 C4
Mawbey Rd CHERT KT16 ....55 H5
Mawson CI RYNPK SW20 ....43 J3
Mawson La CHSWK W4 ....18 D3
Maxine CI SHST GU47 ....49 M8
Maxton Wk CRAWW RH11 * 176 E9
Maxwell CI CROY/NA CR0 ....44 D1
Maxwell Dr BF/WBF KT14 ....55 N9
Maxwell Rd ASHF TW15 ....23 M8
   FUL/PGN SW6 ....19 M5
   WDR/YW UB7 ....14 A2
Maxwell Wy CRAWE RH10 ......177 K2
Mayall Rd BRXN/ST SW9 ....30 C1
May Bate Av KUTN/CMB KT2 ......8 C2
Maybelle CI RDKG RH5 ....156 C1
Mayberry PI BRYLDS KT5 ....41 M8
Maybourne Ri
   WOKS/MYFD GU22 ....92 B4
Maybrick CI SHST GU47 ....49 K8
Maybury CI FRIM GU16 ....68 F3
   KWD/TDW/WH KT20 ....79 J8
Maybury HI
   WOKN/KNAP GU21 ....11 J1
Maybury Rd
   RCHPK/HAM TW10 ....26 C5
Maybury St TOOT SW17 ....29 H8
May CI BOP GU35 ....164 B7
   CHSGTN KT9 ....59 M5
   GODL GU7 ....150 A2
   SHST GU47 ....49 P9
May Crs ASHV GU12 ....108 G5
Maycross Av MRDN SM4 ....43 K5
Mayday Rd THHTH CR7 ....45 J7
Maydwell Av SWTR RH13 ....190 C8
Mayefield Rd THHTH CR7 ....45 H5
Mayell CI LHD/OX KT22 ....97 J3
Mayes CI CRAWE RH10 ....177 M6
   WARL CR6 ....82 G7
Mayes La HORS RH12 ....191 M1
Mayfair Av WHTN TW2 ....25 K3
   WPK KT4 ....42 E9
Mayfair CI BECK BR3 ....47 H2
   SURB KT6 ....41 L8
Mayfield CRAWE RH10 ....177 N5
   LHD/OX KT22 ....97 J1
   LING RH7 ....162 F3
   RFNM GU10 ....146 C1
Mayfield Av ADL/WDHM KT15 ..55 M8
   ASHF TW15 ....23 N1
   CLAP SW4 ....29 N1
   PGE/AN SE20 * 46 B2
   PUR/KEN CR8 ....81 J1
   RCHPK/HAM TW10 ....17 J2
   WOT/HER KT12 ....57 P3
Mayfield CI ASHTD KT21 ....77 J8
   ASHV GU12 ....89 H6
   BLKW GU17 ....67 P4
   CAT SE6 ....31 P8
   CRAWE RH10 ....177 N5
   ESH/CLAY KT10 ....58 B7
   GODL GU7 ....131 L6
   HORS RH12 ....182 F6
   HSLWW TW4 ....25 H2
   LIPH GU30 ....182 F6
   MFD/CHID GU8 ....8 F2
   PUR/KEN CR8 ....81 P3
   RCHPK/HAM TW10 ....26 B5
   RYNPK SW20 ....42 G5
   WOT/HER KT12 ....57 P3
Mayfield Crs THHTH CR7 ....45 H6
Mayfield Gdns GT/LBKH KT23 ..96 A7
Mayfield Gn GT/LBKH KT23 ......96 A7
Mayfield Rd BELMT SM2 ....61 P5
   FARN GU14 ....68 B9
   SAND/SEL CR2 ....63 M7
   WEY KT13 ....56 B2
   WIM/MER SW19 ....43 K2
   WOT/HER KT12 ....57 J3
Mayflower CI CRAWE RH10 ....177 M4
Mayflower Dr YTLY GU46 ....66 E1
Mayford CI BAL SW12 ....29 J3
   BECK BR3 ....46 D4
   WOKS/MYFD GU22 ....92 B2
Mayford Rd BAL SW12 ....29 J3
Mayhurst Av
   WOKS/MYFD GU22 ....72 G5
Mayhurst CI
   WOKS/MYFD GU22 ....72 G5
Mayhurst Crs
   WOKS/MYFD GU22 ....72 G5
Maynard CI CRAWE RH10 ......176 D8
   FUL/PGN SW6 ....19 M5
Mayo Rd CROY/NA CR0 ....45 M6
   WOT/HER KT12 ....39 J8
Maynooke Av SYD SE26 ....31 L7
Maypole Rd EGRIN RH19 ....180 C1
   EGRIN RH19 ....181 K5
Mayroyd Av SURB KT6 ....59 N1
Mays CI WEY KT13 ....56 B8
Mays Cnr BRAK RG12 *..............32 C7
Mays Hill Rd HAYES BR2 ....47 L3
Maysoule Rd BTSEA SW11 ....19 P9
Mays Rd HPTN TW12..................8 C2
May St WKENS W14 ....19 K3
Maytree CI GU GU1 ....111 P2
Maytree Rd CAR SM5 ....44 C4
Maytrees WOKN/KNAP GU21 ...71 J6
Maytree Wk
   BRXS/STRHM SW2 * 30 B5
Maywater CI SAND/SEL CR2 .....63 M9
Maywood CI BECK BR3 * 47 H1
Maywood Dr CBLY GU15 ....69 K1
Maze Rd RCH/KEW TW9 ....17 N5
McAlmont Rdg GODL GU7 ......131 K6
McCarthy Rd FELT TW13 ....24 E8
Mc Carthy Wy EWKG RG40 ......48 D1
McDonough CI CHSGTN KT9 ....59 L3
McDougall Ct RCH/KEW TW9 ....17 N7
McGrigor Barracks
   ALDT GU11 ....108 D3
McIndoe Rd EGRIN RH19 ....162 C9
McIntosh CI WLGTN SM6 ....62 G6
McIver CI EGRIN RH19 ....161 N8
McKay CI ALDT GU11 ....108 A3
McKay Rd RYNPK SW20 ....42 F1
McKenzie Wy
   HOR/WEW KT19.....................59 N8
McLeod's Ms SKENS SW7 ....19 M1
McNair Rd NWDGN UB2 ....16 A1
Mc Naughton Ct FARN GU14 ....87 N4
McRae La MTCM CR4 ....44 B8
Mead Av REDH RH1 ....140 C4
Mead CI CRAN GU6 ....171 H1
   REDH RH1 ....120 C2
Mead Ct EGH TW20 ....21 P9
   WOKN/KNAP GU21 ....71 L6
Mead Crs GT/LBKH KT23 ....96 A5
   SUT SM1 ....62 C3
Mead Dr COUL/CHIP CR5 ....80 G3
Meade CI CHSWK W4 ....17 N4
Mead End ASHTD KT21 ....77 M5
Meades CI LING RH7 ....162 F5
The Meades LING RH7 ....162 G3
   WEY KT13 * 56 F5
Meadfield Av DTCH/LGLY SL3 ..12 E1
Meadfield Rd DTCH/LGLY SL3 ..12 F1
Meadfoot Rd
   STRHM/NOR SW16 ....44 E2
Mead Crs GT/LBKH KT23 ....96 A5
Meadhurst Pk SUN TW16 ....23 P9
Meadhurst Rd CHERT KT16 * 37 M9
Meadlands Dr
   RCHPK/HAM TW10 ....26 C5
Meadow Ap CRAWE RH10 ......160 B9
Meadow Av CROY/NA CR0 ....46 D3
Meadowbank BRYLDS KT5 ....41 M6
   FNM GU9 * 4 E5
Meadowbank CI
   FUL/PGN SW6 ....18 G5
Meadowbank Gdns
   HEST TW5 ....15 J6
Meadowbank Rd LTWR GU18 ...52 C8
Meadowbrook CI
   DTCH/LGLY SL3 ....13 J7
Meadowbrook Rd
   DORK RH4 ....116 C6
Meadow CI ASHV GU12 ....89 H6
   BLKW GU17 ....67 P4
   CAT SE6 ....31 P8
   CRAWE RH10 ....176 E1
   ESH/CLAY KT10 ....58 E1
   GODL GU7 ....131 L6
   HORS RH12 ....191 N8
   HSLWW TW4 ....25 H2
   LIPH GU30 ....182 F6
   MFD/CHID GU8 ....8 F2
   PUR/KEN CR8 ....81 P3
   RCHPK/HAM TW10 ....26 B5
   RYNPK SW20 ....42 G5
   WOT/HER KT12 ....57 P3
Meadow Ct EPSOM KT18 ....78 B2
   STA TW18 ....22 B6
Meadowcroft CI
   CRAWW RH11 ....176 C6
   EGRIN RH19 ....180 B1
Meadow Croft CI HORL RH6 ...159 L7
Meadow Dr RPLY/SEND GU23 ..93 K3
Meadow Farm La
   HORS RH12 ....192 E3
Meadow Gdns STA TW18 ....22 B6
Meadow Gate Av FARN GU14 ...88 B6
Meadow Hi COUL/CHIP CR5 .....80 E2
   NWMAL KT3 ....42 C5
Meadowlands COB KT11 ....75 J2
   CRAWW RH11 ....176 F2
   OXTED RH8 ....104 B7
   RGUE GU4 ....113 N1
Meadow La EDEN TN8 ....144 F4
   LHD/OX KT22 ....96 C2
Meadowlea CI WDR/YW UB7 ....13 P4
Meadow Ri COUL/CHIP CR5 .....80 F2
   WOKN/KNAP GU21 ....71 N8
Meadow Rd ASHF TW15 ....23 N8
   ASHTD KT21 ....77 L5
   DTCH/LGLY SL3 ....12 C1
   ESH/CLAY KT10 ....58 B3
   FARN GU14 ....68 D3
   FELT TW13 ....24 F5
   HAYES BR2 ....47 N6
   RPLY/SEND GU23 ....113 N3
   SUT SM1 ....62 C3
   VW GU25 ....35 L6
   WIM/MER SW19 ....43 L6
Meadows End SUN TW16 ....39 J2
Meadowside GT/LBKH KT23 .....96 A6
   HORL RH6 ....140 D9
   TWK TW1 ....26 C3
   WOT/HER KT12 ....57 J3
Meadowside Rd BELMT SM2.....61 J7
Meadows Leigh CI WEY KT13 ...56 E2
The Meadows CRAN GU6 ....112 A8
   RFNM GU10 ....165 J2
   WARL CR6 ....82 D6
Meadow Stile CROY/NA CR0 ......2 C4
Meadowsweet CI
   NWMAL KT3 ....42 C6
The Meadow CRAWE RH10 .....160 B9
Meadow V HASM GU27 ....184 B4
Meadow Vw FLEETS GU52 ......106 E1
McMenamin CI
The Meads CHEAM SM3 ....61 H2
   EGRIN RH19 ....180 D4
   HASM GU27 ....184 A4
   HASM GU27 ....184 A4
   WEY KT13 ....56 F5
The Mead ASHTD KT21 ....77 L8
   BECK BR3 ....47 J3
   DORK RH4 * 137 J1
   FARN GU14 * 88 D4
   LIPH GU30 ....182 E5
   WLGTN SM6 ....62 G5
   WWKM BR4 ....47 K9
Meadvale HORS RH12 ....191 N8
Meadvale Rd CROY/NA CR0 ......45 P8
   CROY/NA CR0 ....64 E1
   HAYES BR2 ....47 N7
Meadway ASHF TW15 ....22 G9
   BECK BR3 ....47 J2
   BRYLDS KT5 ....41 P7
   EHSLY KT24 ....94 A5
   ESH/CLAY KT10 ....58 B7
   FRIM GU16 ....69 H6
   HORL RH6 ....159 M1
   HOR/WEW KT19......................78 A2
   LHD/OX KT22 ....76 D3
   RYNPK SW20 ....42 G5
   STA TW18 ....37 J1
   WARL CR6 ....82 C5
   WHTN TW2 ....25 L4
Meadway CI STA TW18 ....37 J1
Meadway Dr
   ADL/WDHM KT15...................55 N6
   WOKN/KNAP GU21 ....71 M5
The Meadway HORL RH6 ....159 M1
Meaford Wy PGE/AN SE20 ....46 B1
Meare CI KWD/TDW/WH KT20 ..98 G3
Meath Green Av HORL RH6 .....140 A8
Meath Green La HORL RH6 .....140 A5
Medawar Rd GUW GU2 ....111 K6
Medcroft Gdns
   MORT/ESHN SW14 ....18 A7
Mede CI STWL/WRAY TW19 ......21 J4
Mede Fld LHD/OX KT22 ....96 A7
Medfield St PUT/ROE SW15 ......27 M3
Medhurst Ct CHD/PIR GU24 .....53 M7
Medina Av ESH/CLAY KT10 ......58 C2
Medlake Rd EGH TW20 ....21 P9
Medland CI WLGTN SM6 ....44 C9
Medlar CI CRAWW RH11 ....176 F2
   FNM GU9 ....112 A3
Medlar Dr BLKW GU17 ....68 B5
Medonte CI FLEETN GU51 ....87 H7
Medora Rd
   BRXS/STRHM SW2 ....30 A2
Medway CRAWE RH10 ....179 H6
Medway CI CROY/NA CR0 ....46 C2
Medway Dr EGRIN RH19 ....180 C5
   FARN GU14 ....68 A8
   FROW RH18 ....181 M9
Medway Rd CRAWW RH11 ......176 C6
Medwin Wy HORS RH12 ....192 B8
Melbourne CI WLGTN SM6 ....62 E4
Melbourne Rd TEDD TW11 ....26 B9
   WIM/MER SW19 ....43 L2
   WLGTN SM6 ....62 D4
Melbourne Ter
   FUL/PGN SW6 * 19 M5
Melbury CI
   HORS RH12 * 192 E5
Melbury Av NWDGN UB2 ....16 B1
Melbury CI BF/WBF KT14 ....73 L3
   ESH/CLAY KT10 ....58 B7
Melbury Ct WKENS W14 ....19 K1
Melbury Gdns RYNPK SW20 .....42 F2
Meldon CI FUL/PGN SW6 * 19 M6
Meldone CI BRYLDS KT5 ....41 P7
Meldrum CI OXTED RH8 ....123 M3
Melford CI CHSGTN KT9 ....59 M4
Melford Rd EDUL SE22 ....31 H4
Melfort Av THHTH CR7 ....45 K4
Melfort Rd THHTH CR7 ....45 K4
Melksham CI SWTR RH13 ....192 D8

Meller Cl *CROY/NA* CR0 62 G2
Mellersh Cl *FLEETS* GU52 106 E2
Mellersh Hill Rd *SHGR* GU5 132 F7
Mellison Rd *TOOT* SW17 29 H8
Melliss Av *RCH/KEW* TW9 17 P6
Mellor Cl *WOT/HER* KT12 39 P8
Mellow Cl *BNSTD* SM7 79 M3
Mellows Rd *WLGTN* SM6 62 F4
Melody Rd *BH/WHM* TN16 84 A7
WAND/EARL SW18 28 F2
Melrose *BRAK* RG12 32 D9
Melrose Av *FARN* GU14 87 N2
MTCM CR4 44 D1
STRHM/NOR SW16 45 H4
WHTN TW2 25 J3
WIM/MER SW19 28 C5
Melrose Gdns *HMSMTH* W6 18 G1
NWMAL KT3 42 B4
WOT/HER KT12 57 L4
Melrose Rd *BARN* SW13 18 D7
BH/WHM TN16 84 A5
COUL/CHIP CR5 80 D4
WAND/EARL SW18 28 C2
WEY KT13 56 C4
WIM/MER SW19 43 L3
Melrose Vls *BECK* BR3 * 46 G3
Melsa Rd *MRDN* SM4 43 N7
Melton Flds *HOR/WEW* KT19 60 B7
Melton Pl *HOR/WEW* KT19 60 B7
Melton Rd *REDH* RH1 120 E1
Melville Av *FRIM* GU16 69 H7
RYNPK SW20 42 E1
SAND/SEL CR2 63 P4
Melville Rd *BARN* SW13 18 E6
Melville Ter *FNM* GU9 * 4 E4
Melvin Rd *PGE/AN* SE20 46 C2
Melvinshaw *LHD/OX* KT22 97 J1
Membury Cl *FRIM* GU16 69 J9
Membury Wk *BRAK* RG12 33 H5
Memorial Cl *HEST* TW5 15 P4
Mendip Cl *DTCH/LGLY* SL3 12 E3
HYS/HAR UB3 14 F5
SYD SE26 31 K7
WPK KT4 60 G1
Mendip Rd *BRAK* RG12 32 G6
BTSEA SW11 19 N8
FARN GU14 68 A9
Mendip Wk *CRAWW* RH11 176 E5
Mendora Rd *FUL/PGN* SW6 19 J5
Menin Wy *FNM* GU9 5 K6
Menlo Gdns *NRWD* SE19 45 M1
Meon Cl *FARN* GU14 87 P1
KWD/TDW/WH KT20 98 F2
Meopham Rd *MTCM* CR4 44 E2
Merantun Wy
WIM/MER SW19 43 M2
Mercer Cl *CRAWE* RH10 177 M8
THDIT KT7 40 F8
Mercer Rd *HORS* RH12 192 B2
Mercers Pl *HMSMTH* W6 18 G2
Mercier Rd *PUT/ROE* SW15 28 B1
Mercury Centre
EBED/NFELT TW14 * 24 B1
Mercury Cl *CRAWW* RH11 176 B8
Mercury Rd *BTFD* TW8 17 J3
Merebank *RDKG* RH5 137 K9
Merebank La *WLGTN* SM6 63 H4
Mere Cl *WIM/MER* SW19 28 A3
Meredyth Rd *BARN* SW13 18 E7
Mere End *CROY/NA* CR0 46 D8
Merefield Gdns
KWD/TDW/WH KT20 79 H8
Mere Rd *KWD/TDW/WH* KT20 98 F4
SHPTN TW17 * 38 D7
WEY KT13 56 F2
Mereside Pk *ASHF* TW15 * 23 M7
Merevale Crs *MRDN* SM4 43 N7
Mereway Rd *WHTN* TW2 25 L4
Mereworth Cl *HAYES* BR2 47 M6
Mereworth Dr *CRAWE* RH10 177 N3
Meridian Cl *CRAWW* RH11 176 C8
Meridian Gv *HORL* RH6 140 E9
Meridian Wy *EGRIN* RH19 162 E9
Merivale *FLEETN* GU51 86 D7
Merivale Rd *PUT/ROE* SW15 19 J9
Merland Cl
KWD/TDW/WH KT20 78 G9
Merland Gn
KWD/TDW/WH KT20 78 G9
Merland Ri *EPSOM* KT18 78 G8
Merle Common Rd
OXTED RH8 123 N7
Merlewood *BRAK* RG12 32 F6
Merlewood Cl *CTHM* CR3 81 M9
Merlin Centre
CRAWW RH11 * 176 G1
Merlin Cl *CRAWW* RH11 176 B5
CROY/NA CR0 3 G7
DTCH/LGLY SL3 * 12 F4
MTCM CR4 44 A4
Merlin Gv *BECK* BR3 46 F5
Merlin Rd *FARN* GU14 88 D5
Merlins Cl *FNM* GU9 5 G6
Merlin Wy *EGRIN* RH19 162 F9
FARN GU14 87 P4
Merredene St
BRXS/STRHM SW2 30 A2
Merrick Rd *NWDGN* UB2 15 P2
Merrilands Rd *WPK* KT4 42 G9
Merrilyn Cl *ESH/CLAY* KT10 58 G5
Merrington Rd *FUL/PGN* SW6 19 L4
Merritt Gdns *CHSGTN* KT9 59 J5
Merritt Rd *BROCKY* SE4 31 N1
Merrivale Gdns
WOKN/KNAP GU21 72 A6
Merron Cl *YTLY* GU46 66 G3
Merrow Cha *GU* GU1 112 G5
Merrow Common Rd
RGUE GU4 113 H2
Merrow Copse *GU* GU1 112 F4
Merrow Ct *GU* GU1 * 113 H5
Merrow Cft *GU* GU1 112 G4
Merrow La *RGUE* GU4 92 G9
Merrow Pl *RGUE* GU4 113 H3
Merrow Rd *BELMT* SM2 61 H7
Merrow St *RGUE* GU4 113 H3
Merrow Wy *CROY/NA* CR0 65 J5
GU GU1 * 113 H4
Merrow Woods *GU* GU1 112 F3
Merryacres *MFD/CHID* GU8 149 M6
Merryfield Dr *HORS* RH12 191 P7
Merryhill Rd *BNFD* RG42 32 C2
Merryhills Cl *BH/WHM* TN16 84 B5
Merryhills La *BIL* RH14 188 D5
Merrylands *CHERT* KT16 55 J2
Merrylands Farm
GT/LBKH KT23 95 P4
Merrylands Rd *GT/LBKH* KT23 95 P3
Merryman Dr *CWTH* RG45 49 K3
Merrymeet *BNSTD* SM7 80 B3
Merryweather Ct
NWMAL KT3 42 C6
Merrywood Gv
KWD/TDW/WH KT20 119 H1
Merrywood Pk *CBLY* GU15 69 H4
REIG RH2 119 M3
Mersham Pl *PGE/AN* SE20 46 B2
THHTH CR7 45 M3
Mersham Rd *THHTH* CR7 45 M4
Merstham Rd *REDH* RH1 121 J1
Merthyr Ter *BARN* SW13 18 F4
Merton Av *CHSWK* W4 18 D2
Merton Cl *SHST* GU47 50 B7
Merton Gdns
KWD/TDW/WH KT20 79 H9
Merton Hall Gdns
RYNPK SW20 43 J2
Merton Hall Rd
WIM/MER SW19 43 J2
Merton High St
WIM/MER SW19 43 N1
Merton Pl *WIM/MER* SW19 * 43 N2
Merton Rd *CRAWW* RH11 194 E2
SNWD SE25 45 P6
WAND/EARL SW18 28 D4
WIM/MER SW19 43 M1
Merton Wy *E/WMO/HCT* KT8 40 C5
LHD/OX KT22 76 G8
Mervyn Rd *SHPTN* TW17 38 E8
WEA W13 16 G1
Metcalf Rd *ASHF* TW15 23 L8
Metcalf Wy *CRAWW* RH11 176 G1
Meteor Wy *FARN* GU14 88 C6
WLGTN SM6 62 G6
Meudon Av *FARN* GU14 88 D4
Mews Ct *EGRIN* RH19 180 E5
Mewsend *BH/WHM* TN16 84 B7
The Mews *BECK* BR3 * 46 G2
GU GU1 * 113 H5
HORS RH12 * 191 L6
MFD/CHID GU8 169 L6
REIG RH2 * 119 M4
STRHM/NOR SW16 * 45 H2
TWK TW1 * 26 A2
Mexfield Rd *PUT/ROE* SW15 28 C1
Meyrick Cl *WOKN/KNAP* GU21 71 L5
Meyrick Rd *BTSEA* SW11 19 P8
Michael Crs *HORL* RH6 159 K3
Michael Flds *FROW* RH18 181 K9
Michaelmas Cl *RYNPK* SW20 42 G4
YTLY GU46 67 H4
Michael Rd *FUL/PGN* SW6 19 M6
SNWD SE25 45 N4
Micheldever Wy *BRAK* RG12 33 H7
Michelet Cl *LTWR* GU18 52 B8
Michelham Gdns
KWD/TDW/WH KT20 * 78 G9
TWK TW1 25 N6
Michell Cl *HORS* RH12 191 P8
Mickleham Dr *LHD/OX* KT22 97 J6
Mickleham Gdns *CHEAM* SM3 61 J5
Mickleham Wy *CROY/NA* CR0 65 K6
Mickle Hl *SHST* GU47 49 L8
Micklethwaite Rd
FUL/PGN SW6 19 L4
Middle Av *FNM* GU9 127 P5
Middle Bourne La
RFNM GU10 127 M7
Middle Church La *FNM* GU9 5 F4
Middle Cl *CBLY* GU15 69 L2
COUL/CHIP CR5 81 J9
EW KT17 78 C1
Middle Dartrey Wk
WBPTN SW10 * 19 N5
Middle Farm Pl *EHSLY* KT24 95 M7
Middlefield *FNM* GU9 127 L6
HORL RH6 140 E9
Middlefield Cl *FNM* GU9 127 L5
Middlefields *CROY/NA* CR0 64 E7
Middle Gordon Rd *CBLY* GU15 68 E3
Middle Green Cl *BRYLDS* KT5 41 M7
Middle Hl *ALDT* GU11 108 C4
EGH TW20 21 H8
Middle La *EW* KT17 78 C1
TEDD TW11 25 N9
Middlemarch
MFD/CHID GU8 149 M7
Middlemead Cl
GT/LBKH KT23 96 A5
Middlemead Rd
GT/LBKH KT23 95 P5
Middlemoor Rd *FRIM* GU16 68 G8
Middle Old Pk *FNM* GU9 127 K1
Middle Rd *LHD/OX* KT22 97 H1
STRHM/NOR SW16 44 E3
Middlesex Rd *MTCM* CR4 44 G6
Middle St
BRKHM/BTCW RH3 117 P7
CROY/NA CR0 2 D4
HORS RH12 192 B8
SHGR GU5 134 C1
Middleton Gdns *FARN* GU14 88 A1
Middleton Rd *CBLY* GU15 68 G2
COB KT11 75 K8
HOR/WEW KT19 * 60 B8
HORS RH12 191 P8
MRDN SM4 43 N7
NWMAL KT3 42 A4
Middleton Wy *CRAWW* RH11 176 B6
Middle Wk *WOKN/KNAP* GU21 10 E3
Middle Wy *STRHM/NOR* SW16 44 F3
Midgley Rd *CRAWE* RH10 177 J3
Midholm Rd *CROY/NA* CR0 64 E2
Mid Holmwood La
RDKG RH5 137 J3
Midhope Cl
WOKS/MYFD GU22 72 C8
Midhope Gdns
WOKS/MYFD GU22 10 C7
Midhope Rd
WOKS/MYFD GU22 10 C7
Midhurst Av *CROY/NA* CR0 45 J8
Midhurst Cl *CRAWW* RH11 176 D4
Midhurst Rd *HASM* GU27 184 C5
LIPH GU30 182 F7
Midleton Cl *MFD/CHID* GU8 149 N2
Midleton Industrial Estate Rd
GUW GU2 111 P4
Midleton Rd *GUW* GU2 6 A1
Midmoor Rd *BAL* SW12 29 M4
WIM/MER SW19 43 H2
Mid St *REDH* RH1 121 H5
Midsummer Av *HSLWW* TW4 15 P9
Midsummer Wk
WOKN/KNAP GU21 10 A1
Midway *CHEAM* SM3 43 K8
WOT/HER KT12 57 K1
Midway Av *CHERT* KT16 37 M4
EGH TW20 36 F4
Midway Cl *STA* TW18 22 E6
Miena Wy *ASHTD* KT21 77 K6
Mike Hawthorn Dr *FNM* GU9 5 H2
Milbanke Ct *BRAK* RG12 32 B3
Milbanke Wy *BRAK* RG12 32 B3
Milborne Gv *WBPTN* SW10 19 N3
Milborne Rd *CRAWE* RH10 177 M9
Milbourne La *ESH/CLAY* KT10 58 C5
Milbrook *ESH/CLAY* KT10 58 C5
Milburn Wk *EPSOM* KT18 78 C4
Milden Cl *FRIM* GU16 89 J1
Milden Gdns *FRIM* GU16 89 J1
Mildred Av *HYS/HAR* UB3 14 F2
Mile Pth *WOKS/MYFD* GU22 71 P9
Mile Rd *WLGTN* SM6 44 C9
Miles La *COB* KT11 75 N2
GDST RH9 122 G7
Miles Pl *BRYLDS* KT5 * 41 M5
LTWR GU18 69 P1
Miles Rd *ASHV* GU12 109 K3
HOR/WEW KT19 78 B1
MTCM CR4 44 A4
Miles's Hl *RDKG* RH5 154 D1
Milestone Cl *BELMT* SM2 61 P5
RPLY/SEND GU23 93 L2
Milestone Rd *NRWD* SE19 30 G9
Milford By-Pass Rd
MFD/CHID GU8 149 L3
MFD/CHID GU8 149 L4
Milford Gv *SUT* SM1 61 N3
Milford Ldg *MFD/CHID* GU8 149 N4
Milford Ms
STRHM/NOR SW16 30 A6
Milford Rd *MFD/CHID* GU8 129 N9
Milkhouse Ga *GU* GU1 * 7 F6
Milking La *ORP* BR6 84 C1
Milkwood *RGUE* GU4 * 132 D3
Milkwood Rd *HNHL* SE24 30 C1
Millais *SWTR* RH13 192 F7
Millais Cl *CRAWW* RH11 176 C9
Millais Ct *SWTR* RH13 192 F6
Millais Rd *NWMAL* KT3 42 C8
Millais Wy *HOR/WEW* KT19 60 A3
Millan Cl *ADL/WDHM* KT15 55 M8
The Millbank *CRAWW* RH11 176 C6
Mill Bay La *HORS* RH12 192 A9
Millbottom La *RDKG* RH5 137 K6
Millbourne Rd *FELT* TW13 24 F7
Millbridge Rd *YTLY* GU46 48 F9
Millbrook *GUW* GU2 6 E6
WEY KT13 56 G3
Millbrook Wy *DTCH/LGLY* SL3 13 J7
Mill Cl *BAGS* GU19 51 M6
CAR SM5 * 62 C1
EGRIN RH19 180 D4
GT/LBKH KT23 96 A4
HASM GU27 183 P4
HORL RH6 140 A9
WDR/YW UB7 13 P1
Millcombe Cl
WOKN/KNAP GU21 71 P7
Mill Copse Rd *HASM* GU27 184 C6
Mill Cnr *FLEETN* GU51 87 J2
Mill Cottages *EGRIN* RH19 * 180 D4
HORS RH12 * 189 N5
Millennium Wy *BNFD* RG42 32 D2
Miller Cl *MTCM* CR4 44 B8
Miller Rd *CROY/NA* CR0 45 H9
RGUE GU4 112 G2
WIM/MER SW19 28 G9
Millers Cl *STA* TW18 22 E8
Millers Copse *EPSOM* KT18 78 B8
REDH RH1 141 K6
Miller's Ct *CHSWK* W4 18 D3
Millers Ga *HORS* RH12 192 C4
Miller's La *REDH* RH1 141 K6
Mill Farm Av *SUN* TW16 38 G1
Mill Farm Crs *HSLWW* TW4 24 F4
Mill Farm Rd *SWTR* RH13 192 F6
Mill Fld *BAGS* GU19 51 M6
Millfield *SUN* TW16 38 F2
Millfield La
KWD/TDW/WH KT20 99 L5
Millfield Rd *HSLWW* TW4 24 F4
Millford *WOKN/KNAP* GU21 71 P6
Mill Gdns *SYD* SE26 31 J7
Mill Gn *BNFD* RG42 32 A1
MTCM CR4 * 44 C8
Mill Green Rd *MTCM* CR4 44 C8
Millhedge Cl *COB* KT11 75 N5
Mill Hl *BARN* SW13 18 E8
BRKHM/BTCW RH3 117 P6
EDEN TN8 145 H6
Mill Hill La
BRKHM/BTCW RH3 117 P5
Mill Hill Rd *BARN* SW13 18 F8
Mill House La *CHERT* KT16 36 F5
Millhouse Pl *WNWD* SE27 30 C7
Millington Rd *HYS/HAR* UB3 14 G1
Millins Cl *SHST* GU47 49 P8
Mill La *ASC* SL5 35 H3
BF/WBF KT14 74 C2
BH/WHM TN16 104 G7
BOR GU35 164 A6
BRAK RG12 32 C6
CAR SM5 62 C3
CHOB/PIR GU24 90 D4
CRAWE RH10 160 F9
CRAWW RH11 176 D3
CROY/NA CR0 63 J2
DORK RH4 117 H6
DTCH/LGLY SL3 12 F8
EGH TW20 36 G5
EGRIN RH19 161 L7
EW KT17 60 D7
GODL GU7 131 K9
GUW GU2 6 E6
HORL RH6 158 G1
LHD/OX KT22 96 G2
LING RH7 162 E2
MFD/CHID GU8 149 N7
MFD/CHID GU8 167 P8
MFD/CHID GU8 169 K7
OXTED RH8 123 M3
OXTED RH8 124 D2
RDKG RH5 138 B8
RDKG RH5 154 E5
REDH RH1 120 E2
RFNM GU10 146 E5
RGUE GU4 133 K1
RGUW GU3 132 A4
RPLY/SEND GU23 73 P8
SHGR GU5 132 D7
YTLY GU46 49 H9
Millmead *BF/WBF* KT14 74 B1
GUW GU2 6 D6
Mill Md *STA* TW18 22 C7
Millmead Ct *GUW* GU2 * 6 D7
Millmead Ter *GUW* GU2 6 D7
Millmere *YTLY* GU46 67 H1
Mill Pl *DTCH/LGLY* SL3 12 B7
KUT KT1 9 F6
Mill Plat *ISLW* TW7 16 G8
Mill Plat Av *ISLW* TW7 16 G7
Millpond Ct *ADL/WDHM* KT15 56 A4
Mill Pond Rd *BFOR* GU20 52 B3
Mill Ride *ASC* SL5 33 M2
Mill Rd *COB* KT11 75 L4
CRAWE RH10 177 L4
ESH/CLAY KT10 58 A1
EW KT17 78 D1
KWD/TDW/WH KT20 99 H3
RDKG RH5 137 J6
WDR/YW UB7 13 P1
WHTN TW2 25 K5
WIM/MER SW19 43 N1
Mill Shaw *OXTED* RH8 123 M3
Millshot Cl *FUL/PGN* SW6 18 G6
Millside *CAR* SM5 62 B1
Millside Ct *GT/LBKH* KT23 * 96 A5
Millside Pl *ISLW* TW7 17 H7
Mills Rd *WOT/HER* KT12 57 L4
Mills Rw *CHSWK* W4 18 B2
Mills Sp *WDSR* SL4 20 G3
Millstead Cl
KWD/TDW/WH KT20 98 F3
Mill Stream *FNM* GU9 108 A8
The Millstream *HASM* GU27 183 P5
Mill St *BH/WHM* TN16 105 H7
DTCH/LGLY SL3 13 H5
KUT KT1 8 E6
REDH RH1 120 A6
Millthorpe Rd *HORS* RH12 192 E6
Mill V *HAYES* BR2 47 N4
Mill Vw *CRAN* GU6 * 152 E9
Mill View Cl *EW* KT17 60 D6
Millview Cl *REDH* RH1 119 P3
Mill View Gdns *CROY/NA* CR0 64 D2
Mill Wy *EBED/NFELT* TW14 24 C1
EGRIN RH19 180 D4
LHD/OX KT22 97 M5
Millway *REIG* RH2 119 P5
Millwood *EGRIN* RH19 179 M6
Millwood Rd *HSLW* TW3 25 K1
Milman Cl *BRAK* RG12 33 H3
Milmans St *WBPTN* SW10 19 P4
Milne Cl *CRAWW* RH11 176 B8
Milne Pk East *CROY/NA* CR0 65 K9
Milne Pk West *CROY/NA* CR0 65 K9
Milner Ap *CTHM* CR3 102 A1
Milner Cl *CTHM* CR3 102 A2
Milner Dr *COB* KT11 75 P1
WHTN TW2 25 L3
Milner Rd *CTHM* CR3 102 A2
KUT KT1 8 C7
MRDN SM4 43 P6
THHTH CR7 45 L4
WIM/MER SW19 43 M2
Milnthorpe Rd *CHSWK* W4 18 B4
Milnwood Rd *HORS* RH12 192 B7
Milo Rd *EDUL* SE22 30 G2
Milson Rd *WKENS* W14 19 J1
Milton Av *CROY/NA* CR0 45 M8
DORK RH4 116 D8
SUT SM1 61 P2
Milton Cl *BRAK* RG12 32 C7
DTCH/LGLY SL3 12 E8
SUT SM1 61 P2
Miltoncourt La *DORK* RH4 116 E7
Milton Crs *EGRIN* RH19 180 B2
Milton Dr *SHPTN* TW17 38 A5
Milton Gdns *EPSOM* KT18 78 C3
STWL/WRAY TW19 23 J4
Milton Mount Av
CRAWE RH10 177 M3
Milton Pk *EGH* TW20 * 36 E1
Milton Rd *ADL/WDHM* KT15 55 L5
CRAWE RH10 177 M4
CROY/NA CR0 45 M8
CTHM CR3 101 M1
EGH TW20 21 L8
HNHL SE24 30 C1
HORS RH12 192 B7
HPTN TW12 40 A1
MORT/ESHN SW14 18 B8
MTCM CR4 44 C1
SUT SM1 61 L2
WIM/MER SW19 28 F9
WLGTN SM6 62 E5
WOT/HER KT12 57 M2
Miltons Crs *GODL* GU7 150 A2
Milton St *DORK* RH4 116 D8
Miltons Yd *MFD/CHID* GU8 * 149 N8
Milton Wy *GT/LBKH* KT23 96 C5
WDR/YW UB7 14 B2
Mimosa St *FUL/PGN* SW6 19 K6
Mina Rd *WIM/MER* SW19 43 L2
Minchin Cl *LHD/OX* KT22 96 G2
Mincing La *CHOB/PIR* GU24 53 M7
Minden Rd *CHEAM* SM3 61 J1
PGE/AN SE20 46 B2
Mindleheim Av *EGRIN* RH19 180 G1
Minehead Rd
STRHM/NOR SW16 30 A8
Minehurst Rd *FRIM* GU16 89 H3
Minerva Cl
STWL/WRAY TW19 * 22 D1
Minerva Rd *FARN* GU14 88 D6
KUT KT1 9 F5
Minimax Cl
EBED/NFELT TW14 24 B2
Mink Ct *HSLWW* TW4 15 L7
Minley Cl *FARN* GU14 88 A3
Minley Gv *FLEETN* GU51 87 H4
Minley Rd *FARN* GU14 67 J7
FARN GU14 87 N2
FLEETN GU51 87 H4
Minniedale *BRYLDS* KT5 41 M6
Minorca Av *FRIM* GU16 69 N6
Minorca Rd *FRIM* GU16 69 N7
WEY KT13 56 C3
Minshull Pl *BECK* BR3 * 46 G1
Minstead Cl *BRAK* RG12 33 H4
Minstead Dr *YTLY* GU46 66 G3
Minstead Gdns
PUT/ROE SW15 27 L3
Minstead Wy *NWMAL* KT3 42 C7
Minster Av *SUT* SM1 61 L1
Minster Ct *CBLY* GU15 * 68 B4
Minster Dr *CROY/NA* CR0 3 G7
Minster Gdns
E/WMO/HCT KT8 39 P5
Minsterley Av *SHPTN* TW17 38 G5
Minster Rd *BMLY* BR1 47 P1
GODL GU7 150 C2
Minstrel Gdns *BRYLDS* KT5 41 M5
Minterne Av *NWDGN* UB2 16 A2
Mint Gdns *DORK* RH4 116 G6
Mint La *KWD/TDW/WH* KT20 99 L9
Mint Rd *BNSTD* SM7 79 N5
WLGTN SM6 62 D4
Mint St *GODL* GU7 131 K9
The Mint *GODL* GU7 131 K9
Mint Wk *CROY/NA* CR0 2 D5
WARL CR6 82 D6
WOKN/KNAP GU21 71 L6
Mirabel Rd *FUL/PGN* SW6 19 K5
Misbrooks Green Rd
RDKG RH5 156 D5
Missenden Cl
EBED/NFELT TW14 24 A4
Missenden Gdns *MRDN* SM4 43 N7
Mistletoe Cl *CROY/NA* CR0 46 D9
Mistletoe Rd *YTLY* GU46 67 H4
Misty's Fld *WOT/HER* KT12 39 L9
Mitcham La
STRHM/NOR SW16 29 M8
Mitcham Pk *MTCM* CR4 44 B5
Mitcham Rd *CBLY* GU15 51 J8
CROY/NA CR0 44 F7
TOOT SW17 29 J9
Mitchell Gdns *SWTR* RH13 190 F7
Mitchells Cl *RGUE* GU4 132 C2
Mitchells Rd *CRAWE* RH10 177 J5
Mitchell Wy *BMLY* BR1 47 N2
Mitchley Av *PUR/KEN* CR8 81 M2
Mitchley Gv *SAND/SEL* CR2 82 A2
Mitchley Hl *SAND/SEL* CR2 81 P2
Mitchley Vw *SAND/SEL* CR2 82 A2
Mitre Cl *BELMT* SM2 61 N6
HAYES BR2 47 M3
SHPTN TW17 38 F7
Mixbury Gv *WEY* KT13 56 F5
Mixnams La *CHERT* KT16 37 L4
Mizen Cl *COB* KT11 75 M3
Mizen Wy *COB* KT11 75 M4
Moat Ct *ASHTD* KT21 77 L6
Moated Farm Dr
ADL/WDHM KT15 55 N6
Moat Rd *EGRIN* RH19 180 D1
Moat Side *FELT* TW13 24 D7
Moats La *REDH* RH1 140 G2
The Moat *NWMAL* KT3 42 C2
Moat Wk *CRAWE* RH10 177 M4
Moberly Rd *CLAP* SW4 29 N3
Moffat Rd *THHTH* CR7 45 L3
TOOT SW17 29 H7
Moffatts Cl *SHST* GU47 49 L9
Mogador Rd
KWD/TDW/WH KT20 99 J8
Mogden La *ISLW* TW7 25 N1

Moir CI *SAND/SEL* CR2 ....**64** A7
Mole Abbey Gdns
  E/WMO/HCT KT8...........**40** A4
Mole CI *CRAWW* RH11 ....**176** E3
  FARN GU14 ....**87** P5
Mole Ct *HOR/WEW* KT19......**60** A3
Molember Rd
  E/WMO/HCT KT8............**40** A6
Mole Rd *LHD/OX* KT22 ....**96** D1
  WOT/HER KT12 ....**57** M4
Molesey Av *E/WMO/HCT* KT8 .**39** P6
Molesey CI *WOT/HER* KT12 ....**57** N3
Molesey Dr *CHEAM* SM3.......**61** J1
Molesey Park Av
  E/WMO/HCT KT8............**40** B6
Molesey Park CI
  E/WMO/HCT KT8............**40** C6
Molesey Park Rd
  E/WMO/HCT KT8............**40** B6
Molesey Rd *E/WMO/HCT* KT8 .**39** N6
  WOT/HER KT12 ....**57** M4
Molesford Rd *FUL/PGN* SW6 *..**19** L6
Molesham CI
  E/WMO/HCT KT8............**40** B4
Molesham Wy
  E/WMO/HCT KT8............**40** B4
Moles HI *LHD/OX* KT22 ....**58** D9
Moles Md *EDEN* TN8 ....**144** G3
Mole St *EBDS* RH5.............**155** H5
Mole Valley PI *ASHTD* KT21 ....**77** K8
Mollison Dr *WLGTN* SM6 ....**63** J6
Molly Huggins CI *BAL* SW12....**29** M3
Molyneux Dr *TOOT* SW17 ......**29** L7
Molyneux Rd *BFOR* GU20 ......**52** C5
  GODL GU7 ....**131** H6
  WEY KT13 ....**56** C3
Monahan Av *PUR/KEN* CR8 ....**81** H1
Monarch CI *CRAWW* RH11 ....**176** D8
  EBED/NFELT TW14 ....**23** P3
  WWKM BR4 ....**65** M1
Monarch Ms *WNWD* SE27 .....**30** D8
Monarch Pde *MTCM* CR4 * **44** E1
Monaveen Gdns
  E/WMO/HCT KT8............**40** B4
Monck's Rw *PUT/ROE* SW15 *..**28** C2
Mondial Wy *WDR/YW* UB7.....**14** E5
Money Av *CTHM* CR3 ....**101** M2
Money La *WDR/YW* UB7 ....**13** P1
Money Rd *CTHM* CR3 ....**101** M2
Mongers La *EW* KT17 ....**60** B8
Monivea Rd *BECK* BR3 ....**46** F1
Monkleigh Rd *MRDN* SM4 ....**43** J4
Monks Av *E/WMO/HCT* KT8 ....**39** P6
Monks CI *ASC* SL5 ....**34** B7
  FARN GU14 ....**88** E3
Monks Crs *ADL/WDHM* KT15 ...**55** M4
  WOT/HER KT12 ....**39** K9
Monksdene Gdns *SUT* SM1 ....**61** M2
Monks Dr *ASC* SL5 ....**34** B7
Monksfield *CRAWE* RH10 .....**177** J5
Monks Gn *LHD/OX* KT22 ....**96** C1
Monkshanger *FNM* GU9......**128** A3
Monks La *OXTED* RH8 ....**124** B8
  RDKG RH5 ....**172** C6
Monks Orchard Rd
  BECK BR3 ....**46** C9
Monkton La *FNM* GU9...........**108** A9
Monmouth Av *KUT* KT1 ....**8** A1
Monmouth CI *CHSWK* W4 ......**18** B1
  MTCM CR4 ....**44** G5
Monmouth Gv *BTFD* TW8 ....**17** L2
Monmouth Rd *HYS/HAR* UB3 ..**14** G2
Monro Dr *GUW* GU2 ....**111** P2
Monroe Dr
  MORT/ESHN SW14 ....**26** G1
Monro PI *HOR/WEW* KT19 ......**59** N7
Mons CI *ALDT* GU11.............**88** C8
Monson Rd *REDH* RH1 ....**120** B2
Mons Wk *STA* TW18 ....**21** P8
Montacute CI *FARN* GU14 .....**88** F3
Montacute Rd *CAT* SE6 ....**31** N3
  CROY/NA CR0 ....**65** J7
  MRDN SM4 ....**43** P7
Montague Av
  SAND/SEL CR2 ....**81** L1
Montague CI *CBLY* GU15 ....**68** D3
  LTWR GU18 ....**52** A9
  WOT/HER KT12 ....**39** J8
Montague Dr *CTHM* CR3 ......**101** L2
Montague Rd *CROY/NA* CR0 .....**2** B1
  HSLW TW3 ....**16** B8
  NWDGN UB2 ....**15** N2
  RCHPK/HAM TW10 ....**26** D2
  WIM/MER SW19 ....**43** N1
Montague Ter *HAYES* BR2 ....**47** N5
Montagu Gdns *WLGTN* SM6 ....**62** E3
Montagu Rd *DTCH/LGLY* SL3 ...**12** A7
Montana CI *SAND/SEL* CR2 ......**81** N8
Montana Gdns *CAT* SE6 ....**31** N8
  SUT SM1 ....**61** N4
Montana Rd *RYNPK* SW20 ......**42** G2
  TOOT SW17 ....**29** K6
Montcalm CI *HAYES* BR2 ....**47** P9
Monteagle La *YTLY* GU46 ....**66** F3
Montem Rd *FSTH* SE23...........**31** N3
  NWMAL KT3 ....**42** C5
Montford Rd *SUN* TW16 ....**39** J5
Montfort PI *WIM/MER* SW19...**28** A4
Montfort Ri *REDH* RH1 ....**140** B4
Montgomerie Dr *GUW* GU2 ....**91** N9

Montgomery Av
  ESH/CLAY KT10...................**58** E1
Montgomery CI *MTCM* CR4 * ...**44** G5
  SHST GU47 ....**49** M9
Montgomery Rd *CHSWK* W4 ....**18** A2
  FARN GU14 ....**88** B2
  WOKS/MYFD GU22 ....**10** D5
Monthorne Rd *BTSEA* SW11 ....**29** J2
Montoteu Gdns
  PUT/ROE SW15 ....**27** N1
Montpelier Rd *PUR/KEN* CR8 ...**63** K8
  SUT SM1 ....**61** N3
Montpelier Rw *TWK* TW1 ....**26** A3
Montrave Rd *PGE/AN* SE20 .....**31** K9
Montrell Rd
  BRXS/STRHM SW2 ....**29** P4
Montrose Av *DTCH/LGLY* SL3 ...**12** A3
  WHTN TW2 ....**25** J3
Montrose CI *ASHF* TW15 ....**23** M9
  FLEETN GU51 ....**87** H7
  FRIM GU16 ....**68** G6
Montrose Gdns *LHD/OX* KT22 ..**76** D1
  MTCM CR4 ....**44** B4
  SUT SM1 ....**61** M1
Montrose Rd
  EBED/NFELT TW14 ....**23** N2
Montrose Vls *HMSMTH* W6 * ...**18** E4
Montrose Wy *WEY* KT13 ....**56** D2
Montrose Wy
  DTCH/LGLY SL3 ....**12** B6
  FSTH SE23 ....**31** L4
Montrouge Crs *EW* KT17 ....**78** G5
Mont St Aignan Wy
  EDEN TN8 ....**144** G4
Montserrat Av *NRWD* SE19 .....**30** B8
Montserrat Rd
  PUT/ROE SW15 ....**19** J9
Monument HI *WEY* KT13 ....**56** D3
Monument Rd *WEY* KT13 ....**56** D3
  WOKN/KNAP GU21 ....**72** F4
Monument Wy East
  WOKN/KNAP GU21 ....**72** F4
Monument Wy West
  WOKN/KNAP GU21 ....**72** E4
Moons HI *RFNM* GU10 ....**146** E2
Moon's La *EGRIN* RH19.........**163** J5
  SWTR RH13 ....**192** C9
Moor CI *EWKG* RG40 ....**48** C2
  SHST GU47 ....**50** A8
Moorcroft CI *CRAWW* RH11 ...**176** E4
Moorcroft Rd
  STRHM/NOR SW16 ....**29** P6
Moordale Av *BNFD* RG42 ....**32** B1
Moore CI *ADL/WDHM* KT15 ....**55** M4
  FLEETS GU52 ....**106** C1
  MORT/ESHN SW14 ....**18** A8
  MTCM CR4 * **44** D5
  RFNM GU10 ....**109** H6
Moore Grove Crs *EGH* TW20 ...**36** C1
Mooreland Rd *BMLY* BR1........**47** M1
Moore Park Rd *FUL/PGN* SW6 ..**19** M5
Moore Rd *CHOB/PIR* GU24 .....**70** B1
  FLEETS GU52 ....**106** C1
  NRWD SE19 ....**30** D9
Moores Rd *DORK* RH4 ....**117** H6
Moore Wy *BELMT* SM2...........**61** L7
Moorfield *HASM* GU27.........**184** A5
Moorfield CI *CHSGTN* KT9 ......**59** L4
  GU GU1 ....**112** C1
Moorfields CI *STA* TW18 ....**37** J2
Moorhayes Dr *STA* TW14 ....**37** N4
Moorhead Rd *HORS* RH12 .....**192** G5
Moorholme
  WOKS/MYFD GU22 ....**10** D7
Moorhouse Rd *OXTED* RH8 ...**124** D1
Moorhurst La *RDKG* RH5 ......**156** G5
The Moorings *BF/WBF* KT14 ....**73** N1
  CHSWK W4 * **17** N4
  EGRIN RH19 ....**161** P9
  GT/LBKH KT23 ....**96** A5
  STWL/WRAY TW19 ....**21** H3
Moorland CI *HSLWW* TW4 ....**25** P3
Moorland Rd *CRAWE* RH10 ....**177** M4
  WDR/YW UB7 ....**13** N5
Moorlands CI *FLEETN* GU51 .....**87** H7
  GSHT GU26 ....**165** P7
Moorlands Rd *CBLY* GU15 ......**68** C4
The Moorlands
  WOKS/MYFD GU22 ....**92** D1
Moor La *CHSGTN* KT9 ....**59** M4
  STWL/WRAY TW19 ....**21** P4
  WDR/YW UB7 ....**13** N4
  WOKS/MYFD GU22 ....**92** C2
Moormead Dr *HOR/WEW* KT19..**60** C4
Moor Mead Rd *TWK* TW1 ....**25** P2
Moormede Crs *STA* TW18........**22** C7
Moor Pk *HORL* RH6 * **159** L2
Moor Park Crs
  CRAWW RH11 ....**176** A6
Moor Park Gdns
  KUTN/CMB KT2 ....**42** C1
Moor Park La *FNM* GU9 ....**128** A2
Moor Park Wy *FNM* GU9 ....**128** B3
Moor Pl *BFOR* GU20 ....**52** B4
  EGRIN RH19 ....**180** C1
Moor Rd *FARN* GU14 ....**68** C8
  FRIM GU16 ....**69** H8
  HASM GU27 ....**183** M5
Moorside CI *FARN* GU14 ....**68** C7
Moors La *MFD/CHID* GU8 ......**168** C4
Moorsom Wy *COUL/CHIP* CR5 ..**80** F6
The Moors *RFNM* GU10 ....**109** H7
Moravian Pl *WBPTN* SW10 .....**19** P4
Moray Av *SHST* GU47 ....**67** P1
Mordaunt Dr *CWTH* RG45 .....**49** M6
Morden CI *BRAK* RG12 ....**33** H5
  KWD/TDW/WH KT20 ....**99** H9
Morden Ct *MRDN* SM4 ....**43** M5
Morden Court Pde
  WIM/MER SW19 * **43** M4

Morden Gdns *MTCM* CR4.......**43** P5
Morden Hall Rd *MRDN* SM4....**43** M4
Morden Rd *WIM/MER* SW19 ...**43** M4
Morden Wy *CHEAM* SM3 ....**43** L8
Morecambe CI
  CRAWW RH11 ....**176** C7
More Cir *GODL* GU7 ....**131** L6
More CI *PUR/KEN* CR8 ....**63** H9
  WKENS W14 ....**19** H2
Morecoombe CI
  KUTN/CMB KT2 ....**41** P1
Morecote CI *RGUE* GU4 ....**132** C3
Moreland Av *DTCH/LGLY* SL3 ...**12** G5
Morella CI *ESH/CLAY* KT10 ......**58** B2
Morella CI *VW* GU25 ....**36** A5
Morella Rd *BAL* SW12 ....**29** J3
Moremead Rd *CAT* SE6 ....**31** N7
Morena St *CAT* SE6 ....**131** L6
Moresby Av *BRYLDS* KT5 ....**41** P8
Moretaine Rd *ASHF* TW15 * **22** G3
Moreton Av *ISLW* TW7 ....**16** D6
Moreton CI *FLEETS* GU52 ......**106** F2
  RFNM GU10 ....**165** H2
Moreton Rd *SAND/SEL* CR2 .....**63** M4
  WPK KT4 ....**60** E1
Morgan Rd *BMLY* BR1 ....**47** N1
Moring Rd *STRHM/NOR* SW18 .**29** M9
Moring Rd *TOOT* SW17 ....**29** L7
Morkyns Wk *DUL* SE21 *..........**30** F6
Morland Av *CROY/NA* CR0 ....**3** H1
Morland CI *HPTN* TW12 ....**24** G8
  MTCM CR4 ....**44** B4
  RFNM GU10 ....**146** D1
  SUT SM1 ....**61** N4
Morland's Rd *ALDT* GU11 .....**108** F1
Morley CI *YTLY* GU46 ....**66** F3
Morley Rd *CHEAM* SM3 ....**43** K9
  FNM GU9 ....**5** H6
  SAND/SEL CR2 ....**63** N6
  WEY KT13 ....**57** H3
  TWK TW1 ....**26** C2
Morningside Rd *WPK* KT4 ....**60** F1
Mornington Av *EWKG* RG40 ....**48** D1
  WKENS W14 ....**19** K2
Mornington Crs *HEST* TW5 ......**15** K6
Mornington Rd *ASHF* TW15 ....**23** M8
Mornington Wk
  RCHPK/HAM TW10 ....**26** B7
Morrell Av *HORS* RH12 ....**192** C6
Morris CI *DTCH/LGLY* SL3 ....**12** D2
Morris Rd *CROY/NA* CR0 ....**46** E7
Morris Gdns
  WAND/EARL SW18 ....**28** D3
Morrish Rd
  BRXS/STRHM SW2 ....**29** P3
Morris Rd *FARN* GU14 ....**88** F7
  ISLW TW7 ....**16** E2
  REDH RH1 ....**120** G7
Morston CI
  KWD/TDW/WH KT20 ....**78** F9
Mortimer CI *BAL* SW12 ....**29** N5
Mortimer Crs *WPK* KT4 ....**60** B2
Mortimer Rd *BH/WHM* TN16..**84** A1
  DTCH/LGLY SL3 ....**12** B1
  MTCM CR4 ....**44** B2
  RDKG RH5 ....**156** C6
Mortlake CI *CROY/NA* CR0 ......**62** G2
  MORT/ESHN SW14 ....**18** A8
Mortlake High St
  MORT/ESHN SW14 ....**18** B8
Mortlake Rd *RCH/KEW* TW9 ....**17** P5
Morton *KWD/TDW/WH* KT20 ...**99** H1
Morton CI *CRAWW* RH11 ......**194** E2
  FRIM GU16 ....**69** H9
  WOKN/KNAP GU21 ....**72** A4
Morton Gdns *WLGTN* SM6 .....**62** E4
Morton Ms *ECT* SW5 * **19** M2
Morton Rd *EGRIN* RH19 ....**180** D4
  MRDN SM4 ....**44** A3
  WOKN/KNAP GU21 ....**72** A4
Morval CI *FARN* GU14 ....**88** A3
Morval Rd *BRXS/STRHM* SW2 ..**30** B1
Morven Rd *TOOT* SW17 ....**29** J6
Moselle CI *FARN* GU14 ....**87** P2
Moselle Rd *BH/WHM* TN16 .....**84** C7
Mosford CI *HORL* RH6 ....**140** D8
Mospey Crs *EW* KT17 ....**78** D4
Moss CI *SAND/SEL* CR2 ....**64** D8
Moss Gdns *SAND/SEL* CR2 ......**64** D6
Moss La *GODL* GU7 ....**131** K9
Mosslea Rd *CTHM* CR3 ....**101** K9
  PGE/AN SE20 ....**31** K9
Mossville Gdns *MRDN* SM4 .....**43** K4
Moston CI *HYS/HAR* UB3 ....**15** H3
Mostyn Rd *WIM/MER* SW19 ....**43** K3
Mostyn Ter *REDH* RH1 ....**120** C6
Moth CI *WLGTN* SM6 ....**62** G6
Motspur Pk *NWMAL* KT3 ....**42** D7
Motts Hill La
  KWD/TDW/WH KT20 ....**98** E3
Mouchotte CI *BH/WHM* TN16 ..**83** P1
Moulsham Copse La
  YTLY GU46 ....**66** F1
Moulsham La *YTLY* GU46 ....**66** F1
Moulton Av *HEST* TW5 ....**15** N7
Mountacre CI *SYD* SE26 ....**30** G7
Mount Adon Pk *EDUL* SE22 ....**31** H3
Mount Angelus Rd
  PUT/ROE SW15 ....**27** L3
Mount Ararat Rd
  RCHPK/HAM TW10 ....**26** D1
Mount Ash Rd *SYD* SE26 ....**31** J4
Mount Av *CTHM* CR3 ....**101** L4
Mountbatten CI
  CRAWW RH11 * **176** C7
  NRWD SE19 ....**30** F8
Mountbatten Ri *SHST* GU47 .....**49** K8
Mount CI *CAR* SM5 ....**62** C7
  CRAN GU6......................**153** P7

  CRAWE RH10 ....**177** M4
  LHD/OX KT22 ....**96** F3
  PUR/KEN CR8 ....**81** L5
  WOKS/MYFD GU22 ....**91** P1
The Mount CI *VW* GU25 ....**36** B7
Mount CI *WEY* KT13 ....**56** B5
Mount Ephraim La
  STRHM/NOR SW16 ....**29** N6
Mount Ephraim Rd
  STRHM/NOR SW16 ....**29** N5
Mount Felix *WOT/HER* KT12 ...**39** H9
Mount Gdns *SYD* SE26 ....**31** J6
Mount Hermon CI
  WOKS/MYFD GU22 ....**10** C6
Mount Hermon Rd
  WOKS/MYFD GU22 ....**10** D7
Mounthurst Rd *HAYES* BR2 .....**47** N8
Mount La *BRAK* RG12 ....**32** E4
Mount La *RFNM* GU10 ....**179** H7
Mount Lee *EGH* TW20 ....**21** K8
Mount Nod Rd
  STRHM/NOR SW16 ....**30** A6
Mount Pk *CAR* SM5 ....**62** C7
Mount Park Av
  SAND/SEL CR2 ....**63** K7
Mount Pl *GU* GU1 * **6** C6
Mount Pleasant
  BH/WHM TN16 ....**84** D6
  BRAK RG12 ....**32** E4
  EHSLY KT24 ....**113** P8
  EHSLY KT24 ....**113** P8
  EW KT17 ....**60** D8
  FNM GU9 ....**4** C4
  GUW GU2 ....**6** A4
  RDKG RH5 * **135** H2
  SHST GU47 ....**49** L8
  WEY KT13 ....**56** C2
  WNWD SE27 ....**30** D8
Mount Pleasant CI
  LTWR GU18 ....**52** A8
Mount Pleasant Cottages
  EGH TW20 * **21** J9
Mount Pleasant Rd *ASHV*
  GU12 ....**108** E4
  CTHM CR3 ....**101** L4
  LING RH7 ....**143** J9
  NWMAL KT3 ....**42** A4
Mount Ri *FSTH* SE23 ....**31** K5
  REDH RH1 ....**120** B5
Mount Rd *CHOB/PIR* GU24 .....**71** P1
  CHSGTN KT9 ....**59** M4
  CRAN GU6......................**171** H1
  FELT TW13 ....**24** F6
  MTCM CR4 ....**43** P2
  NRWD SE19 * **30** E9
  NWMAL KT3 ....**42** B4
  WAND/EARL SW18 ....**28** D5
The Mount *BOR* GU35...........**164** D5
  COUL/CHIP CR5 ....**80** C2
  CRAN GU6......................**153** P7
  CRAN GU6......................**171** H1
  ESH/CLAY KT10 ....**58** A5
  EW KT17 ....**60** D7
  FLEETN GU51 ....**86** F5
  GUW GU2 ....**111** P8
  HASM GU27 ....**166** C9
  HORS RH12 ....**175** N2
  KWD/TDW/WH KT20 ....**99** K6
  LHD/OX KT22 ....**96** E3
  NWMAL KT3 ....**42** D4
  VW GU25 ....**36** B5
  WARL CR6.........................**82** A8
  WEY KT13 ....**56** C1
  WOKN/KNAP GU21 ....**72** A4
  WPK KT4 ....**60** F3
Mount Vw *ALDT* GU11 ....**108** C5
  NWDGN UB2 * **15** M2
Mountview *REDH* RH1 ....**120** A7
Mountview Rd *REDH* RH1 .....**120** A7
Mount Vw Rd
  ESH/CLAY KT10 ....**58** A6
Mount Vls *WNWD* SE27 ....**30** C6
Mount Wy *CAR* SM5 ....**62** C7
Mountwood
  E/WMO/HCT KT8...............**40** A4
Mountwood CI
  SAND/SEL CR2 ....**64** D8
Mousehill La *MFD/CHID* GU8 .**149** M4
Mowbray Av *BF/WBF* KT14 .....**74** A1
Mowbray Crs *EGH* TW20 ....**21** M8
Mowbray Dr *CRAWW* RH11 ...**176** C7
Mowbray Gdns *DORK* RH4 ....**117** H5
Mowbray Rd *NRWD* SE19 ....**45** P2
  RCHPK/HAM TW10 ....**26** B6
Moyer PI *CRAN* GU6 ....**153** H8
Moylan Rd *HMSMTH* W6 ....**19** J4
Moyne Rd *CRAWW* RH11 ......**176** C7
Moys CI *CROY/NA* CR0 ....**44** D7
Moyser Rd
  STRHM/NOR SW16 ....**29** L8
Mulcheiney Rd *MRDN* SM4 .....**43** P5
Muckhatch La *EGH* TW20 ....**36** F4
Muggeridge CI
  SAND/SEL CR2 ....**63** N4
Muggeridge's HI *RDKG* RH5 ..**174** D3
Muir CI *WAND/EARL* SW18 .....**29** H2
Muirdown Av
  MORT/ESHN SW14 ....**18** A9
Muirfield CI *CRAWW* RH11 ...**176** A6
Muirfield Rd
  WOKN/KNAP GU21 ....**71** N7

Mulberry Av
  STWL/WRAY TW19...............**23** H4
Mulberry CI *ASHV* GU12 ....**109** J2
  CHEL SW3 * **19** P4
  CWTH RG45 ....**49** N5
  HORS RH12 ....**192** B5
  STRHM/NOR SW16 ....**29** M7
  WEY KT13 ....**56** D2
  WOKN/KNAP GU21 ....**72** C3
Mulberry Crs *BTFD* TW8 ....**17** H5
Mulberry Dr *DTCH/LGLY* SL3 ...**12** C3
Mulberry La *CROY/NA* CR0........**3** K2
Mulberry Ms *WLGTN* SM6 * **62** E5
Mulberry PI *HMSMTH* W6 ....**18** E3
Mulberry Rd *CRAWW* RH11 ...**176** E2
Mulberry Trees *SHPTN* TW17 ...**38** F8
Mulberry Wk *CHEL* SW3 ....**19** P3
Mulgrave Rd *BELMT* SM2........**61** K6
  CROY/NA CR0 ....**2** E6
  FUL/PGN SW6 * **19** H6
  WOKS/MYFD GU22 ....**19** K4
Mulgrave Wy
  WOKN/KNAP GU21 ....**71** C7
Mulholland CI *MTCM* CR4 ......**44** D3
Mullards CI *MTCM* CR4 ....**44** B9
Mullens Rd *EGH* TW20 ....**21** P8
Mullins Pth
  MORT/ESHN SW14 ....**18** B8
Mulroy Dr *CBLY* GU15 ....**69** J2
Multon Rd *WAND/EARL* SW18 ..**28** C3
Mumford Rd *HNHL* SE24 ....**30** C1
Muncaster CI *ASHF* TW15 ....**23** K7
Muncaster Rd *ASHF* TW15 ......**23** L8
  BTSEA SW11 ....**29** J1
Mundania Rd *EDUL* SE22 ....**31** J2
Munday CI *BRFD* RG42............**4** A1
Munday's Boro *RGUW* GU3 ....**130** A1
Munday's Boro Rd
  RGUW GU3 ....**130** B3
Munden St *WKENS* W14 ....**19** J2
Munden St *WKENS* W14 ....**19** K3
Mundford Rd *CLPT* E5 ....**67** D2
Munnings Dns *ISLW* TW7........**25** L1
Munslow Gdns *SUT* SM1 ....**61** N3
Munstead Heath Rd
  MFD/CHID GU8 ....**152** A9
Munstead Pk
  MFD/CHID GU8 ....**151** H1
Munstead View Rd
  SHGR GU5 ....**132** B8
Munster Av *HSLWW* TW4 ....**15** N9
Munster CI *FUL/PGN* SW6 ......**19** K5
Munster Ms *FUL/PGN* SW6 .....**19** J5
Munster Rd *FUL/PGN* SW6 .....**19** J5
  TEDD TW11 ....**26** B9
Murdoch CI *STA* TW18 ....**22** D8
Murfett CI *WIM/MER* SW19 ....**28** C3
Murray Av *BMLY* BR1 ....**47** P4
  HSLW TW3 ....**25** J1
Murray Ct *ASC* SL5 ....**34** C7
  SWTR RH13 ....**192** G6
Murray Rd *CHERT* KT16 ....**55** H5
  EA W5...............................**17** J3
  FARN GU14 ....**88** B4
  RCHPK/HAM TW10 ....**26** A5
  WIM/MER SW19 ....**28** A9
Murray's La *BF/WBF* KT14 ......**73** P3
Murray's Rd *ALDT* GU11 ....**108** F1
Murrell Rd *ASHV* GU12 ....**109** J3
Murrells La *CBLY* GU15 ....**68** C5
Murrell's Wk *GT/LBKH* KT23 ...**96** A3
Murrey Ct *SWTR* RH13 * **192** G6
The Murreys *ASHTD* KT21.......**77** K7
Musard Rd *WKENS* W14 ....**19** J4
Muschamp Rd *CAR* SM5 ....**62** A1
Museum HI *HASM* GU27 ......**184** E4
Musgrave Av *EGRIN* RH19 .....**180** D4
Musgrave Crs *FUL/PGN* SW6 ...**19** L5
Musgrave Rd *ISLW* TW7 ....**16** F6
Musjid Rd *BTSEA* SW11 ....**19** P7
Musquash Wy *HSLWW* TW4 .....**15** L2
Mustard Mill Rd *STA* TW18......**22** C7
Mutton HI *LING* RH7 ....**162** F5
Muybridge Rd *NWMAL* KT3 ....**42** A4
Myers Wy *FRIM* GU16 ....**69** M6
Mylis CI *SYD* SE26 ....**31** J7
Mylne CI *HMSMTH* W6 * **18** E3
Mylor CI *WOKN/KNAP* GU21 ...**72** C3
Mynn's CI *EPSOM* KT18..........**77** P3
Myrna CI *WIM/MER* SW19 ......**44** A1
Myrtle Av *EBED/NFELT* TW14 ...**23** N1
Myrtle CI *DTCH/LGLY* SL3 ....**13** J6
  WDR/YW UB7 ....**14** B2
Myrtle Cottages
  DORK RH4 * **137** H1
Myrtle Dr *BLKW* GU17 ....**67** P4
Myrtle Gv *NWMAL* KT3 ....**42** A2
Myrtle Rd *CROY/NA* CR0 ....**64** C2
  DORK RH4 ....**116** G6
  HPTN TW12 ....**25** K9
  HSLW TW3 ....**16** C7
  SUT SM1 ....**61** N4
Mytchett Farm Pk
  FRIM GU16 ....**89** H5
Mytchett Heath *FRIM* GU16 ....**89** J5
Mytchett Lake Rd *FRIM* GU16 .**89** J6
Mytchett Place Rd
  FRIM GU16 ....**89** J3
Myton Rd *DUL* SE21 ....**30** E6

N

Nailsworth Crs REDH RH1 100 F9
Nairn Cl FRIM GU16 68 G6
Nairne Gv EDUL SE22 30 E1
Naldrett Cl HORS RH12 192 E6
Naldretts La HORS RH12 189 M5
Nallhead Rd FELT TW13 24 D8
Namba Roy Cl
STRHM/NOR SW16 30 A7
Namton Dr
STRHM/NOR SW16 45 H5
Nantes Cl WAND/EARL SW18 19 N9
Napier Av FUL/PGN SW6 19 K8
Napier Cl ALDT GU11 88 G8
CWTH RG45 49 N5
WDR/YW UB7 14 B1
Napier Ct CTHM CR3 101 N2
Napier Dr CBLY GU15 69 J1
Napier Gdns GU GU1 112 F4
Napier Pl WKENS W14 19 K1
Napier Rd ASHF TW15 38 F1
CWTH RG45 49 N5
HAYES BR2 47 P4
ISLW TW7 16 G9
SAND/SEL CR2 63 M6
SNWD SE25 46 B5
WDR/YW UB7 13 P6
WKENS W14 19 K1
Napier Wk ASHF TW15 38 F1
Napier Wy CRAWE RH10 177 J2
Napoleon Av FARN GU14 88 D1
Napoleon Rd TWK TW1 * 26 A3
Napper Cl ASC SL5 33 L3
Napper Pl CRAN GU6 171 H2
Narbonne Av CLAP SW4 29 M2
Narborough St FUL/PGN SW6 19 M7
Narrow La WARL CR6 82 B8
Naseby BRAK RG12 32 D9
Naseby Cl ISLW TW7 16 E6
Naseby Ct WOT/HER KT12 * 57 L1
Naseby Rd NRWD SE19 30 E9
Nash Cl FARN GU14 88 B3
SUT SM1 61 P2
Nash Gdns ASC SL5 33 M3
REDH RH1 120 B3
Nash Gn BMLY BR1 47 N1
Nash Grove La EWKG RG40 48 D1
Nash La HAYES BR2 65 N5
Nash Rd BROCKY SE4 31 M1
CRAWE RH10 177 H8
DTCH/LGLY SL3 12 D3
Nasmyth St HMSMTH W6 18 F1
Nassau Rd BARN SW13 18 D6
Nasturtium Dr
CHOB/PIR GU24 70 G4
Natalie Cl EBED/NFELT TW14 23 N3
Natal Rd STRHM/NOR SW16 29 N9
THHTH CR7 45 M4
Neale Cl EGRIN RH19 162 A9
Neal Ter FSTH SE23 * 31 L4
Neath Gdns MRDN SM4 43 N7
Neb La OXTED RH8 123 J2
Needles Bank GDST RH9 122 B2
Needles Cl HORS RH12 192 A9
Neil Cl ASHF TW15 23 M8
Nelgarde Rd CAT SE6 31 P3
Nella Rd HMSMTH W6 19 H4
Nell Ball BIL RH14 187 K8
Nell Gwynn Av SHPTN TW17 38 F7
Nell Gwynne Av ASC SL5 34 D5
Nell Gwynne Cl
HOR/WEW KT19 59 N9
Nello James Gdns
WNWD SE27 30 E7
Nelson Cl ASHV GU12 108 E5
BH/WHM TN16 84 C6
BRAK RG12 32 G3
CRAWE RH10 177 M6
CROY/NA CR0 2 B2
DTCH/LGLY SL3 12 B2
EBED/NFELT TW14 * 24 A4
FNM GU9 107 P6
WOT/HER KT12 39 K9
Nelson Gdns GU GU1 112 E4
HSLW TW3 25 H2
Nelson Grove Rd
WIM/MER SW19 43 M2
Nelson Rd ASHF TW15 23 H8
CTHM CR3 101 M3
FNM GU9 107 P6
HORS RH12 192 A7
HSLW TW3 25 H2
NWMAL KT3 42 B6
WDR/YW UB7 14 B6
WIM/MER SW19 43 M1
Nelson St ALDT GU11 108 C4
Nelson Wk HOR/WEW KT19 59 N7
Nelson Wy CBLY GU15 68 B4
Nene Gdns FELT TW13 24 G5
Nene Rd HTHAIR TW6 14 D6
Nepean St PUT/ROE SW15 27 M2
Neptune Cl CRAWW RH11 176 B7
Neptune Rd HTHAIR TW6 * 14 E6
Nesbitt Sq NRWD SE19 * 45 N1
Nestle's Av HYS/HAR UB3 15 H1
Netheravon Rd CHSWK W4 18 D3
Netheravon Rd South
CHSWK W4 18 D4
Netherbury Rd EA W5 17 K1
Netherby Pk WEY KT13 56 G4
Netherby Rd FSTH SE23 31 K3
Nethercote Av
WOKN/KNAP GU21 71 M6
Netherfield Rd TOOT SW17 29 K6
Netherhouse Moor
FLEETN GU51 86 E9
The Netherlands
COUL/CHIP CR5 80 E8
Netherleigh Pk REDH RH1 120 G8
Nether Mt GUW GU2 6 B7
Nethern Court Rd
CTHM CR3 102 G3
Netherne Dr
COUL/CHIP CR5 100 E2
Netherne La COUL/CHIP CR5 100 E3
Netherton BRAK RG12 32 C5
Netherton Gv WBPTN SW10 19 N4
Netherton Rd TWK TW1 25 P1
Nether Vell-Mead
FLEETS GU52 106 E2
Netherwood CRAWW RH11 176 D8
Netherwood Pl
WKENS W14 * 19 H1
Netherwood Rd WKENS W14 19 H1
Netley Cl CHEAM SM3 61 H4
CRAWW RH11 194 F2
CROY/NA CR0 65 J6
SHGR GU5 114 E9
Netley Dr WOT/HER KT12 39 P8
Netley Gdns MRDN SM4 43 N8
Netley Rd BTFD TW8 17 L4
MRDN SM4 43 N8
Netley St FARN GU14 88 E7
Nettlecombe BRAK RG12 32 F6
Nettlecombe Cl BELMT SM2 61 M7
Nettlefold Pl WNWD SE27 30 C6
Nettlestead Cl BECK BR3 46 F1
Nettles Ter GU GU1 6 E2
Nettleton Rd HTHAIR TW6 14 D6
Nettlewood Rd
STRHM/NOR SW16 44 F1
Neuchatel Rd CAT SE6 31 N5
Neuman Crs BRAK RG12 32 C7
Nevada Cl FARN GU14 87 P4
NWMAL KT3 42 A5
Nevern Pl ECT SW5 19 L2
Nevern Rd ECT SW5 19 L2
Nevern Sq ECT SW5 19 L2
Nevile Cl CRAWW RH11 176 D8
Neville Av NWMAL KT3 42 B2
Neville Cl BNSTD SM7 79 M3
ESH/CLAY KT10 57 P5
HSLW TW3 16 A7
Neville Duke Rd FARN GU14 68 B8
Neville Gill Cl
WAND/EARL SW18 28 D2
Neville Rd CROY/NA CR0 45 M8
KUT KT1 9 J4
RCHPK/HAM TW10 26 B6
Neville St SKENS SW7 19 P3
Neville Ter SKENS SW7 * 19 P3
Neville Wk CAR SM5 44 A8
Nevil Wk CAR SM5 * 44 A8
Nevinson Cl
WAND/EARL SW18 28 G2
Nevis Rd TOOT SW17 29 K5
New Acres EWKG RG40 * 49 J2
Newall Rd HTHAIR TW6 14 E6
Newark Cl RGUE GU4 92 F9
RPLY/SEND GU23 93 K1
Newark Ct WOT/HER KT12 39 L9
Newark La RPLY/SEND GU23 73 K9
Newark Rd BFOR GU20 52 B3
BLKW GU17 67 J7
CRAWE RH10 177 J3
SAND/SEL CR2 63 M5
New Barn Cl CROY/NA CR0 63 H5
FLEETN GU51 86 D8
New Barn La CTHM CR3 81 N6
RDKG RH5 155 H9
Newbarn La RSEV TN14 85 H5
New Barns Av MTCM CR4 44 F5
New Battlebridge La
REDH RH1 120 D1
New Berry La WOT/HER KT12 57 M4
Newbolt Av CHEAM SM3 60 G4
Newborough Gn NWMAL KT3 42 B5
Newbridge Cl HORS RH12 191 K7
Newbury Gdns
HOR/WEW KT19 60 D3
Newbury Rd CRAWE RH10 177 N5
HAYES BR2 47 N4
WDR/YW UB7 14 B6
New Cswy REIG RH2 119 M8
Newchapel Rd LING RH7 161 P2
New Cl FELT TW13 24 F8
WIM/MER SW19 43 N4
Newcome Gdns
STRHM/NOR SW16 29 P7
Newcomen Rd BTSEA SW11 19 P8
Newcome Pl ASHV GU12 108 F7
Newcome Rd FNM GU9 108 A7
New Coppice
WOKN/KNAP GU21 71 L8
New Cottages DORK RH4 * 116 F8
REIG RH2 * 119 H3
New Cross Rd GUW GU2 111 N3
New Dawn Cl FARN GU14 87 P4
Newdigate
STRHM/NOR SW16 * 30 B7
Newdigate Rd HORS RH12 175 J3
RDKG RH5 156 C2
Newenham Rd
GT/LBKH KT23 96 A6
Newent Cl CAR SM5 44 B9
New Farm Av HAYES BR2 47 N5
New Farthingdale LING RH7 162 F4
Newfield Av FARN GU14 88 A1
Newfield Cl HPTN TW12 40 A2
Newfield Rd ASHV GU12 89 J9
New Forest Ride BRAK RG12 32 G8
Newfoundland Rd
FRIM GU16 69 M8
Newgate CROY/NA CR0 2 D1
Newgate Cl FELT TW13 24 F5
New Green Pl NRWD SE19 30 F9
Newhache LING RH7 162 F3
Newhall Gdns WOT/HER KT12 57 L1
Newhaven Cl HYS/HAR UB3 15 H2
Newhaven Crs ASHF TW15 23 N8
Newhaven Rd SNWD SE25 45 M6
New Haw Rd
ADL/WDHM KT15 55 N5
New Heston Rd HEST TW5 15 P5
Newhouse Cl NWMAL KT3 42 C8
New House Farm La
RGUW GU3 111 J4
New House La REDH RH1 140 F4
New House Ter EDEN TN8 * 144 G3
Newhouse Wk MRDN SM4 43 N8
New Inn La RGUE GU4 112 F2
New Kelvin Av TEDD TW11 25 M9
New Kings Rd FUL/PGN SW6 19 K7
Newlands FLEETS GU52 86 G9
GU GU1 7 K6
Newlands Av THDIT KT7 40 E9
WOKS/MYFD GU22 92 D1
Newlands Cl HORL RH6 140 B8
NWDGN UB2 15 N3
WOT/HER KT12 57 N3
YTLY GU46 67 H3
Newlands Crs EGRIN RH19 180 C1
GU GU1 7 K6
Newlands Dr ASHV GU12 109 K2
DTCH/LGLY SL3 13 J8
Newlands Pk CRAWE RH10 160 F9
SYD SE26 31 K9
Newlands Pl FROW RH18 * 181 L8
Newlands Rd CRAWW RH11 176 F6
FRIM GU16 68 D7
HORS RH12 192 B6
STRHM/NOR SW16 44 G3
The Newlands WLGTN SM6 62 E6
Newlands Wy CHSGTN KT9 59 J4
Newlands Wd CROY/NA CR0 64 F7
Newlands Woods
CROY/NA CR0 * 64 F7
New La RGUE GU4 92 D4
New Lodge Dr OXTED RH8 103 M8
Newman Cl CRAWE RH10 177 M6
Newman Rd BMLY BR1 47 N2
CROY/NA CR0 45 H8
Newmans Ct FNM GU9 107 L8
Newmans Pl ASC SL5 35 H8
Newmarket Rd
CRAWE RH10 177 K8
New Meadow ASC SL5 33 M2
New Mile Rd ASC SL5 34 B3
Newminster Rd MRDN SM4 43 N7
New Moorhead Dr
HORS RH12 193 H4
Newnham Cl THHTH CR7 45 L3
New North Rd REIG RH2 119 K8
New Pde ASHF TW15 * 23 J7
DORK RH4 * 117 H6
GT/LBKH KT23 * 96 C6
New Park Rd ASHF TW15 23 M8
BRXS/STRHM SW2 29 P4
CRAN GU6 153 H9
New Pl BFOR GU20 * 52 E1
New Place Gdns LING RH7 143 L9
New Pond Rd RGUW GU3 131 L4
Newport Rd ASHV GU12 108 E5
BARN SW13 18 E6
HTHAIR TW6 14 C6
New Rd ASC SL5 33 P1
BAGS GU19 51 P6
BLKW GU17 68 A4
BRAK RG12 32 F3
BTFD TW8 * 17 K4
CWTH RG45 49 N4
DTCH/LGLY SL3 12 B6
DTCH/LGLY SL3 12 E1
E/WMO/HCT KT8 40 A4
EBED/NFELT TW14 23 N2
EBED/NFELT TW14 24 C4
ESH/CLAY KT10 58 C3
FELT TW13 24 F8
FLEETS GU52 87 H9
GDST RH9 122 G7
HASM GU27 184 A5
HORL RH6 160 C1
HSLW TW3 16 B9
HTWY RG27 66 C1
HYS/HAR UB3 14 E5
KUTN/CMB KT2 41 N1
KWD/TDW/WH KT20 98 G3
MFD/CHID GU8 149 M4
MFD/CHID GU8 150 D7
MFD/CHID GU8 167 P3
MTCM CR4 44 C9
OXTED RH8 123 P1
RCHPK/HAM TW10 26 B7
RDKG RH5 154 F6
RFNM GU10 109 H8
RGUE GU4 114 A2
RGUE GU4 132 F3
RSEV TN14 105 P4
SHGR GU5 133 P1
SHGR GU5 134 E1
SHPTN TW17 38 C4
SHST GU47 49 L9
STA TW18 21 P8
WEY KT13 56 E4
Newry Rd TWK TW1 16 G9
Newsham Rd
WOKN/KNAP GU21 71 M6
New Site ADL/WDHM KT15 * 56 A3
Newstead Cl GODL GU7 131 K7
Newstead Hall HORL RH6 159 N2
Newstead Ri CTHM CR3 102 B6
Newstead Wk MRDN SM4 43 N8
Newstead Wy
WIM/MER SW19 28 A7
New St BH/WHM TN16 104 G7
CRAWE RH10 177 K4
STA TW18 22 D7
SWTR RH13 192 C8
Newton Av EGRIN RH19 180 E5
Newton Ct WDSR SL4 20 F2
Newton Gv CHSWK W4 18 C1
Newton La WDSR SL4 20 G2
Newton Rd CRAWE RH10 177 J1
FARN GU14 88 F1
ISLW TW7 16 F7
PUR/KEN CR8 80 E1
WDR/YW UB7 14 A6
WIM/MER SW19 43 J1
Newtonside Orch
WDSR SL4 * 20 F2
Newton's Yd
WAND/EARL SW18 28 D1
Newton Wy RFNM GU10 108 G7
Newton Wood Rd
ASHTD KT21 77 M5
New Town CRAWE RH10 160 C9
Newtown Rd LIPH GU30 182 F7
SHST GU47 49 M9
New Wy GODL GU7 131 J9
New Wickham La EGH TW20 36 E1
New Wokingham Rd
CWTH RG45 49 L3
New Years La RSEV TN14 85 K5
New Zealand Av
WOT/HER KT12 39 J9
Nexus Pk ASHV GU12 89 H7
Niagara Av EA W5 17 J2
Nicholas Gdns
WOKS/MYFD GU22 73 J5
Nicholas Rd CROY/NA CR0 62 G3
Nicholes Rd HSLW TW3 16 A9
Nichol La BMLY BR1 47 N1
Nicholsfield BIL RH14 188 C6
Nicholson Ms EGH TW20 * 21 M8
KUT KT1 41 L5
Nicholson Rd CROY/NA CR0 3 K1
Nicholson Wk EGH TW20 21 M8
Nicola Cl SAND/SEL CR2 63 L5
Nicosia Rd WAND/EARL SW18 29 H3
Niederwald Rd SYD SE26 31 M7
Nigel Fisher Wy CHSGTN KT9 59 J6
Nigel Playfair Av
HMSMTH W6 18 F3
Nightingale Av EHSLY KT24 94 F5
Nightingale Cl
BH/WHM TN16 84 A4
CAR SM5 62 C1
CHSWK W4 18 A4
COB KT11 57 M9
CRAWW RH11 176 F3
EGRIN RH19 180 C4
FARN GU14 87 N1
HOR/WEW KT19 77 N1
Nightingale Crs BRAK RG12 32 E6
EHSLY KT24 94 F5
Nightingale Dr FRIM GU16 89 J4
HOR/WEW KT19 59 P5
Nightingale Gdns SHST GU47 49 M9
Nightingale La BAL SW12 29 J3
CRAWE RH10 179 K6
RCHPK/HAM TW10 26 D3
Nightingale Ms KUT KT1 * 8 C6
Nightingale Pl WBPTN SW10 19 N4
Nightingale Rd ASHV GU12 109 L3
CAR SM5 62 B2
E/WMO/HCT KT8 40 B6
EHSLY KT24 95 H5
ESH/CLAY KT10 57 P4
GODL GU7 131 L7
GU GU1 7 F2
HORS RH12 192 C7
HPTN TW12 25 H9
SAND/SEL CR2 64 D9
WOT/HER KT12 * 39 L8
Nightingales CRAN GU6 171 H2
Nightingale Shott EGH TW20 21 L9
Nightingale Sq BAL SW12 29 K3
The Nightingales
STWL/WRAY TW19 23 J4
Nightingale Wk BAL SW12 29 L2
Nightingale Wy REDH RH1 121 N5
Nightjar Cl RFNM GU10 107 H6
Nimbus Rd HOR/WEW KT19 60 B8
Nimrod Rd
STRHM/NOR SW16 29 L9
Nineacres Wy
COUL/CHIP CR5 80 G5
Nine Elms Cl
EBED/NFELT TW14 24 A4
Ninehams Cl CTHM CR3 81 M9
Ninehams Gdns CTHM CR3 81 M9
Ninehams Rd
BH/WHM TN16 104 B1
CTHM CR3 101 M1
Nine Mile Ride CWTH RG45 32 C9
EWKG RG40 48 B3
Nineteenth Rd MTCM CR4 44 G5
Ninth Av
KWD/TDW/WH KT20 * 99 K6
Niton Rd RCH/KEW TW9 * 17 N8
Niton St FUL/PGN SW6 19 H5
Niven Cl CRAWE RH10 177 N6
Noahs Ct CRAWE RH10 * 179 H7
Nobel Dr HYS/HAR UB3 14 G5
Noble Cnr HEST TW5 * 16 A6
Nobles Wy EGH TW20 36 C1
Noke Dr REDH RH1 120 C4
Nonsuch Court Av EW KT17 60 F8
Nonsuch Pl CHEAM SM3 * 61 H6
Nonsuch Wk BELMT SM2 61 H8
Noons Corner Rd RDKG RH5 135 P5
Norbiton Av KUT KT1 9 J4
Norbiton Common Rd
NWMAL KT3 41 P4
Norbury Av HSLW TW3 25 L1
STRHM/NOR SW16 45 H2
Norbury Cl
STRHM/NOR SW16 45 J2
Norbury Court Rd
STRHM/NOR SW16 44 G3
Norbury Crs
STRHM/NOR SW16 45 J3
Norbury Cross
STRHM/NOR SW16 44 G4
Norbury Hl
STRHM/NOR SW16 45 J1
Norbury Ri
STRHM/NOR SW16 44 G4
Norbury Rd REIG RH2 119 K5
THHTH CR7 45 L3
Norbury Vls KUT KT1 * 9 G5
Norbury Wy GT/LBKH KT23 96 C5
Norcroft Gdns EDUL SE22 31 H3
Norcutt Rd WHTN TW2 25 M4
Norfolk Av SAND/SEL CR2 64 A8
Norfolk Cha BNFD RG42 33 H1
Norfolk Cl CRAWW RH11 176 B9
HORL RH6 159 K2
TWK TW1 * 26 A2
Norfolk Farm Cl
WOKS/MYFD GU22 72 G4
Norfolk Farm Rd
WOKS/MYFD GU22 73 H4
Norfolk Gdns
WOKN/KNAP GU21 * 71 M8
Norfolk House Rd
STRHM/NOR SW16 29 N6
Norfolk La RDKG RH5 137 H4
Norfolk Rd DORK RH4 116 G7
ESH/CLAY KT10 58 E4
FELT TW13 24 D4
HORS RH12 192 C8
RDKG RH5 137 J7
THHTH CR7 45 L4
WIM/MER SW19 44 A1
Norgrove St BAL SW12 29 K4
Norheads La BH/WHM TN16 83 N7
Norhyrst Av SNWD SE25 45 P4
Nork Gdns BNSTD SM7 79 J3
Nork Ri BNSTD SM7 79 H5
Nork Wy BNSTD SM7 79 H4
Norlands La EGH TW20 37 J3
Norley V PUT/ROE SW15 27 M4
Norman Av EW KT17 78 D1
FELT TW13 24 F5
SAND/SEL CR2 63 L8
TWK TW1 26 A3
Normanby Cl PUT/ROE SW15 28 C1
Norman Cl EPSOM KT18 78 F8
Norman Colyer Ct
HOR/WEW KT19 * 60 B8
Norman Crs HEST TW5 15 M5
Normand Gdns WKENS W14 * 19 J4
Normand Ms WKENS W14 19 J4
Normand Rd WKENS W14 19 K4
Normandy HORS RH12 192 B9
Normandy Cl CRAWE RH10 177 L7
EGRIN RH19 * 180 E3
FRIM GU16 69 N8
SYD SE26 31 M6
Normandy Gdns HORS RH12 192 B9
Normandy Wk EGH TW20 * 21 P8
Normanhurst Cl
CRAWE RH10 177 J5
Normanhurst Dr TWK TW1 26 A1
Normanhurst Rd
BRXS/STRHM SW2 30 A5
WOT/HER KT12 57 M1
Norman Keep BNFD RG42 33 H2
Norman Rd ASHF TW15 23 N9
SUT SM1 61 L4
THHTH CR7 45 K6
WIM/MER SW19 43 N1
Normansfield Av KUT KT1 8 A1
Normans La EDEN TN8 144 C5
Norman's Rd HORL RH6 141 L8
Normanton Av
WAND/EARL SW18 28 D5
Normanton Rd
SAND/SEL CR2 63 N5
Normanton St FSTH SE23 31 L5
Normington Cl
STRHM/NOR SW16 30 B8
Norrels Dr EHSLY KT24 95 H6
Norrels Ride EHSLY KT24 95 H6
Norris Br FARN GU14 87 L7
Norris Hill Rd FLEETS GU52 87 K8
Norris Rd STA TW18 22 C7
Norroy Rd PUT/ROE SW15 19 H9
Norstead Pl PUT/ROE SW15 27 M5
North Acre BNSTD SM7 79 K5
Northampton Cl BRAK RG12 32 F4
Northampton Rd
CROY/NA CR0 64 A1
Northanger Rd
STRHM/NOR SW16 29 P9
North Av CAR SM5 62 C6
FNM GU9 107 P7
RCH/KEW TW9 17 N6
WOT/HER KT12 56 G7
North Beta Rd FARN GU14 88 D5
Northborough Rd
STRHM/NOR SW16 44 G3
Northbourne GODL GU7 131 M5
HAYES BR2 47 N8
Northbrook Copse
BRAK RG12 33 H7
Northbrook Rd ALDT GU11 108 D6
CROY/NA CR0 45 M6
Northcliffe Cl WPK KT4 60 C2
North Cl ASHV GU12 108 G5
CRAWE RH10 177 J4
EBED/NFELT TW14 23 N2
FARN GU14 68 C8
MRDN SM4 43 J5
RDKG RH5 137 J2
North Common WEY KT13 * 56 E3
Northcote ADL/WDHM KT15 55 P3
Northcote Av BRYLDS KT5 41 N8
ISLW TW7 25 P1
Northcote Crs EHSLY KT24 94 E5
Northcote La SHGR GU5 133 J8
Northcote Rd ASHV GU12 89 J8
CROY/NA CR0 45 M7
EHSLY KT24 94 E5
FARN GU14 88 A1

NWMAL KT3 .....42 A4
TWK TW1 .....25 P1
Northcott BRAK RG12 .....22 B7
Northcroft Cl EGH TW20 .....20 G8
Northcroft Gdns EGH TW20 .....20 G8
Northcroft Rd EGH TW20 .....20 G8
HOR/WEW KT19 .....60 C6
Northcroft Vls EGH TW20 .....20 G8
North Cross Rd EDUL SE22 .....30 G1
North Dene HEST TW5 .....16 B5
Northdown Cl HORS RH12 .....192 E6
Northdown La GU GU1 .....112 C8
Northdown Rd BELMT SM2 .....61 L8
GDST RH9 .....102 G5
Northdowns CRAN GU6 .....171 H2
North Downs Crs
CROY/NA CRO 65 H8
North Downs Rd
CROY/NA CRO 65 H8
North Downs Wy
BRKHM/BTCW RH3 .....118 G3
GDST RH9 .....102 F8
KWD/TDW/WH KT20 .....117 M3
OXTED RH8 .....103 N3
RDKG RH5 .....115 N6
REDH RH1 .....101 M7
RFNM GU10 .....128 C3
RGUE GU4 .....112 G9
RGUW GU3 .....129 P2
Northdown Ter
EGRIN RH19 * 162 C9
North Dr BECK BR3 .....47 H5
CHOB/PIR GU24 .....90 E2
HSLW TW3 .....16 C7
STRHM/NOR SW16 .....29 M7
VW GU25 .....35 L6
North End CROY/NA CRO 2 C3
EGRIN RH19 * 162 A9
North End Crs WKENS W14 .....19 K2
North End La ASC SL5 .....34 C8
North End Rd FUL/PGN SW6 .....19 L5
WKENS W14 .....19 K2
Northernhay Wk MRDN SM4 .....43 J5
Northern Perimeter Rd
HTHAIR TW6 .....14 E6
Northern Perimeter Rd West
HTHAIR TW6 .....14 N6
Northey Av BELMT SM2 .....61 H8
North Eyot Gdns
HMSMTH W6 .....18 D3
North Farm La FARN GU14 .....88 A8
Northfield LTWR GU18 .....52 B9
MFD/CHID GU8 .....168 A9
RGUE GU4 .....132 C4
Northfield Cl ASHV GU12 .....108 F5
FLEETS GU52 * 87 H9
HYS/HAR UB3 .....15 H1
Northfield Ct ST A TW18 .....37 M2
Northfield Crs CHEAM SM3 .....61 J3
Northfield Pde
HYS/HAR UB3 * 15 J1
Northfield Pk HYS/HAR UB5 .....14 C1
Northfield Pl WEY KT13 .....56 D6
North Field Rd HEST TW5 .....15 M4
Northfield Rd COB KT11 .....75 J2
FLEETS GU52 .....87 H9
STA TW18 .....37 M2
Northfields ASHTD KT21 .....77 L8
EW KT17 .....60 C9
WAND/EARL SW18 .....28 F1
North Fryerne YTLY GU46 .....49 H9
North Gdns WIM/MER SW19 .....43 P1
Northgate Av CRAWE RH10 .....177 J4
THHTH CR7 .....45 L4
Northgate Pl CBLY GU15 .....69 J1
Northgate Pl CRAWE RH10 .....177 J4
Northgate Rd CRAWE RH10 .....176 D5
North Gate Rd FARN GU14 .....88 B5
North Gn BRAK RG12 .....32 F2
North Heath Cl HORS RH12 .....192 C5
North Heath La HORS RH12 .....192 C5
North Holmes Cl HORS RH12 .....192 G5
North Hyde Gdns
HYS/HAR UB3 .....15 J1
North Hyde La NWDGN UB2 .....15 N3
North Hyde Rd HYS/HAR UB3 .....14 C1
North Hyde Whf
NWDGN UB2 * 15 L2
Northington Cl BRAK RG12 .....33 H7
Northlands RDKG RH5 * 156 G3
Northlands Rd HORS RH12 .....191 L1
HORS RH12 .....192 D3
North La ALDT GU11 .....108 F3
North Lodge MFD/CHID GU8 * 167 N1
North Lodge
PUT/ROE SW15 * 28 A1
North Lodge Dr ASC SL5 .....33 L1
North Looe EW KT17 * 78 G2
North Md CRAWE RH10 .....177 H8
REDH RH1 .....120 B3
Northmead FARN GU14 .....88 D3
North Moors GU GU1 .....112 C1
North Munstead La
GODL GU7 .....150 F9
Northolt Rd WDR/YW UB7 .....13 P6
North Pde CHSGTN KT9 .....59 M4
HORS RH12 .....192 B7
North Pk IVER SLO 13 J1
North Park La REDH RH1 .....102 A9
North Pas WAND/EARL SW18 .....28 D1
North Pl TEDD TW11 .....25 N9
WIM/MER SW19 .....44 B1
North Pole La HAYES BR2 .....65 H5
North Rd ALDT GU11 .....88 F8
ASC SL5 .....33 K2
ASHV GU12 .....109 H2
BMLY BR1 .....47 N1
BTFD TW8 .....17 L1
CRAWE RH10 .....177 K4

EA W5 .....17 K1
EBED/NFELT TW14 .....23 N2
GUW GU2 .....111 P2
HEST TW5 .....15 L4
KEN/KEW TW9 .....17 P1
REIG RH2 .....119 K8
SURB KT6 .....41 K7
WDR/YW UB7 .....14 B1
WIM/MER SW19 .....28 F9
WOKN/KNAP GU21 .....11 G1
WOT/HER KT12 .....57 L4
Northrop Rd HTHAIR TW6 .....14 G6
North Side RFNM GU10 .....109 J7
North Side BMLY BR1 .....47 N2
North Side Wandsworth Common
WAND/EARL SW18 .....28 F1
Northspur Rd SUT SM1 .....61 L2
North Station Ap
REDH RH1 * 121 H7
Northstead Rd
BRXS/STRHM SW2 .....30 B5
North St BMLY BR1 .....47 N2
CAR SM5 .....62 B3
CRAWE RH10 .....179 H7
DORK RH4 .....116 C7
EGH TW20 .....21 L8
GODL GU7 .....131 L6
GU GU1 .....6 C5
HORS RH12 .....192 D1
ISLW TW7 .....16 G8
LHD/OX KT22 .....96 G2
REDH RH1 .....120 B4
Northumberland Av
ISLW TW7 .....16 F6
Northumberland Cl
BNFD RG42 .....33 H1
STWL/WRAY TW19 .....23 H2
Northumberland Crs
EBED/NFELT TW14 .....23 P2
Northumberland Gdns
MTCM CR4 .....44 G6
North Verbena Gdns
HMSMTH W6 * 18 E3
North Vw WIM/MER SW19 .....27 N8
North View Crs EPSOM KT18 .....78 G6
Northway GODL GU7 .....131 H6
GUW GU2 .....111 N5
HORL RH6 .....159 J4
RYNPK SW20 .....43 J4
WLGTN SM6 .....62 E3
North Weald La
KUTN/CMB KT2 .....26 D6
Northwick HTWY GU27 .....66 C1
North Wk CROY/NA CRO 65 H5
Northwood Av PUR/KEN CR8 .....81 J2
WOKN/KNAP GU21 .....71 K7
Northwood Pk
CRAWE RH10 * 177 K1
Northwood Rd CAR SM5 .....62 C5
FSTH SE23 .....31 N4
HTHAIR TW6 .....13 P6
THHTH CR7 .....45 L3
North Worple Wy
MORT/ESHN SW14 .....18 B8
Norton Av BRYLDS KT5 .....41 P8
Norton Cl RGUW GU3 .....91 K7
Norton Gdns
STRHM/NOR SW16 .....44 G3
Norton Pk ASC SL5 .....34 C6
Norton Rd CBLY GU15 .....69 L4
Norwich Av CBLY GU15 .....68 G5
Norwich Rd CRAWE RH10 .....177 K7
THHTH CR7 .....45 L4
Norwood Cl EHSLY KT24 .....95 N8
NWDGN UB2 .....16 A2
WHTN TW2 .....25 L5
Norwood Crs HTHAIR TW6 .....14 E6
Norwood Farm La COB KT11 .....57 J9
Norwood Gdns NWDGN UB2 .....15 P2
Norwood Green Rd
NWDGN UB2 .....16 A2
Norwood High St
WNWD SE27 .....30 D7
Norwood Hl HORL RH6 .....158 A1
Norwoodhill Rd HORL RH6 .....158 C5
Norwood Park Rd
WNWD SE27 .....30 D8
Norwood Rd EHSLY KT24 .....95 N8
HNHL SE24 .....30 C4
NWDGN UB2 .....15 N1
NWDGN UB2 .....16 A2
Notley End EGH TW20 .....36 A1
Notson Rd SNWD SE25 .....46 B5
Nottingham Ct
WOKN/KNAP GU21 .....71 M7
Nottingham Rd ISLW TW7 .....16 F7
SAND/SEL CR2 .....63 L4
TOOT SW17 .....29 J4
Nova Ms MRDN SM4 .....43 J8
Nova Rd CROY/NA CRO 2 D1
Novello St FUL/PGN SW6 .....19 L6
Nowell Rd BARN SW13 .....18 E4
Nower Cl DORK RH4 .....116 C7
The Nower RSEV TN14 .....85 K9
RSEV TN14 .....85 P5
Nowhurst La HORS RH12 .....191 H5
Noyna Rd TOOT SW17 .....29 J6
Nuffield Dr SHST GU47 .....50 B8
Nugent Cl DTCH/LGLY SL3 .....49 M4
Nugent Cl MFD/CHID GU8 .....169 L5
Nugent Rd GUW GU2 .....111 K6
SNWD SE25 .....45 P4
Nunappleton Wy
OXTED RH8 .....123 N3
Nuneaton BRAK RG12 .....32 G7
Nunns Pd RDKG RH5 * 156 B6
Nuns Wk VW GU25 .....36 B6
Nursery Av CROY/NA CRO 64 D1
Nursery Cl ADL/WDHM KT15 .....55 K8
CROY/NA CRO 64 D1

EBED/NFELT TW14 .....24 C3
EW KT17 .....60 C8
FLEETN GU51 .....87 K8
FRIM GU16 .....69 H9
MTCM CR4 .....98 F5
RDKG RH5 .....156 B7
WOKN/KNAP GU21 .....72 A5
Nursery Gdns HSLWW TW4 .....24 C1
RGUE GU4 .....132 F2
STA TW18 .....37 M3
SUN TW16 .....39 H3
Nursery Hl SHGR GU5 .....133 H9
Nurserylands
CRAWW RH11 .....176 D5
Nursery La HORL RH6 .....158 G2
Nursery Pl WDSR SL4 .....20 G2
Nursery Rd GODL GU7 .....131 M6
KWD/TDW/WH KT20 .....98 F5
MTCM CR4 .....44 A5
SUN TW16 .....38 G3
SUT SM1 .....61 M3
THHTH CR7 .....45 M3
WIM/MER SW19 .....43 J1
WIM/MER SW19 .....43 J1
WOKN/KNAP GU21 .....71 K6
Nursery Wy OXTED RH8 * 123 M3
STWL/WRAY TW19 .....21 J2
Nutbourne FNM GU10 .....116 F7
Nutcombe La DORK RH4 .....116 F7
GSHT GU26 .....185 P1
Nutcroft Gv LHD/OX KT22 .....96 E2
Nutfield Cl CAR SM5 .....62 A2
Nutfield Marsh Rd
REDH RH1 .....120 G2
Nutfield Rd COUL/CHIP CR5 .....80 C5
EDUL SE22 .....30 G1
REDH RH1 .....120 D1
REDH RH1 .....120 E3
THHTH CR7 .....45 K5
Nuthatch Cl RFNM GU10 .....107 H7
Nuthatch Gdns REIG RH2 .....119 N8
Nuthatch Wy CRAWE RH10 .....179 K6
Nuthurst BRAK RG12 .....32 G6
Nuthurst Av
BRXS/STRHM SW2 .....30 A5
CRAN GU6 .....153 H9
Nutley Cl CRAWW RH11 .....176 D4
Nutley BRAK RG12 .....32 C9
Nutley Cl YTLY GU46 .....67 H3
Nutley La REIG RH2 .....119 K4
Nutmeg Cl FARN GU14 .....87 N2
Nutshell La FNM GU9 .....107 N8
Nutty La SHPTN TW17 .....38 E5
Nutwell St TOOT SW17 .....29 H8
Nutwood Av
BRKHM/BTCW RH3 .....118 A6
Nutwood Cl
BRKHM/BTCW RH3 .....118 A6
Nyefield Pk
KWD/TDW/WH KT20 .....98 E6
Nylands Av RCH/KEW TW9 .....17 N7
Nymans Cl HORS RH12 .....192 C7
Nymans Ct CRAWE RH10 .....177 L8
Nymans Gdns RYNPK SW20 .....42 F4
Nyon Gv FSTH SE23 .....31 N5

Oakapple Cl CRAWW RH11 .....194 E1
SAND/SEL CR2 .....82 B3
Oak Av CHOB/PIR GU24 .....90 C1
CROY/NA CRO 46 E9
EGH TW20 .....36 B2
HEST TW5 .....15 M5
HPTN TW12 .....24 G9
SHST GU47 .....49 P8
WIM/MER SW19 * 44 C1
Oakbank CROY/NA CRO 65 H5
LHD/OX KT22 .....96 C3
WOKS/MYFD GU22 .....92 A4
Oakbank Av WOT/HER KT12 .....39 P8
Oakbury Rd FUL/PGN SW6 .....19 M7
Oak Cl CRAWE RH10 .....160 A9
CROY/NA CRO 131 L5
KWD/TDW/WH KT20 .....117 P1
MFD/CHID GU8 .....167 P7
SUT SM1 .....61 N1
Oakcombe Cl NWMAL KT3 .....42 B1
Oak Cnr RDKG RH5 .....156 B1
Oak Cottage La RGUW GU3 .....110 C1
Oak Cottages HASM GU27 * 185 P4
Oak Cft CRAWE RH10 .....176 G1
FNM GU9 .....5 F6
Oak Cft EGRIN RH19 .....180 F3
Oakcroft Cl BF/WBF KT14 .....73 K3
Oakcroft Rd BF/WBF KT14 .....73 K3
CHSGTN KT9 .....59 M3
Oakcroft Vls CHSGTN KT9 .....59 M3
Oakdale BRAK RG12 .....32 F7
Oakdale La EDEN TN8 .....124 G4
Oakdale Rd HOR/WEW KT19 .....60 B7
STRHM/NOR SW16 .....29 P8
WEY KT13 .....56 C2
Oakdale Wy MTCM CR4 .....44 C8
Oak Dell CRAWE RH10 .....177 M4
Oakdene ASC SL5 .....34 B5
CHOB/PIR GU24 .....53 M8
KWD/TDW/WH KT20 .....79 J9
Oakdene Av THDIT KT7 .....40 G6
Oakdene Cl
BRKHM/BTCW RH3 .....118 A7
GT/LBKH KT23 .....96 C7
Oakdene Dr BRYLDS KT5 .....42 A2
Oakdene Ms CHEAM SM3 .....43 M9
Oakdene Rd
BRKHM/BTCW RH3 .....117 P7
COB KT11 .....75 K3
GODL GU7 .....150 C1

GT/LBKH KT23 .....95 P4
REDH RH1 .....120 B5
RGUE GU4 .....132 A4
Oak Dr KWD/TDW/WH KT20 .....117 P1
Oaken Coppice ASHTD KT21 .....77 N8
Oaken Copse CBLY GU15 .....69 L2
FLEETS GU52 .....107 H2
Oaken Copse Crs FARN GU14 .....68 D9
Oak End RDKG RH5 .....156 B1
Oak End Wy
ADL/WDHM KT15 .....73 J1
Oakengates BRAK RG12 .....32 C9
Oaken La ESH/CLAY KT10 .....58 E3
Oakenshaw Cl SURB KT6 .....41 L8
Oak Farm Cl BLKW GU17 .....67 N3
Oakfield BIL RH14 .....187 K7
WOKN/KNAP GU21 .....71 L5
Oakfield Cl NWMAL KT3 .....42 D6
WEY KT13 .....56 D5
Oakfield Dr REIG RH2 .....119 L3
Oakfield Gdns BECK BR3 .....46 G6
CAR SM5 .....44 A9
Oakfield Gld WEY KT13 .....56 E2
Oakfield Rd ASHF TW15 .....23 L7
ASHTD KT21 .....77 L7
BLKW GU17 .....67 N4
COB KT11 .....75 K2
CROY/NA CRO 2 C1
EDEN TN8 .....144 F1
PGE/AN SE20 .....46 B1
WIM/MER SW19 .....28 A6
Oakfields BF/WBF KT14 .....73 M3
CBLY GU15 .....68 D5
CRAWE RH10 .....177 N4
GUW GU2 .....111 J3
RDKG RH5 .....172 F3
WOT/HER KT12 .....39 J9
Oakfield St WBPTN SW10 .....19 M4
Oak Gdns CROY/NA CRO 64 G1
Oak Grange Rd RGUE GU4 .....133 M9
Oak Gv BIL RH14 .....188 D6
CRAN GU6 .....171 J2
SUN TW16 .....39 K1
WWKM BR4 .....65 J1
Oak Grove Crs CBLY GU15 .....68 D2
Oak Grove Rd PGE/AN SE20 .....46 C2
Oakhall Dr SUN TW16 .....24 A6
Oakham Cl CAT SE6 * 31 N5
Oakham Dr HAYES BR2 .....47 N5
Oakhaven CRAWE RH10 .....176 G7
Oakhill ESH/CLAY KT10 .....58 G5
Oak Hill EW KT17 .....60 C8
RGUE GU4 .....112 G1
RGUW GU3 .....110 G3
SURB KT6 .....41 L8
Oakhill Cl ASHTD KT21 .....77 J7
Oak Hill Crs SURB KT6 .....41 L8
Oakhill Gdns WEY KT13 .....56 G1
Oak Hill Gv SURB KT6 .....41 L7
Oakhill Pl WAND/EARL SW18 .....28 F3
Oak Hill Rd SURB KT6 * 41 L7
Oakhill Rd ADL/WDHM KT15 .....55 K5
ASHTD KT21 .....77 J7
BECK BR3 .....47 J3
BOR GU35 .....164 E6
PUT/ROE SW15 .....28 C1
REIG RH2 .....119 M6
STRHM/NOR SW16 .....44 G2
SUT SM1 .....61 M2
SWTR RH13 .....192 D8
Oakhurst CHOB/PIR GU24 .....53 L7
CSHT GU26 .....165 N8
Oakhurst Cl TEDD TW11 .....25 M8
Oakhurst Gdns EGRIN RH19 .....180 B1
Oakhurst La BIL RH14 .....188 B4
Oakhurst Ri CAR SM5 .....62 A7
Oakhurst Rd HOR/WEW KT19 .....60 A5
Oakington Av HYS/HAR UB3 .....14 F2
Oakington Dr SUN TW16 .....39 L3
Oakland Av FNM GU9 .....108 A7
Oaklands GDST RH9 .....122 E9
HASM GU27 .....184 D3
HORL RH6 .....159 M1
LHD/OX KT22 .....96 D4
PUR/KEN CR8 .....81 L3
Oaklands Av ESH/CLAY KT10 .....40 D9
ISLW TW7 .....16 F4
THHTH CR7 .....45 J5
WWKM BR4 .....65 H1
Oaklands Cl ASC SL5 .....33 P1
CHSGTN KT9 .....59 K3
RGUE GU4 .....132 C4
Oaklands Ct ADL/WDHM KT15 .....55 M2
Oaklands Dr ASC SL5 .....33 P1
REDH RH1 .....120 D7
Oaklands Gdns PUR/KEN CR8 .....81 L3
Oaklands La BH/WHM TN16 .....84 C4
CWTH RG45 .....49 J3
Oaklands Rd BMLY BR1 .....47 L1
MORT/ESHN SW14 .....18 B8
Oaklawn Rd LHD/OX KT22 .....77 H1
Oaklea ASHV GU12 .....109 J1
Oak Leaf Cl HOR/WEW KT19 * 78 B1
Oakleigh BECK BR3 .....47 H9
Oakleigh Av SURB KT6 .....41 N9
Oakleigh Ct OXTED RH8 .....103 L8
Oakleigh Rd HORS RH12 .....192 E6
Oakleigh Wy MTCM CR4 .....44 D8
SURB KT6 .....41 N9

Oakley Av CROY/NA CRO 62 G3
Oakley Cl ADL/WDHM KT15 .....55 P3
EGRIN RH19 .....180 G4
ISLW TW7 .....16 D6
Oakley Dell RGUE GU4 .....112 G3
Oakley Dr BY FLEETN GU51 .....86 G3
Oakley Gdns BNSTD SM7 .....79 M4
Oakley Rd GBLY GU15 .....68 D4
SNWD SE25 .....46 B6
WARL CR6 .....82 A7
Oak Ldg HASM GU27 * 184 F6
Oak Lodge Cl WOT/HER KT12 .....57 L4
Oak Lodge Dr REDH RH1 .....140 C4
WWKM BR4 .....47 J9
Oak Lodge La
BH/WHM TN16 .....105 H5
Oak Md GODL GU7 .....131 K5
Oakmead Av HAYES BR2 .....47 N7
Oakmead Gn EPSOM KT18 .....78 A4
Oakmead Pl MTCM CR4 .....44 A3
Oakmead Rd BAL SW12 .....29 L4
CROY/NA CRO 44 F7
Oak Park Gdns
WIM/MER SW19 .....28 A4
Oakridge CHOB/PIR GU24 .....70 F2
Oak Rd BH/WHM TN16 .....105 H5
COB KT11 .....75 M4
CRAWW RH11 .....176 F6
CTHM CR3 .....101 N2
FARN GU14 .....88 E4
LHD/OX KT22 .....76 G8
NWMAL KT3 .....42 B3
REIG RH2 .....119 M4
Oak Rw MTCM CR4 .....44 E3
NRWD SE19 .....30 F8
WPK KT4 .....60 F3
Oaks Cl HORS RH12 .....192 C2
LHD/OX KT22 .....96 G1
Oaksford Av SYD SE26 .....31 J6
Oakshade Rd LHD/OX KT22 .....76 C3
Oakshaw Rd
WAND/EARL SW18 .....28 E3
Oakshaw OXTED RH8 .....103 K7
Oakside La HORL RH6 .....140 E9
Oaks La CROY/NA CRO 64 C2
RDKG RH5 .....137 H4
Oaks Pk BNSTD SM7 * 80 B1
The Oaks Pk RDKG RH5 * 156 C5
Oaks Rd CROY/NA CRO 64 B4
RGUE GU4 .....132 G1
REIG RH1 .....119 P4
STWL/WRAY TW19 .....22 C1
WOKN/KNAP GU21 .....10 C4
The Oaks BF/WBF KT14 .....73 L3
BRAK RG12 .....32 H1
DORK RH4 * 137 H1
EPSOM KT18 .....78 C3
FELT TW13 * 24 F5
FLEETN GU51 .....86 A7
MFD/CHID GU8 * 168 A7
MRDN SM4 * 43 J5
STA TW18 .....22 C7
SURB KT6 .....41 L8
WOKN/KNAP GU21 .....10 C4
YTLY GU46 .....67 H3
Oaks Wy CAR SM5 .....62 B6
EPSOM KT18 .....78 F8
PUR/KEN CR8 .....81 J3
RFLY/SEND GU23 .....93 L4
SURB KT6 .....59 L1
Oak Tree Cl ASHV GU12 .....89 H6
ASHV GU12 .....108 F6
BOR GU35 .....164 C7
EGRIN RH19 * 162 B9
RGUE GU4 .....92 A8
RGUE GU4 .....92 C9
VW GU25 .....36 B7
WOKN/KNAP GU21 .....71 H7
Oak Tree Dr EGH TW20 .....21 H8
GU GU1 .....112 A1
Oak Tree La HASM GU27 .....183 N4
MFD/CHID GU8 .....169 L6
Oak Tree Rd MFD/CHID GU8 .....169 H1
WOKN/KNAP GU21 .....71 H7
Oaktrees ASHV GU12 .....109 H5
FNM GU9 .....107 M8
Oaktree Wy SHST GU47 .....49 L8
Oak Tree Vw FNM GU9 .....107 M8
Oakview Gv CROY/NA CRO 46 E9
Oak Wk HORS RH12 .....195 L1
Oak Wy ASHTD KT21 .....77 N5
CRAWE RH10 .....177 H1
CROY/NA CRO 46 D7
EBED/NFELT TW14 .....23 P6
FARN GU14 .....88 E2
REIG RH2 .....119 P6
Oakway HORS RH12 .....192 B7
HAYES BR2 .....47 K3
RFNM GU10 .....126 A9
RYNPK SW20 .....42 G5
Oakway Dr FRIM GU16 .....68 G7
GUW GU2 .....111 N3
WLGTN SM6 .....62 E5
Oakwood FLEETS GU52 .....106 G2
GUW GU2 .....111 N3
WLGTN SM6 .....62 F6
Oakwood Av BECK BR3 .....47 J3
HAYES BR2 .....47 K3
HOR/WEW KT19 .....59 N7
MTCM CR4 .....43 P3
PUR/KEN CR8 .....81 J1
Oakwood Cl EHSLY KT24 .....94 G7
REDH RH1 .....120 C5
Oakwood Ct CHOB/PIR GU24 .....70 G5
WKENS W14 .....19 K1

Oakwood Dr *EHSLY* KT24 ....94 G7
  NRWD SE19 ....30 E9
Oakwood Gdns *SUT* SM1 ....61 L1
  WOKN/KNAP GU21 ....70 C2
Oakwood La *WKENS* W14 ....19 K1
Oakwood Pl *CROY/NA* CR0 ....45 J7
Oakwood Ri *CTHM* CR3 ....101 N5
Oakwood Rd *BFOR* GU20 ....52 E5
  BRAK RG12 ....32 G3
  CROY/NA CR0 ....45 J7
  HORL RH6 ....140 C9
  RYNPK SW20 ....36 A6
  VW GU25 ....36 A6
  WOKN/KNAP GU21 ....71 L8
Oareborough *BRAK* RG12 ....32 G5
Oarsman Pl *E/WMO/HCT* KT8 ....40 E5
Oast House Cl
  STWL/WRAY TW19 ....21 K3
Oasthouse Dr *FLEETN* GU51 ....87 J3
Oast House La *FNM* GU9 ....107 P9
Oast La *ALDT* GU11 ....108 D7
Oast Rd *OXTED* RH8 ....123 M1
Oates Cl *HAYES* BR2 ....47 L4
Oates Wk *CRAWE* RH10 ....177 J8
Oatfield Rd
  KWD/TDW/WH KT20 ....98 F7
Oatlands *CRAWW* RH11 ....176 D6
  HORL RH6 ....140 D9
Oatlands Av *WEY* KT13 ....56 F4
Oatlands Cha *WEY* KT13 ....56 C2
Oatlands Cl *WEY* KT13 ....56 E3
Oatlands Dr *WEY* KT13 ....56 D3
Oatlands Gn *WEY* KT13 ....56 E2
Oatlands Mere *WEY* KT13 ....56 F2
Oatlands Rd
  KWD/TDW/WH KT20 ....79 J8
Oatsheaf Pde *FLEETN* GU51 * 86 F7
Oban Rd *SNWD* SE25 ....45 M5
Obelisk Wy *CBLY* GU15 ....62 E2
Oberon Wy *CRAWW* RH11 ....176 B8
  SHPTN TW17 ....38 A4
Oberstein Rd *BTSEA* SW11 ....19 P9
Oborne Cl *HNHL* SE24 ....30 C1
Observatory Rd
  MORT/ESHN SW14 ....18 A9
Occam Rd *GU* GU2 ....111 K5
Occupation La *EA* W5 ....17 K2
Ockenden Cl
  WOKS/MYFD GU22 * 11 F6
Ockenden Gdns
  WOKS/MYFD GU22 * 11 F6
Ockenden Rd
  WOKS/MYFD GU22 ....10 E6
Ockfields *MFD/CHID* GU8...149 N3
Ockford Dr *GODL* GU7 ....150 B3
Ockford Rdg *GODL* GU7 ....150 A2
Ockford Rd *GODL* GU7 ....150 B3
Ockham Dr *EHSLY* KT24 ....94 H4
Ockham Rd North
  RPLY/SEND GU23 ....94 D2
Ockham Rd South
  EHSLY KT24 ....94 G7
Ockley Ct *RGUE* GU4 ....92 F9
Ockley Rd *CRAN* GU6 ....153 P6
  CROY/NA CR0 ....45 H8
  RDKG RH5 ....155 J5
  STRHM/NOR SW16 ....29 P7
Ockleys Md *GDST* RH9 ....102 C9
O'connor Rd *ALDT* GU11 ....88 F8
Octagon Rd *WOT/HER* KT12 ....56 G8
Octavia *BRAK* RG12 ....32 C9
Octavia Cl *MTCM* CR4 ....44 A6
Octavia Rd *ISLW* TW7 ....16 F8
Octavia Wy *STA* TW18 ....22 D9
Odard Rd *E/WMO/HCT* KT8 ....40 A5
Odeon Pde *ISLW* TW7 * 16 E7
Odiham Rd *RFNM* GU10 ....106 F6
O'Gorman Av *FARN* GU14 ....88 D5
Oil Mill La *HMSMTH* W6 ....18 E3
Okeburn Rd *TOOT* SW17 ....29 P8
Okehurst Rd *BIL* RH14 ....189 M9
Okingham Cl *SHST* GU47 ....49 P8
Old Acre *BF/WBF* KT14 ....73 L3
Oldacre *CHOB/PIR* GU24 ....70 F1
Old Av *BF/WBF* KT14 ....73 J3
  WEY KT13 ....56 C5
Old Avenue Cl
  WOKN/KNAP GU21 ....73 J2
Old Bakery Ct *CRAN* GU6 ....153 P7
Old Barn Cl *BELMT* SM2 ....61 J6
Old Barn Dr *RDKG* RH5 ....156 C5
Old Barn La *CTHM* CR3 ....81 P5
  RFNM GU10 ....165 L1
Old Barn Rd *EPSOM* KT18 ....78 A6
Old Barn Vw *GODL* GU7 * 150 B2
Old Bisley Rd *FRIM* GU16 ....69 J6
Old Bracknell Cl *BRAK* RG12 ....32 D4
Old Bracknell La East
  BRAK RG12 ....32 D4
Old Bracknell La West
  BRAK RG12 ....32 C4
Old Brickfield Rd *ALDT* GU11...108 D7
Old Bridge St *KUT* KT1 ....8 A3
Old Brighton Rd North
  CRAWW RH11 ....194 F3
Old Brighton Rd South
  CRAWW RH11 ....158 G8
  CRAWW RH11 ....194 E5
Old Brompton Rd *ECT* SW5 ....19 L3
Oldbury *BRAK* RG12 ....32 A4
Oldbury Cl *FRIM* GU16 ....69 H8
  HORS RH12 ....192 F3
Oldbury Rd *CHERT* KT16 ....37 J8
Old Charlton Rd *SHPTN* TW17...38 E6
Old Chertsey Rd
  CHOB/PIR GU24 ....53 P8
Old Chestnut Av
  ESH/CLAY KT10 ....58 A5
Old Church La *FNM* GU9...127 P6

Old Church Pth
  ESH/CLAY KT10 ....58 B3
Old Church St *CHEL* SW3 ....19 P4
Old Claygate La
  ESH/CLAY KT10 ....58 G5
Old Common Rd *COB* KT11 ....75 K1
Old Common Rd *COB* KT11 ....75 K1
Old Compton La *FNM* GU9...128 A4
Old Convent *EGRIN* RH19 * 180 D1
Oldcorne Hollow *HTWY* RG27...66 E3
Old Cote Dr *HEST* TW5 ....16 A4
Old Ct *ASHTD* KT21 ....77 L8
Old Court Rd *GU* GU2 ....111 N6
Old Ctyd *BMLY* BR1 * 47 P2
Old Cove Rd *FLEETN* GU51 ....87 H4
Old Crawley Rd *HORS* RH12...193 H4
Old Cross Tree Wy
  ASHV GU12..........109 L6
Old Dairy Ms *BAL* SW12 ....29 K4
Old Dean Rd *CBLY* GU15 ....51 P9
Old Deer Pk *RCH/KEW* TW9 * ...17 M8
Old Deer Park Gdns
  RCH/KEW TW9 ....17 L8
Old Denne Gdns
  HORS RH12..........192 B3
Old Devonshire Rd *BAL* SW12 ...29 L3
Old Dock Cl *RCH/KEW* TW9 * ...17 N6
Old Dr *SHGR* GU5 ....114 E9
Olde Farm Dr *BLKW* GU17 ....67 M3
Old Elstead Rd
  MFD/CHID GU8 ....149 M2
Old Lane *PUR/KEN* CR8 ....81 J1
Old Esher Cl *WOT/HER* KT12 * .57 M4
Old Esher Rd *WOT/HER* KT12 .57 M4
Old Farleigh Rd
  SAND/SEL CR2 ....64 C8
  WARL CR6 ....82 F4
Old Farm Cl *HSLW* TW3 ....15 P9
Old Farm Dr *BRAK* RG12 ....32 E1
Old Farmhouse Dr
  LHD/OX KT22 ....76 D4
Old Farm Pl *ASHV* GU12..........109 H2
Old Farm Rd *GU* GU1 ....112 B2
  HPTN TW12 ....24 G9
Old Farnham La *FNM* GU9..........107 N8
  RFNM GU10 ....126 E4
Old Ferry Dr
  STWL/WRAY TW19..........21 H2
Oldfield Gdns *ASHTD* KT21 ....77 K8
Oldfield Rd *HORL* RH6 ....159 J3
  HPTN TW12 ....40 A2
  WIM/MER SW19 ....28 B9
Oldfields Rd *CHEAM* SM3 ....61 L1
Oldfieldwood
  WOKS/MYFD GU22..........11 K3
Old Forge Crs *SHPTN* TW17 ....38 D7
Old Forge End *SHST* GU47 ....67 M1
Old Fox Cl *CTHM* CR3 ....101 K1
Old Frensham Rd
  RFNM GU10 ....127 P7
Old Green La *CBLY* GU15 ....68 E1
Old Guildford Rd *FRIM* GU16...89 L2
  HORS RH12 ....191 M7
Old Haslemere Rd
  HASM GU27..........184 D5
Old Heath Wy *FNM* GU9 * 107 N7
Old Hi *WOKS/MYFD* GU22 ....72 B9
Old Holbrook *HORS* RH12 ....72 D2
Old Hollow *CRAWE* RH10 ....178 A3
Old Horsham Rd
  CRAWW RH11..........176 E7
  RDKG RH5..........137 J8
Old Hospital Cl *TOOT* SW17 * ...29 J4
Old House Cl *EW* KT17 ....60 D8
  WIM/MER SW19 ....28 A9
Old House Gdns *TWK* TW1 * ...26 B2
Oldhouse La *CHOB/PIR* GU24 ...52 C7
  CHOB/PIR GU24 ....70 C2
Old House Ms *HORS* RH12 * ..192 B3
Old Kiln Cl *RFNM* GU10 ....165 L1
Old Kiln La
  BRKHM/BTCW RH3 ....118 A5
  RFNM GU10 ....165 K1
Old Kingston Rd *WPK* KT4 ....60 A2
Old Lands Hi *BRAK* RG12 ....32 F2
Old La *ALDT* GU11 ....108 G3
  BH/WHM TN16 ....104 D8
  COB KT11 ....74 C9
  OXTED RH8 ....123 M1
  RFNM GU10 ....146 B8
Old Lane Gdns *COB* KT11 ....95 H2
Old Lodge La *GODL* GU7 * 150 A1
Old Lodge La *PUR/KEN* CR8 ....81 H5
Old London Rd *EPSOM* KT18 ...78 E7
  RDKG RH5 ....97 J8
Old Malden La *WPK* KT4 ....60 C1
Old Malt Wy
  WOKN/KNAP GU21 ....10 B3
Old Manor Cl *CRAWW* RH11...176 D3
Old Manor Dr *ISLW* TW7 ....25 K2
Old Manor Gdns *RGUE* GU4 ...112 G1
Old Manor Yd *ECT* SW5 * 19 M2
Old Martyrs *CRAWW* RH11 ....176 A1
Old Merrow St *RGUE* GU4 ....112 G2
Old Mill La *REDH* RH1 ....100 D8
Old Millmeads *HORS* RH12...192 B5
Old Mill Pl *HASM* GU27..........184 A3
  STWL/WRAY TW19 ....22 A1
Old Mill Rd *KUT* KT1 ....9 G7
Old Nursery Pl *ASHF* TW15..........23 J8
Old Oak Av *COUL/CHIP* CR5...80 A8
Old Oak Cl *COB* KT11 ....75 L1
Old Orch *BF/WBF* KT14 ....74 B1
  SUN TW16 ....39 J3
Old Orchards *CRAWE* RH10...177 N6
The Old Orch *FNM* GU9..........127 K6
Old Palace Rd *CROY/NA* CR0......2 A2
  GUW GU2 ....111 N6
  WEY KT13 ....56 D2
Old Palace Yd *RCH/KEW* TW9 .26 D1
Old Park Av *BAL* SW12 ....29 K2

Old Park Cl *FNM* GU9..........107 L8
Old Park La *FNM* GU9..........107 K7
Old Park Ms *HEST* TW5 ....15 P5
Old Parvis Rd *BF/WBF* KT14 ...73 N1
Old Pasture Rd *FRIM* GU16 ....69 H5
Old Pharmacy Ct
  CWTH RG45 *..........49 N5
Old Pond Cl *FRIM* GU16..........68 D7
Old Portsmouth Rd
  CBLY GU15 ....69 J4
  MFD/CHID GU8 ....148 E8
  RGUW GU3 ....131 P4
Old Pottery Cl *REIG* RH2..........119 M7
Old Pound Cl *ISLW* TW7 ....16 C6
Old Pumphouse Cl
  FLEETN GU51 *..........87 H5
The Old Quarry *HASM* GU27 ..184 A6
Old Rectory Cl
  KWD/TDW/WH KT20..........98 E4
Old Rectory Dr *ASHV* GU12..........109 J1
Old Rectory Gdns *FARN* GU14..88 F3
  GODL GU7..........150 E2
Old Rectory La *EHSLY* KT24 ....94 F7
Old Redstone Dr *REDH* RH1 ..120 C6
Old Reigate Rd *DORK* RH4..........117 L5
  BRKHM/BTCW RH3 ....118 B7
Old Rd *ADL/WDHM* KT15 ....55 K6
  BRKHM/BTCW RH3 ....118 D4
  EGRIN RH19 ....180 E3
Old Sawmill La *CWTH* RG45 ....49 N3
Old School Cl *ASHV* GU12..........109 J3
  BECK BR3 ....46 D3
  FLEETN GU51 *..........86 C6
Old School Ct
  STWL/WRAY TW19..........21 K3
Old School La
  BRKHM/BTCW RH3 ....117 N8
  YTLY GU46 ....66 G2
Old School Ms *WEY* KT13 ....56 F2
Old School Pl *LING* RH7 ....143 K9
  WOKS/MYFD GU22 ....92 C1
Old Schools La *EW* KT17 ....60 D7
Old School Sq *THDIT* KT7 ....40 F7
Old Slade La *DTCH/LGLY* SL3 ...13 K9
Old Station Cl *CRAWE* RH10...179 J4
Old Station Gdns
  TEDD TW11 * 25 P9
Old Station La
  STWL/WRAY TW19..........21 L2
Old Station Rd
  HYS/HAR UB3 *..........14 C1
Old Station Wy *GODL* GU7 ....131 L7
Oldstead *BRAK* RG12 ....32 F6
The Old Surrey Ms
  GDST RH9 *..........122 C1
Old Swan Yd *CAR* SM5..........62 B3
Old Town *CROY/NA* CR0 ....2 B5
Old Town Ms *FNM* GU9 * 5 L4
Old Tye Av *BH/WHM* TN16 ....84 C5
Old Welmore *YTLY* GU46 ....67 J3
Old Westhall Cl *WARL* CR6 ....82 C8
Old Wickhurst La
  HORS RH12..........191 L9
Old Wokingham Rd
  CWTH RG45 ....49 N2
Old Woking Rd *BF/WBF* KT14 ...73 L2
Oldwood Cha *FARN* GU14 ....87 M4
Old York Rd
  WAND/EARL SW18 ....28 E1
Oleander Cl *CWTH* RG45 ....49 K2
Oliver Av *SNWD* SE25 ....45 P4
Oliver Cl *ADL/WDHM* KT15 ....55 H6
  CHSWK W4 ....17 P4
Oliver Gv *SNWD* SE25 ....45 P5
Olive Rd *EA* W5 ....17 K1
  WIM/MER SW19 ....43 N1
Oliver Rd *ASC* SL5 ....34 B5
  HORS RH12 ....191 P9
  NWMAL KT3 ....42 A1
  SUT SM1 ....61 P3
Olivier Rd *CRAWE* RH10 ....177 N6
Ollerton *BRAK* RG12 ....32 C9
Olley Cl *WLGTN* SM6 ....62 G6
Olveston Wk *MRDN* SM4 ....43 P7
Olyffe Dr *BECK* BR3 ....47 J2
Olympia Wy *WKENS* W14 ....19 J1
Omega Rd *WOKN/KNAP* GU21...72 B4
Omega Wy *EGH* TW20 ....36 C2
One Tree La *FSTH* SE23 ....31 K2
One Tree Hill Rd *RGUE* GU4 ..112 F7
Ongar Cl *ADL/WDHM* KT15 ....55 H5
Ongar Hi *ADL/WDHM* KT15 ....55 J5
Ongar Pl *ADL/WDHM* KT15 ....55 J6
Ongar Rd *ADL/WDHM* KT15 ....55 J4
  FUL/PGN SW6 ....19 L3
Onslow Av *BELMT* SM2 ....61 L6
  RCH/KEW TW9 ....26 D2
Onslow Cl *WOKS/MYFD* GU22 ...11 H1
Onslow Crs
  WOKS/MYFD GU22 ....11 H1
Onslow Dr *ASC* SL5 ....34 A1
Onslow Gdns *SAND/SEL* CR2 ...82 A4
  SKENS SW7 ....19 P3
  THDIT KT7 ....40 E9
  WLGTN SM6 ....62 E6
Onslow Ms East *SKENS* SW7 ...19 P3
Onslow Ms West
  SKENS SW7 *..........19 P2
Onslow Rd *ASC* SL5 ....35 H4
  CROY/NA CR0 ....45 J8
  GU GU1 ....7 F3
  NWMAL KT3 ....42 D5
  RCHPK/HAM TW10 ....26 C3
  WOT/HER KT12 ....57 J3
Onslow Sq *SKENS* SW7 ....19 P2
Onslow St *GU* GU1 ....6 D5
Ontario Cl *HORL* RH6..........160 B2

Ontario Wy *LIPH* GU30..........182 F7
Openfields *BOR* GU35..........164 B5
Openview *WAND/EARL* SW18 ...28 F4
Opladen Wy *BRAK* RG12 ....32 E6
Opossum Wy *HSLWW* TW4 ......15 L8
Opus Pk *GU* GU1 *..........112 B1
The Orangery
  RCHPK/HAM TW10 ....26 B5
Oratory La *CHEL* SW3 * 19 P3
Orbain Rd *FUL/PGN* SW6 ....19 J5
Orbit Cl *EWKG* RG40 ....48 D3
Orchard Av *ADL/WDHM* KT15...55 K9
  ASHF TW15 ....23 K9
  CROY/NA CR0 ....64 E1
  EBED/NFELT TW14 ....23 N1
  HEST TW5 ....15 N5
  MTCM CR4 ....44 C7
  NWMAL KT3 ....42 C3
  THDIT KT7 ....40 G9
Orchard Cl *ASHF* TW15 ....23 J9
  ASHTD KT21 ....77 K9
  ASHV GU12 ....109 J1
  BNSTD SM7 ....79 M3
  CHOB/PIR GU24 ....52 D5
  EDEN TN8 ....144 F3
  EHSLY KT24 ....95 H4
  FARN GU14 ....88 C7
  FNM GU9 ....108 C8
  FSTH SE23 ....31 K2
  GU GU1 ....112 F5
  HOR/WEW KT19 * 59 P5
  HORL RH6 ....140 B9
  LHD/OX KT22 ....96 D2
  MFD/CHID GU8 ....129 M9
  RGUW GU3 ....110 B5
  RYNPK SW20 ....42 G5
  WOKS/MYFD GU22 ....11 K2
  WOT/HER KT12 ....39 J8
Orchard Cottages
  KUTN/CMB KT2 * 9 H3
Orchard Ct *BRAK* RG12 * 32 E3
  WLGTN SM6 * 62 D4
  WPK KT4 * 42 G9
Orchard Dr *EDEN* TN8 ....144 F3
  RFNM GU10 ....146 C1
  WEY KT13 ....56 C1
Orchard End *CTHM* CR3 ....101 N2
  GT/LBKH KT23 ....96 C4
  RFNM GU10 ....146 C2
  WEY KT13 ....56 E1
Orchardfield Rd *GODL* GU7 ....131 M9
Orchard Gdns *ALDT* GU11..........108 E6
  CHSGTN KT9 ....59 J4
  CRAN GU6..........171 J1
  EHSLY KT24 ....94 G7
  EPSOM KT18 ....78 A4
  SUT SM1 ....61 L4
Orchard Ga *ESH/CLAY* KT10 ....40 D9
  SHST GU47 ....49 M9
Orchard Gv *CROY/NA* CR0 ....46 E1
  PGE/AN SE20 ....46 A1
Orchard Hi *BFOR* GU20 ....52 D6
  HORS RH12..........189 M3
Orchard La *E/WMO/HCT* KT8 ....40 C5
  RYNPK SW20 ....42 G2
Orchard Lea Cl
  WOKS/MYFD GU22 ....73 J4
Orchardleigh *LHD/OX* KT22 ....97 H2
The Orchard Mains
  WOKS/MYFD GU22 ....72 A9
Orchard Ri *CROY/NA* CR0 ....46 E9
  KUTN/CMB KT2 ....42 A3
  RCHPK/HAM TW10 ....17 P9
Orchard Rd *BTFD* TW8 ....17 J4
  CHSGTN KT9 ....59 L3
  DORK RH4 ....117 H8
  FARN GU14 ....88 C3
  FNM GU9 ....108 C8
  GUW GU2 ....111 J2
  HORL RH6 ....160 C1
  HPTN TW12 ....24 G9
  HSLW TW3 ....16 D9
  KUT KT1 ....8 D5
  RCH/KEW TW9 ....17 N9
  REIG RH2 ....119 M5
  RGUE GU4 ....132 C2
  SAND/SEL CR2 ....82 B3
  SHGR GU5 ....132 D8
  SUN TW16 ....39 K1
  SUT SM1 ....61 L4
  SWTR RH13 ....192 D9
  TWK TW1 ....25 P2
  WDSR SL4 ....20 C3
Orchards Cl *BF/WBF* KT14 ....73 L3
Orchard Sq *WKENS* W14 * 19 J3
The Orchards *CRAWW* RH11 ...176 A6
Orchard St *CRAWE* RH10..........176 G5
  THDIT KT7 ....41 H9
The Orchard *CHSWK* W4 ....18 B2
  EW KT17 ....60 D8
  EWKG RG40 ....48 D3
  HORL RH6 ....159 K1
  LTWR GU18 ....52 B9
  RDKG RH5 ....137 J2
  SWTR RH13 ....192 C6
  VW GU25 ....36 D5
  WEY KT13 ....56 D5
  WOKN/KNAP GU21 ....71 P5
  WOKS/MYFD GU22 ....72 C4
Orchard Wy *ADL/WDHM* KT15...55 M4
  ALDT GU11 ....108 E6
  ASHF TW15 ....22 G5
  CBLY GU15 ....68 C6
  CROY/NA CR0 ....46 E9
  DORK RH4 ....117 H8
  ESH/CLAY KT10 ....58 C5
  KWD/TDW/WH KT20 ....98 G2
  OXTED RH8 ....123 N4
  REIG RH2 ....119 M5
  RGUW GU3 * 91 K4
  RGUW GU3 ....110 B5

Ontario Wy column continues → right column:
RPLY/SEND GU23 ....92 G5
  SUT SM1 ....61 P3
Orchid Cl *CHSGTN* KT9 ....59 J6
Orchid Ct *EGH* TW20 * 21 N7
Orchid Dr *CHOB/PIR* GU24 ....70 G4
Orde Cl *CRAWE* RH10..........177 N2
Ordnance Cl *FELT* TW13 ....24 B5
Ordnance Rd *ALDT* GU11..........108 F3
Oregano Wy *GUW* GU2 ....91 N9
Oregon Av *GU* GU1 ....112 G2
Oregon Wk *EWKG* RG40 ....48 B2
Orestan La *EHSLY* KT24 ....95 L7
Orford Gdns *TWK* TW1 ....25 N5
Orford Rd *CRAWE* RH10..........177 M2
  MTCM CR4 ....44 F5
Oriel Dr *BARN* SW13 ....18 G4
Oriel Rd *CBLY* GU15 ....68 A1
Oriental Cl *WOKS/MYFD* GU22..11 F3
Oriental Rd *ASC* SL5 ....34 D5
  WOKS/MYFD GU22 ....11 F4
Orion *BRAK* RG12 ....32 C9
Orlando Gdns
  HOR/WEW KT19 ....60 B8
Orltons La *HORS* RH12..........175 L1
Ormanton Rd *SYD* SE26 ....31 H7
Ormathwaites Cnr
  BNFD RG42 ....32 G1
Orme Cottages *GDST* RH9 * ..122 D6
Ormeley Rd *BAL* SW12 ....29 L4
Orme Rd *KUT* KT1 ....41 P3
  SUT SM1 ....61 M5
Ormerod Gdns *MTCM* CR4 ....44 C2
Ormond Av *HPTN* TW12 ....40 B2
Ormond Crs *HPTN* TW12 ....40 B2
Ormond Dr *HPTN* TW12 ....40 B1
Ormonde Av *HOR/WEW* KT19 ..60 B7
Ormonde Pl *WEY* KT13 * 56 F5
Ormonde Rd *GODL* GU7..........131 L7
  MORT/ESHN SW14 ....18 A8
  WOKN/KNAP GU21 ....72 A5
Ormond Rd
  RCHPK/HAM TW10 ....26 C1
Ormsby *BELMT* SM2 * 61 M6
Ormside Wy *REDH* RH1 ....120 D1
Orpin Rd *REDH* RH1 ....120 E1
Orpwood Cl *HPTN* TW12 ....24 G8
Orville Rd *BTSEA* SW11 ....19 P7
Orwell Cl *FARN* GU14 ....68 A3
Orwell Gdns *REIG* RH2..........119 N7
Osborne Av
  STWL/WRAY TW19..........23 H4
Osborne Cl *BECK* BR3 ....46 E5
  FELT TW13 ....24 E8
Osborne Dr *FLEETS* GU52 ....87 H8
  LTWR GU18 ....52 A9
Osborne Gdns *THHTH* CR7 ....45 L3
Osborne La *BNFD* RG42 ....32 A2
Osborne Ms *WDSR* SL4 ....21 H1
Osborne Pl *SUT* SM1 ....61 P4
Osborne Rd *CBLY* GU15 ....68 F3
  EGH TW20 ....21 N9
  FARN GU14 ....88 E7
  HSLW TW3 ....15 P8
  KUTN/CMB KT2 ....41 L1
  REDH RH1 ....120 C2
  THHTH CR7 ....45 L3
  WOT/HER KT12 ....39 J9
Osborne Ter *TOOT* SW17 * 29 K8
Osborne Wy *CHSGTN* KT9 ....59 M4
Osborn La *FSTH* SE23 ....31 M3
Osborn Rd *FNM* GU9..........127 P1
Osier Pl *EGH* TW20 ....21 P9
Osiers Rd *WAND/EARL* SW18 ...19 L9
Osier Wy *BNSTD* SM7 ....79 J3
  MTCM CR4 ....44 B6
Osman Rd *HMSMTH* W6 * 18 G1
Osmani's Cl *BNFD* RG42 ....33 K1
Osmond Gdns *WLGTN* SM6 ...62 E4
Osmunda Bank *EGRIN* RH19 .162 D6
Osmund Cl *CRAWE* RH10..........177 P5
Osnaburgh Hi *CBLY* GU15 ....68 D3
Osney Cl *CRAWW* RH11..........176 F6
Osney Wk *MRDN* SM4..........43 P7
Osprey Gdns *SAND/SEL* CR2 ...64 D8
Ospringe Cl *PGE/AN* SE20 ....46 C1
Ostade Rd *BRXS/STRHM* SW2 .30 A2
Osten Ms *SKENS* SW7 * 19 M1
Osterley Av *ISLW* TW7 ....16 E6
Osterley Crs *ISLW* TW7 ....16 E6
Osterley Gdns *THHTH* CR7 ....45 L2
Osterley La *ISLW* TW7 ....16 C1
Osterley Park Rd
  NWDGN UB2 *..........15 P1
Osterley Rd *ISLW* TW7 ....16 E5
Oswald Cl *BNFD* RG42 ....32 F1
  LHD/OX KT22 ....96 C4
Oswald Rd *BAL* SW12 ....33 H1
Otford Cl *CRAWW* RH11..........194 F2
  PGE/AN SE20 ....46 C2
Othen Crs *BROCKY* SE4 ....31 N2
Othello Gv *BNFD* RG42 ....32 G2
Otterbourne Pl
  EGRIN RH19 *..........180 A2
Otterbourne Rd *CROY/NA* CR0...2 C3
Otterburn Gdns *ISLW* TW7 ....16 F5
Otterburn St *TOOT* SW17 ....29 J9
  CWTH RG45 ....54 C5
Otterden St *CAT* SE6 ....31 P9
Ottermead La *CHERT* KT16 ....54 C5
Otto Cl *SYD* SE26 ....31 J4
Ottways Av *ASHTD* KT21 ....77 K8
Ottways La *ASHTD* KT21 ....77 L8
Otway Cl *CRAWW* RH11..........176 C7
Ouseley Rd *BAL* SW12 ....29 J4
  STWL/WRAY TW19..........21 H5
Outdowns *EHSLY* KT24..........115 K1
Outram Pl *WEY* KT13 ....56 E3
Outram Rd *CROY/NA* CR0 ....3 K3
Outwood La
  KWD/TDW/WH KT20 ....99 M2
  REDH RH1 ....121 M5

Oval Rd CROY/NA CR0 ....3 F3
The Oval BNSTD SM7 ....79 L3
  GODL GU2 ....131 M6
  GUW GU2 ....111 N6
  RGUW GU3 ....111 H4
Ovenden Rd RSEV TN14 ....85 P9
Overbrae BECK BR3 ....31 P9
Overbrook EHSLY KT24 ....94 D9
  GODL GU7 ....131 N8
Overbury Av BECK BR3 ....47 H4
Overbury Crs CROY/NA CR0 ....65 J8
Overdale ASHTD KT21 ....77 J5
  RDKG RH5 ....117 J6
  REDH RH1 ....121 L4
Overdale Av NWMAL KT3 ....42 A3
Overdale Ri FRIM GU16 ....68 G5
Overdale Rd EA W5 * 17 J1
Overdene Dr CRAWW RH11 ....176 D5
Overdown Rd CAT SE6 ....31 P7
Overford Cl CRAN GU6 ....171 H1
Overford Dr CRAN GU6 ....171 H1
Overhill WARL CR6 ....82 C8
Overhill Cottages
  MTCM CR4 * 44 C3
Overhill Rd EDUL SE22 ....31 H3
  ISLW TW7 ....16 F6
Overhill Wy BECK BR3 ....47 K6
Overlord Cl CBLY GU15 ....50 E9
Overstand Cl BECK BR3 ....46 G6
Overstone Gdns
  CROY/NA CR0 ....46 F8
Overstone Rd HMSMTH W6 ....18 G2
Overthorpe Cl
  WOKN/KNAP GU21 ....71 L6
Overton Cl ALDT GU11 ....108 E3
  ISLW TW7 ....16 F6
Overton Rd BELMT SM2 ....61 L6
Overton Shaw EGRIN RH19 ....162 D9
Overton's Yd CROY/NA CR0 ....2 C5
Oveton Wy GT/LBKH KT23 ....96 A6
Ovett Cl NRWD SE19 ....30 F9
Ovington Ct
  WOKN/KNAP GU21 ....71 M5
Owen Cl CROY/NA CR0 ....45 M6
Owen Pl LHD/OX KT22 * 97 H2
Owen Rd BFOR GU20 ....52 D4
  GODL GU7 ....131 M7
Owens Wy FSTH SE23 ....31 M3
Owlbeech Wy SWTR RH13 ....192 E6
Owl Cl SAND/SEL CR2 ....64 D8
Owletts CRAWE RH10 ....177 N4
Owlscastle Cl HORS RH12 ....192 C5
Owlsmoor Rd SHST GU47 ....49 P6
Ownstead Gdns
  SAND/SEL CR2 ....63 P9
Ownsted Hl CROY/NA CR0 ....65 J9
Oxberry Av FUL/PGN SW6 ....19 J7
Oxdowne Cl COB KT11 ....76 B3
Oxenden Cl RFNM GU10 ....108 G6
Oxenden Rd RFNM GU10 ....108 G6
Oxenhope BRAK RG12 ....32 C5
Oxford Av HEST TW5 ....16 A3
  HYS/HAR UB3 ....15 H5
  RYNPK SW20 ....43 J5
Oxford Cl ASHF TW15 ....38 E1
  MTCM CR4 ....44 E4
Oxford Crs NWMAL KT3 ....42 B7
Oxford Gdns CHSWK W4 ....17 N3
Oxford Ga WKENS W14 * 19 J2
Oxford Rd CAR SM5 ....62 A5
  CRAWE RH10 ....177 J9
  FARN GU14 ....88 E6
  HPTN TW12 ....25 L8
  NRWD SE19 ....30 E9
  PUT/ROE SW15 ....19 J9
  REDH RH1 ....120 A7
  SHST GU47 ....50 A7
  SWTR RH13 ....192 D8
Oxford Rd North CHSWK W4 ....17 P3
Oxford Rd South CHSWK W4 ....17 N3
Oxford Rw SUN TW16 * 39 L4
Oxford Ter GU GU1 ....7 F6
Oxford Ter FELT TW13 ....24 E7
Oxleigh Cl WWMAL KT3 ....42 C6
Oxshott Ri COB KT11 ....75 N3
Oxshott Rd LHD/OX KT22 ....76 F5
Oxshott Wy COB KT11 ....75 N4
Oxted Cl MTCM CR4 ....43 P4
Oxted Gn MFD/CHID GU8 ....149 M5
Oxted Rd GDST RH9 ....122 F2
Oxtoby Wy
  STRHM/NOR SW16 ....44 F2
Oyster La BF/WBF KT14 ....55 P9

P

Pacific Cl EBED/NFELT TW14 ....24 A4
Packway FNM GU9 ....128 A6
Padbrook OXTED RH8 ....103 N9
Padbury Cl
  EBED/NFELT TW14 ....23 N4
Paddenswick Rd
  HMSMTH W6 ....18 E1
Paddock Cl CBLY GU15 ....69 J2
  MFD/CHID GU8 * 168 B2
  OXTED RH8 ....123 M2
  RDKG RH5 ....137 K9
  SYD SE26 ....31 L7
  WPK KT4 ....42 F9
Paddock Gdns EGRIN RH19 ....180 D4
  NRWD SE19 ....30 F9
Paddock Gv RDKG RH5 ....137 K9
Paddockhurst Rd
  CRAWW RH11 ....176 D6

Paddocks Cl COB KT11 ....75 L3
Paddocks Md
  WOKN/KNAP GU21 ....71 L5
Paddocks Rd RGUE GU4 ....112 E1
The Paddocks EA W5 * 17 K1
  GT/LBKH KT23 ....96 B6
  RGUW GU3 ....110 C5
  WEY KT13 * 56 A9
  WEY KT13 * 56 G2
Paddocks Wy ASHTD KT21 ....77 L7
  CHERT KT16 ....37 M9
The Paddock
  BH/WHM TN16 ....104 C6
  BOR GU35 ....164 B6
  BRAK RG12 ....32 E4
  CRAN GU6 ....153 P8
  CRAWE RH10 ....177 N4
  CWTH RG45 ....49 L3
  DORK RH4 ....116 B8
  GODL GU7 ....150 E1
  GSHT GU26 ....165 K7
  GU GU1 ....113 H4
  HASM GU27 ....184 B2
  RFNM GU10 * 127 J6
  VW GU25 ....36 C7
Paddock Wk WARL CR6 ....82 B8
Paddock Wy HASM GU27 ....167 H9
  LIPH GU30 ....182 E5
  OXTED RH8 ....123 M2
  WOKN/KNAP GU21 ....72 D4
Padley Cl CHSGTN KT9 ....59 M4
Padstow Cl DTCH/LGLY SL3 * 12 C1
Padstow Wk
  EBED/NFELT TW14 ....24 A5
Padua Rd PGE/AN SE20 ....46 C2
Padwick Rd SWTR RH13 ....192 E8
Pageant Wk CROY/NA CR0 ....3 G5
Page Cl FELT TW13 ....24 E5
Page Crs CROY/NA CR0 ....63 K4
Pagehurst Rd CROY/NA CR0 ....46 A8
Pages Cl REBED/NFELT TW14 ....23 N2
Pages Yd CHSWK W4 * 18 C4
Paget Av SUT SM1 ....61 P2
Paget Cl CBLY GU15 ....69 K1
  HPTN TW12 ....25 N5
Paget La ISLW TW7 ....16 D8
Paget Pl KUTN/CMB KT2 * 27 H9
  THDIT KT7 ....40 F9
Paget Rd DTCH/LGLY SL3 ....12 D2
Pagewood Cl CRAWE RH10 ....177 N7
Pagoda Av RCH/KEW TW9 ....17 N8
Pain's Cl MTCM CR4 ....44 G4
Pains Cl COB KT11 * 75 H3
  OXTED RH8 ....124 A3
Pains Hill Pk COB KT11 * 75 H2
Paisley Rd CAR SM5 ....43 P9
Pakenham Cl BAL SW12 ....29 K4
Pakenham Rd BRAK RG12 ....32 F8
Palace Dr WEY KT13 ....56 D2
Palace Gdns West WEY KT13 ....56 D2
Palace Gn CROY/NA CR0 ....64 F6
Palace Ms FUL/PGN SW6 * 19 K5
Palace Rd ADL/WDHM KT15 ....55 M7
  BH/WHM TN16 ....104 E1
  BMLY BR1 ....47 P2
  BRXS/STRHM SW2 ....30 A4
  E/WMO/HCT KT8 ....40 C4
  KUT KT1 ....41 K5
  NRWD SE19 ....45 P1
Palace Sq NRWD SE19 ....45 P1
Palace Vw BMLY BR1 ....47 P4
  CROY/NA CR0 ....64 F3
Pale La HTWY RG27 ....86 A5
Palemead Cl FUL/PGN SW6 ....19 H6
Palestine Gv WIM/MER SW19 ....43 P2
Palewell Common Dr
  MORT/ESHN SW14 ....27 J1
Palewell Pk
  MORT/ESHN SW14 ....27 J1
Palgrave Rd SHB W12 ....18 D1
Pallingham Dr CRAWE RH10 ....177 M8
Palliser Rd WKENS W14 ....19 J3
Palmer Av CHEAM SM3 ....60 G3
Palmer Cl EKRG RG40 ....49 J1
  HEST TW5 ....16 A6
  HORL RH6 ....140 B8
  REDH RH1 ....120 C6
  WWKM BR4 ....65 K1
Palmer Rd CRAWE RH10 ....177 M6
  KUT KT1 * 8 B5
Palmer's La CRAWE RH10 ....177 M6
Palmersfield Rd BNSTD SM7 ....79 L3
Palmers Gv E/WMO/HCT KT8 ....40 A5
Palmers Rd
  MORT/ESHN SW14 ....18 A4
  STRHM/NOR SW16 ....45 H3
Palmerston Cl FARN GU14 ....87 P4
  WOKN/KNAP GU21 ....72 E3
Palmerston Gv
  WIM/MER SW19 ....43 L1
Palmerston Rd ACT W3 ....18 A1
  CAR SM5 ....62 B3
  CROY/NA CR0 ....45 M6
  HSLWW TW4 ....16 C6
  MORT/ESHN SW14 ....18 A4
  SUT SM1 ....61 N4
  WHTN TW2 ....25 N2
  WIM/MER SW19 ....43 L1
Palmers Whf KUT KT1 * 8 B5
Palm Gv EA W5 ....17 L1
Pampisford Rd PUR/KEN CR8 ....63 J9
Pams Wy HOR/WEW KT19 ....60 B4
Pankhurst Cl ISLW TW7 ....16 F8
Pankhurst Dr BRAK RG12 ....32 F6
Pankridge St RFNM GU10 ....106 D7
Panmuir Rd RYNPK SW20 ....42 F2
Panmure Rd SYD SE26 ....31 J6
Pannell Cl EGRIN RH19 ....180 C2

Pannells RFNM GU10 ....127 P8
Pannells Cl CHERT KT16 ....37 K9
Pannells Ct GU GU1 ....7 G5
Pan's Gdns CBLY GU15 ....69 H4
Pantile Rd WEY KT13 ....56 F3
Pantile Rw DTCH/LGLY SL3 ....12 E2
Pantiles CBR GU35 * 164 E6
Pantiles Cl WOKN/KNAP GU21 ....71 P7
Panton Cl CROY/NA CR0 ....2 B1
Papercourt La
  RPLY/SEND GU23 ....93 K2
Paper Ms DORK RH4 ....117 H6
Papermill Cl CAR SM5 ....62 C3
Papworth Wy
  BRXS/STRHM SW2 ....30 B3
Parade Cl RPLY/SEND GU23 ....92 G3
Parade Ct EHSLY KT24 * 94 C6
Parade Ms BRXS/STRHM SW2 ....30 C5
The Parade ASHV GU12 * 109 J2
  BH/WHM TN16 * 104 A1
  BTSEA SW11 * 19 P9
  CAR SM5 * 62 B4
  CRAWE RH10 ....177 H4
  CROY/NA CR0 ....44 G7
  CROY/NA CR0 ....63 H4
  EGRIN RH19 * 162 A9
  EPSOM KT18 ....78 B2
  ESH/CLAY KT10 ....58 E5
  FRIM GU16 * 68 E8
  GUW GU2 ....91 P9
  HORS RH12 * 191 P7
  KUT KT1 * 8 E4
  KWD/TDW/WH KT20 * 79 J8
  LHD/OX KT22 * 97 H2
  PGE/AN SE20 * 46 C2
  RCH/KEW TW9 * 17 N8
  STA TW18 * 22 A8
  SUN TW16 ....39 H1
  SUT SM1 * 61 K2
  SYD SE26 * 31 J7
  VW GU25 * 36 B4
  WOKN/KNAP GU21 * 10 C4
Paradise Rd
  RCHPK/HAM TW10 ....26 D1
Paragon Gv BRYLDS KT5 ....41 M7
Parbury Ri CHSGTN KT9 ....59 L5
Parbury Rd FSTH SE23 ....31 M2
Parchmore Rd THHTH CR7 ....45 K3
Parchmore Wy THHTH CR7 ....45 K3
Pares Cl WOKN/KNAP GU21 ....10 A1
Parfitts Cl FNM GU9 ....4 C4
Parfour Dr PUR/KEN CR8 ....81 L5
Parfrey St HMSMTH W6 ....18 G4
Parham Rd CRAWW RH11 ....176 C4
Parish Cl ASHV GU12 ....109 K5
  FNM GU9 ....107 L8
Parish La CRAWE RH10 ....195 J4
  SYD SE26 ....31 L9
Parish Rd FARN GU14 ....88 D7
Park Av CAR SM5 ....62 C5
  CBLY GU15 ....68 G7
  CTHM CR3 ....101 N4
  EDEN TN8 ....144 F3
  EGH TW20 ....36 G9
  HSLW TW3 ....25 J2
  MFD/CHID GU8 ....130 C8
  MORT/ESHN SW14 ....18 B9
  MTCM CR4 ....44 D1
  REDH RH1 ....140 D4
  SHPTN TW17 ....38 G4
  STA TW18 ....22 C9
  STWL/WRAY TW19 ....21 J1
  WWKM BR4 ....65 J1
Park Av East EW KT17 ....60 E5
Park Av West EW KT17 ....60 E5
Park Barn Dr GUW GU2 ....111 L4
Park Barn East GUW GU2 ....111 M4
Park Barn Pde GUW GU2 ....111 L4
Park Cha GODL GU7 ....150 D2
  GU GU1 ....7 G3
Park Cl ADL/WDHM KT15 ....55 M8
  BRKHM/BTCW RH3 ....137 P1
  CAR SM5 ....62 B5
  EGH TW20 ....21 P8
  ESH/CLAY KT10 ....58 B4
  HPTN TW12 ....25 N9
  HSLW TW3 ....25 K1
  KUTN/CMB KT2 ....9 D4
  LHD/OX KT22 ....96 G1
  OXTED RH8 ....103 M8
  WEY KT13 ....57 H1
  WKENS W14 ....19 K1
Park Copse RDKG RH5 ....117 K7
Park Corner Dr EHSLY KT24 ....94 G8
Park Ct BF/WBF KT14 * 73 L2
  DUL SE21 ....30 E6
  NWMAL KT3 ....42 B5
  SYD SE26 * 31 J9
  WOKS/MYFD GU22 ....10 E6
Park Crs ASC SL5 ....34 A4
  EGH TW20 ....21 P8
  FROW RH18 ....181 M9
  WHTN TW2 ....25 M3
Park Dr ACT W3 ....18 A1
  ASC SL5 ....34 F8
  CRAN GU6 ....153 J8
  MORT/ESHN SW14 ....27 J1
  SHGR GU5 ....132 D7
  WEY KT13 ....56 G3
  WOKS/MYFD GU22 ....10 E6
Park End BMLY BR1 ....47 N2
Parker Cl CAR SM5 ....62 B5
Parker Ct CRAWE RH10 ....177 N6
Parke Rd BARN SW13 ....18 E6
  SUN TW16 ....39 J5
Parker Rd CROY/NA CR0 ....2 D6
Parkers Cl ASHTD KT21 ....77 L8
Parker's Hl ASHTD KT21 ....77 L8
Parker's La ASHTD KT21 ....77 M8
Park Farm Cl HORS RH12 ....192 C3

Park Farm Rd
  KUTN/CMB KT2 ....41 L1
Parkfield GODL GU7 ....150 D2
  HORS RH12 ....192 D7
Parkfield Av FELT TW13 ....24 B6
  MORT/ESHN SW14 ....18 C9
Parkfield Cl CRAWW RH11 ....176 C5
Parkfield Crs FELT TW13 ....24 B6
Parkfield Pde FELT TW13 * 24 B6
Parkfield Rd FELT TW13 ....24 B6
Parkfields CROY/NA CR0 ....46 F9
  LHD/OX KT22 ....58 D9
  PUT/ROE SW15 ....18 G9
  YTLY GU46 ....67 H3
Parkfields Av RYNPK SW20 ....42 F2
  CAR SM5 ....62 C5
Parkfields Cl CAR SM5 ....62 C5
Parkfields Rd KUTN/CMB KT2 ....26 E8
Park Gdns KUTN/CMB KT2 ....26 E8
Parkgate Cl KUTN/CMB KT2 ....9 C9
Park Gate Ct HPTN TW12 * 25 K8
  WOKS/MYFD GU22 * 10 D6
Parkgate Gdns
  MORT/ESHN SW14 ....27 J1
Parkgate Rd CAR SM5 ....62 F2
  RDKG RH5 ....156 C2
  REIG RH2 ....119 M6
Park Gn GT/LBKH KT23 ....96 A4
Park Hall Rd DUL SE21 ....30 E6
  REIG RH2 ....119 L3
Parkham St BTSEA SW11 ....19 P6
Park HI CAR SM5 ....62 B5
  CLAP SW4 ....29 N1
  FLEETS GU52 ....106 F1
  FSTH SE23 ....31 J5
  RCHPK/HAM TW10 ....26 E4
Parkhill Cl BLKW GU17 ....67 P4
Park Hill Cl CAR SM5 ....62 A4
Park Hill Ri CROY/NA CR0 ....3 J5
Parkhill Rd BLKW GU17 ....67 P4
  CROY/NA CR0 ....63 N3
  EW KT17 ....60 D9
  HAYES BR2 ....47 N3
Park Hill Rd CROY/NA CR0 ....3 J6
  WLGTN SM6 ....62 D6
  WOKS/MYFD GU22 ....11 G4
Park Horsley EHSLY KT24 * 95 H5
Park House Dr REIG RH2 ....119 K7
Park House Gdns TWK TW1 ....26 B1
Parkhurst HOR/WEW KT19 ....60 B1
Parkhurst Flds RFNM GU10 ....165 J2
Parkhurst Gv HORL RH6 ....140 A9
Parkhurst Rd GUW GU2 ....111 N4
  HORL RH6 ....140 A9
  SUT SM1 ....61 P3

Park La ASHTD KT21 ....77 M7
  CAR SM5 ....62 C4
  CBLY GU15 * 68 E3
  CHEAM SM3 ....61 J5
  COUL/CHIP CR5 ....100 F1
  CROY/NA CR0 ....2 E4
  DTCH/LGLY SL3 ....12 B8
  HYS/HAR UB3 ....15 J2
  LING RH7 ....143 L8
  MFD/CHID GU8 ....166 F4
  RCH/KEW TW9 ....17 K9
  RDKG RH5 ....115 J8
  REIG RH2 ....119 J3
  RGUE GU4 ....113 H2
  TEDD TW11 ....25 N9
Park La East REIG RH2 ....119 J4
Park Lawn Rd WEY KT13 ....56 G2
Parkleigh Rd WIM/MER SW19 ....43 M3
Park Ley Rd CTHM CR3 ....82 D9
Parkleys RCHPK/HAM TW10 ....26 C7
Parkleys Pde
  KUTN/CMB KT2 * 26 C7
Parklion Av EPSOM KT18 * 78 B2
Parkmead PUT/ROE SW15 ....27 N2
Park Ms STWL/WRAY TW19 ....23 J3
Parkpale La
  BRKHM/BTCW RH3 ....137 N3
Park Pde ACT W3 * 17 N1
  CRAN GU6 * 153 J8
Park Pl ACT W3 ....18 A2
  BMLY BR1 * 47 P2
  FLEETS GU52 ....106 F1
  HORS RH12 * 192 B6
  HPTN TW12 ....25 N9
  WOKS/MYFD GU22 ....10 E6
Park Ri HORS RH12 ....192 A6
  LHD/OX KT22 ....96 G1
Park Rise Cl LHD/OX KT22 ....97 H1
Park Rise Rd FSTH SE23 ....31 M4
Park Rd ALDT GU11 ....108 D7
  ASHF TW15 ....23 L8
  ASHTD KT21 ....77 K6
  BECK BR3 ....46 F1
  BMLY BR1 ....47 P2
  BNSTD SM7 ....79 N5
  BRAK RG12 ....32 D4
  BRYLDS KT5 ....41 M7
  CBLY GU15 ....68 E5
  CHEAM SM3 ....61 J5
  CHSWK W4 ....18 B4

  CTHM CR3 ....101 N3
  E/WMO/HCT KT8 ....40 C5
  E/WMO/HCT KT8 ....41 J2
  EGH TW20 ....21 M7
  EGRIN RH19 ....162 D6
  EGRIN RH19 ....180 C2
  ESH/CLAY KT10 ....58 B3
  FARN GU14 ....88 G6
  FELT TW13 ....24 E7
  FNM GU9 ....127 P1
  FROW RH18 ....181 M9
  GODL GU7 ....131 K7
  GU GU1 ....6 E3
  HASM GU27 ....184 D4
  HORL RH6 ....160 D3
  HORS RH12 ....193 L1
  HPTN TW12 ....25 K8
  HSLW TW3 ....25 J3
  ISLW TW7 ....17 H6
  KUT KT1 ....8 A3
  KUTN/CMB KT2 ....26 E8
  LING RH7 ....143 L2
  NWMAL KT3 ....42 B5
  OXTED RH8 ....103 M8
  PUR/KEN CR8 ....81 L4
  RCHPK/HAM TW10 ....26 E4
  REDH RH1 ....120 B3
  SHGR GU5 ....134 B3
  SHPTN TW17 ....38 C9
  SHST GU47 ....67 N1
  SNWD SE25 ....45 N5
  STWL/WRAY TW19 ....21 K1
  SUN TW16 ....39 K1
  SWTR RH13 ....190 E1
  TEDD TW11 ....40 F1
  TWK TW1 ....26 B2
  WARL CR6 ....83 L3
  WIM/MER SW19 ....43 P1
  WLCTN SM6 ....62 C3
  WOKS/MYFD GU22 ....11 G4
Park Rd North CHSWK W4 ....18 B4
Park Rw FNM GU9 ....5 F2
Parkshot RCH/KEW TW9 ....17 K9
Park Side ADL/WDHM KT15 ....55 M8
Parkside BECK BR3 * 47 H3
  CHEAM SM3 ....61 J5
  CRAWE RH10 ....177 H5
  EGRIN RH19 ....180 B2
  FNM GU9 ....107 N8
  HPTN TW12 ....25 L8
  WIM/MER SW19 ....28 A8
Parkside Cl EHSLY KT24 ....95 H5
  PGE/AN SE20 ....46 C1
Parkside Crs BRYLDS KT5 ....42 A7
Parkside Gdns
  COUL/CHIP CR5 ....80 D6
  WIM/MER SW19 ....28 A7
Parkside Ms HORS RH12 * 192 C8
  WARL CR6 ....82 C8
Parkside Pl EHSLY KT24 ....94 G5
Parkside Rd ASC SL5 ....34 C7
  HSLW TW3 ....25 J1
Parkstead Rd PUT/ROE SW15 ....27 M1
Parkstone Dr CBLY GU15 ....68 E4
Park St BAGS GU19 ....51 N6
  CBLY GU15 ....68 E2
  CROY/NA CR0 ....2 D3
  DTCH/LGLY SL3 ....13 H6
  HORS RH12 ....192 C6
  SWTR RH13 ....190 D7
  TEDD TW11 ....25 M9
Park Ter CAR SM5 * 62 A2
  RSEV TN14 * 105 P4
  WPK KT4 ....42 E9
Park Ter East SWTR RH13 ....192 C9
Park Ter West SWTR RH13 ....192 C9
The Park CAR SM5 ....62 B4
  GT/LBKH KT23 ....96 A5
Parkthorne Rd BAL SW12 ....29 N3
Park Vw ADL/WDHM KT15 * 55 N4
  BAGS GU19 ....51 M6
  CRAWW RH11 ....176 F6
  EW KT17 * 78 D2
  GT/LBKH KT23 ....96 A5
  HORL RH6 ....159 K1
  NWMAL KT3 ....42 D4
Park View Ct
  WOKS/MYFD GU22 ....10 E7
Park View Dr MTCM CR4 ....43 P3
Park View Gdns
  EGRIN RH19 ....162 C9
Parkview Rd CROY/NA CR0 ....46 A9
Park View Rd CTHM CR3 ....102 F2
  REDH RH1 ....140 C3
Parkview V RGUE GU4 ....112 G2
Parkville Rd FUL/PGN SW6 ....19 K5
Park Wk ASHTD KT21 ....77 L8
Park Wy CRAWE RH10 ....177 M8
  E/WMO/HCT KT8 ....40 C4
  EBED/NFELT TW14 ....24 C3
  GT/LBKH KT23 ....96 A3
  HORS RH12 ....192 B9
Parkway CBLY GU15 ....68 E5
  CROY/NA CR0 ....65 J7
  CWTH RG45 ....49 L4
  DORK RH4 ....116 G6
  GU GU1 ....112 C4
  RYNPK SW20 ....43 H5
  WEY KT13 ....55 H5
The Parkway HEST TW5 ....15 L5
Parkwood BECK BR3 * 47 H3
Parkwood Av ESH/CLAY KT10 ....40 C9
Park Wood Cl BNSTD SM7 ....79 H4
Park Wood Gv SUN TW16 ....39 J4
Park Wood Rd BNSTD SM7 ....79 H4
Parkwood Rd
  BH/WHM TN16 ....104 C1
  ISLW TW7 ....16 F6
  REDH RH1 ....120 G4

WIM/MER SW19 ....28 C8
Park Wood Vw BNSTD SM7....78 G5
Park Works Rd REDH RH1.....121 H4
Parlaunt Rd DTCH/LGLY SL3 ...12 E1
  IVER SL0 ....13 H1
Parley Dr WOKN/KNAP GU21...72 A7
Parliamentary Rd
  CHOB/PIR GU24 ....90 A1
Parnell Cl SHB W12 ....18 F1
Parnell Gdns WEY KT13............96 B6
Parnham Av LTWR GU18 ....52 D9
Parr Av EW KT17 ....60 F7
Parr Cl LHD/OX KT22...................76 F9
Parris Cft RDKG RH5.................137 J1
Parrs Cl SAND/SEL CR2 ....63 M7
Parr's Pl HPTN TW12 ....40 A1
Parry Cl EW KT17 ....60 E6
  SWTR RH13 ....193 H6
Parry Dr WEY KT13......................56 E6
Parry Gn North
  DTCH/LGLY SL3 ....12 D2
Parry Gn South
  DTCH/LGLY SL3 ....12 E2
Parry Rd SNWD SE25 ....45 N4
Parsonage Cl WARL CR6 ....82 E5
Parsonage La DORK RH4..........116 G6
Parsonage Rd CRAN GU6.........152 G9
  EGH TW20 ....21 J8
  HORS RH12 ....192 D6
Parsonage Sq DORK RH4..........116 G6
Parsonage Wy FRIM GU16........68 G7
  HORS RH12 ....192 D6
Parsons Cl FLEETS GU52.........106 F1
  HASM GU27 ....18 M2
  HORL RH6...............................140 A9
Parsons Fld SHST GU47 ....49 M9
Parsonsfield Cl BNSTD SM7......78 H9
Parsonsfield Rd BNSTD SM7 ....79 H5
Parsons Gn FUL/PGN SW6 ....19 L6
  GU GU1 ....112 B3
  HASM GU27 ....184 D2
Parsons Green La
  FUL/PGN SW6 ....19 L6
Parsons La GSHT GU26 ....165 M5
Parson's Md CROY/NA CRO 2 B4
  E/WMO/HCT KT8 ....40 C4
Parthenia Rd FUL/PGN SW6 .....19 L6
Parthia Cl EPSOM KT18 ....78 F8
Partridge Av YTLY GU46............66 F2
Partridge Cl FRIM GU16 ....107 H6
  RFNM GU10..............................107 H6
Partridge Knoll
  PUR/KEN CR8 ....81 K1
Partridge La HORS RH12 ....175 K1
  RDKG RH5................................158 B9
  RDKG RH5................................157 L4
Partridge Md BNSTD SM7 ....78 G4
Partridge Pl CRAWE RH10 ......179 K5
Partridge Wy HPTN TW12 ....24 C9
Parvis Rd BF/WBF KT14 ....78 N1
Paschal Rd CBLY GU15 ....51 H9
Passfield Rd LIPH GU30 ....182 B2
Pastens Rd OXTED RH8 ....124 J2
Paston Cl WLGTN SM6 ....62 E2
The Pasture CRAWE RH10 ....177 M5
Pasture Wood Rd
  RDKG RH5................................135 M7
Patching Cl CRAWW RH11 ....176 C4
Patchings SWTR RH13 ....192 F7
Paterson Cl FRIM GU16 ....69 L5
Pater St KENS W8 ....19 L1
Pates Manor Dr
  EBED/NFELT TW14 ....23 N3
Pathfield MFD/CHID GU8 ....168 A7
Pathfield Cl HORS RH12 ....189 N3
Pathfield Rd HORS RH12 ....189 N3
  STRHM/NOR SW16 ....29 N9
Pathfields SHGR GU5 ....134 C2
Pathfields Cl HASM GU27 ....184 E3
Path Link CRAWE RH10 ....177 H4
Pathway WIM/MER SW19 ....43 M2
The Pathway
  RPLY/SEND GU23 ....93 K5
Patio Cl CLAP SW4......................29 N2
Patmore La WOT/HER KT12......57 H5
Patrick Gdns BNFD RG42............32 G1
Patrington Cl CRAWW RH11 ....176 D8
Par AV YTLY GU46......................66 C3
Pattenden Rd CAT SE6 ....31 N4
Patten Rd WAND/EARL SW18 ...29 H3
Patterdale Cl CRAWW RH11 ....176 B4
Patterson Rd NRWD SE19 ....30 C9
Paul Cl ALDT GU11 ....108 A6
Paul Gdns CROY/NA CRO 3 J4
Pauline Crs WHTN TW2 ....25 K4
Paul's Fld HTWY RG27 ....43 H9
Pauls Md CBLY GU15 ....143 L8
Paul's Pl ASHTD KT21 ....77 P8
Paultons Sq CHEL SW3 ....19 P4
Paultons St CHEL SW3 ....19 P4
The Pavement EA W5 * 17 L1
  TEDD TW11 * 41 H1
  WIM/MER SW19 * 27 J2
  WNWD SE27 * 30 D7
Pavilion Gdns STA TW18............37 M1
Pavilion Rd ALDT GU11..............87 N9
  KTBR SW1X 19 N2
The Pavilions End CBLY GU15 ...68 F5
The Pavilions CRAWW RH11 .....194 F4
Pavilion Wy EGRIN RH19 ....180 D3
Pawley Cl RFNM GU10 ....109 H7
Pawleyne Cl PGE/AN SE20 ....46 C2
Pawmers Md FLEETS GU52 .....106 E3
Pawson's Rd CROY/NA CRO 45 L7
Pax Cl CRAWW RH11 ....176 B7
Paxton Cl RCH/KEW TW9..........17 M7
  WOT/HER KT12 * 39 L8
Paxton Gdns
  WOKN/KNAP GU21 ....73 J2

Paxton Av WNWD SE27 ....30 F7
Paxton Rd BMLY BR1 ....47 N1
  CHSWK W4 ....18 C4
  FSTH SE23 ....31 M6
Payne Cl CRAWE RH10 ....177 N3
Paynesfield Av
  MORT/ESHN SW14 ....18 B8
Paynesfield Rd
  BH/WHM TN16 ....84 A9
Paynes Wk HMSMTH W6 ....19 J4
Peabody Av BELGR SW1V..........46 C9
Peabody Cottages
  HNHL SE24 * 30 D3
Peabody Est FUL/PGN SW6 * 19 L4
  HMSMTH W6 * 19 J4
  HNHL SE24 ....30 C3
Peabody Hl DUL SE21 ....30 C4
Peabody Rd FARN GU14.............88 F6
Peace Cl SNWD SE25 ....45 N5
Peacemaker Cl
  CRAWW RH11 ....176 B7
Peaches Cl BELMT SM2 ....61 J6
Peach Tree La FARN GU14 ....68 C9
Peacock Av
  EBED/NFELT TW14 ....23 N4
Peacock Gdns CROY/NA CRO....64 E8
Peakfield RFNM GU10 ....146 F5
Peak Hl SYD SE26.......................31 K7
Peak Hill Av SYD SE26 ....31 K7
Peak Hill Gdns SYD SE26 ....31 K7
Peak Rd GUW GU2 ....111 N2
Peaks Hl PUR/KEN CR8 ....62 G8
Peaks Hill Ri PUR/KEN CR8 ....62 G8
The Peak SYD SE26 ....31 K6
Peaked Rd CROY/NA CRO...........45 H7
Pear Av SHPTN TW17..................38 G4
Pearce Cl MTCM CR4 ....44 C3
Pearcefield Av FSTH SE23 ....31 K4
Pearfield Rd FSTH SE23 ....31 M6
Pearl Ct WOKN/KNAP GU21 ......71 L5
Pearmain Cl SHPTN TW17..........38 C4
Pear Av SHPTN TW17 * 38 C4
Pearscroft Ct FUL/PGN SW6 .....19 M7
Pearscroft Rd FUL/PGN SW6.....19 M7
Pearson Rd CRAWE RH10.........177 L5
Pears Rd HSLW TW3 ....16 D8
Pear Tree Av FLEETN GU51 ....86 F5
Pear Tree Cl ADL/WDHM KT15...55 L4
  MTCM CR4 ....44 A3
Peartree Cl SANL CR2 ....82 B3
Pear Tree Hl REDH RH1 * 140 C5
Pear Tree La REDH RH1 ....146 C1
Pear Tree Rd
  ADL/WDHM KT15......................55 L4
  ASHF TW15 ....23 M8
Pear Tree Rd HORS RH12..........192 C4
Peaslake La SHGR GU5 ....134 F7
Peat Common
  MFD/CHID GU8 ....148 D2
Peat Moor Cl FLEETN GU51 ....86 E5
Peatmoor Cl FLEETN GU51 ....86 E5
Peatmore Av
  WOKS/MYFD GU22 ....73 L5
Peatmore Cl
  WOKS/MYFD GU22 ....73 L5
Peatmore Dr CHOB/PIR GU24 ...90 C1
Pebble Cl
  KWD/TDW/WH KT20 ....114 E4
Pebble Hl EHSLY KT24 ....114 C4
Pebblehill Rd
  BRKHM/BTCW RH3 ....118 C5
Pebble La EPSOM KT18 ....97 N2
Peckarmans Wd SYD SE26.........31 H6
Peddlars Gv YTLY GU46.............67 J2
Peek Crs WIM/MER SW19 ....28 A8
Peeks Brook La HORL RH6 ....159 P5
Pegasus Av ASHV GU12 ....108 G3
Pegasus Ct BTFD TW8 * 17 M3
Pegasus Cl FUL/PGN SW6 ....19 L6
Pegasus Rd CROY/NA CRO.........63 J5
  FARN GU14 * 88 D9
  FARN GU14 * 68 D5
Pegasus Wy EGRIN RH19 ....162 F9
Peggotty Pl SHST GU47 ....50 A7
Pegg Rd HEST TW5 ....15 M5
Pegler Wy CRAWE RH10 ....176 G5
Pegwell Cl CRAWW RH11 ....176 C7
Peket Cl STA TW18 ....37 J2
Pelham Ct CRAWW RH11 ....176 F3
  HORS RH12 * 192 A8
Pelham Dr CRAWW RH11 ....176 D9
Pelham Pl CRAWW RH11 ....176 D9
  RFNM GU10.............................127 L1
Pelham Rd PGE/AN SE20 ....46 C3
  WIM/MER SW19 ....28 C5
Pelhams Cl ESH/CLAY KT10 ......58 A3
Pelham St SKENS SW7 ....19 P2
Pelhams Wk ESH/CLAY KT10 ....58 A2
Pelham Wy GT/LBKH KT23 ....96 H6
Pellant Rd FUL/PGN SW6 ....19 J5
Pellatt Rd EDUL SE22 ....30 G1
Pelling Hl WDSR SL4 ....20 A2
Pelton Av BELMT SM2 ....61 M8
Pemberley Cha
  HOR/WEW KT19........................59 P4
Pemberley Cl
  HOR/WEW KT19........................59 P4
Pemberton Rd
  E/WMO/HCT KT8 ....40 C4
Pemberton Rd
  E/WMO/HCT KT8 ....40 C4
Pembley Gn CRAWE RH10 ....160 F9
Pembridge Av WHTN TW4..........24 G4
Pembridge Rd BKYLDS KT5.......41 P6
  WOT/HER KT12 * 57 M5
Pembroke Broadway
  CBLY GU15 ....68 E3
Pembroke Cl ASC SL5 ....34 D4
Pembroke Gdns KENS W8 ....19 K1
  WOKS/MYFD GU22 ....11 H5

Pembroke Gardens Cl
  KENS W8 ....19 K1
Pembroke Ms KENS W8 ....19 L1
Pembroke Pl ISLW TW7 ....16 E7
  KENS W8 ....19 L1
Pembroke Rd CRAWE RH10......177 M2
  ECT SW5 ....19 L2
  MTCM CR4 ....44 C3
  SNWD SE25 ....45 N5
  WOKS/MYFD GU22 ....11 H4
Pembroke Sq KENS W8 ....19 L1
Pembroke Wk KENS W8 ....19 L1
Pembrook Ms BTSEA SW11 * 19 P9
Pembury Av WPK KT4 ....42 E9
Pembury Cl COUL/CHIP CR5 ......80 C5
  HAYES BR2 ....47 M9
Pembury Pl HYS/HAR UB3 ....14 F4
Pembury Rd SNWD SE25 ....45 N5
Pemdevon Rd CROY/NA CRO 45 J4
Pemerich Cl HYS/HAR UB3 *......15 H3
Penard Rd NWDGN UB2 ....16 A1
Penates ESH/CLAY KT10.............58 D3
Penbury Rd NWDGN UB2 ....15 P3
Pendarves Rd RYNPK SW20 ....42 G2
Pendell Av HYS/HAR UB3 ....15 H5
Pendell Ms REDH RH1 * 120 B6
Pendell Rd REDH RH1 ....121 K2
Pendennis Cl BF/WBF KT14........73 L3
Pendennis Rd
  STRHM/NOR SW16 ....29 N7
Penderel Rd HSLW TW3 ....25 H1
Pendine Pl BRAK RG12 ....32 D6
Pendlebury BRAK RG12...............32 C8
Pendle Rd STRHM/NOR SW16....29 K9
Pendleton Cl REDH RH1.............120 C7
Pendleton Rd REDH RH1...........119 P8
Pendragon Wy CBLY GU15 ....69 M4
Penfold Cl CROY/NA CRO............63 J2
Penfold Cft FNM GU9 ....128 B3
Penfold Rd CRAWE RH10 ....177 L9
Penge La PGE/AN SE20 ....46 C1
Penge Rd SNWD SE25 ....46 A4
Pengilly Rd FNM GU9 ....128 A3
Penhurst WOKN/KNAP GU21......72 D3
Peninsular Cl CBLY GU15 ....69 K1
  EBED/NFELT TW14 ....23 N7
Penistone Rd
  STRHM/NOR SW16 ....44 C1
Penlee Cl EDEN TN8 ....144 G3
Penmans Cl KENS W8 ....19 M2
The Pennards SUN TW16 ....39 L4
Penn Cl CRAWW RH11..............176 C2
Penn Ct CRAWW RH11 ....176 C5
Pennefather's Rd
  ALDT GU11 ....108 B3
Penner Cl WIM/MER SW19 ....28 B5
Penners Gdns SURB KT6.............41 L8
Pennine Cl CRAWW RH11 ....176 E5
Pennine Wy FARN GU14 ....67 P9
  HYS/HAR UB3 ....14 F5
Pennings Av GUW GU2 ....111 M2
Pennington Dr WEY KT13 ....56 C2
Penn Rd DTCH/LGLY SL3 ....12 D6
Penns Rd FUL/PGN SW6 ....88 F6
Penns Yd FNM GU9 ....5 H5
Pennycroft CROY/NA CRO...........64 E7
Penny Dr RGUW GU3 ....111 H4
Pennyfield COB KT11 ....75 J2
Penny La SHPTN TW17................38 G8
Pennymead Dr EHSLY KT24........95 H7
Pennymead Pl THDIT KT7 ....40 G8
Penny Oak La BRAK RG12...........32 G3
Penny Oaks Dr WDR/YW UB7 ....13 M7
Penny Ri FSTH SE23.....................31 M6
Pennys La ORP BR6 ....65 L6
Penny V FSTH SE23 ....31 K5
Penny Wy BOR GU35 ....164 D7
  BRAK RG12 ....32 G3
  FNM GU9 * 107 H7
  LTWR GU18 ....69 H1
Penrith Pl STRHM/NOR SW16 ....30 C5
Penrith Rd NWMAL KT3 ....42 B5
  THHTH CR7 ....45 L3
Penrith St STRHM/NOR SW16 ....29 M9
Penrose Ct EGH TW20 ....21 H9
Penrose Rd LHD/OX KT22 ....76 C6
Penryn Dr BOR GU35 ....164 F6
Pensford Av RCH/KEW TW9 ....17 N7
Pensford Rd CWTH RG45 ....49 M2
Penshurst Cl CRAWE RH10........177 N4
Penshurst Gn HAYES BR2............47 M6
Penshurst Ri FRIM GU16 ....69 H6
Penshurst Rd THHTH CR7 ....45 L6
Penshurst Wy BELMT SM2 ....61 L6
Pentelow Gdns
  EBED/NFELT TW14 ....24 B2
Pentland Av SHPTN TW17 ....38 C6
Pentland Cl MTCM CR4 ....44 D4
Pentland St
  WAND/EARL SW18.....................28 F2
Pentlow St PUT/ROE SW15 ....18 G7
Pentney Rd BAL SW12 ....29 M4
  WIM/MER SW19 ....43 J2
Penton Av STA TW18 ....37 K1
Penton Hall Dr STA TW18 ....37 L2
Penton Hook Rd STA TW18 ....37 K1
Pentreath Av GUW GU2 ....111 M6
Penwerris Av ISLW TW7 ....16 C5
Penwith Dr HASM GU27.............183 N6
Penwith Rd
  WAND/EARL SW18.....................28 E5
Penwith Wk
  WOKS/MYFD GU22 ....10 A7
Penwood End
  CROY/NA CRO * 91 P1
Penwortham Rd
  SAND/SEL CR2..........................63 M8

STRHM/NOR SW16 ....29 L9
Penywern Rd ECT SW5 ....19 L3
Peperham Rd HASM GU27........184 D2
Peper Harow La
  MFD/CHID GU8 ....130 C7
Peperharow Rd GODL GU7 ....131 J7
Pepperbox La SHGR GU5..........152 B8
Pepper Cl CTHM CR3 ....101 M5
Peppercorn Cl THHTH CR7 ....45 M3
Peppermead Sq LEW SE13 * 31 P1
Peppers Rd HORS RH12 * 192 C7
Pepys Cl ASHTD KT21 ....77 N6
  DTCH/LGLY SL3 ....12 E3
Pepys Rd RYNPK SW20 ....42 G3
Percheron Dr
  WOKN/KNAP GU21 ....71 J8
Percival Rd FELT TW13 ....24 A5
  MORT/ESHN SW14 ....27 H1
Percival Wy HOR/WEW KT19......60 A2
Percy Av ASHF TW15 ....23 K8
Percy Bryant Rd SUN TW16 ....38 G1
Percy Bush Rd
  WDR/YW UB7............................14 B1
Percy Gdns WPK KT4 ....42 B9
Percy Rd GUW GU1 ....111 P3
  HORS RH12 ....192 A1
  HPTN TW12 ....40 A1
  ISLW TW7 ....16 G9
  MTCM CR4 ....44 C8
  PGE/AN SE20 ....46 D2
  SNWD SE25 ....45 N6
  WHTN TW2 ....25 J4
Percy Wy WHTN TW2 ....25 K4
Peregrine Cl BRAK RG12..............32 D6
  CRAN GU6................................153 H8
Peregrine Gdns
  CROY/NA CRO 64 E1
Peregrine Rd SUN TW16 ....38 G2
Peregrine Wy
  WIM/MER SW19 ....42 G1
Perham Rd WKENS W14...............19 J3
Perifield DUL SE21 ....30 D4
Perimeter Rd East
  HORL RH6................................159 L5
Perimeter Rd North
  HORL RH6................................158 C5
Perimeter Rd South
  HORL RH6................................159 J7
Perleybrooke La
  WOKN/KNAP GU21 ....71 N6
Perowne St ALDT GU11.............108 B4
Perran Bd BRXS/STRHM SW2....30 C5
Perrers Rd HMSMTH W6 ....18 F1
Perrin Cl ASHF TW15 ....23 J8
Perrin Ct WOKN/KNAP GU21......72 F4
Perring Rd FARN GU14 ....68 A8
Perring Rd FARN GU14 ....68 A8
Perrior Rd GODL GU7 ....131 L6
Perry Av EGRIN RH19 ....162 D9
Perry Cl GODL GU7 ....131 M8
Perry Dr FLEETN GU51.................86 D6
Perryfield Rd CRAWW RH11 ......176 G6
Perryfield Wy
  RCHPK/HAM TW10 ....26 A5
Perry Hl CAT SE6 ....31 N5
  RGUW GU3................................91 L8
Perryhill Dr SHST GU47 ....49 K8
Perry How WPK KT4 ....42 D1
Perrylands HORL RH6 ....158 C5
Perrylands La HORL RH6 ....160 A2
Perrymead St FUL/PGN SW6 ......19 M6
Perry Oak Dr HTHAIR TW6 ....13 P7
Perry Oaks Dr WDR/YW UB7......13 M7
Perry Ri FSTH SE23 ....31 M6
Perrys La ORP BR6 ....67 M9
Perry V FSTH SE23 ....31 K5
Perry Wy BOR GU35 ....164 D7
  BRAK RG12 ....32 G3
  FNM GU9 * 107 H7
  LTWR GU18 ....69 H1
Persant Rd CAT SE6 ....32 A5
Persfield Ms EW KT17 * 60 D8
Persfield Rd EW KT17 * 60 E8
Pershore Gv CAR SM5 ....43 P7
Perth Cl CRAWW RH11 ....176 D2
  RYNPK SW20 ....42 E3
Perth Rd BECK BR3......................47 J3
Perth Wy HORS RH12 ....192 E6
Petauel Rd TEDD TW11................25 M8
Petavel Rd TEDD TW11................25 M9
Peter Av OXTED RH8 ....103 K9
Peterborough Ms
  FUL/PGN SW6 ....19 L7
Peterborough Rd CAR SM5 * 43 P7
  CRAWE RH10 ....177 H9
  FUL/PGN SW6 ....19 L8
  GUW GU2 ....111 P3
Peterborough Vls
  FUL/PGN SW6 ....19 M6
Petergate BTSEA SW11 ....19 N9
Peterhead Ms DTCH/LGLY SL3....12 E3
Peterhouse Cl SHST GU47 ....50 B7
Petersfield Av STA TW18 ....22 F8
Petersfield Crs
  COUL/CHIP CR5 ....80 C5
Petersfield Ri PUT/ROE SW15 .....27 N4
Petersfield Rd STA TW18 ....22 F8
Petersham Av BF/WBF KT14 ....74 A1
Petersham Cl BF/WBF KT14 ....74 A1
  RCHPK/HAM TW10 ....26 C5
  SUT SM1....................................61 K4
Petersham La SKENS SW7 ....19 N1
Petersham Ms SKENS SW7..........19 N1
Petersham Rd
  RCHPK/HAM TW10 ....26 C6
Petersham Ter
  CROY/NA CRO * 62 G2
Petersmead Cl
  KWD/TDW/WH KT20 ....98 G3

Peterstow Cl
  WIM/MER SW19 ....28 B5
Peterwood Wy CROY/NA CRO....63 H1
Petley Rd HMSMTH W6...............18 G4
Petridge Rd REDH RH1 ....140 B1
Petters Rd ASHTD KT21 ....77 P5
Pettiward Cl PUT/ROE SW15 ......18 G9
Petts La SHPTN TW17 ....38 C5
  FRIM GU16 ....69 H8
Petworth Ct CRAWW RH11 ....176 C8
Petworth Dr HORS RH12 ....192 E5
Petworth Gdns RYNPK SW20 .....42 F4
Petworth Rd HASM GU27 ....184 E5
  MFD/CHID GU8 ....149 N6
  MFD/CHID GU8 ....168 B7
Pevensey Cl CRAWE RH10........177 M6
  ISLW TW7 ....16 C5
Pevensey Rd FELT TW13 ....24 F4
  TOOT SW17 ....28 G7
Pevensey Wy FRIM GU16............69 J8
Peverel Rd CRAWW RH11 ....176 B6
Peveril Dr TEDD TW11..................25 L8
Pewley Bank GU GU1 ....7 H6
Pewley Hl GU GU1 ....7 G6
Pewley Point GU GU1 ....7 H7
Pewley Wy GU GU1 ....7 H7
Pewsey V BRAK RG12 ....33 H6
Pharaoh Cl MTCM CR4................44 B9
Pheasant Cl PUR/KEN CR8 ....81 K2
Pheasant Copse
  FLEETN GU51 ....86 D5
Phelps Wy HYS/HAR UB3 ....15 H2
Philanthropic Rd REDH RH1 ......120 D6
Philbeach Gdns ECT SW5 ....19 L3
Philip Gdns CROY/NA CRO 64 F1
Philip Rd STA TW18 ....22 G9
Philip's Cl MTCM CR4 ....44 C9
Philips Crs BOR GU35 ....164 C6
Phillimore Gardens Cl
  KENS W8 ....19 L1
Phillimore Ter KENS W8 * 19 L1
Phillimore Wk KENS W8 ....19 L1
Phillips Cl BOR GU35 ....164 C6
  CRAWE RH10 ....177 H8
  GODL GU7................................150 B2
  RFNM GU10..............................108 G6
Phillips Hatch SHGR GU5...........132 C5
Philpot La CHOB/PIR GU24 ....72 A1
Phipp's Bridge Rd
  WIM/MER SW19 ....43 P3
Phoenix Cl WWKM BR4 ....65 K1
Phoenix Ct BTFD TW8 ....17 J4
  GU GU1 ....6 E6
Phoenix La EGRIN RH19............181 K5
Phoenix Pk BTFD TW8 * 17 K3
Phoenix Rd PGE/AN SE20 ....31 K9
Phyllis Av NWMAL KT3.................42 F6
Pickering BRAK RG12 ....32 C6
Pickering Gdns SNWD SE25 ....45 P7
Picket Post Cl BRAK RG12 ....33 H4
Pickets St BAL SW12 ....29 K3
Picketts La REDH RH1 ....140 E5
Pickford St ALDT GU11 ....108 D4
Pickfield Cl EGRIN RH19 ....180 E2
Pickhurst Gn HAYES BR2.............47 M7
Pickhurst La HAYES BR2 ....47 M8
Pickhurst Md HAYES BR2.............47 M8
Pickhurst Pk HAYES BR2 ....47 L5
Pickhurst Ri WWKM BR4 ....47 L9
Pickhurst Rd
  BH/WHM TN16 * 168 B8
Pickins Piece DTCH/LGLY SL3 ...12 E7
Pickwick Cl HSLWW TW4 ....24 G4
Pickwick Gdns CBLY GU15 ....69 K4
Pickwick Rd DUL SE21 ....30 E3
Picquets Wy BNSTD SM7.............79 J5
Picton Cl CBLY GU15 ....69 L1
Piermont Rd EDUL SE22 ....31 J1
Pierrefondes Av FARN GU14 ....88 D2
Pier Ter RBED/NFELT TW14 ....18 M9
Pigbush La BIL RH14 ....188 C3
Pigdown La EDEN TN8................145 P9
Pigeonhouse La
  COUL/CHIP CR5.........................99 N5
Pigeon Ln HPTN TW12 ....25 H7
Pigeon Pass CRAWE RH10........179 K6
Pike Cl ALDT GU11 ....108 E4
Pikes HI EW KT17 ....78 C2
Pikes La LING RH7 ....143 L4
Pilcot Rd HTWY RG27..................86 B9
Pilgrim Cl MRDN SM4...................43 M8
Pilgrim Hl WNWD SE27 ....30 D7
Pilgrims Cl FNM GU9 ....116 G3
  RDKG RH5................................116 G3
  SHGR GU5................................134 C1
Pilgrims' La CTHM CR3...............101 H6
  OXTED RH8 ....104 A4
Pilgrims Pl ASHF TW15 * ....22 ?
  REIG RH2 ....119 L3
Pilgrims Vw ASHV GU12 ....109 L6
Pilgrims Wy BOR GU35 ....164 B6
  CHOB/PIR GU24 ....70 G5
  RDKG RH5................................117 H2
  REIG RH2 ....119 K3
  RGUE GU4................................112 G7
  SAND/SEL CR2...........................63 P5
  SHGR GU5................................134 C1
Pilsden Cl WIM/MER SW19 * 27 P4
Pimms Cl RGUE GU4 ....112 E1
Pinckards MFD/CHID GU8 ....167 P6
Pincott La EHSLY KT24 ....94 D9
Pincott Rd WIM/MER SW19 ....43 L5
Pine Av CBLY GU15 ....143 N5
  CHOB/PIR GU24 ....90 F1
  WWKM BR4 ....47 M9
Pine Bank GSHT GU26 ....165 P9
Pine Cl ADL/WDHM KT15 ....55 M9
  ASHV GU12................................89 J9
  CBLY GU15................................68 A1

CRAWW RH11..........176 F2
PGE/AN SE20.............46 C2
PUR/KEN CR8............81 L6
WOKN/KNAP GU21.......72 A6
Pine Coombe CROY/NA CR0 ..64 D3
Pinecote Dr ASC SL5.......34 F8
Pine Ct FRIM GU16 *.......89 J4
Pine Crs CAR SM5..........61 P9
Pine Dean GT/LBKH KT23 ..16 B8
Pine Dr BLKW GU17.........48 A2
EWKG RG40.................48 E2
Pinefields ADL/WDHM KT15 *..55 M3
Pinefields CI CWTH RG45......49 M4
Pine Gdns BRYLDS KT5........41 N7
BORH RH6...................159 K2
Pine Gv BFOR GU20..........52 D5
EDEN TN8...................144 F3
EGRIN RH19................162 A9
FLEETS GU52...............107 H1
RFNM GU10................128 A7
WEY KT13...................56 D4
WIM/MER SW19...............28 C8
Pine Grove WEY KT13 *......56 L4
Pinehill RI SHST GU47.......49 M9
Pinehill Rd CWTH RG45......49 M5
HORS RH12................192 B6
Pinehurst ASC SL5..........34 D6
Pinehurst CI
KWD/TDW/WH KT20...........99 L2
Pinehurst Cottages
FARN GU14.................88 D5
Pinel CI VW GU25..........36 C5
Pineleeos Ct
MORT/ESHN SW14 *.........18 A3
Pine Mount Rd CBLY GU15 ..68 F4
Pine Pk RGUW GU3 *........90 C9
Pine PI EW KT17............79 H3
Pine Rdg CAR SM5...........62 C7
Pine Ridge Dr RFNM GU10..127 M8
Pine Rd WOKS/MYFD GU22 ..72 A9
Pine Shaw CRAWE RH10....177 M4
Pines Rd FLEETS GU51......86 F5
LIPH GU30................182 B6
The Pines CBLY GU15.......69 H1
HORS RH12................193 H5
NRWD SE19 *...............30 C9
PUR/KEN CR8................62 L8
SUN TW16..................39 J4
WOKN/KNAP GU21..........72 D3
Pinetops SWTR RH13 *.....193 H6
Pine Tree HI
WOKS/MYFD GU22...........73 H5
The Trees STA TW18 *......22 D8
Pinetrees CI CRAWE RH10..160 C9
Pine Vw BOR GU35..........164 C5
Pine View CI FNM GU9.....108 C5
HASM GU27................184 D2
RGUE GU4..................133 K2
Pine Wk BNSTD SM7.........80 B6
BRYLDS KT5...............41 N7
CAR SM5...................61 P9
COB KT11..................75 M3
CTHM CR3.................101 N2
EHSLY KT24................95 H8
GT/LBKH KT23...............96 B5
Pine Wy EGH TW20..........20 C9
Pine Way CI EGRIN RH19...180 D4
Pine Wd SUN TW16..........39 J2
Pinewood Av
ADL/WDHM KT15............55 N7
CWTH RG45................49 N3
Pinewood CI CROY/NA CR0 ..64 C2
HORS RH12................191 J7
SHST GU47.................49 K9
WOKN/KNAP GU21..........72 E4
Pinewood Crs FARN GU14 ..87 N2
Pinewood Dr STA TW18 *.....22 D8
Pinewood Gdns BAGS GU19 ..51 L6
Pinewood Gv
ADL/WDHM KT15............55 N7
Pinewood MI FLEETN GU51 ..86 G5
Pinewood Ms
STWL/WRAY TW19............22 G2
Pinewood Pk
ADL/WDHM KT15............55 M9
FARN GU14.................67 N9
Pinewood Rd ASHV GU12..109 M3
FELT TW13.................24 C6
HAYES BR2.................47 N5
VW GU25...................35 N4
Pinfold Rd
STRHM/NOR SW16............29 P8
Pingiestone CI WDR/YW UB7 ..14 A5
Pinkcoat CI FELT TW13.......24 C6
Pinkhurst La SWTR RH13....193 M8
Pinkwell Av HYS/HAR UB3 ..14 F2
Pinkwell La HYS/HAR UB3 ..14 E2
Piper Rd KUT KT1............9 H6
Pipers CI COB KT11.........75 M4
Pipers Cft FLEETS GU52...106 F2
Pipers End SWTR RH13.....190 F7
VW GU25...................36 B4
Pipers Gdns CROY/NA CR0..46 E8
Piper's Green
BH/WHM TN16..............105 L8
Pipers La BH/WHM TN16...105 M7
Pipers Patch FARN GU14 ..88 D3
Pipewell Rd CAR SM5.......44 A7
Pippbrook Gdns DORK RH4..117 H6
Pippin CI CROY/NA CR0.....46 G8
Pippins CI WDR/YW UB7 ..13 P1
Pippins Ct ASHF TW15......23 L9
Pipsons CI YTLY GU46.......67 H2
Piquet Rd PGE/AN SE20.....46 C3
Pirbright Crs CROY/NA CR0..65 J5
Pirbright Rd FARN GU14 ..88 C4
RGUW GU3.................90 C9
WAND/EARL SW18............28 C4

Pirbright Ter
CHOB/PIR GU24 *..........90 F3
Pisley La RDKG RH5.........155 H7
Pitcairn Rd MTCM CR4.......44 B1
Pitchfont La OXTED RH8....103 N6
Pitfield Rd GU GU1.........112 C5
Pitfold CI HASM GU27......183 P4
Pitlake CROY/NA CR0.........2 B3
Pitland St RDKG RH5.......135 L8
Pit La EDEN TN8............144 C1
Pitson CI ADL/WDHM KT15 ..55 P3
Pitt Crs WIM/MER SW19......28 E7
Pitt La RFNM GU10.........146 D6
Pitt PI EW KT17.............78 C3
Pitt Rd EW KT17.............78 C3
THHTH CR7.................45 L6
Pittsmead Av HAYES BR2....47 N8
Pittville Gdns SNWD SE25...46 A4
Pitt Wy FARN GU14..........88 B2
Pit Wood Gn
KWD/TDW/WH KT20...........78 G9
Pixham La DORK RH4........117 J4
Pixholme Gv DORK RH4......117 J5
Pixton Wy CROY/NA CR0.....64 F6
Place Farm Rd REDH RH1...121 M1
Placehouse La
COUL/CHIP CR5.............81 H8
Plaistow Cv BMLY BR1.......47 P1
Plaistow La BMLY BR1.......47 N1
Plaistow Rd BIL RH14......188 D9
MFD/CHID GU8..............169 K8
MFD/CHID GU8..............186 C5
Plaistow St LING RH7......143 J9
The Planes CHERT KT16......37 N8
Plane St SYD SE26..........31 J6
Plane Tree Crs FELT TW13 ..24 C6
Plantagenet CI
WPK KT4...................60 B3
Plantagenet Pk BNFD RG42..33 H2
Plantain Crs CRAWW RH11 ..176 D9
Plantation La WARL CR6.....82 E8
The Plat EDEN TN8..........145 H4
HORS RH12................191 P8
Platt Meadow RGUE GU4....113 H2
The Platt LING RH7.........162 F4
Plawsfield Rd BECK BR3.....46 D2
Plaws HI SHGR GU5.........134 F7
Playfair St HMSMTH W6 *....18 C3
Playfield Crs EDUL SE22....30 F1
Playgreen Wy CAT SE6.......31 P7
Playground CI BECK BR3....46 D2
Pleasance Rd PUT/ROE SW15 ..27 N1
The Pleasance
PUT/ROE SW15..............18 F9
Pleasant Gv CROY/NA CR0...64 F2
Pleasant PI WOT/HER KT12..57 M5
Plesman Wy WLGTN SM6 *....62 G7
Plevna Rd HPTN TW12.......40 B2
Pleydell Av HMSMTH W6.....18 D1
Pleydell Gdns NRWD SE19 *..30 C9
Plough CI CRAWW RH11....176 C5
Ploughlands BNFD RG42....32 E1
Plough La COB KT11.........75 J5
CRAN GU6..................154 B7
CROY/NA CR0...............62 G3
EDUL SE22..................30 G2
HORS RH12................192 D5
TEDD TW11..................25 P8
WIM/MER SW19..............28 G7
WLGTN SM6.................63 H3
Plough Lane CI WLGTN SM6 ..62 G4
Ploughmans End ISLW TW7 ..25 L1
Plough Rd BTSEA SW11......19 P8
HOR/WEW KT19.............60 B6
HORL RH6..................160 D1
LING RH7..................162 F2
YTLY GU46..................67 J1
Plough Ter BTSEA SW11.....19 P9
Plover CI CRAWW RH11.....176 F3
STA TW18...................22 C6
Plovers RI CHOB/PIR GU24 ..70 E9
Plovers Rd SWTR RH13....192 F7
Plum CI FELT TW13..........24 B4
Plum Garth BTFD TW8.......17 K2
Plummer La MTCM CR4.......44 B2
Plummer Rd CLAP SW4.......29 M2
Plumpton Wy CAR SM5......62 A2
Plymouth Rd BMLY BR1......47 P2
Pockford Rd MFD/CHID GU8..168 C7
Pocock Av WDR/YW UB7......14 B1
Podmore Rd
WAND/EARL SW18............19 N9
Pointers HI DORK RH4......116 C9
Pointers Rd COB KT11.......74 F6
The Pointers ASHTD KT21...77 L9
Point Pleasant
WAND/EARL SW18............19 L9
Polden CI FARN GU14........68 A9
Polecroft La CAT SE6.......31 N5
Polesden Gdns RYNPK SW20 ..42 F4
Polesden La
RPLY/SEND GU23............93 K3
Polesden Rd GT/LBKH KT23 ..96 B9
Polesden Vw GT/LBKH KT23 ..96 B7
Poles La CRAWW RH11......158 F9
Polesteeple HI
BH/WHM TN16..............84 B6
Police Station Rd
WOT/HER KT12..............57 L5
Polkerris Wy FLEETS GU52..107 H2
Pollard CI WDSR SL4........20 C1
Pollard Gv CBLY GU15.......69 L4
Pollard Rd MRDN SM4.......43 P6
WOKS/MYFD GU22............11 K1
Pollardrow Av BNFD RG42 ..32 B2
Pollards CRAWW RH11......176 D6
Pollards Crs
STRHM/NOR SW16............44 G4
Pollards Dr SWTR RH13....192 E8

Pollards HI East
STRHM/NOR SW16............45 H4
Pollards HI North
STRHM/NOR SW16............45 H4
Pollards HI South
STRHM/NOR SW16............44 G4
Pollards HI West
STRHM/NOR SW16............44 G4
Pollards Oak Crs OXTED RH8..123 N3
Pollards Oak Rd OXTED RH8..123 N3
Pollards Wood HI
OXTED RH8................123 N1
Pollards Wood Rd
OXTED RH8................123 P2
STRHM/NOR SW16............29 P8
Pollyanthus Wy CWTH RG45..49 M1
Poncl CI BIL RH14.........188 C6
WOT/HER KT12.............57 J3
Pond Copse La BIL RH14 ..188 C5
Pond Cottage La BECK BR3 ..46 G9
Pond Cft YTLY GU46.........67 J2
Pond Farm CI
KWD/TDW/WH KT20...........98 F4
Pondfield Rd GODL GU7.....131 M7
HAYES BR2..................47 L9
HORS RH12................189 N2
PUR/KEN CR8................81 K5
Pond Head La DORK RH4....154 E9
Pond Hill Gdns
CHEAM SM3.................61 J5
Pond La RFNM GU10.........146 B4
SHGR GU5.................134 E6
Pond Md EDUL SE22 *.......30 F1
Pond Meadow GUW GU2....111 L5
Pond Moor Rd BRAK RG12...32 C6
Pond Piece LHD/OX KT22 ..76 B2
Pond Rd BOR GU35.........164 D7
EGH TW20..................21 P9
FARN GU14.................88 D5
WOKS/MYFD GU22...........71 N9
Pondside CI HYS/HAR UB3 ..14 F5
Ponds La SHGR GU5.........134 B5
The Ponds WEY KT13........56 F5
Pondtail CI FLEETN GU51 ..87 J7
HORS RH12................192 C5
Pondtail Copse HORS RH12..192 C4
Pondtail Dr HORS RH12....192 C3
Pondtail Gdns FLEETN GU51 ..87 J7
Pondtail Rd FLEETN GU51 ..87 J7
HORS RH12................192 B5
Pondview CI FLEETN GU51 ..87 J7
Pond Wy EGRIN RH19.......180 G2
TEDD TW11..................25 P9
Pond Wood Rd
CRAWE RH10...............177 K3
Poneys CI BRAK RG12 *......32 E5
Ponsonby Rd PUT/ROE SW15..27 N3
Pony Cha COB KT11..........75 P2
Pook HI MFD/CHID GU8....167 M8
Pool CI BECK BR3...........39 P6
E/WMO/HCT KT8.............39 J5
Poole Court Rd HEST TW5 ..15 N7
Pool End CI SHPTN TW17....38 C5
Poole Rd HOR/WEW KT19....60 B5
WOKN/KNAP GU21..........11 G4
Pooles La WBPTN SW10 *....19 N5
Pooley Av EGH TW20........21 N8
Pooley Green Rd EGH TW20 ..21 N8
Pool Rd ALDT GU11.........108 E7
E/WMO/HCT KT8.............39 J5
Pootings Rd EDEN TN8.....125 K8
Pope CI EBED/NFELT TW14 ..24 A4
WIM/MER SW19 *............28 G9
Pope's Av WHTN TW2.......25 M5
Popes CI DTCH/LGLY SL3....12 C5
Popes Gv CROY/NA CR0.....64 F2
WHTN TW2..................25 M6
Pope's La EA W5............17 K1
OXTED RH8................123 M6
Popes Md HASM GU27 *......184 F6
Popham CI BRAK RG12.......33 H7
FELT TW13..................24 F6
Popham Gdns
RCH/KEW TW9 *..............17 P2
Popinjays Rw CHEAM SM3 *..61 H4
Poplar Av BFOR GU20.......52 A3
LHD/OX KT22...............44 B2
MTCM CR4..................44 B2
NWDGN UB2.................16 B1
Poplar CI BRAK RG12........32 F4
CRAWW RH11...............176 F2
DTCH/LGLY SL3.............13 J6
FRIM GU16..................89 J4
Poplar Court Bde TWK TW1 *..26 B2
Poplar Crs HOR/WEW KT19 ..60 A5
Poplar Dr EW KT17..........79 H3
Poplar Farm CI
HOR/WEW KT19.............60 A5
Poplar Gdns NWMAL KT3 ..42 B3
Poplar Gv WOKS/MYFD GU22..10 D7
Poplar Gv NWMAL KT3......42 B3
Poplar Rd ASHF TW15........23 M8
CHEAM SM3.................43 K9
LHD/OX KT22...............97 H2
RGUE GU4.................132 G3
WIM/MER SW19..............43 J3
Poplar Rd South
WIM/MER SW19..............43 L4
Poplars CI FARN GU14.......87 N2
The Poplars ASC SL5........34 A6
SWTR RH13................192 D7
Poplar Wk CROY/NA CR0......2 C2
CTHM CR3.................101 N3
FNM GU9..................107 P7

Poplar Wy FELT TW13........24 C6
Poppy CI MTCM CR4..........44 C9
Poppyhills Rd CBLY GU15 ..51 H9
Poppy La CROY/NA CR0......46 C8
Porchester ASC SL5.........34 A5
Porchester Rd KUT KT1......9 K4
Porchfield CI BELMT SM2 ..61 M8
Porridge Pot Aly GUW GU2 ..6 D7
Portal CI WNWD SE27.......30 B6
Porten Houses WKENS W14 *..19 J1
Porten Rd WKENS W14.......19 J1
Porters Wy WDR/YW UB7 ..14 B1
Portesbery Rd CBLY GU15 ..68 F3
Portesbery Hill Dr CBLY GU15..68 F1
Porthcawe Rd SYD SE26....31 M7
Port HI ORP BR6............85 M1
Portia Gv BNFD RG42........32 B2
The Porticos WBPTN SW10 *..19 P4
Portinscale Rd
PUT/ROE SW15..............28 B1
Portland Av NWMAL KT3 ..42 D8
Portland Cottages
CROY/NA CR0 *.............44 B7
Portland Crs FELT TW13.....23 N7
Portland Dr FLEETS GU52 ..106 F2
REDH RH1..................100 E9
Portland PI EW KT17 *......78 C1
SNWD SE25..................46 A5
Portland Rd ASHF TW15......23 H6
DORK RH4..................116 G6
EGRIN RH19................180 D3
KUT KT1....................9 F6
MTCM CR4..................44 A3
NWDGN UB2.................15 P1
SNWD SE25..................46 B5
Portland Ter FNM GU9 *....127 P1
GU GU1 *....................7 H5
RCH/KEW TW9 *..............7 K5
Portley La CTHM CR3.......101 N1
Portley Wood Rd CTHM CR3..101 P1
Portman Av
MORT/ESHN SW14...........18 A3
Portman CI BNFD RG42......32 C2
Portman Rd KUT KT1..........9 G4
Portmore Park Rd WEY KT13..56 C2
Portmore Quays WEY KT13 ..56 B3
Portmore Wy WEY KT13 *....56 C2
Portnall Dr VW GU25........35 K6
Portnall Ri VW GU25.........35 M6
Portnall Rd VW GU25........35 M6
Portnalls Rd COUL/CHIP CR5..80 D5
Portnalls CI COUL/CHIP CR5..80 E5
Portnalls Rd COUL/CHIP CR5..80 D5
Portsmouth Av THDIT KT7 ..40 C4
Portsmouth Rd CBLY GU15 ..73 F3
COB KT11...................74 F3
ESH/CLAY KT10..............58 A5
FRIM GU16..................68 G5
GODL GU7.................149 P3
KUT KT1....................8 D6
LIPH GU30.................182 E9
LIPH GU30.................183 K3
MFD/CHID GU8..............166 E1
PUT/ROE SW15..............27 N4
RPLY/SEND GU23............74 C7
SHGR GU5..................149 P3
Portugal Gdns WHTN TW2 *..25 K5
Portugal Rd
WOKN/KNAP GU21..........11 F2
Port Wy CHOB/PIR GU24 ..70 G9
Portway EW KT17............78 D2
Portway Crs EW KT17........60 D7
Postboys Rw COB KT11 *.....75 J3
Post House La GT/LBKH KT23..96 A5
Post Rd NWDGN UB2.........16 C1
Postmill CI CROY/NA CR0....64 C2
Potley Hill Rd YTLY GU46....67 K3
Potter CI MTCM CR4 *.......44 D3
Potteries La FRIM GU16......89 H4
The Potteries CHERT KT16...55 J5
FARN GU14.................87 P1
Potterne CI WIM/MER SW19..28 A4
Potters CI CROY/NA CR0.....46 E8
MFD/CHID GU8..............149 N2
Potters Crs CfT SWTR RH13..192 D8
Potters Ga FNM GU9.........4 A5
Potters Gv NWMAL KT3......42 A5
Potters HI RPLY/SEND GU23..92 F5
Potters La BIL RH14........188 C5
WOKN/KNAP GU21..........72 E9
MTCM CR4..................44 C3
Potters Wy REIG RH2........119 N9
Potters Rd FUL/PGN SW6 ..19 N6
Pottery La RFNM GU10......127 K7
Pottery Rd BTFD TW8 *......17 L1
Poulcott STWL/WRAY TW19..21 K2
Poulett Gdns TWK TW1.......25 N5
Poulter Pk MTCM CR4 *......44 A7
Poulton Av SUT SM1.........61 P2
Pound CI BIL RH14.........188 C5
BOR GU35.................164 C6
GODL GU7.................131 L9
SURB KT6...................41 J9
Pound Ct ASHTD KT21.......77 M7
RGUW GU3................111 H3
Pound Crs LHD/OX KT22.....96 D4
Pound Farm La ASHV GU12..109 M5
ESH/CLAY KT10.............40 D3
Pound Fld GU GU1............6 E1
Poundfield Gdns
WOKS/MYFD GU22...........72 G9
Poundfield La BIL RH14....187 N4
Pound HI RGUW GU3........111 H3
Pound Hill PI CRAWE RH10..177 M5
Pound La BFOR GU20.........52 C5
GODL GU7.................131 L9
HOR/WEW KT19.............60 B9
RGUW GU3................111 H4
RSEV TN14..................85 P3

Povey Cross Rd HORL RH6 ..158 C3
Powderham Ct
WOKN/KNAP GU21..........71 K7
Powder Mill La WHTN TW2 ..24 G4
Powell CI GUW GU2.........111 M7
HORL RH6..................140 A9
Power Rd CHSWK W4.........18 A1
Powers Ct TWK TW1..........26 C3
Pownall Gdns HSLW TW3.....16 B9
Pownall Rd HSLW TW3.......16 B9
Poyle Gdns BRAK RG12......32 F2
Poyle Pk DTCH/LGLY SL3 ..13 J8
Poyle Rd DTCH/LGLY SL3 ..13 J8
GU GU1 *....................7 G7
RFNM GU10................109 J7
Poynders Rd CLAP SW4......29 M3
Poynes Rd HORL RH6.......140 A8
Poynings Rd CRAWW RH11..176 A6
The Poynings IVER SL0......13 K2
Prague PI BRXS/STRHM SW2..29 P1
Prairie CI ADL/WDHM KT15..55 M2
Prairie Rd ADL/WDHM KT15..55 M2
Pratts La WOT/HER KT12 ..57 M3
Prebend Gdns CHSWK W4 ..18 D2
The Precinct CRAN GU6....153 H8
Premier Pde HORL RH6 *....159 L1
Prentice CI FARN GU14......88 E1
Prentis Rd STRHM/NOR SW16..29 N7
Presburg Rd NWMAL KT3 ..42 C6
Prescott BRAK RG12.........32 B8
Prescott Rd DTCH/LGLY SL3..13 J7
Presentation Ms
BRXS/STRHM SW2...........30 A5
Prestbury Crs BNSTD SM7 ..80 B5
Preston CI WHTN TW2........25 M6
Preston Dr HOR/WEW KT12..39 L9
Preston Gv ASHTD KT21......77 J6
Preston La
KWD/TDW/WH KT20...........78 G9
PIN RCHPK/HAM TW10...26 D1
Preston Rd NRWD SE19......30 C9
RYNPK SW20................42 E1
SHPTN TW17.................38 C6
Prestons Rd HAYES BR2.....65 N2
Prestwick Ct STWL/WRAY TW19 *..21 K4
Prestwick La CHOB/PIR GU24 *..70 G4
Prestwick Ter SWTR RH13 *..192 D7
Prestwood CI CRAWW RH11..176 A6
NWDGN UB2.................15 N3
Prestwick La HASM GU27 ..167 H9
Prestwood Gdns
CROY/NA CR0................45 L8
Prestwood La CRAWW RH11..175 P1
Pretoria Rd CHERT KT16......55 J7
STRHM/NOR SW16............29 L9
Pretty La COUL/CHIP CR5 ..100 E1
Prettymans La EDEN TN8 ..145 L2
Prey Heath CI
WOKS/MYFD GU22...........92 A4
Prey Heath Rd
WOKS/MYFD GU22...........91 P4
Price CI TOOT SW17 *........29 J6
Price Rd CROY/NA CR0......63 K4
Prices La REIG RH2.........119 L8
Prickley Wd HAYES BR2......47 M9
Prideaux Gdns RDKG RH5 *..155 L8
Priddles Crossing ASC SL5....34 L1
Pridham Rd THHTH CR7 *....45 M5
Priest Croft CI CRAWW RH11..176 C6
Priestfield Rd FSTH SE23...31 M6
Priest HI EGH TW20..........21 H5
OXTED RH8................103 P9
Priest La CHOB/PIR GU24 ..70 C4
Priestley Gdns
WOKS/MYFD GU22...........72 E9
Priestley Rd GUW GU2......111 K6
MTCM CR4..................44 C3
Priestley Wy CRAWE RH10..159 K9
Priests Br MORT/ESHN SW14..18 C8
Priestwood Av BNFD RG42..32 B2
Priestwood Court Rd
BNFD RG42.................32 B2
Priestwood Sq BNFD RG42..32 B2
Priestwood Ter BNFD RG42..32 B2
Primrose Av HORL RH6.....159 L3
HORL RH6..................159 L3
Primrose CI CRAWW RH11 ..176 E8
WLGTN SM6.................44 D9
Primrose Copse HORS RH12..192 C3
Primrose Dr CHOB/PIR GU24..70 D9
WDR/YW UB7................13 P2
Primrose Gdns FARN GU14 ..88 A4
Primrose La CROY/NA CR0 ..46 C9
Primrose Rdg GODL GU7....150 A2
Primrose Wk WOT/HER KT12..57 L4
Primrose Wk BRAK RG12 *...32 C6
EW KT17...................60 D6
Primrose Wy SHGR GU5....132 D8
SHST GU47.................49 M8
Prince Albert Dr ASC SL5 ..33 M5
Prince Albert Sq REDH RH1..140 C1
Prince Andrew Wy ASC SL5..33 M3
Prince Charles Wy
WLGTN SM6.................62 D2
Prince Consort Dr ASC SL5 ..33 M5
Prince Consort Rd
SKENS SW7..................19 P1
Prince George's Av
RYNPK SW20................42 G3
Prince Georges Rd
WIM/MER SW19..............43 P2
Prince of Wales Rd
REDH RH1..................141 J4
SUT SM1....................61 P1

Prince of Wales Ter
CHSWK W4 18 C3
Prince Regent Rd *HSLW* TW3 16 C8
Prince Rd *SNWD* SE25 45 N6
Princes Av *ACT* W3 17 N1
ALDT GU11 108 E1
CAR SM5 62 B6
GODL GU7 131 J6
SAND/SEL CR2 82 B4
SURB KT6 59 N1
Princes Cl *BAGS* GU19 51 N8
HPTN TW12 25 L7
SAND/SEL CR2 82 B4
Prince's Dr *LHD/OX* KT22 76 E1
Princes Gdns *RGUW* GU3 * 91 L7
SKENS SW7 19 P1
Princes Ga *SKENS* SW7 * 19 P1
Princes Gate Ms *SKENS* SW7 19 P1
Princes Ms *HMSMTH* W6 * 18 F3
Princes Rd *ASHF* TW15 23 J8
EGH TW20 21 L9
FELT TW13 24 A6
HPTN TW12 25 L7
KUTN/CMB KT2 9 H2
MORT/ESHN SW14 18 B8
PGE/AN SE20 31 L9
RCH/KEW TW9 17 M6
RCHPK/HAM TW10 26 E1
REDH RH1 120 C8
WEY KT13 56 D4
WIM/MER SW19 28 D9
Princess Anne Rd
HORS RH12 189 N4
Princess Gdns
WOKS/MYFD GU22 11 K1
Princess Margaret Rd
HORS RH12 189 N3
Princess Mary's Rd
ADL/WDHM KT15 55 N3
Princess Rd *CRAWW* RH11 176 F5
CROY/NA CR0 45 L7
WOKS/MYFD GU22 11 K1
Prince's St *RCH/KEW* TW9 17 L7
SUT SM1 61 P3
Princess Wy *CBLY* GU15 68 E3
REDH RH1 120 C4
Princes Wy *ALDT* GU11 108 C4
CROY/NA CR0 63 H4
WIM/MER SW19 28 B4
WWKM BR4 65 M3
Princethorpe Rd *SYD* SE26 31 L7
Pringle Gdns *PUR/KEN* CR8 63 H8
STRHM/NOR SW16 29 M7
Prior Av *BELMT* SM2 62 A6
Prior Croft Cl *CBLY* GU15 69 J4
Prior End *CBLY* GU15 69 J3
Prioress Rd *WNWD* SE27 30 C6
Prior Rd *CBLY* GU15 69 K4
Priors Cl *FARN* GU14 68 D8
Priors Ct *WOKN/KNAP* GU21 71 N7
Priors Cft *WOKS/MYFD* GU22 72 E9
Priorsfield Rd *GODL* GU7 130 G5
Priors Hatch La *GODL* GU7 130 F4
Priors Keep *FLEETS* GU52 87 J7
Prior's La *BLKW* GU17 67 L3
Priors Md *GT/LBKH* KT23 96 C5
The Priors *ASHTD* KT21 77 K8
Priors Wk *CRAWE* RH10 177 J5
Priors Wd *CWTH* RG45 49 H5
HASM GU27 184 A4
Priorswood *RGUW* GU3 130 F3
Priory Av *CHEAM* SM3 61 H3
CHSWK W4 18 C1
Priory Cl *ASC* SL5 34 G8
BECK BR3 46 E4
DORK RH4 116 G9
FLEETN GU51 86 D7
HORL RH6 140 B9
HPTN TW12 39 P2
SUN TW16 39 J1
WIM/MER SW19 * 43 M2
WOKN/KNAP GU21 73 H2
WOT/HER KT12 57 J2
Priory Ct *CBLY* GU15 * 68 B3
DORK RH4 * 117 H9
Priory Crs *CHEAM* SM3 61 H3
NRWD SE19 45 L1
Priory Dr *REIG* RH2 119 L7
Priory Gdns *ASHF* TW15 23 N8
BARN SW13 18 D8
CHSWK W4 * 18 C2
HPTN TW12 39 P1
SNWD SE25 45 P5
Priory Gn *STA* TW18 22 E8
Priory La *BRAK* RG12 32 E1
E/WMO/HCT KT8 40 A5
PUT/ROE SW15 27 L1
RFNM GU10 146 G4
Priory Ms *STA* TW18 22 E8
Priory Rd *ASC* SL5 33 K2
ASC SL5 34 G8
CHEAM SM3 61 H3
CHSGTN KT9 59 L2
CHSWK W4 18 B1
CROY/NA CR0 45 J8
HPTN TW12 39 P1
HSLW TW3 25 K1
RCH/KEW TW9 17 N4
REIG RH2 119 L7
WIM/MER SW19 43 P1
Priory St *FARN* GU14 88 F3
The Priory *CROY/NA* CR0 * 63 J2
GDST RH9 122 B2
Priory Wk *BRAK* RG12 33 H5
WBPTN SW10 19 N3
Priory Wy *NWDGN* UB2 15 M1
WDR/YW UB7 14 A4
Probert Rd
BRXS/STRHM SW2 30 B1
Probyn Rd *BRXS/STRHM* SW2 30 C5
Proctor Cl *CRAWE* RH10 177 M7
MTCM CR4 44 C2
Proctor Gdns *GT/LBKH* KT23 96 B5
Proctors Cl
EBED/NFELT TW14 24 B4
Profumo Rd *WOT/HER* KT12 57 M4
Progress Wy *CROY/NA* CR0 63 H1
Promenade Approach Rd
CHSWK W4 18 C5
Promenade De Verdun
PUR/KEN CR8 62 F9
The Promenade *CHSWK* W4 18 C6
Propeller Rd *FARN* GU14 88 D5
Prospect Av *FARN* GU14 88 D1
Prospect Cl *HEST* TW5 15 P6
SYD SE26 31 J7
Prospect Cottages
WAND/EARL SW18 19 L9
Prospect Crs *WHTN* TW2 25 K2
Prospect La *EGH* TW20 20 F8
Prospect Pl *CHSWK* W4 18 B3
CRAWW RH11 176 F5
EW KT17 78 C2
HAYES BR2 47 P4
RYNPK SW20 42 F1
STA TW18 22 C8
Prospect Rd *ASHV* GU12 109 J1
FARN GU14 88 C3
RFNM GU10 146 B1
SURB KT6 41 J7
Prossers *KWD/TDW/WH* KT20 99 H1
Prothero Rd *FUL/PGN* SW6 19 J5
Providence La *HYS/HAR* UB3 14 F5
Providence Pl *BF/WBF* KT14 * 73 L3
Providence Ter
CRAWE RH10 * 179 H7
Provincial Ter
PGE/AN SE20 * 46 D1
Prune Hl *EGH* TW20 36 C1
Prunus Cl *CHOB/PIR* GU24 70 E2
Puckridge Gate Rd
ALDT GU11 87 P9
Puckridge Hill Rd
ALDT GU11 108 A1
Puckshill *WOKN/KNAP* GU21 71 K6
Puckshott Wy *HASM* GU27 184 E2
Pudding La *HORL* RH6 158 B4
Puddledock La
BH/WHM TN16 125 L3
Puffin Cl *CROY/NA* CR0 46 D6
Puffin Hl *CRAWE* RH10 * 179 K6
Puffin Rd *CRAWW* RH11 * 176 A6
Pulborough Rd
WAND/EARL SW18 28 C3
Pulborough Wy *HSLWW* TW4 15 L9
Pullman Gdns
PUT/ROE SW15 27 P2
Pullman La *GODL* GU7 150 B2
Pullmans Pl *STA* TW18 22 D8
Pulton Pl *FUL/PGN* SW6 19 L5
Pump Aly *BTFD* TW8 17 K5
Pump House Cl *HAYES* BR2 47 M3
Pumping Station Rd
CHSWK W4 18 C5
Pump La *ASC* SL5 34 E2
Punchbowl La *RDKG* RH5 117 K6
Punch Copse Rd
CRAWE RH10 177 J4
Purbeck Av *NWMAL* KT3 42 D7
Purbeck Cl *REDH* RH1 100 E9
Purbeck Dr
WOKN/KNAP GU21 72 D3
Purberry Gv *EW* KT17 60 D8
Purberry Shot *EW* KT17 * 60 D8
Purbrook Ct *BRAK* RG12 32 G7
Purcell Cl *PUR/KEN* CR8 81 L3
Purcell Crs *FUL/PGN* SW6 19 H4
Purcell Rd *CRAWW* RH11 176 C8
CWTH RG45 49 M2
Purley Bury Av *PUR/KEN* CR8 63 L9
Purley Bury Cl *PUR/KEN* CR8 63 L9
Purley Cl *CRAWE* RH10 177 N8
Purley Downs Rd
PUR/KEN CR8 63 L8
Purley Hl *PUR/KEN* CR8 81 K1
Purley Knoll *PUR/KEN* CR8 63 H9
Purley Oaks Rd
SAND/SEL CR2 63 M8
Purley Pde *PUR/KEN* CR8 * 63 J9
Purley Park Rd *PUR/KEN* CR8 63 K8
Purley Ri *PUR/KEN* CR8 81 H1
Purley Rd *SAND/SEL* CR2 63 M6
Purley V *PUR/KEN* CR8 81 K2
Purley Wy *CROY/NA* CR0 45 H9
CROY/NA CR0 63 J3
FRIM GU16 68 G8
Purmerend Cl *FARN* GU14 87 N2
Pursers Cross Rd
FUL/PGN SW6 * 19 K6
Pursers Hollow *SHGR* GU5 134 F6
Pursers La *SHGR* GU5 134 F4
Purton Rd *HORS* RH12 192 A6
Putney Br *PUT/ROE* SW15 19 J8
Putney Bridge Ap
PUT/ROE SW15 19 J8
Putney Bridge Rd
PUT/ROE SW15 19 J9
Putney Common
PUT/ROE SW15 18 G8
Putney Ex *PUT/ROE* SW15 * 19 H9
Putney Heath
PUT/ROE SW15 27 N2
Putney Heath La
PUT/ROE SW15 28 A2
Putney High St
PUT/ROE SW15 19 J9
Putney Hl *PUT/ROE* SW15 28 A3
Putney Park Av
PUT/ROE SW15 18 E9
Putney Park La
PUT/ROE SW15 18 F9
Puttenham Heath Rd
RGUW GU3 130 D1
Puttenham Hl *RGUW* GU3 110 C9
Puttenham La
MFD/CHID GU8 130 C4
Puttenham Rd *RFNM* GU10 129 L1
Puttock Cl *HASM* GU27 183 N5
Pye Cl *CTHM* CR3 101 M3
Pyecombe Ct *CRAWW* RH11 176 C8
Pyegrove Cha *BRAK* RG12 32 G8
Pyestock Crs *FARN* GU14 87 M3
Pylbrook Rd *SUT* SM1 61 L2
Pyle Hl *WOKS/MYFD* GU22 92 C5
Pymers Md *DUL* SE21 30 D4
Pyne Rd *SURB* KT6 41 N9
Pyrcroft La *WEY* KT13 56 D4
Pyrcroft Rd *CHERT* KT16 37 K8
Pyrford Common Rd
WOKS/MYFD GU22 73 J5
Pyrford Heath
WOKS/MYFD GU22 73 K5
Pyrford Rd *BF/WBF* KT14 73 L3
Pyrford Woods Cl
WOKS/MYFD GU22 73 K4
Pyrford Woods Rd
WOKS/MYFD GU22 73 K4
Pyrland Rd
RCHPK/HAM TW10 26 E2
Pyrmont Gv *WNWD* SE27 30 C6
Pyrmont Rd *CHSWK* W4 17 N4
Pytchley Crs *NRWD* SE19 30 D9

Q

The Quadrangle *GUW* GU2 111 N6
HNHL SE24 * 30 D1
WBPTN SW10 * 19 N6
Quadrant Ct *BRAK* RG12 32 G4
Quadrant Rd *RCH/KEW* TW9 17 K9
THHTH CR7 45 K5
The Quadrant *ASHV* GU12 109 J2
BELMT SM2 61 N5
GU GU1 * 6 D5
RCH/KEW TW9 17 L9
RYNPK SW20 43 J2
Quadrant Wy *WEY* KT13 56 B3
Quail Cl *HORS* RH12 192 C3
Quail Gdns *CROY/NA* CR0 64 E8
Quaker La *NWDGN* UB2 16 A1
Quakers Wy *RGUW* GU3 111 J1
Qualitas *BRAK* RG12 32 B9
Quality St *REDH* RH1 100 D8
Quantock Cl *CRAWW* RH11 176 E5
DTCH/LGLY SL3 12 E3
HYS/HAR UB3 14 F5
Quarrendon St *FUL/PGN* SW6 19 L6
Quarr Rd *CAR* SM5 43 P7
Quarry Bank *LTWR* GU18 51 P9
Quarry Cl *HORS* RH12 192 E4
LHD/OX KT22 97 K1
OXTED RH8 123 L1
Quarry Gdns *LHD/OX* KT22 97 K1
Quarry Hl *GODL* GU7 150 A1
Quarry Hill Pk *REIG* RH2 119 N2
Quarry La *YTLY* GU46 67 J3
Quarry Park Rd *SUT* SM1 61 K5
Quarry Ri *EGRIN* RH19 162 F9
SUT SM1 61 K5
Quarry Rd *GDST* RH9 102 C8
GODL GU7 130 G6
OXTED RH8 123 L1
WAND/EARL SW18 28 F2
Quarry St *GU* GU1 6 E7
The Quarry
BRKHM/BTCW RH3 118 B3
GU GU1 * 7 F4
Quarterbrass Farm Rd
HORS RH12 192 C3
Quartermaine Av
WOKS/MYFD GU22 92 D2
Quarter Mile Rd *GODL* GU7 150 D2
Quarters Rd *FARN* GU14 88 E5
Quebec Av *BH/WHM* TN16 105 H6
Quebec Cl *HORL* RH6 160 B1
LIPH GU30 182 F7
Quebec Gdns *BLKW* GU17 67 P4
Quebec Sq *BH/WHM* TN16 105 H6
Queen Adelaide Rd
PGE/AN SE20 31 K9
Queen Alexandra's Wy
HOR/WEW KT19 59 N9
Queen Anne Av *HAYES* BR2 47 N4
Queen Anne Dr
ESH/CLAY KT10 58 E6
Queen Anne's Cl *WDSR* SL4 20 A6
WHTN TW2 25 L6
Queen Anne's Gdns
CHSWK W4 18 C1
MTCM CR4 * 44 B4
Queen Anne's Ga *FNM* GU9 107 P7
Queen Anne's Gv *CHSWK* W4 18 C1
Queen Annes Ms
LHD/OX KT22 * 97 H1
Queen Anne's Ride
WDSR SL4 20 B3
Queen Anne's Ter
LHD/OX KT22 * 97 H1
Queen Caroline Est
HMSMTH W6 18 G3
Queen Caroline St
HMSMTH W6 18 G3
Queendale Ct
WOKN/KNAP GU21 71 M5
Queen Eleanor's Rd
GUW GU2 111 M6
Queen Elizabeth Dr
ALDT GU11 108 B4
Queen Elizabeth Gdns
MRDN SM4 43 L5
Queen Elizabeth Rd
CBLY GU15 50 F8
HORS RH12 189 N3
KUTN/CMB KT2 9 F4
Queen Elizabeth's Dr
CROY/NA CR0 65 K8
Queen Elizabeth's Wk
WLGTN SM6 62 F3
Queen Elizabeth Wk
BARN SW13 18 E6
Queen Elizabeth Wy
WOKS/MYFD GU22 72 D8
Queenhill Rd *SAND/SEL* CR2 64 B8
Queenhythe Rd *RGUE* GU4 92 B8
Queen Mary Av *CBLY* GU15 68 C3
MRDN SM4 43 H6
Queen Mary Cl *CHSGTN* KT9 59 N2
FLEETN GU51 86 F5
WOKS/MYFD GU22 * 72 G5
Queen Mary Rd *NRWD* SE19 30 C9
SHPTN TW17 38 E3
Queen Mary's Av *CAR* SM5 62 B6
Queen Mary's Dr
ADL/WDHM KT15 55 K8
Queens Acre *CHEAM* SM3 61 H6
Queen's Av *ALDT* GU11 108 D1
BF/WBF KT14 73 P1
FELT TW13 24 D7
Queensberry Ms West
SKENS SW7 19 P2
Queensberry Pl *SKENS* SW7 * 19 P2
Queensberry Wy
SKENS SW7 * 19 P2
Queensbridge Pk *ISLW* TW7 25 L2
Queensbury Pl *BLKW* GU17 67 N5
Queens Cl *CHOB/PIR* GU24 70 G6
ESH/CLAY KT10 * 58 B3
FARN GU14 88 D7
KWD/TDW/WH KT20 98 E4
WDSR SL4 20 F1
WLGTN SM6 62 D4
Queens Club Gdns
WKENS W14 19 J4
Queens Club Ter
WKENS W14 * 19 K4
Queens Ct *BELMT* SM2 * 61 L9
FNM GU9 107 M7
WEY KT13 56 G4
WOKS/MYFD GU22 10 E6
Queens Court Ride *COB* KT11 75 J2
Queens Crs *DORK* RH4 * 116 G8
RCHPK/HAM TW10 26 E1
Queens Dr *BRYLDS* KT5 41 N8
GODL GU7 131 H6
GUW GU2 111 N2
LHD/OX KT22 58 C9
THDIT KT7 40 G7
Queen's Elm Sq *CHEL* SW3 19 P3
Queen's Gdns *HEST* TW5 15 N6
Queens Garth *FSTH* SE23 * 31 K5
Queensgate *COB* KT11 75 M1
Queens Ga *HORL* RH6 159 K4
SKENS SW7 * 19 N2
Queensgate Gdns
PUT/ROE SW15 18 F9
Queens Gate Gdns
SKENS SW7 19 N1
Queen's Gate Ms *SKENS* SW7 19 N1
Queen's Gate Pl *SKENS* SW7 19 N1
Queen's Gate Place Ms
SKENS SW7 19 N1
Queen's Gate Rd *FARN* GU14 88 D8
Queen's Gate Ter *SKENS* SW7 19 N1
Queenshill Ldg *ASC* SL5 34 B4
Queens Hill Ri *ASC* SL5 34 C4
Queens Keep *TWK* TW1 * 26 B2
Queensland Av
WIM/MER SW19 43 M2
Queens La *FNM* GU9 107 M7
Queensmead *FARN* GU14 88 D4
LHD/OX KT22 * 58 C9
Queen's Md *MFD/CHID* GU8 168 A7
Queensmead Av *EW* KT17 60 F8
Queen's Mead Rd *HAYES* BR2 47 M3
Queensmere Cl
WIM/MER SW19 28 A5
Queensmere Rd
WIM/MER SW19 28 A5
Queensmill Rd *FUL/PGN* SW6 19 H5
Queens Pde *SWTR* RH13 * 192 C9
Queens Park Gdns
FELT TW13 24 A6
Queen's Park Rd *CTHM* CR3 101 N3
Queens Pine *BRAK* RG12 32 G7
Queen's Pl *ASC* SL5 34 A4
MRDN SM4 43 L5
WOT/HER KT12 56 G4
Queens Prom *KUT* KT1 41 K5
Queen's Ride *BARN* SW13 18 F8
Queen's Ri *RCHPK/HAM* TW10 26 E2
Queens Ride *CWTH* RG45 49 L2
Queens Rd *ALDT* GU11 108 B4
ASC SL5 34 D6
BECK BR3 46 E3
BELMT SM2 61 L8
BMLY BR1 47 N3
CBLY GU15 68 D4
CHOB/PIR GU24 70 E9
EGH TW20 21 L9
EGRIN RH19 180 D3
FARN GU14 88 F7
FELT TW13 24 C4
FLEETS GU52 86 G8
FNM GU9 107 N8
GU GU1 7 F3
HORL RH6 159 K1
HPTN TW12 25 J7
HSLW TW3 16 B8
KUTN/CMB KT2 9 J1
MORT/ESHN SW14 18 B8
MRDN SM4 43 L5
MTCM CR4 43 P4
NWMAL KT3 42 D5
RCHPK/HAM TW10 26 E2
TEDD TW11 25 N9
THDIT KT7 40 F6
TWK TW1 25 N4
WEY KT13 56 F4
WIM/MER SW19 28 E8
WLGTN SM6 62 D4
WOKN/KNAP GU21 71 J7
WOT/HER KT12 57 J3
Queens Sq *CRAWE* RH10 176 G5
Queen's Ter *ISLW* TW7 16 G9
THDIT KT7 * 40 G7
Queensthorpe Ms *SYD* SE26 * 31 L7
Queensthorpe Rd *SYD* SE26 31 L7
Queen St *ASHV* GU12 108 F4
CHERT KT16 37 L9
CROY/NA CR0 2 C7
GODL GU7 131 L9
SHGR GU5 134 E1
SWTR RH13 192 C9
Queensville Rd *CLAP* SW4 29 N3
Queens Wk *ASHF* TW15 22 G7
Queens Wy *FELT* TW13 24 D7
Queensway *CRAN* GU6 171 J1
CRAWE RH10 177 H5
CROY/NA CR0 63 H4
EGRIN RH19 180 D2
FRIM GU16 69 J9
REDH RH1 120 B4
SUN TW16 39 K3
SWTR RH13 192 B9
WOT/HER KT12 57 K4
WWKM BR4 65 N3
Queensway North
WOT/HER KT12 57 L4
Queensway South
WOT/HER KT12 57 L4
Queenswood Av *HEST* TW5 15 P7
HPTN TW12 25 J9
THHTH CR7 45 J6
WLGTN SM6 62 F3
Queenswood Rd *FSTH* SE23 31 M6
WOKN/KNAP GU21 71 K8
Quennell Cl *ASHTD* KT21 77 M8
Quennells Hl *RFNM* GU10 127 J7
Quentins Dr *BH/WHM* TN16 * 84 F5
Quentins Wk
BH/WHM TN16 * 84 F5
Quentin Wy *VW* GU25 35 P5
Querrin St *FUL/PGN* SW6 19 N7
Quick Rd *CHSWK* W4 18 C3
Quicks Rd *WIM/MER* SW19 43 M1
Quiet Cl *ADL/WDHM* KT15 55 L3
The Quillot *WOT/HER* KT12 57 H4
Quince Cl *ASC* SL5 34 D5
Quince Dr *CHOB/PIR* GU24 71 H4
Quincy Rd *EGH* TW20 21 M8
Quintilis *BRAK* RG12 32 B9
Quintin Av *RYNPK* SW20 43 J2
Quinton Cl *BECK* BR3 47 J4
HEST TW5 15 K5
WLGTN SM6 62 D3
Quinton Rd *THDIT* KT7 40 G9
Quinton St *WAND/EARL* SW18 28 F5
Quintrell Cl
WOKN/KNAP GU21 71 P6

R

Rabies Heath Rd
REDH RH1 122 A5
Raby Rd *NWMAL* KT3 42 B5
Raccoon Wy *HSLWW* TW4 15 L7
Racecourse Rd *LING* RH7 162 E1
Racecourse Wy *HORL* RH6 159 J5
Rachaels Lake Vw
BNFD RG42 32 G1
Rackfield *HASM* GU27 183 N3
Rackham Cl *CRAWW* RH11 176 G7
Rackham Ms
STRHM/NOR SW16 29 M9
Rackstraw Rd *SHST* GU47 49 P8
Racquets Court Hl
GODL GU7 131 J7
Racton Rd *FUL/PGN* SW6 19 L4
Radar Rd *FARN* GU14 87 P6
Radbourne Av *EA* W5 17 J2
Radbourne Rd *BAL* SW12 29 M3
Radcliffe Cl *FRIM* GU16 69 H9
Radcliffe Gdns *CAR* SM5 62 A6
Radcliffe Rd *CROY/NA* CR0 3 K4
Radcliffe Wy *BNFD* RG42 32 A2
Radcot Av *DTCH/LGLY* SL3 12 F1
Radford Cl *FNM* GU9 108 A9
Radford Rd *CRAWE* RH10 159 M8
Radical Ride *EWKG* RG40 48 D2
Radipole Rd *FUL/PGN* SW6 19 K6
Radius Pk
EBED/NFELT TW14 * 15 H9
Rad La *SHGR* GU5 134 G3
Radlet Av *SYD* SE26 31 J6
Radley Cl *EBED/NFELT* TW14 24 A4
Radley Ms *KENS* W8 19 L1
Radnor Cl *MTCM* CR4 44 G6
Radnor Gdns *TWK* TW1 25 N5
Radnor La *SHGR* GU5 135 J6
Radnor Rd *BRAK* RG12 33 H4
SHGR GU5 134 F7
TWK TW1 25 N5
WEY KT13 56 C2
Radnor Ter *WKENS* W14 19 K2
Radnor Wk *CROY/NA* CR0 46 E8
Radnor Wy *DTCH/LGLY* SL3 12 C2
Radolphs
KWD/TDW/WH KT20 99 H2
Radstock Wy *REDH* RH1 100 G9

Radstone Ct
WOKS/MYFD GU22 ....10 E6
Raeburn Av BRYLDS KT5 ....41 P7
Raeburn Cl KUT KT1 ....8 B1
Raeburn Ct
WOKN/KNAP GU21 * 71 N8
Raeburn Wy SHST GU47 ....67 P2
Rae Rd FARN GU14 ....88 D6
Rafford Wy BMLY BR1 ....47 P3
Raf Gate Rd FARN GU14 ....88 D6
Rag Hill Rd BH/WHM TN16 ....104 B1
Raglan Cl ASHV GU12 ....108 E5
FRIM GU16 ....69 H8
HSLWW TW4 ....24 F1
REIG RH2 ....119 N3
Raglan Ct CROY/NA CR0 ....63 K4
Raglan Rd REIG RH2 ....119 N3
WOKN/KNAP GU21 ....71 L7
Raikes La RDKG RH5 ....135 K4
Railey Rd CRAWE RH10 ....177 H5
Railshead Rd ISLW TW7 ....17 H9
Railton Rd GUW GU2 ....111 P1
HNHL SE24 ....30 B1
Railway Ap CHERT KT16 * 37 K9
EGRIN RH19 ....180 C2
TWK TW1 ....25 P3
WLGTN SM6 * 62 D5
Railway Cottages
BNSTD SM7 * 79 K3
OXTED RH8 * 123 N4
WIM/MER SW19 * 28 E7
Railway Rd TEDD TW11 ....25 M7
Railway Side BARN SW13 ....18 C8
Railway Ter BH/WHM TN16 ....105 H5
FELT TW13 ....24 B4
STA TW18 ....22 A8
Railway Vw DTCH/LGLY SL3 * ..12 D8
Rainbow Ct
WOKN/KNAP GU21 ....71 L5
Rainham Cl BTSEA SW11 ....29 H2
Rainville Rd HMSMTH W6 ....18 G4
Rake La MFD/CHID GU8 ....149 N5
Rakers Rdg HORS RH12 ....192 C5
Raleigh Av WLGTN SM6 ....62 F3
Raleigh Ct CRAWE RH10 * 159 K9
STA TW18 ....22 D7
Raleigh Dr BRYLDS KT5 ....42 A9
ESH/CLAY KT10 ....58 D4
HORL RH6 ....160 B1
Raleigh Gdns
BRXS/STRHM SW2 ....30 A2
MTCM CR4 ....44 B4
Raleigh Rd FELT TW13 ....24 A5
NWDGN UB2 ....15 N3
PGE/AN SE20 ....46 D1
RCH/KEW TW9 ....17 M8
Raleigh Wk CRAWE RH10 ....177 H7
Raleigh Wy CBLY GU15 ....69 H5
FELT TW13 ....24 D8
Ralliwood Rd ASHTD KT21 ....77 N8
Ralph Perring Ct BECK BR3 ....46 G5
Ralphs Cross GT/LBKH KT23 * ..96 C6
Ralphs Ride BRAK RG12 ....32 G4
Rama Cl STRHM/NOR SW16 ....44 G1
Rambler Cl
STRHM/NOR SW16 ....29 M7
Rambler La DTCH/LGLY SL3 ....12 A1
Ramblers Wy CRAWW RH11 ....194 E1
Rame Cl TOOT SW17 ....29 K8
Ramilles Cl BRXS/STRHM SW2 ..29 P2
Ramillies Cl ALDT GU11 ....88 C8
Ramillies Rd CHSWK W4 ....18 B1
Ramones Ter MTCM CR4 * 44 E5
Ramornie Cl WOT/HER KT12 ....57 P3
Ram Pas KUT KT1 ....8 B5
Ramsay Cl CBLY GU15 ....51 K9
Ramsay Rd ACT W3 ....18 A1
BFOR GU20 ....52 E4
Ramsbury Cl BRAK RG12 ....32 A7
Ramsdale Rd TOOT SW17 ....29 K8
Ramsdell Rd FLEETN GU51 ....86 D4
Ramsden Ga BAL SW12 * 29 L3
Ramsden Rd BAL SW12 ....29 K3
GODL GU7 ....150 C1
Ramsey Cl HORL RH6 ....159 J1
HORS RH12 ....192 C5
Ramsey Pl CTHM CR3 ....101 L2
Ramsey Rd THHTH CR7 ....45 H7
Ramslade Rd BRAK RG12 ....32 E6
Rams La MFD/CHID GU8 ....169 M9
Ram St WAND/EARL SW18 ....28 E1
Randal Crs REIG RH2 ....119 L7
Randall Cl DTCH/LGLY SL3 ....12 D3
Randalls Crs LHD/OX KT22 ....76 G9
Randalls Park Av
LHD/OX KT22 ....76 G9
Randalls Park Dr
LHD/OX KT22 ....96 G1
Randalls Rd LHD/OX KT22 ....76 E9
Randalls Wy LHD/OX KT22 ....96 G1
Randle Rd RCHPK/HAM TW10 ..26 B7
Randlesdown Rd CAT SE6 ....31 P7
Randle's La ORP BR6 ....85 P3
Randolph Cl COB KT11 ....76 A4
KUTN/CMB KT2 * 27 H8
WOKN/KNAP GU21 ....71 L6
Randolph Dr FARN GU14 ....87 N4
Randolph Rd DTCH/LGLY SL3 ..12 C1
EW KT17 ....78 D3
Ranelagh Av BARN SW13 ....18 E7
FUL/PGN SW6 ....19 K8
Ranelagh Crs ASC SL5 ....33 L2
Ranelagh Dr BRAK RG12 ....32 E4
TWK TW1 ....17 H9
Ranelagh Gdns CHSWK W4 ....18 A5
FUL/PGN SW6 ....19 J8
Ranelagh Pl NWMAL KT3 ....42 C6
Ranelagh Rd REDH RH1 ....120 A5
Ranfurly Rd SUT SM1 ....61 L1
Range Ride CBLY GU15 ....68 B1
Range Rd EWKG RG40 ....48 F2
FARN GU14 ....87 N6
The Range SHGR GU5 ....132 E9
Range Vw SHST GU47 ....50 A9
Range Wy SHPTN TW17 ....38 C8
Rankine Cl FNM GU9 ....108 C8
Ranmere St BAL SW12 ....29 L4
Ranmore Av CROY/NA CR0 ....3 K6
Ranmore Cl CRAWW RH11 ....194 F2
REDH RH1 ....120 C2
Ranmore Common Rd
RDKG RH5 ....116 D4
Ranmore Pl WEY KT13 * 56 E4
Ranmore Rd BELMT SM2 ....61 H7
RDKG RH5 ....116 E5
Rannoch Rd HMSMTH W6 ....18 G4
Ransome Cl CRAWW RH11 ....176 A8
Ranyard Cl CHSGTN KT9 ....59 M2
Rapallo Cl FARN GU14 ....88 E3
Raphael Dr THDIT KT7 ....40 F9
Rapley Cl CBLY GU15 ....51 H9
Rapley Gn BRAK RG12 ....32 E7
Rapley's Fld CHOB/PIR GU24 ..90 E3
Rapsley La WOKN/KNAP GU21 ..71 H7
Rashleigh Ct FLEETS GU52 ....107 H2
Rasset Md FLEETS GU52 ....106 E3
Rastell Av BRXS/STRHM SW2 ..29 N5
Ratcliffe Rd FARN GU14 ....68 B8
Rathbone Sq CROY/NA CR0 * ..2 C7
Rathfern Rd CAT SE6 ....31 N4
Rathgar Cl REDH RH1 ....140 C1
Rathlin Rd CRAWW RH11 ....176 E8
Rathmell Dr CLAP SW4 ....29 N2
Ravelin Cl RFNM GU10 ....106 D9
Raven Cl CRAWE RH10 ....179 K6
YTLY GU46 ....66 F2
Ravendale Rd SUN TW16 ....39 H3
Ravenfield Rd TOOT SW17 ....29 J6
Raven La CRAWW RH11 ....176 F3
Ravenna Rd PUT/ROE SW15 ....28 A1
Ravens Ait SURB KT6 * 41 K6
Ravensbourne Av HAYES BR2 ..47 K2
STWL/WRAY TW19 ....23 H4
Ravensbourne Pk
BROCKY SE4 ....31 P3
Ravensbourne Park Crs
CAT SE6 ....31 N3
Ravensbourne Rd BMLY BR1 ..47 N4
CAT SE6 ....31 N3
TWK TW1 ....26 B2
Ravensbury Av MRDN SM4 ....43 N6
Ravensbury Gv MTCM CR4 ....43 P5
Ravensbury La MTCM CR4 ....43 P5
Ravensbury Rd
WAND/EARL SW18 ....28 E5
Ravensbury Ter
WAND/EARL SW18 ....28 E5
Ravenscar Rd SURB KT6 ....59 M1
Ravens Cl HAYES BR2 ....47 M3
REDH RH1 ....120 B4
WOKN/KNAP GU21 ....71 J5
Ravenscourt SUN TW16 ....39 H2
Ravenscourt Av
HMSMTH W6 ....18 E2
Ravenscourt Gdns
HMSMTH W6 ....18 D2
Ravenscourt Pk
HMSMTH W6 ....18 E2
Ravenscourt Pl HMSMTH W6 ..18 F2
Ravenscourt Rd
HMSMTH W6 ....18 F2
Ravenscourt Sq HMSMTH W6 ..18 E1
Ravenscroft Cl ASHV GU12 ....109 L3
Ravenscroft Rd BECK BR3 ....46 C3
CHSWK W4 ....18 A2
WEY KT13 ....56 E9
Ravensdale Gdns NRWD SE19 ..45 M1
Ravensdale Ms STA TW18 ....22 E9
Ravensdale Rd ASC SL5 ....34 A6
HSLWW TW4 ....15 N8
Ravensfield EGH TW20 ....20 G9
Ravensfield Gdns
HOR/WEW KT19 ....60 C4
Ravenshead Cl
SAND/SEL CR2 ....64 C9
Ravenslea Rd BAL SW12 ....29 J3
Ravensmead Rd HAYES BR2 ....47 K1
Ravensmede Wy CHSWK W4 ..18 D2
Ravenstone Rd CBLY GU15 ....69 M3
Ravenstone St BAL SW12 ....29 K4
Ravens Wold PUR/KEN CR8 ....81 L4
Ravenswood Av CWTH RG45 ..49 J4
SURB KT6 ....59 M1
WWKM BR4 ....47 J9
Ravenswood Cl COB KT11 ....75 M4
Ravenswood Ct
KUTN/CMB KT2 * 26 G9
WOKS/MYFD GU22 ....10 D5
Ravenswood Crs WWKM BR4 ..47 J9
Ravenswood Dr CBLY GU15 ....69 J3
Ravenswood Gdns ISLW TW7 ..16 E6
Ravenswood Rd BAL SW12 ....29 L3
CROY/NA CR0 ....2 A6
Rawlins Cl SAND/SEL CR2 ....64 F6
Rawlinson Rd CBLY GU15 ....68 B2
Rawnsley Av MTCM CR4 ....43 P6
Raworth Cl CRAWE RH10 * 177 M7
Raygnoldes FLEETS GU52 ....106 E3
Ray La LING RH7 ....142 G6
Rayleigh Av TEDD TW11 ....25 M9
Rayleigh Ct KUT KT1 ....9 H4
Rayleigh Ri SAND/SEL CR2 ....63 N5
Rayleigh Rd WIM/MER SW19 ..43 K2
Raymead Av THHTH CR7 ....45 J6
Raymead Cl LHD/OX KT22 ....96 E2
Raymead Wy LHD/OX KT22 ....96 E2
Raymer Wk HORL RH6 ....140 E9
Raymond Av HNWL W7 ....16 G1
Raymond Cl DTCH/LGLY SL3 ..13 J6
SYD SE26 ....31 K8
Raymond Crs GUW GU2 ....111 M6
Raymond Rd BECK BR3 ....46 E5
DTCH/LGLY SL3 ....12 E2
WIM/MER SW19 ....28 C9
Raymond Wy
ESH/CLAY KT10 * 58 G5
Rayners Cl DTCH/LGLY SL3 ....12 G5
Rayner's Rd PUT/ROE SW15 ....28 B1
Raynham Rd HMSMTH W6 ....18 F2
Ray Rd E/WMO/HCT KT8 ....40 B6
Rays Rd WWKM BR4 ....47 J8
Raywood Cl WDR/YW UB7 ....14 E5
Rdffye Ct HORS RH12 ....192 F6
The Readens BNSTD SM7 ....80 A5
Reading Arch Rd REDH RH1 ..120 B5
Reading Rd BLKW GU17 ....67 M4
FARN GU14 ....88 E6
HTWY RG27 ....48 B9
SUT SM1 ....61 N4
Reading Rd North
FLEETN GU51 ....86 E6
Reading Rd South
FLEETN GU51 ....86 F7
Read Rd ASHTD KT21 ....77 K6
Reads Rest La
KWD/TDW/WH KT20 ....79 K8
Reapers Cl HORS RH12 ....192 C5
Reapers Wy ISLW TW7 ....25 L1
Rebecca Cl FLEETS GU52 ....106 E3
Reckitt Rd CHSWK W4 ....18 C3
Recovery St TOOT SW17 ....29 H8
Recreation Cl FARN GU14 ....68 B7
Recreation Rd GU GU1 ....6 D2
HAYES BR2 ....47 M3
NWDGN UB2 ....15 N2
RFNM GU10 ....146 B1
SYD SE26 ....31 L7
Recreation Wy MTCM CR4 ....44 G4
Rectory Cl ASHTD KT21 ....77 M8
BF/WBF KT14 ....74 A2
BRAK RG12 ....32 E5
CRAN GU6 ....153 P6
GODL GU7 ....150 E2
RDKG RH5 ....155 K9
RGUE GU4 ....113 H3
RYNPK SW20 ....42 G3
SHGR GU5 ....132 D7
SHPTN TW17 ....38 C4
SHST GU47 ....49 K9
SURB KT6 ....41 J9
Rectory Gdn CRAN GU6 * 152 G9
Rectory Gdns BECK BR3 * 46 G2
Rectory Gn BECK BR3 ....46 F2
Rectory Gv CROY/NA CR0 ....2 A4
FELT TW13 ....24 G7
Rectory La ASHTD KT21 ....77 M7
BF/WBF KT14 ....74 A2
BFOR GU20 ....52 C6
BH/WHM TN16 ....104 C3
BH/WHM TN16 ....105 N4
BNSTD SM7 ....80 B4
BRAK RG12 ....32 D5
BRKHM/BTCW RH3 ....118 D3
CRAWW RH11 ....176 C3
GT/LBKH KT23 ....95 P6
HORL RH6 ....158 A5
LIPH GU30 ....182 G3
RFNM GU10 ....126 B9
SHGR GU5 ....134 B1
SURB KT6 ....41 J9
TOOT SW17 ....29 K8
WLGTN SM6 ....62 E3
Rectory Orch
WIM/MER SW19 ....28 B7
Rectory Pk SAND/SEL CR2 ....81 N2
Rectory Rd BARN SW13 ....18 E7
BECK BR3 ....46 G2
COUL/CHIP CR5 ....99 P5
FARN GU14 ....88 E3
HEST TW5 ....15 K7
NWDGN UB2 ....15 P1
SUT SM1 ....61 L2
Rectory Rw BRAK RG12 ....32 D5
Red Admiral St HORS RH12 ....192 D5
Red Anchor Cl CHEL SW3 * 19 P4
Redan Gdns ASHV GU12 ....108 E4
Redan Hill Est ASHV GU12 * 108 E4
Redan Rd ASHV GU12 ....108 E4
Redan St WKENS W14 ....19 H1
Redbarn Cl PUR/KEN CR8 ....63 K9
Redberry Gv SYD SE26 ....31 K6
Redbridge Cottages
RHWH RH17 * 195 P8
Redbridge La RHWH RH17 ....195 L7
Redcliffe Cl ECT SW5 ....19 M3
Redcliffe Gdns WBPTN SW10 ..19 M3
Redcliffe Ms WBPTN SW10 ....19 M3
Redcliffe Pl WBPTN SW10 ....19 N4
Redcliffe Rd WBPTN SW10 ....19 N3
Redcliffe Sq WBPTN SW10 ....19 M3
Redcliffe St WBPTN SW10 * 19 M4
Redclose Av MRDN SM4 ....43 L6
Redcote Pl DORK RH4 ....117 K5
Red Cottage Ms
DTCH/LGLY SL3 ....12 A1
Redcourt WOKS/MYFD GU22 ....73 H4
Redcrest Gdns CBLY GU15 ....69 H3
Redcroft Wk CRAN GU6 ....171 H1
Red Deer Cl SWTR RH13 ....192 G7
Reddington Cl SAND/SEL CR2 ..63 M7
Reddington Dr
DTCH/LGLY SL3 ....12 D2
Redding Wy
WOKN/KNAP GU21 ....71 J7
Redditch BRAK RG12 ....32 F8
Redditch Cl CRAWW RH11 ....176 B9
Reddons Rd BECK BR3 ....46 E1
Reddown Rd COUL/CHIP CR5 ..80 F7
Rede Ct WEY KT13 ....56 D2
Redehall Rd HORL RH6 ....160 C3
Redesdale Gdns ISLW TW7 ....16 G5
Redfern Av HSLWW TW4 ....25 H3
Redfield La ECT SW5 ....19 L2
Redfield Ms ECT SW5 ....19 L2
Redfields La FLEETS GU52 ....106 E5
Redford Av COUL/CHIP CR5 ....80 D4
HORS RH12 ....192 A6
THHTH CR7 ....45 H5
WLGTN SM6 ....62 G5
Redford Cl FELT TW13 ....24 A5
Redgarth Ct EGRIN RH19 ....162 A9
Redgate Dr HAYES BR2 ....65 P1
Redgate Ter PUT/ROE SW15 ....28 A2
Redgauntlet EWKG RG40 ....48 C3
Redgrave Cl SNWD SE25 ....45 P7
Redgrave Dr CRAWE RH10 ....177 N6
Redgrave Rd PUT/ROE SW15 ..19 H9
Redhearne Flds RFNM GU10 ..165 H1
Redhill Rd COB KT11 ....74 D2
Red House La
MFD/CHID GU8 ....148 D1
WOT/HER KT12 ....57 J1
Redhouse Rd
BH/WHM TN16 ....104 A1
Red House Rd CROY/NA CR0 ....44 F7
Redkiln Cl SWTR RH13 ....192 E7
Redkiln Wy SWTR RH13 ....192 E7
Redland Gdns
E/WMO/HCT KT8 * 39 P5
Redlands COUL/CHIP CR5 ....80 G5
Redlands La RDKG RH5 ....136 G4
RFNM GU10 ....106 E7
Redlands Wy
BRXS/STRHM SW2 ....29 P3
Red La BOR GU35 ....164 E4
ESH/CLAY KT10 ....58 G5
OXTED RH8 ....123 P4
RDKG RH5 ....137 N3
Redleaves Av ASHF TW15 ....23 L9
Redlees Cl ISLW TW7 ....16 G9
Red Lion Ct HSLW TW3 * 16 B8
Red Lion La CHOB/PIR GU24 ....53 L7
FNM GU9 ....5 F6
Red Lion Rd CHOB/PIR GU24 ....53 L7
SURB KT6 ....59 M1
Red Lion Sq
WAND/EARL SW18 * 28 D1
Red Lion St
RCHPK/HAM TW10 ....26 C1
Red Lodge Rd WWKM BR4 ....47 J9
Redmayne CBLY GU15 ....69 L4
Redmead Rd HYS/HAR UB3 ....14 G2
Redmore Rd HMSMTH W6 * 18 F2
Red Oaks RFNM GU10 * 146 B1
Red Post Hl HNHL SE24 ....30 E1
Red River Ct HORS RH12 * 192 A5
Red Rd LTWR GU18 ....70 A1
Redroofs Cl BECK BR3 ....47 H2
Redstart Cl CROY/NA CR0 ....65 K8
Redstone Hl REDH RH1 ....120 C5
Redstone Hollow REDH RH1 ..120 C6
Redstone Mnr REDH RH1 ....120 C5
Redstone Pk REDH RH1 ....120 C5
Redstone Rd REDH RH1 ....120 C6
Redvers Buller Rd ALDT GU11 ..88 E8
Redvers Rd BRAK RG12 ....32 D6
WARL CR6 ....82 D7
Redway Dr WHTN TW2 ....25 K3
Redwing Av GODL GU7 ....131 K4
Redwing Cl SAND/SEL CR2 ....64 D9
SWTR RH13 ....192 E7
Redwing Gdns BF/WBF KT14 ..73 M1
Redwing Ri RGUE GU4 ....113 H3
Redwing Rd WLGTN SM6 ....62 G5
Redwood EGH TW20 ....37 J3
Redwood Cl CRAWE RH10 ....177 H3
PUR/KEN CR8 ....81 L3
Redwood Dr ASC SL5 ....35 H7
CBLY GU15 ....69 M4
Redwood Gv RGUE GU4 ....132 G2
Redwood Ms ASHF TW15 * 38 F1
Redwood Mt REIG RH2 ....119 L2
Redwoods ADL/WDHM KT15 ....55 L5
Redwoods Wy FLEETS GU52 ..107 H2
Reece Ms SKENS SW7 ....19 P2
Reed Cl ALDT GU11 ....88 F9
Reed Dr REDH RH1 ....120 C8
Reedham Dr PUR/KEN CR8 ....81 H2
Reedham Park Av
PUR/KEN CR8 ....81 J5
Reedings CRAWW RH11 ....176 A7
Reed Pl WOKN/KNAP GU21 ....73 J2
Reedsfield Cl ASHF TW15 ....23 L6
Reedsfield Rd ASHF TW15 ....23 L7
Reed's Hl BRAK RG12 ....32 D6
The Reeds Rd RFNM GU10 ....146 G3
Rees Gdns CROY/NA CR0 ....45 P7
Reeve Rd REDH RH1 ....119 N9
Reeves Cnr CROY/NA CR0 ....2 B4
Reeves Rd ASHV GU12 ....108 E5
Regal Ct MTCM CR4 ....44 B4
Regal Crs WLGTN SM6 ....62 D2
Regal Dr EGRIN RH19 ....180 E3
Regalfield Cl GUW GU2 ....111 N1
Regan Cl GUW GU2 ....91 P9
Regency Cl HPTN TW12 ....24 G8
Regency Ct
ADL/WDHM KT15 * 55 P3
Regency Dr BF/WBF KT14 ....73 K2
Regency Gdns
WOT/HER KT12 ....39 M9
Regency Ms BECK BR3 ....47 J2
Regency Ter SKENS SW7 * 19 P3
Regency Wk CROY/NA CR0 ....46 E7
Regent Cl ADL/WDHM KT15 ....55 N7
FLEETN GU51 ....86 G7
HEST TW5 ....15 K6
REDH RH1 ....100 E9
Regent Ct BAGS GU19 ....51 P7
GUW GU2 * 111 P3
Regent Crs REDH RH1 ....120 B3
Regent Pde BELMT SM2 * 61 N5
Regent Pk LHD/OX KT22 * 76 G7
Regent Pl WIM/MER SW19 ....28 F8
Regent Rd BRYLDS KT5 ....41 M6
HNHL SE24 ....30 C2
Regents Cl CRAWW RH11 ....176 F9
CTHM CR3 ....81 N7
SAND/SEL CR2 ....63 N5
Regents Ms HORL RH6 ....159 K1
Regents Pl SHST GU47 ....49 N9
Regent St CHSWK W4 ....17 N3
FLEETN GU51 ....86 G7
Regents Wk ASC SL5 ....34 C7
Regent Wy FRIM GU16 ....69 H7
Regiment Cl FARN GU14 * 87 N4
Regina Rd NWDGN UB2 ....15 N2
SNWD SE25 ....46 A4
Reid Av CTHM CR3 ....101 M1
Reid Cl COUL/CHIP CR5 ....80 D5
Reigate Av SUT SM1 ....43 M9
Reigate Cl CRAWE RH10 ....177 N2
Reigate Hl REIG RH2 ....119 M1
Reigate Hill Cl REIG RH2 ....119 L2
Reigate Rd
BRKHM/BTCW RH3 ....118 D4
DORK RH4 ....117 L5
EPSOM KT18 ....79 H6
EW KT17 ....60 D8
EW KT17 ....78 G4
HORL RH6 ....158 G2
LHD/OX KT22 ....97 J3
REIG RH2 ....119 N5
Reigate Wy WLGTN SM6 ....62 G4
Reindorp Cl GUW GU2 ....111 N6
Rembrandt Ct
HOR/WEW KT19 ....60 D5
Rendle Cl CROY/NA CR0 ....45 P6
Renfree Wy SHPTN TW17 ....38 C8
Renfrew Rd HEST TW5 ....15 M7
KUTN/CMB KT2 ....42 A1
The Renmans ASHTD KT21 ....77 M5
Renmuir St TOOT SW17 ....29 J9
Rennie Cl ASHF TW15 ....22 G6
Rennie Ter REDH RH1 ....120 C6
Renown Cl CROY/NA CR0 ....2 B2
Renton Cl
BRXS/STRHM SW2 * 30 A2
Replingham Rd
WAND/EARL SW18 ....28 C4
Reporton Rd FUL/PGN SW6 ....19 J6
Repton Av HYS/HAR UB3 ....14 F2
Repton Cl SUT SM1 ....62 A4
Repton Ct BECK BR3 ....47 H2
Reservoir Cl THHTH CR7 ....45 M4
Reservoir Rd FARN GU14 ....87 P6
Restmor Wy WLGTN SM6 ....62 C1
Restwell Av CRAN GU6 ....152 E6
Retreat Rd RCH/KEW TW9 ....26 C1
The Retreat BARN SW13 ....18 C8
BRYLDS KT5 ....41 M7
CRAN GU6 * 152 F8
EGH TW20 ....21 J9
THHTH CR7 ....45 M5
WPK KT4 ....60 F2
Revell Cl LHD/OX KT22 ....96 B2
Revell Dr LHD/OX KT22 ....96 B2
Revell Rd KUT KT1 ....41 P3
SUT SM1 ....61 K5
Revelstoke Av FARN GU14 ....88 D1
Revelstoke Rd
WAND/EARL SW18 ....28 D5
Revesby Cl CHOB/PIR GU24 ....70 D2
Revesby Rd CAR SM5 ....44 A7
Rewell St FUL/PGN SW6 * 19 N5
Rewley Rd CAR SM5 ....43 P7
Rex Av ASHF TW15 ....23 K9
Reynard Cl HORS RH12 ....192 G5
Reynard Dr NRWD SE19 ....45 P1
Reynolds Av CHSGTN KT9 ....59 L6
Reynolds Cl CAR SM5 ....44 B9
WIM/MER SW19 ....43 P2
Reynolds Gn SHST GU47 ....67 P2
Reynolds Pl CRAWW RH11 ....176 F4
RCHPK/HAM TW10 ....26 E2
Reynolds Rd CHSWK W4 ....18 A1
CRAWW RH11 ....176 F4
NWMAL KT3 ....42 B8
PECK SE15 ....31 K1
Reynolds Wy CROY/NA CR0 ....3 H7
Rheingold Wy WLGTN SM6 ....62 G7
Rhine Banks FARN GU14 ....87 P2
Rhodes Cl EGH TW20 ....21 P8
Rhodes Ct EGH TW20 * 21 P8
Rhodes Wy CRAWE RH10 ....177 J7
Rhododendron Cl ASC SL5 ....33 N1
Rhododendron Ride
EGH TW20 ....20 E8
Rhododendron Rd
FRIM GU16 ....69 K8
Rhododendron Wk ASC SL5 ....33 N1
Rhodrons Av CHSGTN KT9 ....59 L4
Rialto Rd MTCM CR4 ....44 C3
Ribble Pl FARN GU14 ....88 A1
Ribblesdale Rd
STRHM/NOR SW16 ....29 L8
Ricardo Ct SHGR GU5 ....132 D8
Ricardo Rd WDSR SL4 ....20 G2
Ricards Rd WIM/MER SW19 ....28 C8
Rices Hl EGRIN RH19 ....180 D2
Richard Cl FLEETN GU51 ....86 E8
Richards Cl ASHV GU12 * 109 J1
HYS/HAR UB3 ....14 F4
Richards Cottages CAR SM5 * ..62 B4
Richards Fld HOR/WEW KT19 ..60 B7
Richards Rd COB KT11 ....76 B3
Richbell Cl ASHTD KT21 ....77 K7
Richborough Ct
CRAWW RH11 * 176 F5
Richens Cl HSLW TW3 ....16 D7
Richford Ga HMSMTH W6 * 18 G1
Richings Wy IVER SL0 ....13 K1
Richland Av COUL/CHIP CR5 ....80 C4
Richlands Av EW KT17 ....60 E3
Richmond Av
EBED/NFELT TW14 ....23 P2
RYNPK SW20 ....43 J2
Richmond Cl BH/WHM TN16 ....83 P8
EPSOM KT18 ....78 C3
FARN GU14 ....87 P4

FLEETS GU52 ....86 F9
FRIM GU16 ....69 H7
GT/LBKH KT23 ....96 C4
Richmond Ct *CRAWE* RH10 ..177 H6
Richmond Crs *STA* TW18 * 22 C8
Richmond Dr *SHPTN* TW17 ....38 E7
Richmond Gn *CROY/NA* CRO ..62 C2
Richmond Hl
RCHPK/HAM TW10 ....26 D2
Richmond Pde *TWK* TW1 * 26 B4
Richmond Rd
KUTN/CMB KT2 ....8 E2
MORT/ESHN SW14 ....27 H1
Richmond Rd
BH/WHM TN16 ....84 B7
COUL/CHIP CR5 ....80 D4
CROY/NA CRO 62 C2
GODL GU8 ....131 K7
HORS RH12 ....192 B6
ISLW TW7 ....16 C9
KUTN/CMB KT2 ....26 C8
RYNPK SW20 ....42 F2
SHST GU47 ....50 A9
STA TW18 ....22 C8
THHTH CR7 ....45 K5
TWK TW1 ....26 A3
Richmond Wy *EGRIN* RH19 ..180 E3
GT/LBKH KT23 ....96 B3
Richmondwood *ASC* SL5 ......35 H9
Rickard Cl *BRXS/STRHM* SW2 ..30 B4
WDR/YW UB7 ....13 P1
Rickards Cl *SURB* KT6 ....59 L1
Ricketts Hill Rd
BH/WHM TN16 ....84 B7
Rickett St *FUL/PGN* SW6 ......19 L4
Rickfield *CRAWW* RH11 ......176 D6
Rickford Hl *RGUW* GU3 ......91 K6
Rickman Cl *BRAK* RG12 ......32 E7
Rickman Crs
ADL/WDHM KT15 ....55 M2
Rickman Hl *COUL/CHIP* CR5 ..80 D6
Rickman Hill Rd
COUL/CHIP CR5 ....80 D7
Rickman's La *BIL* RH14 ......187 L8
Ricksons La *EHSLY* KT24 ......94 D7
Rickwood *HORL* RH6 ....140 D9
Rickwood Pk *RDKG* RH5 * ..156 C3
Rickyard *GUW* GU2 ....111 K5
The Riddings *CTHM* CR3 ......101 P5
Riddlesdown Av
PUR/KEN CR8 ....81 L1
Riddlesdown Rd
PUR/KEN CR8 ....63 L8
PUR/KEN CR8 ....81 N4
Ride La *SHGR* GU5 ....133 P6
Riders Wy *GDST* RH9 ....122 C2
The Ride *BIL* RH14 ....187 P8
BTFD TW8 ....17 H3
Ride Wy *CRAN* GU6 ....153 L2
Rideway Cl *CBLY* GU15 ....68 D4
Ridge Cl *BRKHM/BTCW* RH3 ..117 P9
WOKS/MYFD GU22 ....91 P1
Ridgegate Cl *REIG* RH2 ......119 P3
Ridge Gn *REDH* RH1 ....120 C8
Ridge Green Cl *REDH* RH1 ..120 C8
Ridgehurst Dr *HORS* RH12 ..191 N9
Ridgelands *LHD/OX* KT22 ......96 D4
Ridge Langley *SAND/SEL* CR2 ..64 A8
Ridgemead Rd *EGH* TW20 ......20 G6
Ridge Moor Cl *GSHT* GU26 ..165 P6
Ridgemount *GUW* GU2 ....6 A3
WEY KT13 ....56 C1
Ridgemount Av
COUL/CHIP CR5 ....80 D6
CROY/NA CRO 46 D1
Ridge Mount Rd *ASC* SL5 ......34 C9
Ridgemount Wy *REDH* RH1 ..119 P7
Ridge Pk *WLGTN* SM6 ....62 F8
Ridge Rd *CHEAM* SM3 ....43 K9
MTCM CR4 ....44 D1
Ridgeside *CRAWE* RH10 ......177 J5
The Ridges *RGUW* GU3 ....113 N2
The Ridge *ASC* SL5 * 34 G8
BRYLDS KT5 ....41 N6
COUL/CHIP CR5 ....80 G3
CTHM CR3 ....103 L5
EPSOM KT18 ....78 A7
HORS RH12 ....189 P2
LHD/OX KT22 ....96 D4
PUR/KEN CR8 ....62 F8
WHTN TW2 ....25 L3
WOKS/MYFD GU22 ....11 J3
Ridge Wy *EDEN* TN8 ....144 G1
FELT TW13 ....24 F6
WU GU25 ....36 C6
Ridgeway *EGRIN* RH19 ....180 D4
HAYES BR2 ....65 N1
HOR/WEW KT19 ....78 B1
WOT/HER KT12 ....39 H9
Ridgeway Cl *CRAN* GU6 ......153 K9
DORK RH4 ....116 G9
LTWR GU18 ....52 A9
WOKS/MYFD GU21 ....72 D6
Ridgeway Ct *REDH* RH1 * ..120 A6
Ridgeway Dr *DORK* RH4 ......136 C1
Ridgeway Gdns
WOKN/KNAP GU21 ....72 D6
Ridgeway Rd *DORK* RH4 ......116 G9
ISLW TW7 ....16 E5
REDH RH1 ....120 B5
Ridgeway Rd North
ISLW TW7 ....16 E5
The Ridgeway *ACT* W3 ......17 N1
BRAK RG12 ....32 E4
CHOB/PIR GU24 ....70 F9
CRAN GU6 ....153 J9
EW KT17 ....60 D8
HORL RH6 ....159 K3
HORS RH12 ....192 A6
LHD/OX KT22 ....76 C3
LHD/OX KT22 ....96 D3
LTWR GU18 ....52 B8
The Ridge Wy *SAND/SEL* CR2 ..63 N8

Ridgewell Cl *SYD* SE26 ....31 N7
Ridgewood Dr *FRIM* GU16 ....69 M5
Ridgley Rd *MFD/CHID* GU8 ..167 P7
Ridgmount Rd
WAND/EARL SW18 ....28 E1
Ridgway *RCHPK/HAM* TW10 * ..26 C2
WIM/MER SW19 ....42 C1
WOKS/MYFD GU22 ....73 K4
Ridgway Gdns
WIM/MER SW19 ....43 H1
Ridgway Hill Rd *FNM* GU9 ..127 L6
Ridgway Pde *FNM* GU9 * 127 L6
Ridgway Pl *WIM/MER* SW19 ..28 B9
Ridgway Rd *FNM* GU9 ......127 N6
WOKS/MYFD GU22 ....73 K4
The Ridgway *BELMT* SM2 ..61 P6
Riding Court Rd
DTCH/LGLY SL3 ....12 A4
The Ridings *ADL/WDHM* KT15 ..55 J5
ASHTD KT21 ....78 B9
BH/WHM TN16 ....84 C6
BRYLDS KT5 ....41 N6
COB KT11 ....76 A1
CRAWE RH10 ....177 N4
*EWKT24 ....94 C5
EPSOM KT18 ....78 C3
EW KT17 ....60 D7
FRIM GU16 ....69 K5
IVER SL0 ....13 K2
KWD/TDW/WH KT20 ....79 K9
REDH RH1 ....119 P3
RPLY/SEND GU23 ....93 L3
SUN TW16 ....24 A7
The Riding *CRAN* GU6 ....153 H8
WOKN/KNAP GU21 ....72 F3
Ridlands Gv *OXTED* RH8 ......124 C5
Ridlands La *OXTED* RH8 ......124 C5
Ridlands Ri *OXTED* RH8 ......124 C1
Ridley Av *WEA* W13 ....17 H1
Ridley Cl *FLEETS* GU52 * 86 F9
Ridley Rd *HAYES* BR2 ....47 M4
WARL CR6 ....82 C7
WIM/MER SW19 ....43 M1
Ridsdale Rd *PGE/AN* SE20 ....46 B2
WOKN/KNAP GU21 ....71 P6
Riesco Dr *CROY/NA* CRO 64 C5
Rifle Wy *FARN* GU14 ....87 N4
Rigault Rd *FUL/PGN* SW6 ......19 J7
Rigby Cl *CROY/NA* CRO 63 J2
Riggindale Rd
STRHM/NOR SW16 ....29 N8
Riley St *WBPTN* SW10 ....19 P5
Rillside *CRAWE* RH10 ....177 M7
Rily Wk *EGRIN* RH19 ....180 G2
Rimbault Cl *ALDT* GU11 ......88 F8
Rimmer Cl *CRAWW* RH11 ....194 E2
Rinaldo Rd *BAL* SW12 ....29 L3
Ring Cl *BMLY* BR1 ....47 P1
Ringer's Rd *BMLY* BR1 ....47 N4
Ringford Rd
WAND/EARL SW18 ....28 C1
Ringley Av *HORL* RH6 ....159 K2
Ringley Oak *HORS* RH12 ......192 E6
Ringley Park Av *REIG* RH2 ..119 P6
Ringley Park Rd *REIG* RH2 ..119 N5
Ringley Rd *HORS* RH12 ......192 E6
Ringmead *BRAK* RG12 ....32 C7
Ringmer Av *FUL/PGN* SW6 ..19 J6
Ringmore Dr *RGUE* GU4 ......112 G2
Ringmore Ri *FSTH* SE23 ....31 J3
Ring Rd North *HORL* RH6 ....159 L4
Ring Rd South *HORL* RH6 ....159 M5
Ringstead Rd *CAR* SM1 ....61 P5
The Ring *BRAK* RG12 ....32 E4
Ringway *NWDGN* UB2 ....15 N3
Ringwold Cl *BECK* BR3 ....46 E1
Ringwood *BRAK* RG12 ....32 B6
REDH RH1 ....120 B2
Ringwood Cl *ASC* SL5 ....34 A5
CRAWE RH10 ....177 H7
Ringwood Gdns
PUT/ROE SW15 ....27 M5
FARN GU14 ....68 A9
Ringwood Wy *HPTN* TW12 ..25 H7
Ripley By-Pass
RPLY/SEND GU23 ....93 J6
Ripley La *RPLY/SEND* GU23 ..94 B4
Ripley Rd *HPTN* TW12 ....40 A1
RPLY/SEND GU23 ....93 N6
Ripley Wy *HOR/WEW* KT19 ..59 N9
Ripon Cl *CBLY* GU15 ....69 M5
GUW GU2 ....111 M2
Ripon Gdns *CHSGTN* KT9 ......59 K4
Ripon Rd *BLKW* GU17 ....67 N4
Ripplesmere *BRAK* RG12 ......32 F6
Ripplesmore Cl *SHST* GU47 ..49 M9
Ripston Rd *ASHF* TW15 ....23 N8
Risborough Dr *WPK* KT4 ....42 E8
Riseldine Rd *FSTH* SE23 ....31 M2
Rise Rd *ASC* SL5 ....34 E7
The Rise *CRAWE* RH10 ....177 N4
CWTH RG45 ....49 K4
EGRIN RH19 ....180 E3
EHSLY KT24 ....94 G6
EW KT17 ....60 D8
KWD/TDW/WH KT20 ....98 G1
SAND/SEL CR2 ....64 A2
Ritchie Cl *CRAWE* RH10 ......177 M9
Ritchie Rd *CROY/NA* CRO 46 B7
Ritherdon Rd *TOOT* SW17 ....29 K5
River Av *THDIT* KT7 ....40 G8
Riverbank *DORK* RH4 * 116 F7
E/WMO/HCT KT8 ....40 A4

River Bank *THDIT* KT7 ....40 F6
Riverbank Wy *BTFD* TW8 ......17 J4
Rivercourt Rd *HMSMTH* W6 ..18 F2
Riverdale Dr *WAND/EARL* SW18 ..28 E4
Riverdale Gdns *TWK* TW1 ....26 B1
Riverdale Rd *FELT* TW13 ......24 F7
TWK TW1 ....26 B2
Riverfield Rd *STA* TW18 * 22 C9
River Gdns *CAR* SM5 ....62 C1
EBED/NFELT TW14 ....24 C1
River Grove Pk *BECK* BR3 ....46 F2
Riverhead Dr *BELMT* SM2 ....61 M8
River Hl *COB* KT11 ....75 K4
Riverholme Dr
HOR/WEW KT19 ....60 B7
River La *COB* KT11 ....75 N5
FNM GU9 ....127 J6
LHD/OX KT22 ....76 D9
RCHPK/HAM TW10 ....26 C4
River Md *CRAWW* RH11 ......176 D2
HORS RH12 ....192 A9
Rivermead *BF/WBF* KT14 ......74 C2
E/WMO/HCT KT8 ....40 A4
SURB KT6 * 41 K6
Rivermead Cl
ADL/WDHM KT15 * 55 N6
TEDD TW11 ....26 A8
Rivermead Rd *CBLY* GU15 ....68 D6
River Mt *WOT/HER* KT12 ......39 H8
River Mount Gdns *GUW* GU2 ..112 A8
Rivernook Cl *WOT/HER* KT12 ..39 L6
River Park Av *STA* TW18 ......22 A7
Riverpark Gdns *HAYES* BR2 ..47 K1
River Reach *TEDD* TW11 ......26 B9
River Rd *STA* TW18 ....37 K2
YTLY GU46 ....66 F1
River Rw *FNM* GU9 ....127 K5
Rivers Cl *FARN* GU14 ....88 G6
Riversdale Rd *THDIT* KT7 ......40 G6
Riversdell Cl *CHERT* KT16 ....37 K8
Riverside *CHERT* KT16 * 37 L3
DORK RH4 ....117 K5
EDEN TN8 ....144 G4
FROW RH18 ....181 K6
GU GU1 ....112 B3
HORL RH6 ....159 K3
HORS RH12 ....191 P8
RCH/KEW TW9 * 17 M4
STWL/WRAY TW19 ....21 H3
SUN TW16 ....39 M3
TWK TW1 ....26 A4
Riverside Av
E/WMO/HCT KT8 ....40 C4
LTWR GU18 ....52 C9
Riverside Cl *CHOB/PIR* GU24 ..70 F9
KUT KT1 ....41 K5
STA TW18 ....37 K1
WLGTN SM6 ....62 D2
Riverside Dr *CHSWK* W4 ......18 C5
ESH/CLAY KT10 ....58 A5
MTCM CR4 ....43 P6
RCHPK/HAM TW10 ....26 C8
SHGR GU5 ....132 E6
STA TW18 ....22 B8
STA TW18 ....37 K1
Riverside Gdns *HMSMTH* W6 ..18 F3
WOKS/MYFD GU22 ....72 F1
Riverside Ms *CROY/NA* CRO * ..62 G2
Riverside Pl
STWL/WRAY TW19 ....22 G2
Riverside Rd *STA* TW18 ....37 K1
STWL/WRAY TW19 ....21 P2
TOOT SW17 ....28 G7
WOT/HER KT12 ....57 M3
The Riverside
E/WMO/HCT KT8 ....40 D4
Rivewood Cl *ISLW* TW7 ....16 E8
Riverside Vis *SURB* KT6 * 41 J7
Riverside Wk *ISLW* TW7 ....16 E8
KUT KT1 ....8 B4
Riverside Wy *CBLY* GU15 ......68 B5
Riversmeet *RFNM* GU10 ......128 E9
River Ter *HMSMTH* W6 ....18 G3
River Vw *ADL/WDHM* KT15 * ..55 N4
Riverview *GU* GU1 * 6 C2
Riverview Gdns *BARN* SW13 ..18 F3
COB KT11 ....75 J2
River View Gdns *TWK* TW1 ..25 N5
Riverview Pk *CAT* SE6 ....31 P5
Riverview Rd *CHSWK* W4 ......17 P5
HOR/WEW KT19 ....60 A3
River Wk *SUN* TW16 ....39 M3
WOT/HER KT12 ....39 J7
River Wy *FELT* TW13 ....24 F6
HOR/WEW KT19 ....60 B4
Riverway *STA* TW18 ....37 K2
Rivett-Drake Rd *GUW* GU2 ..111 N1
Rivey Cl *BF/WBF* KT14 ....73 K3
Road House Est
WOKS/MYFD GU22 * 72 E9
Roakes Av *ADL/WDHM* KT15 ..55 M1
Robert Cl *WOT/HER* KT12 ......57 K4
Robertsbridge Rd *CAR* SM5 ..43 P8
Roberts Cl *CHEAM* SM3 ....61 H6
STWL/WRAY TW19 ....22 F2
THHTH CR7 ....45 M4
Roberts Ct *CHSGTN* KT9 * 59 K4
Roberts Rd *ALDT* GU11 ....108 C6
BIL RH14 ....187 P7
Robert St *CROY/NA* CRO 2 D5
Roberts Wy *EGH* TW20 ....36 A1
Robin Cl *ADL/WDHM* KT15 ....55 P4
ASHV GU12 ....89 H9

CRAWW RH11 ....176 F3
EGRIN RH19 ....180 D1
HPTN TW12 ....24 F8
Robin Gdns *REDH* RH1 ......120 C8
Robin Gv *BTFD* TW8 ....17 J4
Robin Hl *GODL* GU7 ....131 K6
Robin Hill Dr *CBLY* GU15 ......69 J5
Robin Hood Cl *FARN* GU14 ..88 G4
WOKN/KNAP GU21 ....71 J7
Robin Hood Cl
WOKN/KNAP GU21 ....71 M7
Robin Hood Crs
WOKN/KNAP GU21 ....71 K7
Robin Hood La *HORS* RH12 ..191 M5
PUT/ROE SW15 ....27 K7
RGUE GU4 ....92 D4
SUT SM1 ....61 L4
Robinhood La *MTCM* CR4 ......44 E4
Robin Hood Rd
PUT/ROE SW15 ....27 K7
WOKN/KNAP GU21 ....71 M7
Robin Hood Wy
PUT/ROE SW15 ....27 K7
Robin Hood Wy (Kingston By-Pass)
PUT/ROE SW15 ....27 K7
Robinia Cl *PGE/AN* SE20 ......46 A2
Robin La *SHST* GU47 ....49 N8
Robin Rw *CRAWE* RH10 ......179 K6
Robins DI *WOKN/KNAP* GU21 ..71 J4
Robins Gv *WWKM* BR4 ....65 N2
Robins Grove Crs *YTLY* GU46 ..66 F2
Robinson Cl
WOKS/MYFD GU22 ....72 G9
Robinson Rd *CRAWW* RH11 ..176 C6
WIM/MER SW19 ....29 H9
Robinsway *WOT/HER* KT12 ..57 L3
Robinswood Ct
HORS RH12 * 192 B6
Robin Wy *GUW* GU2 ....111 P1
STA TW18 ....22 C6
Robin Willis Wy *WDSR* SL4....20 F2
Robinwood Pl
RCHPK/HAM TW10 ....26 C9
Robson Rd *WNWD* SE27 ....30 C6
Roby Dr *BRAK* RG12 ....32 F8
Robyns Wy *EDEN* TN8 ....145 H5
Rochelle Cl *BTSEA* SW11 ......19 P9
Robinson Cl
WOKS/MYFD GU22 ....72 G9
Roche Rd
STRHM/NOR SW16 ....44 G2
FELT TW13 ....24 A5
Rochester Cl
STRHM/NOR SW16 * 44 C1
Rochester Gdns *CROY/NA* CRO ..3 H5
CTHM CR3 ....101 N2
Rochester Gv *FLEETS* GU51 ..86 F7
Rochester Ms *EA* W5 * 17 J2
Rochester Pde *FELT* TW13 * ..24 B6
Rochester Rd *CAR* SM5 ....62 B3
EGH TW20 ....22 A8
Roche Wk *ARDN* SM4 ....43 J6
Rochford Wy *CROY/NA* CRO ..45 H7
Rockall Ct *DTCH/LGLY* SL3 ....12 F1
Rock Av *MORT/ESHN* SW14 ..18 A9
Rockbourne Rd *FSTH* SE23 ..31 L4
Rock Cl *MTCM* CR4 ....43 P4
Rockdale Dr *GSHT* GU26 ......165 N8
Rockell's Pl *EDUL* SE22 ....31 J2
The Rockery *FARN* GU14 ......87 P6
Rocket Rd *FARN* GU14 ....87 P6
Rockfield Cl *OXTED* RH8 ......123 M1
Rockfield Rd *OXTED* RH8 ....123 N1
Rockfield Wy *SHST* GU47 * ..49 P8
Rock Gdns *ALDT* GU11 ....108 B5
Rockhampton Rd
SAND/SEL CR2 ....63 N5
STRHM/NOR SW16 ....30 B7
Rock Hl *SYD* SE26 ....30 F9
Rockingham Cl
PUT/ROE SW15 ....18 D9
Rockland Rd *PUT/ROE* SW15 ..19 J9
Rockmount Rd *NRWD* SE19 ..30 E9
Rockshaw Rd *REDH* RH1 ....100 E7
Rocks La *BARN* SW13 ....18 E4
The Rocks *EGRIN* RH19 ......181 H5
Rockwell Gdns *NRWD* SE19 ..30 E7
Rockwood Pk *EGRIN* RH19 * ..180 B6
Rocky La *REIG* RH2 ....100 G6
Rocombe Crs *FSTH* SE23 * 31 K3
Roden Gdns *CROY/NA* CRO ..45 N7
Rodenhurst Rd *CLAP* SW4 ....29 N3
Rodmel Ct *FARN* GU14 ....88 B5
Rodmill La *BRXS/STRHM* SW2 ..29 P3
Rodney Cl
NWMAL KT3 ....42 C6
WOT/HER KT12 ....57 L2
Rodney Gdns *WWKM* BR4 ....65 N3
Rodney Pl *WIM/MER* SW19 ..43 N2
Rodney Rd *HSLW* TW3 ....15 J9
MTCM CR4 ....44 C4
NWMAL KT3 ....42 C6
WOT/HER KT12 ....57 L2
Rodney Wy *DTCH/LGLY* SL3 ..13 H6
GU GU1 ....112 E4
Rodona Rd *WEY* KT13 ....56 F9
Rodway Rd *BMLY* BR1 ....47 P2
PUT/ROE SW15 ....27 H3
Rodwell Rd *EDUL* SE22 ....30 G2
Roebuck Cl *ASHTD* KT21 ....77 K9
FELT TW13 ....24 C7
REIG RH2 ....119 L5
SWTR RH13 ....192 E8
Roebuck Rd *CHSGTN* KT9 ....59 N4
Roedean Crs *PUT/ROE* SW15 ..18 B9
Roedeer Copse *HASM* GU27 ..183 P4
Roehampton Cl
PUT/ROE SW15 ....18 E9
Roehampton Ga
PUT/ROE SW15 ....27 K2
Roehampton High St
PUT/ROE SW15 ....27 M3

Roehampton La
PUT/ROE SW15 ....27 N3
Roehampton V
PUT/ROE SW15 ....27 L6
Roffes La *CTHM* CR3 ....101 M5
Roffey Cl *HORL* RH6 ....159 J1
PUR/KEN CR8 ....81 K5
Roffey Pk *HORS* RH12 * 193 K4
Roffey's Cl *CRAWE* RH10 ....160 B8
Roffords *WOKN/KNAP* GU21 ..71 P6
Rogers Cl *COUL/CHIP* CR5 ....81 K7
Rogers La *WARL* CR6 ....82 E7
Rogers Md *GDST* RH9 ....122 B3
Rogers Rd *TOOT* SW17 ....28 G7
Rojack Rd *FSTH* SE23 ....31 L4
Rokeby Cl *BRAK* RG12 ....32 F3
Rokeby Pl *RYNPK* SW20 ......42 F1
PUR/KEN CR8 ....81 L3
Roke Cl *MFD/CHID* GU8 ......149 M7
PUR/KEN CR8 ....81 L3
Roke La *MFD/CHID* GU8 ....149 M7
Roke Lodge Rd
PUR/KEN CR8 ....81 K2
Roke Rd *PUR/KEN* CR8 ....81 L4
Rokers La *MFD/CHID* GU8 ..130 D6
Rokes Pl *YTLY* GU46 ....66 E2
Roland Gdns *SKENS* SW7 ....19 N3
Roland Wy *WBPTN* SW10 ....19 N5
WPK KT4 ....60 D1
Rollesby Rd *CHSGTN* KT9 ....59 N5
Rolleston Rd *SAND/SEL* CR2 ..63 N6
Rollit Crs *HSLW* TW3 ....25 H1
Rolliscourt Av *NRWL* SE24 ..30 D1
Romana Ct *STA* TW18 * 22 D7
Roman Cl *EBED/NFELT* TW14 ..24 D1
Roman Farm Wy *GUW* GU2 ..111 K4
Romanfield Rd
BRXS/STRHM SW2 ....30 A3
Romanhurst Av *HAYES* BR2 ..47 L5
Romanhurst Gdns *BECK* BR3 ..47 L4
Roman Ride *CWTH* RG45 ......49 H4
Roman Ri *NRWD* SE19 ....30 E9
Roman Rd *CHSWK* W4 ....18 C2
DORK RH4 ....116 G9
EDEN TN8 ....145 H8
Romans Wy
WOKS/MYFD GU22 ....73 L4
Roman Wy *BNFD* RG42 ....33 H2
CROY/NA CRO 2 B3
FNM GU9 ....128 A1
Romany Gdns *CHEAM* SM3 ..43 J8
The Romany *FARN* GU14 ....87 L6
Romayne Cl *FARN* GU14 ......88 C2
Romberg Rd *TOOT* SW17 ......29 K6
Romeo Hl *BNFD* RG42 ....33 H2
Romeyn Rd
STRHM/NOR SW16 ....30 A4
Rommany Rd *WNWD* SE27 ..30 E7
Romney Cl *ASHF* TW15 ....23 M8
CHSGTN KT9 ....59 L3
Romney Rd *FARN* GU14 ....88 A6
NWMAL KT3 ....42 B7
Romola Rd
BRXS/STRHM SW2 ....30 C4
Romsey Cl *ALDT* GU11 ....108 E8
BLKW GU17 ....67 N2
DTCH/LGLY SL3 ....12 D1
Ronald Cl *BECK* BR3 ....46 F6
Ronalds Rd *BMLY* BR1 ....47 N2
Ronelean Rd *SURB* KT6 ....59 M2
Ronneby Cl *WEY* KT13 ....56 G2
Ronson Wy *LHD/OX* KT22 ....96 C1
Roodlands La *EDEN* TN8 ....125 P8
Rookeries Cl *FELT* TW13 ......24 E5
Rookery Cl *LHD/OX* KT22 ....96 E4
Rookery Dr *DORK* RH4 ....116 A9
REDH RH1 ....141 K7
Rookery Rd *STA* TW18 ....22 B8
The Rookery
STRHM/NOR SW16 * 30 A9
Rookery Wy
KWD/TDW/WH KT20 ....99 K7
Rook La *CTHM* CR3 ....101 J4
Rookley Cl *BELMT* SM2 ....61 M8
Rooks Hl *SHGR* GU5 ....151 P2
Rooksmead Rd *SUN* TW16 ....39 H3
Rook Wy *HORS* RH12 ....192 D4
Rookwood Av *NWMAL* KT3 ..42 E5
SHST GU47 ....50 A8
WLGTN SM6 ....62 F3
Rookwood Cl *REDH* RH1 ....100 D9
Rookwood Ct *GUW* GU2 ......112 A8
Rookwood Pk *HORS* RH12 ..191 P7
Roothill La
BRKHM/BTCW RH3 ....137 N2
Ropeland Wy *HORS* RH12 ..192 D3
Roper Wy *MTCM* CR4 ....44 C3
Rorkes Drift *FRIM* GU16 ......89 H3
Rosa Av *ASHF* TW15 ....23 K7
Rosalind Franklin Cl
GUW GU2 ....111 L6
Rosaline Rd *FUL/PGN* SW6 ....19 J5
Rosaline Ter *FUL/PGN* SW6 * ..19 J5
Rosamond St *SYD* SE26 ....31 J6
Rosamund Cl *SAND/SEL* CR2 ..63 N4
Rosamund Rd *CRAWE* RH10 ..177 L7
Rosary Cl *HSLW* TW3 ....15 N7
Rosary Gdns *ASHF* TW15 ....23 L7
SKENS SW7 ....19 N2
YTLY GU46 ....66 F1
Rosaville Rd *FUL/PGN* SW6 ..19 K5
Roseacre *OXTED* RH8 ....123 N4
Roseacre Cl *SHPTN* TW17 ....38 C6
Roseacre Gdns *RGUE* GU4 ..133 K2
Roseary Cl *WDR/YW* UB7 ....13 P2
Rose Av *MRDN* SM4 ....43 N6

MTCM CR4 ....44 B2
Rosebank *EPSOM* KT18 ......78 A3
PGE/AN SE20 * 46 C1
Rosebank Cl *TEDD* TW11 .....25 P9
Rosebank Cottages
REIG RH2 * 119 M7
Rosebery Av *EW* KT17 ....78 C3
NWMAL KT5 ....42 D3
THHTH CR7 ....45 L3
Rosebery Cl *MRDN* SM4 ......43 H7
Rosebery Crs
WOKS/MYFD GU22 ....72 D9
Rosebery Gdns *SUT* SM1 .....61 M3
Rosebery Pde *EW* KT17 ....60 D6
Rosebery Rd *CLAP* SW4 ....29 P2
HSLW TW3 ....13 L5
KUT KT1 ....9 K5
SUT SM1 ....61 K5
Rosebery Sq *KUT* K1 ....9 J5
Rosebery Rd *WHTN* TW2 ....25 L3
Rosebriar Cl
WOKS/MYFD GU22 ....73 L5
Rosebriars *CTHM* CR3 ....81 N9
ESH/CLAY KT10 ....58 C4
Rosecourt Rd *CROY/NA* CRO ..44 D9
Rosebury Rd *FUL/PGN* SW6 ..19 M7
Rose Bushes *EW* KT17 ....78 G5
Rosecroft Cl *BH/WHM* TN16 ..84 D7
Rosecroft Gdns *WHTN* TW2 ...25 L4
Rosedale *ASHTD* KT21 ....77 J7
ASHV GU12 ....108 E4
Rosedale Cl *CRAWW* RH11 ...176 D7
Rosedale Gdns *BRAK* RG12 ...32 C6
Rosedale Rd *EW* KT17 ....60 E4
RCH/KEW TW9 ....17 J9
Rosedene Av *CROY/NA* CRO ...44 A6
MRDN SM4 ....43 A6
STRHM/NOR SW16 ....30 A6
Rosedene Gdns *FLEETN* GU51 .86 F5
Rosedene La *SHST* GU47 ....67 P1
Rosedew Rd *HMSMTH* W6 .....19 H4
Rose End *WPK* KT4 ....43 H9
Rosefield Cl *CAR* SM5 ....62 A4
Rosefield Gdns *CHERT* KT16 ..55 H5
Rosefield Rd *STA* TW18 ....22 D7
Rose Gdns *FA* W5 ....17 K1
FARN GU14 ....87 P4
FELT TW13 ....24 B5
STWL/WRAY TW19 ....22 G3
Rosegarth Pk *NWMAL* TW4 ...24 C1
Rose Hl *DORK* RH4 ....116 G8
SUT SM1 ....61 M1
Rosehill *ESH/CLAY* KT10 ......58 C5
HPTN TW12 ....40 A2
Rose Hill Arch Ms
DORK RH4 * 116 G7
Rosehill Av *SUT* SM1 ....43 N1
WOKN/KNAP GU21 ....72 A5
Rosehill Court Pde
MRDN SM4 * 43 N8
Rosehill Farm Meadow
BNSTD SM7 ....79 M4
Rosehill Gdns *SUT* SM1 ....61 M1
Rose Hill Pk West *SUT* SM1 ...43 N9
Rosehill Rd *BH/WHM* TN16 ...84 A6
WAND/EARL SW18 ....28 D2
Rose La *RPLY/SEND* GU23 .....95 P2
Roselare Cl *BH/WHM* TN16 ..105 H5
Roseleigh Cl *TWK* TW1 ....26 C2
Rosemary Av *ASHV* GU12 ......89 J7
E/WMO/HCT KT8 ....40 A4
HSLW TW4 ....15 M7
Rosemary Cl *CROY/NA* CRO ...45 H1
FARN GU14 ....87 P2
OXTED RH8 ....123 N4
Rosemary Ct *HORL* RH6 * 140 A9
Rosemary Crs *RGUW* GU3 ...111 M1
Rosemary Gdns *BLKW* GU17 ..67 N3
CHSGTN KT9 ....59 L5
Rosemary La *BLKW* GU17 .....67 N3
CRAN GU6 ....188 B2
EGH TW20 ....36 F4
HORL RH6 ....158 B5
HORL RH6 ....159 L2
MORT/ESHN SW14 ....18 A9
RFNM GU10 ....127 J9
Rosemary Rd *TOOT* SW17 .....28 E6
Rosemead *CHERT* KT16 ....37 M8
Rosemead Av *FELT* TW13 ......24 A5
MTCM CR4 ....44 H4
Rosemead Cl *REDH* RH1 ......119 P7
Rosemont Rd *NWMAL* KT3 .....42 A4
RCHPK/HAM TW10 ....26 D1
Rosemount Av *BF/WBF* KT14 ..73 L2
Rosendale Rd *DUL* SE21 ....30 D4
Roseneath Ct *CTHM* CR3 * ..102 A5
Roseneath Dr
MFD/CHID GU8 ....168 A7
Roseneath Rd *BTSEA* SW11 ...29 K2
Rosenthorpe Rd *PECK* SE15 ..31 L1
The Rosery *CROY/NA* CRO 46 D7
Roses Cottages *DORK* RH4 * .116 G7
Rose Sq *CHEL* SW3 * 19 P3
Rosethorn Cl *BAL* SW12 ....29 M3
Rosetrees *GU* GU1 ....112 E6
Rose Vw *ADL/WDHM* KT15 * ..55 N4
Roseville Av *HSLW* TW3 ....15 J3
Roseville Rd *HYS/HAR* UB3 ...15 J3
Rosevine Rd *RYNPK* SW20 ....42 G2
Rose Wk *BRYLDS* KT5 ....41 P6
CRAWW RH11 * 176 E2
FLEETN GU51 ....86 F5
PUR/KEN CR8 ....62 F9
REIG RH2 ....65 J1
Rosewarne Cl
WOKN/KNAP GU21 ....71 N7
Roseway *DUL* SE21 ....30 E7
Rosewell Cl *PGE/AN* SE20 ....46 B1
Rose Wd *WOKS/MYFD* GU22 ..11 Q7
Rosewood Cl *KUTN/CMB* KT2 ..9 H1

Rosewood Dr *SHPTN* TW17 ...38 B6
Rosewood Gv *SUT* SM1 ....61 N1
Rosewood Ter
PGE/AN SE20 * 46 C1
Rosewood Wy
CHOB/PIR GU24 ....70 E2
Roskell Rd *PUT/ROE* SW15 ...19 H8
Roslin Rd *ACT* W3 ....17 P1
Roslyn Cl *MTCM* CR4 ....43 P3
Ross Cl *CRAWE* RH10 ....177 J8
HYS/HAR UB3 ....14 F2
Rossdale *SUT* SM1 ....62 A4
Rossdale Rd *PUT/ROE* SW15 ..18 G9
Rosset Cl *BRAK* RG12 ....32 C5
Rossetti Gdns
COUL/CHIP CR5 ....81 H6
Rossignol Gdns *CAR* SM5 .....62 C1
Rossindel Rd *HSLW* TW3 ......25 J1
Rossiter Cl *DTCH/LGLY* SL3 ..12 C2
Rossiter Ldg *GU* GU1 * 112 F1
Rossiter Rd *BAL* SW12 ....29 L4
Rosslea *BFOR* GU20 ....52 A3
Rosslyn Av *BARN* SW13 ....18 C8
EBED/NFELT TW14 ....24 B2
Rosslyn Cl *SUN* TW16 ....23 P9
Rosslyn Pk *WEY* KT13 ....56 F3
Rosslyn Rd *TWK* TW1 ....26 B2
Rossmore Cl *CRAWE* RH10 ..177 N1
Ross Pde *WLGTN* SM6 ....62 D5
Ross Rd *COB* KT11 ....75 L2
SNWD SE25 ....45 M4
WHTN TW2 ....25 K4
WLGTN SM6 ....62 D5
Rosswood Gdns *WLGTN* SM6 .62 D5
Rostella Rd *TOOT* SW17 ....28 G8
Rostrevor Gdns *NWDGN* UB2 .15 N3
Rostrevor Rd *FUL/PGN* SW6 ..19 K6
WIM/MER SW19 ....28 C8
Rothbury Gdns *ISLW* TW7 .....16 C5
Rother Cl *SHST* GU47 ....67 P1
Rother Crs *CRAWW* RH11 ....176 C6
Rotherfield Rd *CAR* SM5 ....62 C3
Rotherhill Av
STRHM/NOR SW16 ....29 N9
Rothermere Rd
CROY/NA CRO 63 H4
Rother Rd *FARN* GU14 ....88 A1
Rothervale *HORL* RH6 ....140 D8
Rotherwood Cl
WIM/MER SW19 ....43 J2
Rotherwood Rd
PUT/ROE SW15 ....19 H8
Rothesay Av
RCHPK/HAM TW10 ....17 P9
RYNPK SW20 ....43 J3
Rothesay Rd *SNWD* SE25 .....45 M5
Rothes Rd *DORK* RH4 ....117 H6
Rothschild St *DUL* SE24 ....30 C1
Rothschild St *WNWD* SE27 ....30 C7
Rotten Green Rd
FLEETN GU51 ....86 E1
Rotunda Est *ALDT* GU11 * 108 D4
Rougemont Av *MRDN* SM4 ....43 L7
Roughets La *REDH* RH1 ....101 N9
Rough Fld *EGRIN* RH19 ....162 C8
Roughlands
WOKS/MYFD GU22 ....73 J4
Rough Rew *RDKG* RH5 ....137 H1
Rough Wy *HORS* RH12 ....192 C8
Rounce La *CHOB/PIR* GU24 ...70 D2
Roundals La *MFD/CHID* GU8 .168 D4
Round Cl *YTLY* GU46 ....67 H3
Round Gv *CROY/NA* CRO 46 D8
Roundhay Cl *FSTH* SE23 ....31 L5
Round Hl *SYD* SE26 ....31 J5
Roundhill *WOKS/MYFD* GU22 ..11 K7
Roundhill Dr
WOKS/MYFD GU22 ....11 K6
Roundhill Wy *COB* KT11 ....58 B9
GUW GU2 ....111 M5
Round Oak Rd *WEY* KT13 .....56 B3
Roundshead Dr *BNFD* RG42 ..32 F1
Rounds Hl *BRAK* RG12 * 32 B2
Roundthorn Wy
WOKN/KNAP GU21 ....71 M5
Roundway *CBLY* GU15 ....69 L2
EGH TW20 ....21 P8
Roundway Cl *CBLY* GU15 ......69 L2
The Roundway
ESH/CLAY KT10 ....58 F3
Roundwood Vw *BNSTD* SM7 ..79 H4
Roundwood Wy *BNSTD* SM7 ..79 H4
Roupell Rd
BRXS/STRHM SW2 * 30 A4
Rouse Gdns *DUL* SE21 ....30 F7
Routh Rd *WAND/EARL* SW18 ..29 H1
Rowallan Rd *FUL/PGN* SW6 ...19 J5
Rowan Av *EGH* TW20 ....21 P8
Rowan Ct *RFNM* GU10 ....127 L8
Rowan Cl *CBLY* GU15 ....59 H1
CRAWE RH10 ....177 J5
FLEETN GU51 ....87 J6
GU GU1 ....111 P2
HORS RH12 ....192 C5
NWMAL KT3 ....42 C3
REIG RH2 ....119 N7
STRHM/NOR SW16 ....44 H4
Rowan Crs
STRHM/NOR SW16 ....44 H4
Rowan Dl *FLEETS* GU52 ....106 F1
Rowan Dr *CWTH* RG45 ....49 N2
Rowan Gdns *CROY/NA* CRO 3 K7
Rowan Gv *COUL/CHIP* CR5 ...100 D1
Rowan Md *EPSOM* KT18 * 78 B2
Rowan Rd *BTFD* TW8 ....17 H1
HMSMTH W6 ....19 H2
STRHM/NOR SW16 ....44 H4
WDR/YW UB7 ....13 P2
Rowans Cl *FARN* GU14 ....68 A7

Rowanside Cl *BOR* GU35 ....164 F7
The Rowans *GSHT* GU26 .....165 N9
SUN TW16 ....24 A8
WOKS/MYFD GU22 ....10 D6
Rowan Ter *PGE/AN* SE20 * ...46 A2
Rowan Wy *HORS* RH12 ....193 H5
Rowbarns Wy *EHSLY* KT24 ..115 H1
Rowberry Cl *FUL/PGN* SW6 ...19 H5
Rowbill Av *ALDT* GU11 ....108 B6
Rowbury *GODL* GU7 ....131 N6
Rowcroft Cl *ASHV* GU12 ....89 J9
Rowdon Av *BECK* BR3 ....46 E2
HOR/WEW KT19 ....59 K6
Rowdown Crs *CROY/NA* CRO ..65 K7
Rowe La *CHOB/PIR* GU24 .....90 G4
Rowfant Cl *CRAWE* RH10 ....177 N5
Rowfant Rd *TOOT* SW17 ....29 K5
Row Hl *ADL/WDHM* KT15 ......55 K5
Rowhill Av *ALDT* GU11 ....108 B6
Rowhill Crs *ALDT* GU11 ....108 B6
Rowhills *FNM* GU9 ....107 P6
Rowhills Cl *FNM* GU9 ....108 B6
Rowhook Rd *HORS* RH12 .....190 G1
Rowhurst Av
ADL/WDHM KT15 ....55 M5
Rowland Cl *CRAWE* RH10 ....160 F7
Rowland Gv *SYD* SE26 ....31 J6
Rowland Rd *CRAN* GU6 ....152 C9
Rowlands Rd *HORS* RH12 ....192 F4
Rowland Wy *ASHF* TW15 ....38 E1
WIM/MER SW19 ....43 M2
Row La *SHGR* GU5 ....134 A8
Rowley Cl *BRAK* RG12 ....32 G4
WOKS/MYFD GU22 ....73 L5
Rowley Cottages
WKENS W14 * 19 K2
Rowley Ct *CTHM* CR3 ....101 J2
Rowlheys Pl *WDR/YW* UB7 ...14 A1
Rowlls Rd *KUT* KT1 ....9 G6
Rowly Dr *CRAN* GU6 ....152 D7
Rowly Edge *CRAN* GU6 ....152 D6
Rowntree Rd *WHTN* TW2 ......25 M4
Rowplatt La *EGRIN* RH19 .....161 M9
The Row *EDEN* TN8 * 144 F7
Row Town *ADL/WDHM* KT15 ..55 K6
Rowbee Cox Rd *FARN* GU14 ..87 L6
Roxborough Av *ISLW* TW7 .....16 F5
Roxburgh Cl *CBLY* GU15 ....69 L4
Roxburgh Rd *WNWD* SE27 ....30 C8
Roxby Pl *FUL/PGN* SW6 ....19 L4
Roxford Cl *SHPTN* TW17 ....38 C6
Roxton Gdns *CROY/NA* CRO ..64 F5
Royal Av *WEY* KT14 ....60 C1
Royal Circ *WNWD* SE27 ....30 B6
Royal Cl *WPK* KT4 ....60 C1
Royal Dr *EPSOM* KT18 ....78 F7
Royal Earlswood Pk
REDH RH1 ....120 C9
Royale Cl *ALDT* GU11 ....108 E7
Royal Ms *BELT* SW1 * 12 F3
Royal Oak Cl *YTLY* GU46 ....67 J2
Royal Oak Dr *EWKG* RG40 ....49 M1
Royal Oak Pl *EDUL* SE22 ....31 J2
Royal Oak Rd
WOKN/KNAP GU21 ....72 A7
Royal Orchard Cl
WAND/EARL SW18 ....28 B3
Royal Pde *FUL/PGN* SW6 * ...19 J5
Royal Rd *TEDD* TW11 ....25 L8
Royce Rd *CRAWE* RH10 ......159 K9
Roycroft Cl
BRXS/STRHM SW2 * 30 B4
Roycroft La *EWKG* RG40 ....48 C1
Roydon Ct *WOT/HER* KT12 ....57 J3
Roy Gv *HPTN* TW12 ....25 J9
Royston Av *BF/WBF* KT14 .....74 A1
SUT SM1 ....61 P2
WLGTN SM6 ....62 F3
Royston Cl *CRAWE* RH10 ....177 K1
HEST TW5 ....15 K6
WOT/HER KT12 ....39 J9
Royston Rd *BF/WBF* KT14 ....74 A1
PGE/AN SE20 ....46 D2
RCHPK/HAM TW10 ....26 D1
The Roystons *BRYLDS* KT5 ...41 N6
Rubastic Rd *NWDGN* UB2 .....15 L1
Rubens St *CAT* SE6 ....31 N5
Rubus Cl *CHOB/PIR* GU24 .....70 E2
Ruckmans La *RDKG* RH5 .....173 J4
Rudd Hall Ri *CBLY* GU15 ....68 F5
Ruden Wy *EW* KT17 ....78 F4
Rudge Ri *ADL/WDHM* KT15 ...55 K4
Rudgwick Rd *CRAWW* RH11 .176 C4
Rudloe Rd *BAL* SW12 ....29 M3
Rudsworth Cl *DTCH/LGLY* SL3 .13 H4
Ruffetts Cl *SAND/SEL* CR2 .....64 B6
The Ruffetts *SAND/SEL* CR2 ..64 B6
Ruffetts Wy
KWD/TDW/WH KT20 ....79 J7
Rufford Cl *FLEETS* GU52 ....86 D9
Rufwood *CRAWE* RH10 ....179 H3
Rugby Cl *SHST* GU47 ....50 A8
Rugby La *BELMT* SM2 ....61 H7
Rugby Rd *WHTN* TW2 ....25 K1
Ruggles-Brise Rd *ASHF* TW15 .22 G8
Rugosa Rd *CHOB/PIR* GU24 ..70 E2
Ruislip St *TOOT* SW17 ....29 J7
Rumbold Rd *FUL/PGN* SW6 ...19 M5
Rumsey Cl *HPTN* TW12 ....24 G9
Runcorn Cl *CRAWW* RH11 ...176 B9
Runes Cl *MTCM* CR4 ....43 P6
Runnemede Rd *EGH* TW20 ....21 M8
Runnymede *WIM/MER* SW19 ..43 P2
Runnymede Cl *WHTN* TW2 .....25 J2
Runnymede Ct *EGH* TW20 .....21 M8
Runnymede Crs
STRHM/NOR SW16 ....44 F2
Runnymede Gdns
WHTN TW2 ....25 J2
Runtley Wood La *RGUE* GU4 ..92 D5
Rupert Ct *E/WMO/HCT* KT8 * ..40 A1

Rupert Rd *CHSWK* W4 ....18 C1
GUW GU2 ....6 B5
Rural Wy *REDH* RH1 ....120 C5
STRHM/NOR SW16 ....44 D1
Ruscoe Dr *WOKS/MYFD* GU22 .11 H5
Ruscombe Wy
EBED/NFELT TW14 ....24 A3
Rusham Park Av *EGH* TW20 ..21 L9
Rusham Rd *BAL* SW12 ....29 J2
EGH TW20 ....21 L9
Rushams Rd *HORS* RH12 .....192 A8
Rush Common Ms
BRXS/STRHM SW2 * 30 A2
Rush Cft *GODL* GU7 ....131 N5
Rushden Cl *NRWD* SE19 ....45 M1
Rushdene Wk *BH/WHM* TN16 .84 B6
Rushden Wy *FNM* GU9 ....107 P2
Rushett Cl *THDIT* KT7 ....41 H9
Rushett Dr *DORK* RH4 ....137 H1
Rushett La *CHSGTN* KT9 ....77 K1
Rushett Rd *THDIT* KT7 ....41 H8
Rushetts Pl *CRAWW* RH11 ...176 E2
Rushetts Rd *CRAWW* RH11 ..176 E2
REIG RH2 ....119 P8
Rushey Cl *NWMAL* KT3 ....42 B5
Rushey Grn *CAT* SE6 * 31 P1
Rushfold Rd *BROCKY* SE4 .....31 N2
Rushfords *LING* RH7 ....143 L7
Rushmead
RCHPK/HAM TW10 ....26 A6
Rushmead Cl *CROY/NA* CRO ...3 J7
Rushmere Cl *WPK* KT4 ....60 E1
Rushmere Pl *EGH* TW20 ....21 K8
WIM/MER SW19 ....28 A8
Rushmon Pl *CHEAM* SM3 * 61 J5
Rushmon Vis *NWMAL* KT3 * ..42 D5
Rushmoor Cl *FLEETS* GU52 ...86 C8
GU GU1 ....111 M2
Rushmoor Rd *ALDT* GU11 ....108 A5
Rushmoor Wk *FARN* GU14 ....88 B3
Rushmore Cl *NRSV* TN14 .....85 P3
Rushmore Gv *NRWD* SE19 ....30 FB
Rusholme Rd *PUT/ROE* SW15 .28 A2
Rushton Av *GDST* RH9 ....122 C9
Rushworth Rd *REIG* RH2 ......119 J4
Rushy Meadow La *CAR* SM5 ..62 A1
Ruskin Av *EBED/NFELT* TW14 ..24 A1
RCH/KEW TW9 ....17 N5
Ruskin Cl *CRAWE* RH10 ......177 M2
Ruskin Ct *CWTH* RG45 * 49 K5
Ruskin Dr *WPK* KT4 ....60 F1
CROY/NA CRO 2 D3
STA TW18 ....22 C9
Ruskin Wk *HNHL* SE24 ....30 D1
Ruskin Wy *WIM/MER* SW19 ..43 P3
Rusper Rd *CRAWW* RH11 ....176 C4
HORS RH12 ....175 J2
HORS RH12 ....192 E3
RDKG RH5 ....156 G4
Ruspers Keep *CRAWW* RH11 .176 C4
Russel Cl *BECK* BR3 ....47 H4
Russell Cl *BRAK* RG12 ....32 D7
KWD/TDW/WH KT20 ....98 E5
WOKN/KNAP GU21 ....72 A4
Russell Ct *BLKW* GU17 ....67 P3
LHD/OX KT22 ....97 H2
Russell Dr *STWL/WRAY* TW19 .22 G2
Russell Gdns
RCHPK/HAM TW10 ....26 B5
WDR/YW UB7 ....14 C3
WKENS W14 * 19 J1
Russell Green Cl
PUR/KEN CR8 ....63 J8
Russell Hill *PUR/KEN* CR8 .....63 H8
Russell Hill Pl *PUR/KEN* CR8 ..63 J9
Russell Hill Rd *PUR/KEN* CR8 ..63 J8
Russell Kerr Cl *CHSWK* W4 * ..18 A5
Russell Rd *MTCM* CR4 ....44 A4
SHPTN TW17 ....54 B8
WHTN TW2 ....25 N2
WIM/MER SW19 ....43 L1
WKENS W14 ....19 J1
WOKN/KNAP GU21 ....72 A4
WOT/HER KT12 ....39 J7
Russells *KWD/TDW/WH* KT20 .99 H2
Russell's Crs *HORL* RH6 ......159 K2
Russells Wy *CRAWE* RH10 ...177 K6
SUT SM1 ....61 M4
Russet Av *SUN* TW16 ....39 K9
Russet Cl *HORL* RH6 ....159 M1
RFNM GU10 ....108 A2
STWL/WRAY TW19 ....22 C2
Russet Dr *CROY/NA* CRO 46 E9
Russet Gdns *CBLY* GU15 ......68 E5
Russet Gld *FNM* GU9 ....107 P6
Russets Cl
WOKN/KNAP GU21 ....72 D4
Russetts Dr *FLEETN* GU51 ....86 E4
Russet Wy *HORS* RH12 ....192 E3
Russ Hl *RDKG* RH5 ....157 M8
Russington Rd *SHPTN* TW17 ..38 F7
Rusthall Av *CHSWK* W4 ....18 B1
Rusthall Cl *CROY/NA* CRO 46 D6
Rustic Av *STRHM/NOR* SW16 ..44 D1
Rustic Gln *FLEETS* GU52 .....106 F1
Rustington Wk *MRDN* SM4 ....43 P8
Ruston Av *BRYLDS* KT5 ....41 P8
Ruston Cl *CRAWE* RH10 ......177 M8
Ruston Wy *ASC* SL5 ....33 N3
Rutford Rd
STRHM/NOR SW16 ....29 P8
Ruth Cl *FARN* GU14 ....87 N2
Rutherford Cl *BELMT* SM2 .....61 P5
Rutherford Wy
CRAWE RH10 ....159 K9
Rutherwick Cl *HORL* RH6 .....159 J1
Rutherwick Ri
COUL/CHIP CR5 ....80 G6

Rutherwyke Cl *EW* KT17 ....60 E5
Rutherwyk Rd *CHERT* KT16 ...37 J8
Rutland Cl *ALDT* GU11 ....108 C3
ASHTD KT21 ....77 L6
DORK RH4 ....116 B8
MORT/ESHN SW14 ....17 P8
REDH RH1 ....120 B1
Rutland Dr *MRDN* SM4 ....43 L8
RCHPK/HAM TW10 ....26 C4
Rutland Ga *HAYES* BR2 ....47 M5
Rutland Gv *HMSMTH* W6 ....18 F3
Rutland Pk *CAT* SE6 ....31 N1
Rutland Rd *HYS/HAR* UB3 .....14 F2
WHTN TW2 ....25 L5
WIM/MER SW19 ....44 A1
Rutland Wk *CAT* SE6 ....31 L1
Rutlish Rd *WIM/MER* SW19 ...43 L2
Rutter Gdns *MTCM* CR4 ....43 P5
Rutton Hill Rd
MFD/CHID GU8 ....166 F3
Ruvigny Gdns
PUT/ROE SW15 ....19 H8
Ruxbury Rd *CHERT* KT16 ....37 H7
Ruxley Cl *HOR/WEW* KT19 ....59 P6
Ruxley Crs *ESH/CLAY* KT10 ...59 P5
Ruxley La *HOR/WEW* KT19 ....59 P5
Ruxley Ms *HOR/WEW* KT19 ...59 P5
Ruxley Rdg *ESH/CLAY* KT10 ..58 G4
Ruxley Towers
ESH/CLAY KT10 * 58 G6
Ruxton Cl *COUL/CHIP* CR5 ....80 E4
Ryan Dr *BTFD* TW8 ....17 J1
Ryan Mt *SHST* GU47 ....49 L9
Rydal Cl *CBLY* GU15 ....69 M3
CRAWW RH11 ....176 A12
FARN GU14 ....87 P4
PUR/KEN CR8 ....81 M2
Rydal Dr *FLEETS* GU52 ....106 E1
PUT/ROE SW15 ....27 K8
Rydal Gdns *HSLW* TW3 ....25 J2
PUT/ROE SW15 ....27 K8
Rydal Mt *HAYES* BR2 * 47 M5
Rydal Pl *LTWR* GU18 ....52 B9
Rydal Rd *STRHM/NOR* SW16 ..29 N8
Rydal Wy *EGH* TW20 ....36 F1
RPLY/SEND GU23 ....95 N1
Ryde Heron
WOKN/KNAP GU21 ....71 L6
Ryde Lands *CRAN* GU6 ....153 H9
Rydens Av *WOT/HER* KT12 ....57 L1
Rydens Cl *WOT/HER* KT12 .....57 L1
Rydens Gv *WOT/HER* KT12 ....57 M3
Rydens Pde
WOKS/MYFD GU22 ....72 F9
Rydens Pk *WOT/HER* KT12 ....57 M1
Rydens Rd *WOT/HER* KT12 ....57 K2
Rydens Wy
WOKS/MYFD GU22 ....72 F9
Ryde Pl *TWK* TW1 ....26 B2
Ryders Wy *HORS* RH12 ....192 E3
Rydes Av *GUW* GU2 ....111 M2
Ryde's Hill Crs *RGUW* GU3 ...111 M3
Ryde's Hill Rd *GUW* GU2 ......111 M3
The Ryde *STA* TW18 ....37 L9
Ryde Vale Rd *BAL* SW12 ....29 L5
Rydon's La *COUL/CHIP* CR5 ...81 L9
Rydon's Wd Cl
COUL/CHIP CR5 ....81 L9
Rye Ash *CRAWE* RH10 ....177 K4
Rybeck Rd *FLEETS* GU52 .....106 C1
Rye Brook Rd *LHD/OX* KT22 ..76 G2
FARN GU14 ....87 M4
FLEETN GU51 * 87 J1
GUW GU2 ....111 L4
Ryecotes Med *DUL* SE21 ......30 F4
Rye Cft *FLEETS* GU52 ....106 E2
Ryecroft Av *WHTN* TW2 ....25 J4
Ryecroft Dr *HORS* RH12 ......191 P7
Ryecroft Gdns *BLKW* GU17 ...68 A4
Ryecroft Rd
STRHM/NOR SW16 ....30 B9
Ryecroft St *FUL/PGN* SW6 ....19 M6
Ryedale *EDUL* SE22 ....31 J2
Ryefield Rd *NRWD* SE19 ....30 D9
Rye Gv *CHOB/PIR* GU24 ....52 E8
CRAN GU6 * 153 L1
Ryeland Cl *FLEETN* GU51 * 87 J1
Ryelands *CRAWW* RH11 ......176 D6
HORL RH6 * 140 E9
Ryelands Cl *CTHM* CR3 ....101 N1
Ryelands Ct *LHD/OX* KT22 .....76 G2
Ryelaw Rd *FLEETS* GU52 .....106 C2
Ryersh La *RDKG* RH5 ....156 B5
Ryersh La *RDKG* RH5 ....156 B5
Rye Wk *PUT/ROE* SW15 ....28 A1
Ryfold Rd *WIM/MER* SW19 ....28 B7
Ryland Cl *FELT* TW13 ....24 A7
Rylandes Rd *SAND/SEL* CR2 ..64 B7
Ryle Rd *FNM* GU9 ....107 M5
Rylett Crs *SHB* W12 ....18 C1
Rylston Rd *FUL/PGN* SW6 .....19 K4
Rymer Rd *CROY/NA* CRO 45 M3
Rymer St *HNHL* SE24 ....30 C2
Rysted La *BH/WHM* TN16 ....106 C6
Ryst Wood Rd *FROW* RH18 ..181 N9
Rythe Cl *CHSGTN* KT9 ....59 H5
Rythe Ct *THDIT* KT7 ....40 G8
Rythe Rd *ESH/CLAY* KT10 .....58 D4
The Rythe *LHD/OX* KT22 ....96 B8
Ryvers Ende *DTCH/LGLY* SL3 ..12 D1
Ryvers Rd *DTCH/LGLY* SL3 ....12 D1
Ryves Av *YTLY* GU46 ....66 F3
Ryves Cottages *MTCM* CR4 * .44 C3

S

Sable Cl HSLWW TW4 15 L8
Sabre Ct ALDT GU11 108 A4
Sachel Court Rd CRAN GU6 170 A8
Sackville Av HAYES BR2 47 N9
Sackville Cl EGRIN RH19 162 B9
Sackville Ct EGRIN RH19 * 180 E3
Sackville Est
STRHM/NOR SW16 29 P6
Sackville La EGRIN RH19 162 A9
Sackville Rd BELMT SM2 61 L6
Saddleback Rd CBLY GU15 50 G9
Saddleback Wy FLEETN GU51 87 H3
Saddlebrook Pk SUN TW16 38 G1
Saddler Cnr SHST GU47 67 M1
Saddler Rw CRAWE RH10 176 G8
Saddlers Ms KUT KT1 * 8 A3
Saddlers Scarp GSHT GU26 165 K7
Saddlers Wy EPSOM KT18 78 B8
Saddlewood CBLY GU15 68 E4
Sadler Cl MTCM CR4 44 B3
Sadlers Cl RGUE GU4 113 H4
Sadlers Ride
E/WMO/HCT KT8 40 C3
Saffron Cl CRAWW RH11 176 D8
CROY/NA CR0 44 G7
Saffron Platt GUW GU2 111 N1
Saffron Rd BRAK RG12 32 D5
Saffron Wy SURB KT6 41 K9
Sage Wk BNFD RG42 32 F1
Sage Yd SURB KT6 * 41 M9
Sailors La MFD/CHID GU8 166 A1
Sainfoin Rd TOOT SW17 29 K5
Sainsbury Rd NRWD SE19 30 F8
St Agatha's Dr
KUTN/CMB KT2 26 E9
St Agatha's Gv CAR SM5 44 B9
St Agnes Rd EGRIN RH19 180 D1
St Aidan's Rd EDUL SE22 31 J2
St Albans Av CHSWK W4 18 B1
FELT TW13 24 E8
WEY KT13 56 C2
St Albans Cl RGUW GU3 111 H4
St Albans Farm
HSLWW TW4 * 24 D1
St Alban's Gdns TEDD TW11 25 P8
St Alban's Gv CAR SM5 44 A8
KENS W8 19 M1
St Albans Rd KUTN/CMB KT2 26 D9
REIG RH2 119 L3
SUT SM1 61 K3
St Albans Ter HMSMTH W6 * 19 J4
St Amunds Cl CAT SE6 31 P7
St Andrew Av
CHOB/PIR GU24 91 H1
St Andrews BRAK RG12 32 A7
CRAN GU6 * 152 E9
HORL RH6 * 159 L2
St Andrews Cl CWTH RG45 49 K3
REIG RH2 119 M6
SHPTN TW17 38 F5
STWL/WRAY TW19 21 K2
THDIT KT7 41 H9
WDSR SL4 20 F2
WOKN/KNAP GU21 72 A6
St Andrew's Ct
WAND/EARL SW18 28 F5
St Andrews Gdns COB KT11 75 L2
St Andrews Ga
WOKS/MYFD GU22 10 E5
St Andrews Ms BAL SW12 29 N4
St Andrews Rd CAR SM5 62 A2
COUL/CHIP CR5 80 D5
CRAWW RH11 176 A6
CROY/NA CR0 2 C7
SURB KT6 41 K7
WKENS W14 19 J4
St Andrew's Sq SURB KT6 41 K7
St Andrew's Wk COB KT11 75 K4
St Andrews Wy FRIM GU16 69 H9
OXTED RH8 124 C2
St Anne's Av
STWL/WRAY TW19 22 G3
St Annes Bvd REDH RH1 120 C3
St Anne's Dr REDH RH1 120 C4
St Annes Gld BAGS GU19 51 M6
St Annes Mt REDH RH1 * 120 C4
St Annes Ri REDH RH1 120 C4
St Annes Rd CRAWE RH10 177 M1
GODL GU7 131 N8
St Annes Wy REDH RH1 * 120 C4
St Anns WOKS/MYFD GU22 * 10 C6
St Ann's Cl CHERT KT16 37 K6
St Ann's Crs
WAND/EARL SW18 28 E2
St Ann's Hl
WAND/EARL SW18 28 E1
St Ann's Hill Rd CHERT KT16 36 G7
St Ann's Park Rd
WAND/EARL SW18 28 F2
St Anns Rd BARN SW13 * 18 D7
CHERT KT16 37 K7
St Anns Wy BH/WHM TN16 * 84 F5
CROY/NA CR0 63 K5
St Anthonys Cl BNFD RG42 32 C2
TOOT SW17 29 H5
St Anthony's Wy
EBED/NFELT TW14 15 H9
St Arvans Cl CROY/NA CR0 3 H5
St Aubin Cl CRAWW RH11 * 176 C9
St Aubyns DORK RH4 * 117 H9
St Aubyn's Av HSLW TW3 25 H1
WIM/MER SW19 28 C8
St Aubyn's Rd NRWD SE19 30 G9
St Augustine's Av
SAND/SEL CR2 63 L6
St Augustine's Cl
ASHV GU12 108 F5
St Austins GSHT GU26 * 165 N8
St Barnabas Av
CHOB/PIR GU24 90 G2
St Barnabas Cl BECK BR3 47 J3
St Barnabas' Gdns
E/WMO/HCT KT8 40 A6
St Barnabas Rd MTCM CR4 44 C1
SUT SM1 61 P4
St Bartholomew's Cl
SYD SE26 31 K7
St Bartholomew's Ct GU GU1 7 J6
St Benedict's Cl ALDT GU11 108 C5
St Benets Cl TOOT SW17 * 29 H5
St Benet's Gv MRDN SM4 43 N8
St Bernards CROY/NA CR0 3 G6
St Bernards Cl WNWD SE27 30 E7
St Bernards Rd
DTCH/LGLY SL3 12 A1
St Blaise Av BMLY BR1 47 P3
St Brelades Cl DORK RH4 116 G9
St Brelades Ct EDEN TN8 * 144 E2
St Brelades Rd
CRAWW RH11 176 C9
St Catherines WEY KT13 * 56 D2
WOKS/MYFD GU22 72 A8
St Catherines Cl CHSGTN KT9 59 K5
TOOT SW17 * 29 H5
St Catherines Ct FELT TW13 24 B4
St Catherine's Cross
REDH RH1 121 N5
St Catherine's Dr GUW GU2 111 P9
St Catherine's Hl GUW GU2 112 A9
St Catherine's Pk GU GU1 7 J6
St Catherines Rd
CRAWE RH10 177 M2
FRIM GU16 69 J7
St Chad Av
WOKS/MYFD GU22 91 J2
St Chads Cl SURB KT6 41 J8
St Charles Pl WEY KT13 56 C4
St Christophers LING RH7 * 143 K9
St Christophers Cl
HASM GU27 * 184 B4
HORS RH12 192 B6
ISLW TW7 16 E6
St Christophers Gdns
ASC SL5 33 M2
St Christopher's Ms
WLGTN SM6 62 E4
St Christophers Pl
FARN GU14 88 B4
St Christopher's Rd
FARN GU14 88 C4
HASM GU27 184 B4
St Clair Cl OXTED RH8 123 J1
REIG RH2 119 N5
St Clair Dr WPK KT4 60 F2
St Clair's Rd CROY/NA CR0 3 G4
St Clement Rd
CRAWW RH11 176 C9
St Clements Yd EDUL SE22 * 30 G1
St Cloud Rd WNWD SE27 30 D7
St Crispins Wy CHERT KT16 54 G7
St Cross Rd FNM GU9 5 G2
FRIM GU16 69 J9
RFNM GU10 106 D9
St Cuthbert's Cl EGH TW20 21 J9
St Cyprian's St TOOT SW17 29 J7
St David's COUL/CHIP CR5 81 H6
St David's Cl FARN GU14 68 B8
FNM GU9 108 A7
REIG RH2 119 N4
WWKM BR4 47 H8
St David's Dr EGH TW20 36 A1
St Denis Rd WNWD SE27 30 E7
St Deny's Cl
WOKN/KNAP GU21 * 71 K7
St Dionis Rd FUL/PGN SW6 19 K7
St Dunstans Cl HYS/HAR UB3 15 H2
St Dunstan's Hl SUT SM1 61 J3
St Dunstan's La BECK BR3 47 J7
St Dunstan's Rd FELT TW13 24 A6
HMSMTH W6 19 H3
HSLWW TW4 15 K7
SNWD SE25 45 P5
St Edmunds Cl
CRAWW RH11 176 G2
TOOT SW17 29 H5
St Edmund's La WHTN TW2 25 J3
St Edmunds Sq BARN SW13 18 G4
St Edwards Cl CROY/NA CR0 65 K9
EGRIN RH19 180 B2
St Elizabeth Dr EPSOM KT18 78 A3
St Faith's Rd HNHL SE24 30 C4
St Fillans WOKS/MYFD GU22 * 11 K2
St Francis Gdns
CRAWE RH10 160 D8
St George Av CHOB/PIR GU24 91 H2
St Georges HORL RH6 * 159 L2
St George's Av WEY KT13 56 E5
St George's Cl FNM GU9 * 108 D8
HORL RH6 159 L1
WEY KT13 56 E4
St Georges Ct CRAWE RH10 176 G4
St George's Gdns EW KT17 78 D3
SURB KT6 59 P1
SWTR RH13 192 D6
St George's Gv TOOT SW17 28 G6
St George's La ASC SL5 34 B4
St Georges Ms CHSWK W4 * 18 A4
FNM GU9 5 F2
St Georges Pde CAT SE6 * 31 N5
St Georges Rd
ADL/WDHM KT15 55 N3
ASHV GU12 108 D5
BECK BR3 47 H2
CBLY GU15 68 F2
FELT TW13 24 E7
FNM GU9 5 J5
KUTN/CMB KT2 9 H1
MTCM CR4 44 D4
RCH/KEW TW9 17 M8
REDH RH1 140 F4
TWK TW1 26 A1
WEY KT13 56 F5
WIM/MER SW19 28 C9
WLGTN SM6 62 D4
St Georges Sq NWMAL KT3 * 42 C4
St George's Wk CROY/NA CR0 2 D4
St Georges Yd FNM GU9 5 F3
St Gerards Cl CLAP SW4 29 M1
St German's Rd FSTH SE23 31 M4
St Gothard Rd WNWD SE27 30 E7
St Helena Ter
RCH/KEW TW9 * 26 C1
St Helens THDIT KT7 * 40 E8
St Helens Crs SHST GU47 49 M9
STRHM/NOR SW16 45 H2
St Helen's Rd
STRHM/NOR SW16 45 H3
St Helier Av MRDN SM4 43 N8
St Helier Cl CRAWW RH11 176 D9
St Heliers Av HSLWW TW4 25 H1
St Hilda's Av ASHF TW15 23 H8
St Hilda's Cl CRAWE RH10 * 177 M2
HORL RH6 159 L1
TOOT SW17 29 H5
WOKN/KNAP GU21 71 K6
St Hilda's Rd BARN SW13 18 F4
St Hill Rd EGRIN RH19 180 A5
St Hughes Cl TOOT SW17 * 29 H5
St Hugh's Cl CRAWE RH10 177 M2
St Hugh's Rd PGE/AN SE20 * 46 B1
St Ives CRAWE RH10 * 177 M4
St James Av EW KT17 60 D9
FNM GU9 127 P1
SUT SM1 61 L4
St James Cl EPSOM KT18 78 C3
NWMAL KT3 42 D6
WOKN/KNAP GU21 71 N7
St James Ga CTHM CR3 * 102 A2
St James Ms WEY KT13 56 D3
St James Rd CAR SM5 62 A2
EWKG RG40 48 C1
FLEETN GU51 86 F7
KUT KT1 8 C5
MTCM CR4 44 C1
PUR/KEN CR8 81 K2
SURB KT6 41 K7
SUT SM1 61 L5
St James's Av BECK BR3 46 E4
HPTN TW12 25 K8
St James's Cl TOOT SW17 * 29 J5
TOOT SW17 * 29 K8
St James's Cottages
RCHPK/HAM TW10 * 26 C1
St James's Ct KUT KT1 * 8 D7
St James's Dr BAL SW12 29 J4
St James's Pk CROY/NA CR0 45 L8
St James's Pl CRAN GU6 152 F9
St James Sq SURB KT6 41 J8
St James's Rd CROY/NA CR0 45 L8
EGRIN RH19 180 C2
HPTN TW12 25 J8
St James's Rw CHSGTN KT9 * 59 K5
St James St HMSMTH W6 18 G3
St James Ter BAL SW12 * 29 K4
FNM GU9 5 H1
St Joan Cl CRAWW RH11 176 G2
St John Cl FUL/PGN SW6 * 19 L5
SWTR RH13 192 D9
St John's RDKG RH5 137 J2
St Johns Av EW KT17 78 D1
LHD/OX KT22 97 H1
PUT/ROE SW15 28 A1
St Johns Church Rd
RDKG RH5 135 P1
St Johns Cl BH/WHM TN16 * 84 F5
FUL/PGN SW6 * 19 L5
LHD/OX KT22 97 J1
St Johns Cottages
PGE/AN SE20 * 46 C1
St Johns Ct EGH TW20 21 M8
FARN GU14 * 87 P2
GDST RH9 * 122 F9
ISLW TW7 16 F7
St John's Crs HORS RH12 191 M7
St John's Dr
WAND/EARL SW18 28 E4
WOT/HER KT12 39 L9
St John's Gv BARN SW13 * 18 D7
FNM GU9 127 M6
RCH/KEW TW9 * 17 L9
St John's Hl PUR/KEN CR8 81 J6
St John's Hill Gv BTSEA SW11 19 P9
St John's Hill Rd
WOKN/KNAP GU21 71 N8
St John's Lye (Festival Path)
WOKN/KNAP GU21 71 M8
St John's Meadow LING RH7 142 D5
St Johns Ms
WOKN/KNAP GU21 71 N7
St Johns Ri BH/WHM TN16 * 84 F5
WOKN/KNAP GU21 71 P8
St John's Rd
ASC SL5 33 P1
CAR SM5 62 A2
CRAWW RH11 176 F5
CROY/NA CR0 2 B5
DORK RH4 116 C8
E/WMO/HCT KT8 40 D5
EGRIN RH19 180 D1
FARN GU14 88 A3
FELT TW13 24 G7
FNM GU9 127 M5
GUW GU2 111 M6
ISLW TW7 16 F7
KUT KT1 8 A4
LHD/OX KT22 97 J1
NWDGN UB2 15 N1
NWMAL KT3 42 A4
PGE/AN SE20 46 C1
RCH/KEW TW9 17 L9
REDH RH1 120 B7
SHST GU47 67 M1
SUT SM1 61 L1
WIM/MER SW19 43 J1
WOKN/KNAP GU21 71 N8
St John's Road Rd
WOKN/KNAP GU21 71 P7
St John's St GODL GU7 131 M7
St John's Terrace Rd
REDH RH1 120 B7
St John's Vls KENS W8 19 M1
St John's Wy
ADL/WDHM KT15 55 L1
St Joseph's Rd ALDT GU11 108 C5
St Jude's Cl EGH TW20 21 H8
St Jude's Rd EGH TW20 21 H7
St Julian's Cl
STRHM/NOR SW16 * 30 B7
St Julian's Farm Rd
WNWD SE27 30 B7
St Katharines Rd CTHM CR3 102 A5
St Kitts Ter NRWD SE19 30 F8
St Lawrence Wy CTHM CR3 101 M3
St Leonards Dr CRAWE RH10 177 K8
St Leonard's Gdns HEST TW5 15 N5
St Leonard's Rd CROY/NA CR0 2 A6
EPSOM KT18 78 G8
ESH/CLAY KT10 58 F5
MORT/ESHN SW14 18 A8
SURB KT6 41 K6
SWTR RH13 192 E9
THDIT KT7 40 G7
St Leonards Wk IVER SL0 13 K1
STRHM/NOR SW16 45 H1
St Louis Rd WNWD SE27 30 D7
St Luke's Cl SNWD SE25 46 B7
St Lukes Ct
WOKN/KNAP GU21 * 72 G3
St Luke's Rd CTHM CR3 81 P7
WDSR SL4 20 F2
St Luke's Sq GU GU1 7 J5
St Margaret's GU GU1 7 J1
RCHPK/HAM TW10 * 27 H8
St Margarets Av ASHF TW15 23 L8
BH/WHM TN16 * 84 F5
CHEAM SM3 61 J2
EGRIN RH19 162 D6
St Margarets Ct
PUT/ROE SW15 * 18 F9
St Margaret's Crs
PUT/ROE SW15 * 27 N1
St Margarets Dr EPSOM KT18 78 B3
TWK TW1 26 A1
St Margaret's Gv TWK TW1 25 P2
St Margarets La KENS W8 * 19 M1
St Margarets Ms
RCHPK/HAM TW10 * 27 H8
St Margaret's Rd
COUL/CHIP CR5 100 D1
EGRIN RH19 162 E9
TWK TW1 17 H9
St Mark Av CHOB/PIR GU24 91 H3
St Marks Cl FARN GU14 88 E6
FUL/PGN SW6 19 L6
St Mark's Gv WBPTN SW10 19 M5
St Mark's Hl SURB KT6 41 L7
St Mark's La HORS RH12 192 D4
St Marks Pl FNM GU9 * 107 M7
WIM/MER SW19 * 28 C9
St Marks Rd EPSOM KT18 78 G7
HAYES BR2 47 P4
MTCM CR4 44 B3
SNWD SE25 46 A5
TEDD TW11 41 H1
St Martha's Av
WOKS/MYFD GU22 92 D1
St Marthas Ct RGUE GU4 * 132 F2
St Martin's Av EPSOM KT18 78 C3
St Martins Cl EHSLY KT24 94 G9
EW KT17 * 78 D2
WDR/YW UB7 13 N1
St Martin's Ct ASHF TW15 22 F8
St Martins Dr WOT/HER KT12 57 L2
St Martin's La BECK BR3 47 H6
St Martins Meadow
BH/WHM TN16 105 N3
St Martins Ms DORK RH4 116 G7
WOKS/MYFD GU22 73 L5
St Martin's Wy TOOT SW17 28 F6
St Mary Abbot's Pl KENS W8 19 K1
St Mary Abbots Ter
WKENS W14 * 19 K1
St Mary Av WLGTN SM6 62 C2
St Marys WEY KT13 * 56 F2
St Mary's Av HAYES BR2 47 L4
NWDGN UB2 16 B2
STWL/WRAY TW19 22 G3
TEDD TW11 * 25 N9
St Mary's Cl CHSGTN KT9 59 M6
EW KT17 60 D6
LHD/OX KT22 96 D3
OXTED RH8 103 L9
SHST GU47 49 N9
SUN TW16 39 J5
St Mary's Ct BH/WHM TN16 105 H6
SHB W12 * 18 D1
St Mary's Crs ISLW TW7 16 D5
STWL/WRAY TW19 22 G3
St Mary's Dr CRAWE RH10 177 L3
EBED/NFELT TW14 23 M3
St Mary's Gdns BAGS GU19 51 N6
HORS RH12 192 B9
St Mary's Ga KENS W8 19 M1
St Mary's Gn BH/WHM TN16 84 A7
St Mary's Gv BARN SW13 18 F8
BH/WHM TN16 84 A7
CHSWK W4 17 P4
RCH/KEW TW9 17 M9
St Mary's Hl ASC SL5 34 C6
St Mary's Mt CTHM CR3 101 P4
St Mary's Pl KENS W8 19 M1
St Mary's Rd ASC SL5 34 B7
ASHV GU12 109 J1
CBLY GU15 68 E2
E/WMO/HCT KT8 40 D6
LHD/OX KT22 97 H2
REIG RH2 119 M6
SAND/SEL CR2 63 M8
SNWD SE25 45 N4
SURB KT6 41 J8
WEY KT13 56 F3
WIM/MER SW19 28 B8
WOKN/KNAP GU21 72 A6
WPK KT4 60 C1
St Marys Ter GUW GU2 * 6 E6
St Marys Wy GUW GU2 111 L3
St Matthew's Av SURB KT6 41 L9
St Matthew's Rd
BRXS/STRHM SW2 30 A1
REDH RH1 120 B4
St Maur Rd FUL/PGN SW6 19 K6
St Michael's Av RGUW GU3 91 J9
St Michaels Cl FLEETN GU51 87 J7
WOT/HER KT12 57 L1
WPK KT4 60 D1
St Michael's Rd ALDT GU11 108 D5
ASHF TW15 23 K8
CBLY GU15 * 68 D3
CROY/NA CR0 2 D2
CTHM CR3 101 M2
EGRIN RH19 180 D1
FARN GU14 88 D1
SHST GU47 49 K9
WLGTN SM6 62 E5
WOKN/KNAP GU21 73 H3
St Mildred's Rd GU GU1 112 D4
St Monica's Rd
KWD/TDW/WH KT20 99 K1
St Nazaire Cl EGH TW20 * 21 P8
St Nicholas Av GT/LBKH KT23 96 B5
St Nicholas Cl FLEETN GU51 86 F6
St Nicholas Crs
WOKS/MYFD GU22 73 L5
St Nicholas Dr SHPTN TW17 38 C8
St Nicholas Glebe TOOT SW17 29 K9
St Nicholas Hl LHD/OX KT22 97 H2
St Nicholas Rd SUT SM1 61 M4
THDIT KT7 40 F7
St Nicholas Wy SUT SM1 61 M3
St Nicolas Av CRAN GU6 153 H9
St Nicolas Cl CRAN GU6 153 H9
St Normans Wy EW KT17 60 E8
St Olaf's Rd FUL/PGN SW6 19 J5
St Olave's Cl STA TW18 37 K1
St Olave's Wk
STRHM/NOR SW16 44 E3
St Omer Barracks
ALDT GU11 108 F1
St Omer Rdg GU GU1 112 E6
St Omer Rd GU GU1 112 E6
St Oswald's Rd
STRHM/NOR SW16 45 K2
St Paul's Cl ADL/WDHM KT15 55 L3
ASHF TW15 23 M8
CAR SM5 44 A8
CHSGTN KT9 59 K3
HSLW TW3 15 N7
HYS/HAR UB3 14 F3
RFNM GU10 109 H7
St Paul's Rd BTFD TW8 17 K4
RCH/KEW TW9 17 M8
STA TW18 22 A8
THHTH CR7 45 L4
WOKS/MYFD GU22 11 H3
St Paul's Rd East DORK RH4 117 H8
St Paul's Rd West
DORK RH4 116 G8
St Peters CHERT KT16 * 54 G2
St Peters Av BH/WHM TN16 * 84 F5
St Peter's Cl STA TW18 22 C9
TOOT SW17 29 H5
WDSR SL4 20 F1
WOKS/MYFD GU22 72 G9
St Peters Ct E/WMO/HCT KT8 40 A5
St Peter's Gdns RFNM GU10 127 K7
WNWD SE27 30 B6
YTLY GU46 67 H2
St Peter's Gv HMSMTH W6 18 E2
St Peters Md ASHV GU12 109 K4
St Peters Pk FNM GU9 108 A6
St Peter's Rd CRAWW RH11 176 F5
CROY/NA CR0 63 M3
E/WMO/HCT KT8 40 A5
HMSMTH W6 * 18 E3
KUT KT1 9 H5
TWK TW1 26 A1
WOKS/MYFD GU22 92 F1
St Peter's Sq HMSMTH W6 18 E2
St Peter's St SAND/SEL CR2 63 M4
St Peter's Ter FUL/PGN SW6 19 J5
St Peter's Vls HMSMTH W6 18 E2
St Peter's Wy CHERT KT16 55 J3
FRIM GU16 69 H9
HYS/HAR UB3 14 F3
St Philip's Av WPK KT4 60 F1
St Philip's Rd SURB KT6 41 K7
St Pier's La LING RH7 162 E1
St Pinnock Av STA TW18 37 L2
St Richards Ms
CRAWE RH10 * 177 J5
St Sampson Rd
CRAWW RH11 176 C9
St Saviour Av
CHOB/PIR GU24 91 H1
St Saviours Pl GU GU1 * 6 D3
St Saviour's Rd
BRXS/STRHM SW2 30 A1
Saints Cl WNWD SE27 30 C7
St Sebastian's Cl EWKG RG40 49 J1
St Simon's Av PUT/ROE SW15 27 P1
St Stephens Av ASHTD KT21 77 L6
St Stephens Cl HASM GU27 184 D3
St Stephens Ct GDST RH9 122 E9
St Stephen's Crs THHTH CR7 45 J4
St Stephen's Gdns TWK TW1 26 B2

St Stephen's Rd *HSLW* TW3...25 H2
St Stephen's Wk
SKENS SW7 *...19 N2
St Swithun's Cl *EGRIN* RH19 *...180 E2
St Theresa Cl *EPSOM* KT18...78 A3
St Theresa's Rd
EBED/NFELT TW14...15 H9
St Thomas Cl *SURB* KT6...41 M9
WOKN/KNAP GU21...72 A6
St Thomas' Rd *CHSWK* W4...18 A5
St Thomas's Dr *RGUE* GU4 *...114 A2
St Thomas's Ms *GU* GU1...7 J6
St Thomas's Wy
FUL/PGN SW6...19 K5
St Thomas Wk
DTCH/LGLY SL3...13 H5
St Vincent Cl *CRAWE* RH10...177 N6
WNWD SE27...30 C8
St Vincent Rd *WHTN* TW2...25 K2
WOT/HER KT12...57 K2
St Winifred's Rd
BH/WHM TN16...84 D7
TEDD TW11...26 A9
Salamanca *CWTH* RG45...49 J4
Salamander Cl
KUTN/CMB KT2...26 B8
Salamander Quay *KUT* KT1 *...8 B3
Salbrook Rd *REDH* RH1...140 C4
Salcombe Dr *MRDN* SM4...43 H9
Salcombe Rd *ASHF* TW15...23 H7
Salcot Crs *CROY/NA* CR0...65 J8
Salcott Rd *BTSEA* SW11...29 J1
CROY/NA CR0...62 G2
Salehurst Rd *BROCKY* SE4...31 N2
CRAWE RH10...177 P5
Salem Pl *CROY/NA* CR0...2 B6
Salerno Cl *ALDT* GU11...108 C4
Salesian Vw *FARN* GU14...88 G7
Salford Rd *BRXS/STRHM* SW2...29 N4
Salisbury Av *SUT* SM1...61 K5
Salisbury Cl *WPK* KT4...60 D2
Salisbury Gdns
WIM/MER SW19 *...43 J1
Salisbury Gv *FRIM* GU16...89 J4
Salisbury Pavement
FUL/PGN SW6 *...19 L5
Salisbury Pl *BF/WBF* KT14...55 N9
Salisbury Rd *ASHV* GU12...109 J4
BLKW GU17...67 N3
BNSTD SM7...79 M4
CAR SM5...62 B5
CRAWE RH10...177 J9
CROY/NA CR0...46 A7
FARN GU14...88 E3
FELT TW13...24 D4
GDST RH9...122 C2
HOR/WEW KT19...60 B3
HSLWW TW4...15 L8
NWDGN UB2 *...15 N2
NWMAL KT3...42 B4
RCH/KEW TW9...17 L9
WIM/MER SW19...43 J1
WOKS/MYFD GU22...72 C8
Salisbury Ter *FRIM* GU16...89 J4
Salix Cl *GT/LBKH* KT23...96 B3
SUN TW16...39 K1
Salmons La *CTHM* CR3...81 N9
Salmons La West *CTHM* CR3...81 N9
Salmons Rd *CHSGTN* KT9...59 L5
EHSLY KT24...95 L9
Saltash Cl *SUT* SM1...61 K3
Saltbox Hl *BH/WHM* TN16...83 P2
Salt Box Rd *RGUW* GU3...91 N9
Saltdean Cl *CRAWE* RH10...176 C8
Salterford Rd *TOOT* SW17...29 K9
Salterns Rd *CRAWE* RH10...177 M8
Salter's Hl *NRWD* SE19...30 E8
Saltire Gdns *BNFD* RG42...32 C2
Salt La *MFD/CHID* GU8...150 C6
Saltram Rd *FARN* GU14...88 C5
Salvador *TOOT* SW17...29 H8
Salvation Pl *LHD/OX* KT22...96 G4
Salvington Rd *CRAWW* RH11...176 C8
Salvin Rd *PUT/ROE* SW15...19 H8
Salwey Cl *BRAK* RG12...32 D7
Samaritan Cl *CRAWW* RH11...176 B7
Samarkand Cl *CBLY* GU15...69 K4
Samels Ct *HMSMTH* W6...18 E3
Samian Pl *BNFD* RG42...32 A1
Samos Rd *PGE/AN* SE20...46 B3
Samphire Cl *CRAWW* RH11...176 D8
Sampleoak La *RGUE* GU4...133 J3
Samuel Gray Gdns
KUTN/CMB KT2...8 C2
Samuel Lewis Trust Dwellings
WKENS W14 *...19 J2
San Carlos Ap *ALDT* GU11...108 E4
Sanctuary Rd
STWL/WRAY TW19...23 K2
Sandal Rd *NWMAL* KT3...42 C5
Sandalwood *GUW* GU2...6 A5
Sandalwood Av *CHERT* KT16...55 H2
Sandalwood Rd *FELT* TW13...24 C6
Sandbourne Av
WIM/MER SW19...43 M4
Sandcross La *REIG* RH2...119 K8
Sandell's Av *ASHF* TW15...23 M7
Sanders Cl *HPTN* TW12...25 K8
Sandersfield Rd *BNSTD* SM7...79 L4
Sanders Pde
STRHM/NOR SW16 *...29 P9
Sanderstead Cl *CLAP* SW4...29 M3
Sanderstead Court Av
SAND/SEL CR2...82 A2
Sanderstead Hl
SAND/SEL CR2...63 N9
Sanderstead Rd
SAND/SEL CR2...63 M6
Sandes Pl *LHD/OX* KT22...76 G7
Sandfield Gdns *THHTH* CR7...45 K4
Sandfield Pl *THHTH* CR7...45 L4
Sandfield Rd *THHTH* CR7...45 K4
Sandfields *RPLY/SEND* GU23...93 H4
Sandfield Ter *GU* GU1...6 E4
Sandford Ct *ALDT* GU11...108 B5
Sandford Down *BRAK* RG12...33 H6
Sandford Rd *ALDT* GU11...108 B5
FNM GU9...107 M7
HAYES BR2...47 N5
Sandford St *FUL/PGN* SW6...19 M5
Sandgate La
WAND/EARL SW18...29 H4
Sandhawes Hl *EGRIN* RH19...162 F8
Sandheath Rd *GSHT* GU26...165 M4
Sand Hl *FARN* GU14...68 D9
Sandhill La *CRAWE* RH10...179 K5
Sandhills *WLGTN* SM6...62 F3
Sandhills Ct *VW* GU25...36 C6
Sandhills La *VW* GU25...36 D6
Sandhills Rd *REIG* RH2...119 L7
The Sandhills *WBPTN* SW10 *...19 N4
Sandhurst Av *BRYLDS* KT5...41 P8
Sandhurst Cl *SAND/SEL* CR2...63 N7
Sandhurst La *BLKW* GU17...67 M2
Sandhurst Rd *CWTH* RG45...49 M6
EWKG RG40...48 F1
YTLY GU46...67 J2
Sandhurst Wy *SAND/SEL* CR2...63 N6
Sandiford Rd *CHEAM* SM3...61 K1
Sandiland Crs *HAYES* BR2...65 M1
Sandilands *CROY/NA* CR0...64 A2
Sandilands Rd *FUL/PGN* SW6...19 M6
Sandlands Gv
KWD/TDW/WH KT20...98 E3
Sandlands Rd
KWD/TDW/WH KT20...98 E3
Sandon Cl *ESH/CLAY* KT10...40 D8
Sandow Crs *HYS/HAR* UB3...15 H1
Sandown Av *ESH/CLAY* KT10...58 C4
Sandown Cl *BLKW* GU17...67 P3
HEST TW5...15 J6
Sandown Ct *BELMT* SM2 *...61 M6
SYD SE26 *...31 J6
Sandown Crs *ALDT* GU11...108 D7
Sandown Dr *CAR* SM5...62 C7
FRIM GU16...68 F6
Sandown Ga *ESH/CLAY* KT10...58 D1
Sandown Rd *COUL/CHIP* CR5...80 C5
ESH/CLAY KT10...58 C3
SNWD SE25...46 B6
Sandpiper Cl *CRAWW* RH11...176 A7
Sandpiper Rd *SAND/SEL* CR2...64 D9
SUT SM1...61 K4
Sandpit Hall Rd
CHOB/PIR GU24...71 N1
Sandpit Heath *RGUW* GU3...111 K1
Sandpit Rd *REDH* RH1...120 A6
Sandpits Rd *CROY/NA* CR0...64 D3
RCHPK/HAM TW10...26 C5
Sandra Cl *HSLW* TW3...25 J1
Sandringham Av
RYNPK SW20...43 J2
Sandringham Cl
WIM/MER SW19 *...28 A4
WOKS/MYFD GU22...73 L5
Sandringham Dr *ASHF* TW15...22 G7
Sandringham Gdns
HEST TW5...15 J6
Sandringham Pk *COB* KT11...75 P1
Sandringham Pl
E/WMO/HCT KT8...40 A5
Sandringham Rd
CRAWW RH11...176 E9
CROY/NA CR0...45 L6
HTHAIR TW6...23 H1
WPK KT4...60 E2
Sandringham Wy *FRIM* GU16...69 H8
Sandrock *HASM* GU27...184 D4
Sandrock Hill Rd
RFNM GU10...127 K7
Sandrock Pl *CROY/NA* CR0...64 D3
Sandrock Rd *DORK* RH4...116 B9
Sandroyd Wy *COB* KT11...76 A2
Sands Cl *RFNM* GU10...128 F3
Sands End La *FUL/PGN* SW6...19 M6
Sands Rd *RFNM* GU10...128 E3
Sandy Cl *WOKS/MYFD* GU22...72 G6
Sandycombe Rd
EBED/NFELT TW14...24 B4
RCH/KEW TW9...17 N7
Sandycoombe Rd *TWK* TW1...26 B2
Sandy Ct *COB* KT11...75 P2
Sandy Cft *EW* KT17...60 G8
Sandy Dr *COB* KT11...58 A9
EBED/NFELT TW14...23 P4
Sandy Hill Rd *FNM* GU9...107 L7
WLGTN SM6...62 E7
Sandy Holt *COB* KT11...75 P2
Sandy La *ASC* SL5...33 L2
ASC SL5...34 G6
BELMT SM2...61 J7
BH/WHM TN16...105 H5
BRAK RG12...32 E2
BRKHM/BTCW RH3...118 C5
CBLY GU15...68 G2
CHOB/PIR GU24...53 L7
COB KT11...75 P1
CRAWE RH10...179 H3
E/WMO/HCT KT8...41 H2
EGRIN RH19...180 D2
FARN GU14...87 N1
FLEETS GU52...106 G2
GODL GU7...131 K7
GSHT GU26...166 A9
HASM GU27...183 M3
HASM GU27...184 F1
KWD/TDW/WH KT20...99 L3
MFD/CHID GU8...149 L4
MTCM CR4...44 C2
OXTED RH8...103 J9
OXTED RH8...103 P7
RCHPK/HAM TW10...26 B5
REDH RH1...120 F6
REDH RH1...121 K3
REIG RH2...118 F6
RFNM GU10...146 F3
RFNM GU10...147 K6
RGUW GU3...110 D2
RGUW GU3...131 N1
RPLY/SEND GU23...92 G3
SHGR GU5...133 P3
SHGR GU5...134 C2
SHST GU47...49 K8
TEDD TW11...40 G1
VW GU25...36 C6
WOKS/MYFD GU22...11 K4
WOKS/MYFD GU22...73 L5
WOT/HER KT12...39 K7
Sandy La North *WLGTN* SM6...62 F4
Sandy La South *WLGTN* SM6...62 E7
Sandy Md *HOR/WEW* KT19...59 N8
Sandy Rd *ADL/WDHM* KT15...55 L5
Sandy Wy *COB* KT11...76 A1
CROY/NA CR0...64 F2
WOKS/MYFD GU22...72 G6
WOT/HER KT12...39 H9
San Feliu Ct *EGRIN* RH19...180 G1
Sanger Av *CHSGTN* KT9...59 M4
Sanger Dr *RPLY/SEND* GU23...92 G2
Sangers Dr *HORL* RH6...159 J2
Sangley Rd *SNWD* SE25...45 N5
Sangora Rd *BTSEA* SW11...19 P9
Sankey La *FLEETN* GU51...87 K3
Santina Cl *FNM* GU9...107 P6
Santos Rd *PUT/ROE* SW15...28 D1
Sanway Cl *BF/WBF* KT14...74 A3
Sanway Rd *BF/WBF* KT14...74 A3
Sappho Ct *WOKN/KNAP* GU21...71 L5
Sapte Cl *CRAN* GU6...153 K9
Saracen Cl *CROY/NA* CR0...45 M7
Sarah Wy *FARN* GU14...88 D3
Sarel Wy *HORL* RH6...140 D8
Sargent Cl *CRAWE* RH10...177 J9
Sark Cl *CRAWW* RH11...176 D9
HEST TW5...16 A5
Sarsby Dr *STWL/WRAY* TW19...21 M5
Sarsen Av *HSLW* TW3...15 P7
Sarsfeld Rd *BAL* SW12...29 J4
Sarum *BRAK* RG12...32 A9
Sarum Gn *WEY* KT13...56 G2
Saturn Cl *CRAWW* RH11...176 B7
Saunders Cl *CRAWE* RH10...177 L5
Saunders Copse
WOKS/MYFD GU22...91 P2
Saunders La
WOKS/MYFD GU22...91 M2
Saunton Av *HYS/HAR* UB3...15 H5
Saunton Gdns *FARN* GU14...88 C1
Savernake Wk *CRAWE* RH10...177 J8
Savernake Wy *BRAK* RG12...33 H7
Savery Dr *SURB* KT6...41 J8
Savile Cl *NWMAL* KT3...42 C6
THDIT KT7...40 F9
Savile Gdns *CROY/NA* CR0...3 K4
Saville Crs *ASHF* TW15...23 N9
Saville Gdns *CBLY* GU15...69 K3
Saville Rd *CHSWK* W4...18 B1
TWK TW1...25 N4
Saville Rw *HAYES* BR2...47 M9
Savill Gdns *RYNPK* SW20...42 E4
Savona Cl *WIM/MER* SW19...43 H1
Savoy Av *HYS/HAR* UB3...14 G3
Savoy Gv *BLKW* GU17...67 P5
Sawkins Cl *WIM/MER* SW19...28 A5
Sawtry Cl *CAR* SM5...43 P8
Sawyer's Hl
RCHPK/HAM TW10...26 E3
Saxby Rd *BRXS/STRHM* SW2...29 P3
Saxby's La *LING* RH7...143 L8
Saxley *HORL* RH6...140 E9
Saxon Av *FELT* TW13...24 G5
Saxonbury Av *SUN* TW16...39 K4
Saxonbury Cl *MTCM* CR4...43 P4
Saxonbury Gdns *SURB* KT6...41 J9
Saxon Cl *SURB* KT6...41 K7
Saxon Crs *HORS* RH12...192 A6
Saxon Cft *FNM* GU9...5 G5
Saxon Dr *BNFD* RG42...33 H2
Saxonfield Cl
BRXS/STRHM SW2...30 A3
Saxon Hl *BH/WHM* TN16 *...105 H6
Saxon Rd *ASHF* TW15...23 N9
BMLY BR1...47 M1
CRAWE RH10...177 P6
CROY/NA CR0...45 M6
WOT/HER KT12...57 M2
Saxons *KWD/TDW/WH* KT20...99 H1
Saxon Wy *REIG* RH2...119 K4
WDR/YW UB7...13 N4
WDSR SL4...20 G2
Sayers Cl *FRIM* GU16...68 G9
LHD/OX KT22...96 C4
SWTR RH13...192 D8
The Sayers *EGRIN* RH19...180 B2
Sayes Ct *ADL/WDHM* KT15...55 M4
Sayes Court Farm Dr
ADL/WDHM KT15...55 M4
Sbac Tr *ALDT* GU11...88 A9
Scallows Cl *CRAWE* RH10...177 K4
Scallows Rd *CRAWE* RH10...177 K4
Scampton Rd *HTHAIR* TW6...23 J2
Scarborough Cl *BELMT* SM2...61 K8
BH/WHM TN16...84 A7
Scarborough Rd *HTHAIR* TW6...23 M2
Scarbrook Rd *CROY/NA* CR0...2 C6
Scarlet Oaks *CBLY* GU15...68 G5
Scarlett Cl *WOKN/KNAP* GU21...71 M7
Scarlett's Rd *ALDT* GU11...108 C3
Scarsdale Pl *KENS* W8...19 M1
Scarsdale Vls *KENS* W8...19 L1
Scarth Rd *BARN* SW13...18 D8
Scawen Cl *CAR* SM5...62 C3
Scholars Rd *BAL* SW12...29 M4
Scholars Wk *GUW* GU2...6 B4
School Cl *CHOB/PIR* GU24...70 F4
GU GU1...112 B3
HORS RH12...192 F4
School Fld *EDEN* TN8...144 G3
School Hl *CWTH* RG45...49 P5
HORS RH12...191 N2
REDH RH1...100 E8
RFNM GU10...127 K7
RFNM GU10...129 K1
SHST GU47...49 L8
School House La *TEDD* TW11...41 H1
School La *ADL/WDHM* KT15...55 L3
BAGS GU19...51 M7
BFOR GU20...52 D5
CHOB/PIR GU24...90 E2
DORK RH4...116 D8
EGH TW20...21 M8
EGRIN RH19...181 J5
EHSLY KT24...94 D9
FROW RH18...181 L9
KUT KT1...8 A3
LHD/OX KT22...96 D2
MFD/CHID GU8...130 E7
MFD/CHID GU8...168 A7
RDKG RH5...97 J7
RFNM GU10...126 B8
RFNM GU10...127 P7
RGUE GU4...114 A2
RGUW GU3...109 P2
RGUW GU3...130 C1
RPLY/SEND GU23...94 D2
SHPTN TW17...38 D7
SURB KT6...41 N9
YTLY GU46...66 F2
School Pas *KUT* KT1...9 G5
School Rd *ASC* SL5...34 D6
ASHF TW15...23 L9
BFOR GU20...52 A3
E/WMO/HCT KT8...40 D5
GSHT GU26...165 L8
HASM GU27...184 A5
HPTN TW12...25 K9
HSLW TW3...16 C8
KUT KT1...8 A3
RFNM GU10...146 B1
WDR/YW UB7...13 P4
School Road Av *HPTN* TW12...25 K9
Schroder Ct *EGH* TW20...20 G8
Schubert Rd *PUT/ROE* SW15...28 C1
Scillonian Rd *GUW* GU2...111 N7
Scizdons Climb *GODL* GU7...131 M9
Scoles Crs *BRXS/STRHM* SW2...30 B4
Scope Wy *KUT* KT1...41 L5
Scords La *BH/WHM* TN16...125 N3
Scory Cl *CRAWW* RH11...176 D8
Scotia Rd *BRXS/STRHM* SW2...30 B3
Scotland Bridge Rd
ADL/WDHM KT15...55 L9
Scotland Cl *ASHV* GU12...109 J1
Scotland Farm Rd
ASHV GU12...109 J1
Scotland Hl *SHST* GU47...49 L9
Scotland La *HASM* GU27...184 D5
Scotlands Cl *HASM* GU27...184 C5
Scotlands Dr *HASM* GU27...184 C5
Scots Cl *STWL/WRAY* TW19...22 G4
Scotsdale Cl *BELMT* SM2...61 J6
Scotshall La *WARL* CR6...83 J4
Scott Cl *GUW* GU2...111 N3
HOR/WEW KT19...60 A4
STRHM/NOR SW16...45 H2
WDR/YW UB7...14 B2
Scott Farm Cl *THDIT* KT7...41 H9
Scott Gdns *HEST* TW5...15 M5
Scott Rd *CRAWE* RH10...177 J8
Scotts Av *HAYES* BR2...47 K3
SUN TW16...38 G1
Scott's Ct *FARN* GU14...68 D9
Scotts Dr *HPTN* TW12...40 B1
Scotts Farm Rd
HOR/WEW KT19...60 A5
Scott's Grove Cl
CHOB/PIR GU24...71 K2
Scott's Grove Rd
CHOB/PIR GU24...71 H3
Scott's Hl *HORL* RH6...141 M9
Scott's La *HAYES* BR2...47 K4
Scotts Rd *BMLY* BR1...47 N1
NWDGN UB2...15 L1
Scotts Wy *SUN* TW16...38 G1
Scott Ter *BNFD* RG42...32 G2
Scott Trimmer Wy *HEST* TW5...15 N7
Scutari Rd *EDUL* SE22...31 J1
Scylla Crs *HTHAIR* TW6...23 L3
Scylla Pl *WOKN/KNAP* GU21 *...71 N8
Scylla Rd *HTHAIR* TW6...23 L2
Seabrook Dr *WWKM* BR4...65 L1
Seacourt Rd *DTCH/LGLY* SL3...12 F2
Seafire Wy *FARN* GU14...88 A8
Seaford Rd *CRAWW* RH11...194 D1
HTHAIR TW6...22 G1
Seaforth Av *NWMAL* KT3...42 F6
Seaforth Gdns
HOR/WEW KT19...60 D3
Seagrave Rd *FUL/PGN* SW6...19 L4
Sealand Rd *HTHAIR* TW6...23 K2
Seale La *RFNM* GU10...128 F1
RGUW GU3...129 P1
Seale Rd *MFD/CHID* GU8...129 K5
Seaman's Gn *RDKG* RH5...156 C4
Searchwood Rd *WARL* CR6...82 B7
Searle Hl *REIG* RH2...119 L7
Searle Rd *FNM* GU9...5 G7
Searle's Vw *HORS* RH12...192 E5
Seaton Cl *PUT/ROE* SW15...27 N3
WHTN TW2...25 L2
Seaton Dr *ASHF* TW15...23 H5
Seaton Rd *CBLY* GU15...68 D3
HYS/HAR UB3...14 F2
MTCM CR4...44 A3
WHTN TW2...25 K2
Sebastopol Rd *ALDT* GU11...108 D4
Second Av *ADL/WDHM* KT15...55 M7
KWD/TDW/WH KT20 *...99 K6
MORT/ESHN SW14...18 C8
WOT/HER KT12...39 K7
Second Cl *E/WMO/HCT* KT8...40 B5
Second Cross Rd *WHTN* TW2...25 L5
Seddon Hl *BNFD* RG42...32 D1
Seddon Rd *MRDN* SM4...43 P6
Sedgefield Cl *CRAWE* RH10...177 P4
Sedgehill Rd *CAT* SE6...31 P8
Sedgemoor *FARN* GU14...68 D9
Sedgewick Cl *CRAWE* RH10...177 M5
Sedgewood Cl *HAYES* BR2...47 M8
Sedleigh Rd
WAND/EARL SW18...28 C2
Sedlescombe Rd
FUL/PGN SW6...19 K4
Seebys Oak *SHST* GU47...67 P2
Seeley Dr *DUL* SE21...30 F7
Seely Rd *TOOT* SW17...29 K9
Seething Wells La *SURB* KT6...41 J7
Sefton Cl *CHOB/PIR* GU24...70 F2
Sefton Rd *CROY/NA* CR0...46 A9
HOR/WEW KT19...60 B8
Sefton St *PUT/ROE* SW15...18 G7
Segrave Cl *WEY* KT13...56 C6
Segsbury Gv *BRAK* RG12...32 G5
Sekhon Ter *FELT* TW13...25 H6
Selborne Av *ALDT* GU11...108 E7
Selborne Cl *BLKW* GU17...67 N2
Selborne Gdns *FNM* GU9...127 L6
Selborne Rd *CROY/NA* CR0...3 H6
NWMAL KT3...42 C3
Selbourne Av
ADL/WDHM KT15...55 M8
SURB KT6...59 M1
Selbourne Cl
ADL/WDHM KT15...55 M8
CRAWE RH10...177 N1
Selbourne Rd *RGUE* GU4...112 E2
Selbourne Sq *GDST* RH9...122 C1
Selby Cl *CHSGTN* KT9...59 L6
Selby Gn *CAR* SM5...44 A8
Selby Rd *ASHF* TW15...23 M9
CAR SM5...44 A8
PGE/AN SE20...46 A3
Selbys *LING* RH7...143 L8
Selby Wk *WOKN/KNAP* GU21...71 P7
Selcroft Rd *PUR/KEN* CR8...81 K1
Selham Cl *CRAWW* RH11...176 D4
Selhurst Cl *WIM/MER* SW19...28 A4
WOKN/KNAP GU21...72 D4
Selhurst New Rd *SNWD* SE25...45 N7
Selhurst Pl *CROY/NA* CR0...45 N7
Selhurst Rd *SNWD* SE25...45 N6
Selkirk Rd *TOOT* SW17...29 H7
WHTN TW2...25 K5
Sellar's Hl *GODL* GU7...131 K6
Sellincourt Rd *TOOT* SW17...29 H8
Sellindge Cl *BECK* BR3...46 F1
The Sells *GU* GU1...7 K6
Selsdon Av *SAND/SEL* CR2...63 M5
Selsdon Cl *SURB* KT6...41 L6
Selsdon Crs *SAND/SEL* CR2...64 C8
Selsdon Park Rd
SAND/SEL CR2...64 A9
Selsdon Rd *ADL/WDHM* KT15...55 L9
SAND/SEL CR2...63 M4
WNWD SE27...30 C6
Selsey Rd *CRAWW* RH11...176 D9
Selsfield Rd *CRAWE* RH10...179 H9
Seltops Cl *CRAN* GU6...171 J1
Selwood Cl
STWL/WRAY TW19 *...22 F2
Selwood Gdns
STWL/WRAY TW19...22 F2
Selwood Pl *SKENS* SW7...19 P3
Selwood Rd *CHEAM* SM3...43 K9
CHSGTN KT9...59 K3
CROY/NA CR0...64 B1
WOKS/MYFD GU22...72 F9
Selwood Ter *SKENS* SW7...19 P3
Selworthy Rd *CAT* SE6...31 N6
Selwyn Av *RCH/KEW* TW9...17 M8
Selwyn Cl *CRAWE* RH10...177 M2
HSLWW TW4...15 N9
Selwyn Dr *YTLY* GU46...66 F2
Selwyn Rd *NWMAL* KT3...42 B6
Semaphore Rd *GU* GU1...7 G7
Semley Rd *STRHM/NOR* SW16...44 G3
Semper Cl *WOKN/KNAP* GU21...71 L6
Send Barns La
RPLY/SEND GU23...93 J4
Send Cl *RPLY/SEND* GU23...92 G3
Send Hl *RPLY/SEND* GU23...92 G5
Send Marsh Rd
RPLY/SEND GU23...93 J3
Send Parade Cl
RPLY/SEND GU23 *...92 G3
Send Rd *RPLY/SEND* GU23...92 G3
Seneca Rd *THHTH* CR7...45 L5
Senga Rd *WLGTN* SM6...44 C9
Senhouse Rd *CHEAM* SM3...61 H2
Sepen Meade *FLEETS* GU52...106 E2
Sequoia Pk *CRAWW* RH11...176 G7
Serrin Wy *HORS* RH12...192 D5
Service Rd *HORL* RH6...159 K5
Service Yard H *BRAK* RG12 *...32 D3
Setley Wy *BRAK* RG12...33 H4
Settrington Rd *FUL/PGN* SW6...19 M7
The Sett *YTLY* GU46...66 F3
Seven Acres *CAR* SM5...62 A1
Seven Arches Ap *WEY* KT13...56 B6
Seven Hills Cl *WEY* KT13...56 G7
Seven Hills Rd
WOT/HER KT12...56 G7
Seven Hills Rd South
COB KT11...74 G2
Sevenoaks Cl *BELMT* SM2...61 L8
Sevenoaks Rd *BROCKY* SE4...31 N2
Seventh Av
KWD/TDW/WH KT20 *...99 K6
Severn Cl *SHST* GU47...49 N9
Severn Crs *DTCH/LGLY* SL3...12 F3

Severn Dr ESH/CLAY KT10 .....58 G1
  WOT/HER KT12 .....57 M1
Severn Rd CRAWE RH10 .....177 M6
  FARN GU14 .....88 A3
Seward Rd BECK BR3 .....46 D3
Sewer's Farm Rd RDKG RH5 .135 P7
Sewill Cl HORL RH6 .....158 C5
Seymour Av CTHM CR3 .....101 L3
  EW KT17 .....60 C7
  MRDN SM4 .....43 H8
Seymour Cl E/WMO/HCT KT8 .40 C6
Seymour Ct COB KT11 .....75 H2
Seymour Dr CBLY GU15 .....51 K9
Seymour Gdns BRYLDS KT5 ....41 M6
  FELT TW13 .....24 C7
  TWK TW1 .....26 A3
Seymour Ms EW KT17 .....60 E8
  WOKS/MYFD GU22 .....71 P9
Seymour Pl SNWD SE25 .....46 B5
  WOKS/MYFD GU22 .....71 P9
Seymour Rd BOR GU35 .....164 F7
  CAR SM5 .....62 C4
  CHSWK W4 .....18 A1
  CRAWW RH11 .....176 D9
  E/WMO/HCT KT8 .....40 C6
  GODL GU7 .....150 A1
  HPTN TW12 .....25 K8
  KUT KT1 .....8 B2
  MTCM CR4 .....44 C8
  WAND/EARL SW18 .....28 C3
  WIM/MER SW19 .....28 A6
Seymour Vls PGE/AN SE20 .....46 B2
Seymour Vs PGE/AN SE20 .....46 B2
Seymour Wy WBPTN SW10 .....19 N4
Seymour Wy SUN TW16 .....39 J3
Shabden Cottages
  COUL/CHIP CR5 * 100 B1
Shackleford Rd
  MFD/CHID GU8 .....130 D6
  MFD/CHID GU8 .....148 C1
  WOKS/MYFD GU22 .....72 E9
Shackleton La ASHV GU12 .489 H9
  FSTH SE23 .....31 J5
Shackleton Rd CRAWE RH10..177 L4
Shackstead La GODL GU7 .....150 B1
Shadbolt Cl WPK KT4 .....60 D1
Shadyhanger GODL GU7 .....131 L7
Shady Nook FNM GU9 .....107 M8
Shaef Wy TEDD TW11 .....40 C1
Shaftesbury Av
  EBED/NFELT TW14 .....24 B2
  NWDGN UB2 .....16 A2
Shaftesbury Cl BRAK RG12 .....32 F6
Shaftesbury Crs STA TW18 .....37 N4
Shaftesbury Ms KENS W8 .....19 L1
Shaftesbury Mt BLKW GU17 .....67 N5
Shaftesbury Rd BECK BR3 .....46 F3
  CAR SM5 .....43 P8
  CHOB/PIR GU24 .....70 F5
  CRAWE RH10 .....177 N7
  RCH/KEW TW9 .....17 L8
  WOKS/MYFD GU22 .....11 J4
Shaftesbury Ter
  HMSMTH W6 * 19 J3
Shaftesbury Wy WHTN TW2 ...25 L6
Shakespeare Av
  EBED/NFELT TW14 .....24 B2
Shakespeare Gdns
  FARN GU14 .....87 P2
Shakespeare Rd
  ADL/WDHM KT15 .....55 P3
  HNHL SE24 .....30 C1
Shakespeare Ter
  RCH/KEW TW9 * 17 N8
Shakespeare Wy BNFD RG42 ..32 G2
  FELT TW13 .....24 D7
Shalbourne Ri CBLY GU15 .....68 F3
Shalcomb St WBPTN SW10 ...19 N4
Shalden Rd ASHV GU12 .....108 F6
Shaldon Dr MRDN SM4 .....43 J6
Shaldon Wy FLEETN GU51 ....86 D7
  WOT/HER KT12 .....57 L2
Shalford La RGUE GU4 .....132 C1
Shalford Rd GU GU1 .....112 B8
Shalstone Rd
  MORT/ESHN SW14 .....17 P8
Shalston Vls SURB KT6 .....41 M7
The Shambles GU GU1 .....6 E5
Shamrock Cl FRIM GU16 .....68 F8
  LHD/OX KT22 .....96 D1
Shamrock Rd CROY/NA CRO ..45 H7
Shandon Rd CLAP SW4 .....29 M1
Shandys Cl HORS RH12 .....191 P9
Shanklin Ct ASHV GU12 .....108 E5
Shannon Cl HEST TW5 .....15 M3
Shap Crs CAR SM5 .....44 B9
Shardcroft Av HNHL SE24 .....30 C1
Shardeloes Rd BROCKY SE4 * .31 N1
Shardland Cl THHTH CR7 .....45 L2
Sharney Av DTCH/LGLY SL3 ...12 F1
Sharon Cl CRAWE RH10 .....177 K8
  GT/LBKH KT23 .....96 A4
  HOR/WEW KT19 .....78 A2
  SURB KT6 .....41 J9
Sharon Rd CHSWK W4 .....18 B3
Sharpthorne Cl
  CRAWW RH11 .....176 C5
Shawbury Rd EDUL SE22 .....30 C1
Shaw Cl CHERT KT16 .....54 C5
  EW KT17 .....60 D9
  SAND/SEL CR2 .....81 J1
Shaw Crs SAND/SEL CR2 .....81 N1
Shaw Dr WOT/HER KT12 .....39 L8
Shawfield La ASHV GU12 .....109 H4
Shawfield Rd ASHV GU12 .....109 H5
Shawford Rd
  HOR/WEW KT19 .....60 B5
Shaw Gv KWD/TDW/WH KT20..99 K6
Shawley Crs EPSOM KT18 .....78 G7
Shawley Wy EPSOM KT18 .....78 F7
Shaw Pk CWTH RG45 .....49 M6
Shaw Rd BH/WHM TN16 .....84 A9

Shaw's Cottages FSTH SE23 ...31 M6
Shaws Rd CRAWE RH10 .....177 H4
Shaw Wy WLGTN SM6 .....62 G6
Shaxton La CROY/NA CRO 65 J7
Sheaf Cottages THDIT KT7 * ...40 E9
Shearing Dr MRDN SM4 .....43 H8
Shearwater Rd SUT SM1 .....61 K4
Sheath La LHD/OX KT22 .....76 B2
Sheaths Cottages
  THDIT KT7 * 41 H8
Sheen Common Dr
  RCHPK/HAM TW10 .....17 N9
Sheen Court Rd
  RCHPK/HAM TW10 .....17 N9
Sheendale Rd RCH/KEW TW9 .17 M9
Sheenewood SYD SE26 .....31 J8
Sheen Gate Gdns
  MORT/ESHN SW14 .....18 A9
Sheen La MORT/ESHN SW14 ..18 A9
Sheen Pk RCH/KEW TW9 .....17 M9
Sheen Rd RCHPK/HAM TW10 ..17 L9
Sheen Wd MORT/ESHN SW14 .17 N9
Sheepbarn La WARL CR6 .....83 N1
Sheepcote Cl HEST TW5 .....15 J5
Sheephatch La RFNM GU10 .128 D8
Sheephouse FNM GU9 .....5 J7
Sheephouse Gn RDKG RH5 ..135 P1
Sheephouse La RDKG RH5 ...135 P1
  RDKG RH5 .....156 A6
Sheephouse Wy NWMAL KT3 .42 C8
Sheeplands Av GU GU1 .....112 G3
Sheep Wk REIG RH2 .....119 K2
Sheepwalk THHTH TW17 .....38 B8
Sheep Walk Ms
  WIM/MER SW19 .....28 A9
Sheerwater Av
  ADL/WDHM KT15 .....73 K1
Sheerwater Rd
  ADL/WDHM KT15 .....73 J1
Sheet's Heath La
  CHOB/PIR GU24 .....70 G8
Sheet Street Rd WDSR SL4 ...20 A2
Sheffield Cl CRAWE RH10 .....177 L7
  FARN GU14 .....88 B3
Sheffield Rd HTHAIR TW6 .....23 M2
Sheffield Wy HTHAIR TW6 .....23 N1
Shelburne Dr HSLWW TW4 ...24 G4
Shelbury Rd EDUL SE22 .....31 J1
Sheldon Cl CRAWE RH10 .....177 N6
  PGE/AN SE20 .....46 B2
  REIG RH2 .....119 M6
Sheldon Ct GU GU1 * 7 J4
Sheldon St CROY/NA CRO.....2 C6
Sheldrick Cl MTCM CR4 .....43 P3
Shelford Ri NRWD SE19 .....45 N1
Shelgate Rd BTSEA SW11 .....29 J1
Shelley Av BRAK RG12 .....32 C3
Shelley Cl BNSTD SM7 .....79 H4
  COUL/CHIP CR5 .....81 H6
  CRAWE RH10 .....177 M3
  DTCH/LGLY SL3 .....13 L6
  FLEETN GU51 .....86 C7
Shelley Ct CBLY GU15 .....68 E3
Shelley Crs HEST TW5 .....15 K6
Shelley Dr HORS RH12 .....191 K7
  HORS RH12 .....192 A7
Shelley Ri FARN GU14 .....88 A4
Shelleys La RSEV TN14 .....85 L5
Shelley Wk YTLY GU46 .....66 F3
Shelley Wy WIM/MER SW19 ..28 C9
Shellfield Cl
  STWL/WRAY TW19 .....13 N8
Shellwood Rd RDKG RH5 ....137 J2
Shellwood Rd REIG RH2 .....138 B5
Shelly Ri FARN GU14 .....88 B1
Shellys Ct SWTR RH13 * 192 F1
Shelson Av FELT TW13 .....24 A7
Shelson Pde FELT TW13 * 24 A6
Shelton Av WARL CR6 .....82 C7
Shelton Cl GUW GU2 .....91 N9
  WARL CR6 .....82 C6
Shelton Rd WIM/MER SW19 ..43 L2
Shelvers Av
  KWD/TDW/WH KT20 .....98 G1
Shelvers HI
  KWD/TDW/WH KT20 .....98 G1
Shelvers Sp
  KWD/TDW/WH KT20 .....98 G1
Shelvers Wy
  KWD/TDW/WH KT20 .....98 G1
Shenfield Cl COUL/CHIP CR5 ..80 D8
Shenley Rd HEST TW5 .....15 N6
Shenstone Cl EWKG RG40 ....48 E1
Shenstone Pk ASC SL5 .....34 E5
Shepherds & Flock Round
  RFNM GU10 .....128 A2
Shepherd Cl CRAWE RH10 ..176 G8
  FELT TW13 .....24 F7
Shepherd's Bush Rd
  HMSMTH W6 .....18 G2
Shepherds Cha BAGS GU19 ...51 N7
Shepherds Cl SHPTN TW17 ...38 D7
Shepherdsgrove La
  EGRIN RH19 .....163 L7
Shepherds HI BRAK RG12 .....32 E2
  GUW GU2 .....111 N3
  HASM GU27 .....184 D4
  REDH RH1 .....100 E6
Shepherds La BFOR GU20 ....52 C4
  BNFD RG42 .....32 C1
  GUW GU2 .....111 M2
Shepherds' Wk EPSOM KT18..97 P1
  FARN GU14 .....68 A9
Shepherds Wy CWTH RG45 ...49 J5
  HORS RH12 .....192 F5
  LIPH GU30 .....182 G4
  RFNM GU10 .....128 E9
  RGUE GU4 .....112 C9
  SAND/SEL CR2 .....64 D6

Shepiston La WDR/YW UB7 ...14 D2
  REDH RH1 .....120 B7
Shires Cl ASHTD KT21 .....77 K8
The Shires RCHPK/HAM TW10..26 D7
Shires Wy YTLY GU46 .....49 H9
Shirley Av BELMT SM2 .....61 K8
  COUL/CHIP CR5 .....81 K8
  CROY/NA CRO 46 C9
  REDH RH1 .....140 B1
  SUT SM1 .....62 A3
Shirley Church Rd
  CROY/NA CRO 64 D2
Shirley Cl HSLW TW3 .....25 K1
Shirley Crs BECK BR3 .....46 E5
Shirley Dr HSLW TW3 .....25 K1
Shirley Hills Rd
  CROY/NA CRO 64 D4
Shirley Oaks Rd
  CROY/NA CRO 46 D9
Shirley Park Rd
  CROY/NA CRO 46 B9
Shirley Rd WOKN/KNAP GU21 .71 J6
Shirley Rd CROY/NA CRO 46 C7
  WLGTN SM6 .....62 E7
Shirley Rw SNWD SE25 * 46 A3
Shirley Wy CROY/NA CRO 64 F2
Shoe La ALDT GU11 .....88 C9
Shophouse La SHGR GU5 ....133 P1
Shord HI PUR/KEN CR8 .....81 M5
Shore Cl EBED/NFELT TW14 ..24 F8
  HPTN TW12 .....24 F8
Shore Gv FELT TW13 .....25 H5
Shoreham Cl CROY/NA CRO ..47 H5
  WAND/EARL SW18 .....28 E1
Shoreham Rd CRAWE RH10..177 M8
Shoreham Rd East
  HTHAIR TW6 .....23 H1
Shoreham Rd West
  HTHAIR TW6 .....23 H1
Shoreham Wy HAYES BR2 ....47 N2
Shore's Rd WOKN/KNAP GU21.72 D1
Shorrolds Rd FUL/PGN SW6 ..19 L5
Shortacres REDH RH1 .....121 H4
Short Cl CRAWW RH11 .....194 C1
Shortcroft Rd EW KT17 .....60 D7
Short Dale Rd ALDT GU11 ...108 E8
Short Gallop CRAWE RH10 * .177 N4
Shortheath Crest FNM GU9..127 K7
Shortheath Rd FNM GU9 ....127 L7
Shortlands HMSMTH W6 .....19 H2
  HYS/HAR UB3 .....14 F4
Shortlands Gv HAYES BR2 ....47 K4
Shortlands Rd BLKW GU17....67 N2
  KUTN/CMB KT2 .....9 G1
Short La OXTED RH8 .....123 P3
  STWL/WRAY TW19 .....23 H5
Short Rd CHSWK W4 .....18 C4
  STWL/WRAY TW19 .....23 H5
Shortsfield Cl HORS RH12 ...192 B3
Shorts Rd CAR SM5 .....62 A3
Short St ALDT GU11 .....108 C4
Shortwood Av STA TW18 .....22 E6
Shotfield WLGTN SM6 .....62 D5
Shott Cl SUT SM1 .....61 N4
Shottendane Rd
  FUL/PGN SW6 * 19 L6
Shottermill HORS RH12 .....192 F5
Shottermill Ph HASM GU27 * .183 P8
Shottfield Av
  MORT/ESHN SW14 .....18 C9
Shovelstrode La
  EGRIN RH19 .....181 K1
Shrewsbury Av
  MORT/ESHN SW14 .....18 A9
Shrewsbury Cl SURB KT6 .....59 L1
Shrewsbury Rd BECK BR3 ....46 E4
  CAR SM5 .....44 A8
  EBED/NFELT TW14 .....23 M2
  REDH RH1 .....120 B5
Shrewton Rd TOOT SW17 * ...44 A1
Shrivenham Cl SHST GU47 ...49 P9
Shropshire Cl MTCM CR4 .....44 G5
Shropshire Gdns BNFD RG42 .33 H1
Shrubbery Rd
  STRHM/NOR SW16 .....29 P7
The Shrubbery FARN GU14 * .87 P3
  SURB KT6 * 41 L9
Shrubbs HI CHOB/PIR GU24...53 J7
Shrubbs Hill La ASC SL5 .....35 J5
Shrubbs La RFNM GU10 .....127 K9
Shrubland Gv WPK KT4 .....60 G2
Shrubland Rd BNSTD SM7 ....79 L4
Shrublands Av CROY/NA CRO .64 G3
Shrublands Cl SYD SE26 .....31 K6
Shrublands Dr LTWR GU18 ...52 B9
Shuters Sq WKENS W14 * 19 J3
Shuttleworth Rd
  BTSEA SW11 .....19 P7
Sian Cl FLEETS GU52 .....107 H1
Sibthorp Rd MTCM CR4 * 44 B3
Sibton Rd CAR SM5 .....44 A8
Sickle Rd HASM GU27 .....184 G5
Sidbury Cl ASC SL5 .....34 G6
Sidbury St FUL/PGN SW6 .....19 J6
Siddeley Dr HSLWW TW4 .....15 N8
Siddons Rd CROY/NA CRO 45 J1
  FSTH SE23 .....31 M5
Sidestrand Rd ALDT GU11 ....88 A8
Sideways La HORL RH6 .....158 F3
The Sidings ALDT GU11 .....108 E3
  STA TW18 * 22 D7
Sidlaws Rd FARN GU14 .....67 P9
Sidmouth Av ISLW TW7 .....16 E7
Sidney Gdns BTFD TW8 .....17 K4
Sidney Rd BECK BR3 .....46 E3
  SNWD SE25 .....46 A6
  TWK TW1 .....26 A1
  WOT/HER KT12 .....57 K2
Signal Ct LING RH7 .....143 L8

Sigrist Sq KUTN/CMB KT2 .....8 E3
Silbury Av MTCM CR4 .....44 A2
Silchester Dr CRAWW RH11 ..176 D8
Silistria Cl WOKN/KNAP GU21 .71 J7
Silkham Rd OXTED RH8 .....103 K7
Silkin Wk CRAWW RH11 * 194 C1
Silkmore La EHSLY KT24 .....94 E7
  RPLY/SEND GU23 .....94 E7
Silo Cl GODL GU7 .....131 M5
Silo Dr GODL GU7 .....131 M5
Silo Rd GODL GU7 .....131 M5
Silverbeck Wy
  STWL/WRAY TW19 .....22 D1
Silver Birch Cl
  ADL/WDHM KT15 .....73 J1
  CAT SE6 .....31 N6
  FLEETS GU52 .....106 F1
Silver Birches Wy
  MFD/CHID GU8 .....148 F1
Silver Cl KWD/TDW/WH KT20..99 J4
Silver Crs CHSWK W4 .....18 A2
Silverdale FLEETS GU52 .....86 G9
  FSTH SE23 .....31 L7
Silverdale Av LHD/OX KT22 ...76 C3
  WEY KT13 .....57 H2
Silverdale Cl
  BRKHM/BTCW RH3 .....117 P9
  SUT SM1 .....61 K3
Silverdale Ct STA TW18 * 22 E8
Silverdale Dr SUN TW16 .....39 K3
Silver Dene PUT/ROE SW15 * .27 P1
Silver Dr FRIM GU16 .....69 L5
Silverglades YTLY GU46 .....66 G4
Silverhall St ISLW TW7 .....16 G8
Silver HI SHST GU47 .....50 A9
Silverlands Cl CHERT KT16 * ..55 H2
Silver La PUR/KEN CR8 .....80 F1
  WWKM BR4 .....65 K1
Silverlea Gdns HORL RH6 ...159 M2
Silverleigh Rd THHTH CR7 ....45 H5
Silver Park Cl FLEETS GU52 ..87 H3
Silversmiths Wy
  WOKN/KNAP GU21 .....72 A7
Silversted La BH/WHM TN16..105 H1
Silverstone Cl REDH RH1 ....120 B3
Silverstone Dr HTHAIR TW6 ...14 F1
Silver Tree Cl WOT/HER KT12 .57 J5
Silverwood CRAWE RH10 * .160 G9
Silverwood Cl BECK BR3 .....46 G1
  CROY/NA CRO 64 F7
Silvester Rd EDUL SE22 .....30 G1
Silvister Rd WLGTN SM6 .....62 E3
Silwood BRAK RG12 .....32 A9
Silwood Cl ASC SL5 .....34 D3
  ASC SL5 .....34 F4
Silwood Rd ASC SL5 .....34 E4
Simmil Rd ESH/CLAY KT10 ....58 E4
Simmonds Cl BNFD RG42 .....32 A2
Simmondstone La
  RFNM GU10 .....164 G1
Simmons Cl DTCH/LGLY SL3 * .12 C4
Simmons Cl SURB KT6 .....58 G4
Simmons Pl STA TW18 .....22 B8
Simms Cl CAR SM5 .....62 A1
Simone Dr PUR/KEN CR8 .....81 L5
Simons Cl CHERT KT16 .....54 C5
Simons Wk EGH TW20 .....36 A1
Simplemarsh Rd
  ADL/WDHM KT15 .....55 L3
Simpson Rd HSLWW TW4 .....24 G2
  RCHPK/HAM TW10 .....26 A4
Simpson's Rd HAYES BR2 ....47 N3
Simpson Wy SURB KT6 .....41 J7
Sinclair Cl CRAWE RH10 .....177 M7
Sinclair Dr BELMT SM2 .....61 M7
Sincots Rd REDH RH1 .....120 B5
Sine Cl FARN GU14 .....68 D8
Singles Cross RSEV TN14 * ...85 J4
Singles Cross La RSEV TN14 ...85 N4
Single St BH/WHM TN16 .....84 F4
Singleton Rd CROY/NA CRO ..45 L8
Singleton Cl HORS RH12 .....191 L7
Sinhurst Rd CBLY GU15 .....68 D4
Sion Rd TWK TW1 .....26 B3
Sipson Cl WDR/YW UB7 .....14 C4
Sipson La HYS/HAR UB3 .....14 B1
Sipson Rd WDR/YW UB7 .....14 B1
Sipson Wy WDR/YW UB7 .....14 C5
Sir Abraham Dawes Cottages
  PUT/ROE SW15 * 19 J9
Sir Cyril Black Wy
  WIM/MER SW19 .....43 K1
Sirdar Rd MTCM CR4 .....29 K9
Sir Thomas Moore Est
  CHEL SW3 .....19 P4
Siskin Av CRAWE RH10 .....179 K6
Siskin Cl HORS RH12 .....192 D5
Sispara Gdns
  WAND/EARL SW18 .....28 C2
Sissinghurst Cl CRAWE RH10..177 N4
Sissinghurst Rd
  CROY/NA CRO 46 A8
Sistova Rd BAL SW12 .....29 L4
Siward Rd HAYES BR2 .....47 N4
Six Penny Cl EDEN TN8 .....144 G5
Sixteenth Av
  KWD/TDW/WH KT20 * 99 K6
Sixth Av
  KWD/TDW/WH KT20 .....99 K6
Sixth Cross Rd WHTN TW2....25 K6
Skeena Hi WAND/EARL SW18 .28 B3
Skelbrook St
  WAND/EARL SW18 .....28 E5
Skelgill Rd PUT/ROE SW15....19 K9

Skelton Flds *BNFD* RG42	32	E1
Skelwith Rd *HMSMTH* W6	18	G4
Skerne Rd *KUTN/CMB* KT2	8	C3
Skeynes Rd *EDEN* TN8	144	F4
Skid Hill La *WARL* CR6	85	M4
Skiffington Cl		
BRXS/STRHM SW2	30	B4
Skiff La *BIL* RH14	188	D9
Skimpedhill La *BRAK* RG12	32	C3
Skinners La *ASHTD* KT21	77	K7
EDEN TN8	145	H3
HEST TW5	16	B6
MFD/CHID GU8	168	C6
Skipton Dr *HYS/HAR* UB3	14	E1
Skipton Wy *HORL* RH6	140	D8
Skyes Dr *STA* TW18	22	E8
Skylark Vw *HORS* RH12	192	C3
Skyport Dr *WDR/YW* UB7	13	P5
Slade Ct *CHERT* KT16	55	H5
Slade Rd *CHERT* KT16	55	H5
CHOB/PIR GU24	70	D9
Slagrove Pl *LEW* SE13	31	P1
Slaidburn La *BRAK* RG12	32	G8
Slaidburn St *WBPTN* SW10	19	N4
Slattery Rd *FELT* TW13	24	D4
Slaugham Ct *CRAWW* RH11	176	C8
Sleets Rd *HORS* RH12	191	M7
Slim Cl *ALDT* GU11	88	G8
Slim Rd *CBLY* GU15	68	E2
Slines New Rd *CTHM* CR3	82	D9
Slines Oak Rd *CTHM* CR3	82	G8
Slinfold Wk *CRAWW* RH11	176	D9
Slip of WG GU4	153	H8
Slipshatch Rd *REIG* RH2	119	K9
Slipshoe St *REIG* RH2	119	K5
The Slip *BH/WHM* TN16	104	G6
Sloane Wk *CROY/NA* CR0	6	F7
Slocock Hl *WOKN/KNAP* GU21	72	A6
Sloughbrook Cl *HORS* RH12	192	D1
Slough La		
BRKHM/BTCW RH3	118	G4
EPSOM KT18	98	A5
Slyfield Gn *GU* GU1	112	C1
Smaldon Cl *WDR/YW* UB7	14	C1
Smallberry Av *ISLW* TW7	16	C1
Smallfield Rd *HORL* RH6	159	L1
HORL RH6	160	F1
Smallmead *HORL* RH6	159	L1
Smalls Hill Rd *REIG* RH2	158	G6
Smalls Md *CRAWW* RH11	176	F5
Smallwood Rd *TOOT* SW17	28	G7
Smart's Heath La		
WOKS/MYFD GU22	91	N3
Smart's Heath Rd		
WOKS/MYFD GU22	91	N3
Smeaton Rd		
WAND/EARL SW18	28	D3
Smitham Bottom La		
PUR/KEN CR8	80	F1
Smitham Downs Rd		
COUL/CHIP CR5	80	G2
Smithbarn *SWTR* RH13	192	F7
Smitham La *HORL* RH6	160	D8
Smith Cl *CRAWE* RH10	176	G8
The Smithers		
BRKHM/BTCW RH3	117	P7
Smithfield La *BOR* GU35	164	D2
Smith Rd *REIG* RH2	119	K8
Smiths La *EDEN* TN8	124	G4
Smith Sq *BRAK* RG12	32	F2
Smith St *BRYLDS* KT5	41	M7
Smithwood Av *CRAN* GU6	152	E5
Smithwood Cl		
WIM/MER SW19	28	B5
Smithwood Common Rd		
CRAN GU6	152	E4
Smithy Cl		
KWD/TDW/WH KT20	99	K6
Smithy La *BOR* GU35	164	B9
KWD/TDW/WH KT20	99	K6
Smithy's Gn *BFOR* GU20	52	D5
Smoke La *REIG* RH2	119	N8
Smolletts *EGRIN* RH19	180	B3
Smugglers' La *RDKG* RH5	173	M4
Smugglers' Wy *RFLM* GU10	128	C5
WAND/EARL SW18	19	M9
Snag La *RSEV* TN14	85	H1
Snailslynch *FNM* GU9	5	J3
Snatts Hl *OXTED* RH8	105	M9
Snell Hatch *CRAWW* RH11	176	E5
Snellings Rd *WOT/HER* KT12	57	L4
Snipe La *HASM* GU27	184	B9
Snowbury Rd *FUL/PGN* SW6	19	M7
Snowdenham La *SHGR* GU5	132	C8
Snowdenham Links Rd		
SHGR GU5	132	B7
Snowdon Crs *HYS/HAR* UB3	14	E1
Snowdon Rd *FARN* GU14	68	A9
Snowdon Rd West		
HTHAIR TW6	23	M2
Snowdown Cl *PGE/AN* SE20	46	C2
Snowdrop Cl *CRAWW* RH11	176	D9
HPTN TW12	24	G3
Snowdrop Wy		
CHOB/PIR GU24	70	G6
Snowerhill Rd		
BRKHM/BTCW RH3	118	D9
Snow Hl *CRAWE* RH10	160	G7
Snowhill La *CRAWE* RH10	160	G4
Snows Paddock *BFOR* GU20	52	B2
Snows Ride *BFOR* GU20	52	B3
Snowy Fielder Waye		
ISLW TW7	17	H7
Snoxhall Fld *CRAN* GU6	170	G4
Soames Wk *NWMAL* KT3	42	C2
Soane Cl *CRAWW* RH11	176	B7
Soham Rd		
EBED/NFELT TW14	24	G8
Soldiers Ri *EARG* GU14	49	H2
Solecote *GT/LBKH* KT23	96	A5
Sole Farm Av *GT/LBKH* KT23	95	P5
Sole Farm Cl *GT/LBKH* KT23	95	P4
Sole Farm Rd *GT/LBKH* KT23	95	P5
Solna Av *PUT/ROE* SW15	27	P1
Solomons Court Rd		
BNSTD SM7	79	P6
Solway Cl *HSLWW* TW4	15	N8
Somerfield Cl		
KWD/TDW/WH KT20	79	J8
Somergate *HORS* RH12	191	N6
Somersbury La *CRAN* GU6	172	A1
Somers Cl *REIG* RH2	119	L4
RYNPK SW20	42	F3
Somerset Cl *CHSGTN* KT9	59	K8
RYNPK SW20	42	F3
Somerset Cl *HOR/WEW* KT19	60	C8
NWMAL KT3	42	C7
WOT/HER KT12	57	K4
Somerset Gdns		
STRHM/NOR SW16	45	H4
TEDD TW11	25	M8
Somerset Gv *BNFD* RG42	33	H1
Somerset Rd *BTFD* TW8	17	J4
CHSWK W4	18	B1
FARN GU14	88	E6
KUT KT1	9	G5
REIG RH2	119	P7
TEDD TW11	25	M8
WIM/MER SW19	28	B6
Somerset Wy *WKENS* W14 *	19	J1
Somerset Waye *HEST* TW5	15	N4
Somers Rd *BRXS/STRHM* SW2	30	A3
Somers Rd *BRXS/STRHM* SW2	30	A2
REIG RH2	119	L4
Somerswey *RGUE* GU4	132	C4
Somerton Av *RCH/KEW* TW9	17	P8
Somerton Cl *PUR/KEN* CR8	81	J5
Somertons Cl *GUW* GU2	111	N1
Somerville Av *BARN* SW13	18	G4
Somerville Crs *YTLY* GU46	67	J2
Somerville Dr *CRAWE* RH10	177	M2
Somerville Rd *COB* KT11	76	A3
PGE/AN SE20	46	D1
Sondes Farm *DORK* RH4 *	116	F7
Sondes Place Cottages		
DORK RH4 *	116	F7
Sondes Place Dr *DORK* RH4	116	F7
Sonia Gdns *HEST* TW5	16	A5
Sonninge Cl *SHST* GU47	49	P9
Sonning Gdns *HPTN* TW12	24	F9
Sonning Rd *CROY/NA* CR0	46	A7
Soper Cl *FSTH* SE23	31	L4
Soper Dr *CTHM* CR3	101	M3
Sopwith Av *CHSGTN* KT9	59	L8
Sopwith Rd *HEST* TW5	15	L5
Sopwith Wy *KUTN/CMB* KT2	8	B3
Sorbie Cl *WEY* KT13	56	E5
Sorrel Bank *CROY/NA* CR0	64	E8
Sorrel Cl *CRAWW* RH11	176	D9
Sorrel Dr *LTWR* GU18	69	P1
Sorrel Rd *HORS* RH12	192	D1
Sorrento Rd *SUT* SM1	61	M2
Souldern Rd *WKENS* W14 *	19	H1
South Albert Rd *REIG* RH2	119	K4
Southall La *HEST* TW5	15	K3
Southampton Cl *BLKW* GU17	67	N3
Southampton Gdns		
MTCM CR4	44	G4
Southampton Rd		
HTHAIR TW6	23	J2
Southampton St *FARN* GU14	88	D7
South Atlantic Dr		
ALDT GU11	108	E3
South Av *CAR* SM5	62	C6
EGH TW20	21	P9
RCH/KEW TW9 *	17	N7
WOT/HER KT12	56	C8
South Bank *BH/WHM* TN16	105	H6
SURB KT6	41	L7
Southbank *THDIT* KT7	40	H8
South Bank Ter *SURB* KT6 *	41	L7
South Beta Rd *FARN* GU14	88	D5
South Black Lion La		
HMSMTH W6	18	E3
South Bolton Gdns		
WBPTN SW10	19	M3
The South Border		
PUR/KEN CR8	62	G9
Southborough Cl *SURB* KT6	41	K9
Southborough Rd *SURB* KT6	41	K9
Southborough Rd (The Lane)		
SURB KT6	41	L9
Southbourne *HAYES* BR2	47	N8
Southbridge Pl *CROY/NA* CR0	2	C7
Southbridge Rd *CROY/NA* CR0	2	C7
Southbrook *CRAWW* RH11	194	F1
Southbrook Rd		
STRHM/NOR SW16	44	G2
Southby Dr *FLEETN* GU51	87	H6
South Cl *CRAWE* RH10	177	J4
FELT TW13	24	E4
WDR/YW UB7	14	B1
WOKN/KNAP GU21	71	N4
South Close Gn *REIG* RH2	100	D9
Southcombe St *WKENS* W14	19	J2
Southcote *WOKN/KNAP* GU21	72	B4
Southcote Av *BRYLDS* KT5	41	P8
FELT TW13	24	B5
Southcote Dr *CBLY* GU15	69	J3
Southcote Rd *REDH* RH1	120	E1
SAND/SEL CR2	63	N8
SNWD SE25	46	B6
Southcroft *EGH* TW20	20	D8
Southcroft Av *WWKM* BR4	65	J1
Southcroft Rd		
STRHM/NOR SW16	29	J9
South Croxted Rd *DUL* SE21	30	E6
Southdean Gdns		
WIM/MER SW19	28	C5
Southdown Av *HNWL* W7	16	G1
Southdown Cl *HORS* RH12	192	F5
Southdown Dr *RYNPK* SW20	43	H1
Southdown Rd *CAR* SM5	62	C7
CTHM CR3	102	F2
RYNPK SW20	43	H2
WOT/HER KT12	57	N3
South Down Wy *DORK* RH4	117	J3
South Dr *BELMT* SM2	61	J8
BNSTD SM7	62	A5
CHOB/PIR GU24	90	C1
COUL/CHIP CR5	80	F4
RDKG RH5	117	J7
VW GU25	35	N8
South Eden Park Rd		
BECK BR3	47	H6
South Edwardes Sq *KENS* W8	19	K1
South End *CROY/NA* CR0	2	D7
GT/LBKH KT23	96	B6
KENS W8 *	19	M1
Southend La *CAT* SE6	31	N7
Southend Rd *BECK* BR3	46	C1
South End Rd *WKENS* W8	19	M1
Southerland Cl *WEY* KT13	56	E3
Southern Av		
EBED/NFELT TW14	24	B4
REDH RH1	140	C3
SNWD SE25	45	P4
Southern Down *FELT* TW13 *	24	D4
Southern Perimeter Rd		
HTHAIR TW6	22	F1
HTHAIR TW6	23	L2
Southern Rd *CBLY* GU15	68	E2
Southern La *COUL/CHIP* CR5	99	N4
Southern Wy *FARN* GU14	87	P4
FNM GU9	5	H5
Southerton Rd		
HMSMTH W6 *	18	G2
Southey Rd *WIM/MER* SW19	43	L1
Southey St *PGE/AN* SE20	46	D1
South Farm La *BAGS* GU19	52	A7
Southfield Gdns *TWK* TW1	25	N7
Southfield Pl *WEY* KT13	56	D6
Southfield Rd *CHSWK* W4	18	B1
Southfields *E/WMO/HCT* KT8	40	E7
Southfields Av *ASHF* TW15	23	L9
Southfields Ms		
WAND/EARL SW18 *	28	D2
Southfields Rd *CTHM* CR3	102	C4
GDST RH9	103	H5
WAND/EARL SW18	28	D1
South Gdns *WIM/MER* SW19	43	P1
South View Rd *ASHTD* KT21	77	K8
South Gate Av *FELT* TW13	23	N7
Southgate Dr *CRAWE* RH10	176	C7
Southgate Pde		
CRAWE RH10 *	176	C7
Southgate Rd *CRAWE* RH10	176	C7
South Gv *CHERT* KT16	37	K7
FLEETN GU51	87	J3
SWTR RH13	192	C9
South Hl *GODL* GU7	131	M9
GU GU1	7	F6
South Hill Rd *BRAK* RG12	32	D7
HAYES BR2	47	L4
South Holmes Rd		
SWTR RH13	192	G6
South Kensington Station Ar		
SKENS SW7 *	19	P2
Southlands *EGRIN* RH19	180	D4
Southlands Av *HORL* RH6	160	C2
Southlands Cl *ASHV* GU12	109	J5
COUL/CHIP CR5	81	H6
Southlands Dr		
WIM/MER SW19	28	A5
Southlands La *OXTED* RH8	123	H5
Southlands Rd *HSLW* TW3	25	L1
South La *ASHV* GU12	109	K5
KUT KT1	8	C7
NWMAL KT3	42	B5
South La West *NWMAL* KT3	42	B5
South Lodge Av *MTCM* CR4	44	G5
South Lodge Rd		
WOT/HER KT12	57	J7
South Lynn Crs *BRAK* RG12	32	D6
South Md *CROY/NA* CR0	60	D6
REDH RH1	120	B2
South Meadow *CWTH* RG45	49	P6
Southmead Rd *ALDT* GU11	108	D6
WIM/MER SW19	28	B4
Southmont Rd		
ESH/CLAY KT10	58	C1
South Munstead La		
SNWD SE25	45	N3
South Norwood Hl		
SNWD SE25	45	N3
South Oak Rd		
STRHM/NOR SW16	30	A7
South Pde *CHEL* SW3	19	P5
CHSWK W4	18	B1
HORL RH6 *	140	B9
REDH RH1 *	100	E8
WLGTN SM6	62	E5
South Park Hill Rd		
SAND/SEL CR2	63	M4
South Park La *REDH* RH1	122	A6
South Park Ms *FUL/PGN* SW6	19	M8
South Park Rd		
WIM/MER SW19	28	D9
South Pier Rd *HORL* RH6	159	L5
REDH RH1 *	41	M8
South Rdg *WEY* KT13	56	D8
South Ri *CAR* SM5	62	A7
South Rd *ASHV* GU12	109	H2
CHOB/PIR GU24	70	D5
CWTH RG45	49	L5
EA W5	17	K2
EGH TW20	21	H9
EWKG RG40	48	D4
FELT TW13	24	E8
FSTH SE23	31	L5
GUW GU2	111	P3
LIPH GU30	182	F9
REIG RH2	119	P7
WDR/YW UB7	14	C1
WEY KT13	56	D9
WHTN TW2	25	G8
WIM/MER SW19	28	G9
WOKN/KNAP GU21	72	A4
Southsea Rd *KUT* KT1	41	L5
South Side *HMSMTH* W6	18	D1
RFNM GU10	109	H7
Southside Common		
WIM/MER SW19	28	A9
South Station Ap *REDH* RH1	121	H7
South St *BMLY* BR1	47	N3
DORK RH4	116	C8
EPSOM KT18	84	B3
FARN GU14	88	G6
FNM GU9	5	G3
GODL GU7	131	K9
HORS RH12	192	B8
ISLW TW7	16	C4
STA TW18	22	C8
South Ter *DORK* RH4	116	E7
SURB KT6	41	L7
South V *NRWD* SE19	30	F9
South Vale Rd *SURB* KT6	59	L1
South View Cl *CRAWE* RH10	160	F9
Southview Cl *TOOT* SW17	29	K8
South View Ct *NRWD* SE19 *	45	L1
WOKS/MYFD GU22	10	D5
Southview Gdns *WLGTN* SM6	62	E6
South View Rd *ASHTD* KT21	77	K8
South View Rd *BOR* GU35	164	E6
CTHM CR3	101	H4
WARL CR6	82	B9
Southviews *SAND/SEL* CR2	64	D7
Southville Cl		
EBED/NFELT TW14	23	P3
HOR/WEW KT19	60	B7
Southville Crs		
EBED/NFELT TW14	23	P4
Southville Rd		
EBED/NFELT TW14	23	P4
THDIT KT7	40	G8
South Wk *ASHV* GU12	108	F4
REIG RH2 *	119	M5
WWKM BR4	65	L9
Southwark Cl *CRAWW* RH11	176	E9
YTLY GU46	66	G2
Southwater Cl *BECK* BR3	47	H1
CRAWW RH11	176	E9
South Wy *CAR* SM5	61	P9
CROY/NA CR0	64	E2
Southway *CBLY* GU15	68	D4
GU GU1	111	L5
HAYES BR2	47	M8
RYNPK SW20	43	H5
WLGTN SM6	62	F4
Southway Pk *GUW* GU2 *	111	N3
Southways Pk		
CRAWE RH10 *	158	G9
Southwell Gdns *SKENS* SW7	19	N2
Southwell Park Rd		
CBLY GU15	68	D3
Southwell Rd *CROY/NA* CR0	45	J7
South Western Rd *TWK* TW1	25	J7
Southwick Cl *EGRIN* RH19	180	C1
Southwick Ct *BRAK* RG12	32	C7
Southwold Rd *FARN* GU14	32	A9
Southwood Av *CHERT* KT16	54	G6
COUL/CHIP CR5	80	E4
KUTN/CMB KT2	42	A2
Southwood Cha *CRAN* GU6	171	J2
Southwood Dr *BRYLDS* KT5	42	A9
Southwood Gdns		
ESH/CLAY KT10	58	G2
Southwood La *FARN* GU14	87	J4
Southwood Rd *FARN* GU14	67	J7
FARN GU14	88	A3
South Worple Wy		
MORT/ESHN SW14	18	B8
Sovereign Cl *PUR/KEN* CR8	63	H8
Sovereign Ct		
E/WMO/HCT KT8	39	P5
Sovereign Dr *CBLY* GU15	69	L1
Space Waye		
EBED/NFELT TW14	24	C1
Spa Cl *NRWD* SE19	45	N2
Spa Dr *EPSOM* KT18	77	N3
Spa Hl *THHTH* CR7	45	M2
Spalding Rd *TOOT* SW17	29	L8
Spanish Rd		
WAND/EARL SW18	28	E1
Sparks Cl *HPTN* TW12	24	F9
Sparrow Dr		
EBED/NFELT TW14	24	D3
Sparrow Farm Dr		
EBED/NFELT TW14	24	D3
Sparrow Farm Rd *EW* KT17	60	E3
Sparrowhawk Cl		
RFNM GU10	107	H6
Sparrow Rw *CHOB/PIR* GU24	53	H5
Sparrows Md *REDH* RH1	120	C2
Sparvell Rd		
WOKN/KNAP GU21	71	H9
Sparvells *HTWY* RG27	48	B9
Sparts La *BOR* GU35	164	C3
Speakers Ct *CROY/NA* CR0 *	2	E1
Spear Ms *ECT* SW5	19	L2
Speart La *HEST* TW5	15	N5
Speedbird Wy *WDR/YW* UB7	13	M9
Speedwell Cl *RGUE* GU4	112	G2
Speedwell Wy *HORS* RH12	192	D5
Speer Rd *THDIT* KT7	40	F7
Speirs Cl *NWMAL* KT3	42	D7
Speke Rd *THHTH* CR7	45	M2
Speldhurst Cl *HAYES* BR2	47	M6
Speldhurst Rd *CHSWK* W4	18	B1
Spelthorne Gv *SUN* TW16	39	H1
Spelthorne La *ASHF* TW15	38	E1
Spence Av *BF/WBF* KT14	74	A3
Spencer Cl *EPSOM* KT18	78	C8
FLEETS GU52	107	J1
FNM GU9	88	C1
WOKN/KNAP GU21	72	C5
Spencer Gdns *EGH* TW20	21	J8
MORT/ESHN SW14	27	H1
Spencer Hl *WIM/MER* SW19	28	B8
Spencer Hill Rd		
WIM/MER SW19	43	J1
Spencer House *SURB* KT6 *	41	L8
Spencer Ms *HMSMTH* W6	19	H4
Spencer Pk		
WAND/EARL SW18	28	C1
Spencer Pl *CROY/NA* CR0	45	M8
Spencer Rd *BMLY* BR1	47	M4
BNFD RG42	32	B2
BTSEA SW11	19	P9
CHSWK W4	18	A5
COB KT11	75	K4
CTHM CR3	101	M1
DTCH/LGLY SL3	12	D1
E/WMO/HCT KT8	40	C5
ISLW TW7	16	C6
MTCM CR4	44	C4
RYNPK SW20	42	F2
SAND/SEL CR2	63	N4
WHTN TW2	25	H6
Spencers La *HORL* RH6	158	C5
Spencers Pl *HORS* RH12	192	A6
Spencers Rd *CRAWW* RH11	176	F6
HORS RH12	192	A7
Spencer St *NWDGN* UB2 *	15	M1
Spenser Av *WEY* KT13	56	C7
Spenser Ms *DULE* SE21	30	E4
Spenser Rd *HNHL* SE24	30	C1
Spiceall *RGUW* GU3	131	H2
Spicer Cl *WOT/HER* KT12	39	L7
Spicers Flg *LHD/OX* KT22	76	D2
Spices Yd *CROY/NA* CR0	2	C7
Spiers Wy *HORL* RH6	159	L3
Spindle Wy *CRAWE* RH10	177	J6
Spindlewood Gdns		
CROY/NA CR0	3	F7
Spindlewoods		
KWD/TDW/WH KT20	98	F2
Spinis *BRAK* RG12	32	A9
Spinner Gn *BRAK* RG12	32	C6
Spinney Cl *BECK* BR3	47	H5
COB KT11	75	M8
CRAWE RH10	179	K3
HORS RH12	192	G4
NWMAL KT3	42	C6
WPK KT4	43	H6
Spinneycroft *LHD/OX* KT22	76	D4
Spinney Dr		
EBED/NFELT TW14	23	M3
Spinney Gdns *NRWD* SE19	30	G8
Spinney Hl *ADL/WDHM* KT15	55	K4
Spinney Oak *CHERT* KT16	55	H5
The Spinney *ASC* SL5	34	E6
BARN SW13 *	18	F4
CBLY GU15	69	L2
CHEAM SM3	61	J3
CRAWW RH11	176	E7
EPSOM KT18	84	D8
EWKG RG40	48	D3
FLEETN GU51	86	D7
GSHT GU26	165	K7
GT/LBKH KT23	96	B6
HASM GU27	183	N5
HASM GU27	184	D2
HORL RH6	140	C8
LHD/OX KT22	76	C1
PUR/KEN CR8	63	K9
RPLY/SEND GU23	93	N7
STRHM/NOR SW16	30	A6
SUN TW16	39	J2
YTLY GU46	66	G1
The Spinning Wk *SHGR* GU5	134	C1
Spital Heath *RDKG* RH5	117	J6
Spitfire Est *HEST* TW5 *	15	L3
Spitfire Wy *HEST* TW5	15	L3
Spoil La *RFNM* GU10	109	H7
Spokane Cl *ALDT* GU11	108	B6
Spook Hl *RDKG* RH5	137	H3
Spooners Rd *HORS* RH12	192	C4
Spooner Wk *WLGTN* SM6	62	F4
Spout Hl *CROY/NA* CR0	64	C4
Spout La *EDEN* TN8	124	G5
STWL/WRAY TW19	22	D1
Spout La North		
STWL/WRAY TW19	22	C1
Spratts La *ADL/WDHM* KT15	55	J3
Spreighton Rd		
E/WMO/HCT KT8	40	B5
Spring Av *EGH* TW20	21	K9
Spring Bottom La		
REDH RH1	101	L7
Springclose La *CHEAM* SM3	61	J5
Spring Copse *CRAWE* RH10	160	D9
Springcopse Rd *REIG* RH2	119	N6
Spring Cottages *SURB* KT6 *	41	K8
Springcross Av *BLKW* GU17	67	P5
Springdale *EWKG* RG40	48	C4
Springfarm Rd *HASM* GU27	183	P5
Springfield *EGRIN* RH19	162	C8
LTWR GU18	52	C9
FNM GU9	128	C8
Springfield Cl		
WOKN/KNAP GU21	71	K7
Springfield Crs *HORS* RH12	192	A8

Springfield Dr LHD/OX KT22 ....76 E8
Springfield Gdns WWKM BR4 ..65 H1
Springfield St FARN TW16 ......39 J2
Springfield La FLEETN GU51 ...88 E6
 SWTR RH13 ....195 N6
 WEY KT13 ....56 D3
Springfield Mdw WEY KT13....56 D3
Springfield Pk HORS RH12 * .192 B7
Springfield Park Rd
 HORS RH12 ....192 A8
Springfield Rd ASHF TW15 .....23 J8
 ASHV GU12 ....109 J1
 CBLY GU15 ....69 J3
 CRAWW RH11.....................176 F6
 DORK RH4 ....116 B8
 DTCH/LGLY SL3 ....12 F5
 EDEN TN8............................144 H4
 EW KT17 ....60 G8
 GU GU1 ....7 G4
 HORS RH12 ....192 B8
 KUT KT1 ....41 L5
 SYD SE26 ....31 J8
 TEDD TW11 ....25 P8
 WHTN TW2 ....25 H4
 WIM/MER SW19 ....28 C8
 WLGTN SM6 ....62 E4
Springfields CI CHERT KT16 ...37 M9
Springfield Wy
 MFD/CHID GU8 ....148 F1
Spring Gdns ASC SL5 ....34 B5
 BH/WHM TN16 ....84 A7
 CBLY GU15 ....69 J3
 CRAWE RH10 ....160 D9
 E/WMO/HCT KT8...................40 C6
 EWKG RG40 * 48 D4
 FARN GU14 ....68 C9
 WLGTN SM6 ....62 E4
Spring Gv CHSWK W4 ....17 N3
 GODL GU7 ....131 L5
 GT/LBKH KT23 ....96 B3
 HPTN TW12 ....40 B2
 MTCM CR4 ....44 D2
Spring Grove Crs HEST TW5 ....16 C6
Spring Grove Rd HSLW TW3 ...16 C6
 RCHPK/HAM TW10 ....26 E1
Springhaven CI GU GU1..........112 E5
Springhill MFD/CHID GU8 .....148 F1
Spring HI SYD SE26 ....31 K7
Springholm CI
 BH/WHM TN16 ....84 A7
Springhurst CI CROY/NA CRO...64 A7
Springlakes Est
 ASHV GU12 * 108 G3
Spring La FNM GU9.................107 L7
 OXTED RH8..........................123 K2
 SNWD SE25 ....30 B8
 SWTR RH13 ....190 D7
Spring La West FNM GU9.......107 L8
Spring Meadow BRAK RG12 ...32 F2
Spring Park Av CROY/NA CRO..64 D3
Springpark Dr BECK BR3 ....47 J2
Spring Park Rd CROY/NA CRO..64 D3
Spring Pl Cot
 CRAWE RH10 * 177 M5
Spring Ri EGH TW20 ....21 K9
Spring Rd FELT TW13 ....24 A6
Spring St EW KT17 ....60 D7
Springvale Av BTFD TW8..........17 K3
Springvale Ms WKENS W14.......19 H1
Spring Wy ECRIN RH19 ....162 F8
Springwell Rd HEST TW5 ....15 M6
 RDKG RH5 ....156 C1
 STRHM/NOR SW16 ....30 D4
Springwood MFD/CHID GU8...149 P3
Spring Woods FLEETS GU52 ....86 F8
 SHST GU47 ....49 N8
 VW GU25 ....35 P5
Sprucedale Gdns
 CROY/NA CRO 64 D3
 PUR/KEN CR8 ....62 G7
Spruce Dr LTWR GU18 ....70 A1
Spruce Rd BH/WHM TN16 ......84 B5
Spruce Wy FLEETN GU51 ....87 K6
Spur Dr KWD/TDW/WH KT20...99 H1
Spurfield E/WMO/HCT KT8 ......40 B4
Spurgeon Av NRWD SE19 ....45 M2
Spurgeon CI CRAWW RH11 * ..176 F4
Spurgeon Rd NRWD SE19 ....45 M2
Spur Rd EBED/NFELT TW14 .....24 C1
 ISLW TW7 ....16 C5
Spurs CI ALDT GU11 ....88 H7
The Spur WOKN/KNAP GU21 ...71 H7
Spy La BIL RH14.......................188 D6
Square Dr HASM GU27 ....184 D9
The Square BH/WHM TN16 .....84 A4
 BRAK RG12 ....32 F4
 CAR SM5 ....62 C4
 CRAWE RH10 ....176 G5
 GUW GU2 ....111 M7
 HMSMTH W6 ....18 C3
 LING RH7 ....143 J9
 RCHPK/HAM TW10 ....26 D1
 WDR/YW UB7 ....13 M6
Squerryes Mede
 BH/WHM TN16 * 104 C3
Squire's Bridge Rd
 SHPTN TW17 ....38 B5
Squires CI CRAWW RH11 ....179 H3
Squires Ct WIM/MER SW19 * ...43 M3
Squires Hill La RFNM GU10 ...128 E8
Squire's Rd SHPTN TW17........38 B5
Squire Wk ASHF TW15 ....38 F1
Squirrel CI CRAWW RH11.......176 F2
 HSLWW TW4 ....15 L8
 SHST GU47 ....49 M9
Squirrel La FARN GU14 ....88 C2
Squirrel Rdg CRAWE RH10 * ..179 J4

Squirrels CI GODL GU7 ....131 K4
Squirrels Drey CWTH RG45 .....49 K4
Squirrels Gn GT/LBKH KT23 ....96 A3
 WPK KT4 ....60 D1
Squirrel's Wy EPSOM KT18 .....78 B4
Squirrel Wd BF/WBF KT14......73 M1
Stable CI CRAWE RH10 ....177 M6
Stable Cft BAGS GU19 ....51 M7
Stable Ms REIG RH2 ....119 L5 *
 WNWD SE27 ....30 D8
The Stables COB KT11 ....75 P3
Stable Vw YTLY GU46 ....67 H1
Stacey's Farm Rd
 MFD/CHID GU8 ....148 E1
Stackfield Rd CRAWW RH11 ...176 B6
Stadium St WBPTN SW10.........19 N5
Staff College Rd CBLY GU15 ....68 D2
Staffhurst Wood Rd
 OXTED RH8..........................124 A8
Stafford CI CHEAM SM3 ....61 J5
 CTHM CR3 ....101 P3
Stafford Gdns CROY/NA CRO...63 H4
Stafford Lake
 CHOB/PIR GU24 ....70 G7
Stafford Pl
 RCHPK/HAM TW10 ....26 E3
Stafford Rd CRAWW RH11 .....176 D2
 CROY/NA CRO 63 J3
 CTHM CR3 ....101 P3
 NWMAL KT3 ....42 A4
 WLGTN SM6 ....62 E5
Staffords PI HORL RH6............159 L2
Stafford St KENS W8 ....19 L1
Staff Rd ASHV GU12 ....108 E4
Stagbury Av
 COUL/CHIP CR5 ....80 A8
Stagbury CI COUL/CHIP CR5 ...80 A8
Stagelands CRAWW RH11 ......176 E3
Stag Hi GUW GU2 ....111 N6
Stag La PUT/ROE SW15 ....27 L6
Stag Leys ASHTD KT21 ....77 L9
Stag Leys CI BNSTD SM7 ....80 A4
Stags Wy ISLW TW7 ....16 F4
Stainash Crs STA TW18 ....22 E8
Stainash Pde STA TW18 * 22 E8
Stainbank Rd MTCM CR4 ....44 D4
Stainbry CI WDR/YW UB7 ....14 A1
Staines Av CHEAM SM3 ....61 H1
Staines By-Pass
 STWL/WRAY TW19...................22 B6
Staines La CHERT KT16.............37 L7
Staines Lane CI CHERT KT16 ....37 L6
Staines Rd CHERT KT16 ....23 N3
 EBED/NFELT TW14 ....24 E1
 HSLWW TW4 ....24 E1
 STA TW18 ....37 K3
 STWL/WRAY TW19...................21 L4
 WHTN TW2 ....25 K6
Staines Rd East SUN TW16 ......39 J1
Staines Rd West ASHF TW15 ....38 E1
 SUN TW16 ....39 H1
Stainford CI ASHF TW15............23 N8
Stainton Wk
 WOKN/KNAP GU21 * 72 A7
Staiths Wy
 KWD/TDW/WH KT20................78 F9
Stake La FARN GU14..................88 E2
Stakescorner Rd RGUW GU3..131 N4
Stambourne Wy NRWD SE19 ...45 N1
 WWKM BR4 ....65 H2
Stamford Brook Av
 HMSMTH W6 ....18 D1
Stamford Brook Gdns
 HMSMTH W6 ....18 D1
Stamford Brook Rd
 HMSMTH W6 ....18 D1
Stamford Cottages
 BRXS/STRHM SW2 * 29 P4
Stamford Dr HAYES BR2 ....47 M5
Stamford Green Rd
 EPSOM KT18 ....77 P2
Stamford Rd WOT/HER KT12 ...57 M2
Stanborough CI HPTN TW12 ....24 V9
Stanborough Rd HSLW TW3 .....16 D8
Stanbridge CI CRAWW RH11 ...176 B6
Standard Rd HSLWW TW4 ....15 N8
Standen CI EDEN TN8 ....161 P9
Standen PI HORS RH12............192 F3
Standen Rd
 WAND/EARL SW18..................28 D3
Standinghall La
 CRAWE RH10 ....178 B7
Standish Rd HMSMTH W6 ....18 B2
Standon La RDKG RH5 ....172 F1
Stane CI WIM/MER SW19 ....43 M1
Stane St RDKG RH5 ....155 L6
 RDKG RH5 ....173 K1
Stanford CI HPTN TW12 ....24 G9
Stanford Orch HORS RH12 * ...191 N3
Stanford Rd KENS W8................19 M1
 STRHM/NOR SW16 ....44 G3
Stanfords PI LING RH7.............162 C1
 The Stanfords EW KT17 ....78 B3
Stanford Wy HORS RH12.........191 L7
 STRHM/NOR SW16 ....44 F3
Stanger Rd SNWD SE25 ....46 A5
Stangrove Rd EDEN TN8 ....144 G4
Stan HI RDKG RH6 ....157 P4
Stanhoe Av HAYES BR2 ....47 N9
Stanhope Gdns SKENS SW7 ....19 M2
Stanhope Gv BECK BR3 ....46 F6
Stanhope Heath
 STWL/WRAY TW19...................22 F2
Stanhope Ms East
 SKENS SW7 ....19 N2
Stanhope Ms South
 SKENS SW7 ....19 N2

Stanhope Ms West
 SKENS SW7 ....19 N2
Stanhope Rd CAR SM5 ....62 C5
 CBLY GU15 ....68 C3
 CROY/NA CRO 3 G6
Stanhopes OXTED RH8...........103 P8
Stanhope Ter TWK TW1 * 25 N3
Stanhope Wy
 STWL/WRAY TW19...................22 F2
Stanier CI CRAWE RH10 ....177 L6
 WKENS W14 ....19 K3
Staniland Dr WEY KT13 ....56 B9
Stanley Av BECK BR3 ....47 J2
 NWMAL KT3 ....42 E6
Stanley CI COUL/CHIP CR5 .....81 H6
 CRAWE RH10 ....177 H7
Stanley Dr FARN GU14 * 87 N4
Stanley Gdns MTCM CR4 * 29 K9
 SAND/SEL CR2 ....82 A1
 WLGTN SM6 ....62 E5
 WOT/HER KT12 ....57 L8
Stanley Gardens Rd
 TEDD TW11 ....25 M8
Stanley Gv
 DTCH/LGLY SL3 ....12 D2
 CTHM CR3 ....101 J7
Stanley HI CHOB/PIR GU24 ......90 C2
Stanley Park Rd CAR SM5 ....62 D5
 WLGTN SM6 ....62 D5
Stanley Rd ACT W3....................17 P1
 ASHF TW15 ....23 J8
 BELMT SM2 ....61 M5
 CAR SM5 ....62 D5
 CROY/NA CRO 45 J8
 HSLW TW3 ....16 C9
 MORT/ESHN SW14 ....17 P9
 MRDN SM4.............................43 L5
 MTCM CR4 ....44 C1
 WHTN TW2 ....25 L6
 WIM/MER SW19 ....43 J1
 WOKN/KNAP GU21...................11 F2
Stanley Sq CAR SM5 ....62 C6
Stanley St CTHM CR3..............101 C2
Stanley Ws SWTR RH13...........192 C8
Stanmore CI ASC SL5................34 A5
Stanmore Gdns
 RCH/KEW TW9 ....17 M8
 SUT SM1 ....61 N2
Stanmore Rd RCH/KEW TW9...17 M8
Stanmore Ter BECK BR3 ....46 G3
Stannet Wy WLGTN SM6 ....62 E3
Stansfield Rd HSLWW TW4 ......15 K7
Stanstead CI HAYES BR2 ....47 M6
Stanstead Gv CAT SE6 ....31 L4
Stanstead Rd CTHM CR3........101 N4
 FSTH SE23 ....31 L3
Stansted Rd HTHAIR TW6.........23 J2
Stanthorpe Rd
 STRHM/NOR SW16 ....29 P8
Stanton Av TEDD TW11 ....25 M9
Stanton CI CRAN GU6 ....152 E9
 HOR/WEW KT19 ....60 A4
 WPK KT4 ....43 H9
Stanton Dr FLEETN GU51 ....86 E7
Stanton Rd BARN SW13............18 D7
 CROY/NA CRO 45 J8
 RYNPK SW20 ....43 H3
Stantons Whf SHGR GU5 ....132 E6
Stanton Wy DTCH/LGLY SL3 ....12 C2
 SYD SE26 ....31 N7
Stanway Cottages
 CHERT KT16 * 37 L8
Stanwell CI
 STWL/WRAY TW19...................22 G2
Stanwell Gdns
 STWL/WRAY TW19...................22 G2
Stanwell Moor Rd
 STWL/WRAY TW19...................13 M6
 WDR/YW UB7 ....13 M6
Stanwell New Rd STA TW18 .....22 E7
Stanwell Pl
 STWL/WRAY TW19...................13 H7
Stanwell Rd ASHF TW15 ....23 H7
 DTCH/LGLY SL3 ....12 B8
 EBED/NFELT TW14 ....23 M3
Stanwick Rd WKENS W14 ....19 K2
Staplecross CI CRAWW RH11..176 D9
Staplefield Rd
 BRXS/STRHM SW2 * 29 P4
Stapleford CI KUT KT1 ....9 J5
 WIM/MER SW19 ....28 B3
Staple Hi CHOB/PIR GU24 ....53 K5
Staplehurst CI REIG RH2 ....119 N9
Staplehurst CI REDH RH1 ......119 N9
Staplehurst Rd CAR SM5 ....62 A6
 REDH RH1 ....119 N9
Staple La RGUE GU4...............114 A4
Stapleton Gdns CROY/NA CRO.63 J4
Stapleton Rd TOOT SW17 ....29 K6
Star And Garter Hl
 RCHPK/HAM TW10 ....26 D4
Starborough CI EDEN TN8 .....144 D9
Star CI SWTR RH13 ....192 F6
Star HI RFNM GU10 ....146 C9
Star Hill Dr RFNM GU10 ....146 C9
Star La ASHV GU12 ....109 H4
 COUL/CHIP CR5 ....100 C3
Star Post Rd CBLY GU15 ....50 D7
Star Rd ISLW TW7 ....16 D7
 WKENS W14 ....19 K4
Starrock La COUL/CHIP CR5 ....80 C9
Starrock Rd COUL/CHIP CR5 ...80 D8
Starveall CI BF/WBF KT14 ....74 B1
Starwood CI BF/WBF KT14 ....55 N9
Starwood Ct DTCH/LGLY SL3 ...12 A1
Staten Gdns TWK TW1 ....25 N4
Statham Ct BNFD RG42 ....32 A2
Station Ap ASHV GU12 ....89 J8
 BECK BR3 ....46 E2

BELMT SM2 ....61 J6
BELMT SM2 ....61 M8
BF/WBF KT14 ....73 L1
BLWV GU17.............................68 A4
CAT SE6 ....31 N8
COUL/CHIP CR5 ....80 D7
COUL/CHIP CR5 ....80 F5
CROY/NA CRO 3 G4
CTHM CR3 ....83 J5
DORK RH4 ....117 J5
EDEN TN8.............................144 D4
EHSLY KT24 ....94 C6
ESH/CLAY KT10 ....58 F2
EW KT17 ....60 F8
FUL/PGN SW6 * 19 J8
GODL GU7 ....131 K9
GU GU1 ....6 C5
GU GU1 ....7 G4
HAYES BR2 ....47 N9
HOR/WEW KT19 ....78 B2
HORL RH6.............................159 L1
HPTN TW12 ....40 A2
HYS/HAR UB3.........................15 H1
KUT KT1 ....9 J3
LHD/OX KT22 ....96 G1
MFD/CHID GU8 ....167 N3
OXTED RH8 ....103 L8
PUR/KEN CR8 ....63 J9
RCH/KEW TW9 ....17 N6
SAND/SEL CR2 ....64 A7
SHPTN TW17 * 38 E7
STA TW18 ....22 D8
STRHM/NOR SW16 ....29 N8
SUN TW16 ....39 J1
VW GU25 ....36 B5
WEY KT13 ....56 C5
WOKS/MYFD GU22 ....10 D5
WOKN/KNAP GU21 ....11 H1
Station Ap East REDH RH1 .....120 B7
Station Ap West REDH RH1 ....120 B7
Station Av CTHM CR3 ....102 A4
 HOR/WEW KT19 ....60 C7
 NWMAL KT3 ....42 C4
 WOT/HER KT12 ....57 J7
Station Buildings
 HAYES BR2 ....*
Station CI HPTN TW12 ....40 B2
 SWTR RH13 ....192 C8
Station Crs ASHF TW15.............22 G7
Station Est BECK BR3 ....46 D5
Station Estate Rd
 EBED/NFELT TW14 ....24 C4
Station Garage Ms
 STRHM/NOR SW16 * 29 N9
Station Gdns CHSWK W4 ....18 A4
Station Hill ASC SL5 ....34 A4
 CRAWE RH10 ....177 L4
 FNM GU9 ....5 H4
 HAYES BR2 ....65 H1
Station La MFD/CHID GU8 .....167 N4
 MFD/CHID GU8 ....167 M3
Station Pde BAL SW12 * 29 J4
 BECK BR3 ....46 D5
 BELMT SM2 ....61 N5
 BMLY BR1 ....47 N2
 CHSWK W4 ....18 A2
 CHSWK W4 ....18 A3
 EBED/NFELT TW14 * 24 C3
 EHSLY KT24 * 94 C6
 RCH/KEW TW9 ....17 N6
 VW GU25 ....36 B6
Station Ri WNWD SE27 ....30 C5
Station Rd ADL/WDHM KT15 ...55 L5
 ALDT GU11 ....108 D4
 ASC SL5 ....34 C7
 ASHF TW15 ....23 J7
 BAGS GU19 ....51 N5
 BARN SW13 ....18 D7
 BELMT SM2 ....61 L8
 BF/WBF KT14 * 73 L1
 BH/WHM TN16 ....105 M5
 BIL RH14..............................188 E2
 BMLY BR1 ....47 N2
 BRAK RG12 ....32 E4
 BRKHM/BTCW RH3 ....118 B4
 CAR SM5 ....62 B3
 CHERT KT16 ....37 K9
 CHOB/PIR GU24....................71 M1
 CHSGTN KT9..........................59 M5
 COB KT11 ....75 M6
 CRAWE RH10 ....176 G6
 CRAWE RH10 ....175 H4
 CROY/NA CRO 2 E1
 CTHM CR3 ....81 P7
 CTHM CR3 ....102 E2
 DORK RH4 ....116 F7
 EDEN TN8.............................144 D4
 EDEN TN8.............................144 G2
 EGH TW20 ....21 M8
 EGRIN RH19 ....180 C2
 EGRIN RH19 ....162 B6
 ESH/CLAY KT10 ....58 D4
 FARN GU14 ....88 D3
 FRIM GU16..............................89 H7
 FROW RH18..........................181 N3
 GDST RH9 ....122 E9
 GODL GU7 ....131 M6
 HORL RH6.............................159 K2
 HAYES BR2 ....47 L8
 HORL RH6.............................159 L1
 HORS RH12 ....189 N1
 HORS RH12 ....192 A2
 HPTN TW12 ....40 B2
 HSLW TW3 ....16 C9
 HYS/HAR UB3.........................14 G2
 KUT KT1 ....8 C3

KUTN/CMB KT2 ....9 H3
LHD/OX KT22 ....96 G1
LING RH7 ....143 L9
LIPH GU30 ....182 E8
NRWD SE19 ....31 H9
NWMAL KT3 ....42 F6
PUR/KEN CR8 ....81 L3
REDH RH1 ....100 E8
REDH RH1 ....120 B4
RFNM GU10 ....126 A9
RGUE GU4 ....132 C2
SHGR GU5 ....132 D6
SHGR GU5 ....134 F1
SHPTN TW17 ....38 E6
SNWD SE25 ....45 P5
STWL/WRAY TW19...................21 L2
SUN TW16 ....39 J1
SWTR RH13 ....192 D8
TEDD TW11 ....25 P9
THDIT KT7 ....40 F8
TWK TW1 ....25 N4
WIM/MER SW19 ....43 N2
WOKN/KNAP GU21 ....10 D5
WWKM BR4 ....47 J9
Station Rd East ASHV GU12 ....89 H8
 OXTED RH8 ....103 L9
Station Rd North REDH RH1 ..100 E8
Station Rd South REDH RH1 ..100 E8
Station Rd West OXTED RH8 ..103 L9
Station Vw RGUE GU4 ....132 C2
 GU GU1 ....6 C4
Station Wy BRAK RG12............32 E3
 CHEAM SM3 ....61 J5
 CRAWE RH10 ....176 G6
Station Yd ASHF TW15 ....23 J7
 KWD/TDW/WH KT20 ....99 K1
 PUR/KEN CR8 * 81 K1
 TWK TW1 ....25 P3
Staunton Rd
 KUTN/CMB KT2 ....41 M1
Staveley Gdns CHSWK W4.......18 B6
Staveley Rd ASHF TW15 ....23 N9
 CHSWK W4 ....18 A4
Staveley Wy
 WOKN/KNAP GU21 ....71 L6
Staverton CI BNFD RG42 ....32 D1
Stavordale Rd CAR SM5 ....43 N8
Stayne End VW GU25 ....35 N5
Stayton Rd SUT SM1 ....61 L2
Steadfast Rd KUT KT1 ....8 C3
Steam Farm La
 EBED/NFELT TW14 ....15 H9
Steele Rd CHSWK W4 ....18 A1
 ISLW TW7 ....16 C9
Steeles Rd ALDT GU11 ....108 D2
Steel's La ESH/CLAY KT10 ....76 G2
Steep Hi CHOB/PIR GU24 ....53 J6
 CROY/NA CRO 3 G7
 STRHM/NOR SW16 ....29 N6
Steeple CI FUL/PGN SW6 ....19 J8
 WIM/MER SW19 ....28 B7
Steeple Heights Dr
 BH/WHM TN16 ....84 B6
Steeple Point ASC SL5 ....34 B4
Steepways CSHT GU26............165 L5
Steeres HI HORS RH12 ....175 H4
Steerforth Copse SHST GU47 ...50 A7
Steerforth St
 WAND/EARL SW18...................28 E5
Steers La CRAWE RH10 ....159 M8
Steers Md MTCM CR4 ....44 B2
Stella Rd TOOT SW17 ....29 J9
Stembridge Rd PGE/AN SE20...46 B3
The Stennings EGRIN RH19 ...162 B9
Stepbridge Pth
 WOKN/KNAP GU21 ....10 B4
Stepgates CHERT KT16.............37 M8
Stepgates CI CHERT KT16 * 37 M8
Stephen CI CRAWW RH11 ......176 C2
 EGH TW20 ....21 P9
Stephendale Rd FNM GU9 .....127 P1
 FUL/PGN SW6 ....19 M8
Stephenson Dr EGRIN RH19 ..180 E5
Stephenson PI CRAWE RH10...177 L5
Stephenson Rd WHTN TW2 .....25 H3
Stephenson Wy
 CRAWE RH10 ....177 L5
Stepney CI CRAWE RH10 ....177 M7
The Steps EHSLY KT24 * 95 M7
Sterling Av SHPTN TW17 ....38 C4
Sterling Buildings
 HORS RH12 * 192 B8
Sterling Centre BRAK RG12 .....32 F4
Sterling Pk CRAWE RH10 * 159 L9
Sterling PI BTFD TW8 ....17 L2
Sterndale Rd WKENS W14 * 19 H1
Sternhold Av
 BRXS/STRHM SW2 ....29 N5
Sterry Dr HOR/WEW KT19 ....60 C3
 THDIT KT7 ....40 E7
Steucers La FSTH SE23 ....31 M4
Steve Biko La CAT SE6 ....31 P7
Steve Biko Wy HSLW TW3 ....16 B8
Stevenage Rd CRAWW RH11..176 B9
 FUL/PGN SW6 ....19 H6
Stevens CI BECK BR3 ....31 P9
 EW KT17 ....78 C1
 HPTN TW12 ....24 G9
Stevens HI YTLY GU46 ....67 J3
Stevens' La ESH/CLAY KT10 .....58 G6
Stevens PI PUR/KEN CR8 ....81 M2
Stewards Ri RFNM GU10 ....127 K6
Stewart KWD/TDW/WH KT20 ...99 H1
Stewart Av SHPTN TW17 ....38 C5
Stewart CI HPTN TW12 ....24 F9
 WOKN/KNAP GU21 ....71 M6
Stewarts Gv CHEL SW3..............19 P3
Steyning CI CRAWW RH11 ......176 B9
 PUR/KEN CR8 ....81 K5
Steyning Wy HSLWW TW4 ....15 L9
Stile Gdns HASM GU27 ....184 A4

Stile Hall Gdns CHSWK W4 .....17 N3
Stile Pth SUN TW16 .....39 J4
Stile Rd DTCH/LGLY SL3 .....12 B2
Stillers MFD/CHID GU8 * 168 A7
Stillingfleet Rd BARN SW13 .....18 E5
Stillness Rd FSTH SE23 .....31 M2
Stilwell Cl YTLY GU46 .....67 J2
Stirling Av SHPTN TW17 * 38 G4
Stirling Cl ASHV GU12 .....109 H1
  BNSTD SM7 .....79 K6
  CRAWE RH10 .....177 L6
  FARN GU14 .....88 C4
  FRIM GU16 .....68 G6
  STRHM/NOR SW16 .....44 E2
Stirling Gv HSLW TW3 .....16 C7
Stirling Rd ACT W3 .....17 P1
  GUW GU2 .....6 C4
  WHTN TW2 .....25 H3
Stirling Wk EGRN RH19 .....162 G9
  FARN GU14 .....87 P8
  SWTR RH13 .....192 D8
Stirrup Wy CRAWE RH10 .....177 N4
Stites Hill Rd CTHM CR3 .....81 M5
Stoatley Hollow HASM GU27 .....184 B2
Stoatley Ri HASM GU27 .....184 B2
Stoatley River HASM GU27 .....184 B2
Stoats Nest Rd
  COUL/CHIP CR5 .....80 G4
Stockbridge Dr ALDT GU11 .....108 E8
Stockbridge Wy YTLY GU46 .....67 H4
Stockbury Rd CROY/NA CR0 .....46 C7
Stockers La
  WOKS/MYFD GU22 .....72 D9
Stockfield HORL RH6 * 140 D9
Stockfield Rd ESH/CLAY KT10 .....58 E4
  STRHM/NOR SW16 .....30 A6
Stockhams Cl SAND/SEL CR2 .....63 M8
Stock Hi BH/WHM TN16 .....84 B5
Stockhurst Cl PUT/ROE SW15 .....18 G7
Stockley Farm Rd
  WDR/YW UB7 .....14 D1
Stockley Rd WDR/YW UB7 .....14 D1
Stockport Rd
  STRHM/NOR SW16 .....44 F2
Stocks Cl HORL RH6 .....159 L2
Stockton Av FLEETN GU51 .....86 E5
Stockton Pk FLEETN GU51 .....86 F5
Stockton Rd REIG RH2 .....119 L8
Stockwell Cl BMLY BR1 .....47 P3
Stockwell Rd EGRN RH19 .....180 D5
Stockwood Wy FNM GU9 .....108 B7
Stocton Cl GU GU1 .....6 D1
Stocton Rd GU GU1 .....6 D1
Stodart Rd PGE/AN SE20 .....46 C2
Stoford Cl WIM/MER SW19 .....28 B4
Stoke Cl COB KT11 .....75 P5
Stoke Cottages
  LHD/OX KT22 * 96 D1
Stoke Flds GU GU1 .....6 E4
Stokeford Cl BRAK RG12 .....33 H6
Stoke Gv GU GU1 * 7 F3
Stoke Hills FNM GU9 .....5 J1
Stoke Ms GU GU1 * 7 F3
Stokenchurch St
  FUL/PGN SW6 .....19 M6
Stoke Park Ct GU GU1 * 7 F3
Stoke Ridings
  KWD/TDW/WH KT20 * 99 H3
Stoke Rd COB KT11 .....75 N5
  GU GU1 .....7 F2
  KUTN/CMB KT2 .....42 A1
  WOT/HER KT12 .....57 L2
Stokesby Rd CHSGTN KT9 .....59 M5
Stokes Cl CRAWE RH10 .....177 M8
Stokesheath Rd
  LHD/OX KT22 .....58 C9
Stokes Ridings
  KWD/TDW/WH KT20 * 99 J1
Stokes Rd CROY/NA CR0 .....46 D1
Stompond La WOT/HER KT12 .....57 J1
Stonards Brow SHGR GU5 .....133 H9
Stondon Pk FSTH SE23 .....31 M3
Stonebanks WOT/HER KT12 .....39 J8
Stonebridge Ct
  HORS RH12 * 191 P8
Stonebridge Flds RGUE GU4 .....132 B3
Stonecot Cl MRDN SM4 .....43 J9
Stonecot HI MRDN SM4 .....43 J9
Stonecourt Cl HORL RH6 .....159 M1
Stone Crs EBED/NFELT TW14 .....24 A3
Stonecroft Wy CROY/NA CR0 .....44 G9
Stonecrop Cl CRAWW RH11 .....176 D8
Stonecrop Rd RGUE GU4 .....112 G3
Stonedene Cl BOR GU35 .....164 E7
  FROW RH18 .....181 N9
Stonegate CBLY GU15 .....69 L2
Stone Hall Gdns KENS W8 * 19 M1
Stone Hall Pl KENS W8 * 19 M1
Stone Hatch CRAN GU6 .....170 D8
Stonehill Cl GT/LBKH KT23 .....96 A5
  MORT/ESHN SW14 .....27 J1
Stonehill Ga ASC SL5 * 34 D7
Stonehill Pk BOR GU35 .....164 E7
Stonehill Rd BOR GU35 .....164 E7
  CHERT KT16 .....54 C5
  CHSWK W4 .....17 N3
  LTWR GU18 .....52 A8
  MORT/ESHN SW14 .....27 H1
Stonehills Ct DUL SE21 .....30 F6
Stone House Gdns
  CTHM CR3 .....101 N5
Stonehouse Ri FRIM GU16 .....68 F8
Stonehouse Rd SUD GU7 .....182 G6
Stoneings La RSEV TN14 .....85 K7
Stoneleigh Av WPK KT4 .....60 D2
Stoneleigh Broadway
  EW KT17 .....60 E4

Stoneleigh Ct EGRN RH19 .....180 E1
Stoneleigh Ct FRIM GU16 .....69 H7
Stoneleigh Crs
  HOR/WEW KT19 .....60 E4
Stoneleigh Pk WEY KT13 .....56 E5
Stoneleigh Park Av
  CROY/NA CR0 .....46 D7
Stoneleigh Park Rd
  HOR/WEW KT19 .....60 D5
Stoneleigh Rd CAR SM5 .....44 B8
  OXTED RH8 .....124 C1
Stone Park Av BECK BR3 .....46 G5
Stonepark Dr FROW RH18 .....181 M9
Stonepit Cl GODL GU7 .....131 H9
Stone Pl WPK KT4 .....60 E1
Stoners Cl HORL RH6 .....158 G4
Stones La DORK RH4 .....116 C8
Stone's Rd EW KT17 .....60 C9
Stone St ASHV GU12 .....108 F6
  CROY/NA CR0 .....63 J4
Stoneswood Rd OXTED RH8 .....123 P2
Stoney Bottom GSHT GU26 .....165 M8
Stoney Brook GUW GU2 .....111 L4
Stoneybrook HORS RH12 .....191 N9
Stoney Cl YTLY GU46 .....67 H4
Stoney Cft COUL/CHIP CR5 .....100 E2
Stoneyfield Rd
  COUL/CHIP CR5 .....81 H6
Stoneyfields FNM GU9 .....128 A4
Stoneylands Ct EGH TW20 .....21 L8
Stoneylands Rd EGH TW20 .....21 L8
Stoney La NRWD SE19 .....30 C9
Stoney Rd BNFD RG42 .....32 C2
Stonnell's Rd BTSEA SW11 .....29 J1
Stonny Cft ASHTD KT21 .....77 M6
Stonor Rd WKENS W14 .....19 K2
Stony Hi ESH/CLAY KT10 .....57 P6
Stookes Wy YTLY GU46 .....66 F4
Stopham Rd WKENS W14 .....177 M8
Stormont Wy CHSGTN KT9 .....59 J4
Stornaway Rd
  DTCH/LGLY SL3 .....12 G2
Storrington Rd CROY/NA CR0 .....3 K1
Storr's La RGUW GU3 .....91 J4
Stott Cl WAND/EARL SW18 .....28 G1
Stoughton Av CHEAM SM3 .....61 H4
Stoughton Cl PUT/ROE SW15 .....27 M4
Stoughton Rd GUW GU2 .....111 N2
Stour Av NWDGN UB2 .....16 A1
Stourhead Cl FARN GU14 .....88 C3
  WIM/MER SW19 .....28 A3
Stourhead Gdns
  RYNPK SW20 .....42 E4
Stourton Av FELT TW13 .....24 G7
Stovolds Hi CRAN GU6 .....169 P3
Stovold's Wy ALDT GU11 .....108 B8
Stowell Av CROY/NA CR0 .....65 K8
Strachan Pl RYNPK SW20 .....27 P3
Stradella Rd HNHL SE24 .....30 D2
Strafford Rd HSLW TW3 .....15 P8
  TWK TW1 .....25 P3
Straight Rd WDSR SL4 .....20 C3
Strand Cl CRAWE RH10 .....177 N7
  EPSOM KT18 .....78 B8
Strand-on-the-Green
  CHSWK W4 .....17 H3
Strangways Ter WKENS W14 .....19 K1
Stratfield BRAK RG12 .....32 A9
Stratford Cl NWMAL KT3 .....42 B5
Stratford Gv PUT/ROE SW15 .....19 H9
Stratford Rd ASHV GU12 .....109 H7
  HTHAIR TW6 .....23 L2
  KENS W8 .....19 L2
  NWDGN UB2 .....15 N2
  THHTH CR7 .....45 J5
Strathan Cl
  WAND/EARL SW18 .....28 B2
Strathavon Cl CRAN GU6 .....152 E5
Strathblaine Rd BTSEA SW11 .....28 G1
Strathbrook Rd
  STRHM/NOR SW16 .....45 H1
Strathcona Av EHSLY KT24 .....95 N8
Strathcona Gdns
  WOKN/KNAP GU21 .....71 J8
Strathdale
  STRHM/NOR SW16 .....30 A8
Strathdon Dr TOOT SW17 .....28 G6
Strathearn Av HYS/HAR UB3 .....15 H5
  WHTN TW2 .....25 H4
Strathearn Rd SUT SM1 .....61 L4
  WIM/MER SW19 .....28 D8
Strathmore Cl
  BRXS/STRHM SW2 .....29 P1
Strathmore Ct CTHM CR3 .....101 N1
Strathmore Rd
  CRAWW RH11 .....176 D2
  CROY/NA CR0 .....45 L8
  TEDD TW11 * 25 L7
  WIM/MER SW19 .....28 D6
Strathville Rd
  WAND/EARL SW18 .....28 E1
Strathyre Av
  STRHM/NOR SW16 .....45 J4
Stratton Av WLGTN SM6 .....62 F7
Stratton Cl HEST TW5 .....15 P6
  WIM/MER SW19 * 43 H3
  WOT/HER KT12 .....39 L9
Stratton Rd SUN TW16 .....39 H3
  WIM/MER SW19 * 43 J3
Stratton Wk FARN GU14 .....68 C9
Strawberry Cl
  CHOB/PIR GU24 .....90 D1
Strawberry Flds
  CHOB/PIR GU24 .....70 G4
Strawberry Hill Rd TWK TW1 .....25 N6
Strawberry La CAR SM5 .....62 B2
Strawberry Ri
  CHOB/PIR GU24 .....70 G4
Strawberry V TWK TW1 .....25 N6
Straw Cl CTHM CR3 .....101 L3

Stream Cl BF/WBF KT14 .....74 A1
Stream Farm Cl RFNM GU10 .....127 P6
Streamline Ms EDUL SE22 .....31 J4
Stream Pk EGRN RH19 .....161 P9
Streamside FLEETN GU51 .....86 G7
Streamside Cl HAYES BR2 .....47 N5
Stream Valley Rd
  RFNM GU10 .....127 N7
Streatfield EDEN TN8 .....145 H4
Streatham Cl
  STRHM/NOR SW16 * 29 P5
Streatham Common
  STRHM/NOR SW16 .....44 F1
Streatham Common North
  STRHM/NOR SW16 .....30 A8
Streatham Common South
  STRHM/NOR SW16 .....29 P9
Streatham Ct
  STRHM/NOR SW16 .....29 P8
Streatham Gn
  STRHM/NOR SW16 .....29 P7
Streatham High Rd
  STRHM/NOR SW16 .....29 P7
Streatham Pl
  BRXS/STRHM SW2 .....29 P4
Streatham Rd MTCM CR4 .....44 D1
Streatham V
  STRHM/NOR SW16 .....44 E1
Streatbourne Rd
  TOOT SW17 .....29 K5
Streatleigh Pde
  STRHM/NOR SW16 * 29 P5
Streeters Cl GODL GU7 .....131 N7
Streeters La WLGTN SM6 .....62 F2
Streetfield Rd SWTR RH13 .....190 E7
Street Hi CRAWE RH10 .....177 P6
Streets Heath
  CHOB/PIR GU24 .....52 F9
The Street ASHTD KT21 .....77 M7
  BIL RH14 .....187 K8
  BRKHM/BTCW RH3 .....118 B5
  CRAN GU6 .....153 P6
  EHSLY KT24 .....94 D8
  EHSLY KT24 .....95 M8
  FLEETN GU51 .....106 E1
  HORL RH6 .....158 B5
  LHD/OX KT22 .....96 D2
  MFD/CHID GU8 .....130 D6
  MFD/CHID GU8 .....148 D8
  RDKG RH5 .....156 C6
  RFNM GU10 .....109 H9
  RFNM GU10 .....127 J7
  RFNM GU10 .....146 B5
  RFNM GU10 .....146 F5
  RGUE GU4 .....113 L1
  RGUE GU4 .....113 J8
  RGUE GU4 .....132 C1
  RGUW GU3 .....130 B1
  RGUW GU3 .....131 H3
  SHGR GU5 .....132 E6
  SWTR RH13 .....190 E6
Stretton Rd CROY/NA CR0 .....45 N8
  RCHPK/HAM TW10 .....26 B5
Strickland Cl CRAWW RH11 .....176 B6
Strickland Rw
  WAND/EARL SW18 .....28 C3
Stringer's Av RGUE GU4 .....92 B9
Stringhams Copse
  RPLY/SEND GU23 .....93 K4
Strodes College La EGH TW20 .....21 L8
Strode St EGH TW20 .....21 M7
Strood La ASHV GU12 .....191 K3
Stroud Crs PUT/ROE SW15 .....27 L6
Stroude Rd EGH TW20 .....21 M9
  VW GU25 .....36 C5
Strouds Cl WPK KT4 .....42 D8
Stroud Green Wy
  CROY/NA CR0 .....46 C7
Stroud La FLEETN GU51 .....106 C1
  SHGR GU5 .....152 D2
Stroudley Cl CRAWE RH10 .....177 L6
Stroud Rd SNWD SE25 .....46 A7
  WIM/MER SW19 .....28 C4
Stroudwater Pk WEY KT13 .....56 D5
Strudgate Cl CRAWE RH10 .....177 L7
Strudwicks Fld CRAN GU6 .....153 J8
Stuart Av HAYES BR2 .....47 N9
  WOT/HER KT12 .....57 J1
Stuart Cl CRAWE RH10 .....177 M6
  FARN GU14 .....88 C2
  REIG RH2 .....119 L8
Stuart Crs CROY/NA CR0 .....64 F2
Stuart Gv TEDD TW11 .....25 M8
Stuart Pl MTCM CR4 .....44 B2
Stuart Rd RCHPK/HAM TW10 .....26 B5
  REIG RH2 .....119 L8
  THHTH CR7 .....45 L5
  WARL CR6 .....82 B9
  WIM/MER SW19 .....28 C4
Stuart Wy EGRN RH19 .....180 E3
  STA TW18 .....22 E9
Stubbs Folly SHST GU47 .....67 P1
Stubbs Hi ORP BR6 .....85 N2
Stubbs La
  KWD/TDW/WH KT20 .....99 K8
Stubbs Moor Rd FARN GU14 .....88 C2
Stubbs Wy WIM/MER SW19 .....43 P2
Stubfield HORS RH12 .....191 P7
Stubpond La LING RH7 .....161 L5
Stubs Cl DORK RH4 .....117 J9
Stubs Hi DORK RH4 .....117 J9
Stucley Rd ISLW TW7 .....16 G6
Studdridge St FUL/PGN SW6 .....19 L7
Studios Rd SHPTN TW17 .....38 A4
Studland Rd BF/WBF KT14 .....74 B2
  KUTN/CMB KT2 .....26 D9

SYD SE26 .....31 L8
Studland St HMSMTH W6 .....18 F2
Studley Grange Rd HNWL W7 .....16 E1
Stumblets CRAWE RH10 .....177 M3
Stumps Hill La BECK BR3 .....31 P9
Sturdee Cl FRIM GU16 .....68 G7
Sturt Av HASM GU27 .....184 A5
Sturt Ct RGUE GU4 .....112 G3
Sturt Rd FNM GU9 .....107 M7
  FRIM GU16 .....89 H2
  HASM GU27 .....184 B6
Sturt's La
  KWD/TDW/WH KT20 .....98 D7
Stychens Cl REDH RH1 .....121 L4
Stychens La REDH RH1 .....121 L4
Styles Cl EDEN TN8 .....125 M9
Styles End GT/LBKH KT23 .....96 B7
Styles Wy BECK BR3 .....47 J6
Styventon Pl CHERT KT16 .....37 K8
Subrosa Dr REDH RH1 .....120 D1
Subrosa Pk REDH RH1 .....120 D1
Succomb's Hi WARL CR6 .....82 B9
Succombs Pl WARL CR6 .....82 B9
Sudbourne Rd
  BRXS/STRHM SW2 .....29 P1
Sudbrook Gdns
  RCHPK/HAM TW10 .....26 D6
Sudbrook La
  RCHPK/HAM TW10 .....26 D4
Sudbury Gdns CROY/NA CR0 .....3 H7
Sudlow Rd WAND/EARL SW18 .....19 L9
Suffield Cl SAND/SEL CR2 .....82 D1
Suffield La RGUW GU3 .....129 P5
Suffield Rd PGE/AN SE20 .....46 C3
  SNWD SE25 .....46 D5
  WPK KT4 .....60 D1
Suffolk Cl BAGS GU19 .....53 N7
  HORL RH6 .....159 K2
Suffolk Combe BNFD RG42 .....33 H1
Suffolk Dr RGUE GU4 .....92 G7
Suffolk Rd BARN SW13 .....18 D5
  SNWD SE25 .....46 A5
  WPK KT4 .....60 D1
Suffolk Vls
  WAND/EARL SW18 * 28 D3
Sugden Rd THDIT KT7 .....40 G9
Sulina Rd BRXS/STRHM SW2 .....29 P3
Sulivan Ct FUL/PGN SW6 .....19 L7
Sulivan Rd FUL/PGN SW6 .....19 L8
Sullington HI CRAWW RH11 .....176 G7
Sullington Md HORS RH12 .....191 M7
Sullivan Cl E/WMO/HCT KT8 .....40 B4
  FARN GU14 .....88 A5
Sullivan Dr CRAWW RH11 .....176 B9
Sullivan Rd CBLY GU15 .....68 D3
Sullivans Reach
  WOT/HER KT12 .....39 J8
Sultan St BECK BR3 .....46 D3
Sumburgh Rd BAL SW12 .....29 K2
Summer Av E/WMO/HCT KT8 .....40 E6
Summerene Cl
  STRHM/NOR SW16 .....44 E1
Summerfield ASHTD KT21 .....77 K8
Summerfield La RFNM GU10 .....146 D2
  SURB KT6 .....59 K1
Summerfield Pl
  CHERT KT16 * 55 H5
Summerfields Cl
  ADL/WDHM KT15 .....55 L4
Summer Gdns CHOB/PIR CR0 .....3 H7
  E/WMO/HCT KT8 .....40 E6
Summerhayes Cl
  WOKN/KNAP GU21 .....72 C3
Summerhays COB KT11 .....75 M2
Summerhill GODL GU7 .....131 K7
Summerhill Wy MTCM CR4 .....44 C2
Summerhouse Av HEST TW5 .....15 N6
Summerhouse Cl GODL GU7 .....150 C3
Summerhouse La
  WDR/YW UB7 .....13 P4
Summerhouse Rd
  GODL GU7 .....131 K7
Summerlands CRAN GU6 .....153 H8
Summerlay Cl
  KWD/TDW/WH KT20 .....99 J1
Summerley St
  WAND/EARL SW18 .....28 E5
Summers Av WEY KT13 * 56 F5
Summersbury Dr RGUE GU4 .....132 C4
Summersbury Hall
  RGUE GU4 * 132 C4
Summers Cl BELMT SM2 .....61 L7
  WEY KT13 .....56 C9
Summers La GODL GU7 .....150 D5
Summer's Rd GODL GU7 .....131 N5
Summerstown TOOT SW17 .....28 F6
Summersvere Cl
  CRAWE RH10 * 177 K2
Summerswood Cl
  PUR/KEN CR8 .....81 M5
Summer Trees SUN TW16 .....39 K2
Summerwood Rd ISLW TW7 .....25 P3
Summit Av FARN GU14 .....87 N4
Summit Cl EWKG RG40 .....48 D3
  WOKN/KNAP GU21 .....71 K6
Summit Cl LHD/OX KT22 .....97 G4
Summer Pl ADL/WDHM KT15 .....55 L4
  SKENS SW7 * 19 P2
Sumner Place Ms SKENS SW7 .....19 P2
Sumner Rd CROY/NA CR0 .....2 C1
Sumner Rd South
  CROY/NA CR0 .....2 C1
Summnit Pl WEY KT13 .....56 C6
Sun Bow HASM GU27 .....184 A5
Sunbury Av
  MORT/ESHN SW14 .....18 B9
Sunbury Cl WOT/HER KT12 .....39 J7
Sunbury Ct SUN TW16 .....39 M3

Sunbury Court Rd SUN TW16 .....39 L3
Sunbury La BTSEA SW11 .....19 P6
  WOT/HER KT12 .....39 J7
Sunbury Rd CHEAM SM3 .....61 H3
  FELT TW13 .....24 A6
Sunbury Wy FELT TW13 .....24 D8
Suncroft Pl SYD SE26 .....31 K6
Sundale Av SAND/SEL CR2 .....64 C8
Sunderland Mt FSTH SE23 * 31 L5
Sunderland Rd EA W5 .....17 K1
  FSTH SE23 .....31 L5
Sundew Cl CRAWW RH11 .....176 D9
  LTWR GU18 .....52 B8
Sundial Av SNWD SE25 .....45 P3
Sundon Crs VW GU25 .....35 P5
Sundown Av SAND/SEL CR2 .....63 P9
Sundown Rd ASHF TW15 .....23 M8
Sundridge La RSEV TN14 .....85 H7
Sundridge Pde BMLY BR1 * 47 P1
Sundridge Rd CROY/NA CR0 .....3 K1
  WOKS/MYFD GU22 .....72 E8
Sun HI WOKS/MYFD GU22 .....91 P1
Sun Inn Rd MFD/CHID GU8 .....169 L6
Sunken Rd CROY/NA CR0 .....64 C4
Sunkist Wy WLGTN SM6 .....62 G7
Sunlight Cl WIM/MER SW19 * 28 F8
Sunmead Cl LHD/OX KT22 .....97 F2
Sunmead Pde LHD/OX KT22 * 96 G2
Sunmead Rd SUN TW16 .....39 J4
Sunna Gdns SUN TW16 .....39 K3
Sunning Av ASC SL5 .....34 E8
Sunningdale Av FELT TW13 .....24 F5
Sunningdale Cl SURB KT6 .....59 L1
Sunningdale Ct
  CRAWW RH11 .....176 C7
Sunningdale Gdns KENS W8 * 19 L1
Sunningdale Pk ASC SL5 * 34 F6
Sunningdale Rd SUT SM1 .....61 K2
Sunninghill Cl ASC SL5 .....34 F6
Sunninghill Pk ASC SL5 * 34 E6
Sunninghill Rd ASC SL5 .....34 D6
  BFOR GU20 .....52 A2
Sunningvale Av
  BH/WHM TN16 .....84 A4
Sunningvale Cl
  BH/WHM TN16 .....84 B5
Sunny Av CRAWE RH10 .....179 H3
Sunny Bank ASC SL5 .....34 A5
Sunny Bank EPSOM KT18 .....78 F5
  SNWD SE25 .....46 A3
  WARL CR6 .....82 G7
Sunnybank Ms ASHV GU12 * 109 K3
Sunnybank Rd FARN GU14 .....87 M9
Sunnycroft Rd HSLW TW3 .....16 B8
  SNWD SE25 .....46 A4
Sunnydell La FNM GU9 .....127 L7
Sunnydene Rd PUR/KEN CR8 .....81 K2
Sunnydene St SYD SE26 .....31 M7
Sunny Down
  MFD/CHID GU8 .....149 M7
Sunny Hi MFD/CHID GU8 .....149 M7
Sunnyhill Cl CRAWE RH10 .....179 H3
Sunny Hill Rd ALDT GU11 .....107 P4
Sunnyhill Rd
  STRHM/NOR SW16 .....29 P7
Sunnyhurst Cl SUT SM1 .....61 L2
Sunnymead CRAWE RH10 * 179 J3
  CRAWE RH10 .....176 C5
Sunnymead Av MTCM CR4 .....44 F4
Sunnymead Rd
  PUT/ROE SW15 .....27 N1
Sunnymede Av CAR SM5 .....61 P9
  HOR/WEW KT19 .....60 C7
Sunny Nook Gdns
  SAND/SEL CR2 .....63 M5
Sunny Ri CTHM CR3 .....101 M4
Sunnyside CAT SE6 * 31 N3
  FLEETN GU51 .....86 E5
  GODL GU7 * 131 L7
  WIM/MER SW19 .....28 B9
  WOKN/KNAP GU21 * 71 H8
  WOT/HER KT12 .....39 L6
Sunnyside Rd BOR GU35 .....164 F7
  TEDD TW11 .....25 L7
Sunnyview Cl ALDT GU11 .....108 E5
Sunray Av BRYLDS KT5 .....59 P1
Sun Ray Est SHST GU47 .....49 P8
Sunrise Cl FELT TW13 .....24 G6
Sun Rd WKENS W14 .....19 K4
Sunset Gdns NRWD SE19 .....45 N3
Sunset Rd WIM/MER SW19 .....28 F8
Sunshine Wy MTCM CR4 .....44 B3
Sunvale Av HASM GU27 .....183 N6
Sunvale Cl HASM GU27 .....183 N6
Surbiton Ct SURB KT6 .....41 J7
Surbiton Crs SURB KT6 .....41 L5
Surbiton Hall Cl KUT KT1 .....41 L5
Surbiton Hill Pk BRYLDS KT5 .....41 M6
Surbiton Hill Rd SURB KT6 .....41 L5
Surbiton Rd CBLY GU15 .....51 J8
  KUT KT1 .....41 L5
Surrenden Ri CRAWW RH11 .....194 F2
Surrey Av CBLY GU15 .....68 C4
Surrey Ct BNFD RG42 .....33 H1
Surrey Gdns COB KT11 .....95 H3
Surrey Gv SUT SM1 .....61 P2
Surrey Hills Av
  KWD/TDW/WH KT20 .....118 A2
Surrey Hills Wy
  KWD/TDW/WH KT20 .....118 A2
Surrey Ms NRWD SE27 .....30 F7
Surrey Rd PECK SE15 .....31 L1
  WWKM BR4 .....47 H9
Surrey St CROY/NA CR0 .....2 C4
Surrey Wy GUW GU2 .....6 A1
Surridge Ct BAGS GU19 .....51 N1
Surridge Gdns NRWD SE19 .....30 E9
Sussex Av ISLW TW7 .....16 E8
Sussex Border Pth
  CRAWE RH10 .....178 E1

EDEN TN8 ....163 P4
EGRIN RH19 ....163 J7
EGRIN RH19 ....179 L4
EGRIN RH19 ....180 F2
HASM GU27 ....148 C5
HORL RH6 ....158 F4
HORL RH6 ....159 P4
HORS RH12 ....175 H4
LIPH GU30 ....182 F9
MFD/CHID GU8 ....185 N5
MFD/CHID GU8 ....188 F7
RDKG RH5 ....172 F6
RDKG RH5 ....174 A3
Sussex Cl NWMAL KT3 ....42 C5
REIG RH2 ....119 P6
TWK TW1 ....26 A2
WOKN/KNAP GU21 ....71 J7
Sussex Gdns CHSGTN KT9 ....59 K5
FLEETN GU51 ....87 H3
NWMAL KT3 ....42 C5
Sussex Pl HMSMTH W6 ....18 G3
NWMAL KT3 ....42 C5
Sussex Rd CAR SM5 ....62 B5
MTCM CR4 ....44 C6
NWDGN UB2 ....15 M1
NWMAL KT3 ....42 C5
SAND/SEL CR2 ....63 M5
WOKN/KNAP GU21 ....71 J7
WWKM BR4 ....47 H2
Sussex Ter PGE/AN SE20 * 46 C1
Sutherland Av
BH/WHM TW16 ....84 B6
HYS/HAR UB3 ....15 J2
RGUE GU4 ....92 C8
SUN TW16 ....39 J3
Sutherland Dr RGUE GU4 ....112 E2
Sutherland Gdns
MORT/ESHN SW14 ....18 C8
SUN TW16 ....39 H3
WPK KT4 ....42 F9
Sutherland Gv TEDD TW11 ....25 M8
WAND/EARL SW18 ....28 C3
CROY/NA CR0 ....2 C5
Sutton Av WOKN/KNAP GU21 ....71 L8
Sutton Cl BECK BR3 ....47 H2
CHSWK W4 ....18 A4
Sutton Common Rd
CHEAM SM3 ....43 K8
SUT/CR BELMT SM2 ....61 N6
CHSWK W4 * 18 A4
Sutton Court Rd CHSWK W4 ....18 A4
SUT SM1 ....61 N5
Sutton Dene HSLW TW3 ....16 B6
Sutton Gdns CROY/NA CR0 ....45 P6
REDH RH1 ....140 A6
Sutton Green Rd RGUE GU4 ....92 C6
Sutton Gv SUT SM1 ....61 P4
Sutton Hall HEST TW5 ....16 A5
Sutton La BNSTD SM7 ....79 M4
CHSWK W4 ....18 A3
DTCH/LGLY SL3 ....12 F4
HSLW TW3 ....15 P7
RDKG RH5 ....135 K5
Sutton La South CHSWK W4 ....18 A4
Sutton Park Rd SUT SM1 ....61 M5
Sutton Pl DTCH/LGLY SL3 ....12 F4
SHGR 135 H5
Sutton Rd CBLY GU15 ....51 J8
HEST TW5 ....15 P6
Sutton Wy HEST TW5 ....15 P6
Swabey Rd DTCH/LGLY SL3 ....12 E2
Swaby Rd WAND/EARL SW18 ....28 F5
Swaffield Rd
WAND/EARL SW18 ....28 F3
Swain Cl STRHM/NOR SW16 ....29 L9
Swain Rd THHTH CR7 ....45 L6
Swains La MTCM CR4 ....44 D5
Swaledale BRAK RG12 ....32 C6
Swaledale Cl CRAWW RH11 ....176 F8
Swaledale Gdns
FLEETN GU51 ....87 H3
Swale Rd FARN GU14 ....87 P1
Swallands Rd CAT SE6 ....31 P6
Swallow Cl MFD/CHID GU8 ....149 M5
STA TW18 ....22 C7
YTLY GU46 ....66 F2
Swallowdale SAND/SEL CR2 ....64 D7
Swallowfield EGH TW20 ....20 G9
EGH 162 F2
Swallow Gdns
STRHM/NOR SW16 ....29 N8
Swallow La RDKG RH5 ....137 H4
Swallow Ri
WOKN/KNAP GU21 ....71 J6
Swallow Rd CRAWW RH11 ....176 F8
Swallow St CRAWE RH10 ....179 K6
Swallowtail Rd HORS RH12 ....192 D4
Swanage Rd
WAND/EARL SW18 ....28 F2
Swan Barn Rd HASM GU27 ....184 E4
The Swan Centre
TOOT SW17 * 29 H6
Swan Cl CROY/NA CR0 * 45 N8
FELT TW13 ....24 G8
Swancote Gn BRAK RG12 ....32 D6
Swan Ct GU GU1 ....112 B3
Swandon Wy
WAND/EARL SW18 ....19 M3
Swan Island TWK TW1 * 25 P6
Swan La EDEN TN8 ....144 G1
GU GU1 ....6 E5
HORL RH6 ....158 G1
SHST GU47 ....67 M2
Swan Mill Gdns DORK RH4 ....117 J5
Swanns Meadow
GT/LBKH KT23 ....96 A6
Swann Wy HORS RH12 ....191 M7
Swan Pl BARN SW13 ....18 D7

Swan Rdg EDEN TN8 ....145 H1
Swan Rd FELT TW13 ....24 F7
Swanscombe Rd CHSWK W4 ....18 C3
Swansea Rd HTHAIR TW6 ....15 L2
Swans Ghyll FROW RH18 ....181 K8
Swan St ISLW TW7 ....17 H8
The Swansway WEY KT13 * 56 C2
Swanton Gdns
WIM/MER SW19 ....28 A4
Swan Wk HORS RH12 * 192 B8
SHPTN TW17 ....38 G8
Swan Wy FLEETN GU51 ....86 D8
Swanwick Cl PUT/ROE SW15 ....27 L3
Swanworth La RDKG RH5 ....97 H8
Swaynesland Rd
OXTED RH8 ....124 D5
Swayne's La EGH GU1 ....113 J5
Sweeps Ditch Cl STA TW18 ....37 L2
Sweeps La EGH TW20 ....21 L8
Sweetbriar CWTH RG45 * 49 J3
Sweet La SHGR GU5 ....134 F5
Sweetwater Cl SHGR GU5 ....133 H9
Sweetwater La
MFD/CHID GU8 ....149 P9
SHGR GU5 ....133 H9
Swievelands Rd
BH/WHM TW16 ....83 P8
Swift La BAGS GU19 ....51 P6
CRAWW RH11 ....176 C3
Swift Rd FELT TW13 ....24 F6
FNM GU9 ....107 M7
NWDGN UB2 ....15 P1
Swift's Cl RFNM GU10 ....128 D4
Swift St FUL/PGN SW6 ....19 K6
Swinburne Crs CROY/NA CR0 ....46 C7
Swinburne Rd
PUT/ROE SW15 ....18 E9
Swindon Rd HORS RH12 ....192 A6
HTHAIR TW6 ....23 M2
Swinfield Cl FELT TW13 ....24 F7
Swingate Rd FNM GU9 ....127 N5
Swinley Rd ASC SL5 ....33 L5
Swiss Cl RFNM GU10 ....127 K9
Swissland Hl EGRIN RH19 ....162 D6
Switchback La RFNM GU10 ....127 K9
Within Cha BNFD RG42 ....32 C1
Swordfish Wy FARN GU14 ....88 A4
Swyncombe Av BTFD TW8 ....17 H2
Sycamore Av EA W5 ....17 K1
HORS RH12 ....193 H5
Sycamore Cl CAR SM5 ....62 B3
CRAWW RH11 ....176 D3
FELT TW13 ....24 B6
FRIM GU16 ....68 C7
LHD/OX KT22 ....96 F2
SAND/SEL CR2 ....63 N4
SHST GU47 ....67 M1
Sycamore Ct WEY KT13 ....57 H2
Sycamore Crs FLEETN GU51 ....86 D3
Sycamore Dr ASHV GU12 ....89 H8
EGRIN RH19 ....180 F2
FRIM GU16 ....68 C6
RFNM GU10 ....127 L7
Sycamore Gdns MTCM CR4 ....43 P5
Sycamore Gv NWMAL KT3 ....42 C4
PGE/AN SE20 ....46 A1
Sycamore Ri BRAK RG12 ....32 F4
Sycamore Rd FARN GU14 ....88 D5
GU GU1 ....6 E2
RFNM GU10 ....127 L7
The Sycamores BLKW GU17 * 67 M3
Sycamore Wk EGH TW20 ....20 G9
REIG RH2 ....119 N3
Sycamore Wy THHTH CR7 ....45 M2
Sydcote DUL SE21 * 30 D5
Sydenham Av SYD SE26 ....31 J8
Sydenham Hi FSTH SE23 ....31 J5
Sydenham Pk SYD SE26 ....31 K6
Sydenham Park Rd
FSTH SE23 ....31 K6
Sydenham Ri FSTH SE23 ....31 K3
Sydenham Rd CROY/NA CR0 ....2 C2
GU GU1 ....7 F6
SYD SE26 ....31 L8
Sydenham Station Ap
SYD SE26 ....31 K7
Sydney Av PUR/KEN CR8 ....81 H1
Sydney Crs ASHF TW15 ....23 L9
Sydney Ms SKENS SW7 ....19 P2
Sydney Pl GU GU1 ....7 G4
SKENS SW7 ....19 P2

Sylvia Ct CHOB/PIR GU24 ....70 G4
Syon Gate Wy BTFD TW8 ....16 G5
Syon La ISLW TW7 ....16 G5
Syon Pk ISLW TW7 * 17 H8
Syon Park Gdns ISLW TW7 ....16 F5
Syon Pl FARN GU14 ....88 A4
Sythwood WOKN/KNAP GU21 ....71 P6
Szabo Crs RGUW GU3 ....110 B5

T

Tabarin Wy EW KT17 ....78 G5
Tableer Av CLAP SW4 ....29 M1
Tabor Gdns CHEAM SM3 ....61 K5
Tabor Gv WIM/MER SW19 ....43 J1
Tabor Rd HMSMTH W6 ....18 F1
Tachbrook Rd
EBED/NFELT TW14 ....24 A3
NWDGN UB2 ....15 M2
Tadema Rd WBPTN SW10 ....19 N5
Tadley Cl FLEETN GU51 ....86 D3
Tadmor Cl SUN TW16 ....39 H5
Tadome Rd
KWD/TDW/WH KT20 ....98 G1
Tadpole La RFNM GU10 ....107 H5
Tadworth Av NWMAL KT3 ....42 D5
Tadworth Cl
KWD/TDW/WH KT20 ....99 H2
Taffy's How MTCM CR4 ....44 A4
Tainters Hl EDEN TN8 * 145 K9
Tait Rd CROY/NA CR0 ....45 N8
Talbot Av DTCH/LGLY SL3 ....12 C1
Talbot Cl FRIM GU16 ....89 J3
REIG RH2 ....119 M6
Talbot La HORS RH12 ....192 B9
Talbot Pl BAGS GU19 ....51 N6
DTCH/LGLY SL3 ....12 A6
Talbot Rd ASHF TW15 ....22 G8
CAR SM5 ....62 C4
FNM GU9 ....4 E7
ISLW TW7 ....17 J9
LING RH7 ....162 C1
NWDGN UB2 ....15 N2
THHTH CR7 ....45 M5
WHTN TW2 ....25 K4
Talcott Pth
BRXS/STRHM SW2 * 30 B4
Taleworth Cl ASHTD KT21 ....77 K9
Taleworth Pk ASHTD KT21 ....77 K9
Taleworth Rd ASHTD KT21 ....77 K8
Talgarth Dr FARN GU14 ....88 F5
Talgarth Rd HMSMTH W6 ....19 H3
Talisman Cl CWTH RG45 ....49 H4
Talisman Sq SYD SE26 ....31 H7
Talisman Wy EW KT17 ....78 G5
Tall Elms Cl HAYES BR2 ....47 M6
Tallis Cl CRAWW RH11 ....176 C8
Tall Trees DTCH/LGLY SL3 ....13 H3
REIG RH2 ....180 E3
STRHM/NOR SW16 ....45 H4
Tally Ho OXTED RH8 ....124 C2
Talma Gdns WHTN TW2 ....25 M3
Talmage Cl FSTH SE23 ....31 J3
Talman Cl CRAWW RH11 * 176 B6
Tamar Cl CRAWE RH10 ....177 M6
Tamarind Cl GUW GU2 ....91 N9
Tamar Wy DTCH/LGLY SL3 ....12 D1
Tamerton Sq
WOKS/MYFD GU22 ....10 C1
Tamesis Gdns WPK KT4 ....60 C1
Tamian Wy HSLWW TW4 ....15 L5
Tamworth BRAK RG12 ....32 F8
Tamworth Dr FLEETN GU51 ....87 H3
Tamworth La MTCM CR4 ....44 D4
Tamworth Pk MTCM CR4 ....44 D5
Tamworth Pl CROY/NA CR0 ....2 C4
Tamworth St FUL/PGN SW6 ....19 K4
Tanbridge Pk HORS RH12 ....191 P9
Tanbridge Pl HORS RH12 ....192 A9
Tandridge Gdns
SAND/SEL CR2 ....81 P2
Tandridgehill La GDST RH9 ....102 F8
Tandridge La LING RH7 ....142 F5
OXTED RH8 ....122 G4
Tandridge Rd WARL CR6 ....82 D8
Tanfield Rd CROY/NA CR0 ....2 C7
Tangier Rd GU GU1 ....112 G6
RCHPK/HAM TW10 ....17 N9
Tangier Wy
KWD/TDW/WH KT20 ....79 J6
Tangle Oak EGRIN RH19 ....161 M8
Tanglewood EWKG RG40 ....48 C2
Tanglewood Cl CHERT KT16 ....53 P2
CROY/NA CR0 ....64 C2
WOKS/MYFD GU22 ....74 C3
Tanglewood Ride
CHOB/PIR GU24 ....70 D1
Tanglewood Wy FELT TW13 ....24 F5
Tangley Gv PUT/ROE SW15 ....27 L3
Tangley La RGUW GU3 ....111 M1
Tangley Park Rd
HPTN TW12 * 24 G8
Tangyn av SHPTN TW17 ....38 C6
Tangmere Gv
KUTN/CMB KT2 ....26 B8
Tangmere Rd CRAWW RH11 ....176 C5
Tanhouse Rd OXTED RH8 ....123 K3
Tanhurst La RDKG RH5 ....154 D2
Tanker Rd FARN GU14 ....88 D6
Tankerton Rd SURB KT6 ....59 M1
Tankerton Ter
CROY/NA CR0 * 45 H8

Tankerville Rd
STRHM/NOR SW16 ....44 F1
Tanners Cl WOT/HER KT12 ....39 K7
Tanners Dean LHD/OX KT22 ....97 K2
Tannersfield RGUE GU4 ....132 C4
Tanner's Hl
BRKHM/BTCW RH3 ....117 P7
Tanners La HASM GU27 ....184 D1
Tanners Meadow
BRKHM/BTCW RH3 ....117 P9
Tanners Yd BAGS GU19 * 51 N6
Tannery Cl CROY/NA CR0 ....46 D6
SWTR RH13 ....190 D7
Tannery La RPLY/SEND GU23 ....93 J2
SHGR GU5 * 133 N4
The Tannery REDH RH1 ....120 A5
Tannsfeld Rd SYD SE26 ....31 L8
Tansy Cl RGUE GU4 ....112 G3
Tantallon Rd BAL SW12 ....29 K4
Tanyard Av CRAWE RH10 ....177 M8
Tanyard Cl CRAWE RH10 ....177 M8
SWTR RH13 ....190 G7
Tanyard La SHGR GU5 ....132 D6
Tanyard Wy HORL RH6 ....140 D3
Tapestry Cl BELMT SM2 ....61 M6
Taplow Ct MTCM CR4 ....44 A5
Tapner's Rd REIG RH2 ....138 D2
Tapping Cl KUTN/CMB KT2 ....9 H1
Tara Pk COUL/CHIP CR5 ....80 B9
Tarbat Ct SHST GU47 ....49 P9
Tarbert Rd EDUL SE22 ....30 F1
Target Cl EBED/NFELT TW14 ....23 P2
Target Hl BNFD RG42 ....32 F1
Tarham Cl HORL RH6 ....140 A8
Tarleton Gdns FSTH SE23 ....31 J4
Tarmac Wy WDR/YW UB7 ....13 M5
Tarnbrook Wy BRAK RG12 ....32 G8
Tarn Cl FARN GU14 ....88 A5
Tarn Rd GSHT GU26 ....165 N8
Tarragon Cl FARN GU14 ....87 N3
Tarragon Dr GUW GU2 ....91 N9
Tarragon Gv SYD SE26 ....31 L9
Tarrant Gn BNFD RG42 ....32 E1
Tarrant Pl BF/WBF KT14 * 73 K2
Tarrington Cl
STRHM/NOR SW16 * 29 N7
Tartar Hl COB KT11 ....75 K2
Tartar Rd COB KT11 ....75 L2
Tasker Cl HYS/HAR UB3 ....14 G5
Tasso Rd HMSMTH W6 ....19 J4
Tate Cl LHD/OX KT22 ....97 J3
Tate Rd SUT SM1 ....61 L4
Tates Wy HORS RH12 ....189 N3
Tatnell Rd FSTH SE23 ....31 M6
Tatsfield La BH/WHM TW16 ....104 D1
Tattenham Corner Rd
EPSOM KT18 ....78 E7
Tattenham Crs EPSOM KT18 ....78 F7
Tattenham Gv EPSOM KT18 ....78 F7
Tattenham Wy
KWD/TDW/WH KT20 ....79 J6
Taunton Av CTHM CR3 ....101 P3
HSLW TW3 ....16 C7
RYNPK SW20 ....42 F3
Taunton Cl CHEAM SM3 ....43 J8
COUL/CHIP CR5 ....81 J8
Tavern Cl CAR SM5 ....44 A8
Tavistock Cl STA TW18 ....37 P1
Tavistock Crs MTCM CR4 ....44 G5
Tavistock Gdns FARN GU14 ....68 D9
Tavistock Gv CROY/NA CR0 ....45 L8
Tavistock Rd CAR SM5 ....43 P9
CROY/NA CR0 ....2 E2
FLEETN GU51 ....86 E7
HAYES BR2 ....47 N5
Tawfield BRAK RG12 ....32 A8
Tawny Cl FELT TW13 ....24 B5
Tawny Rw SHST GU47 ....49 P9
Tayben Av WHTN TW2 ....25 M1
Tay Cl FARN GU14 ....88 A1
Tayles Hill Dr EW KT17 ....78 E5
Taylor Av RCH/KEW TW9 ....17 P7
Taylor Cl HPTN TW12 ....25 K8
HSLW TW3 ....16 C6
Taylor Rd ASHTD KT21 ....77 J5
MTCM CR4 ....44 A1
WIM/MER SW19 ....28 F9
WLGTN SM6 ....62 C4
Taylors Ct FELT TW13 ....24 B5
Taylors Cl LING RH7 ....143 J9
Taylor's La SYD SE26 ....31 J7
Taylor Wk CRAWW RH11 ....176 F5
Taymount Ri FSTH SE23 ....31 K5
Taynton Dr REDH RH1 ....120 F1
Teal Cl HORS RH13 ....192 B5
SAND/SEL CR2 ....64 F7
Teal Ct DORK RH4 ....116 G6
Tealing Dr HOR/WEW KT19 ....60 B8
Teasel Cl CRAWW RH11 ....176 E8
CROY/NA CR0 ....46 E9
Teazlewood Pk LHD/OX KT22 ....76 G6
Tebbit Cl BRAK RG12 ....32 F4
Teck Cl ISLW TW7 ....16 G7
Tedder Cl CHSGTN KT9 ....59 J4
Tedder Rd SAND/SEL CR2 ....64 D6
Teddington
HOR/WEW KT19 ....59 N9
Teddington Pk TEDD TW11 ....25 N8
Teddington Park Rd
TEDD TW11 ....25 N7
Tedham La GDST RH9 ....142 B6
Tees Cl FARN GU14 ....88 A1
Teesdale CRAWW RH11 ....176 E4
Teesdale Av ISLW TW7 ....16 G6
Teesdale Gdns ISLW TW7 ....16 G6
SNWD SE25 ....45 N3
Teevan Cl CROY/NA CR0 ....46 A8
Teevan Rd CROY/NA CR0 ....46 A8
Tegg's La WOKS/MYFD GU22 ....73 K5
Tekels Av CBLY GU15 ....68 G3

Tekels Wy CBLY GU15 ....68 G5
Telconia Cl BOR GU35 ....164 F7
Telegraph La ESH/CLAY KT10 ....58 F3
Telegraph Pas
BRXS/STRHM SW2 ....29 P3
Telegraph Rd PUT/ROE SW15 ....27 N3
Telegraph Tr WLGTN SM6 ....62 C9
Telephone Pl WKENS W14 * 19 K4
Telferscot Rd BAL SW12 ....29 N4
Telford Av BAL SW12 ....29 N4
BRXS/STRHM SW2 ....29 N4
Telford Cl NRWD SE19 ....30 C9
Telford Ct GU GU1 ....7 J4
Telford Dr WOT/HER KT12 ....39 L8
Telham Ct CRAWW RH11 * 176 C8
Telford Rd WHTN TW2 ....25 H3
Tellisford ESH/CLAY KT10 ....58 B3
Temperley Rd BAL SW12 ....29 K3
Tempest Rd EGH TW20 ....21 P9
Templar Cl SHST GU47 ....49 L9
Templar Pl HPTN TW12 ....40 A1
Templars Av CROY/NA CR0 ....64 F2
Temple Bar Rd
WOKN/KNAP GU21 ....71 M8
Temple Cl CRAWE RH10 ....177 N6
Templecombe Ms
WOKS/MYFD GU22 ....11 H2
Templecombe Wy
MRDN SM4 ....43 J6
Templedene Av STA TW18 ....37 N1
Temple Field Cl
ADL/WDHM KT15 ....55 M5
Temple Gdns STA TW18 ....37 K2
Templeman Cl PUR/KEN CR8 ....81 J5
Templer Av FARN GU14 ....88 B6
Temple Rd CHSWK W4 ....18 A1
CROY/NA CR0 ....2 E7
EA W5 ....17 K1
HOR/WEW KT19 ....78 B1
HSLW TW3 ....16 B9
RCH/KEW TW9 ....17 M7
Temple Sheen Rd
MORT/ESHN SW14 ....18 A9
Templeton Cl THHTH CR7 ....45 M2
Templeton Pl ECT SW5 ....19 L2
Temple Wy BNFD RG42 ....32 A2
Tempsford Cl
REDH RH1 * 120 B2
Ten Acre WOKN/KNAP GU21 ....71 N7
Ten Acre La EGH TW20 ....36 G3
Ten Acres Cl LHD/OX KT22 ....96 D4
Tenbury Ct
BRXS/STRHM SW2 ....29 N4
Tenby Dr ASC SL5 ....34 D6
Tenby Rd FRIM GU16 ....69 J8
Tenchley's La OXTED RH8 ....124 D2
Tenham Av
BRXS/STRHM SW2 ....29 N5
Tenniel Cl GUW GU2 ....111 P3
Tennison Cl COUL/CHIP CR5 ....81 N5
Tennison Rd SNWD SE25 ....45 P5
Tennyson Av NWMAL KT3 ....42 F6
EBED/NFELT TW14 ....24 B2
HORS RH12 ....192 D4
Tennyson Ri EGRIN RH19 ....180 B2
Tennyson Rd
ADL/WDHM KT15 ....56 A3
ASHF TW15 ....23 H8
HSLW TW3 ....16 C7
PGE/AN SE20 ....46 D1
WIM/MER SW19 ....28 F9
Tennysons La HASM GU27 ....184 F6
Tenterden Gdns
CROY/NA CR0 ....46 A8
Tenterden Rd CROY/NA CR0 ....46 A8
Tenth Av
KWD/TDW/WH KT20 * 99 G6
Term Rd CRAWW RH11 ....176 A6
Terrace La RCH/KEW TW9 ....26 F1
Terrace La BARN SW13 ....18 D6
Terrace Rd WOT/HER KT12 ....39 K8
The Terrace ADL/WDHM KT15 ....56 A4
ASC SL5 ....34 D6
BARN SW13 ....18 B5
CBLY GU15 ....68 B3
CWTH RG45 ....49 P4
FARN GU14 * 88 F4
FSTH SE23 ....31 M3
WOKS/MYFD GU22 * 92 E1
Terrace Vis HMSMTH W6 * 19 H3
Terra Cotta Rd GDST RH9 ....122 C9
Terrace St RCH/KEW TW9 ....17 M9
Terrapin Rd TOOT SW17 ....29 L6
Terry Rd CRAWW RH11 ....194 E1
Tesimond Dr YTLY GU46 ....66 E3
Testard Rd GUW GU2 ....6 C6
Testers Cl OXTED RH8 ....124 A3
Tetcott Rd WBPTN SW10 ....19 N5
Tetty Wy HAYES BR2 ....47 N3
Teviot Cl GUW GU2 ....111 N2
Tewkesbury Av FSTH SE23 ....31 J3
Tewkesbury Cl BF/WBF KT14 ....55 P9
Tewkesbury Rd CAR SM5 ....43 P9
Teynham Gn HAYES BR2 ....47 N6
Thackeray Cl ISLW TW7 ....17 J7
WIM/MER SW19 ....43 H1
Thackeray St KENS W8 ....19 M1
Thakeham Cl SYD SE26 ....31 J8
Thames Av CHERT KT16 ....37 L4
WBPTN SW10 ....19 N6
Thames Bank
MORT/ESHN SW14 ....18 A7
Thames Cl CHERT KT16 ....37 M8
FARN GU14 ....88 A1

HPTN TW12 .....40 B3
Thames Down Link
CHSGTN KT9 .....60 A3
EPSOM KT18 .....77 M3
Thames Eyot TWK TW1 * 25 P5
Thamesfield Ct SHPTN TW17 ..38 E8
Thamesfield Ms
SHPTN TW17 * 38 E8
Thamesgate CI STA TW18 .....37 M3
Thamesgate CI
RCHPK/HAM TW10 .....26 A7
Thameside TEDD TW11 .....41 K1
Thames Lock SHPTN TW17 * ..56 C1
Thames Md WOT/HER KT12 ..39 J8
Thames Meadow
E/WMO/HCT KT8 .....40 A4
WOT/HER KT12 .....38 F9
Thames Pth CHSWK W4 .....18 D6
EGH TW20 .....21 K5
RCH/KEW TW9 .....17 J7
STA TW18 .....22 B6
WEY KT13 .....56 D1
Thames PI PUT/ROE SW15...19 H8
Thamespoint TEDD TW11 * ..41 K1
Thames Quay WBPTN SW10 *.19 N6
Thames Reach KUT KT1 * 8 B2
Thames Rd CHSWK W4 .....17 P4
DTCH/LGLY SL3 .....12 F2
Thames Side KUT KT1 .....8 C3
STA TW18 .....37 N6
THDIT KT7 .....41 H7
Thames St HPTN TW12 .....40 B3
KUT KT1 .....8 C4
STA TW18 .....22 C8
SUN TW16 .....39 K4
WEY KT13 .....56 C2
WOT/HER KT12 .....39 H8
Thamesvale CI HSLW TW3 ...16 A7
Thames Village CHSWK W4 ..18 A6
Thanescroft Gdns
CROY/NA CRO 3 H6
Thanet PI CROY/NA CRO.....2 C7
Tharp Rd WLGTN SM6 .....62 F4
Thatcher CI CRAWE RH10 ..176 G8
Thatchers Ct HORL RH6 .....140 D8
HORS RH12 .....192 D6
Thatchers La GUW GU2 .....91 K7
Thatchers Wy ISLW TW7 .....25 L1
Thaxted PI RYNPK SW20 .....43 H1
Thaxton Rd WKENS W14 .....19 K4
Thayers Farm Rd BECK BR3..46 E2
Theal CI SHST GU47 .....49 P9
Theatre Rd FARN GU14 .....88 D7
The Beverly MRDN SM4 .....43 H7
Thelma Gv TEDD TW11 .....25 P9
Thelton Av HORS RH12 .....191 J7
Theobald Rd CROY/NA CRO ..2 A2
Theobalds Wy FRIM GU16 ..69 L5
Thepps CI REDH RH1 .....121 H8
Therapia La CROY/NA CR0 ..44 G8
Therapia Rd EDUL SE22 .....31 K2
Theresa Rd HMSMTH W6 ....18 E2
Theresa's Wk SAND/SEL CR2..63 M7
Thesiger Rd PGE/AN SE20 ..46 C1
Thetford Rd ASHF TW15 .....23 H7
NWMAL KT3 .....42 C6
Theydon CI CRAWE RH10 ..177 K7
Thibet Rd SHST GU47 .....49 N9
Thicket Crs SUT SM1 .....61 N3
Thicket Gv PGE/AN SE20 ....46 A1
Thicket Rd PGE/AN SE20 ....46 A1
SUT SM1 .....61 N3
Thicket Ter PGE/AN SE20 * ..46 A1
Thickthorne La STA TW18 ...37 N1

Third Av
KWD/TDW/WH KT20 * 99 K6
Third CI E/WMO/HCT KT8 ...40 B5
Third Cross Rd WHTN TW2...25 L5
Thirlmere CI EGH TW20 .....36 F1
FARN GU14 .....88 A3
Thirlmere Crs FLEETS GU52..106 E1
Thirlmere Rd CRAWE RH11 ..176 A7
STRHM/NOR SW16 .....29 N7
Thirsk Ct ASHV GU12 .....108 F4
Thirsk Rd MTCM CR4 .....44 C5
SNWD SE25 .....45 M5
Thirteenth Av
KWD/TDW/WH KT20 * 99 K6
Thistlecroft Rd
WOT/HER KT12 .....57 L3
Thistledene BF/WBF KT14 ...75 K8
THDIT KT7 .....40 E7
Thistledown V BIL RH14 * ..188 A6
Thistle Gv WBPTN SW10 * ...19 L3
Thistle Wy HORL RH6 .....141 L9
Thistlewood Crs
CROY/NA CRO 83 K1
Thistley CI CH ISLW TW7 .....16 D5
Thistley La CRAN GU6 .....153 H8
Thistledown V BIL RH14 ....188 A6
Thomas Av CTHM CR3 .....101 L1
Thomas Baines Rd
BTSEA SW11 .....19 P8
Thomas Dean Rd SYD SE26 * .31 N7
Thomas Dr BNFD RG42 * ...32 C1
Thomas La EW KC RG40 .....48 C1
Thomas PI KENS W8 * 19 M1
Thomas Wall CI SUT SM1 ....61 M4
Thompson Av RCH/KEW TW9 ..17 P8
Thompson CI CHEAM SM3 ...43 L9
DTCH/LGLY SL3 .....12 E2
Thompson Rd EDUL SE22 ...30 G2
HSLW TW3 .....16 B9
Thompsons CI
CHOB/PIR GU24 .....90 D3
Thompson's La
CHOB/PIR GU24 .....90 C3
Thomson Crs CROY/NA CRO ..45 J9
Thorburn Cha SHST GU47 ...68 A2
Thorburn Wy
WIM/MER SW19 * 43 P2

Thorkhill Gdns THDIT KT7 ...40 G9
Thorkhill Rd THDIT KT7 .....41 H9
Thorley CI BF/WBF KT14 .....73 L5
Thorley Gdns BF/WBF KT14...73 L5
Thornash CI
WOKN/KNAP GU21 .....72 A4
Thornash Rd
WOKN/KNAP GU21 .....72 A4
Thornash Wy
WOKN/KNAP GU21 .....72 A4
Thorn Bank GUW GU2 .....111 N7
Thornbury Av ISLW TW7 .....16 D5
Thornbury CI CWTH RG45 ...49 M4
Thornbury Rd CLAP SW4 ....29 P2
ISLW TW7 .....16 D5
Thorncliffe Rd CLAP SW4 ....29 P2
NWDGN UB2 .....15 P3
Thorn CI RFNM GU10 .....128 E7
Thorncombe St EDUL SE22 ..30 F1
Thorncombe St
MFD/CHID GU8 .....151 J4
Thorn Ct BELMT SM2 * 61 M6
Thorncroft EGH TW20 .....36 A1
Thorncroft CI
COUL/CHIP CR5 .....81 J8
Thorncroft Rd SUT SM1 .....61 M3
Thorndean St
WAND/EARL SW18 .....28 F5
Thorndike CI WBPTN SW10 ..19 N5
Thorndon Gdns
HOR/WEW KT19 .....60 C3
Thorndown La BFOR GU20 ..52 D6
Thorndyke CI CRAWE RH10 ..177 N6
Thorne CI ASHF TW15 .....38 E1
CWTH RG45 .....49 L2
Thorneloe Gdns
CROY/NA CR0 .....63 K4
Thorne's CI BECK BR3 .....47 J4
Thorne St BARN SW13 .....19 D5
Thorney Crs BTSEA SW11 * ..19 P5
Thorneycroft CI
WOT/HER KT12 .....39 L7
Thorney Hedge Rd
WOT/HER KT12 .....17 P2
Thorney Mill Rd WDR/YW UB7..13 M1
Thornfield Gn BLKW GU17 ..68 B5
Thornhill BRAK RG12 .....32 G5
Thornhill Av SURB KT6 .....59 L1
Thornhill Rd ALDT GU11 ...108 F2
CROY/NA CR0 .....45 L8
SURB KT6 .....59 L1
Thornhill Vw GSHT GU26 *..165 N8
Thornhill Wy SHPTN TW17...38 C8
Thornlaw Rd WNWD SE27 ..30 B7
Thornleas PI EHSLY KT24 ....94 G6
Thorn Rd RFNM GU10 .....127 K9
Thornsett PI PGE/AN SE20 ..46 B3
Thornsett Rd PGE/AN SE20 ..46 B3
WAND/EARL SW18 .....28 E5
Thorn's Meadow
BH/WHM TN16 .....105 M3
Thornton Av BAL SW12 .....29 N4
CHSWK W4 .....18 C2
CROY/NA CR0 .....45 H7
WDR/YW UB7 .....14 B1
Thornton CI GUW GU2 .....111 N2
HORL RH6 .....159 H1
WDR/YW UB7 .....14 B1
Thornton Crs COUL/CHIP CR5..81 J8
Thornton Dene BECK BR3 ....46 G3
Thornton Gdns BAL SW12 ...29 N4
Thornton Hl WIM/MER SW19..43 J1
Thornton PI HORL RH6 .....159 H1
Thornton Rd BAL SW12 .....29 N3
CAR SM5 .....43 P9
MORT/ESHN SW14 .....18 B3
THHTH CR7 .....45 J4
WIM/MER SW19 .....28 D8
Thornton Rw THHTH CR7 ....45 J6
Thornville Gv MTCM CR4 ....43 N5
Thornyhurst Rd FRIM GU16 ..89 J3
Thorold CI SAND/SEL CR2 ...64 D8
Thorold Rd FNM GU9 .....5 G3
Thorpe By-pass EGH TW20 ..36 F4
Thorpe CI CROY/NA CRO.....65 M6
SYD SE26 * 31 L7
Thorpe Lea Rd EGH TW20 ...37 K4
Thorpe Pk CHERT KT16 * 36 F4
Thorpe Rd CHERT KT16 .....37 H6
EGH TW20 .....22 A9
KUTN/CMB KT2 .....41 L1
Thorpes CI GUW GU2 .....111 N2
Thorpeside CI EGH TW20 ....37 J3
Thorpewood Av SYD SE26 ...31 J5
Thorsden CI
WOKS/MYFD GU22 .....10 D7
Thorsden Ct
WOKS/MYFD GU22 .....10 D6
Thorsden Wy NRWD SE19 *..30 H8
Thrale Rd STRHM/NOR SW16..29 M8
Three Acres HORS RH12 ....191 P9
Three Arches Pk
REDH RH1 * 120 B9
Three Arch Rd REDH RH1 ..120 C9
Three Bridges Rd
CRAWE RH10 * 177 J5
Three Castles Pth ASC SL5..33 L4
ASC SL5 .....34 E1
HTWY RG27 .....66 E1
WDSR SL4 .....33 J1
Three Gates GU GU1 .....112 G4
Three Gates La HASM GU27..184 E8
Three Mile Rd CRAN GU6 ..154 B2
Three Pears Rd GU GU1 ....113 J5
Threestile Rd HORS RH12 ..191 N1
Three Stiles Rd FNM GU9 .....5 G2
Threshers Cnr FLEETS GU51..87 J3
Threshfield BRAK RG12 .....32 C6
Thrift La BH/WHM TN16 * 85 J6
Thrift V RGUE GU4 .....113 H2

Thrigby Rd CHSGTN KT9 .....59 M5
Throgmorton Rd YTLY GU46..66 E3
Throwley Rd SUT SM1 .....61 M3
Throwley Wy SUT SM1 .....61 M3
Thrupp CI MTCM CR4 .....44 D3
Thrupps Av WOT/HER KT12..57 M4
Thrupps La WOT/HER KT12..57 M4
Thundery HI RFNM GU10 ...129 H1
Thurbans Rd FNM GU9 .....127 L6
Thurbarns HI RDKG RH5 ...156 D5
Thurlby Rd WNWD SE27 .....30 B7
Thurleigh Av BAL SW12 .....29 K2
Thurleigh Rd BAL SW12 .....29 J2
Thurleston Av MRDN SM4 ...43 J6
Thurlestone CI SHPTN TW17 *.38 E7
Thurlestone Pde
SHPTN TW17 * 38 E7
Thurlestone Rd WNWD SE27..30 B6
Thurloe PI SKENS SW7 .....19 P2
Thurloe Place Ms
SKENS SW7 .....19 P2
Thurloe St SKENS SW7 .....19 P2
Thurlow HI DUL SE21 .....30 D4
Thurlow Park Rd
DUL SE21 .....30 C5
Thurlow Wk CRAN GU6 .....171 H2
Thurlton Ct
WOKN/KNAP GU21 .....10 D1
Thurne Wy HORS RH12 .....189 N3
Thurnham Wy
KWD/TDW/WH KT20 .....79 H9
Thursby Rd
WOKN/KNAP GU21 .....71 N7
Thursley Crs CROY/NA CR0 ..65 K6
Thursley Gdns
WIM/MER SW19 .....28 A5
Thursley Rd MFD/CHID GU8..148 C7
RFNM GU10 .....147 M9
Thurso St TOOT SW17 .....28 G7
Thurstan Rd RYNPK SW20 ...42 F1
Thyme Ct FARN GU14 .....87 N2
GU GU1 .....112 F2
Tibbenham PI CAT SE6 .....31 P5
Tibbets CI WIM/MER SW19 ..28 A3
Tibbet's Ride PUT/ROE SW15..28 A3
Ticehurst CI CRAWE RH10 ..177 P5
Ticehurst Rd FSTH SE23 .....31 M5
Tichborne CI BLKW GU17 ....67 P3
Tichbourne CI FRIM GU16 ...69 J3
Tichmarsh HOR/WEW KT19...60 A8
Tickenor Dr EWKG RG40 .....48 D2
Tidenham Gdns CROY/NA CR0 ..3 H9
Tideswell Rd CROY/NA CRO..64 C2
PUT/ROE SW15 .....18 G9
Tideway CI
RCHPK/HAM TW10 .....26 A7
Tidwells Lea BNFD RG42 .....32 G2
Tiepigs La WWKM BR4 .....65 L1
Tierney Rd BRXS/STRHM SW2..29 P4
Tierney Ter
BRXS/STRHM SW2 * 29 P4
Tiger La HAYES BR2 .....47 P5
Tilburstow Hill Rd GDST RH9..122 C3
Tilbury Wk DTCH/LGLY SL3 ..12 F1
Tildesley Rd PUT/ROE SW15..28 P7
Tile Barn CI FARN GU14 .....88 A2
Tilehouse Rd RGUE GU4 ....112 C9
Tilehurst La RDKG RH5 .....117 L8
Tilehurst Rd CHEAM SM3 ....61 J4
WAND/EARL SW18 .....28 G4
Tiler's Wy REDH RH1 .....119 N9
Tilford Av CROY/NA CR0 .....65 J7
Tilford Gdns WIM/MER SW19..28 A4
Tilford Rd FNM GU9 .....5 J5
GSHT GU26 .....166 A6
RFNM GU10 .....147 M8
RFNM GU10 .....147 M8
Tilford St RFNM GU10 .....146 G9
Tilgate Common REDH RH1..121 L4
Tilgate Dr CRAWE RH10 ....195 H1
Tilgate Forest Ldg
CRAWE RH10 * 194 F6
Tilgate Pde CRAWE RH10 ..177 H8
Tilgate PI CRAWE RH10 .....177 H8
Tilgate Wy CRAWE RH10 ...177 H8
Tilletts La HORS RH12 .....191 M2
Tilley La EPSOM KT18 .....98 A3
Tilling bourne Rd RGUE GU4..132 C2
Tillingdown HI CTHM CR3 ..102 B2
Tillingdown La CTHM CR3 ..102 B5
Tillotson CI CRAWE RH10 ..177 N6
Tilney Rd NWDGN UB2 .....15 L2
Tilson Gdns
BRXS/STRHM SW2 .....29 P3
Tilt CI COB KT11 .....75 N5
Tilthams Corner Rd
GODL GU7 .....131 P5
Tilt Meadow COB KT11 .....75 N5
Tilton St FUL/PGN SW6 .....19 J4
Tilt Rd COB KT11 .....75 M5
Tilt Vw COB KT11 * 75 M5
Tiltwood Dr CRAWE RH10 ..179 K2
Timber Bank FRIM GU16 .....89 J2
Timber CI FNM GU9 * 4 E2
GT/LBKH KT23 .....96 C7
WOKS/MYFD GU22 .....73 K4
Timbercroft HOR/WEW KT19 ..60 C3
Timberham Farm Rd
HORL RH6 .....158 C4
Timber HI ASHTD KT21 .....77 L8
Timber Mill Rd CTHM CR3 ..102 A4
Timberlands CRAWE RH11..194 E1
Timberley PI CWTH RG45 ....49 K5
Timberling Gdns
SAND/SEL CR2 .....63 M8
Timbermill CT HASM GU27..184 A4
Timberslip Dr WLGTN SM6 ..62 F7
Timbertop Rd BH/WHM TN16..84 A7
Times Sq SUT SM1 * 61 M4

Timeline Gn BRAK RG12 .....33 H3
Timperley Gdns REDH RH1..120 A3
Timsway STA TW18 .....22 C6
Tindal CI YTLY GU46 .....67 H2
Tindale CI SAND/SEL CR2 ....63 M9
Tinefields CAR SM5 * 44 C8
Tinsey CI EGH TW20 .....21 N8
Tinsley CI CRAWE RH10 .....177 L2
SNWD SE25 .....46 B5
Tinsley Gn CRAWE RH10 ....159 L9
Tinsley La CRAWE RH10 ....177 K2
Tinsley La North
CRAWE RH10 .....159 L9
Tinsley La South
CRAWE RH10 .....177 K3
Tintagel CI EW KT17 .....78 D3
Tintagel Dr FRIM GU16 .....69 H7
Tintagel Rd EWKG RG40 .....48 E1
Tintagel Wy
WOKS/MYFD GU22 .....11 H2
Tintells La EHSLY KT24 .....94 D8
Tintern CI PUT/ROE SW15 ...28 B1
WIM/MER SW19 .....43 N1
Tintern Rd CAR SM5 .....43 P9
CRAWE RH11 .....176 D7
Tipton Dr CROY/NA CR0 .....3 H7
Tirlemont Rd SAND/SEL CR2..63 L6
Tirrell Rd CROY/NA CR0 .....45 L7
Tisbury Rd
STRHM/NOR SW16 .....44 G3
Tisted CI FLEETS GU51 .....86 E4
Titan CI BTFD TW8 * 17 M3
Titchfield Rd CAR SM5 .....43 P9
Titchfield Wk CAR SM5 .....43 P8
Titchwell Rd
WAND/EARL SW18 .....28 G3
Tite HI EGH TW20 .....21 J8
Tithe Barn CI KUTN/CMB KT2..8 G1
Tithe CI WOT/HER KT12 * 39 J7
Tithe Ct DTCH/LGLY SL3 .....12 E2
Tithe La STWL/WRAY TW19 ..21 L2
Tithe Orch FRIM RH19 * 161 M8
Tithepit Shaw La WARL CR6..82 B6
Titlarks Hill Rd ASC SL5 .....35 H9
Titmus Dr CRAWE RH10 ....176 G7
Titness Pk ASC SL5 * 34 G4
Titsey HI WARL CR6 .....103 M4
Titsey Rd OXTED RH8 .....103 P7
Tiverton Rd HSLW TW3 .....16 B7
Tiverton Wy CHSGTN KT9 ...59 J4
Tivoli Rd HSLW TW4 .....24 C1
WNWD SE27 * 30 D8
Toad La BLKW GU17 .....68 A4
HSLWW TW4 .....15 P9
Toby Wy SURB KT6 .....59 P1
Todds CI HORL RH6 .....140 D8
Toftwood CI CRAWE RH10..177 M6
Toland Sq PUT/ROE SW15...27 M1
Tolldene CI
WOKN/KNAP GU21 .....71 L6
Tollers La COUL/CHIP CR5 ...81 H8
Toll Gdns BRAK RG12 .....32 G4
Tollgate GU GU1 .....113 H4
Tollgate Av REDH RH1 .....140 D7
Tollgate Dr DUL SE21 .....30 F5
Tollgate Hi CRAWE RH11 ...194 F2
Tollgate Rd DORK RH4 .....137 H1
Tollhouse La WLGTN SM6 ...62 E7
Tolpuddle Wy YTLY GU46 ...67 K3
Tolson Rd ISLW TW7 .....16 G8
Tolvaddon WOKN/KNAP GU21..71 N6
Tolverne Rd RYNPK SW20 ...42 G2
Tolworth CI SURB KT6 .....59 P5
Tolworth Park Rd SURB KT6..59 M1
Tolworth Ri North
BRYLDS KT5 .....42 A8
Tolworth Ri South
BRYLDS KT5 .....42 A9
Tolworth Rd SURB KT6 .....59 L1
Tomlin CI HOR/WEW KT19 ...60 D9
Tomlins Av FRIM GU16 .....69 H6
Tomlinscote Wy FRIM GU16..69 J6
Tomlinson CI CHSWK W4 ....17 P3
Tomlinson Dr EWKG RG40 ..48 F2
Tomtit Crs CRAWE RH10 ....179 K6
Tonbridge CI BNSTD SM7 ...80 B3
Tonbridge Rd
E/WMO/HCT KT8 .....39 N5
Tonfield Rd CHEAM SM3 .....43 K8
Tongham Mdw RFNM GU10..128 E1
Tongham Rd RFNM GU10 ..128 E1
Tonsley HI WAND/EARL SW18..28 E1
Tonsley PI WAND/EARL SW18..28 E1
Tonsley Rd WAND/EARL SW18..28 E1
Tonsley St WAND/EARL SW18..28 E1
Tonstall Rd HOR/WEW KT19..60 B8
MTCM CR4 .....44 B3
Tooting Bec Gdns
STRHM/NOR SW16 .....29 N7
Tooting Bec Rd TOOT SW17..29 K6
Tooting Gv TOOT SW17 .....29 H8
Tooting High St TOOT SW17..29 H9
Tooting Market TOOT SW17 *..29 J7
Tootswood Rd HAYES BR2...47 L6
Top Common Rd BRAK RG12..32 F1
Topiary Sq RCH/KEW TW9 ...17 M8
The Topiary ASHTD KT21 ....77 J9
FARN GU14 * 88 A4
Toplady PI FNM GU9 .....107 N7
Top Pk BECK BR3 .....47 N5
Topsham Rd TOOT SW17 ....29 J6
Top Terrace Rd FARN GU14..88 C7
Torcross Dr FSTH SE23 .....31 K5
Torin Ct EGH TW20 .....21 H8
Torland Dr LHD/OX KT22 ....76 D5
Tor La WEY KT13 .....56 E9
Tormead Cl SUT SM1 .....61 L5
Tormead Rd GU GU1 .....7 K2
Toronto Dr HORL RH6 .....160 B2
Torrens Rd BRXS/STRHM SW2..30 A1
Torridge Rd DTCH/LGLY SL3..12 F4
THHTH CR7 .....45 K6

Torridon CI
WOKN/KNAP GU21 .....71 P6
Torridon Rd
ESH/CLAY KT10 .....58 E5
Torrington Rd
ESH/CLAY KT10 .....58 E5
Torrington Sq
CROY/NA CR0 * 45 M8
Torrington Wy MRDN SM4 ...43 L8
Tor Rd FNM GU9 .....4 B4
Tor Rd PGE/AN SE20 .....46 D1
Torwood La CTHM CR3 .....101 P5
Torwood Rd PUT/ROE SW15..27 M1
Totford La RFNM GU10 .....129 N2
Totland CI FARN GU14 .....88 C1
Tottenham Rd GODL GU7 ..131 L7
Tottenham Wk SHST GU47 ...49 P8
Totterdown St TOOT SW17...29 J7
Totton Rd THHTH CR7 .....45 J4
Tournai CI ALDT GU11 .....88 G8
Tournay Rd FUL/PGN SW6 ..19 K5
Tovil CI PGE/AN SE20 .....46 A3
Tower CI EGRIN RH19 .....180 C1
HORL RH6 .....159 J2
WOKN/KNAP GU21 .....10 C2
Tower Ct EGRIN RH19 * 180 D1
Tower Gdns ESH/CLAY KT10..58 H9
Tower Gv WEY KT13 .....56 G1
Tower HI DORK RH4 .....117 H9
FARN GU14 .....88 C3
Towerhill SHGR GU5 .....134 G2
Tower Hill RI SHGR GU5 ....134 E2
Tower Hill Rd DORK RH4 ...117 H9
Tower Ri RCH/KEW TW9 .....17 L8
Tower Rd CGSHT GU26 .....165 P7
HORS RH12 .....193 M2
KWD/TDW/WH KT20 * 98 G3
LIPH GU30 .....182 E6
WHTN TW2 .....25 M6
Towers Dr CWTH RG45 .....49 M5
Towers PI RCHPK/HAM TW10..26 B3
The Towers PUR/KEN CR8....81 L4
Towers Wk WEY KT13 .....56 D5
Tower Vw CROY/NA CR0 .....46 C9
Towfield Rd FELT TW13 .....24 G5
Town Barn Rd CRAWE RH11..176 F6
Townend CTHM CR3 .....101 N2
Town End CI CTHM CR3 .....101 N2
GODL GU7 * 131 L9
Town End Pde KUT KT1 * 8 B4
Town End St GODL GU7 ....131 L9
Town Farm Wy
STWL/WRAY TW19 * 22 G3
Townfield Rd DORK RH4 ....116 G8
Town Field Wy ISLW TW7 ....16 G7
Towngate COB KT11 .....75 N4
Townhall Av CHSWK W4 .....18 B3
Town HI LING RH7 .....143 L7
Townholm Crs HNWL W7 * ..16 F1
Town La STWL/WRAY TW19 ..22 G2
Townley Rd EDUL SE22 .....30 F1
Town Md CRAWE RH11 * ...176 E6
REDH RH1 .....121 M4
Town Meadow BTFD TW8 ...17 K3
Townmead Rd FUL/PGN SW6..19 P7
RCH/KEW TW9 .....17 P7
Town Quay STA TW18 * 22 B8
Townsend La
WOKS/MYFD GU22 .....92 F1
Townsend Rd ASHF TW15 ...23 H8
Townsend La
RCH/KEW TW9 .....17 M9
Townshend Ter
RCH/KEW TW9 .....17 M9
Townshott CI GT/LBKH KT23..96 A6
Townside PI CBLY GU15 .....68 F2
Town Sq BRAK RG12 .....32 D3
Town Tree Rd ASHF TW15 ...23 K8
Town Whf ISLW TW7 * 17 H8
Towpath SHPTN TW17 .....38 C9
WOT/HER KT12 * 39 K5
Towpath Wy CROY/NA CR0..45 P5
Towton Rd WNWD SE27 .....30 D5
Toynbee Rd RYNPK SW20 ...43 J2
Toy's Hi BH/WHM TN16 .....125 N2
EDEN TN8 .....125 L7
The Tracery BNSTD SM7 ....79 M4
Tracious CI
WOKN/KNAP GU21 .....71 P5
Trafalgar Av WPK KT4 .....43 H9
Trafalgar Chambers
CHEL SW3 * 19 P3
Trafalgar Ct COB KT11 * 75 J2
FNM GU9 * 5 J5
Trafalgar Dr WOT/HER KT12..57 K2
Trafalgar Gdns KENS W8 * ..19 M1
Trafalgar Rd HORS RH12 ...192 B6
WHTN TW2 .....25 L3
Trafalgar Wy CBLY GU15 .....68 F3
CROY/NA CR0 .....45 J8
Trafford Rd FRIM GU16 .....68 F8
THHTH CR7 .....45 H6
Tramway Pth MTCM CR4 ....44 A5
Tranmere Rd
WAND/EARL SW18 .....28 F5
WHTN TW2 .....25 J3
Tranquil Dl
BRKHM/BTCW RH3 .....118 D3
Transport Av BTFD TW8 .....16 G3
Transport Rd FARN GU14 ....88 C8
Trap La NWMAL KT3 .....172 C1
Trasher Md RDKG RH5 .....137 J1
Travellers Wy HEST TW5 .....15 L7
Travis La SHST GU47 .....67 N1
Treadcroft Dr HORS RH12 ..192 D5
Treadwell Rd EPSOM KT18 ..78 D4
Treaty Centre HSLW TW3 * ...16 B8
Trebor Av FNM GU9 .....5 J6
Trebovir Rd ECT SW5 .....19 L2

Tredenham Cl FARN GU14 ....88 E7
Tredown Rd SYD SE26 ......31 K8
Tredwell Rd NRWD SE27 ....30 C7
Tree Av HASM GU27 ....184 A2
Treebourne Rd
  BH/WHM TN16 ....84 A6
Treebys Av RGUE 92 B8
Tree Cl RCHPK/HAM TW10 ...26 C1
Treelands RDKG RH5.......137 J1
Treen Av BARN SW13 ....18 C3
Treeside Cl WDR/YW UB7...13 P2
Treeside Dr FNM GU9 ......108 A7
Treetops GDST RH9........122 E8
Tree Tops Av CBLY GU15....51 J9
Treeview CRAWW RH11......194 F1
Tree View Cl NRWD SE27.....45 N2
Tree View Ct REIG RH2 * ...119 P5
Treeway REIG RH2 ....119 M2
Trefoil Cl HORS RH12 ......122 E2
Trefoil Crs CRAWW RH11....176 D9
Trefoil Rd WAND/EARL SW18 ..28 F1
Tregaron Gdns NWMAL KT3...42 C5
Tregarth Pl LHD/OX KT22 ...97 J1
Tregarths Pl
  WOKN/KNAP GU21 .....71 M6
Tregolls Dr FARN GU14 .....88 E4
Tregunter Rd WBPTN SW10 ..19 N4
Trehaven Pde REIG RH2 ....119 M8
Trehern Rd
  MORT/ESHN SW14 ......18 B8
Trelawn Cl CHERT KT16 .....54 A8
Trelawne Dr CRAN GU6 ....171 H1
Trelawney Av DTCH/LGLY SL3 ..12 B9
Trelawney Gv WEY KT13 ....56 C5
Trelawn Rd
  BRXS/STRHM SW2 ......30 B1
Treloar Gdns NRWD SE19....30 E9
Tremaine Rd PGE/AN SE20...46 B3
Tremayne Wk CBLY GU15 ....69 L4
Trenance WOKN/KNAP GU21..71 N6
Trenchard Cl WOT/HER KT12..57 L4
Trenear Cl SWTR RH13 .....192 D8
Trenham Dr WARL CR6......82 B7
Trenholme Rd PGE/AN SE20..46 B1
Trenholme Ter PGE/AN SE20..46 B1
Trent Av W5 ....17 J1
Trent Cl CRAWW RH11 .....176 C7
  FARN GU14 ....88 A1
Trentham Crs
  WOKS/MYFD GU22 .....92 C1
Trentham Rd REDH RH1 ....120 B7
Trentham St
  WAND/EARL SW18......28 D4
Trenton Cl FRIM GU16 ......69 J6
Trent Rd BRXS/STRHM SW2...30 A1
  DTCH/LGLY SL3 ....12 F4
Trent Wy WPK KT4 ....60 G2
Treport St WAND/EARL SW18 ..28 E3
Tresham Crs YTLY GU46.....66 E2
Tresillian Wy
  WOKN/KNAP GU21 .....71 N6
Tresta Wk WOKN/KNAP GU21..71 N4
Trevanion Rd WKENS W14 * ..19 J3
Trevanne Plat CRAWE RH10..177 N4
Trevelyan Rd TOOT SW17....29 H9
Trevelyan BRAK REIG RH2....119 J2
Trevereux Rd OXTED RH8...124 E3
Treville St PUT/ROE SW15...27 N3
Treviso Rd FSTH SE23 ......31 L5
Trevithick Cl
  EBED/NFELT TW14 ......24 A4
Trevor Cl HAYES BR2 ....47 M8
  ISLW TW7 ....25 N1
Trevor Rd WIM/MER SW19....43 J1
Trevose Av BF/WBF KT14....73 K3
Trewenna Dr CHSGTN KT9...59 K4
Trewince Rd RYNPK SW20...42 G2
Trewint St WAND/EARL SW18..28 F5
Trewsbury Rd SYD SE26.....31 L8
Treyford Cl CRAWW RH11...176 C5
The Triangle NWMAL KT3....42 A3
  WOKN/KNAP GU21 .....72 A7
Trident Pl CHEL SW3 * 19 P4
Trident Wy NWDGN UB2 ....15 K1
Trigg's Cl WOKS/MYFD GU22..10 A7
Trigg's La WOKN/KNAP GU21..72 A7
Trig St RDKG RH5.........156 D4
Trilby Rd FSTH SE23 ....31 L5
Trimmers Cl FNM GU9 .....107 M7
Trimmers Fld FNM GU9 ....128 A4
Trimmers Wd GSHT GU26...165 N5
Trindledown BNFD RG42 ....32 C1
Trindles Rd REDH RH1 .....121 H7
Tringham Cl CHERT KT16....54 A4
  WOKN/KNAP GU21 .....71 J7
Trinity SHST GU47 ....50 B9
Trinity Church Rd
  BARN SW13 ....18 F4
Trinity Churchyard GU GU1 *..7 F4
Trinity Cl CRAWE RH10 ....177 M3
  HSLWW TW4 ....15 N8
  SAND/SEL CR2.........63 N6
  STWL/WRAY TW19 ......23 J2
Trinity Crs ASC SL5 ....34 G6
  TOOT SW17 ....29 J5
Trinity Flds FNM GU9 .....107 L8
Trinity Hl FNM GU9 ......107 L8
Trinity Ms PGE/AN SE20 * ...46 C2
Trinity Pde HSLW TW3 * 16 B8
Trinity Ri BRXS/STRHM SW2 ..30 B3
Trinity Rd RCH/KEW TW9 * ..17 M8
  TOOT SW17 ....29 J5
  WAND/EARL SW18......28 F3
  WIM/MER SW19 ....28 C9
  WOKN/KNAP GU21 .....71 H7
Tritton Av CROY/NA CRO 62 G3
Tritton Rd WNWD SE27.....30 E6
Tritons KWD/TDW/WH KT20..98 D6
Triumph Cl HYS/HAR UB3...14 E5
Trodds La GU GU1 ....113 K6

Trojan Wy CROY/NA CRO 63 H2
Troon Cl CRAWW RH11.....176 A6
Trossachs Rd EDUL SE22....30 F1
Trotsford Meadow
  BLKW GU17 ....67 N4
Trotsworth Av VW GU25.....36 C5
Trotters La CHOB/PIR GU24...71 P1
Trotter Wy HOR/WEW KT19...77 H1
Trotton Cl CRAWE RH10....177 M8
Trotts La BH/WHM TN16 ....104 G7
Trott St BTSEA SW11........19 P6
Trotwood Cl SHST GU47 ....50 A9
Trout Rd HASM GU27 ......183 P4
Trouville Rd CLAP SW4......29 M2
Trowers Wy REDH RH1 .....120 D2
Trowlock Av TEDD TW11 ....26 C9
Trowlock Island TEDD TW11 ..26 C9
Trowlock Wy TEDD TW11....26 B9
Troy Cl KENS W8 ....19 L1
Troy La EDEN TN8 ....144 D1
Troy Rd NRWD SE19 ....30 E9
Trubshaw Rd NWDGN UB2...16 A1
Trumball Rd BNFD RG42 ....32 C1
Trumpers Wy HNWL W7.....16 F1
Trumpetshill Rd REIG RH1...118 E6
Trumpsgreen Av VW GU25...36 B5
Trumps Green Cl VW GU25...36 C6
Trumpsgreen Rd VW GU25...36 A9
Trumps Mill La VW GU25 ....36 D6
Trundle Md HORS RH12 ....192 B5
Trunk Rd FARN GU14.......87 N3
Trunley Heath Rd SHGR GU5..152 A9
Truslove Rd WNWD SE27....30 A1
Truss Hill Rd ASC SL5......34 C6
Trussley Rd HMSMTH W6....18 G1
Tryplets FLEETS GU52......106 D3
Trys Hill Longcross Rd
  CHERT KT16..........54 C2
Trystings Cl ESH/CLAY KT10..58 G3
Tucker Rd CHERT KT16 .....55 H5
Tuckers Dr CRAN GU6......152 E9
Tuckey Gv RPLY/SEND GU23..93 K4
Tudor Av HPTN TW12 ......25 H4
  WPK KT4 ....60 F2
Tudor Cir GODL GU7 ......131 L6
Tudor Cl ASHF TW15 ......23 H7
  BNSTD SM7 ....79 J4
  BRXS/STRHM SW2 * 30 A2
  CHEAM SM3 ....61 H4
  CHSGTN KT9 ....59 L4
  COB KT11 ....75 P2
  COUL/CHIP CR5 ....81 J7
  CRAWE RH10 ....177 N6
  EGRIN RH19 ....180 E4
  GSHT GU26..........165 N9
  GT/LBKH KT23 ....95 P4
  HORL RH6 ....160 C1
  HPTN TW12 ....25 K4
  SAND/SEL CR2.........63 N6
  WLGTN SM6 ....62 E6
  WOKS/MYFD GU22 .....11 G5
Tudor Ct KUTN/CMB KT2 ....26 D8
  MRDN SM4 ....43 H7
  MRDN SM4 ....43 K8
  WHTN TW2 * 25 N3
  YTLY GU46 ....67 H3
Tudor Dr KUTN/CMB KT2 ....26 D8
  MRDN SM4 ....43 H7
Tudor Gdns BARN SW13 ....18 C8
  TWK TW1 ....25 N4
  WWKM BR4 ....65 J2
Tudor La WDSR SL4 ....21 H3
Tudor Pl NRWD SE19 * 45 P1
  WIM/MER SW19 ....44 A1
Tudor Rd ASHF TW15.......23 N9
  BECK BR3 ....47 J4
  GODL GU7 ....131 L6
  HPTN TW12 ....40 A1
  HSLW TW3 ....16 D9
  KUTN/CMB KT2 ....9 H1
  NRWD SE19 ....45 P1
  PGE/AN SE20 ....46 D4
  SNWD SE25 ....46 B6
The Tudors REIG RH2 * 119 N2
Tudor Wk LHD/OX KT22 ....76 D9
Tudor Wy FLEETS GU52.....106 C2
Tuesley Cnr GODL GU7 ....150 C1
Tuesley La GODL GU7 .....150 C1
Tufton Gdns E/WMO/HCT KT8..40 B3
Tugela Rd CROY/NA CRO 45 M3
Tugela St CAT SE6 ....31 N5
Tuggles Plat HORS RH12 ...191 M3
Tulip Cl CROY/NA CRO 46 D9
  HPTN TW12 ....24 G9
Tulip Ct HORS RH12 * 192 B6
Tulip Wy WDR/YW UB7.....13 N3
Tulleth Rd CRAWE RH10 ...177 L9
Tulls La BOR GU35 ....164 A9
Tull St MTCM CR4 ....44 B8
Tulse Cl BECK BR3 ....47 J4
Tulse Hl BRXS/STRHM SW2...30 C4
Tulsemere Rd NRWD SE27...30 D5
Tulyar Cl KWD/TDW/WH KT20..78 F9
Tumber St EPSOM KT18 ....98 A5
Tumblewood Rd BNSTD SM7..79 J5
Tumbling Bay WOT/HER KT12..39 J7
Tummons Gdns SNWD SE25..45 N3
Tunbridge Crs LIPH GU30...182 E5
Tunbridge La LIPH GU30 ...182 E5
Tunley Rd BAL SW12.......29 K5
Tunnel Link Rd HTHAIR TW6..23 K1
Tunnel Rd FARN GU14 ......88 B4
Tunnel Rd East WDR/YW UB7..14 D5
Tunnel Rd West
  WDR/YW UB7 ....14 C6
Tunnel Av MEATH NWMAL...176 D6
Tunstall Rd CROY/NA CRO....3 F6
Tunstall Wy GU GU1 * 7 E6
Tunworth Cl FLEETS GU51...86 E3
Tunworth Crs PUT/ROE SW15..27 L2
Tupwood La CTHM CR3.....102 A9
Tupwood Scrubs Rd
  CTHM CR3 ....82 A9
  GDST RH9 ....102 A8

Turene Cl BTSEA SW11 .....19 N9
Turf Hill Rd CBLY GU15 .....51 H9
Turle Rd STRHM/NOR SW16..44 G2
Turing Dr BRAK RG12 ......32 C6
Turkey Oak La NRWD SE19...45 N2
Turle Rd STRHM/NOR SW16..44 G3
Tumberry BRAK RG12.......32 A7
Turner Av MTCM CR4 ......44 B2
  WHTN TW2 ....25 K6
Turner Cl RGUE GU4 ......112 D2
Turner Ct EGRIN RH19 ....162 F9
Turner Pl SHST GU47 ......67 P2
Turner Rd BH/WHM TN16 ...84 A1
  NWMAL KT3 ....42 B8
Turners Cl STA TW18 ......22 E8
Turner's Green La
  HTWY RG27 ....86 D2
Turners Hill Rd CRAWE RH10..160 C9
  CRAWE RH10 ....179 N2
  EGRIN RH19 ....179 P6
Turners La WOT/HER KT12...57 K5
Turners Md MFD/CHID GU8..148 C3
Turners Meadow Wy
  BECK BR3 ....46 F2
Turners Wy CROY/NA CRO....63 J1
Turneville Rd WKENS W14 ...19 K4
Tumey Rd DUL SE21 ....30 D3
Turnham Cl GUW GU2 .....112 A9
Turnham Green Ter
  CHSWK W4 ....18 C2
Turnham Rd BROCKY SE4 ...31 M1
Turnoak Av
  WOKS/MYFD GU22 .....72 C9
Turnoak La
  WOKS/MYFD GU22 .....72 C9
Turnpike La SUT SM1......61 N4
Turnpike Link CROY/NA CRO...3 K4
Turnpike Pl CRAWW RH11...176 C3
Turnpike Wy ISLW TW7 .....16 G6
Turnstone Cl SAND/SEL CR2..64 E8
Turnstone End YTLY GU46...66 F3
Turnville Cl LTWR GU18 ....52 A2
Turpin Rd EBED/NFELT TW14..24 A2
Turpins Ri BFOR GU20 .....52 B3
Turpin Wy WLGTN SM6 .....62 D6
Turtledove Av CRAWE RH10..179 K6
Tuscany Gdns CRAWE RH10..177 H3
Tushmore Av CRAWE RH10 * ..177 J3
Tushmore Crs CRAWE RH10..177 H3
Tushmore La CRAWE RH10...177 H2
Tussock Cl CRAWW RH11...176 D7
Tuxford Cl CRAWE RH10....177 M7
Tweed Cl FARN GU14.......88 A1
Tweeddale Rd CAR SM5.....43 P9
Tweed La
  BRKHM/BTCW RH3 ....137 M9
  CRAWW RH11 ....176 C2
Tweed Rd DTCH/LGLY SL3...12 F4
Tweedsmuir Cl FARN GU14...87 P4
Tweedy Rd BMLY BR1 ......47 N2
Twelve Acre Cl GT/LBKH KT23..95 P4
Twelve Acres Crs FARN GU14..87 P2
Twelve Av
  KWD/TDW/WH KT20 *...99 K6
Tweseldown Rd
  FLEETS GU52 ....107 H2
Twickenham Br TWK TW1....26 C1
Twickenham Cl CROY/NA CRO..63 H2
Twickenham Rd FELT TW13...25 J6
  ISLW TW7 ....16 G9
  RCH/KEW TW9 ....26 B1
  TEDD TW11 ....25 P8
Twilley St WAND/EARL SW18..28 E3
Twining Av WHTN TW2......25 K6
Twinoaks COB KT11 ....76 B2
Twisell Thorne FLEETS GU52..106 E2
Twitten La EGRIN RH19 ....161 M8
The Twitten CRAWW RH11...176 F5
  LING RH7 * 143 K9
Two Ways BIL RH14 ....188 D6
Twycross Rd GODL GU7 ....131 K6
Twyford La WARL CR6 ......82 C8
Twyford Rd CAR SM5.......43 P9
Twyhurst Ct EGRIN RH19 ...162 C9
Twyne Cl CRAWW RH11 ....176 C7
Twyner Cl HORL RH6.......140 F9
Twynersh Av CHERT KT16....37 K7
Tybenham Rd
  WIM/MER SW19 ....43 L4
Tychbourne Dr RGUE GU4...112 G2
Tydcombe Rd WARL CR6....82 C8
Tylden Wy HORS RH12 .....192 E4
Tylecroft Rd
  STRHM/NOR SW16......44 G3
Tylehost GUW GU2 ....112 A2
Tyler Gdns ADL/WDHM KT15..55 N5
Tyler Rd CRAWE RH10 .....176 G8
Tylers Cl GDST RH9 ....122 B1
Tylers Ct CRAN GU6 * 152 C9
Tylney Av NRWD SE19 .....30 G8
Tylston Meadow LIPH GU30..182 E5
Tymperley Ct SWTR RH13 * ..192 D3
Tynamara KUTN/CMB KT2 *...8 B8
Tyndalls GSHT GU26.......165 N8
Tynedale Cl CRAWW RH11...176 F1
Tyne Cl CRAWE RH10 .....177 M6
  FARN GU14 ....88 A1
Tynedale Rd
  BRKHM/BTCW RH3 ....117 P9
Tynemoth Rd MTCM CR4....44 D7
Tynemouth St FUL/PGN SW6..19 N7
Tynley Gv RGUE GU4.......92 B8
Tyrawley Rd FUL/PGN SW6..19 M6
Tyrwhitt Av GUW GU2 .....111 P1
Tyson Gdns FSTH SE23 * ...31 K3
Tyson Rd FSTH SE23 ......31 K3
Tythebarn Cl RGUE GU4....92 F9
Tythebarns La
  RPLY/SEND GU23 ......93 L6
Tytherton BRAK RG12......32 E3

U

Uckfield Gv MTCM CR4 .....44 C2
Uckfield La EDEN TN8 .....145 N8
Udney Park Rd TEDD TW11...25 P8
Uffington Dr BRAK RG12 ....32 G5
Uffington Rd WNWD SE27...30 B7
Ullathorne Rd
  STRHM/NOR SW16......29 M7
Ullswater Av FARN GU14....88 A4
Ullswater Cl FNM GU9 .....107 L8
  KUTN/CMB KT2 * 8 B2
  LTWR GU18..........52 B8
Ullswater Crs
  COUL/CHIP CR5 ....80 C5
  PUT/ROE SW15 ....27 J7
Ullswater Rd BARN SW13....18 E5
  LTWR GU18..........52 C6
  WNWD SE27 ....30 C6
Ulstan Cl CTHM CR3 ......102 G3
Ulva Rd PUT/ROE SW15 ....19 H9
Ulverscroft Rd EDUL SE22...31 H1
Ulwyn Av BF/WBF KT14.....74 A2
Umbria St PUT/ROE SW15...27 M2
Underhill Cl GODL GU7 ....150 D1
Underhill La FNM GU9 ....127 M6
Underhill Park Rd REIG RH2..119 L2
Underhill Rd EDUL SE22....31 H1
  RDKG RH5 ....156 G3
Underwood BRAK RG12.....32 A7
  CROY/NA CRO 65 J4
Underwood Av ASHV GU12..108 G5
Underwood Cl CRAWE RH10..179 J3
Underwood Ct CTHM CR3...101 N5
Underwood Rd CTHM CR3...101 N5
  HASM GU27 ....184 A3
Undine St TOOT SW17 .....29 J8
Union Cl SHST GU47 ......50 A9
Union Rd CROY/NA CRO 45 L8
  FRIM GU16 ....69 M8
  FARN GU14 ....88 C3
Union St ALDT GU11 ......108 C4
  CHOB/PIR GU24 ....90 A1
  FARN GU14 ....88 C3
  KUT KT1 ....8 D5
Unity Cl CROY/NA CRO 65 H7
  WNWD SE27 ....30 D8
University Rd
  WIM/MER SW19 ....28 G9
Unstead La SHGR GU5 ....132 A6
Unwin Av EBED/NFELT TW14..13 P8
Unwin Rd ISLW TW7 ....16 E8
  SKENS SW7 ....19 P1
Upavon Gdns BRAK RG12...33 H6
Upcerne Rd WBPTN SW10...19 N5
Updown Hl BFOR GU20.....52 D5
Upfield CROY/NA CRO 64 B1
  HORL RH6 ....159 K3
Upfield Cl HORL RH6 .....159 K4
Upfold Cl CRAN GU6......152 B5
Upfold La CRAN GU6 .....152 F7
Upfolds Gn RGUE GU4 ....112 G1
Upham Park Rd CHSWK W4..18 C2
Upland Rd BELMT SM2.....61 P8
  CBLY GU15 ....68 F1
  CTHM CR3 ....82 G9
  EDUL SE22 ....31 H1
  SAND/SEL CR2.........63 M4
Uplands ASHTD KT21 ......77 K9
  BECK BR3 ....46 G3
Uplands Cl HASM GU27....184 E2
  MORT/ESHN SW14......26 C1
  SHST GU47 ....49 M9
Uplands Dr LHD/OX KT22...76 D3
Uplands Rd FNM GU9 .....128 A4
  PUR/KEN CR8 ....81 L6
Upland Wy EPSOM KT18....78 G7
Uppark Gdns HORS RH12...192 E4
Upper Beulah Hl NRWD SE19..45 N2
Upper Bourne La
  RFNM GU10 ....127 L8
Upper Bourne V
  RFNM GU10 ....127 L8
Upper Bridge Rd REDH RH1..120 A5
Upper Brighton Rd
  SURB KT6 ....41 L8
Upper Broadmoor Rd
  CWTH RG45 ....49 N4
Upper Butts BTFD TW8.....17 J4
Upper Charles St CBLY GU15..68 E3
Upper Chobham Rd
  CBLY GU15 ....69 K4
Upper Church La FNM GU9...5 F4
Upper Cl FROW RH18 .....181 L9
Upper College Ride
  CBLY GU15 ....50 G9
Upper Court Rd CTHM CR3..102 C3
  HOR/WEW KT19 ....60 A7
Upper Dartrey Wk
  WBPTN SW10 * 19 N5
Upper Dr BH/WHM TN16 ...84 A7
Upper Dunnymans
  BNSTD SM7 ....79 K3
Upper Edgeborough Rd
  GU GU1 ....7 K5
Upper Elmers End Rd
  BECK BR3 ....46 E5
Upper Elms Rd
  ALDT GU11 ....108 C5
Upper Fairfield Rd
  LHD/OX KT22 ....97 H1
Upper Farm Rd
  E/WMO/HCT KT8........39 P5

Upper Forecourt HORL RH6..159 L5
Upper Gordon Rd CBLY GU15..68 F3
Upper Gn East MTCM CR4...44 B4
Upper Gn West MTCM CR4...44 B3
Upper Grotto Rd TWK TW1 ..25 N5
Upper Gv SNWD SE25 .....45 N5
Upper Guildown Rd
  GUW GU2 ....111 P8
Upper Hale Rd FNM GU9...107 M7
Upper Halliford Rd
  SHPTN TW17 ....38 G4
Upper Ham Rd
  RCHPK/HAM TW10 .....26 C7
Upper Harestone CTHM CR3..102 A7
Upper High St EW KT17.....78 C2
Upper House La SHGR GU5..152 C3
Upper Kiln DORK RH4 * 117 J9
Upper Manor Rd GODL GU7..131 L6
  MFD/CHID GU8 ....149 M3
Upper Mt HASM GU27 .....184 G1
Upper Mulgrave Rd
  BELMT SM2 ....61 J6
Upper Old Park La FNM GU9..107 K9
Upper Park Rd BMLY BR1....47 P2
  CBLY GU15 ....68 F3
  KUTN/CMB KT2 ....26 F9
Upper Pth DORK RH4 * 117 J9
Upper Pillory Down CAR SM5..80 C2
Upper Pines BNSTD SM7 ...80 B6
Upper Pinewood Rd
  ASHV GU12 ....109 L3
Upper Queen St GODL GU7..131 L9
Upper Richmond Rd
  PUT/ROE SW15 ....18 F9
Upper Richmond Rd West
  RCHPK/HAM TW10 .....17 N9
Upper Rd WLGTN SM6 .....62 F4
Upper Rose Hl DORK RH4...117 H8
Upper St Michael's Rd
  ALDT GU11 ....108 D6
Upper Sawleywood
  BNSTD SM7 * 79 K3
Upper School Dr
  HASM GU27 ....184 A5
Upper Selsdon Rd
  SAND/SEL CR2.........63 P7
Upper Shirley Rd
  CROY/NA CRO 64 C2
Upper South Vw FNM GU9...5 G2
Upper Springfield
  MFD/CHID GU8 ....129 M9
Upper Sq ISLW TW7 ....16 G8
Upper Stanford Rd
  CHOB/PIR GU24 ....90 F5
Upper St FLEETS GU51 .....86 F6
  SHGR GU5 ....114 B9
Upper Sunbury Rd
  HPTN TW12 ....39 P2
Upper Sutton La HEST TW5...16 A6
Upper Teddington Rd KUT KT1..41 J2
Upper Terrace Rd FARN GU14..88 C7
Upper Tooting Pk
  TOOT SW17 ....29 J5
Upper Tooting Rd
  TOOT SW17 ....29 J7
Upper Tulse Hl
  BRXS/STRHM SW2 ......30 A3
Upper Union St ALDT GU11..108 B4
Upper Union Ter
  ALDT GU11 ....108 C4
Upper Vann La
  MFD/CHID GU8 ....168 F2
Upper Vernon Rd SUT SM1...61 P4
Upper Verran Rd CBLY GU15..69 H5
Upper Village Rd ASC SL5...34 C6
Upper Wk VW GU25 ....36 C5
Upper Wy FNM GU9 ......127 M5
Upper West St REIG RH2...119 K5
Upper Weybourne La
  FNM GU9 ....107 P6
Upper Whistler Wk
  WBPTN SW10 * 19 N5
Upper Woodcote Village
  PUR/KEN CR8 ....80 F2
Upshire Gdns BRAK RG12...33 H5
Upshott La
  WOKS/MYFD GU22 .....73 K6
Upton WOKN/KNAP GU21...71 P6
Upton Cl FARN GU14.......88 B5
Upton Dene BELMT SM2 ....61 M6
Upton Rd HSLW TW3 ......15 P8
  THHTH CR7 ....45 M7
Upwood Rd
  STRHM/NOR SW16......44 G2
Urmston Dr WIM/MER SW19..28 A4
Usherwood Cl
  KWD/TDW/WH KT20....118 A2
Usk Rd BTSEA SW11.......19 N9
Uvedale Cl CROY/NA CRO....65 K9
Uvedale Crs CROY/NA CRO...65 K9
Uvedale Rd OXTED RH8....103 M9
Uxbridge Rd WBPTN SW10..19 N5
  HPTN TW12 ....25 H8
  SURB KT6 ....41 K5

V

Vachery La CRAN GU6 .....171 J3
Vaillant Rd WEY KT13 ......56 E3
Vale Lane HAYES BR2......47 L4
Vale Cl COUL/CHIP CR5....81 H2
  RFNM GU10 ....127 N9
  TWK TW1 * 25 P6
  WEY KT13 ....56 F2

WOKN/KNAP GU21 10 C1
Vale Cottages
PUT/ROE SW15 * 27 K6
Vale Ct WEY KT13 56 F2
Vale Crs PUT/ROE SW15 27 K7
Vale Cft ESH/CLAY KT10 58 F6
Vale Dr HORS RH12 192 A8
Vale Farm Rd
WOKN/KNAP GU21 10 C4
Valentyne Cl CROY/NA CR0 65 L9
Vale Rd ASHV GU12 89 J8
CBLY GU15 68 C4
ESH/CLAY KT10 58 E7
MTCM CR4 44 F4
SUT SM1 61 M3
WEY KT13 56 F2
WPK KT4 60 D2
Vale Rd North SURB KT6 59 L1
The Vale CHEL SW3 19 P4
COUL/CHIP CR5 80 G3
CROY/NA CR0 64 D1
EBED/NFELT TW14 24 C2
HEST TW5 15 N4
SUN TW16 * 24 B9
Vale Wood Dr RFNM GU10 127 P9
Vale Wood La GSHT GU26 165 M7
Valewood Rd HASM GU27 184 D6
Valiant Wy FARN GU14 87 P7
Valley End Rd
CHOB/PIR GU24 53 H5
Valleyfield Rd
STRHM/NOR SW16 30 A8
Valley Gdns WIM/MER SW19 43 P1
Valley La FNM GU9 127 N6
Valley Rd FRIM GU16 69 L8
HAYES BR2 47 L3
PUR/KEN CR8 81 M4
STRHM/NOR SW16 30 A7
Valley Side LIPH GU30 182 E5
Valley Vw BH/WHM TN16 84 A7
GODL GU7 131 K9
SHST GU47 67 L1
Valley View Gdns
PUR/KEN CR8 81 N4
Valley Wk CROY/NA CR0 64 C1
Vallis Wy CHSGTN KT9 59 K3
Valnay St TOOT SW17 29 J8
Valonia Gdns
WAND/EARL SW18 28 C2
Valroy Cl CBLY GU15 68 F2
Vampire Wy FARN GU14 88 A7
Vanbrugh Cl CRAWW RH11 176 B8
Vanbrugh Dr WOT/HER KT12 39 L8
Vanbrugh Rd CHSWK W4 18 B1
Vancouver Cl
HOR/WEW KT19 60 A9
Vancouver Ct HORL RH6 160 B1
Vancouver Dr
CRAWW RH11 176 G2
Vancouver Rd FSTH SE23 31 M5
RCHPK/HAM TW10 26 B7
Vanderbilt Rd
WAND/EARL SW18 28 E4
Van Dyck Av NWMAL KT3 42 B8
Vandyke BRAK RG12 32 A7
Vandyke Cl PUT/ROE SW15 28 A2
REDH RH1 120 B3
Vanguard Cl CROY/NA CR0 2 A2
Vanguard Wy CROY/NA CR0 3 J7
EDEN TN8 124 E5
EDEN TN8 144 C7
EGRIN RH19 163 L7
HTHAIR TW6 14 G7
LING RH7 163 M4
OXTED RH8 103 N6
WARL CR6 82 F2
WLGTN SM6 62 G6
Vanneck Sq PUT/ROE SW15 * 27 M1
Vanners CRAWE RH10 177 H4
Vanners Pde BF/WBF KT14 * 74 A2
Vann Farm Rd RDKG RH5 155 M8
Vann Lake RDKG RH5 155 N8
Vann Lake Rd RDKG RH5 155 N9
Vann La MFD/CHID GU8 168 C2
Vanston Pl FUL/PGN SW6 19 L5
Vantage Pl KENS W8 19 L1
Vant Rd TOOT SW17 29 J8
Vapery La CHOB/PIR GU24 90 D1
Vardens Rd BTSEA SW11 19 P9
Varley Wy MTCM CR4 43 P3
Varna Rd FUL/PGN SW6 19 J5
HPTN TW12 * 40 B2
Varney Cl FARN GU14 88 A2
Varsity Dr TWK TW1 25 N1
Varsity Rw
MORT/ESHN SW14 18 A7
Vaughan Av HMSMTH W6 18 D2
Vaughan Rd THDIT KT7 41 H8
Vaughan Wy DORK RH4 116 G7
Vaux Crs WOT/HER KT12 57 K5
Vauxhall Gdns SAND/SEL CR2 63 L5
Veals Md MTCM CR4 44 A2
Vectis Gdns TOOT SW17 29 L9
Vectis Rd TOOT SW17 29 L9
Vegal Crs EGH TW20 21 H8
Vellum Dr CAR SM5 62 C2
Velmead Cl FLEETS GU52 87 H8
Velmead Rd FLEETS GU52 86 G8
Vencourt Pl HMSMTH W6 18 E3
Venner Rd SYD SE26 31 K9
Ventnor Rd BELMT SM2 61 M6
Ventnor Ter ASHV GU12 108 E5
Venton Cl WOKN/KNAP GU21 71 P6
Vera Rd FUL/PGN SW6 19 J6
Verbania Wy EGRIN RH19 180 G2
Verbena Cl WDR/YW UB7 13 P3
Verbena Gdns HMSMTH W6 18 E3
Verdayne Av CROY/NA CR0 46 D9
Verdayne Gdns WARL CR6 82 C5
Verdun Rd BARN SW13 18 E5
Vereker Dr SUN TW16 39 J4
Vereker Rd WKENS W14 * 19 J3
Verge Wk ALDT GU11 108 C7
Vermont Rd NRWD SE19 30 E9
SUT SM1 61 M2
WAND/EARL SW18 28 E2
Vermont Woods EWKG RG40 48 C2
Verner Cl BOR GU35 164 B7
The Verne FLEETS GU52 106 G1
Verney Rd DTCH/LGLY SL3 12 E2
Vernon Av RYNPK SW20 43 H3
Vernon Cl CHERT KT16 55 H5
HOR/WEW KT19 60 A5
HORS RH12 192 F6
Vernon Dr ASC SL5 33 M3
CTHM CR3 101 L2
Vernon Rd FELT TW13 24 A5
MORT/ESHN SW14 18 B8
SUT SM1 61 N4
Vernon St WKENS W14 19 J2
Vernon Wk
KWD/TDW/WH KT20 79 H9
Vernon Wy GUW GU2 111 M4
Verona Dr SURB KT6 59 L1
Veronica Dr FLEETN GU51 106 D1
Veronica Gdns MTCM CR4 44 E2
Veronica Rd TOOT SW17 29 L6
Verralls WOKS/MYFD GU22 11 K3
Verran Rd BAL SW12 * 29 L3
CBLY GU15 68 F6
Versailles Rd PGE/AN SE20 46 A1
Verulam Av PUR/KEN CR8 80 E1
Veryan WOKN/KNAP GU21 71 N6
Vesey Cl FARN GU14 88 C2
Vestris Rd FSTH SE23 31 L5
Vevers Rd REIG RH2 119 M8
Vevey St FSTH SE23 31 N5
Vibart Gdns
BRXS/STRHM SW2 30 A3
Vibia Cl STWL/WRAY TW19 22 G3
Viburnum Ct CHOB/PIR GU24 70 E2
Vicarage Av EGH TW20 21 N9
Vicarage Cl EWKG RG40 48 D3
FNM GU9 127 P6
GT/LBKH KT23 96 A5
KWD/TDW/WH KT20 99 J4
LING RH7 143 K9
WPK KT4 42 C9
Vicarage Ct BECK BR3 * 46 E4
EGH TW20 21 N9
Vicarage Crs BTSEA SW11 19 P7
EGH TW20 21 N8
Vicarage Dr BECK BR3 46 G2
MORT/ESHN SW14 27 J1
Vicarage Farm Rd HEST TW5 15 N6
Vicarage Flds WOT/HER KT12 39 L7
Vicarage Gdns ASC SL5 34 A6
FLEETS GU52 106 F2
GSHT GU26 165 M8
MTCM CR4 44 A4
Vicarage Ga GUW GU2 111 N7
Vicarage Gate Ms
KWD/TDW/WH KT20 * 99 J4
Vicarage Hl BH/WHM TN16 105 H6
FNM GU9 127 P6
Vicarage La FNM GU9 5 F4
FNM GU9 127 P6
HASM GU27 184 A4
HORL RH6 140 B9
LHD/OX KT22 97 H2
RDKG RH5 156 C6
RPLY/SEND GU23 92 G6
STA TW18 37 M4
STWL/WRAY TW19 21 K4
YTLY GU46 66 G1
Vicarage Ms CHSWK W4 * 18 C4
Vicarage Rd BFOR GU20 51 L6
BLKW GU17 68 A4
CHOB/PIR GU24 53 K9
CRAWE RH10 179 H4
CROY/NA CR0 63 J2
E/WMO/HCT KT8 41 J2
EGH TW20 21 N8
KUT KT1 8 C4
LING RH7 143 K9
MORT/ESHN SW14 27 H1
STA TW18 22 B7
SUN TW16 24 A9
SUT SM1 61 L3
TEDD TW11 25 P8
WHTN TW2 25 K2
WHTN TW2 25 M5
WOKS/MYFD GU22 92 D1
YTLY GU46 66 G1
Vicarage Wk BTSEA SW11 * 19 P6
Vicarage Wy DTCH/LGLY SL3 13 H5
Vicars Oak Rd NRWD SE19 30 F9
Vickers Cl CROY/NA CR0 63 H6
Vickers Dr North WEY KT13 56 A8
Vickers Dr South WEY KT13 56 A9
Vickers Rd ASHV GU12 109 H1
Victoria Av CBLY GU15 68 C3
E/WMO/HCT KT8 40 B4
HSLW TW3 25 H1
SAND/SEL CR2 63 L8
SURB KT6 41 K7
WLGTN SM6 62 C2
Victoria Cl E/WMO/HCT KT8 40 A4
HORL RH6 159 K1
WEY KT13 56 F2
Victoria Cottages
RCH/KEW TW9 17 M6
Victoria Ct BAGS GU19 51 N8
RGUE GU4 * 132 C2
Victoria Crs NRWD SE19 30 F9
WIM/MER SW19 * 43 K1
Victoria Dr BLKW GU17 67 N4
WIM/MER SW19 28 A4
Victoria Gdns BH/WHM TN16 84 A4
FLEETN GU51 * 86 F6
HEST TW5 15 N6
Victoria Gv KENS W8 19 N1
Victoria Hill Rd FLEETN GU51 86 E6
Victoria La HYS/HAR UB3 14 F3
Victoria Ms FLEETN GU51 * 86 F6
WAND/EARL SW18 28 F4
Victoria Pde FLEETN GU51 * 86 F6
RCH/KEW TW9 * 17 N6
Victoria Pl EW KT17 78 C1
RCHPK/HAM TW10 26 C1
Victoria Rd ADL/WDHM KT15 55 P3
ALDT GU11 108 C4
ASC SL5 34 B6
COUL/CHIP CR5 80 F4
CRAN GU6 152 G9
CRAWW RH11 176 F5
EDEN TN8 144 G5
FARN GU14 88 D3
FELT TW13 24 C4
FLEETN GU51 86 E6
FNM GU9 5 G4
GODL GU7 131 L9
GU GU1 7 G4
HORL RH6 159 K1
KENS W8 19 N1
KUT KT1 9 G5
MORT/ESHN SW14 18 B8
MTCM CR4 44 A1
NWDGN UB2 15 P1
REDH RH1 120 C6
SHST GU47 50 A8
STA TW18 22 B6
SURB KT6 41 K7
SUT SM1 61 P4
TEDD TW11 25 P9
TWK TW1 26 A3
WEY KT13 56 F2
WOKN/KNAP GU21 71 K6
WOKS/MYFD GU22 10 D4
Victoria St EGH TW20 21 H9
SWTR RH13 192 C8
Victoria Ter DORK RH4 * 116 G7
Victoria Tr ALDT GU11 87 P8
Victoria Vls RCH/KEW TW9 17 M8
Victoria Wy EGRIN RH19 180 E4
WEY KT13 56 F2
WOKN/KNAP GU21 10 D4
Victor Rd PGE/AN SE20 46 D1
TEDD TW11 25 M8
Victors Dr HPTN TW12 * 24 F9
Victor Wy FARN GU14 87 N7
Victory Av MRDN SM4 43 N6
Victory Park Rd
ADL/WDHM KT15 55 N3
Victory Pl NRWD SE19 * 30 F9
Victory Rd CHERT KT16 37 L9
HORS RH12 192 A7
WIM/MER SW19 43 N1
Victory Wy HEST TW5 15 L3
View Cl BH/WHM TN16 84 A5
Viewfield Rd
WAND/EARL SW18 28 C2
Viewlands Av
BH/WHM TN16 85 J9
View Ter LING RH7 162 F4
Viggory La
WOKN/KNAP GU21 71 P4
Vigilant Cl SYD SE26 31 H7
Vigo La YTLY GU46 66 G3
Viking BRAK RG12 32 A6
Village Cl WEY KT13 56 F2
Village Gdns EW KT17 60 D8
Village Green Av
BH/WHM TN16 84 C6
Village Green Wy
BH/WHM TN16 84 C6
Village Rd EGH TW20 36 G4
Village Rw BELMT SM2 61 L6
Village St RDKG RH5 156 G3
The Village EWKG RG40 48 C6
WDSR SL4 * 20 A5
Village Wy ASHF TW15 23 J7
BECK BR3 46 G5
HNHL SE24 30 E2
SAND/SEL CR2 82 A2
YTLY GU46 67 H1
Villiers Av BRYLDS KT5 41 M6
WHTN TW2 24 G4
Villiers Cl BRYLDS KT5 41 M5
Villiers Gv BELMT SM2 61 H7
Villiers Rd BECK BR3 46 D3
ISLW TW7 16 E7
KUT KT1 9 F7
The Villiers WEY KT13 * 56 F5
Vinall Gdns HORS RH12 191 L6
Vincam Cl WHTN TW2 25 H3
Vincennes Est WNWD SE27 30 E7
Vincent Av BRYLDS KT5 41 P9
CAR SM5 61 P9
Vincent Cl CHERT KT16 37 J8
ESH/CLAY KT10 58 B2
GT/LBKH KT23 96 B3
HAYES BR2 47 P5
SWTR RH13 192 D8
WDR/YW UB7 14 C4
Vincent Dr DORK RH4 116 G8
SHPTN TW17 38 G4
Vincent La DORK RH4 116 G7
Vincent Ri BRAK RG12 32 G4
Vincent Rd ACT W3 18 A1
CHERT KT16 37 J8
COB KT11 75 N5
COUL/CHIP CR5 80 E5
CROY/NA CR0 45 N8
DORK RH4 116 G7
HSLWW TW4 15 M8
ISLW TW7 16 D6
KUT KT1 9 J6
Vincent Rw HPTN TW12 25 K9
Vincents Cl COUL/CHIP CR5 80 B9
Vincent Sq BH/WHM TN16 84 A2
Vincent Wk DORK RH4 * 116 G7
Vine Cl ALDT GU11 88 C9
BRYLDS KT5 41 M7
RFNM GU10 127 L9
RGUW GU3 91 K6
STWL/WRAY TW19 22 D1
SUT SM1 61 N2
WDR/YW UB7 14 C2
Vine House Cl FRIM GU16 89 J4
Vine Pl HSLW TW3 16 B9
Vineries Cl WDR/YW UB7 14 C4
The Vineries CAT SE6 * 31 P4
Vine Rd BARN SW13 18 D8
E/WMO/HCT KT8 40 C5
Vine Rw RCHPK/HAM TW10 * 26 D1
Viners Cl WOT/HER KT12 39 L7
Vine Sq WKENS W14 * 19 K3
Vine St ALDT GU11 108 C5
Vine Wy RFNM GU10 127 L8
Vineyard Cl CAT SE6 31 P4
KUT KT1 9 F6
Vineyard Hill Rd
WIM/MER SW19 28 D7
Vineyard Pth
MORT/ESHN SW14 18 B8
Vineyard Rd FELT TW13 24 B6
Vineyard Rw
E/WMO/HCT KT8 41 J2
The Vineyard
RCHPK/HAM TW10 26 C1
SUN TW16 * 39 J4
Viney Bank CROY/NA CR0 64 F7
Vintney St FLEETN GU51 86 D4
Viola Av EBED/NFELT TW14 24 D2
STWL/WRAY TW19 23 H5
Viola Cft BNFD RG42 33 H2
Violet Cl WLGTN SM6 44 C9
Violet Gdns CROY/NA CR0 63 K4
Violet La CROY/NA CR0 63 K4
Virginia Av VW GU25 36 A6
Virginia Cl ASHTD KT21 77 K7
NWMAL KT3 42 A5
STA TW18 37 N4
WEY KT13 56 E5
Virginia Dr VW GU25 36 A6
Virginia Gdns FARN GU14 88 E5
Virginia Pk VW GU25 * 36 C5
Virginia Pl COB KT11 75 J3
Virginia Rd THHTH CR7 45 L2
Viscount Cl ASHV GU12 109 H1
Viscount Gdns BF/WBF KT14 74 A1
Viscount Rd
STWL/WRAY TW19 22 G3
Viscount Wy HTHAIR TW6 14 G9
Viveash Cl HYS/HAR UB3 15 H1
Vivian Cl FLEETS GU52 87 H9
Vivien Cl CHSGTN KT9 59 L6
Vivienne Cl CRAWW RH11 176 G2
TWK TW1 26 C2
Voewood Cl NWMAL KT3 42 D7
Vogan Cl REIG RH2 119 M8
Volta Wy CROY/NA CR0 45 H9
Voss Ct STRHM/NOR SW16 29 P9
Vulcan Cl CRAWW RH11 176 F9
Vulcan Wy CROY/NA CR0 65 L8
FARN GU14 87 N7
SHST GU47 67 L1

W

Waddington Av
COUL/CHIP CR5 81 J8
Waddington Cl
COUL/CHIP CR5 81 K8
CRAWW RH11 176 D8
Waddington Wy NRWD SE19 45 L2
Waddon Rd CROY/NA CR0 63 K2
Waddon Cl CROY/NA CR0 63 J2
Waddon Court Rd
CROY/NA CR0 63 J3
Waddon Marsh Wy
CROY/NA CR0 63 H1
Waddon New Rd
CROY/NA CR0 2 A5
Waddon Park Av
CROY/NA CR0 63 J3
Waddon Wy CROY/NA CR0 63 J5
Wade's La TEDD TW11 25 P8
Wadham SHST GU47 50 B8
Wadham Cl CRAWE RH10 177 M2
SHPTN TW17 38 E8
Wadham Rd PUT/ROE SW15 19 J9
Wadhurst Cl PGE/AN SE20 46 B3
Wadhurst Rd CHSWK W4 18 B1
Wadlands Brook Rd
EGRIN RH19 162 C7
Wagbullock Ri BRAK RG12 32 E7
Wagg Cl EGRIN RH19 180 F2
Waggon Cl GUW GU2 111 L4
Waggoners Hollow
BAGS GU19 51 N7
Waggoners Wy GSHT GU26 165 K8
Waggoners Wells Rd
GSHT GU26 165 K9
Wagtail Cl HORS RH12 192 B3
Wagtail Gdns SAND/SEL CR2 64 D8
Wagtail Wk BECK BR3 47 J6
Waights Ct KUTN/CMB KT2 8 E2
Wain End HORS RH12 192 C5
Wainford Cl WIM/MER SW19 28 A4
Wainwright Gv ISLW TW7 16 D9
Wainwrights CRAWE RH10 176 G8
Wakefield Cl BF/WBF KT14 74 A1
Wakefield Gdns NRWD SE19 45 N1
Wakefield Rd
RCHPK/HAM TW10 26 C1
Wakefords Copse
FLEETS GU52 107 H3
Wakefords Cnr
FLEETS GU52 * 107 H2
Wakefords Pk FLEETS GU52 107 H3
Wakehams Green Dr
CRAWE RH10 177 N2
Wakehurst Dr CRAWE RH10 176 G8
Wakehurst Ms HORS RH12 191 N9
Wakehurst Rd BTSEA SW11 29 J1
Wakely Cl BH/WHM TN16 84 A7
Walburton Rd PUR/KEN CR8 80 E2
Walbury BRAK RG12 32 G5
Waldeck Gv WNWD SE27 30 C6
Waldeck Rd CHSWK W4 17 N4
MORT/ESHN SW14 18 A8
Waldegrave Gdns TWK TW1 25 N5
Waldegrave Pk TWK TW1 25 N7
Waldegrave Rd NRWD SE19 45 P1
TWK TW1 25 N7
Waldegrove CROY/NA CR0 3 J6
Waldemar Av FUL/PGN SW6 19 J6
Waldemar Rd
WIM/MER SW19 28 D8
Walden Cottages
RGUW GU3 110 A3
Walden Gdns THHTH CR7 45 H5
Waldenshaw Rd FSTH SE23 31 K4
Waldens Park Rd
WOKN/KNAP GU21 72 A6
Waldens Rd
WOKN/KNAP GU21 10 A3
Waldo Cl CLAP SW4 29 M1
Waldo Pl WIM/MER SW19 44 A1
Waldorf Cl SAND/SEL CR2 63 K7
Waldorf Hts BLKW GU17 67 P4
Waldram Crs FSTH SE23 31 K4
Waldram Park Rd FSTH SE23 31 L4
Waldron Gdns HAYES BR2 47 K4
Waldron Hl BRAK RG12 33 H2
Waldronhyrst CROY/NA CR0 63 K3
Waldron Ms CHEL SW3 19 P4
Waldron Rd
WAND/EARL SW18 28 F6
The Waldrons CROY/NA CR0 2 C7
OXTED RH8 123 M2
Waldy Ri CRAN GU6 153 H8
Wales Av CAR SM5 62 B4
Walesbeech CRAWE RH10 177 K6
Waleton Acres
WLGTN SM6 * 62 E5
Waley's La RDKG RH5 173 L2
Walford Rd RDKG RH5 137 H2
Walham Green Ct
FUL/PGN SW6 * 19 M5
Walham Gv FUL/PGN SW6 19 L5
Walham Ri WIM/MER SW19 28 B9
Walham Yd FUL/PGN SW6 19 L5
Walker Cl EBED/NFELT TW14 24 A3
HPTN TW12 24 G9
Walker Rd CRAWE RH10 177 L7
Walkerscroft Md DUL SE21 30 D4
Walker's Pl PUT/ROE SW15 * 19 J9
Walker's Rdg CBLY GU15 68 G3
Walkfield Dr EPSOM KT18 78 F6
Walking Bottom SHGR GU5 134 E7
The Walk OXTED RH8 122 G4
Wallace Cl RGUW GU3 111 J1
SHPTN TW17 38 F5
Wallace Crs CAR SM5 62 B4
Wallace Flds EW KT17 78 D1
Wallace Sq COUL/CHIP CR5 100 F2
Wallace Wk ADL/WDHM KT15 55 N3
Wallace Wy ALDT GU11 108 B3
Wallage La CRAWE RH10 178 E5
Wallcroft Cl BNFD RG42 32 A1
The Walled Gdn BIL RH14 188 C3
BRKHM/BTCW RH3 118 B6
KWD/TDW/WH KT20 99 H2
Waller La CTHM CR3 101 P3
Wallgrave Rd ECT SW5 19 M2
Wall Hill Rd FROW RH18 181 J6
Wallingford Cl BRAK RG12 32 G5
Wallington Rd CBLY GU15 51 J8
Wallis Cl BTSEA SW11 19 P8
Wallis Ct CRAWE RH10 * 177 J1
Wallis Ms LHD/OX KT22 * 96 G2
Wallis Wy SWTR RH13 192 F6
Wallorton Gdns
MORT/ESHN SW14 18 B9
Walmer Cl CWTH RG45 49 N4
FRIM GU16 69 H9
Walnut Av WDR/YW UB7 14 C1
Walnut Cl ALDT GU11 108 C6
CAR SM5 62 B4
EPSOM KT18 78 D4
YTLY GU46 67 H4
Walnut Dr
KWD/TDW/WH KT20 99 J4
Walnut Gv BNSTD SM7 79 H3
Walnut La CRAWW RH11 176 E2
Walnut Ms BELMT SM2 61 N6
The Walnuts FLEETS GU52 106 D1
HORS RH12 * 192 B6
Walnut Tree Av MTCM CR4 * 44 A4
Walnut Tree Cl BARN SW13 18 D6
BNSTD SM7 79 J1
GU GU1 6 C4
Walnut Tree Gdns
GODL GU7 131 L6
Walnut Tree La BF/WBF KT14 73 P1
Walnut Tree Pk GU GU1 * 6 C2
Walnut Tree Rd BTFD TW8 17 L4
HEST TW5 * 15 P4
SHPTN TW17 38 E4
Walpole Av COUL/CHIP CR5 80 B8
RCH/KEW TW9 17 M7
Walpole Crs TEDD TW11 25 N8
Walpole Gdns CHSWK W4 18 A3
WHTN TW2 25 M5
Walpole Pl TEDD TW11 25 N8
Walpole Rd CROY/NA CR0 2 E3
SURB KT6 41 L8
TEDD TW11 25 N8
WDSR SL4 20 G3
WHTN TW2 25 M5
WIM/MER SW19 28 G9

Walrus Rd FARN GU14 ...87 P7
Walsham Rd
EBED/NFELT TW14 ...24 C3
Walsh Av BNFD RG42 ...32 G1
Walsh Crs CROY/NA CR0 ...83 L1
Walsingham Gdns
HOR/WEW KT19 ...60 C3
Walsingham Rd CLAP SW4 ...29 K2
CROY/NA CR0 ...65 J8
MTCM CR4 ...44 B6
Walter's Md ASHTD KT21 ...77 L6
Walter's Rd SNWD SE25 ...45 N5
Walter St KUTN/CMB KT2 ...8 D3
Walters Wy FSTH SE23 ...31 L2
Walters Yd BMLY BR1 ...47 N3
Waltham Av GUW GU2 ...111 P2
HYS/HAR UB3 ...14 E1
Waltham Cl SHST GU47 ...49 P8
Waltham Rd CAR SM5 ...43 P9
CTHM CR3 ...102 B2
NWDGN UB2 ...15 N1
Walton Av CHEAM SM3 ...61 K2
NWMAL KT3 ...42 D5
Walton Bridge Rd
SHPTN TW17 ...38 G8
Walton Ct WOKN/KNAP GU21 ..72 E4
Walton Dr ASC SL5 ...33 P2
SWTR RH13 ...193 H6
Walton Gdns FELT TW13 ...24 A7
Walton Gn CROY/NA CR0 ...65 H7
Walton Heath CRAWE RH10 ..177 N3
Walton La WEY KT13 ...56 E1
WOT/HER KT12 ...38 E9
Walton Pk WOT/HER KT12 ...57 M1
Walton Park La
WOT/HER KT12 ...57 N1
Walton Rd EPSOM KT18 ...98 A1
WOKN/KNAP GU21 ...11 G2
WOT/HER KT12 ...39 M6
Walton St
KWD/TDW/WH KT20 ...98 E4
Walton Ter
WOKN/KNAP GU21 ...72 F4
Walton Wy MTCM CR4 ...44 E5
Wanborough Dr
PUT/ROE SW15 ...27 N4
Wanborough Hl RGUW GU3 ..110 C8
Wanborough La CRAN GU6 ...153 K8
Wandle Bank CROY/NA CR0 ...62 G2
WIM/MER SW19 ...28 G9
Wandle Cl ASHV GU12 ...109 J5
CRAWE RH10 ...177 M6
Wandle Ct HOR/WEW KT19 ...60 A3
Wandle Court Gdns
CROY/NA CR0 ...62 G2
Wandle Rd CROY/NA CR0 ...2 C6
MRDN SM4 ...43 P6
TOOT SW17 ...29 H5
WLGTN SM6 ...62 D1
Wandle Side CROY/NA CR0 ...63 H2
WLGTN SM6 ...62 D2
Wandle Wy MTCM CR4 ...44 B6
WAND/EARL SW18 ...28 E4
Wandon Rd FUL/PGN SW6 ...19 M5
Wandsdyke Cl FRIM GU16 ...69 H8
Wandsworth Br
WAND/EARL SW18 ...19 N8
Wandsworth Bridge Rd
FUL/PGN SW6 ...19 M6
Wandsworth Common West Side
WAND/EARL SW18 ...28 F1
Wandsworth High St
WAND/EARL SW18 ...28 D1
Wanmer Ct REIG RH2 * ...119 L4
Wansdown Pl FUL/PGN SW6 ...19 M5
Wansford Gn
WOKN/KNAP GU21 ...71 M6
Wanstraw Gv BRAK RG12 ...32 G8
Wantage Cl BRAK RG12 ...32 G6
CRAWE RH10 ...177 M8
Wantage Rd SHST GU47 ...49 P9
Wapiti Wy FARN GU14 ...87 P7
The Waplings
KWD/TDW/WH KT20 * ...98 F4
Wapshott Rd STA TW18 ...22 B9
Warbank Cl CROY/NA CR0 ...65 L8
Warbank Crs CROY/NA CR0 ...65 L8
Warbank La KUTN/CMB KT2 ...42 D1
Warblers Gn COB KT11 ...75 P3
Warboys Ap KUTN/CMB KT2 ...26 G9
Warboys Rd KUTN/CMB KT2 ...26 G9
Warburton Cl EGRIN RH19 ...180 F2
Warburton Rd WHTN TW2 ...25 J4
Warbury La
WOKN/KNAP GU21 ...71 J5
War Coppice Rd REDH RH1 ...101 M7
Ward Cl SAND/SEL CR2 ...63 N4
Ward La WARL CR6 ...82 C5
Wardle Cl BAGS GU19 ...51 N6
Wardley St WAND/EARL SW18 ..28 E3
Wardo Av FUL/PGN SW6 ...19 J6
The Wardrobe
RCH/KEW TW9 * ...26 C1
Wards Pl EGH TW20 ...21 P9
Wards Stone Pk BRAK RG12 ...32 G8
Ward St GU GU1 ...7 F5
Wareham Cl HSLW TW3 ...16 B9
Wareham Rd BRAK RG12 ...33 H6
Warenne Hts REDH RH1 ...119 P7
Warenne Rd LHD/OX KT22 ...96 C2
Warfield Rd BRAK RG12 ...32 E2
EBED/NFELT TW14 ...23 P3
HPTN TW12 ...40 B2
Wargrove Dr SHST GU47 ...49 P9
Warham Rd SAND/SEL CR2 ...63 L4
Waring St WNWD SE27 ...30 D7
Warkworth Gdns ISLW TW7 ...16 G5
Warlingham Rd THHTH CR7 ...45 K5
Warltersville Wy HORL RH6 ...159 M3
Warmington Rd HNHL SE24 ...30 D2
Warminster Rd SNWD SE25 ...46 A3
Warminster Sq SNWD SE25 ...46 A3
Warminster Wy MTCM CR4 ...44 D2
Warner Av CHEAM SM3 ...61 J1
Warner Cl CRAWE RH10 ...177 M9
HPTN TW12 ...24 G8
HYS/HAR UB3 ...14 F5
Warner Rd BMLY BR1 ...47 M1
Warners La SHGR GU5 ...134 A3
Warnham Court Ms
HORS RH12 * ...172 F7
Warnham Court Rd CAR SM5 ..62 B6
Warnham Rd CRAWE RH10 ...177 K7
HORS RH12 ...191 L6
HORS RH12 ...192 A5
Warpole Pk WEY KT13 ...56 C6
Warramill Rd GODL GU7 ...131 N8
Warren Av BELMT SM2 ...61 K8
BMLY BR1 ...47 L1
RCHPK/HAM TW10 ...17 P9
SAND/SEL CR2 ...64 D6
Warren Cl DTCH/LGLY SL3 ...12 C1
EGRIN RH19 ...161 M9
ESH/CLAY KT10 ...58 B3
FLEETS GU52 ...87 H8
SHST GU47 ...49 L9
Warren Cnr RFNM GU10 ...106 G7
Warren Cutting
KUTN/CMB KT2 ...42 B1
Warren Down BNFD RG42 ...32 A2
Warren Dr CRAWW RH11 ...176 D4
KWD/TDW/WH KT20 ...99 K2
Warren Dr North BRYLDS KT5 ..41 P9
Warren Dr South BRYLDS KT5 ..42 A9
Warreners La WEY KT13 ...56 F7
Warren Fm WOKS/MYFD GU22 ..73 M8
Warren Hl EPSOM KT18 ...78 B5
Warren La EWKG RG40 ...48 B4
LHD/OX KT22 ...76 C1
OXTED RH8 ...123 N5
WOKS/MYFD GU22 ...73 L7
Warren Lodge Dr
KWD/TDW/WH KT20 ...99 J4
Warren Md BNSTD SM7 ...78 G4
Warrenne Rd
BRKHM/BTCW RH3 ...118 A8
Warrenne Wy REIG RH2 ...119 L5
Warren Pk KUTN/CMB KT2 ...27 H9
KWD/TDW/WH KT20 * ...118 A2
WARL CR6 ...82 D7
Warren Park Rd SUT SM1 ...61 P5
Warren Ri FRIM GU16 ...68 G5
NWMAL KT3 ...42 B2
Warren Rd ADL/WDHM KT15 ...55 L8
ASHF TW15 ...38 G1
BNSTD SM7 ...79 H4
CROY/NA CR0 ...3 H1
GODL GU7 ...131 L6
GU GU1 ...7 J5
HAYES BR2 ...65 N1
KUTN/CMB KT2 ...27 H9
PUR/KEN CR8 ...81 K1
REIG RH2 ...119 M4
WHTN TW2 ...25 L2
WIM/MER SW19 ...29 H9
Warren Rw ASC SL5 ...33 M3
The Warren ASHTD KT21 ...77 M9
BRAK RG12 * ...33 H5
CAR SM5 ...61 P7
EHSLY KT24 ...115 H1
FNM GU9 ...108 A6
HEST TW5 ...15 P5
HOR/WEW KT19 ...60 B3
KWD/TDW/WH KT20 ...99 J3
LHD/OX KT22 ...76 C1
Warren Wy WEY KT13 ...56 E5
Warren Wood Cl HAYES BR2 ...65 N1
Warrington Cl CRAWW RH11 ..176 B9
Warrington Ms ALDT GU11 ...108 A6
Warrington Rd CROY/NA CR0 ...2 A6
RCHPK/HAM TW10 ...26 C1
Warrington Sp WDSR SL4 ...20 G3
Warwick BRAK RG12 ...32 G8
Warwick Av EGH TW20 ...36 G2
STA TW18 ...22 F9
Warwick Chambers
KENS W8 * ...19 L1
Warwick Cl ALDT GU11 ...108 E6
CBLY GU15 ...69 K5
HPTN TW12 ...40 C1
RDKG RH5 ...137 H6
Warwick Deeping
CHERT KT16 ...54 G4
Warwick Dr BARN SW13 ...18 F8
Warwick Gdns ASHTD KT21 ...77 J6
THDIT KT7 ...40 F6
THHTH CR7 * ...45 J5
WKENS W14 ...19 K1
Warwick Gv BRYLDS KT5 ...41 M8
Warwick La
WOKN/KNAP GU21 ...71 N8
Warwick Pl THDIT KT7 * ...40 G7
Warwick Rd ASHF TW15 ...23 H8
ASHV GU12 ...89 H6
COUL/CHIP CR5 ...80 E3
FARN GU14 ...87 P7
HSLWW TW4 ...15 K8
KUT KT1 ...8 A2
NWDGN UB2 ...15 P1
NWMAL KT3 ...42 A4
PGE/AN SE20 ...46 B4
RDKG RH5 ...137 J7
REDH RH1 ...120 B4
SUT SM1 ...61 N4
THDIT KT7 ...40 F6
THHTH CR7 ...45 J4
WHTN TW2 ...25 M4
WKENS W14 ...19 K2
Warwicks Bench GU GU1 ...7 F7
Warwick's Bench La GU GU1 ..112 C8
Warwick Vls EGH TW20 * ...36 G2
Warwick Wold Rd
REDH RH1 ...101 J9
Wasdale Cl SHST GU47 ...49 P7
Washington Cl REIG RH2 ...119 L3
Washington Gdns
EWKG RG40 ...48 E1
Washington Rd BARN SW13 ...18 E5
CRAWW RH11 ...176 B8
KUT KT1 ...9 H5
WPK KT4 ...60 F1
Washneys Rd ORP BR6 ...85 L2
Washpond La WARL CR6 ...83 J7
Washponds Cottages
WARL CR6 * ...83 J7
Wasp Green La REDH RH1 ...141 K5
Wassand Cl CRAWE RH10 ...177 K5
Wastdale Rd FSTH SE23 ...31 L4
Watchetts Dr CBLY GU15 ...68 E6
Watchetts Lake Cl CBLY GU15 ..68 F5
Watchetts Rd CBLY GU15 ...68 D5
Watchfield Ct CHSWK W4 * ...18 A3
Watchmoor Point
CBLY GU15 * ...68 D4
Watchmoor Rd CBLY GU15 ...68 D4
Watcombe Rd SNWD SE25 ...46 B6
Watercress Wy
WOKN/KNAP GU21 ...71 P6
Waterden Rd GU GU1 ...7 H4
Waterer Gdns
KWD/TDW/WH KT20 ...79 J7
Waterer Ri WLGTN SM6 ...62 F5
Waterers Ri
WOKN/KNAP GU21 ...71 K6
Waterfall Cl VW GU25 ...35 M4
Waterfall Cottages
WIM/MER SW19 ...28 G9
Waterfall Rd WIM/MER SW19 ..28 G9
Waterfall Ter TOOT SW17 ...29 H9
Waterfield EPSOM KT18 ...78 F8
Waterfield Cl SWTR RH13 ...192 D7
Waterfield Cottages
MORT/ESHN SW14 * ...17 P9
Waterfield Dr WARL CR6 ...82 B8
Waterfield Gdns
CRAWW RH11 ...176 B7
SNWD SE25 ...45 N5
Waterfield Gn
KWD/TDW/WH KT20 ...78 F9
Waterfields LHD/OX KT22 ...77 H8
Waterford Cl COB KT11 ...57 N9
Waterford Rd FUL/PGN SW6 ...19 M6
Waterham Rd BRAK RG12 ...32 D7
Waterhouse La
KWD/TDW/WH KT20 ...99 K1
PUR/KEN CR8 ...81 L8
REDH RH1 ...121 P3
Waterhouse Md SHST GU47 ...67 P1
Waterlakes EDEN TN8 ...144 G5
Waterlands La HORS RH12 ...190 F2
Water La CHOB/PIR GU24 ...70 E8
COB KT11 ...75 N4
EDEN TN8 ...144 B6
FARN GU14 ...68 G9
FNM GU9 ...128 B1
GDST RH9 ...122 D9
GT/LBKH KT23 ...95 N6
KUT KT1 ...8 C3
MFD/CHID GU8 ...150 A8
OXTED RH8 ...103 N6
RCH/KEW TW9 ...26 C1
RDKG RH5 ...135 K5
SHGR GU5 ...113 M9
TWK TW1 ...25 P4
Water Lea CRAWE RH10 ...177 K6
Waterloo Cl CBLY GU15 ...69 K1
EBED/NFELT TW14 ...24 A4
Waterloo Pl CAR SM5 * ...62 B2
CWTH RG45 * ...49 M5
RCH/KEW TW9 ...17 N4
Waterloo Rd ASHV GU12 ...108 E5
CWTH RG45 ...49 L5
HOR/WEW KT19 ...78 B1
SUT SM1 ...61 P4
Waterloo Ter WEY KT13 * ...56 C3
Waterlow Rd REIG RH2 ...119 N6
Watermans Cl
KUTN/CMB KT2 * ...8 D1
Waterman St PUT/ROE SW15 ..19 H8
Watermead
EBED/NFELT TW14 ...23 P4
KWD/TDW/WH KT20 ...98 F1
WOKN/KNAP GU21 ...71 M5
Watermead La MTCM CR4 ...44 B7
Watermeadow La
FUL/PGN SW6 ...19 N7
Watermens Sq
PGE/AN SE20 * ...46 C1
Watermill Cl
RCHPK/HAM TW10 ...26 B6
Water Mill Wy FELT TW13 ...24 G5
Watermill Wy
WIM/MER SW19 ...43 N2
Waterperry La
CHOB/PIR GU24 ...53 M8
Water Rede FLEETS GU52 ...106 E3
Waters Dr STA TW18 ...22 C7
Water's Edge FUL/PGN SW6 * ..19 H6
Watersedge HOR/WEW KT19 ...60 A3
Waterside EGRIN RH19 ...180 G2
HORL RH6 ...140 C8
Waterside Cl CRAWW RH11 ...176 B7
GODL GU7 ...131 N8
SURB KT6 ...59 L1
Waterside Ct FLEETN GU51 ...87 H4
Waterside Dr WOT/HER KT12 ..39 K6
Waterside La GODL GU7 ...150 B1
Waterside Ms FLEETN GU51 ...87 H4
GU GU1 ...112 A3
Waterside Rd GU GU1 ...112 C2
NWDGN UB2 ...16 A1
Waterside Wy TOOT SW17 ...28 F7
WOKN/KNAP GU21 ...71 P7
Waterslade REDH RH1 ...120 A5
Watersmeet Cl RGUE GU4 ...92 E9
Watersplash Cl KUT KT1 ...8 D6
Water Splash La ASC SL5 ...34 E2
Watersplash La HEST TW5 ...15 K3
Watersplash Rd SHPTN TW17 ..38 C5
Waters Rd KUT KT1 ...9 K5
Waters Sq KUT KT1 ...9 K6
Water Tower Hl CROY/NA CR0 ..3 F7
Waterway Rd LHD/OX KT22 ...96 G2
Waterworks Rd
BRXS/STRHM SW2 ...29 P2
Watery La CHOB/PIR GU24 ...53 K8
FLEETS GU52 ...106 E3
HYS/HAR UB3 ...14 F3
RYNPK SW20 ...43 K3
Wates Wy MTCM CR4 ...44 B7
Watford Cl GU GU1 ...7 K3
Wathen Rd DORK RH4 ...117 H6
Watlings Cl CROY/NA CR0 ...46 E7
Watlington Gv SYD SE26 ...31 M8
Watney Rd
MORT/ESHN SW14 ...18 A8
Watneys Rd MTCM CR4 ...44 F6
Watson Av CHEAM SM3 ...61 J1
Watson Cl CRAWE RH10 ...177 M8
WIM/MER SW19 ...29 H9
Watson Rd DORK RH4 ...116 C8
Wattendon Rd PUR/KEN CR8 ..81 K5
Watts Cl
KWD/TDW/WH KT20 * ...99 H2
Watts Common Rd
ALDT GU11 ...88 A8
Watt's La
KWD/TDW/WH KT20 ...99 H2
TEDD TW11 ...25 P8
Watts Lea WOKN/KNAP GU21 ...71 N4
Watt's Md
KWD/TDW/WH KT20 ...99 H2
Watts Rd FARN GU14 ...88 B2
THDIT KT7 ...40 G8
Wavel Pl SYD SE26 ...30 G7
Wavendene Av EGH TW20 ...36 G1
Wavendon Av CHSWK W4 ...18 B3
Waverleigh Rd CRAN GU6 ...171 H2
Waverley BRAK RG12 ...32 A6
Waverley Av BRYLDS KT5 ...41 P7
FLEETN GU51 ...86 F4
PUR/KEN CR8 ...81 N5
SUT SM1 ...61 M1
WHTN TW2 ...24 G4
Waverley Cl CBLY GU15 ...69 H4
E/WMO/HCT KT8 ...40 A6
FNM GU9 * ...5 J4
HYS/HAR UB3 ...14 F2
Waverley Ct HORS RH12 * ...192 A8
WOKS/MYFD GU22 ...10 D5
Waverley Dr ASHV GU12 ...89 J9
CBLY GU15 ...68 G3
CHERT KT16 ...55 H2
VW GU25 ...35 N5
Waverley Gdns ASHV GU12 ...89 J9
Waverley La FNM GU9 ...5 K4
Waverley Pl LHD/OX KT22 * ...97 H2
Waverley Rd BAGS GU19 ...51 N6
COB KT11 ...76 B3
EW KT17 ...60 F4
FARN GU14 ...88 F4
SNWD SE25 ...46 B5
WEY KT13 ...56 C4
Waverley Wy CAR SM5 ...62 A5
Waverton Rd
WAND/EARL SW18 ...28 F3
Wavertree Rd
BRXS/STRHM SW2 ...30 A4
Waye Av HEST TW5 ...15 J6
Wayland Cl BRAK RG12 ...33 H5
Waylands STWL/WRAY TW19 ...21 K2
Waylett Pl WNWD SE27 ...30 C6
Wayman Rd FARN GU14 ...68 A8
Wayneflete Tower Av
ESH/CLAY KT10 ...58 A2
Waynflete Av CROY/NA CR0 ...2 A6
Waynflete La FNM GU9 ...4 B4
Waynflete St
WAND/EARL SW18 ...28 F5
Ways End CBLY GU15 ...68 G4
Wayside CRAWW RH11 ...176 B7
CROY/NA CR0 * ...65 H5
MORT/ESHN SW14 ...18 A9
RDKG RH5 * ...156 C6
Wayside Ct TWK TW1 ...26 B2
Wayside Dr EDEN TN8 ...145 H2
The Way REIG RH2 ...119 P4
Weald Cl RGUE GU4 ...132 C2
Weald Dr CRAWE RH10 ...177 K6
Wealdstone Rd CHEAM SM3 ...61 K1
The Weald EGRIN RH19 ...162 E9
Weald Wy REDH RH1 ...101 N8
REIG RH2 ...119 N9
Weapon Rd FARN GU14 ...88 D5
Weare St RDKG RH5 ...155 P7
RDKG RH5 ...173 K4
Weasdale Ct
WOKN/KNAP GU21 ...71 M5
Weatherall Cl
ADL/WDHM KT15 ...55 M4
Weatherhill Cl HORL RH6 ...160 A1
Weatherhill Rd HORL RH6 ...160 B1
Weather Wy BRAK RG12 ...32 E3
Weaver Cl CRAWW RH11 * ...176 B6
Weaver Moss SHST GU47 ...67 M1
Weavers Cl ISLW TW7 ...16 F9
Weavers Down LIPH GU30 * ..182 A7
Weavers Gdns RFNM GU10 ...127 K6
Weavers Ter
FUL/PGN SW6 * ...19 L4
Weaver Wk WNWD SE27 ...30 C7
Webb Cl BAGS GU19 ...51 N8
BNFD RG42 ...32 A1
CRAWW RH11 ...194 E1
DTCH/LGLY SL3 ...12 B2
Webb Rd MFD/CHID GU8 ...149 K5
Webb's Rd BTSEA SW11 ...29 J1
Webster Cl COB KT11 ...76 B3
Websters Cl
WOKS/MYFD GU22 ...71 N9
Weddell Rd CRAWE RH10 ...177 J8
Wedgwoods
BH/WHM TN16 * ...104 A1
Wedgwood Wy NRWD SE19 ...45 L1
Weekley Sq BTSEA SW11 * ...19 P8
Weighbridge Rd
ADL/WDHM KT15 ...55 M7
Weighton Rd PGE/AN SE20 ...46 B3
Weihurst Gdns SUT SM1 ...61 P4
Weimar St PUT/ROE SW15 ...19 J8
Weir Av FARN GU14 ...88 C4
Weirbrook CRAWE RH10 ...177 K8
Weir Cl FARN GU14 ...88 C4
Weir Pl STA TW18 ...37 J2
Weir Rd BAL SW12 ...29 M4
CHERT KT16 ...37 M8
FARN GU14 ...87 L5
WIM/MER SW19 ...28 E6
WOT/HER KT12 ...39 J7
Weiss Rd PUT/ROE SW15 ...19 H8
Welbeck BRAK RG12 ...32 A6
Welbeck Cl EW KT17 ...60 E6
FARN GU14 ...88 B3
NWMAL KT3 ...42 D6
Welbeck Rd CAR SM5 ...44 A9
SUT SM1 ...61 P1
Welcomes Cottages
CTHM CR3 * ...102 G3
Welcomes Rd PUR/KEN CR8 ...81 L4
Weldon Cl FLEETS GU52 ...107 H1
Weldon Dr E/WMO/HCT KT8 ...39 P5
Weldon Wy REDH RH1 ...100 F9
Welford Pl WIM/MER SW19 ...28 B7
Welham Rd TOOT SW17 ...29 K8
Welhouse Rd CAR SM5 ...44 A9
Welland Cl DTCH/LGLY SL3 ...12 E4
Wellburn Cl SHST GU47 ...67 M1
Well Cl CBLY GU15 ...68 D4
STRHM/NOR SW16 ...30 A7
WOKN/KNAP GU21 ...72 A6
Weller Cl CRAWE RH10 ...177 N6
Weller Dr CBLY GU15 ...68 E5
Wellers Cl BH/WHM TN16 ...104 G7
Wellesford Cl BNSTD SM7 ...79 K6
Wellesley Av HMSMTH W6 ...18 F1
IVER SL0 ...13 K1
Wellesley Cl ASHV GU12 ...89 H8
BAGS GU19 ...51 L6
Wellesley Court Rd
CROY/NA CR0 * ...2 E4
Wellesley Crs WHTN TW2 ...25 M5
Wellesley Dr CWTH RG45 ...49 J4
Wellesley Gdn FNM GU9 ...107 N7
Wellesley Ga ASHV GU12 * ...108 D5
Wellesley Gv CROY/NA CR0 ...2 E3
Wellesley Pde WHTN TW2 * ...25 M6
Wellesley Rd ALDT GU11 ...107 P3
BELMT SM2 ...61 N5
CHSWK W4 ...17 N3
CROY/NA CR0 ...2 D1
RFNM GU10 ...147 L6
WHTN TW2 ...25 L6
Welley Av STWL/WRAY TW19 ...12 C9
Welley Rd STWL/WRAY TW19 ..12 C9
Well Farm Rd CTHM CR3 ...82 A8
Wellfield EGRIN RH19 ...181 H4
Wellfield Gdns CAR SM5 ...62 A8
Wellfield Rd
STRHM/NOR SW16 ...29 P7
Wellhouse La
BRKHM/BTCW RH3 ...118 B8
Wellhouse Rd BECK BR3 ...46 F5
Wellington Av ALDT GU11 ...108 B4
FLEETN GU51 ...87 H5
HSLW TW3 ...25 H1
VW GU25 ...35 P7
WPK KT4 ...60 G2
Wellington Cl CRAWE RH10 ...177 P2
SHST GU47 ...49 N9
WOT/HER KT12 ...39 H9
Wellington Crs NWMAL KT3 ...42 A4
Wellington Dr BRAK RG12 ...32 F6
PUR/KEN CR8 ...63 H8
Wellington Gdns
ALDT GU11 * ...108 B5
HPTN TW12 ...25 L7
Wellingtonia Av EWKG RG40 ...48 F5
Wellingtonia Wy EDEN TN8 ...144 G3
Wellington La FNM GU9 ...107 P7
Wellington Pl COB KT11 ...76 A1
GODL GU7 * ...131 L6
Wellington Rd ASHF TW15 ...23 H8
CROY/NA CR0 ...45 K8
CTHM CR3 ...101 L2
CWTH RG45 ...49 N5
EA W5 ...17 J2
EBED/NFELT TW14 ...23 P1
HORS RH12 ...192 C8
HPTN TW12 ...25 L7
SHST GU47 ...49 M9
WIM/MER SW19 ...28 D5
Wellington Rd North
HSLWW TW4 ...15 P8
Wellington Rd South
HSLWW TW4 ...15 P9
Wellington St ALDT GU11 ...108 C4
Wellington Ter SHST GU47 ...49 N9
WOKN/KNAP GU21 * ...71 L7
Wellington Town Rd
EGRIN RH19 ...162 C9
Wellington Wy FARN GU14 ...87 P8
HORL RH6 ...140 B8
WEY KT13 ...56 B8
Well La HASM GU27 ...184 E4
MFD/CHID GU8 * ...167 L3
MORT/ESHN SW14 ...27 H1
WOKN/KNAP GU21 ...72 A6
Wellmeadow Rd HNWL W7 ...16 G2
Well Pth WOKN/KNAP GU21 ...72 A6
Well Rd RFNM GU10 ...106 C8

Wells Cl *BH/WHM* TN16 ....104 G7
  GT/LBKH KT23 ....96 B4
  HORS RH12 ....191 N8
  SAND/SEL CR2 ....69 N4
Wells Cottages *FNM* GU9 ....127 L6
Wells La *ASC* SL5 ....34 B5
  RGUW GU3 ....110 C2
Wells Lea *EGRIN* RH19 ....162 C9
Wells Meadow *EGRIN* RH19 ..162 C9
Wells Park Rd *SYD* SE26 ......31 H6
Wells Pl *REDH* RH1 ....120 D1
  WAND/EARL SW18 ....28 F3
Wells Rd *CRAWE* RH10 * 177 H9
  EPSOM KT18 ....77 N3
  RGUE GU4 ....112 C2
Wells Wy *SKENS* SW7 ....19 P1
Well Wy *EPSOM* KT18 ....77 N4
Wellwood Cl *COUL/CHIP* CR5 ..80 C3
  SWTR RH13 ....192 G6
Wellwynds Rd *CRAN* GU6 .....171 H1
Welstead Wy *CHSWK* W4 ....18 D1
Weltje Rd *HMSMTH* W6 ....18 E3
Welwyn Av
  EBED/NFELT TW14 ....24 A2
Welwyn Cl *CRAWW* RH11 ......176 B8
Wembley Pk *HPTN* TW12 ....40 A2
Wembury Pk *LING* RH7 ....161 N6
Wendela Cl
  WOKS/MYFD GU22 ....11 F6
Wendley Dr *ADL/WDHM* KT15 ..55 K8
Wendling Rd *CAR* SM5 ....43 P9
Wendover Dr *FRIM* GU16 ....69 L5
  NWMALL KT3 ....42 D7
Wendover Pl *STA* TW18 ....36 C6
Wendover Rd *HAYES* BR2 * 47 P5
  STA TW18 ....22 A8
Wendron Cl
  WOKN/KNAP GU21 ....71 N7
The Wend *COUL/CHIP* CR5 .....80 F3
Wendy Crs *GUW* GU2 ....111 N5
Wendock Cl *CRAWW* RH11 .....176 D7
Wenlock Edge *DORK* RH4 * 117 J9
Wensleydale *CRAWW* RH11 ....176 F8
Wensleydale Dr *CBLY* GU15 ...69 M3
Wensleydale Gdns
  HPTN TW12 ....40 B1
Wensleydale Rd *HPTN* TW12 ..40 A1
Wentworth Av *ASC* SL5 ....33 L5
Wentworth Cl *ASHF* TW15 .....23 L7
  ASHV GU12 ....89 J8
  CWTH RG45 ....49 N7
  FNM GU9 ....108 B8
  HAYES BR2 * 65 N1
  MRDN SM4 ....43 L8
  RPLY/SEND GU23 ....93 M1
  SURB KT6 ....59 K1
  YTLY GU46 ....67 H3
Wentworth Crs *ASHV* GU12 ....89 J9
  HYS/HAR UB3 ....14 F1
Wentworth Dene *WEY* KT13 ...56 D4
Wentworth Dr *CRAWE* RH10 ..177 N4
  VW GU25 ....35 M5
Wentworth Wy *ASC* SL5 ....33 L3
  NWDGN UB2 ....15 L2
  SAND/SEL CR2 ....82 A4
Werndee Rd *SNWD* SE25 ....46 A5
Werter Rd *PUT/ROE* SW15 .....19 P9
Wesley Av *HSLW* TW3 ....15 N7
Wesley Cl *CRAWW* RH11 .....176 D8
  HORL RH6 ....140 C8
  REIG RH2 ....119 K6
Wesley Dr *EGH* TW20 ....21 M9
Wessels *KWD/TDW/WH* KT20 ..99 H1
Wessex Av *WIM/MER* SW19 ....43 L3
Wessex Cl *ESH/CLAY* KT10 ....58 F1
  KUTN/CMB KT2 ....9 K3
Wessex Ct *BECK* BR3 * 46 E2
Wessex Pl *FNM* GU9 ....5 H5
Wessex Ter *MTCM* CR4 * 44 A6
Westacres *ESH/CLAY* KT10 ....57 P6
Wes Av *CRAWE* RH10 ....177 J3
  FNM GU9 ....107 P8
  REDH RH1 ....140 B2
  WLGTN SM6 ....62 C4
  WOT/HER KT12 ....56 G8
West Bank *DORK* RH4 ....116 F8
Westbank Rd *HPTN* TW12 .....25 K9
West Barnes La *NWMAL* KT3 ..42 E6
Westbourne Av *CHEAM* SM3 ...61 J1
  CROY/NA CR0 ....45 J7
Westbourne Rd
  CROY/NA CR0 ....45 P7
  FELT TW13 ....24 A6
  SHST GU47 ....68 A1
  STA TW18 ....37 M1
  SYD SE26 ....31 L9
Westbridge Rd *BTSEA* SW11 ..19 P6
Westbrook *FROW* RH18 * 181 K8
Westbrook Av *HPTN* TW12 .....39 P1
Westbrook Gdns *BRAK* RG12 ..32 E2
Westbrook Hl
  MFD/CHID GU8 ....129 L9
Westbrook Rd *GODL* GU7 ....131 J4
  HEST TW5 ....15 P5
  STA TW18 ....37 M1
  THHTH CR7 ....45 M2
Westbury Av *ESH/CLAY* KT10 ..58 F5
  FLEETN GU51 ....87 K7
Westbury Cl *CTHM* CR3 * 81 P7
  CWTH RG45 ....49 M3
  FLEETN GU51 ....87 J7
  SHPTN TW17 * 37 P7
Westbury Gdns *FLEETN* GU51 ..87 K7
  FNM GU9 ....4 D8
Westbury Pl *BTFD* TW8 ....17 K4
Westbury Rd *CROY/NA* CR0 ...45 M7
  FELT TW13 ....24 E4
  NWMAL KT3 ....42 B5

PGE/AN SE20 ....46 D2
Westbury Ter
  BH/WHM TN16 ....104 G6
Westbury Wy *ASHV* GU12 ......89 L4
Westcar La *WOT/HER* KT12 ....57 K5
Westcliffe Vls *KUT* KT1 * 9 G5
West Cl *ASHF* TW15 ....23 H7
  FNM GU9 ....107 P7
Westcombe Av *CROY/NA* CR0 ..44 G7
Westcombe Cl *BRAK* RG12 ....32 F8
West Common Rd
  HAYES BR2 ....65 N1
Westcoombe Av
  RYNPK SW20 ....42 D2
Westcote Rd
  STRHM/NOR SW16 ....29 M8
Westcott Cl *CRAWW* RH11 ....194 F2
  CROY/NA CR0 ....65 H7
Westcott Gn *BNFD* RG42 ......32 F1
Westcott Rd *DORK* RH4 ....116 F7
  PUR/KEN CR8 ....61 P9
Westcott St *DORK* RH4 ....116 B8
Westcott Wy *BELMT* SM2 ......60 G8
Westcroft Gdns *MRDN* SM4 ...43 K4
Westcroft Ms *HMSMTH* W6 * ..18 E2
Westcroft Rd *CAR* SM5 ....62 C3
West Cromwell Rd *ECT* SW5 ..19 L3
West Cross Wy *BTFD* TW8 .....17 H4
Westdean Cl
  WAND/EARL SW18 ....28 A2
Westdene Mdw *CRAN* GU6 ...152 D9
Westdene Wy *WEY* KT13 ......56 G2
West Down *GT/LBKH* KT23 ....96 B7
Westdown Rd *CAT* SE6 ....31 P3
West Drayton Park Av
  WDR/YW UB7 ....14 A1
West Dr *ADL/WDHM* KT15 .....55 M8
  ASC SL5 ....35 K6
  BELMT SM2 ....61 H7
  CAR SM5 ....61 P8
  KWD/TDW/WH KT20 ....79 H7
  TOOT SW17 ....29 L7
West End Gdns
  ESH/CLAY KT10 ....57 P4
West End Gv *FNM* GU9 ....4 C4
West End La *ESH/CLAY* KT10 ..57 P4
  HASM GU27 ....185 L2
  HYS/HAR UB3 ....14 E5
  RFNM GU10 ....146 B3
Westerdale Dr *FRIM* GU16 .....69 K5
Westerfolds Cl
  WOKS/MYFD GU22 ....72 C6
Westerham Cl
  ADL/WDHM KT15 ....55 N5
  BELMT SM2 * 61 L8
Westerham Hl
  BH/WHM TN16 ....104 F2
Westerham Rd
  BH/WHM TN16 ....105 L5
  OXTED RH8 ....103 N9
Westerley Crs *SYD* SE26 * 31 N7
Westerman
  ADL/WDHM KT15 ....55 N8
Western Av *CHERT* KT16 ....37 L4
  CHOB/PIR GU24 ....90 C1
  EGH TW20 ....36 F4
Western Cl *CHERT* KT16 * 37 L4
Western Dr *SHPTN* TW17 ......38 F6
Western La *BAL* SW12 ....29 K3
Western Perimeter Rd
  HTHAIR TW6 ....13 M8
Western Pl *DORK* RH4 * 116 G7
Western Rd *ALDT* GU11 ....108 A5
  BNFD RG42 ....32 A2
  MTCM CR4 ....44 A2
  NWDGN UB2 ....15 L2
  SUT SM1 ....61 K3
Western Ter *HMSMTH* W6 * ...18 E3
West Farm Av *ASHTD* KT21 ...77 J7
West Farm Cl *ASHTD* KT21 ...77 J8
West Farm Dr *ASHTD* KT21 ...77 K8
Westfield *REIG* RH2 ....119 M2
  SHGR GU5 ....134 G5
Westfield Av *SAND/SEL* CR2 ..81 M2
  WOKS/MYFD GU22 ....92 C1
Westfield Cl *FUL/PGN* SW6 * ..19 N5
  SUT SM1 ....61 K3
Westfield Common
  WOKS/MYFD GU22 ....92 C2
Westfield Dr *GT/LBKH* KT23 ..96 B2
Westfield Gv
  WOKS/MYFD GU22 ....72 C9
Westfield La *RFNM* GU10 ....127 J7
Westfield Pde
  ADL/WDHM KT15 * 55 P8
Westfield Rd *BECK* BR3 ....46 F3
  CBLY GU15 ....68 D6
  CRAWW RH11 ....176 E5
  CROY/NA CR0 ....2 A5
  GU GU1 ....112 C1
  MTCM CR4 ....44 A3
  SURB KT6 ....41 K6
  SUT SM1 ....61 K3
  WOKS/MYFD GU22 ....92 C2
  WOT/HER KT12 ....39 N8
Westfields *BARN* SW13 ....18 D8
Westfields Av *BARN* SW13 ....18 C8
Westfield Wy
  WOKS/MYFD GU22 ....92 C2
West Flexford La
  RGUW GU3 ....110 E6
West Fryerne *YTLY* GU46 ......67 H1
West Gdns *EW* KT17 ....60 C8
  WIM/MER SW19 ....29 H9
Westgate Est
  EBED/NFELT TW14 * 23 J1
Westgate Rd *BECK* BR3 ....47 J2
  SNWD SE25 ....46 B5
Westgate Ter *WBPTN* SW10 ..19 M3
Westglade *FARN* GU14 ....87 P3
West Gn *YTLY* GU46 ....66 F1

CRAWW RH11 ....176 F5
West Green Dr
  CRAWW RH11 ....176 F5
West Gv *WOT/HER* KT12 ......57 K3
West Hall Br *WBF* KT14 * 73 N5
Westhall Pk *WARL* CR6 ....82 C8
West Hall Rd *RCH/KEW* TW9 ..17 P6
Westhall Rd *WARL* CR6 ....82 A7
Westhay Gdns
  MORT/ESHN SW14 ....26 G1
West Heath *CHOB/PIR* GU24 ..90 D3
West Heath Rd *FARN* GU14 ...88 B3
West Hl *EGRIN* RH19 ....162 D6
  HOR/WEW KT19 ....78 A1
  MFD/CHID GU8 ....148 D1
  ORP BR6 ....84 D1
  OXTED RH8 ....123 K1
  PUT/ROE SW15 ....28 A3
  SAND/SEL CR2 ....63 N7
  WAND/EARL SW18 ....28 A3
West Hill Av *HOR/WEW* KT19 ..78 A1
West Hill Bank *OXTED* RH8 ..123 K1
West Hill Cl *CHOB/PIR* GU24 ..71 H9
  MFD/CHID GU8 ....148 D1
West Hill Rd *PUT/ROE* SW15 ..28 C2
  WOKS/MYFD GU22 ....10 B7
West Hoathly Rd
  EGRIN RH19 ....180 B8
Westhorpe Rd
  PUT/ROE SW15 ....18 G8
Westhumble St *RDKG* RH5 ...117 H2
The West Hundreds
  FLEETN GU51 ....86 D4
Westland Cl
  STWL/WRAY TW19 * 23 H2
Westland Dr *HAYES* BR2 ......65 M1
Westlands Cl *HYS/HAR* UB3 ...15 J2
Westlands Ter *BAL* SW12 .....29 M2
Westlands Wy *OXTED* RH8 ...103 K7
West La *EGRIN* RH19 ....180 C3
  RDKG RH5 ....135 M1
Westlea Rd *HNWL* W7 ....16 C1
Westleas *HORL* RH6 ....140 A8
Westlees Cl *RDKG* RH5 ....137 J1
West Leigh *EGRIN* RH19 ......180 E4
Westleigh Av *COUL/CHIP* CR5 ..80 C5
  PUT/ROE SW15 ....27 P1
Westmacott Dr
  EBED/NFELT TW14 ....24 B4
West Md *FNM* GU9 * 4 E3
  HOR/WEW KT19 ....60 C5
Westmead *FARN* GU14 ....88 D4
  PUT/ROE SW15 ....27 N3
Westmead Dr *REDH* RH1 ....140 G2
West Mead *SUT* SM1 ....61 P3
West Meads *GUW* GU2 ....111 M6
  HORL RH6 ....159 M1
Westminster Av *THHTH* CR7 ..45 K3
Westminster Cl
  EBED/NFELT TW14 ....24 B4
  FLEETN GU51 ....86 G5
  TEDD TW11 ....25 P8
Westminster Ct
  WOKS/MYFD GU22 * 92 F1
Westminster Rd
  CRAWE RH10 ....177 M6
  SUT SM1 ....61 P1
Westmont Cl *BECK* BR3 ....47 J1
Westmont Rd *ESH/CLAY* KT10 ..58 C1
Westmoreland Dr
  BELMT SM2 ....61 M7
Westmoreland Pl
  HAYES BR2 * 47 N4
Westmoreland Rd
  BARN SW13 ....18 D6
  HAYES BR2 ....47 J8
Westmoreland Ter
  PGE/AN SE20 * 46 B1
Westmore Rd *BH/WHM* TN16 ..84 A9
Westmorland Cl
  HOR/WEW KT19 ....60 C8
  TWK TW1 ....26 A2
Westmorland Dr *BNFD* RG42 ..33 H1
  CBLY GU15 ....69 K5
Westmorland La *RGUW* GU3 ..110 A3
Westmorland Wy *MTCM* CR4 ..44 F5
West Mt *GUW* GU2 * 6 C7
West Oak *BECK* BR3 ....47 K2
Weston Av *ADL/WDHM* KT15 ..55 L5
  E/WMO/HCT KT8 ....39 N5
  ESH/CLAY KT10 ....40 E8
Weston Cl *COUL/CHIP* CR5 ....81 H9
  GODL GU7 ....131 L7
Weston Fids *SHGR* GU5 ....133 N1
Weston Gdns *ISLW* TW7 ....16 D6
Weston Gn *THDIT* KT7 ....40 E9
West Gn
  ESH/CLAY KT10 ....40 D9
Weston Gv *BAGS* GU19 ....51 P7
  BMLY BR1 ....47 M1
Weston Lea *EHSLY* KT24 ......94 F5
Weston Pk *KUT* KT1 ....8 D5
  THDIT KT7 ....40 E9
Weston Park Cl *THDIT* KT7 * ..40 E9
Weston Rd *BMLY* BR1 ....47 M2
  CHSWK W4 ....18 A1
  EW KT17 ....60 C9
  GUW GU2 ....111 N4
Weston Wy
  WOKS/MYFD GU22 ....73 J5
Weston Yd *SHGR* GU5 ....133 N1
Westover Cl *BELMT* SM2 ......61 M7
Westover Rd *FLEETN* GU51 ...87 H6
  WAND/EARL SW18 ....28 F2
Westow Hl *NRWD* SE19 ....30 F9
Westow St *NRWD* SE19 ....30 F9
West Pde *HORS* RH12 ....192 B6

West Park Av *RCH/KEW* TW9 ..17 N6
West Park Cl *HEST* TW5 ....15 P4
West Park Rd *CRAWE* RH10 ..160 C9
  HOR/WEW KT19 ....77 M1
  LING RH7 ....161 J5
  RCH/KEW TW9 ....17 P6
West Parkside *WARL* CR6 .....82 G5
West Pl *NWDGN* UB2 * 16 B2
  WIM/MER SW19 ....27 P8
West Rd *HTHAIR* TW6 ....14 C6
West Rng *RFNM* GU10 ....109 H9
West Rd *CBLY* GU15 ....68 F3
  CHSGTN KT9 ....59 J9
  CLAP SW4 ....29 N1
  EBED/NFELT TW14 ....23 N1
  FARN GU14 ....68 C8
  GU GU1 ....7 H4
  KUTN/CMB KT2 ....42 A2
  REIG RH2 ....119 M6
  WDR/YW UB7 ....14 B1
  WEY KT13 ....56 D7
West Sheen V *RCH/KEW* TW9 ..17 M9
West Side Common
  WIM/MER SW19 ....27 P9
Westside
  CHOB/PIR GU24 * 70 E2
West St *BMLY* BR1 ....47 N2
  CAR SM5 ....62 B3
  CRAWW RH11 ....2 D7
  CROY/NA CR0 ....6 D7
  DORK RH4 ....116 C7
  EGRIN RH19 ....180 D3
  EW KT17 ....60 C8
  FNM GU9 ....4 D4
  HASM GU27 ....184 D4
  HOR/WEW KT19 ....78 A2
  HORS RH12 ....192 B8
  LING RH7 ....162 F3
  REIG RH2 ....119 K5
  SUT SM1 ....61 P4
  WOKN/KNAP GU21 ....10 E3
West Street La *CAR* SM5 ....62 B3
West Street Pl *CROY/NA* CR0 ..2 D7
West Temple Sheen
  MORT/ESHN SW14 ....26 G1
West Vw *EBED/NFELT* TW14 ..23 M4
West View Av *CTHM* CR3 ......81 P7
Westview Cl *REDH* RH1 ....120 A8
West View Gdns
  EGRIN RH19 ....180 D3
West View Rd *BOR* GU35 ....164 F7
  WARL CR6 ....82 B8
Westville Rd *THDIT* KT7 ....40 G8
Westward Ho *GU* GU1 ....112 C3
Westwates Cl *BRAK* RG12 .....32 F2
West Wy *CAR* SM5 ....61 N7
  CRAWE RH10 ....177 K4
  CROY/NA CR0 ....64 E1
  HEST TW5 ....15 P6
  SHPTN TW17 ....38 B7
  SWTR RH13 ....190 E7
West Wy Gdns
  CROY/NA CR0 ....64 D1
Westway Gdns *REDH* RH1 ...120 C2
Westways *BH/WHM* TN16 ....104 G6
  EDEN TN8 ....144 G3
  HOR/WEW KT19 ....60 D3
Westwell Rd
  STRHM/NOR SW16 ....29 P9
Westwell Road Ap
  STRHM/NOR SW16 ....29 P9
Westwick Gdns *HEST* TW5 ....15 K7
Westwood Av
  ADL/WDHM KT15 ....55 L1
  NRWD SE19 ....45 L1
Westwood Cl *ESH/CLAY* KT10 ..58 C2
Westwood Gdns *BARN* SW13 ..18 B8
Westwood La *RGUW* GU3 ....110 A3
  RGUW GU3 ....110 A3
Westwood Pk *FSTH* SE23 ......31 H8
Westwood Rd *BARN* SW13 ....18 C8
  COUL/CHIP CR5 ....80 F7
Wetherby Gdns *ECT* SW5 .....19 N3
  FARN GU14 ....88 C7
Wetherby Ms *ECT* SW5 ....19 N3
Wetherby Wy *CHSGTN* KT9 ...59 L6
Wettern Cl *SAND/SEL* CR2 ....63 N8
Wetton Pl *EGH* TW20 ....21 M9
Wexfenne Gdns
  WOKS/MYFD GU22 ....73 M5
Wexford Rd *BAL* SW12 ....29 J2
Wey Av *CHERT* KT16 ....37 L4
Weybank *RPLY/SEND* GU23 ...93 M5
Weybank Cl *FNM* GU9 ....5 H2
Weybarton *BF/WBF* KT14 ......74 B2
Weybourne Pl *SAND/SEL* CR2 ..81 M8
Weybourne Rd *FNM* GU9 ....108 A9
Weybourne St
  WAND/EARL SW18 ....28 F5
Weybridge Md *WEY* KT13 .....56 D2
Weybridge Pk *WEY* KT13 .....56 D4
Weybridge Rd
  ADL/WDHM KT15 ....55 P2
  THHTH CR7 ....45 J5
Weybrook Dr *RGUE* GU4 .....113 H2
Wey Cl *ASHV* GU12 ....109 J5
  BF/WBF KT14 * 73 M2
  CBLY GU15 ....68 D3
Weycombe Rd *HASM* GU27 ..184 D2

Wey Ct *ADL/WDHM* KT15 ......55 P7
  GODL GU7 ....131 N7
Wey Ct *HOR/WEW* KT19 ....60 A3
Weycrofts *BNFD* RG42 ....32 B1
Weydon Farm La *FNM* GU9 ....5 F7
Weydon Hill Cl *FNM* GU9 ......5 F7
Weydon Hill Rd *FNM* GU9 .....5 F7
Weydon Mill La *FNM* GU9 .....4 E6
Weydown Cl *GUW* GU2 ....91 M9
  WIM/MER SW19 ....28 B4
Weydown La *GUW* GU2 * 91 M9
Weydown Rd *HASM* GU27 ....184 C5
Wey Hl *HASM* GU27 ....184 B4
Weyland Cl *LIPH* GU30 ....182 F5
Weylands Pk *WEY* KT13 ....56 F5
Weylea Av *RGUE* GU4 ....112 E2
Wey Lodge Cl *LIPH* GU30 * ..182 G6
Wey Manor Rd
  ADL/WDHM KT15 ....55 P7
Weymead Cl *CHERT* KT16 .....37 N9
Weymouth Av *EA* W5 ....17 J1
Weymouth Ct *BELMT* SM2 * ..61 M6
Wey Rd *GODL* GU7 ....131 N8
  WEY KT13 ....56 B2
Weyside *BF/WBF* KT14 ....74 B3
Weyside Gdns *GU* GU1 ....111 P3
Weyside Rd *GU* GU1 ....111 P4
Wey South Pth *CRAN* GU6 ...152 C8
  GUW GU2 ....6 F2
  MFD/CHID GU8 ....169 P9
  SHGR GU5 ....132 C4
  SHGR GU5 ....152 D4
Weysprings *HASM* GU27 .....184 A3
Weyview Cl *GU* GU1 ....112 A3
Wey View Ct *GU* GU1 ....6 C5
Weywood Cl *FNM* GU9 ....108 B7
Weywood La *FNM* GU9 ....108 A7
Wharf Bridge Rd *SLSW* TW7 ..17 H8
Wharfedale Gdns
  STRHM/NOR SW16 ....45 H3
Wharfedale St *WBPTN* SW10 ..19 M3
Wharfenden Wy *FRIM* GU16 ..89 H1
Wharf La *RPLY/SEND* GU23 ...92 G3
  TWK TW1 ....25 P4
Wharf Rd *ASHV* GU12 ....109 J2
  FRIM GU16 ....89 H1
  GU GU1 ....7 G5
  STWL/WRAY TW19 ....21 H3
Wharf St *GODL* GU7 ....131 N9
Wharf Wy *FRIM* GU16 ....89 H1
Wharncliffe Gdns
  SNWD SE25 ....45 N3
Wharncliffe Rd *SNWD* SE25 ..45 M3
Wharton Rd *BMLY* BR1 ....47 P2
Whateley Rd *EDUL* SE22 .....30 C1
  GUW GU2 ....91 N9
  PGE/AN SE20 ....46 D1
Whatley Av *RYNPK* SW20 .....43 H4
Whatman Rd *FSTH* SE23 ......31 L3
Whatmore Cl
  STWL/WRAY TW19 ....21 J7
Wheatash Rd
  ADL/WDHM KT15 ....55 M1
Wheatfield Wy *HORL* RH6 ...140 D9
  KUT KT1 ....8 D6
Wheathill Rd *PGE/AN* SE20 ...46 B3
Wheat Knoll *PUR/KEN* CR8 ...81 L5
Wheatlands *HEST* TW5 ....16 A4
Wheatlands Rd *TOOT* SW17 ..29 K6
Wheatley *BRAK* RG12 ....32 A6
Wheatley Rd *ALDT* GU11 ....108 B3
  ISLW TW7 ....16 F8
Wheatsheaf Cl *CHERT* KT16 ..55 H5
  HORS RH12 ....192 D5
  WOKN/KNAP GU21 ....10 D1
Wheatsheaf La *FUL/PGN* SW6 ..18 G5
  STA TW18 ....37 J4
Wheatsheaf Pde *WDSR* SL4 * ..20 F1
Wheatsheaf Ter
  FUL/PGN SW6 * 19 K5
Wheatstone Cl *CRAWE* RH10 ..159 L9
  WIM/MER SW19 ....43 P2
Wheeler Av *OXTED* RH8 .....103 K9
Wheeler La *MFD/CHID* GU8 ..149 M6
Wheeler Rd *CRAWE* RH10 ...177 L7
Wheelers La
  BRKHM/BTCW RH3 ....117 P7
  EPSOM KT18 ....78 A3
  HORL RH6 ....160 B2
Wheelers Wy *EGRIN* RH19 ...161 M9
Wheelwrights La
  GSHT GU26 ....165 K7
Wheelwrights Pl
  DTCH/LGLY SL3 * 12 G5
Whelan Wy *WLGTN* SM6 ......62 F2
Whellock Rd *CHSWK* W4 ......18 C1
Wherwell Rd *GU* GU1 ....6 C6
Whetstone Rd *FARN* GU14 ...88 A7
Whimbrel Cl *PUR/KEN* CR8 ...63 M9
Whinfell Cl
  STRHM/NOR SW16 ....29 N8
Whin Holt *FLEETS* GU52 ......86 G9
Whins Cl *CBLY* GU15 ....68 D4
Whins Dr *CBLY* GU15 ....68 D4
Whistler Cl *ASC* SL5 ....34 C9
Whipley Cl *RGUE* GU4 ....92 G9
Whistler Cl *CRAWE* RH10 ...177 J8
Whistler Gv *SHST* GU47 ....67 N1
Whistlers Av *BTSEA* SW11 * ..19 P5
Whistler Wk *WBPTN* SW10 * ..19 P6
Whistley Cl *BRAK* RG12 ....32 C4
Whitby Gdns *SUT* SM1 ....61 P1
Whitby Rd *SUT* SM1 ....61 P1
Whitchurch Cl *ALDT* GU11 ..108 F8
Whitchurch Rd *CRAWW* RH11 ..176 E6
Whitcome Ms
  RCH/KEW TW9 ....17 P6
White Acres Rd *FRIM* GU16 ...89 H3
Whitebeam Dr *REIG* RH2 ....119 M6

Whitebeams Gdns
  FARN GU14.....................87 N4
White Beam Wy
  KWD/TDW/WH KT20..........98 E1
Whiteberry Rd RDKG RH5 ..136 B6
White Bridge Av MTCM CR4 ..43 P5
White Bridge Cl
  EBED/NFELT TW14 ....24 A2
White City CWTH RG45.........49 H4
White Cottage Cl FNM GU9...107 P8
Whitecroft Cl BECK BR3........47 K5
Whitecroft Wy BECK BR3......47 J5
Whitefield Av PUR/KEN CR8...81 P5
Whitefield Cl
  WAND/EARL SW18.............28 B2
Whitegates
  WOKS/MYFD GU22............72 D9
Whitegate Wy
  KWD/TDW/WH KT20..........78 F9
Whitehall Crs CHSGTN KT9....59 K4
Whitehall Dr CRAWW RH11...176 B5
Whitehall Farm La VW GU25...36 C4
Whitehall Gdns CHSWK W4...17 P4
Whitehall La EGH TW20.........36 D1
  REIG RH2 ....119 K9
  STWL/WRAY TW19...........21 K7
Whitehall Pde EGRIN RH19 *..180 D2
Whitehall Park Rd
  CHSWK W4...................17 P4
Whitehall Pl CAR SM5...........62 D3
Whitehall Rd THHTH CR7......45 J6
White Hart Ct HORS RH12...192 B6
White Hart La BARN SW13......18 C7
  RGUW GU3.................110 G4
White Hart Mdw
  RPLY/SEND GU23............93 N1
White Hart Rw CHERT KT16 *..37 L8
Whitehaven Cl HAYES BR2....47 N5
Whitehead Cl
  WAND/EARL SW18.............28 F3
White Hermitage
  STWL/WRAY TW19 *..........21 H1
White Heron Ms
  TEDD TW11....................25 N9
White Hl BFOR GU20............20 B3
  COUL/CHIP CR5...............99 P3
  SAND/SEL CR2................80 G4
Whitehill Cl CBLY GU15........68 F1
Whitehill La REDH RH1........101 M7
  RPLY/SEND SEND23.........94 E3
Whitehorse La SNWD SE25....45 N5
Whitehorse Rd CROY/NA CR0..45 L8
  HORS RH12.................192 G4
White House Gdns
  YTLY GU46...................66 G1
White House La RGUE GU4....92 B9
White House Wk FNM GU9...107 J7
White Knights Rd WEY KT13...56 E6
White Knobs Wy CTHM CR3 ..102 A5
Whitelands Dr ASC SL5..........33 M2
White La BH/WHM TN16.......103 P3
  RFNM GU10.................109 L7
  RGUE GU4..................112 G7
Whiteley Rd NRWD SE19.......30 E8
Whiteleys Wy FELT TW13.......25 H6
White Lion Wk GU GU1 *.........6 E6
White Lion Wy YTLY GU46....67 H1
White Ldg NRWD SE19..........45 M1
White Lodge Cl BELMT SM2 ...61 N6
White Lodge Gdns
  REDH RH1...................140 C4
Whitemore Rd GU GU1........112 B1
White Oak Dr BECK BR3........47 J3
Whiteoaks BNSTD SM7..........79 M2
White Pillars
  WOKS/MYFD GU22 *..........72 A9
Whitepost Hl REDH RH1......120 A5
White Post La RFNM GU10 ..127 L9
White Rd CBLY GU15............68 B2
White Rose La
  WOKS/MYFD GU22..........10 A4
Whites Rd FARN GU14..........88 G6
Whitestile Rd BTFD TW8........17 J3
Whitethorn Av
  COUL/CHIP CR5..............80 C4
Whitethorn Cl ASHV GU12...109 K5
Whitethorn Gdns
  CROY/NA CR0................64 B1
White Wy GT/LBKH KT23.......96 B6
Whitewood Cottages
  BH/WHM TN16...............84 A9
Whitewood La GDST RH9.....142 B7
Whitfield Cl GUW GU2..........111 N2
  HASM GU27.................184 D1
Whitfield Rd HASM GU27.....184 D2
Whitford Gdns MTCM CR4.....44 B4
Whitgift Av SAND/SEL CR2.....63 L4
Whitgift Ct SROY/NA CR0 ....2 C6
Whitgift St CAR SM5.............43 P9
Whitlet Cl FNM GU9................4 E5
Whitley Rd STWL/WRAY TW19..25 H2
Whitley Rd YTLY GU46..........67 H4
Whitley Wy FARN GU14.........88 A6
Whitlock Dr
  WAND/EARL SW18.............28 B3
Whitmead Cl SAND/SEL CR2..63 M5
Whitmead La RFNM GU10....128 G8
Whitmoor La RGUE GU4........92 B6
Whitmoor Rd BAGS GU19.......51 N7
Whitmoor Vale Rd
  GSHT GU26..................165 J4
Whitmore Cl SHST GU47........49 P9
Whitmore Gn FNM GU9.......108 A8
Whitmore La ASC SL5............34 G6
Whitmore Rd BECK BR3.........46 F4

Whitmores Cl EPSOM KT18 *..78 A4
Whitmore V CSHT GU26.......165 J5
Whitmore Vale Rd
  GSHT GU26..................165 L7
Whitnell Wy
  PUT/ROE SW15 *.............27 P1
Whitstable Cl BECK BR3........46 F2
Whitstable Pl CROY/NA CR0...63 L3
Whittaker Av
  RCH/KEW TW9 *..............26 C1
Whittaker Rd CHEAM SM3.....61 K2
Whittell Gdns SYD SE26........31 K6
Whittingstall Rd
  FUL/PGN SW6.................19 K6
Whittington College
  EGRIN RH19 *................161 P8
Whittington Rd
  CRAWE RH10................176 C8
Whittlebury Cl CAR SM5........62 B6
Whittle Cl ASHV GU12........109 H1
  EWKG RG40...................48 C2
  SHST GU47....................49 L8
Whittle Crs FARN GU14.........68 B9
Whittle Rd HEST TW5...........15 L5
Whittle Wy CRAWE RH10....159 K8
Whitton Dene HSLW TW3.......25 J2
Whitton Manor Rd ISLW TW7..25 K2
Whitton Rd BRAK RG12..........33 H4
  HSLW TW3...................16 B9
  WHTN TW2...................25 M2
Whitton Waye HSLW TW3.......25 H2
Whitworth Rd
  CRAWW RH11...............158 C9
  SNWD SE25...................45 N4
Whopshott Av
  WOKN/KNAP GU21..........72 A5
Whopshott Cl
  WOKN/KNAP GU21..........71 P5
Whopshott Dr
  WOKN/KNAP GU21..........72 A5
Whynstones Rd ASC SL5........34 A6
Whyte Av ASHV GU12.........108 F7
Whytebeam Vw CTHM CR3....81 P7
Whytecliffe Rd North
  PUR/KEN CR8.................63 K9
Whytecliffe Rd South
  PUR/KEN CR8.................81 J1
Whytecroft HEST TW5...........15 M5
Whyteleafe Hl CTHM CR3......81 N8
Whyteleafe Rd CTHM CR3....101 N1
Wickers Oake NRWD SE19 *...30 C7
Wicket Hl RFNM GU10.........127 L7
The Wickets ASHF TW15......23 H7
The Wicket CROY/NA CR0......64 G4
Wickham Av CHEAM SM3......60 G4
  CROY/NA CR0................64 E1
Wickham Cha WWKM BR4 *...47 K8
Wickham Cl FLEETS GU52....106 B1
  HORL RH6...................140 B9
  NWMAL KT3...................42 D6
Wickham Ct WWKM BR4 *.....65 K3
Wickham Court Rd
  WWKM BR4....................65 J1
Wickham Crs WWKM BR4......65 J1
Wickham La EGH TW20.........36 E1
Wickham Pl FLEETS GU52......86 E9
Wickham Rd BECK BR3.........47 H4
  CBLY GU15....................50 C9
  CROY/NA CR0.................64 D1
  FLEETS GU52.................86 E9
Wickham V BRAK RG12.........32 A7
Wickham Wy BECK BR3........47 K4
Wickhurst La HORS RH12.....191 M7
Wick La EGH TW20..............34 G7
Wick Rd EGH TW20..............35 P1
  TEDD TW11....................41 H1
Wide Wy STRHM/NOR SW16..44 F4
Widgeon Wy HORL RH6.......192 B5
Widmore Rd BMLY BR1..........47 P7
Wigan Rd FARN GU14...........67 P7
Wiggie La RDKG RH5...........137 J1
Wigley Rd FELT TW13............24 E5
Wigmore La RDKG RH5.......156 B3
Wigmore Rd CAR SM5...........61 P1
Wilberforce Cl
  CRAWW RH11...............194 F2
Wilberforce Wy BRAK RG12...32 F6
  WIM/MER SW19...............28 A9
Wilbury Av BELMT SM2..........61 K8
Wilbury Rd
  WOKN/KNAP GU21..........10 B4
Wilcot Cl CHOB/PIR GU24......70 C5
Wilcot Gdns CHOB/PIR GU24..70 C5
Wilcox Gdns SHPTN TW17.....38 A4
Wilcox Rd SUT SM1 *............61 M3
  TEDD TW11....................25 K7
Wildacre Cl BIL RH14..........188 A7
Wild Acres BF/WBF KT14........55 N9
Wild Briar EWKG RG40..........48 D2
Wildcroft Dr RDKG RH5........137 K1
Wildcroft Rd PUT/ROE SW15..27 P3
Wildcroft Wd
  MFD/CHID GU8..............149 L6
Wilderness Ri EGRIN RH19...162 F7
Wilderness Rd FRIM GU16......68 G6
  OXTED RH8...................123 L1
The Wilderness
  E/WMO/HCT KT8..............40 C6
  HPTN TW12 *..................25 J7
Wilders Cl BNFD RG42............32 A7
  FRIM GU16....................68 F5
Wildfield Cl RGUW GU3........111 H4
Wildgoose Dr HORS RH12....191 H1
Wildridings North
  DTCH/LGLY SL3...............12 E2
Wildridings South
  DTCH/LGLY SL3...............12 E2

Wildridings Rd BRAK RG12....32 C6
Wild Ridings Sq BRAK RG12...32 C5
Wildwood Cl CRAN GU6 *.....171 J2
  EHSLY KT24...................95 H5
  WOKS/MYFD GU22...........73 K4
Wildwood Ct PUR/KEN CR8...81 M4
Wildwood Gdns YTLY GU46....66 G4
Wildwood La CRAN GU6.......170 G6
Wilford Rd DTCH/LGLY SL3....12 C2
Wilfred St WOKN/KNAP GU21..10 A4
Wilhelmina Av
  COUL/CHIP CR5...............80 E8
Wilkes Rd BTFD TW8 *..........17 M3
Wilkins Cl HYS/HAR UB3.......15 H3
  MTCM CR4....................44 A2
Wilks Gdns CROY/NA CR0......46 E9
Willats Cl CHERT KT16 *........37 K7
Willcocks Cl CHSGTN KT9......59 L2
Willdens Av ALDT GU11.......108 B4
Willett Rd THHTH CR7...........45 J6
Willey Broom La CTHM CR3..101 J5
Willey Farm La CTHM CR3....101 L6
Willey La CTHM CR3...........101 M5
William Booth Rd
  PGE/AN SE20...................46 A2
William Ellis Cl WDSR SL4....20 F1
William Evans Rd
  HOR/WEW KT19................59 N9
William Evelyn Ct
  RDKG RH5...................135 P1
William Farthing Cl
  ALDT GU11 *.................108 C4
William Gdns PUT/ROE SW15..27 N1
William Morris Wy
  CRAWW RH11...............194 E2
  FUL/PGN SW6.................19 N8
William Rd CTHM CR3.........101 M2
  GU GU1.......................11 K4
  SUT SM1.......................61 N4
  WIM/MER SW19...............43 J1
Williams Cl CRAN GU6.........153 P7
  FUL/PGN SW6.................19 J5
Williams Dr HASM GU27 *....184 B8
Williams Gv SURB KT6...........41 J7
Williams La
  MORT/ESHN SW14............18 A8
  NWDGN UB2...................14 A3
Williamson Cl HASM GU27 ..184 C1
Williams Rd NWDGN UB2.....15 N2
Williams Ter CROY/NA CR0....63 H4
William St CAR SM5.............62 A2
Williams Wy CRAWE RH10 ..177 L5
  FLEETN GU51..................87 J6
Willingham Wy KUT KT1.........9 H5
Willington Cl CBLY GU15.......68 D2
Willis Av BELMT SM2.............62 B3
Willis Cl EPSOM KT18...........77 P2
Willis Rd CROY/NA CR0..........45 L8
Willmore End
  WIM/MER SW19...............43 M2
Willoughby Av CROY/NA CR0..63 H3
Willoughby Rd BRAK RG12....32 D4
  DTCH/LGLY SL3...............12 F1
  KUTN/CMB KT2.................9 J1
  TWK TW1......................26 B1
Willow Av BARN SW13...........18 D7
Willow Bank
  WOKS/MYFD GU22...........92 C2
Willowbank Gdns
  KWD/TDW/WH KT20..........98 F2
Willow Brean HORL RH6.......140 A9
Willowbrook HPTN TW12 *.....25 J8
Willowbrook Rd NWDGN UB2..15 P1
  STWL/WRAY TW19............23 H4
The Willow Centre
  MTCM CR4....................44 B6
Willow Cl ADL/WDHM KT15 ...55 K9
  BTFD TW8....................17 J4
  CRAWE RH10................177 H3
  DTCH/LGLY SL3...............12 C5
  EGRIN RH19.................162 C9
  FRIM GU16....................68 G3
  LIPH GU30...................182 G7
  RDKG RH5...................137 J9
Willow Cnr HORL RH6..........158 C5
Willow Ct FRIM GU16............68 F7
  HORL RH6...................140 D7
Willow Crs FARN GU14..........88 D9
  FLEETE GU51..................86 D6
Willowdene Cl WHTN TW2.....25 K3
Willow Dr BRAK RG12...........32 E2
  RGUW GU3..................110 C5
  RPLY/SEND SW15............93 L4
Willowford YTLY GU46...........67 H2
  LIPH GU30...................182 G7
Willow Gn CHOB/PIR GU24....70 C2
Willowhayne Dr
  WOT/HER KT12.................39 K8
Willowhayne Gdns WPK KT4...60 G3
Willow La BLKW GU17............67 M4
  MTCM CR4....................44 B6
Willow Md DORK RH4..........116 G6
  EGRIN RH19.................180 E3
  MFD/CHID GU8..............149 M7
Willowmead STA TW18..........37 M2
Willowmead Cl
  WOKN/KNAP GU21..........71 N5
Willow Mt CROY/NA CR0 *......3 H6
Willow Pk ASHV GU12.........109 H4
Willow Rdg CRAWE RH10....177 N7
Willow Rd DTCH/LGLY SL3....13 J7
  GODL GU7...................131 M5
  HORS RH12.................192 A6
  NWMAL KT3...................41 P3
  REDH RH1...................140 F5
  WLGTN SM6...................62 D6
Willows Av MRDN SM4..........43 M8
Willows End SHST GU47........49 M9
Willows Pth EPSOM KT18......77 P3

The Willows BECK BR3 *.......46 G2
  BF/WBF KT14.................74 A2
  ESH/CLAY KT10...............58 E5
  GUW GU2.....................91 M9
  LTWR GU18....................52 C9
  MFD/CHID GU8..............167 P7
  RFNM GU10.................128 E1
  RGUE GU4..................113 H3
  WEY KT13.....................56 C2
Willow Ter PGE/AN SE20 *.....31 J9
Willow Tree Cl
  WAND/EARL SW18.............28 C4
Willow Tree Wk BMLY BR1....47 P2
Willowtree Wy
  STRHM/NOR SW16............45 J2
Willow V GT/LBKH KT23.........96 B3
Willow Vw WIM/MER SW19....43 P2
Willow Wk CHEAM SM3.........61 K2
  KWD/TDW/WH KT20.........117 P1
  REDH RH1...................120 D7
  SHGR GU5...................134 C1
Willow Wy ASHV GU12........108 G6
  BF/WBF KT14.................55 N9
  FNM GU9....................107 P8
  EGRIN RH19.................122 B3
  GU GU1.......................112 A3
  HOR/WEW KT19...............60 B5
  SHST GU47....................49 J9
  SUN TW16....................39 J5
  SYD SE26.....................31 J6
  WHTN TW2...................25 J5
  WOKS/MYFD GU22...........72 A7
Willow Wood Crs SNWD SE25..45 N7
Willow Wren Whf
  NWDGN UB2 *................15 K2
Wills Crs HSLW TW3.............25 J1
Wilson Rd EGH TW20............20 G8
Wilmar Gdns WWKM BR4.......47 H9
Wilmer Cl
  RCHPK/HAM TW10............26 E8
Wilmerhatch La EPSOM KT18..77 J7
Wilmington Av CHSWK W4.....18 B5
Wilmington Cl CRAWW RH11..194 E2
Wilmot Cottages
  BNSTD SM7 *..................79 M4
Wilmot Rd CAR SM5..............62 B4
  PUR/KEN CR8.................81 J1
Wilmots Cl REIG RH2..........119 N4
Wilmot's La REDH RH1........141 M6
Wilmot Wy BNSTD SM7.........79 L4
  CBLY GU15....................69 H5
Wilna Rd WAND/EARL SW18...28 F3
Wilson Av MTCM CR4...........44 A8
Wilson Cl CRAWE RH10.......177 K6
  SAND/SEL CR2 *..............63 M4
Wilson Dr CHERT KT16..........54 F4
Wilson Rd ASHV GU12.........108 F5
  CHSGTN KT9..................59 M5
Wilsons KWD/TDW/WH KT20..98 H1
Wilsons Rd BOR GU35.........164 E6
  HMSMTH W6...................18 G3
Wilson Wk HMSMTH W6 *......18 G1
Wilstrode Av BNFD RG42.......32 A3
Wilton Av CHSWK W4............18 C3
Wilton Cl WDR/YW UB7..........14 A1
Wilton Ct FARN GU14...........88 E4
Wilton Crs WIM/MER SW19....43 K2
  WOT/HER KT12.................39 M9
Wilton Gdns E/WMO/HCT KT8..40 A3
  WIM/MER SW19...............43 K2
Wilton PI ADL/WDHM KT15....55 P7
Wilton Rd CBLY GU15............68 C5
  HSLWW TW4...................15 M8
  REDH RH1...................120 B6
  WIM/MER SW19...............44 A1
Wiltshire Av CRWR RG45.......49 M8
Wiltshire Gdns WHTN TW2.....25 K4
Wiltshire Rd THHTH CR7........45 J4
Wilverley Crs NWMAL KT3......42 C7
Wilwood Rd BNFD RG42.........32 A2
Wimbart Rd
  BRXS/STRHM SW2 *..........30 A3
Wimbledon Br
  WIM/MER SW19...............28 C9
Wimbledon Hill Rd
  WIM/MER SW19...............28 B9
Wimbledon Park Rd
  WIM/MER SW19...............28 A6
Wimbledon Park Side
  WIM/MER SW19...............27 P9
Wimbledon Rd CBLY GU15.....51 H8
  TOOT SW17...................28 G7
Wimblehurst Rd HORS RH12..192 A5
Wimborne Av NWDGN UB2....16 A2
Wimborne Cl EW KT17............78 C4
  WPK KT4.......................42 G9
Wimborne Wy BECK BR3.......46 E3
Wimbushes EWKG RG40........48 B3
Wimland Hl HORS RH12.......175 J9
Wimland Rd HORS RH12......174 G6
  HORS RH12.................175 J8
Wimpole Cl KUT KT1..............9 G5
Wimshurst Cl CROY/NA CR0...44 G8
Wincanton Cl CRAWE RH10..177 N5
Wincanton Rd
  WAND/EARL SW18.............28 C3
Winchcombe Cl FLEETN GU51..86 G6
Winchcombe Rd CAR SM5......43 P8
Winchelsea Cl
  PUT/ROE SW15...............27 N2
Winchelsey Ri SAND/SEL CR2..63 P5
Winchendon Rd
  FUL/PGN SW6.................19 K5
  TEDD TW11....................25 L7

Winchester Av HEST TW5.......15 P4
Winchester Cl DTCH/LGLY SL3..13 J6
  ESH/CLAY KT10...............58 A3
  HAYES BR2....................47 M4
  KUTN/CMB KT2.................41 P1
Winchester Pk HAYES BR2.....47 M4
Winchester Rd ASHV GU12...109 J3
  CRAWE RH10................177 H9
  FELT TW13....................24 G6
  HAYES BR2....................47 M4
  HYS/HAR UB3.................14 G5
  RFNM GU10.................147 L5
  TWK TW1......................26 B3
  WOT/HER KT12.................39 J9
Winchester St FARN GU14.....88 E7
Winchet Wy HORS RH12 *....193 P4
The Winches HORS RH12......193 P4
Winchfield Cl FLEETN GU51...86 E4
Winchfield Ct HTWY RG27......85 J1
Winchfield Rd SYD SE26........31 M8
Winchgrove Rd BNFD RG42....32 C1
Winchilsea Crs
  E/WMO/HCT KT8..............40 C1
Winchstone Cl SHPTN TW17...38 B5
Windall Cl NRWD SE19..........45 N2
Windborough Rd CAR SM5.....62 C6
Windermere Av
  WIM/MER SW19...............43 M4
Windermere Cl
  EBED/NFELT TW14............23 P4
  EGH TW20.....................36 A8
  FARN GU14....................88 A4
  STWL/WRAY TW19 *..........22 F1
Windermere Ct
  ASHV GU12 *.................109 H2
Windermere Rd
  COUL/CHIP CR5...............80 G4
  CROY/NA CR0...................3 K1
  EA W5..........................17 J1
  LTWR GU18....................52 B8
  PUT/ROE SW15................27 K7
  STRHM/NOR SW16............44 E2
  WIM/MER SW19...............43 M4
  WWKM BR4....................65 L1
Windermere Wy FNM GU9 ...107 L8
Windfield Cl SYD SE26..........31 L7
Windgates RGUE GU4...........93 J1
Windham Av CROY/NA CR0....65 A9
Windham Rd RCH/KEW TW9...17 M8
The Windings SAND/SEL CR2..63 P9
Winding Wood Dr
  CBLY GU15....................69 K4
Windlebrook Gn BNFD RG42..32 C2
Windle Cl BFOR GU20...........52 D5
Windlesham Cl BFOR GU20....52 C3
Windlesham Gv
  WIM/MER SW19...............28 A4
Windlesham Rd BNFD RG42...32 B2
  CHOB/PIR GU24...............52 E9
Windley Cl FSTH SE23...........31 K5
Windmill Av EW KT17............60 D8
Windmill Cl CTHM CR3.........101 L1
  EGRIN RH19.................181 H4
  EW KT17........................16 D2
  HORL RH6...................159 L1
  ISLW TW7 *....................16 E2
  SUN TW16.....................38 G1
  SURB KT6......................41 J9
  SWTR RH13..................192 F7
Windmill Dr CRAWE RH10....176 C6
Windmill Dr BOR GU35........164 E5
  CLAP SW4.....................29 L1
  LHD/OX KT22.................97 H3
  REDH RH1...................119 P3
Windmill End EW KT17..........78 D1
Windmill Fld BFOR GU20.......52 D5
Windmill La EGRIN RH19......162 C9
  EW KT17.......................78 D1
  ISLW TW7......................16 D2
  THDIT KT7.....................41 H8
Windmill Pas CHSWK W4 *.....18 C1
Windmill Ri KUTN/CMB KT2....41 P1
Windmill Rd ASHV GU12......108 B3
  BNFD RG42....................32 B2
  CHSWK W4....................18 C2
  CROY/NA CR0.................45 L8
  EA W5..........................17 J2
  HPTN TW12....................25 J7
  MTCM CR4....................44 E6
  WAND/EARL SW18.............28 G2
  WIM/MER SW19...............27 N8
Windmill Rd West
  SHPTN TW17...................38 G3
Windmill Shott EGH TW20......21 J9
Windmill Ter SHPTN TW17.....38 G8
Windmill Wy REDH RH1.......119 P3
Windrush Av DTCH/LGLY SL3..12 F1
Windrush Cl BTSEA SW11 *.....19 P9
  CHSWK W4...................18 A5
  CRAWW RH11...............176 C7
  SHGR GU5...................132 D7
Windrush Hts SHST GU47......49 M9
Windrush La FSTH SE23........31 L6
Windsor Av CHEAM SM3........61 J2
  E/WMO/HCT KT8..............40 A4
  NWMAL KT3...................42 A5
  WIM/MER SW19...............43 N1
Windsor Cl CRAWW RH11....176 F9
  FARN GU14....................88 A7
  GUW GU2....................111 M7
  WNWD SE27...................30 D7
Windsor Court Rd
  CHOB/PIR GU24...............53 L7
Windsor Dr ASHF TW15.........22 G7
Windsor Gdns ASHV GU12...109 H5
  CROY/NA CR0..................2 A9
  HYS/HAR UB3.................14 F1
Windsor Great Pk ASC SL5 *....34 F1
Windsor Gv WNWD SE27.......30 D7

Windsor Park Rd
HYS/HAR UB3 ......15 H5
Windsor Pl CHERT KT16 * 37 L7
EGRIN RH19 ......180 F3
Windsor Ride ASC SL5 ......33 K6
BFOR GU20 ......32 C9
CHOB/PIR GU24 ......50 C9
EWKG RG40 ......48 E2
Windsor Rd ASC SL5 ......33 P3
CHOB/PIR GU24 ......53 L7
EGH TW20 ......21 L6
FARN GU14 ......87 P7
FARN GU14 ......88 F6
HSLWW TW4 ......5 K7
KUTN/CMB KT2 ......8 D1
NWDGN UB2 ......15 P1
RCH/KEW TW9 ......17 M7
SUN TW16 ......39 J1
TEDD TW11 ......25 L8
THHTH CR7 ......45 J5
WDSR SL4 ......21 H3
WPK KT4 ......60 C5
Windsor St CHERT KT16 ......37 L7
Windsor Wk WEY KT13 ......56 D4
Windsor Wy ALDT GU11 ......108 D4
FRIM GU16 ......69 H8
WKENS W14 ......19 H2
WOKS/MYFD GU22 ......72 C5
Winds Rdg RPLY/SEND GU23...92 G5
Windways MFD/CHID GU8...169 L4
Windycroft Cl PUR/KEN CR8....44 G7
Windyridge CRAWW RH11 ...176 D6
Windy Ridge Cl
WIM/MER SW19 ......28 A8
Windy Wd COOL GU7 ......150 B1
Winern Giebe BF/WBF KT14 ...73 P2
Winery La KUT KT1 ......9 F6
Winey Cl CHSGTN KT9 ......59 J6
Winfield Gv RDKG RH5 ....156 G3
Winfrith Rd
WAND/EARL SW18 ......28 F3
Wingate Cl ALDT GU11 ....108 B4
Wingate Crs CROY/NA CRO 44 G7
Wingate Rd HMSMTH W6 ....18 F1
Wingfield Cl
ADL/WDHM KT15 ......55 M8
Wingfield Gdns FRIM GU16 ...69 M5
Wingfield Rd KUTN/CMB KT2 ..26 E9
Wingford Rd
BRXS/STRHM SW2 ......29 P2
Wingrave Rd HMSMTH W6 ...18 G4
Wings Cl FNM GU9 ......107 M8
SUT SM1 ......61 L3
Winifred Rd COUL/CHIP CR5...25 H7
HPTN TW12 ......25 H7
WIM/MER SW19 ......43 L2
Winkfield Rd ASC SL5 ......34 A2
Winkworth Rd SMT 79 L3
Winnington Wy
WOKN/KNAP GU21 ......71 P7
Winnipeg Cl LIPH GU30 ...182 F7
Winscombe BRAK RG12 ...32 N6
Winsford Rd CAT SE6 ......31 N6
Winsham Gv BTSEA SW11 ....29 K1
Winslade Rd
BRXS/STRHM SW2 ......29 P1
Winslow Rd HMSMTH W6 ...18 G4
Winslow Wy FELT TW13 ....38 D1
WOT/HER KT12 ......57 L2
Winstanley Cl COB KT11 ....75 K3
Winstanley Rd BTSEA SW11 ...19 P8
Winston Cl FRIM GU16 ......89 H1
Winston Dr COB KT11 ......75 N5
Winston House SURB KT6 * ...41 L6
Winston Wk RFNM GU10 ....127 N1
Winston Wy
WOKS/MYFD GU22 ......72 F9
Winterbourne HORS RH12 ...192 E3
Winterbourne Gv WEY KT13 ...56 E5
Winterbourne Rd CAT SE6 ...31 N4
THHTH CR7 ......45 J5
Winter Box Wk
RCHPK/HAM TW10 ......26 E1
Winterbrook Rd HNHL SE24 ...30 D2
Winterdown Gdns
ESH/CLAY KT10 ......57 P5
Winterdown Rd
ESH/CLAY KT10 ......57 N5
Winterfold CRAWE RH10 ...177 K8
Winterfold G
WIM/MER SW19 ......28 B5
Winterhill Wy RGUE GU4 ...112 F1
Wintersells Rd BF/WBF KT14...55 P8
Winters Rd THDIT KT7 ......41 H8
Winterstoke Rd CAT SE6 ....31 N4
Winston Ct SWTR RH13 ...192 C8
Winterton Pl WBPTN SW10 ...19 N4
Winterwell Rd
BRXS/STRHM SW2 ......29 P1
Winthorpe Rd
PUT/ROE SW15 ......19 J9
Winton Crs YTLY GU46 ......67 H5
Winton Rd ALDT GU11 ....108 C5
FNM GU9 ......5 J1
Winton Wy
STRHM/NOR SW16 ......30 B8
Wireless Rd BH/WHM TN16....84 B4
Wire Mill La LING RH7 ....161 M4
Wisbeach Rd CROY/NA CRO...45 M6
Wisborough Ct
CRAWW RH11 ......176 C8
Wisborough Rd
SAND/SEL CR2 ......63 P7
Wise La WDR/YW UB7 ......13 J2
Wiseton Rd TOOT SW17 ....29 H4
Wishanger La BOR GU35 ...164 E1
Wishbone Wy
WOKN/KNAP GU21 ......71 M5
Wishmoor Cl CBLY GU15...50 G9
Wishmoor Rd CBLY GU15...50 G9
Wisley Gdns FARN GU14...87 P5

Wisley La RPLY/SEND GU23 ...74 A5
Wisley Rd BTSEA SW11 ......29 J1
Wistaria La YTLY GU46 ......66 G3
Wiston Ct CRAWW RH11 ...176 C8
Witham Rd ISLW TW7 ......16 D6
PGE/AN SE20 ......46 C4
Witherby Cl SAND/SEL CR2 ...63 N4
Wither Dl HORL RH6 ......140 A9
Witherslack Cl BOR GU35...164 E7
Withey Brook HORL RH6...158 G3
Witheygate Av STA TW18 ...22 E9
Withey Mdw HORL RH6...158 G3
Withies La RGUW GU3 ......131 J3
The Withies LHD/OX KT22 ...77 H9
WOKN/KNAP GU21 ......71 L6
Withybed Cnr
BRAK RG12 ......98 F3
Withy Cl LTWR GU18 ......52 C8
Withypitts CRAWE RH10 ...179 H8
Withypitts East
CRAWE RH10 ......179 H8
Witley Crs CROY/NA CRO 65 J5
Witley Gdns NWDGN UB2...15 P2
Witney Pth FSTH SE23 * 31 L6
Wittenham Rd BRAK RG12 ...33 H2
Wittering Cl KUTN/CMB KT2 ...26 C8
Wittmead Rd FRIM GU16 ...89 H3
Mivenhoe Ct HSLW TW3...15 J9
Wiverton Rd SYD SE26 ......31 K9
Wix Hl EHSLY KT24 ......114 D1
Woburn Av FARN GU14 ......88 F3
PUR/KEN CR8 ......63 J9
Woburn Cl FRIM GU16 ......69 J7
WIM/MER SW19 ......28 F9
Woburn Hl ADL/WDHM KT15...55 N1
Woburn Pk
ADL/WDHM KT15 * 55 P1
Woburn Rd CAR SM5 ......44 A9
CRAWW RH11 ......176 D7
CROY/NA CRO 2 D1
Wodeland Av GUW GU2 ......6 B7
Woffington Cl
E/WMO/HCT KT8 ......41 J2
Woking Cl PUT/ROE SW15 ...18 D9
Wokingham Rd BNFD RG42 ...32 B2
CWTH RG45 ......49 J3
Wold Cl CRAWW RH11 ...176 C7
Woldhurstlea Cl
CRAWW RH11 ......176 D7
Woldingham Rd CTHM CR3...82 B9
The Wold CTHM CR3 ......102 G2
Wolfe Cl HAYES BR2 ......47 N7
Wolfe Rd ASHV GU12 ......108 E5
Wolfington Rd WNWD SE27...30 C7
Wolf's Hl OXTED RH8 ......123 N2
Wolf's Rd OXTED RH8 ......123 P1
Wolfs Wd OXTED RH8 ......123 N3
Wolseley Av
WAND/EARL SW18 ......28 D5
Wolseley Gdns CHSWK W4 ...17 N4
Wolseley Rd ALDT GU11 ...108 C5
CHSWK W4 ......17 J4
GODL GU7 ......131 L7
MTCM CR4 ......44 C8
Wolsey Cl HSLW TW3 ......16 C3
KUTN/CMB KT2 ......41 P2
NWDGN UB2 ......16 C1
RYNPK SW20 ......42 F1
WPK KT4 ......60 E8
Wolsey Crs CROY/NA CRO ...65 J8
MRDN SM4 ......43 K8
Wolsey Dr KUTN/CMB KT2 ...26 D8
WOT/HER KT12 ......39 M9
Wolsey Gv ESH/CLAY KT10...58 B3
Wolsey Rd ASHF TW15 ......23 H7
E/WMO/HCT KT8 ......40 D5
ESH/CLAY KT10 ......58 B3
HPTN TW12 ......25 J9
SUN TW16 ......39 H1
Wolsey Wk
WOKN/KNAP GU21 ......10 E3
Wolsey Wy CHSGTN KT9 ...59 N4
Wolstonbury Cl
CRAWW RH11 ......176 F1
Wolvens La DORK RH4 ...136 A2
RDKG RH5 ......136 E8
Wolverton Av KUTN/CMB KT2...9 J2
Wolverton Cl HORL RH6...159 J3
Wolverton Gdns
HMSMTH W6 ......19 H2
HORL RH6 ......159 J2
Wolves Hl RDKG RH5 ......156 B8
Wonersh Common Rd
SHGR GU5 ......132 F6
Wonersh Wy BELMT SM2...61 H7
Wonford Cl
KWD/TDW/WH KT20 ......98 E6
NWMAL KT3 ......42 C2
Wonham La
BRKHM/BTCW RH3 ......118 D6
Wonham Wy SHGR GU5 ...134 F2
Wontford Rd PUR/KEN CR8...81 J4
Wontner Rd BAL SW12 ......29 L1
Woodall Cl CHSGTN KT9 ...59 J6
The Woodbarn FNM GU9 * ...5 H5
Woodbastwick Rd SYD SE26...31 L9
Woodberry Cl
MFD/CHID GU8 ......167 P6
SUN TW16 ......24 B9
Woodbine Cl SHST GU47...68 B1
Woodbine Gv PGE/AN SE20...46 B1
Woodbine La WPK KT4 ......60 F2
Woodbines Av KUT KT1 ......8 C7
Woodborough Rd
PUT/ROE SW15 ......18 F2
Woodbourne FNM GU9 ...108 A7
Woodbourne Av
STRHM/NOR SW16 ......29 N6
Woodbourne Cl YTLY GU46...67 H2
Woodbourne Dr
ESH/CLAY KT10 ......58 F5

Woodbourne Gdns
WLGTN SM6 ......62 D6
Woodbridge Av LHD/OX KT22...76 G7
Woodbridge Ct
HORS RH12 * 192 F5
Woodbridge Cr CBLY GU15...68 F7
Woodbridge Gv LHD/OX KT22...76 G7
Woodbridge Hl GUW GU2...111 P4
Woodbridge Hill Gdns
GUW GU2 * 111 N4
Woodbridge Mdw GU GU1 ...6 C1
Woodbridge Rd BLKW GU17...67 M3
GU GU1 ......7 E5
Woodbury Av EGRIN RH19...180 G3
Woodbury Cl BH/WHM TN16...84 D7
CROY/NA CRO 3 K4
EGRIN RH19 ......180 G3
Woodbury Dr BELMT SM2 ...61 N8
Woodbury St TOOT SW17 ...29 H8
Woodby Dr ASC SL5 ......34 F8
Wood Cl REDH RH1 ......140 C5
Woodcock Dr
CHOB/PIR GU24 ......53 J6
Woodcock Hl LING RH7 ...161 N6
Woodcock La
CHOB/PIR GU24 ......53 H6
Woodcombe Cl CRAN GU6...152 E8
HORL RH6 ......140 C1
RGUW GU3 ......111 P9
Woodcote Av THHTH CR7 ...45 K5
WLGTN SM6 ......62 D7
Woodcote Cl EPSOM KT18...78 B3
KUTN/CMB KT2 ......26 E8
Woodcote End EPSOM KT18...78 B4
Woodcote Gn FLEETN GU51...86 D7
WLGTN SM6 ......62 E7
Woodcote Green Rd
EPSOM KT18 ......78 A5
Woodcote Grove Rd
COUL/CHIP CR5 ......80 F4
Woodcote House Ct
EPSOM KT18 * 78 B4
Woodcote Hurst
EPSOM KT18 ......78 A6
Woodcote Pk
COUL/CHIP CR5 * 80 D2
Woodcote Park Av
PUR/KEN CR8 ......62 E9
Woodcote Park Rd
EPSOM KT18 ......78 A5
Woodcote Pl ASC SL5 ......33 P2
WNWD SE27 * 30 C9
Woodcote Rd FROW RH18...181 K9
EPSOM KT18 ......78 A4
PUR/KEN CR8 ......80 F2
WLGTN SM6 ......62 E4
Woodcote Side EPSOM KT18...77 P4
Woodcote Valley Rd
PUR/KEN CR8 ......80 F2
Woodcot Gdns FARN GU14...87 P9
Woodcott Ter ASHV GU12...108 F6
Woodcourt CRAWW RH11...194 F1
Wood Crest BELMT SM2 * ...61 N6
Woodcrest Rd
CRAWW RH11 ......176 A1
THHTH CR7 ......45 K6
Woodcroft Rd RFNM GU10...127 K8
Wooden Bridge Ter
WNWD SE27 * 30 C6
Wood End CWTH RG45 ....49 K5
HORS RH12 ......195 K5
Woodend ESH/CLAY KT10 ...58 C1
FARN GU14 ......88 F4
LHD/OX KT22 ......97 J3
NRWD SE19 ......30 D9
SUT SM1 ......61 N1
Woodend Cl CRAWE RH10...177 K3
WOKN/KNAP GU21 ......71 N8
Woodend Dr ASC SL5 ......34 B6
Woodend Pk COB KT11 ...75 M4
Woodend Rd FRIM GU16 ...69 L9
Woodenhill BRAK RG12 ...32 A8
Woodend Cl SNWD SE25 ...45 N5
Woodfield ASHTD KT21 ...77 K6
Woodfield Av CAR SM5 ...62 C5
STRHM/NOR SW16 ......29 N6
Woodfield Cl ASHTD KT21...77 K6
COUL/CHIP CR5 ......80 E8
CRAWE RH10 ......177 N1
NRWD SE19 ......45 L1
REDH RH1 ......120 A4
Woodfield Gdns
NWMAL KT3 ......42 D6
Woodfield Gv
STRHM/NOR SW16 ......29 N6
Woodfield Hl COUL/CHIP CR5..80 D8
Woodfield La ASHTD KT21 ...77 K6
CRAWE RH10 ......177 J3
ESH/CLAY KT10 ......58 C2
HORS RH12 ......189 N3
HSLWW TW4 ......15 K7
The Woodfields
SAND/SEL CR2 ......63 P9
Woodfield Rd REDH RH1 ...120 A4
Woodford Gn BRAK RG12 ...33 H5
Woodgate FLEETN GU51...87 J4
Woodgate Av CHSGTN KT9...59 K4
Woodgate Dr
STRHM/NOR SW16 ......44 F1
Woodgates Cl SWTR RH13...192 F6
Woodgavil BNSTD SM7 ......79 K5
Wooger Cl RGUE GU4 ......112 G3
Woodger Cl RGUE GU4 ......112 G3
Woodhall Av DUL SE21 ......30 G6
Woodhall Dr DUL SE21 ......30 G6
Woodhall La BFOR GU20 ...52 E1

Woodham La
ADL/WDHM KT15 ......73 J1
WOKN/KNAP GU21 ......72 F2
Woodham Park Rd
ADL/WDHM KT15 ......55 K9
Woodham Park Wy
ADL/WDHM KT15 ......55 K9
Woodham Rl
WOKN/KNAP GU21 ......72 C4
Woodham Waye
WOKN/KNAP GU21 ......72 C4
Woodhatch Rd REDH RH1...119 P9
Woodhatch Spinney
COUL/CHIP CR5 ......80 G5
Woodhaven Ms
WOT/HER KT12 * 57 J3
Woodhaw EGH TW20 ......21 N7
Woodhayes HORL RH6 ...140 D9
Woodhayes Rd RYNPK SW20...42 C1
WIM/MER SW19 ......27 P3
Woodhill RPLY/SEND GU23...93 H6
Woodhill Cl RPLY/SEND GU23..93 H5
Woodhill La SHGR GU5 ...133 J9
Woodhouse Cl HYS/HAR UB3..15 H1
Woodhouse La SHGR GU5...135 J5
Woodhouse St BNFD RG42...32 A2
Woodhurst La OXTED RH8...123 L1
Woodhurst Pk OXTED RH8...123 L1
Woodhyrst Gdns
PUR/KEN CR8 ......81 K4
Wooding Gv CRAWW RH11...194 E1
Woodland Av CRAN GU6 ...153 J9
Woodland Cl EHSLY KT24...94 D3
HOR/WEW KT19 * 60 C5
NRWD SE19 ......30 F9
SWTR RH13 ......192 G6
Woodland Ct OXTED RH8...103 K8
Woodland Dr BNFD RG42 ...32 E1
Woodland Dr CRAWE RH10...179 J3
EDEN TN8 ......145 H2
EHSLY KT24 ......94 D3
RDKG RH5 ......155 P7
RFNM GU10 ......127 M7
Woodland Gdns ISLW TW7...16 E8
Woodland Hl NRWD SE19 ...30 F9
Woodland La SWTR RH13...193 N7
OXTED RH8 ......103 K8
Woodland Rd NRWD SE19...30 F8
THHTH CR7 ......45 H5
Woodlands ADL/WDHM KT15...56 A2
ASHTD KT21 * 77 M7
CRAWE RH10 ......177 N3
CWTH RG45 ......49 M6
FLEETN GU51 ......85 K5
RPLY/SEND GU23 ......93 K5
RYNPK SW20 ......42 G6
WOKS/MYFD GU22 ......10 C6
YTLY GU46 ......67 H5
Woodlands Av BF/WBF KT14...73 L1
FNM GU9 ......108 B2
NWMAL KT3 ......42 B2
REDH RH1 ......120 B6
WPK KT4 ......60 D7
Woodlands Cl ASC SL5 ......33 J7
ASHV GU12 ......109 J1
CHERT KT16 ......54 F8
CRAN GU6 ......153 J9
CRAWE RH10 ......179 J4
ESH/CLAY KT10 ......58 F6
FARN GU14 ......88 D3
Woodlands Copse
ASHTD KT21 ......77 K5
Woodlands Ct REDH RH1 * ...120 B7
SHST GU47 ......50 B8
WOKS/MYFD GU22 ......10 D7
Woodlands Dr GDST RH9...122 E8
SUN TW16 ......39 K2
Woodlands Gdns
EPSOM KT18 ......78 G6
Woodlands Gv
COUL/CHIP CR5 ......80 D6
ISLW TW7 ......16 E7
Woodlands La
CHOB/PIR GU24 ......52 F6
COB KT11 ......76 A6
HASM GU27 ......184 A3
Woodlands Pde ASHF TW15...23 M9
Woodlands Pk
ADL/WDHM KT15 ......55 K4
GU GU1 ......112 F9
KWD/TDW/WH KT20 ......99 P2
WOKN/KNAP GU21 ......72 G2
Woodlands Ride ASC SL5 ...33 P7
Woodlands Rd BARN SW13...18 D8
BF/WBF KT14 ......73 K3
CBLY GU15 ......50 B8
EGRIN RH19 ......162 F8
EHSLY KT24 ......94 B2
EPSOM KT18 ......78 B4
FARN GU14 ......87 P1
GU GU1 ......7 E1
ISLW TW7 ......16 B1
LHD/OX KT22 ......96 C3
MFD/CHID GU8 ......168 C2
REDH RH1 ......120 B7
SURB KT6 ......41 K8
VW GU25 ......36 A5
Woodlands Rd East VW GU25...35 P4
Woodlands Rd West
VW GU25 ......36 A4
The Woodlands
ESH/CLAY KT10 ......58 C1
HORL RH6 ......160 B5
ISLW TW7 ......16 F7
NRWD SE19 ......45 L1
WLGTN SM6 ......62 D7

Woodlands Wy ASHTD KT21...77 N5
KWD/TDW/WH KT20 ......118 A5
PUT/ROE SW15 ......28 C1
Woodland Vw GODL GU7 ...131 L4
Woodland Wk
HOR/WEW KT19 ......59 N5
Woodlands Wy BRYLDS KT5...59 P3
CROY/NA CRO 46 E9
KWD/TDW/WH KT20 ......99 J2
MRDN SM4 ......43 K5
MTCM CR4 ......44 C1
PUR/KEN CR8 ......81 N1
REDH RH1 ......101 N8
SWTR RH13 ......192 F6
WEY KT13 ......56 F4
WWKM BR4 ......65 J2
Wood La CTHM CR3 ......101 N4
FARN GU14 ......88 C4
FLEETN GU51 ......87 J6
ISLW TW7 ......16 C3
KWD/TDW/WH KT20 ......79 K6
RFNM GU10 ......109 L9
WEY KT13 ......56 F7
WOKN/KNAP GU21 ......71 N4
Woodlawn Cl PUT/ROE SW15...28 C1
Woodlawn Crs WHTN TW2...25 J5
Woodlawn Dr FELT TW13...24 E5
Woodlawn Gv
WOKN/KNAP GU21 ......72 A3
Woodlawn Rd FUL/PGN SW6..19 H5
Woodleigh FLEETN GU51...86 G7
Woodley Cl TOOT SW17 ...44 B1
Woodley La SUT SM1 ......61 J2
Wood Lodge La WWKM BR4 ...65 J2
Woodmancote Gdns
BF/WBF KT14 ......73 L2
Woodmancourt GODL GU7 ...131 J5
Woodman Rd
COUL/CHIP CR5 ......80 E5
Woodmans Hl CRAWW RH11..194 F1
Woodmansterne La
BNSTD SM7 ......79 M4
CAR SM5 ......80 B1
Woodmansterne Rd
CAR SM5 ......62 A6
COUL/CHIP CR5 ......80 E4
STRHM/NOR SW16 ......44 E1
Woodmansterne St
BNSTD SM7 ......80 A4
Woodmere Av CROY/NA CRO...46 D8
Woodmere Cl CROY/NA CRO...46 D8
Woodmere Gdns
CROY/NA CRO 46 D8
Woodmere Wy BECK BR3 ...47 K6
Wood Moor EWKG RG40...48 D2
Woodnook Rd
STRHM/NOR SW16 ......29 L8
Woodpecker Cl COB KT11...75 N1
RFNM GU10 ......107 H6
Woodpecker La RDKG RH5...157 H2
Woodpecker Mt
CROY/NA CRO 64 E7
Woodpeckers
MFD/CHID GU8 ......149 M5
Woodpecker Wy
CRAWE RH10 ......179 K5
WOKS/MYFD GU22 ......92 B3
Woodplace Cl
COUL/CHIP CR5 ......80 E8
Woodplace La
COUL/CHIP CR5 ......80 E9
Woodquest Av HNHL SE24...30 C1
Woodridge Cl BRAK RG12 ...32 K4
Wood Riding
WOKS/MYFD GU22 ......73 J4
Wood Ridings WEY KT13 * ...56 C5
Wood Rd BH/WHM TN16 ...84 C3
Wood Rd CU GU9 * 113 J9
CBLY GU15 ......68 D7
FNM GU9 ......107 N7
GODL GU7 ......131 M6
GSHT GU26 ......165 N5
SHPTN TW17 ......38 C5
Woodrough Copse
SHGR GU5 ......132 E8
Woodroyd Av HORL RH6...159 J3
Woodroyd Gdns HORL RH6...159 J4
Woodruff Av GU GU1 ......112 E2
Woods Hill La EGRIN RH19...181 J5
Woods Hill La EGRIN RH19...181 J5
Woodshore Cl VW GU25...35 P7
Woodside BLKW GU17 ......67 N5
CBLY GU15 ......68 E3
EHSLY KT24 ......94 E6
KWD/TDW/WH KT20 ......99 K8
LHD/OX KT22 ......96 B2
SWTR RH13 ......192 G6
WIM/MER SW19 ......28 B1
WOT/HER KT12 ......57 K3
Woodside Cl BRYLDS KT5 ...42 A8
CTHM CR3 ......101 N4
EWKG RG40 ......48 D3
RDKG RH5 ......157 H4
WOKN/KNAP GU21 ......71 K6
Woodside Court Rd
CROY/NA CRO 46 A8
Woodside Crs HORL RH6...160 B3
Woodside Gdns FLEETN GU51..87 J5
Woodside Pk SNWD SE25 ...46 A7
Woodside Pl ALDT GU11...88 B8
Woodside Rd BH/WHM TN16..84 C3
COB KT11 ......76 A2
CRAWE RH10 ......177 J3
FNM GU9 ......108 A7
GUW GU2 ......111 M4

KUTN/CMB KT2 ...8 D1
MFD/CHID GU8 ...167 N6
NWMAL KT3 ...42 B3
PUR/KEN CR8 ...80 C2
RDKG RH5
RSEV TN14 ...105 P4
SNWD SE25 ...46 B7
SUT SM1
Woodside Wy CROY/NA CRO ...46 C7
MTCM CR4 ...44 D2
REDH RH1 ...120 C6
REDH RH1 ...140 C2
VW GU25 ...35 P4
Woodlands HORL RH6 ...140 F9
Woodspring Rd
WIM/MER SW19 ...28 B5
Woodstock EGRIN RH19 ...180 B1
RGUE GU4 ...93 M8
Woodstock Av CHEAM SM3 ...43 K8
DTCH/LGLY SL3 ...12 G1
HNWL W7 ...16 G1
ISLW TW7 ...15 G1
Woodstock Cl CRAN GU6 ...171 J2
HORS RH12 ...192 C5
WOKN/KNAP GU21 ...10 C2
Woodstock Dr
Woodstock Gv GODL GU7 ...131 L6
Woodstock La North
SURB KT6 ...59 J1
Woodstock La South
ESH/CLAY KT10 ...59 H4
Woodstock Ri CHEAM SM3 ...43 K9
Woodstock Rd CAR SM5 ...62 C4
CHSWK W4 ...18 C2
COUL/CHIP CR5 ...80 D5
CROY/NA CRO ...44 C8
Woodstocks FARN GU14 ...88 E1
Woodstock Wy MTCM CR4 ...44 E3
Woodstone Av KT17 ...60 E4
Wood St ASHV GU12 ...109 J9
CHSWK W4 ...18 C3
EGRIN RH19 ...180 C2
KUT KT1
MTCM CR4 ...44 C8
REDH RH1 ...100 E9
Woodsway LHD/OX KT22 ...76 D2
Woodsyre SYD SE26 ...30 C7
Woodthorpe Rd ASHF TW15 ...22 D2
PUT/ROE SW15 ...18 F9
Wood V FSTH SE23 ...31 J4
Woodvale Av SNWD SE25 ...45 P4
Woodview CHSGTN KT9 ...71 J1
Woodville Cl KUTN/CMB KT2 ...27 J7
SAND/SEL CR2 ...82 B3
Woodville Gdns SURB KT6 * ...41 J8
TEDD TW11 ...25 P7
Woodville Rd
WIM/MER SW19 ...43 N2
Woodward Cl
ESH/CLAY KT10 ...58 F5
Woodwarde Rd EDUL SE22 ...30 F2
Woodwards CRAWW RH11 ...194 E1
Woodway CBLY GU15 ...68 D3
WOKS/MYFD GU22
Woodyard La DUL SE21 ...30 F3
Woodyers Cl SHGR GU5 ...132 F6
Woolacombe Wy
HYS/HAR UB3 ...14 G2
Woolborough Cl
CRAWE RH10 ...177 H4
Woolborough La
CRAWE RH10 ...177 J2
REDH RH1 ...141 H5
Woolborough Rd
CRAWE RH10 ...176 G4
Woolford Cl BNFD RG42 ...33 K1
Woolfords La
MFD/CHID GU8 ...148 B5
Woolhampton Wy
BRAK RG12 ...32 F6
Woolhams CTHM CR3 ...101 P6
Woollards Rd ASHV GU12 ...109 J2
Woolmead Rd FNM GU9 ...5 G3
The Woolmead FNM GU9
Woolmer Hill Rd
HASM GU27 ...183 M3

Woolmer La LIPH GU30 ...182 F2
Woolneigh St FUL/PGN SW6 ...19 M8
Wool Rd RYNPK SW20 ...27 N9
Woolsack Wy GODL GU7 ...131 M9
Woolstone Rd FSTH SE23 ...31 M5
Wootton Cl EPSOM KT18 ...78 C5
Worbeck Rd PGE/AN SE20 ...46 B3
Worcester Cl CROY/NA CRO ...64 F1
FARN GU14 ...68 D9
MTCM CR4 ...44 C3
Worcester Ct WOT/HER KT12 ...57 L1
Worcester Dr ASHF TW15 ...23 L9
CHSWK W4 ...18 C1
Worcester Gdns WPK KT4 ...60 C2
Worcester Park Rd WPK KT4 ...60 A2
Worcester Rd BELMT SM2 ...61 L8
CRAWE RH10 ...177 H9
GUW GU2 ...111 M3
REIG RH2 ...119 L4
WIM/MER SW19 ...28 C8
Worcestershire Lea
BNFD RG42 ...33 H1
Wordsworth Cl CRAWE RH10 ...177 L3
Wordsworth Av
PUR/KEN CR8 ...81 M4
YTLY GU46 ...66 F4
Wordsworth Cl
CRAWE RH10 ...177 L3
Wordsworth Dr CHEAM SM3 ...60 C3
Wordsworth Md REDH RH1 ...120 D3
Wordsworth Pl HORS RH12 ...192 D3
Wordsworth Ri EGRIN RH19 ...180 B2
Wordsworth Rd
ADL/WDHM KT15 ...55 P3
FELT TW13 ...24 C7
PGE/AN SE20 ...46 D1
WLGTN SM6 ...62 E5
Wordsworth Wy
ADL/WDHM KT15 ...14 A2
Works Rd ADL/WDHM KT15 ...55 M7
World's End COB KT11 ...75 J3
EPSOM KT18 * ...78 B5
Worlds End Est
WBPTN SW10 * ...19 P5
Worlds End Rd BRAK RG12 ...33 H7
Worlds End Pas
WBPTN SW10 * ...19 P5
Worlidge St HMSMTH W6 ...18 G3
Wormley La MFD/CHID GU8 ...167 P2
Worple Av ISLW TW7 ...25 P1
STA TW18 ...22 E9
WIM/MER SW19 ...43 H1
Worple Rd EPSOM KT18 ...78 C3
ISLW TW7 ...25 P1
LHD/OX KT22 ...97 H3
RYNPK SW20 ...42 G3
STA TW18 ...37 M1
WIM/MER SW19 ...43 J1
Worple Road Ms
WIM/MER SW19 ...43 J1
Worplesdon Hill Heath House Rd
WOKS/MYFD GU22 ...91 J2
Worplesdon Rd RGUW GU3 ...91 M9
Worple St MORT/ESHN SW14 ...18 B8
The Worple
STWL/WRAY TW19 ...21 L2
Worple Wy
RCHPK/HAM TW10 ...26 D1
Worsfold Cl RPLY/SEND GU23 ...92 F3
Worslade Rd TOOT SW17 ...28 C7
Worsley Bridge Rd CAT SE6 ...31 N8
Worsley Rd FNM GU16 ...68 G9
Worsopp Dr CLAP SW4 ...29 M1
Worsted Gn REDH RH1 ...100 F9
Worsted La EGRIN RH19 ...180 C4
Worthfield Cl
HOR/WEW KT19 ...60 B6
Worthing Rd HEST TW5 ...15 P4
HORS RH12 ...192 A9
Worthington Cl MTCM CR4 ...44 D5
Worthington Rd SURB KT6 ...41 M9
Worth Park Av CRAWE RH10 ...177 M4
Worth Rd CRAWE RH10 ...177 M5
Worth Wy CRAWE RH10 ...177 N6
Wortley Rd CROY/NA CRO ...45 J8
Worton Gdns ISLW TW7 ...16 D7
Worton Rd ISLW TW7 ...16 F8
Worton Wy ISLW TW7 ...16 D7
Wotton Dr RDKG RH5 ...135 N2
Wotton Wy BELMT SM2 ...60 G8
Wrabness Wy STA TW18 ...37 M2

Wray Cl EGRIN RH19 ...181 J5
Wray Common Rd REIG RH2...119 N4
Wrayfield Av REIG RH2 ...119 N4
Wrayfield Rd CHEAM SM3 ...61 H2
Wraylands Dr REIG RH2 ...119 P3
Wray La REIG RH2 ...119 N1
Wraymead Rd REIG RH2 ...119 M4
Wray Mill Pk REDH RH1 ...119 P3
Wray Park Rd REIG RH2 ...119 N4
Wray Rd BELMT SM2 ...61 K7
Wraysbury Cl HSLWW TW4 ...24 F1
Wraysbury Gdns STA TW18 ...22 B7
Wraysbury Rd STA TW18 ...22 B7
STWL/WRAY TW19 ...21 P6
Wrecclesham Hl
RFNM GU10 ...127 J8
Wrecclesham Rd FNM GU9 ...127 K5
The Wrekin FARN GU14 ...88 G6
Wren Av NWDGN UB2 ...15 P2
Wren Cl HORS RH12 ...192 C3
SAND/SEL CR2 ...64 D8
YTLY GU46 * ...66 F3
Wren Ct ASHV GU12 ...109 K3
CRAWE RH10 * ...177 H8
Wren Crs ADL/WDHM KT15 ...55 P4
Wren Dr WDR/YW UB7 ...13 P1
Wren's Av ASHF TW15 ...23 M8
Wren's Hl LHD/OX KT22 ...76 C4
Wren St CRAWE RH10 ...176 G6
Wren Wy FARN GU14 ...68 B9
Wright Cl CRAWE RH10 * ...177 L9
Wright Gdns SHPTN TW17 ...38 C6
Wright Rd HEST TW5 ...15 L5
Wrights La KENS W8 * ...19 L1
Wrights Rd SNWD SE25 ...45 N4
Wright's Rw CAR SM5 ...62 B3
Wrotham Hl MFD/CHID GU8 ...169 M8
Wroughton Rd BTSEA SW11 ...29 J2
Wroxham BRAK RG12 ...32 B6
Wrythe Cl CAR SM5 ...44 B9
Wrythe Gn CAR SM5 ...62 B2
Wrythe Green Rd CAR SM5 ...62 B2
Wrythe La CAR SM5 ...43 P9
Wulwyn Side CWTH RG45 ...49 L4
Wyatt Cl FELT TW13 ...24 F3
Wyatt Dr BARN SW13 ...18 F4
Wyatt Park Rd
BRXS/STRHM SW2 ...30 A5
Wyatt Rd STA TW18 ...22 D8
Wyatt's Cl GODL GU7 ...131 N7
Wyche Gv SAND/SEL CR2 ...63 L6
Wych Elm Ri GU GU1 ...112 C8
Wychelm Rd LTWR GU18 ...52 C9
Wych Hl WOKS/MYFD GU22 ...72 A8
Wych Hill La
WOKS/MYFD GU22 ...72 C8
Wych Hill Pk
WOKS/MYFD GU22 ...10 A7
Wych Hill Ri
WOKS/MYFD GU22 ...72 B8
Wychwood Av BIL RH14 ...188 A7
Wychwood Av BRAK RG12 ...33 H5
THHTH CR7 ...45 K4
Wychwood Cl ASHV GU12 ...109 H4
SUN TW16 ...23 K9
Wychwood Pl CBLY GU15 ...51 K8
Wycliffe Rd WIM/MER SW19 ...28 E9
Wycombe Rd
WAND/EARL SW18 ...28 F2
Wycliffe Gdns REDH RH1 ...120 E1
Wye Cl ASHF TW15 ...23 L7
CRAWW RH11 ...194 F2
Wye St BTSEA SW11 ...19 P8
Wyeths Ms EW KT17 * ...78 D2
Wyeth's Rd EW KT17 ...78 D2
Wyfold Rd FUL/PGN SW6 ...19 J6
Wyke Av ASHV GU12 ...109 M3
Wyke Cl ISLW TW7 ...16 F4
Wyke Gdns HNWL W7 ...16 F1
Wykeham Cl WDR/YW UB7 ...14 C4
Wykeham Rd FNM GU9 ...5 G1
GU GU1 ...113 H4
Wyke La ASHV GU12 ...109 M3
Wyke Rd RYNPK SW20 ...42 G3
Wykwood LIPH GU30 ...182 G6
Wylam BRAK RG12 ...32 B6
Wylands Rd DTCH/LGLY SL3 ...12 E3
Wyldewood ASC SL5 ...34 D7
Wyleu St FSTH SE23 ...31 M3

Wylie Rd NWDGN UB2 ...16 A1
Wymering Ct FARN GU14 ...88 F2
Wymond St PUT/ROE SW15 ...18 G8
Wyncote Wy SAND/SEL CR2 ...64 D7
Wyndham Av COB KT11 ...75 J2
Wyndham Cl BELMT SM2 ...61 L6
YTLY GU46 ...67 H1
Wyndham Crs CRAN GU6 ...152 D9
HSLWW TW4 ...24 C2
Wyndham Rd KUTN/CMB KT2...41 M1
WEA W13 ...17 H1
WOKN/KNAP GU21 ...71 P7
Wyndham St ASHV GU12 ...108 E5
Wyneham Rd HNHL SE24 ...30 E1
Wynell Rd FSTH SE23 ...31 L5
Wynfields FRIM GU16 ...89 H4
Wynlea Cl CRAWE RH10 ...179 H3
Wynne Gdns FLEETS GU52 ...107 H1
Wynnstay Gdns KENS W8 * ...19 L1
Wynsham Wy BFOR GU20 ...52 G4
Wynter St BTSEA SW11 ...19 N9
Wynton Gdns SNWD SE25 ...45 N6
Wynton Gv WOT/HER KT12 ...57 J2
Wyphurst Rd CRAN GU6 ...152 G8
Wyre Gv HYS/HAR UB3 ...15 J2
Wysemead HORL RH6 ...140 E9
Wyvern Cl ASHV GU12 * ...109 H1
BRAK RG12 ...32 C5
Wyvern Est NWMAL KT3 * ...42 E4
Wyvern Pl ADL/WDHM KT15 *...55 M3
Wyvern Rd PUR/KEN CR8 ...63 J8

Y

Yaffle Rd WEY KT13 ...56 E8
Yale Cl HSLWW TW4 ...24 C1
SHST GU47 ...50 B7
Yarborough Rd
WIM/MER SW19 ...43 P2
Yarbridge Cl BELMT SM2 * ...61 M8
Yardley BRAK RG12 ...32 B6
Yardley Cl REIG RH2 ...119 M3
Yard Md EGH TW20 ...21 M6
Yarm Cl LHD/OX KT22 ...97 J3
Yarm Court Rd LHD/OX KT22 ...97 J3
Yarmouth Cl CRAWE RH10...177 K7
Yarm Wy LHD/OX KT22 ...97 J3
Yarrow Cl HORS RH12...192 C2
Yateley Rd YTLY GU46 ...67 K1
Yatesbury Cl FNM GU9 ...127 K6
Yattendon Rd HORL RH6 ...159 L1
Yaverland Dr BAGS GU19 ...51 M7
Yeats Cl REDH RH1 ...119 N8
Yeend Cl E/WMO/HCT KT8 ...40 A5
Yeldham Rd HMSMTH W6 ...19 H3
Yeldham Vls HMSMTH W6 * ...19 H3
Yellowcress Dr
CHOB/PIR GU24 ...70 C5
Yelverton Rd BTSEA SW11 ...19 P7
Yenston Cl MRDN SM4 ...43 L7
Yeomanry Ct EW KT17 ...78 D1
Yeomans HTWY RG27 ...66 C1
Yeomans Cl FARN GU14 ...88 A2
RFNM GU10 ...109 H6
Yeomans La LIPH GU30 ...182 D6
Yeomans Pl BOR GU35 ...164 B6
Yeomans Ter
WOKN/KNAP GU21 * ...71 K6
Yeomans Wy CBLY GU15 ...68 G3
Yeoman Wy REDH RH1 ...140 D1
Yeoveney Cl
STWL/WRAY TW19 ...22 A5
Yeovil Cl FARN GU14 ...88 F6
Yeovil Rd SHST GU47 ...50 A8
Yeovilton Pl KUTN/CMB KT2 ...26 C8
Yetminster Rd FARN GU14 ...88 F6
Yewbank Cl PUR/KEN CR8...81 M4
Yew Cnr BRAK RG12 ...32 E4
Yewens MFD/CHID GU8 ...168 A6
Yewlands Cl BNSTD SM7 ...79 M4
Yew La EGRIN RH19 ...162 A9
Yew Pl WEY KT13 * ...57 H2
The Yews ASHF TW15 * ...23 L7
BF/WBF KT14 * ...74 A1

Yew Tree Bottom Rd
EW KT17 ...78 F6
Yew Tree Cl COUL/CHIP CR5 ...80 D8
FARN GU14 * ...87 N4
HORL RH6 ...140 C8
WPK KT4 ...42 C9
Yew Tree Dr CTHM CR3 ...101 P5
GU GU1 ...91 P9
Yew Tree Gdns EPSOM KT18...78 A4
Yew Tree La REIG RH2 ...119 M2
Yewtree Rd BECK BR3 ...46 F4
Yew Tree Rd DORK RH4 ...116 C5
HORL RH6 ...158 B5
MFD/CHID GU8 ...149 L6
Yewtrees EGH TW20 ...36 G4
Yew Trees SHPTN TW17 ...38 B5
Yew Tree Wk EHSLY KT24 ...95 M7
FRIM GU16 ...68 G2
HSLWW TW4 ...24 C1
PUR/KEN CR8 ...63 L8
Yockley Cl CBLY GU15 ...69 M5
Yolland Cl FNM GU9 ...107 N7
York Av EGRIN RH19 ...180 F3
MORT/ESHN SW14 ...27 H1
York Cl BF/WBF KT14 ...74 A1
MRDN SM4 ...43 M5
SWTR RH13 ...192 E7
York Crs ALDT GU11 ...108 B5
Yorke Gdns REIG RH2 ...119 L4
Yorke Ga CTHM CR3 ...101 M2
Yorke Rd REIG RH2 ...119 L4
York Gdns WOT/HER KT12 ...57 M1
York Hl STRHM/NOR SW16 ...30 C6
York Pde BTFD TW8 * ...17 K3
York Pl BTSEA SW11 ...19 N9
CBLY GU15 ...68 F1
York Rd ALDT GU11 ...108 B5
ASHV GU12 ...109 J3
BELMT SM2 ...61 L5
BH/WHM TN16 ...83 P8
BTFD TW8 ...17 K3
BTSEA SW11 ...19 N9
CBLY GU15 ...68 F1
CRAWE RH10 ...177 H9
CROY/NA CRO ...45 J8
EA W5 ...17 J1
FARN GU14 ...88 B6
FNM GU9 ...5 H7
GU GU1 ...7 G2
HSLW TW3 ...16 B8
KUTN/CMB KT2 ...9 G1
RCHPK/HAM TW10 ...26 E1
SAND/SEL CR2 ...64 D8
TEDD TW11 ...25 M7
WEY KT13 ...56 E4
WIM/MER SW19 ...28 E9
WOKS/MYFD GU22 ...10 B6
Yorkshire Pl BNFD RG42 ...32 G1
Yorkshire Rd MTCM CR4 ...44 G6
York St MTCM CR4 ...44 C8
TWK TW1 ...25 P4
York Terrace La CBLY GU15 * ...68 F2
Yorktown Rd SHST GU47 ...67 N1
York Wy CHSGTN KT9 ...59 L6
FELT TW13 ...24 G6
SHST GU47 ...49 L9
Youlden Cl CBLY GU15 ...69 J3
Youlden Dr CBLY GU15 ...69 J3
Youngs Dr ASHV GU12 ...109 H4
Young St LHD/OX KT22 ...96 F4
Youngstroat La
CHOB/PIR GU24 ...54 C8
Yukon Rd BAL SW12 ...29 L3

Z

Zealand Av WDR/YW UB7 ...13 P5
Zennor Rd BAL SW12 ...29 M4
Zermatt Rd THHTH CR7 ...45 L5
Zig Zag Rd PUR/KEN CR8 ...81 L5
Zinnia Dr CHOB/PIR GU24 ...70 G5
Zion Pl THHTH CR7 ...45 M5
Zion Rd THHTH CR7 ...45 M5

Index - featured places

AA Southwood
FARN GU14 ...87 N3
Abbey Business Park
FNM GU9 ...128 C5
Abbey Industrial Estate
MTCM CR4 ...44 B6
Abbeylands School
ADL/WDHM KT15 ...55 L4
Abbey Mill Business Park
GODL GU7 ...130 E9
Abbey Mills
WIM/MER SW19 ...43 N2
Abbey Moor Golf Club
ADL/WDHM KT15 ...55 L2
The Abbey School
FNM GU9 ...5 K6
Abbey Trading Estate
SYD SE26 ...31 M8
Abbotsbury First School
MRDN SM4 ...43 M6
Abbots Hospital
GU GU1 ...7 F5

ABC Cinema
ALDT GU11 ...108 C4
ESH/CLAY KT10 ...58 B3
KUTN/CMB KT2 ...8 E4
PUT/ROE SW15 ...19 J8
STA TW18 ...22 B7
STRHM/NOR SW16 ...29 P5
Aberdour School
KWD/TDW/WH KT20 ...79 K7
Abingdon Common First School
FNM GU9 ...128 D9
Abinger Common First School
RDKG RH5 ...135 M4
Abinger Hammer
Village School
RDKG RH5 ...135 H1
Abro Industrial Estate
ALDT GU11 ...108 F3
Acre Road Health Clinic
KUTN/CMB KT2 ...9 F1
Acting School
GUW GU2 ...6 D7

Acumen (Anglo School)
NRWD SE19 ...45 N1
Adamsrill Primary School
FSTH SE23 ...31 M6
Addington Business Centre
CROY/NA CRO ...65 L8
The Addington Golf Club
CROY/NA CRO ...64 E5
Addington Palace Golf Club
CROY/NA CRO ...64 E5
Addison Primary School
WKENS W14 ...19 H1
Addlestone Cemetery
ADL/WDHM KT15 ...55 L1
ADT Technology College
PUT/ROE SW15 ...28 C1
Adult Education Centre
CBLY GU15 ...68 D3
FNM GU15 ...4 E4
GODL GU7 ...131 L8
GU GU1 ...7 G5

Airborne Forces Museum
ALDT GU11 ...108 C1
Airbus Coach Station
FARN TW6 ...14 B8
Airedale
Physiotherapy Clinic
CHSWK W4 ...18 D3
Airlinks Golf Club
HEST TW5 ...15 L2
Air Links Industrial Estate
HEST TW5 ...15 L3
Airport Gate
Business Centre
WDR/YW UB7 ...14 B5
Airport Industrial Estate
BH/WHM TN16 ...84 B4
Albany Clinic
WIM/MER SW19 ...43 M1
Albany Park
Canoe & Sailing Centre
KUTN/CMB KT2 ...26 C9

Albany Park
Industrial Estate
FRIM GU16 ...68 D7
Albemarle Primary School
WIM/MER SW19 ...28 B5
Alderbrook Primary School
BAL SW12 ...29 L3
Aldershot & Farnham
County Court
ALDT GU11 ...108 D4
Aldershot Health Centre
ALDT GU11 ...108 B4
Aldershot Military Museum
ALDT GU11 ...88 E8
Aldershot Military Stadium
ALDT GU11 ...88 E9
Aldershot Town FC
ALDT GU11 ...108 E4
Aldro School
MFD/CHID GU8 ...130 C6
Alexander Barracks
CHOB/PIR GU24 ...90 B1

Alexander House Hotel
   CRAWE RH10 ....179 K6
Alexandra Infant School
   KUTN/CMB KT2 ....9 H1
   PGE/AN SE20 ....46 D1
Alexandra Junior School
   HSLW TW3 ....16 B3
   SYD SE26 ....31 L9
Alfred Mizen First School
   MTCM CR4 ....44 F4
The All England Lawn Tennis
   & Croquet Club
   WIM/MER SW19 ....28 A6
Alleyns School
   EDUL SE22 ....30 F1
Allfarthing JMI School
   WAND/EARL SW18 ....28 F2
All Hallows RC
   Comprehensive School
   FNM GU9 ....108 B7
All Saints Benhilton School
   SUT SM1 ....61 M2
All Saints CE First School
   WIM/MER SW19 ....43 N1
All Saints CE Infant School
   LHD/OX KT22 ....76 C8
   RFNM GU10 ....147 M1
All Saints CE Junior School
   FLEETN GU51 ....86 D7
   NRWD SE19 ....45 N2
All Saints CE Primary School
   FUL/PGN SW6 ....19 J7
   PUT/ROE SW15 ....18 C8
Al Muntada Islamic School
   FUL/PGN SW6 ....19 K6
The Alton School
   PUT/ROE SW15 ....27 L3
Ambleside Junior School
   WOT/HER KT12 ....39 L9
Amen Corner Business Park
   BRAK RG12 ....32 A3
American Community School
   EGH TW20 ....36 A2
The American
   Community School
   COB KT11 ....57 M8
American Golf at Sunbury
   SHPTN TW17 ....38 E5
Amesbury School
   GSHT GU26 ....183 P1
Amy Johnson
   Primary School
   WLGTN SM6 ....62 G6
The Andrew Ewing
   Primary School
   HEST TW5 ....15 P5
Anerley Primary School
   PGE/AN SE20 ....46 A2
Anerley School
   PGE/AN SE20 ....46 A2
The Angel Posting House
   & Livery Hotel
   GU GU1 ....6 E6
Animal Care College
   ASC SL5 ....34 A4
Ansells Farm
   Community Centre
   FLEETN GU51 ....87 J3
Apex Retail Park
   FELT TW13 ....24 C6
Apostolic Nuncio
   WIM/MER SW19 ....27 P6
Applegarth Primary School
   CROY/NA CR0 ....65 H5
Aquarius Golf Club
   PECK SE15 ....31 K1
The Archbishop
   Lanfranc School
   CROY/NA CR0 ....44 G7
Archbishop Tenisons
   CE School
   CROY/NA CR0 ....3 J6
Archdeacon Cambridge's
   CE Primary School
   WHTN TW2 ....25 M5
Archway Theatre
   HORL RH6 ....159 K2
Arena Leisure Centre
   CBLY GU15 ....68 E2
Arlington Business Park
   BRAK RG12 ....32 D3
Army Golf Club
   ALDT GU11 ....88 A9
Army Medical Services
   Museum
   FRIM GU16 ....89 K6
Army Training Regiment
   CHOB/PIR GU24 ....90 C1
Arndale Health Centre
   WAND/EARL SW18 ....28 D3
Arnhem Barracks
   ALDT GU11 ....108 C3
Arrow Industrial Estate
   FARN GU14 ....88 B5
Arts Centre
   HORS RH12 ....192 B8
Arts Centre & Staines
   Theatre
   STA TW18 ....22 B7
Art School
   BECK BR3 ....46 E6
Arts Link Theatre Cinema
   CBLY GU15 ....68 F2
Arts Theatre
   PUT/ROE SW15 ....19 H9
Arun House
   HORS RH12 ....192 C4
Arunside Primary School
   HORS RH12 ....191 N6
Ascot Heath Junior School
   ASC SL5 ....33 N1

Ascot Racecourse
   ASC SL5 ....33 P4
Ashburnham Primary School
   WBPTN SW10 ....19 P5
Ashburton High School
   CROY/NA CR0 ....46 B8
Ashburton Primary School
   CROY/NA CR0 ....46 B8
Ashby Mill School
   CLAP SW4 ....29 P1
The Ashcombe School
   DORK RH4 ....117 H5
Ashdown Forest
   Health Centre
   FROW RH18 ....181 K8
Ashdown House School
   FROW RH18 ....181 P7
Ashford CE Primary School
   ASHF TW15 ....23 L9
Ashford Clinic
   ASHF TW15 ....23 H5
Ashford High School
   ASHF TW15 ....23 H6
Ashford High School
   ASHF TW15 ....23 H6
Ashford Hospital A & E
   STWL/WRAY TW19 ....23 J5
Ashford Industrial Estate
   ASHF TW15 ....23 M7
Ashford Manor Golf Club
   ASHF TW15 ....23 J9
Ashford Park Primary School
   ASHF TW15 ....22 F7
The Ashford
   & St Peters Hospital
   CHERT KT16 ....55 H2
Ashford Sports Club
   ASHF TW15 ....22 G7
Ashford Sports Club
   STWL/WRAY TW19 ....23 J4
Ash Grange CP School
   ASHV GU12 ....109 K4
Ashgrove School
   BMLY BR1 ....47 P3
Ashley Centre
   Shopping Precinct
   HOR/WEW KT19 ....78 B2
Ashley Primary School
   WOT/HER KT12 ....39 J9
Ash Manor School
   ASHV GU12 ....109 H6
Ashtead Clinic
   ASHTD KT21 ....77 L6
Ashtead Cricket Club
   ASHTD KT21 ....77 L7
Ashtead Hospital
   ASHTD KT21 ....77 L9
Ashton House School
   ISLW TW7 ....16 D6
Ashurst Wood
   Primary School
   EGRIN RH19 ....181 K5
Ash Vale Health Centre
   ASHV GU12 ....109 K2
Aspen House Secondary
   & Primary School
   BRXS/STRHM SW2 ....29 P4
Assembly Rooms
   KUT KT1 ....41 L5
The Astolat Industrial Estate
   RGUW GU3 ....132 A4
Aston Clinic
   NWMAL KT3 ....42 C5
Astra Business Centre
   REDH RH1 ....140 C6
Atheiney Primary School
   CAT SE6 ....31 P6
Athelstan House School
   HPTN TW12 ....40 A2
Atkinson Morley Hospital
   RYNPK SW20 ....42 F1
Atlas Medical Centre
   HORL RH6 ....159 K5
Atlas Transport Estate
   BTSEA SW11 ....19 N7
Atwood Primary School
   SAND/SEL CR2 ....82 A3
Audley Primary School
   CTHM CR3 ....101 N1
Auriol Junior School
   HOR/WEW KT19 ....60 D3
The Avenue Primary School
   BELMT SM2 ....61 L8
Avon Trading Estate
   WKENS W14 ....19 K2
BAA Heathrow Visitor Centre
   HTHAIR TW6 ....14 D6
Back Care Clinic
   WPK KT4 ....42 E9
Baden Powell House
   SKENS SW7 ....19 N2
Badshot Lea
   Village Infant School
   FNM GU9 ....108 C8
Bagshot School
   BAGS GU19 ....51 N6
Baldwins Hill
   Primary School
   EGRIN RH19 ....162 B9
Balfour Business Centre
   NWDGN UB2 ....15 M1
Balgowan Primary School
   BECK BR3 ....46 E3
Balham Health Centre
   BAL SW12 ....29 L5
Balham Leisure Centre
   TOOT SW17 ....29 K5
Balham Preparatory School
   TOOT SW17 ....29 J7
Bandon Hill Cemetery
   WLGTN SM6 ....62 F4
Bandon Hill Primary School
   WLGTN SM6 ....62 F5

Banstead Athletic FC
   KWD/TDW/WH KT20 ....78 G9
Banstead Clinic
   BNSTD SM7 ....79 L4
Banstead County
   Junior School
   BNSTD SM7 ....79 K4
Banstead County
   Primary School
   BNSTD SM7 ....79 K4
Banstead Downs Golf Club
   BELMT SM2 ....61 L9
Banstead Sports Centre
   KWD/TDW/WH KT20 ....78 G9
Banstead Village Clinic
   BNSTD SM7 ....79 M4
Barfield School
   RFNM GU10 ....128 D2
Barn Elms Athletics Track
   BARN SW13 ....18 F7
Barn Elms
   Water Sports Centre
   BARN SW13 ....18 G7
Barnes Hospital
   MORT/RSHN SW14 ....18 C4
Barnes Sports Club
   BARN SW13 ....18 D7
Barnett Wood Infant School
   ASHTD KT21 ....77 K6
Barnsbury County School
   WOKS/MYFD GU22 ....92 B1
Barnwood County
   First School
   GUW GU2 ....111 K4
Barons Court Theatre
   WKENS W14 ....19 J3
Barrow Hedges
   Primary School
   CAR SM5 ....62 A6
Barrow Hills Golf Club
   CHERT KT16 ....54 A1
Barrow Hills School
   MFD/CHID GU8 ....149 M8
Barwell Business Park
   CHSGTN KT9 ....59 K6
Baston School
   HAYES BR2 ....65 P1
Bath Factory Estate
   HNHL SE24 ....30 D2
Battersea Sports Centre
   BTSEA SW11 ....19 P8
Battersea Tutorial College
   TOOT SW17 ....29 K5
Beacon Hill County
   Primary School
   GSHT GU26 ....165 M5
Beatrix Potter
   Primary School
   WAND/EARL SW18 ....28 F4
Beauclerc Infant School
   SUN TW16 ....39 L4
Beaufort Primary School
   WOKN/KNAP GU21 ....71 M5
Beaumont Junior School
   ALDT GU11 ....108 A4
Beaumont Primary School
   PUR/KEN CR8 ....81 H3
Beaver Industrial Estate
   LIPH GU30 ....182 F8
The Beavers Community
   Primary School
   HSLWW TW4 ....15 L8
Beckenham Business Centre
   BECK BR3 ....31 M9
Beckenham Crematorium
   SNWD SE25 ....46 C4
Beckenham Cricket Club
   BECK BR3 ....47 H1
Beckenham Hospital
   BECK BR3 ....46 F3
Beckenham Leisure Centre
   BECK BR3 ....46 E2
Beckenham RFC
   BECK BR3 ....46 E5
Beckenham Town FC
   BECK BR3 ....46 G6
Beckmead School
   BECK BR3 ....64 G4
Bective House Clinic
   PUT/ROE SW15 ....19 K9
Beddington Infants School
   WLGTN SM6 ....62 E2
Beddington Medical Centre
   CROY/NA CR0 ....62 G3
Beddington Park
   Primary School
   CROY/NA CR0 ....62 F2
Beddington Trading Estate
   CROY/NA CR0 ....44 G9
Bedelsford Special School
   KUT KT1 ....8 D7
Bedfont Health Clinic
   EBED/NFELT TW14 ....23 P3
Bedfont Industrial Park
   EBED/NFELT TW14 ....23 N6
Bedfont J & I School
   EBED/NFELT TW14 ....23 N4
Bedfont Lakes Country Park
   EBED/NFELT TW14 ....23 M5
Bedington Infant School
   WLGTN SM6 ....62 E3
Beech House School
   SAND/SEL CR2 ....63 P8
Beechnut Industrial Estate
   ASHV GU12 ....108 D5
Beecholme First School
   MTCM CR4 ....44 D2
Beechwood School
   STRHM/NOR SW16 ....29 P5

Belfry Shopping Centre
   REDH RH1 ....120 B4
Bellerby Theatre
   GU GU1 ....6 E4
Belleville Primary School
   BTSEA SW11 ....29 J1
Belle Vue Infant School
   ASHV GU12 ....108 F4
Bell Farm Junior School
   WOT/HER KT12 ....57 L3
Bell Industrial Estate
   CHSWK W4 ....18 A2
Belmont Preparatory
   School
   RDKG RH5 ....135 L7
Belmont Primary School
   CHSWK W4 ....18 B2
Bensham Manor School
   THHTH CR7 ....45 L6
Benson Primary School
   CROY/NA CR0 ....64 E2
The Bentall Shopping Centre
   KUT KT1 ....8 B4
Bentley Industrial Centre
   RFNM GU10 ....126 A9
Bentley Trimmings
   Business Park
   RFNM GU10 ....126 B8
Berkeley Primary School
   HEST TW5 ....15 M4
The Berkshire Golf Club
   ASC SL5 ....51 L1
Bertram House School
   TOOT SW17 ....29 K5
The Berystede Hotel
   ASC SL5 ....34 C7
Betchworth Park Golf Club
   RDKG RH5 ....117 L6
Bethlem Royal Hospital
   BECK BR3 ....46 G8
Beulah J & I School
   THHTH CR7 ....45 L3
Bevendean Pre-preparatory
   School
   LHD/OX KT22 ....76 C2
Beverley School
   NWMAL KT3 ....42 E6
Beverley Trading Estate
   MRDN SM4 ....43 H8
Bewbush Leisure Centre
   CRAWW RH11 ....176 C9
Bewbush Medical Centre
   CRAWW RH11 ....176 B8
Bewbush Middle School
   CRAWW RH11 ....176 B8
Bewhurst County
   First School
   CRAWW RH11 ....176 C8
Biggin Hill Airport
   BH/WHM TN16 ....84 B2
Biggin Hill Business Park
   BH/WHM TN16 ....84 B4
Biggin Hill Primary School
   BH/WHM TN16 ....84 C5
Bilton Industrial Estate
   BRAK RG12 ....32 A5
Bingham Hotel
   RCHPK/HAM TW10 ....26 D2
Binscombe Medical Centre
   GODL GU7 ....131 K5
Birches Industrial Estate
   EGRIN RH19 ....161 P9
Birch Hill Medical Centre
   BRAK RG12 ....32 D8
Birch Hill Primary School
   BRAK RG12 ....32 D8
Bishop Challoner School
   HAYES BR2 ....47 K3
Bishop David Brown School
   WOKN/KNAP GU21 ....73 H1
Bishop Gilpin
   Primary School
   WIM/MER SW19 ....28 C8
Bishop Perrin
   CE Primary School
   WHTN TW2 ....25 J3
Bishop Reindorp CE School
   GU GU1 ....112 A2
Bishopsgate School
   EGH TW20 ....20 F6
Bishop's Table Hotel
   FNM GU9 ....4 E3
Bishop Thomas Grant School
   STRHM/NOR SW16 ....30 A8
Bishop Wand
   CE Secondary School
   SUN TW16 ....39 H1
Blackburn Trading Estate
   STWL/WRAY TW19 ....23 J2
Blackbushe Airport
   BLKW GU17 ....66 E5
Blackbushe Business Park
   YTLY GU46 ....66 G4
Blackbushe Business Park
   YTLY GU46 ....67 K2
Blackdown Primary School
   FRIM GU16 ....69 N8
Blackwater & Hawley
   Leisure Centre
   BLKW GU17 ....67 P5
Blackwater Industrial Estate
   CBLY GU15 ....68 A3
Blackwater Trading Estate
   ASHV GU12 ....108 G6
Blackwell Primary School
   EGRIN RH19 ....162 D9
Bleach's Yard
   Industrial Estate
   LIPH GU30 ....182 F8
Blenheim Business Centre
   MTCM CR4 ....44 B2

Blenheim High School
   HOR/WEW KT19 ....60 B8
Blenheim Shopping Centre
   PGE/AN SE20 ....46 C1
Bletchingley Golf Club
   REDH RH1 ....121 M4
Bloomsbury College
   FUL/PGN SW6 ....19 L5
Blossom House School
   RYNPK SW20 ....42 G1
Bluebell Railway
   EGRIN RH19 ....179 P9
Bocketts Farm Park
   LHD/OX KT22 ....96 F5
Bohunt Community School
   LIPH GU30 ....182 E6
Bohunt Manor
   LIPH GU30 ....182 E7
Bolingbroke Hospital
   BTSEA SW11 ....29 H1
Bolingbroke Primary School
   BTSEA SW11 ....29 H1
Bond First School
   MTCM CR4 ....44 B3
Bond Road School
   MTCM CR4 ....44 B3
Bonneville Primary School
   CLAP SW4 ....29 M2
Bookham Grange Hotel
   GT/LBKH KT23 ....95 N3
Bookham Industrial Estate
   GT/LBKH KT23 ....95 P3
Borers Business Park
   CRAWE RH10 ....160 D9
Borough Hall
   GODL GU7 ....131 L8
Boston Business Park
   HNWL W7 ....16 E1
Boston University
   ECT SW5 ....19 N2
Boundary Business Centre
   WOKN/KNAP GU21 ....72 E4
Boundary Business Park
   MTCM CR4 ....43 P3
Bourne Business Park
   ADL/WDHM KT15 ....55 N1
Bourne Hall Health Centre
   EW KT17 ....60 D7
Bourne Hall Museum
   EW KT17 ....60 D7
Bourne Mill Industrial Estate
   FNM GU9 ....128 A2
The Bourne School
   RFNM GU10 ....127 P6
Bourne Tennis Club
   FNM GU9 ....127 N5
Bousfield Primary School
   ECT SW5 ....19 M3
Bowling Alley
   BRAK RG12 ....32 D3
   BRXS/STRHM SW2 ....29 P5
   CRAWE RH10 ....176 G4
   CRAWW RH11 ....176 B8
   EGRIN RH19 ....180 D2
   EPSOM KT18 ....78 C3
   FELT TW13 ....24 C5
   SURB KT6 ....41 P4
   SUT SM1 ....61 M4
Boxgrove Primary School
   GU GU1 ....112 F4
Box Hill Country Park
   KWD/TDW/WH KT20 ....117 L3
Box Hill School
   RDKG RH5 ....97 H7
Brackenbury Health Centre
   HMSMTH W6 ....18 F1
Brackenbury Primary School
   HMSMTH W6 ....18 F1
Bracknell Business Centre
   BRAK RG12 ....32 B3
Bracknell College
   BRAK RG12 ....32 E2
Bracknell College of FE
   BRAK RG12 ....32 E2
Bracknell Sports Centre
   BRAK RG12 ....32 G3
Bracknell Sports Centre
   BRAK RG12 ....32 E2
Bracknell Town FC
   BRAK RG12 ....32 D3
Brakenhale School
   BRAK RG12 ....32 D5
Brambletye Junior School
   REDH RH1 ....120 C7
Brambletye School
   EGRIN RH19 ....181 H6
The Bramley
   Business Centre
   SHGR GU5 ....132 D6
Bramley CE Infant School
   SHGR GU5 ....132 E7
Bramley Golf Club
   SHGR GU5 ....132 C6
Bramley School
   KWD/TDW/WH KT20 ....98 E5
Brandlehow Primary School
   PUT/ROE SW15 ....19 K9
Breaside
   Pre-preparatory School
   BMLY BR1 ....47 N1
Brentford Business Centre
   BTFD TW8 ....17 J5
The Brentford Clinic
   BTFD TW8 ....17 L4
Brentford County Court
   BTFD TW8 ....17 K5
Brentford FC (Griffin Park)
   BTFD TW8 ....17 K4
Brentford Fountain
   Leisure Centre
   CHSWK W4 ....17 M3

Brentford Health Centre
 BTFD TW8 ....17 J4
Brentford Medical Centre
 BTFD TW8 ....17 K5
Brentford School for Girls
 BTFD TW8 ....17 K4
Brent Knoll School
 FSTH SE23 ....31 L6
Brent Park
 Industrial Estate
 NWDGN UB2 ....15 K1
Brentwaters Business Park
 BTFD TW8 ....17 J5
Brewery Mews
 Business Centre
 ISLW TW7 ....16 F8
Brickfields Industrial Park
 BRAK RG12 ....32 C3
Bridge House Hotel
 REIG RH2 ....119 M1
Bridge Industrial Estate
 HORL RH6 ....159 L1
The Bridge Leisure Centre
 SYD SE26 ....31 N8
Bridge Medical Centre
 CRAWE RH10 ....177 K4
Bright Sparks School
 STRHM/NOR SW16 ....29 P7
Brigstock Medical Centre
 THHTH CR7 ....45 K6
Bristow Infant School
 CBLY GU15 ....68 D6
Britannia Industrial Estate
 DTCH/LGLY SL3 ....13 J7
British Transport Police
 CU CU1 ....6 C4
The Brit School
 SNWD SE25 ....45 M7
Brixton College for Further
 Education
 BRXS/STRHM SW2 ....30 A1
Broadbridge Heath
 Retail Park
 HORS RH12 ....191 M7
Broadbridge Heath Stadium
 HORS RH12 ....191 M8
Broadfield East
 Middle School
 CRAWW RH11 ....176 F9
Broadfield Health Centre
 CRAWW RH11 ....176 E9
Broadford Park
 Business Centre
 RGUE GU4 ....132 B3
Broadlands
 Business Campus
 HORS RH12 ....174 B7
 HORS RH12 ....193 N2
Broadmead Primary School
 CROY/NA CR0 ....45 M7
The Broadmere
 Primary School
 WOKN/KNAP GU21 ....73 H2
Broadmoor County
 Primary School
 CWTH RG45 ....49 P5
Broadmoor Hospital
 CWTH RG45 ....50 A4
Broadwater Park Golf Club
 GODL GU7 ....131 N6
Broadwater Primary School
 TOOT SW17 ....28 G7
Broadwater School
 GODL GU7 ....131 N5
Broadway Shopping Centre
 HMSMTH W6 ....18 G3
Broadway Squash
 & Fitness Centre
 HMSMTH W6 ....19 J4
Brockenhurst Hotel
 ASC SL5 ....34 B7
Brockham School
 BRKHM/BTCW RH3 ....117 P7
Brocklebank Health Centre
 WAND/EARL SW18 ....28 E3
Brockley Primary School
 BROCKY SE4 ....31 N1
Brockwell Lido
 HNHL SE24 ....30 C2
Brockwell Primary School
 BRXS/STRHM SW2 ....30 A4
Bromley Cemetery
 BMLY BR1 ....47 M1
Bromley College of Further
 & Higher Education
 BMLY BR1 ....47 N2
Bromley County Court
 BMLY BR1 ....47 N2
Bromley FC
 HAYES BR2 ....47 P6
Bromley Hospital
 HAYES BR2 ....47 P5
Bromley Mall Indoor Market
 BMLY BR1 ....47 N3
Bromley Road Infant School
 BECK BR3 ....47 H2
Brompton Cemetery
 WBPTN SW10 ....19 M4
Brompton Medical Centre
 CHEAM SM3 ....43 J9
Brookfield Primary School
 LIPH GU30 ....183 H8
Brookham School
 LIPH GU30 ....183 H8
Brooklands Airfield
 WEY KT13 ....56 B8
Brooklands Business Park
 WEY KT13 ....56 A8
Brooklands College
 WEY KT13 ....56 B5
Brooklands Museum
 WEY KT13 ....56 C7

Brooklands School
 REIG RH2 ....119 M3
Brook Lane Business Centre
 BTFD TW8 ....17 K3
Brookmead Industrial Estate
 MTCM CR4 ....44 E7
The Brook Trading Estate
 ASHV GU12 ....108 C3
Brookwood Cemetery
 CHOB/PIR GU24 ....91 H2
Brookwood County
 Primary School
 CHOB/PIR GU24 ....70 G2
Broomfield Infant School
 RCH/KEW TW9 ....17 M6
Broomsleigh Business Park
 CAT SE6 ....31 N8
Broomwood Hall School
 BAL SW12 ....29 K3
Browning Barracks
 ALDT GU11 ....108 C1
Brunel University
 ISLW TW7 ....16 E5
 TWK TW1 ....17 H9
Brunel University
 (Osterley Campus) Track
 ISLW TW7 ....16 E5
Buchan Country Park
 HORS RH12 ....194 A2
Buckingham Primary School
 HPTN TW12 ....24 G8
Buckland Infant School
 CHSGTN KT9 ....59 M4
Buckland Primary School
 STA TW18 ....37 N1
Bullsbridge Industrial Estate
 NWDGN UB2 ....15 K2
The Burford Bridge Hotel
 RDKG RH5 ....117 J2
Burghwood Clinic
 BNSTD SM7 ....79 K5
Burhill Golf Club
 WOT/HER KT12 ....57 J7
Burhill Infant School
 WOT/HER KT12 ....57 M5
Burlington Primary School
 NWMAL KT3 ....42 D5
Bumhill Business Centre
 BECK BR3 ....46 G2
Burns Hotel
 ECT SW5 ....19 M2
Bumtwood School
 TOOT SW17 ....28 C5
Burpham Foundation
 Primary School
 RGUE GU4 ....112 E1
Burstow Business Centre
 HORL RH6 ....141 K8
Burstow Lodge
 Business Centre
 HORL RH6 ....159 L3
Burstow Primary School
 HORL RH6 ....160 B1
Burvale Cemetery
 WOT/HER KT12 ....57 J5
Burwood Park
 School & College
 WOT/HER KT12 ....57 H5
Burys Court School
 REIG RH2 ....138 C2
Busbridge CE Junior School
 GODL GU7 ....150 E1
Busbridge Infant School
 GODL GU7 ....150 E2
Bushey Middle School
 RYNPK SW20 ....42 F4
The Bush Hotel
 FNM GU9 ....5 G3
Bushy Hill Junior School
 RGUE GU4 ....113 H3
Business Aviation Centre
 ALDT GU11 ....88 B8
Bute House Preparatory
 School for Girls
 HMSMTH W6 ....18 G2
Butterfly House
 BTFD TW8 ....17 H6
Byfleet Business Centre
 BF/WBF KT14 ....55 P9
Byfleet CP School
 BF/WBF KT14 ....55 P9
Byfleet Industrial Estate
 BF/WBF KT14 ....55 P9
Byron Primary School
 COUL/CHIP CR5 ....80 G6
Cable House School
 WOKN/KNAP GU21 ....72 C4
California Chalet
 & Touring Park
 EWKG RG40 ....48 B2
California Country Park
 EWKG RG40 ....48 A2
Calthorpe Park School
 FLEETN GU51 ....86 C7
Camberley County
 Infant School
 CBLY GU15 ....68 D3
Camberley Cricket Club
 CBLY GU15 ....68 F5
Camberley Health Centre
 CBLY GU15 ....68 D5
Camberley Heath Golf Club
 CBLY GU15 ....68 G5
Camberley Magistrates Court
 CBLY GU15 ....68 F2
Camberley RFC
 CBLY GU15 ....68 E5
Camberley Town FC
 CBLY GU15 ....68 D5
Camberwell New Cemetery
 FSTH SE23 ....31 L2

Cambridge Military Hospital
 ALDT GU11 ....108 D3
Cambridge Park Bowling
 & Sports Club
 TWK TW1 ....26 B2
Cambridge School
 HMSMTH W6 ....18 F2
Camden Junior School
 CAR SM5 ....62 B3
Camesdale County
 First School
 HASM GU27 ....184 A5
Cameron House School
 CHEL SW3 ....19 P4
Campana Finishing School
 RFNM GU10 ....128 C4
Camphill Industrial Estate
 ADL/WDHM KT15 ....55 M9
Camphill Road First School
 BF/WBF KT14 ....73 M1
Campion House College
 ISLW TW7 ....16 D5
Camp Road Industrial
 Estate
 FARN GU14 ....88 E7
Canbury Business Centre
 KUTN/CMB KT2 ....8 E3
Canbury 2000 Business Park
 KUTN/CMB KT2 ....8 E3
Canbury Medical Centre
 KUTN/CMB KT2 ....9 F2
Canbury School
 RCHPK/HAM TW10 ....26 G9
The Canning School
 KENS W8 ....19 L1
Cannizaro House Hotel
 WIM/MER SW19 ....27 P9
The Canons Leisure Centrel
 MTCM CR4 ....44 B5
Capital Business Centre
 MTCM CR4 ....44 B6
Caplan Estate
 MTCM CR4 ....44 E2
Cardinal Newman RC School
 WOT/HER KT12 ....57 M2
Cardinal Road Infant School
 FELT TW13 ....24 C4
Carew Manor School
 WLGTN SM6 ....62 F2
Cargo Terminal
 HORL RH6 ....158 C5
Carlisle Infant School
 HPTN TW12 ....25 J9
The Carlton Mitre Hotel
 E/WMO/HCT KT8 ....40 E4
Carlyle Business Centre
 CHERT KT16 ....37 L8
Carnwath Road
 Industrial Estate
 FUL/PGN SW6 ....19 M8
Carrier Business Park
 CRAWE RH10 ....177 L4
Carshalton AFC
 CAR SM5 ....62 A2
Carshalton College of FE
 CAR SM5 ....62 B2
Carshalton
 High School for Boys
 CAR SM5 ....61 P1
Carshalton
 High School for Girls
 CAR SM5 ....62 A2
Carshalton War
 Memorial Hospital
 CAR SM5 ....62 B4
Carwarden House School
 FRIM GU16 ....69 J5
The Cassel Hospital
 RCHPK/HAM TW10 ....26 C7
Cassidy Medical Centre
 FUL/PGN SW6 ....19 L5
Castleview
 Combined School
 DTCH/LGLY SL3 ....12 B2
The Caterham Dene
 Hospital
 CTHM CR3 ....101 P3
Caterham
 Preparatory School
 CTHM CR3 ....101 P6
Caterham School
 CTHM CR3 ....101 P6
Catford Cyphers
 Cricket Club
 CAT SE6 ....31 N5
Catherington
 Special School
 CRAWW RH11 ....176 G1
Cator Park School for Girls
 BECK BR3 ....46 E1
Cavendish School
 CHSWK W4 ....18 C5
The Cedars Primary School
 HEST TW5 ....15 J5
Centaurs Business Centre
 BTFD TW8 ....16 G4
Centaurs RFC
 ISLW TW7 ....16 F4
Central Estate
 ALDT GU11 ....108 D4
Central London Golf Club
 TOOT SW17 ....28 C5
Central Medical Centre
 MRDN SM4 ....43 N5
Centre Court
 Shopping Centre
 WIM/MER SW19 ....28 C9
Chaffinch Business Park
 BECK BR3 ....46 D4
Chalk Lane Hotel
 EPSOM KT18 ....78 B4

Chambers Business Park
 WDR/YW UB7 ....14 C4
Chancellors Wharf Dev
 BARN SW13 ....18 G3
Chandler Junior School
 MFD/CHID GU8 ....149 M7
Chandlers Field
 Primary School
 E/WMO/HCT KT8 ....40 A6
Chandos Business Centre
 WLGTN SM6 ....62 E5
Charing Cross Hospital
 HMSMTH W6 ....19 H4
Charing Cross & Westminster
 Medical School
 HMSMTH W6 ....19 H3
Charles Darwin School
 BH/WHM TN16 ....84 D4
Charles Kingsleys
 CE Primary School
 HTWY RG27 ....48 A9
Charlwood Place
 HORL RH6 ....158 B6
Charlwoods
 Industrial Estate
 EGRIN RH19 ....162 D9
Charlwood Village
 Infant School
 HORL RH6 ....158 C5
Charterhouse School
 GODL GU7 ....131 J6
Charterhouse School
 Students Residences
 GODL GU7 ....131 H6
The Charter School
 EDUL SE22 ....30 E1
Charters School
 ASC SL5 ....34 D8
Chartfield School
 PUT/ROE SW15 ....27 N1
Chartham Park Golf Club
 EGRIN RH19 ....162 B6
Chase Bridge
 Primary School
 WHTN TW2 ....25 M2
Chatsworth J & I School
 HSLW TW3 ....16 C9
Cheam Common
 Infant School
 WPK KT4 ....60 F1
Cheam Common Junior
 School
 WPK KT4 ....60 F2
Cheam Fields
 Primary School
 CHEAM SM3 ....61 J4
Cheam High School
 CHEAM SM3 ....61 J3
Cheam Leisure Centre
 CHEAM SM3 ....61 H3
Cheam Park Farm
 Junior School
 CHEAM SM3 ....61 J2
Cheam Sports Club
 BELMT SM2 ....61 H6
Cheapside
 CE Primary School
 ASC SL5 ....34 E2
Chelsea Centre & Theatre
 WBPTN SW10 ....19 P5
The Chelsea Club
 Leisure Centre
 FUL/PGN SW6 ....19 M4
Chelsea College
 of Art & Design
 CHEL SW3 ....19 P3
 FUL/PGN SW6 ....19 N7
Chelsea FC (Stamford Bridge)
 FUL/PGN SW6 ....19 M5
Chelsea Fields
 Industrial Estate
 WIM/MER SW19 ....43 P2
Chelsea Village Hotel
 WBPTN SW10 ....19 M5
Chelsea & Westminster
 Hospital
 WBPTN SW10 ....19 N4
Chelsea Wharf
 WBPTN SW10 ....19 P5
Chennestone
 Community School
 SUN TW16 ....39 K3
Cherry Lane Primary School
 WDR/YW UB7 ....14 B2
Cherry Lodge Golf Club
 BH/WHM TN16 ....84 E6
Chertsey Business Centre
 CHERT KT16 ....37 L8
Chertsey Cemetery
 ADL/WDHM KT15 ....55 L1
Chertsey Hall
 CHERT KT16 ....37 L8
Chertsey Museum
 CHERT KT16 ....37 L7
Chertsey Recreation Centre
 CHERT KT16 ....37 K9
Chertsey Town FC
 CHERT KT16 ....37 K7
Chessington Community
 College & Sports Centre
 CHSGTN KT9 ....59 K6
Chessington Cricket Club
 CHSGTN KT9 ....59 J6
Chessington Golf Club
 CHSGTN KT9 ....59 K6
Chessington
 World of Adventures
 CHSGTN KT9 ....59 J9
Chestnut Grove School
 BAL SW12 ....29 K4
Chesworth Junior School
 SWTR RH13 ....192 D7

Chiddingfold Golf Club
 MFD/CHID GU8 ....186 A1
Chilworth CE Infant School
 RGUE GU4 ....133 H2
Chinthurst School
 KWD/TDW/WH KT20 ....98 G3
Chipstead Golf Club
 COUL/CHIP CR5 ....80 B7
Chipstead RFC
 COUL/CHIP CR5 ....100 B3
Chipstead Valley
 Primary School
 COUL/CHIP CR5 ....80 C5
Chiswick & Bedford Park
 Preparatory School
 CHSWK W4 ....18 C2
Chiswick Business Park
 CHSWK W4 ....17 P2
Chiswick Community School
 CHSWK W4 ....18 B5
Chiswick House
 CHSWK W4 ....18 B4
Chiswick FC
 CHOB/PIR GU24 ....71 M1
Chobham Golf Club
 WOKN/KNAP GU21 ....71 K4
Chobham RFC
 CHOB/PIR GU24 ....53 L8
Chobham St Lawrence
 CE F & M School
 CHOB/PIR GU24 ....53 L9
Christchurch
 CE Infant School
 VW GU25 ....35 N4
Christchurch Junior School
 CHERT KT16 ....55 H5
Christ Church
 CE Infant School
 NWMAL KT3 ....42 C4
Christ Church
 CE Junior School
 NWMAL KT3 ....42 B4
Christ Church
 CE Primary School
 BRXS/STRHM SW2 ....30 A4
Christ Church
 CE Primary School
 BRYLDS KT5 ....41 N7
Christ Church
 Primary School
 FSTH SE23 ....31 L5
Christ Church
 Primary School
 PUR/KEN CR8 ....63 K8
Christian Meeting Hall
 BECK BR3 ....46 G2
Christs School
 RCHPK/HAM TW10 ....26 E1
Christ the King
 RC First School
 STWL/WRAY TW19 ....22 G2
Chrysalis Theatre
 BAL SW12 ....29 K4
Chrysanthemum Clinic
 CHSWK W4 ....18 A5
Church Crookham
 Junior School
 FLEETS GU52 ....106 C2
Churchfields Primary School
 BECK BR3 ....46 D4
Church Hill House Hospital
 BRAK RG12 ....32 C6
Churchill Business Park
 BH/WHM TN16 ....105 H6
Churchill CE Primary School
 BH/WHM TN16 ....104 C5
Churchill College
 RYNPK SW20 ....42 G3
The Churchill Medical Centre
 KUTN/CMB KT2 ....9 G3
Churchill Theatre
 HAYES BR2 ....47 N1
The Church School
 BTFD TW8 ....17 L4
Cineworld Cinema
 FELT TW13 ....24 C5
City Business Centre
 SWTR RH13 ....192 C9
The City Business Centre
 CRAWW RH11 ....176 D1
City of London
 Freemans School
 ASHTD KT21 ....77 P8
Civic Centre & Bromley
 Palace
 BMLY BR1 ....47 P3
Civil Service College
 ASC SL5 ....34 F6
Clandon CE Infant School
 RGUE GU4 ....113 L2
Clandon Regis Golf Club
 RGUE GU4 ....113 N2
Clapham Park School
 CLAP SW4 ....29 N1
Clare House Primary School
 BECK BR3 ....47 J3
Claremont Fan Court School
 ESH/CLAY KT10 ....58 B5
Clarence Road School
 SWTR RH13 ....192 C9
Clarendon Primary School
 ASHF TW15 ....23 J6
Clarendon Special School
 HPTN TW12 ....25 J9
Claygate Primary School
 ESH/CLAY KT10 ....58 E6
Clayponds Hospital
 BTFD TW8 ....17 L2
Clayton Barracks
 ALDT GU11 ....108 F2
Cleves Junior School
 WEY KT13 ....57 H3

Clewborough House
  Preparatory School
  CBLY GU15 ....69 K3
Clewborough House School
  at Cheswycks
  FRIM GU16 ....89 K2
Clifton Hill School
  CTHM CR3 ....101 M4
Clifton Primary School
  NWDGN UB2 ....15 N2
Clockhouse Industrial Estate
  EBED/NFELT TW14 ....23 L4
Cobham Bus Museum
  COB KT11 ....74 E1
The Cobham Health Centre
  COB KT11 ....75 K2
Cobham RFC
  COB KT11 ....75 M1
Colgate Primary School
  SWTR RH13 ....193 P4
Coliseum Business Centre
  CBLY GU15 ....68 C5
College Fields
  Business Centre
  WIM/MER SW19 ....44 A2
College Library
  & Civic Centre
  SUT SM1 ....61 M4
The College
  of Richard Collyer
  HORS RH12 ....192 C7
The College of St Barnabas
  LING RH7 ....162 D4
Collingwood Town Infant School
  SHST GU47 ....50 A9
Collingwood College
  CBLY GU15 ....51 J9
Collingwood
  Preparatory School
  WLGTN SM6 ....62 D4
Collis Primary School
  TEDD TW11 ....26 A9
Collyer Sixth Form College
  HORS RH12 ....192 C6
Colnbrook
  CE Combined School
  DTCH/LGLY SL3 ....13 H5
Colnbrook Sports Club
  DTCH/LGLY SL3 ....13 K6
Coln Industrial Estate
  DTCH/LGLY SL3 ....13 H5
Coloma Convent Girls School
  CROY/NA CR0 ....64 D2
Colours Sports Club
  SUT SM1 ....61 N4
Coltwood Business Centre
  ALDT GU11 ....108 D4
Comfort Inn Hotel
  HYS/HAR UB3 ....14 C3
  KENS W8 ....19 L2
Commonwealth Institute
  KENS W8 ....19 K1
Compton Place
  Business Centre
  CBLY GU15 ....68 C4
Concorde Business Park
  BH/WHM TN16 ....84 B4
Coney Hill School
  HAYES BR2 ....65 M1
Connaught Business Centre
  CROY/NA CR0 ....63 L6
  MTCM CR4 ....44 B6
Connaught County
  Junior School
  BAGS GU19 ....51 N7
The Connaught School
  ASHV GU12 ....108 G7
Conrad London Hotel
  WBPTN SW10 ....19 N6
Consulate
  General of Monaco
  SKENS SW7 ....19 P1
Consulate of Burkina Faso
  BTSEA SW11 ....19 N8
Coombe Girls School
  NWMAL KT3 ....42 B3
Coombe Hill Golf Club
  KUTN/CMB KT2 ....42 B1
Coombe Hill J & I School
  NWMAL KT3 ....42 B2
Coombe Wood Golf Club
  KUTN/CMB KT2 ....41 P1
Copthorn CE Junior School
  CRAWE RH10 ....160 C9
The Copthorne
  Business Centre
  CRAWE RH10 ....160 C9
Copthorne Fairway
  Infant School
  CRAWE RH10 ....160 C9
Copthorne Golf Club
  CRAWE RH10 ....160 D9
Copthorne Hotel
  Effingham Park Gatwick
  CRAWE RH10 ....160 G8
Copthorne Hotel
  London Gatwick
  CRAWE RH10 ....178 B1
Copthorne Junior School
  CRAWE RH10 ....160 C9
Copthorne
  Preparatory School
  CRAWE RH10 ....160 E8
Copthorne Squash Club
  CRAWE RH10 ....178 B1
Copthorne Tara Hotel
  KENS W8 ....19 M1
Cordwalles Junior School
  CBLY GU15 ....51 H9
Corinthian Casuals FC
  CHSGTN KT9 ....59 N2

Cornhill Sports Club
  BECK BR3 ....31 P8
Corpus Christi
  RC Primary School
  BRXS/STRHM SW2 ....30 A1
Cosmic Cycle
  HORS RH12 ....192 A6
Cottesmore Golf
  & Country Club
  CRAWW RH11 ....194 B3
Cottesmore School
  CRAWW RH11 ....194 C2
Coulsdon 6th Form College
  COUL/CHIP CR5 ....81 J8
Coulsdon CE Primary School
  COUL/CHIP CR5 ....81 H7
The Coulsdon Eye Clinic
  COUL/CHIP CR5 ....80 E4
Coulsdon High School
  COUL/CHIP CR5 ....81 K9
Coulsdon Manor Hotel
  Golf Club
  COUL/CHIP CR5 ....81 H5
Country Gardens Estate
  BFOR GU20 ....52 C1
County Mall
  CRAWE RH10 ....177 H5
County Oak Retail Park
  CRAWE RH10 ....176 C1
Court Farm Industrial Estate
  STWL/WRAY TW19 ....23 J2
Courtfield Medical Centre
  ECT SW5 ....19 M2
Court Lodge County
  First School
  HORL RH6 ....159 J1
Court Moor School
  FLEETS GU52 ....86 F9
Courtwood Primary School
  CROY/NA CR0 ....64 F8
Cove Cricket Club
  FARN GU14 ....88 A3
Cove Infant School
  FARN GU14 ....88 A1
Cove Junior School
  FARN GU14 ....88 A2
Cove Secondary School
  FARN GU14 ....88 A2
Cowarth Park School
  CHOB/PIR GU24 ....53 H3
Coxmoor Farm Light
  Industrial Estate
  RFNM GU10 ....106 B4
Crane Infant School
  FELT TW13 ....24 G5
Crane Junior School
  FELT TW13 ....24 F5
Cranford Community
  College
  HEST TW5 ....15 K4
Cranford Infant School
  HSLWW TW4 ....15 J7
Cranford Junior School
  HSLWW TW4 ....15 K7
Cranford Park Junior School
  HYS/HAR UB3 ....15 H2
Cranleigh Health Centre
  CRAN GU6 ....170 G1
Cranleigh Leisure Centre
  CRAN GU6 ....170 G1
Cranleigh
  Preparatory School
  CRAN GU6 ....152 G8
Cranleigh School
  CRAN GU6 ....152 F7
Cranleigh Village Hospital
  CRAN GU6 ....153 H9
Cranley Townhouse Hotel
  ECT SW5 ....19 M3
Cranmer School
  MTCM CR4 ....44 B6
Cranmore School
  EHSLY KT24 ....94 E9
The Craven Clinic
  HMSMTH W6 ....18 F2
Crawley College
  CRAWE RH10 ....177 H5
Crawley College Annexe
  CRAWE RH10 ....176 F4
Crawley Down
  CE Infant School
  CRAWE RH10 ....179 J3
Crawley Down CE School
  CRAWE RH10 ....179 J3
Crawley Down
  Health Centre
  CRAWE RH10 ....179 H3
Crawley Health Clinic
  CRAWE RH10 ....177 H5
Crawley Hospital
  CRAWW RH11 ....176 F5
The Crawley
  Lawn Tennis Club
  CRAWE RH10 ....177 L3
Crawley Leisure Centre
  Athletics Arena
  CRAWE RH10 ....177 J6
Crawley Museum
  (Goffs Park House)
  CRAWW RH11 ....176 E6
Crawley RFC
  CRAWW RH11 ....176 D1
Crawley Ridge
  Primary School
  CBLY GU15 ....69 H2
Crawley Swimming Pool
  CRAWE RH10 ....177 H4
Crawley Town FC
  CRAWW RH11 ....176 F9
Crockham Hill County
  Primary School
  EDEN TN8 ....124 G4

Crofton Leisure Centre
  BROCKY SE4 ....31 P2
Crofton School
  BROCKY SE4 ....31 P2
Croham Hurst Golf Club
  SAND/SEL CR2 ....63 P5
Croham Hurst School
  SAND/SEL CR2 ....63 P4
Cromwell Hospital
  KENS W8 ....19 L2
Crondall Primary School
  RFNM GU10 ....106 D8
Crookham CE Infants School
  FLEETS GU52 ....106 F7
Cross Farm Infant School
  FRIM GU16 ....88 G1
Crouch Industrial Estate
  LHD/OX KT22 ....76 G8
Crowne Plaza Hotel
  WDR/YW UB7 ....14 C2
The Crown Hotel
  CHERT KT16 ....37 L7
Crown Lane Primary School
  WNWD SE27 ....30 C8
Crown Wood Primary School
  BRAK RG12 ....32 F7
Crowthorne Business Centre
  CWTH RG45 ....49 N2
Crowthorne CE Primary
  School
  CWTH RG45 ....49 M4
Croydon Airport
  Industrial Estate
  CROY/NA CR0 ....63 J6
Croydon Cemetery
  THHTH CR7 ....45 H6
Croydon Clocktower Cinema
  CROY/NA CR0 ....2 D5
Croydon College
  CROY/NA CR0 ....2 E4
Croydon Fairfield Halls
  Cinema
  CROY/NA CR0 ....2 E5
Croydon FC
  SNWD SE25 ....46 C6
Croydon High School Gdst
  SAND/SEL CR2 ....64 B9
Croydon Indoor
  Bowling Club
  SAND/SEL CR2 ....63 L4
Croydon Road
  Industrial Estate
  SNWD SE25 ....46 C5
Croydon Sports Arena
  SNWD SE25 ....46 C6
Crystal Palace
  NRWD SE19 ....31 H9
Crystal Palace
  Athletics Stadium
  NRWD SE19 ....31 H9
Crystal Palace FC
  (Selhurst Park)
  SNWD SE25 ....45 N5
Crystal Palace Museum
  NRWD SE19 ....30 G9
Cuaco Sports Ground
  BECK BR3 ....31 P9
Cuddington Cemetery
  WPK KT4 ....60 F1
Cuddington CP School
  HOR/WEW KT19 ....60 D2
Cuddington Golf Club
  BNSTD SM7 ....79 J2
Cudham CE Primary School
  BH/WHM TN16 ....84 E5
Culvers House
  Primary School
  MTCM CR4 ....44 C9
Cumnor House School
  SAND/SEL CR2 ....63 K7
Cypress Infant School
  SNWD SE25 ....45 N3
Cypress Junior School
  SNWD SE25 ....45 N3
Cyprus College of Art
  WNWD SE27 ....30 C7
Dairy Meadow
  Primary School
  NWDGN UB2 ....15 P1
D'Albiac House
  HTHAIR TW6 ....14 C7
Dalmain Primary School
  FSTH SE23 ....31 M4
Danesfield Manor School
  WOT/HER KT12 ....57 K1
Danes Hill School
  LHD/OX KT22 ....76 D3
Danetree School
  HOR/WEW KT19 ....60 A6
Dapdune Wharf
  GU GU1 ....6 C2
Darell Primary School
  RCH/KEW TW9 ....17 N8
Darley Dene Infant School
  ADL/WDHM KT15 ....55 N3
Darwin Centre
  SKENS SW7 ....19 N1
David Game Tuitorial College
  SKENS SW7 ....19 P2
David Livingstone
  Primary School
  THHTH CR7 ....45 L2
David Lloyd Leisure Centre
  KENS W8 ....19 M2
Davidson J & I School
  CROY/NA CR0 ....45 P8
The Dawnay County
  Primary School
  GT/LBKH KT23 ....96 A6
Day Hospital
  PUR/KEN CR8 ....63 J9

Days Inn Hotel
  FLEETN GU51 ....86 D3
Deerswood School
  CRAWW RH11 ....176 D3
Defence Evaluation Research
  Agency
  FARN GU14 ....88 C5
Defence Research Agency
  FARN GU14 ....88 C5
Denbies Wine Estate
  RDKG RH5 ....117 H3
Denmead School
  HPTN TW12 ....40 A1
Desmond Anderson
  F & M School
  CRAWE RH10 ....176 C9
De Stafford College
  CTHM CR3 ....101 P1
Deutsche Schule
  RCHPK/HAM TW10 ....26 C4
Devonshire Primary School
  BELMT SM2 ....61 N6
Diana Fountain
  E/WMO/HCT KT8 ....40 F3
Dockwell's Industrial Estate
  EBED/NFELT TW14 ....24 C1
Dogmersfield
  CE Primary School
  HTWY RG27 ....86 A8
Dolphin School
  BTSEA SW11 ....29 J1
Donyngs Recreation Centre
  REDH RH1 ....120 A4
Doods Brow School
  REDH RH1 ....121 H4
Dorchester Primary School
  WPK KT4 ....42 C9
The Dorking Business Park
  DORK RH4 ....116 G6
Dorking Cemetery
  DORK RH4 ....117 J5
Dorking FC (Meadowbank)
  RDKG RH4 ....116 G6
Dorking General Hospital
  DORK RH4 ....116 G8
Dorking Golf Club
  DORK RH4 ....117 J8
Dorking Halls
  DORK RH4 ....117 J6
Dorking Lawn Tennis &
  Squash Club
  DORK RH4 ....116 C9
Dorking Museum
  DORK RH4 ....116 G7
Dorking RFC
  BRKHM/BTCW RH3 ....117 P5
Dorking Swimming & Sports
  Centre
  DORK RH4 ....117 J6
Douglas Bader Foundation
  PUT/ROE SW15 ....27 M2
Dovers Green School
  REIG RH2 ....119 N9
Down House -
  Home of Charles Darwin
  ORP BR6 ....84 D1
Downsend School
  LHD/OX KT22 ....77 K9
Downsend School -
  Ashtead Lodge
  ASHTD KT21 ....77 L7
Downsview Primary School
  NRWD SE19 ....45 L1
Downs Way County Primary
  School
  OXTED RH8 ....103 L7
Drift Golf Club
  COB KT11 ....94 G3
Drummond Shopping Centre
  CROY/NA CR0 ....2 C4
Duff Miller College
  SKENS SW7 ....19 N1
Duke of Kent School
  CRAN GU6 ....153 N2
Duke's Dene Golf Club
  WARL CR6 ....82 D9
Dukes Head Hotel
  CAR SM5 ....62 D3
Dulwich College
  DUL SE21 ....30 F4
Dulwich College Preparatory
  School
  DUL SE21 ....30 F6
Dulwich College Track
  DUL SE21 ....30 F5
Dulwich Hamlet Junior
  School
  DUL SE21 ....30 E2
Dulwich Medical Centre
  EDUL SE22 ....31 H1
Dulwich Picture Gallery
  DUL SE21 ....30 E3
Dulwich & Sydenham Hill
  Golf Club
  DUL SE21 ....31 H5
Dulwich Village
  CE Infant School
  DUL SE21 ....30 F2
Dundonald First School
  WIM/MER SW19 ....43 K1
Dunnings Squash Club
  EGRIN RH19 ....180 D5
Dunottar School
  REIG RH2 ....119 P6
Dunraven School
  (Lower School)
  STRHM/NOR SW16 ....30 A6
Dunraven School
  (Upper School)
  STRHM/NOR SW16 ....30 A6
Dunsfold Aerodrome
  MFD/CHID GU8 ....170 A6

Duppas Junior School
  CROY/NA CR0 ....63 K4
Dysart School
  KUTN/CMB KT2 ....26 C7
Dysart Special School
  SURB KT6 ....41 L8
Eagle House School
  SHST GU47 ....49 L7
Eagle Trading Estate
  MTCM CR4 ....44 B7
Ealing Park Health Centre
  ....17 K2
Ealing Road Trading Estate
  BTFD TW8 ....17 K3
Eardley Primary School
  STRHM/NOR SW16 ....29 N8
Earl's Court Exhibition Centre
  ECT SW5 ....19 L3
Earlsfield Primary School
  WAND/EARL SW18 ....28 F5
Earlswood Infant School
  REDH RH1 ....120 C6
Earth Galleries
  SKENS SW7 ....19 P1
East Berkshire Golf Club
  CWTH RG45 ....49 J4
East Court
  EGRIN RH19 ....180 E1
Eastern Business Centre
  BRAK RG12 ....32 F3
Eastern Business Park
  HTHAIR TW6 ....15 H7
East Grinstead Health Clinic
  EGRIN RH19 ....180 D1
East Grinstead Sports Club
  EGRIN RH19 ....180 B6
East Molesey Cricket Club
  E/WMO/HCT KT8 ....40 C4
East Sheen Cemetery
  RCHPK/HAM TW10 ....26 F1
East Sheen Primary School
  MORT/ESHN SW14 ....18 C4
East Surrey College
  REDH RH1 ....120 C1
East Surrey Hospital
  REDH RH1 ....120 D9
East Surrey Museum
  CTHM CR3 ....101 P4
Eastwick Infant School
  GT/LBKH KT23 ....96 B3
Eastwick Junior School
  GT/LBKH KT23 ....96 B4
Ebbisham County
  Infants School
  EPSOM KT18 ....78 A3
Ebbisham Sports Club
  HOR/WEW KT19 ....78 A1
Ecclesbourne Primary
  School
  THHTH CR7 ....45 L6
Echelford Primary School
  ASHF TW15 ....23 L8
Eclipse Estate
  HOR/WEW KT19 ....78 A2
Edenbridge & District War
  Memorial Hospital
  EDEN TN8 ....144 G6
Edenbridge Golf
  & Tennis Centre
  EDEN TN8 ....144 E3
Edenbridge Leisure Centre
  EDEN TN8 ....144 F3
The Edenbridge
  Medical Centre
  EDEN TN8 ....144 G4
Edenbridge Primary School
  EDEN TN8 ....144 G4
Edenham High School
  CROY/NA CR0 ....46 E8
Edenvale Child Health Clinic
  TOOT SW17 ....44 C1
Eden Valley School
  EDEN TN8 ....144 G3
Eden Walk Shopping Centre
  KUT KT1 ....8 D5
Edes Business Park
  WLGTN SM6 ....62 C1
Edgebarrow School
  CWTH RG45 ....49 M6
Edgebarrow Sports Centre
  CWTH RG45 ....49 N6
Edgeborough School
  RFNM GU10 ....146 F1
The Edge Sports Centre
  HASM GU27 ....183 N2
Edward Pauling School
  FELT TW13 ....24 A4
Eelmoor Road
  Depot Trading Estate
  FARN GU14 ....88 C5
Effingham Cricket Club
  EHSLY KT24 ....95 K4
Effingham Golf Club
  EHSLY KT24 ....95 M8
Effingham Park Golf Club
  CRAWE RH10 ....160 G8
Effra Primary School
  BRXS/STRHM SW2 ....30 B1
Effra Road Retail Park
  BRXS/STRHM SW2 ....30 B1
Egham Business Village
  EGH TW20 ....36 G3
Egham Cricket Club
  EGH TW20 ....21 N9
Egham Sports Centre
  EGH TW20 ....21 N9
Egham Town FC
  EGH TW20 ....21 P9

Electrical Trades
Union College
ESH/CLAY KT10 ....58 A3
The Electric Theatre
GU U1 ....6 D5
Elers Clinic
HYS/HAR UB3 ....14 F2
Eliot Bank Primary School
FSTH SE23 ....31 J5
Elizabeth Barracks
CHOB/PIR GU24 ....90 A1
Ellingham Primary School
CHSGTN KT9 ....59 K6
Elliott Foundation School
PUT/ROE SW15 ....27 P2
Elliott Industrial Park
KUT KT1 ....9 G7
Elmbridge Leisure Centre
WOT/HER KT12 ....39 K6
Elmbridge Museum
WEY KT13 ....56 C3
Elm Court School
WNWD SE27 ....30 C5
Elm House Business Centre
MFD/CHID GU8 ....129 P9
Elmhurst
Preparatory School
BECK BR3 ....46 D5
Elmhurst School
CROY/NA CRO 63 M3
The Elmsleigh Centre
Shopping Precinct
STA TW18 ....22 B7
Elmwood Primary School
CROY/NA CRO 45 K8
Elm Wood Primary School
WNWD SE27 ....30 E6
Elthorne Park High School
HNWL W7 ....16 F1
Elthorne Sports Centre
HNWL W7 ....16 F1
Emanuel School
WAND/EARL SW18 ....28 C1
Embassy of Armenia
KENS W8 ....19 M1
Embassy of Bahrain
SKENS SW7 ....19 N1
Embassy of Bulgaria
SKENS SW7 ....19 N1
Embassy of Guatemala
WBPTN SW10 ....19 M4
Embassy of Iraq
SKENS SW7 ....19 N1
Embassy of Morocco
SKENS SW7 ....19 N1
Embassy of Oman
SKENS SW7 ....19 N1
Embassy of Paraguay
SKENS SW7 ....19 M1
Embassy of
Republic of Gabon
SKENS SW7 ....19 N1
Embassy of Thailand
SKENS SW7 ....19 N1
Embassy of Yemen
SKENS SW7 ....19 P2
Ember Sports Club
ESH/CLAY KT10 ....40 C9
Emerson College
FROW RH18 ....181 N8
Endsleigh Industrial Estate
NWDGN UB2 ....15 N2
Englefield Green County
Infant School
EGH TW20 ....21 H8
Ensham Secondary School
TOOT SW17 ....29 J8
Enterprise Industrial Estate
ASHV GU12 ....89 H8
Epsom Business Park
EW KT17 ....60 C9
Epsom Cemetery
EPSOM KT18 ....78 C5
Epsom College
EW KT17 ....78 E3
Epsom County
& Magistrates Court
EPSOM KT18 ....78 B2
Epsom County Primary
School
HOR/WEW KT19 ....60 B9
Epsom Downs Racecourse
EPSOM KT18 ....78 D6
Epsom & Ewell High School
HOR/WEW KT19 ....60 A5
Epsom General Hospital
EPSOM KT18 ....78 A4
Epsom Golf Club
EW KT17 ....78 A4
Epsom Health Clinic
EPSOM KT18 ....78 C2
Epsom Sports Club
EPSOM KT18 ....78 B4
Ernest Bevin School
TOOT SW17 ....29 H6
Escotts County
Primary School
EGRIN RH19 ....180 F2
Esher Church School
(Primary)
ESH/CLAY KT10 ....40 E8
Esher College
THDIT KT7 ....40 E8
Esher RFC
WOT/HER KT12 ....57 N1
Eversley Cricket Club
HTWY RG27 ....48 D9
Eversley Medical Centre
THHTH CR7 ....45 J7
Evolution House
RCH/KEW TW9 ....17 L7

Ewell Athletics Track
HOR/WEW KT19 ....60 B5
Ewell Castle School
EW KT17 ....60 E7
Ewell Grove Infant School
EW KT17 ....60 D7
Ewhurst CE Infant School
CRAN GU6 ....153 N7
Express by Holiday Inn
CRAWE RH10 ....177 K5
WAND/EARL SW18 ....19 M9
WIM/MER SW19 ....43 P1
HMSMTH W6 ....18 F2
Fairfax Industrial Estate
ASHV GU12 ....108 G4
Fairfield Industrial Estate
KUT KT1 ....9 G7
Fairfield Medical Centre
GT/LBKH KT23 ....96 B6
Fairholme J & I School
EBED/NFELT TW14 ....23 N4
Fairlawn Primary School
FSTH SE23 ....31 K3
Fairoaks Airport
CHOB/PIR GU24 ....54 D9
Fairview Industrial Estate
OXTED RH8 ....123 K1
OXTED RH8 ....123 N4
Fairview Medical Centre
STRHM/NOR SW16 ....44 G2
Falconbrook JMI School
BTSEA SW11 ....19 P7
Falcon Hotel
FARN GU14 ....88 E6
Falkner House School
SKENS SW7 ....19 N3
Farleigh Court Golf Club
WARL CR6 ....82 D6
Farleigh Primary School
WARL CR6 ....82 D6
Farleigh Rovers FC
WARL CR6 ....82 F5
Farlington School
HORS RH12 ....191 J4
Farm Lane Trading Estate
FUL/PGN SW6 ....19 L4
Farnborough
Aerospace Centre
FARN GU14 ....88 B7
Farnborough Airport
FARN GU14 ....88 B6
Farnborough
Business Centre
FARN GU14 ....88 B5
Farnborough College of
Technology
ASHV GU12 ....108 D5
FARN GU14 ....88 E5
FARN GU14 ....88 E5
Farnborough Gate
Retail Park
FARN GU14 ....68 E9
Farnborough Hill School
FARN GU14 ....88 E2
Farnborough
Recreation Centre
FARN GU14 ....88 D4
Farnborough RFC
FARN GU14 ....88 C1
Farnborough Town FC
FARN GU14 ....68 C8
Farncombe
CE Infant School
GODL GU7 ....131 L6
Farncombe Cricket Club
GODL GU7 ....131 M6
Farnell House
Medical Centre
HSLW TW3 ....16 B6
Farnham Business Centre
FNM GU9 ....5 H2
FNM GU9 ....5 J5
Farnham Business Park
FNM GU9 ....4 D7
Farnham Castle Keep
FNM GU9 ....4 E1
Farnham College
FNM GU9 ....5 H6
Farnham Golf Club
RFNM GU10 ....128 F3
Farnham Health Centre
FNM GU9 ....5 G2
Farnham Hospital
FNM GU9 ....5 K1
Farnham House Hotel
RFNM GU10 ....126 G5
Farnham Museum
FNM GU9 ....4 E4
Farnham Park Golf Club
FNM GU9 ....127 M1
Farnham Retail Park
FNM GU9 ....128 A2
Farnham Sports Club
FNM GU9 ....5 H3
Farnham Trading Estate
FNM GU9 ....128 B1
Faygate Business Centre
HORS RH12 ....193 L1
Featherstone
Primary School
NWDGN UB2 ....15 N1
Featherstone Road
Health Clinic
NWDGN UB2 ....15 N1
Featherstone School
NWDGN UB2 ....15 M2
Felbridge Primary School
EGRIN RH19 ....161 N8
Felnex Trading Estate
WLGTN SM6 ....62 C1

Feltham Airparcs
Leisure Centre
FELT TW13 ....24 E5
Feltham Athletics Arena
EBED/NFELT TW14 ....24 B3
Felthambrook
Industrial Estate
FELT TW13 ....24 C6
Feltham Community College
FELT TW13 ....24 E5
Feltham Hill Infant School
FELT TW13 ....23 P6
Feltham Hill Junior School
FELT TW13 ....24 A6
Feltham & Hounslow Boro FC
EBED/NFELT TW14 ....24 B3
Feltonfleet School
COB KT11 ....74 G2
Fenstanton J & I School
BRXS/STRHM SW2 ....30 B4
Fernfell Golf & Country Club
CRAN GU6 ....153 J6
Fernhill Primary School
FARN GU14 ....68 B7
Fern Hill Primary School
KUTN/CMB KT2 ....26 D9
Fernhill Secondary School
FARN GU14 ....68 B7
Ferrier Industrial Estate
WAND/EARL SW18 ....19 M9
Fetcham Social
& Sports Club
LHD/OX KT22 ....96 E1
Fetcham Village
Infant School
LHD/OX KT22 ....96 D2
Fielding Primary School
WEA W13 ....17 H1
Film House Cinema
RCH/KEW TW9 ....26 C1
Finchampstead
CE Primary School
EWKG RG40 ....48 C6
Finchampstead Sports Club
EWKG RG40 ....48 C6
Finns Industrial Park
RFNM GU10 ....106 B4
Finton House School
TOOT SW17 ....29 J5
Fircroft Primary School
TOOT SW17 ....29 J5
First Quarter Business Park
HOR/WEW KT19 ....60 C9
Fishing Club House
FROW RH18 ....180 G8
Five Ways Business Centre
FELT TW13 ....24 E7
Fleet Business Park
FLEETS GU52 ....107 H3
Fleet Community Hospital
FLEETN GU51 ....86 E5
Fleet Cricket Club
FLEETN GU51 ....86 E7
Fleet Town FC
FLEETN GU51 ....86 E7
Flexlands School
CHOB/PIR GU24 ....53 M9
Flora Gardens
Primary School
HMSMTH W6 ....18 F2
Flutters Leisure Centre
FUL/PGN SW6 ....19 L5
Folly Hill Infant School
FNM GU9 ....107 L8
Follys End
Christian High School
SNWD SE25 ....45 N7
Fonthill Lodge School
EGRIN RH19 ....180 B5
Fontigarry Farm
Business Park
REIG RH2 ....139 N5
The Foot Clinic
WIM/MER SW19 ....28 B8
The Foot Health Centre
COUL/CHIP CR5 ....80 F4
Fordbridge Medical Centre
ASHF TW15 ....23 J7
Fordwater Trading Estate
ADL/WDHM KT15 ....37 N9
Forestdale Primary School
CROY/NA CRO 64 E7
Forest End Medical Centre
BRAK RG12 ....32 D7
Foresters Primary School
WLGTN SM6 ....62 F5
Forest Hill Business Centre
FSTH SE23 ....31 K5
Forest Hill Industrial Estate
FSTH SE23 ....31 K5
Forest Hill School
FSTH SE23 ....31 L6
Forest Hills Pools
FSTH SE23 ....31 K6
Forest Row Business Park
FROW RH18 ....181 J8
Forest Row
CE Infant School
FROW RH18 ....181 L7
The Forest School
SWTR RH13 ....192 E9
Forge Close Clinic
HAYES BR2 ....47 N9
Forge Lane Primary School
FELT TW13 ....24 E7
Forge Wood
Industrial Estate
CRAWE RH10 ....177 L1
Four Elms Primary School
EDEN TN8 ....125 M9
Foxborough Primary School
DTCH/LGLY SL3 ....12 E3

Foxbridge Golf Club
BIL RH14 ....187 P9
Fox Hill Primary School
BRAK RG12 ....32 D6
Foxhills Golf Club & Hotel
CHERT KT16 ....54 D3
France Hill School
CBLY GU15 ....68 E5
Franciscan Primary School
TOOT SW17 ....29 K7
Franklin Industrial Estate
PGE/AN SE20 ....46 C2
Freehold Industrial Estate
HSLWW TW4 ....24 D1
Freemantles School
CHERT KT16 ....37 J8
Frensham Common
& Country Park
RFNM GU10 ....147 H6
Frensham Heights
Primary School
RFNM GU10 ....146 D2
Frensham Pond Hotel
RFNM GU10 ....146 F8
Frensham Pond Sailing Club
RFNM GU10 ....146 F7
The Friary Centre
GU U1 ....6 D5
Frimley Business Park
FRIM GU16 ....68 D8
Frimley CE Junior School
FRIM GU16 ....68 G9
Frimley Green
Medical Centre
FRIM GU16 ....89 H1
Frimley Hall Hotel
CBLY GU15 ....69 H2
Frimley Park Hospital
FRIM GU16 ....68 F6
Froebel College
PUT/ROE SW15 ....27 M2
Frogmore Community School
BLKW GU17 ....67 K3
Frogmore County
Infant School
BLKW GU17 ....67 M4
Frogmore Junior School
BLKW GU17 ....67 M3
Fulham Clinic
FUL/PGN SW6 ....19 K4
Fulham Cross School
FUL/PGN SW6 ....19 J7
Fulham FC (Craven Cottage)
BARN SW13 ....18 G6
Fulham Medical Centre
FUL/PGN SW6 ....19 M5
Fulham Palace
FUL/PGN SW6 ....19 J7
Fulham Preparatory School
FUL/PGN SW6 ....19 J7
Fulham Primary School
FUL/PGN SW6 ....19 L4
Fulham & South Kensington
Institute
WBPTN SW10 ....19 N3
Fullbrook School
ADL/WDHM KT15 ....55 L9
Fuller Smith
& Turner Sports Club
CHSWK W4 ....18 C6
Fulwell Golf Club
HPTN TW12 ....25 L7
Furzedown Primary School
TOOT SW17 ....29 L9
Furzefield Primary School
REDH RH1 ....100 F8
Gaflac Sports Ground
Pavilion
SUN TW16 ....39 J2
Gardener Industrial Estate
BECK BR3 ....31 M8
Garfield Primary School
WIM/MER SW19 ....28 F9
Garratt Park Secondary
Special School
WAND/EARL SW18 ....28 E6
The Garth Hill School
BRAK RG12 ....32 E2
Garth Primary School
MRDN SM4 ....43 P6
The Garth Road
Industrial Centre
MRDN SM4 ....42 G8
Gatton Manor Hotel Golf
& Country Club
RDKG RH5 ....172 G1
Gatton Park Business Centre
REDH RH1 ....120 D1
Gatwick Gate
Industrial Estate
HORL RH6 ....159 H7
Gatwick Industrial Estate
HORL RH6 ....158 C6
Gatwick Manor Golf Club
HORL RH6 ....159 H9
Gatwick Medical Centre
HORL RH6 ....159 L5
Gatwick Park Hospital
HORL RH6 ....159 H2
Gatwick Worth Hotel
CRAWE RH10 ....178 A6
Gatwick Zoo
HORL RH6 ....158 A6
Genesis Business Centre
SWTR RH13 ....192 E7
Genesis Business Park
WOKS/MYFD GU22 ....72 C4
George Abbot School
GU U1 ....112 G9
Georgian House Hotel
HASM GU27 ....184 D3

Gibbs Green Special School
WKENS W14 ....19 K3
Gilbert Scott Primary School
SAND/SEL CR2 ....64 E6
The Glades Shopping Centre
BMLY BR1 ....47 N3
Glebelands School
CRAN GU6 ....152 C9
Glebe School
WWKM BR4 ....47 K9
Glen Lecky Health Centre
PUT/ROE SW15 ....19 H9
Glenbrook Primary School
CLAP SW4 ....29 N2
Glendower
Preparatory School
SKENS SW7 ....19 N2
Glenesk School
EHSLY KT24 ....94 F5
Glenlyn Medical Centre
E/WMO/HCT KT8 ....40 C6
Glenthorne High School
CHEAM SM3 ....43 L9
Glyn Technology School
EW KT17 ....60 D9
Goal Farm Golf Club
CHOB/PIR GU24 ....90 D1
The Godalming
Badminton Club
GODL GU7 ....150 C2
Godalming Business Centre
GODL GU7 ....131 M9
Godalming College
GODL GU7 ....150 C2
Godalming County
Junior School
GODL GU7 ....131 M8
Godalming & Guildford FC
GODL GU7 ....131 N7
Godalming Leisure Centre
GODL GU7 ....131 N6
Godalming Museum
GODL GU7 ....131 K9
Godolphin & Latymer School
HMSMTH W6 ....18 F2
Goldhawk Industrial Estate
SHB W12 ....18 F1
Goldsworth CP School
WOKN/KNAP GU21 ....72 A7
Goldsworth Park
Health Centre
WOKN/KNAP GU21 ....71 N6
Goldsworth Park
Trading Estate
WOKN/KNAP GU21 ....71 N5
Goldsworth Rd
Industrial Estate
WOKN/KNAP GU21 ....10 A4
Golf Driving Range
REDH RH1 ....120 C8
Gonville Primary School
THHTH CR7 ....45 H6
Goodrich J & I School
EDUL SE22 ....31 H2
Good Shepherd
RC Primary School
CROY/NA CRO 65 H6
Gordonbrook Primary School
BROCKY SE4 ....31 P1
Gordons School
CHOB/PIR GU24 ....70 E1
Gorringe Park Middle School
MTCM CR4 ....44 C2
Gorse Ride Junior School
EWKG RG40 ....48 C2
Gosbury Hill Health Centre
CHSGTN KT9 ....59 L3
Gosden House School
SHGR GU5 ....132 C5
Gossops Green Clinic
CRAWW RH11 ....176 C7
Gossops Green F & M School
CRAWW RH11 ....176 D6
Grace Business Centre
MTCM CR4 ....44 B7
Granard Primary School
PUT/ROE SW15 ....27 N2
Grand Avenue
Primary School
BRYLDS KT5 ....42 A8
Grange CP School
ADL/WDHM KT15 ....55 L8
Grange Hotel
BRAK RG12 ....32 E3
Grange Junior School
FARN GU14 ....68 C8
Granton Primary School
STRHM/NOR SW16 ....44 E1
Grasshoppers RFC
ISLW TW7 ....16 F4
Grassroots School
HPTN TW12 ....40 A2
Graveney School
TOOT SW17 ....29 L9
Grayshott
CE Primary School
GSHT GU26 ....165 L8
Grayshott Clinic
GSHT GU26 ....165 L7
Graywood
CE Infant School
HASM GU27 ....166 C9
Great Bookham
County Infant School
GT/LBKH KT23 ....96 A3
Great Hollands Health Centre
BRAK RG12 ....32 B7
Great Hollands J & I School
BRAK RG12 ....32 A6
Great Hollands
Recreation Centre
BRAK RG12 ....32 A9

Great West Trading Estate
BTFD TW8 ....17 H4

Greenacre School for Girls
BNSTD SM7 ....79 N2

Green Business Centre
EGH TW20 ....21 P7

Green Dragon School
BTFD TW8 ....17 L3

Greenfield School
WOKS/MYFD GU22 ....10 C7

Green Lane Infant School
CODL GU7 ....131 L4

Green Lane Primary School
WPK KT4 ....42 F8

Greenmead Primary School
PUT/ROE SW15 ....27 N1

The Green School for Girls
ISLW TW7 ....16 G5

Greenshaw High School
SUT SM1 ....61 N1

Greenvale Primary School
SAND/SEL CR2 ....64 D9

Greenvale School
FSTH SE23 ....31 M6

Greenway Primary School
HORS RH12 ....192 A7

Greenwood First School
MTCM CR4 ....44 F4

Green Wrythe
Primary School
CAR SM5 ....43 P7

Gresham Industrial Estate
ASHV GU12 ....108 G4

Gresham Primary School
SAND/SEL CR2 ....81 P1

Gresham Way
Industrial Estate
WIM/MER SW19 ....28 E6

Greville Primary School
ASHTD KT21 ....77 M6

Grey Court School
RCHPK/HAM TW10 ....26 C6

Greyhound Hotel
CAR SM5 ....62 B4

Grist Memorial Sports Club
E/WMO/HCT KT8 ....40 E6

Grovebell Industrial Estate
RFNM GU10 ....127 K6

Grove County
Primary School
FRIM GU16 ....68 G6

Grove House School
WNWD SE27 ....30 C5

Grovelands School
WOT/HER KT12 ....39 K7

Grove Park Primary School
CHSWK W4 ....18 A4

Grove Road Primary School
HSLW TW3 ....16 A9

The Groves Medical Centre
NWMAL KT3 ....42 C4

Grove Village Medical Centre
EBED/NFELT TW14 ....23 P4

Guildford Business Park
GUW GU2 ....6 A1

Guildford Castle
GU GU1 ....7 F6

Guildford Cathedral
GUW GU2 ....6 A3

Guildford College of Further
& Higher Education
GU GU1 ....7 F1

Guildford County School
GU GU2 ....6 B6

Guildford Crematorium
GODL GU7 ....131 P5

Guildford Cricket Ground
(Surrey CCC)
GU GU1 ....6 D2

Guildford Discovery
GU GU1 ....7 F5

Guildford Golf Club
GU GU1 ....112 G5

Guildford Grove
Primary School
GUW GU2 ....111 L5

Guildford High School
GU GU1 ....7 G3

Guildford Hockey
& Cricket Club
GU GU1 ....6 D3

Guildford House Gallery
GU GU1 ....7 F6

Guildford Industrial Estate
GUW GU2 ....111 N4

Guildford Lido
GU GU1 ....112 B4

Guildford Museum
GUW GU2 ....6 E7

Guildford Natural
Health Centre
GU GU1 ....6 E6

The Guildford Nuffield
Hospital
GUW GU2 ....111 L5

Guildford Road
Industrial Estate
FNM GU9 ....5 K1

Guildford Rowing Club
GU GU1 ....112 B8

Guildford Spectrum
GU GU1 ....112 C4

Guildford Spectrum
Athletics Stadium
GU GU1 ....112 C3

Guillemont County
Junior School
FARN GU14 ....87 N1

Gumley House Convent School
ISLW TW7 ....16 G8

Gunnersbury Catholic School
BTFD TW8 ....17 J3

Gunnersbury Park Museum
ACT W3 ....17 N1

Gym Club
LHD/OX KT22 ....96 G3

Hackbridge Primary School
WLGTN SM6 ....44 C9

Hakim Qureshi Clinic
NWDGN UB2 ....15 N1

Hale Primary School
FNM GU9 ....107 M7

Haling Manor High School
CROY/NA CR0 ....63 K6

Hall Grove Farm
Industrial Estate
BAGS GU19 ....51 P4

Hall Grove School
BAGS GU19 ....52 A4

Halliford Health Clinic
SHPTN TW17 ....38 G5

Halliford School
SHPTN TW17 ....38 E8

Halls Business Centre
HYS/HAR UB3 ....15 J1

Hall School Wimbledon
PUT/ROE SW15 ....27 M6

Halsford Park
Primary School
EGRIN RH19 ....180 A1

Halstead
Preparatory School
WOKN/KNAP GU21 ....72 D4

Ham Health Clinic
RCHPK/HAM TW10 ....26 B6

Ham House (NT)
RCHPK/HAM TW10 ....26 B4

Hamilton Road
Industrial Estate
WNWD SE27 ....30 E7

Hamm Court
WEY KT13 ....56 B2

Hammersmith Apollo
HMSMTH W6 ....18 G3

Hammersmith Cemetery
HMSMTH W6 ....19 H3

Hammersmith
Industrial Estate
HMSMTH W6 ....18 G4

Hammersmith
New Cemetery
RCH/KEW TW9 ....17 P7

Hammersmith Palais
HMSMTH W6 ....18 G2

Hammersmith Physio
& Sports Injury Clinic
HMSMTH W6 ....18 G2

Hammersmith
& West London College
WKENS W14 ....19 H2

Hammerwood Park
EGRIN RH19 ....181 P1

Hammond Junior School
LTWR GU18 ....52 A8

Ham & Petersham
Cricket Club
RCHPK/HAM TW10 ....26 C7

Hampton Cemetery
HPTN TW12 ....40 A1

Hampton
Community College
HPTN TW12 ....25 H8

Hampton Court Palace
E/WMO/HCT KT8 ....40 F4

Hampton Farm
Industrial Estate
FELT TW13 ....24 F6

Hampton FC
HPTN TW12 ....40 B2

Hampton Hill Junior School
HPTN TW12 ....25 K8

Hampton Infant School
HPTN TW12 ....39 P1

Hampton Junior School
HPTN TW12 ....40 A1

The Hampton Medical Centre
HPTN TW12 ....40 A1

Hampton Open Air Pool
HPTN TW12 ....40 C1

Hampton Road
Industrial Park
CROY/NA CR0 ....45 L7

Hampton School
HPTN TW12 ....25 H8

Hampton Wick Infant School
KUT KT1 ....8 A1

Hamsey Green County
Junior School
WARL CR6 ....82 B5

Hamsey Green Infant School
WARL CR6 ....82 B5

Handcross Park School
RHWH RH17 ....194 G8

Handcross Primary School
RHWH RH17 ....194 F9

Hankley Common Golf Club
RFNM GU10 ....147 N3

Hanworth Business Park
CHERT KT16 ....37 K9

Hanworth Trading Estate
FELT TW13 ....24 F6

Happy Valley Golf Club
CTHM CR3 ....101 K3

Harland Primary School
WIM/MER SW19 ....43 N3

Harlington
Community School
HYS/HAR UB3 ....14 F2

Harmans Water Junior
and Infants School
BRAK RG12 ....32 G4

Harrington Hall Hotel
SKENS SW7 ....19 N2

Harris City
Technology College
NRWD SE19 ....45 P2

Harrodian School
BARN SW13 ....18 D5

Hart Shopping Centre
FLEETN GU51 ....86 F6

Hart Sports Centre
FLEETN GU51 ....86 C7

Haseltine Primary School
CAT SE6 ....31 N7

Haslemere Hall
HASM GU27 ....184 D3

Haslemere Hospital
& Health Centre
HASM GU27 ....184 E3

Haslemere Industrial Estate
EBED/NFELT TW14 ....24 B1
HASM GU27 ....184 E5

Haslemere Museum
HASM GU27 ....184 E3

Haslemere
Preparatory School
HASM GU27 ....184 E5

Haslemere Primary School
MTCM CR4 ....43 P3

Hastings Clinic
BRXS/STRHM SW2 ....30 A1

Hatch Ride Primary School
CWTH RG45 ....49 M2

Havelock Primary School
NWDGN UB2 ....15 P1

Havenbury Industrial Estate
DORK RH4 ....116 G6

Hawes Down Clinic
WWKM BR4 ....65 K1

Hawes Down School
WWKM BR4 ....47 K9

Hawkedale Gm School
SUN TW16 ....39 H4

The Hawker Centre
KUTN/CMB KT2 ....26 C8

Hawkins Clinic
EW KT17 ....78 G4
PUT/ROE SW15 ....19 H9

Hawkins Clinic
RYNPK SW20 ....42 D2

Hawley CP School
BLKW GU17 ....68 A5

Hawley Lane
Industrial Estate
FARN GU14 ....68 D8

Hawley Place School
BLKW GU17 ....68 A7

The Hawthorns
Pre-preparatory School
REDH RH1 ....121 K2

The Hawth Theatre, Cinema
& Conference Complex
CRAWE RH10 ....177 J6

Hayes Grove Priory Hospital
HAYES BR2 ....65 N1

Hayes Primary School
HAYES BR2 ....47 P9

The Hayes Primary School
PUR/KEN CR8 ....81 K5

Hayes School
HAYES BR2 ....65 P1

Haysbridge Business Centre
GDST RH9 ....142 C7

Hazelhurst School
RYNPK SW20 ....43 H2

Hazelwick School
CRAWE RH10 ....177 K3

Hazelwood School
OXTED RH8 ....123 N2

Headley Park Country Club
BOR GU35 ....164 A2

Heath Business Centre
HSLW TW3 ....16 C9
REDH RH1 ....140 D6

Heathcote Medical Centre
KWD/TDW/WH KT20 ....99 H2

Heath End County
Secondary School
FNM GU9 ....108 A8

Heathermount School
ASC SL5 ....34 D7

Heather Ridge County
Infants School
CBLY GU15 ....69 M4

Heatherside Schools
FLEETS GU52 ....86 G8

Heatherwood Hospital
ASC SL5 ....33 N4

Heathfield Junior School
WHTN TW2 ....25 H4

Heathfield School
ASC SL5 ....33 K3

Heathland School
HSLWW TW4 ....24 G2

Heathmere Primary School
PUT/ROE SW15 ....27 M4

Heathpark Golf Club
WDR/YW UB7 ....14 C1

Heathrow Airport
HTHAIR TW6 ....14 D7

Heathrow Airport
Central Bus
& Coach Station
HTHAIR TW6 ....14 C8

Heathrow International
Trading Estate
HSLWW TW4 ....15 K8

Heathrow Medical Centre
HYS/HAR UB3 ....14 F3

Heathrow Primary School
WDR/YW UB7 ....14 B4

Heathrow World
Cargo Centre
HTHAIR TW6 ....23 J1

Heathside School
WEY KT13 ....56 B4

Heavers Farm
Primary School
SNWD SE25 ....45 P6

Heber Primary School
EDUL SE22 ....30 C2

Heliport Industrial Estate
BTSEA SW11 ....19 P7

Helix Business Park
CBLY GU15 ....68 D5

Helston Court
Business Centre
WIM/MER SW19 ....27 N8

Henderson Hospital
BELMT SM2 ....61 L7

Henry Cavendish
Primary School
BAL SW12 ....29 M4

Henry Compton School
FUL/PGN SW6 ....19 H6

Henry Tyndale School
FARN GU14 ....88 E1

Hermitage County
First School
WOKN/KNAP GU21 ....71 L8

The Hermitage School
WOKN/KNAP GU21 ....71 L8

Herne Hill School
HNHL SE24 ....30 D1

Herne Hill Stadium
(Cycle Centre)
DUL SE21 ....30 E2

The Herons Swimming
& Fitness Centre
HASM GU27 ....184 A4

Heron Way Primary School
SWTR RH13 ....192 F9

Hersham Trading Estate
WOT/HER KT12 ....57 N1

Heston Community School
HEST TW5 ....16 A5

Heston Community
Sports Hall
HEST TW5 ....16 A5

Heston Industrial Mall
HEST TW5 ....15 P5

Heston Infant School
HEST TW5 ....16 A5

Heston Junior School
HEST TW5 ....16 A4

Heston Park Cricket Club
HEST TW5 ....15 P4

Heston Swimming Baths
HEST TW5 ....15 P4

Hever Castle and Gardens
EDEN TN8 ....145 P6

Hever CE Primary School
EDEN TN8 ....145 P7

Hever Golf Club
EDEN TN8 ....145 P4

Hewitts Industrial Estate
CRAN GU6 ....152 E9

Highclere Hotel
ASC SL5 ....34 D6

High Commission
of Bangladesh
SKENS SW7 ....19 N1

High Commission
of Dominica
ECT SW5 ....19 M2

High Commission
of Grenada
ECT SW5 ....19 M3

Highfield Infant School
HAYES BR2 ....47 L5

Highfield Junior School
HAYES BR2 ....47 L5

Highfield School
LIPH GU30 ....183 H8
WAND/EARL SW18 ....29 H3

High View Primary School
BTSEA SW11 ....19 P9

Highview Primary School
WLGTN SM6 ....62 G4

Hillbrook Primary School
TOOT SW17 ....29 J7

Hillcroft College
SURB KT6 ....41 L7

Hillcrest Primary School
CTHM CR3 ....101 N3

Hillcross Primary School
MRDN SM4 ....43 K5

Hill's Cemetery
HORS RH12 ....191 N8

Hill School
BH/WHM TN16 ....104 F3

Hilly Fields Medical Centre
BROCKY SE4 ....31 P1

Hinchley Wood School
ESH/CLAY KT10 ....58 C1

Hindhead Golf Club
GSHT GU26 ....165 L5

Hitherfield Primary School
STRHM/NOR SW16 ....30 B5

HM Customs
HTHAIR TW6 ....14 D6

HM Prison
BRXS/STRHM SW2 ....29 P2
WAND/EARL SW18 ....28 C2

HM Young Offender
Institution
FELT TW13 ....23 N9

Hobbs Industrial Estate
LING RH7 ....161 L5

Hockley Industrial Centre
REDH RH1 ....120 B6

Hoebridge Golf Centre
WOKS/MYFD GU22 ....72 G8

Hoe Bridge School
WOKS/MYFD GU22 ....72 F8

Hogan Business Centre
WOKN/KNAP GU21 ....10 C4

Hogarth Business Park
CHSWK W4 ....18 C4

The Hogarth Hotel
ECT SW5 ....19 M2

Hogarth Primary School
CHSWK W4 ....18 C3

Hogarth's House
CHSWK W4 ....18 C3

Holbeach Primary School
CAT SE6 ....31 P3

Holborn College
WKENS W14 ....19 J4

Holbrook County
Primary School
HORS RH12 ....192 C3

Holbrook Recreation Centre
HORS RH12 ....192 D3

Holiday Inn
CRAWW RH11 ....176 G3
FARN GU14 ....88 D7
GUW GU2 ....111 M6
HORL RH6 ....159 H2
SKENS SW7 ....19 N2
SUT SM1 ....61 N4
WDR/YW UB7 ....14 C5
WDR/YW UB7 ....14 G3

Hollybush Business Centre
CRAWE RH10 ....160 A8

Hollybush Industrial Park
ALDT GU11 ....108 C1

The Hollyfield School
SURB KT6 ....41 L6

Holly Lodge CP School
ASHV GU12 ....89 H7

Hollymount Primary School
RYNPK SW20 ....42 G2

Holly Spring J & I School
BRAK RG12 ....32 G3

Holmesdale School
REIG RH2 ....119 M3

Holmethorpe
Industrial Estate
REDH RH1 ....120 D2

Holy Cross Convent School
NWMAL KT3 ....42 B5

Holy Cross Hospital
HASM GU27 ....184 A3

Holy Cross
Preparatory School
KUTN/CMB KT2 ....42 A1

Holy Cross Primary School
FUL/PGN SW6 ....19 L6

Holy Family
RC Primary School
ADL/WDHM KT15 ....55 L4

Holy Family RC School
DTCH/LGLY SL3 ....12 D3

Holy Ghost
RC Primary School
BAL SW12 ....29 J3

Holy Trinity CE First School
WIM/MER SW19 ....28 D9

Holy Trinity CE Junior School
GU GU1 ....7 K6
WLGTN SM6 ....62 E3

Holy Trinity
CE Primary School
ASC SL5 ....34 G7
BRXS/STRHM SW2 ....30 A3
CHOB/PIR GU24 ....70 C2
FSTH SE23 ....31 K5
RCHPK/HAM TW10 ....17 N9

The Holy Trinity CE School
CRAWW RH11 ....176 D7

Homefield
Preparatory School
SUT SM1 ....61 L4

Home Park Golf Club
E/WMO/HCT KT8 ....41 J6

Hones Yard Business Park
FNM GU9 ....5 J4

Honeywell Primary School
BTSEA SW11 ....29 J2

Hong Kong & Shanghai
Sports Club
BECK BR3 ....31 M9

Honor Oak Crematorium
FSTH SE23 ....31 L1

Honor Oak Gallery
FSTH SE23 ....31 L2

Hook Rise South
Industrial Park
CHSGTN KT9 ....59 N2

The Hop Kiln
FNM GU9 ....5 F6

Horley Anderson Centre
HORL RH6 ....159 H1

Horley Health Centre
HORL RH6 ....159 H1

The Horniman Museum
& Gardens
FSTH SE23 ....31 J4

Horniman Primary School
FSTH SE23 ....31 J4

Hornsby House School
BAL SW12 ....29 K4

Horsell CE Junior School
WOKN/KNAP GU21 ....72 A5

Horsell Village County
Infant School
WOKN/KNAP GU21 ....10 A2

Horsham Cricket
& Sports Club
HORS RH12 ....192 A9

Horsham FC
SWTR RH13 ....192 C9

Horsham Hospital
HORS RH12 ....192 B7

Horsham Museum
HORS RH12 ....192 B9

Horsham Swimming Centre *HORS* RH12 ...192 B7
Horsham Trading Estate *HORS* RH12 ...192 D6
Horsham YMCA FC *SWTR* RH13 ...192 C9
Horsley Sports Club *EHSLY* KT24 ...95 H7
Horton Country Park *HOR/WEW* KT19 ...59 N7
Horton Hospital *HOR/WEW* KT19 ...60 A9
Horton Park Golf & Country Club *HOR/WEW* KT19 ...60 A6
Horton Trading Estate *DTCH/LGLY* SL3 ...12 F8
Hoskins Place Industrial Estate *CBLY* GU15 ...68 D5
Hotel Ibis *HTHAIR* TW6 ...14 C6
CRAWE RH10 ...159 H9
Hotham Primary School *PUT/ROE* SW15 ...19 H9
Hounslow Business Park *HSLW* TW3 ...16 A9
Hounslow Cemetery *HSLWW* TW4 ...24 G3
Hounslow College Independent School *FELT* TW13 ...24 E7
Hounslow Cricket Club *HSLW* TW3 ...15 P7
Hounslow Heath Golf Club *HSLWW* TW4 ...24 E1
Hounslow Heath Infant School *HSLWW* TW4 ...15 N8
Hounslow Heath Junior School *HSLWW* TW4 ...15 N8
Hounslow Manor School *HSLW* TW3 ...16 B8
Hounslow Manor Sports Hall *HSLW* TW3 ...16 B8
Hounslow & Spelthorne Community & Mental Health NHS Trust *STA* TW18 ...22 D8
Hounslow Town Primary School *HSLW* TW3 ...16 C8
Howard of Effingham School *EHSLY* KT24 ...95 N7
Howard Primary School *CROY/NA* CRO ...63 L3
Hubbard School *EGRIN* RH19 ...180 D2
Humphries Industrial Estate *BRAK* RG12 ...32 D5
Hurlands Business Centre *FNM* GU9 ...128 L1
Hurlingham Business Park *FUL/PGN* SW6 ...19 L8
Hurlingham & Chelsea School *FUL/PGN* SW6 ...19 L8
Hurlingham House *FUL/PGN* SW6 ...19 K8
Hurlingham Private School *PUT/ROE* SW15 ...19 K9
Huron University *SKENS* SW7 ...19 P1
Hurst Green School *OXTED* RH8 ...123 N3
Hurst Lodge School *ASC* SL5 ...34 B9
Hurst Park School *E/WMO/HCT* KT8 ...40 A4
Hurtmore Golf Club *GODL* GU7 ...130 F6
Hurtwood House *CRAN* GU6 ...154 B2
Hurtwood Inn Hotel *SHGR* GU5 ...134 F7
Hyland Business Centre *REDH* RH1 ...120 B5
The Hythe School *STA* TW18 ...22 A8
Ibstock Place School *PUT/ROE* SW15 ...27 K2
Ifield Community College *CRAWW* RH11 ...176 D4
Ifield F & B School *CRAWW* RH11 ...176 D5
Ifield Golf & Country Club *CRAWW* RH11 ...176 D5
Ifield Golf & Country Club *RDKG* RH5 ...157 H8
Imber Court Trading Estate *E/WMO/HCT* KT8 ...40 D7
Imberhorne Business Centre *EGRIN* RH19 ...162 A9
Imberhorne School *EGRIN* RH19 ...180 A1
The Imber Sports Centre *EGRIN* RH19 ...162 C9
Immanuel CE Primary School *STRHM/NOR* SW16 ...29 P9
Imperial College *SKENS* SW7 ...19 P1
Imperial College Athletic Ground *WDR/YW* UB7 ...14 E4
Imperial College of Science *FUL/PGN* SW6 ...19 L4
Imperial College of Science Technology & Medicine *ASC* SL5 ...34 F4

Independent Business Park *EGRIN* RH19 ...161 P9
Indoor Sports Centre *STA* TW18 ...22 D7
The Industrial Estate *EDEN* TN8 ...144 F2
Innkeeper's Lodge Hotel *ASC* SL5 ...35 H4
BECK BR3 ...46 G7
DTCH/LGLY SL3 ...12 D3
FRIM GU16 ...68 G5
GODL GU7 ...150 B1
REDH RH1 ...120 C5
SAND/SEL CR2 ...63 L7
WDSR SL4 ...20 F1
WEY KT13 ...56 G2
WOT/HER KT12 ...57 J2
Institut Francais *SKENS* SW7 ...19 P2
International School of London *ACT* W3 ...17 N2
International Trading Estate *NWDGN* UB2 ...15 K1
Inwood Business Centre *HSLW* TW3 ...16 B9
The Islamic Grammar School *WAND/EARL* SW18 ...28 C3
Isleworth Blue CE Primary School *ISLW* TW7 ...16 G8
Isleworth Cemetery *ISLW* TW7 ...16 G8
Isleworth Recreation Centre *ISLW* TW7 ...16 G8
Isleworth & Syon School for Boys *ISLW* TW7 ...16 E5
Isleworth Town Primary School *ISLW* TW7 ...16 F7
Ismaili Centre *SKENS* SW7 ...19 P2
Ithaca College *TWK* TW1 ...25 N2
Ivybridge Primary School *ISLW* TW7 ...25 N1
Ivybridge Retail Park *ISLW* TW7 ...25 N1
Ivydene Industrial Estate *EGRIN* RH19 ...181 J4
Jack & Jill School *HPTN* TW12 ...25 H9
WHTN TW2 ...25 M5
Jack Tizzard School *FUL/PGN* SW6 ...19 H4
Jacques Prevert School *WKENS* W14 ...19 H2
James Allens Preparatory Girls School *EDUL* SE22 ...30 E1
James Dixon Primary School *PGE/AN* SE20 ...46 A1
James Searle Industrial Estate *HORS* RH12 ...192 D6
Jenner Health Centre *FSTH* SE23 ...31 M4
The Jigsaw School *FRIM* GU16 ...88 G4
John Betts Primary School *HMSMTH* W6 ...18 E1
John Fisher School *PUR/KEN* CR8 ...62 G8
John Nightingale School *E/WMO/HCT* KT8 ...39 P4
John Nike Athletics Stadium *BRAK* RG12 ...32 E6
John Paul II RC School *WIM/MER* SW19 ...28 A3
John Ruskin College *SAND/SEL* CR2 ...64 E6
Johnsons Industrial Estate *HYS/HAR* UB3 ...15 J1
Joseph Hood Primary School *RYNPK* SW20 ...43 J3
Joseph Tritton Primary School *BTSEA* SW11 ...19 N9
Jubilee Hall Clinic *CRAWE* RH10 ...177 K6
Julians Primary School *STRHM/NOR* SW16 ...30 B7
Jurys Inn Hotel *CROY/NA* CRO ...2 D3
Jury's Kensington Hotel *SKENS* SW7 ...19 P2
Kangley Business Centre *SYD* SE26 ...31 N8
Kelsey Park School *BECK* BR3 ...46 G4
Kelvin Business Centre *CRAWE* RH10 ...177 J2
Kelvin Grove Primary School *SYD* SE26 ...31 J4
Kempton Park Racecourse *SUN* TW16 ...39 K1
Kendall Court Business Centre *CBLY* GU15 ...68 B4
Kenley Primary School *PUR/KEN* CR8 ...81 N5
Kenley Sports Club *PUR/KEN* CR8 ...81 L3
Kensington Avenue Primary School *THHTH* CR7 ...45 J2
Kensington & Chelsea College *WBPTN* SW10 ...19 N5
Kensington Preparatory School *FUL/PGN* SW6 ...19 K6

Kensington Wharf *WBPTN* SW10 ...19 P5
Kenyngton Manor Primary School *SUN* TW16 ...24 B9
Keston Junior School *COUL/CHIP* CR5 ...81 J8
Keston Church *COUL/CHIP* CR5 ...81 J8
Kew Bridge Steam Museum *BTFD* TW8 ...17 M3
Kew College *RCH/KEW* TW9 ...17 N5
Kew Gardens (Royal Botanic Gardens) *RCH/KEW* TW9 ...17 L6
Kew Palace *RCH/KEW* TW9 ...17 L5
Kew Retail Park *RCH/KEW* TW9 ...17 P6
Kilmorie Primary School *FSTH* SE23 ...31 M5
Kiln Park Business Centre *EW* KT17 ...60 C9
Kimpton Industrial Estate *CHEAM* SM3 ...61 K1
King Athelstan Primary School *KUT* KT1 ...9 F6
King Edwards School *MFD/CHID* GU8 ...167 N2
King Fahad Academy (Girls Upper School) *EA* W5 ...17 J2
Kingfield School *WOKS/MYFD* GU22 ...72 E9
The Kingfisher Sports Centre *KUT* KT1 ...8 E5
King Henry's Reach Development *BARN* SW13 ...18 G4
Kings Acre Primary School *CLAP* SW4 ...29 P1
The Kings Centre *ALDT* GU11 ...108 C4
Kings College *GUW* GU2 ...111 L5
King's College School *WIM/MER* SW19 ...27 P9
Kings College of Medicine & Dentistry *DUL* SE21 ...30 E2
Kings Court First School *WDSR* SL4 ...20 C3
Kingscroft School *STA* TW18 ...22 D9
Kingsdale School *DUL* SE21 ...30 F6
Kingsfield Business Centre *REDH* RH1 ...120 C6
Kingsgate Business Centre *KUTN/CMB* KT2 ...8 D3
Kingsgrove Industrial Estate *FARN* GU14 ...88 C4
Kings House School *RCHPK/HAM* TW10 ...26 E1
Kingsley Primary School *CROY/NA* CRO ...45 H9
Kings Mall Shopping Centre *HMSMTH* W6 ...18 G2
Kingsmeadow Athletics Centre *KUT* KT1 ...9 J7
Kingsmead Shopping Centre *FARN* GU14 ...88 D4
Kings Road Industrial Estate *HASM* GU27 ...184 D6
Kings School of English *BECK* BR3 ...46 F3
Kingston Business Centre *CHSGTN* KT9 ...59 L2
Kingston Cemetery *KUT* KT1 ...9 H6
Kingston College of Further Education *KUT* KT1 ...8 C6
Kingston Crematorium *KUT* KT1 ...9 H7
Kingston Crown Court *KUT* KT1 ...8 C6
Kingston Grammar School *KUT* KT1 ...9 F4
Kingston Hospital *KUTN/CMB* KT2 ...9 K2
Kingston Hospital NHS Trust *KUTN/CMB* KT2 ...9 K2
Kingstonian FC *KUT* KT1 ...9 K7
Kingston Lodge Hotel *KUTN/CMB* KT2 ...41 P1
Kingstons Industrial Estate *ASHV* GU12 ...108 G4
Kingston University *KUT* KT1 ...8 E7
KUT KT1 ...41 L5
KUTN/CMB KT2 ...27 J8
King Street College *HMSMTH* W6 ...18 G2
Kingsway Business Centre *HPTN* TW12 ...39 P2
Kingswood CE Junior School *WOKN/KNAP* GU21 ...72 G3
Kingswood Golf Club *KWD/TDW/WH* KT20 ...99 L4
Kingswood House School *HOR/WEW* KT19 ...77 P2
Kingswood Primary School *KWD/TDW/WH* KT20 ...99 K8
WNWD SE27 ...30 E7
KLC School of Design *WBPTN* SW10 ...19 N6

Knaphill Junior School *WOKN/KNAP* GU21 ...71 J7
Knaphill Lower School *WOKN/KNAP* GU21 ...71 H7
Knockholt CE Primary School *RSEV* TN14 ...85 M6
Knolmead Primary School *WPK* KT4 ...60 A1
Knowle Park Infant School *STA* TW18 ...22 D8
Knowl Hill School *CHOB/PIR* GU24 ...90 E2
Ladycross Business Park *EGRIN* RH19 ...163 H5
Lady Edens School *KENS* W8 ...19 M1
The Lady Eleanor Holles School *HPTN* TW12 ...25 J8
Lady Margaret School *FUL/PGN* SW6 ...19 L6
Ladymead Retail Centre *GU* GU1 ...112 A4
Ladywell Cemetery *BROCKY* SE4 ...31 N1
Laine Theatre Arts *EW* KT17 ...78 C2
Laker Industrial Estate *BECK* BR3 ...31 M8
Lakeside Business Park *SHST* GU47 ...67 L1
Lakeside Country Club *FRIM* GU16 ...89 J1
Lakeside Industrial Estate *DTCH/LGLY* SL3 ...13 J5
DTCH/LGLY SL3 ...13 L4
Lakeside International Hotel *FRIM* GU16 ...89 J1
Lakeside Primary School *FRIM* GU16 ...69 H7
Laleham CE Primary School *STA* TW18 ...37 N3
Laleham Golf Club *CHERT* KT16 ...37 M5
Lambeth Cemetery *TOOT* SW17 ...28 F8
Lambeth College *CLAP* SW4 ...29 M1
Lambeth Crematorium *TOOT* SW17 ...28 F7
Lambs Business Park *GDST* RH9 ...122 B9
Lamont Business Centre *CROY/NA* CRO ...44 G8
Lampton School *HEST* TW5 ...16 A6
Langbourne Primary School *DUL* SE21 ...30 F6
Langford Primary School *FUL/PGN* SW6 ...19 M7
Langley Grammar School *DTCH/LGLY* SL3 ...12 D2
Langley Green First School *CRAWW* RH11 ...176 C1
Langley Health Centre *DTCH/LGLY* SL3 ...12 E3
Langley Park Girls School & Sports Centre *BECK* BR3 ...47 K7
Langley Park Golf Club *BECK* BR3 ...47 H6
Langley Park School for Boys *BECK* BR3 ...47 H7
Langleywood School *DTCH/LGLY* SL3 ...12 C1
Langshott County Infant School *HORL* RH6 ...159 M1
Langshott Manor Hotel *HORL* RH6 ...140 F9
The Lansbury Estate *WOKN/KNAP* GU21 ...71 K7
La Retraite RC Girls School *BAL* SW12 ...29 M3
Larmenier Infant School *HMSMTH* W6 ...19 H2
Latchmere J & I School *KUTN/CMB* KT2 ...26 E9
Latymer Upper School *HMSMTH* W6 ...18 E2
Laurel Clinic *EA* W5 ...17 J2
Lavender Golf Club *ASC* SL5 ...33 L4
Lawn Tennis Club *HORL* RH6 ...159 J1
REDH RH1 ...120 B3
Lawson Hunt Industrial Park *HORS* RH12 ...191 L6
Lazards Sports Club *SUN* TW16 ...39 K2
Leatherhead Business Park *LHD/OX* KT22 ...77 H8
Leatherhead Clinic *LHD/OX* KT22 ...97 J1
Leatherhead Cricket Club *LHD/OX* KT22 ...96 G2
Leatherhead FC *LHD/OX* KT22 ...96 G2
Leatherhead Golf Club *LHD/OX* KT22 ...76 G5
Leatherhead Hospital *LHD/OX* KT22 ...97 J2
Leatherhead Industrial Estate *LHD/OX* KT22 ...96 G1
Leatherhead Institute *LHD/OX* KT22 ...97 H1
Leatherhead Leisure Centre & Water Park *LHD/OX* KT22 ...96 G3

Leatherhead Museum *LHD/OX* KT22 ...97 H2
L'ecoles Des Petits *FUL/PGN* SW6 ...19 M7
Leechpool Lane Primary School *SWTR* RH13 ...192 F6
Leigh Close Industrial Estate *NWMAL* KT3 ...42 B5
Leigh Primary School *REIG* RH2 ...138 E2
Leighton House Museum & Art Gallery *WKENS* W14 ...19 K1
Le Meridien Hotel *HORL* RH6 ...159 H3
Le Meridien Hotel & Travelodge *WDR/YW* UB7 ...14 D5
Lena Gardens Primary School *HMSMTH* W6 ...18 G1
Lewin Mead Community Mental Health Centre *STRHM/NOR* SW16 ...29 N9
Lewis Clinic *CAR* SM5 ...62 C3
Liberty Middle School *MTCM* CR4 ...44 A3
Library & Community Centre *BTSEA* SW11 ...19 P5
Library & Council Building *CRAWE* RH10 ...177 H5
The Licensed Victuallers School *ASC* SL5 ...33 L3
Lido *STRHM/NOR* SW16 ...29 M7
Lifecare NHS Trust *CTHM* CR3 ...101 N3
Lightwater Country Park *LTWR* GU18 ...51 P8
Lightwater Village School *LTWR* GU18 ...52 A3
Lillian Bishop School of English *SKENS* SW7 ...19 P2
Lillie Road Fitness Centre *FUL/PGN* SW6 ...19 H4
Limes Business Centre *HORL* RH6 ...158 C5
Limpsfield CE Infant School *OXTED* RH8 ...103 P9
Limpsfield Chart Golf Club *OXTED* RH8 ...104 A9
Limpsfield Grange School *OXTED* RH8 ...103 N7
Limpsfield Lawn Tennis Club *OXTED* RH8 ...103 N8
Linden Bridge School *WPK* KT4 ...60 C2
Linden Lodge School *WIM/MER* SW19 ...28 B3
Lindon Bennett School *FELT* TW13 ...24 E8
Lingfield Park Racecourse *LING* RH7 ...162 E2
Lingfield Primary School *LING* RH7 ...143 K9
Lingfield Squash & Leisure Club *LING* RH7 ...162 E1
The Link Day Primary School *CROY/NA* CRO ...62 G3
The Link Secondary School *CROY/NA* CRO ...63 H3
Links Primary School *TOOT* SW17 ...29 K9
Linsford Business Park *FRIM* GU16 ...89 H4
Lionel Road Primary School *BTFD* TW8 ...17 L2
Lion House School *PUT/ROE* SW15 ...19 H9
Lion & Lamb Yard Shopping Centre *FNM* GU9 ...4 E2
Lion Retail Park *WOKS/MYFD* GU22 ...11 J1
Liphook CE Junior School *LIPH* GU30 ...182 D6
Liphook Infant School *LIPH* GU30 ...182 D6
Little Eden & Eden High School *FELT* TW13 ...24 E7
Liphook School *LIPH* GU30 ...182 G8
Littlehaven Infant School *HORS* RH12 ...192 E5
Little Mead Industrial Estate *CRAN* GU6 ...152 E9
Littleton CE Infant School *SHPTN* TW17 ...38 C4
Little Wandsworth School *TOOT* SW17 ...29 K5
Lloyds Register Cricket Club *DUL* SE21 ...30 E4
Lodge School *PUR/KEN* CR8 ...80 F1
Lombard Business Park *CROY/NA* CRO ...45 H8
WAND/EARL SW18 ...28 G2
WIM/MER SW19 ...43 N3
London Academy of Music & Dramatic Art *HMSMTH* W6 ...19 H3
London Broncos RLFC (Griffin Park) *BTFD* TW8 ...17 K4

London Electronics College
ECT SW5 .... 19 L3
London Executive College
TOOT SW17 .... 29 K6
Manby Lodge Infant School
WEY KT13 .... 56 D3
Mancroft Primary School
EGH TW20 .... 21 M9
Mandeville Primary School
WPK KT4 .... 42 D9
Manor Drive Health Centre
RYNM GU10 .... 109 H9
The Manor Hotel
RGUE GU4 .... 113 M6
Manor House School
EHSLY KT24 .... 95 N7
Manor Mead School
SHPTN TW17 .... 38 D6
Manor Park Industrial Estate
ASHV GU12 .... 108 E5
Manor Park Primary School
SUT SM1 .... 61 N4
Manor Primary School
FARN GU14 .... 88 D1
The Manor School
FARN GU14 .... 74 A3
Maple Grove Business Centre
HSLWW TW4 .... 15 L9
Maple Industrial Estate
FELT TW13 .... 24 B5
Maple Infant School
SURB KT6 .... 41 K6
Marble Hill House
TWK TW1 .... 26 B3
Marden Lodge Primary School
CTHM CR3 .... 82 B9
Margaret Roper
RC Primary School
PUR/KEN CR8 .... 63 H8
Marion Vian Primary School
BECK BR3 .... 46 D6
Marish First School
DTCH/LGLY SL3 .... 12 D1
Marist Convent Senior School
ASC SL5 .... 34 D6
Marist Junior School
ASC SL5 .... 34 D5
The Marist RC Primary School
BF/WBF KT14 .... 73 K2
The Marjory Kinnon School
EBED/NFELT TW14 .... 23 P1
Market Trading Estate
NWDGN UB2 .... 15 K2
Markington Hotel & Conference
Centre
SAND/SEL CR2 .... 63 L5
Marlborough County
Infant School
ALDT GU11 .... 88 E8
Marlborough Cricket Club
DUL SE21 .... 31 H4
Marlborough Primary School
ISLW TW7 .... 16 C6
Marlborough Trading Estate
RCH/KEW TW9 .... 17 P6
Marriott Hotel
DTCH/LGLY SL3 .... 12 D3
Marsh Farm Business Centre
RFRM GU10 .... 106 D5
Mary Boone School
WKENS W14 .... 19 J2
Marymount
International School
KUTN/CMB KT2 .... 42 A1
Mary Wallace Theatre
TWK TW1 .... 25 P4
Master Robert Hotel
HEST TW5 .... 15 P6
Maswell Park Health Centre
HSLW TW3 .... 25 K1
The Matthew Arnold School
STA TW18 .... 22 F9
Maybury Business Centre
WOKS/MYFD GU22 .... 11 J3
Maybury Infant School
WOKN/KNAP GU21 .... 11 F2
Mayday University Hospital
THHTH CR7 .... 45 K7
Mayfield Junior School
FARN GU14 .... 88 C1
McKay Trading Estate
DTCH/LGLY SL3 .... 13 J7
The Mead Infant School
HOR/WEW KT19 .... 60 D2
Meadlands Primary School
RCHPK/HAM TW10 .... 26 B7
Meadowbrook
Industrial Centre
CRAWE RH10 .... 177 K2
Meadowcroft County Infant
School
CHERT KT16 .... 55 K2
The Meadows (Superstores)
SHST GU47 .... 68 A3
Meadow Vale Primary
School
BNFD RG42 .... 32 B1
The Meads Primary School
EGRIN RH19 .... 180 D4
Meath Green County
Infant School
HORL RH6 .... 140 B8
Meath Green Junior School
HORL RH6 .... 140 B8
Meath School
CHERT KT16 .... 55 H6
Melcombe Primary School
HMSMTH W6 .... 19 H4
Melrose Special School
MTCM CR4 .... 44 A4
Merland Rise Primary School
EPSOM KT18 .... 78 G8
Merlin School
PUT/ROE SW15 .... 28 A1
Merrist Wood College
RGUW GU3 .... 91 J8
Merrist Wood Golf Club
RGUW GU3 .... 91 J9
Merrow Business Centre
RGUE GU4 .... 113 H2
Merrow CE Infant School
RGUE GU4 .... 113 H3
Merstham Primary School
REDH RH1 .... 100 E8
Merton Abbey First School
WIM/MER SW19 .... 43 M2
Merton Adult College
RYNPK SW20 .... 43 J4
Merton College
MRDN SM4 .... 43 K6
Merton Industrial Park
WIM/MER SW19 .... 43 N2
Merton Park Primary School
WIM/MER SW19 .... 43 K3
Merton Road
Industrial Estate
WAND/EARL SW18 .... 28 D3
Metro Business Centre
SYD SE26 .... 31 N9
Metro Industrial Centre
ISLW TW7 .... 16 E7
Metropolitan Police FC
E/WMO/HCT KT8 .... 40 D7
Metropolitan Police
Hayes Sports Club
HAYES BR2 .... 65 M1
Micklefield School
REIG RH2 .... 119 L4
Middle Hill Health Clinic
ALDT GU11 .... 108 C3
Midleton Industrial Estate
GUW GU2 .... 6 A1
Milbourne Lodge School
ESH/CLAY KT10 .... 58 D5
Milford Golf Club
MFD/CHID GU8 .... 149 P3
Milford Hospital
GODL GU7 .... 150 B4
Milford School
MFD/CHID GU8 .... 149 N3
Military Cemetery
CHOB/PIR GU24 .... 90 F1
Millais School
SWTR RH13 .... 192 E8
Milbourne Lodge
Junior School
ESH/CLAY KT10 .... 58 C4
Millennium Bailey's Hotel
SKENS SW7 .... 19 N2
Millennium Gloucester Hotel
SKENS SW7 .... 19 P1
Mill Farm Business Park
HSLWW TW4 .... 24 F3
Mill Green Business Park
MTCM CR4 .... 44 B8
Mill Lane Trading Estate
CROY/NA CR0 .... 63 H2
Mill Ride Golf Club
ASC SL5 .... 33 M2
Milo Hawkins Clinic
GU GU1 .... 7 F5
Milton Mount School
CRAWE RH10 .... 177 M3
Mitcham Cricket Club
MTCM CR4 .... 44 A5
Mitcham Golf Club
MTCM CR4 .... 44 C6
Mitcham Industrial Estate
MTCM CR4 .... 44 C2
Mitcham Road
Crematorium
THHTH CR7 .... 44 G6
Mole Business Park
LHD/OX KT22 .... 96 G1
Molesey Hospital
E/WMO/HCT KT8 .... 40 A6
Molesey Lock
E/WMO/HCT KT8 .... 40 E4
Mollison Drive Health Centre
WLGTN SM6 .... 62 G6
Monks Hill Sports Centrel
SAND/SEL CR2 .... 64 D6
Monks Orchard Primary
School
CROY/NA CR0 .... 46 D6
Monument Bridge East
Industrial Estate
WOKN/KNAP GU21 .... 72 F4
Moore Place Golf Club
ESH/CLAY KT10 .... 58 A4
Moor House School
RDKG RH5 .... 123 M3
Moor Lane Junior School
CHSGTN KT9 .... 59 M4
Morden Cemetery
MRDN SM4 .... 42 G7
Morden First School
MRDN SM4 .... 43 L6
Morden Hall Medical Centre
WIM/MER SW19 .... 43 L6
Morden Park Pool
MRDN SM4 .... 43 K7
Morden Road Clinic
WIM/MER SW19 .... 43 M4
More House School
ISLW TW7 .... 16 F2
RFNM GU10 .... 146 F2
Mortimer School
STRHM/NOR SW16 .... 29 N5
Mortlake Cemetery
MORT/ESHN SW14 .... 18 C8
Mortlake Crematorium
RCH/KEW TW9 .... 17 P7
Moss Lane Primary School
GODL GU7 .... 131 K9
Mount Alvernia Hospital
GU GU1 .... 7 H6
Mount Carmel
RC Primary School
EA W5 .... 17 J1
The Mount Infant School
NWMAL KT3 .... 41 P4
Mount Medical Centre
FELT TW13 .... 24 F5
Murky Puddle Theatre
NWMAL KT3 .... 42 D4
Muschamp Primary School
CAR SM5 .... 62 A1
Museum of Fulham Palace
FUL/PGN SW6 .... 19 H7
Museum of Richmond
RCH/KEW TW9 .... 26 C1
Museum of Rugby &
Twickenham Stadium Tours
WHTN TW2 .... 25 M2
The Musical Museum
BTFD TW8 .... 17 L4
Mytchett Primary School
FRIM GU16 .... 89 H3
National Physical Laboratory
TEDD TW11 .... 25 M9
Natural History Museum
SKENS SW7 .... 19 P1
Natural Therapy Clinic
TOOT SW17 .... 29 L8
Nature Reserve
CROY/NA CR0 .... 64 E9
Natwest Sports Club
BECK BR3 .... 31 N9
NEC Harlequins RFC
(The Stoop
Memorial Ground)
WHTN TW2 .... 25 M3
Nelson Hospital
WIM/MER SW19 .... 43 K3
Nelson Primary School
WHTN TW2 .... 25 J2
Nelson Trading Estate
WIM/MER SW19 .... 43 N3
New Addington Pools
& Fitness Centre
CROY/NA CR0 .... 65 J8
New Brentford Cemetery
HSLW TW3 .... 15 P7
New Chiswick Pool
CHSWK W4 .... 18 C5
Newdigate Endowed
CE Infant School
RDKG RH5 .... 156 G3
New Haw Therapy Clinic
ADL/WDHM KT15 .... 55 M8
Newhouse Farm
Business Centre
HORS RH12 .... 193 H3
New Kings Primary School
FUL/PGN SW6 .... 19 K7
Newland House School
TWK TW1 .... 25 N7
Newlands CP School
YTLY GU46 .... 66 G3
New Life School
EGRIN RH19 .... 180 C1
New Monument School
WOKS/MYFD GU22 .... 72 C4
Newport Junior School
ASHV GU12 .... 108 F5
New School
FUL/PGN SW6 .... 19 K6
New Scotland Hill
Primary School
SHST GU47 .... 49 L7
New Victoria Hospital
KUTN/CMB KT2 .... 42 C1
New Victoria Theatre
WOKN/KNAP GU21 .... 10 D3
New Zealand Golf Club
WOKN/KNAP GU21 .... 73 J1
Nightingale Industrial Estate
HORS RH12 .... 192 C7
Nightingale School
TOOT SW17 .... 29 H5
Nomad Theatre
EHSLY KT24 .... 95 M4
Nonsuch
High School for Girls
EW KT17 .... 61 H6
Nonsuch Industrial Estate
EW KT17 .... 60 C7
Nonsuch Primary School
EW KT17 .... 60 F4
Norbury Complementary
Therapy Clinic
STRHM/NOR SW16 .... 45 H2
Norbury Health Centre
STRHM/NOR SW16 .... 45 H1
Norbury Manor
Primary School
STRHM/NOR SW16 .... 44 D2
Norbury Manor
Secondary Girls School
STRHM/NOR SW16 .... 45 H2
Norbury Trading Estate
STRHM/NOR SW16 .... 45 H3
Normand Park
Primary School
WKENS W14 .... 19 K4
Norman Park
Athletics Track
HAYES BR2 .... 47 P7
North Clinic
BMLY BR1 .... 47 N2
Northcote Lodge School
BTSEA SW11 .... 29 H2
North Croydon
Medical Centre
THHTH CR7 .... 45 K7
North Downs Golf Club
GDST RH9 .... 102 G5
North East Surrey
College of Technology
EW KT17 .... 60 E9
North East Surrey
Crematorium
NWMAL KT3 .... 42 G7
North Farnborough County
Infant School
FARN GU14 .... 88 F2
North Feltham Trading Estate
EBED/NFELT TW14 .... 15 K9
Northfields Prospect Business
Centre
WAND/EARL SW18 .... 19 K9
Northgate F & M School
CRAWE RH10 .... 177 H3
North Hants Golf Club
FLEETN GU51 .... 86 G3
North Heath Lane
Industrial Estate
HORS RH12 .... 192 C4
North Heath Primary School
HORS RH12 .... 192 C5
North Holmwood
Cricket Club
RDKG RH5 .... 137 J3
Northlands Business Park
HORS RH12 .... 173 K7
North Lodge Industrial Park
LIPH GU30 .... 182 C9
Northolmes Junior School
HORS RH12 .... 192 F5
North Terminal
HORL RH6 .... 159 H4
Northtown Trading Estate
ASHV GU12 .... 108 G5
North Weylands
Industrial Estate
WOT/HER KT12 .... 57 N1
The Norwegian School
WIM/MER SW19 .... 42 G1
Norwood Green
Infant School
NWDGN UB2 .... 15 N3
Norwood Green
Junior School
NWDGN UB2 .... 15 N3
Norwood Heights
Shopping Centre
NRWD SE19 .... 30 F9
Norwood Park
Primary School
WNWD SE27 .... 30 D7
Norwood School
WNWD SE27 .... 30 D8
Notre Dame
Preparatory School
WOT/HER KT12 .... 57 H9
Notre Dame Senior School
LING RH7 .... 162 E1
Novello Theatre
ASC SL5 .... 34 D6
Novotel Hotel
HMSMTH W6 .... 19 H2
WDR/YW UB7 .... 14 C2
Nower Lodge School
DORK RH4 .... 116 G8
Nutfield Cemetery
REDH RH1 .... 120 F4
Nutfield Church
CE Primary School
REDH RH1 .... 121 H6
Nutfield Priory Hotel
REDH RH1 .... 120 E5
Nutley Dean Business Park
HORS RH12 .... 139 J7
Oak Farm Community School
FARN GU14 .... 88 C1
Oakfield Junior School
LHD/OX KT22 .... 96 C3
Oakfield Preparatory School
EGRIN RH19 .... 30 E5
Oakfield Road
Industrial Estate
PGE/AN SE20 .... 46 B1
Oakfield School
WOKS/MYFD GU22 .... 73 K4
Oak Hill Health Centre
SURB KT6 .... 41 L7
Oakhyrst Grange School
CTHM CR3 .... 101 M6
Oakland Primary School
BH/WHM TN16 .... 84 A5
Oaklands County
J & I School
CRWG RG45 .... 49 L3
Oaklands School
ISLW TW7 .... 16 D8
Oak Lane Cemetery
TWK TW1 .... 25 P3
Oak Lane Medical Centre
TWK TW1 .... 26 A3
Oak Lodge JMI School
WWKM BR4 .... 47 H8
Oak Lodge School
BAL SW12 .... 29 J3
Oak Park Golf Club
RFNM GU10 .... 106 E8
The Oaks F & M School
CRAWE RH10 .... 177 J8
Oaks Sports Park
CAR SM5 .... 62 B9
Oak Tree Clinic
WOKN/KNAP GU21 .... 71 K7
Oakview Business Park
MFD/CHID GU8 .... 168 A1

Oakwood
　Independent School
　PUR/KEN CR8 ......81 K2
Oakwood Industrial Park
　CRAWE RH10 ......177 K2
Oakwood School
　HORL RH6 ......159 L1
Oakwood Sports Centre
　HORL RH6 ......159 M1
Oatlands Park Hotel
　WEY KT13 ......56 E2
Oatlands School
　WEY KT13 ......56 F3
Occupational Health Centre
　CROY/NA CR0 ......2 E6
Odeon Cinema
　BECK BR3 ......46 G3
　ESH/CLAY KT10 ......58 B3
　HAYES BR2 ......78 C2
　KENS W8 ......19 L1
　KUTN/CMB KT2 ......8 E4
　RCHPK/HAM TW10 ......26 C1
　STRHM/NOR SW16 ......29 P2
　WIM/MER SW19 ......43 L1
Odeon Multiplex
　GU GU1 ......6 D5
Old Barnes Cemetery
　BARN SW13 ......18 F7
Old Bam Theatre
　CRAWW RH11 ......176 C3
Old Beckenhamian RFC
　WWKM BR4 ......65 K2
Old Bromilans Cricket Club
　HAYES BR2 ......47 P6
Old Cemetery
　EDUL SE22 ......31 J2
The Old Cottage Hospital
　EW KT17 ......78 D2
Oldfield House
　Special School
　HPTN TW12 ......39 P2
Oldfields Trading Estate
　SUT SM1 ......61 L2
Old Palace School
　CROY/NA CR0 ......2 B5
Old Thorns Hotel, Golf
　& Country Club
　LIPH GU30 ......182 A7
Old Tiffinians Sports Ground
　E/WMO/HCT KT8 ......40 E6
Old Vicarage School
　RCHPK/HAM TW10 ......26 D2
Old Wilsonians Sports Club
　WWKM BR4 ......47 L9
Olympia
　WKENS W14 ......19 J1
Ongar Place Infant School
　ADL/WDHM KT15 ......55 L5
On Sai Clinic
　ECT SW5 ......19 M2
Onslow County
　Infant School
　GUW GU2 ......111 M7
The Open University
　EGRIN RH19 ......180 D2
Orange Tree Theatre
　TWK TW1 ......17 L9
Orchard Business Centre
　REDH RH1 ......140 C5
　SYD SE26 ......31 N8
Orchard House School
　CHSWK W4 ......17 P2
Orchard Infant School
　REIG RH2 ......119 L8
The Orchard Junior School
　HSLW TW3 ......16 A9
The Orchard School
　E/WMO/HCT KT8 ......40 D6
Orchard Way Primary School
　CROY/NA CR0 ......46 E8
Oriel Primary School
　FELT TW13 ......24 F6
Orleans House Gallery
　TWK TW1 ......26 A4
Orleans Infant School
　TWK TW1 ......26 A3
Orleans Park School
　TWK TW1 ......26 A3
Osteopathic Clinic
　HOR/WEW KT19 ......60 B4
Osterley Four Pillars Hotel
　ISLW TW7 ......16 F5
Osterley RFC
　NWDGN UB2 ......16 B1
Our Lady Immaculate
　RC Primary School
　BRYLDS KT5 ......41 P9
Our Lady and St Johns
　RC Primary School
　BTFD TW8 ......17 J3
Our Lady of the Rosary
　RC Primary School
　STA TW18 ......22 D9
Our Lady of Victories
　RC Primary School
　SKENS SW7 ......19 N2
　PUT/ROE SW15 ......19 H9
Our Lady Queen of Heaven
　Catholic Primary School
　CRAWW RH11 ......176 E3
Our Lady Queen of Heaven
　RC Primary School
　WIM/MER SW19 ......28 A3
Our Lady & St Philip Neri
　RC Primary School
　FSTH SE23 ......31 L6
Our Ladys Preparatory School
　CWTH RG45 ......49 L4
Outwood Windmill
　REDH RH1 ......141 M5

Oval Primary School
　CROY/NA CR0 ......3 G2
Overton Grange School
　BELMT SM2 ......61 M6
Owismoor Primary School
　SHST GU47 ......50 A8
Oxshott Village Sports Club
　LHD/OX KT22 ......76 C3
Oxted Health Centre
　OXTED RH8 ......103 M8
Oxted & Limpsfield Hospital
　OXTED RH8 ......103 K8
Oxted School
　OXTED RH8 ......103 M8
Pachesham Park Golf Centre
　LHD/OX KT22 ......76 E7
Paddock School
　PUT/ROE SW15 ......18 D9
Painshill Landscape Garden
　COB KT11 ......75 H5
Palmerston Business Centre
　SUT SM1 ......61 N4
Palm House
　RCH/KEW TW9 ......17 M6
Papplewick School
　ASC SL5 ......33 P2
Paragon Hotel
　FUL/PGN SW6 ......19 L4
Parayhouse School
　WBPTN SW10 ......19 N5
Parchmore Medical Centre
　THHTH CR7 ......45 L4
Parish CE Primary School
　BMLY BR1 ......47 N1
Park Crematorium
　ASHV GU12 ......108 F8
Park Farm Industrial Estate
　FRIM GU16 ......68 E7
Park Hall Trading Estate
　WNWD SE27 ......30 D6
Park Hill Junior School
　CROY/NA CR0 ......3 K6
Park Hill School
　KUTN/CMB KT2 ......9 J1
Parkhouse Middle School
　WIM/MER SW19 ......28 C7
Park Mead Infant School
　CRAN GU6 ......153 J8
Park Mead Junior School
　CRAN GU6 ......153 H8
Park Mews
　Small Business Centre
　HNHL SE24 ......30 D2
Park Primary School
　ALDT GU11 ......108 E7
Park Recreation Centre
　HORS RH12 ......192 B8
Park School
　WOKS/MYFD GU22 ......11 G4
Parkside Hospital
　WIM/MER SW19 ......28 A6
Parkside School
　COB KT11 ......76 A7
Park Walk Primary School
　WBPTN SW10 ......19 P4
Parkway Trading Estate
　HEST TW5 ......15 L4
Park Wood Golf Club
　BH/WHM TN16 ......104 C2
Parliant Park
　Combined School
　DTCH/LGLY SL3 ......12 F1
Parsonage Business Park
　HORS RH12 ......192 D6
Parsons Green Health Clinic
　FUL/PGN SW6 ......19 L6
Parsons Mead School
　ASHTD KT21 ......77 L8
Passfield Mill Business Park
　LIPH GU30 ......182 A11
Passport Language Schools
　BMLY BR1 ......47 P2
The Patrick Doody
　Clinic & Health Centre
　WIM/MER SW19 ......43 L1
Pattinson Clinic
　RCHPK/HAM TW10 ......26 D2
The Paul Robeson Theatre
　HSLW TW3 ......16 B8
The Pavilion Leisure Centre
　BMLY BR1 ......47 N3
Pavilion Restaurant
　RCH/KEW TW9 ......17 L2
Paxton Primary School
　NRWD SE19 ......30 C9
Payne Clinic
　EW KT17 ......78 E2
Peacock Cinema
　WOKN/KNAP GU21 ......10 C3
The Peacocks
　Shopping Centre
　WOKN/KNAP GU21 ......10 C3
Peall Road Industrial Estate
　CROY/NA CR0 ......45 H7
Peaslake School
　SHGR GU5 ......134 G6
Pelham Court
　Business Centre
　CRAWW RH11 ......176 E4
Pelham Primary School
　WIM/MER SW19 ......43 L1
Pennthorpe School
　HORS RH12 ......189 M3
Pennyhill Park
　Hotel & Country Club
　CBLY GU15 ......51 K7
Penwortham
　Primary School
　STRHM/NOR SW16 ......29 L9
Perrymount Primary School
　FSTH SE23 ......31 L5

Perrywood Business Park
　REDH RH1 ......140 D4
Peterborough
　Primary School
　FUL/PGN SW6 ......19 L7
Pewley Down Infant School
　GU GU1 ......7 G6
Phoenix College
　MRDN SM4 ......43 M6
Pickhurst Infant School
　HAYES BR2 ......47 L7
Pickhurst Junior School
　HAYES BR2 ......47 M7
Pierrepont School
　RFNM GU10 ......147 H3
The Pilgrims Way
　Primary School
　FNM GU9 ......4 E7
Pilton Estate
　CROY/NA CR0 ......2 B3
Pine Ridge Golf Club
　FRIM GU16 ......69 M6
Pine Ridge Infant School
　CBLY GU15 ......51 J8
The Pines Junior School
　RGUW GU3 ......111 L3
The Pines Trading Estate
　RGUW GU3 ......111 J3
Pine Trees Business Park
　STA TW18 ......22 B8
Pinewood Infant School
　FARN GU14 ......67 P9
Pinewood Leisure Centre
　EWKG RG40 ......49 M1
Pinkwell Primary School
　WDR/YW UB7 ......14 E2
Pioneers Industrial Park
　CROY/NA CR0 ......44 C9
Pippins School
　DTCH/LGLY SL3 ......13 K6
Pirbright Camp
　CHOB/PIR GU24 ......70 B9
Pirbright Primary School
　CHOB/PIR GU24 ......90 E2
Piries Place
　HORS RH12 ......192 B8
Pitwood Park
　Industrial Estate
　KWD/TDW/WH KT20 ......79 H9
Pixham School
　DORK RH4 ......117 J5
Plaistow Infant School
　BIL RH14 ......187 L7
Playhouse Cinema
　EPSOM KT18 ......78 B3
Playhouse Theatre
　EPSOM KT18 ......78 A2
Plaza Cinema
　OXTED RH8 ......103 L9
Plough Industrial Estate
　LHD/OX KT22 ......76 G9
Polka Theatre for Children
　WIM/MER SW19 ......28 D5
Polygon Business Centre
　DTCH/LGLY SL3 ......13 K7
Pond Meadow School
　GUW GU2 ......111 L4
Pools in the Park
　RCH/KEW TW9 ......17 K9
The Popes Grotto Hotel
　TWK TW1 ......25 P5
Poplar First School
　WIM/MER SW19 ......43 L4
Portesbery School
　CBLY GU15 ......68 F2
Portland Medical Centre
　SNWD SE25 ......46 B6
Potley Hill County
　Primary School
　BLKW GU17 ......67 L3
Potters Gate
　CE Primary School
　FNM GU9 ......4 D3
Potters Industrial Park
　FLEETS GU52 ......107 J1
Potters International Hotel
　ALDT GU11 ......108 B2
Pound Hill Middle School
　CRAWE RH10 ......177 M4
The Pountney Clinic
　HSLW TW3 ......16 A8
Powell Corderoy CP School
　DORK RH4 ......116 F8
Premier Cinema
　DORK RH4 ......117 J6
Premier Lodge
　COB KT11 ......75 L1
　CRAWW RH11 ......176 E6
　CROY/NA CR0 ......63 J5
　HOR/WEW KT19 ......60 C4
　WHTN TW2 ......25 K4
　CRAWE RH10 ......159 H9
　RFNM GU10 ......79 J8
Preston Cross
　Hotel & Country Club
　GT/LBKH KT23 ......95 N6
Preymead Industrial Estate
　FNM GU9 ......108 D7
PR for Schools
　SYD SE26 ......31 K6
Pride of the Valley Hotel
　RFNM GU10 ......164 E6
Princes Hall
　ALDT GU11 ......108 C4
Princes Mead
　Shopping Centre
　FARN GU14 ......88 D4
Princess of Wales
　Conservatory
　RCH/KEW TW9 ......17 M5
Princess Square
　Shopping Centre

BRAK RG12 ......32 D3
Prins Willem-Alexander
　School
　WOKS/MYFD GU22 ......72 G6
Prior Heath Infant School
　CBLY GU15 ......69 J3
Priors Field School
　GODL GU7 ......130 F4
Priory CE Middle School
　WIM/MER SW19 ......28 D6
Priory Hospital Group
　KWD/TDW/WH KT20 ......99 L8
Priory Retail Park
　WIM/MER SW19 ......43 P1
Priory School
　BNSTD SM7 ......79 L4
The Priory School
　DORK RH4 ......116 F8
Priory Special School
　SNWD SE25 ......45 P5
Progress Business Park
　CROY/NA CR0 ......63 H1
Prospect House School
　PUT/ROE SW15 ......28 A3
Public Record Office Museum
　RCH/KEW TW9 ......17 P5
Purley Community
　Health Clinic
　PUR/KEN CR8 ......63 J9
Purley & District
　War Memorial Hospital
　PUR/KEN CR8 ......63 J9
Purley Downs Golf Club
　PUR/KEN CR8 ......63 J9
Purley John Fisher RFC
　COUL/CHIP CR5 ......81 J9
Purley Oaks Primary School
　SAND/SEL CR2 ......63 M6
Purley Pool
　PUR/KEN CR8 ......63 J9
Purley Secretarial
　& Language College
　PUR/KEN CR8 ......63 J9
Purley Sports Club
　WLGTN SM6 ......62 F8
Putney Animal Hospital
　PUT/ROE SW15 ......19 H9
Putney Exchange
　Shopping Centre
　PUT/ROE SW15 ......19 H9
Putney High School
　PUT/ROE SW15 ......28 A1
Putney Hospital
　PUT/ROE SW15 ......19 H8
Putney Leisure Centre
　PUT/ROE SW15 ......18 G9
Putney Lower Common
　Cemetery
　PUT/ROE SW15 ......18 F7
Putneymead Medical Centre
　PUT/ROE SW15 ......18 G9
Putney Park School
　PUT/ROE SW15 ......18 F9
Putney School of Art
　PUT/ROE SW15 ......19 J9
Putney Vale Cemetery
　PUT/ROE SW15 ......27 M5
Putney Vale Crematorium
　PUT/ROE SW15 ......27 M5
Puttenham CE Infant School
　RGUW GU3 ......130 B1
Puttenham Golf Club
　RGUW GU3 ......130 D1
Pyrcroft Primary School
　CHERT KT16 ......37 J7
Pyrford County Middle School
　WOKS/MYFD GU22 ......73 K5
Quality Hotel
　DTCH/LGLY SL3 ......12 F4
Quarryside Business Park
　REDH RH1 ......120 D1
Quebec House
　BH/WHM TN16 ......105 H6
Queen Charlottes & Chelsea
　Hospital
　HMSMTH W6 ......18 E1
Queen Charlotte's Cottage
　RCH/KEW TW9 ......17 M5
Queen Eleanor's
　CE Junior School
　GUW GU2 ......111 M6
Queen Elizabeth Foundation
　BNSTD SM7 ......79 N5
Queen Elizabeth Hospital
　BNSTD SM7 ......79 N7
Queen Elizabeth II
　Silver Jubilee School
　SWTR RH13 ......192 L1
Queen Marys
　Hospital for Children
　CAR SM5 ......62 B7
Queen Marys
　Hospital School
　CAR SM5 ......62 B8
Queen Mary's
　University Hospital
　PUT/ROE SW15 ......27 M2
Queen's Building
　HTHAIR TW6 ......14 D8
Queens CE Primary School
　RCH/KEW TW9 ......17 M5
Queen's Club
　WKENS W14 ......19 J3
Queens Gate School
　SKENS SW7 ......19 N2
Queens Manor
　Primary School
　FUL/PGN SW6 ......18 G5
Queens Medical Centre
　RCHPK/HAM TW10 ......26 E1
Queensmill School
　FUL/PGN SW6 ......19 L7

Queen's Road Cemetery
　CROY/NA CR0 ......45 L7
Queens Sports Centre
　GODL GU7 ......131 H6
Queen Victoria Hospital
　EGRIN RH19 ......162 E9
The Radisson
　Edwardian Hotel
　HYS/HAR UB3 ......14 E5
Radisson Edwardian
　Vanderbilt Hotel
　SKENS SW7 ......19 N2
Railton Road Clinic
　BRXN/ST SW9 ......30 C1
Rainbow Industrial Estate
　RYNPK SW20 ......42 F3
Rainbow Leisure Centre
　EW KT17 ......78 C1
Rainbow
　Natural Health Centre
　REDH RH1 ......120 B6
The Raleigh School
　EHSLY KT24 ......94 E5
Ram Brewery
　& Visitor Centre
　WAND/EARL SW18 ......28 C1
Ranelagh School
　BRAK RG12 ......32 E4
Rathfern Primary School
　CAT SE6 ......31 N4
The Ravensbourne School
　HAYES BR2 ......47 P5
Ravensbourne Trust
　COUL/CHIP CR5 ......80 E6
Ravenscourt Park Preparatory
　School
　HMSMTH W6 ......18 E2
Ravenstone Primary School
　BAL SW12 ......29 K4
Raynes Park High School
　NWMAL KT3 ......42 F4
Raynes Park Sports Ground
　RYNPK SW20 ......42 E3
Raynes Park Vale FC
　RYNPK SW20 ......43 H6
RCA
　SKENS SW7 ......19 N1
Redcliffe School
　WBPTN SW10 ......19 N5
Redfields Business Park
　FLEETS GU52 ......106 A1
Redhill Aerodrome
　REDH RH1 ......140 G1
Redhill Business Centre
　REDH RH1 ......120 B4
Redhill FC
　REDH RH1 ......120 B9
Redhill & Reigate Golf Club
　REDH RH1 ......119 P8
The Redlands
　Primary School
　RDKG RH5 ......137 H1
Red Lion Business Park
　SURB KT6 ......59 M1
Redstone Cemetery
　REDH RH1 ......120 D6
Reedham Park School
　PUR/KEN CR8 ......81 J3
Reed Place Business Park
　SHPTN TW17 ......38 D3
Reeds School
　COB KT11 ......76 A1
Refuse Disposal Centre
　KUT KT1 ......9 G7
Regal Cinema
　CRAN GU6 ......152 F9
Regina Coeli
　RC Primary School
　CROY/NA CR0 ......63 K6
Reigate College
　REIG RH2 ......119 M4
Reigate Day Hospital
　REIG RH2 ......119 P5
Reigate Grammar School
　REIG RH2 ......119 N5
Reigate Heath Golf Club
　REIG RH2 ......118 G5
Reigate Hill Golf Club
　REIG RH2 ......100 C8
Reigate Manor Hotel
　REIG RH2 ......119 M2
Reigate Parish
　Infant School
　REIG RH2 ......119 N5
Reigate Priory
　Junior School
　REIG RH2 ......119 L5
Reigate Priory & Museum
　REIG RH2 ......119 L5
Reigate St Marys
　Preparatory & Choir School
　REIG RH2 ......119 N5
Reigate Screen Cinema
　REIG RH2 ......119 L5
The Renaissance
　London Hotel
　HTHAIR TW6 ......14 E6
The Retail Business Centre
　BTFD TW8 ......17 J3
Reynard Mills Trading Estate
　BTFD TW8 ......17 J3
Rhoda McGaw
　Theatre & Cinema
　WOKN/KNAP GU21 ......10 D3
RHS Gardens Wisley
　RPLY/SEND GU23 ......74 A7
Ricards Lodge High School
　WIM/MER SW19 ......28 C8
Richard Atkins Primary School
　BRXS/STRHM SW2 ......29 P3

272 Index - featured places

Richings Park Golf
& Country Club
DTCH/LGLY SL3 .....13 H2
Richings Park Sports Club
IVER SL0 .....13 K1
Richmond Adult
& Community College
RCH/KEW TW9 .....17 K9
Richmond Adult
& Community College
TWK TW1 .....25 N4
The Richmond Clinic
RCHPK/HAM TW10 .....17 M9
Richmond College
KENS W8 .....19 M1
Richmond College
RCHPK/HAM TW10 .....26 D3
Richmond FC
RCH/KEW TW9 .....17 K9
Richmond Gate Hotel
RCHPK/HAM TW10 .....26 D3
The Richmond Golf Club
RCHPK/HAM TW10 .....26 D5
The Richmond Green
Medical Centre
RCH/KEW TW9 .....26 C1
The Richmond Hill Hotel
RCHPK/HAM TW10 .....26 D2
Richmond House School
HPTN TW12 .....24 G8
Richmond Magistrates Court
RCH/KEW TW9 .....17 K9
Richmond Park Golf Club
PUT/ROE SW15 .....27 K3
Richmond Road Medical Centre
KUTN/CMB KT2 .....8 D1
Richmond Theatre
RCH/KEW TW9 .....17 K9
Richmond upon Thames
College
WHTN TW2 .....25 M3
Riddlesdown High School
SAND/SEL CR2 .....81 N3
The Ridgeway
Community School
FNM GU9 .....127 N6
Ridgeway Primary School
SAND/SEL CR2 .....63 N7
Rikkyo School
BIL RH14 .....188 G2
Ripley CE School
RPLY/SEND GU23 .....93 M1
Ripley Court School
RPLY/SEND GU23 .....93 N1
Ripley Cricket Club
RPLY/SEND GU23 .....73 N9
Ritz Cinema
HORS RH12 .....192 C8
River Brent Business Park
NWDGN UB2 .....16 E1
Riverdene Industrial Estate
WOT/HER KT12 .....57 M4
River Gardens
Business Centre
EBED/NFELT TW14 .....15 K9
River Mole Business Park
ESH/CLAY KT10 .....40 A9
Riversdale Primary School
WAND/EARL SW18 .....28 D4
Riverside Business Centre
WAND/EARL SW18 .....28 E4
The Riverside Business Centre
GU GU1 .....6 C3
Riverside Business Park
WIM/MER SW19 .....43 N2
Riverside Community
Health Care
WKENS W14 .....19 H1
Riverside Park
Industrial Estate
FNM GU9 .....5 J2
Riverside Studios Cinema
HMSMTH W6 .....18 F3
Riverside Wandle
Trading Estate
MTCM CR4 .....44 B8
Riverview CE Primary School
HOR/WEW KT19 .....60 A3
Riverway Industrial Estate
GODL GU7 .....132 A5
Roan Industrial Estate
MTCM CR4 .....44 A2
Robin Hood Infant School
SUT SM1 .....61 L4
Robin Hood Junior School
SUT SM1 .....61 M4
Robin Hood Lane
Health Centre
SUT SM1 .....61 L4
Robin Hood Primary School
KUTN/CMB KT2 .....27 J8
Robins Camberly Cinema
CBLY GU15 .....68 D3
The Roche School
WAND/EARL SW18 .....28 D1
Rockmount School
NRWD SE19 .....30 D9
Rodborough School
MFD/CHID GU8 .....149 N5
Rodd Estate
SHPTN TW17 .....38 E6
Roehampton Church Estate
PUT/ROE SW15 .....27 N3
Roehampton Golf Club
PUT/ROE SW15 .....18 D9
Roehampton Institute
PUT/ROE SW15 .....27 L1
WAND/EARL SW18 .....28 B2
The Roehampton
Priory Hospital
PUT/ROE SW15 .....18 D9

Roehampton
Recreation Centre
PUT/ROE SW15 .....27 M3
Roffey Social & Sports Club
HORS RH12 .....192 F5
Rokeby School
KUTN/CMB KT2 .....42 A1
Roke Primary School
PUR/KEN CR8 .....81 L3
Roker Park Golf Club
RGUW GU3 .....91 K9
Roman Industrial Estate
CROY/NA CR0 .....45 N8
Romans Business Park
FNM GU9 .....5 J1
Ronald Rose Primary School
WIM/MER SW19 .....28 A3
Rosary RC Infant School
HEST TW5 .....15 P4
Rosebery School
EPSOM KT18 .....78 A3
Roselands Clinic
NWMAL KT3 .....42 A5
Rosemead
Preparatory School
DUL SE21 .....30 D5
Rosendale Primary School
DUL SE21 .....30 D3
Rosslyn Park RFC
PUT/ROE SW15 .....18 D9
The Rotunda
KUTN/CMB KT2 .....8 E4
Rowan High School
CLAP SW4 .....29 N2
Rowans School
RYNPK SW20 .....42 E1
Rowfant Business Centre
CRAWE RH10 .....178 F5
Rowledge CE
(Controlled) Primary School
FARN GU10 .....146 A1
Rowley Industrial Park
ACT W3 .....17 P1
Royal Aircraft Estab
FARN GU14 .....88 D5
The Royal Alexandra
& Albert School
REIG RH2 .....100 A9
Royal Army Medical Corps
ALDT GU11 .....108 F2
Royal Ascot Golf Club
ASC SL5 .....34 B3
The Royal Ballet School
RCHPK/HAM TW10 .....27 J4
The Royal Berkshire Hotel
ASC SL5 .....34 F4
Royal Botanic Gardens
Kew School
RCH/KEW TW9 .....17 M5
Royal Brompton
& National Heart Hospitals
CHEL SW3 .....19 P3
Royal College of Music
SHB W12 .....18 E1
SKENS SW7 .....19 P1
Royal Grammar School
GU GU1 .....7 F4
Royal Holloway
University of London
EGH TW20 .....21 J9
EGH TW20 .....36 B2
Royal Holloway
University of London
(Hall of Residence)
EGH TW20 .....21 J7
Royal Hospital
RCH/KEW TW9 .....17 L8
Royal Hospital
for Neuro-Disability
WAND/EARL SW18 .....28 B2
Royal Hospital & Home
PUT/ROE SW15 .....27 N1
The Royal Kent
CE Primary School
LHD/OX KT22 .....76 C3
Royal Logistics
Corps Museum
FRIM GU16 .....69 M8
Royal Marsden Hospital
BELMT SM2 .....61 N8
CHEL SW3 .....19 P5
Royal Mid-Surrey Golf Club
RCH/KEW TW9 .....17 K8
Royal Military Academy
CBLY GU15 .....68 B2
Royal Military
School of Music
ISLW TW7 .....25 L2
Royal Russell School
CROY/NA CR0 .....64 B5
The Royal School for Girls
HASM GU27 .....166 B9
Royal & Sun Alliance
Sports Club
HORS RH12 .....192 D4
Royal Surrey
County Hospital
GUW GU2 .....111 L5
Royal Wimbledon Golf Club
WIM/MER SW19 .....27 N8
Royston Primary School
BECK BR3 .....46 D2
RSPCA HQ
HORS RH12 .....192 B9
Rudgwick Medical Centre
HORS RH12 .....189 M3
Rudgwick Primary School
HORS RH12 .....189 N3
Rufus Business Centre
WAND/EARL SW18 .....28 E5

Runnymede Hospital
CHERT KT16 .....55 H2
Runnymede Hotel & Spa
EGH TW20 .....21 N6
Runnymede (NT)
STWL/WRAY TW19 .....21 H4
Rural Life Centre
RFNM GU10 .....147 J1
Ruskin House School
HNHL SE24 .....30 D1
Rusper Primary School
HORS RH11 .....175 H4
The Russell JMI School
RCHPK/HAM TW10 .....26 C5
The Russell School
RCHPK/HAM TW10 .....26 C4
Rutherford Way
Industrial Estate
CRAWE RH10 .....159 K9
Rutlish School
RYNPK SW20 .....43 K3
Rydens School
WOT/HER KT12 .....57 L2
Rydes Hill
Preparatory School
GUW GU2 .....111 M3
Rydon Business Centre
LHD/OX KT22 .....76 G9
Ryebrook Business Park
LHD/OX KT22 .....76 G9
Ryelands Primary School
SNWD SE25 .....46 B6
Ryvers Combined School
DTCH/LGLY SL3 .....12 B1
Sackville Community College
EGRIN RH19 .....180 F2
Sacred Heart High School
HMSMTH W6 .....18 G2
Sacred Heart Junior School
HMSMTH W6 .....19 H2
Sacred Heart
RC Primary School
NWMAL KT3 .....42 A5
PUT/ROE SW15 .....27 M1
TEDD TW11 .....41 H1
Safari Cinema
CROY/NA CR0 .....45 K8
St Agathas
RC Primary School
KUTN/CMB KT2 .....26 E9
St Albans RC Aided
Primary School
E/WMO/HCT KT8 .....40 B6
St Andrews
CE Combined School
CRAWE RH10 .....177 K6
St Andrews CE Infant School
FNM GU9 .....5 F4
St Andrews CE School
CROY/NA CR0 .....2 A6
St Andrews Primary School
COB KT11 .....75 L2
St Andrews RC School
LHD/OX KT22 .....77 J9
St Andrews School
WOKN/KNAP GU21 .....10 B1
St Annes Catholic
Primary School
BNSTD SM7 .....79 L5
CHERT KT16 .....37 L9
St Annes CE Primary School
WAND/EARL SW18 .....28 E1
St Annes Primary School
STWL/WRAY TW19 .....23 H3
St Annes Special School
MRDN SM4 .....43 M6
St Anns Heath Junior School
VW GU25 .....36 D6
St Anselms RC Primary School
NWDGN UB2 .....15 P1
TOOT SW17 .....29 K6
St Anthonys Hospital
WPK KT4 .....43 H9
St Anthonys
RC Primary School
EDUL SE22 .....30 G2
PGE/AN SE20 .....46 B2
St Augustines
Primary School
WKENS W14 .....19 J4
St Barnabas & Philip
CE Primary
KENS W8 .....19 L1
St Bartholomews
CE Primary School
SYD SE26 .....31 K7
St Bartholomews
Middle School
HASM GU27 .....184 D3
St Bartholomews
Primary School
HASM GU27 .....184 D2
St Bedes CE Junior School
RPLY/SEND GU23 .....93 H4
St Bedes RC Infant School
BAL SW12 .....29 N4
St Bede's School
REDH RH1 .....120 A2
St Bernadettes
RC Primary School
FARN GU14 .....88 C2
St Boniface
RC Primary School
TOOT SW17 .....29 J8
St Catherine's Hospice
CRAWE RH10 .....176 G7
St Catherines
RC Middle School
NWMAL KT3 .....42 G6
St Catherines School
CBLY GU15 .....68 E4
SHGR GU5 .....132 D6

TWK TW1 .....25 N5
St Cecilias RC Primary School
WPK KT4 .....61 H1
St Chads RC Primary School
SNWD SE25 .....45 N6
St Charles RC Primary School
WEY KT13 .....56 C2
St Christophers School
BECK BR3 .....47 J3
EPSOM KT18 .....78 C3
St Clare Business Park
HPTN TW12 .....25 K9
St Clements
RC Primary School
EW KT17 .....60 D7
St Cuthbert Mayne
RC Primary School
CRAN GU6 .....153 H9
St Cuthberts CE Primary School
EGH TW20 .....36 A1
St Cuthbert With St Matthias
CE Primary School
ECT SW5 .....19 M3
St Davids College
WWKM BR4 .....47 H8
St Davids Health Centre
STWL/WRAY TW19 .....22 G3
St Davids School
LHD/OX KT22 .....56 C1
PUR/KEN CR8 .....63 H9
St Dominics School
MFD/CHID GU8 .....168 B2
St Dunstans
CE Primary School
CHEAM SM3 .....61 J6
St Dunstans College
CAT SE6 .....31 N4
St Dunstans
RC Primary School
WOKS/MYFD GU22 .....11 G3
St Ebba's Hospital
HOR/WEW KT19 .....60 A7
St Edmunds
RC Primary School
GODL GU7 .....150 E1
WHTN TW2 .....25 J3
St Edmunds School
GSHT GU26 .....165 N8
St Elizabeths
RC Primary School
RCHPK/HAM TW10 .....26 E2
St Elpheges
RC Primary School
WLGTN SM6 .....62 G5
St Faiths CE Primary School
WAND/EARL SW18 .....28 E1
St Francesca Cabrini Primary
School
FSTH SE23 .....31 K2
St Francis of Assisi
Primary School
CRAWE RH10 .....177 H6
St Francis RC Primary School
ASC SL5 .....34 A7
St Francis RC School
CTHM CR3 .....101 P1
St Francis Xavier College
BAL SW12 .....29 L2
St Georges Business Park
WEY KT13 .....56 C7
St Georges College
ADL/WDHM KT15 .....55 P2
St Georges College
Junior School
ADL/WDHM KT15 .....56 A2
St George's College Track
WEY KT13 .....56 D2
St George's Hill Golf Club
WEY KT13 .....56 E9
St Georges Hospital
TOOT SW17 .....29 H8
St Georges Industrial Estate
CBLY GU15 .....68 D5
KUTN/CMB KT2 .....26 B8
St Georges School
ASC SL5 .....34 B5
St Giles CE (Aided)
Infant School
ASHTD KT21 .....77 M7
St Giles School
CROY/NA CR0 .....63 K5
St Helier Hospital
SUT SM1 .....43 N9
St Hilary's School
GODL GU7 .....150 C1
St Hill Manor
EGRIN RH19 .....180 B7
St Hugh of Lincoln
Rcp School
WOKN/KNAP GU21 .....71 K8
St Ignatius
RC Primary School
SUN TW16 .....39 J2
St James CE Primary School
MFD/CHID GU8 .....148 D1
WEY KT13 .....56 E2
St James
Independent School
TWK TW1 .....25 P5
St James Medical Centre
CROY/NA CR0 .....45 M8
St James RC Primary School
WHTN TW2 .....25 M6
St James the Great
RC Primary School
THHTH CR7 .....45 K3
St John Fisher
RC Primary School
NWMAL KT3 .....42 G6
St John Rigby
Catholic College
WWKM BR4 .....65 K3

St Johns Beaumont School
STWL/WRAY TW19 .....21 H5
St Johns Catholic
Primary School
HORS RH12 .....191 P6
St Johns CE Infant School
CTHM CR3 .....102 B5
RFNM GU10 .....165 H2
St Johns CE Primary School
KUT KT1 .....8 C1
PGE/AN SE20 .....46 C1
CROY/NA CR0 .....64 D1
St John's CE Walham Green
FUL/PGN SW6 .....19 J6
St Johns CP School
WOKN/KNAP GU21 .....71 L7
St John's Hospital Day Centre
BTSEA SW11 .....19 P9
St Johns Junior School
CTHM CR3 .....102 B6
St Johns Primary School
REDH RH1 .....120 A7
St Johns School
LHD/OX KT22 .....97 H1
St John the Baptist
CE Junior School
KUT KT1 .....8 B1
St John the Baptist
RC School
WOKS/MYFD GU22 .....72 E8
St Joseph
RC Primary School
DORK RH4 .....116 G7
St Josephs Catholic
Primary Redhill
REDH RH1 .....120 A4
St Josephs Catholic
Primary School
ALDT GU11 .....108 C6
EPSOM KT18 .....78 A3
St Josephs College
STRHM/NOR SW16 .....30 C9
St Josephs Primary School
PUT/ROE SW15 .....28 D1
St Josephs RC Infant School
NRWD SE19 .....30 D9
St Josephs RC Junior School
NRWD SE19 .....30 D9
St Josephs
RC Primary School
BRAK RG12 .....32 F3
KUT KT1 .....9 F5
St Josephs School
CRAN GU6 .....153 J6
St Judes CE Junior School
EGH TW20 .....21 H9
St Jude's CE Prim School
HNHL SE24 .....30 C2
St Lawrence Business Centre
FELT TW13 .....24 C5
St Lawrence Catholic School
FELT TW13 .....24 C5
St Lawrence Primary School
E/WMO/HCT KT8 .....40 D4
St Lawrence Primary School
EHSLY KT24 .....95 M7
St Leonards
CE Primary School
STRHM/NOR SW16 .....29 N8
St Leonards Community
Infant & Nursery School
SWTR RH13 .....192 C8
St Lukes CE Primary School
KUTN/CMB KT2 .....9 F2
WNWD SE27 .....30 D8
St Lukes School
THHTH CR7 .....45 J5
St Margaret Clitherow
Primary School
BRAK RG12 .....32 B8
St Margarets Business Centre
TWK TW1 .....25 P3
St Margarets
CE F & M School
CRAWW RH11 .....176 D4
St Marks
CE Aided Primary School
GODL GU7 .....150 A1
St Marks CE Primary School
FARN GU14 .....88 F7
HAYES BR2 .....47 N4
SNWD SE25 .....46 A5
St Marks RC School
MTCM CR4 .....44 B3
St Martin-in-the-Fields
BRXS/STRHM SW2 .....30 C4
St Martins CE Junior School
EPSOM KT18 .....78 B4
St Martins CE Primary School
DORK RH4 .....116 F6
St Martins House
Business Centre
EHSLY KT24 .....94 G9
St Martins Walk Shopping Centre
DORK RH4 .....116 H6
St Mary CE Primary School
PUT/ROE SW15 .....19 H8
St Mary Magdalens RC Primary
School
MORT/ESHN SW14 .....18 B8
St Marys CE First School
MFD/CHID GU8 .....130 E7
St Marys CE Infant School
LHD/OX KT22 .....97 J2
RFNM GU10 .....146 G5
St Marys CE Junior School
OXTED RH8 .....103 L8
STWL/WRAY TW19 .....23 H2
THDIT KT7 .....41 H9

St Mary's Cemetery
  BTSEA SW11 .... 29 H1
  HORS RH12 .... 192 B9
St Marys CE Primary School
  BF/WBF KT14 .... 74 A2
  CHSGTN KT9 .... 59 L5
  EGRIN RH19 .... 180 C1
  HORS RH12 .... 192 A9
  MFD/CHID GU8 .... 168 A8
  TWK TW1 .... 25 P3
St Marys High School
  CROY/NA CR0 .... 2 D1
St Marys Infant School
  CAR SM5 .... 62 A3
St Marys Primary School
  WKENS SW14 .... 19 H1
St Marys RC Infant School
  CAR SM5 .... 62 B3
St Marys RC Primary School
  BECK BR3 .... 47 J1
  CHSWK W4 .... 18 B3
  CLAP SW4 .... 29 M1
  CROY/NA CR0 .... 2 E1
  ISLW TW7 .... 16 C8
  WIM/MER SW19 .... 43 L1
St Marys & St Peters
  CE Primary School
  TEDD TW11 .... 25 M8
St Marys School Ascot
  ASC SL5 .... 34 B8
St Marys Tutorial College
  GUW GU2 .... 112 A8
St Marys University College
  TWK TW1 .... 25 N6
St Matthews CE (Aided)
  Infant School
  COB KT11 .... 75 K7
St Matthews
  CE Primary School
  REDH RH1 .... 120 B3
  RYNPK SW20 .... 42 E2
  SURB KT6 .... 41 L8
St Michaels Abbey
  FARN GU14 .... 88 E2
St Michaels
  CE First School
  RDKG RH5 .... 97 J7
St Michaels
  CE Infant School
  ALDT GU11 .... 108 D6
St Michaels
  CE Junior School
  ALDT GU11 .... 108 D6
St Michaels
  CE Primary School
  ASC SL5 .... 34 D6
  BRAK RG12 .... 32 C6
  SHST GU47 .... 49 J9
  WAND/EARL SW18 .... 28 C3
St Michaels RC School
  ASHF TW15 .... 23 K8
St Michaels & St Martins RC
  Primary School
  HSLWW TW4 .... 15 P8
St Michaels Sydenham
  CE Primary School
  SYD SE26 .... 31 M7
St Nicholas CE F & M School
  SHPTN TW17 .... 38 D7
St Nicholas Centre
  SUT SM1 .... 61 M4
St Nicholas Middle School
  CRAN GU6 .... 152 G9
St Nicholas School
  FLEETS GU52 .... 106 E4
  PUR/KEN CR8 .... 81 H2
  REDH RH1 .... 100 T9
St Nicolas CE Infant School
  GUW GU2 .... 6 C7
St Nicolas School
  MFD/CHID GU8 .... 169 L5
St Omer Barracks
  ALDT GU11 .... 108 F2
St Osmunds
  RC Primary School
  BARN SW13 .... 18 D6
St Patricks Catholic Primary
  School
  FARN GU14 .... 88 D7
St Pauls Catholic College
  SUN TW16 .... 39 J2
St Pauls CE Aided
  Primary School
  DORK RH4 .... 117 H1
St Pauls CE Infant School
  RFNM GU10 .... 109 J7
St Pauls CE Junior School
  KUTN/CMB KT2 .... 9 J1
St Pauls CE Primary School
  ADL/WDHM KT15 .... 55 L3
  BTFD TW8 .... 17 K4
  CHSGTN KT9 .... 59 L3
St Pauls Girls School
  HMSMTH W6 .... 19 H2
St Pauls Preparatory School
  BARN SW13 .... 18 E3
St Paul's Primary School
  HMSMTH W6 .... 18 G3
St Pauls RC Primary School
  THDIT KT7 .... 40 E8
St Peter & St Paul
  CE Primary School
  CTHM CR3 .... 101 J5
  MTCM CR4 .... 44 B5
St Peter's
  Catholic Primary School
  EGRIN RH19 .... 180 B2
St Peters Catholic School
  GU GU1 .... 112 G4
St Peters CE Primary School
  FARN GU14 .... 88 E3
  YTLY GU46 .... 67 H2
St Peters CE Middle School
  WDSR SL4 .... 20 E2
St Peters
  CE Primary School
  GDST RH9 .... 122 G4
  HMSMTH W6 .... 18 E3
St Peters CE (Aided) Primary
  School
  FNM GU9 .... 127 K7
St Peters Primary School
  SAND/SEL CR2 .... 63 M5
St Peters
  RC Primary School
  LHD/OX KT22 .... 77 J9
St Philips School
  CHSGTN KT9 .... 59 K5
St Philips School
  SKENS SW7 .... 19 N2
St Phillips Infant School
  SYD SE26 .... 31 J7
St Philomenas
  RC High School
  CAR SM5 .... 62 B4
St Polycarps
  RC Primary School
  FNM GU9 .... 5 J5
St Raphaels Hospice
  WPK KT4 .... 61 H1
St Richards with St Andrews
  CE Primary School
  RCHPK/HAM TW10 .... 26 A6
St Robert Southwell
  Primary School
  HORS RH12 .... 192 F4
St Sebastians
  CE Primary School
  EWKG RG40 .... 49 J1
St Stephens
  CE Junior School
  TWK TW1 .... 25 P2
St Stephens
  CE Primary School
  GDST RH9 .... 122 F8
St Teresas Preparatory
  School
  EHSLY KT24 .... 95 M8
St Teresas School
  RDKG RH5 .... 115 M3
St Thomas of Canterbury
  RC Middle School
  MTCM CR4 .... 44 C4
St Thomas of Canterbury
  RC Primary School
  FUL/PGN SW6 .... 19 K5
  GU GU1 .... 112 F5
St Walter & St John
  Sports Ground
  TOOT SW17 .... 29 H4
St Wilfrids RC School
  CRAWW RH11 .... 176 E6
St William of York
  Primary School
  FSTH SE23 .... 31 M4
Salesian College
  CHERT KT16 .... 37 L9
  FARN GU14 .... 88 C6
Salesian RC School
  CHERT KT16 .... 55 J1
Salfords Primary School
  REDH RH1 .... 140 C2
Salfords Industrial Estate
  REDH RH1 .... 140 C4
Sampson Business Park
  CBLY GU15 .... 68 D5
The Samuel Cody School
  ALDT GU11 .... 88 D8
Sandcross Junior School
  REIG RH2 .... 119 K8
Sanderstead Junior School
  SAND/SEL CR2 .... 63 M7
Sandfield CP School
  GU GU1 .... 6 E4
Sandhurst College Town
  County Junior School
  SHST GU47 .... 50 A9
Sandhurst
  Comprehensive School
  SHST GU47 .... 49 P9
Sandhurst Sports Club
  SHST GU47 .... 67 N1
Sandown Golf Centre
  ESH/CLAY KT10 .... 58 B2
Sandown Industrial Park
  ESH/CLAY KT10 .... 58 A1
Sandown Park Racecourse
  ESH/CLAY KT10 .... 58 B2
Sandy Lane Infant School
  BNFD RG42 .... 32 E1
Sandy Lane Junior School
  BNFD RG42 .... 32 E2
Sangers County
  Middle School
  HORL RH6 .... 159 J1
Satellite Business Village
  CRAWE RH10 .... 177 H1
Savill Garden
  (Windsor Great Park)
  EGH TW20 .... 20 D9
Saxon Business Centre
  WIM/MER SW19 .... 43 N3
Saxon CP School
  SHPTN TW17 .... 38 B6
Sayer Clinic
  CROY/NA CR0 .... 63 H3
Sayes Court Junior School
  ADL/WDHM KT15 .... 55 M4
School of Art
  RCH/KEW TW9 .... 17 L9
School of Art & Design
  REIG RH2 .... 119 P5
Science Museum
  SKENS SW7 .... 19 P1

Science Museum
  IMAX Cinema
  SKENS SW7 .... 19 P1
Scott Broadwood
  Infant School
  RDKG RH5 .... 156 C6
Scott Broadwood School
  RDKG RH5 .... 155 K8
The Scott Gallery
  HORL RH6 .... 159 K2
Screen Cinema
  WOT/HER KT12 .... 39 J9
Seaton House School
  BELMT SM2 .... 61 P8
Secombe Centre
  SUT SM1 .... 61 L4
The Selhurst Medical Centre
  SNWD SE25 .... 45 M7
Sellincourt School
  TOOT SW17 .... 29 H9
Selsdon High School
  SAND/SEL CR2 .... 64 D6
Selsdon Park Hotel
  & Golf Club
  SAND/SEL CR2 .... 64 C9
Selsdon Primary School
  SAND/SEL CR2 .... 64 C7
Selsdon Road
  Industrial Estate
  SAND/SEL CR2 .... 63 M6
Semaphore Tower
  COB KT11 .... 74 F6
Send CE Infant School
  RPLY/SEND GU23 .... 93 H4
Send Cricket Club
  RPLY/SEND GU23 .... 93 H4
Sergeant Industrial Estate
  WAND/EARL SW18 .... 28 E2
Servite RC Primary School
  WBPTN SW10 .... 19 N4
Seymour F & M School
  CRAWW RH11 .... 176 E9
Shalford Infant School
  RGUE GU4 .... 132 C2
Shalford Mill (NT)
  RGUE GU4 .... 132 C1
Shannon Corner Retail Park
  NWMAL KT3 .... 42 E5
Shawfield Primary School
  ASHV GU12 .... 109 J3
Shawley Primary School
  EPSOM KT18 .... 78 C7
Sheen Lane Health Centre
  MORT/ESHN SW14 .... 18 A8
Sheen Mount
  Primary School
  RCHPK/HAM TW10 .... 26 G1
Sheen School
  MORT/ESHN SW14 .... 18 C9
Sheen Sports Centre
  MORT/ESHN SW14 .... 18 C9
Shelley Catholic
  Primary School
  HORS RH12 .... 191 L7
Shepperton Business Park
  SHPTN TW17 .... 38 E6
Shepperton Health Centre
  SHPTN TW17 .... 38 D6
Shepperton Studios
  SHPTN TW17 .... 38 B4
Sheraton Skyline Hotel
  & Conference Centre
  HYS/HAR UB3 .... 14 F5
Shere CE Infant School
  SHGR GU5 .... 134 C1
Sheringdale Primary School
  WAND/EARL SW18 .... 28 C4
Sherwood First School
  MTCM CR4 .... 44 E5
Sherwood Park School
  WLGTN SM6 .... 62 F2
Shillinglee Park Golf Club
  MFD/CHID GU8 .... 186 C4
The Ship Hotel
  WEY KT13 .... 56 D2
Shirley Clinic
  CROY/NA CR0 .... 46 C9
Shirley High School
  CROY/NA CR0 .... 64 D2
Shirley Park Golf Club
  CROY/NA CR0 .... 64 B1
Shirley Wanderers RFC
  WWKM BR4 .... 65 J3
Shortlands Golf Club
  HAYES BR2 .... 47 L2
Shortwood Infant School
  STA TW18 .... 22 E6
Shotfield Health Clinic
  WLGTN SM6 .... 62 D5
Shottermill County
  Primary School
  HASM GU27 .... 184 A3
Shrewsbury House School
  SURB KT6 .... 59 K1
Silverglade Business Park
  CHSGTN KT9 .... 77 J1
Silvermere Golf Club
  COB KT11 .... 74 D2
Silver Wing Industrial Estate
  CROY/NA CR0 .... 63 H5
Sinclair House School
  FUL/PGN SW6 .... 19 J6
Singlegate First School
  WIM/MER SW19 .... 43 P1
Sir Greville Sprat Stadium
  GODL GU7 .... 131 H7
Sir John Lillie Primary School
  HMSMTH W6 .... 19 J4
Sir William Perkins School
  CHERT KT16 .... 37 K9
The Sixth Form College
  FARN GU14 .... 88 D9

Skimped Hill Health Centre
  BRAK RG12 .... 32 D3
Sky Business Park
  FELT TW20 .... 36 G3
Slinfold CE Primary School
  SWTR RH13 .... 190 E6
Slinfold Park Golf
  & Country Club
  SWTR RH13 .... 190 C6
Sloane Hospital
  BECK BR3 .... 47 K2
Slough Community
  Mental Health Centre
  DTCH/LGLY SL3 .... 12 E2
Slyfield Industrial Estate
  GU GU1 .... 92 B9
Smallberry Green
  Primary School
  ISLW TW7 .... 16 C7
Smallwood Primary School
  TOOT SW17 .... 28 C7
Smitham Primary School
  COUL/CHIP CR5 .... 80 E5
Smithbrook Clinic
  CRAN GU6 .... 152 A9
Snowhill Business Centre
  CRAWE RH10 .... 161 H8
South Bookham School
  GT/LBKH KT23 .... 96 C7
Southborough School
  SURB KT6 .... 59 L2
South Croydon
  Medical Centre
  SAND/SEL CR2 .... 63 L6
South Croydon Sports Club
  SAND/SEL CR2 .... 63 L7
Southern Clinic
  REIG RH2 .... 119 N6
South Farnborough
  County Junior School
  FARN GU14 .... 88 F5
South Farnborough
  Infant School
  FARN GU14 .... 88 F7
South Farnham School
  FNM GU9 .... 128 A4
The Southfields Clinic
  WAND/EARL SW18 .... 28 D2
Southfields Community
  School
  WAND/EARL SW18 .... 28 D4
Southgate F & M School
  CRAWE RH10 .... 176 G7
Southgate West
  F & M School
  CRAWW RH11 .... 176 F7
South Hill Park
  Arts Centre Cinema
  BRAK RG12 .... 32 D8
Southlands College
  PUT/ROE SW15 .... 18 D9
South London Crematorium
  MTCM CR4 .... 44 E3
South London Tamil School
  CROY/NA CR0 .... 45 L8
South London Theatre
  WNWD SE27 .... 30 D6
Southmead Primary School
  WIM/MER SW19 .... 28 B4
South Norwood
  Country Park
  SNWD SE25 .... 46 C5
South Norwood Hill
  Medical Centre
  SNWD SE25 .... 45 N3
South Norwood
  Medical Centre
  SNWD SE25 .... 45 N5
South Norwood
  Primary School
  SNWD SE25 .... 46 A5
South Nutfield Cricket Club
  REDH RH1 .... 121 H7
South Park Hotel
  SAND/SEL CR2 .... 63 N3
South Terminal
  HORL RH6 .... 159 N5
South Thames College
  PUT/ROE SW15 .... 28 A1
South Thames College /
  Wandsworth Adult College
  PUT/ROE SW15 .... 27 L2
Southville Junior School
  EBED/NFELT TW14 .... 24 A4
Southwark Sports Ground
  DUL SE21 .... 30 G4
South West Middlesex
  Crematorium
  FELT TW13 .... 24 F4
South West Surrey
  Business Centre
  GU GU1 .... 7 G4
Southwood Golf Club
  FARN GU14 .... 88 A5
Sparrow Farm County
  Junior School
  EW KT17 .... 60 F4
Sparrow Farm Junior School
  EBED/NFELT TW14 .... 24 D3
Sparrow Farm
  Nursery School
  EBED/NFELT TW14 .... 24 D3
Spectators Viewing Area
  HTHAIR TW6 .... 14 D8
Speldhurst Clinic
  ASHF TW15 .... 23 N9
Spelthorne Leisure Centre
  STA TW18 .... 22 D8
Spelthorne Museum
  STA TW18 .... 22 B8
Spelthorne Primary School
  ASHF TW15 .... 23 N9

Spelthorne
  Sixth Form College
  ASHF TW15 .... 23 J7
Spelthorne Sports Club
  ASHF TW15 .... 38 F1
Spring Copse Business Park
  SWTR RH13 .... 190 C7
Springfield Hospital
  TOOT SW17 .... 29 H6
Springfield Primary School
  SUN TW16 .... 38 G2
Spring Grove Primary School
  ISLW TW7 .... 16 D7
Springlake Country Club
  ASHV GU12 .... 108 G2
Spring Park Primary School
  CROY/NA CR0 .... 64 G2
Springwell Infant School
  HEST TW5 .... 15 N5
Springwell Junior School
  HEST TW5 .... 15 N5
Sprint Industrial Estate
  BF/WBF KT14 .... 55 P9
Spurgeons College
  SNWD SE25 .... 45 N3
Squash & Badminton Club
  WIM/MER SW19 .... 43 J1
Squerryes Court
  Manor House & Gardens
  BH/WHM TN16 .... 104 G8
Squirrels Trading Estate
  HYS/HAR UB3 .... 15 H1
Staff College
  CBLY GU15 .... 68 G2
Stafford Cross Business Park
  CROY/NA CR0 .... 63 H4
Staines County Court
  STA TW18 .... 22 D7
Staines Preparatory School
  STA TW18 .... 22 D8
Staines RFC
  FELT TW13 .... 24 B8
Staines Town FC
  STA TW18 .... 37 L1
Stamford Clinic
  HMSMTH W6 .... 18 E2
Stamford Green County
  Primary School
  HOR/WEW KT19 .... 77 P1
Stammerham
  Business Centre
  HORS RH12 .... 174 D4
Stanford Middle School
  STRHM/NOR SW16 .... 44 F2
Stanhill Court Hotel
  HORL RH6 .... 157 N3
Stanley Infant School
  TEDD TW11 .... 25 M7
Stanley Junior School
  TEDD TW11 .... 25 M7
Stanley Park High School
  CAR SM5 .... 62 C5
Stanley Park Junior School
  CAR SM5 .... 62 B6
Stanley Technical
  Boys High School
  SNWD SE25 .... 45 P4
Stanton Square
  Industrial Estate
  CAT SE6 .... 31 N7
Stanway School
  DORK RH4 .... 117 H4
Starborough Castle
  EDEN TN8 .... 144 D8
Starhurst School
  RDKG RH5 .... 117 J9
Station Industrial Estate
  FLEETN GU51 .... 87 H4
Station Yard
  KWD/TDW/WH KT20 .... 99 K1
Stepgates Community School
  CHERT KT16 .... 37 M8
Stewart Fleming
  Primary School
  PGE/AN SE20 .... 46 C4
Stilness Primary School
  BROCKY SE4 .... 31 M2
Stirling Way
  Industrial Estates
  CROY/NA CR0 .... 44 G8
Stoke Hill CP School
  GU GU1 .... 112 A2
Stompond Lane Track
  WOT/HER KT12 .... 57 J1
Stoughton County
  Junior School
  GUW GU2 .... 111 P2
Stowford College
  BELMT SM2 .... 61 N6
Strand on the Green
  J & I School
  CHSWK W4 .... 17 N4
Strathmore School
  RCHPK/HAM TW10 .... 26 C4
Strawberry Hill Golf Club
  WHTN TW2 .... 25 M6
Streatham Cemetery
  TOOT SW17 .... 29 H6
Streatham & Clapham
  High School
  STRHM/NOR SW16 .... 29 M6
Streatham & Clapham
  High School
  Preparatory Site
  BRXS/STRHM SW2 .... 30 A4
Streatham
  & Croydon RFC
  THHTH CR7 .... 45 J6
Streatham Ice Rink
  STRHM/NOR SW16 .... 29 P8
Streatham Modern School
  STRHM/NOR SW16 .... 29 P9

Streatham Park Cemetery
MTCM CR4 ....44 E3
Streatham Swimming Pool
STRHM/NOR SW16 ......29 P8
Streatham Vale Sports Club
STRHM/NOR SW16 ......44 E1
Streatham Wells
Primary School
BRXS/STRHM SW2 ......30 A5
Streete Court School
GDST RH9 ....122 E1
Strodes College
EGH TW20 ....21 L8
Stubbs Industrial Estate
ALDT GU11 ....108 G1
Studholme Medical Centre
ASHF TW15 ....23 J7
The Study
Preparatory School
WIM/MER SW19 ....28 A8
The Study School
NWMAL KT3 ....42 C6
Sturt Priory Hospital
KWD/TDW/WH KT20 ......98 E6
Sudbourne Primary School
BRXS/STRHM SW2 ....30 A1
Sulivan Primary School
FUL/PGN SW6 ....19 L7
Summit Business Park
SUN TW16 ....39 J1
Sunbury Business Centre
SUN TW16 ....38 G2
Sunbury Court
SUN TW16 ....39 M3
Sunbury Health Centre
SUN TW16 ....39 J3
Sunbury Leisure Centre
SUN TW16 ....39 H2
Sunbury Lock
WOT/HER KT12 ....39 K4
Sunbury Manor School
SUN TW16 ....39 H2
Sun Life Trading Estate
EBED/NFELT TW14 ....15 J8
Sunningdale Golf Club
ASC SL5 ....34 G9
Sunningdale Ladies Golf Club
ASC SL5 ....34 F9
Sunningdale School
ASC SL5 ....34 E7
Sunnydown School
CTHM CR3 ....101 P1
Sunnyhill Primary School
STRHM/NOR SW16 ....30 A7
Surbiton Business Centre
SURB KT6 ....41 K7
Surbiton Cemetery
BRYLDS KT5 ....41 N5
Surbiton Golf Club
ESH/CLAY KT10 ....59 H3
Surbiton High School
KUT KT1 ....41 L5
Surbiton Hospital
SURB KT6 ....41 L7
Surbiton Natural
Health Centre
SURB KT6 ....41 L7
Surex Swimming Pools
WHTN TN16 ....84 B4
Surrey Business Park
EW KT17 ....60 C9
Surrey County Hall
KUT KT1 ....8 C7
Surrey Heath Museum
CBLY GU15 ....68 F2
Surrey History Centre
WOKN/KNAP GU21 ....10 A5
Surrey Institute
of Art & Design
EPSOM KT18 ....78 B3
FNM GU9 ....4 E3
HOR/WEW KT19 ....32 D7
Surrey Probation Service
GU GU1 ....6 D4
The Surrey
& Sussex Crematorium
CRAWE RH10 ....159 N9
Surrey Welfare Court Service
GU GU1 ....6 D5
Sussex Manor Business Park
CRAWE RH10 ....177 K1
Sutton Alternative
Health Centre
SUT SM1 ....61 M4
Sutton Arena
CAR SM5 ....43 P8
Sutton Bowling Club
BELMT SM2 ....61 L7
Sutton Cemetery
CHEAM SM3 ....61 K1
Sutton General Hospital
BELMT SM2 ....61 M8
Sutton Grammar School
for Boys
SUT SM1 ....61 N4
Sutton Green Golf Club
WOKS/MYFD GU22 ....92 C2
Sutton High Junior School
SUT SM1 ....61 M5
Sutton High School
for Girls GDST
SUT SM1 ....61 L5
Sutton United FC
SUT SM1 ....61 L3
Sutton West Centre
SUT SM1 ....61 L4
Swaffield Primary School
WAND/EARL SW18 ....28 F2
Swallow International Hotel
ECT SW5 ....19 M2
Swan Business Centre
CHSWK W4 ....18 B2

The Swan Centre
LHD/OX KT22 ....97 H1
Swansmere School
WOT/HER KT12 ....39 L9
Swan Walk Shopping Centre
HORS RH12 ....192 B8
Swedish School
BARN SW13 ....18 E4
Swinley CP School
CRAWE RH10 ....177 J7
Swinley Forest Golf Club
ASC SL5 ....34 A6
Swinley Forest Golf Club
ASC SL5 ....33 P8
Sybil Elgar School
NWDGN UB2 ....15 P1
Sydenham Girls School
SYD SE26 ....31 J6
Sydenham High School
SYD SE26 ....31 J8
Sydenham (Junior)
High School
SYD SE26 ....31 J7
Syon House
BTFD TW8 ....17 J6
Syon Park
BTFD TW8 ....17 J7
Syon Park School
ISLW TW7 ....17 H6
Sythwood Primary School
WOKN/KNAP GU21 ....71 P5
Tabard Theatre
CHSWK W4 ....18 C2
Taberner House
CROY/NA CR0 ....2 D5
TA Centre
CHERT KT16 ....37 L8
HORS RH12 ....192 B9
Tadworth Primary School
KWD/TDW/WH KT20 ......99 H2
Tait Road Industrial Estate
CROY/NA CR0 ....45 M8
Talavera Primary School
ALDT GU11 ....108 C3
Tamian Industrial Estate
WHTN TW4 ....15 L9
Tamworth Manor
High School
STRHM/NOR SW16 ....44 F4
Tanbridge House School
HORS RH12 ....191 N8
HORS RH12 ....192 A9
Tanbridge Retail Park
HORS RH12 ....192 A9
Tandem Centre
WIM/MER SW19 ....43 P2
Tandridge Golf Club
OXTED RH8 ....123 J2
Tatsfield Primary School
BH/WHM TN16 ....104 B1
Tattenham Health Centre
EPSOM KT18 ....78 F7
Taverstock Infant School
FLEETN GU51 ....86 D7
TAVR Centre
KUT KT1 ....41 K5
Teddington Business Park
TEDD TW11 ....25 N8
Teddington Cemetery
TEDD TW11 ....25 M7
Teddington Clinic
TEDD TW11 ....25 M9
Teddington Lock
TEDD TW11 ....26 A7
Teddington Memorial
Hospital
TEDD TW11 ....25 M9
Teddington Pool
& Fitness Centre
TEDD TW11 ....25 P8
Teddington School
TEDD TW11 ....26 C9
The Teddington Theatre Club
E/WMO/HCT KT8 ....40 D6
Telferscott Primary School
BAL SW12 ....29 M4
Temperate House
RCH/KEW TW9 ....17 M7
Tennis Centre
HASM GU27 ....183 N1
Tennis Club
FLEETS GU52 ....106 F3
HAYES BR2 ....47 P5
Thames Christian College
BTSEA SW11 ....19 P8
Thames Ditton Infant School
THDIT KT7 ....40 F7
Thames Ditton Junior School
THDIT KT7 ....40 F8
The Thames Lodge Hotel
STA TW18 ....22 B8
Thamesmead School
SHPTN TW17 ....38 F7
Thatched House Hotel
SUT SM1 ....61 K5
Theatre Centre
BECK BR3 ....47 H3
Theatre Magenta
LHD/OX KT22 ....76 G9
Theatre of the Dispossessed
WIM/MER SW19 ....28 A4
The Theatre on the Hill
CTHM CR3 ....101 N2
Therapia Trading Estate
CROY/NA CR0 ....44 F8
Therfield School
LHD/OX KT22 ....76 G8
Thomas Becket
RC Primary School
SNWD SE25 ....46 A7
Thomas Bennett
Community College
CRAWE RH10 ....176 G8

Thomas London Independent
Day School
KENS W8 ....19 M1
Thomas's Preparatory School
BTSEA SW11 ....19 P6
Thomson House
FARN GU14 ....88 E2
Thorn Chase School
GU GU1 ....112 G5
Thorncroft Manor
LHD/OX KT22 ....96 G3
Thorney Park Golf Club
IVER SL0 ....13 M1
Thornton Heath
Health Centre
THHTH CR7 ....45 L5
Thornton Heath Pools
& Fitness Centre
SNWD SE25 ....46 A6
SNWD SE25 ....45 L5
Thornton Road
Industrial Estate
CROY/NA CR0 ....44 G7
Thorpe CE Infant School
EGH TW20 ....36 G4
Thorpe Cricket Club
EGH TW20 ....36 D5
Thorpe Industrial Park
EGH TW20 ....37 H2
Thorpe Lea Primary School
EGH TW20 ....37 H2
Thorpe Park
EGH TW20 ....37 J5
Three Bridges Cricket Club
CRAWE RH10 ....177 K5
Three Bridges FC
CRAWE RH10 ....177 K5
Three Bridges First School
CRAWE RH10 ....177 K4
Three Bridges Middle School
CRAWE RH10 ....177 J5
Three Bridges
Primary School
NWDGN UB2 ....16 B1
Thurlow Park School
WNWD SE27 ....30 C5
Tiffin Girls School
KUTN/CMB KT2 ....26 D9
Tiffin School
KUTN/CMB KT2 ....9 F4
Tilgate Forest
Business Centre
CRAWW RH11 ....194 C1
Tilgate Forest Golf Centre
CRAWE RH10 ....177 K9
Tilgate Park
CRAWE RH10 ....195 J1
Tillingbourne Junior School
RGUE GU4 ....132 F3
Times Square Shopping
Centre
SUT SM1 ....61 M4
Tobias School of Art
EGRIN RH19 ....180 D5
Tollgate Primary School
CROY/NA CR0 ....46 C7
Tolworth CP School
SURB KT6 ....41 M9
Tolworth Girls School & Centre
for Continuing Education
SURB KT6 ....59 M2
Tolworth Recreation Centre
CHSGTN KT9 ....59 M2
Tolworth Tower
SURB KT6 ....41 P9
Tomlinscote School
FRIM GU16 ....69 H6
Tooting Bec Athletics Track
TOOT SW17 ....29 L7
Tooting Leisure Centre
TOOT SW17 ....29 G7
Tooting & Mitcham United FC
MTCM CR4 ....44 C2
Tormead School
GU GU1 ....7 K2
Tower Hill Primary School
FARN GU14 ....88 B4
Tower House School
MORT/ESHN SW14 ....18 A9
Tower Industrial Estate
SNWD SE25 ....46 A5
Town Farm Primary School
STWL/WRAY TW19 ....22 G3
Townmead Business Centre
FUL/PGN SW6 ....19 N8
Toyhorse International
Stud Farm
BIL RH14 ....189 M6
Traditions Golf Club
WOKS/MYFD GU22 ....73 L4
Trafalgar Community
Infant School
HORS RH12 ....192 A6
Trafalgar Junior School
WHTN TW2 ....25 L5
Travel Inn
ALDT GU11 ....108 A4
BAGS GU19 ....51 N4
BRAK RG12 ....32 D3
CHSGTN KT9 ....59 J8
EGRIN RH19 ....161 P8
EPSOM KT18 ....78 A3
FARN GU14 ....88 A4
FUL/PGN SW6 ....19 J8
GU GU1 ....112 B4
HORL RH6 ....159 J3
HORL RH6 ....192 C7
OXTED RH8 ....104 C6
REDH RH1 ....140 C3
SAND/SEL CR2 ....64 A4
SHST GU47 ....67 P1
WOKN/KNAP GU21 ....72 A6

Travelodge
BTSEA SW11 ....19 N8
HEST TW5 ....15 L4
HEST TW5 ....15 N4
HORL RH6 ....159 H7
LIPH GU30 ....182 C5
RDKG RH5 ....117 K6
The Treaty Centre
HSLW TW3 ....16 B8
Trident Business Centre
TOOT SW17 ....29 J8
Trident Industrial Estate
DTCH/LGLY SL3 ....13 J8
Trilakes Country Park
YTLY GU46 ....67 J1
Trinity St Marys
Primary School
BAL SW12 ....29 K4
Trinity School
CROY/NA CR0 ....64 C1
Trinity Trading Estate
HYS/HAR UB3 ....15 J1
Trumps Green County
Infant School
VW GU25 ....36 B7
Tudor Lodge Health Centre
WIM/MER SW19 ....28 A3
Tudors Business Centre
KWD/TDW/WH KT20 ......99 K2
Turners Hill CE Primary
School
CRAWE RH10 ....179 H8
Turney School
DUL SE21 ....30 D3
Tweeddale Infant School
CAR SM5 ....43 P8
Tweeddale Junior School
CAR SM5 ....43 P8
Tweseldown Infant School
FLEETS GU52 ....107 H2
Twickenham Cemetery
WHTN TW2 ....25 J4
Twickenham Golf Club
FELT TW13 ....25 H6
Twickenham Park
Health Centre
WHTN TW2 ....26 B2
Twickenham Stadium
WHTN TW2 ....25 M2
Twickenham Trading Estate
TWK TW1 ....25 N2
Two Bridges Business Park
SAND/SEL CR2 ....63 M5
Two Rivers Retail Park
STA TW18 ....22 B7
Tyrrells Wood Golf Club
LHD/OX KT22 ....97 M4
UCI Cinema
BRAK RG12 ....32 D3
SUT SM1 ....61 M4
CHEL SW3 ....19 P4
CRAWE RH10 ....176 G4
HMSMTH W6 ....18 F2
The Ullswater Business Park
COUL/CHIP CR5 ....80 C5
Ullswater Trading Centre
COUL/CHIP CR5 ....80 G5
Unicorn School
RCH/KEW TW9 ....17 M6
Unicorn Trading Estate
HASM GU27 ....184 C6
United Services
Sports Ground
CHSWK W4 ....18 C6
University of London
Athletics Ground
NWMAL KT3 ....42 E6
University of Surrey
GUW GU2 ....111 N5
University of Westminster
CHSWK W4 ....18 A6
University Vandals RFC
WOT/HER KT12 ....38 E8
Uplands CP School
SHST GU47 ....49 M9
Upper Tooting
Independent High School
TOOT SW17 ....29 H5
Ursuline High School
RYNPK SW20 ....43 H1
The Vale Medical Centre
FSTH SE23 ....31 M5
Valence School
BH/WHM TN16 ....105 K6
Vale Primary School
EPSOM KT18 ....78 B8
The Vale School
SKENS SW7 ....19 N1
Valley End CE Infant School
CHOB/PIR GU24 ....52 G5
Valley End Cricket Club
CHOB/PIR GU24 ....52 G6
The Valley Gardens
EGH TW20 ....35 M3
Valley Primary School
HAYES BR2 ....47 M3
Velmead Community Centre
FLEETS GU52 ....106 D2
Vencourt Hotel
HMSMTH W6 ....18 E2
Vestry Hall
MTCM CR4 ....44 B4
Vicarage Lane Clinic
HASM GU27 ....184 A4
Victoria & Albert Museum
SKENS SW7 ....19 P1
Victoria Clinic
WOKN/KNAP GU21 ....10 E2
Victoria Junior School
FELT TW13 ....24 C4
Victor Seymour Infant School
CAR SM5 ....62 B2

Victory Business Centre
ISLW TW7 ....16 F9
The Vine Clinic
KUTN/CMB KT2 ....26 D9
Vine Medical Centre
E/WMO/HCT KT8 ....40 C4
The Vineyard
Primary School
RCHPK/HAM TW10 ....26 D2
Virgo Fidelis
Convent Schools
NRWD SE19 ....30 D9
Viscount Industrial Estate
DTCH/LGLY SL3 ....13 J8
Vulcan Business Centre
CROY/NA CR0 ....65 L7
Waddon Clinic
CROY/NA CR0 ....63 J4
Waddon Infant School
CROY/NA CR0 ....63 J4
The Waldegrave Clinic
TEDD TW11 ....25 N8
Waldegrave Girls School
WHTN TW2 ....25 L6
Waldorf School
of SW London
STRHM/NOR SW16 ....29 M5
Waldorf Steiner School
of SW London
STRHM/NOR SW16 ....29 N7
Wallace Fields County
Infant School
EW KT17 ....78 E2
Wallace Fields Junior School
EW KT17 ....78 E1
Wallbrook Business Centre
HSLWW TW4 ....15 K8
Wallington County Grammar
School
WLGTN SM6 ....62 D3
Wallington
High School for Girls
WLGTN SM6 ....62 D7
Walsh CE F & M School
ASHV GU12 ....109 H5
Walton Business Centre
WOT/HER KT12 ....39 K8
Walton Casuals FC
WOT/HER KT12 ....39 K6
Walton Community Hospital
WOT/HER KT12 ....57 K1
Walton Heath
Golf Club Shop
KWD/TDW/WH KT20 ......98 F5
Walton & Hersham FC
WOT/HER KT12 ....57 J1
Walton Leigh School
WEY KT13 ....56 G3
Walton-on-Thames
Cricket Club
WOT/HER KT12 ....39 H9
Walton on the Hill
CE Junior School
KWD/TDW/WH KT20 ......98 F4
Walton on the Hill
Primary School
KWD/TDW/WH KT20 ......98 F4
Walton Swimming Pool
WOT/HER KT12 ....39 K9
Wandle Primary School
WAND/EARL SW18 ....28 E4
Wandle Recreation Centre
WAND/EARL SW18 ....28 E2
Wandle Trading Estate
MTCM CR4 ....44 B8
Wandsworth Adult College
TOOT SW17 ....29 H7
The Wandsworth
Arndale Centre
WAND/EARL SW18 ....28 E2
Wandsworth Cemetery
WAND/EARL SW18 ....28 F4
Wandsworth Community
Health Trust
CROY/NA CR0 ....29 K8
Wandsworth County Court
WAND/EARL SW18 ....28 E1
Wandsworth Trading Estate
WAND/EARL SW18 ....28 E3
Warehouse Theatre
CROY/NA CR0 ....2 E4
Warfield Primary School
BNFD RG42 ....32 G1
Warlingham Park School
WARL CR6 ....82 G5
Warlingham RFC
& John Fisher Sports Club
WARL CR6 ....82 B5
Warlingham School
WARL CR6 ....82 B5
Warlingham Sports Club
WARL CR6 ....82 D6
War Memorial Sports Ground
SUT SM1 ....62 A3
Warner Village Cinema
CROY/NA CR0 ....63 H1
Warner Village Cinema
EW KT17 ....19 L5
Warnham CE Primary School
HORS RH12 ....191 N2
Warren Mead Infant School
BNSTD SM7 ....78 C4
Warren Mead Junior School
BNSTD SM7 ....78 C4
Warsop Trading Estate
EDEN TN8 ....145 H5
Warwick Quadrant
& Harlequin Theatre,
Cinema & Library
REDH RH1 ....120 C4
The Warwick School
REDH RH1 ....120 D4

The Watchetts Junior School
  CBLY GU15 ....68 E6
Waterden Road Private
  Medical Clinic
  GU GU1 ....7 H4
Waterfield First School
  CRAWW RH11 ....176 B7
Waterfront Business Park
  FLEETN GU51 ....86 E7
Waterfront Business Park
  FLEETN GU51 ....87 H5
Waterloo Hotel
  CWTH RG45 ....49 L4
Watermans Arts, Cinema
  & Theatre Centre
  BTFD TW8 ....17 L4
Watermans Business Park
  STA TW18 ....22 B7
Watermeads High School
  MRDN SM4 ....43 P7
Watermill Museum
  LING RH7 ....144 A5
Waterside Business Centre
  ISLW TW7 ....17 H9
The Waterside Trading
  Centre
  HNWL W7 ....16 E1
Waterside Trading Estate
  ADL/WDHM KT15 ....56 A3
Wattenden Primary School
  PUR/KEN CR8 ....81 J5
The Waveil
  Secondary School
  ALDT GU11 ....88 D8
Waverley Abbey CE School
  RFNM GU10 ....128 E8
Waverley Abbey House
  FNM GU9 ....128 D5
Waverley
  Lower Secondary School
  EDUL SE22 ....31 J1
Waverley School
  PECK SE15 ....31 K1
The Weald
  CE Primary School
  RDKG RH5 ....156 C1
Wellington Business Park
  CWTH RG45 ....49 J5
Wellington College
  CWTH RG45 ....49 L6
Wellingtonia Avenue
  (Arboretum)
  CWTH RG45 ....48 G5
Wellington Primary School
  HSLW TW3 ....15 P7
Wellington Shopping Centre
  ALDT GU11 ....108 A8
Wellington Sports Centre
  CWTH RG45 ....49 K5
Wentworth Golf Club
  VW GU25 ....35 N6
West Ashtead Primary School
  ASHTD KT21 ....77 L9
Westbourne Primary School
  SUT SM1 ....61 L2
West Byfleet Golf Club
  BF/WBF KT14 ....73 K2
West Byfleet Health Centre
  BF/WBF KT14 ....73 L2
West Byfleet
  Physiotherapy Clinic
  BF/WBF KT14 ....73 L1
West Byfleet Primary School
  BF/WBF KT14 ....73 M1
Westcott CE First School
  DORK RH4 ....116 C8
Westcroft Leisure Centre
  CAR SM5 ....62 C3
West Dene School
  PUR/KEN CR8 ....81 H2
West Drayton Cricket Club
  WDR/YW UB7 ....13 N2
Westend County
  Infant School
  ALDT GU11 ....108 B5
West End Sports
  & Social Club
  ESH/CLAY KT10 ....57 P5
Westerham Golf Club
  BH/WHM TN16 ....105 K6

West Ewell County
  Infant School
  HOR/WEW KT19 ....60 B4
Westfield Primary School
  WOKS/MYFD GU22 ....92 C1
Westfields Primary School
  BARN SW13 ....18 D7
  YTLY GU46 ....66 F3
West Green First School
  CRAWW RH11 ....176 F5
West Hill Golf Club
  CHOB/PIR GU24 ....91 H1
West Hill Primary School
  WAND/EARL SW18 ....28 D1
West Hill School
  LHD/OX KT22 ....76 C7
West Kent Golf Club
  ORP BR6 ....84 C1
Westland Heliport
  BTSEA SW11 ....19 P8
West London County Court
  WKENS W14 ....19 J2
West London
  Magistrates Court
  HMSMTH W6 ....19 H3
West Middlesex
  University Hospital
  ISLW TW7 ....16 G7
Westmoor Community Clinic
  PUT/ROE SW15 ....27 M3
West Norwood Clinic
  WNWD SE27 ....30 D5
West Norwood Crematorium
  WNWD SE27 ....30 D6
Weston Green School
  THDIT KT7 ....40 E9
West Park Hospital
  HOR/WEW KT19 ....77 L1
West Ramp Coach Park
  WDR/YW UB7 ....14 C6
West Surrey Golf Club
  MFD/CHID GU8 ....150 A6
West Thames College
  ISLW TW7 ....16 E6
West Thornton
  Primary School
  CROY/NA CR0 ....45 H8
The Westway Clinic
  REDH RH1 ....120 A4
West Wickham
  Swimming Baths
  WWKM BR4 ....47 J9
Westwood
  High School for Girls
  NRWD SE19 ....45 L1
Weybourne County
  Infant School
  FNM GU9 ....108 A8
Weybridge Business Park
  ADL/WDHM KT15 ....56 A3
Weybridge Cricket Club
  WEY KT13 ....56 G1
Weybridge Hospital
  & Primary Care Centre
  WEY KT13 ....56 C3
Weydon County
  Secondary School
  FNM GU9 ....127 K6
Weydown Industrial Estate
  HASM GU27 ....184 C3
Weyfield Primary School
  GU GU1 ....112 B2
Wey House School
  SHGR GU5 ....132 C5
Wey Retail Park
  BF/WBF KT14 ....74 A1
White Hart Industrial Estate
  BLKW GU17 ....68 A3
The White Horse Hotel
  DORK RH4 ....117 H7
Whitehorse Manor
  Primary School
  THHTH CR7 ....45 M5
Whitgift School
  SAND/SEL CR2 ....63 L4
Whitgift Shopping Centre
  CROY/NA CR0 ....2 D3
Whitton Health Centre
  WHTN TW2 ....25 K4

Whitton Health Clinic
  WHTN TW2 ....25 J4
Whitton School
  WHTN TW2 ....25 J5
Whitton Sports & Fitness Centre
  WHTN TW2 ....25 J5
Whyteleafe Business Village
  CTHM CR3 ....81 P6
Whyteleafe FC
  CTHM CR3 ....81 P8
Whyteleafe Primary School
  CTHM CR3 ....81 P7
Wickham Theatre
  WWKM BR4 ....65 K2
Wide Way Health Clinic
  MTCM CR4 ....44 F4
Wildridings CP School
  BRAK RG12 ....32 C5
The Wildwood Golf Club
  CRAN GU6 ....170 D9
William Byrd School
  HYS/HAR UB3 ....14 E4
William Cobbett Junior School
  FNM GU9 ....108 A8
William Morris Academy
  HMSMTH W6 ....19 H3
William Morris Middle School
  MTCM CR4 ....44 F4
Willington School
  WIM/MER SW19 ....28 C9
Willow Business Centre
  MTCM CR4 ....44 B6
Willow Business Park
  SYD SE26 ....31 K6
Wilsons School
  WLGTN SM6 ....62 G5
Wimbledon Chase
  Middle School
  RYNPK SW20 ....43 J2
Wimbledon College
  High School
  WIM/MER SW19 ....43 H1
Wimbledon Common
  Golf Club
  WIM/MER SW19 ....27 N8
Wimbledon Common Pre-
  preparatory School
  WIM/MER SW19 ....27 P9
Wimbledon
  (Gap Road) Cemetery
  WIM/MER SW19 ....28 E7
Wimbledon High School
  WIM/MER SW19 ....28 B9
Wimbledon House School
  WIM/MER SW19 ....43 L2
Wimbledon
  Magistrates Court
  WIM/MER SW19 ....28 D9
Wimbledon Park
  Athletics Track
  WIM/MER SW19 ....28 C5
Wimbledon Park Golf Club
  WIM/MER SW19 ....28 C6
Wimbledon Park
  Primary School
  WIM/MER SW19 ....28 D5
Wimbledon Recreation Centre
  WIM/MER SW19 ....28 E9
Wimbledon RFC
  RYNPK SW20 ....42 D1
Wimbledon School of Art
  WIM/MER SW19 ....43 J2
Wimbledon School of English
  WIM/MER SW19 ....28 B9
Wimbledon Stadium
  TOOT SW17 ....28 E7
Wimbledon Stadium
  Business Centre
  WIM/MER SW19 ....28 E6
Wimbledon Theatre
  WIM/MER SW19 ....43 L1
Windlemere Golf Club
  CHOB/PIR GU24 ....52 E9
Windlesham Golf Club
  BAGS GU19 ....51 P5
Windlesham Village
  Infant School
  BFOR GU20 ....52 B3

The Windmill
  on the Common Hotel
  CLAP SW4 ....29 L1
Windmill School
  BRXS/STRHM SW2 ....29 P1
Windmill Trading Estate
  MTCM CR4 ....44 E6
Windmill Trading Estate
  SUN TW16 ....38 F2
Winkworth Arboretum (NT)
  MFD/CHID GU8 ....151 H6
The Winston Churchill School
  WOKN/KNAP GU21 ....71 L7
Winterbourne
  Junior Girls School
  THHTH CR7 ....45 J5
Wishmore Cross School
  CHOB/PIR GU24 ....53 L8
The Wisley Golf Club
  RPLY/SEND GU23 ....73 P6
Wispers School
  HASM GU27 ....184 D1
Witley Common
  Information Centre (NT)
  MFD/CHID GU8 ....149 J8
Witley Industrial Estate
  NWDGN UB2 ....15 P2
Woking Arts Council
  WOKN/KNAP GU21 ....10 D4
Woking Athletics Track
  WOKN/KNAP GU21 ....72 C2
Woking Business Park
  WOKN/KNAP GU21 ....72 F4
Woking College
  WOKS/MYFD GU22 ....72 E9
Woking Community Hospital
  WOKS/MYFD GU22 ....10 E5
Woking FC
  WOKS/MYFD GU22 ....72 D9
Woking Golf Club
  WOKS/MYFD GU22 ....71 N9
Woking High School
  WOKN/KNAP GU21 ....72 B4
Woking Hospice
  WOKS/MYFD GU22 ....10 E5
Woking Leisure Centre
  & Swimming Pool
  WOKS/MYFD GU22 ....10 E7
Woking Nuffield Hospital
  WOKN/KNAP GU21 ....72 C3
Woking St John's
  Crematorium
  WOKN/KNAP GU21 ....71 L8
Woldingham School
  GDST RH9 ....102 E5
Wolf Fields Primary School
  NWDGN UB2 ....15 P2
Wolfson Medical Centre
  RYNPK SW20 ....42 E1
Wonersh & Shamley Green
  CE Infant School
  SHGR GU5 ....133 H8
Woodbridge Business Park
  GU GU1 ....6 C1
Woodbrook School
  BECK BR3 ....46 F2
Woodcote High School
  COUL/CHIP CR5 ....80 F2
Woodcote House School
  BFOR GU20 ....52 B4
Woodcote Park Golf Club
  COUL/CHIP CR5 ....80 E3
Woodcotes Primary School
  COUL/CHIP CR5 ....80 F3
Wooden Hill County
  Primary School
  BRAK RG12 ....32 A8
Woodentops School
  BAL SW12 ....29 N4
Woodfield School
  REDH RH1 ....100 G9
Woodlands Park Hotel
  COB KT11 ....76 C6
Woodlands School
  LHD/OX KT22 ....97 J2
Wood Lane School
  FUL/PGN SW6 ....19 N6
Woodlea Primary School
  CTHM CR3 ....102 F2

Woodmansterne
  Primary School
  BNSTD SM7 ....80 B3
Woodmansterne
  Primary School
  STRHM/NOR SW16 ....44 F2
Woodmansterne Sports Club
  BNSTD SM7 ....80 A4
Woodside Health Centre
  SNWD SE25 ....46 B6
Woodside Junior School
  CROY/NA CR0 ....46 A8
Wood Street County Infant School
  RGUW GU3 ....111 J3
Woodville Junior School
  LHD/OX KT22 ....77 H9
Woolmer Hill Athletics Track
  HASM GU27 ....183 N2
Woolmer Hill School
  HASM GU27 ....183 N3
Working & Horsell
  Cricket Club
  WOKN/KNAP GU21 ....10 A3
World Business Centre
  Heathrow
  HTHAIR TW6 ....14 E6
Worlds End Place
  WBPTN SW10 ....19 N5
Worple Primary School
  ISLW TW7 ....16 G9
Worplesdon CP School
  RGUW GU3 ....111 K1
Worplesdon Golf Club
  WOKS/MYFD GU22 ....91 L2
Worsley Bridge
  Junior School
  BECK BR3 ....46 G1
Worton Hall
  Industrial Estate
  ISLW TW7 ....16 E9
Wosley Place
  Shopping Centre
  WOKN/KNAP GU21 ....10 D3
Wray Common
  County Middle School
  REIG RH2 ....119 P4
Wray Common
  Primary School
  REDH RH1 ....119 P4
Wraysbury Medical Centre
  STWL/WRAY TW19 ....21 J2
Wraysbury Primary School
  STWL/WRAY TW19 ....21 K2
Wrencote
  CROY/NA CR0 ....2 D6
Wyke CP School
  RGUW GU3 ....109 P2
Wyke Green Golf Club
  ISLW TW7 ....16 F4
Yateley Common
  Country Park
  BLKW GU17 ....67 K5
Yateley Health Centre
  YTLY GU46 ....67 H2
Yateley Infant School
  YTLY GU46 ....67 H2
Yateley Manor
  Preparatory School
  YTLY GU46 ....67 H2
Yateley School
  YTLY GU46 ....66 G3
Yattendon School
  HORL RH6 ....140 C9
Yehudi Menuhin School
  COB KT11 ....76 A8
Ye Olde King's Head Hotel
  HORS RH12 ....192 B9
YMCA Community
  & Sports Centre
  REDH RH1 ....120 C8
York Clinic
  WOKN/KNAP GU21 ....10 D4
York House Medical Centre
  WOKS/MYFD GU22 ....10 E5
York Town Industrial Estate
  CBLY GU15 ....68 C3
Yvonne Arnaud Theatre
  GU GU1 ....6 E7
Zennor Road Industrial Estate
  BAL SW12 ....29 M4

Acknowledgements

The Post Office is a registered trademark of Post Office Ltd. in the UK and other countries.

Schools address data provided by Education Direct.

Petrol station information supplied by Johnsons

Tele Atlas One-way street data provided by © Tele Atlas N.V.

Garden centre information provided by:

Garden Centre Association  Britains best garden centres

Wyevale Garden Centres